THE ROYAL HORTICULTURAL SOCIETY
NEW
ENCYCLOPEDIA *of*
HERBS
& THEIR USES

"… and what I have been preparing to say is, that in Wildness is the preservation
of the world. Every tree sends its fibres forth in search of the Wild. The
cities import it at any price. Men plough and sail for it. From the forest and
wilderness come the tonics and barks which brace mankind …"

Henry David Thoreau WALDEN, OR LIFE IN THE WOODS, 1854

THE ROYAL HORTICULTURAL SOCIETY

NEW

ENCYCLOPEDIA *of*

HERBS

& THEIR USES

DENI BOWN

London, New York, Munich, Melbourne, Delhi

London, New York, Munich, Melbourne, Delhi

REVISED EDITION 2002
In memory of Laura Langley (1939–1997), my editor on the first edition

Senior Art Editor Ursula Dawson, Alison Lotinga
Senior Editor Joanna Chisholm

Senior Managing Editor Anna Kruger
Senior Managing Art Editor Lee Griffiths
Designers Ann Thompson
Editorial Assistance Helen Fewster, Victoria Heyworth-Dunne,
Georgina Hobbs, Fiona Wild
DTP Designer Louise Waller
Production Mandy Inness
Picture Research Brenda Clynch

DELHI OFFICE
Project Editor Dipali Singh **Project Designer** Elizabeth Thomas
Managing Editor Ira Pande **Managing Art Editor** Shuka Jain

FIRST EDITION
To PJ, who understands the sense in which this is a life's work,
and to our daughters, Anna and Dani, and sons, Will, Robin, and Ben

Project Editor Laura Langley
Editor Claire Folkard **Additional editorial assistance** Maureen Rissik
Project Art Editor Rachel Gibson **Designer** Julian Holland
Additional design assistance Gillian Andrews, Ursula Dawson,
Sasha Kennedy, Rachael Parfitt **DTP Designer** Chris Clark
Managing Editor Francis Ritter **Managing Art Editor** Gillian Allan
Picture Research Anna Lord

Photographer Deni Bown **Additional photographers** Andrew de Lory, Christine
Douglas, Neil Fletcher, Nancy Gardiner, Tony Rodd, Matthew Ward, Steven Wooster
Illustrators Karen Cochrane, Martine Collings, Valerie Hill

Colour reproduction by GRB Editrice, Italy
Printed and bound by Mohndruck GmbH, Gütersloh, Germany

see our complete catalogue at
www.dk.com

CONTENTS

AUTHOR'S INTRODUCTION

Herbs may have ancient roots but they are not a thing of the past. A resurgence of interest in herbs began with the hippies in the 1960s and 1970s, and in the last decade has come of age. The often-quoted statistics that 80 per cent of the world's population relies on traditional plant-based medicine, and that 25 per cent of prescription drugs contain plant extracts, are only the tip of the iceberg in terms of current trends. Since 1995, when *The Royal Horticultural Society Encyclopedia of Herbs and Their Uses* was first published, the market for "botanicals" (medicinal herbs) in the United States alone has grown by 100 per cent annually, and there have been comparable increases in many other countries. By medicinal herbs we are not talking simply about herbs taken as medicines but also about those used in the food industry, dietary supplements, and teas. In addition, there has been similar growth in herbs for skin- and hair-care products, and aromatics – everything from perfumery to room fragrances. Sales of culinary herbs have expanded too as more people travel widely, enjoy ethnic and regional food, and watch TV cookery programmes.

Now that the popular fascination with herbs has been translated into increased consumption, my job as an author and photographer is less concerned with persuading an audience to try growing and using herbs than with drawing attention to what happens when we try herbs, like them, and want more. Where will future supplies come from to meet such a rapidly expanding demand? How can we tell whether the herbal products we buy are what they say they are? Issues now are not whether herbs work, but their quality, safety, efficacy, and conservation: some 80 per cent of medicinal herbs are still harvested from the wild, and many, unfortunately, are becoming scarce through over-collection.

In this revised encyclopedia I have included many new herbs that have become better known since the first edition was published, and have updated and expanded the information on those that already had entries. There are also more varieties and cultivars described. These variants widen the scope of the plant in cultivation, in terms of size, habit, colour, flavour, or cropping potential – characteristics of interest to gardeners, landscape designers, and commercial growers alike. New features have also been added on wildflower gardening and the cultivation of native herbs, reflecting a greater awareness that conservation begins at home.

Although I hope we shall always find nostalgia and romance in herbs, and be struck by the beauty and power of plants, today's global herb trade demands different realities. We need to deepen our knowledge of herbs as living organisms, and face to the full our responsibilities when wild-collecting, cultivating, harvesting, processing, buying or selling, and using herbs. If, as they say, green is the colour of hope, and of healing, then the future is definitely bright green, and herbal. Nail your colour to the mast, join a herb society, and read all about it!

the *world* of
HERBS

HERBS THROUGH THE AGES

A SULTAN'S DIVAN
Islamic gardens were often enclosed, and contained a pool and scented flowers.

THE HISTORY OF HERB-growing is woven into the histories of peoples and civilizations. Wild plants depended upon from earliest times for food, medicine, fibre, and other raw materials were taken into cultivation and were joined by others from farther afield as people travelled as a result of trade, warfare, or migration. Some herbs have been collected and cultivated for so long that truly wild plants can no longer be found. Ginger (*Zingiber officinale*) is possibly the oldest known herb, having been distributed during early human migrations that began 6000 years ago. As there are no written records from this time, evidence comes from linguistics; the word for ginger has entered many different languages from an ancestral language, "proto-Austronesian", which was spoken over a vast area, from Taiwan and New Zealand to Madagascar and the eastern Pacific. In most parts of the world herbs are still grown mainly as field crops, or on a small scale as catch-crops among vegetables and ornamentals, as they were thousands of years ago.

Some of the earliest herb gardens were planted about 4000 years ago in Egypt. Herb-growing was often associated with temples, which required herbs and sacred flowers for daily worship and ritual. Olives (*Olea europea*) and pomegranates (*Punica granatum*) were introduced to Egypt at a very early date. Queen Hatshepsut (d.1482BC) imported frankincense (*Boswellia sacra*) and myrrh (*Commiphora myrrha*) from Arabia, and cornflowers (*Centaurea cyanus*), poppies (*Papaver* spp.), mandrakes (*Mandragora* spp.), figs (*Ficus* spp.), and lotuses (*Nymphaea lotus*) appear in many wall paintings. Chamomile (*Chamaemelum nobile*) was identified by pollen analysis as the main herb constituent in the embalming oil used to mummify Rameses II, d.1224BC.

ISLAMIC AND CHRISTIAN GARDENS

The present-day concept of a herb garden (an open area with divisions for different kinds of herbs) has developed largely from ancient Egyptian, Christian, and Islamic religious traditions. Wherever cultivation is closely associated with buildings, it tends to be orderly, making economic use of space. In Islam, paradise is seen as an enclosed garden, with cool shade and water, and exquisite flowers and fruits. Islamic gardens contained roses (*Rosa* spp.), jasmine (*Jasminum* spp.), lilies (*Lilium* spp.), and trees such as apricots (*Prunus armeniaca*), pomegranates, and almonds (*Prunus dulcis*), often hedged with myrtle (*Myrtus communis*).

Early Christian monasteries resembled Roman villas in design. They also inherited Roman garden style, which was essentially geometric and formal. Favourite plants in Roman times included rosemary (*Rosmarinus officinalis*), bay (*Laurus nobilis*), and myrtle, together with hedges and topiary, grown as much for their scent and beauty as for their usefulness. Monastic gardening also owed much to Egyptian, Syrian, and Persian traditions, in which useful plants were grown in enclosures to protect them from animals, provide shade, and make the best use of water supplies in a dry climate.

SELF-SUFFICIENT MONASTERIES

The first Christian monastery was founded by St Anthony in El Faiyum, northern Egypt, in AD305. He made a small enclosed garden with a water supply to provide the basic necessities. Monastic cultivation became so firmly established that when St Benedict founded the Benedictine order at Monte Cassino in Italy in AD540, gardening was second only to prayer

MEDIEVAL GARDEN
In this illustration from Roman de la Rose *(c.1400), a doctor selects herbs for medicinal use. Herb gardens had a range of species, which might include culinary and decorative plants.*

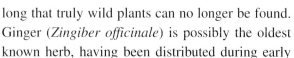

in the monastic regime. Expanding on St Jerome's instructions a century earlier to "hoe your ground, set out cabbages…", he specified in the *Regula Monachorum* – the foundation of monastic rule to this day – that vegetables, fruit, grapes, herbs, dye plants, and aromatics for incense should be grown. A plan drawn up in the 9th century at St Gall, a Swiss Benedictine monastery, shows a rectangular garden with 16 beds of "herbs both beautiful and health-giving," such as sage (*Salvia* spp.) and rosemary, and a larger garden with 18 beds of vegetables and herbs. Monasteries were largely self-sufficient in produce, placing special emphasis on herbs to heal the sick. They also made great use of herbs for flavouring a vegetarian diet and were expert in the brewing and distillation of ale, wine, liqueurs such as Benedictine, and the cosmetic Carmelite water which was based on *Melissa officinalis*.

PHYSIC GARDENS

Herb gardening grew in popularity during the 13th century, often as a result of instruction by infirmary sisters. Most large houses grew a wide variety of herbs for household use, while small properties were surrounded by a mixture of orchard, grass, and kitchen garden in which vegetables, herbs, and flowers were grown.

In the 16th century, herb gardens were planted by universities for teaching botany and medicine – subjects that were inextricably linked until separated by advances in science during the 18th century. The first of these "physic gardens" was founded at the University of Padua in 1545. By the end of the 17th century, there were physic gardens at universities throughout Europe. The demands of teaching influenced how the herbs were laid out – in Edinburgh, for example, medicinal herbs were grown in alphabetical order. As new species were brought back by colonial explorers and botanical knowledge expanded, physic gardens embraced a far more extensive range of plants and became the botanic gardens that we know today.

DEVELOPMENT OF THE FORMAL GARDEN

The 17th and 18th centuries saw great changes in style. Some of the finest formal herb gardens in the world were created in France, at châteaux such as Villandry, where the reconstructed box parterres and *potager* are unparalleled in grandeur. Landscape gardening, with an abhorrence of unnatural symmetry, became fashionable during the 18th century, and as the industrial revolution got under way, nostalgia for the cottage garden and rural idyll increased the popularity of informal style. Today we see an eclectic approach, choosing formal or informal as taste and situation permit. Both approaches have a long and fascinating history. Even the windowbox has its pedigree; it first appeared as a space-saving device in cramped Elizabethan London.

During the colonial era, Europeans settled in many parts of the world, taking seeds and cuttings of indispensable plants with them. Through trial and error, settlers learned which of their plants thrived. The Dutch, who were acknowledged as the finest gardeners in Europe at the time, were the first to plant box (*Buxus sempervirens*), on Shelter Island, Long Island, New York, in 1652, but in New England, box hedges failed

to survive the severe winters and were replaced by the hardier wormwood (*Artemisia* spp.) and ornamental quince (*Chaenomeles speciosa*).

GARDENS AROUND THE WORLD

The story is similar in Canada, Australia, New Zealand, and South Africa, where the traditional European style of herb garden is also enduringly popular – so much so that the Plants Naturally Nursery of Victoria, Australia, created a herb garden at London's Chelsea Flower Show in 1987. In Cape Town, there are formal public gardens west of Government Avenue where the kitchen gardens of the Dutch East India Company were set out in the 17th century, and where the first non-native species were planted in southern Africa. Many of the herbs nurtured by colonists escaped into the wild and have become pernicious weeds that threaten the survival of native plants and ecosystems. The Aztecs of Mexico used some 3000 herbs and had sophisticated systems of cultivation and botanical classification. The "floating gardens" of Xochimilco are of great antiquity, their irrigated plots dating back to the 6th century AD. Cortés wrote to Charles V of Spain in 1522 that Montezuma's gardens at Huaxtepec (present-day Oaxtepec) were the finest he had seen; they boasted cacao (*Theobroma cacao*) and vanilla (*Vanilla* spp.), brought from the coastal tropics.

HERB GROWING IN CHINA

Herb growing in China has belonged more to rural industry than to the noble art of gardening. Both Chinese medicine and Chinese gardens follow abstract concepts (the theory of the five elements, for example), the ultimate goal of both being to create harmony. Chinese (and Japanese) gardens are stylized scenes from nature, with a disciplined use of plants, and therefore they are never designed symmetrically.

THE KNOT GARDEN
The rectangles and trellises of medieval times developed into elaborate patterns of knot gardens and parterres.

CORN CULTIVATION
Pre-Incan people in Mexico are known to have cultivated chillies, cotton, and squashes as early as 2500BC. These multipurpose crops were joined by corn and coca.

HERBS IN MYTH AND LEGEND

Folk medicine has always been closely allied to ritual and magic. In most cultures, curing the sick, fumigating buildings with incense, and perfuming the body (or embalming it when dead) were once considered divine acts to be performed according to religious rituals. Plants of great beauty and fragrance came to be regarded as sacred for their importance in mediating between sickness and health, humanity and divinity, death and eternal life. Most of these plants had medicinal properties, too, since fragrance is usually due to volatile oils that have a wide range of curative effects.

SACRED CORN
As a staple crop, corn (Zea mays) was synonymous with life to the ancient civilizations of Central and South America and elevated to the status of deity. This vessel originated from the Mochica people of Peru AD100–800; their advanced agricultural system included irrigation.

The use of incense has long been important in ritual; frankincense (*Boswellia sacra*) and myrrh (*Commiphora myrrha*) were burned in the temples of ancient Babylon, Egypt, Rome, Greece, India, and China, and were traded throughout these regions from Arabia. The trees were protected by legendary multi-coloured winged serpents, and their resins were once worth their weight in gold.

THE LOTUS AND THE ROSE

Scented blue and white lotus flowers (from *Nymphaea caerulea*, a narcotic in ancient Egypt, and the night-blooming *N. lotus*, respectively) were the favourite flowers offered 4000 years ago by Egyptians to their gods and used for garlands in funeral rites. The lotus was revered as symbol of the Nile, giver of life, and sacred to Isis, goddess of fertility. Egyptian lotuses are quite different from the sacred lotus (*Nelumbo nucifera*), which is Asian in origin and was not known in Egypt before 500BC. This species is sacred in Indian, Chinese, and Tibetan cultures. The lotus germinates in mud and unfolds its immaculate flowers in the sunlight; it is seen as analogous to the growth of consciousness, purity, and enlightenment.

Roses are to Islam what the sacred lotus is to Hinduism and Buddhism. The original sacred rose was the white, pink-budded damask rose, *Rosa* × *damascena*. One legend gives its origin as drops of sweat, fallen from Mohammed as he ascended into heaven. Accounts of the creation of red and white roses are found in ancient Greek, Roman, and Christian legends. In one Roman myth, the goddess Venus, on her way to meet Adonis, pricked her foot on a thorn of a white rose, turning it red with her blood.

Inevitably, the rose also found favour in Christian imagery. The Virgin Mary is known as the *Rosa Mystica*, symbolized by a white rose, while the red rose represents the blood of Christ, its five petals denoting his wounds. In one legend, the Virgin lays her veil on a rosebush to dry, and the red roses beneath it turn white. *Rosa* × *damascena* was closely associated with the Virgin Mary because of its colouring – the dark pink buds representing human flesh and blood, and its open white petals symbolizing the divine spirit.

SYMBOLISM OF THE LILY
The Madonna lily is closely associated with the Virgin Mary as a symbol of purity. Early Christians believed that the life cycle of the lily symbolized the life of the soul.

CLASSICAL MYTHS

A number of pagan symbols and myths became absorbed into Christianity. It may be no coincidence that the Romans dedicated the white Madonna lily, *Lilium candidum*, to Juno, goddess of all that is essentially female, and that both she and the Virgin Mary were known as "queen of heaven." According to Greek myth, the lily originated in drops of milk, spilled from the breast of Hera, queen of the gods, as she suckled the infant Hercules – drops that also spread through the sky to form the Milky Way.

Myrtle (*Myrtus communis*) was dedicated to Venus, often depicted wearing a crown of myrtle, and who was on occasion worshipped as Myrtilla, from the Latin name of the plant. Venus is identified with the Greek goddess Aphrodite, and linked with Ishtar, the Babylonian and Assyrian goddess of love and fertility. To this day myrtle is carried in wedding bouquets. In ancient Greece, winning athletes in the Olympic games were crowned with bay (*Laurus nobilis*), as were victorious warriors and poets – hence the title "poet laureate". Ancient Greeks hung a branch of bay over the door of a sick person to fend off evil and death. This led to the garlanding of newly qualified doctors with a bay wreath, the *bacca laureus*, which gave us "baccalaureate" (university degree).

THE LOTUS IN HINDUISM AND BUDDHISM
In Hindu legend, the sacred lotus was created from the navel of the supreme being. Inside the flower sat Brahma, who turned the lotus into a new world. In Buddhist mythology, Buddha first appeared floating on a lotus, and is depicted on a stylized lotus "throne" with the soles of his feet resting on his thighs – a posture known in yoga as the "lotus position".

HERBS IN WITCHCRAFT

Henbane (*Hyoscyamus niger*), deadly nightshade (*Atropa bella-donna*), and mandrake (*Mandragora officinarum*) all feature in European witchcraft and sorcery. The image of witches on broomsticks has origins in the use of these plants which, when rubbed into the skin or inhaled, cause intoxicating sensations of flying. Mandrake was one of the most magical and feared plants in the world. Believing that the root resembled human form and would shriek and cause death if uprooted, herb gatherers carried out the task by tying a dog to the plant. Outbreaks of lycanthropy (supposed transformation of a human being into a wolf) have also been associated with ointments made from nightshades, aconite (*Aconitum napellus*), and narcotic herbs such as cannabis (*Cannabis sativa*) and opium (*Papaver somniferum*).

HERBS IN NORTHERN LEGEND

Elder (*Sambucus nigra*) is a magical plant in many cultures. It is sacred to the gypsies, and is planted in the courtyards of synagogues in the Israeli town of Safad, where it was probably associated with occult practices. According to German folklore, one's hat must be doffed whenever an elder tree is passed. In Denmark one should always ask permission of Hylde-Moer (elder mother) before harvesting the tree, and never make a cradle from elder wood, lest Hylde-Moer strangle the baby in revenge. Hawthorn, or may (*Crataegus laevigata* and *C. monogyna*), has been associated with fertility rites since earliest times. The customs of going "a-Maying", and of crowning the May queen with hawthorn, are pre-Christian, harking back to the pagan fertility festival of Beltane, which began when the hawthorn came into bloom. The white flowers are regarded in British folklore as omens of death or disaster if brought into the house – perhaps as a memory of the human sacrifices required as part of the May Day ritual, or maybe subconsciously because their scent contains the chemical trimethylamine, which also occurs during the process of putrefaction.

Mistletoe (*Viscum album*) was sacred to the Druids during pre-Christian times in Gaul, Britain, and Ireland. It could be cut only with a golden knife at a certain phase of the moon, and could not touch the ground. Branches (the original Golden Bough) were carried to announce the New Year. In Norse mythology, Balder, a gentle god, was killed by a dart of mistletoe; now it may grow only in tree tops, and those meeting under it kiss as a sign of love. In German folklore, mistletoe bestows the power to see ghosts and make them speak.

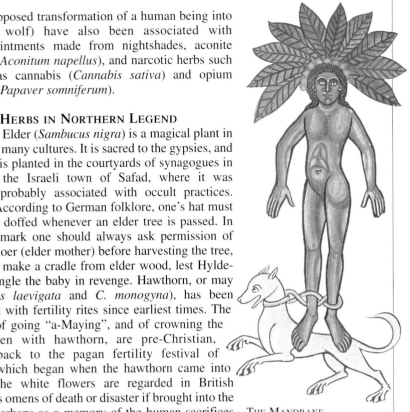

THE MANDRAKE
This illustration refers to the superstition of tying a dog to the plant to avoid hearing its shrieks when uprooted.

GOING A-MAYING
In ancient times the Queen of the May was put to death to ensure a good harvest.

HERBS IN PRINT

K nowledge of herbs has been handed down from generation to generation for thousands of years. In the 1970s a grave was found in northern Iraq, belonging to a Neanderthal man who, 60,000 years ago, was buried surrounded by flowers. The plant fragments were analyzed and found to be mostly herbs still used by local people; one of them was yarrow (*Achillea millefolium*). For much of human history, traditions of herbal use have thus been oral, often divulged only to the initiated, for ritual or healing purposes. In some cultures, such as those of Amazonian peoples, they remain so to this day.

KREÜTERBUCH (HERBAL)
The title page of the Kreüterbuch *of Pierandrea Mattioli, or Matthiolus (1501–77), who was physician to the Emperor Maximilian II. It was published in 1586, by which time Mattioli had died of the plague.*

Oral knowledge can disappear within a generation when alien pressures cause traditional cultures to break down. The threat to habitats such as the tropical rainforest is not just that plant species become extinct day by day, but also that local skill in their uses is lost.

ANCIENT HERBAL RECORDS
Chinese herbalism is widely regarded as the oldest in the world, because it has the longest unbroken history of recorded knowledge; several ancient Chinese herbals are still in regular use today. Ayurvedic medicine is ancient and well recorded, too; herbs are mentioned in the *Rig Veda*, a sacred Hindu text dating from at least 2000BC. It is known that there were Chaldean herbalists c.5000BC, and Assyrian clay tablets from c.2500BC describe some 250 herbs. The ancient Egyptians undoubtedly had a sophisticated knowledge of herbs by 3000BC, but there is little written evidence to amplify archaeological finds, though herbs are illustrated in tomb wall paintings and carvings dating back to c.2000BC. The illustrations are more decorative and symbolic than an aid to identification, indicating familiarity with herbs in everyday use. All that remains is the Ebers papyrus (c.1500BC), which records long usage of herbs such as elder and wormwood, and a few fragments from the 2nd century AD, some of which were written in Greek. Egyptian herbal traditions passed to the Copts, who were early Christian descendants of the ancient Egyptians.

HERBALS IN MANUSCRIPT
Before the invention of printing in 1440, herbals were written and illustrated by hand. They were often copied many times, giving rise to errors and different versions. Early herbals combine myth and magic with the descriptive and practical. They contain information that is in itself ancient, and often show foreign influences that were communicated via trade and travel. The *Leech Book of Bald* (c.AD900) includes, for example, a detailed knowledge of native plants and Syrian prescriptions sent to King Alfred from the Patriarch of Jerusalem, alongside magical charms that are common to many ancient cultures. A herbal written in the 13th century by the physicians of Myddfai, Wales, presents herbal knowledge that dates back to the Druids. The Druids, in their turn, were influenced by ancient Greek medicine and the works of Hippocrates. One of the best examples of early printed herb illustration is the *Herbarius zu Teusch*, printed at Mainz in 1485 and widely copied. The drawings by Leonhard Fuchs in *Neue Kreüterbuch*

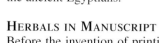

"HEALING HERBS"
From the Illustrated Family Library, *Leipzig, 1901.*

14

(1543) and *De historia Stirpium* (1545) were copied throughout Europe in the 16th century. In the late 17th century, herbals were joined by still-room books, which collected recipes, notes, and advice for the running of a large household. Much information concerned the use of herbs. Gardening books also began to appear, as new plants were introduced from the colonies. By the 18th century, botany and medicine were developing as sciences in their own right, requiring specialized textbooks. Separation of these various subject areas continued through the 19th century. This can clearly be seen in *The Universal Herbal* by Thomas Green (1816), which is subtitled "Botanical, Medical, and Agricultural Dictionary. Specifying the uses to which they are or may be applied, whether as Food, as Medicine, or in the Arts and Manufactures. Adapted to the use of the Farmer – the Gardener – the Husbandman – the Botanist – the Florist – and Country Housekeepers in General". The increase in knowledge in the 20th and 21st centuries has produced an era of specialization, with databases, websites, CD-Roms and scientific journals for the student of medical herbalism and ethnobotany, but the herbal in book form remains an important way to learn how to use plants.

HERBS IN MANUSCRIPT AND PRINT

WESTERN HERBALS

c.300BC *Enquiry into Plants* (*Historia Plantarum*) and *Growth of Plants* (*De Causis Plantarum*) by Theophrastus, a Greek philosopher and writer. Listing a total of 500 herbs, and based on Aristotle's botanical writings, with Theophrastus's own observations.

AD77 *Natural History* (*Historia Naturalis*) by Pliny the Elder, a Roman natural historian and writer. 37 volumes of fact and fantasy, including medicinal uses of plants; origin of the Doctrine of Signatures.

AD100 *De Materia Medica* by Dioscorides, a Greek physician. The most influential Western herbal of all time, and a standard reference work for 1500 years. It describes some 600 herbs, many of which remain today in modern pharmacopoeias.

PARADISUS TERRESTRIS
The first three words on this 1629 title-page are a pun on the author's name: Paradisi in Sole *translates as Park-in-sun.*

c.AD150 *De Simplicibus* by Galen, a Greek physician from the Middle East. His works, which codified existing medical knowledge and propounded the theory of "humours", were standard medical texts in Europe and the Arab world until the Renaissance.

c.900 *Leech Book of Bald* Manual of a Saxon doctor, and the earliest European herbal written in the vernacular.

c.1000 *Canon of Medicine* by Avicenna, the great physician of the Islamic world. Based on Galen, written in Arabic, translated into Latin, it was a standard text until the 17th century.

c.1250 *De Proprietatibus Rerum* by Bartolomaeus Anglicus. 19 volumes of natural history, the 17th constituting the only original herbal written in England during the Middle Ages.

1525 *Banckes's Herbal* The first printed English herbal. An anonymous compilation of earlier herbals,

including the 10th-century Aemilius Macer's herbal (*De Virtutibus Herbarum*), a poem on the virtues of 77 herbs, and the famous discourse on rosemary sent by the French Countess of Hainault to her daughter, Philippa, Edward I's queen.

1551–68 *A New Herball* (in three parts) by William Turner. The first English herbal to take a scientific approach, illustrated with more than 400 outstanding woodcuts, most of which were reproduced from drawings by Leonhard Fuchs in Swiss herbals.

1570 *Herbal* by Paracelsus (Theophrastus Bombastus von Hohenheim), a Swiss physician and alchemist. It expounded the Doctrine of Signatures (see p.44).

1597 *The Herball or Generall Historie of Plants* by John Gerard, an eminent Elizabethan herbalist and gardener. Based on Dodoens' *Cruÿdboeck* (1554), and extended by Thomas Johnson in 1633, it has delightful descriptions of plants from all over the world.

1629 *Paradisus Terrestris*; **1640** *Theatrum Botanicum* by John Parkinson. The latter is the largest herbal in English. Less well known than the former, which is more of a gardening book, describing 3800 herbs, divided into 17 groups, though one group consists of "stragglers" that the author had neglected to include elsewhere!

1652 *The English Physician* by Nicholas Culpeper, English herbalist and astrologer. One of the best-selling herbals of all time, containing astrological, often flippant, descriptions of 398 herbs. It promoted the Doctrine of Signatures and was castigated as "ignorant" by physicians of the day. *The English Physician Enlarged* came out in 1653, followed by many later revisions.

1656 *The Art of Simpling* by William Coles. "An Introduction to the Knowledge and Gathering of Plants," including the first account of herbs for treating animals.

1710 *Botanologia. The English Herbal or History of Plants* by William Salmon. The last major herbal before the disciplines of botany and medicine parted company.

1838 *Flora Medica* by John Lindley. A worldwide survey of medicinal plants, written by an eminent botanist and horticulturist, typical of the new scientific approach.

1866 *A Botanic Guide to Health* by Albert Coffin. He brought Physiomedicalism from America to England, leading to the founding in 1864 of the National Institute of Medical Herbalists.

1931 *A Modern Herbal* by Mrs M. Grieve. Second perhaps only to Culpeper's herbal in its popularity. It describes over 1000 herbs.

PEPPER PLANT
Illustration of Capsicum *species in an English 17th-century manuscript.*

CHINESE HERBALS

c.1000BC *Yellow Emperor's Classic of Internal Medicine* First treatise on principles of health, by Huang Di (Yellow Emperor), founding father of Chinese medicine, who lived c.2697–2595BC.

AD25–220 *Shen Nong Canon of Herbs* Attributed to Shen Nong, god of husbandry and legendary emperor, said to have lived c.3000BC. It lists 252 drugs from plants.

c.659 *Tang Materia Medica* by Su Ying. 54 volumes of Chinese plants. It was commissioned by the government during the Tang dynasty.

1590 *Compendium of Materia Medica* by Li Shi Zhen. 52 volumes describing nearly 2000 drugs, mainly of plant origin. Revised in 1765 by Zhao Xue Min, who added a further 900.

1970 *The Atlas of Commonly Used Chinese Traditional Drugs* by the Chinese Academy of Medical Science. A product of the Communist revival of traditional medicine after the Kuomintang era. It listed 248 drugs from plants and animals.

AMERICAN HERBALS

1569 *Joyfull Newes Out of the Newe Founde Worlde* by Nicolas Monardes, a Spanish doctor. The first American herbal, translated into English, Latin, Italian, Flemish, and French to provide information on the herbs of the Americas.

1672 *New England's Rarities Discover'd* by John Josselyn. The first account of useful European plants that thrived when transported to and grown in North America, written to help settlers garden in unfamiliar surroundings.

1672 *The American Physitian* by William Hughes. Particularly famous for its account of chocolate.

1715 *The South-Sea Herbal* by James Petiver. The first account in the English language of herbs native to Peru and Chile.

1835 *New Guide to Health, Or, Botanic Family Physician*; **1841** *The Thomsonian Materia Medica* by Samuel Thomson. Native American herbs and therapies formulated by him as Physiomedicalism.

HERBS THAT CHANGED THE WORLD

The lives of people and plants are more entwined than is often realized. Our passion for aromatics and flavourings inspired exploration and was a significant factor in colonial expansion. Some herbs have such power to change our physiological functioning that they have assumed social and religious importance, and in some cases revolutionized medicine, creating fortunes for those who harvest, process, and trade them. The foxglove (*Digitalis* spp.) is a European wildflower and folk remedy that became a vital drug. Wars have been fought over opium, and conflict continues over both it and coca. The Swiss physician and alchemist Paracelsus (c.1493–1541) wrote that "All substances are poisons; there is none which is not a poison. The right dose differentiates a poison and a remedy."

QUININE CULTIVATION
Quinine (Cinchona *spp.) trees under cultivation in Java. Demand for the bark to combat malaria prompted the search for alkaloid-rich species, and plantations were established in many parts of SE Asia. Synthetic anti-malarial drugs were developed after the Second World War, and mosquito populations were decimated by spraying with DDT, but resistance to synthetic drugs has since increased.*

A WONDER DRUG
Catharanthus roseus *was screened in the 1960s as a cure for diabetes, but its effect on white blood cells has led to its use in treating cancers.*

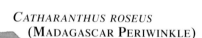

AMMI VISNAGA (KHELLA)
The anti-asthmatic
The aromatic fruits of *Ammi visnaga* have been used for medicinal purposes in Egypt since ancient times, mainly to treat kidney stones. They contain various furanochromones, including khellin, that relax smooth (visceral) muscle. Khellin was first isolated in 1879, but in 1946 an Egyptian pharmacologist discovered that extracts of the herb also had a powerful effect on the bronchioles and coronary arteries and gave good control of asthmatic symptoms. Over 670 compounds were synthesized before the production of sodium cromoglycate, a bischromone that prevents release of the anti-allergenic substances responsible for an asthmatic attack.

CATHARANTHUS ROSEUS (MADAGASCAR PERIWINKLE)
The fight against cancer
The Madagascar or rosy periwinkle is frequently cited as an example of a "wonder drug", and also to demonstrate the importance of screening tropical plants for active constituents. The analysis of its alkaloids began in the 1920s; recent counts put the total at over 75. Of these, vincristine and vinblastine are now well established in the treatment of acute leukaemia, Hodgkin's disease, and other cancers that were previously incurable.

CHONDRODENDRON TOMENTOSUM (PAREIRA)
Arrow poison and muscle relaxant
Extract from the stems of the large rainforest liana, *Chondrodendron tomentosum*, is one of the main toxic ingredients of curare, a black gum that causes instantaneous muscular paralysis. In many parts of South America native people hunt with darts tipped with curare, which kills the prey but leaves the flesh untainted. Curare was first used as an adjunct to general anaesthesia in 1942, and is now essential in all surgical procedures. It cannot be synthesized, however, and stocks must be collected in the wild.

CINCHONA SPECIES (QUININE)
The first anti-malarial drug
During the era of colonial expansion, cinchona bark was in great demand to prevent and treat malaria, and by the end of the 17th century vast quantities were being shipped from Peru and Bolivia. In 1820 the alkaloid quinine was isolated. By then, wild stocks were seriously depleted, so there was fierce competition between the British and the Dutch to cultivate supplies and find high-yielding strains. *Cinchona ledgeriana* proved to be the highest in alkaloid content, but failed to thrive in cultivation. Dutch plantations in Java succeeded in grafting *C. ledgeriana* seedlings on to more vigorous rootstocks and thus gained a world monopoly of the quinine trade.

CLAVICEPS PURPUREA (ERGOT)
St Anthony's fire, childbirth, and LSD
Outbreaks of poisoning by ergot, a fungus that affects grain crops such as rye, have been recorded throughout history. It causes hallucinations and unbearable burning sensations. Before the causes were understood, sufferers were executed as witches. Medically significant alkaloids of ergot were isolated between 1906 and 1920, notably ergonovine and ergotamine; these drugs have greatly improved the management of labour, postpartum haemorrhage, and migraine. Another ergot derivative, lysergic acid diethylamide (LSD), was extracted in 1943 and attracted a great deal of attention in the 1970s as a potent hallucinogenic. Though not addictive, it can cause psychosis, suicide, homicide, abortion, and congenital abnormalities.

COLCHICUM AUTUMNALE (AUTUMN CROCUS)
Cure for gout and key to genetic engineering
The poisonous properties of *Colchicum* spp. were probably known in ancient Egypt, and were used medicinally in ancient Greece to relieve the pain of gout, and as a poison. The extreme toxicity of the plant earned it names such as "vegetable arsenic". The active constituent is the toxic alkaloid colchicine. It remains a standard treatment for gout, and its effects on cells have revolutionized plant breeding. If applied to plant cells when they are dividing, chromosome numbers can be manipulated, rendering sterile hybrids fertile, and bringing improvements – such as increased size and vigour – in food plants and ornamentals.

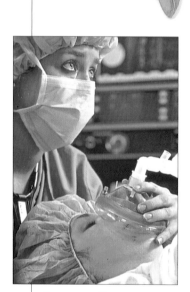

PAREIRA IN SURGERY
Before the use in surgery of tubocurarine, from pareira, muscle relaxation was obtained only by deep anaesthesia, which carried considerable risk.

DIOSCOREA
*Leaves and (right) dried root of
Dioscorea villosa, one of several
species of this genus from which
saponins are extracted for conversion
into steroid hormones.*

DIOSCOREA SPECIES (MEXICAN YAM)
Blueprint for the oral contraceptive
The discovery of hormones came very late in the history of medicine. It took until 1934 to isolate cortisone, after which plants were investigated for saponins that could be converted cheaply into steroids and other drugs. Extraction of the hormone diosgenin from Mexican yams was first carried out in the early 1940s by Russell Marker, who produced several kilograms of diosgenin when its market value was $80,000 per kilo. Large-scale cultivation of yams for steroidal drugs – corticosteroids, anabolic agents, and sex hormones – became a major industry in Mexico and put an affordable contraceptive pill on the market.

ERYTHROXYLUM COCA (COCA)
Local anaesthetic; origin of a famous soft drink
The chewing of coca leaves by the early peoples of Peru has been dated to at least AD500; small bags of coca leaves have been found in the funeral urn of a mummified potentate from the pre-Inca Nazca period. The first detailed description of coca was given by Nicolas Monardes in 1565. The alkaloid cocaine was isolated in 1860 and was used as a local anaesthetic in 1884 in the first painless cataract operation. Social use of cocaine and coca-leaf products was popularized during the 19th century, and widely used among the intelligentsia. Coca wine became a craze, and many alcohol-free imitations appeared with the onset of Prohibition in the US. One of the most popular was made by John Pemberton, who in 1886 produced the "Intellectual Beverage and Temperance Drink", *Coca-Cola*. Only decocainized coca extracts have been used to make it since the sale of cocaine was banned in 1902. Cocaine has also been largely replaced in surgery by synthetics such as procaine.

COCA LEAVES
*Fresh leaves of the coca
plant (Erythroxylum coca)
are harvested to extract the
powerful alkaloid cocaine.*

FILIPENDULA ULMARIA (MEADOWSWEET)
Plant aspirin
The analgesic salicin was first isolated from meadowsweet leaves in 1827. Salicylic acid was made in 1838, and synthesized in 1859, but proved suitable only for the external treatment of skin conditions. It did, however, provide the basis for acetylsalicylic acid, which was first produced in 1899, and named aspirin after *Spiraea ulmaria*, which was the old name for *Filipendula ulmaria*. Aspirin is the world's most widely used drug, and probably the cheapest. It is recommended for over 40 different complaints and may also help to prevent heart attack and stroke.

PAPAVER SOMNIFERUM (OPIUM POPPY)
The irreplaceable painkiller
Opium is as old as medicine itself, and there has never been another painkiller to equal it. Its uses were inscribed on clay tablets by Sumerians in 4000BC, and it was known to the ancient Greeks. Opium is the world's greatest painkiller and is still the drug of choice for relieving severe pain in serious accidents and terminal illnesses. It is also one of the most addictive substances known. By the 19th century, international trade in opium was of major economic importance. When China tried to tackle the social problems of addiction by banning imports, Britain declared war and defeated the Chinese in the Opium Wars of the 1840s, gaining Hong Kong in the process. Morphine is the principal alkaloid of the 20 or more in opium, and it has potent analgesic, euphoric, and narcotic effects. It was the first alkaloid to be isolated in the history of chemistry, a feat achieved in 1806. Opioid alkaloids, which also include codeine and methadone, cannot be synthesized. Hence the growing and processing of opium for the pharmaceutical industry continues to be a trade of major importance within the world.

RAUVOLFIA SERPENTINA (RAUVOLFIA)
The first tranquillizer
The earliest known mention of rauvolfia is in *Charaka Samhita*, a major Hindu medical treatise that was written in 600BC, a time when rauvolfia was used for snake bite and "moon disease" (insanity). The most important alkaloid in the plant, reserpine, was isolated in 1952, and the term "tranquillizer" was coined the following year, when the effects of reserpine on the central nervous system were described. Alkaloids extracted from rauvolfia have also revolutionized the management of psychotic patients and led to advances in the development of drugs to treat high blood pressure.

OPIUM
PIPE
*Introduced into
China from Java
in the 17th century,
opium brought serious
social problems.*

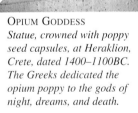

OPIUM GODDESS
*Statue, crowned with poppy
seed capsules, at Heraklion,
Crete, dated 1400–1100BC.
The Greeks dedicated the
opium poppy to the gods of
night, dreams, and death.*

RAUVOLFIA
*Calming herb used in India and
the Far East. Its chemistry was
first described in 1887 by Dutch
scientists in Java.*

WHAT IS A HERB?

A ll plants are classified according to their relationships, in much the same way as we have a family tree to trace our origins. Relationships are established by shared characteristics, especially of reproductive parts. The binomial system that we use today gives each plant a name in two Latinized words: the first is the name of the genus, and the second denotes the species. This system of classification was largely the work of the Swedish botanist Carl Linnaeus and, though later amended, is still accepted worldwide as the standard way to identify plants.

UPPSALA UNIVERSITY
The Orangery in the gardens at Uppsala University, near Stockholm, Sweden. Carl Linnaeus was here from 1741 as a professor of medicine and later of botany. While at Uppsala he established his system of plant classification in several books, including Species Plantarum *(1753), and replanted the physic garden, which had been founded in 1655, accordingly.*

Traditionally, the plant kingdom consists of six divisions. These are flowering plants or angiosperms, which include herbaceous perennials, annuals, biennials, and many trees and shrubs; naked-seeded plants or gymnosperms, embracing conifers and related groups, such as cycads and ginkgo; ferns, clubmosses, and horsetails or pteridophytes; mosses and liverworts or bryophytes; fungi and lichens; and lastly, algae, including seaweeds. More recent systems classify fungi as a kingdom separate from plants and animals. Further subdivisions separate these main groups into classes and orders, and then into families, genera, and species.

DEFINING A HERB

The term "herb" also has more than one definition. Botanists describe a herb as a small, seed-bearing plant with fleshy, rather than woody, parts (from which we get the term "herbaceous"). In this book, the term refers to a far wider range of plants. In addition to herbaceous perennials, herbs include trees, shrubs, annuals, vines, and more primitive plants, such as ferns, mosses, algae, lichens, and fungi. They are valued for their flavour, fragrance, medicinal and healthful qualities, economic and industrial uses, pesticidal properties, and colouring materials (dyes).

Many people are sceptical about the effectiveness of herbal remedies, but there is no doubt that herbs contain ingredients that have a measurable effect on the body. Related herbs may have similar chemistry, but each herb, regardless of the family it belongs to, or which part is used, has unique constituents that are as

CARL LINNAEUS (1707–78)
The great Swedish botanist, from Robert Thornton's The Temple of Flora *(1797–1807). Above his head is* Linnaea borealis, *a plant species named after him.*

individual as a fingerprint, though the proportions of the constituents may fluctuate. These fluctuations are dependent on season, weather, soil type and fertility, time of day, and even phase of the moon, which is why there are optimum times for harvesting to ensure high levels of active constituents. The chemistry of most

PLANT CLASSIFICATION

Plant classes and orders are further classified into even smaller groups, to describe finer differences:

Family (group of related genera): e.g. Boraginaceae.

Genus (group of related species, indicated by the first part of the Latin name): e.g. *Borago, Symphytum*.

Species (group of plants that are alike and naturally breed with each other,

denoted by the second part of the Latin name): e.g. "*asperum*" and "*officinale*" are species of the genus *Symphytum* and are written as *Symphytum asperum, Symphytum officinale*.

Hybrid (cross between two species, which may happen in the wild, but more usually occurs accidentally or artificially in cultivation). A hybrid is indicted by a "×": e.g. *Symphytum × uplandicum* (Russian comfrey)

is a cross between *Symphytum asperum* and *Symphytum officinale*.

Subspecies (subsp.),**variety** (var.), and **form** (forma, f.) are subdivisions within a species or natural hybrid, that differ consistently in small but distinct ways from the type, e.g. *Symphytum officinale* var. *ochroleucum* is a white-flowered variant of common comfrey. These natural variants are often rare in the wild but common in cultivation, having attractive differences in habit and/or flower colour.

Cultivar (a variant, produced and maintained by cultivation, that has desirable characteristics of habit, colour, flavour, etc.), e.g. *Symphytum × uplandicum* 'Variegatum' has large golden blotches on its dark green leaves, while those of the species are plain green.

Symphytum asperum *(far left)*, Symphytum officinale *(left)*

Symphytum × uplandicum

Symphytum officinale *var.* ochroleucum

Symphytum × uplandicum *'Variegatum'*

RHUBARB'S EARLY HISTORY

Among the most important medicinal herbs is rhubarb root (*Rheum officinale* and *R. palmatum*), a laxative drug known in China as *da huang*. Records show that dried roots were exported from China along caravan routes to Europe as early as 114BC. Due to Chinese, and later Russian, monopolies, plants did not reach the West until the 1750s. Before this, great efforts were made to find suitable substitutes. *Rheum rhaponticum* was found in the Rhodope Mountains, Bulgaria, in about 1608, and was soon cultivated as a medicinal plant.

herbs is very complex. Some widely used herbs are poorly understood. Research into the chemistry of herbs intensified in the 1990s, following successful clinical trials and increasing concern about interactions between herbal remedies and other drugs.

HOW PLANT INGREDIENTS WORK

Herbal medicines differ greatly from the compounds isolated or synthesized from them. The whole plant (and extracts derived from it) contains many ingredients that work together, and which may produce a quite different effect (known as a synergistic effect) from that of a constituent if given on its own. An example is meadowsweet (*Filipendula ulmaria*), which contains salicylates (substances akin to aspirin). Meadowsweet contains healing ingredients, plus buffering substances that protect the mucous membranes from the corrosive effects of salicylates. The complex chemistry of the herb as a whole appears to lower the risk of side-effects, whereas the compounds in isolation may be surprisingly toxic.

ACTIVE PLANT CONSTITUENTS

While the gardener and cook favour herbs rich in aromatic volatile oils, those containing other compounds are often of greater interest to herbalists. Some of the main active constituents found in herbs are:

Acids Sour, often antiseptic and cleansing, e.g. citric acid in *Citrus* species.

Alkaloids Bitter, based on alkaline nitrogenous compounds, grouped into various classes depending on structure, e.g. tropane alkaloids, common in the family Solanaceae. Alkaloids affect the central nervous system, and in excess are extremely toxic.

Bitters Various compounds with a very bitter taste that stimulates the liver and gall bladder, improving appetite and digestion, e.g. *Gentiana lutea*.

Coumarins Antibacterial, anticoagulant, typically with a smell of new-mown hay, e.g. *Melilotus officinalis*. Similar in effect to flavonoids but toxic in excess. Furanocoumarins sensitize skin to sunlight.

Flavonoids Bitter or sweet, anti-inflammatory, antibiotic, and antioxidant. Present in most plants, and typically orange or yellow (as in safflower, *Carthamus tinctorius*), but may also be red-purple anthocyanidins, as in bilberry and blueberry fruits (*Vaccinium* spp.).

Glycosides Four main kinds: cardiac – affecting heart contractions, e.g. *Digitalis* spp.; cyanogenic – bitter, anti-spasmodic, sedative, affecting heart rate and respiration, e.g. *Prunus serotina*; mustard oil – acrid, extremely irritant, e.g. *Sinapis alba*; sulphur – acrid, stimulant, antibiotic, e.g. *Allium sativum*.

Gums and mucilages Bland, sticky or slimy, soothing and softening, e.g. marsh mallow (*Althaea officinalis*).

Quinones Bitter, with anti-bacterial and anti-fungal effects. Anthraquinones are laxative, e.g. *Rheum* species.

Resins Often bound with oils and gums – acrid, astringent, antiseptic, healing, e.g. *Commiphora myrrha*.

Saponins Sweet, stimulant, hormonal; often anti-inflammatory or diuretic; soapy in water, e.g. *Saponaria officinalis*.

Tannins Astringent, often antiseptic, checking bleeding and discharges, e.g. *Potentilla erecta*. They bind with other molecules, helping to detoxify tissues and the digestive system.

Terpenoids Bitter and pharmacologically complex. Often present as saponins (*see above*) or as constituents of volatile oils. Classed according to number of carbon groups (isoprene units): monoterpenoids (two units) as in menthol; sesquiterpenoids (three units), common in the family Asteraceae, e.g. feverfew, *Tanacetum parthenium*; and triterpenoids (six units), e.g. madecassic acid in *Centella asiatica*.

Volatile oils Aromatic, antiseptic, fungicidal, irritant, and stimulant, e.g. *Thymus vulgaris*. Potentially highly toxic when isolated as essential oils.

LEGAL RESTRICTIONS

A number of herbs discussed in this book are potentially dangerous. They are subject to legal restrictions regarding formulation, use, and sale, in three main categories:
• Poisonous therapeutic herbs
• Herbs that may be hazardous as garden plants
• Herbs that have become pernicious weeds outside their country of origin

Restrictions on Therapeutic Use

There are legal restrictions on the use, supply, and sale of many herbs intended for therapeutic use. They may apply to the whole herb, or to specific parts, preparations, or substances derived from it. Some herbs and their extracts are regarded as too toxic for general use and are subject to legislative control. These regulations differ from country to country, and are very complex. Restrictions also concern individuals permitted to prescribe, administer, supply, and sell certain herbs and preparations,

and the permitted doses, concentrations, and preparations. An indication of a restricted herb is shown in the A–Z of Herbs (pp.92–411) by the warning note in the entry concerned; detailed information may be obtained from the appropriate department of your government.

Restrictions on Cultivation

A number of countries have legal restrictions on the cultivation of certain herbs. They concern those plants from which illegal drugs are produced, plus species that have been introduced and have spread widely, becoming weeds and threatening local flora and fauna. Laws and regulations governing dangerous drugs and plants are too complex to detail in this book. Readers are advised to obtain more information from the appropriate regulatory body on any herb that carries a warning after the HARVEST information in the A–Z of Herbs (pp.92–411).

ANCIENT USES *Meadowsweet* (Filipendula ulmaria) *is a herb with very ancient uses besides its medicinal applications. It was one of three herbs sacred in Druid worship, and because of its sweet smell was strewn on floors in the Middle Ages. Meadowsweet contains salicylates that relieve the pain of peptic ulcers, while other constituents protect and heal damaged tissues.*

HERBS IN THE WILD

PEOPLE ALL OVER THE WORLD have picked and uprooted herbs from the wild since ancient times. Of the 250,000 species of flowering plants in the world, more than 20,000 – about 10 per cent of the world total – are recorded as herbs. In addition to flowering plants, other kinds such as mosses, fungi, and seaweeds have herbal uses. Many herbs were taken into cultivation so long ago that they differ significantly from their wild ancestors, having been hybridized for thousands of years. A high

SURINAM RAINFOREST
Tropical rainforests provide rich habitats for plant species with therapeutic properties.

proportion of medicinal herbs have always been harvested from the wild. Knowledge of where certain herbs grow, the best time to gather them, and taboos about harvesting have formed an important oral tradition among healers in many different cultures. These traditions were successful in balancing supply and demand, allowing wild stocks to regenerate. Commercial pressures tend to disrupt this relationship, leading to unregulated harvesting that is unsustainable or habitat loss from development.

CULTIVATION OF GINSENG
The American species, Panax quinquefolius, *being grown commercially in South Korea. This species was introduced in the 18th century to supplement the depleted native* P. ginseng.

The early 20th century brought great optimism that science would conquer disease. In reality, most countries are too poor to benefit fully from medical advances, and they lack the basic infrastructure of reliable supplies of electricity and clean water that is necessary for modern medical services. Some 80 per cent of the world's people still rely on traditional, plant-based medicine for primary health care. This reliance continues to a certain extent in developed countries as well; despite major advances in developing synthetic drugs, plant extracts are still present in a high proportion of Western drugs. Research takes its quota of plants, too, as pharmaceutical companies turn to them in the search for new compounds to treat incurable conditions.

CHANGES IN ATTITUDES TO HERBAL MEDICINE

The most noticeable change in developed countries in the 20th century has, however, been in the interest shown by the ordinary person. From being regarded as "old-fashioned" and distrusted, herbs such as ginseng and guaraná are now hailed as wonder drugs. Change began in the 1960s, when the "hippie" movement advocated a return to more natural living, initiating "alternative" medicine and therapies. The growth of the conservation movement and the establishment of companies using mainly natural products in an environmentally friendly way were also major factors. As a result, an increasingly wide range of herbs is now available fresh, dried, and as ingredients of cosmetics, perfumes, and over-the-counter medicines. Jojoba oil (from *Simmondsia chinensis*) was unheard of 20 years ago; it was promoted as a substitute for sperm whale

RAINFOREST MEDICINE
In the Putomayo River region of Colombia, a brujo *(stem collector) of the Siona tribe is making a ritual drink from* ayahuasca *or* yagé *(Banisteriopsis caapi), mixed with* chagropanga *(Diploterys cabrerana). Ayahuasca is a rainforest vine with potent hallucinogenic, laxative, and emetic effects.*

oil in industrial high-performance lubricants as part of the campaign to save whales, and went on to become a revolutionary new emollient in skin- and hair-care products. Fortunately, the jojoba plant has been micropropagated, but many others are now perilously close to extinction, or so reduced in the wild that only a narrow genetic base remains for regeneration.

SAVING THE PLANTS THAT SAVE LIVES

Protecting herbs from over-exploitation requires international co-operation and a pooling of expertise. Ecologists, horticulturists and plant breeders, health professionals and traditional healers, and policy makers and communicators must all explain the importance of conservation if the message is to reach the public. Protection of plants in the wild may take one or more forms, in which the individual contribution is as important as the commercial or national one.

Conservation *in situ* – reserves and national parks that are established in the regions where species are at risk. Collecting of wild herbs can be strictly controlled, and depleted species reintroduced.

Conservation collections – this may include seed banks, where seed is stored against shortages; cryopreservation (a technique for low-temperature storage of tissues for cell culture); or the establishment of collections of living plants for study and propagation.

Cultivation – whether in the garden or on a commercial scale, cultivation of herbs reduces pressure on wild populations. On a commercial level it encourages plant breeders to improve vigour and quality, and develop techniques for propagation, harvesting, and processing.

PROTECTING WILD HERBS FOR THE FUTURE

Many herbs are protected under one of the following different categories:

Rare – species with very restricted distribution and/or a very small population.

RECORDING THE FLORA
This herbarium (dried plant collection) is owned by a mining company in Linhares Forest Reserve, Brazil. There is pressure on industries to show concern for their environment.

Vulnerable – seriously depleted or under threat from over-collection and/or habitat destruction.

Endangered – in danger of extinction, because remaining populations are too small to breed successfully or to survive further losses.

Extinct – no longer known to exist in the wild.

There are protected plant species that fall within these categories in most countries. Details are available from conservation organizations, botanic gardens, and appropriate government departments. Species that are protected at international level are monitored by the IUCN (International Union for the Conservation of Nature) and are listed in CITES (Convention on International Trade in Endangered Species of Wild Fauna and Flora). CITES is enforced by customs controls and by compulsory documentation of imports and exports. It is further monitored by TRAFFIC (Trade Records Analysis of Flora and Fauna in Commerce), an organization that was established in 1976 to support legislation. The IUCN publishes "Red Data Books" that list and describe the rarest species in particular areas, and these are also freely available to the public.

JOJOBA
The jojoba plant, Simmondsia chinensis, *is native to desert regions of northern Mexico and southwestern United States. It is cultivated on a large scale in the USA and the Middle East for its oil, which is in great demand as an emollient for cosmetic products. As only female plants produce oil-bearing nuts, plants are increased by micropropagation to ensure the optimum ratio of females to males.*

COLLECTING HERBS

Collecting from the wild has a varying impact on plant populations, according to the type of plant sought and the part harvested. Weed species are least at risk, and harvesting a few leaves, fruits, flowers, and seeds from common herbs has a low impact on populations.

Characteristics of Herbs at Risk:
• slow-growing
• low reproduction rate

• naturally few leaves and flowers
• endemic species, with localized distribution

Causes of Damaging Effects:
• whole plant is taken or (in the case of trees especially) cut down for harvesting of any parts
• stripped for bark (bark-ringing usually kills a tree)
• dug up for tubers, rhizomes, or roots

Observe the Law
• Do not pick or uproot protected species. In some countries it is illegal to pick or uproot any wild plant without the landowner's permission, or at all.
• Do not bring plants or seeds into the country without first checking whether it is legal to do so. Most countries have strict quarantine regulations and plant controls to prevent the spread of pests, diseases, and weeds.

NORTH AMERICA

There is an extraordinary range of environments in this huge land mass, from arctic tundra, various kinds of forest and extensive prairies, to semi-desert and subtropical swamps, with the Rocky Mountains and Appalachians running through the west and east respectively. Many of the characteristic landscapes, habitats, and plants of the United States are preserved in an outstanding system of National Parks that was originated by John Muir (1838–1914), an explorer, naturalist, and visionary conservationist who presented the case for saving wilderness areas to Theodore Roosevelt in 1903.

Despite widespread active conservation campaigning and legislation, the United States and Canada are battling against the odds to save their native plants. Here, as elsewhere in the world, urbanization is a major cause of habitat loss; leisure pursuits and removal of wild plants for the herb trade are others. There is also a psychological barrier; both the United States and Canada have a strong pioneering tradition of exploiting natural resources in a land that at first seemed infinitely bounteous.

The majority of important North American medicinal herbs are woodland species and were originally native American remedies. Indigenous uses had little impact on wild populations, involving small amounts and careful use of the resource. As settlers adopted these remedies, commercial collecting began, with dire consequences for many plant populations. Demand for native American herbs was fostered by Shaker communities, who traded

MOUNT RAINIER NATIONAL PARK
Thanks to the excellent system of national parks, the rich forests and alpine meadows that are characteristic of the Cascade Range in the Pacific Northwest are protected and preserved.

WILD HYDRANGEA
The wild hydrangea (Hydrangea arborescens) has long been used in traditional North American medicine as a remedy for kidney disorders. Unfortunately the roots are used, so the shrub is destroyed by harvesting.

NORTH AMERICAN MEDICINE BAG
This medicine bag of the early 1900s contains herbs for a range of ailments. The packaging prevents the herbs from mixing with each other and drying out, and also maintains the air of mystique that surrounds the power of the healer.

extensively in dried herbs and remedies from about 1830 onwards, and by Samuel Thomson's Physiomedical movement, based largely on indigenous medicine, which was taken to Britain by Dr Albert Isaiah Coffin in 1838 and eventually gained some three million followers.

Trees and shrubs account for a high proportion of the plants used in native American medicine and its derivatives, including birches (*Betula* spp.), red cedar (*Juniperus virginiana*), pines (*Pinus* spp.), cascara sagrada (*Rhamnus purshiana*), sassafras (*Sassafras albidum*), sweet gum (*Liquidambar styraciflua*), seven barks (*Hydrangea arborescens*), and arborvitae (*Thuja occidentalis*). Often the bark is harvested, causing terminal injury. Species with a limited distribution, such as *Rhamnus purshiana*, are very vulnerable. A herb marketing guide, published in 1977, stated that "the end of the cascara business in the Northwest is in sight, because every tree stripped is killed...The demand for this bark since 1903 has been a boon to many small farmers and homesteaders in Oregon and Washington."

THREATENED FOREST SPECIES

Plants of the forest floor include several important herbs used both in North America and by herbalists abroad, such as black cohosh (*Actaea racemosa*), goldenseal (*Hydrastis canadensis*), and birthroot (*Trillium erectum*). Trilliums are in great demand, being collected for both the horticultural and herb trades. In most cases it is the roots that are used, so many plants are destroyed during collection. Slow-growing, uncommon species, such as American ginseng (*Panax quinquefolius*), are especially threatened by uprooting. This species was discovered near Montreal in 1716 after a search initiated by Jesuit missionaries who knew the value of ginseng in China. A thriving export trade quickly developed. However, in 1752 a huge quantity of roots was collected out of season and carelessly dried, causing the Chinese to reject the consignment and cease trading. American traders took advantage of the Canadian disaster, and by the 1890s there were such shortages that experiments in cultivation were started – though often of wild-collected roots.

Panax quinquefolius has been on CITES Appendix II since its inception in 1975. Exports of wild-collected plants have fallen greatly, but collecting still goes on in the southern Appalachians, the Ozarks, and the Pacific Northwest, often of scarce species such as *Echinacea angustifolia*, *Sanguinaria canadensis*, and *Rhamnus purshiana*. As long ago as 1913 one herb trader reported that *Hydrastis canadensis* had long been scarce; it was added to CITES Appendix II in 1997.

Today, as in the past, collecting is mostly done by rural people working for wholesale distributors who pay very little. In some cases, wild-collecting threatens other species that are harvested instead. This has happened with wild quinine (*Parthenium integrifolium*), which is taken as an echinacea substitute, and with much rarer *Echinacea* species that have been harvested commercially, in error or deliberately, as substitutes for the main medicinal species, *E. purpurea*, *E. pallida*, and *E. angustifolia*. As a consequence, most echinaceas have become increasingly rare in the wild.

Attempts are made to regulate collection of wild plants; the US National Forests, for example, have lists of plants that may not be collected within their boundaries, and issue permits for others. Fruits of *Serenoa repens* are wild-collected, mostly in Florida, where it is claimed there is no impact on plant populations.

CULTIVATION AS A SOLUTION

Where regulation fails, cultivation will often succeed. Herbs such as *Panax quinquefolius*, *Lobelia inflata*, *Passiflora incarnata*, *Scutellaria lateriflora*, *Echinacea purpurea,* and *E. pallida* are increasingly cultivated.

TRADITIONAL CEREMONY
This 19th-century engraving shows a native American, with a pipe of peace on forked sticks, preparing for a peace ceremony. Herbs would be used on such occasions as much as in medicine.

Some are more difficult; lady's slipper orchids (*Cypripedium* spp.) do not transplant easily and can be raised from seed only in laboratory conditions. Jojoba (*Simmondsia chinensis*) takes three years from seed before male and female plants can be told apart; only female plants yield the oil-rich seeds; and seven females to one male are needed for successful fruiting. Efficient, large-scale cultivation has been achieved through micropropagation of known female and male plants.

CALIFORNIA POPPIES
The California poppy (Eschscholzia californica) *is more familiar as a garden annual than as a herb. Shown here growing in Antelope State Park, California, it is named for that state and is the state's official flower.*

MAJOR HERBS OF THE REGION

Aletris farinosa
UNICORN ROOT
Rhizomes used as a digestive tonic; now endangered in Canada, largely because trail bikes have destroyed most of its sites.

Ceanothus americanus
NEW JERSEY TEA
Used in treating skin cancer by native Americans, and by settlers as a substitute for tea.

Chionanthus virginicus
FRINGE TREE
One of the best remedies for liver and gall bladder disorders.

Eschscholzia californica
CALIFORNIA POPPY
Sedative herb, familiar as a garden annual.

Hamamelis virginiana
WITCH HAZEL
Astringent used in eye lotions, skin toners, and healing creams.

Hydrastis canadensis
GOLDENSEAL
A tonic herb used mainly for digestive and menstrual complaints. Anti-bacterial.

Ledum groenlandicum
LABRADOR TEA
Characteristic shrub of northern forests, used as a substitute for tea during the 18th century.

Lobelia inflata
LOBELIA
A respiratory stimulant and anti-asthmatic, used in cough medicines and anti-smoking mixtures.

Panax quinquefolius
AMERICAN GINSENG
So similar to Korean ginseng (*P. ginseng*) that it is now cultivated in China.

Passiflora incarnata
PASSIONFLOWER
One of the best known herbal tranquillizers.

Phytolacca americana
POKEBERRY
Native American remedy for rheumatism, now important to the pharmaceutical industry for anti-viral compounds, and in the control of water snails that cause schistosomiasis.

Podophyllum peltatum
MAYAPPLE
Source of anti-cancer drugs.

Rhamnus purshiana
CASCARA SAGRADA
Well-known laxative, used as food, medicine, and dye plant by native people.

Sanguinaria canadensis
BLOODROOT
Originally an expectorant. Now valued as a dental plaque inhibitor.

Sassafras albidum
SASSAFRAS
Probably the first American plant drug to reach Europe, c.1560.

Scutellaria lateriflora
VIRGINIA SKULLCAP
Important herbal sedative.

Senna marilandica
WILD SENNA
Native American laxative.

Serenoa repens
SAW PALMETTO
Tonic herb that benefits the prostate gland.

Simmondsia chinensis
JOJOBA
Emollient oil, widely used in cosmetics and lubricants.

Smilax glauca
WILD SARSAPARILLA
Tonic and flavouring for soft drinks.

Thuja occidentalis
ARBORVITAE
Made into anti-rheumatic tea by loggers, now used to treat catarrh and cystitis.

Ulmus rubra
SLIPPERY ELM
Inner bark is used to make a soothing remedy for serious digestive complaints, such as ulcers.

CENTRAL AND SOUTH AMERICA

This vast region is unparalleled in the richness of its flora. Brazil alone has some 55,000 species of flowering plants, compared with about 20,000 in the US (excluding Hawaii), and less than 1450 in the UK. The Amazon region contains the world's largest area of tropical rainforest, renowned for its role in the global ecosystem. Here, it is often said, lies our greatest hope of finding new drugs to combat diseases. In most parts of the world, the main concern is to protect specific plants, but in this vast and complex wilderness, where countless species are yet to be discovered, it is the unknown that needs as much conservation as the known.

SOUTH AMERICAN
RAINFOREST
*This forest in Itatiaia
National Park, in Rio de
Janeiro State, eastern Brazil,
is home to vast numbers of
different plant species.*

Tropical forests of various kinds stretch from lowland Amazonia to the lower slopes of the Andes, the Guiana Highlands, and the Caribbean, through Central America to southern Mexico. Elsewhere there are temperate montane forests, high plateaus, dry woodlands, and grasslands, with a Mediterranean-type climate prevailing through most of Mexico and central Chile, and cool temperate conditions at the southern tip of the continent. Many familiar plants come from the drier regions, including Mexican marigolds (*Tagetes* spp.), sages (such as *Salvia greggii* and *S. hispanica*), and corn (*Zea mays*). The region is also home to some of the world's most important edible and medicinal plants, such as peppers and squashes (*Capsicum* and *Cucurbita* spp.), cocoa (*Theobroma cacao*), and papaya (*Carica papaya*). Some southern South American species have odd affinities: the aromatic *Drimys winteri*, of Chile and western Argentina, is related to the Australian pepper tree (*Tasmannia lanceolata*), indicating that these widely separated regions were

NATIVE AMAZONIAN
*The blowpipe is used for shooting darts tipped with curare,
which paralyzes and kills rapidly (even in tiny amounts) but
leaves the flesh of the animal untainted.*

once a single land mass. In the 16th century, when Europeans began colonizing Central and South America, the region was inhabited by numerous Indian tribes. There were about 1000 tribes in Brazil alone, more than a third of which are now extinct. Surviving tribes that have been studied show a detailed knowledge of the plants in their area. The massive loss of native tribes, plant species, and uniquely rich habitats in these regions is of great concern.

THE DISCOVERY OF MODERN DRUGS

Botanical discoveries in the New World have had a profound impact on world trade and culture. Amerigo Vespucci (c.1454–1512), a Florentine navigator after whom the two continents were named, came across Colombian tribes chewing coca leaves (*Erythroxylum coca*), a practice known from at least 2000BC. The alkaloid cocaine proved a valuable topical anaesthetic, but also a disastrously addictive narcotic drug. It has been estimated that 688,500 hectares (1.7 million acres) of rainforest in Peru alone have been destroyed for coca cultivation since the early 20th century. Curare, containing strychnine, from *Strychnos nux-vomica*, and ipecac (from *Cephaelis ipecacuanha*) were among other early finds, as was quinine (*Cinchona* spp.), a cure for malaria that, ironically, enabled Europeans to survive in the tropics and conquer the people who taught them about it. *Chondrodendron tomentosum*, a rainforest liana, is an ingredient of curare among tribes in Colombia, Peru, and Ecuador. It contains tubo-

curarine, a potent muscle relaxant that plays a vital role in modern surgery; it cannot be synthesized, so the pharmaceutical industry relies on wild-collected plants.

CONSERVATION OF THE RAINFORESTS

Research into the vegetation of Brazil, and its neighbours in the Amazon region, has a deservedly high profile, and there is international pressure to halt destruction of remaining rainforests. No less important is how forest people use the plants in their particular region, which may differ considerably from those encountered by tribes in other areas. Unfortunately, this knowledge forms part of an oral tradition and is fast disappearing as Western medicine is introduced to even the remotest areas. Statistics of rainforest destruction in this part of the world are especially depressing. On the positive side, painstaking work is being done by universities and botanical gardens, often in conjunction with medical institutes and conservation charities, to survey plant resources and set up protected areas and cultivation projects for vulnerable species. Costa Rica was among the first countries in the region to gain widespread support for national parks. Others, such as the Dominican Republic, find that eco-tourism can help make conservation pay. As long ago as 1701, demand for lignum vitae (*Guaiacum officinale*) had so reduced wild stocks that the republic of Martinique listed it as a protected species. Over-collection of the tree for its fine wood and medicinal resin during the 18th and 19th centuries reduced its populations elsewhere, but it is now protected by the Dominican Republic, Guadeloupe, Colombia, Puerto Rico, Costa Rica, El Salvador, and Nicaragua. Research has shown that these slow-growing, long-lived trees are easily grown from seed and adapt to cultivation in many regions.

PAPAYA
The papaya (Carica papaya) *is thought to have originated in Peru. It is valued as a fruit, a remedy for digestive disorders, and as a source of papain for commercial uses.*

MAKING CURARE
Pulping and drying the fruit of Strychnos nux-vomica *to extract the poisonous seeds as an ingredient of curare arrow poison. Alexander von Humboldt (1769–1859) gave the first detailed description of curare, which causes instantaneous muscular paralysis.*

MAJOR HERBS OF THE REGION

Agave americana
CENTURY PLANT
An important fibre, food, and medicinal plant. Industrial leaf waste yields steroid drug precursors.

Anacardium occidentale
CASHEW
Native to Brazil and the Caribbean, but now a major crop throughout the tropics for food, medicinal, and industrial products; bark extracts used by Amazon tribes as a contraceptive.

Bixa orellana
LIPSTICK TREE
Mexican culinary herb, used worldwide as a colorant for foods and cosmetics.

Capsicum species
CHILLI PEPPER
Used for flavouring by the Aztecs and now of global importance as a spice. Also important medicinally, and a key remedy in 19th-century American Physiomedicalism.

Carica papaya
PAPAYA
Source of papain, an enzyme that tenderizes meat and helps digestion of proteins.

Cephaelis ipecacuanha
IPECAC
A potent emetic, which in the correct dose is an excellent expectorant, used in over-the-counter cough remedies.

Chenopodium ambrosioides
WORMSEED
Medicinally used to expel worms, and important in Mexican cooking as the herb epazote.

Cinchona species
PERUVIAN BARK
Source of anti-malarial quinine.

Datura species
THORN APPLE
Rich in tropane alkaloids.

Dioscorea macrostachya
MEXICAN YAM
Source of hormone diosgenin

for oral contraceptives until it was synthesized in 1970.

Erythroxylum coca
COCA
Leaves chewed to relieve fatigue and hunger in S America; alkaloid cocaine extracted for anaesthetics by pharmaceutical industry and as an illegal narcotic by drug dealers.

Guaiacum officinale
LIGNUM VITAE
National flower of Jamaica, endangered species, and fine lumber tree, also famed as a cleansing, tonic herb.

Ilex paraguariensis
MATÉ
Stimulant herb and popular tea in S America, now endangered in the wild.

Peumus boldus
BOLDO
An economically important Chilean tree, used medicinally for liver and gall bladder

complaints, and often added to diet formulas.

Pfaffia paniculata
BRAZILIAN GINSENG
Tonic aphrodisiac, increasingly popular in over-the-counter herbal remedies.

Pilocarpus species
JABORANDI
Source of pilocarpine, used to treat glaucoma.

Pimenta dioica
ALLSPICE
Clovelike spice, grown mainly in Jamaica.

Piscidia piscipula
JAMAICA DOGWOOD
Contains rotenone, a powerful insecticide, and pain-killing compounds. Used locally to stupefy fish, leaving them easy to catch yet safe to eat.

Strychnos nux-vomica
STRYCHNINE
Highly toxic seeds used in curare and rodent poisons, but

with tonic properties in minute, accurately measured doses.

Tabebuia species
PAU D'ARCO
Medicinal bark contains immunostimulant properties.

Theobroma cacao
CACAO
Used to make the Aztec beverage *chocolatl*. Now a universal flavouring and food (cocoa solids); with rich emollient oils (cocoa butter).

Vanilla planifolia
VANILLA
Fermented pods provide alcoholic tinctures for perfumes, as well as one of the world's most popular flavourings.

Zea mays
CORN
Familiar as a staple food, but less well known for its medicinal flowers, which have a soothing, cooling effect, described in Aztec herbals.

EUROPE

The landmass that is called Europe stretches from Arctic regions in the Nordic countries to hot, dry regions bordering on the Mediterranean, and its central areas have a typical continental climate of hot, dry summers and cold winters. With the exception of the Low Countries (The Netherlands, Belgium, and Luxembourg), mountains are a feature of almost every country in the region, with a distinctive flora that has evolved in response to their differences in topography and climate. Plants such as bearberry (*Arctostaphylos uva-ursi*) and juniper (*Juniperus communis*) are found both in Scandinavia and northern North America.

WILD HERBS IN SPAIN
Holm oaks (Quercus ilex) *with Spanish lavender* (Lavandula stoechas)*, growing wild in Spain. The essential oil from the latter is rich in camphor and has insect-repellent properties.*

YELLOW GENTIAN
The yellow gentian (Gentiana lutea) *grows wild in lime-rich meadows above 600m (2000ft) in central and southern Europe. The roots contains bitter glycosides.*

The northern and upland areas of Europe were once clad in evergreen and mixed forests. Large natural woodlands remain in E Europe, but elsewhere most of them have disappeared under the axe and the plough. The now bare landscape of Scotland was until the last few hundred years covered by Caledonian forest, dominated by pines (*Pinus sylvestris*). European woodland trees and shrubs include a number of important herbs, such as beech (*Fagus sylvatica*), oak (*Quercus robur*), alder buckthorn (*Rhamnus frangula*), and small-leafed lime (*Tilia cordata*), which is now rare in the north of its range. There were mixed forests of evergreen oaks, pines, and mastic trees (*Pistacia lentiscus*) in Mediterranean countries before deforestation, erosion, and overgrazing reduced the region to thorny scrubland. Human activity has degraded the vegetation in the area, but the aromatic, drought-resistant maquis that now predominates is home to some of the most widely used herbs in the world – lavender, olive, sage, thyme, savory, oregano, rosemary, and bay.

TRADITIONAL EUROPEAN HERBS
European herbalism is eclectic, derived largely from ancient Greek and Roman traditions, which were in turn influenced by theories and practices from ancient Egypt, Assyria, India, and the Arab world. Herbs from the East therefore took their place long ago beside native European plants in the medicine of the region. Outstanding among European herbs are yellow gentian (*Gentiana lutea*) of alkaline alpine pastures; arnica (*Arnica montana*), an inhabitant of acidic alpine soils; the pasque flower (*Pulsatilla vulgaris*), which thrives on dry, calcareous hillsides; and Cretan dittany

CRETAN DITTANY
This dittany (Origanum dictamnus) *is native to the mountains of Crete. It is also cultivated as a crop and is prized as an ornamental.*

GREATER PLAINTAIN
Though European in origin, greater plantain (Plantago major) *has now spread worldwide. This common weed is valued by herbalists for its anti-bacterial properties.*

MAJOR HERBS OF THE REGION

Aconitum napellus
MONKSHOOD
Extremely poisonous herb, used in homeopathy for shock.

Aesculus hippocastanum
HORSE CHESTNUT
Familiar as an ingredient of shampoos for dark hair, and used medicinally for circulatory problems.

Alchemilla species
LADY'S MANTLE
Herbs used to alleviate disorders of the female reproductive system.

Arnica montana
ARNICA
Healing herb, popular in Germany for heart conditions.

Artemisia absinthium
WORMWOOD
A bitter, aromatic herb, with a tonic effect on the digestive system, traditionally used to flavour alcoholic aperitifs, such as absinthe.

Atropa bella-donna
DEADLY NIGHTSHADE
Source of tropane alkaloids, used in surgical procedures and to control travel sickness.

Borago officinalis
BORAGE
Cucumber-flavoured leaves traditionally added to alcoholic summer drinks; seeds contain oil that helps regulate hormonal functions.

Calendula officinalis
POT MARIGOLD
Soothing, anti-inflammatory herb for digestive and skin problems.

Chamaemelum nobile
CHAMOMILE
Popular tisane, taken as a mild sedative and digestive; also used to lighten fair hair.

Crocus sativus
SAFFRON
The world's most expensive herb by weight; only the stigmas and styles are used.

Digitalis species
FOXGLOVE
Source of cardiac glycosides.

Filipendula ulmaria
MEADOWSWEET
Contains painkilling salicylates and antacids that help heal ulcers.

Common foxglove

Foeniculum vulgare
FENNEL
Like the closely related dill (*Anethum graveolens*), a popular culinary herb that also relieves indigestion.

Gentiana lutea
YELLOW GENTIAN
A very bitter herb, valued for treating gastrointestinal disorders.

Humulus lupulus
HOPS
Sedative medicinal herb, grown worldwide as a flavouring for beers.

Juniperus communis
JUNIPER
Flavouring for gin and useful remedy for cystitis and rheumatism.

Laurus nobilis
BAY
Important flavouring for sweet and savoury foods; an ingredient of bouquet garni.

Lavandula species
LAVENDER
The oil of this classic herb is used in perfumery, aromatherapy, and medicine.

Mentha spicata
SPEARMINT
Clean, refreshing flavour for sweet and savoury foods and for oral hygiene products.

Oenothera biennis
EVENING PRIMROSE
Oil is used to help regulate hormonal functions and to relieve skin problems.

Origanum species
OREGANO
Warm, pungent flavour widely used in Italian and Greek cuisine.

Petroselinum crispum
PARSLEY
Leaves are used as a garnishing and culinary herb; seeds have diuretic effects.

Pimpinella anisum
ANISE
Favourite flavouring for alcoholic drinks in the Mediterranean region.

Rhamnus frangula
ALDER BUCKTHORN
Non-griping laxative.

Salvia officinalis
SAGE
Popular culinary herb, used medicinally for digestive problems and excessive perspiration.

Silybum marianum
MILK THISTLE
Contains silymarin, which detoxifies the liver.

Taraxacum officinale
DANDELION
One of the finest herbal diuretics.

Thymus vulgaris
THYME
Favourite culinary herb and source of thymol, a potent antiseptic used in oral hygiene products.

Urginea maritima
SQUILL
Common ingredient of many cough medicines.

Urtica dioica
NETTLE
A traditional detoxifying herb, rich in minerals and vitamins.

Valeriana officinalis
VALERIAN
Sedative; the roots when dried attract cats.

Vinca major
PERIWINKLE
Source of alkaloids that have hypotensive and vasodilatory effects.

(*Origanum dictamnus*), found wild only in the mountains of Crete. All have specific cultivation requirements and have been over-collected for medicinal use, and as ornamentals. Arnica is rare and protected in many areas, and difficult to grow at low altitudes. Pasque flowers are increasingly rare in the wild due to both over-collection and loss of habitat; they have been greatly reduced in England due to the extensive ploughing up of chalk downland for the commercial production of arable crops.

Saffron (*Crocus sativus*) has been domesticated since the late Bronze Age, probably first on Crete. Most European saffron now comes from Spain, where some 4000 hectares (9884 acres) are under cultivation. Historically, high-quality saffron was grown in cooler parts of Europe, such as Saffron Walden in England, where growers were known as "crokers". The English saffron industry declined after 300 years because of cheap imports, though the lower prices were commonly achieved by adulterating the saffron stigmas with petals from safflower (*Carthamus tinctorius*).

Many herbs are weeds in their own right, and have often been inadvertently introduced to other countries. Some European herbs have become weeds in other parts of the world. These include chickweed (*Stellaria media*), dandelion (*Taraxacum officinale*), shepherd's purse (*Capsella bursa-pastoris*), goosegrass (*Galium aparine*), nettle (*Urtica dioica*), and greater plantain (*Plantago major*).

AFRICA

This vast continent ranges from Mediterranean coastal areas in the north, which were fertile agricultural areas in Roman times, through the harsh, desiccated Saharan and Kalahari deserts to "safari country" – dry savannah, grassland, and open woodland, with short, unreliable rainy seasons. In contrast, central Africa is dominated by equatorial rainforests that extend along the Congo Basin and fringe the W African coast from Cameroon through to the Gambia. Tropical rainforest also occurs on the island of Madagascar, which has been cut off from the mainland so long that it has evolved unique plant and animal species.

CENTRAL AFRICAN LANDSCAPE
Dry woodland covers vast areas of central Africa. Kiaat trees (Pterocarpus angolensis), *important locally for lumber, occur in lowland forest, here in the Chote National Park, Namibia.*

TRADITIONAL COLLECTOR
The modern "witch doctor" (here in Zimbabwe, near the Victoria Falls) protects supplies of wild herbs for his medicines in the same way that his predecessors did. Traditional collecting is restricted by taboos that ensure plants have time to recover and reproduce to ensure future supplies.

In Cape Province, in the extreme south of South Africa, the prevailing pattern of hot, dry summers and winter rain supports one of the richest floras in the world. The Table Mountain massif rises abruptly from the south coast, creating innumerable ecological niches for plants. African rainforests are home to such important medicinal plants as *Catharanthus roseus*, *Physostigma venenosum*, *Rauvolfia vomitoria*, and various species of *Strophanthus* and *Voacanga*, but a surprising number of herbs come from Africa's drylands and montane woodlands, which are equally threatened by urbanization and poor land management. Much of the continent is arid, and dry regions are especially vulnerable to overgrazing, deforestation, and burning, which lead to the spread of deserts and famines. Africa has the highest rate of urbanization in the world, with urban populations doubling every 14 years and yet it is still dependent on wild plants for primary health care.

CULTURAL CHANGES IN TRADITIONAL MEDICINE
Collecting herbs was once a local activity, carried out by traditional healers, known as inyangas (herbalists), sangomas (diviners), and Cape "bossiedokters". Harvesting was governed by age-old codes of practice

– "taboos" – that served to balance resources and demand. Now it has become part of the cash economy, and wild herbs are regarded as "free for all". It has been estimated that 80 per cent of African plants have medicinal uses, and a very high proportion of people in Africa – some 70–80 per cent – rely on plants for their health care. There are, too, some 30 traditional practitioners for every qualified doctor. Whereas traditional herb gathering had little impact on populations of wild plants, commercial collecting can be compared to a swarm of locusts, which damages or kills every specimen in its path. An example is *Harpagophytum procumbens*, which is now traded

ROOIBOS TEA
Plantations of Aspalathus linearis, *the source of rooibos tea, growing in the arid Cedarberg Mountains, in the west of Cape Province. The rooibos tea industry expanded greatly during the Second World War, because of shortages of oriental tea, and following research in the 1980s into its beneficial properties.*

MAJOR HERBS OF THE REGION

Agathosma species
BUCHU
Versatile aromatic herbs, popular in teas for minor ailments, and as insect-repellents.

Artemisia afra
WILDE ALS, WILD WORMWOOD
A favourite African remedy for bronchial and skin complaints.

Aspalathus linearis
ROOIBOS
Desert shrub made into a tea by the Hottentots, now a major crop for caffeine-free drinks.

Catharanthus roseus
MADAGASCAR PERIWINKLE
Alkaloids for cancer chemotherapy, especially childhood leukaemia.

Euphorbia tirucallii
MILK BUSH
Zimbabwean succulent with acrid latex that removes warts, repels mosquitoes, and also yields fuel hydrocarbons.

Harpagophytum procumbens
DEVIL'S CLAW
A veld plant, valued as a remedy for arthritis and digestive problems.

Devil's claw

Hypoxis hemerocallidea
syn. *H. rooperi*
AFRICA POTATO, *INKOMFE*
Tuberous grassland species used as a traditional remedy for prostate problems, urinary infections, and testicular cancer. Contains rooperol, which has shown anti-inflammatory, anti-cancer, and anti-HIV effects in clinical trials.

Pausinystalia johimbe
JOHIMBE
The bark of this West African tree contains johimbine, a potent alkaloid that acts as a sexual stimulant.

Pelargonium species
Favourite ornamental, medicinal, and perfume plants.

Physostigma venenosum
CALABAR BEAN
Source of physostigmine, an alkaloid used in ophthalmology. Seeds were used in "ordeal by poison".

Prunus africana
AFRICAN CHERRY
Multiple-use tree for local people, now internationally important for bark extracts to treat prostate disorders.

Ricinus communis
CASTOR BEAN
Originally from E Africa and best known as a purgative, this shrub is now grown worldwide for products in the paint, paper, and fibre industries.

Strophanthus species
Traditionally used as arrow poison, important now as a source of cardiac glycosides.

Tetradenia riparia
IBOZA
Used to relieve fevers and bronchial infections.

Voacanga africana
Source of drugs used in cerebrovascular disorders.

ALOE PLANT
Aloes are a common feature of African landscapes. There are hundreds of different species, and most have medicinal uses. The southern Cape area was once well known for Cape aloes, extracted from Aloe ferox, *first exported in 1761.*

worldwide; in 1984 commercial collectors harvested 66 per cent of known plants in Botswana for their tubers, a rate that was obviously not sustainable. Local demand can be ruthless, too; *Warburgia salutaris*, a tree related to *Canella winterana*, is regarded in Africa as a cure-all, though it is almost unknown elsewhere. A warning of its decline through bark-ringing and the need for cultivation was made in 1946, but only in the 1990s, with extinction looming, was there any attempt made to protect and cultivate it.

PROBLEMS IN CONSERVATION
One problem in Africa is that conservation areas and botanical gardens suffer the same fate as wild places, with declining medicinal plants almost impossible to establish before being "harvested". As ever, slow-growing species exploited for bark, roots, and bulbs or tubers are most at risk, especially if they have a restricted distribution. Cultivation of herbs in Africa is also thwarted by low prices and poverty, which make it almost impossible to cultivate them as cheaply as they can be collected. There is also a widespread belief that cultivated plants have no "power". As a result, most African herbs still come from the wild, and it is only *in extremis*, when stocks are so depleted, that those concerned – collectors, users, administrators, and scientists – discuss the problems and agree strategies to conserve through cultivation.

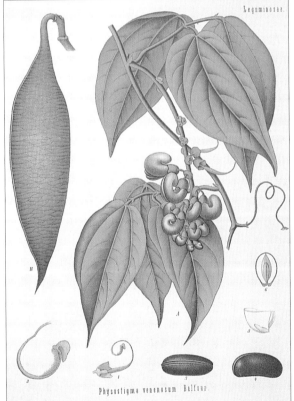
CALABAR BEAN
A plate from Köhler's Medizinal-Pflanzen *of 1888–90, illustrating* Physostigma venenosum. *This tropical climber grows to 15m (50ft) and bears pink, pea-like flowers, as seen here. The brownish-black seeds, shown at the foot of this plate, contain valuable alkaloids.*

THE MIDDLE EAST

Stretching from Northern Africa to Pakistan and Arabia, the Middle East is a region of extremes, with the Hindu Kush, Elburz, and Taurus Mountains to the north, and the arid Syrian Desert and Arabian Peninsula in the centre and to the south. Cool uplands are home to several ancestors of garden roses: the damask rose (*Rosa × damascena*) was long cultivated in Persia before its introduction to Europe by Crusaders returning from the Holy Land. Roses are of supreme importance in Islam; ten tonnes of rosewater are required to wash the walls of the holy city of Mecca during the annual hajj or pilgrimage.

TURKISH PINE
Regarded as a cure-all in Turkish folk medicine, Pinus halepensis *subsp.* brutia *occurs from Turkey to Lebanon and the eastern Black Sea coast.*

DISTILLATION OF ROSE OIL
The distillation process was an invention of early Arab scientists, and most of the world's rosewater still comes mainly from Turkey and Iran.

Western areas of the Middle East (Israel, Lebanon, Syria, and southern Turkey) are similar in climate and vegetation to coastal zones of the Mediterranean in southern Europe and N Africa, with hot dry summers and winter rain. Characteristic shrubs include the olive (*Olea europaea*), fig (*Ficus carica*), myrtle (*Myrtus communis*), and oleander (*Nerium oleander*). Forests of oak and pine once covered much of this area, but thousands of years of deforestation and overgrazing have changed the Middle Eastern landscape and flora.

In desert regions, such as Oman, evergreen *Salvadora persica* grows from cliffs and rocks along coasts and wadis, its bright green foliage surviving only where out of reach of camels. Away from water sources, the land supports drought-resistant frankincense trees (*Boswellia sacra*), myrrh (*Commiphora* spp.), and gum arabic (*Acacia senegal*). Succulents and bulbous plants abound, surviving drought through swollen water-storing foliage and stems. Plants rendered unpalatable by spines or toxins are also common, and where numerous are often indicators of overgrazing.

THE FRUITFUL DESERT

Western Asia and adjoining Mediterranean regions constitute a so-called "Vavilov Centre" – one of the several centres of botanical diversity that have given rise to almost all the world's major crops. Named after the Russian scientist and botanist N.I. Vavilov, who originated the theory in the 1920s, Vavilov Centres consist of only a quarter of the Earth's arable land, but are extremely varied in topography and climate. These "evolutionary cradles" were home to ancient civilizations, such as Assyria (now Iraq), that first

HINDU KUSH MOUNTAINS, AFGHANISTAN
The western continuation of the Himalayas extends more than 800km (500 miles) in northern Pakistan and Afghanistan, from the Dasht-i-Margo (Desert of Death) to the Pamir Knot.

brought edible and medicinal plants into cultivation. Nearly all the world's major crops have a very narrow genetic base, making them prone to epidemics. The conservation of the habitats and plant species within Vavilov Centres is especially important, because the wild ancestors of crop plants contain genes that may prove vital in breeding resistance to pests and diseases. Crops originating in the Middle East include oats, barley, flax, sesame, safflower, cabbages, onions, garlic, alfalfa, grapes, figs, olives, almonds, and pomegranates. All have medicinal uses.

PROGRESS IN CONSERVATION

Reafforestation, and restrictions on trade in endangered bulbous species, are priorities for Middle Eastern countries. Israel has led the way in greening the desert, as part of a pledge made in 1948 when the state was created. Steps are being taken to document the rich floral heritage of the Middle East. The *Flora of Turkey* was completed in 1988, and two other major floras, *Flora Iranica* and *Flora of Arabia*, are in progress. As a result of work on the Arabian flora, the Royal Botanic Garden Edinburgh is involved in a major conservation programme on the island of Socotra. This island off the coast of Yemen has been separated from the mainland for so long that 300 of its c.750 plant species are endemic. Once protected by their isolation, these unique plants are now threatened by development following construction of the island's first major port and airport. The programme will advise the Yemeni government on sustainable development that will safeguard Socotra's delicate dry tropical ecosystem.

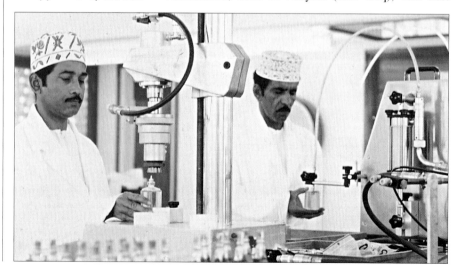

MAJOR HERBS OF THE REGION

Acacia senegal
GUM ARABIC
Resin is used in medicated pastilles and chewing gum, and as a food additive.

Allium cepa
ONION
Food and flavouring, with anti-infective compounds.

Allium sativum
GARLIC
Pungent flavouring and potent antibiotic.

Taking sap from aloe leaves

Aloe perryi
SOCOTRINE ALOE
Purgative, anti-inflammatory sap.

Ammi majus
BISHOPSWEED
Has specific effects on skin pigmentation.

Anethum graveolens
DILL
Important culinary and medicinal herb in the Middle East since biblical times, improving digestion and relieving indigestion.

Astragalus gummifer
TRAGACANTH
Mucilaginous herb, used mainly as a stabilizing and thickening agent.

Boswellia sacra
FRANKINCENSE
Legendary perfume and incense with relaxant, antiseptic, and decongestant effects.

Brassica juncea and *Sinapis alba*
MUSTARD
Pungent spice and condiment, also used externally to stimulate the circulation.

Cannabis sativa
HEMP
Hallucinogenic herb and fibre

plant with analgesic, anti-emetic, and sedative properties.

Carthamus tinctorius
SAFFLOWER
Circulatory stimulant and source of fine cooking oil and dyes; burned to make kohl.

Carum carvi
CARAWAY
Pungent digestive herb, popular in Jewish cuisine, named after Caria, an ancient region of SW Asia.

Catha edulis
QAT, KHAT
Leaves and stems chewed as a stimulant drug, used by Muslim communities worldwide.

Cedrus species
CEDAR
Wood repels insects; oil used in perfumery and aromatherapy.

Commiphora wightii
GUGGUL
Contains unique saponins that lower cholesterol and relieve arthritis.

Commiphora myrrha
MYRRH
Potent antiseptic used in oral hygiene products.

Coriandrum sativum
CORIANDER
One of the oldest known herbs, cultivated for over 3000 years; leaves and seeds have quite different aromas.

Cuminum cyminum
CUMIN
Characteristic flavour in Middle Eastern dishes; used in Ayurvedic medicine to improve liver function.

Ferula assa-foetida
ASAFOETIDA
Unpleasant-smelling gum resin

Frankincense resin

Henna powder

and much used in Arab medicine and ritual.

Prunus dulcis
ALMOND
Source of sweet, emollient, laxative oil, and bitter oil for food flavouring.

Punica granatum
POMEGRANATE
Fruits made into cordial (grenadine) and syrup for flavouring Middle Eastern

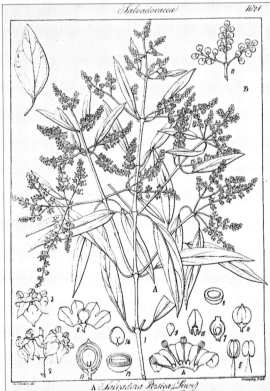

Cedar of Lebanon

gives characteristic flavour to curries and Worcestershire sauce.

Ficus carica
FIG
Probably Arabian in origin, valued medicinally for its prolific, gently laxative fruits.

Lawsonia inermis
HENNA
Powdered henna yields a red dye for hair, skin, and nails.

Medicago sativa
ALFALFA
Detoxicant, diuretic herb, best known in the form of sprouted seeds for salads.

Morus nigra
BLACK MULBERRY
Multi-purpose tree with edible fruits, medicinal properties, and industrial uses.

Papaver somniferum
OPIUM POPPY
The world's most important painkiller.

Peganum harmala
SYRIAN RUE
Source of Turkey red dye for tarbooshes (men's caps),

dishes; medicinally used to expel tapeworms.

Rosa × *damascena*
DAMASK ROSE
Oil and extracts used in perfumery, cosmetics, and food flavouring.

Salvadora persica
TOOTHBRUSH TREE
Roots used for dental hygiene; seeds are "mustard seeds" of the New Testament parable.

Sesamum indicum
SESAME
Source of oil, paste, and seeds, used especially in Middle Eastern dishes.

Trachyspermum ammi
AJOWAN
Bitter seeds with a thyme-like aroma, used in Middle Eastern cuisine (especially with breads and legumes).

Trigonella foenum-graecum
FENUGREEK
Important in Middle Eastern cuisine and spice mixes.

Vitis vinifera
GRAPE
Ancient culinary and medicinal uses.

Toothbrush tree

THE INDIAN SUBCONTINENT

Mountainous regions are nearly always rich in plant life, being relatively inaccessible and providing an array of habitats as contours and altitude change. The Indian subcontinent has the world's highest mountain range, the Himalayas, home to some 9000 plant species, and extensive tropical ranges, such as the Western Ghats, with about 1500 endemic species. Rainforest and rugged mountains continue in Sri Lanka; 30 per cent of species on the island are endemic, notably cinnamon (*Cinnamomum verum*), which has been traded since biblical times.

WOODFORDIA FRUTICOSA
Woodfordia *flowers are used in many Ayurvedic remedies, especially for dysentery and liver diseases.*

COLLECTING CARDAMOM
The capsules ripen during the dry season and are either sun-dried on mats, which takes about five days, and produces a superior, whiter product, or dried with hot-air machines in two days.

As in China, traditional medicine in the Indian subcontinent has an ancient history, with written texts dating from c.2500BC. The system of medicine is known as Ayurveda (literally, "life knowledge") and uses some 600 indigenous herbs. Unani and Siddha systems are similarly dependent on many local plants, as are India's hundreds of tribal groups. Some 200 species are in common use, many of them trees from the rich forests of the region: kino, or bastard teak (*Pterocarpus marsupium*); neem (*Azadirachta indica*); and various myrobalans (*Phyllanthus emblica*, *Terminalia bellirica*, and *T. chebula*). Myrobalan fruits are key ingredients of a rejuvenative tonic, known as the *triphala*, which is a recurrent combination in Tibetan medicine as well. *Terminalia arjuna*, a heart tonic, is also commonly used, as is sandalwood (*Santalum album*). Though originally from SE Asia, sandalwood is naturalized in parts of India and Sri Lanka, and is central to Hindu practices and traditional medicine.

ENDANGERED SPECIES

More medicinal plant species are endangered in this region than in any other. One of the most threatened is *Saussurea costus*, a thistle-like alpine, found in the

HIMALAYAN FOOTHILLS IN NEPAL
These steep hillsides were once forested, protecting watersheds and influencing rainfall. Now terraced for food cultivation, they are subject to problematic flash floods and erosion.

Himalayas from Pakistan to Himachal Pradesh, and used in both Ayurvedic and Chinese medicine. Another is *Rauvolfia serpentina*, a small woodland shrub, already well known in 1563, when a Portuguese account published in Goa described it as "the foremost and most praiseworthy Indian medicine". In both these species the roots are used, which means destroying the plants. India has banned their export, and both species are so rare in the wild from over-collection that they are protected by international legislation. Shortages of *Rauvolfia serpentina* have led to intensive efforts to cultivate it for the pharmaceutical industry, and inevitably also to the exploitation of at least four other *Rauvolfia* species, which may be threatened in their turn by over-collection.

Protection by international legislation is also given to the Indian mandrake (*Podophyllum hexandrum*) and Himalayan yew (*Taxus wallichiana*), both of which provide anti-cancer drugs, and to the Himalayan yam (*Dioscorea deltoidea*), which has the highest steroid content of any yam. All have been over-collected for the pharmaceutical industry. Excessive local demand has endangered red sandalwood (*Pterocarpus santalinus*), an anti-diabetic and colouring agent, spikenard (*Nardostachys jatamansi*), which has a restricted distribution on Himalayan slopes, and *kutki*

(*Picrorhiza kurrooa*), a bitter tonic popular in Ayurvedic and Unani medicine. The last two were given international protection in 1997.

Increasingly scarce in some areas, *Gloriosa superba* is endangered in Bangladesh. Its flame-like lilies were first seen in the West in 1690, since when it has been in great demand as an ornamental, and more recently as a source of colchicine.

CONSERVATION AND CULTIVATION WORK

India, Bangladesh, and Sri Lanka give priority to research programmes concerning the distribution, abundance, uses, and efficacy of medicinal plants, and are aiming to increase conservation and cultivation. There has been an all-India survey of the many hundreds of tribal groups, and monitoring units for medicinal plants are set up in each state under the Ministry of Health and Family Welfare. It has been estimated that 90 per cent of medicinal herbs used in India are wild-collected.

To reduce pressures on wild plants, the Foundation for the Revitalization of Local Health Traditions (FRLHT) has established more than 30 community projects for the conservation, cultivation, and propagation of herbs. Sri Lanka has an integrated health policy of traditional (Ayurvedic) and Western medicine, and established a Ministry of Indigenous Medicine in 1980. Areas for conservation and cultivation are well advanced; botanical gardens grow many of the 600 native medicinal plants; in addition, some 400 Forest Reserves and 50 Protected Areas have localized reservations for medicinal plants.

GRINDING MUSTARD SEEDS IN JAISALMER
Indian mustard (Brassica juncea) *is a common crop in the Indian subcontinent. It is increasingly important as an ingredient of French mustard, replacing* B. nigra.

MAJOR HERBS OF THE REGION

Andrographis paniculata
Controls bacillary dysentery.

Berberis species
DARUHARIDRA
Main remedy for diarrhoea and dysentery.

Centella asiatica
GOTU KOLA
Key rejuvenative herb in Ayurvedic medicine.

Cinnamomum verum
CINNAMON
Important culinary spice, traded since earliest times.

Commiphora wightii
GUGGULU
Source of myrrh, now exploited for cholesterol-lowering saponins.

Coptis teeta
Important detoxicant and anti-pyretic, often used as a substitute for the equally rare *C. chinensis*.

Coscinium fenestratum
CALUMBA WOOD
A bitter tonic in Ayurvedic medicine, and source of an anti-tetanus drug.

Dioscorea deltoidea
YAM
This small Himalayan species is exceptionally rich in steroidal saponins.

Elettaria cardamomum
CARDAMOM
Seeds are characteristic of Indian desserts.

Gloriosa superba
FLAME LILY
Highly toxic roots contain colchicine, used to treat gout and in genetic engineering.

Jasminum sambac
ARABIAN JASMINE
A sacred Hindu flower, grown all over the subcontinent for its perfume and to flavour tea.

Indian mandrake

Nardostachys grandiflora
SPIKENARD
Aromatic roots yield perfume oil, traded since biblical times.

Nelumbo nucifera
SACRED LOTUS
A tonic for heart energy in Ayurvedic medicine.

Phyllanthus emblica
AMALAKI
Astringent fruits used in Ayurvedic tonics.

Picrorhiza kurrooa
KUTKI
Important Ayurvedic tonic for the liver.

Piper nigrum
PEPPER
The most widely used spice.

Plantago indica
BLACK PSYLLIUM
A bulk laxative and anti-inflammatory.

Podophyllum hexandrum
INDIAN MANDRAKE
Himalayan woodland plant with valuable anti-tumour compounds.

Rauvolfia serpentina
INDIAN SNAKEROOT
Source of alkaloids for sedatives and hypertension.

Santalum album
SANDALWOOD
Aromatic oil used in Ayurvedic medicine,

aromatherapy, perfumery, and incense.

Saussurea costus
COSTUS, KUTH
Perfumery and medicinal herb, important in both Ayurvedic and Chinese medicine.

Swertia chirata
CHIRETTA
Himalayan gentian-like plant with bitter, digestive properties.

Terminalia species
MYROBALAN
Fruits are used in Ayurvedic and Tibetan medicine for their rejuvenative properties.

Withania somnifera
ASHWAGANDHA
The "ginseng" of Ayurvedic medicine.

Woodfordia fruticosa
Flowers yield a liver remedy, a tragacanth-like gum, and dye.

CHINA AND ITS NEIGHBOURS

The vastness of China is legendary; its sheer size is encapsulated in the phrase "for all the tea in China". One-fifth of the world's human population lives there, and ten per cent of all known plant species are found in the country's wide range of habitats. These range from tundra, deserts, and grasslands to forests of every description – coniferous, bamboo, oak, rich deciduous woodlands, and tropical rainforest. Of the 35,000 species of plants growing in these varied habitats, some 5000 are used in traditional Chinese medicine, which yield 634,900 tonnes of raw materials annually and provide 40 per cent of all China's medication.

HERBS IN FOLKLORE
The Chinese goddess Ma-kou, with her basket of medicinal plants, from Henri Doré's Recherches sur les superstitions en Chine, *1918.*

Written records of medical knowledge in China began over 2000 years ago. In the early 20th century, the wisdom of these ancient remedies was questioned, and during the Kuomintang era practitioners of traditional Chinese medicine were marginalized. As advances in chemistry took place, Chinese scientists began to isolate the chemical compounds in herbs, leading to the discovery of ephedrine, from *Ephedra sinica*. In 1949, with the establishment of the People's Republic of China, traditional medicine once again received official recognition. Evidence gained in the 1950s convinced the authorities that to provide an effective health system for the entire population, China should combine Western medicine with traditional methods, which were cheaper and more readily available. As a consequence, colleges of traditional Chinese medicine were established by Mao Tse-tung, training both graduates in Western medicine and paramedics

CHINA'S SPECTACULAR LIMESTONE PINNACLES
An extraordinary landscape, at Yangshou in central China. Every kind of plant habitat can be found in China from the vast Plateau of Tibet and mountains in the north to tropical Hainan.

("barefoot doctors") to serve the rural population. In addition, scientific research began to give equal prominence to Chinese herbs and Western-style drugs.

CULTIVATION OF MEDICINAL HERBS

Integrating traditional with Western medicine had the effect of increasing the demand for herbs. In order to meet demand, when in fact supplies were diminishing through loss of habitats and over-collection, China pioneered a national programme of medicinal plant cultivation. Some 324,000 ha (800,000 acres) were devoted to herbs, controlled by the Chinese Crude Drugs Company in each province. Greatest demand is for *Angelica polymorpha* var. *sinensis*, *Atractylodes macrocephala*, *Cinnamomum cassia*, *Coptis chinensis*, *Paeonia suffruticosa*, *Panax ginseng*, *P. pseudoginseng* var. *notoginseng*, and *Rehmannia glutinosa*. Some herbs are inherently more difficult to cultivate than others. Success in cultivating fungi, such as *Wolfiporia cocos*, and the saprophytic orchid *Gastrodia elata*, is a considerable achievement.

THE GROWING DEMAND FOR GINSENG

The best-known Chinese herb is undoubtedly ginseng. This ancient Taoist tonic herb has featured in Chinese formulas for over 3000 years. It was known in Europe from the 9th century onwards, notably when presented to Louis XIV (1638–1715) by the King of Siam, but became widely used in the West only as a result of Soviet research into "adaptogens" during the 1950s. *Panax ginseng*, a slow-growing woodland perennial with a very limited natural distribution, was near-

MARITIME HARVEST
Seaweed (Gelidium amansii) *being collected off the coast of Japan, to be dried for use in the pharmaceutical and food industries.*

extinct in the wild by the 19th century, and collection was forbidden during the reign of Tao Kuang (1821–51). Scarcity of Chinese ginseng prompted the discovery of American ginseng (*Panax quinquefolius*) in the 18th century. The latter has been imported from Canada and the USA ever since, and is now cultivated in China using tissue culture.

ORNAMENTAL CHINESE HERBS

Some Chinese herbs are popular garden plants, introduced to cultivation in the West by missionaries and explorers from the 18th century onwards. Fruits of the familiar forsythia are an important remedy for acute infections, often combined with the flowers and stems of Japanese honeysuckle (*Lonicera japonica*). Peonies have been cultivated in China for 1000 years as favourite flowers of the emperors, and for their medicinal roots. When Western plant collectors searched for tree peonies (*Paeonia suffruticosa*) in China at the beginning of the 20th century, they found few remaining in the wild. The British plant hunter Reginald Farrer found wild plants on only one hillside in Kansu in 1914, and it was not until 1925, when more were found by the American collector, Dr Joseph Rock, that seeds were collected. He sent the seeds to the Arnold Arboretum in Boston, which some years later returned seed to him in China so that he could re-establish peonies in the wild.

One of China's most distinctive species is *Ginkgo biloba*, the sole survivor of a large group of plants that was wiped out during the last ice age, 160 million years ago. Known in China as a sacred tree around Buddhist temples, it was introduced to the West in 1727, where it gained fame as a "living fossil". Though long thought to be extinct in the wild, ginkgos have in fact been found in two remote areas of China. Fortunately, ginkgos are very easily cultivated, and popular as ornamentals worldwide.

THE ASIAN RHUBARB TRADE

Purgatives were once regarded as cure-alls, and far more important in medicine than they are today. The borderlands between China and Russia are home to medicinal rhubarbs (*Rheum* spp.), which have an ancient history. Dried rhubarb roots have been traded overland across Asia and Europe since earliest times. Names were given to rhubarbs – Turkey, Russian, Chinese, East Indian – referring to the route taken, rather than to the origin of the species or roots. Live plants were unknown in the West until the 18th century due to Chinese and Russian trade monopolies. After seed was introduced to European botanical gardens in about 1750, large areas were devoted to the cultivation of medicinal rhubarb.

JAPANESE KAMPO MEDICINE

Chinese medicine reached Japan in AD400 and was known as *kampo* from *kan*, the word for ancient China, and *po*, medicine. The first written account, *Ishimpo*, by Yasuyori Tamba, appeared in the 10th century and was largely derived from Chinese texts, but over the centuries *kampo* was absorbed into Japanese culture to become a unique system. In the Meiji era (1868–1912), European medicine increased in influence and *kampo* fell into decline. The revival began in 1950 with the founding of the Japan Society for Oriental Medicine. In

TRADITIONAL CHINESE MEDICINE
Weighing out remedies in Yunnan, China. Traditional procedures are combined with Western practices.

1967 the first four kampo formulas were approved as prescription drugs, and another 42 formulas were added over the next decade.

All *kampo* preparations are now available through National Health Insurance and more than 75 per cent of Japanese physicians use a combination of Western and *kampo* medicine, depending on the patient. Although most of the herbs used in *kampo* would be familiar to a Chinese herbalist, they are dispensed in traditional formulas, rather than according to a practitioner's presciption. The method of diagnosis is also different, based on *sho*, a system of four procedures: observation; listening; questioning; and palpation. Standards for cultivation, harvesting, and processing of *kampo* herbs are extremely high, as are research facilities devoted to quality control and clinical investigations.

MAJOR HERBS OF THE REGION

Angelica polymorpha var. **sinensis**
CHINESE ANGELICA, DANG GUI
Major tonic for women.

Artemisia annua
QING HAO
Effective anti-malarial drug.

Cinnamomum camphora
CAMPHOR
Used in moth repellents and liniments.

Dioscorea nipponica
YAM
Commercial source of steroidal compounds.

Eleutherococcus senticosus
SIBERIAN GINSENG
Substitute for rarer ginsengs.

Ephedra sinica, E. equisetina
EPHEDRA, MA HUANG
Source of ephedrine; helps relieve bronchial congestion.

Ginkgo biloba
Contains unique flavonoids that improve circulation to the brain.

Glycyrrhiza uralensis
LICORICE
Tonic, harmonizing herb, used in almost all Chinese formulas.

Mentha arvensis var. **piperascens**
JAPANESE PEPPERMINT
Major source of menthol, used in oral hygiene products.

Paeonia lactiflora
PEONY
Circulatory tonic and remedy for childhood eczema.

Panax ginseng
GINSENG
Archetypal adaptogenic herb.

Rheum species
RHUBARB
Important laxative herbs.

SOUTHEAST ASIA

Until recently, most of SE Asia was covered in dense tropical rainforests, which were rich in lumber trees and the source of some of the world's most important spice plants; both nutmeg and cloves, for example, originated in the Moluccas ("Spice Islands"). The creeping, aromatic rhizomes of the ginger family are common on the rainforest floor. A number of other plant families, important for their medicinal uses, have their greatest diversity of species in this region, including the Apocynaceae, a source of cardiac and tranquillizing alkaloids.

NUTMEG AND MACE
Nutmeg and mace come from Myristica fragrans, *a SE Asian tree originally found in tropical rainforests that have now largely been destroyed.*

The rate of trees being cut from rainforest is, however, by no means balanced by their natural regeneration, though species vary greatly in their vulnerability to harvesting. In SE Asia, for example, *Aquilaria malaccensis* is found only in primary forest and is nowhere abundant. It is felled for its resinous wood, but this varies considerably in quality, and, of the great many trees that are felled in the process, some yield little or nothing, and stumps rarely resprout. Severe depletion of populations has occurred in many forests. By contrast, *Melaleuca leucadendra* grows in disturbed areas, forming dense stands, and is widely cultivated, resprouting readily when felled for oil extraction. Threatened tree species such as *Aquilaria malaccensis* are an urgent priority for conservation.

RAINFOREST INTERIOR
Irreplaceable tropical rainforests, such as this one in Vietnam, are increasingly at risk from agricultural and urban development.

PROTECTING THE ENVIRONMENT

Like many developing countries, Indonesia has a rising population, with a corresponding loss of habitats, especially of tropical rainforest, through urban development, agricultural expansion, and mining. As a result, there are serious shortages of herbs both for traditional medicine (known as *jamu*) and for an enlarging export market in pharmaceutical materials. The hundreds of widely scattered islands that make up Indonesia present a considerable challenge for programmes of conservation, cultivation, and education. Various nature reserves and living collections of medicinal and industrial plants have been established, and the Department of Health is encouraging the cultivation of herbs in gardens for home use.

REVIVING TRADITIONAL MEDICINE

The flora of SE Asia is one of the richest on Earth, numbering more than 35,000 species. There are 8000 species in Malaysia alone, of which some 1230 are used medicinally. Most parts of SE Asia have nevertheless been strongly influenced by Chinese medicine, which uses herbs of Chinese origin. Towards the end of the 20th century, conservation issues focused attention on national plant resources and generated interest in utilizing them better and documenting the knowledge of largely oral traditions. Thailand's policy is to make traditional remedies available throughout the country, especially in rural areas where medical services are limited. Drug co-operatives have been set up in 45,000 villages, with 1000 villages involved in cultivating about 50 of the most commonly used medicinal plants. The hill tribes of northern Thailand, many of which are refugees from Burma and Laos, have invaluable knowledge of plant life in the Golden Triangle, which should be preserved at all costs.

There has been a resurgence of interest in indigenous herbs in Malaysia, too, following a government-backed initiative in 1998 to research and develop the medicinal plant industry. Traditional Malay herbs include important tonics for men and women, such as the slender rainforest tree known as *tongkat ali* (*Eurycoma longifolia*), a male aphrodisiac, and *kacip fatimah* (*Labisia pumila*), which is taken after childbirth to contract the uterus.

In response to recommendations from the World Health Organization (WHO), traditional medicine in Indochina is being promoted and scientifically investigated. Several important books were published in the 20th century, including *Medicinal Plants of Vietnam, Cambodia, and Laos* (Nguyen van Duong, 1993). Vietnamese folk medicine has an exceptional history. The first Vietnamese pharmacopoiea (*Thuóc nam*), describing some 650 indigenous herbs, was written in the 14th century. Another major work is the 66-volume *Y ton Tam Linh*, which was published in the 18th century. During the Second World War, when supplies of quinine (see *Cinchona*, p.169) were cut off, malaria patients in Vietnam were successfully treated with extracts of *Dichroa febrifuga*, a common shrub that has been used as an anti-malarial in the region for many thousands of years.

REGIONAL FLAVOURS

The distinctive character of SE Asian cuisine is based on herbs and spices that for the most part are native to the region. As more and more people enjoy Thai, Malaysian, and Vietnamese food, these are becoming more familiar. Many supermarkets now stock fresh ginger (*Zingiber officinale*), lemon grass (*Cymbopogon citratus*), and galangal (*Alpinia galanga*). Chillies (*Capsicum* spp.) are such a vital ingredient that it is hard to believe that they were introduced from South America only 300 years ago. There are numerous varieties known as 'Thai Hot', characteristically bearing narrow, pointed, very pungent fruits.

Less well known are the large, strap-shaped leaves of pandan (*Pandanus amaryllifolius*), a common herb in Thai and Malaysian gardens and markets. Sections of leaf are added to rice when cooking, pounded or raked with the tines of a fork to flavour cakes and desserts, or used to wrap morsels of meat, frequently in the form of miniature baskets, before being fried.

The ginger family, Zingiberaceae, has its centre of distribution in tropical Asia, and is rich in aromatic species that are little known elsewhere. Resurrection lilies (*Kaempferia* spp.) are small, low-growing plants with camphor-scented rhizomes, which are crushed and added to various dishes, especially fish curries. The leaves are finely sliced in salads. Another unusual ginger is Chinese key or *krachai*

(*Boesenbergia pandurata*). The long, finger-like roots are an especially popular flavouring for soups and curries in Thailand.

Some Vietnamese who fled their country in the 1970s and 1980s took herbs with them. Some 20–30 different ones are grown by Vietnamese communities in the United States for use in home cooking and restaurant menus. Unusually, the majority are used raw, gathered immediately before the meal as garnish or salad, and eaten in large sprigs, rather than chopped. They include Vietnamese coriander or *rau răm* (*Persicaria odorata*) and young leaves of wild pepper or *lá lót* (*Piper lolot*).

TRADITIONAL MEDICINE
A Beluga-Kenyah tribesman in Borneo, Sarawak, gathers a rainforest herb to soothe and heal wounds. The practice of traditional medicine is dying out in many tribal areas as people turn to Western medicine and ways of life change. These ancient traditions are quickly lost unless the younger generation shows interest in learning.

A CHILLI SELLER IN PAKXÉ, LAOS
Though South American in origin, and introduced to SE Asia only 300 years ago, chilli peppers (Capsicum spp.) are now a vital ingredient of both commercial and domestic cuisines in Laos and other parts of the region.

MAJOR HERBS OF THE REGION

Alpinia galanga
GALANGAL
Gingerlike flavouring.

Aquilaria malaccensis
EAGLEWOOD
Tonic herb and flavouring for Malaysian curries.

Cananga odorata
YLANG-YLANG
The "queen of perfumes".

Croton tiglium
PURGING CROTON
Drastic purgative.

Hydnocarpus kurzii
CHAULMOOGRA
Unique oil used for skin diseases, such as leprosy.

Cananga odorata

Melaleuca leucadendra
CAJUPUT
Antiseptic oil used in cough

medicines, soaps, and aromatherapy.

Myristica fragrans
NUTMEG AND MACE
Both spices are used worldwide.

Strychnos nux-vomica
STRYCHNINE
Deadly poison; stimulant in minute amounts.

Styrax benzoin
BENZOIN
Ingredient of friar's balsam.

Syzygium aromaticum
CLOVES
Important spice, and cure for toothache.

AUSTRALASIA

The plant life of Australasia owes its character to the region's ancient geological history, when part of the southern continental mass of Gondwanaland collided with the landmass of Laurasia to the north of it. This joined what is now known as New Guinea and the islands to the north of Australia with a land bridge that permitted movement of plant and animal species. The area of interchange, known as Wallace's Line, runs between Borneo and Sulawesi in SE Asia, and explains some odd distributions in the plant life of these regions.

ARID LANDSCAPE
White gum trees and red rocks, Hamersley Ranges, Western Australia. This deceptively barren land supports a rich flora, including some 450 species of eucalyptus.

The rich variety of Australian plant life has provided food and healing plants for thousands of years. It is characterized by species that have adapted to increasing aridity; much of Australia is subject to bushfires, and many plants have developed oils and resins to encourage a rapid burning of aerial parts that leaves woody tissues and underground parts unharmed. Eucalyptus trees, whose oils and resins are of major importance in medicine and industry, are a prime example. Species of this genus in northern tropical parts of Australia have lower oil and resin contents than those in the south, and so are largely replaced in Aboriginal medicine by tea trees (*Melaleuca* spp.).

ABORIGINAL USE OF HERBS

The early Aboriginal people of Australia were hunters and gatherers who lived in an extraordinary range of environments, from the tropical north and harsh interior deserts to relatively cool and moist, coastal southern parts where there are lush forests of tree ferns. They travelled vast distances on foot, and in the process acquired an intimate knowledge of the land and its plants, on which their lives depended.

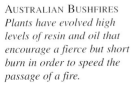

AUSTRALIAN BUSHFIRES
Plants have evolved high levels of resin and oil that encourage a fierce but short burn in order to speed the passage of a fire.

Their uses of native plants are poorly documented, as many oral traditions were lost before records could be made. It is known, however, that a very wide range of herbs – some 150 different species – were used just to treat inflamed wounds and eyes, which can worsen rapidly in hot climates. Both native people and early settlers made extensive use of eucalypt gum, or kino, to control infections, bleeding, and diarrhoea. The vast distances travelled by Aboriginal people are traditionally eased by the chewing of *pituri*, which can be likened to tobacco in effects and, coincidentally, is made from plants of the nightshade family

(Solanaceae), notably *Duboisia hopwoodii*, that also contain the alkaloid nicotine. *Pituri* relieves hunger and increases endurance on long journeys. Its pain-numbing effects are also utilized during the circumcision of boys in initiation rituals.

BUSHFOODS

When early European settlers arrived in Australia, they were confronted by very different plants from those in Europe. As a result, they gave familiar names to any plant that resembled those back home, so today there are desert raisins, bush potatoes and bananas, native cherries, pears, and plums that are unrelated to their namesakes. They brought seeds of favourite edible and medicinal plants, many of which did so well that they escaped from cultivation and became established in the wild. By trying out the new, and introducing the old, Australians today have a rich heritage of herbal plants, and one of the finest cuisines to be found in the world.

In the 1990s, nutritional research into native foods and flavourings at the University of Sydney gave rise to the bushfoods industry. The new industry prompted research into the cultivation, selection, and breeding of native food plants, and pioneered the planting of native species on farmland that had previously grown introduced crops. It grew rapidly: the first Australian Native Bushfood Conference was held in Brisbane in 1996, and soon bush flavours and foods, with their evocative Aboriginal names, were available on all continents. More widely, it stimulated interest in indigenous culture, native plants, and their ecosystems.

MAORIS AND POLYNESIANS

Research into Maori uses of herbs shows that native species such as New Zealand flax (*Phormium tenax*) and manuka (*Leptospermum scoparium*), now familiar worldwide as ornamentals, were used in a wide range of remedies, including those for gunshot wounds. Herbal medicines were administered by the Tohunga, who was both doctor and spiritual leader. Rituals and vapour baths were an integral part of the healing process. New Zealand's plants have little in common with those of Australia (there are no eucalypts or melaleucas, for example). In northern parts they resemble those of SE Asia, while central regions are temperate, and the cool, wet southern zone has many unique alpine species.

The Polynesian islands were the last places on Earth to be settled; migrants first came from Asia about 1000BC, reaching the Hawaiian islands in about AD400. The most important plant sustaining these settlers was taro (*Colocasia esculenta*), of which there are over 1000 varieties. Migrations of people across the Pacific can be traced through the genetics of this ancient crop plant. It became the staple food on many islands and was used widely for medicinal purposes, treating everything from boils to heart complaints.

CONTROLLING ALIEN SPECIES

Native species in Australia and New Zealand are threatened by the introduction of plants from elsewhere. Both countries have strict regulations governing the import of seeds and plants, and enforce control of established exotics. Serious alien weeds include herbs such as fennel (*Foeniculum vulgare*), horehound (*Marrubium vulgare*), and pennyroyal (*Mentha pulegium*).

MAJOR HERBS OF THE REGION

Abrus precatorius
JEQUIRITY
Tropical northern species, used by Aboriginals as body ornaments; and cure for trachoma (sandy blight).

***Acacia* species**
WATTLE
Floral emblem of Australia, source of tanbark, and traditional remedy for diarrhoea.

Acronychia acidula
LEMON ASPEN
Greenish-yellow, grape-sized fruits have a strong, very tart, lemon–eucalyptus flavour. About 20 lemon aspen fruits equal six lemons.

Acronychia oblongifolia
SOUTHERN LEMON ASPEN, YELLOW WOOD
Similar to lemon aspen but grows in cooler forests, in Victoria and New South Wales.

Apium prostratum
SEA CELERY
Coastal, parsley-like plant. Shiny, slightly succulent leaves and stems resemble celery in flavour; var. *filiforme* is best.

Atriplex nummularia
OLD MAN SALTBUSH
Rich source of vitamin C, used by settlers to cure scurvy.

***Backhousia* species**
MYRTLES
Lemon myrtle (*B. citriodora*) has lemon-scented leaves, flowers, and seeds. Used fresh or dried, often powdered.

Leaves of aniseed myrtle (*B. anisata*) can be used to give anise-like flavours, and nutmeg myrtle (*B. myrtifolia*) has nutmeg-flavoured leaves.

Capparis canescens
NATIVE CAPER
Fruits contain mustard oils and can be used as a substitute for mustard.

Colocasia esculenta
TARO
Staple food and all-purpose medicine of many Oceanic islands, notably in the Hawaiian group.

Dodonaea viscosa
STICKY HOP BUSH
Astringent leaves chewed for toothache and put on stings.

***Duboisia* species**
CORKWOOD
Known to Aboriginals as *pituri*, a narcotic stimulant chewed on long journeys, now an important source of tropane alkaloids for the pharmaceutical industry.

Eremocitrus glauca
WILD LIME, DESERT LIME, NATIVE KUMQUAT
Fruits resemble miniature limes in appearance and flavour. Ten wild limes equal one West Indian lime.

***Eucalyptus* species**
GUM TREE
Rich in resinous, tannin-rich kino, long used as a healing astringent, and aromatic oils now used worldwide in cough

medicines, cold remedies, and liniments.

Melaleuca alternifolia
TEA TREE
Oil used as an antibacterial and anti-fungal treatment, and is popular in aromatherapy.

Pandanus tectorius
SCREW PINE
A multipurpose plant on Pacific islands, providing food, medicine, and perfume, and materials for thatch and weaving.

Phormium tenax
NEW ZEALAND FLAX
Maori uses include decoctions for battle injuries, and as a binding for splints.

***Prostanthera* species**
MINT BUSH
Rich in antibiotic, fungicidal oils, and popular as ornamental plants.

Santalum lanceolatum
PLUMBUSH
Important to Aboriginals for edible fruits and medicinal leaves, bark, and roots.

Santalum spicatum
SANDALWOOD
Source of native Australian sandalwood oil.

Tasmannia lanceolata
MOUNTAIN PEPPERBERRY
All parts have an aromatic, hot, peppery flavour. Dried berries resemble peppercorns; powdered dried leaves are stronger than white pepper.

BUSHFOODS PLANTATION
*Native herbs and spices are now being grown commercially to supply the expanding bushfoods industry. This plantation of lemon myrtle (*Backhousia citriodora*) is in a subtropical northern region of New South Wales.*

USING HERBS

HERBS FOR USE
Good-quality, dried herbs and aromatic plants, ready for processing.

A COMMON MISAPPREHENSION is that herbs are small, green, leafy plants with a strong aroma. In both economic and medicinal terms they include an astonishing diversity of plants, from mighty rainforest trees to seaweeds and fungi. No less surprising is the range of parts used as well as some of the uses for which they are harvested. One part of a herb often has quite different properties from the others. In *Hibiscus sabdariffa*, for example, only the calyx of the flower provides the flavouring and the colouring, which is used in herb teas. Chinese medicine also has many examples of specific usages, such as orange peel from *Citrus reticulata*, the peel from unripe fruits being a quite different drug to peel taken from ripe fruits. Methods of preparation and storage also affect the properties of a herb. Volatile oils evaporate easily when exposed to light or heat, and while certain herbs must be used fresh, others are best when dried. This section looks at various uses of herbs, past and present, with some suggestions for modern adaptations.

SAFFRON CROCUS
Saffron consists only of the scarlet stigmas and style (collectively known as the pistil) of Crocus sativus; *other parts of the flower are useless for colouring or medicinal purposes. The pistils of other kinds of crocus cannot be used as a substitute.*

If you are planning to use any herb for culinary, medicinal, or any other purpose, it is essential to make sure that you have the right plant. Common names are often misleading, since the same common name may apply to different species. Do not be tempted to substitute with a similar herb, even if related, particularly for medicinal use; subspecies and varieties may differ in chemistry, although cultivars with minor variations from the species may not do so. Be sure to use only the part specified, and to harvest and process herbs only in the ways recommended in the A–Z of Herbs (see pp.92–411).

PARTS OF THE HERB

The A–Z of Herbs distinguishes which parts of each herb are used for specific purposes. The term whole plant usually refers to the parts above the ground (aerial parts). Leaves and stems (stalks) are the most commonly used parts. Green tissues are where photosynthesis occurs, and many compounds, such as volatile oils and alkaloids, are present. Leaves and stalks are at their best in late spring and summer.

In many plants the flower forms the reproductive part. The corolla (petals) is often colourful and fragrant to attract pollinators. Petals are protected by a ring of

PARTS OF THE PLANT
This herbal medicine stall in Kaili, western China, shows how specific parts are sold for use in traditional remedies. On sale are whole plants, fruits, bundles of leafy stems, dried bark, and underground parts, including bulbs, rhizomes, and tubers.

sepals, forming the calyx, which often has a strong aroma. In the centre are the female organ, the pistil, and/or the male part, or stamens. In many plants the seeds are surrounded by a fruit, which protects them as they develop. The underground parts of a plant are storage organs of various types, usually rich in nutrients that are most concentrated when the plant is dormant. They include roots, rhizomes (often thickened stems bearing buds that produce shoots), tubers (thickened stems), corms (thickened stem bases), and bulbs (fleshy leaf bases). All types have an outer layer of peel or bark, which may often have different properties from the inner tissues, as well as from the bark of parts above ground. Tree trunks and branches consist of heartwood in the centre, surrounded by sapwood, which is protected by inner and outer layers of bark. The hard tissue contains lignin, a complex aromatic compound, rich in resins, gums, and oils. Removing sections of bark from a tree or shrub makes it very vulnerable to infection; if removed in a complete ring around the trunk, the plant will almost certainly die.

USING HERBS SAFELY

It is often said that herbal remedies are safe because they are natural. This is not necessarily the case. Any herb, whether used internally or externally, can cause unpleasant reactions in some people. All herbs are toxic in excess and can cause unpredictable reactions when mixed with other herbs or medications. The information in this book is for general interest only and should not be taken as a recommendation for use.

Self-medication with herbal remedies should only be used for minor complaints such as coughs and colds, stomach upsets, or cuts and bruises. Do not exceed the dose. Babies, pregnant women, and the elderly should not take any herbal remedies unless they have been prescribed by a qualified practitioner. Do not take herbal remedies in conjunction with other medication, whether bought over the counter or prescribed by your doctor, without checking with a qualified practitioner that it is safe to do so.

Take great care with inhalant remedies, which are rich in essential oils. These oils are concentrated – it takes the peel of 85 lemons to produce 30g (1oz) of lemon oil – and can be highly toxic, internally and externally, when undiluted. Essential oils are also widely available for use in food flavouring, potpourris, and aromatherapy. Avoid taking herbal remedies for conditions such as obesity, exhaustion, and nervous tension; these are often better treated with a change of lifestyle. Diet formulas, tonics, and sedatives based on herbs often contain potent ingredients.

Think of herbs in terms of improving health rather than curing ailments. Used regularly and in moderation as part of a balanced diet and lifestyle, herbs can boost immunity and give a sense of well being. Grow them to use in cooking, salads, or teas, for skin and hair preparations, and to enjoy their colours and fragrance.

FRANKINCENSE RESIN
Frankincense (Boswellia sacra) *on sale in a Somali market. It is collected by shaving off plates of bark, and either scraping off the gum resin that oozes and solidifies on a wound, or allowing it to drip onto palm leaf mats, where it solidifies. Harvesting methods are the same today as in antiquity, but prices have changed; in Roman times, frankincense was as costly as gold.*

POISONOUS HERBS

Herbs vary greatly in toxicity, from food-cum-medicinal plants such as globe artichoke (*Cynara cardunculus* subsp. *cardunculus*) to deadly nightshade (*Atropa bella-donna*), but it goes without saying that if they can do good, they must contain substances that in excess can poison. This is true even of everyday culinary herbs such as thyme, marjoram, rosemary, and mint – they all contain volatile oils that are extremely poisonous in large amounts. Although quite safe when used fresh or dried in the quantities given in recipes, poisonous herbs are potentially dangerous in the form of essential oils, which need very careful measuring and dosage, even for external use. Many poisonous herbs are commonly grown as ornamentals. These include:
• Monkshoods (*Aconitum* spp.)
• Box (*Buxus sempervirens*)
• Madagascar periwinkle (*Catharanthus roseus*)

Opium poppies

• Meadow saffron (*Colchicum* spp.)
• Lily of the valley (*Convallaria majalis*)
• Daphnes (*Daphne* spp.)
• Foxgloves (*Digitalis* spp.)
• Glory lilies (*Gloriosa* spp.)
• Opium poppies (*Papaver somniferum*)
• Pokeweeds (*Phytolacca* spp.)
• Castor oil plant (*Ricinus communis*)
• Variegated nightshade (*Solanum dulcamara* 'Variegatum')
• Yew (*Taxus baccata*)

The following may cause skin irritation when handled:
• Cowslip (*Primula veris*)
• Primrose (*Primula vulgaris*)
• Rue (*Ruta graveolens*)

Warning labels are provided in some countries to alert gardeners to these dangers, but anyone planting herbs must also consider the safety of children and animals.

CULINARY HERBS

Herbs make all the difference to food; the cuisine of a region is characterized as much by the herbs it uses as by the staple foods. We tend to differentiate between herbs, spices, and flavourings, but the differences are small: "herbs" usually refers to aromatic leafy parts; "spices" to pungent seeds, roots, and bark; and "flavourings" to commodities that are often used in the same ways as herbs and spices but are foods in their own right, such as coffee, chocolate, nuts, citrus fruits, onion, garlic, and horseradish. Both leaves and seeds are used in some plants, such as fennel, dill, and coriander.

FIVE-SPICE POWDER
This powder is found all over China and Vietnam. It is made from star anise (Illicium verum), *cloves* (Syzygium aromaticum), *Sichuan pepper or fagara* (Zanthoxylum simulans), *cassia* (Cinnamomum cassia), *and fennel seeds* (Foeniculum vulgare).

SELLING HERBS
Markets all over the world are a marvellous place to see local herbs. Here in Essaouira, Morocco, spearmint is traded in large quantities for making the country's favourite mint tea.

Another category is the salad herb, or "pot-herb". It includes watercress, sorrel, dandelion, arugula, and chicory. Though most commonly added to salads, salad herbs can also be used in soups and stews. All herbs and spices have very distinctive aromas and flavours, but undergo subtle changes when combined with foods and/or other flavourings. Fragrant mixtures have come to characterize the cooking of certain regions – bouquet garni (parsley, thyme, bay leaf) in France, *garam masala* (cumin, coriander, cardamom, cloves, mace, cinnamon, bay leaf, black pepper) in northern India, and five-spice powder (see above) in China. Mint affects the taste buds very differently in Moroccan mint tea, mint sauce (an accompaniment for roast lamb), mint julep (an alcoholic drink), *harissa* (a Tunisian paste made from mint, chillies, cumin, coriander, caraway seeds, and garlic), *tabbouleh* (a Middle Eastern salad of mint, parsley, and bulghur wheat) and *tzatziki* (a mint, cucumber, and yogurt dip).

AIDING THE DIGESTION OF FOOD

Herbs add colour as well as flavour. Soups made from pale ingredients are much more appetizing when flecked green with finely chopped parsley or chives. Yellow is an especially appetizing colour – at its most subtle in saffron, and at its brightest in turmeric. Although seldom seen in the form of seeds, annatto is a colouring appreciated every day in butter, margarine, and "red" cheeses, which would otherwise be cream-coloured. Paprika gives a glorious brick-red colour to dishes such as goulash. It is made from dried, powdered red peppers (*Capsicum annuum*), as is cayenne, but can be used in much larger quantities because it lacks cayenne's fiery alkaloid, capsaicin. Herbs and spices also increase the vitamin and mineral content of food, and improve digestion. The bitter element in herbs and spices serves to "prime" the digestive system, stimulating the liver and gall bladder, improving digestion, especially of fats, and helping the elimination of toxins. Aperitifs with a hint of bitterness, and raw foods such as salads and crudités, are traditionally eaten for this purpose. Essential oils are the key components in both the flavour and beneficial effects of herbs and spices, and many are strongly antiseptic, protecting against harmful micro-organisms. Fennel, dill, and caraway contain carminative oils that almost instantly relieve gas. They are particularly good with foods that many people find hard to digest – fennel with oily fish, for example, or dill with cucumbers, or caraway with coleslaw or rich meats.

BENEFICIAL EFFECTS OF HERBS

Peppermint has a soothing, mildly anaesthetic effect on the digestive tract, hence the popularity of after-dinner mints and peppermint tea. Perilla, which is used with raw fish dishes in Japan, contains antidotes to seafood poisoning. Garlic is an excellent gastric disinfectant, well worth taking in capsule form, as well as in food, while travelling to prevent bouts of diarrhoea and vomiting. The therapeutic side of culinary herbs used to be more important than it is today. Sloe gin originally contained pennyroyal and valerian to calm the fraught

COOKING WITH HERBS AND SPICES

Use the freshest possible herbs and spices, since aromatic essential oils evaporate readily. For optimum flavour, grow your own herbs and buy spices whole, grinding them in small quantities.

the kitchen means that the volatile oils are in the air, not in the food!
• Garlic, spices, and tougher herbs, such as bay leaves, can be added at the beginning to let their flavours permeate.

Herbs in salads
• Add pot-herbs, such as arugula, sorrel, dandelion, or nasturtium leaves, to salads for a piquant flavour.
• Fresh herbs contain valuable vitamins essential in a healthy diet, such as watercress, which has high levels of iron.

Herbs in hot dishes
• Add herbs towards the end of cooking to give the best flavour and retain a fresh colour. A lovely aroma in

Flavouring with herbs
• Add herbs or spices to oils, vinegars, and mustard to flavour garnishes, dressings, and marinades.
• Prepare a quantity in advance to allow flavours to permeate (vinegar or oil with a sprig of herb added will keep for up to a year).
• Steeping in oil or vinegar is a way of using herbs with strong flavours, such as lavender, that cannot easily be added directly to food (especially to salads).

housewife, which gave it the name "mother's ruin". In the Middle Ages, a hot purgative porridge was made with rough grain, fat, and tansy, and nettle soup was consumed to "spring clean" the body of wastes accumulated in winter through lack of exercise and stodgy food. Medicinal meals remain important in traditional Chinese and Ayurvedic practice. In warm countries, eating hot spices, such as chilli, ginger, and pepper, serves to raise the metabolic rate and increase perspiration, effectively cooling the body, and speeding the excretion of toxins. Spices act as preservatives too, and are of great importance in warm regions where food deteriorates rapidly. Some herbs and spices are

almost universally popular. As well as pepper, ginger, cinnamon, nutmeg, and cloves, garlic is a favourite flavouring in most cuisines. Chillies and cayenne were unknown outside South America before Columbus discovered the New World in 1492 but are now characteristic of N African, Indian, and Asian dishes, and important in temperate countries, too.

Flavourings and digestive benefits are not all we get from herbs. Research into the nutritional benefits of herbs is adding a new dimension to their culinary uses. Rosemary, purslane (*Portulaca oleracea*), and green tea are rich in antioxidants, which help to maintain vitality and slow the ageing process.

COLLECTING SAFFRON
Saffron flowers (Crocus sativus) *are collected by hand in southern Europe. The stigmas and style from each crocus are also later separated by hand. Saffron has been used in cooking since the 10th century BC.*

PEPPER HARVEST
Pepper being gathered in the kingdom of Quilon, Kerala, India; an illustration from the French 15th-century Livre des Merveilles. *From very early times pepper, cinnamon, cloves, nutmeg, and ginger have been traded worldwide, causing intense competition between commercial rivals and nations.*

MEDICINAL HERBS

Herbs have been an essential factor in health care throughout the ages and in all cultures. They are prepared in a number of ways to extract their active ingredients for internal and external use. Western herbalists today are trained in anatomy and physiology, as any doctor is, but they prescribe herbs to correct underlying imbalances, rather than to give temporary relief. Most prescriptions call for several herbs, which work together to greater effect, known as a "synergistic effect".

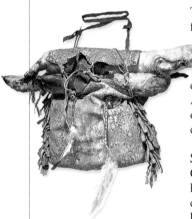

There are a variety of systems of herbal medicine, followed by practitioners in different parts of the world. In tribal cultures, herbal remedies are part of shamanism (spirit worship), in which illness is attributed to evil spirits. Early European herbals often attribute disease to malevolent goblins; Amazonian medicine men diagnose the magical cause of a complaint through hallucinogenic drugs and dancing. Herbs are used as talismans, as well as cures.

SYSTEMS OF HERBAL MEDICINE

Chinese herbalists see illness as a symptom of disharmony in the balance between opposite cosmic energies (*yin*: female, dark, cold; *yang*: male, light, hot), and elements (wood, fire, earth, metal, and water). Energy (*qi*) flows through channels called meridians. Over 700 prescriptions are commonly used by Chinese herbalists, and the materia medica describes over 5500 herbs. Ayurvedic practitioners similarly view the patient as a microcosm of all-pervading forces: *prana* (breath/life), *agni* (spirit/fire), and *soma* (love/harmony), which interact with the elements of earth, water, fire, air, and ether, flowing through energy centres or *chakras*. The elements are combined into three humours, *vata* (wind), *pitta* (fire/bile), and *kapha*

PLAINS INDIANS
This medicine bundle belonged to the native American Crow people. During ceremonial dances it was opened to gain supernatural powers, which would ensure the fertility and growth of the tribe.

(phlegm), which make up the individual's health profile and determine the kind of herb and foods prescribed. Ayurveda ("science of living") uses some 500 herbs.

Western herbalism is essentially eclectic. Historically influenced by ancient Egyptian, Assyrian, and Indian practices, it was for many centuries dominated by early Greek theories of elements (fire, air, earth, water), humours (sanguine, choleric, melancholic, phlegmatic), and essential body fluids (blood, yellow bile, black bile, phlegm). Herbs and foods were categorized as hot, dry, cold, and damp, and prescribed to balance the body's systems. The medicine of Hippocrates (468–377BC) and Galen (AD200) evolved this system, on which Unani (Islamic) medicine is still based. For several centuries European herbalism was influenced by the Doctrine of Signatures, developed by the Swiss alchemist and physician, Paracelsus (c.1493–1541), which taught that healing herbs were given a symbolic colour or shape by God to indicate their use. In the 19th century came Samuel Thomson's Physiomedicalism, a system that combined aspects of native American medicine with traditional European healing of the late 18th century. Physiomedicalism emphasized warmth as a healing force, and aimed to restore vitality through herbs that stimulated or sedated the nervous system, and had astringent or relaxing effects on tissues. Homeopathy is quite different from herbalism, using minute doses of a herb that in healthy people produces symptoms similar to those of the illness being treated. It is based on the theory that "like cures like", formulated by Samuel Hahnemann in 1796.

FLOWER REMEDIES AND AROMATHERAPY

The Bach Flower Remedies were devised in the 1930s by Dr Edward Bach (1886–1936), a practising homeopath. There are 38 Flower Remedies, in which the healing energies of plants are transferred to water

TREATING YOURSELF WITH HERBAL REMEDIES

Using commercial or home-made herbal remedies is fine for occasional minor problems, but not advisable for serious or persistent complaints. The following herbs, however, are useful to have in a simple herbal medicine chest, along with commercial remedies such as decongestants for colds and cough mixtures for particular kinds of cough: chesty (productive or "wet"); or dry and irritant (they need different remedies):

Allium sativum
GARLIC
Capsules taken for colds, influenza, and mucus.

Carum carvi
CARAWAY
Seeds chewed for indigestion.

Foeniculum vulgare
FENNEL
Drunk as a tea for indigestion.

Hamamelis virginiana
WITCH HAZEL
Applied externally for bruises and sore eyes.

Lavandula species
LAVENDER
Essential oil applied sparingly direct to the skin for minor burns and scalds.

Matricaria recutita
GERMAN CHAMOMILE
Drunk as a tea or infusion to ease nervous tension and insomnia.

Melaleuca alternifolia
TEA TREE
Essential oil applied sparingly direct to the skin to treat cold sores.

Melissa officinalis
LEMON BALM
Drunk as a tea for stress-related stomach upsets (especially in children).

Stellaria media
CHICKWEED
Applied as an external ointment for skin irritations.

Symphytum officinale
COMFREY
Applied as an external ointment for minor injuries and bruising.

Szygium aromaticum
CLOVE
Essential oil applied sparingly direct for toothache while awaiting dental treatment.

Tilia species
LIME
Drunk as lime flower tea to ease nervous tension and sleeplessness.

Zingiber officinale
GINGER
Taken in capsule form to ease nausea and travel sickness.

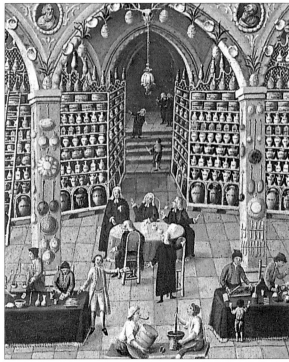

MEDIEVAL WESTERN MEDICAL PRACTICE
An anonymous French 18th-century painting illustrating the reception room of a master apothecary. The apothecary would stock a great range of herbal and other popular medicines.

through the power of sunlight. Bach flower remedies were followed in the 1970s by the California Flower Essences, produced by the Flower Essence Society (FES), and in the 1990s by the Australian Bush Flower Essences, developed by naturopath Ian White. As in homeopathic preparations, no molecules of the original materials remain in flower remedies.

Aromatherapy is the use of essential oils in massage, inhalations, baths, natural room fragrances, and perfumes to maintain and improve health and vitality. The beneficial effects of plant aromas have been known and used since ancient times, but underwent methodical evaluation and scientific research during the 20th century. The term "aromatherapy" was first used in 1928 by Rene Gattefossé, a French chemist and perfumier who discovered by chance that lavender oil could heal burns. His research was followed by the work of Jean Valnet, a French army doctor who treated soldiers with essential oils. His *Practice of Aromatherapy* (1964) remains a standard text. The use of aromatherapy for massage was popularised by Marguerite Maury, an Austrian biochemist who researched the effects of oils when absorbed through the skin. Although clinical aromatherapy, in which essential oils are prescribed internally, is sometimes used, most practitioners strongly advise against internal use, and emphasize that when applying essential oils externally, they should be diluted in a vegetable oil.

HERBAL PREPARATIONS

Herbal remedies are prepared in a number of ways. Some are taken internally, others applied to the skin.

Compresses are made by soaking a clean cloth in an infusion, decoction, or diluted tincture.

Decoctions are made by simmering the herb for at least 15 minutes and straining. Decoctions are best for tough parts, such as bark or roots. Standard quantities are 60g (2½oz) of fresh herb or 30g (1¼oz) of dried herb to 500ml (18fl oz) of water. Infusions and decoctions must be taken the same day.

Fluid extracts are prepared from one part herb to one part alcohol, according to pharmaceutical grades, giving a concentrated, preserved extract.

Infusions are prepared by pouring near-boiling water over the herb and covering for 5–10 minutes. This method is best for leaves and flowers. Standard quantities are 75g (3oz) of fresh herb or 30g (1¼oz) of dried herb to 500ml (18fl oz) of water.

Macerations are prepared by steeping the herb in water at room temperature for 12 hours, and then strained or pressed. Standard quantities are 25g (1oz) of dried herb to 500ml (18fl oz) of water.

Oils are made in three ways: by heating 250g (9oz) of dried herb or 750g (27oz) of fresh herb in 500ml (18fl oz) of oil in a bowl over boiling water for 2–3 hours; by filling a jar with fresh herb and oil, covering and leaving for 2–3 weeks; or by adding 25–50 drops of essential oil to 100ml (5 tbs) oil.

Ointments are made by heating herbs in petroleum jelly or solid fat in a bowl over boiling water for about 2 hours, and straining into jars. Standard quantities are 60g (2½oz) of dried herb to 500g (18oz) of fat.

Poultices consist of a pulp or paste made by heating chopped fresh, dried, or powdered herbs with a little water. They are applied bearably hot, and replaced as

necessary. Research has shown that the healing constituents of comfrey penetrate deeply into the tissues when applied in this way. The simplest poultice is a dock leaf applied to a nettle sting!

Powders consist of ground dried herbs and are used to make pills, capsules, or pastes. Powders may be taken with milk or water, or mixed with oil or honey.

Syrups are concentrated sugar solutions that help preserve infusions and decoctions and add a soothing, palatable element to herbal preparations. Standard quantities are 500ml (18fl oz) of liquid to 500g (18oz) of sweetening agent.

Teas (tisanes) are infusions made from aromatic herbs, such as lime flowers, fennel, or chamomile. They may be sweetened but should not have milk added.

Tinctures are made like macerations, but using one part herb to four parts alcohol, which both preserves and extracts the constituents. They store well and are more concentrated than infusions and decoctions.

WILD INGREDIENTS
This medicinal herb stall in São Paulo, Brazil, reveals a considerable range of dried herbal products that are derived from wild plants.

GATHERING IN CHINA
The first step in preparing any traditional remedy is gathering the herbal material. Often, the herbs will have been cultivated, but sometimes they must be collected from where they are growing wild.

COSMETIC HERBS

The ancient Egyptians valued cosmetics and perfumery so highly that they were buried with their beauty products, such as kohl and eye pencils, which were kept in ornate vases. Perfumes in the tomb of Tutankhamun were still faintly fragrant after more than 3000 years. The most common ingredients were frankincense and myrrh, which were mixed with sesame, almond, olive, or balanos oil. Gum resins such as myrrh were added for their aroma and as fixatives for elusive scents. Lily oil was made with myrrh, cardamom, sweet flag, cinnamon, and the petals of 2000 lilies.

The earliest forms of perfumes were unguents, which were based on animal fat, heated with aromatic plant ingredients. When cold, they were either used as ointment or formed into cones that were worn on the head, so that they melted gradually, anointing the body and clothes with scented grease. The ancient Egyptians also had prototypes of most skin preparations that we use today: depilatories made from gum, cucumber, fig juice, and other ingredients; incense-based deodorants; cleansing creams of oil and lime; and hair tonics made from juniper berries, fir oil, or lettuce.

ANCIENT EGYPTIAN COSMETICS
These elegant containers were used by the Egyptians to store cosmetics and beauty preparations.

FRANKINCENSE RESIN
Resin from Boswellia sacra *has been used in perfumery for thousands of years. The Egyptians added it to anti-wrinkle cream, for which purpose it is still used today. It is also included as a base note in many perfumes.*

YLANG-YLANG
The fragrant flowers of ylang-ylang (Cananga odorata) *are shown here having been freshly picked on the island of Mayotte, off Madagascar.*

THE POPULARITY OF BATH OILS

Perfumed oils were known to the ancient civilizations of Egypt, Persia, and India. The ancient Greeks studied the art of perfumery and passed on their love of cosmetics and scents to the Romans, who in turn influenced most of Europe. The Romans developed different kinds of perfume: solid and liquid unguents, and powder perfumes. These were especially popular after bathing, which was a major social function in Roman times. Essential oils became available after techniques of distillation were perfected by the Arabs in the Middle Ages. Body oils to perfume and moisturize the skin after bathing are as popular today as in ancient times. Although bath preparations are now mostly made with synthetics, one of the few dispersable natural oils is Turkey red oil (sulphonated castor oil). To make your own natural bath oil, add 50 drops of essential oil to 50ml (2fl oz) Turkey red oil (available from suppliers of essential oils).

THE DEVELOPMENT OF FRAGRANCES

Lavender, which scented the hot water of Roman public baths and was introduced to far corners of the empire, became closely associated with both personal and domestic cleanliness. The first recipe for lavender water dates from 1615. Lavender was soon widely used as a strewing herb and in bags to freshen the air, among fabrics to repel moths, and in wax to prevent woodworm in furniture. The unpleasant smell of soap, which until the 1800s was made by boiling animal fat with wood ash, was disguised by adding lavender oil.

The making of household fragrances and cleaning and hygiene preparations took a great deal of time before the days of mass production, and recipes for these items of domestic economy were handed down from mother to daughter. Large houses had a still-room in which herbs, spices, and other raw materials were concocted into powders, polishes, washballs, sachets ("sweet bags"), floral waters, and potpourri. Pomanders and nosegays or tussie-mussies of aromatic herbs were carried against infection.

The first toilet water was "Hungary water", made in the 14th century from rosemary macerated in alcohol. The sophisticated perfumes we know today were developed in France towards the end of the 18th century. Eau de Cologne, made from essential oils and alcohol, was first produced in Cologne in 1709. One of the earliest of floral scents was orange blossom water or neroli, introduced c.1725. From 1850 Oriental fragrances came into popularity, such as vetiver, patchouli, vanilla, and benzoin. Synthetic essences were introduced at the end of the 19th century, but natural oils still predominate in quality perfumes.

A perfume is made up of three main kinds of scent: top notes, derived from ingredients with fresher, sharper scents (lemon, lime, basil, bergamot, coriander, lavender, chamomile); middle or "heart" notes, from herbs and spices with pervasive perfumes (clary sage,

clove, ginger, jasmine, lemon grass, rose, nutmeg, ylang-ylang); and base notes, mostly from woods, roots, resins, and gums, such as frankincense, myrrh, sandalwood, cinnamon, and cedarwood. The art of perfumery is to combine scents of differing intensity and duration. Formulas for famous fragrances are closely guarded secrets, but the main ingredients of some are known. Chanel No. 5, for example, has top notes of bergamot, lemon, and neroli, middle notes of rose, jasmine, and ylang-ylang, and base notes of cedarwood, vetiver, and vanilla.

BODY PAINTING AND MAKEUP

Ancient Britons painted their bodies with woad, a blue dye obtained by fermenting *Isatis tinctoria*, and native North Americans had a sophisticated repertoire of body pigments based on plant dyes, fats, and oils. Face painting as we know it came via the Romans from the ancient Egyptians and Persians. Red colourings were usually produced by red ochre, a natural mineral soil; today such colorants are mainly derived from annatto (*Bixa orellana*). Trends in makeup through the ages have been set by courts and upper classes; Mary Queen of Scots bathed in wine, and ladies of the Spanish court improved their complexions with almond paste and creams of vanilla and cacao. Beauty products became so popular and elaborate that in 1770 a bill was introduced to the English parliament to dissolve a marriage if the man was deceived into it by "scents, paints, cosmetic washes…" A similar law was passed in Pennsylvania; cosmetics were frowned on in Puritan New England but flourished in colonies of French origin. Body painting is still traditional among many tribal peoples all over the world.

HENNA FOR DECORATION
This Indian girl is using a henna (Lawsonia inermis) *paste to decorate the hands of her friend for a special occasion, probably a religious ceremony such as a marriage.*

SOME PLANT INGREDIENTS USED IN COSMETICS AND PERFUMERY

Aloe vera
ALOE VERA
A "miracle" herb used for soothing and healing sunburn and to moisturize irritated or sensitive skin.

Calendula officinalis
POT MARIGOLD
An antiseptic, soothing, anti-inflammatory herb, for healing very dry, sensitive skin, especially after sunburn.

Citrus species
CITRUS FRUITS
Contain antioxidants and vitamin C to repair damaged skin, and AHAs (alpha-hydroxy acids) to peel away old tissues.

Chamaemelum nobile
CHAMOMILE
A healing, anti-inflammatory herb that also conditions the hair and lightens fair hair.

Cucumis sativus
CUCUMBER
A cooling herb that has an astringent, softening effect on the skin.

Fucus species
SEAWEED
Rich in minerals and vitamins to condition skin and hair.

Hamamelis virginiana
WITCH HAZEL
Perhaps the most widely used astringent, present in most toning lotions.

Krameria lappacea
RHATANY ROOT
A powerful astringent that improves gum health.

Mentha × piperita
PEPPERMINT
Antiseptic, cooling, mildly anaesthetic and deodorant

essential oil, added to almost all oral hygiene preparations, and to face masks, foot lotions, shampoos, and conditioners.

Mentha spicata
SPEARMINT
Potent antiseptic and deodorant with a cooling, refreshing taste owing to its mild anaesthetic effects. Used in almost all oral hygiene products, often in the form of menthol, a part of the essential oil.

Oenothera biennis
EVENING PRIMROSE
Oil is used to soften and replenish dry skin; seeds are ground for use in facial scrubs.

Prunus armeniaca
APRICOT
Skin-softening enzymes are found in the pulp, and extra-

moisturizing oil containing vitamin B15, which speeds skin regeneration.

Prunus dulcis
SWEET ALMOND OIL
A fine, emollient oil, which is extensively used in moisturizers and is an ingredient of cold creams.

Rosa species
ROSE
Astringent, tonic, healing extracts, such as rosewater, are used in skin products.

Rosmarinus officinalis
ROSEMARY
Circulatory stimulant that improves scalp and hair health.

Sambucus nigra
ELDERFLOWER
Soothes irritated and inflamed skin.

Sanguinaria canadensis
BLOODROOT
Anti-bacterial extracts added to oral hygiene preparations.

Simmondsia chinensis
JOJOBA
A rapidly absorbed liquid wax, similar to the skin's own oils.

Symphytum officinale
COMFREY
A potent healing agent, containing allantoin, which speeds the formation of new cells.

Theobroma cacao
COCOA BUTTER
Yields a rich, softening oil, used to moisturize the skin.

Thymus vulgaris
THYME
Contains thymol, one of the strongest natural antiseptics.

CULTIVATING HERBS

A RICH HARVEST
A wide selection of freshly gathered herbs, ready for drying and use.

THE GROWING OF HERBS is a rich and varied pastime, combining the delights of the flower garden and the productivity of the vegetable plot with the fascinating allure of the ancient myths connected with many of them. Herbal plants include trees, shrubs, fungi, lichens, mosses, and seaweeds, as well as annuals and perennials. They come from every climatic zone and are used in all cultures. In this section you will find many suggestions for growing herbs in a variety of situations, as well as advice for their propagation,

harvest, and storage. Even without a garden, plenty of herbs can be grown in pots that are small enough for a windowsill, or in containers to hang from walls. Perhaps you may wish to produce fresh parsley all year, or supply your own raw materials for home-made potpourri, cosmetics, or tisanes. Maybe you aspire to an entire herb garden, a peaceful retreat with soft colours, sweet fragrances, and the hum of bees. Whatever you want from your garden, the advice in these pages will help you achieve your aims.

The A–Z of Herbs (see pp.92–411) gives detailed information on how each herb is grown. This section covers more general stages for the home gardener, from planning a garden to storing the produce.

DESIGN FOR A SMALL SPACE
Culinary herbs grouped in pots, as here, can be moved to catch the sun. Using a wheelbarrow to display the herbs gives them extra height and adds visual interest to the planting design.

CHOOSING SUITABLE PLANTS
A successful herb garden is one that is planned with regard to the site and growing conditions, its purpose, and the plants that are suited to it. Not every herb described in the A–Z of Herbs is suitable for growing at home, and some are not cultivated at all, being either wild-collected or extremely difficult. These include some rainforest trees, such as angostura (*Galipea*

officinalis), and lichens, such as oak moss (*Evernia prunastri*). In these cases, practical information on their care and cultivation may not be available, but growing conditions can be deduced from their natural habitats, and trial and error may bring success. Some herbs are weeds, and though cultivated by specialists for the herb trade are problematic as garden plants. Between these extremes are numerous herbs that are easily grown, productive, and attractive for the garden.

HERBS IN SMALL GARDENS
It is fun to allocate a special part of the garden to herbs. A popular choice is to make a small bed of culinary herbs within easy reach of the kitchen. Another possibility is a collection of herbs for making teas, planted in a bed or pots around the garden table, or sitting area. The "tea garden" could include fragrant lemon balm (*Melissa officinalis*), chamomile (*Matricaria recutita*), lemon verbena (*Aloysia triphylla*), or peppermint (*Mentha × piperita*). Growing herbs in containers makes it easy to rearrange them, and saves space, especially with an invasive herb such as mint. Herbs can also be grown with other plants in the border. Tall annuals such as sunflowers (*Helianthus annuus*) can provide focal points, and smaller ones are useful for filling gaps and giving colour as well as culinary ingredients.

SCENT AND COLOUR
Colour can come from flowers, such as borage (*Borago officinalis*), poppies (*Papaver rhoeas*), and pot marigolds (*Calendula officinalis*), or from foliage, such as red shiso (*Perilla frutescens* var. *crispa*) or bronze basil (*Ocimum basilicum* 'Dark Opal'). Purple-leafed, shrubby herbs, as in *Salvia officinalis* 'Purpurascens', combine well with silver artemisias. Many herbs have golden-leafed forms that brighten up borders and containers. They tend to scorch in full sun so are ideal for partial shade, where they also show up well.

Favourite scented herbs are something to appreciate at every opportunity, so plant them close to where you sit, or near entrances and doorways. Citrus trees make excellent pot plants for the patio or conservatory and fill the air with fragrance when flowering. Yellow evening primroses (*Oenothera biennis*) or white Madonna lilies (*Lilium candidum*) planted near a window will scent the air on summer evenings. Lavender and scented-leafed pelargoniums are perfect beside paths or seats, so that you can enjoy them to the full.

CLIMBERS AND CREEPERS

Make the most of herbs that are natural climbers, such as the golden hop (*Humulus lupulus* 'Aureus'), jasmine (*Jasminum officinale*), and passionflower (*Passiflora incarnata*). They can be planted to climb over a garden shed or old tree stump. Some herbs are low-growing creepers and can be grown in very small spaces. These include creeping thymes (*Thymus* spp.), basil thyme (*Acinos arvensis*), and creeping savory (*Satureja spicigera*), which all prefer full sun; and parsley piert (*Aphanes arvensis*), or Corsican mint (*Mentha requienii*), which thrive in partial shade.

THE HERB KITCHEN GARDEN

Kitchen gardens mix business with pleasure, producing food for the family and herbs to delight the senses. These plots make sense in terms of husbandry, since a changing mixture of short-lived plants is less likely to suffer from pests and diseases than a large amount of one crop. Salad crops and tomatoes could have parsley (*Petroselinum crispum*) or basil (*Ocimum basilicum*) planted nearby, ready to combine in cooking or salads.

GROWING WITHOUT A GARDEN

The would-be herb gardener without a garden is at no great disadvantage. Many herbs are quite small plants, easily grown in almost any type of container. Mounting herb pots on to walls or fences, or placing them at the edges of steps, takes minimal space. Containerized plants can also be changed from year to year, and the growing season extended with pots under cover in winter. Elderly and disabled gardeners find pots easier to manage than plants in open ground, provided that there is help with lifting and repotting.

GARDEN MICROCLIMATES

As with any cultivated plant, herbs do best when provided with conditions closest to those in the natural habitat. Gardens create a succession of microclimates, and much of the skill of gardening is in identifying the right place for a plant. Hedges, walls, and fences can provide shelter from winds, excessively wet winters, and frost; walls and paving retain warmth, improving survival chances of slightly tender herbs; and sunny slopes or banks, especially on stony soil, are ideal for Mediterranean herbs, such as rosemary (*Rosmarinus officinalis*). Herbs that like sharp drainage can be further accommodated by adding grit or sharp sand to the soil. Given the additional warmth and protection of a cold frame or greenhouse, an even wider range of herbs can be grown. Cuttings are easier to root in warm, sheltered conditions, and tender herbs, such as scented-leafed pelargoniums and balm of Gilead (*Cedronella canariensis*), which need frost-free, fairly dry conditions during winter, also benefit from protection.

GROWING TEMPERATURES

Plants from different climatic zones (for zone information see pp.94–95) differ in their requirements regarding soil, water, humidity, light levels, and temperature. Most critical is the temperature range tolerated. The maximum tolerated by many plants, unless they have special adaptations, is 35°C (96°F), but minimum temperatures vary greatly from plant to plant. For this reason, the hardiness of a plant is the first thing to consider before trying to grow it. Minimum temperatures should be taken as night-time lows; most plants prefer a rise in temperature during the day.

Fully hardy Requires minimum -15°C (5°F). Some plants from Mediterranean climates, such as *Lavandula*, *Salvia*, *Thymus*, and *Rosmarinus* spp., tolerate low temperatures occasionally, but may succumb to prolonged cold, especially in wet weather. Similarly, desert species are hardier in sunny, dry conditions. *Aloe vera*, for instance, tolerates 2°C (36°F) if kept on the dry side in winter.

Frost hardy Requires minimum -5°C (23°F). In temperate regions frost-hardy species, such as *Aloysia triphylla*, may be grown in a sheltered position outdoors, or in containers that can be moved indoors or out, according to conditions.

Half hardy Requires minimum 0°C (32°F). Though tolerant of lower temperatures than tender plants, half-hardy plants are usually grown only for summer bedding and containers in temperate areas. They need 13–21°C (55–70°F) for propagation and early growth, and must therefore be kept under cover initially.

Tender Warm (minimum 18°C/64°F); intermediate (minimum 13°C/55°F); cool (minimum 10°C/50°F). In temperate regions tender plants are grown under cover all year, since nights are too cold, even in summer, for them to thrive outdoors. "Under cover" may mean indoors, or in a greenhouse or conservatory where the minimum temperature that they require can be maintained, with a rise during the day of 5–10°C (9–18°F).

STRIKING COLOURS AND SHAPES
Warm, vibrant colours and strong foliage give impact to the herb garden. The dominant angelica is framed by feathery bronze fennel, bold alliums, mounds of Alchemilla mollis, *and spiky irises. Purple sage and Spanish lavender give rich, long-lasting colour.*

BLENDING DIFFERENT STYLES
This formal diamond pattern sits well in what is otherwise an informal garden border.

STYLE AND SITE

While there are few more pleasurable experiences than harvesting herbs from your own herb garden, you do not need a herb garden in order to grow herbs. Herbs may be cultivated and enjoyed in a variety of situations to suit personal preferences and resources. They can be grown in containers or a patch of ground near the kitchen, or mixed in with flowers and vegetables elsewhere in the garden. A special herb garden does have its advantages, though. It brings plants with similar uses together, making harvesting easier and combining usefulness with visual impact, subtle colours, and delightful aromas. A herb garden is also an asset to any property.

CHAMOMILE

The non-flowering lawn chamomile (*Chamaemelum nobile* 'Treneague') needs light, fertile, well-drained soil, and diligent weeding. Although often recommended for planting as a lawn, it can be slow-growing and difficult to establish and maintain on a large scale. A more practical alternative is to plant a small area, which will be easier to look after, perhaps setting it within an area of paving, or between stones in a path, where footsteps will release its fragrance.

DECIDING ON THE STYLE

Having decided to make a herb garden, you will need to consider the style at an early stage. Whether formal or informal, the design should complement the rest of the garden, and the style of your home. An informal garden would be the obvious choice for a cottage on the side of a hill, whereas a formal design would be more appropriate for a city apartment with a paved courtyard. Suggestions for styles to suit a range of situations are given in the section Designing a Herb Garden (see pp.70–91), and these can be adapted to individual tastes and circumstances. Costs and maintenance should be taken into account at the planning stage. Formal herb gardens are often labour intensive and expensive to construct and may be tedious to keep in pristine condition if there are long lengths of dwarf hedging to clip or paths to weed. An informal herb design usually needs less initial structural work and is easier to maintain, as the tasks can be spread over time. A combination of formal overall structure and informal planting can work well if the formal element is simple and spacious.

FORMAL DESIGNS

Formal gardens, such as knot gardens and parterres, are usually based on geometric patterns and framed by low hedges or paths. They are satisfying to construct, looking mature soon after planting. For maximum impact, each small bed is planted with one kind of herb, giving bold blocks of colour and texture. In general,

AN INFORMAL COUNTRY GARDEN
Lavandula angustifolia 'Hidcote Blue', interspersed with a golden-leafed ivy and grey-white eryngiums, is planted here in cottage-garden style.

tall, invasive, or sprawling herbs spoil the pattern and proportion of a formal herb garden, and may damage dwarf hedges. Where used as focal points, large shrubs and trees are trained or clipped into an appropriate shape for the planting position. A standard bay (*Laurus nobilis*), perhaps in a handsome container, is the classic centrepiece in any formal herb garden. Formal designs are most impressive when viewed from above, and ideally sited where they can be overlooked from an upper window or a slope.

At its simplest, a formal design may take the form of a cartwheel with a different herb planted in each segment, or a group of species of one genus. Formal and informal can also be combined by choosing a simple formal outline, such as a circle or rectangle divided into four parts by straight paths, and planting like a herbaceous border.

INFORMAL DESIGNS

An informal herb garden is a good solution for an irregularly shaped plot, as it depends more for its success on the plants themselves, and on plant groupings. There is far greater scope here for a mixture of elements, such as a water feature for aquatic herbs, or a paved area for creeping ones. Plants of varying heights and habits are more suited to an informal setting than a formal one. Herbs with dramatic shapes can be planted to great effect. Possibilities include prostrate blue rosemary (*Rosmarinus officinalis* Prostratus Group) overhanging a wall, or angelica (*Angelica archangelica*) as an architectural feature in the border. Informal plantings give more scope for using interesting colours and textures in striking ways – perhaps a tapestry of various creeping thymes (*Thymus* spp.) beside a path or patio, or the tall spires of foxgloves (*Digitalis purpurea*) in a corner lit by low shafts of sunlight.

INFORMAL PLANTING IN A FORMAL SHAPE
A central urn and bed, surrounded by a geometric brick path, provides a formal structure for relaxed, informal plantings of mixed herbs.

ASSESSING THE SITE

After deciding on style, the next step is to assess the site and work out the size, shape, and aspect. You will need to determine the kind of soil and weather patterns the area is subject to, the direction it faces, and other important details, such as slope, drainage, and surrounding features. Make allowances for seasonal changes; deciduous trees look innocuous in winter, but for much of the year they cast heavy shade, and in autumn drop their leaves on to plants and features below. The ideal site is sunny, open but sheltered, with neutral to alkaline, well-drained, fertile soil. As far as possible, it should be free from perennial weeds and overhanging trees, and have good access from the house so that the herbs can be harvested in less than perfect weather. If your proposed site has serious disadvantages, it is worth considering professional help to landscape, clear, and drain the area, improve soil condition, lay paths, and do any other construction work that requires skill and experience. If the site is overgrown or neglected, it may take an entire growing season to ensure the area is completely free from weeds and ready for planting.

PREPARING THE GROUND

If the ground is infested with perennial weeds, clear it as far in advance of planting as possible, and allow it to lie fallow for several weeks to allow any weeds that

HEIGHT AS A FOCAL POINT
This combination of open ground planting and small containers at varying levels creates an interesting focal point and gives prominence to the mix of unusual leaf shapes.

PREPARING AND MARKING OUT THE SITE

1 Use a fork to dig up the roots of perennial weeds. Hold the main stem close to the ground, so that the whole root system is removed.

2 Having prepared the soil, the design for the bed can be marked out. Use string and stakes, measure to scale, and include any paths or paving.

have been missed to resurface. Digging them out is hard work but is environmentally friendly and usually more successful than using weedkiller. When the ground is "clean", fork in well-rotted organic matter, such as garden or mushroom compost, and rake the soil to a fine, level tilth. Heavy feeding with manure is not recommended for most herbs, since it produces soft growth, lacking in aroma and with little resistance to pests, diseases, and cold. On heavy clay soils, improve drainage by the addition of sand or gritty material. This can be done immediately in and around the planting holes rather than throughout the whole garden. Though many Mediterranean herbs enjoy alkaline conditions, the majority thrive in neutral or slightly acid soil. If the pH is below 6.5, add a dressing of lime in the recommended quantity when preparing the soil for planting. For large areas, especially on ground that has been badly infested with weeds, it may be worth covering the prepared area with geotextile membrane and planting through holes, cut in a cross shape, so that they fold back to cover the soil around the plant. When the area is planted, mulch with chipped bark or gravel.

MAKING A PLAN

To draw up a plan, first measure the site accurately. Be sure to include factors such as the spread of existing trees, and take account of any changes in ground level. Note where shade is cast at different times of the day and at different seasons; this will determine the best sites for garden seats, as well as for herbs that have specific requirements for full sun or shade. Whether your design is formal or informal in style, the herbs should ideally be planted within arm's length for convenient harvesting. In large beds or borders, plan to provide stepping stones for access so that the soil is not compacted by being stepped on to reach the herbs. Stones or paving should be laid before planting so that you have a surface to walk on while preparing and laying out the garden. When all the measurements have been made, transfer them to graph paper, working to scale, and including the surrounding features such as trees or boundaries. This will be your master plan; if you have several different designs to consider, draw each one on tracing paper, laid over the master plan. Decide which herbs will best suit your design (see Choosing and Planting Herbs, pp.52–53), and make notes on their cultivation requirements, habit, colour, and eventual height and spread.

CHOOSING AND PLANTING HERBS

If you aim to create a herb garden, the ideal plan of attack would be to spend the autumn and winter planning the design and compiling orders for seeds and plants. Then, when spring is in the air, you will be ready to start work out of doors, preparing the site and transferring your plans from paper to ground. There are many excellent books on herbs and herb gardens, as well as on more general garden design, and it is worth spending time to consider various options. It will also pay to explore the huge range of herbs now available. Every year new varieties come on to the market, offering interesting variations in terms of colour, scent, flavour, and habit.

PREPARING THE SITE
The amount of time this may take depends on the size and complexity of the proposed garden and the state of the ground (see Style and Site, pp.50–51). If the design is large and ambitious, or the existing area a wilderness, it may be necessary to spend the entire first year preparing the site. In the meantime, your garden can begin with herbs grown in containers; you can also raise herbs from seed, acquire surplus plants and cuttings from friends, and buy stock plants to grow on or use for propagating.

CHOOSING SUITABLE HERBS
Perhaps the most enjoyable stage in planning a herb garden is deciding which herbs to grow. Be sure, though, that they are suitable for the conditions and the design of your garden. Herbs should be grown in conditions that, as far as possible, resemble their natural habitat. Many popular culinary and aromatic herbs are Mediterranean in origin; these mainly prefer ample sunshine, mild winters, and free-draining soil. Some herbs prefer a damp, shaded position, however, or even wet soil. Sweet flag (*Acorus calamus*) and bog bean (*Menyanthes trifoliata*) are true aquatics and can be grown in mud or shallow water. Most variegated and golden-leafed cultivars do best in a site that receives morning or evening sun and shade at midday, since full

SPECIALIST HERB NURSERY
Well-established herb nurseries offer the widest range of culinary, medicinal, and aromatic plants for the herb garden, and expert advice on cultivation. Specialist nurseries are listed in gardening magazines, books on herbs, local herb societies, and websites.

sun often scorches the colourful foliage. Find out about your chosen plant's natural habitat in the A–Z of Herbs (see pp.92–411) and try to match it with a niche in the garden. For example, primroses (*Primula vulgaris*) love shady banks and can be sited at the foot of a slope which stays damp all year; the houseleek (*Sempervivum tectorum*), an inhabitant in the wild of rock faces, will happily grow out of a wall.

BUYING HERBS
Most garden centres sell various herbs, though they are not always where you expect to find them. The section devoted to herbs will include a good range of culinary herbs. Medicinal herbs such as valerian (*Valeriana officinalis*), rue (*Ruta graveolens*), and catnip (*Nepeta cataria*) are often sold alongside culinary herbs with little or no explanation of their uses. An interesting selection of thymes (*Thymus* spp.) is usually found among the alpines, and the water-gardening section may have herbs such as sweet flag (*Acorus calamus*), watercress (*Nasturtium officinale*), watermint (*Mentha aquatica*), and *Houttuynia*. Ornamental cultivars of herbal trees and shrubs such as elder (*Sambucus nigra*), and perennials such as bergamot (*Monarda* spp.) and *Echinacea* are often well represented in other sections. Some herbs are not good buys for planting out from pots since they dislike root disturbance. These include borage (*Borago officinalis*), chervil (*Anthriscus cerefolium*), dill (*Anethum graveolens*), and poppies (*Papaver*), which are better grown from seed, sown where the plants are to flower. Wildflower centres are another good resource. Here you will find seeds for meadows or other natural plantings (see pp.56–57), and native herbs that have most likely been grown from local seed. This ensures that the plants are well adapted to conditions in your area.

SPECIALITY HERB NURSERIES
Speciality herb nurseries offer a much wider choice and may be able to give better advice than garden centres. Most stock an interesting selection of medicinal herbs and dye plants, as well as larger sizes of culinary herbs. Plants are often of better quality, too, due to the staff's greater interest and knowledge. If you are planning a thyme collection or lavender hedge, for instance, it is well worth visiting a herb nursery at flowering time to make your selection. There is a surprising range of colours and habits to choose from, and decisions are much more easily reached when the cultivars are in front of you and looking at their best.

POINTS TO LOOK FOR WHEN BUYING
When making your selection, check plants for pests and diseases, and choose the one that has the best shape and condition. Try to ignore flowers, which may mislead you into buying an inferior specimen. Concentrate instead on the number of growths or new shoots, and look for richly coloured, vigorous foliage. Ensure that the specimen is not potbound, since it may take many months for it to send out new roots from a very compressed rootball. In the meantime the plant will be almost as dependent upon watering as if it were still containerized.

CHECKING THE DESIGN
Place all the pots of herbs in the positions they will occupy in the bed; this will enable you to check the spacing and the overall effect before you commit to planting. Often it is more effective to plant in groups of uneven numbers, such as three or five, rather than in even numbers or singly. Leave room for a few annuals, too, such as pot marigolds (Calendula officinalis) *and perilla, and make sure you grow enough of herbs such as basil* (Ocimum spp.) *or parsley* (Petroselinum crispum) *that you use in generous quantities, so that the plants are not over-harvested even during the growing season.*

EASY TO GROW

Herbs for Dry, Sunny Positions
CULINARY
Artemisia dracunculus, Ocimum basilicum, Origanum vulgare, Rosmarinus officinalis, Salvia officinalis, Satureja montana, Thymus vulgaris.
AROMATIC
Artemisia abrotanum, Helichrysum italicum, Lavandula spp.*, Santolina chamaecyparissus, Teucrium chamaedrys.*
MEDICINAL
Calendula officinalis, Hyssopus officinalis, Nepeta cataria, Sempervivum tectorum, Verbascum thapsus.

Herbs for Moist Shade
CULINARY
Allium schoenoprasum, Levisticum officinale, Mentha spicata, Myrrhis odorata, Petroselinum crispum.
AROMATIC
Galium odoratum, Houttuynia cordata, Mentha requienii.
MEDICINAL
Ajuga reptans, Melissa officinalis, Mentha × piperita, Sambucus nigra, Symphytum officinale.

Herbs for a Bog or Pond
Acorus spp.*, Cardamine pratensis, Filipendula ulmaria, Iris versicolor, Mentha aquatica.*

PRINCIPLES OF PLANTING

Container-grown herbs can be planted out all year round, but will establish more quickly in autumn or spring when there is more dependable rainfall. If they have been kept under cover during the winter or bought from under cover at a nursery, they will need hardening off in a cold frame or unheated greenhouse before planting out in spring. Culinary and medicinal herbs should be planted away from possible contamination by pets, roadside pollution, and agricultural sprays. A number of commonly grown herbs, such as foxgloves (*Digitalis* spp.), castor oil plants (*Ricinus communis*), lily of the valley (*Convallaria majalis*), monkshoods (*Aconitum* spp.), opium poppy (*Papaver somniferum*), meadow saffron (*Colchicum autumnale*), and box (*Buxus sempervirens*), are highly poisonous and need careful siting in gardens used by children.

PLANTING METHODS

Water well before planting, since dry rootballs are difficult to wet thoroughly when underground. Bare roots can be submerged in water for several hours, so they have a thorough soaking. To avoid trampling and compacting the surrounding soil, which restricts root growth, stand on a board in order to reach the planting position. If you are following a planting plan, first set out the herbs in their positions, as shown above. Space them according to their expected height and spread so that they have room to reach their full potential – an angelica (*Angelica archangelica*) only 15cm (6in) high when planted will eventually exceed 2m (6ft) in height and 1.2m (4ft) in width. Seedlings of smaller herbs may be planted out more densely and thinned in stages.

Planting out is best done on a calm, damp day to minimize stress to the plants; sunny, windy days increase moisture loss. Incorporate some organic soil conditioner or concentrated organic fertilizer, such as dried poultry manure or fish meal. Coarse sand may also be added to heavy soils for herbs that need fast drainage. Firm the soil gently around the plant and water thoroughly to settle the soil and provide ample moisture for new root growth. After planting, pinch out the tips of shrubby herbs to encourage a bushy habit.

PLANTING OUT HERBS
Planting holes should be big enough to take some organic fertilizer or soil conditioner as well as the plants. Some extra plants will improve the coverage until they are all larger.

PLANTING INVASIVE HERBS IN OPEN GROUND

Some very useful garden herbs can be a nuisance because of their tendency to overwhelm neighbouring plants. These include mints (*Mentha* spp.), woodruff (*Galium odoratum*), and tansy (*Tanacetum vulgare*). Restrict their spread by planting in sunken containers, hidden below ground. Use a large pot, old bucket, or heavy-duty plastic bag, making drainage holes as necessary. Lift and divide the plant each spring and re-plant a small division, filling the container with fresh soil, potting mix, or a mixture of the two.

1 Dig a hole large enough to take the container. Make drainage holes if required and fill with a soil and compost mixture.

2 Plant the herb (this is peppermint, *Mentha × piperita*), adding enough soil to cover the pot. Water thoroughly to establish.

HERBS IN CONTAINERS

Any herb grown in a container needs more care than those in the open ground. Almost any container is suitable, provided that it has a drainage hole to prevent waterlogging, but is covered with crocks to prevent loss of soil mix. However, watertight containers can be used for herbs that enjoy wet conditions, such as galingale (*Cyperus longus*). Terracotta pots are well suited to Mediterranean herbs, and they age beautifully to complement the subtle colours of flowers and foliage. The disadvantages are that they dry out quickly in warm weather and must be brought under cover in winter unless they are frost-resistant.

A STRAWBERRY JAR
This is a popular and practical container for growing herbs in a confined area. It allows for seasonal flexibility, since most of the plants are replaced regularly.

HERBS ON DIFFERENT LEVELS
A display of herbs in terracotta pots makes an attractive feature for small spaces. The gold-variegated and purple sages (Salvia officinalis 'Icterina' and 'Purpurascens') add a touch of colour to the area.

Rectangular Versailles tubs or half-barrels are effective for more formal plantings, perhaps of a clipped bay or box. Mature shrubs and trees trained as standards give height to the containerized garden. A large container or group of smaller ones can provide a focal point for a herb garden or add interest beside a garden seat or entrance. An entire herb garden may consist of containers, on walls, steps, and windowsills, as well as at ground level. Where space is at a premium, a number of different herbs can be grown in a very small area, using a half-barrel, cartwheel, or windowbox. A strawberry jar (a pot with planting pockets) is an attractive container for growing a selection of herbs. It is convenient for regularly used culinary herbs, but can also be planted with interesting collections, such as home remedies .

WHY GROW HERBS IN CONTAINERS?
One advantage of growing herbs in pots is that they can be sited conveniently for easy harvesting. Another is that containers can be kept looking good all year, since unsightly plants can simply be replaced, and invasive herbs, given separate containers, are easily controlled. Tender herbs can be positioned somewhere warm and sheltered, and brought under cover in bad weather. Herbs with special soil requirements are not a problem, since they can be grown using suitable soil mix. Succulent herbs that appeal to slugs, such as basil (*Ocimum* spp.) and purslane (*Portulaca oleracea*), are also more easily protected when grown in pots.

PLANTING AND SITING
The key to success with containers of herbs is to plant the appropriate kind and number of plants in each pot. If they are over-planted, the containers become top-heavy, dry out quickly, and soon exhaust nutrients. When choosing herbs for a mixed planting in a single container, consider eventual size and habit carefully. Dwarf cultivars (such as *Origanum vulgare* 'Compactum') or naturally small-growing herbs, such as houseleeks (*Sempervivum tectorum*) and heartsease (*Viola tricolor*), are good choices. Prostrate or trailing herbs are useful for softening outlines. Large, deep-rooted herbs, such as angelica (*Angelica* spp.), lovage (*Levisticum officinale*), and fennel (*Foeniculum vulgare*), are unsuitable for containers in the long term. Use a soil-based mix for herbs in pots, since it is relatively heavier than soilless mixes and retains moisture better. It is also easier to re-wet if it does dry out. Containers tend to dry out more quickly as the growing season advances, and may be given additional water by standing them in trays. In order to reduce evaporation, place containers in a sheltered position, so that they are protected from the wind. Spiky herbs, such as standard hollies and agaves planted as specimens, are wind-resistant, but can be hazardous in confined spaces.

SUGGESTED CONTAINER PLANTS

Specimen Shrubs and Trees
Aloysia triphylla
Buxus sempervirens and cultivars
Citrus spp.
Eucalyptus globulus
Ilex aquifolium 'Ferox Argentea'
Juniperus communis
Laurus nobilis and cultivars
Myrtus communis 'Variegata'
Olea europaea
Pelargonium spp. and hybrids
Phyllostachys nigra and cultivars
Pinus sylvestris 'Aurea'
Punica granatum var. *nana*

Centerpieces for Large Containers
Agave americana 'Variegata'
Helianthus annuus 'Teddy Bear'
Laurus nobilis and cultivars
Ricinus communis 'Impala'
Zea mays 'Variegata'

Compact Herbs
Arctostaphylos uva-ursi
Buxus sempervirens 'Suffruticosa'
Buxus sempervirens 'Kingsville Dwarf'
Dianthus chinensis cultivars
Hedera helix 'Erecta'
Hyssopus officinalis subsp. *aristatus*
Lavandula angustifolia 'Nana Alba'

Myrtus communis subsp. *tarentina*
Ocimum basilicum 'Well-Sweep Miniature Purple'
Ocimum minimum
Origanum vulgare 'Compactum'
Pinus mugo var. *pumilio*
Salvia officinalis 'Compacta'
Santolina chamaecyparissus var. *nana*
Sempervivum tectorum
Tagetes patula cultivars
Thymus serpyllum 'Elfin'
Thymus vulgaris 'Erectus'

Trailing Herbs
Acinos arvensis
Cytisus scoparius subsp. *maritimus*
Fragaria vesca
Glechoma hederacea 'Variegata'
Hedera helix cultivars
Rosmarinus officinalis Prostratus Group
Thymus herba-barona
Vinca minor and cultivars

Aquatic Herbs
Acorus spp.
Cyperus longus
Houttuynia cordata
Iris versicolor
Mentha aquatica
Menyanthes trifoliata
Nasturtium officinale

AN ELEGANT STANDARD
Growing a standard box (Buxus sempervirens) in a container allows room around it for bushy or creeping herbs, such as thymes (Thymus spp.).

AN ATTRACTIVE CONTRAST
A pot of ornamental alliums set against a bed of pink chives (Allium schoenoprasum) and silver-leafed thyme (Thymus vulgaris 'Silver Posie').

soaking. In the growing season, feed every two weeks with an organic liquid fertilizer. In the winter, bring the containers under cover. Frost-proof pots may be left outdoors, but in severe weather you may need to wrap them with insulating material (such as old carpet, hessian, or bubblewrap) to protect the roots from freezing. Fleece can be used to cover both containers and plants, since it lets in sufficient light. In the spring, check the condition of each plant.

If a plant is potbound (has outgrown the container) there will be roots protruding through the base of the pot, pale foliage, and weak new growth. A potbound plant can either be transferred into a larger pot, or split for replanting in the original pot. Cutting back the herbs after they have been repotted will stimulate new growth, remove any pests on the foliage, and compensate for any root damage. If repotting is impractical, the container can be top-dressed by replacing the top 2.5–5cm (1–2in) with fresh soil mix and well-rotted organic matter. Bay trees thrive in relatively small containers and, provided they are not too top-heavy, are better top-dressed than repotted.

HIGH-LEVEL HERB GARDENS
Growing herbs on balconies, roof gardens, window ledges, and in hanging baskets is a challenge, since the restricted space limits choice, and extra air movement accelerates drying out. In confined spaces, the habit of a plant can be put to practical use. Where a large barrel will fit, several evergreen herbs with different habits make the best use of available space and give a pleasing display all year. Try combining a climber such as jasmine (*Jasminum officinale*), trained on a fan-shaped trellis, with dwarf white lavender (*Lavandula angustifolia* 'Nana Alba') or rock hyssop (*Hyssopus officinalis* subsp. *aristatus*) around the base, and a prostrate rosemary (*Rosmarinus officinalis* Prostratus Group) or creeping savory (*Satureja spicigera*) to soften the front. If you intend to grow herbs on a window ledge, the choice of plant depends on its position. Woody-stemmed herbs with resilient foliage, such as sage (*Salvia* spp.), thyme (*Thymus* spp.), rosemary (*Rosmarinus* spp.), and bay (*Laurus nobilis*), are more wind-resistant than soft-stemmed ones such as chives (*Allium schoenoprasum*), chervil (*Anthriscus cerefolium*), and parsley (*Petroselinum crispum*).

CARE AND MAINTENANCE
Regular watering is essential. Check soil moisture daily, especially in hot or windy conditions. Water in the evening or early morning, giving the pot a thorough

PLANTING A WINDOWBOX

Herbs for Windowboxes
Dianthus chinensis cultivars
Glechoma hederacea 'Variegata'
Hedera helix cultivars
Hyssopus officinalis subsp. *aristatus*
Lavandula angustifolia 'Nana Alba'
Origanum vulgare 'Compactum'
Rosmarinus officinalis 'Benenden Blue'
Rosmarinus officinalis Prostratus Group
Salvia officinalis 'Compacta'
Salvia viridis cultivars
Santolina chamaecyparissus var. *nana*
Tagetes patula cultivars

Tanacetum parthenium 'Golden Moss'
Thymus vulgaris and cultivars
Vinca minor and cultivars
Viola tricolor

A GOLDEN COMBINATION
Golden marjoram and golden feverfew combine well with yellow-flowered bedding plants in this windowbox.

WILDFLOWER GARDENING WITH HERBS

Creating your own area of wild garden has a special appeal. Also, the plants form a natural community and are more resistant to pests and diseases as a result. This eliminates the need for fertilizers and sprays, even of an organic kind. Planting with wild herbs attracts wildlife that thrives in certain habitats, so in time the area will become a mini nature reserve. Visually, wild areas are restful on the eye and an enticing retreat from more formal garden areas. They will also provide organic herbs for harvesting, and an abundance of craft materials and wild flowers for cutting.

SUN-BAKED CONDITIONS
The best way of gardening in an arid area is to plant native species that are adapted to extreme heat and drought. Here desert plants bloom in a garden in Tucson, Arizona.

ENVIRONMENTAL CONSIDERATIONS

Whether you plant native or non-native herbs, there is a chance that they may seed into the wild and disrupt local plant populations. If you live near an ecologically sensitive area, or farmland, check with regional advisers before planting. For native herbs, it is best to purchase seeds or plants that originated locally. These days, seeds of familiar wild flowers may have been produced in a different region or country, and have subtle differences in adaptations to soils, climate, pests, diseases, and pollinators. Specialist wildflower nurseries can advise on suitable strains for your area. Non-native herbs pose another threat. Some Eurasian species have proved extremely invasive elsewhere. These include purple loosestrife, a major weed of North American wetlands, and hemlock and horehound, which are destroying Australian ecosystems.

IDENTIFYING YOUR HABITAT

Having checked for restrictions in your area, you then need to assess conditions in your garden. Existing trees and shrubs that give dappled shade provide a woodland setting. Moist or wet soil, perhaps in a boggy hollow or beside water, is ideal for aquatic herbs. Open sunny areas can be planted as annual or perennial meadows, or as a prairie. Areas on poor dry soil can support drought-tolerant plants that enjoy arid conditions

When you have identified a suitable area, list the herbs you would like to grow, and check their requirements as to soil, exposure, and hardiness. Keep in mind their final height and spread, especially if you are including trees and shrubs in the scheme.

PREPARATION, PURCHASING, AND PLANTING

You can create a wildflower garden by clearing an area, or by adapting a suitably planted site. Areas already planted will need some "spot" clearance to make space for new plants. Wildflower areas may be started from seeds or young plants, though just scattering seed into a planted area is unlikely to succeed, since seedlings are unlikely to compete with surrounding vegetation. Wildflower nurseries offer "plugs" (young plants grown in "cells" rather than pots), which are an excellent way of introducing wild flowers to a planted area. You can raise your own plugs from packets of seed, or seed collected locally, providing you do not collect from protected species. Sow seeds in multi-cell trays and thin to the strongest seedling. Whatever the weather when planting out, water well to settle the soil around the roots. When established, wildflower areas need little maintenance.

A BANK OF WILD FLOWERS
In this garden a meadow-style planting covers a steep bank, providing an attractive, low-maintenance solution to a difficult area, which also benefits wildlife.

AN ANNUAL MEADOW

You may not aspire to a field of poppies and cornflowers among grain, but a mass of brightly coloured annual herbs is easily achieved. In addition to poppies and cornflowers, these could include pot marigolds, California poppies, safflower, and painted sage, with Queen Anne's lace or dill as "fillers". For best results, clear the area completely and rake over before and after sowing. When the meadow has finished flowering, seed heads provide interest for many months. Collect seeds as they ripen or leave for the birds. The following spring, remove debris to prevent a build up of fertility, because annuals flower better on relatively poor soil. Then weed, rake over, and re-sow. You should need less seed in successive years as natural regeneration takes place.

A PERENNIAL MEADOW OR PRAIRIE

Grasslands vary the world over, according to the mix of species, and are rich in colourful, interesting herbs. A European meadow or native American prairie can be planted on a garden scale, either from seed or plugs. Wildflower nurseries sell a range of mixes for different conditions, and can advise on quantities.

Do not be tempted to let your meadow or prairie bloom in its first year. This weakens the perennials and allows grasses and weeds to get the upper hand. Instead, mow at intervals on the highest blade setting to encourage the young plants to concentrate on roots and shoots. In subsequent years, cut after flowering and remove the hay. An existing lawn can be turned into a perennial meadow or prairie by removing patches of turf and planting young perennials into it. Mow lightly once if grasses threaten to overwhelm the herbs. American prairies benefit from being burnt every few years.

European meadow herbs include summer-flowering clover, yarrow, agrimony, wild carrot, lady's bedstraw, melilot, sorrel, and toadflax. For spring interest, add cowslips, and for late colour, plant bulbs of meadow saffron. A native American prairie might include coneflowers, *Eupatorium*, *Liatris*, and *Monarda* species, anise hyssop, butterflyweed, false indigo, and wild quinine.

A WOODLAND HERB AREA

A few trees and shrubs create woodland conditions in which you can grow a wide range of herbs that enjoy a cool, moist root run, and some shade. Small woodlanders include primroses, violets, ramsons, ramps, woodruff, and lungwort, and colony-forming birthroot, Indian turnip, ginseng, and wild gingers. Intersperse these with taller plants, such as Solomon's seal, foxgloves, monkshoods, and Culver's root. Woodland herbs thrive in leafmould. If your area has not yet built up a layer of leaf litter, plant young herbs in pockets of compost-enriched soil.

A WETLAND AREA

To make a bog garden, excavate an area to a depth of 45cm (18in) and line with heavy-duty, black polythene. Replace the soil, enriching it with compost, leafmould, or well-rotted manure. A small pond is easily made using a pre-formed or butyl pond liner.

Herbs that enjoy wet conditions include watercress, bog bean, and blue flag, while beebalm, meadowsweet, valerian, and Chinese rhubarb grow lush in humus-rich, moist soil. Water mint and houttuynia make good ground cover in boggy soil, and large areas could support moisture-loving trees and shrubs, such as alder, willow, and sweet gale.

A DESERT, COASTAL, OR GARRIGUE AREA

Many herbs grow naturally in poor soils and arid conditions, and can bring interest, fragrance, and useful

ingredients to areas that are too dry for other garden plants. For example, classic culinary herbs, such as rosemary, sage, thyme, oregano, and savory, cover stony Mediterranean hillsides. A garrigue-style garden is the answer for areas subject to drought. To complete the picture, add colourful lavender and *Cistus*, with bay, boxwood, or olive for contrast, underplanted with mandrakes and orris. Dry sandy areas can be turned into desert gardens by annual sowings of California poppies and flax, punctuated by *Eucalyptus*, agaves, and *Aloe vera*. Herbs such as samphire, sea holly, sea buckthorn, and *Rosa rugosa* thrive in coastal situations, tolerating sandy soils and salt. Though drought-tolerant herbs survive long dry periods when established, they should be started during the coolest, rainiest time of the year, and watered in after planting.

LOW-MAINTENANCE WOODLAND
Woodland areas create the ideal habitat for herbs, such as lungwort (Pulmonaria officinalis), *Solomon's seal* (Polygonatum odoratum), *and wake robin* (Trillium erectum), *which naturally are shade-loving. They grow and flower early in the year when the trees are still bare, while in summer benefit from shade and a cool, moist root run.*

WETLAND HERBS
Wet or boggy areas of the garden give scope for planting aquatic and moisture-loving herbs, such as meadowsweet (Filipendula ulmaria), *sweet flag* (Acorus calamus), *and skunk cabbage* (Symplocarpus foetidus).

GROWING UNDER COVER

There are herbs for all tastes that can be grown in various situations under cover or indoors. The additional warmth and shelter are ideal for tender subjects and extend the growing season for hardy and marginal plants. Whether in a greenhouse, in a conservatory, or on a windowsill, the herbs will be close at hand for harvesting and for the enjoyment of their fragrance. It is also easy to make changes when plants are past their best.

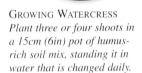

GROWING WATERCRESS
Plant three or four shoots in a 15cm (6in) pot of humus-rich soil mix, standing it in water that is changed daily.

WINDOWSILL HERBS
Arranged on a kitchen windowsill, pots of sweet marjoram (Origanum majorana), *chives* (Allium schoenoprasum), *purple sage* (Salvia officinalis 'Purpurascens'), *and mint* (Mentha spicata) *are at hand for culinary use.*

LIGHT AND WARMTH

Although the covered environment offers protection against the elements, it may cut down the amount of available light. Most herbs thrive in bright light, and therefore need a sunny position with 12–14 hours of daylight per day and as much overhead light as possible. Variegated plants need more light than others, since they have a smaller green area for photosynthesis. Plants receiving directional light can be turned each time they are watered to counteract one-sided growth. A fan heater, designed for use in humid conditions, can control temperature and also function as a cooling fan for summer. Most tender plants come from tropical regions where humidity rises as the temperature increases. Humid conditions can be created by misting plants in the morning, or by standing containers on a layer of moisture-retentive material, such as gravel, sand, or capillary matting. Greenhouses may be damped down by splashing water on the floor and shelving. If the humidity is too low, tender plants may develop brown tips on leaves and become prone to red spider mite; if it is too high, plants may develop fungal diseases, such as grey mould (*Botrytis*).

HERBS INDOORS

One of the easiest ways to grow culinary herbs is in pots on a windowsill. The only limiting factors are size and the length of time that any herb can be kept in good condition in lower light levels. Pots of seedlings for cutting, such as salad cress, can be bought from supermarkets, or they may be raised from seed. Rocket (*Eruca vesicaria* subsp. *sativa*), coriander (*Coriandrum sativum*), and dill (*Anethum graveolens*) are especially suitable for cropping as seedlings: rocket seeds sprout within three to four days; coriander takes about five or six days; and dill is usually up within about ten days. Herbs such as parsley (*Petroselinum crispum*), thyme (*Thymus vulgaris*), sage (*Salvia officinalis*), rosemary (*Rosmarinus officinalis*), savory (*Satureja* spp.), and basil (*Ocimum basilicum*) can be grown as single plants in pots, or in a hanging basket or wall-mounted container. Baskets tend to dry out easily, but moisture retention can be improved by adding granules that absorb water. Nasturtiums (*Tropaeolum majus*) can trail to give colour. Seed onions or "sets" (*Allium cepa*) and cloves of garlic (*A. sativum*), left whole as a bulb or separated, can be planted several to a pot at any time from autumn to spring. Within about three weeks they will sprout tasty leaves that can be snipped when they reach 5cm (2in) long. Tall-growing herbs will soon outgrow a windowsill, but even giants such as lovage (*Levisticum officinale*) and fennel (*Foeniculum vulgare*) will provide useful amounts of flavouring at the seedling stage. Many of these culinary herbs require a cold period and are therefore unlikely to thrive indefinitely in the warmth and relatively low light of even the sunniest windowsill. Aim to replace single plants two or three times a year, and seedlings every month or so.

HERBS FOR THE GREENHOUSE

The greenhouse is an ideal place to raise culinary herbs in variety and quantity. Light levels are good, and even unheated greenhouses enable out-of-season crops to be grown. Clumps of chives (*Allium schoenoprasum*), French tarragon (*Artemisia dracunculus*), and mint (*Mentha* spp.) can be lifted, divided, and potted up for early spring crops, or for winter use, under glass where frost-free temperatures can be maintained. Discard forced plants in spring, or plant them out and do not harvest again for an entire growing season to allow them time to recover. Sown in late summer or early autumn, herbs such as chervil (*Anthriscus cerefolium*), cilantro, and parsley will continue to grow throughout the winter if protected from severe cold.

THE GREENHOUSE IN SUMMER

The best use of a greenhouse in the summer is to grow tender herbs that often give disappointing results in the open ground in cool summers. A wider range of plants can also be grown. Basil (*Ocimum basilicum*) rarely thrives outdoors in cold areas but it luxuriates in warmth and light under glass. Growing several different cultivars gives visual interest and a choice of flavours. *Perilla frutescens* is another herb that benefits from extra warmth, and has purple-leafed cultivars. Chilli peppers (*Capsicum* spp.) enjoy temperatures above 21°C (70°F) and bear more reliably under glass in cool regions. If the greenhouse gets too hot and sunny, shade can be provided by climbing herbs, such as grapes (*Vitis vinifera*), cucumbers (*Cucumis sativus*), or loofah (*Luffa cylindrica*).

ORNAMENTAL HERBS INDOORS

A garden room or conservatory is a refuge in which to sit and enjoy the fragrance and beauty of herbs in all weathers and seasons. A few large, well-chosen plants with a long period of interest may give more pleasure and need less maintenance than an assortment of smaller ones. Citrus trees make attractive specimens, with glossy, evergreen leaves, delightfully fragrant

blossoms, and colourful fruits. The variegated lemon (*Citrus limon* 'Variegata') is one of the finest for indoor cultivation, with its yellow-edged leaves and striped young fruits. Variegated myrtle (*Myrtus communis* 'Variegata') also offers greater interest than its plain green counterpart and, being less hardy, is a suitable candidate for cosseting under glass.

Scented-leafed pelargoniums are very varied in leaf shape, texture, and aroma and are excellent for indoors. They tolerate hard pruning and dry conditions and are easily propagated when they become too woody or leggy. Site them near entrances so that their fragrance fills the air as you pass. The brilliant green, velvety peppermint pelargonium (*Pelargonium tomentosum*) is happy in partial shade. Tender sages (*Salvia* spp.) and lavenders (*Lavandula* spp.) are similarly generous with scent and colour; the pineapple sage, *Salvia elegans* 'Scarlet Pineapple', produces scarlet flowers in midwinter in the northern hemisphere. For an even more exotic touch, try growing pots of ginger (*Zingiber officinale*) or turmeric (*Curcuma longa*) from fresh rhizomes. They make elegant foliage plants, with cane-like stems several feet tall, and conveniently die down in the autumn to make space for plants brought in from the garden. Complete your tropical paradise with the heavy fragrance of patchouli (*Pogostemon cablin*) and Arabian jasmine (*Jasminum sambac*), which at room temperature flowers on and off all year.

PESTS AND DISEASES

Ventilation and hygiene are of paramount importance in controlling pests and diseases. To keep fungal diseases at bay, remove dead leaves and flowers regularly, and open windows on nice days, or use a fan. Spring clean the area at the change of each season. Keep glass clean inside and out to ensure maximum light. If containers of plants are brought in from the garden in the autumn, remove dead parts, check for pests and diseases, and treat appropriately. Ample warmth encourages the growth of pests as well as plants.

SOME COMMON AILMENTS

Inspect indoor herbs regularly, especially under the leaves and around the growing tips, for any telltale signs of pests or diseases. Common pests such as red spider mite, aphid, and whitefly can be controlled by organic sprays or by introducing predators that will attack them. Improved air circulation helps to control fungal diseases.

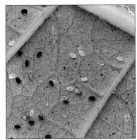
Whitefly nymphs

Adult whitefly

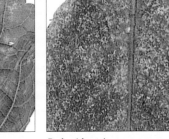
Red spider mite

BIOLOGICAL PEST CONTROL

Most people are averse to using chemical sprays on culinary herbs, especially when growing indoors, but a biological control, which may not eliminate the pest altogether but reduces it to acceptable levels, can be used. The term means the use of predators, parasites, and diseases that affect a particular pest. These agents may sound alarming, but they are smaller than the pests, and work invisibly. There are now biological controls for aphid, whitefly, red spider mite, mealybugs, some scale insects, thrips, caterpillars, and vine weevil grubs.

For best results, introduce the control before plants become heavily infested, since it may take a few weeks to have a noticeable impact. Make sure you order enough predators for the area, or they may not keep pace with the pests. Most predators and parasites need a minimum day-time temperature of 21°C (70°F) and bright light in order to breed successfully. If pest populations get out of hand in early spring before conditions are suitable for controls, cut back affected plants, discard foliage, and repot or apply a generous amount of fertilizer to encourage healthier growth. Do not use pesticides after controls have been introduced, other than those specified in the instructions, because even organic pest controls may harm predators.

GREENHOUSE SUN AND SHADE
This grapevine (Vitis vinifera) *fruits well in warmth and has been trained along the roof of the greenhouse to benefit from the sunlight and to provide shade for foliage plants.*

ROUTINE GARDEN CARE

However well the herb garden is designed and planted initially, it needs regular care to look good from year to year. General maintenance is obviously important, but plants need individual attention, too. Tasks such as dead-heading and pruning also give you the opportunity to enjoy the textures and habits of herbs at close quarters. The delightful scents produced by many herbs when moved or cut add to the enjoyment of routine garden care in the herb garden.

VARIEGATION
The pale areas of variegated plants, such as Teucrium × lucidrys *'Variegatum', tend to scorch if planted in full sun. Most variegated plants produce plain green shoots occasionally. These encourage reversion and must be removed promptly.*

WATERING
Many Mediterranean herbs, such as thymes (*Thymus* spp.) and rosemary (*Rosmarinus officinalis*), are naturally drought-resistant when established and need watering only in periods of prolonged drought. Newly planted herbs need regular watering until strong new growth is apparent and the root system has extended beyond the original rootball. It is better to water thoroughly and less frequently rather than little and often, which encourages production of shallow surface roots. The best time to water is in the evening; this minimizes evaporation.

FEEDING AND MULCHING
Few popular culinary herbs are rich feeders, but heavy cropping – of chives (*Allium schoenoprasum*), for example – increases their nutritional requirements. An annual mulch of bulky organic fertilizer, such as soil mix or shredded bark soil conditioner, replenishes nutrients, and inhibits weeds. This should be spread in spring after rain and when the ground has warmed up; covering dry, frozen earth retards growth. On damp, heavy soils, feed and mulch only established herbs that thrive in humus-rich, moist conditions, such as mint (*Mentha* spp.), bergamot (*Monarda didyma*), and angelica (*Angelica archangelica*). Spread a layer of gritty material around Mediterranean and grey-leafed herbs to help prevent fungal disease and rot. Heavy manuring is not recommended for herbs. Excessive nitrogen encourages sappy growth that lacks flavour and is more prone to frost damage, pests, and diseases.

WEEDING
Removing weeds from the herb garden ensures that growth is not suppressed by competition for light, nutrients, and moisture. It also provides the opportunity to check the condition of your herbs and to enjoy their aromas and details of foliage and flowers. Take special care when weeding near rue (*Ruta graveolens*), since contact with the leaf oil in bright sun (or sometimes even in bright light) can cause severe and painful blistering of the skin.

VARIEGATION AND REVERSION
Most variegated herbs are propagated from green-leafed species that have produced a freak variegated shoot. These "sports", or mutations, may be caused by environmental factors or by a particular virus. They are usually less vigorous than their plain green counterparts, which is an advantage in invasive species, such as ground elder (*Aegopodium podagraria*). Sometimes, variegated plants develop shoots that revert to plain green. These are more vigorous and should be removed, or the entire plant will eventually revert to plain green. Some variegated herbs, such as pineapple mint (*Mentha suaveolens* 'Variegata'), also put out the odd plain cream shoot. Again, these are best removed as they scorch easily. Reverted shoots of culinary herbs can be used for flavouring.

DEAD-HEADING
Some herbs flower for longer or grow more vigorously if their faded flower heads are removed promptly, saving the energy that would otherwise be put into seed production. This is particularly true of annuals, such as pot marigold (*Calendula officinalis*) and German chamomile (*Matricaria recutita*). Vigilant dead-heading is required for herbs that self-sow freely, such as red plantain (*Plantago major* 'Rubrifolia'). Dandelions grown for their roots and leaves should have flower buds removed as they appear. Individual flower heads may be picked off or cut with pruners; flower heads of shrubby herbs, such as lavender (*Lavandula* spp.), are best removed en masse with about 2.5cm (1in) of growth.

CONTROLLING GROWTH
A number of commonly grown herbs are invasive. These include mint (*Mentha* spp.), periwinkle (*Vinca* spp.), and woodruff (*Galium odoratum*). If grown in the open ground rather than containers, it is advisable to remove excess growth as it appears, especially if nearby plants are threatened. Some shrubs and trees produce suckers from stems or roots, which may spoil the appearance of the plant. In grafted specimens, suckers resemble the more vigorous stock in foliage, and will dominate if allowed to grow. *Prunus* spp. tend to develop suckers if their roots are disturbed by digging. When small, suckers can be rubbed out easily with a thumb, but when further developed they should be cut off with a knife close to the stem or root.

PREVENTION OF SELF-SOWING
*Remove the seed heads of angelica (*Angelica archangelica, *above) before the seeds ripen to prevent an invasion of seedlings that will smother small garden plants.*

PRUNING AND COPPICING

MAINTAINING HEALTHY GROWTH
Prune Mediterranean herbs, such as this cotton lavender (Santolina chamaecyparissus), *hard in spring in order to encourage new growth. Trim the plant again after flowering.*

COPPICING SHRUBS
To encourage colourful growth, cut back plants such as this willow (Salix alba subsp. vitellina 'Britzensis') *to almost ground level at the first sign of growth in spring.*

PRUNING GRAPE VINES
All grape vines should be pruned when dormant, otherwise they "bleed" (ooze sap) and are weakened. Cut back stems that have fruited to two or three buds from the main stem.

PRUNING

Pruning is an important part of routine care, stimulating vigorous fresh growth and creating well-shaped, manageable plants. Herbs that are grown for their fresh young foliage may be cut back hard once or twice during the growing season to produce a supply of new leaves. Mints (*Mentha* spp.) and lemon balm (*Melissa officinalis*) should be cut back before flowering and then again in late summer. It is best to leave chives (*Allium schoenoprasum*) and marjoram (*Oregano* spp.) until after flowering, since the flowers are both attractive and also make useful flavourings. Remove the first flowering stems of sorrel (*Rumex acetosa*) as they appear, to prolong leaf production. Unlike other Mediterranean herbs, thyme (*Thymus* spp.) dislikes hard pruning and should be trimmed lightly after flowering.

Most deciduous trees are pruned when dormant in late autumn and early winter. Care is needed with those that "bleed" (exude sap) excessively if pruned towards the end of dormancy. Examples are horse chestnut (*Aesculus*), birch (*Betula*), walnut (*Juglans*), and *Prunus* spp., which are best pruned in midsummer. The majority of evergreen trees require little pruning other than the removal of dead wood. Most conifers dislike hard pruning and do not regenerate well. Box (*Buxus*) needs clipping once or twice in the growing season when grown as a hedge or topiary.

Pruning a shrub enhances the shape of the plant and encourages better foliage, flowers, and fruits. Elder (*Sambucus nigra*) should be pruned hard in winter as it comes into growth very early in the year. Hard pruning is particularly necessary for elder cultivars, since they will produce larger, more colourful leaves in response to it. Many trees, shrubs, and climbers, especially those grown for their fruits, such as grapes (*Vitis* spp.), blackcurrants (*Ribes nigrum*), and blackberries or raspberries (*Rubus* spp.), need specialized pruning. The A–Z of Herbs (pp. 92–411) gives details of pruning for individual species.

TRAINING

Various shrubs and climbers described in this book can be trained against a wall, pillar, or pergola to give interest and height in the herb garden and extend the range of plants grown in a small space. Walls act as storage heaters, offering considerable protection to borderline-hardy plants. It is important to establish a framework for training when planting, using durable materials, and to tie in new growths when they are still soft and pliable. A judicious combination of pruning and training is needed throughout the growing season to discipline growth; a plant should not be allowed to become so heavy and wide-spreading that it damages its supports and swamps nearby plants.

AUTUMN CLEARANCE

Cutting down the dead foliage of herbaceous perennials may look neater, but leaving this natural layer until spring helps to protect the dormant crowns from frost and wind, and provides hibernation places for beneficial insects. Remove dead leaves that fall on thymes and other small, evergreen herbs, since they may encourage fungal disease.

WINTER PROTECTION

The hardiness of many common culinary herbs varies according to the species or cultivar. In cold areas, protect marginally hardy herbs with a layer of insulating material, or lift them and bring under cover. In spring, they can be cut back and planted out again, or used as a source of cuttings to propagate new plants. This works especially well for scented-leafed pelargoniums.

TRANSPLANTING

Even with careful planning it is sometimes necessary to move a plant to avoid overcrowding or to create a more pleasing association. For perennials, shrubs, and trees, this is best undertaken in autumn or early spring. Large plants should be lifted carefully to minimize root damage, and they may need to have their roots wrapped in hessian or plastic sheeting to protect the rootball during transit. Annuals usually need thinning out so that they have sufficient room to develop without hindrance.

Transplant on a damp, rainy day, but do not tread on the soil. Water the plants well afterwards, since annuals tend to "bolt" (flower prematurely) when severely stressed by disturbance and shortage of water. Chervil (*Anthriscus cerefolium*) and dill (*Anethum graveolens*) are particularly prone to bolting. Flax (*Linum usitatissimum*), borage (*Borago officinalis*), and California poppies (*Eschscholzia californica*) do not transplant well under any conditions.

CLIPPED BAY TREES
Bays trained as standards (as here) or in other formal shapes should be clipped in summer, to maintain an attractive, tidy shape.

PROPAGATING HERBS

Herbs may be propagated by a wide variety of methods, depending on the kind of plant. For information on individual species and cultivars, see the Propagation information given in the A–Z of Herbs (see pp.92–411). Many herbs are easy to grow from seed or can be propagated by splitting the roots or from cuttings. Some can be grown from the pips of the fruit, or from shoots produced from the root or rhizome.

PLANTING OUT IN OPEN GROUND
When seedlings are sufficiently advanced, they can be planted out at the recommended spacing and depth. Firm the soil gently around the roots and water in well.

PLANTING IN PAVING
Sow seeds in moist soil in the cracks of a patio or path to add interest.

RAISING HERBS FROM SEED

To give your herbs a head start, sow in pots or trays of seed compost and prick out individually when large enough to handle. Where larger quantities are required, sow in a prepared bed of fine soil in the open. Seeds of small, creeping herbs, such as wild thyme (*Thymus serpyllum*) may also be sown directly into cracks between paving stones where it would be difficult to insert plants. Spring and autumn are the best times to sow most seeds.

Notably cold-tolerant annuals such as borage (*Borago officinalis*), pot marigolds (*Calendula officinalis*), cornflowers (*Centaurea cyanus*), and poppies (*Papaver* spp.) can be sown in spring to flower in summer, or in early autumn for flowering the following spring. Biennials such as evening primrose (*Oenothera biennis*), angelica (*Angelica archangelica*), and caraway (*Carum carvi*) should be sown in late summer or early autumn to flower the following summer. Thin out seedlings after germination and again after a few weeks so that only the strongest are left to grow on. Short-lived, hardy herbs that are used in large quantities, such as coriander (*Coriandrum sativum*) or parsley (*Petroselinum crispum*), should be sown at intervals of 3–4 weeks from early spring to early autumn for a regular supply of young leaves. Dill (*Anethum graveolens*) and chervil (*Anthriscus cerefolium*) must be sown *in situ* as they tend to "bolt" (flower prematurely) if the roots are disturbed. In cold areas, basil (*Ocimum* spp.) should not be sown until late spring when there is ample warmth and light. Seeds need a minimum temperature of 13°C (55°F) and good ventilation to prevent damping off and fungal diseases such as grey mould (*Botrytis*).

Perennials should be sown in warmth in spring, growing the seedlings in pots until they are large enough to be hardened off and planted out. Seeds of some hardy herbaceous perennials, trees, and shrubs need stratifying (subjecting to a period of cold) in order to break their dormancy. Soak the seeds overnight, put them in a plastic bag containing a mixture of moist peat and sand, and place the bag in a refrigerator for 4–12 weeks at 1–5°C (34–41°F). As an alternative, they may be sown in containers of soil, covered with a layer of sharp sand to prevent mudsplash, and left outdoors through the winter. Seeds needing stratification include those of aconite (*Aconitum napellus*), beech (*Fagus* spp.), birch (*Betula* spp.), and primrose (*Primula vulgaris*); also *Adonis*, *Euonymus*, and many *Viburnum* species. Alternate periods of warmth and cold are required for successful germination of *Trillium* and *Paeonia* species. Hard-coated seeds, such as those of *Galega officinalis*, *Baptisia tinctoria*, and *Paeonia* spp., germinate more quickly if the seed coat is scarified (nicked or abraded with sandpaper) before sowing so that the seed can more readily absorb moisture.

SAVING SEED

If you save seed from garden plants, bear in mind that certain herbs may cross-pollinate, giving rise to seedlings that differ from the mother plant. When various kinds of thyme (*Thymus* spp.), marjoram (*Origanum* spp.), mint (*Mentha* spp.), and lavender (*Lavandula* spp.) are grown near each other, the chances of hybridization are high. Closely related genera may interbreed if they are grown together and flower at the same time; dill and fennel (*Foeniculum vulgare*) are known to cross, resulting in plants that are indeterminate in flavour. More successful from home-grown seed are coriander, pot marigold, sweet cicely (*Myrrhis odorata*), angelica, caraway, and borage. Seed should be gathered as soon as it is ripe, cleaned, and stored in envelopes (not plastic bags) in a dry, dark place at 1–5°C (34–41°F). Remember: when propagating from gathered seed, most cultivars do not come true from seed. Some annuals and biennials, such as poppies, pot marigolds, and foxgloves (*Digitalis* spp.), produce a percentage of plants resembling the mother plant, but this tends to decrease each year. Very few variegated cultivars come true from seed; an exception is variegated rue (*Ruta graveolens* 'Variegata').

SOWING SEEDS IN CONTAINERS

1 Sprinkle the dried seeds evenly over the surface of firmed seed soil mix. Space out larger seeds individually by hand. Cover lightly with sieved soil.

2 Once the seedlings are large enough to handle, tap the container to loosen the soil. Lift the seedlings out, holding them by the leaves, not the stems.

GRAPEVINE GROWN FROM PIPS
A grapevine (Vitis vinifera) *is easily grown from pips and should fruit successfully, but it will not come true from seed. However, it is valuable for its decorative qualities as well.*

PLANTS FROM PRODUCE

An interesting range of herbs can be propagated from produce bought in a greengrocer's shop. Many suppliers sell pots of growing herbs, such as parsley (*Petroselinum crispum*), basil (*Ocimum basilicum*), and coriander (*Coriandrum sativum*), which consist of numerous seedlings crowded together. These can be split into three or four smaller clumps, potted up separately, and grown on for planting out in either containers or the herb garden. (If the seedlings are growing in cotton fibre, rather than soil, it is easier to cut the rootball using scissors; some seedlings inevitably get damaged, but the majority will soon put out new roots and leaves). Bunches of watercress (*Nasturtium officinale*) can be treated as cuttings destined for the garden pond and will thrive for a short time in a jar of water on the windowsill. Fresh roots of ginger (*Zingiber officinale*), galingal (*Alpinia galanga*), and turmeric (*Curcuma longa*) rapidly produce handsome new shoots if planted in a pot of moist soil and kept above 21°C (70°F). Spring is the best time to start rhizomes into growth. Bulbs of garlic (*Allium sativum*), split into separate cloves, should be planted out 15cm (6in) apart in autumn, or raised in pots and then planted out the following spring. Alternatively, the cloves will sprout garlic-flavoured leaves if potted up 2.5cm (1in) apart. Fresh chilli peppers (*Capsicum* spp.) contain viable seeds from which useful and ornamental plants can easily be grown, given

COLLECTING AND SAVING SEED

1 Dry out all seed heads in a warm environment on absorbent paper to remove any moisture. As they dry, they will split open and begin to release their seeds.

2 When the seed heads are dry, shake out the seeds on to clean paper and clear away any debris. Store the seeds in a labelled envelope in a cool, dry place.

sufficient warmth and light. In addition, they may be commercial cultivars from other countries that are not otherwise available.

GROWING FROM PIPS

A number of trees and shrubs are easily raised from pips. A plant propagated in this way will not be exactly the same as the parent; pips from a 'Pinot Noir' grape, for instance, will grow into grape vines but the fruits may differ considerably from the original variety. Oranges, tangerines, lemons, and limes make very handsome trees with fragrant foliage, regardless of whether they flower or fruit successfully. The best time to plant citrus pips is in the spring. They take 3–4 weeks to germinate when kept at 16–21°C (60–70°F). Most citruses produce polyembryonic pips, resulting in two or three seedlings from each pip. These seedlings can be grown on together or separated.

Pomegranate seeds (*Punica granatum*) need about 21°C (70°F) for germination. They can be obtained from ripe fruits in the autumn and sown the following spring. Wash and dry a few seeds extracted from the pink pulp, or store a fruit whole through the winter – the skin shrinks and hardens but the seeds remain plump. Golden loquat fruits (*Eriobotrya japonica*) ripen in the spring, germinating readily from fresh pips sown in sandy soil and kept above 18°C (64°F). Young loquats make exceptionally fine pot plants. A papaya, or pawpaw (*Carica papaya*), is probably the most exotic tree you can grow easily from a pip. It needs 22–28°C (72–82°F) for germination. Use biodegradable pots for seeds and young papayas so that they can be potted on without root disturbance.

Seedlings grown under cover are prone to damping off, a condition caused by various fungi that are soil- or water-borne. The roots of the seedlings rot and the plants collapse. It is a virulent disease, especially prevalent in overcrowded seedlings and peat-based soil mixes, and usually spreads rapidly to all plants in the same container. There is no cure, but watering with a copper-based fungicide may help prevent infection. The best protection against damping off is to use clean containers, sterilized, peat-free soil, and clean water.

PROPAGATING GINGER
A good crop of ginger (Zingiber officinale) *can be produced in warm conditions by planting rhizomes bought from a supermarket.*

VEGETATIVE PROPAGATION

Of the various methods of propagation that you can use, one of the most popular and reliable is by taking cuttings. This applies to herbs as much as to other plants and is often the quickest way to increase perennials. The secret of rooting cuttings successfully is to know which part of the plant to take cuttings from, and when. Also important is understanding how to treat cuttings: some require warmth while others prefer cool conditions.

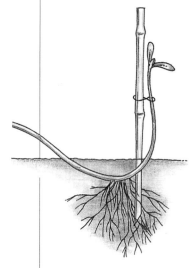

SIMPLE LAYERING
This form of propagation is best carried out on the pliable stem of a shrub between autumn and spring. The layer should have rooted by the following autumn and can then be detached from the parent and potted up until sufficiently established to plant out in open ground.

TYPES OF CUTTINGS

Use a clean sharp knife or pruners for taking cuttings and insert them as soon as possible in open, well-drained soil, or a mixture of peat and sand, or vermiculite. Adding perlite to the soil improves drainage for Mediterranean herbs. Warmth is needed for rooting: 18–25°C (64–77°F) for cool temperate species; 25–32°C (77–90°F) for warm-growing and tropical ones. Humidity is important for leafy cuttings; this can be provided by a propagator or by sealing the pot in a plastic bag. Pinching out the growing tip, and cutting the ends off large leaves, will further reduce wilting.

Hardwood (ripewood) cuttings are taken from mature wood at the end of the growing season from both evergreen subjects, such as hollies, and deciduous trees and shrubs, for example poplars and roses. Cuttings of deciduous species will be leafless. Hardwood cuttings are slow to root but are easily kept in good condition as they do not wilt.

Softwood cuttings are taken from young, immature, non-flowering growth during the growing season. They may be tip cuttings in shrubby herbs, such as hyssop (*Hyssopus officinalis*), and pelargoniums, or basal in herbaceous plants, such as marjoram (*Origanum* spp.), tansy (*Tanacetum vulgare*), and violet (*Viola* spp.). Remove lower leaves, which will rot if inserted into the soil. Softwood cuttings of most mints (*Mentha* spp.) root easily in water. Pelargonium cuttings should be left for a day so that the cut surfaces dry off; this helps prevent rot and improves rooting. Most softwood cuttings wilt easily, and may need to be kept under cover and misted to retain turgidity.

Semi-ripe cuttings are taken from half-ripened wood during the growing season from plants such as artemisias, box (*Buxus* spp.), *Citrus* spp., *Helichrysum*, lavender (*Lavandula* spp.), myrtle (*Myrtus*), rosemary (*Rosmarinus officinalis*), and thyme (*Thymus* spp.). This method also works best for conifers.

Stem cuttings can be taken from any section of the plant stem during the growing season, for example lemon balm (*Melissa officinalis*) and sage (*Salvia* spp.).

Basal cuttings are taken from the base of a plant, on or just below ground level, as it begins new growth in spring. Used mainly for herbaceous perennials, such as gland bellflower (*Adenophora* spp.). "Irishman's cuttings" are cuttings that already have some roots and so "take" very easily. Hop (*Humulus lupulus*) provides Irishman's cuttings in early spring.

Root cuttings are small sections taken from a semi-mature or mature root from plants such as horseradish (*Armoracia rusticana*) and goldenseal (*Hydrastis canadensis*).

Leaf cuttings consist of detached, healthy, mature leaves taken from the plant during the growing season, for example lady's smock (*Cardamine pratensis*).

Stem-tip (soft tip) cuttings are taken from the tip of a non-flowering shoot at any time during the growing season. They may be either greenwood or softwood cuttings. Greenwood cuttings consist of the soft tips of new growth, often with a "heel" of older wood, taken when the main flush of spring growth has slowed down. This method works well for patchouli (*Pogostemon cablin*) and winter cherry (*Withania somnifera*). Heel cuttings are taken with a sliver of wood at the base from such plants as *Helichrysum italicum*. They are obtained by gently pulling a greenwood or semi-ripe side shoot from the main stem. Nodal greenwood cuttings are taken just beneath a node or leaf joint.

Leaf-bud cuttings consist of short sections of stem, bearing a leaf bud or pair of buds and a leaf, taken during the growing season.

Eye cuttings are small, mature, leafless stem sections, each with a bud, or eye, taken in late winter, for example grape vine (*Vitis vinifera*).

LAYERING

In this method of propagation a stem or shoot is induced to form roots while still attached to the parent plant. Choose a strong, flexible shoot, of jasmine (*Jasminum* spp.), for example, that will easily bend to the ground. Make a small cut in the underside of the shoot, and insert it into the soil so that the growing tip protrudes above the surface. Secure the shoot tip to a cane, and anchor the buried section with a large stone. The following autumn, if the layer has rooted, it can be severed from the main plant and potted up or transplanted.

Air layering is used mainly for warm-growing trees and shrubs, for example fig (*Ficus carica*), *Magnolia* spp., *Tabebuia* spp., and cocoa (*Theobroma cacao*). Choose a healthy shoot, 1–2 years old, and make a slit 15–40cm (6–15in) from the growing tip. Pack the slit and surrounding area with moist sphagnum moss and wrap in plastic, secured at each end with garden twine. Air layering is best done in the spring; rooting may take up to two years. When the roots can be seen through the plastic, cut the new plant from the parent and pot separately.

Mound layering is a useful method for shrubby herbs, such as thyme, that are prone to becoming woody and sparse with age. In spring, mound free-draining soil

TAKING STEM-TIP CUTTINGS OF PERENNIALS

1 Fill a pot with well-drained soil mix. Trim the lower leaves off non-flowering shoots. Make a hole with a dibber and insert a cutting. Gently firm the soil mix around the cutting, pressing with your fingers.

2 Insert stakes around the pot edge, then cover with a plastic bag, and seal, to keep an even temperature and conserve moisture. Alternatively, put the pot in the bag, inflate the bag, and seal.

DIVISION OF RHIZOMATOUS PLANTS

1 Shake the clumps of rhizomes to remove any loose soil. Using your hands, or a hand fork, split each clump into manageable pieces, checking for signs of disease.

2 Discard any old rhizomes, then detach the young rhizomes from the clump and neatly trim off their ends. Dust the cut areas with sulphur powder to prevent rot.

MOUND LAYERING HERBS
To stimulate rooting from the lower stems, in spring mound up 7–12cm (3–5in) of sandy soil over the crown of the plant, covering the lower stems, except for the tips of the shoots. By late summer the shoots should be well rooted.

over the base of the plant, leaving the tips of the shoots above the surface. This stimulates new shoots to develop roots. By late summer, the shoots should be sufficiently well rooted to detach and pot separately.

DIVISION
Clumps of herbaceous perennials need dividing every few years, or when they become too large. This can be done by lifting the plant and splitting it into smaller pieces by hand, or with a spade if the roots are too tough. The best time to divide herbs is when growth is minimal, from autumn to early spring, choosing mild weather to avoid frost damage. To minimize disturbance, divide sensitive plants in early spring when new buds are visible. Water transplanted or divided plants well, even in damp weather, to settle the soil round the roots.

OFFSETS
Most herbs with storage organs increase naturally by producing offsets from the mature bulb or corm. Offsets can be detached during dormancy and planted separately to grow on as new plants. The term "offsets" also refers to plantlets that are formed at the ends of stolons and runners (horizontal stems). These usually form roots while still attached to the parent plant, or root rapidly when detached and potted separately.

SUCKERS
Removing rooted suckers is a very easy method of propagation for herbs such as *Alnus glutinosa* and *Rosa rugosa*. It is not suitable for propagating grafted plants that are not growing on their own roots.

GRAFTING AND BUDDING
These are more specialized methods of propagation for woody plants in which a section of stem (a scion) from the desired plant is united with a rootstock or stock of a different plant. If the scion consists of a short piece of stem with a single bud, the method is referred to as "budding". The aim is to produce a new plant with

certain characteristics, such as a greater resistance to root disease. Grafting is usually carried out from late winter to early spring; budding is done mostly in summer.

SPORES
Non-flowering plants, such as ferns, mosses, fungi, horsetails, and algae, reproduce by means of minute, dust-like spores. They need constant moisture for germination. To propagate a fern such as *Adiantum capillus-veneris* in this way, select a frond that has ripe brown sporangia on the underside of the leaf blade, and position it over a piece of clean white paper to gather the spores. These can then be sown in a container of moist, sterile soil mix and covered with plastic wrap. Germination takes 1–3 months. Spray the surface of the soil mix regularly with water. Pot on the ferns when they are large enough to handle.

MICROPROPAGATION
This technique requires sterile laboratory conditions and is used commercially to propagate identical plants of the same cultivar in a short time. It is an important method of producing virus-free stock from infected plants, and of "bulking up" rare species for re-introduction to the wild or for the horticultural trade.

DIVISION OF PERENNIAL PLANTS

1 Lift the plant to be divided, taking care to insert the fork far enough away from the plant so that the roots are not damaged. Carefully shake off any surplus soil by hand or holding the plant with the fork.

2 Divide the plant into smaller pieces by hand or with a sharp knife, retaining only healthy, vigorous sections, each with several new shoots. Replant the divided sections. Firm in and water thoroughly to settle them.

HARVESTING YOUR HERBS

Gathering herbs is a delight and an adventure. It brings us into contact with the remarkable plants on which so many people in the world depend for their health and physical well being. However, harvesting herbs is also a practical undertaking, and needs careful preparation and organization if the best results are to be achieved.

HARVESTING WILD HERBS

In many countries it is an offence to pick any parts of certain rare plants, or uproot any plant without the landowner's permission. You should therefore harvest only those that you know are permitted, common, and plentiful, and which you can identify with certainty. Special care is needed with some groups of plants such as the parsley family (Apiaceae), which even experts find hard to identify. However common they may be, respect wild plants and pick only a few of their leaves, flowers, or fruits to ensure that the plants survive. Avoid destructive harvesting – uprooting or removing bark – and ensure that wild plants are not polluted by vehicle exhausts, agricultural sprays, or animals.

CUTTING

Rather than cutting garden herbs at random, take the opportunity to pinch out or prune the plant at the same time, removing unwanted shoots and encouraging bushiness. Harvesting time is also a good opportunity to remove reverted shoots of variegated plants.

HARVEST FROM THE GARDEN
A mix of bay leaves, rosemary, lavender, basil, sage, and parsley. Sharp scissors or pruners are essential for a clean cut from the parent plant. The shallow trug ensures that the herbs are kept in their optimum condition for storing.

TIMING

The A–Z of Herbs (see pp.92–411) tells you the best time of the year to harvest the various parts of a particular herb. If you intend to process and store the herbs for future use, choose a dry, overcast morning, after any dew or rain has dried.

EQUIPMENT

You will need ordinary garden tools (including a sharp knife, scissors, or pruners) and it is advisable to wear gloves. Some herbs can trigger an allergic reaction, and a few (such as rue) may cause blistering if the sap contacts skin in the presence of sunlight.

POINTS TO REMEMBER

Gather small quantities at a time, handle them as little as possible, and process them quickly to protect the active constituents from deterioration. Aromatic herbs are especially vulnerable – any scent they leave in the air or on your hands indicates that their volatile oils are being lost. Always try to harvest material from only clean, healthy plants in the peak of condition. The active constituents and properties will then be at their highest levels. Avoid damaged or diseased parts, and any that are immature, ageing, or out of season – these factors also imply low levels of active constituents. Gather only one kind of herb at a time to avoid transfer of odours and mistakes in identification. Lay the cut parts carefully in a single layer in a shallow container, and use or process them quickly; even a small heap generates heat which will lead to wilting and deterioration of the herb.

WHICH PARTS, AND WHEN?

It is important to harvest the correct part of the plant for the purpose you intend: the leaves and seeds of coriander (*Coriandrum sativum*), for example, have quite different aromas and uses. In some cases, unusual plant parts are used – stigmas and styles of the saffron crocus (*Crocus sativus*), peel of tangerines (*Citrus reticulata*), or spores of the puffball fungus (*Lycoperdon perlatum*). The most commonly used parts of plants are described on the opposite page, together with the best times to harvest them.

COMMERCIAL HARVESTING
Many herbs are grown on a commercial scale and can be harvested like other crops. Here a planting of lavender is being cut in southern Spain. The oil will be extracted from the cut flowers for use in perfume manufacture.

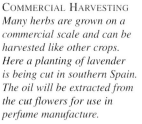

WHOLE PLANT
This is also known as the aerial parts, and means the parts growing above the soil, which are usually cut off near ground level as the plant begins to flower.

LEAVES AND STEMS
Individual leaves or sprigs are generally harvested when young since foliage tends to toughen when flowering begins. Large leaves may be picked individually. Cut stems or branches of small-leafed herbs and remove the leaves from them later.

FLOWERS
Occasionally picked when in bud, but for most purposes flowers are at their best when just opened. Large blooms can be picked individually, with or without stalks; small ones, such as elder (*Sambucus nigra*) are separated from the stalks after picking. In the case of some herbs, such as lavender (*Lavandula* spp.), the whole flower head is cut and may be used whole or separated into florets. For certain uses, only specific parts may be required; the petals (as in pot marigold, *Calendula officinalis*), or the flower head or corolla (as in borage, *Borago officinalis*).

FRUITS AND BERRIES
Harvested mostly when ripe, but before they become squishy. They may be picked individually or in bunches, depending on habit of growth and intended use.

SEEDS
Harvested in pods or seed heads when fully developed but before completely ripe and shedding. If gathered intact, with some stem attached, the ripening process will continue for a time after harvesting and the seeds can be shaken free into paper bags.

ROOTS, RHIZOMES, TUBERS, AND BULBS
In most cases, these are harvested during autumn after the aerial parts have died down. It is often possible to avoid destroying the whole plant by carefully lifting and removing a portion of the underground parts. Bulbous plants will often produce small offsets that can be replanted.

RIPE SEED HEADS
Seed capsules of poppies (Papaver *spp.*) contain hundreds of seeds that are shed through holes at the top when they are ripe. Use the seeds in baking, and enjoy the dried empty capsules for their ornamental shapes.

BARK AND WOOD
The required age of the shrub or tree, and the time to harvest the bark or wood, may vary greatly. Wherever possible, remove only a few branches from each plant or grow them on a coppice basis. Cut the branch cleanly and remove bark later to avoid introducing infection. Do not bark-ring trees (that is, remove a band of the bark going around the trunk or branch), since this usually kills them. Remove lichen and mosses from the bark before it is processed.

SAP, GUM, AND RESIN
Sap from trees is usually collected in the spring as it rises. Gum and resin may be harvested by cutting grooves diagonally in the bark. Resin also often exudes naturally and can be scraped off the tree at any time.

PREPARING FOR PROCESSING
The purpose of storing herbs is to preserve the constituents – and thereby the flavour, aroma, and therapeutic properties – as fully as possible for later use. Exactly how this is done depends on the part used and the purpose for which it is intended. With few exceptions, herbs are best used freshly harvested. Certain constituents, such as the alkaloids in *Papaver somniferum*, remain potent for many years, but the majority are easily destroyed by the enzymatic processes at work within the cut plant, and by exposure to light, heat, and air. As a rule, stocks of preserved herbs should be replaced every year, since a certain amount of deterioration will inevitably take place, especially when they are stored at room temperature in the home.

CLEANING THE HARVEST
Check that all parts harvested are clean and free of dirt and insects. Avoid washing leaves, flowers, fruits, and seed heads, since this lengthens the time of air-drying and encourages deterioration. Underground parts, however, should be thoroughly washed to remove soil and sand, dried on kitchen paper, and then sliced into manageable pieces.

RESIN COLLECTION
The sticky aromatic substance from mastic trees (Pistacia lentiscus) *was the original chewing gum, chewed to sweeten the breath. The industry is now centred on the Greek island of Chios.*

PRESERVING HERBS

Most of the techniques used for preserving and storing herbs are traditional and are easily carried out at home. Extraction of the constituents (through distillation, pressing, or by solvent extraction, for example) is much more complex and requires equipment and expertise that is rarely available on a domestic scale. In many countries, too, it is an offence to be in possession of an unlicensed still.

SIMPLE DRYING
A drying rack can be readily made from an old slatted shelf or a mesh-covered wooden frame. Lay the herbs on it in a single layer and keep in a warm place, out of direct sunlight.

AIR-DRYING
Here long-stemmed seed heads of lovage (Levisticum officinale) *are hung up to dry in a shed. When dry, the seeds can be carefully shaken into a paper bag or onto a sheet of clean paper.*

AIR-DRYING

Hanging herbs up or spreading them out to dry is the most widely used method of preservation. In many countries they are simply left on mats in the sun or strung under the house eaves. The ideal place is dry and well ventilated, free from dust and fumes, and constantly at 20–32°C (68–90°F). To maximize air circulation, hang whole plants, stems, and seed heads in small bundles, and thread sliced roots and fungi on strings. Solitary flower heads, such as chives (*Allium schoenoprasum*) and roses (*Rosa* spp.), can be dried by slotting the stems through a wire mesh drying rack, or by laying them on it. Speed is of the essence in air-drying. Herbs should be dry in 24–48 hours, otherwise enzymes in the plant tissues continue to break down the chemical constituents, and factors such as moisture, air, light, and heat bring about further deterioration. If the leaves turn black or mouldy, the drying process has been too slow and the herb is not worth keeping.

Fragile seed heads of herbs such as fennel, dill, and caraway should be cut with sufficient stalk to tie in bundles. Hang the bundles upside down over clean paper or inside a paper bag to catch the seeds as they fall. Onions and garlic are traditionally harvested with the foliage attached, which is then braided into ropes and sun-dried. Large leaves, flowers, fruits, or petals can be arranged in a single layer on racks covered with wire mesh or muslin. On a small scale, a cake-cooling rack, spread with kitchen paper, can be used. Heat or air movement may be boosted by a fan.

MICROWAVE-DRYING

For this method herbs can be washed before being dried, if required. Then spread the herbs in a single layer on kitchen paper in the microwave oven, and dry according to the temperature guidelines provided by the manufacturer. On average, this should only take about 2–3 minutes, but progress should be checked every 30 seconds, re-arranging the parts to ensure even drying. Cool first, before storing as for air-dried herbs.

OVEN-DRYING

This is recommended only for underground plant parts that need long drying and tolerate higher temperatures than fragile leaves and flowers. Slice the roots or rhizomes and spread out thinly on a baking tray. Dry at 50–60°C (120–140°F) (less for fan ovens) for 2–3 hours, depending on the size of the root material.

FREEZE-DRYING

This method produces excellent retention of flavour in soft-leafed herbs, such as parsley, mint, basil, and chives. Pack sprigs, whole leaves, or chopped herbs into labelled plastic bags or boxes. There is no need to defrost before use as the leaves crumble easily when still frozen; chopped herbs can be thawed quickly in a sieve before use.

Herbs can also be added when making ice cubes (see illustration, right). Iced borage flowers, or sprigs of mint or lemon balm, may also be put directly into drinks to impart flavour and interest.

CONTAINERS

Food-grade plastic bags and plastic boxes or tubs are recommended for frozen herbs, but for other purposes are best avoided, as they encourage humidity. The best containers are dark glass or ceramic jars and bottles. Lids should be airtight to prevent the entry of moisture, moulds, and bacteria, which cause rapid deterioration. Clear glass containers can be used, but they let in light, which causes bleaching and oxidation of the contents. For this reason, clear glass containers should be kept in a dark cupboard. If recycling containers, make sure that they are scrupulously clean by sterilizing them in the oven or in pans of boiling water. Containers of preserved herbs should be stored in a cool, dry place, out of direct sunlight.

STORING DRIED HERBS

When quite dry, herbs should be packed into containers and labelled with name and date. In the case of aromatic herbs, keep the pieces as large as possible to avoid loss of volatile oils through exposure to air. At this stage, blends can be created for bouquets garnis, special recipes, potpourris, and teas. If large quantities of dried herbs are being processed, it may be advisable

DRYING AERIAL PARTS AND LEAVES

1 Dry small-leafed herbs on the stem, in a well-aired place. When the leaves are brittle, rub them off the stems on to paper and leave whole or crumble, as preferred.

2 Transfer dried herbs from the paper to a storage container, seal, and label with name and date. Coloured glass, used here, helps to prevent oxidization.

to wear a face mask to avoid inhaling dust. All dried herbs have a tendency to absorb moisture from the air, so use containers that are only just big enough, in order to exclude as much air as possible. Once opened, check the contents regularly before use in case the remaining herbs are turning mouldy. Certain herbs, such as the marsh mallow (*Althaea officinalis*) and lady's mantle (*Alchemilla* spp.), are especially prone to the problem of moisture absorption and should be stored with especial care to avoid this.

HERB OILS AND VINEGARS

The flavours of many fresh herbs can be preserved in oils or vinegars to enhance salad dressings and marinades. They also look attractive and make lovely gifts. Choose a good-quality oil, such as sunflower, or olive for a stronger flavour. Loosely fill a clear glass jar with the herb, pour in the oil, and seal. Leave the jar in a sunny place for at least two weeks, shaking daily. Strain the contents to remove the steeped herb, and refill into clean jars or bottles, adding a sprig of the fresh herb for identification. Basil (*Ocimum* spp.) leaves can be preserved by packing in jars of oil; the leaves can be used in sauces and cooked dishes, and the oil in salad dressings.

For herb vinegars, it is best to crush the herb lightly, first. Warm either wine or cider vinegar, and proceed as for herb oil. Do not use containers with metal lids to hold vinegar, because the acid will corrode the lids and taint the contents.

⚠ **WARNING** Preserving herbs in oil carries the risk of botulism (a rare but serious form of food poisoning). The organisms that cause botulism are common in soil and fresh water and may be transferred to plants during harvesting or rain splash. Storing freshly cut herbs in a neutral to slightly acid medium (pH7–4.5), where air is excluded, and in temperatures above 3°C (38°F), creates conditions for these organisms to multiply. Home-made herb-flavoured vinegars do not carry this risk because the acidity of vinegar is below pH4.5. Commercially, herb-flavoured oils are made using specially acidified oil.

HERB JUICE

Some herbs, such as *Galium aparine*, are used in the form of juice. The fresh herb is liquidized or put through an electric juice extractor. It can then be sieved and frozen in small plastic tubs. Yields are small, so large quantities of herb are required, and it may take a number of batches to produce the required amount.

PRESERVING IN SUGAR

In sufficient concentration, sugar or honey make a useful preservative for certain herbs, such as *Glycyrrhiza uralensis*, and will also disguise unpleasant flavours. For syrup, the sugar content should never be less than 65 per cent; unrefined sugar is often preferred. The fresh herb may be simmered in the sugar solution, or sugar (or honey) added to an infusion, decoction, or tincture of the herb, and then heated until it has dissolved. Honey is used in processing certain Chinese herbs for its soothing effects. Rosehips (*Rosa* spp.) should be minced and infused in boiling water, brought to the boil briefly, and left to stand for about 15 minutes; the infusion is strained through a fine sieve to remove the irritant seed hairs before adding sugar.

PREPARING ROOTS FOR STORAGE

1 Always try to remove only part of the root, so that the plant can re-grow. Wash the parts well to remove all soil.

2 Cut the root parts into pieces with a sharp knife. Dry in a low oven until crisp, and cool completely before packing in boxes.

Angelica stems and ginger rhizomes are traditionally preserved by crystallizing. It is a long process, and recipes must be followed exactly for success.

HERBAL WINES

Alcohol is an excellent preservative, drawing out active constituents and prohibiting the growth of micro-organisms. Recipes for herbal wines can be found in books on wine-making; favourites include elderflower and elderberry (*Sambucus nigra*), cowslip (*Primula veris*), and dandelion (*Taraxacum officinale*).

OTHER ALCOHOLIC DRINKS

Elderflower "champagne" and ginger beer are only slightly alcoholic, since they are fermented for only a very short time. Based on hops (*Humulus lupulus*), beers are essentially herbal, too. Home-made ale can be flavoured with nettles (*Urtica dioica*) or ground ivy (*Glechoma hederacea*). A mint liqueur can easily be made by macerating leaves of spearmint (*Mentha spicata*) or peppermint (*M. × piperita*) in vodka or grappa for a week, and adding sugar after straining. It is important to follow herbal recipes with alcohol exactly in order to achieve the right concentration, upon which the benefits and flavour depend.

POT MARIGOLDS
Whole heads of pot marigolds (Calendula) are difficult to dry successfully so the petals are stripped from the centre of the flower, which is discarded.

MAKING HERB ICE CUBES

1 Culinary herbs, such as borage, pineapple mint, and parsley (all shown here) can be frozen in ice cubes to provide flavourings or to add to cold summer drinks.

2 Put individual flowers, leaves, or sprigs, or chopped herbs, into ice-cube trays, and fill with water as usual. Ice cubes of chopped herbs may be added whole to dishes, or be defrosted before use.

FREEZING HERBS
Freezing is a simple way to store herbs, and is convenient for small quantities of sprigs, leaves, or chopped herbs. Use plastic boxes or freezer bags and label clearly.

DESIGNING A HERB GARDEN

A RAISED BORDER
Natural stone is used to edge an attractive raised herb bed and add height to this border.

A HERB GARDEN CAN BE designed to suit almost any size or shape. It does not necessarily need to be located in a sunny, open position; there are herbs, for instance, that will thrive in shade, in heavy wet ground, and even in water. The most popular kind of herb garden is a small bed or border of culinary herbs lying within easy reach of the kitchen. You can, however, equally well devote your herb garden to plants for medicinal uses or to those that come from different parts of the world. You may wish to choose a single genus of herbs to grow, or perhaps plants characteristic of an old medieval monastery garden. There is no limit to the possibilities and themes with which you can experiment. Part of the fun, too, of creating a herb garden is in researching and tracking down the plants, which will make you quite an expert by the time you have finished.

In this section you will find ideas and suggestions for formal and informal plantings in town and country settings, and designs for containers and a *potager*.

A NEAT DESIGN
Designed as a low-allergen garden, this formal design makes good use of a restricted space. Different colours and textures make the geometric divisions more interesting, and there are containers, climbers, and tall, narrow plants to give height.

When planning a new garden, it is important to take in the practical considerations. Whatever your style and interests, don't get too carried away; instead, work on something you know you will be able to achieve in terms of space, time, energy, and money.

The section Cultivating Herbs (see pp.48–69) gives you fuller information on all stages of planning and making a herb garden. Make the best use of available space, and keep within the bounds of your gardening experience. Write down the factors that you will have to take into account in your plan: dimensions, soil type and conditions, existing contours, and the amount of sun and wind the garden is likely to receive at different times of day and during the year. Pinpoint the extreme positions (sunniest, windiest, shadiest, most sheltered, and so on) and problems, such as perennial weeds. Surrounding features are important, too – a tree could provide support for hops or give shade for woodland herbs, but it should not overhang a planting site for thymes. Access and viewpoint are also important. If you want to pick herbs through the year, all-weather paths or stepping stones should be part of the plan, and you will not want the bed to be too far from the house door. Or maybe you are thinking more of a place to relax, in which case a sitting area, perhaps a fragrant arbour, might be more of a priority.

FORMAL OR INFORMAL STYLE?
Once these practical matters have been thought through, the next stage is to consider the style. The basic choice is between formal and informal designs, but you will need to consider how best to fit the style of the herb garden to the rest of your garden. Formal gardens are geometric, usually subdivided by paths or dwarf hedges into symmetrical compartments. They may be square, rectangular, circular, star-shaped, or triangular in outline, or may combine several shapes, but the overall aim is to make a pattern. It is ideal for filling space, be it a bare courtyard or patio, an unwanted area of grass, or a new garden full of builder's rubble. An informal herb garden is better suited to adapting space, such as an existing border, or to finding a niche for particular herbs – Mediterranean herbs on a dry, sunny bank, for example.

FORMAL DESIGNS
On a large scale that involves bulk quantities of hedging herbs and/or paving materials, a formal herb garden can be a major undertaking and expense, especially if professional construction is needed. However, formal gardens are very easily planted and maintained and look interesting from the moment of completion, unlike informal borders that depend on plant growth for effect. A formal garden is more than just an aesthetic exercise,

A CLASSIC FORMAL HERB GARDEN
*This garden has symmetrical beds, outlined with clipped box hedges (*Buxus sempervirens*). The element of height is provided by the topiary, the hedge, and the rose-draped trellis.*

though; the resulting small divisions provide a neat, practical basis for growing herbs. You can grow each herb in its own compartment, or use the divisions to show different features, such as medicinal herbs arranged by ailment (heart complaints, digestive problems, and such like), or by region of traditional use, as at the Garden of World Medicine at the Chelsea Physic Garden in London. Alternatively, the pattern can be emphasized by restricting your choice of plants to certain colours. You can use the same herb in different colours, or you might alternate differently coloured herbs, such as grey-leafed artemisias with purple-leafed sage or perilla.

INFORMAL DESIGNS

An informal design may begin with a geometric outline but will not have the planned symmetry of the formal garden. It depends for aesthetic effect on plant grouping and combinations. An informal herb garden can take on the look of a cottage garden, herbaceous border, or rock or scree garden. This more relaxed arrangement gives scope for incorporating whatever plants and features are already in the garden, whereas a formal herb garden requires much more of a start from scratch. There are interesting climbing herbs for existing walls and fences, such as variegated bittersweet and akebia. Ground covers among trees and shrubs can be provided by spreading herbs. Both sweet woodruff and variegated ground elder combine well with spring-flowering bulbs, producing fresh new foliage as the bulbs' leaves begin to look unhappy. Where evergreen cover is preferred, ivy can be used either as a climber or for carpeting the ground, even in heavy shade. Herbs that

are particular about growing conditions can be accommodated in special places to suit them – acid-loving wintergreen and witch hazel in a raised peat bed, perhaps, or meadowsweet, sweet flag, and skunk cabbage in nutrient-rich mud beside a pool.

HERBS WITH OTHER PLANTS

Informal herb gardening gives scope for combining herbs with other kinds of plants altogether. Many herbs are good garden plants in their own right and have subtle colours that are easy to place among shrubs and other perennials. Examples include the late-flowering soapwort, and cultivars of feverfew, which are excellent for cutting, and the various lavenders, foxgloves, and sages, whose colours and habits complement roses so well. White gardens catch the imagination of plant lovers for their peaceful atmosphere, and an example is given on pages 86–87. Many herbs are suitable for this colour scheme, having silver-grey foliage or white flowers: artemisia, Queen Anne's lace, lavender, hyssop, myrtle, marjoram, roses, lilies, irises, and thyme, to name but a few. Other herbs, such as emerald-green parsley and purple-black basil, have bold colours and striking textures that do not look out of place among beds and summer containers, and provide a useful crop in the process. In France, herbs are traditionally grown alongside fruit and vegetables in an ornamental garden, known as a *potager* (see pp.76–77). This combines many aspects of convenience and good husbandry in a small space, tailor-made for today's average-sized urban garden. Ideas for these and other herb gardens, both formal and informal, are given on the following pages.

HERBS AS GARDEN PLANTS
Herbs such as lavender make excellent garden plants in their own right, as well as having special properties. Here, the deep purple of Lavandula angustifolia 'Hidcote' is edging a border dominated by spiky, grey-blue sea holly (Eryngium).

A FRENCH-STYLE *POTAGER*
Herbs, vegetables, and fruit here attractively mingle among the flowers. Growing different kinds of plants together in a potager-style garden reduces pests and diseases, and encourages beneficial insects, such as ladybirds and hoverflies, whose larvae feed on aphid.

FORMAL GARDEN DESIGNS

A herb garden designed to a formal pattern allows you to grow plants in a pleasing and ordered way. It is easily managed and gives access to the herbs, while creating a haven of restful colours and scents. Choose herbs not only for their aroma or uses but also to make interesting combinations of colour, texture, and habit: the soft pinks and blues of lavender, rosemary, rue, and hyssop, or the fresh, clean appeal of gold-variegated sage (*Salvia officinalis* 'Icterina'), marjoram (*Origanum vulgare* 'Gold Tip'), and lemon balm (*Melissa officinalis* 'Aurea') with white double feverfew (*Tanacetum parthenium* 'Tom Thumb White Stars').

Salvia officinalis 'Icterina' and *Tanacetum parthenium* 'Tom Thumb White Stars'
The golden-variegated leaves of this sage complement the white flowers and bright green foliage of dwarf double feverfew, and both reach about the same height.

GEOMETRIC GARDEN

The plants in the small beds are chosen for their neat habit of growth, to maintain the shape of the beds. It is best to plant tall herbs, such as the hemp agrimony (*Eupatorium cannabinum*) and angelica (*Angelica archangelica*), around the edge, rather than in the middle, since they may swamp other plants. The most self-contained tall herb is fennel (*Foeniculum vulgare*), with its feathery foliage and stiff upright habit. Colour combinations of both flowers and foliage can create pleasing contrasts, such as the bright blue borage flowers (*Borago officinalis*) that mingle attractively with the pale pink flower heads of the marjoram (*Origanum vulgare*). Choosing different cultivars would entirely change the effect.

A FRAGRANT COLLAGE
The rich mixture of colour, texture, and fragrance that a herb garden can provide is almost unlimited. The combination of both aromatic and colourful plants seen here produces a delightful array of colour and scent.

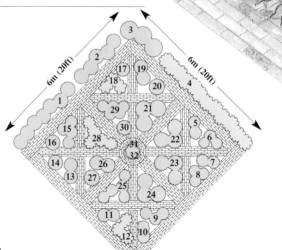

PLANTING PLAN

1. Digitalis lanata × 7

2. Eupatorium cannabinum × 5

3. Angelica archangelica × 3

4. Oenothera biennis × 12

5. Lavandula angustifolia 'Rosea' × 2

6. Lavandula angustifolia 'Hidcote' × 3

7. Helichrysum italicum subsp. *serotinum* × 2

8. Allium schoenoprasum × 3

9. Artemisia pontica × 3

10. Salvia officinalis 'Purpurascens' × 2

11. Origanum vulgare × 2

12. Borago officinalis × 3

13. Monarda didyma × 1

14. Mentha spicata × 2

15. Mentha × *piperita* × 4

16. Allium cepa Proliferum Group × 1

17. Foeniculum vulgare 'Purpureum' × 1

18. Calendula officinalis × 3

19. Origanum vulgare 'Gold Tip' × 2

20. Melissa officinalis 'Aurea' × 1

21. Calamintha nepeta × 3

22. Rosmarinus officinalis × 3

23. Hyssopus officinalis × 3

24. Mentha suaveolens 'Variegata' × 3

25. Thymus serpyllum 'Pink Chintz' × 5

26. Thymus vulgaris × 2

27. Santolina chamaecyparissus × 1

28. Petroselinum crispum × 5

29. Tanacetum parthenium 'Tom Thumb White Stars' × 5

30. Salvia officinalis 'Icterina' × 1

31. Laurus nobilis × 1

32. Chamaemelum nobile 'Flore Pleno' × 1

6m (20ft)

6m (20ft)

KEY ⬤ Perennial ⬤ Annual/Biennial ▨ Evergreen

Origanum vulgare 'Gold Tip' and *Melissa officinalis* 'Aurea'
The fresh new growth of gold-tipped marjoram and golden lemon balm shows up well early in the growing year.

Lavandula angustifolia 'Rosea' and 'Hidcote'
Growing the pink and deep purple lavenders together gives more visual interest while providing a choice of colour for cutting.

Artemisia pontica and *Salvia officinalis* 'Purpurascens'
The filigree foliage of Roman wormwood contrasts attractively with the broad velvety leaves of purple sage.

Helichrysum italicum subsp. *serotinum* and *Allium schoenoprasum*
Chives are useful for edging, and their plain green foliage associates well with the silvery leaves of the curry plant.

73

KNOT GARDEN

Knot gardens were the favourite style of Elizabethan England, expressing the confident, adventurous *joie de vivre* of the age. Composed of intricate geometric patterns, dwarf hedges of evergreen herbs and/or paths were laid out on a raised square. Two kinds were devised: closed knots, with no access and compartments containing coloured sand or gravel; and open knots, with paths forming part of the pattern, and the compartments filled with sweet-smelling plants. They were not herb gardens as such, but most of the fragrant plants so beloved by Elizabethans happen to be what we now categorize as herbs: rosemary, hyssop, sage, and lavender made excellent small, fragrant hedges upon which the washing was spread out to dry.

DWARF BOX HEDGES

Box was widely used, too, though the unpleasant scent it produced when it was cut was considered a drawback. Knots were traditionally made in groups of four, which might be alike or different in pattern. One is sufficient for most gardeners today, bearing in mind the amount of very careful trimming that a dwarf hedge needs. The pattern can be as simple or complex as you like; the only limitation is that dwarf hedges reach 23–30cm (9–12in) wide, and paths need to be about 45cm (18in) across. The pattern you choose can also be symbolic: the initial letters of a name, for example.

OPEN KNOT GARDEN DESIGN

Here the colour contrast of the grey of cotton lavender (Santolina chamaecyparissus) *with the purple lavender* (Lavandula) *sections inside the hedges of box* (Buxus sempervirens) *is an integral part of the design. Small paths allow for maintenance and trimming. Knot gardens are often best appreciated when the whole pattern can be seen from above – through an upper-storey house window, for example.*

CONTRASTS IN HEDGING

Elements of the design, especially of a closed knot, can be emphasized by hedging in a different colour. Three different types have been used in this design, which could have coloured gravel or other material in the spaces between the hedges. The outer hedge of box (Buxus sempervirens) *encloses repeating patterns in hedge germander* (Teucrium × lucidrys) *and silvery santolina. Be careful to buy the correct species of germander, since the hedge type may be labelled as* T. chamaedrys, *the more spreading wall germander. Hedge germander has an upright habit and small, glossy leaves.*

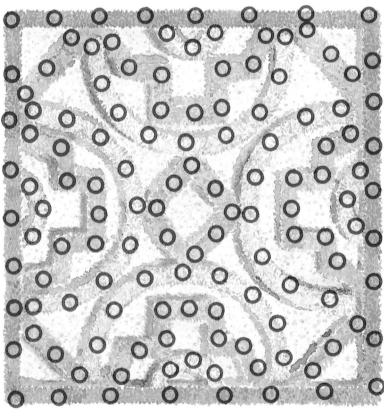

PLANTING PLAN

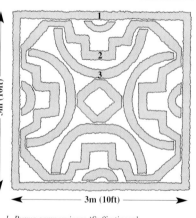

3m (10ft)

3m (10ft)

1. *Buxus sempervirens* 'Suffruticosa'
2. *Teucrium × lucidrys*
3. *Santolina chamaecyparissus*

KEY ▢ Evergreen

INVESTING IN YOUR GARDEN

Box is the best all-purpose dwarf hedge for knot gardens, as it is for any situation where compact, low hedging is required. It is slower growing but longer-lived than other similar hedging plants, and therefore usually more expensive.

COLOUR WHEEL RAISED BED

Dividing a garden into geometric beds gives a sense of order, separates access from growing space, and simplifies planting and routine tasks. Raised beds were a feature of gardens during medieval and Renaissance times; in recent years they have undergone a revival as part of the organic movement, when it was discovered by experimentation that soil condition was greatly improved if left undisturbed. William Lawson (*The Countrie Housewife's Garden*, 1617) regarded raised beds as essential for plants other than trees, because they need drier conditions. This garden is a simple example of something that can be made for the elderly and less able in a confined space. There is ample room for seating in the central circular area, and paths are wide enough for wheelchair access. Gardeners with impaired vision might prefer a design chosen more for its range of aromas, with the added delight of texture too – the occasional silky marsh mallow or spiky houseleek among the sage and thyme. A central water feature might be a fine alternative to a tree.

WHEEL OF COLOUR

Having fun with colour appeals to gardeners of all ages; this particular planting plan is based mainly on short-lived, colourful herbs, so that changes can be made each year to provide interest and challenge.

CHOOSING MATERIALS

The materials most suited to the garden are either ready-made timber or pre-cast edging, if the bed is up to about 30cm (12in) high, or bricks. In theory, any shape is possible, but geometric ones are easiest when a group of beds is designed as a unit.

ADVANTAGES OF HEIGHT

Raising the beds clear of pathways makes it much easier to tend the herbs. A bed built higher still, to a convenient working height, opens up the rewarding pastime of herb gardening to the elderly and less able.

PLANTING PLAN

1. *Tropaeolum majus* 'Empress of India' × 3
2. *Tagetes patula* × 3
3. *Tanacetum parthenium* 'Aureum' × 3
4. *Petroselinum crispum* 'Afro' × 3
5. *Ruta graveolens* 'Jackman's Blue' × 3
6. *Salvia officinalis* 'Purpurascens' × 3
7. *Monarda didyma* × 5
8. *Tropaeolum majus* 'Empress of India' × 7
9. *Calendula officinalis* × 9
10. *Tagetes patula* × 7
11. *Melissa officinalis* 'Aurea' × 3
12. *Tanacetum parthenium* 'Aureum' × 5
13. *Rumex scutatus* × 5
14. *Petroselinum crispum* 'Afro' × 5
15. *Hyssopus officinalis* × 5
16. *Ruta graveolens* 'Jackman's Blue' × 5
17. *Lavandula angustifolia* 'Imperial Gem' × 5
18. *Salvia officinalis* 'Purpurascens' × 5

11m (35ft)

11m (35ft)

KEY ● Perennial ◌ Annual/Biennial ▨ Evergreen

75

VEGETABLE *POTAGER*

In gardens where space is at a premium, many people forego the pleasure of growing their own fresh produce. But shortage of space can be a challenge, as gardeners in France have shown by devising the *potager* – an ornamental, formal garden in which herbs mingle with fruit and vegetables.

GARDEN OF VARIETY

The area is divided into neat little beds that can be at ground level, or raised up. Raised beds allow easy access for both cultivation and harvesting. Crop rotation will happen automatically, since you will almost certainly vary what you grow each year, just for the fun of trying out new planting combinations.

THE IMPORTANCE OF HEIGHT

The skilful use of height adds another dimension to simple geometric designs, which otherwise depend largely on colourful planting for visual interest. In this design, height is provided by a mulberry tree and climbing herbs and vegetables trained on tall supports such as teepees or stakes. As an alternative to the cucumbers (Cucumis sativus) *and miniature pumpkins* (Cucurbita pepo) *shown here, try climbing beans, vining nasturtiums, or a loofah gourd* (Luffa cylindrica).

Tropaeolum majus and Allium porrum 'Musselburgh'
Choose a compact, bushy nasturtium (*Tropaeolum majus*), rather than a climbing one, for this kind of planting. If they spread into the bed, the bases of the leeks (*Allium porrum* 'Musselburgh') should blanch beautifully under cover of the nasturtium leaves.

Brassica oleracea 'Red Drumhead' and Petroselinum crispum
Towards the end of the growing season, the red cabbages (*Brassica oleracea* 'Red Drumhead') mature beneath the flowering stems of the parsley (*Petroselinum crispum*).

PLANTING PLAN

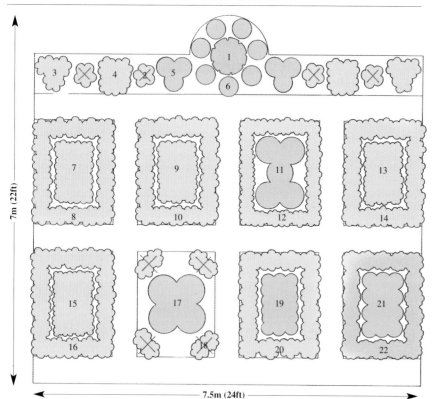
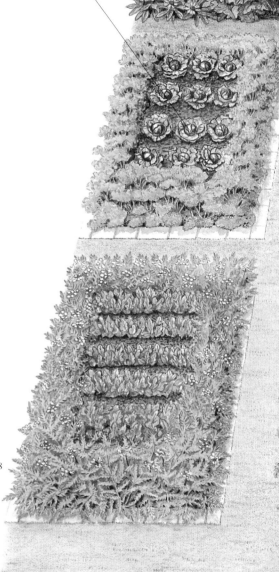

7m (22ft)

7.5m (24ft)

1. *Morus nigra* × 1
2. *Cucumis sativus* 'Telegraph Improved' × 4
3. *Calendula officinalis* × 6
4. *Beta vulgaris* Cicla Group × 12
5. *Allium schoenoprasum* × 3
6. *Fragaria vesca* × 7
7. *Brassica oleracea* 'Red Drumhead' × 12
8. *Petroselinum crispum* × 18

9. *Allium porrum* 'Musselburgh' × 16
10. *Tropaeolum majus* Whirlybird Series × 18
11. *Asparagus officinalis* × 5
12. *Tagetes patula* 'Favourite Mixed' × 24
13. *Atriplex hortensis* 'Rubra' × 12
14. *Phaseolus vulgaris* 'Purple Teepee' × 18

15. *Raphanus sativus* 'Cherry Belle' × 24
16. *Anthriscus cerefolium* × 18
17. *Foeniculum vulgare* × 4
18. *Cucurbita pepo* 'Butternut' × 8
19. *Lactuca sativa* 'Cocarde' × 16
20. *Origanum vulgare* 'Aureum' × 8
21. *Rumex acetosa* × 6
22. *Lavandula angustifolia* 'Munstead' × 18

KEY ● Perennial ✿ Annual/Biennial ▦ Evergreen

Tagetes patula and **Asparagus officinalis**
Some plant combinations fulfil a practical purpose as well as being colourful. The golden French marigold (*Tagetes patula*) is used in companion planting to deter soil pests and whitefly from vegetables such as asparagus, as shown here.

Lactuca sativa 'Cocarde' and **Origanum vulgare** 'Aureum'
This red oakleaf lettuce, 'Cocarde', produces deeply cut, bronze leaves that are ornamental as well as edible. Grow them with a golden marjoram such as *Origanum vulgare* 'Aureum', a herb that is excellent both in flavour and in its effect as a garden plant.

Lavandula angustifolia '**Munstead**' and **Rumex acetosa**
The broad, bright green leaves of sorrel are not especially ornamental in themselves, but the foliage makes a lush contrast to the purple spikes of the lavender bushes.

INFORMAL GARDEN DESIGNS

Fortunately, informal herb gardens can be made in many styles, adapted to suit the conditions in your garden, and the next few pages offer some suggestions for these. The plan below is really several small herb gardens in one, including incorporating requirements for moisture-loving herbs, ramblers, and creepers. On pages 80–81 are contrasting gardens for sun and shade, suitable for urban or country conditions.

INDIVIDUAL GARDEN AREAS

Each of the mini-gardens shown here has its own character. Groupings have been planned for scent, colour, and culinary use. The ideal setting for this garden, which has seven separate areas, would be in paving or gravel, which need little maintenance, and give all-weather access. Stone also makes an attractive, warm, well-drained setting for the plants. Alternatively, the areas containing the creeping herbs, containers, and arbour could be paved or gravelled, and the pool, bog garden, and borders surrounded by lawn.

Humulus lupulus 'Aureus' and *Lonicera japonica* 'Halliana'
The golden hops and honeysuckle shown here are well suited to an arbour, and in combination provide both ample shade and a pleasant fragrance in summer, when the heavily scented honeysuckle comes into flower.

PLANTING PLAN

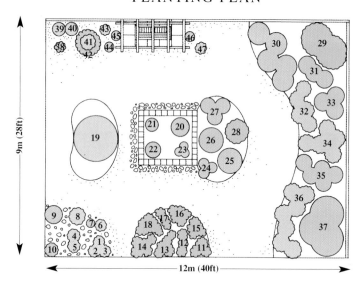

9m (28ft)

12m (40ft)

1. *Thymus pulegioides* 'Bertram Anderson' × 1
2. *Thymus pseudolanuginosus* × 1
3. *Thymus serpyllum* var. *coccineus* × 1
4. *Thymus serpyllum* 'Russetings' × 1
5. *Thymus serpyllum* 'Snowdrift' × 1
6. *Thymus serpyllum* 'Pink Chintz' × 1
7. *Mentha requienii* × 3
8. *Satureja spicigera* × 1
9. *Mentha pulegium* × 1
10. *Thymus herba-barona* × 3
11. *Anethum graveolens* × 3
12. *Borago officinalis* × 3
13. *Papaver rhoeas* × 5
14. *Centaurea cyaneus* × 5
15. *Ocimum basilicum* × 9
16. *Calendula officinalis* × 5
17. *Coriandrum sativum* × 5
18. *Satureja hortensis* × 5

19. *Chamaemelum nobile* 'Treneague' (25 per sq m)
20. *Typha latifolia* 'Variegata' × 1
21. *Menyanthes trifoliata* × 1
22. *Nymphaea alba* × 1
23. *Acorus gramineus* 'Variegatus' × 3
24. *Ranunculus ficaria* f. *flore pleno* × 3
25. *Symplocarpus foetidus* × 1
26. *Symphytum × uplandicum* 'Variegatum' × 1
27. *Filipendula ulmaria* 'Aurea' × 3
28. *Myrica gale* × 1
29. *Sambucus nigra* 'Guincho Purple' × 2
30. *Allium schoenoprasum* 'Forescate' × 3
31. *Saponaria officinalis* 'Rubra Plena' × 1
32. *Salvia officinalis* 'Tricolor' × 3

33. *Foeniculum vulgare* 'Purpureum' × 3
34. *Ruta graveolens* 'Jackman's Blue' × 5
35. *Salvia officinalis* 'Purpurascens' × 3
36. *Lavandula angustifolia* 'Hidcote' × 5
37. *Cynara cardunculus* subsp. *cardunculus* × 3
38. *Petroselinum crispum* 'Afro' × 1
39. *Pelargonium* 'Graveolens' × 1
40. *Pelargonium crispum* 'Variegatum' × 1
41. *Laurus nobilis* × 1
42. *Perilla frutescens* var. *crispa* × 5
43. *Rosmarinus officinalis* Prostratus Group × 2
44. *Mentha spicata* var. *crispa* × 1
45. *Humulus lupulus* 'Aureus' × 1
46. *Lonicera japonica* 'Halliana' × 1
47. *Myrtus communis* 'Variegata' × 1

Chamaemelum nobile 'Treneague'
Establishing a chamomile lawn on a large scale is very difficult (which is why chamomile lawns are such a rarity), but the relatively small area suggested here is much more realistic – and bare patches that appear after winter can easily be replanted.

KEY ● Shrub ● Perennial ◉ Annual/Biennial ▨ Evergreen

Papaver rhoeas and ***Borago officinalis***
This planting is entirely devoted to annuals so that it can be cleared in winter and given a new look each spring, rearranging the different herbs or changing varieties. The blue borage and red poppies shown here could be changed to white borage and pastel poppies for the following year.

A PLACE FOR EVERYTHING
Taller perennials and shrubs are planted against the boundary wall or hedge, which displays them to best advantage; moisture-loving herbs are amply supplied with nutrient-rich mud and water in an aquatic environment. Tender herbs, invasive ones, or favourites for cutting are best in pots, which can be moved and replanted according to need. A group of pots could also house a speciality collection, perhaps of scented-leafed pelargoniums.

Thymus serpyllum 'Pink Chintz' and ***Mentha requienii***
These creeping herbs are suited to an open, sunny area, where they are not in danger of being overgrown and where their fragrance can be released by being crushed underfoot.

79

MEDITERRANEAN HERB BED

The wide range of herbal plants available to the gardener allows even the most extreme planting situations to be considered when planning a herb garden. The design illustrated here would suit a baking hot, very dry bed that is exposed to the sun all day. It is all a question of selecting the right plants for the conditions – in a sunny location (such as shown at right) you could create a predominantly silver herb garden, full of the aromas of the Mediterranean.

USING SILVER PLANTS

This hot weather garden would be best against a patio wall, where the aromatic scents would be close at hand. The containers are optional but add an even more exotic element, with tall, rustling eucalyptus, spiky agave, and velvet-leafed, tender lavender. Spiny foliage, silver-grey hairy leaves, and pungent aromas are common survival mechanisms in dry, bright environments, protecting the plants against high levels of ultraviolet light and desiccation. The planting is enlivened by the colours of California poppies (*Eschscholzia californica*), which flower all summer.

SILVER-LEAFED PLANTS
This grouping of Lavandula angustifolia, Artemisia ludoviciana *'Silver Queen', and* Tanacetum densum subsp. amani *is a variation on the combinations suggested in the planting plan below. In the background, the brilliant purple of the lavender sets off the silver foliage of the artemisia, which has spread sideways to fill the available space. Cascading over the wall in front is the finely cut foliage of the tanacetum, which has bright yellow flowers. As a contrast to these small-leafed plants, there are dramatic clumps of giant thistles at the back, and the broad, downy leaves of self-sown mullein (Verbascum spp.) in the foreground.*

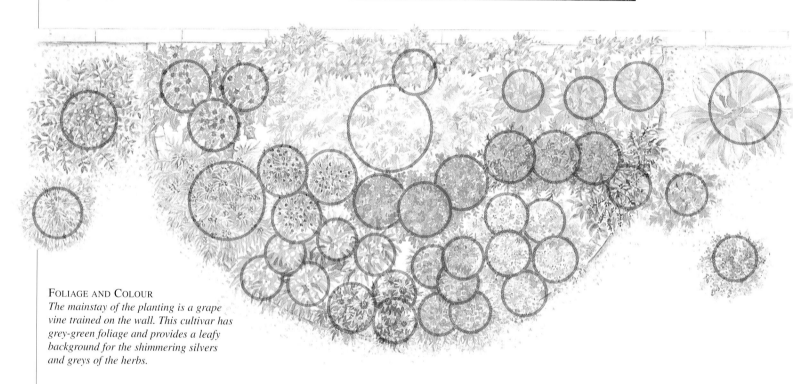

FOLIAGE AND COLOUR
The mainstay of the planting is a grape vine trained on the wall. This cultivar has grey-green foliage and provides a leafy background for the shimmering silvers and greys of the herbs.

PLANTING PLAN

1. *Lavandula lanata* × 1
2. *Eucalyptus globulus* × 1
3. *Silybum marianum* × 3
4. *Vitis vinifera* 'Incana' × 1
5. *Artemisia absinthium* 'Lambrook Silver' × 1
6. *Tanacetum balsamita* subsp. *balsametoides* × 3
7. *Helichrysum italicum* × 1
8. *Lavandula stoechas* subsp. *pedunculata* × 3
9. *Ruta graveolens* × 3
10. *Rosmarinus officinalis* × 3

11. *Salvia officinalis* 'Berggarten' × 1
12. *Iris germanica* var. *florentina* × 5
13. *Eryngium maritimum* × 3
14. *Eschscholzia californica* × 5
15. *Thymus vulgaris* 'Silver Posie' × 5
16. *Agave americana* × 1
17. *Pelargonium* 'Mabel Grey' × 1
18. *Acinos arvensis* × 3

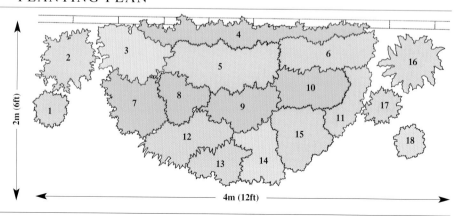

2m (6ft)

4m (12ft)

| KEY ● Shrub ● Perennial ◉ Annual/Biennial ▢ Evergreen

WOODLAND HERB GARDEN

Many interesting herbs that have medicinal properties, and are also very ornamental, originated in a woodland habitat. As a result, they thrive in moist, sheltered conditions, and tolerate shade. In such cool, humid conditions they evolved delicate, often fern-like leaves, or developed a carpeting habit to cover the humus-rich ground beneath trees. An exception to this pattern is the foxglove (*Digitalis* spp.), which is specially adapted to growing in woodland clearings. Foxglove seeds need light to germinate and can remain dormant for years until a clearing appears in the trees, whereupon thousands of young plants come up one year and flower en masse in the next. This biennial pattern means that at first you need to replant foxgloves annually to supplement those that self-sow and to guarantee flowers each year. Herb Robert (*Geranium robertianum*) and sweet Cicely (*Myrrhis odorata*) often self-sow prolifically, whereas periwinkle (*Vinca*) and woodruff (*Galium odoratum*) are rampant spreaders. Remember that, if your woodland is not to become a jungle, you will need to be ruthless about weeding out seedlings and runners.

PLANTING PLAN

1. *Sambucus nigra* 'Marginata' × 1
2. *Myrrhis odorata* × 3
3. *Mentha suaveolens* 'Variegata' × 3
4. *Vinca major* × 5
5. *Valeriana officinalis* × 1
6. *Aconitum napellus* × 1
7. *Trillium erectum* × 3
8. *Geranium robertianum* × 1
9. *Ajuga reptans* 'Atropurpurea' × 3
10. *Digitalis lanata* × 3
11. *Melissa officinalis* × 1
12. *Convallaria majalis* × 5
13. *Galium odoratum* × 1
14. *Persicaria bistorta* × 3
15. *Aegopodium podagraria* 'Variegatum' × 1

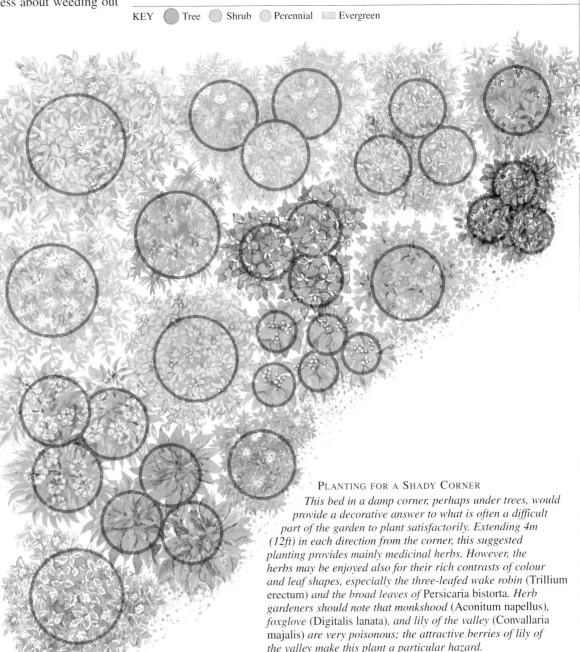

4m (12ft) / 4m (12ft)

KEY ● Tree ● Shrub ○ Perennial ▨ Evergreen

Sambucus nigra* and *Geranium robertianum
The variegated leaves of this elder (*Sambucus nigra* 'Marginata') are encouraged by cutting it back hard, even to the ground, in autumn, as it comes into leaf in late winter. Pink-flowered herb Robert (*Geranium robertianum*) makes a delicate contrast.

Alchemilla mollis* and *Geranium robertianum
The rounded, lobed leaves of lady's mantle (*Alchemilla mollis*) complement the ferny, red-tinged foliage and pink flowers of herb Robert (*Geranium robertianum*).

PLANTING FOR A SHADY CORNER

*This bed in a damp corner, perhaps under trees, would provide a decorative answer to what is often a difficult part of the garden to plant satisfactorily. Extending 4m (12ft) in each direction from the corner, this suggested planting provides mainly medicinal herbs. However, the herbs may be enjoyed also for their rich contrasts of colour and leaf shapes, especially the three-leafed wake robin (*Trillium erectum*) and the broad leaves of* Persicaria bistorta. *Herb gardeners should note that monkshood (*Aconitum napellus*), foxglove (*Digitalis lanata*), and lily of the valley (*Convallaria majalis*) are very poisonous; the attractive berries of lily of the valley make this plant a particular hazard.*

DESIGNS FOR A PURPOSE

These gardens show designs for various purposes. Plants for fragrance and potpourri are shown below, in a diagonal mirror-image plan; a design for colour contrasts in a small, rectangular bed, perhaps under a house wall; and a circular island bed with a brick path, planted with a variety of culinary herbs to supply your kitchen year-round.

POTPOURRI HERB BED

The plants in this plan are only suggestions and can be changed as you wish – a peppermint geranium substituted for a rose-scented one, for example, or green-leafed instead of purple-leafed sage. You might choose the white button flowers of double chamomile (*Chamaemelum nobile* 'Flore Pleno') rather than those of *Tanacetum parthenium* 'Tom Thumb White Stars'. Different annuals may be grown each year: 'Dark Opal' basil, cornflowers, and nutmeg flowers (*Nigella sativa*), perhaps, with pansies for their beautiful colours. Essential potpourri ingredients include lavender and roses; almost any kind can be used, but *Lavandula angustifolia* 'Hidcote' has very deep purple, strongly scented flowers, and *Rosa gallica* var. *officinalis* is favoured for its fragrant, deep red buds and petals. A lemon or orange tree is useful for its blossoms and leaves, as well as for its fruits.

A PLANTING WITH MANY POSSIBILITIES
This planting offers many combinations of scents and colours. The rich scents of the pink and red plants may be combined with those of the grey-leafed sage or thyme; sharp yellows and golds with the musky aromas of hops or coriander. Though attractive in its own right, Iris germanica var. florentina is grown for its rhizomes. The powder, or orris, made from the dried root produces one of the few aromatic fixatives that can be grown at home.

Coriandrum sativum **and** ***Agastache foeniculum***
Coriander seeds are easily grown as a perfume fixative. The plant has pretty white flowers, seen here with the purple spikes of anise/lavender hyssop, which has an unusual fragrance of patchouli and mint.

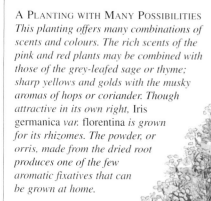

PLANTING PLAN

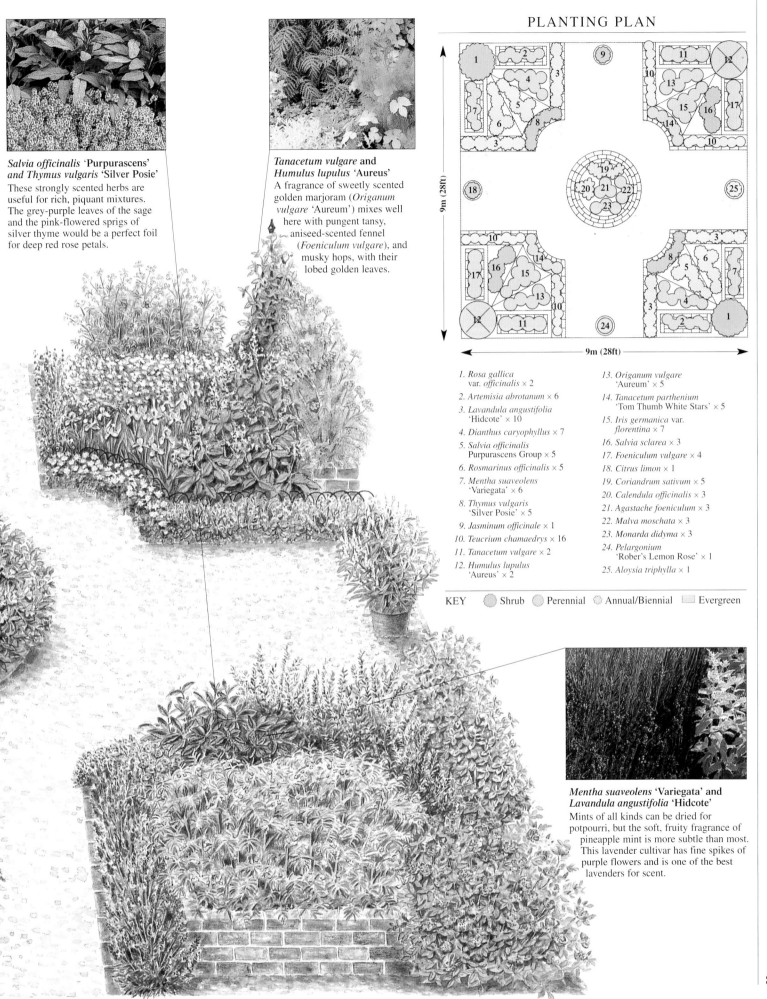

Salvia officinalis 'Purpurascens' *and Thymus vulgaris* 'Silver Posie'

These strongly scented herbs are useful for rich, piquant mixtures. The grey-purple leaves of the sage and the pink-flowered sprigs of silver thyme would be a perfect foil for deep red rose petals.

Tanacetum vulgare and *Humulus lupulus* 'Aureus'

A fragrance of sweetly scented golden marjoram (*Origanum vulgare* 'Aureum') mixes well here with pungent tansy, aniseed-scented fennel (*Foeniculum vulgare*), and musky hops, with their lobed golden leaves.

1. *Rosa gallica* var. *officinalis* × 2
2. *Artemisia abrotanum* × 6
3. *Lavandula angustifolia* 'Hidcote' × 10
4. *Dianthus caryophyllus* × 7
5. *Salvia officinalis* Purpurascens Group × 5
6. *Rosmarinus officinalis* × 5
7. *Mentha suaveolens* 'Variegata' × 6
8. *Thymus vulgaris* 'Silver Posie' × 5
9. *Jasminum officinale* × 1
10. *Teucrium chamaedrys* × 16
11. *Tanacetum vulgare* × 2
12. *Humulus lupulus* 'Aureus' × 2

13. *Origanum vulgare* 'Aureum' × 5
14. *Tanacetum parthenium* 'Tom Thumb White Stars' × 5
15. *Iris germanica* var. *florentina* × 7
16. *Salvia sclarea* × 3
17. *Foeniculum vulgare* × 4
18. *Citrus limon* × 1
19. *Coriandrum sativum* × 5
20. *Calendula officinalis* × 3
21. *Agastache foeniculum* × 3
22. *Malva moschata* × 3
23. *Monarda didyma* × 3
24. *Pelargonium* 'Rober's Lemon Rose' × 1
25. *Aloysia triphylla* × 1

KEY   ⬤ Shrub   ◯ Perennial   ◉ Annual/Biennial   ▨ Evergreen

Mentha suaveolens 'Variegata' and *Lavandula angustifolia* 'Hidcote'

Mints of all kinds can be dried for potpourri, but the soft, fruity fragrance of pineapple mint is more subtle than most. This lavender cultivar has fine spikes of purple flowers and is one of the best lavenders for scent.

REPEATING BORDER PATTERN

This design for a formal herb border has bold, simple shapes, in units that can be repeated, or half-repeated, as required. It uses colourful evergreen herbs, giving year-round interest and needing little maintenance. Borders such as this can be laid at the edge of a garden or along a house wall, and are useful for any awkward space. Alternatively, they can stand independently on either side of an entrance, or flank the sides of a knot garden. The use of standards, tall, clipped shrubs, or topiary has been a popular device since Elizabethan times to give height and an air of dignity to an otherwise uniformly low planting. In some situations, such as in front of house windows, standards may be unsuitable and smaller, perhaps globe-shaped, clipped shrubs may be preferable.

PREPARING AND CARING FOR YOUR BORDERS

When you are planning and constructing the borders, remember to allow enough space for the hedging plants. They may be only a few centimetres wide on arrival, but will reach 23–30cm (9–12in), depending on how closely you keep them trimmed. Maintenance consists of an annual mulch of compost in late spring; trimming the hedges with care and precision in spring and after flowering, or in the case of box (*Buxus sempervirens*), two or three times during the growing season, and similarly cutting back the sages (*Salvia* spp.). Though perennial, sages and lavenders tend to become woody after three or four years and may need replacing. This can be done by taking cuttings in summer or early autumn and growing them on in pots for planting out the following spring. Periodic replacement also gives an opportunity of choosing completely different herbs for hedging or filling.

BORDER WITH DIAMOND MOTIF
If you are adapting an existing border that is narrower than the one in this plan, you could omit the inner hedge of lavender (Lavandula angustifolia). *Bay trees* (Laurus nobilis) *could be replaced by box* (silver box, Buxus sempervirens *'Elegantissima', would be most effective), and the outer hedge of rock hyssop by dwarf white lavender* (L. × intermedia *'Alba'). Other good combinations would be broad-leafed thyme* (Thymus pulegioides) *and golden marjoram* (Origanum vulgare *'Aureum'), or* T. vulgaris *with a white-variegated marjoram.*

PLANTING WITH CONTRASTING COLOURS
A formal border at Hollington Nurseries, Berkshire, England, planted with Lavandula angustifolia, *hedges of rich dark red* Berberis thunbergii *f.* atropurpurea, *and a centrepiece of* Thymus vulgaris *'Silver Posie', from which arise the standards of contrasting silver willow* (Salix alba var. sericea). *The green, silver, and purple colour design works well, but other combinations can be equally effective.*

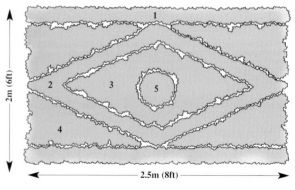

PLANTING PLAN

2m (6ft)

2.5m (8ft)

1. *Hyssopus officinalis* subsp. *aristatus* × 20
2. *Lavandula angustifolia* 'Hidcote' × 16
3. *Salvia officinalis* 'Icterina' × 8
4. *Salvia officinalis* 'Purpurascens' × 14
5. *Laurus nobilis* × 1

KEY ▢ Evergreen

CIRCULAR BED

Many of the popular culinary herbs take up little space and can be grown in quite a small area. A circular bed about 5m (15ft) across will provide an excellent range of fresh herbs for cooking and salads, with plenty to dry and freeze for winter use. It is advisable to start with more than one specimen of each herb, even though a single plant of the larger herbs, such as fennel (*Foeniculum vulgare*) and rosemary (*Rosmarinus officinalis*), would eventually be enough. Putting in several plants of the same kind helps avoid planting different herbs too close together, gives a mature look very quickly, and ensures plenty of harvestable herbs within a few weeks of planting. Coriander (*Coriandrum sativum*) and dill (*Anethum graveolens*) tend to have very short life cycles, which is fine if you are growing them for seed, but you will need two or three sowings a season to ensure a supply of young leaves. Though parsley (*Petroselinum crispum*) is biennial, it is best to make two plantings, in early spring and in late summer, for a year-round supply. Avoid giant herbs, such as angelica, which take over.

PLANTING PLAN

1. *Myrtus communis* × 1
2. *Petroselinum crispum* 'Afro' × 5
3. *Artemisia dracunculus* × 5
4. *Thymus* × *citriodorus* × 6
5. *Borago officinalis* × 5
6. *Coriandrum sativum* × 9
7. *Rosmarinus officinalis* × 1
8. *Mentha spicata* × 3
9. *Thymus vulgaris* × 7
10. *Salvia officinalis* × 1
11. *Origanum vulgare* 'Compactum' × 7
12. *Ocimum basilicum* × 3
13. *Anethum graveolens* × 5
14. *Rumex acetosa* × 7
15. *Foeniculum vulgare* × 1
16. *Allium schoenoprasum* × 5
17. *Satureja montana* × 4

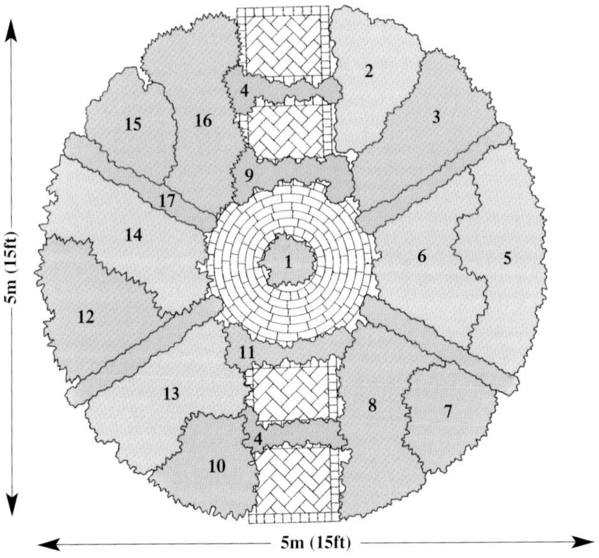

5m (15ft)

5m (15ft)

KEY ⬭ Shrub ⬭ Perennial ⬭ Annual/Biennial ▢ Evergreen

A DECORATIVE AND USEFUL PLANTING

*Many of the herbs in this plan are quite hardy. One exception is basil (*Ocimum basilicum*), which in cold areas can be grown outdoors only during the summer. Also, myrtle (*Myrtus communis*) and tarragon (*Artemisia dracunculus*) need protection in hard winters, and rosemary (*Rosmarinus officinalis*) is susceptible to cold, wet conditions in heavy soils. The various thymes and compact marjoram (*Origanum vulgare* 'Compactum') look good when planted in gaps between the paving stones.*

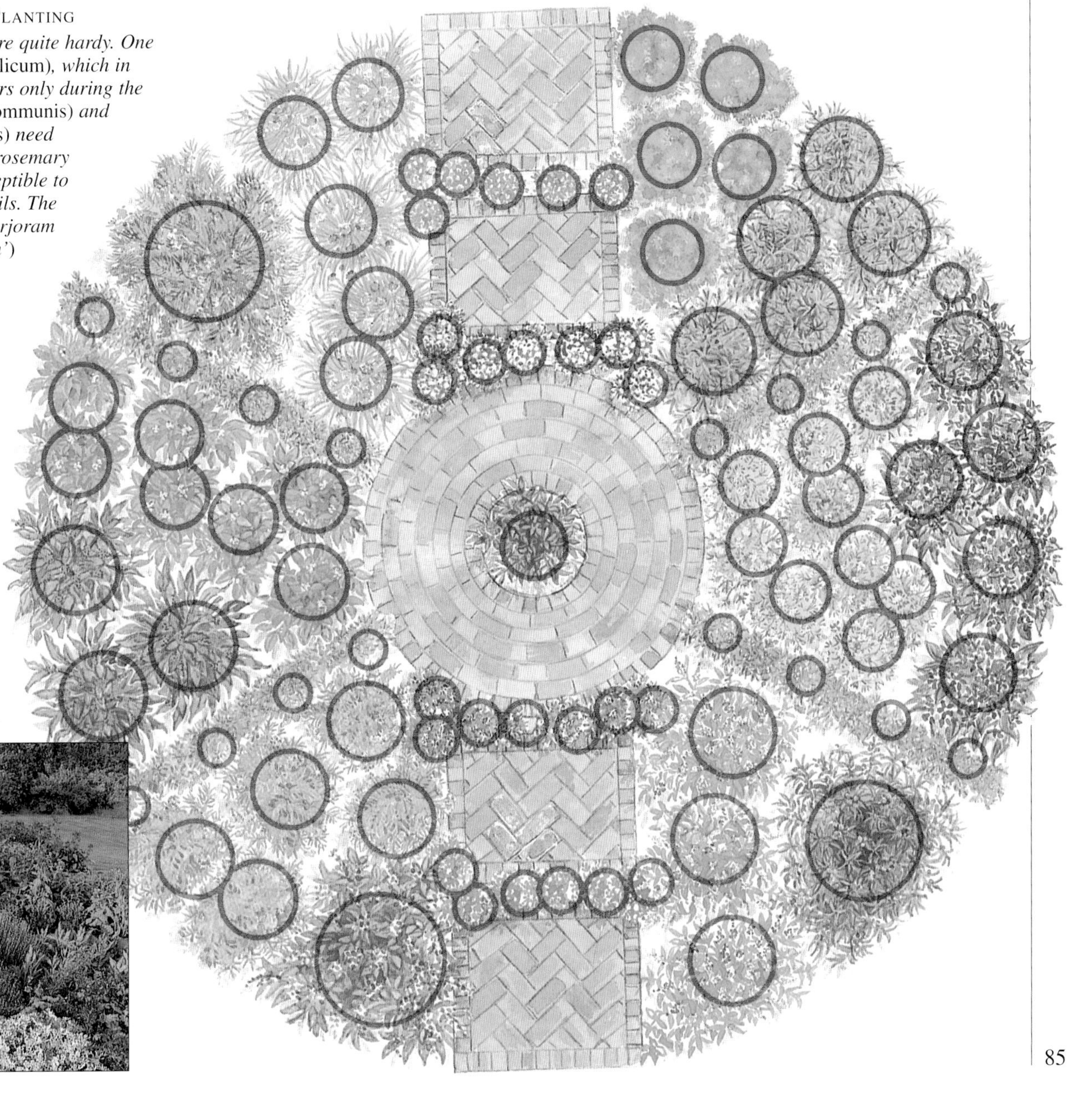

AN INFORMAL CULINARY BED

This culinary herb bed in a country setting has a relaxed feel in the evening sun. There is also space to add additional ornamental plants.

HERBS AMONG THE FLOWERS

Combining herbs with flowers or other plants can give you the best of all worlds in your garden. The fragrant white border shown below is wonderful on a warm summer evening; the rose garden blends scents and warm shades of colour; and the curved border allows plenty of choice and contrast, with herbs and flowers to last all year.

WHITE BED WITH HERBS
The best site for this kind of planting is against a dark green hedge, against which white flowers show up well. A number of herbs naturally have white flowers, such as orris (*Iris germanica* var. *florentina*) and Madonna lilies (*Lilium candidum*), and many others have white-flowered cultivars. These include some of the most popular culinary herbs, such as sage (*Salvia officinalis*), which you will find in this plan; there are also white-flowered chives (*Allium schoenoprasum*), marjorams (*Origanum* spp.), and thymes (*Thymus* spp.).

Rosa × alba '**Alba Semiplena**' **and** *Crambe cordifolia*
Clouds of tiny crambe flowers provide a contrasting background for the heavy, scented blooms of the white rose of York.

A MIXED BORDER
The plants in this plan are perennials and shrubs, with the exception of Lavatera trimestris *'Mont Blanc' and* Nicotiana sylvestris, *which are grown as annuals, and* Lunaria annua *'Alba Variegata', a biennial with variegation that may not be apparent in young plants.*

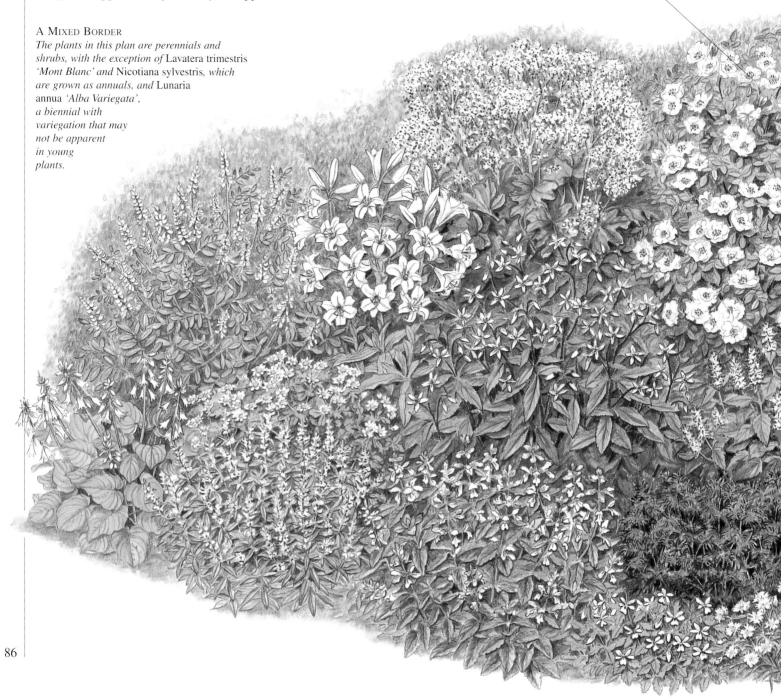

Artemisia 'Powis Castle'
and *Lavatera trimestris*
'Mont Blanc'
Simple white mallow flowers
are delightful among the finely
cut, silver leaves of this
compact wormwood.

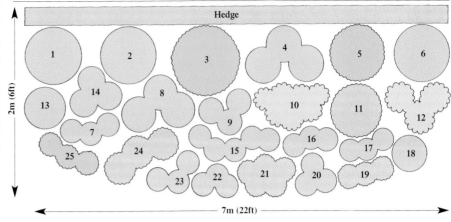

PLANTING PLAN

Hedge

2m (6ft)

7m (22ft)

Ruta graveolens
'Jackman's Blue' and
Aquilegia
The darting flowers of a
white aquilegia overhang
a neat blue-grey mound
of rue.

Taxus baccata – for hedge
1. *Galega officinalis* 'Alba' × 1
2. *Crambe cordifolia* × 1
3. *Rosa alba* 'Alba Semiplena' × 1
4. *Nicotiana sylvestris* × 3
5. *Philadelphus* 'Belle Etoile' × 1
6. *Veronicastrum virginicum*
   f. *album* × 1
7. *Tanacetum parthenium* 'Aureum'
   × 3
8. *Gillenia trifoliata* × 3

9. *Agastache foeniculum*
   'Alabaster' × 3
10. *Lavatera trimestris*
    'Mont Blanc' × 7
11. *Artemisia* 'Powis Castle' × 1
12. *Lunaria annua* 'Alba Variegata'
    × 3
13. *Hosta* 'Royal Standard' × 1
14. *Lilium candidum* × 3
15. *Artemisia pontica* × 5
16. *Iris germanica* var. *florentina* × 3
17. *Aquilegia* × 3

18. *Galium odoratum* × 1
19. *Ruta graveolens* 'Jackman's
    Blue' × 3
20. *Geranium dalmaticum*
    'Album' × 3
21. *Lavandula* × *intermedia*
    'Alba' × 5
22. *Dianthus* 'Mrs. Sinkins' × 3
23. *Viola cornuta* 'Alba' × 3
24. *Salvia officinalis* 'Albiflora' × 3
25. *Hyssopus officinalis*
    f. *albus* × 3

KEY ◯ Shrub ◯ Perennial ◯ Annual/Biennial ⚘ Bulb ▨ Evergreen

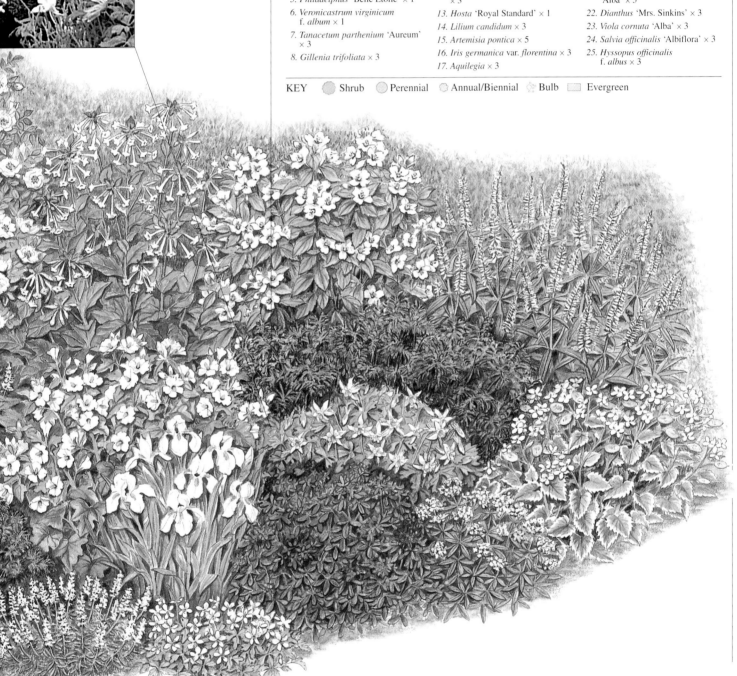

MIXED BORDER WITH HERBS

A specifically made herb garden is a great asset, but not essential – herbs grown alongside other plants in the garden will still smell as sweet! There are a number of things to consider when planting in this way. Height is obviously important, so make sure that any herbs you are adding are a suitable size for their companions. Low-growing savory (*Satureja spicigera*) and parsley (*Petroselinum crispum*) have been planted here as edging, backed by neat, compact dwarf dahlias that are unlikely to smother them. Consider colour and texture, too; try putting lacy coriander (*Coriandrum sativum*) among the magenta spikes of field gladioli to give interesting plant associations. In late winter, pansies (*Viola × wittrockiana*) and chicory (*Cichorium intybus*) will brighten the border.

UNUSUAL COMBINATIONS

Culinary herbs flourish in a mixed border of perennials and bedding plants. This choice of ornamentals includes some interesting plant associations, but other plants of your own preference could easily be substituted.

PLANTING PLAN

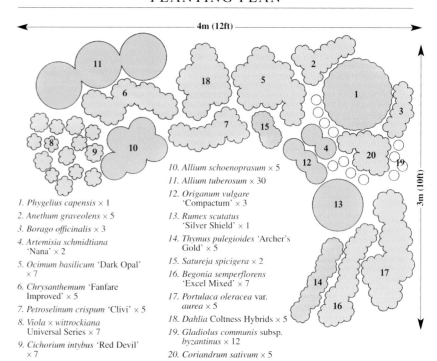

4m (12ft)

3m (10ft)

1. *Phygelius capensis* × 1
2. *Anethum graveolens* × 5
3. *Borago officinalis* × 3
4. *Artemisia schmidtiana* 'Nana' × 2
5. *Ocimum basilicum* 'Dark Opal' × 7
6. *Chrysanthemum* 'Fanfare Improved' × 5
7. *Petroselinum crispum* 'Clivi' × 5
8. *Viola × wittrockiana* Universal Series × 7
9. *Cichorium intybus* 'Red Devil' × 7
10. *Allium schoenoprasum* × 5
11. *Allium tuberosum* × 30
12. *Origanum vulgare* 'Compactum' × 3
13. *Rumex scutatus* 'Silver Shield' × 1
14. *Thymus pulegioides* 'Archer's Gold' × 5
15. *Satureja spicigera* × 2
16. *Begonia semperflorens* 'Excel Mixed' × 7
17. *Portulaca oleracea* var. *aurea* × 5
18. *Dahlia* Coltness Hybrids × 5
19. *Gladiolus communis* subsp. *byzantinus* × 12
20. *Coriandrum sativum* × 5

KEY   ● Perennial   ✿ Annual/Biennial   ❀ Bulb   ▣ Evergreen

***Begonia semperflorens* 'Excel Mixed' and *Thymus pulegioides* 'Archer's Gold'**
The greenish-gold foliage of this compact thyme, excellent for both aromatic and culinary use, is a good foil for the bright mixed colours of the hybrid begonias.

HERBS IN A ROSE GARDEN

The rich colours and exquisite scents of roses are glorious highlights of summer, but the plants can present a rather uninspiring picture for the rest of the year. Adding a selection of aromatic herbs is an ideal solution to this problem; their finely cut, often velvety, greyish foliage provides a contrast to the mainly broad, dark green rose leaves, and their small, pastel-coloured flowers complement rather than compete with the opulence of the roses. All the herbs in this planting are closely related and their flowers range from white to pink and purple-blue. Their similarity in appearance contributes to the harmony of shapes and colours. Purple-leafed sage (*Salvia officinalis* 'Purpurascens') is particularly effective with pale pink roses, whereas the white-flowered sage (*Salvia officinalis* 'Albiflora') is a better choice beside salmon-yellow.

PLANTING PLAN

1. *Rosa* 'Madame Alfred Carrière' × 2
2. *Rosa gallica* 'Versicolor' × 1
3. *Rosa* × *centifolia* 'Muscosa' × 1
4. *Rosa* 'Madame Isaac Pereire' × 1
5. *Rosa* 'Comte de Chambord' × 1
6. *Rosa* 'Complicata' × 1
7. *Teucrium chamaedrys* × 27
8. *Salvia officinalis* 'Albiflora' × 2
9. *Lavandula angustifolia* 'Folgate' × 3
10. *Hyssopus officinalis* f. *roseus* × 3
11. *Salvia officinalis* 'Purpurascens' × 3
12. *Dianthus caryophyllus* × 14
13. *Lavandula angustifolia* 'Rosea' × 3
14. *Salvia officinalis* 'Berggarten' × 3
15. *Origanum vulgare* × 3

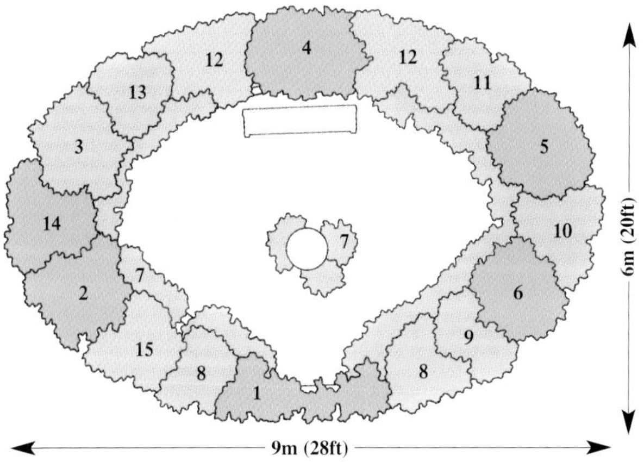

KEY ◯ Shrub ◯ Perennial ▢ Evergreen

6m (20ft)

9m (28ft)

CHOOSING EDGING
*An excellent herb for the inner edging is the small, spreading wall germander (*Teucrium chamaedrys). If you plant the hybrid T. × lucidrys instead, it will need trimming in spring, and again after flowering.*

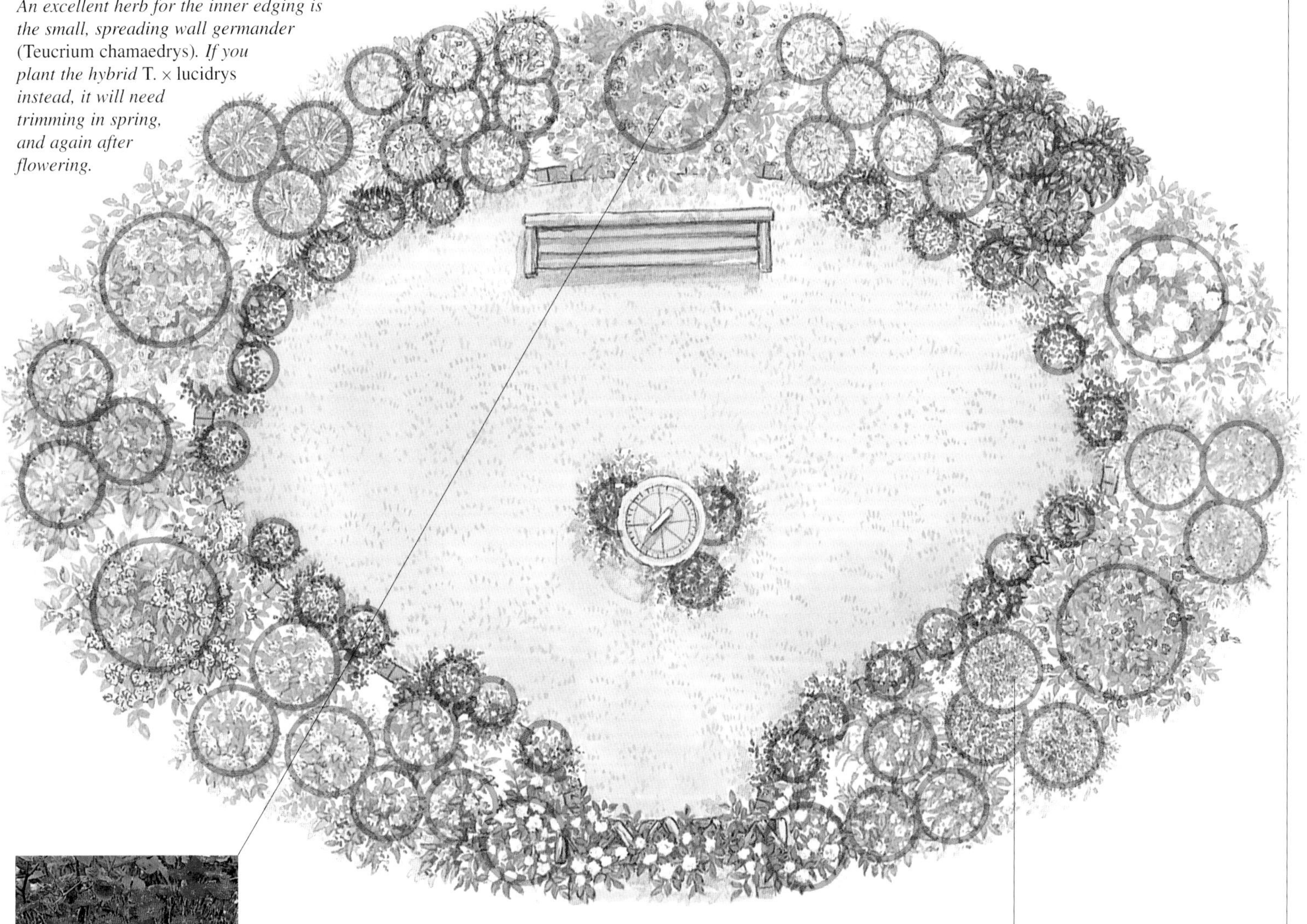

Rosa **'Madame Isaac Pereire'** and *Dianthus caryophyllus*
The brilliant blooms of the pink Bourbon rose contrast eye-catchingly with the deep red of the clove pink and the paler, red-centred pinks in the foreground of this bed.

Rosa gallica **'Versicolor' with** *Lavandula angustifolia* **'Folgate' and foxgloves**
This fragrant pastel display is reminiscent of an old English cottage garden, with elegant spires of pink and white foxgloves (*Digitalis* spp.) waving over a profusion of pink roses and the compact, violet-flowered 'Folgate' lavender.

HERBS IN CONTAINERS

Planting herbs in containers is a practical and ornamental way of displaying your favourites, particularly if garden space is limited. The containers can be positioned easily at hand for harvesting and will change from year to year if you replant them with a different selection of herbs. Hanging baskets can be used, too, and climbers trained on special trellises designed to be stable when inserted into pots.

VARIED CONTAINERS
Grouping herbs in a variety of pots can create an eye-catching display, especially if you take advantage of the differing container heights. If your space includes a balcony or flight of steps, a collection of interesting containers can turn it into a very individual herbary.

CULINARY WINDOWBOX

Providing a sheltered site for the plants and access to a supply of fresh leaves, a windowbox is a great way to grow culinary herbs. Replant the windowbox when the plants become crowded; the bay (*Laurus nobilis*) and rosemary (*Rosmarinus officinalis* 'Severn Sea') will be worth saving, either for larger containers or for planting out in the ground, and the chives (*Allium schoenoprasum*) and marjoram (*Origanum vulgare* 'Gold Tip') can be divided for replanting. All are hardy perennials, except for the parsley (*Petroselinum crispum*) and summer savory (*Satureja hortensis*).

PLANTING PLAN

1. Allium schoenoprasum × 1
2. Petroselinum crispum 'Afro' × 1
3. Laurus nobilis × 1
4. Salvia officinalis × 1
5. Satureja hortensis × 1
6. Rosmarinus officinalis 'Severn Sea' × 1
7. Origanum vulgare 'Gold Tip' × 1

KEY
⬤ Shrub
⬤ Perennial
▢ Evergreen

AN EASY CULINARY SELECTION
This example of herbs suitable for a windowbox includes seven of the most popular culinary herbs. They remain green through the winter, so there is something to enjoy year-round.

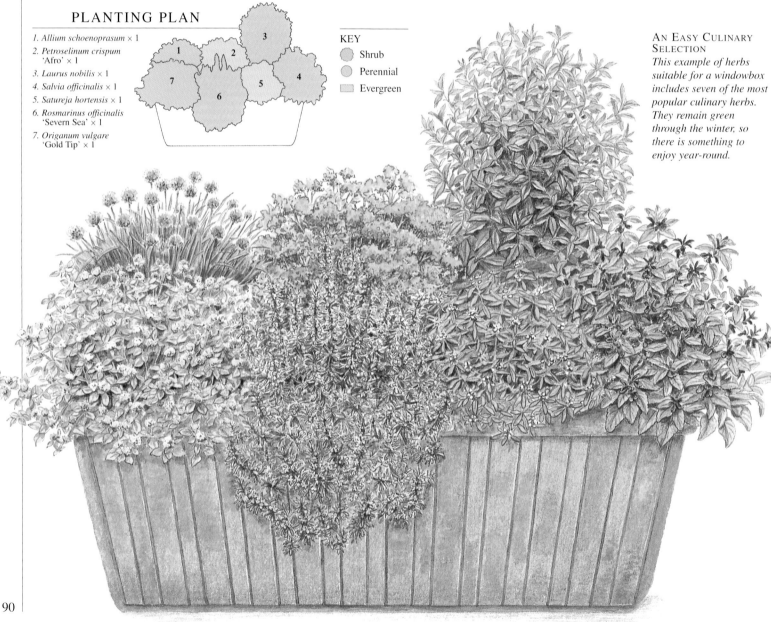

MEDICINAL PLANTER

A pocketed herb planter – known as a strawberry jar because of its original use – makes an interesting display and is useful for someone who would like to try making a few teas and simple remedies. Pocketed planters enable a number of herbs to be grown in a small space, though the large number of herbs growing in a relatively small amount of soil means that pots of this kind will soon become overcrowded. They need to be replanted every spring – especially if they contain mint, which during the year is likely to spread and invade every pocket. Pocketed planters dry out quickly and are then difficult to water, because the soil shrinks and the water merely runs out of the pockets. To make watering easier and more effective, stand the planter in a bowl and water from above and below.

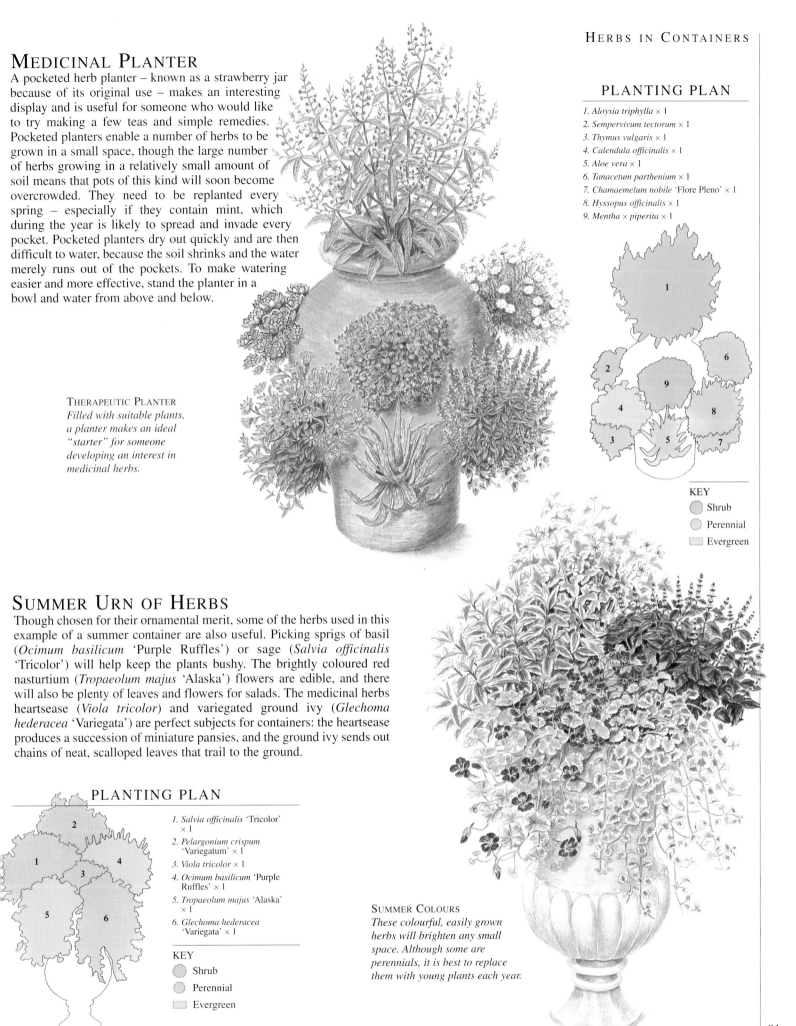

THERAPEUTIC PLANTER
Filled with suitable plants, a planter makes an ideal "starter" for someone developing an interest in medicinal herbs.

PLANTING PLAN

1. Aloysia triphylla × 1
2. Sempervivum tectorum × 1
3. Thymus vulgaris × 1
4. Calendula officinalis × 1
5. Aloe vera × 1
6. Tanacetum parthenium × 1
7. Chamaemelum nobile 'Flore Pleno' × 1
8. Hyssopus officinalis × 1
9. Mentha × piperita × 1

KEY
⬡ Shrub
⬭ Perennial
▢ Evergreen

SUMMER URN OF HERBS

Though chosen for their ornamental merit, some of the herbs used in this example of a summer container are also useful. Picking sprigs of basil (*Ocimum basilicum* 'Purple Ruffles') or sage (*Salvia officinalis* 'Tricolor') will help keep the plants bushy. The brightly coloured red nasturtium (*Tropaeolum majus* 'Alaska') flowers are edible, and there will also be plenty of leaves and flowers for salads. The medicinal herbs heartsease (*Viola tricolor*) and variegated ground ivy (*Glechoma hederacea* 'Variegata') are perfect subjects for containers: the heartsease produces a succession of miniature pansies, and the ground ivy sends out chains of neat, scalloped leaves that trail to the ground.

PLANTING PLAN

1. Salvia officinalis 'Tricolor' × 1
2. Pelargonium crispum 'Variegatum' × 1
3. Viola tricolor × 1
4. Ocimum basilicum 'Purple Ruffles' × 1
5. Tropaeolum majus 'Alaska' × 1
6. Glechoma hederacea 'Variegata' × 1

KEY
⬡ Shrub
⬭ Perennial
▢ Evergreen

SUMMER COLOURS
These colourful, easily grown herbs will brighten any small space. Although some are perennials, it is best to replace them with young plants each year.

A – Z of HERBS

HOW TO USE THIS SECTION

Arranged in alphabetical order by genus, the well-illustrated A–Z of Herbs contains an introductory description of the genus and its distribution, folklore, research, name derivations, and details of relevant species. There is concise information on how the herbs are grown, propagated, and harvested, which is expanded in the feature section Cultivating Herbs (see pp.48–69). The genus introduction is followed by individual plant entries, containing a brief botanical description for every species and its variants, as well as its hardiness rating, information on the parts of the plant used, with their properties, and the ways in which the herb may be exploited (see also Using Herbs, pp.40–47).

WARNINGS AND LEGAL RESTRICTIONS

Warnings on the medicinal use of any herb are given under its entry in this A–Z of Herbs, in the form of an alert appearing in the note on Medicinal Uses. A plant's toxicity and any restrictions that may apply to its cultivation are indicated by a warning at the end of the appropriate genus or species entry. There is also advice on the safe usage of herbs in the Introduction to Using Herbs (see pp.40–41).

HARDINESS RATINGS

The plant's level of hardiness (ability to withstand winter temperatures) is given in the A–Z of Herbs (see pp.96–411) within each plant's description. Thus:

Fully hardy: minimum –15°C (5°F)
Frost hardy: minimum –5°C (23°F)
Half hardy: minimum 0°C (32°F)
Tender: plant may be damaged by temperatures below 5°C (41°F), or whatever other minimum temperature is indicated within that plant's entry

Note: Individual plants may be able to tolerate minimum temperatures slightly lower than those indicated by its rating, depending on local conditions and the maturity, health, and genetic constitution of the plant.

CLIMATIC ZONES

The climates of the world are divided into four main zones and two intermediate ones. The growth and development of plants are influenced to a large extent by the climatic zone that they inhabit.

TROPICAL High temperatures, high humidity, and heavy rainfall throughout the year.

DESERT Daytime temperatures exceeding 38°C (100°F), cold nights, and annual rainfall of less than 25cm (10in).

TEMPERATE Temperature and rainfall more evenly distributed throughout the year, but changeable from day to day, and varying greatly in local conditions.

POLAR Extreme cold, high winds, and low precipitation.

SUBTROPICAL High temperatures throughout the year, but marked seasonal rainfall.

MEDITERRANEAN Hot dry summers and mild moist winters.

Climate also changes with altitude. Within all these zones, temperature drops by 6°C (11°F) for every 1km (3250ft) of increase in altitude.

SYMBOLS

▣ Plant is pictured (within pages containing genus entry)

PLANT DIMENSIONS
↕ Typical height
↔ Typical spread
↕↔ Typical height and spread (if the same)

PARTS OF THE PLANT THAT ARE USED
▥ Bark or wood
✿ Flowers
▨ Fruit, pods
▧ Leaves
⬤ Oil, sap, resin, gum, latex
▩ Rhizomes, bulbs, corms, roots
▨ Seeds
▤ Shoots, stems
▣ Whole plant

USES OF THE PART OF THE PLANT
▮ Medicinal
✓ Culinary
✎ Economic

TENDER PLANTS
▣ Frost tender

A–Z of Herbs

All plants in the A–Z are described within a genus entry (see Plant Classification, p.18). Individual plant entries follow, under their own bold headings, and include sections on hardiness, parts used, properties, and herbal uses for each particular species. The defining characteristic of any variant of a species is described at the end of a species entry.

Anacardium occidentale

red-striped flowers appear all year in terminal panicles, followed by red or yellow fruits that have a kidney-shaped nut at the base. Native to tropical America. ↕ 12m (40ft), ↔ 10m (30ft).
HARDINESS Min. 18°C (64°F).
PARTS USED Leaves, bark, fruits, seeds, oil.
PROPERTIES Reduces fever (leaves) and blood sugar levels (bark), and is diuretic (fruits); the nuts (seeds) are a source of nutrients, and the shell oil is toxic to many disease-causing organisms, such as *Staphylococcus* bacteria.
MEDICINAL USES Internally for diarrhoea (bark and leaf extracts, fruit juice), hypoglycaemia (bark extract), and influenza (fruit juice), and, in W Africa, for malaria (leaf and bark infusions). Externally for leprosy, ringworm, warts, and corns (fresh extract from shells), and, in W Africa, for toothache and sore gums (leaf and bark infusions). Bark extract is considered to have contraceptive properties by native Amazonians.
CULINARY USES Fruits are eaten fresh, cooked, or dried, or made into chutney or jam. Juice is made into soft drinks, such as *cashola*, and distilled as *fenni* and *koniagi*. Nuts are eaten roasted and used in a variety of both sweet and savoury dishes, and also ground when raw to make cashew butter, milk, and cream, as a substitute for dairy produce in special diets.
ECONOMIC USES Shell oil is used in brake linings, synthetic rubbers, and to proof paper and wood against insect attack.
⚠ **WARNING** Oil is a skin irritant; oil vapour is irritant if inhaled.
▥ ▨ ▧ ⬤ ▨ ⬤ ▮ ✓ ✎ ▣

ANACYCLUS
Mount Atlas daisy

Asteraceae

This genus of nine species of annuals and perennials is native to the Mediterranean. *Anacyclus pyrethrum* itself is rarely grown as an ornamental, but the prostrate var. *depressus*, from the Atlas Mountains in Morocco, is popular with rock garden enthusiasts. As a medicinal herb, *A. pyrethrum* has been widely used from medieval times to the present by Arabian,

Asian, and Eur▮
recommended ▮
chewed in the ▮
phlegmatic hur▮
pains in the hea▮
distilling of the▮
thereby preven▮
consumption, t▮
(*The English P*▮
Anacyclus pyre▮
with the insect▮
Tanacetum cin▮
CULTIVATION▮
wet winters.
PROPAGATION▮
softwood cuttir▮
HARVEST Roo▮
and powdered ▮
pastilles, and ti▮

▣ *Anacyclus p▮*
Spain)
Low, rosette-fo▮
divided, grey-g▮
long. Solitary, ▮
(1–2in) across,▮
stalks. They ha▮
petals with a re▮
Algeria, and M▮
(10–12in). var.▮
compact habit ▮
undersides. ↕ 2.▮
HARDINESS F▮
PARTS USED F▮
PROPERTIES A▮
stimulates the s▮
tissues, thereby▮
MEDICINAL US▮
facial neuralgia▮
CULINARY USES▮
in liqueurs.
▣ ⬤ ▮ ▮

Anacyclus pyre▮

2 Genus Introduction
Gives the number of species in the genus, with their distributions. Suitability for garden planting is indicated. The name derivation of the genus is described in many cases. It also discusses historical uses of relevant or related species, occurrence in legend or folklore, and development and research into modern applications.

1 Genus Name
Full name, with family name, and generic common name, if any.

4 Cultivation, Propagation, and Harvest
Gives a brief outline of how the relevant species in the genus described are cultivated, propagated, and harvested, and how their parts are prepared and processed. Where relevant, there are notes on legal restrictions on cultivation, warnings of toxicity or possible allergies, advice on invasive plants, companion planting, and pest and disease problems. Please note that the information given may not apply to species in the genus that are not included in this book.

3 Cross References
Cross references to other genera or species are given throughout the A–Z of Herbs.

ANAGALLIS

Culpeper
...oot dried and
...brain of
...t only easing
...lso hinders the
...ngs and eyes,
...sicks and
...alling sickness"
..., 1653).
...be confused
...which is from
...581).
...in sun. Dislikes

...autumn; by
...rly summer.
...umn, then dried
...ctions,

...ry, pellitory of

...with finely
...4cm (4–5½in)
..., 2.5–5cm
...30cm (12in)
...and white ray
...ative to Spain,
...in), ↔25–30cm
...ow-growing,
...ls with red
...→ 10cm (4in).

...erb that
...d irritates the
...flow to the area.
...r toothache,
...arrh.
...m roots is used

ANAGALLIS
Pimpernel

Primulaceae

A genus of 20 species of low-growing annuals, biennials, and perennials found all over the world. *Anagallis arvensis* (scarlet pimpernel) is a common weed of cultivated ground. The scarce, blue-flowered variety was once thought to be the female form of the scarlet pimpernel. *Anagallis* is from the Greek *anagelas*, "to laugh", from its use in treating depression. Several of the common names relate to weather forecasting: their flowers open and close with changing light and temperature. Once highly regarded as a medicinal herb, with uses dating back to Pliny (AD23–79) and Dioscorides, *A. arvensis* is now little used. It contains irritant saponins, which research shows have anti-viral effects, and cucurbitacins (as found in *Bryonia*, see p.147), which are highly toxic.
CULTIVATION Well-drained to dry or sandy soil in sun. Aphids may attack plants under cover.
PROPAGATION By seed sown in spring at 16–18°C (61–64°F).
HARVEST Whole plants are gathered in summer and used fresh, often as expressed juice, or dried for infusions, liquid extracts, tinctures, and powder.
⚠ **WARNING** Harmful if eaten.

▪ *Anagallis arvensis* (poor man's weatherglass, scarlet pimpernel)
Prostrate annual or biennial with four-angled stems, ovate to lanceolate leaves, 1cm (½in) long, and star-shaped, salmon-red flowers, 5mm (¼in) across, often with purple centres, throughout summer. Native to Europe. ‡ 2.5–5cm (1–2in), ↔ 15–30cm (6–12in). ▪ var. *caerulea* (blue pimpernel) has gentian-blue flowers.
HARDINESS Fully hardy.
PARTS USED Whole plant.
PROPERTIES An acrid mucilaginous herb that lowers fever and has diuretic and expectorant effects.
MEDICINAL USES Traditionally prescribed internally for depression, tuberculosis, liver complaints, epilepsy, dropsy, and rheumatism. No longer considered safe by most medical

A

5 Species Name
The full botanical name is given for each plant as well as any synonyms (former botanical names) and the most usual common names. Synonyms are prefaced by "syn.".

6 Individual Plant Entry
Botanical description of the named species and the country or region from which it originates. Approximate height and spread when fully grown are given at the end of each plant entry (height only for climbers). All measurements are rounded for ease of use.

7 Variants and Cultivars
Varietas, subspecies, forma, and cultivar descriptions follow on from the main plant entry – their names appearing without the generic or species epithet. Only the characteristics that distinguish them from the species are described.

8 Hardiness Rating
Indicates the temperature range required for optimum growth (see box, left).

9 Parts Used
Lists the parts of the plant used, or material extracted, and corresponds to the symbols shown at the end of the individual plant entry.

10 Properties
The herb's properties and effects, for healing or other purposes.

11 Uses of the Herb
How the herb is put to use, under three categories: Medicinal, Culinary, and Economic. Warnings are given of legal restrictions on the therapeutic use of the herb.

12 Symbols
Symbols below the plant description indicate the part of the herb used, the category of use, and whether it is tender. A key to these symbols will be found in the box (far left) on this spread.

Anagallis arvensis   119

A

ABELMOSCHUS

Malvaceae

This genus contains 15 species of bristly or downy, hibiscus-like annuals and perennials (formerly included in *Hibiscus*, see p.235), found in the tropics of Africa and Asia. *Abelmoschus moschatus* is the only species used widely as a herb. It is grown throughout the tropics and virtually all parts are useful, notably the seeds, which are popular as a spice in the East. In cool climates, it can be grown as a half-hardy annual for summer bedding or containers. The name comes from the Arabic *abu-l-mosk*, "father of musk", as the seeds are musk-scented.

CULTIVATION Grow in rich, well-drained soil in sun. Pinch out the growing tips of young plants to encourage bushiness. In spring, cut back plants grown as perennials to 15cm (6in). Plants grown under cover may suffer from whitefly.

PROPAGATION By seed, sown in spring at 24–27°C (75–81°F); also by semi-ripe cuttings in summer.

HARVEST Foliage and pods are picked when young and tender, and flowers as they open, and used fresh. Bark and roots are harvested as required and processed to extract fibre and mucilage. Fruits are cut as they begin to ripen and dried until the seeds are shed. Seeds are stored away from other commodities to avoid persistent musk odour, and are distilled for oil. They are also steeped in vegetable oil for external use.

■ *Abelmoschus moschatus* syn. *Hibiscus abelmoschus* (ambrette, musk mallow, muskseed)
Bushy perennial with palmate leaves, 10–15cm (4–6in) long. Large, sulphur-yellow, hibiscus-like flowers with maroon centres appear in summer, followed by hairy seed pods, 2.5–8cm (1–3in) long, containing grey-brown, kidney-shaped seeds with a strong, musk-like aroma. Native to tropical Asia. ‡ 1–2m (3–6ft), ↔ 45–90cm

(18–36in). 'Oriental Pink' has red-pink, white-centred flowers, 6–8cm (2½–3in) across.
‡ 38–45cm (15–18in), ↔ 23–30cm (9–12in).

HARDINESS Min. 5°C (41°F).

PARTS USED Leaves, bark, roots, flowers, pods, seeds, oil.

PROPERTIES An aromatic stimulant herb that relaxes spasms, especially in the digestive tract. It is also insecticidal and is regarded as an aphrodisiac.

MEDICINAL USES Internally as a digestive and breath-freshener (seeds). Externally for cramps, poor circulation, and aching joints, and in aromatherapy for anxiety and depression (oil).

CULINARY USES Young leaves and new shoots are eaten as vegetables. Leaves are used to clarify sugar. Unripe pods, known as "musk okra", are eaten as a vegetable. Seeds flavour coffee, liqueurs, and breads and are an ingredient of the N African spice mix, *ras-el-hanout*.

ECONOMIC USES Bark is processed into fibre. Root mucilage provides sizing for paper. Flowers are used for flavouring tobacco. Oil is used in food flavouring, vermouth, bitters, perfumery, and cosmetics as a musk substitute; it is free from the faecal note sometimes present in animal musk. Formerly a common ingredient in aftershave lotions but now largely discontinued because it causes photosensitization.

🔲 🔯 🔳 🔲 🔘 🔳 🔳 ▣ ◩ ◩ 🔲

ABIES

Fir

Pinaceae

A genus of about 50 species of large evergreen conifers, distributed throughout subalpine and temperate zones in the northern hemisphere and C America. *Abies* is the original Latin name for these trees. Silver and balsam firs are too large

for most gardens, but *A. balsamea* Hudsonia Group is an attractive dwarf cultivar suitable for small spaces. Many firs are economically important for timber and resin. *Abies alba* was the original Christmas tree, later superseded by the Norway spruce (*Picea abies*) and others. Its medicinal uses have also declined: it was the source of Strassburg turpentine, listed in the *London Pharmacopoeia* until 1788, but it has now been replaced by various species of pine (*Pinus*, see p.318).

CULTIVATION Deep, moist, well-drained, slightly acid soil in sun or shade. Young trees and *A. balsamea* Hudsonia Group are more tolerant of alkaline conditions. Firs are sensitive to atmospheric pollution. They may also be damaged by late spring frosts as the new shoots appear earlier in mild areas than they would in the wild. Planting in light shade, rather than full sun, minimizes damage. Maintain a single leading shoot by cutting out competing shoots flush with the main stem in spring. Firs may be attacked by sap-sucking adelgids, and are prone to die-back and rust caused by fungal infections.

PROPAGATION By seed sown in spring.

HARVEST Leaves and young shoots are collected in spring. Bark is removed throughout the year. Resin is tapped from 60–80-year-old trees, in spring, for distillation of oil. Oleo-resin is collected at any time from blisters on the trunk.

■ *Abies alba* syn. *A. pectinata* (European silver fir, silver fir)
Fast-growing, evergreen conifer with dull grey bark, smooth in young trees, which cracks to form squarish plates in older specimens. Glossy, dark green needles, to 2.5cm (1in) long,

| *Abelmoschus moschatus*

Abies alba

Abies balsamea

Abies balsamea Hudsonia Group

Abrus precatorius

have two silvery white or pale bands on the undersides. Large cylindrical cones are 15cm (6in) long and have conspicuous reflexed bracts. Native to mountains of C and SE Europe. ↕ 45m (150ft), ↔ 20m (70ft).
HARDINESS Fully hardy.
PARTS USED Leaves, resin.
PROPERTIES An aromatic antiseptic herb that acts as a diuretic and expectorant, and irritates the tissues, causing greater blood flow to the area.
MEDICINAL USES Internally and externally as a common ingredient in remedies for coughs and colds. Externally also in bath extracts, rubbing oils and liniments, for rheumatism and neuralgia.
CULINARY USES Source of honeydew honey, regarded as a tonic in parts of Europe. Inner bark made into bread by Lapps and Eskimos.
ECONOMIC USES Oil of turpentine is an important solvent in the paint industry. The residue, known as "rosin oil", is used in the manufacture of varnishes, lacquers, and carbon black (for pigments and ink).

▨ ▢ ▪ ✐ ✎

▣ *Abies balsamea* (balm of Gilead, balsam fir) Conical tree with dark grey bark that becomes fissured in older specimens and flat leaves with two grey to white stripes on the undersurface. Erect cones are purple when young, up to 1.5–2.5cm (½–1in) long, turning brown when mature. Native to C and E Canada, and NE USA. ↕ 15m (45ft), ↔ 5m (15ft). ▣ Hudsonia Group makes a rounded dwarf shrub with a flattish crown and short dense needles. It lacks cones, and is slower growing and more lime-tolerant than the species. ↕↔ 60cm–1m (2–3ft).
HARDINESS Fully hardy.
PARTS USED Leaves, bark, oleo-resin, oil.
PROPERTIES An aromatic, astringent, antiseptic herb that stimulates circulation and acts as a diuretic.
MEDICINAL USES Internally in proprietary mixtures for diarrhoea, but in excess is purgative. Externally, in bath extracts for rheumatic pain, and as a mouthwash. Oleo-resin is known as "Canada balsam" or "spruce gum"; it is used for chewing, and in traditional N American medicine for chest infections, venereal disease, wounds, and burns.
CULINARY USES Shoot tips are used for tea.

ECONOMIC USES Oleo-resin is used in food flavouring, and as a lens cement and a sealing agent for mounting microscope slides. Oil is used in dentistry in sealing preparations, and as a fixative and for fragrance in soaps, cosmetics, and perfumes.

▨ ▨ ▢ ▪ ✐ ✎

ABRUS
Papilionaceae

Seventeen species of tender, deciduous, semi-evergreen, or evergreen, twining shrubs make up this genus, which occurs throughout the tropics in lowland forest. *Abrus precatorius* has acquired numerous common names from its many uses. The name "jequirity" is from the Portuguese translation of the Tupi-Guarani *jekiriti*, "lucky bean". "Indian liquorice" refers to the fact that *A. precatorius* contains glycyrrhizin, a substance 50–60 times sweeter than sugar, which is most commonly found in *Glycyrrhiza* spp. (see p.226). Seeds of *Abrus precatorius* contain abrin, one of the most poisonous plant compounds known. Chewing a raw seed may prove fatal, but the toxin is even more lethal if it enters the bloodstream directly. The seeds are traditionally used in India to weigh gemstones (a single seed equals 1.75g/0.06oz, or 1 carat): the Kohinoor diamond was first weighed by this means. They are also popular worldwide as beads for rosaries, necklaces, and as a charm against illness.
CULTIVATION Rich, well-drained, sandy soil in sun or partial shade. A temperature of 21°C (70°F) is needed in summer for flowering. Tolerates saline conditions. Cut back straggly growth to two or three buds in early spring.
PROPAGATION By seed sown in late winter; by softwood cuttings, at 24°C (75°F). Soak the hard seeds in water for 24 hours before sowing to speed germination.
HARVEST Leaves are picked during the growing season and dried for use in infusions. Ripe seeds are collected in the autumn and ground for pastes.
⚠ **WARNING** Seeds are extremely toxic if eaten.

▣ *Abrus precatorius* (coral pea, crab's eyes, Indian liquorice, jequirity)
Deciduous or semi-evergreen vine with pinnate

leaves, divided into 8–17 or more pairs of leaflets, up to 2cm (¾in) long, tasting of liquorice. Pink-purple, occasionally white, flowers are produced in racemes 3–8cm (1–3in) long, mainly in summer, followed by pods, 5cm (2in) long, containing scarlet, black-tipped seeds. Native to India. ↕ 1–4m (3–13ft), ↔ indefinite.
HARDINESS Min. 16°C (61°F).
PARTS USED Leaves, seeds.
PROPERTIES A liquorice-tasting herb that is soothing (leaves), emetic (seeds and roots), irritant, and abortifacient (seeds).
MEDICINAL USES Internally for sore throats and dry coughs (leaves). Externally for sciatica, hair loss, skin disease, leprosy, nervous debility, and paralysis (seeds). The seeds are extremely poisonous, causing stomach cramps, vomiting, birth deformities, sterility, coma, and death. The roots, rich in glycyrrhizin, have been used as a substitute for liquorice but contain toxic emetic compounds that make this use inadvisable. In some countries the seeds and roots are prohibited from therapeutic use, sale, or supply. For use by qualified practitioners only.

▨ ▩ ▪ ▣

ACACIA
Wattle
Mimosaceae

This genus of 1000 or more evergreen, semi-evergreen, or deciduous trees and shrubs occurs throughout dry tropical to warm temperate regions, especially of Africa and Australia. Wattles are popular as ornamental garden and landscape plants for warmer regions, or as elegant indoor plants under cover in areas with cold winters. Generally fast growing, they are short-lived but flower when young. The name *Acacia* may come from *akakia*, the Arabic name for the plant. Various wattles are cultivated for timber. A number of species contain many valuable compounds, which are used in medicine, flavouring, perfumery, dyes, tanning, adhesives, and insecticides. The acidic leaves of several species, including *A. concinna* (soap pod), are used as a substitute for tamarind in chutneys.

When boiled, the foliage and wood of *A. catechu* produces a dark brown, sticky substance known as "catechu", "cutch", or "cachou", which crystallizes on cooling. *Acacia dealbata* (mimosa, silver wattle) is a source of gum arabic, and the flowers yield "mimosa absolute", used in commercial food flavouring. *Acacia farnesiana* is widely grown for the perfume industry, mostly in the south of France. A substance known as "cassie absolute" is extracted from the flowers. Its violet fragrance is thought superior to violets. Leaves of *A. myrtifolia* (myrtle wattle) have been used as a substitute for hops in brewing. *Acacia nilotica* syn. *A. arabica* is a source of gum arabic or Babul gum, used in the Middle East to make desserts, confectionery, perfumed water, and alcoholic drinks. Some 25 species of *Acacia* yield gum arabic, the most important being *A. senegal*, source of the finest-quality resin, known as "Kordofan gum". Sudan produces 85 per cent of the world's crop, which is collected from the wild. *Acacia victoriae* (elegant wattle) is widely planted by the bushfoods industry for its seeds, which are ground into a rich dark flour, used in baking and as a coffee substitute, known as "wattlecino". Several desert species (such as *A. ancistrocarpa* and *A. trachycarpa*) are used by Australian Aboriginals to treat headaches – twigs and leaves being mashed in water. Infusions or decoctions from bark and roots of some W Australian species, such as *A. bivenosa* subsp. *wayi, A. holosericea, A. monticola,* and *A. tetragonophylla,* are used for coughs, colds, and laryngitis.

CULTIVATION Well-drained, neutral to acid soil in full sun. No regular pruning is required. To keep pot plants bushy, pinch out side shoots. To control size, cut back hard after flowering, removing two-thirds of the main growths. Wattles dislike disturbance, forming long taproots that are sensitive to damage. Repot and transplant only when necessary; trees may take a year to recover. Prone to spider mite and root mealybug when grown under cover. Tortrix moth caterpillars may damage the leaves and new shoots. *Acacia* spp. are noxious weeds in parts of Australia, where sale and introduction are illegal.

PROPAGATION By seed sown in spring at 21°C (70°F): seeds have hard coats, which should be nicked and soaked in water for 24 hours before sowing; by semi-ripe cuttings of lateral shoots in late summer at 16–18°C (61–64°F).

HARVEST Bark and leaves (*A. catechu*) are cut as required for use in infusions and powders. Flowers (*A. farnesiana*) are picked as they open and are dried for use in infusions and baths, or distilled for oil. Seeds and pods are collected when ripe and pressed for oil. Resin (*A. senegal*) is scraped from the trunk and branches in the winter, after the rainy season, as it oozes from the bark; incisions are sometimes made to increase the quantity. Unhealthy trees are the best source of resin, which is processed into powder or dissolved in water.

■ *Acacia catechu* (black catechu)
Deciduous tree with shoots bearing hooked spines at the base, and bipinnate feathery leaves,

Acacia catechu

7.5–15cm (3–6in) long. Pale yellow flowers appear in twos or threes, or in a short spike, in the axils in summer. Native to subtropical forest in SE Asia and India. ‡ up to 25m (80ft), ↔ up to 15m (50ft).
HARDINESS Min. 7°C (45°F).
PARTS USED Leaves, young shoots, bark.
PROPERTIES A bittersweet, antiseptic, astringent herb that checks bleeding and discharges.
MEDICINAL USES Internally for dysentery, chronic diarrhoea, and chronic catarrh. Externally for nose bleeds, haemorrhoids, skin eruptions, bed sores, mouth ulcers, sore throats, and dental infections. Combines well with *Acorus calamus* (see p.101), *Agrimonia eupatoria* (see p.107), *Filipendula ulmaria* (see p.214), *Mentha × piperita* (see p.275), and *Quercus robur* (see p.339), for lower bowel conditions; and with *Commiphora* spp. (see p.177) and *Hamamelis virginiana* (see p.230) as a gargle for oral and dental infections. In India, catechu is used as one of the ingredients of *paan,* a digestive made with betel nuts or leaves.
CULINARY USES Distilled with vodka to make Blavod (black vodka).
ECONOMIC USES Important locally for timber and fuel wood. The bark is used in tanning and as a source of khaki dye.
🔲 📲 🔳 📱 ✏ ✂ 🔲

■ *Acacia farnesiana* (cassie, prickly Moses)
Large shrub or small tree with zigzagged shoots, slender spines 2.5cm (1in) long, and sparse feathery leaves, 7.5cm (3in) long, divided into 4–8 pairs of leaflets and again into 12–20 smaller leaflets. Up to three deep yellow, very fragrant, globose flowers appear in the axils in summer. Native to tropical America. ‡ 3–7m (10–22ft), ↔ 3–5m (10–15ft).
HARDINESS Min. 7°C (45°F).
PARTS USED Bark, flowers, pods, seeds.
PROPERTIES An aromatic, stimulant herb that relieves tension and contains insecticidal compounds (in the flowers). It is reputedly aphrodisiac.
MEDICINAL USES Internally for diarrhoea and skin complaints (bark). Externally in baths for dry skin (flowers).
CULINARY USES Ripe seeds are pressed for cooking oil. Young acid leaves flavour chutneys.

Acacia farnesiana

ECONOMIC USES Bark and pods yield a black dye. Flower extracts are insecticidal. Gum arabic is widely used in the food industry in desserts and confectionery. Flowers are added to potpourris. Solid extract from flowers, "cassie absolute", has a fine violet fragrance, often used in perfumery.
🔲 📲 🔳 📱 ✏ ✂ 🔲

Acacia senegal (gum acacia)
Thicket-forming, large shrub or small tree with a flattened crown, grey branches, and grey-green, bipinnate leaves, each with three curved spines at the base. Pale yellow, fragrant flowers are produced in axillary spikes 5–10cm (2–4in) long. Found from N Africa to India. ‡ 3–9m (10–28ft), ↔ 3–5m (10–15ft).
HARDINESS Min. 15–18°C (59–64°F).
PARTS USED Resin.
PROPERTIES A soothing herb that forms a protective coating over inflamed tissues, reducing irritation and encouraging healing.
MEDICINAL USES Internally in pastilles for sore throats, coughs, and catarrh, and in proprietary mixtures for diarrhoea and dysentery. Externally for burns, sores, and leprosy.
ECONOMIC USES Important in the food industry as a stabilizer (E414) to retard sugar crystallization, and as a flavour fixative and emulsifier. Products such as chewing gum and confectionery are likely to include gum arabic.
🔲 📱 ✏ 🔲

ACANTHOPANAX
Acanthopanax senticosus. See *Eleutherococcus senticosus.*

ACHILLEA
Yarrow

Asteraceae

Over 85 species of quite hardy, often aromatic, commonly mat-forming perennials make up this genus, which occurs in northern temperate regions. Some are semi-evergreen. Achilleas make attractive plants for the border or rock garden, with long-lived flowers that last well in water. Most have a number of cultivars in a range of colours for ornamental plantings. *Achillea* was named after Achilles, who used it to heal his soldiers' wounds after the siege of Troy. *Achillea millefolium* (yarrow) is closely linked to divination, giving rise to sayings and verses in many parts of the world. In China, yarrow stalks are used in consulting the *I Ching* (Book of Changes). Over 40 different constituents have been isolated from yarrow. These include an essential oil, which has anti-inflammatory azulene. The azulene content varies between plants, even in the same habitat. *Achillea ageratum* syn. *A. decolorans* (English or garden mace, also known as maudlin or sweet milfoil) was once used medicinally in similar ways to *Tanacetum balsamita* (alecost, see p.381). The aromatic leaves are good in soups and potato salad. *Achillea erba-rotta* subsp. *moschata* (musk yarrow) is used in perfumery and in the making of *iva* liqueur, wine, and bitters. *Achillea ptarmica* (sneezewort) was once used medicinally and, as the common name suggests, for making snuff.

CULTIVATION Well-drained soil in full sun. Yarrow is prone to mildew in hot dry conditions. It tends to be invasive if not confined in a container. The flowers attract beneficial insects, including hoverflies, ladybirds, and parasitic wasps that prey on garden pests, notably aphids.

PROPAGATION By division in spring; by seed in spring. Variants do not come true from seed.

HARVEST Flowering plants are cut in summer and dried for use in infusions, liquid extracts, lotions, and tinctures.

■ *Achillea millefolium* (carpenter's weed, milfoil, nosebleed, soldier's woundwort, yarrow) Aromatic perennial with tough stems and feathery leaves, 5–15cm (2–6in) long. White to pink flowers, about 6mm (¼in) across, are produced in flat corymbs from early summer to late autumn. Native to northern temperate regions. ↕ 5–30cm (2–12in), ↔ 5–20cm (2–8in), variable in the wild. ■ 'Cerise Queen' has magenta-pink flowers. ↕↔ 60cm (24in). ■ 'Lilac Beauty' syn. 'Lavender Beauty' has lilac-pink flowers. ↕ 80cm (32in). 'Paprika' has

Achillea millefolium 'Cerise Queen'

orange-red flowers that fade with age. ↕↔ 60cm (24in). 'Sammertriese' has dark magenta flower heads, 20cm (8in) across. ↕ 80cm (32in). Cultivars are less invasive than the species.

HARDINESS Fully hardy.

PARTS USED Whole plant.

PROPERTIES An aromatic, bitter, astringent herb that reduces inflammation, promotes perspiration, relieves indigestion, and is a diuretic. It is also effective in lowering blood pressure, relaxing spasms, and arresting haemorrhage.

MEDICINAL USES Internally for feverish illnesses (especially colds, influenza, and measles), catarrh, diarrhoea, dyspepsia, rheumatism, arthritis, menstrual and menopausal complaints, hypertension, and to protect against thrombosis after stroke or heart attack. Externally for wounds, nosebleeds, ulcers, inflamed eyes, and haemorrhoids. Combines well with *Sambucus nigra* (see p.356) and *Mentha × piperita* (see p.275) for fevers, with *Tilia* (see p.391) for high blood pressure, and with *Chamaemelum nobile* (see p.164) for digestive disorders. Used similarly in Ayurvedic medicine and also as a tonic (often combined with *Salvia officinalis*, see p.355) for

the nervous system. Prolonged use of yarrow may cause allergic rashes and make the skin more sensitive to sunlight.

◨ ▪

ACHYRANTHES
Amaranthaceae

This genus of six variable weedy perennials is found mostly in the subtropics and tropics of Eurasia, Australia, and Africa. A few species are used as food or medicinal plants, but they are almost unknown outside their native lands. *Achyranthes bidentata* is cultivated in China on a large scale for the herb trade, mainly in Henan Province. The deep rich soil produces exceptionally large roots, the best quality ones reaching 1–1.2m (3–4ft) in length. This important Chinese herb was first described in medical texts c.AD200. The Chinese name for *A. bidentata* – *huai niu xi* – means "ox knees from the Huai River" and refers to the enlarged nodes on the stem. *Cyathula officinalis* (Sichuan ox knees) is used in similar ways to *A. bidentata*. The seeds of *A. bidentata* are a good substitute for cereal grains in bread-making and have been used for this purpose in India during famine. Young leaves and tops of *A. aspera* (*apamarga*, *latjira*, prickly chaff flower) are eaten like spinach and burned as a source of vegetable salt in Africa. In India the seeds are boiled in milk as a tonic.

CULTIVATION Rich, deep, well-drained soil, ideally sandy and slightly acid, in partial shade.

PROPAGATION By seed sown in late spring.

HARVEST Leaves and stems are picked in summer and crushed for juice or used in tinctures. Roots are lifted in autumn or winter from one- or two-year-old plants and sun-dried for use in decoctions, liquid extracts, pills, and powders. The drying process often involves a stage of stir-frying with rice wine. Fresh root is used in S China.

■ *Achyranthes bidentata* (two-toothed amaranthus)
Slender perennial with velvety, opposite, elliptic leaves, to 12cm (5in) long. In late summer, inconspicuous flowers, accompanied by tiny

Achillea millefolium

Achillea millefolium 'Lilac Beauty'

Achyranthes bidentata

spines, open a few at a time on erect spikes. Native to E and SE Asia; widely naturalized, notably in S USA. ‡ 38cm–1m (15–36in), ↔ 23–45cm (9–18in).

HARDINESS Frost hardy.

PARTS USED Roots (*huai niu xi*), leaves, stems.

PROPERTIES A bitter acrid herb that stimulates the circulatory and digestive systems, liver, and kidneys, lowering blood pressure and relieving pain. Acts mostly on the lower half of the body. Research suggests it dilates the cervix and is therefore inadvisable for use during pregnancy.

MEDICINAL USES Internally for blood in urine, hypertension, low back and joint, menstrual, and postpartum pain, nosebleeds, and bleeding gums.

ACINOS
Basil thyme

Lamiaceae

In this genus there are ten species of annuals or short-lived perennials, closely related to *Calamintha* (see p.149) and resembling thymes in appearance. They are found in dry sunny locations, mainly on chalky soils, throughout Europe, the Mediterranean, and C Asia. One or two species are grown as ornamentals, forming attractive, low-growing trailers for rock gardens, pavings, wall crevices, and containers. The name is derived from the Greek *akinos*, a name used for the plant by Pliny. Although basil thyme is often described as an aromatic herb that can be a substitute for thyme, plants grown today in the UK have little or no aroma. Its medicinal uses are considered obsolete.

CULTIVATION Light dry soil in sun. Prefers sandy and alkaline conditions.

PROPAGATION By seed sown in summer in sandy mix. Self-sows in suitable sites.

HARVEST Flowering plants are cut in summer when in flower and used fresh in infusions, or as a salad herb.

■ *Acinos arvensis* syn. *A. thymoides*, *Clinopodium acinos*, *Satureja acinos* (basil thyme)
Over-wintering annual or short-lived perennial with weak upright stems and lanceolate to ovate

Acinos arvensis

leaves, 7mm–1.5cm (¼–½in) long. Whorls of light purple flowers, with white markings on the lip, appear in summer. Native to N Europe, the Mediterranean, and W Asia. ‡ 15–20cm (6–8in), ↔ 20–30cm (8–12in).

HARDINESS Fully hardy.

PARTS USED Whole plant, oil.

PROPERTIES A stimulant diuretic herb that benefits the digestive system and irritates the tissues, causing a temporary improvement in local blood supply.

MEDICINAL USES Internally, according to old herbals, for shortness of breath, melancholy, and improving the digestion. Externally, oil was once distilled to treat bruises, toothache, sciatica, and neuralgia.

CULINARY USES Once used to flavour jugged hare in England.

ACONITUM
Aconite, monkshood

Ranunculaceae

This genus consists of about 100 species of tuberous perennials that are found throughout northern temperate regions, in woods, thickets, rich grassland, and near water. Monkshoods make handsome border plants, with attractive spring foliage and delphinium-like flowers. The characteristic hooded shape of the flowers allows pollination only by bees. According to Greek myth, *A. napellus* was created by Hecate, goddess of the underworld, from the foaming mouths of Cerberus, the three-headed dog that guarded the gates of Hell. All aconitums contain the alkaloid aconitine, which is one of the most toxic plant compounds known. *Aconitum ferox* is regarded as the most deadly, followed by

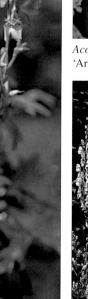

Aconitum carmichaelii

A. napellus, which is one of the most poisonous species in the European flora. Monkshoods were used in making arrow poisons, and a number of species are used medicinally in various parts of the world, having therapeutic effects when used correctly by trained practitioners. *Aconitum carmichaelii* was first mentioned in Chinese medical literature c.AD200. It has two names in Chinese medicine: *wu tou* refers to the fresh root and *fu zi* to the root cooked with salt and sugar. The cooking process makes it safer for internal use. Research has found it to be effective in congestive heart failure.

CULTIVATION Deep, moisture-retentive soil in shade. Plants will also thrive in a sunny position if the soil is sufficiently damp throughout the growing season; they do not flower well in dry conditions. Remove dead flower heads to encourage a second crop of flowers. Monkshoods should be sited out of the reach of children and animals, because even very small amounts can cause poisoning. Taller species require staking.

PROPAGATION By division when dormant; by seed sown in spring.

HARVEST Plants are lifted in autumn and young thick roots are removed before replanting. Roots are processed professionally for use in decoctions, liniments, and tinctures.

⚠ **WARNING** All parts of monkshood are highly toxic if eaten and may cause systemic poisoning if handled. Gloves should always be worn when handling, to avoid absorption of toxins through the skin.

■ *Aconitum carmichaelii* syn. *A. fischeri* (azure monkshood, Sichuan aconite)
Tuberous perennial with glossy, dark green, deeply cut leaves, to 15cm (6in) across. Dense panicles of large, deep purple-blue, hooded

Aconitum carmichaelii 'Arendsii' *Aconitum napellus*

Aconitum napellus subsp. *vulgare* 'Carneum'

flowers appear in late summer and early autumn. Native to C and W China. ‡ 1.5–1.8m (5–6ft), ↔ 30–40cm (12–16in). ▣ 'Arendsii' syn. 'Arends' is larger than the species, and flowers later. 'Kelmscott' has lavender-blue flowers in autumn. ‡ 1.2m (4ft), ↔ 30cm (12in).

HARDINESS Fully hardy.

PARTS USED Roots.

PROPERTIES A sedative painkilling herb that stimulates the heart and kidneys, and has diuretic and anti-rheumatic effects.

MEDICINAL USES Internally as a restorative following shock and trauma, for *yang* energy weakness, and in chronic osteo-arthritis. Dosage is critical, excess causing numbness of lips, tongue, and extremities, vomiting, breathing difficulties, lowering of pulse rate and blood pressure, coma, and death. Not given to pregnant women or patients with severe debilitation. Externally for rheumatism and arthritis, headache, and as a local anaesthetic.

⚠ **WARNING** For use by qualified practitioners only. Medicinal use is subject to legal restrictions in some countries.

▨ ▪

▣ *Aconitum napellus* (aconite, monkshood, wolfsbane)
Tuberous perennial with upright stems and mid-green leaves, to 15cm (6in) across, deeply divided into 5–7 lobes, and further toothed and lobed. Racemes of deep blue, hooded flowers appear in late summer. Native to N and C Europe. ‡ 1.2–1.5m (4–5ft), ↔ 38cm (15in). subsp. *vulgare* 'Albidum' has grey-white flowers; ▣ subsp. *vulgare* 'Carneum' has delicate, flesh-pink flowers and needs cool, rich, moist soil.

HARDINESS Fully hardy.

PARTS USED Roots.

PROPERTIES A sedative painkilling herb that acts on the heart and central nervous system, and also lowers fever.

MEDICINAL USES Internally for facial neuralgia and to relieve the pain of arthritis and gout. Externally for sciatica and arthritis. Used in homeopathy for shock (especially after surgery or childbirth), chickenpox, measles, mumps, croup, toothache and teething, and complaints caused, or made worse, by getting chilled. Excessive external use, or application to broken skin, may lead to systemic poisoning by absorption through the skin.

⚠ **WARNING** For use by qualified practitioners only. Medicinal use is subject to legal restrictions in some countries.

▨ ▪

ACORUS
Sweet flag

Acoraceae

There are two, possibly more, species of rhizomatous aquatic perennials in this genus, which are found wild in N and E Asia, and N America. Variegated forms are popular ornamentals: the larger ones for waterside planting and dwarf varieties as pot plants or aquarium plants. *Acorus calamus* (sweet flag)

Acorus calamus

has been cultivated and traded for over 4000 years, probably reaching E Europe from Mongolia and Siberia during the 13th century, and spreading to W Europe in the 16th century. It was once important as a strewing herb and grown in large quantities in the Norfolk Broads in England, where it was gathered at an annual "gladdon harvest". Calamus candy, made by crystallizing tender slices of the rhizome, was popular in the 18th century as a medicinal pastille to cure coughs and indigestion, and to ward off infection. There are several distinct populations of *A. calamus* in the wild, differing in genetic conformation and in important details of chemistry. Some botanists regard these as separate species. All contain 1–4 per cent of volatile oil (oil of calamus) in the rhizome. The constituents of the oil may include asarone, a tranquillizing and antibiotic compound that is potentially toxic and carcinogenic. Oil from populations in N America and Siberia is asarone-free. Oil of calamus is banned by the US Food and Drug Administration. Doubts about its safety have led to withdrawal from general sale in other countries, including Great Britain, and use is restricted in Australia and New Zealand. *Acorus gramineus* was first mentioned as a medicinal herb in China during the Song dynasty (c.11–12th century).

CULTIVATION Wet soil or shallow water, up to 25cm (10in) deep, in a sunny position. *Acorus gramineus* 'Pusillus' can be grown as a submerged aquatic. Plants grown in aquariums deteriorate if submerged for long periods, especially if grown in tropical conditions. Divide large clumps every 3–4 years to maintain vigour.

PROPAGATION By division of rhizomes in early spring.

HARVEST Plants are lifted at any time, except during the flowering period. The required amount of rhizome is cut and the remainder replanted. The rhizome may be dried for use in decoctions, distilled for oil (*A. calamus*), or used fresh for tinctures, liquid extracts, pastes, and powders.

Acorus calamus 'Variegatus'

Acorus gramineus

Acorus gramineus 'Ogon'

Acorus gramineus 'Pusillus'

▣ *Acorus calamus* (calamus, myrtle flag, sweet flag, sweet rush, sweet sedge)
Semi-evergreen perennial with citrus-scented rhizomes and arching, strap-shaped, tapering leaves to 1.5m (5ft) long. A solitary spadix, 6–8cm (2–3in) long, bearing minute, yellow-green flowers, appears in summer on a flowering stem that resembles a leaf. Native to E Asia and N America; naturalized in Europe. ‡ 90cm (36in), ↔ indefinite. ▣ 'Variegatus' has cream-striped leaves, pink at the base. ‡ 60–90cm (24–36in) ↔ 60cm (24in).

HARDINESS Fully hardy.

PARTS USED Rhizomes, oil.

PROPERTIES An aromatic, bitter, stimulant herb that relaxes spasms and relieves indigestion.

MEDICINAL USES Internally for digestive complaints, bronchitis, and sinusitis. Externally for skin eruptions, rheumatic pains, and neuralgia. An important herb in Ayurvedic medicine, regarded as a restorative for the brain and nervous system, especially after a stroke; also given for bronchial complaints and bleeding disorders. Combined with *Elettaria cardamomum* (see p.200) to help digestion of dairy produce. Used as snuff for nasal congestion, polyps, shock, and coma. Excess causes vomiting.

ECONOMIC USES Calamus oil is used to flavour liqueurs, bitters, soft drinks, cordials, and vinegar.

⚠ **WARNING** Subject to legal restrictions in some countries, especially as oil of calamus.

▨ ▨ ▪ ▱

▣ *Acorus gramineus* (grass-leaved sweet flag, Japanese rush, rock sweet flag)
Very variable, semi-evergreen perennial with branched rhizomes and fans of glossy linear leaves, 8–35cm (3–14in) long. Minute greenish flowers are borne in a spadix, 5–10cm (2–4in) long, in summer. Native to E Asia. ‡ 10–50cm (4–20in), ↔ 10–23cm (4–9in). 'Hakuro-nishiki' is compact, with bright yellow leaves. 'Licorice' (liquorice sweet flag) smells and tastes strongly of liquorice. ‡ 20–30cm (8–12in). ▣ 'Ogon' syn. 'Wogon' has cream-striped leaves. ‡ 25cm (10in), ↔ 10–15cm (4–6in). ▣ 'Pusillus' (dwarf

A

Japanese rush) is the smallest variant, with leaves 4–15cm (1½–6in) long. ‡10cm (4in), ↔ 10–15cm (4–6in). 'Variegatus' has leaves striped cream and yellow. ‡25cm (10in), ↔ 15cm (6in).

HARDINESS Frost hardy.

PARTS USED Rhizomes (*shi chang pu*).

PROPERTIES An aromatic, anti-bacterial tonic herb that stimulates the digestive system, clears the bronchial passages, relieves indigestion, and has mild sedative effects.

MEDICINAL USES An important herb in Chinese medicine for poor appetite, gastritis, catarrh, and depression. Considered to be a warming herb and therefore not given to patients with a tendency to perspire excessively.

CULINARY USES Known as *sekisho* in Japan, rhizomes are roasted or stir-fried. Liquorice sweet flag is used to flavour rice in Thailand.

ACTAEA
Baneberry

Ranunculaceae

This genus of 28 species of perennials is found in moist shady grassland or woodland in northern temperate regions. Several species are grown in borders, especially in woodland settings, for their tall graceful spikes of flowers and their elegantly cut leaves. Sixteen species were formerly classified as the genus *Cimicifuga*. These include species such as *Actaea podocarpa* syn. *Cimicifuga americana* (American bugbane) and *Actaea dahurica* syn. *Cimicifuga dahurica*, an Asian species, used interchangeably with *Actaea foetida* as *sheng ma* in traditional Chinese medicine. The drug *sheng ma* was first noted in a Chinese medical text c.AD25–200. *Actaea racemosa* syn. *Cimicifuga racemosa* has long been used by native N Americans for various female problems, and for this reason it is often referred to as "squaw root". *Actaea pachypoda* syn. *A. alba* ("doll's eyes", white baneberry) is named after its black-eyed, white berries and was used by various tribes for rattlesnake bites, and by the Cherokee to revive the dying, but it is now considered too toxic for medicinal use. The aromatic roots of *A. simplex* syn. *Cimicifuga simplex* (Japanese black snakeroot) are used as a spice and are commonly known in Japan as *sarashina-shôma*.

CULTIVATION Moist, humus-rich, neutral to acid soil in partial shade.

PROPAGATION By seed sown when ripe in a cold frame or nursery bed for germination the following spring; by division in spring.

HARVEST Rhizomes are lifted in autumn and used fresh in tinctures, or used dried for use in decoctions, liquid extracts, and tinctures.

▣ *Actaea foetida* syn. *Cimicifuga foetida* (fetid bugbane)
Tall perennial with a woody rootstock and divided leaves, to 1m (3ft) long, with ovate toothed leaflets and a three-lobed, terminal leaflet. Star-shaped, white flowers are produced in spikes

Actaea foetida

60cm (2ft) long in summer and autumn. Native to Siberia and E Asia. ‡1.2–2m (4–6ft), ↔ 50–80cm (20–32in).

HARDINESS Fully hardy.

PARTS USED Rhizomes (*sheng ma*).

PROPERTIES An anti-infective herb that lowers fevers and relieves pain.

MEDICINAL USES Internally for coughs, colds, headaches, gum disease, and feverish infections, such as measles.

▣ *Actaea racemosa* syn. *Cimicifuga racemosa* (black cohosh, black snakeroot, cohosh bugbane)
Tall perennial with a woody rootstock and broadly ovate leaves, to 40cm (16in) long, divided into three-lobed leaflets with toothed margins. Slender, bottle-brush spikes, to 60cm (2ft) long, of unpleasant-

Actaea racemosa

smelling, white flowers that are borne in summer. Native to eastern N America. ‡1.2–2.2m (4–7ft), ↔ 60cm (24in).

HARDINESS Fully hardy.

PARTS USED Rhizomes.

PROPERTIES A bitter tonic herb that soothes aches and pains, controls coughing, lowers fevers, and stimulates the uterus.

MEDICINAL USES Internally for bronchial complaints (such as whooping cough and asthma), menstrual and menopausal problems, labour and postpartum pains. Often combined with *Menyanthes trifoliata* (see p.278) and *Petroselinum crispum* (see p.310) for arthritic and rheumatic diseases, with *Zanthoxylum americanum* (see p.409) for sciatica and tinnitus, and with *Hypericum perforatum* (see p.240) for menopausal problems. Excess causes nausea and vomiting. Not given during pregnancy and lactation. Used in homeopathy for discomfort in late pregnancy, labour pains, and for headaches and depression.

⚠ **WARNING** This herb is subject to legal restrictions in some countries.

ADENOPHORA
Gland bellflower

Campanulaceae

Closely related to *Campanula*, this genus contains over 40 species of perennials, Eurasian in origin. They are elegant plants for the border, with bell-shaped, sometimes scented flowers. Though well known in the East, where they are grown as ornamentals, vegetables, and medicinal herbs, few are available in the West. *Adenophora* means "gland-bearing" and refers to the cylindrical nectary at the base of the style, hence the common name of gland bellflower. The fragrant *A. liliifolia* is cultivated as a root crop in Japan, and the young shoots of *A. triphylla* var. *japonica* (*ch'andae*, *tsurigane-ninjin*) are a popular vegetable in Korea. Both *A. stricta* and *A. trachilioidis* are used in traditional Chinese medicine for various lung complaints.

CULTIVATION Grow in light, rich, well-drained, moist soil in sun or in partial shade. Plant out when young, since established specimens are

Adenophora stricta

deep-rooted and resent disturbance. *Adenophora* may become invasive.
PROPAGATION By seed sown in autumn; by basal cuttings in early spring. *Adenophora* does not divide well.
HARVEST Roots are lifted in autumn and dried for use in decoctions.

▪ *Adenophora stricta* (fickle ladybell)
Tall perennial with a conical root, upright stems, and oval, toothed, basal leaves, clad in fine white hairs. Narrow racemes of pendulous, blue, bell-shaped flowers, also hairy, open in late summer and autumn. Native to E Asia.
‡ 60–90cm (24–36in), ↔ 30cm (12in).
HARDINESS Fully hardy.
PARTS USED Roots (*nan sha shen*).
PROPERTIES A stimulant herb that acts mainly on the respiratory system and heart.
MEDICINAL USES Internally for dry coughs, chronic bronchitis, and tuberculosis.

ADHATODA

Adhatoda vasica. See *Justicia adhatoda.*

ADIANTUM

Maidenhair fern

Adiantaceae

In this genus there are over 200 species of deciduous, semi-evergreen, or evergreen ferns. The majority are native to tropical America, with a few species in northern temperate regions. Several species are grown as ornamentals. *Adiantum capillus-veneris* is a graceful fern for mild gardens or as a pot plant. *Capillus-veneris* means "Venus's hair" and may refer to the Roman goddess of love, who rose from the waves with miraculously dry hair. The foliage is water-repellent. Medicinal uses of the maidenhair fern have been recorded since Classical times. Dioscorides mentioned "adianton" for asthma; Culpeper valued it as "a good remedy for coughs, asthmas, pleurisy, etc., and on account of its being a gentle diuretic also in jaundice and other impurities of the kidneys"; and Gerard claimed it was a hair restorative. It was once popular as *sirop de capillaire*, a cough mixture made from the rhizomes and fronds, flavoured with orange flowers. The hardier *A. pedatum* from America and Japan is used in similar ways. *Adiantum aethiopicum*, which occurs in Australia, is used by Aboriginals to soothe bronchial complaints.
CULTIVATION Moist, well-drained soil, enriched with leaf mould and bone meal, in a sheltered, humid, shady position. A plant that temporarily dries out will lose most or all of its fronds, although it usually sprouts again from the base.
PROPAGATION By division of rhizomes in early spring; by spores, collected on clean paper and sown in early spring. Spores take about six weeks to germinate.
HARVEST Plants are cut throughout the summer and are used fresh in infusions, powders, and, in Ayurvedic medicine, as milk decoctions.

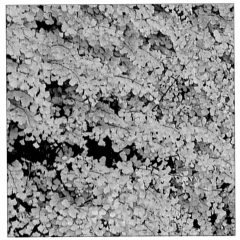

Adiantum capillus-veneris

▪ *Adiantum capillus-veneris* (maidenhair fern)
Evergreen or semi-evergreen, rhizomatous fern with arching fronds, 45–60cm (18–24in) long, of lobed, fan-shaped leaflets. The undersides of mature leaflets carry red-brown sori. Found in temperate and tropical regions worldwide.
‡ 15–35cm (6–14in), ↔ 30cm (12in).
HARDINESS Frost hardy.
PARTS USED Whole plant.
PROPERTIES A bittersweet soothing herb that relieves coughing and is also a diuretic and expectorant.
MEDICINAL USES Internally for bronchitis, dry coughs, catarrh, and pharyngitis. Externally in hair lotions for dandruff and bald spots caused by ringworm. Used in Ayurvedic medicine as a cooling moistening remedy for coughs.
CULINARY USES Source of "capillaire" flavouring, once popular in England as a basis for soft drinks. Fronds were used as a tea substitute in the Arran Islands, off W Scotland.

ADONIS

Ranunculaceae

About 20 species of annuals and herbaceous perennials make up this genus, which occurs in temperate Europe and Asia in a variety of habitats. Several species are valued as ornamentals for their exquisite early flowers. The genus is named after Adonis, the beautiful youth of Greek myth who was killed by a boar. The flowers that sprang from his blood as it touched the earth are planted in Greece to celebrate his return to life each spring. *Adonis vernalis* (spring adonis) is rare and protected in many areas. It contains glycosides that have both tonic and sedative effects on the heart, and is an ingredient of several commercial German preparations for heart complaints and low blood pressure. Spring adonis is also found in Bechterew's Mixture, a Russian formulation for heart conditions of nervous origin.
CULTIVATION Light, well-drained soil, enriched with leafmould, in sun or partial shade. The crown should be planted 2.5cm (1in) below the surface. New growth may be damaged by slugs and snails. Plants die down in summer, so label

Adonis vernalis

them to prevent accidental damage.
PROPAGATION By division in early autumn; by seed sown under cover in summer, as soon as ripe. Germination may be slow and erratic.
HARVEST Plants are cut when in full flower and dried for use in liquid extracts and tinctures. The dried herb does not keep well, and stocks are renewed each year.

▪ *Adonis vernalis* (false hellebore, spring adonis, yellow pheasant's eye)
Clump-forming perennial with a stout rootstock and numerous, finely dissected leaves, to 5cm (2in) long. Solitary yellow flowers resemble large buttercups in early spring. Native to S, C, and E Europe. ‡ 15–40cm (6–16in), ↔ 30–45cm (12–18in).
HARDINESS Fully hardy.
PARTS USED Whole plant.
PROPERTIES A tonic diuretic herb that stimulates the heart.
MEDICINAL USES Internally for cardiac insufficiency, irregular or rapid heartbeat, mitral stenosis, and oedema due to heart failure. Included in many proprietary formulas for heart complaints. Similar in effects to *Digitalis lanata* (see p.193), but not cumulative.
⚠ **WARNING** For use by qualified practitioners only. Medicinal use of this herb is subject to legal restrictions in some countries.

AEGOPODIUM

Apiaceae

There are five to seven species of creeping perennials in this genus, found in woodland, scrub, and on waste ground, throughout Europe and temperate Asia. Most species are invasive weeds. The name *Aegopodium* is derived from the Greek *aigos*, "goat", and *podos*, "foot". The specific epithet *podagraria* derives from the Latin *podagra*, "gout", and refers to the plant's medicinal uses. Goutweed was apparently introduced to the British Isles during medieval times, when it was cultivated in monastery gardens for medicinal purposes. It is often referred to as "bishopweed", "bishopwort", or as "herb Gerard" in old herbals, because of its

Aegopodium podagraria

ecclesiastical connection and its dedication to St Gerard, who was invoked to cure gout.

CULTIVATION Any soil in sun or shade. Too invasive for most gardens, but may be grown in containers for medicinal and culinary use.

PROPAGATION By division of rhizomes in spring or autumn.

HARVEST Roots and leaves are harvested in summer and used fresh, or dried for use in infusions, homeopathic remedies, liquid extracts, medicated oils, and poultices.

■ *Aegopodium podagraria* (goutweed, ground elder)
Herbaceous perennial with a creeping rootstock and strong-smelling, long-stalked leaves, 8–23cm (3–9in) long. Tiny white flowers grow in umbels to 6cm (2½in) across in summer. Native to Europe and temperate Asia; naturalized in N America. ‡ 30–90cm (12–36in), ↔ indefinite.
■ 'Variegatum' has white-marked leaves and is less invasive. ‡ 30–60cm (12–24in), ↔ indefinite.
HARDINESS Fully hardy.
PARTS USED Leaves, roots.

Aegopodium podagraria 'Variegatum'

PROPERTIES A mild sedative herb that has diuretic and anti-inflammatory effects.
MEDICINAL USES Internally for gout or sciatica. Externally for haemorrhoids, gout, stings, or burns. In homeopathy for arthritis and rheumatism.
CULINARY USES Leaves have a distinctive flavour; when young, used in salads and soups and as a vegetable. An ingredient of *grüne suppe* (green soup) in NW Germany.
▨ ▩ ▤ ▱

AEOLLANTHUS
Lamiaceae

This genus includes 35 species of annuals, perennials, and small shrubs, native to tropical and warm parts of Africa, most of which have thick aromatic leaves and an explosive pollination mechanism. Several species have rose-scented flowers and lemon-scented leaves. These are known generally as *nindi*, and include *A. gamwelliae*, *A. heliotropioides*, *A. lamborayi*, *A. myrianthus*, and *A. pubescens*. Oil of *nindi* is used in soaps and perfumes; it is produced mainly in E Africa and in Assam.
CULTIVATION Well-drained to dry, sandy soil in sun.
PROPAGATION By seed sown in sandy soil mix in spring.
HARVEST Whole plant, or leaves and flowers separately, are distilled for oil.

Aeollanthus gamwelliae (ninde, nindi)
Subshrub with branched downy stems and ovate-lanceolate, gland-dotted leaves, to 9cm (3½in) long, with wavy margins and downy undersurfaces. Strongly scented, mauve flowers, 2cm (¾in) long, with woolly calyces appear in much-branched inflorescences. Native to E African mountains. ‡ 1.5m (5ft), ↔ 1m (3ft).
HARDINESS Min. 15–18°C (59–64°F).
PARTS USED Whole plant, leaves, flowers, oil.
PROPERTIES An aromatic herb, rich in essential oils, including geraniol (as in *Pelargonium* 'Graveolens', see p.306).
CULINARY USES Leaves are used to flavour soups and salads.
ECONOMIC USES Oil from leaves and flowers is used in soaps and perfumes, often as a substitute for *palmarosa* oil (from *Cymbopogon martinii*, see p.187).
▨ ▨ ▢ ▨ ▱ ▱ ▨

AESCULUS
Buckeye, horse chestnut
Hippocastanaceae

This genus of 13 species of deciduous trees and shrubs occurs in SE Europe, E Asia, and N America. Horse chestnuts have handsome foliage that turns yellow and gold in autumn, and glossy brown seeds that resemble the eyes of deer; hence the common name "buckeye". The name "horse chestnut" has apparently no connection with the horseshoe-shaped leaf scars visible on the twigs; it may refer to the use of

its fruits as fodder and to treat coughs in horses and cattle. *Aesculus hippocastanum* was introduced to W Europe in the 16th century and rapidly became popular as a fast-growing ornamental and source of "conkers" for games.
CULTIVATION Fertile, well-drained soil in sun or partial shade.
PROPAGATION By seed sown in autumn (species only). The cultivar 'Baumannii' is sterile and is propagated only by grafting on to stocks of the species.
HARVEST Bark and ripe seeds are collected in autumn for use in liquid extracts and decoctions. Seeds are chopped, then roasted before use. Since the active ingredient, escin, is poorly absorbed in its natural state, horse chestnut is processed commercially for better absorption.
⚠ **WARNING** Seeds are harmful if eaten, causing gastroenteritis, kidney failure, and liver disease.

■ *Aesculus hippocastanum* (common horse chestnut)
Large tree with sticky buds and palmate leaves divided into 5–7 obovate leaflets, to 30cm (12in) long. White flowers, each with a yellow to pink basal spot, appear in spikes to 30cm (12in) long in late spring, followed by globose, green-brown, spiny fruits containing 1–3 shiny, red-brown seeds. Found from the Balkans to Himalayas. ‡ 25–40m (80–130ft), ↔ 5–8m (15–25ft).
■ 'Baumannii' has long-lasting, double flowers that do not set seed. 'Hampton Court Gold' has yellow new foliage, pink when unfolding. 'Laciniata' has narrow, irregularly cut leaves and is slower growing. 'Wisselink' has white-marbled leaves.
HARDINESS Fully hardy.
PARTS USED Bark, seeds.
PROPERTIES A bitter, astringent herb that lowers fever and reduces capillary permeability and local oedema. It is diuretic and anti-inflammatory. The

Aesculus hippocastanum

Aesculus hippocastanum 'Baumannii'

main constituent is escin, a complex mixture of saponins, which has a potent, anti-inflammatory effect.

MEDICINAL USES Internally for disorders of the circulatory system, including stroke, heart attack, arteriosclerosis, circulatory insufficiency, varicose veins, phlebitis, chilblains, haemorrhoids, and swelling following severe trauma; injected for swollen joints and fractures.

ECONOMIC USES Used in cosmetics and hair preparations.

AFROMOMUM

Zingiberaceae

Fifty species of rhizomatous perennials make up this genus, which occurs in tropical Africa. Several species are used as spices, including *A. angustifolium* (Madagascar cardamom), which has pleasant-tasting pulp and aromatic seeds, and *A. korarima* (Ethiopian cardamom, *kewrerima*), an important ingredient of Ethiopian spice mixtures for both sweet and savoury dishes. Most important is *A. melegueta*, which was traded by the Portuguese as early as the 13th century. Melegueta pepper is the only major spice that is native to Africa. Known in ancient Rome, it was used during medieval times, with ginger and cinnamon, to flavour hippocras (a spiced wine) and as a pepper substitute – a use that was banned in Britain by George III (1760–1820) as being injurious to health.

CULTIVATION Well-drained, moist soil in high humidity and shade.

PROPAGATION By division of rhizomes as new growth begins.

HARVEST Fruits are collected as they ripen and seeds separated from pulp and dried. Rhizomes are lifted throughout the year.

Afromomum melegueta (grains of paradise, Guinea grains, melegueta pepper)
Rhizomatous perennial with reed-like stems and alternate, narrow, elliptic leaves. Solitary, mauve, trumpet-shaped flowers, up to 13cm (5in) long and 4–9cm (1½–3½in) across, are borne on short stems, followed by pear-shaped, red fruits, 6–10cm (2½–4in) long, containing 60–100

aromatic brown seeds in white pulp. Native to W Africa. ‡ 90cm–1.2m (3–4ft), ↔ indefinite.

HARDINESS Min. 15–18°C (59–64°F).

PARTS USED Rhizomes, seeds.

PROPERTIES A pungent stimulant that benefits the digestion and relieves spasms.

MEDICINAL USES Internally, in W Africa, for a range of conditions, including excessive lactation, painful menstruation, postpartum haemorrhage, infertility (root decoction), and aphrodisiac (seeds); in Nigeria, combined with *Rauvolfia serpentina* (see p.341) for mental disorders, with *Momordica charantia* (see p.279) for cholera (seeds).

CULINARY USES Seeds are used as a condiment and flavouring for meat dishes and bread. Also an ingredient of the N African spice mixture *ras-el-hanout*.

ECONOMIC USES Seed extracts used to flavour soft drinks, liqueurs, cordials, ice creams, and confectionery.

AGASTACHE
Giant hyssop

Lamiaceae

The 30 species of robust aromatic perennials in this genus are native to C and E Asia, N America, and Mexico. Several species are used for flavouring and tea, including *A. mexicana* syn. *Cedronella mexicana* (Mexican giant hyssop, lemon liquorice mint), *A. neomexicana* (wild liquorice mint), and *A. urticifolia* (giant hyssop, sawtooth mountain mint). *Agastache foeniculum* (anise hyssop) has a tidy habit and makes a good, long-flowering border plant. It is an especially rich source of nectar, attracting bees during its six-week flowering period, and was widely planted by beekeepers in N America in the 1870s to produce a fine honey with a slight aniseed flavour. Native Americans used anise hyssop as a tea and a sweetener. *Agastache rugosa* was first noted as a medicinal herb in China in c.AD500. *Agastache* is from the Greek *agan*, "very much", and *stachys*, "ear of wheat", describing the shape of the flower spikes.

CULTIVATION Well-drained soil in sun.

Agastache foeniculum

Agastache foeniculum 'Alabaster'

Agastache foeniculum tolerates poorer soils and drier conditions than *A. rugosa*. Leaves may be affected by powdery mildew in dry conditions.

PROPAGATION By seed sown in spring at 13–18°C (55–64°F); by division in spring; by semi-ripe cuttings in summer.

HARVEST Leaves (*A. foeniculum*, *A. rugosa*) are collected in spring and summer, and flowers in summer, for use fresh or dried as a flavouring, or for teas. Leaves and stems (*A. rugosa*) are cut before flowering and dried for medicinal use.

▪ *Agastache foeniculum* syn. *A. anethiodora*, *Stachys foeniculum* (anise hyssop, anise mint, blue giant hyssop, liquorice mint)
Erect perennial with pointed ovate leaves, 5–8cm (2–3in), with pale undersides and a strong aniseed scent. Light purple flowers, with showy bracts, appear in dense spikes, to 8cm (3in) in summer. Native to N and C America. ‡ 60cm–1.2m (2–4ft), ↔ 30cm (12in). ▪ 'Alabaster' has white flowers. ‡ 45–60cm (18–24in).

HARDINESS Frost hardy.

PARTS USED Leaves, flowers.

PROPERTIES An aromatic, pleasant-tasting herb that increases perspiration and relieves bronchial congestion.

MEDICINAL USES Internally for coughs in the traditional medicine of several native N American tribes.

CULINARY USES Flowers may be added to salads. Leaves are also used for tea.

▪ *Agastache rugosa* syn. *Lophanthus rugosus* (Korean mint, wrinkled giant hyssop)
Short-lived, upright perennial with square stems and pointed leaves, 5–10cm (2–4in) long, which have white hairy undersides and a mint-like aroma. Small purple flowers are produced in spikes to 15cm (6in) long in late summer. Native to E Asia. ‡ 1–1.2m (3–4ft), ↔ 60cm (24in).

HARDINESS Frost hardy.

PARTS USED Leaves, stems (aerial parts are known as *huo xiang*).

PROPERTIES An aromatic, anti-bacterial herb that stimulates the digestive system, relaxes spasms, and also helps to lower fever.

MEDICINAL USES Internally, in traditional Chinese medicine, to improve appetite and to

Agastache rugosa

relieve dyspepsia, nausea, and vomiting; also for the common cold when characterized by chills. Unsuitable for feverish colds. Interchangeable with *Pogostemon cablin* (see p.325).
CULINARY USES Fresh or dried leaves provide flavouring for meat dishes and salads, and make a pleasant tea.

▨ ▨ ▣ ◪

AGATHOSMA

Rutaceae

Native to South Africa, this genus consists of about 135 species of small, tender, evergreen shrubs. Most species are intensely aromatic. Their attractive habit, aroma, and flowers, produced at an early age, make them popular as ornamentals in warmer parts of the world, or as indoor plants in temperate areas. "Buchu", an African word for dusting powder, is used for several *Agathosma* spp., gathered for this and other medicinal and industrial uses. Several species are important and popular herbs in tribal culture, the powdered leaves being mixed with fat to make anointing oil. *Agathosma betulina* syn. *Barosma betulina* (round-leaf buchu) is similar in appearance to *Agathosma crenulata*, though slightly smaller, and is used in identical ways; its aroma is more akin to camphor and peppermint. This species has a restricted natural distribution and is becoming scarce. Plantations have been established to reduce pressure on wild populations. Research has shown that buchus contain a substance that blocks ultraviolet light; it may have applications in skin products.
CULTIVATION Well-drained, acid soil in full sun. Cut back hard in spring to control size.
PROPAGATION By seed sown in spring; by semi-ripe cuttings in summer, in sand, at 13–18°C (55–64°F).
HARVEST Leaves are gathered when the plant is flowering and fruiting, and dried for use in infusions, liquid extracts, tablets, and tinctures.

▣ *Agathosma crenulata* syn. *Barosma crenulata*, *Diosma crenulata* (oval-leaf buchu) Heath-like, evergreen shrub with ovate toothed leaves, to 3.5cm (1¼in) long, bearing conspicuous oil glands that release a strong,

Agathosma crenulata

blackcurrant-like aroma. Five-petalled, white flowers, with purple anthers, appear in spring. Native to South Africa. ↔ 1–2m (3–6ft).
HARDINESS Min. 5°C (41°F).
PARTS USED Leaves.
PROPERTIES A blackcurrant-scented herb that stimulates and cleanses the urinary system and increases perspiration. The active ingredient is diosphenol, or "barosma camphor", which is a potent antiseptic and diuretic.
MEDICINAL USES Internally for urinary tract infections (especially prostatitis and cystitis), digestive problems, gout, rheumatism, coughs, and colds, often combined with *Althaea officinalis* (see p.117). Externally in traditional African medicine as an anti-insect powder and in a vinegar-based lotion for bruises or sprains.
CULINARY USES Used with *Artemisia afra* to flavour brandy and wine in parts of Africa.
ECONOMIC USES Extracts used to give a blackcurrant flavour to foods and drinks by manufacturers and to enhance the blackcurrant aroma of *cassis*.

▨ ▣ ◪ ◪ ▣

AGAVE

Agavaceae

This genus consists of about 300 species of perennial succulents, occurring in arid regions from S USA to S America. Agaves vary greatly in size and can take 5–20 years to reach flowering size. Most are tender, but those that have green or grey-green leaves are usually more hardy. They are widely grown as garden plants in warm countries, and for pots or summer bedding in temperate zones. Many species have edible parts and are used to prepare alcoholic drinks, notably mescal, pulque, and tequila, which are made from *A. angustifolia*, *A. salmiana*, and *A. tequilana*, respectively. *Agave americana* is commonly planted in rows as an effective stock-proof barrier and is used in arid land reclamation. Both *A. americana* and *A. sisalana* (sisal) are important fibre plants and sources of hecogenin, used in the manufacture of steroid drugs. The uses of agaves were developed by the German East Africa Company,

which carried out research after plants were first introduced from C America to Tanganyika (now part of Tanzania) in 1893.
CULTIVATION Well-drained soil in full sun. Prone to attack by mealybugs or root mealybugs. Rot may occur during cool winter temperatures if plants are over-watered.
PROPAGATION By seed sown in spring at 21°C (70°F); by offsets, removed from the parent plant in spring or summer and left for some days to dry off before potting.
HARVEST Parts are harvested and processed as required. Leaves and roots may be used fresh or dried; they last well when dried.
⚠ **WARNING** Skin allergen.

▣ *Agave americana* (century plant, maguey) Large monocarpic succulent with stout roots and rosettes of hard, grey-green, sharply pointed, spine-edged leaves, to 2m (6ft) long. Bell-shaped, creamy yellow flowers, to 10cm (4in) across, appear in panicles in summer on plants about ten years old. Native to Mexico; widely naturalized in India, Africa, and S Europe. ↕ 2m (6ft), reaching 8m (25ft) at flowering. ↔ 3m (10ft). 'Marginata' has yellow-margined leaves. 'Mediopicta' has a central, pale yellow band. 'Striata' has yellow or white stripes down each leaf.
HARDINESS Min. 5°C (41°F).
PARTS USED Whole plant, leaves, roots, sap.
PROPERTIES A healing, anti-inflammatory, diuretic herb with hormonal and insecticidal constituents. It acts mainly on the digestive system, but its intake can also lower fever by increasing perspiration.
MEDICINAL USES Internally for indigestion, flatulence, constipation, jaundice, and dysentery. Externally for burns and minor injuries. Fresh sap in contact with skin may cause skin irritation or dermatitis.
CULINARY USES Sweet sap from the flowering stem is drunk as juice or fermented into pulque. Flower stems and leaf bases are roasted and eaten.
ECONOMIC USES Root extracts are used in soap manufacture, and the coarse fibres are woven into ropes, twine, and mats. Leaf-waste concentrate provides certain precursors for steroid drugs.

▨ ▢ ▣ ▨ ▣ ◪ ◪ ▣

Agave americana

AGLAIA

Meliaceae

A genus of about 250 species of evergreen trees and shrubs, native to Asia and the Pacific Islands. The flowers of *A. odorata* (mock lime) have an exquisite perfume that lasts almost indefinitely when they are dried. It is often grown as a hedge in the tropics and may be planted alternately with *Murraya paniculata* (orange jasmine), which has very similar foliage in a darker shade of green. *Aglaia* is an ancient Greek word meaning "splendid". Little is known about this large genus of tropical trees and shrubs. *Aglaia argentea* is used in Indonesia for feverish illnesses and in preparations to treat leprosy. Mock lime is also used medicinally, but remains primarily a perfume plant.

CULTIVATION Rich, well-drained soil with ample moisture, warmth, and humidity, in sun or partial shade.

PROPAGATION By semi-ripe cuttings in summer.

HARVEST Leaves are picked during the growing season and used fresh or dried in decoctions. Flowers are gathered as they open then dried for infusions and scented articles. Renew dried parts annually for medicinal use.

▣ *Aglaia odorata* (Chinese perfume plant, mock lime)
Elegant shrub or tree with glossy leaves, to 15cm (6in) long, divided into 5–7 leaflets. Tiny, yellow, vanilla-scented flowers are produced in panicles in spring. Native to SE Asia and China. ↕ 15m (50ft), ↔ 10m (30ft).

HARDINESS Min. 15–18°C (59–64°F).

PARTS USED Leaves, flowers.

PROPERTIES An aromatic tonic herb that lowers fevers.

MEDICINAL USES Internally for feverish and convulsive illnesses, and menopausal problems.

CULINARY USES Dried flowers are used to scent tea (China). Young leaves are eaten as a vegetable.

ECONOMIC USES Flowers are used to make joss sticks and potpourris.

▣ ▨ ▪ ▨ ▨ ▣

AGRIMONIA

Agrimony

Rosaceae

A genus of 15 species of rhizomatous perennials found in northern temperate regions and in S America. *Agrimonia* may come from the Greek *arghemon*, an eye disease (albugo), which agrimony was reputed to cure, or from the Latin *agri moenia*, "defender of the fields", after the masses of agrimony found beside fields. *Agrimonia eupatoria* (agrimony) was once an important wound herb, known in Anglo-Saxon times as "garclive". It is an ingredient of *eau d'arquebusade*, a French herbal lotion now used for various complaints, but originally applied to wounds caused by an arquebus, a 15th-century, long-barrelled gun. Agrimony is well behaved in cultivation and may be grown in the border or wildflower meadow. *Agrimonia pilosa* (shaggy speedwell) has been used in Chinese medicine since at least the 14th century. It is used to promote clotting, due to its high vitamin K content, and is often combined with *Bletilla striata* (see p.144) and *Sanguisorba officinalis* (see p.358) in tablets for internal haemorrhage. This combination has also proved beneficial in relieving symptoms of silicosis, a serious lung disease.

CULTIVATION Well-drained soil in sun. Agrimony tolerates dry and alkaline conditions.

PROPAGATION By seed sown in spring.

HARVEST Plants are cut when flowering (avoiding flower spikes that have started to develop spiny burs) then dried for use in infusions, liquid extracts, pills, and tinctures.

Agrimonia eupatoria

▣ *Agrimonia eupatoria* (agrimony, cocklebur, sticklewort)
Perennial with upright, often hairy, stems and downy leaves, divided into 3–6 pairs of leaflets, 2–6cm (¾–2½in) long. Faintly scented, yellow flowers, about 7mm (¼in) across, are produced in long spikes in summer, followed by bristly fruits. Native to Europe, W Asia, and N Africa. ↕ 30–60cm (12–24in), ↔ 20–30cm (8–12in).

HARDINESS Fully hardy.

PARTS USED Whole plant.

PROPERTIES A bitter, mildly astringent, tonic, diuretic herb; it controls bleeding, improves liver and gall bladder function, and has anti-inflammatory effects.

MEDICINAL USES Internally for colitis, dyspepsia, food allergies, diarrhoea, gallstones, cirrhosis, grumbling appendix, urinary incontinence, cystitis, and rheumatism. Not given to patients with stress-related constipation. Externally for sore throat, conjunctivitis, haemorrhoids, minor injuries, and chronic skin conditions.

CULINARY USES Fresh or dried flowering plant makes a pleasant herb tea.

▨ ▪ ▨

AGROPYRON

Agropyron repens. See *Elymus repens*.

AILANTHUS

Simaroubaceae

Five species of handsome, fast-growing, deciduous trees are included in this genus, which is found from E Asia to Australia. *Ailanthus* is from the Amboinese *ai lanto*, "tree of the gods". *Ailanthus altissima* was introduced to Europe in 1751 and is widely planted as a street tree. In France, it is cultivated as a substitute for *A. vilmoriniana*, on which silk moths are raised for the production of shantung silk. *Ailanthus altissima* contains quassinoids, similar to those found in the related *Quassia amara*. Research has shown these to have anti-malarial and anti-cancer effects.

CULTIVATION Fertile, well-drained soil in sun or partial shade. In spring, cut plants grown as

Aglaia odorata

A

Ailanthus altissima

shrubs back hard to encourage production of very large leaves. Tolerates urban pollution. *Ailanthus altissima* is subject to statutory control as a weed in parts of Australia.

PROPAGATION By seed sown in autumn (slow to germinate); by suckers or root cuttings in winter.

HARVEST Bark is removed in spring and dried for decoctions and tinctures.

▣ *Ailanthus altissima* syn. *A. glandulosa* (ailanto, Chinese sumach, tree of heaven) Spreading tree with ash-like leaves to 1m (3ft) long in young specimens. Male and female flowers are borne on separate plants; female trees bear large clusters of dark red, winged fruits in autumn. Native to China. ↕25m (80ft), ↔ 15m (50ft).

HARDINESS Fully hardy.

PARTS USED Bark (*chun pi*).

PROPERTIES A nauseatingly bitter, astringent herb that lowers fever, relaxes spasms, and slows the heart rate. Readily causes vomiting.

MEDICINAL USES Internally for malaria, asthma, palpitations, diarrhoea, dysentery, haemorrhoids, heavy menstruation, and tapeworms.

▥ ▣

AJUGA
Bugle

Lamiaceae

This genus of 50 species of annuals and perennials is found mainly in temperate parts of Eurasia, with some species in Australia and tropical Africa. *Ajuga reptans* (bugle) is an excellent garden plant for moisture-retentive soil in sun or shade, as ground cover, for borders, or for the wildflower garden. It was an ingredient of the "Traumatick Decoction" in the *London Dispensatory* of 1694, and was taken after injury. Bugle was a favourite herb of Nicholas Culpeper, who wrote in *The English Physician Enlarged* (1653), "If the virtues of it make you fall in love with it (as they will if you be wise) keep a syrup of it to take inwardly, an ointment and plaister of it to use outwardly, always by you". He regarded it as both a wound herb and a cure for hangovers. According to Mrs M. Grieve (*A Modern Herbal*,

1931), *A. chamaepitys* "was formerly regarded almost as a specific in gouty and rheumatic affections". Other medicinal bugles include: the Australian *A. australis*, primarily a wound herb, though also used to treat boils and sores; *A. remota*, used in Africa to treat high blood pressure, which contains compounds with potential in both cancer therapy and biological pest control; and the Mediterranean *A. iva*, which has anti-malarial properties.

CULTIVATION *Ajuga chamaepitys* thrives in poor dry soil in full sun. *Ajuga reptans* needs moist soil in sun or partial shade.

PROPAGATION By seed sown in autumn or spring. Germination may be erratic. *Ajuga reptans* and its cultivars may also be divided at any time if kept moist. Cultivars of *A. reptans* do not come true from seed.

HARVEST Leaves (*A. chamaepitys*) are gathered in summer and dried for infusions and liquid extracts. Plants (*A. reptans*) are cut in summer; usually used fresh, in ointments or medicated oils.

▣ *Ajuga chamaepitys* (ground pine, yellow bugle)
Low-growing, pine-scented annual with grey-green leaves deeply divided into linear lobes. Small, tubular, yellow, red-dotted flowers appear singly or in pairs up the leafy stem from late spring to early autumn. Native to Europe and N Africa, on dry bare ground; is rare in Great Britain. ↔15cm (6in).

HARDINESS Fully hardy.

PARTS USED Leaves.

PROPERTIES A stimulant diuretic herb that acts mainly on the urinary system and uterus.

MEDICINAL USES Internally for gout, rheumatism, and menstrual problems.

▨ ▣

▣ *Ajuga reptans* (bugle)
Evergreen, rhizomatous perennial, spreading by stolons, with basal rosettes of oval to spoon-shaped leaves, to 9cm (3½in) long. Deep blue flowers, 1.5cm (½in) long, are produced in whorled spikes in spring and early summer. Native to Europe, NW Africa, Turkey, Iran, and the Caucasus. ↕10–30cm (4–12in), ↔ indefinite. 'Alba' has white flowers. ▣ 'Atropurpurea' (bronze bugle) has dark purple-brown leaves. ▣ 'Burgundy Glow' has silver-green leaves, variegated and suffused with shades of pink. 'Catlin's Giant' has large bronze leaves, to 15cm (6in) long, and flower spikes to 20cm (8in) long. 'Multicolor' syn. 'Rainbow' has bronze leaves, variegated cream and pink. 'Pink Elf' is compact, with deep pink flowers on spikes up to 5cm (2in) high. ▣ 'Variegata' has light green leaves, irregularly variegated grey-green and cream. It has a dense habit and is less vigorous than the species.

HARDINESS Fully hardy.

PARTS USED Whole plant.

PROPERTIES A mild, painkilling, and astringent herb with a slight laxative effect.

MEDICINAL USES Externally for bruises, wounds, and tumours.

▣ ▣

Ajuga chamaepitys

Ajuga reptans 'Atropurpurea'

Ajuga reptans

Ajuga reptans 'Burgundy Glow'

Ajuga reptans 'Variegata'

AKEBIA

Lardizabalaceae

Five evergreen or deciduous, twining perennial climbers are included in this genus, native to China, Japan, and Korea. Several are grown as garden ornamentals for their attractive lobed leaves and small, often scented flowers. The conspicuous edible fruits give added interest but grow only in warm areas where several plants are grown together. The closely related *A. trifoliata* and *A. quinata* differ mainly in having three and five leaflets respectively; *A. quinata* has darker purple fruits. *Akebia* is the Latinized version of *akebi*, the Japanese name for these plants.

CULTIVATION Well-drained soil in sun. Even where hardy, new leaves and flowers may be damaged by severe frost.

PROPAGATION By seed sown in spring or autumn; by semi-ripe cuttings in summer; by layering in winter. They dislike disturbance.

HARVEST Stems are cut in autumn and are dried for use in decoctions and powders. Young leaves are picked in spring and are dried. Fruits are harvested when ripe and are used fresh.

■ *Akebia trifoliata* syn. *A. lobata* (akebia)
Deciduous twining climber with trifoliate leaves, to 10cm (4in) across, bronze when young. Three-petalled, maroon flowers are borne in pendent racemes, to 12cm (5in) long, in spring, followed by sausage-shaped, pale violet fruits, to 13cm (5in) long, containing black seeds in a white pulp. Native to China and Japan. ‡ 10m (30ft).

HARDINESS Fully hardy.

PARTS USED Stems (*mu tong*), leaves, fruits.

PROPERTIES A pungent bitter herb that controls bacterial and fungal infections, stimulates the circulatory and urinary systems and female organs, and is a potent diuretic due to the high content of potassium salts.

MEDICINAL USES Internally for urinary tract infections, rheumatoid arthritis, absence of menstruation, and insufficient lactation. A stew of *mu tong* and pork knuckles is a traditional Chinese method of promoting lactation.

CULINARY USES Dried leaves are used for tea. Fruit pulp is eaten fresh.

▨ ▨ ▨ ▮ ◪

Akebia trifoliata

ALBIZIA

Mimosaceae

There are some 150 species of deciduous, occasionally thorny trees, shrubs, and lianas in this genus, which occurs widely in subtropical regions, from Asia and Africa to Australia, often on poor soils. *Albizia julibrissin* is a graceful tree that tolerates hot dry conditions. It is popular as an ornamental, but susceptible to pests and diseases in urban areas. *Albizia julibrissin* was first mentioned in Chinese medicine in *Omissions from the Materia Medica* (Tang Dynasty, c.AD700). Bark of the related *A. odoratissima*, which bears scented white flowers, is externally used in India and Sri Lanka for ulcers and leprosy.

CULTIVATION Well-drained, moisture-retentive soil in full sun. Tolerates poor, alkaline and saline soils, drought, and windy positions. Size and shape may be controlled by cutting back the previous year's growth to 5–6 buds in spring. Plants may be attacked by webworm, scale insects, and nematodes. In the US the main trunk may be killed by vascular wilt disease, leaving the roots to sucker. Young specimens make attractive foliage plants and may be treated as annuals for the purpose. Mature specimens are hardier and more floriferous in relatively poor soils, and in areas with long hot summers.

PROPAGATION By seed sown when ripe, pre-soaked for 12 hours; by semi-ripe cuttings in summer; by root cuttings in spring; by layering in winter.

HARVEST Bark is removed in spring or late summer, and flowers as they open; both are dried for decoctions.

■ *Albizia julibrissin* (silk tree)
Small, domed to flat-topped, spreading tree with smooth, grey-brown bark and doubly pinnate leaves, to 20cm (8in) long. Yellow-green flower heads with very long stamens are borne in terminal clusters, 7–15cm (3–6in) wide, in summer. Found from Iran to Japan. ‡ 6–10m (20–30ft), ↔ 10m (30ft). var. *alba* has white flowers. f. *rosea* has pink flowers. This species tends to be fast-growing but short-lived and can become weedy through suckering and copious production of seedlings.

Albizia julibrissin

HARDINESS Frost hardy. f. *rosea* is hardier than the species, surviving outdoors in mild parts of Great Britain.

PARTS USED Bark, flowers (*he huan*), leaves.

PROPERTIES A bitter, astringent, sedative herb that is also diuretic and analgesic, with stimulant effects on the circulation, uterus, and appetite (bark); the flowers are tranquillizing and relieve indigestion.

MEDICINAL USES Internally for insomnia and irritability (bark, flowers), boils and carbuncles (bark), breathlessness and poor memory (flowers). Externally for injuries, swellings, and lung abscesses (bark).

CULINARY USES Flowers and young leaves are edible. Dried leaves are used for tea.

▥ ▨ ▨ ▮ ◪

ALCEA

Hollyhock

Malvaceae

In this genus are 60 species of biennials or short-lived perennials, occurring from the Mediterranean to C Asia. Several species are grown for their showy flowers. *Alcea rosea* reached Europe in the 16th century (from either China or the Middle East, perhaps Turkey) and became a popular garden plant and medicinal herb. The name *Alcea* is derived from the Greek *alkaria*, "mallow", and the common name comes from the 16th-century "holy hock" (*hoc* was the Old English word for "mallow"). The hollyhock

Alcea rosea

Alcea rosea 'Chater's Double'

Alcea rosea 'Nigra'

is closely related to marsh mallow (*Althaea officinalis*, see p.117) and was once classified in the same genus. Both have similar properties, but *Alcea rosea* has largely been replaced by its more effective relative.

CULTIVATION Well-drained soil in sun. Rust may damage the foliage and kill the plant. Leaves may be damaged by plant bugs and caterpillars.

PROPAGATION By seed sown *in situ* in spring or late summer. If required, transplant when seedlings have 2–3 leaves.

HARVEST Flowers are picked when open and dried for infusions and syrups.

■ *Alcea rosea* syn. *Althaea rosea* (hollyhock)
Biennial or short-lived perennial with rounded lobed leaves, to 18cm (7in) long. Single or double, hibiscus-like flowers, 5–10cm (2–4in) across, which may be white, pink, purple, or pale yellow, are produced in tall racemes in summer. Native to W Asia. ‡ 1.2–2.5m (4–8ft), ↔ 38–60cm (15–24in). ■ 'Chater's Double' has fully double, peony-like flowers in a variety of colours, including pink, maroon, yellow, and white. ‡ 2–2.5m (6–8ft), ↔ 45–60cm (18–24in). ■ 'Nigra' has very dark maroon-black, single flowers. ‡ 1.5m (5ft), ↔ 45cm (18in).

HARDINESS Fully hardy.

PARTS USED Flowers.

PROPERTIES A soothing herb that relieves irritation and soreness, and has diuretic effects.

MEDICINAL USES Internally for gastritis, coughs, and cystitis. Externally as a gargle for sore throats. Often combined with *Inula helenium* (see p.243), *Tussilago farfara* (see p.395), or *Thymus* spp. (see p.387) in cough syrups.

CULINARY USES Young leaves are edible. Petals and cooked flower buds can be added to salad. Petals may be used for tea.

⊠ ▣ ☑

ALCHEMILLA
Lady's mantle

Rosaceae

In this genus there are 250 species of perennials found throughout northern temperate regions and at high altitudes in the tropics. *Alchemilla alpina* is a handsome foliage plant for rock gardens, though it is not easy to grow, and plants sold under this name are often the similar but more adaptable *A. conjuncta*. *Alchemilla xanthochlora*, a variable aggregate species, resembles the most common lady's mantle, *A. mollis*. "Lady's mantle", the common name for *A. xanthochlora*, refers to the plant's reputation as a herb for female disorders. Historically, *A. xanthochlora* was of greater importance than *A. alpina* as a medicinal herb, but it appears that the latter is more effective. Although widely planted in herb gardens, *A. mollis* has no medicinal uses. *Alchemilla* means "little magical one", because the way the leaves hold water was thought magical.

CULTIVATION Moist, well-drained soil in sun or semi-shade. *Alchemilla xanthochlora* dislikes lime.

PROPAGATION By seed sown in early spring; by division in autumn or spring. Most alchemillas hybridize and self-sow readily.

Alchemilla alpina

HARVEST Whole plants (*A. xanthochlora*) are cut as the flowers begin to open. Leaves (*A. alpina*) are cut after flowering, when the foliage is quite dry. All parts are dried for infusions and liquid extracts.

■ *Alchemilla alpina* (alpine lady's mantle)
Mat-forming perennial with a creeping woody rootstock and long-stalked, round to kidney-shaped leaves, to 3.5cm (1⅜in) long, deeply cut into 5–7 lobes. Leaf undersides are clad in silky hairs. Clusters of tiny, yellow-green flowers appear in summer. Native to NW and C Europe, and Greenland. ↔ 10–20cm (4–8in).

HARDINESS Fully hardy.

PARTS USED Leaves.

PROPERTIES An astringent, anti-inflammatory herb that controls bleeding and discharges.

MEDICINAL USES Internally for menstrual, menopausal, and postpartum problems, and for diarrhoea. Externally as a mouthwash after tooth extraction, douche for vaginal discharge, or skin lotion for sores and minor injuries. Also used in veterinary medicine to treat diarrhoea.

▨ ▣

Alchemilla xanthochlora

■ *Alchemilla xanthochlora* syn. *A. vulgaris* (lady's mantle, lion's foot)
Clump-forming perennial with a woody rootstock, densely hairy stems, and finely toothed, kidney-shaped, yellow-green leaves, 5cm (2in) long, cut into 9–11 lobes. Dense clusters of tiny, yellow-green flowers appear from late spring to early autumn. Native to NW and C Europe and Greece. ↔ 50cm (20in).

HARDINESS Fully hardy.

PARTS USED Whole plant.

PROPERTIES A bitter astringent herb that controls bleeding and discharges.

MEDICINAL USES Internally for excessive or irregular menstruation, menopausal problems, and diarrhoea. Externally for vaginal discharge and vulval itching.

CULINARY USES Leaves are an ingredient of Easter ledger pudding (see also *Persicaria bistorta*, p.309) in N England.

▤ ▣ ☑

ALETRIS
Melanthiaceae

Native to eastern N America and E Asia, this genus consists of ten species of rhizomatous, fibrous-rooted perennials. *Aletris farinosa* is seldom seen in cultivation. Its uses passed to settlers from native N American tribes, notably the Catawba, who made it into a tea to treat dysentery. It was listed as a tonic in the *US Pharmacopoeia* (1831–1926).

CULTIVATION Well-drained, peaty or sandy soil in sun.

PROPAGATION By seed sown in spring.

HARVEST Rhizomes are lifted in late summer after flowering and dried for use in elixirs, liquid extracts, and powders.

Aletris farinosa (colic root, star grass, true unicorn root)
Small perennial with a short thick rhizome and basal rosette of narrow, ribbed, pale yellow-green leaves, to 20cm (8in) long. Tubular white flowers with a mealy surface are borne in spikes during summer. Found from SE USA to Mexico, on acid or sandy soils. ‡ 30–90cm (1–3ft), ↔ 15cm (6in).

HARDINESS Frost hardy.

PARTS USED Rhizomes.

PROPERTIES A bittersweet, soapy-tasting, tonic herb that relieves spasms, especially in the digestive and female pelvic organs.

MEDICINAL USES Internally for flatulent colic, nervous dyspepsia, anorexia, womb prolapse, and menstrual problems. Rhizomes are always used dried; if fresh, they can cause diarrhoea, colic, and dizziness.

⊠ ▣

ALISMA
Alismataceae

This genus of ten species of marginal aquatic perennials occurs in northern temperate regions and in Australia. *Alisma plantago-aquatica* is

grown in water gardens, but the Asian variety appears not to be in cultivation. The specific epithet refers to the similarity of its leaves to *Plantago major* (see p.322) and to its aquatic habitat. *Alisma plantago-aquatica* var. *orientale* has a long history of use in Chinese medicine and is mentioned in texts dating back to AD200.
CULTIVATION Water to 25cm (10in) deep in an open sunny position.
PROPAGATION By seed sown in late summer; by division in spring.
HARVEST Roots are harvested before flowering and dried for decoctions.

Alisma plantago-aquatica var. *orientale* syn. *A. orientale* (Japanese water plantain)
Aquatic perennial with a stout upright stem and long-stalked, narrowly ovate leaves, 5–10cm (2–4in) long. Tall panicles of small, three-petalled, white flowers appear in late summer. Native to China and Japan. ↧↦ 70cm (28in).
HARDINESS Fully hardy.
PARTS USED Roots (*ze xie*).
PROPERTIES A sweet cooling herb that lowers blood pressure, cholesterol, and blood sugar.
MEDICINAL USES Internally for kidney and cardiovascular disease, fluid retention, and acute diarrhoea. Used in traditional Chinese medicine for kidney weakness, which manifests as deafness, tinnitus, and dizziness.
◩ ▣

ALKANNA
Alkanet

Boraginaceae

Some 25–30 perennials occur from S Europe to Iran. *Alkanna tinctoria* is found on limestone screes, pine forests, and coastal sands; it is useful for very dry, sandy, or alkaline soils. Several species, known as "alkanets", are important as dye plants. *Alkanna*, from the Spanish *alcanna*, in turn derives from the Arabic word for henna. Various alkanets are used as colorants, yielding reds, pinks, and flesh tones. *Alkanna tinctoria*

Alkanna tinctoria

was mentioned as the source of a purple dye to adulterate true purples from shellfish in Graeco-Egyptian texts dating to the 3rd century AD. It was used in cosmetics in ancient Greek and Roman times, and as a wine colorant in Europe until banned by the EEC. Alkanet also has medicinal uses. However, like many members of the family Boraginaceae, it contains a liver-damaging pyrrolizidine alkaloid that makes internal use inadvisable.
CULTIVATION Well-drained to dry, alkaline and sandy soils, in sun or partial shade.
PROPAGATION By seed sown in spring; by division in autumn.
HARVEST Roots are lifted in autumn and dried for powders, or macerated fresh in oil or fat.

◪ *Alkanna tinctoria* (dyer's alkanet, dyer's bugloss, Spanish bugloss)
Perennial with a thick, purple-brown root and linear to lanceolate, hairy leaves, to 8cm (3in) long. Funnel-shaped, five-petalled, blue flowers appear in late summer. Native to S Europe and the Middle East. ↥ 10–30cm (4–12in), ↔ 20–30cm (8–12in).
HARDINESS Fully hardy in dry conditions.
PARTS USED Roots.
PROPERTIES An astringent, anti-bacterial herb that encourages healing and relieves itching.
MEDICINAL USES Externally for varicose and indolent ulcers, bed sores, and itching rashes.
ECONOMIC USES Used as a purple colorant for wood, foods, pharmaceuticals, and cosmetics.
⚠ **WARNING** This herb is subject to legal restrictions in some countries.
◩ ▣ ✎

ALLIARIA

Brassicaceae

This genus of five species of perennials or biennials is native to Europe and temperate Asia. *Alliaria petiolata* grows in damp shady places in the wild garden where few herbs will survive,

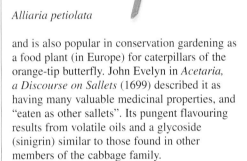
Alliaria petiolata

and is also popular in conservation gardening as a food plant (in Europe) for caterpillars of the orange-tip butterfly. John Evelyn in *Acetaria, a Discourse on Sallets* (1699) described it as having many valuable medicinal properties, and "eaten as other sallets". Its pungent flavouring results from volatile oils and a glycoside (sinigrin) similar to those found in other members of the cabbage family.
CULTIVATION Moist soil in sun or shade.
PROPAGATION By seed sown in spring where the plants are to flower. *Alliaria petiolata* self-sows readily, especially on bare or disturbed ground.
HARVEST Leaves and stems are cut before flowering for use fresh as a juice, and fresh or dried as an infusion or poultice.

◪ *Alliaria petiolata* syn. *A. officinalis*, *Sisymbrium alliaria* (garlic mustard, hedge garlic, Jack-by-the-hedge, sauce alone)
Garlic-smelling biennial with an erect stem and bright green, kidney-shaped leaves, 5–15cm (2–6in) across. Small white flowers open in succession over many weeks in spring, followed by slender, upright, cylindrical pods. Found in the USA, Europe, N Africa, W and C Asia.
↥ 30cm–1.2m (1–4ft), ↔ 30–45cm (12–18in).
HARDINESS Fully hardy.
PARTS USED Leaves, stems.
PROPERTIES A pungent stimulant herb that clears infection, encourages healing, and is expectorant and anti-inflammatory.
MEDICINAL USES Internally for bronchitis, asthma, and eczema. Externally for minor injuries and slow-healing skin problems, neuralgia, rheumatism, and gout.
CULINARY USES Young leaves add a mild garlic flavour to salads, sandwiches, and soups. Traditionally made into a sauce with mint leaves as a sauce for lamb or mutton (England).
◪ ◩ ▣ ✎

ALLIUM
Onion

Alliaceae

Onions form a large genus of about 700 species of mostly strong-smelling, bulbous or rhizomatous biennials and perennials. Alliums

A

are native to the northern hemisphere and South Africa, and vary in hardiness according to origin. Various species have been cultivated since the earliest times and are universally important as vegetables, flavourings, and medicinal plants. Their typical smell is caused by sulphur compounds, which have beneficial effects on the circulatory, digestive, and respiratory systems. It varies in pungency from species to species, and a few are almost odourless. *Allium sativum* (garlic) is the most pungent and highest in therapeutic value. It is also one of the most ancient herbs, recorded in Babylonian times (c.3000BC), found in the tomb of Tutankhamun (c.1370–52BC), and consumed in large quantities by the ancient Greeks and Romans. The pervasive odour of garlic has always caused ambivalence, as in the Muslim legend that, when Satan left the Garden of Eden after the Fall, garlic sprang up from his left footstep and onion from his right. There are many superstitions about garlic: it wards off vampires, causes moles to "leap out of the ground presently" (William Coles, *The Art of Simpling*, 1656), and, if chewed, prevents competitors from getting ahead in races. *Allium sativum* was first mentioned in traditional Chinese medicine c.AD500. In Ayurvedic medicine it is known as *rashona*, "lacking one taste", referring to the absence of sourness, while possessing all five other tastes (pungent root, bitter leaf, astringent stem, saline top of stem, and sweet seed). There are two main kinds of garlic: "hardneck", which has an excellent flavour but is demanding to cultivate, does not store well, and is difficult to braid; and "softneck", which is productive, adaptable, and stores well. *Allium canadense* (Canada onion, meadow garlic/leek, wild garlic) has medicinal properties similar to garlic, as well as spring onion-like leaves and mild-flavoured bulbs and bulbils. There are hundreds of kinds of *A. cepa* worldwide, adapted to latitude and climate, and varying in size, colour, and flavour. *Allium cepa* is often subdivided into three main groups: the Cepa Group (common onion), which has single large bulbs; the Proliferum Group (tree, or Catawissa onion), which produces an inflorescence consisting largely of bulbils; and the Aggregatum Group (shallot, ever-ready onion, and potato, or multiplier, onion), once classified as a separate species, *A. ascalonicum*, which forms clusters of small bulbs. In addition to their culinary and medicinal uses, onions, in the form of their brown or red-purple skins, are used as a dye for Easter eggs in many countries. *Allium fistulosum*, known as *da cong* in Mandarin and *negi* in Japanese, is the most important *Allium* species grown in China, Japan, and SE Asia, and is much used in Chinese, Japanese, and Korean cuisines. Its medicinal uses were first described in Shen Nong's *Canon of Herbs*, c.AD25–200. *Allium tuberosum* is less used in Chinese medicine; it was mentioned c.AD500 in *Ben Jing Ji Zhu* by Tao Hong Jin. *Allium chinense* (baker's garlic, *rakkyo*) is similar to *A. schoenoprasum* in appearance but has brighter green, more angular leaves and shallot-like bulbs. The bulbs have a crisp texture and are used mainly for pickles. *Allium ampeloprasum*

(Levant garlic) has several interesting forms, including: Porrum Group (leeks); 'Perlzwiebel', which produces small solid (unlayered) "pearl onions" for pickling; and the ornamental var. *babingtonii* (British or Welsh leek), which is mildy leek-flavoured and has tall stems of bright purple flowers. The Middle Eastern Kurrat Group was found in ancient Egyptian tombs and is still cultivated today in the Middle East. It is similar to a leek but smaller, with narrower leaves and a more developed bulb, though the young leaves are the parts usually eaten. *Allium ledebourianum* (*asatsuki*, *siu yuk*) from China and Japan has an onion–garlic flavour. It produces chive-like leaves and small fleshy bulbs, known as "fire onions". *Allium scorodoprasum* (rocambole, sand leek) is cultivated to a limited extent in parts of Russia for its small, garlic-flavoured bulbs. Closely related is *Tulbaghia violacea* (see p.395).

CULTIVATION Rich, well-drained soil in full sun. *Allium schoenoprasum* tolerates wetter conditions, heavier soil, and a less open position than most other allium. *Allium tricoccum* and *A. ursinum* prefer moist soil in shade. *Allium fistulosum* may be earthed up, like leeks, to blanch stems. Cut *A. schoenoprasum* down to the ground after flowering to produce fresh leaves. Onion maggot is common in some countries on light soils; downy mildew is prevalent in wet weather; rots may affect both growing and stored bulbs. Onions, garlic, and chives are often recommended in companion planting to deter pests, weeds, and diseases even though they are reputed to affect legumes adversely.

PROPAGATION By seed sown in spring; by bulbils planted in autumn or spring (*A. ampeloprasum*). By seed sown in autumn or spring, or by "sets" (small bulbs), planted in spring (*A. cepa*). Sowing and planting of cultivars of *A. cepa* vary widely in different climates. By seed sown in succession

in spring for summer use, and in summer for autumn and spring use (*A. fistulosum*). By bulbs or individual cloves planted in autumn or winter (*A. sativum*). By seed sown in spring; by division in autumn or spring (*A. schoenoprasum, A. tuberosum*). By seed sown in spring; by bulbs planted when dormant (*A. tricoccum, A. ursinum*).

HARVEST *Allium ampeloprasum*, *A. cepa*, and *A. sativum* are harvested in late summer and early autumn. *Allium cepa* and *A. sativum* are left to dry in the sun before being stored at 3–5°C (37–41°F). *Allium fistulosum* is pulled when the stems are pencil-thick, or left until leek-sized, and used fresh or quickly cooked. *Allium schoenoprasum* is cut as needed in the growing season. It is best used fresh or finely chopped and frozen. *Allium tricoccum*, *A. tuberosum*, and *A. ursinum* are gathered to be used fresh. *Allium tuberosum* is blanched in China using clay pots or straw "tents" to give tender leaves that are eaten raw in finger-length pieces.

■ *Allium ampeloprasum* (Levant garlic, perennial sweet leek, round-headed garlic, Yorktown onion)
Perennial with a two-lobed bulb and axillary bulbs, not enclosed in a papery skin. Purple to pink-white flowers are borne in a dense umbel and appear in summer. Native to the Mediterranean region and the Middle East. ‡ 45cm–1.8m (1½–5½ft), ↔ 5cm (2in). 'Elephant' (elephant garlic) produces giant-sized bulbs with a mild garlic flavour that can be eaten raw, baked, steamed, or stir-fried as a vegetable, or finely chopped as a flavouring.

HARDINESS Fully hardy to frost hardy.
PARTS USED Bulbs.
PROPERTIES Similar to garlic and onion.
CULINARY USES Flavour intermediate between onion and garlic, but milder.
▣ ☑

Allium ampeloprasum

Allium cepa 'Noordhollandse Bloedrode'

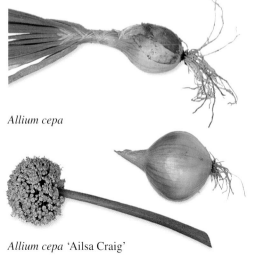

Allium cepa

Allium cepa 'Ailsa Craig'

Allium cepa Proliferum Group

■ *Allium cepa* (onion)
Robust biennial with a bulb, to 10cm (4in) across, and hollow leaves, semi-circular in cross-section, to 40cm (16in) long. An umbel of star-shaped, green-white flowers is produced in summer. Not known in the wild; probably originated in C Asia. ‡1.2m (4ft), ↔15cm (6in). Aggregatum Group (multiplier onion, potato onion, shallot) produces a cluster of smaller bulbs, rather than one large bulb. Aggregatum Group 'Perutile' (everlasting onion, ever-ready onion) forms dense clumps of leaves 30cm (12in) high, similar to but milder and more tender than Welsh onion. ■ 'Ailsa Craig' produces a round bulb with straw-coloured skin and mild flavour. Grown from seed sown in winter, it has long been popular as a large exhibition onion. ‡30–45cm (12–18in), ↔ to 30cm (12in). ■ 'Noordhollandse Bloedrode' ('North Holland Blood Red') is mild flavoured with deep red bulbs and pink flesh. It is easily grown from seed and stores well. ‡30–45cm (12–18in), ↔15–30cm (6–12in). ■ Proliferum Group (Catawissa onion, Egyptian onion, tree onion) produces large bulbils among the flowers, sprouting leaves while still attached to the umbel. ‡1m (3ft), ↔30cm (1ft). ■ 'Sweet Sandwich' has large, globose, brown-skinned bulbs that become exceptionally mild and sweet after about two months in storage. ‡30–45cm (12–18in), ↔15–30cm (6–12in).
HARDINESS Fully hardy to frost hardy.
PARTS USED Bulb, fresh juice.
PROPERTIES A pungent herb that protects against infection, relaxes spasms, and reduces blood pressure, clotting, and blood sugar levels. It is expectorant and diuretic.
MEDICINAL USES Internally for bronchial and gastric infections (liquid extract of bulbs). Externally for acne and boils.
CULINARY USES Cooked or raw, onions are indispensable as a flavouring for most meat and vegetable dishes, sauces, stocks, and chutneys. They are also eaten raw or cooked as a vegetable and as pickles with bread and cheese. Dehydrated onion is an ingredient of salt substitutes. Fermented onion paste, *hrous*, is used in couscous, stews, and soups (Tunisia).

■ *Allium fistulosum* (oriental bunching onion, scallion, spring onion, Welsh onion)
Biennial or perennial with cylindrical bulbs, pencil-thick stems, and hollow leaves, to 30cm (12in) long. Bell-shaped, yellow-white flowers (sometimes entirely replaced by bulbils), subtended by a large spathe, are borne in spherical umbels in summer. Not found in the wild; probably originated in E Asia. ‡1m (3ft), ↔ 15–23cm (6–9in). 'Ishikura' has white, straight, non-bulbous stems. 'Santa Claus' has thick, deep red stems and no bulbs. ■ 'White Lisbon' is a white-stemmed, mild-flavoured cultivar, very hardy and fast-growing. ‡ 20–30cm (8–12in), ↔ up to 15cm (6in).
HARDINESS Fully hardy.
PARTS USED Whole plant, bulb (*cong bai*), roots (*cong xu*).
PROPERTIES A pungent, tonic, antibiotic herb that stimulates the digestion, lowers fever by increasing perspiration, and reduces cholesterol levels. It is also diuretic, anti-inflammatory, and expectorant.
MEDICINAL USES Internally, in traditional Chinese medicine, as a decoction of the fresh plant, for the early stages of the common cold, and for catarrh following respiratory tract infections. Regarded as especially useful for complaints and injuries caused by extreme cold (such as frostbite), and low *yang* energy.
CULINARY USES Leaves are used green or blanched for flavouring in Asian cuisines, and for tying items of food before serving. Lower stems are used like leeks in soups, stews, and omelettes.

■ *Allium sativum* syn. *A. controversum* (garlic)
Perennial with a globose bulb of 5–15 bulblets (cloves), encased in a papery, white or mauve-tinged skin, and flat leaves, to 60cm (24in) long. An umbel of green-white to pink flowers, with a deciduous spathe, appears in summer. Not known in the wild; probably originated in C Asia. ‡30cm–1m (12–36in), ↔ 23–30cm (9–12in). 'Silverskin' is a softneck type with white bulbs and red-purple, strongly flavoured cloves; stores and braids well. 'Spanish Roja' is a hardneck type with large, brown-purple bulbs, containing rich and complex-flavoured cloves.
HARDINESS Fully hardy.
PARTS USED Bulbs (*da suan*).
PROPERTIES A pungent warming herb that wards off or clears bacterial infection, lowers fever by increasing perspiration, reduces blood pressure, cholesterol, and blood sugar levels, and is expectorant. Regarded as rejuvenative, detoxicant, and aphrodisiac in Ayurveda.
MEDICINAL USES Internally to prevent infection and to treat colds, influenza, bronchitis, whooping cough, gastroenteritis, and dysentery. Externally for skin problems, especially acne, and fungal infections. In addition to these traditional uses, garlic has recently been found to reduce glucose metabolism in diabetes, slow the development of arteriosclerosis, and lower the risk of further heart attacks in myocardial infarct patients. It is taken raw (crushed or as juice), as a syrup or tincture, or in capsules.
CULINARY USES Garlic enhances the flavour of most meats, seafood, and many vegetables. It is an essential ingredient of regional dishes in many parts of the world, notably in S Europe, the

Allium cepa 'Sweet Sandwich'

Allium fistulosum 'White Lisbon'

Allium fistulosum

Allium sativum   *Allium schoenoprasum*

Allium schoenoprasum 'Forescate'

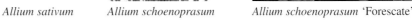

Middle East, the Far East, the West Indies, Mexico, and S America. Raw garlic predominates in sauces, such as *aïoli* (Spain and S France) and *skordaliá* (Greece), and is added as a condiment to butter, oil, vinegar, and salt. Bulbs are baked or roasted whole to produce a creamy, more subtle flavouring; also added to meats during roasting. Young leaves, flower stalks, and flowers taste milder than the bulbs.

■ *Allium schoenoprasum* syn. *A. sibiricum* (chives)
Clump-forming perennial with slender bulbs, 1cm (½in) across, clustered on a rhizome, and cylindrical hollow leaves, to 35cm (14in) long. Pale purple to pink, rarely white, bell-shaped flowers are borne in umbels in summer. ‡10–60cm (4–24in), ↔30cm (12in).
■ 'Forescate' is larger than the species and has pink flowers. ‡45cm (18in), ↔30–45cm (12–18in). 'Grolau' (windowsill chives) has dark green, well-flavoured foliage that keeps well in low light and re-grows rapidly when cut. 'Profusion' has sterile flowers that last well, making an excellent plant for edible flower production. var. *sibiricum* (giant chives, Siberian chives) has a strong, garlic-like flavour.
HARDINESS Fully hardy.
PARTS USED Leaves, bulbs, flowers.
PROPERTIES Similar effects to other allium, but is milder; rarely used medicinally.
CULINARY USES Chives are especially good with potatoes and eggs. Leaves are used to garnish and flavour soups and salads, and in soft cheeses, omelettes, and sauces such as *remoulade* and *ravigote*. Chopped chives and onions flavour Cotswold cheese (England). Individual flowers are added to salads.

Allium tricoccum (ramps, wild leek)
Perennial with slender, onion-like bulbs and elliptic leaves, 20–24cm (8–10in) long, appearing in spring and dying down before the plant blooms. Long-stalked umbels of white flowers are produced in summer. Native to eastern N America. ‡15–45cm (6–18in), ↔10–30cm (4–12in).
HARDINESS Fully hardy.
PARTS USED Leaves, bulbs.
PROPERTIES Similar to *A. sativum*, but milder.
MEDICINAL USES Internally as a spring tonic in native N American medicine, and for colds, sore throat, and worms in children. Externally for earache
CULINARY USES Young leaves and bulbs have a sweet, leek-like flavour. Traditionally baked in the fire or dried for use as a food to reduce acidity. Now used mainly as a flavouring in salads, cream sauces, and soups.

■ *Allium tuberosum* (Chinese chives, cuchay, garlic chives)
Perennial with a stout rhizome, cylindrical bulbs, and flat, solid, keeled leaves, to 35cm (14in) long. Umbels of sweet-scented, white, star-shaped flowers appear in late summer. Native to SE Asia. ‡75cm (30in), ↔45cm (18in).
HARDINESS Fully hardy.
PARTS USED Leaves, roots, flower buds, seeds (*jiu zi*).
PROPERTIES An anti-emetic herb that improves kidney function. It has a mild onion–garlic flavour.
MEDICINAL USES Internally for urinary incontinence, kidney and bladder weakness, stomach chills with vomiting (seeds). Externally with *Gardenia augusta* (see p.220) as a poultice for knee injuries.

CULINARY USES Chopped leaves and flower buds are added to salads, soft cheeses, and stir-fries. Lengthy cooking destroys the flavour. Blanched leaves are served with noodles, chicken, and pork (China). Chopped leaves are added to miso soup (Japan). Seeds are edible, unripe, ripe, or sprouted, and when ripe are pressed for oil.

■ *Allium ursinum* (bear's garlic, ramsons)
Carpeting perennial with a pervasive garlic smell and elliptic leaves, to 28cm (11in) long. Rounded clusters of white, star-like flowers are borne above the foliage in late spring and early summer. Native to Europe and Russia. ‡40cm (16in), ↔30cm (12in).
HARDINESS Fully hardy.
PARTS USED Whole flowering plant, leaves.
PROPERTIES A strong-smelling, pungent herb, similar in flavour and effects to garlic.
MEDICINAL USES Internally for high blood pressure and arteriosclerosis (fresh herb, leaves).
CULINARY USES Leaves are used to taste in salads, sandwiches, omelettes, sauces, and savoury dishes.

ALNUS
Alder

Betulaceae

This genus of 35 species of deciduous trees and shrubs is found mainly in northern temperate regions. Alders are adaptable, fast-growing, and excel in damp situations. *Alnus glutinosa* is very hardy and thrives in wet soils, making it a good choice for bog gardens and waterside places. The piles of wood upon which 16th-century Venice was built are reputedly made from alder, and it has also been used for making dishes, spoons, canoe paddles, cradles, and clogs. A number of different alders are used for timber, dyes, and medicinal purposes. These include: *A. rubra* (Oregon alder, red alder), a western N American

Allium tuberosum

Allium ursinum

Alnus glutinosa

Alnus glutinosa 'Imperialis'

species that is highly prized for smoking fish; *A. rugosa* (speckled alder); and *A. serrulata* (hazel alder, smooth alder) of eastern N America. All were major sources of astringent remedies to native people.
CULTIVATION Rich, moist to wet soil in sun or partial shade.
PROPAGATION By seed sown in autumn or spring; by suckers detached in autumn; by hardwood cuttings in early winter. Trees may be coppiced to minimize damage from harvesting of bark.
HARVEST Bark of young twigs and 2–3-year-old branches is peeled off lengthways when fresh, and dried for decoctions and powders. Leaves are picked in summer and used fresh.

◨ *Alnus glutinosa* (black alder, common alder, European alder)
Bushy tree with purple to grey-brown bark, pendent twigs, and obovate leaves, 3–9cm (1¼–3½in) long. Flowers appear in early spring; male catkins are 2.5–6cm (1–2½in) long, females shorter, followed by ovoid fruits, 1–2cm (½–¾in) long. Native to Europe and Asia. ↕25m (80ft), ↔10m (30ft). 'Aurea' has yellow young leaves. ◨'Imperialis' is a graceful tree with deeply cut leaves. 'Pyramidalis' has upright branches. ↕15m (50ft), ↔5m (15ft).
HARDINESS Fully hardy.
PARTS USED Bark, leaves.
PROPERTIES An astringent tonic herb that encourages healing of damaged tissues.
MEDICINAL USES Internally and externally to control bleeding, and for rheumatism (bark). Externally for throat, mouth, and dental infections, wounds, and scabies (bark); as a poultice for inflammatory conditions such as rheumatism (leaves).
▥ ▨ ▪

ALOE
Aloaceae

Native to South Africa, Arabia, and the Cape Verde Islands, this genus consists of about 325 species of tender evergreen perennials, shrubs, trees, and climbers, many of which are hard to tell apart. Aloes vary greatly in size, but all are architectural plants with thick spiky foliage, often glaucous or patterned, and bold spikes of colourful flowers. Some larger species are grown in gardens in warm climates. *Aloe vera* was mentioned in the Ebers Papyrus, dating from 1552BC, and has been identified in wall paintings in ancient Egypt, where it was used to treat catarrh. Records in ancient Greece date back to the 4th century BC. Its use was described by Dioscorides in *De Materia Medica* (AD70–90). Alexander the Great is said to have conquered Socotra, an island in the Indian Ocean to which several *Aloe* spp. are native, in order to secure supplies of aloes to heal his soldiers' wounds. The aloes mentioned in the Bible do not refer to *Aloe* spp., but to lignin aloes or aloeswood (*Aquilaria malaccensis*, see p.125). The use of *Aloe vera* in Chinese medicine was first mentioned in the 11th century. It appears in Anglo-Saxon medical texts, having been introduced to Europe in the 10th century. Mahatma Gandhi utilized *A. vera*, having discovered its benefits when visiting South Africa, and claimed that it helped him withstand prolonged fasting. Juice extracted from *A. vera* contains aloin, which is highly irritant to the digestive system. Further processing reduces aloin to safe levels. In some countries, such as Japan, there is a limit to the amount of aloin permitted in the juice. Various aloes have similar constituents to *A. vera* and are used in the same ways. These include *A. ferox* (Cape aloe) and *A. perryi* (Socotrine or Zanzibar aloe). "Aloes" or "bitter aloes" is the name given to a purgative drug made from the leaves of several species. *Aloe vera* var. *officinalis* is commonly sold by herb nurseries as *A. vera*. It has orange flowers and greener softer leaves, with longitudinal white spots that persist as the plant matures. Seed and offsets, borne on runners, are readily produced.
CULTIVATION Very well-drained soil in sun. Mealybug may attack pot plants.
PROPAGATION By offsets at any time. *Aloe vera* rarely sets seed.
HARVEST Leaves are cut as required from 2–3-year-old plants. Sap is drained from cut leaves and used fresh, or evaporated to a brown crystalline solid for the preparation of creams, decoctions, lotions, pills, and tinctures.

◨ *Aloe vera* syn. *A. barbadensis* (Barbados aloe, Curaçao aloe)
Clump-forming perennial, suckering at the base, with dense rosettes of thick, spiky, grey-green leaves, red-spotted only in young specimens. Tubular yellow flowers are borne in summer. Origin uncertain. Widely naturalized in Mediterranean regions, India, the West Indies, and tropical and subtropical America. ↕60–90cm (2–3ft), ↔indefinite.

Aloe vera

HARDINESS Min. 10°C (50°F).
PARTS USED Leaves (occasionally), sap (*lu hui*).
PROPERTIES An intensely bitter, purgative herb that controls fungal infection, is anti-inflammatory, and promotes healing. It destroys intestinal parasites and stimulates the uterus.
MEDICINAL USES Internally for chronic constipation (especially following iron medication), poor appetite, digestive problems, colitis, and irritable bowel syndrome. Not given to pregnant women or to patients with haemorrhoids. Leaves are a strong purgative and require great care over dosage. *Aloe vera* juice may cause miscarriage and serious digestive upsets in excess, or if it contains more than 50 parts per million of aloin. To prevent griping in laxative formulations, it is usually combined with *Foeniculum vulgare* (see p.215) or *Tamarindus indica* (see p.380). Externally for burns, scalds, sunburn, wounds, eczema, psoriasis, acne, dermatitis, and ulcers; also in colonic irrigation, and to prevent nail biting.
ECONOMIC USES Used in cosmetic, tanning, skin care, and pharmaceutical preparations.
⚠ **WARNING** This herb, in the form of aloes, is subject to legal restrictions in some countries.
▨ ▢ ▪ ▨ ▣

ALOYSIA
Verbenaceae

There are 37 species of deciduous or evergreen, aromatic shrubs in this genus, which is native to N and S America, and closely related to *Lippia*. *Aloysia* was named after Maria Louisa, Princess of Parma, who died in 1819. *Aloysia triphylla* (lemon verbena) has been a favourite for garden rooms since it was introduced from Chile in 1794. The dried leaves retain their fragrance well and are a useful ingredient for potpourris. Lemon verbena oil was once popular in perfumery, especially in the citrus cologne *eau de verveine*, but expensive. Its use further declined owing to evidence that it may sensitize the skin to sunlight. It has largely been replaced by *Cymbopogon* spp. (see p.187).

CULTIVATION Light, well-drained soil in sun. Cut back main stems to 30cm (12in) and side shoots to two or three buds of the old wood in spring, or remove dead wood in early summer. Plants grown outdoors in cold areas may not show signs of new growth until early summer.

PROPAGATION By softwood or greenwood cuttings in summer.

HARVEST Leaves are picked in summer; used mainly fresh for oil extraction or flavouring, or dried for infusions and potpourris.

▣ *Aloysia triphylla* syn. *Lippia citriodora* (lemon verbena)
Deciduous shrub with lemon-scented, pointed, lanceolate leaves, 10cm (4in) long, in whorls of 3–4. Tiny, pale lilac to white flowers are produced in terminal or axillary panicles in summer. Native to Argentina and Chile.
↨ 3m (10ft).
HARDINESS Frost hardy.
PARTS USED Leaves, oil.
PROPERTIES An astringent aromatic herb, rich in volatile oils, that acts as a mild sedative, relieving spasms, especially of the digestive system, and reducing fever. The essential oil is both insecticidal and bactericidal.
MEDICINAL USES Internally for feverish colds and indigestion. In aromatherapy for nervous or digestive problems; for acne, boils, and cysts.
CULINARY USES Fresh leaves are used in herb teas and to flavour jellies, summer drinks, stuffings for poultry, salads, and salad dressings.
ECONOMIC USES Dried leaves are used in potpourris.
▨ ▢ ▪ ∕ ∕

Aloysia triphylla

ALPINIA
Zingiberaceae

This genus of about 200 species of ginger-scented, rhizomatous perennials is native to Asia and Australia. *Alpinia officinarum* (lesser galingal) is of great importance as a medicinal herb; it has been used in both Ayurvedic and Chinese medicine since very early times (c.AD500 in China), and in Europe since the Middle Ages. *Alpinia galanga* (greater galingal) has less pungent rhizomes and is more important for culinary uses. These tropical galingals are not to be confused with *Cyperus longus* (European galingal, sweet galingale), which has violet-scented roots that are used in perfumery. In addition to *Alpinia officinarum* and *A. galanga*, several other species are used for flavourings and medicines. The Australian *A. caerulea* (native ginger) has ginger-flavoured rhizomes, and *yi zhi*, from the southern Chinese *A. oxyphylla* (black cardamom, sharp-leafed galangal), is a warming digestive and kidney tonic, used in traditional Chinese medicine for diarrhoea, incontinence, and stomach chills.

CULTIVATION Well-drained, humus-rich soil in partial shade with high humidity. Spider mite may attack plants under cover.
PROPAGATION By division of rhizomes as new growth begins.
HARVEST Rhizomes four to six years old are lifted at the end of the growing season and used fresh, or dried for use in decoctions, liquid extracts, and tinctures, or distilled for oil.

▣ *Alpinia galanga* (galangal, greater galingal, Siamese ginger)
Perennial with ginger-scented rhizomes and lanceolate leaves, to 50cm (20in) long. Pale green, orchid-like flowers with a white, pink-striped lip, appear all year, followed by red, three-valved, spherical capsules. Native to SE Asia. ↕ 2m (6ft), ↔ indefinite.
HARDINESS Min. 15–18°C (59–64°F).
PARTS USED Rhizomes, oil.
PROPERTIES An aromatic, bitter, pungent herb that stimulates the digestive system.
CULINARY USES Raw rhizome is a popular ingredient in many Indonesian, Malaysian, and

Alpinia galanga

Alpinia officinarum

Thai dishes for its ginger-like flavour. Oil and extracts are used as flavouring, especially in soft drinks, bitters, and liqueurs, such as Chartreuse. Flower buds, flowers, and fruits are edible, too. Extracts are added to low-alcohol drinks to make them taste more alcoholic.
▢ ▨ ▪ ∕ ▣

▣ *Alpinia officinarum* (galangal, lesser galingal)
Tender perennial with a red-brown, scaly rhizome, to 2cm (1in) thick, lanceolate leaves, to 40cm (16in) long, and panicles of white, red-streaked, orchid-like flowers. Native to China and Vietnam. ↕ 75cm–1.2m (2½–4ft), ↔ indefinite.
HARDINESS Min. 15–18°C (59–64°F).
PARTS USED Rhizomes (*gao liang*), oil.
PROPERTIES A bitter, aromatic, stimulant herb that acts mainly on the digestive system. It also relieves pain, lowers fevers, and controls bacterial and fungal infections.
MEDICINAL USES Internally for digestive upsets, chronic gastritis and gastric ulceration, epigastric and rheumatic pain. Externally for skin infections, skin cancer, and gum disease.
CULINARY USES Rhizome has a pungent, peppery, ginger-like flavour, used to flavour vinegar and liqueurs.
▢ ▨ ▪ ∕ ▣

ALSTONIA
Apocynaceae

A genus of about 43 species of evergreen trees and shrubs with milky sap, found from Africa, C America, and SE Asia to the W Pacific and Australia. Some species have been severely reduced by collection of bark for treating fevers. *Alstonia* is named after the Scottish botanist Charles Alston (1716–60). Alstonia bark is the trade name given to the bark of *A. scholaris* and the Australian *A. constricta* (Australian quinine, fever bark). Both contain indole alkaloids, though their exact constituents differ. *Alstonia scholaris* is so named because the soft timber was once used for making writing slates before paper was widely available. *Alstonia boonei* is used both medicinally and to make domestic items in Ghana. It is called "sky god's tree", as a branch is put up to the sky god in each village. The bark contains alkaloids that act as an antidote to *Strophanthus* poisoning.

CULTIVATION Moist to wet soil in sun or partial shade.
PROPAGATION By hardwood cuttings in moist sand in early spring, at 21°C (70°F).
HARVEST Bark is stripped and dried for liquid extracts, tinctures, decoctions, and powder.

Alstonia scholaris

■ *Alstonia scholaris* (devil tree, dita bark, milky pine)
Evergreen tree with rough grey bark and whorls of leathery leaves, 15–20cm (6–8in) long. Clusters of small, tubular, green-white flowers are followed by paired elongated fruits. Native to SE Asia. ↕12–18m (40–60ft), ↔6–10m (20–30ft).
HARDINESS Min. 15–18°C (59–64°F).
PARTS USED Bark.
PROPERTIES A bitter, astringent, alterative herb that lowers fever, relaxes spasms, stimulates lactation, and expels intestinal worms. It also stimulates the uterus, making it unsafe for pregnant women.
MEDICINAL USES Internally for malaria, chronic diarrhoea, dysentery, and intestinal parasites.
ECONOMIC USES Light, soft timber is used for making masks and coffins.
Ⓜ ◨ ✎ ◧

ALTHAEA
Malvaceae

A genus of about 12 species of annuals and perennials, closely resembling the genus *Malva* (see p.270), that occurs throughout W Europe to C Asia and N Africa. It once included hollyhock (formerly *Althaea rosea*, now *Alcea rosea*, see p.109). The name *Althaea* comes from the Greek *altha*, "to cure", referring to the healing properties of these plants. A few species are grown as border plants; *A. officinalis* is useful for waterlogged ground. The healing properties of *A. officinalis* were first recorded in the 9th century BC, and were widely used in Greek medicine. They are concentrated in the roots. The powdered roots were once used to make soft pastilles (*pâté de guimauve*) for throat infections and coughs – forerunners of the popular confectionery "marsh mallow", which no longer contains extracts of the herb. *Malva sylvestris* (see p.270) and *M. neglecta* have similar properties, but are considered less effective.
CULTIVATION Moist to wet soil in sun. *Althaea officinalis* prefers damp conditions but thrives alongside other plants in the border.
PROPAGATION By seed sown when ripe in late summer; by division in autumn. Germination is erratic.

Althaea officinalis

HARVEST Leaves are dried for infusions, ointments, and liquid extracts. Roots are dried for liquid extracts, ointments, and syrups.

■ *Althaea officinalis* (marsh mallow)
Upright perennial with a fleshy taproot, downy stems, and velvety, round to ovate leaves, 3–8cm (1¼–3in) across. Pale pink flowers, 2–4cm (¾–1½in) across, appear in the axils in summer. Native to Europe to C Russia, W Asia, and N Africa; widely naturalized in N America. ↕1–1.2m (3–4ft), ↔60–90cm (24–36in). var. *alba* has white flowers.
HARDINESS Fully hardy.
PARTS USED Leaves, roots, flowers.
PROPERTIES A sweet mucilaginous herb that soothes and softens tissues, has expectorant effects, and controls bacterial infection.
MEDICINAL USES Internally for inflammation and ulceration of the digestive tract, hiatus hernia, bronchitis, catarrh, asthma, whooping cough, and cystitis (roots); and for urinary tract infections, catarrh, bronchitis, irritating coughs, and cystitis (leaves). Externally for boils, abscesses, eye and skin inflammations, insect bites, splinters, minor injuries, gingivitis, mastitis, and gangrene. Often combined with *Symphytum officinale* (see p.377) for digestive complaints; with *Glycyrrhiza glabra* (see p.226), *Marrubium vulgare* (see p.271), or *Lobelia inflata* (see p.265) for bronchial complaints; and with *Ulmus rubra* for external use. Peeled root is given to children to chew as a traditional aid to teething.
CULINARY USES Root extract may be used as a substitute for egg white in meringue, or mixed with sugar, gum arabic, and egg white to make marsh mallow confectionery. Leaves and flowers are edible.
◧ ✎ ◧ ◨ ✎

Althaea rosea. See *Alcea rosea*.

AMARANTHUS
Amaranthaceae

This genus consists of 60 spinach-like annuals, found worldwide in both temperate and tropical regions. *Amaranthus* is from the Greek *amarantos*, "unfading", referring to the long-lasting flowers. Many species of *Amaranthus* are used as vegetables and pot herbs, and some tropical American species are important locally as grain crops. A few species have attractive foliage and colourful flowers and are grown as ornamentals. Amaranth is the magenta-red pigment found in some species. *Amaranthus*

hypochondriacus is best known as a herb, but it also has nutritious leaves and seeds with high protein levels (15 per cent). Species with similar medicinal uses include: *A. polygamus*, an Indian species with reputedly aphrodisiac seeds; *A. retroflexus* (pigweed, redroot amaranth, wild beet), which originated in tropical America and is now naturalized in the USA and has become an important agronomic weed in warmer areas; and the Chinese *A. spinosus* (careless weed, prickly amaranth), used as an astringent and a febrifuge.
CULTIVATION Rich, well-drained soil in sun. Ample water and humidity intensifies foliage colour. Plants grown under cover may be attacked by aphids.
PROPAGATION By seed sown in spring at 20°C (68°F).
HARVEST Whole plants are cut when coming into flower, and dried for infusions and liquid extracts. Leaves are picked as required and eaten fresh. Seeds are harvested when ripe.

■ *Amaranthus hypochondriacus* syn. *A. hybridus* subsp. *hypochondriacus* (Mercado grain amaranth, prince's feather)
Tall bushy annual with oblong to lanceolate, purple-green leaves, to 15cm (6in) long. Tiny crimson flowers are borne in erect, occasionally flattened, clusters, about 15cm (6in) long, in summer, followed by tiny, red-brown to black seeds. Native to S USA, Mexico, India, and China. ↕1.2–1.5m (4–5ft), ↔45–60cm (18–24in). 'Green Thumb' has divided clusters of yellow-green flowers. ↕60cm (24in), ↔30cm (12in). 'Pygmy Torch' has erect clusters of maroon flowers. ↕30–45cm (12–18in), ↔30cm (12in).
HARDINESS Half hardy.
PARTS USED Whole plant, leaves, seeds.
PROPERTIES An astringent, soothing, cooling herb that controls bleeding.
MEDICINAL USES Internally for diarrhoea and excessive menstruation. Externally for ulcerated mouth and throat, vaginal discharge, wounds, and nosebleeds.
CULINARY USES Leaves are eaten as a vegetable. Seeds are harvested as a grain crop.
ECONOMIC USES The red pigment is used as colouring in foods and medicines.
✎ ◧ ◨ ◨ ✎ ✎

Amaranthus hypochondriacus

A

AMMI

Apiaceae

Ten species of annuals and biennials closely related to *Daucus* (see p.191) make up this genus, which occurs through SW Asia to S Europe and neighbouring Atlantic islands. *Ammi majus* is widely grown in India for the treatment of vitiligo (piebald skin): the active ingredient is psoralene, which stimulates pigment production in skin exposed to ultraviolet light. It also has a long history of use as a contraceptive in various cultures. If a decoction of ground seeds is taken after intercourse, it may prevent implantation of the fertilized ovum. In Morocco, where it is known as *cure-dents du Prophète*, it is used as a gargle for toothache. In the West it is better known as an ornamental. *Ammi visnaga* was mentioned in the Ebers Papyrus c.1550BC. The seeds contain a fatty oil, which includes khellin. Research into khellin in the 1950s led to the formulation of proprietary drugs for the management of asthma attacks.

CULTIVATION Well-drained soil in sun.
PROPAGATION By seed sown in spring.
HARVEST Seeds are gathered when ripe and dried for powders, tinctures, and liquid extracts. Fractions of the fatty oil are extracted for drug formulation.

Ammi copticum. See *Trachyspermum ammi.*

■ *Ammi majus* (bishopsweed, bullwort, Queen Anne's lace)
Tall annual with finely divided leaves, 15–20cm (6–8in) long. Tiny white flowers are borne in umbels, 3–6cm (1¼–2½in) across, in summer, followed by small, ridged, pale brown fruits (seeds). Native to S Europe, Turkey, and N Africa. ↕30–90cm (12–36in), ↔30cm (12in).
HARDINESS Hardy.

Ammi majus

Ammi visnaga

PARTS USED Seeds.
PROPERTIES A tonic diuretic herb that affects skin pigmentation.
MEDICINAL USES Externally, in proprietary preparations, for vitiligo and psoriasis. Excess causes nausea, diarrhoea, and headaches.
CULINARY USES Seeds are used as a condiment.
⚠ **WARNING** Legally restricted in some countries.
▨ ▪ ⧄

■ *Ammi visnaga* syn. *Daucus visnaga* (khella)
Tall stout annual or biennial with triangular–ovate, finely divided, aromatic leaves, to 18cm (7in) long. Tiny, yellow-white flowers appear in summer in long-stalked umbels with 30–150 rays that thicken and remain erect after flowering. Small seeds are oblong–ovoid. Native to E Mediterranean, especially Egypt. ↕45–75cm (18–30in), ↔45cm (18in).
HARDINESS Half hardy.
PARTS USED Seeds.
PROPERTIES An aromatic herb that dilates the bronchial, urinary, and blood vessels without affecting blood pressure.
MEDICINAL USES Internally for asthma, angina, coronary arteriosclerosis, and kidney stones.
CULINARY USES Seeds are an ingredient of *mish*, a soft, yellow-brown, pickled cheese that was popular in ancient Egyptian times and is still made in Egypt today.
⚠ **WARNING** This herb is subject to legal restrictions in some countries.
▨ ▪ ⧄

AMOMUM

Zingiberaceae

This genus includes some 90 species with aromatic rhizomes and reed-like stems that occur in SE Asia. Several species are known as cardamom, and are used for culinary and medicinal purposes. They have aromatic seeds but are not as pleasant in flavour as the true cardamom (*Elettaria cardamomum*, see p.200). In Malaysia, the fruits of *Amomum compactum* syn. *A. kepulaga* (round cardamom) are used as a spice, and chewed as a breath freshener. The seeds of *A. subulatum* (brown/black cardamom, greater cardamom, Nepal cardamom) are widely

used in Afghani cooking. They have a eucalyptus aroma and are used as a cheaper substitute for true cardamom. *Amomum xanthioides* (bastard cardamom) was first mentioned in Chinese medicine during the Ming dynasty (1368–1654).
CULTIVATION Humus-rich soil, with moisture and humidity in partial shade.
PROPAGATION By division as new growth begins.
HARVEST Seeds are harvested when ripe for use in decoctions and for food flavouring.

■ *Amomum xanthioides* syn. *A. villosum* var. *xanthioides* (bastard cardamom, grains of paradise, Tavoy cardamom)
Rhizomatous perennial with reed-like stems and two rows of lanceolate leaves, 20–35cm (8–14in) long. White, purple-spotted, orchid-like flowers appear in globose spikes near the base of the plant, followed by ovoid, three-valved capsules. Native to India, Laos, Cambodia, Thailand, Vietnam, and S China. ↔2–2.5m (6–8ft).
HARDINESS Min. 18°C (64°F).
PARTS USED Seeds (*sha ren*).
PROPERTIES A camphoraceous warming herb that stimulates the appetite, relieves indigestion, and controls nausea and vomiting.
MEDICINAL USES Internally for digestive disturbances, notably in irritable bowel syndrome and pregnancy.
CULINARY USES Used as a substitute for true cardamom in flavouring food and liqueurs.
▨ ▪ ⧄ ▦

AMYGDALUS

Amygdalus communis. See *Prunus dulcis.*

ANACARDIUM

Anacardiaceae

Fifteen species of small to very tall trees make up this genus, which occurs in tropical parts of S and C America, and the West Indies. *Anacardium occidentale* was introduced from Brazil as a crop to India and the Malay Archipelago during the 16th century, but did not reach Europe until 1699. The seeds became known as cashews, after the Portuguese *cajú*. The fruits of *A. occidentale*, known as cashew apples, yield a pleasantly acidic pulp and juice. Shells contain a caustic oil that is extracted before the nuts are removed.
CULTIVATION Well-drained, sandy soil in sun, with ample moisture during the growing season.
PROPAGATION By hardwood cuttings at the end of the growing season.
HARVEST Leaves are picked at any time and dried. Bark is removed as required and used fresh or dried. Fruits are harvested when ripe and processed into fresh pulp and juice. Oil is extracted from the shells, and the seeds ("nuts") are removed and used fresh or roasted.

■ *Anacardium occidentale* (*acajou*, cashew, *marañon*)
Evergreen tree or shrub with ovate leaves to 22cm (9in) long. Sweetly scented, pale green,

Anacardium occidentale

red-striped flowers appear all
year in terminal panicles,
followed by red or yellow
fruits that have a kidney-
shaped nut at the base. Native to tropical
America. ‡ 12m (40ft), ↔ 10m (30ft).
HARDINESS Min. 18°C (64°F).
PARTS USED Leaves, bark, fruits, seeds, oil.
PROPERTIES Reduces fever (leaves) and blood
sugar levels (bark), and is diuretic (fruits); the
nuts (seeds) are a source of nutrients, and the
shell oil is toxic to many disease-causing
organisms, such as *Staphylococcus* bacteria.
MEDICINAL USES Internally for diarrhoea (bark
and leaf extracts, fruit juice), hypoglycaemia
(bark extract), and influenza (fruit juice), and, in
W Africa, for malaria (leaf and bark infusions).
Externally for leprosy, ringworm, warts, and
corns (fresh extract from shells), and, in W Africa,
for toothache and sore gums (leaf and bark
infusions). Bark extract is considered to have
contraceptive properties by native Amazonians.
CULINARY USES Fruits are eaten fresh, cooked,
or dried, or made into chutney or jam. Juice is
made into soft drinks, such as *cashola*, and
distilled as *fenni* and *koniagi*. Nuts are eaten
roasted and used in a variety of both sweet and
savoury dishes, and also ground when raw to
make cashew butter, milk, and cream, as a
substitute for dairy produce in special diets.
ECONOMIC USES Shell oil is used in brake
linings, synthetic rubbers, and to proof paper
and wood against insect attack.
⚠ **WARNING** Oil is a skin irritant; oil vapour is
irritant if inhaled.

ANACYCLUS
Mount Atlas daisy

Asteraceae

This genus of nine species of annuals and
perennials is native to the Mediterranean.
Anacyclus pyrethrum itself is rarely grown as an
ornamental, but the prostrate var. *depressus*,
from the Atlas Mountains in Morocco, is popular
with rock garden enthusiasts. As a medicinal
herb, *A. pyrethrum* has been widely used from
medieval times to the present by Arabian,

Asian, and European physicians. Culpeper
recommended that "the herb or root dried and
chewed in the mouth, purges the brain of
phlegmatic humours; thereby not only easing
pains in the head and teeth, but also hinders the
distilling of the brain upon the lungs and eyes,
thereby preventing coughs, phthisicks and
consumption, the apoplexy and falling sickness"
(*The English Physician Enlarged*, 1653).
Anacyclus pyrethrum should not be confused
with the insecticidal pyrethrum, which is from
Tanacetum cinerariifolium (see p.381).
CULTIVATION Well-drained soil in sun. Dislikes
wet winters.
PROPAGATION By seed sown in autumn; by
softwood cuttings in spring or early summer.
HARVEST Roots are lifted in autumn, then dried
and powdered or made into decoctions,
pastilles, and tinctures.

◼ *Anacyclus pyrethrum* (pellitory, pellitory of
Spain)
Low, rosette-forming perennial with finely
divided, grey-green leaves, 10–14cm (4–5½in)
long. Solitary, daisy-like flowers, 2.5–5cm
(1–2in) across, are produced on 30cm (12in)
stalks. They have yellow centres and white ray
petals with a red stripe below. Native to Spain,
Algeria, and Morocco. ‡30cm (12in), ↔25–30cm
(10–12in). var. *depressus* has a low-growing,
compact habit and white ray petals with red
undersides. ‡ 2.5–5cm (1–2in), ↔ 10cm (4in).
HARDINESS Frost hardy.
PARTS USED Roots.
PROPERTIES A pungent acrid herb that
stimulates the salivary glands and irritates the
tissues, thereby increasing blood flow to the area.
MEDICINAL USES Externally for toothache,
facial neuralgia, and chronic catarrh.
CULINARY USES Essential oil from roots is used
in liqueurs.
🕮 ◼ ✎

Anacyclus pyrethrum

ANAGALLIS
Pimpernel

Primulaceae

A genus of 20 species of low-growing annuals,
biennials, and perennials found all over the
world. *Anagallis arvensis* (scarlet pimpernel) is
a common weed of cultivated ground. The scarce,
blue-flowered variety was once thought to be the
female form of the scarlet pimpernel. *Anagallis*
is from the Greek *anagelas*, "to laugh", from its
use in treating depression. Several of the common
names relate to weather forecasting: their
flowers open and close with changing light and
temperature. Once highly regarded as a medicinal
herb, with uses dating back to Pliny (AD23–79)
and Dioscorides, *A. arvensis* is now little used.
It contains irritant saponins, which research
shows have anti-viral effects, and cucurbitacins
(as found in *Bryonia*, see p.147), which are
highly toxic.
CULTIVATION Well-drained to dry or sandy soil
in sun. Aphids may attack plants under cover.
PROPAGATION By seed sown in spring at
16–18°C (61–64°F).
HARVEST Whole plants are gathered in summer
and used fresh, often as expressed juice, or
dried for infusions, liquid extracts, tinctures,
and powder.
⚠ **WARNING** Harmful if eaten.

◼ *Anagallis arvensis* (poor man's weatherglass,
scarlet pimpernel)
Prostrate annual or biennial with four-angled
stems, ovate to lanceolate leaves, 1cm (½in) long,
and star-shaped, salmon-red flowers, 5mm (¼in)
across, often with purple centres, throughout
summer. Native to Europe. ‡2.5–5cm (1–2in),
↔ 15–30cm (6–12in). ◼ var. *caerulea* (blue
pimpernel) has gentian-blue flowers.
HARDINESS Fully hardy.
PARTS USED Whole plant.
PROPERTIES An acrid mucilaginous herb that
lowers fever and has diuretic and expectorant
effects.
MEDICINAL USES Traditionally prescribed
internally for depression, tuberculosis, liver
complaints, epilepsy, dropsy, and rheumatism.
No longer considered safe by most medical

Anagallis arvensis

Anagallis arvensis var. *caerulea*

herbalists, but of interest to medical researchers. Externally, as pimpernel water, for improving the complexion, especially for freckles.

▨ ▣

ANANAS
Pineapple

Bromeliaceae

A genus of five or six species of rosette-forming, spiny perennials found in a range of habitats in S America. Unlike most bromeliads, which grow epiphytically, members of this genus are terrestrial. The pineapple was cultivated by native S Americans long before European explorers reached the New World. Pineapple fruits were given to Christopher Columbus by Guadeloupe islanders on 4 November 1493. Plants were taken to Madagascar in 1548, and to India in 1590, and then to all parts of the tropics. The fruits became so popular that, on large estates during Victorian times, sunken "pine pits", filled with decaying manure, were constructed for their cultivation to ensure year-round production for the table. These special glasshouses were often 30m (100ft) long and 9m (28ft) wide, containing 600 plants. Pineapple plants are ornamental and are commonly sold as houseplants, though they need higher temperatures and humidity to fruit well, and the spiny foliage is hazardous in confined areas. The main medicinal constituent of pineapple is bromelain, an enzyme that breaks down protein, thus aiding digestion. Bromelain is also strongly anti-bacterial; research shows that it controls digestive infections in intensively reared livestock.

CULTIVATION Well-drained, humus-rich, sandy soil, in sun and high humidity.

PROPAGATION By basal offsets in early summer; by cutting off the "leafy" top of a fruit and allowing it to dry for a day or two before inserting in a mixture of damp peat substitute and either sand or perlite, at 21°C (70°F).

HARVEST Fruits are cut when unripe or ripe, and used fresh or pressed for juice. Bromelain is extracted commercially from stems and foliage for food supplements, tablets, and capsules.

Ananas comosus

■ *Ananas comosus* (pineapple)
Evergreen perennial with a rosette of stiff, slightly recurved, spine-edged leaves, to 1m (3ft) long. An oblong–ovoid inflorescence, 15–30cm (6–12in) long, consisting of pink-flushed bracts and violet-pink flowers, is followed by a golden-yellow, often red-flushed, compound fruit, topped by a tuft of sterile bracts. Native to Brazil. ‡1m (3ft), ↔ 50cm (20in). 'Variegatus' syn. var. *variegatus* has cream-striped, often red-flushed leaves.

HARDINESS Min. 15°C (59°F).

PARTS USED Fruits, stems, leaves.

PROPERTIES An acidic, cooling, soothing herb that improves digestion, has diuretic, laxative, and anthelmintic effects, and acts as a uterine tonic.

MEDICINAL USES Internally, especially in Ayurvedic medicine, for dyspepsia, flatulence, poor digestion, excessive stomach acid (juice of unripe or ripe fruits), menstrual problems (juice of unripe fruits), constipation, and intestinal parasites (juice of foliage). Juice of unripe fruits and foliage is not given to pregnant women because it stimulates the uterus and may cause miscarriage. Bromelain aids digestion (especially of proteins) and controls *E. coli* and other digestive infections.

CULINARY USES Fruits are eaten raw, cooked, candied, or juiced. Young shoots and flower spikes are eaten as a vegetable in producer countries.

ECONOMIC USES Source of bromelain, used in digestive supplements; also for tenderizing meat, clarifying fruit juices, and in the baking and brewing industries.

▨ ▨ ▨ ▣ ✎ ✎ ▣

ANDROGRAPHIS

Acanthaceae

This genus includes 20 species of annuals, perennials, and shrubs distributed in tropical Asia. *Andrographis paniculata* is common in hedgerows on the plains of India and has a long history of use in Ayurvedic medicine. Some of the common names applied to it in India mean "king of bitters"; the entire plant is intensely bitter. In India it is used as a household remedy for fever, notably in Bengal, where the juice from the leaves is mixed with *Cuminum cyminum* (cumin), *Pimpinella anisum* (aniseed), and *Amomum subulatum* (greater cardamom) to make a medicine known as *alui*. *Andrographis echioides* from S India is also used to lower fever. In Vietnam, *A. paniculata* is used in folk medicine as a tonic after childbirth. In Malaysia, where it is known as *hempedu bumi*, it is regarded as a remedy for cardiovascular disease, skin problems, and snake bite. Though not traditionally used in Chinese medicine, *A. paniculata* was described in a herbal published during the Maoist Cultural Revolution as a substitute for *Coptis chinensis* (see p.179).

CULTIVATION Moist, well-drained soil in sun or partial shade and high humidity.

PROPAGATION By seed sown in spring at 18°C (65°F).

HARVEST Leaves and whole plants are collected as required and used fresh in infusions or as juice. Roots are harvested from mature plants for decoctions and tinctures.

■ *Andrographis paniculata* syn. *Justicia paniculata* (*kariyat*)
Upright annual with four-angled stems and smooth narrow leaves, 3–8cm (1¼–3in) long. Panicles of small, tubular, two-lipped, white flowers, with pink to purple markings inside the lower lip, appear in summer, followed by capsules containing numerous seeds. Native to India, S China, Vietnam, Malaysia, and Indonesia. ↔ 30–90cm (1–3ft).

HARDINESS Min. 13–15°C (55–59°F).

PARTS USED Leaves, whole plant, roots.

PROPERTIES An extremely bitter herb that acts as a tonic and alterative. It lowers fever, relieves intermittent fever, improves appetite and digestion, expels intestinal parasites, and has anti-bacterial effects.

MEDICINAL USES Internally for malaria, influenza, syphilis, liver and digestive problems, and dysentery.

▨ ▨ ▨ ▣ ▣

Andrographis paniculata

ANEMARRHENA

Asphodelaceae

The only member of its genus, *A. asphodeloides* resembles an asphodel in appearance, as its name suggests, and is night-flowering. This attractive plant has potential as an ornamental, but is little known in the West. Though neither widespread nor common, it has largely been collected in the wild for medicinal use. *Anemarrhena asphodeloides* was first recorded in traditional Chinese medicine c.AD200. It contains steroidal saponins, including asphonin, that has proven anti-pyretic effects. China is aiming to establish it as a cultivated crop.

CULTIVATION Moist soil in partial shade.
PROPAGATION By division in spring.
HARVEST Rhizomes are lifted in autumn and dried for use in decoctions.

Anemarrhena asphodeloides

Rhizomatous perennial with linear leaves, 20cm (8in) long and 5cm (2in) wide. Small, yellow-white, six-petalled, night-scented flowers are borne in spikes, 1m (3ft) tall, from late summer to autumn, followed by globose capsules, containing one or two triangular black seeds. Native to Japan and N China. ‡45cm–1m (1½–3ft), ↔ indefinite.

HARDINESS Frost hardy.
PARTS USED Rhizomes (*zhi mu*).
PROPERTIES A bitter, mucilaginous, tonic herb that has expectorant and diuretic effects, lowers fever, reduces blood sugar levels, and clears bacterial and fungal infections.
MEDICINAL USES Internally for high fever in infectious diseases, tuberculosis, chronic bronchitis, and urinary problems. Not given to patients with diarrhoea. Excess may cause a sudden drop in blood pressure. Externally as a mouthwash for mouth ulcers. Therapeutic action is slightly altered by cooking with wine or salt.

ANEMONE

Anemone hepatica. See *Hepatica nobilis*.
Anemone pulsatilla. See *Pulsatilla vulgaris*.

ANEMOPSIS

Saururaceae

A genus of one species of herbaceous perennial that occurs in SW USA and Mexico. Though found in arid regions, *A. californica* grows in marshy ground near springs and water courses, thriving in wet clay, alkaline bogs, and saline swamps where few other plants can survive. Though seldom seen in cultivation, it is an excellent subject for the bog garden, or for containers in ponds. It has a long tradition of use in its homelands among Pueblo Indians and people of Spanish descent, and was regularly used by Eclectic physicians and homeopaths in the early 20th century. Towards the close of the 20th century, *A. californica* came to notice as a possible substitute for *Hydrastis canadensis*

Anemopsis californica

(goldenseal) when the latter became increasingly scarce and expensive.

CULTIVATION Constantly moist to wet soil, including heavy clay, in full sun.
PROPAGATION By separation of rooted plantlets that form along the stolons, or by seed sown when ripe in pots of compost that should be stood in water.
HARVEST Roots are dug at any time (though most potent when dormant), wilted, then sliced into small sections and dried for tinctures and powder. Leaves are picked at any time for infusions.

■ *Anemopsis californica* (swamp root, *yerba del manso*, *yerba mansa*)
Low-growing perennial, with a camphor–eucalyptus aroma, that forms large colonies by means of stolons (runners), each plant with broadly elliptic leaves, about 15cm (6in) long, often with a reddish tint to the stalks and margins. Anemone-like flowers, with a conical centre and white, petal-like bracts, appear singly on stalks to 55cm (22in) long, in summer. Native to SW USA and Mexico. ‡15cm (6in), ↔ indefinite.

HARDINESS Fully hardy.
PARTS USED Roots, leaves.
PROPERTIES A healing, diuretic, anti-inflammatory herb with anti-bacterial and anti-fungal effects.
MEDICINAL USES Internally for peptic and duodenal ulcers, cystitis, urethritis, arthritis, and amoebic dysentery. Externally for slow-healing wounds, boils, anal fissure, nappy rash, and muscular or joint aches and pains. Leaves are much weaker than roots but work well for healing baths and washes.

ANETHUM

Dill

Apiaceae

There are two species in this genus, widely distributed in warm parts of Eurasia. *Anethum graveolens* (dill) resembles fennel but is a more slender plant with a single, easily uprooted stem, and a matte, rather than shiny, appearance. Its grey-green leaves have a strong parsley–caraway smell. Dill has been an important medicinal herb in the Middle East since Biblical times; the Talmud (ancient Jewish law) records that it was subject to a tithe. Numerous uses were described by Pliny (AD23–79), and various European writers from the 10th century onwards. According to Culpeper (*The English Physician Enlarged*, 1653), "It stays the hiccough, being boiled in wine … and is used in medicines that serve to expel wind, and the pains proceeding therefrom". Dill also has a long history of both culinary and medicinal use in India. Indian dill, or *satapashpi*, formerly classed as a subspecies of *A. graveolens*, is now considered a separate species, *A. sowa*. It is slightly taller than dill, reaching 1.2m (4ft), and has a white stem and very finely divided leaves. Containing less carvone, it also differs in flavour. The leaves are use to flavour rice and soups, and the pungent seeds are an ingredient of curry powder.

CULTIVATION Well-drained, neutral to slightly acid soil in sun. Dill bolts (flowers prematurely) if overcrowded or in poor dry soil. It should not be grown near fennel because the two may hybridize, producing plants intermediate in flavour and appearance. Dill reputedly has an adverse effect on carrots, but it is beneficial to cabbage if planted nearby. The flowers attract many beneficial insects that prey on aphids.
PROPAGATION By seed sown in spring or summer, thinned to 20cm (8in) apart. For a regular supply of leaves, make successive sowings every 3–4 weeks from early spring to midsummer.
HARVEST Leaves are cut in spring and summer for using fresh or dried. Seeds are gathered in summer and dried for making infusions and concentrated dill water. They are also ground into powder, and distilled for oil.

■ *Anethum graveolens* syn. *Peucedanum graveolens* (dill)
Annual or biennial with usually only one upright hollow stem and glaucous leaves, to 35cm (14in) long, divided into thread-like segments. Umbels of tiny yellow flowers are produced in summer, followed by oval, flattened, aromatic seeds. Native to SW Asia; naturalized in Mediterranean regions and parts of N America. ‡60–90cm

Anethum graveolens

121

A

Anethum graveolens 'Mammoth'

(24–36in), ↔ 15–30cm (6–12in). 'Bouquet' has a bushy habit, blue-green leaves, and compact prolific seed heads. Widely considered the best for seed production. 'Dukat' is vigorous and slow to bolt, with finely flavoured, blue-green leaves. 'Fernleaf' is dwarf and well branched, with luxuriant, dark blue-green foliage. It is slow to bolt; excellent for containers. ‡ 45cm (18in), ↔ 15–30cm (6–12in). 'Hercules' has abundant, flavourful, long-lasting foliage. ‡ 1–1.2m (3–4ft). ■ 'Mammoth' is vigorous, with relatively few, rather green leaves. It quickly runs to seed, with large seed heads; considered best for pickling. ‡ 60–90cm (2–3ft), ↔ 15–30cm (6–12in).

HARDINESS Hardy.
PARTS USED Leaves, seeds, oil.
PROPERTIES A pungent, cooling, aromatic herb that calms and tones the digestive system, controls infection, and has diuretic effects.
MEDICINAL USES Internally for digestive disorders, including indigestion, colic, gas (especially as an ingredient of gripe water for babies), and hiatus hernia.
CULINARY USES Both seeds and leaves are widely used in cooking, especially in Scandinavian cuisine, with eggs, fish, seafood, and potatoes. Sprigs of dill are added to pickles and vinegar; chopped dill is the main flavouring in gravlax (preserved salmon).
ECONOMIC USES Oil is used in proprietary medicines, soaps, detergents, and for flavouring in the food industry.

ANGELICA

Apiaceae

This genus of about 50 biennials and perennials is native to temperate parts of the northern hemisphere. *Angelica* is from the medieval Latin *herba angelica*, "angelic herb", from a belief that it would protect against evil and cure all ills. Its connection with the Feast of the Annunciation and the Archangel Michael may indicate pagan origins, taken over into Christian customs. *Angelica archangelica* became popular in Europe during the 15th century and was rated as the most important of all medicinal herbs by Parkinson (*Paradisi in Sole*, 1629). *Angelica polymorpha* var. *sinensis* (commonly referred to as *A. sinensis*) was first recorded in Chinese medicine in about AD200. Known as *dong quai* or *dang gui*, it is probably the most important Chinese tonic after ginseng and is an ingredient of many Chinese patent medicines in Hong Kong, San Francisco, and Singapore, as well as in China. A number of other angelicas are used in similar ways throughout the world, including: *A. atropurpurea* (American angelica); *A. sylvestris* (European wild angelica); the Chinese *A. anomala*, *A. keiskei*, and *A. pubescens*; and the Indian *A. glauca*. The tonic properties are thought to be highest in *A. glauca* and *A. polymorpha* var. *sinensis*. Known as *choraka* in Ayurvedic medicine, angelicas of various kinds are used mainly as a tonic for women, and are often combined with *Asparagus racemosus* (see p.135). All angelicas contain furanocoumarins, which increase skin photosensitivity and may cause dermatitis.
CULTIVATION Rich moist soil in sun or partial shade. Removing the flower heads before seed develops will prolong the life of short-lived species. The flowers attract many beneficial insects that prey on garden pests.
PROPAGATION By seed sown *in situ* in autumn or spring. Seed is viable for one year only but most plants tend to self-sow freely.
HARVEST Roots are lifted in autumn, leaves gathered before flowering, and seeds harvested as they ripen; all are dried for decoctions. Stalks of *A. archangelica* are cut in early summer.
⚠ **WARNING** Skin allergen.

■ *Angelica archangelica* (angelica)
Robust aromatic biennial or short-lived perennial with thick hollow stems and long-stalked, deeply divided leaves, to 60cm (2ft) long. Tiny, green-white flowers appear in umbels, to 25cm (10in) across, in early summer, followed by ovate ridged seeds. Found in N and E Europe, to Greenland and C Asia. ‡ 1–2.5m (3–8ft), ↔ 1.2m (4ft).
HARDINESS Fully hardy.
PARTS USED Leaves, stems, roots, seeds, oil.
PROPERTIES A bittersweet, aromatic, anti-inflammatory herb that relaxes spasms, increases perspiration, lowers fever, and has expectorant effects. It acts mainly on the bronchial, digestive, urinary, and female reproductive systems.
MEDICINAL USES Internally for digestive problems, including gastric ulcers, anorexia, and migraine sickness (for which it may be combined with *Chamaemelum nobile*, see p.164), bronchitis, catarrh, and influenza (combined with *Achillea millefolium*, see p.99, or *Tussilago farfara*, see p.395), poor circulation (notably Buerger's disease), chronic fatigue, menstrual and obstetric problems. Not given to pregnant women or to patients suffering from diabetes. Externally for rheumatic pain, neuralgia, and pleurisy.
CULINARY USES Foliage is eaten like celery in Greenland and Scandinavia. Young stalks are candied for decorating cakes and other desserts, or may be added to stewed rhubarb, jams, and marmalade. Flower buds, which are enclosed by sheaths, are eaten raw in salads or cooked.
ECONOMIC USES Essential oil from roots and seeds is used to flavour ice creams, confectionery, cordials, vermouth, vodka, and liqueurs. It gives the characteristic flavour to Benedictine.

■ *Angelica polymorpha* var. *sinensis* syn. *A. sinensis* (Chinese angelica, *dong quai*)
Perennial with a short rhizome, upright stems, and pinnately divided, grey-green, often purple-flushed leaves, 20–30cm (8–12in) long. Greenish flowers are produced in umbels in late summer, followed by elliptic notched seeds. Native to E Asia. ‡ 75cm–1.5m (2½–5ft), ↔ 38–90cm (15–36in).
HARDINESS Fully hardy.
PARTS USED Roots (*dong quai*).
PROPERTIES A bittersweet aromatic herb that acts primarily as a tonic, especially for the female reproductive system and liver. It is also a mild laxative, sedative, and painkiller, with some anti-bacterial activity.
MEDICINAL USES Internally for menstrual, postpartum, and menopausal complaints, and anaemia. Not given to pregnant women. Also used as an injection into acupuncture points, for painful injury, neuralgia, angina, and arthritis. Chicken soup with angelica root is a popular Chinese folk remedy after childbirth. An ingredient of the popular tonic *shou wu chih*.

Angelica archangelica

Angelica polymorpha var. *sinensis*

ANIBA
Lauraceae

Forty species of evergreen trees and shrubs make up this genus, which is found in tropical American and West Indian rainforests, with one species in India. Several are used for essential oils, hardwood timber, and medicinal compounds. Native peoples use some species medicinally. Commercially, the most important is *A. roseaodora*, which has been exploited since 1875, when a Frenchman first distilled its exquisite fragrant oil, known as *bois de rose* or rosewood oil. First harvested from the wild in French Guiana, where supplies are now exhausted, stocks are currently taken from the understorey of rainforests in Brazil. One or two plantations have been established, but little natural regeneration takes place. The need for urgent research into the life cycle and cultivation requirements of this rainforest tree was recognized by the Food and Agriculture Organization of the United Nations (FAO) in 1986.
CULTIVATION Moist, well-drained soil in shade, with high humidity.
PROPAGATION By seed sown when ripe; needs light to germinate. Seeds are difficult to harvest.
HARVEST Trees are cut when 10–15 years old and chipped for steam-distillation of oil.

Aniba roseaodora (cara-cara, pau rosa)
Aromatic evergreen tree with a slender habit and leathery elliptic leaves, about 14cm (5½in) long, which have downy, yellow-brown undersides. Insignificant flowers are borne in downy, dull red panicles, to 18cm (7in) long, at various times of the year. Native to Amazonia and the Guianas. ‡ 25m (80ft), ↔ 15m (50ft).
HARDINESS Min. 15–18°C (59–64°F).
PARTS USED Wood, oil.
PROPERTIES Rich in linalol, a volatile oil with a lily fragrance.
ECONOMIC USES Timber is an important hardwood. Oil is used to flavour confectionery, frozen desserts, chewing gum, and baked goods, and to scent pharmaceutical products, detergents, and perfumes.

ANTENNARIA
Cat's ears, catsfoot, pussy-toes
Asteraceae

Approximately 45 species of small, evergreen or semi-evergreen, woolly perennials make up this genus, which is distributed throughout most temperate and warm regions except Africa. The genus name refers to the fluffy appendages on the seeds that resemble insects' antennae. *Antennaria dioica* and its cultivars are popular in rock gardens. Although *A. dioica* is the only species in the genus with widespread use as a medicinal herb, several species in the closely related genus *Gnaphalium* (see p.227) feature in traditional medicine. *Antennaria dioica* was formerly classified as *Gnaphalium dioica*.

Antennaria dioica

CULTIVATION Well-drained soil in sun.
PROPAGATION By seed sown in spring; by division in spring.
HARVEST Whole plants or flower heads are cut before the flowers are fully open, and dried for use in infusions.

■ *Antennaria dioica* (cat's ears, catsfoot, life everlasting, pussy-toes)
Mat-forming, aromatic perennial with grey-green, spoon-shaped leaves, to 4cm (1½in) long. White to pale pink flowers, about 7mm (½in) across, are borne in clusters on upright stalks in late spring and early summer. Native to Europe, N America, and N Asia. ‡ 5–20cm (2–8in), ↔ 25–45cm (10–18in). 'Nyewoods' has a compact habit and pink flowers. ↔ 20cm (8in). ■ 'Rosea' has pink flowers. ‡ 10–15cm (4–6in), ↔ 25cm (10in).
HARDINESS Fully hardy.
PARTS USED Whole plant, flowers.
PROPERTIES An astringent aromatic herb that has diuretic effects and stimulates the liver and gall bladder.

Antennaria dioica 'Rosea'

MEDICINAL USES Internally for liver and gall bladder complaints, hepatitis, and diarrhoea. Externally as a gargle for tonsillitis and a douche for vaginitis.

ANTHEMIS
Asteraceae

This genus includes approximately 100 species of annuals and perennials that mostly form mats or clumps. The majority have finely cut, aromatic foliage and a long flowering period, making them rewarding subjects for the garden. *Chamaemelum nobile* (chamomile) was once classified in this genus. *Anthemis tinctoria* is often grown in herb gardens and is important as a dye plant. It was used for dyeing Turkish carpets before synthetic dyes became popular.
CULTIVATION Well-drained soil in sun. Plants grown in shade or in areas with cloudy summers produce fewer pigments.
PROPAGATION By seed sown in spring; by division in spring; by basal cuttings in spring or late summer. Self-sows freely. Seedlings are fast-growing and flower in the first year.
HARVEST Flower heads are picked as they open and are then dried.

Anthemis nobilis. See *Chamaemelum nobile.*

■ *Anthemis tinctoria* (dyer's chamomile, golden marguerite, ox-eye chamomile)
Clump-forming perennial with upright stems and green, finely divided leaves, 4–7cm (1½–3in) long, which have grey downy undersides. Bright golden-yellow, daisy-like flowers, about 4cm (1½in) across, are produced on long stalks in summer. Native to Europe and W Asia. ‡↔ 60–90cm (2–3ft). 'E.C. Buxton' has lemon-yellow flowers. 'Kelwayi' has medium yellow flowers. ‡↔ 60cm (2ft). 'Sauce Hollandaise' has cream flowers.
HARDINESS Fully hardy.
PARTS USED Flower heads.
PROPERTIES Rich in pigments, including flavones (apigenin and luteolin), and flavonols (quercetagetin and patuletin).

Anthemis tinctoria

A

CULINARY USES Dried flower heads are used for tea.

ECONOMIC USES Used to dye wool a soft golden- or greenish-yellow.

⊠ ✓ ✓

ANTHOXANTHUM
Poaceae

A genus of 18 species of perennial grasses, native to Europe, temperate Asia, and Africa. The South African *A. drogeanum* is fragrant while flowering, whereas the scent of *A. odoratum* intensifies when cut and dried. *Anthoxanthum odoratum* is one of the first grasses to flower in Europe and temperate Asia, and is a major irritant to hay fever sufferers. The flowers are distinguished from most other grasses by having two stamens (not three) and yellow, rather than purple, anthers, hence the name *Anthoxanthum*, from the Greek *xanthos*, "yellow", and *anthos*, "flower". Several species in this genus produce the scent of new-mown hay, because of the coumarin glycosides they contain. These break down to dicoumarol if cut grass becomes damp or is fermented. Dicoumarol is a toxic compound, used in rat poison, but medicinally important as an anti-coagulant.

CULTIVATION Well-drained soil in sun. Can become invasive.

PROPAGATION By seed sown in spring; by division in autumn or spring.

HARVEST Flowers are cut as they open and dried for ornament or tinctures.

■ *Anthoxanthum odoratum* (sweet vernal grass) Tufted perennial grass with aromatic, short, narrowly lanceolate leaves and dense, compact, blunt flower spikes, up to 3cm (1¼in) long, from spring to summer. Native to Eurasia. ‡ 18–50cm (7–20in), ↔ 12–30cm (5–12in).

HARDINESS Fully hardy.

PARTS USED Flowers.

PROPERTIES An aromatic herb that stimulates the circulation and relieves pain and spasms.

MEDICINAL USES Internally, and as a nasal lotion, for hay fever. Externally for painful joints, chilblains, nervous exhaustion, and insomnia.

CULINARY USES Dried leaves can be used for tea.

ECONOMIC USES Dried flowers are added to floral arrangements and potpourris.

⊠ ■ ✓ ✓

ANTHRISCUS
Apiaceae

Annuals, biennials, and perennials make up this genus of 12 species, which is native to Europe, Asia, and N Africa. They are upright plants that resemble parsley in appearance. *Anthriscus cerefolium* (chervil) is one of the best herbs for containers in a cool shady position; it combines well with other shade-loving, culinary herbs, such as *Mentha suaveolens* 'Variegata' (pineapple mint, see p.278) and *Melissa officinalis* 'Aurea' (golden lemon balm, see p.274). Chervil is an indispensable culinary herb that has been used since Roman times. Its medicinal uses are primarily as a "spring tonic" herb, but it is not widely used as such today. According to the herbalist Juliette de Baïracli Levy, it is good for "poor memory and mental depression" (*Herbal Handbook for Everyone*, 1972).

CULTIVATION Rich, light, moisture-retentive soil in partial shade. For a winter crop in cold areas, chervil may be protected with cloches, grown under cover, or grown in a cold frame. It bolts in high temperatures and dry sunny positions. Chervil is reputed to give radishes a sharper flavour if planted beside them. May protect lettuce from ants and aphids, and repel slugs.

PROPAGATION By seed sown at intervals of 3–4 weeks from early spring to early autumn, and thinned to 20cm (8in) apart. Seeds are viable for about a year.

HARVEST Leaves are cut before flowering and usually used fresh. If storage is required, it is better to freeze than to dry them.

■ *Anthriscus cerefolium* (chervil) Aromatic biennial, often grown as an annual, with hollow furrowed stems and delicate, bright green, finely divided leaves, to 15cm (6in) long, that have a subtle anise flavour. Umbels of tiny white flowers are borne in summer, followed by linear fruits. Native

to Europe and W Asia. ‡ 30–60cm (12–24in), ↔ 23–30cm (9–12in).

HARDINESS Fully hardy.

PARTS USED Leaves.

PROPERTIES A bitter aromatic herb that acts as a cleansing tonic, especially for liver and kidney functions, and as an expectorant.

MEDICINAL USES Internally for fluid retention, rheumatism, eczema, and jaundice. Externally for conjunctivitis, inflamed eyelids, and also for haemorrhoids.

CULINARY USES Leaves are added to dishes based on potatoes, eggs, or fish, especially in French cuisine. It is an essential ingredient of *ravigote* sauces and *fines herbes*. The delicate anise flavour does not withstand drying or prolonged cooking; chervil is therefore usually added just before serving. It is also used raw in salads and as a garnish, in sprigs or finely chopped. Flowers and roots are also edible.

✓ ■ ✓

APHANES
Rosaceae

This genus of 20 annuals is closely related to *Alchemilla* (see p.110) and widely distributed in Europe, the Mediterranean, Ethiopia, C Asia, Australia, and N America. *Aphanes arvensis* may be grown as an edging for paths, in gravel, between paving stones, or on walls. Its common names, "parsley piert" (from the French *perce-pierre*) and "breakstone parsley", probably arose from the plant's medicinal uses. Once used as a salad herb and pickled for winter use, *A. arvensis* is rarely eaten today, although it remains important as a medicinal herb.

CULTIVATION Well-drained soil in sun or partial shade. *Aphanes arvensis* tolerates gravelly or stony soils, and acidic and alkaline conditions.

PROPAGATION By seed sown in spring. Plants usually self-sow.

HARVEST Plants are cut when flowering in early summer and used fresh, or dried for infusions, liquid extracts, and tinctures. May also be frozen.

■ *Aphanes arvensis* (breakstone parsley, parsley piert)
Radiating, near-prostrate annual with hairy,

Anthoxanthum odoratum

Anthriscus cerefolium

Aphanes arvensis

fan-shaped, pale green leaves, to 1cm (½in) long. Clusters of minute green flowers appear in summer. Native to Europe, N Africa, and N America. ‡ 2.5cm (1in), ↔ 20cm (8in).
HARDINESS Hardy.
PARTS USED Whole plant.
PROPERTIES An astringent herb that has diuretic effects, and soothes irritated or inflamed tissues.
MEDICINAL USES Internally for kidney and bladder stones, and chronic kidney and liver disorders. Often combined with *Agathosma* spp. (see p.106) or *Cytisus scoparius* (see p.189) for kidney and bladder complaints, and with *Althaea officinalis* (see p.117) to increase demulcent effect for kidney stones.

APIUM

Apiaceae

Perennials, annuals, and biennials are included in this genus of 20 species, which occur in Europe, N America, temperate Asia, and Antarctic regions. *Apium graveolens* (wild celery) has been used as a food and flavouring since earliest times. It was mentioned frequently in ancient Egyptian texts, and garlands made from celery leaves, alternating with blue water lily petals, were found in tombs dating from about 1000BC. *Apium* is the Latinized form of the Celtic *apon*, "water", referring to the natural habitat of the genus, and *graveolens* means "strong-smelling", since all parts have a characteristic strong smell of celery. The cultivated celery var. *dulce*, with its pale succulent stems and mild flavour, was developed during the 17th century in Italy and became popular in the rest of Europe and N America in the 19th century.
CULTIVATION Rich damp soil in a sheltered position in sun or partial shade. Tolerates saline soils. *Apium graveolens* is less prone to pests and diseases than the cultivated variety, but may be damaged by slugs, celery-fly maggots, celery leafspot, and mosaic virus. It fruits better in a warm climate.
PROPAGATION By seed sown in spring at 13–16°C (55–61°F). Seeds sold for cultivation as a vegetable may be treated with fungicides and should not be used for medicinal purposes.
HARVEST Whole plants are harvested when fruiting and liquidized to extract the juice. Roots are dug in autumn and used fresh, or dried for use in tinctures. Seeds are collected as they ripen, and dried for infusions, liquid extracts, and powders, or distilled for oil.

■ *Apium graveolens* (smallage, wild celery)
Strongly aromatic biennial with a bulbous fleshy root, solid grooved stems, and pinnately divided leaves to 50cm (20in) long. Umbels of tiny, green-white flowers are followed by small, grey-brown, ridged seeds. Native to Europe, SW Asia, and N Africa. ‡ 30cm–1m (1–3ft), ↔ 15–30cm (6–12in).
HARDINESS Fully hardy.
PARTS USED Whole plant, roots, seeds, oil.
PROPERTIES An aromatic, bitter, tonic herb that reduces blood pressure, relieves indigestion,

Apium graveolens

stimulates the uterus, and has diuretic and anti-inflammatory effects. Sedative and aphrodisiac effects have also been reported.
MEDICINAL USES Internally for osteo-arthritis, rheumatoid arthritis, gout, and inflammation of the urinary tract. Externally for fungal infections and tumours (oil). It is often combined with *Guaiacum officinale* (see p.229) and *Menyanthes trifoliata* (see p.278) for rheumatic complaints, and with *Taraxacum officinale* (see p.382) to increase its potency. Internally in Ayurvedic medicine for asthma, bronchitis, hiccups, and wind, and as a stimulating nerve tonic. Not given to pregnant women.
CULINARY USES Wild celery is rarely used for culinary purposes because of its bitterness – and toxicity in large amounts – although the seeds may be used in small quantities to flavour soups and stews, or mixed with dehydrated salt.

APOCYNUM

Apocynaceae

Nine poisonous perennials with milky sap are included in this genus, which occurs in N America, E Europe, and Asia. The N American *A. cannabinum* is found on sandy or gravelly soils, especially near water, and is occasionally grown as an ornamental for its striking forked fruits. It is a good subject for the wild garden in N America, being a food plant for milkweed caterpillars. The flowers are pollinated by monarch butterflies. Both *A. cannabinum* and *A. androsaemifolium* are used medicinally, their similar properties being well known to native N Americans long before they were listed in the *Dispensatory of the United States* as "a substitute for digitalis in the treatment of chronic heart disease". The two species may be difficult to identify in the wild as they hybridize, producing atypical offspring.
CULTIVATION Well-drained, moist soil in sun or partial shade. May be invasive.
PROPAGATION By seed sown in autumn; by division in autumn or spring. Seeds require stratification for successful germination.

Apocynum cannabinum

HARVEST Rootstock is lifted in autumn after the plant has seeded, and dried for decoctions, liquid extracts, powders, and tinctures.
⚠ **WARNING** Toxic if eaten.

■ *Apocynum cannabinum* (black Indian hemp, Canadian hemp, dogbane)
Rhizomatous perennial with ovate to lanceolate, pointed leaves, to 15cm (6in) long. Small, green-white, bell-shaped flowers appear in terminal clusters in summer, followed by forked fruits to 20cm (8in) long. Native to NE USA and Canada. ‡↔ 60cm–1.2m (2–4ft).
HARDINESS Fully hardy.
PARTS USED Rhizomes, roots.
PROPERTIES An unpleasantly bitter, stimulant, irritant herb that acts on the heart, respiratory and urinary systems, and the uterus. It has diuretic and expectorant effects, increases perspiration, and causes vomiting.
MEDICINAL USES Internally for heart failure, intermittent fevers, and tumours. Used by the Cherokee for kidney failure. Externally for venereal warts and alopecia. For internal use by qualified practitioners only.
⚠ **WARNING** This herb is subject to legal restrictions in some countries.

AQUILARIA

Thymelaeaceae

A genus of 15 species of tropical shrubs and trees, native to India and Malaysia. *Aquilaria malaccensis*, found in primary forest at low and medium altitudes, is believed to be the aloes of the Bible. According to legend, all trees are descended from a single shoot of it, taken by Adam from the Garden of Eden. The heartwood, known as "agallochum", contains a dark resin (*chuwar*, or *agar attar*) with an odour similar to sandalwood. Known as *jinkoh* in Japan, it is a highly prized and very costly ingredient of incense. *Aquilaria malaccensis* is valued throughout Asia for its decorative, fine-grained, aromatic wood. It also has a long history of use in traditional Chinese, Ayurvedic, and Unani medicine. Similar species include the Chinese *A. sinensis*, which is cultivated as a substitute

Aquilaria malaccensis

for *A. malaccensis*, and *A. crassna* from Cambodia.

CULTIVATION Well-drained, humus-rich soil in partial shade, with ample humidity. Saplings are planted out when 60–80cm (24–32in) tall, in a shady site.

PROPAGATION By seed sown when ripe at 19–25°C (66–77°F). Seeds are short-lived and take 15–30 days to germinate.

HARVEST Heartwood and bark are taken from trees at least 50 years old, and dried for decoctions or distilled for resin.

■ *Aquilaria malaccensis* syn. *A. agallocha* (aloewood, eaglewood, lignin aloes)
Evergreen tree with a smooth pale trunk and thin, leathery, pointed, narrowly oblong leaves, 7–12cm (3–5in) long. Umbels of insignificant, bell-shaped, green to dull yellow flowers are followed by capsules containing red hairy seeds. Native to Malaysia. ‡ up to 40m (130ft), ↔ 3–12m (10–40ft).

HARDINESS Min. 15–18°C (59–64°F).

PARTS USED Bark, wood, resin.

PROPERTIES An astringent, stimulant, tonic herb that relieves spasms, especially of the digestive and respiratory systems, and lowers fevers.

MEDICINAL USES Internally for digestive and bronchial complaints, fevers, and rheumatism (bark, wood).

CULINARY USES Used in Malaysia to flavour curries.

ECONOMIC USES Used for perfumery and incense (resin). Wood is carved as settings for precious stones.

▨ ▣ ▧ ☑ ✎ ▨

ARALIA

Araliaceae

Deciduous or evergreen trees, shrubs, lianas, and rhizomatous perennials make up this genus of about 40 species, distributed through S and E Asia, and N America. *Aralia* is a Latinized version of *aralie*, an old French–Canadian name for these plants. Several shrubby species are grown for their large, exotic-looking, compound leaves. *Aralia racemosa* is a handsome plant,

Aralia nudicaulis

suited to woodland conditions, as is the less ornamental *A. nudicaulis*. These N American aralias were adopted as medicinal herbs by settlers, who learned their uses from native tribes. The Ojibwa made poultices of *A. racemosa* and *Asarum canadense* (see p.134) for fractured limbs. The former was also used as a tea to ease childbirth and for menstrual irregularities. Various tribes took *Aralia nudicaulis* for coughs. *Aralia spinosa* (Hercules club) and *A. hispida* were also used as tonics and to increase perspiration. *Aralia cordata* (Japanese asparagus, *udo*) has lemon-flavoured, new shoots that are blanched and eaten in salads and soups. In traditional Chinese medicine, *A. chinensis* (Chinese angelica tree) is used as a warming, painkilling herb for rheumatoid arthritis.

CULTIVATION Rich moist soil in partial shade.

PROPAGATION By seed sown in spring; by division in spring.

HARVEST Rootstock is lifted in autumn and dried for use in liquid extracts, decoctions, infusions, powders, and poultices.

■ *Aralia nudicaulis* (wild sarsaparilla)
Rhizomatous perennial producing a single, pinnately divided leaf annually. Tiny, green-white flowers are borne in umbels in late spring and early summer, followed by purple-black berries. Native to central and eastern N America. ‡ 15–40cm (6–16in), ↔ 15–30cm (6–12in).

HARDINESS Fully hardy.

PARTS USED Roots.

PROPERTIES A tonic, diuretic, cleansing herb that lowers fever.

MEDICINAL USES Internally for coughs and in blood-purifying tonics. Externally for boils, arthritis, and swellings. Important in homeopathy for cystitis.

CULINARY USES An ingredient of home-made root beer. Also used for tea.

▨ ▣ ☑

■ *Aralia racemosa* (American spikenard, life-of-man)
Rhizomatous perennial with aromatic rootstock and compound leaves, to 75cm (30in) long. Tiny, green-white flowers are borne in umbels in summer followed by purple to brown fruits. Native to N America. ‡ 1–2.2m (3–7ft), ↔ 60cm–2m (2–6ft).

HARDINESS Fully hardy.

PARTS USED Rhizomes, roots.

PROPERTIES A sweet, pungent, tonic herb that acts as an alterative. It also lowers fever and has diuretic and expectorant effects.

MEDICINAL USES Internally for bronchial complaints, rheumatic disorders, gout, skin disease, and blood poisoning. Combines well with *Inula helenium* (elecampane, see p.243) or *Mentha × piperita* (peppermint, see p.277). Externally for sores, wounds, and inflammations. Regarded as a rejuvenative in Ayurvedic medicine.

CULINARY USES Roots have a liquorice flavour, used in root beer. Berries are made into jelly.

▨ ▣ ☑

Aralia racemosa

ARCTIUM

Asteraceae

Occurring widely in temperate Eurasia, this genus consists of about ten species of upright biennials. *Arctium lappa* (burdock) is an imposing plant for the wild garden. *Arctium* is from the Greek *arktos*, "bear", after the rough-coated fruits. The common name "burdock" refers to the fruits (burs), and the large, dock-like leaves. The specific epithet *lappa*, from the Latin *lappare*, "to seize", describes how the burs cling to passing animals. *Arctium lappa* has a number of variants, some of which are classed as different species. The various kinds are used similarly in traditional European medicine. Burdock is cultivated as a vegetable in Japan, where it is known as *gobo*.

CULTIVATION Moist, neutral to alkaline soil in sun or light shade.

PROPAGATION By seed sown in spring. Burdock self-sows freely.

HARVEST Young leaf stalks are cut in spring for use as a vegetable. Roots are lifted in autumn and used fresh as a vegetable or dried for use in decoctions, liquid extracts, tablets, and tinctures. Ripe seeds are collected for use in decoctions.

■ *Arctium lappa* (beggar's buttons, burdock, lappa)
Robust biennial with stout taproots and long-stalked, ovate leaves, to 50cm (20in) long. Purple, thistle-like flowers, to 4cm (1½in) across, are followed by fruits covered in hooked spines, containing beige seeds. Native to Europe and W Asia. ‡ 1.5m (5ft), ↔ 1m (3ft). 'Takinogawa Long' is the most popular cultivar in Japan, with non-fibrous roots, 75–90cm (30–36in) long.

HARDINESS Fully hardy.

PARTS USED Stems, roots, seeds (*niu bang zi*).

PROPERTIES An alterative herb, with bitter foliage and sweet mucilaginous roots, that reduces inflammation and controls bacterial infection. Seed extracts have been shown to lower blood sugar levels.

MEDICINAL USES Internally for

Arctium lappa

skin diseases and inflammatory conditions owing to chronic toxicity (notably eczema, psoriasis, rheumatism, gout, boils, and sores). Often combined with *Rumex crispus* (see p.351) or *Trifolium pratense* (see p.392). In traditional Chinese medicine the seeds are used for similar purposes and to treat colds, pneumonia, and throat infections.

CULINARY USES Stalks of young leaves are scraped and cooked like celery. Roots are eaten raw in salads, cooked like carrots, or added to stir-fries. An ingredient of *kinpira* (burdock root and carrot), pickles, and *tekka* (miso-based condiment) in Japan, and of *namul*, a Korean vegetable dish.

ARCTOSTAPHYLOS

Bearberry

Ericaceae

About 50 species of hardy, deciduous or evergreen shrubs and small trees make up this genus that occurs mainly in western N America. *Arctostaphylos uva-ursi* (bearberry) is widely distributed on acidic, scrubby, rocky, and sandy areas. It is a fast-growing shrublet that can be grown on the rock garden, and on banks to control erosion. The name is from the Greek *arkton staphyle*, "bear's grapes"; the fruits are an important food for bears. Bearberry contains hydroquinones, notably arbutin, which is strongly anti-bacterial. It is effective against a number of pathogens, including *E. coli* and *Staphylococcus aureus*.

CULTIVATION Moist, peaty or sandy, acid (pH5) soil in sun or partial shade.

PROPAGATION By seed sown fresh into a mixture of peat and sand in the autumn; by layering of long branches in early spring; by semi-ripe cuttings with a heel in summer. Dipping seed in boiling water for 20 seconds before sowing speeds germination.

HARVEST Leaves are picked individually at any time during spring and summer, and dried for use in infusions, liquid extracts, medicinal tea bags, and tablets.

■ *Arctostaphylos uva-ursi* (bearberry, mountain box, uva-ursi)
Mat-forming, evergreen shrub with rooting branches and obovate, dark green leaves, about 6cm (2½in) long. Racemes of white, pink-flushed flowers appear from early spring, followed by glossy, spherical, red fruits. Native to N Eurasia and N America. ‡ 10–15cm (4–6in), ↔ 30cm–1.2m (1–4ft). 'Vancouver Jade' has a low arching habit, with glossy foliage and pink flowers. ‡ 15cm (6in), ↔ 45cm (18in).

HARDINESS Fully hardy.

PARTS USED Leaves.

PROPERTIES An astringent, anti-bacterial herb that is an effective urinary antiseptic, possibly with some diuretic action.

MEDICINAL USES Internally for urinary infections (especially cystitis) and vaginitis. Needs alkaline urine to work, therefore acidic fruits and juices may be excluded from the diet

Arctostaphylos uva-ursi

during treatment. Often combined with *Althaea officinalis* (see p.117), *Elymus repens* (see p.201), *Zea mays* (see p.410), and *Agathosma* spp. (see p.106). Recently found useful in treating cystitis in paraplegics (a recurrent condition, frequently resistant to conventional antibiotics). Contains irritant substances and is not given to pregnant women, children, or to patients with kidney disease.

ARECA

Areca palm

Arecaceae

Some 50–60 species of tall evergreen palms belong to this genus, which occurs in India, Malaysia, Australia, and the Solomon Islands. The seeds of *A. catechu* (betel nut palm) have been chewed as a stimulant in India, Pakistan, and SE Asia since ancient times; trees are widely cultivated for the purpose in all these areas. The hard seed is sliced, mixed with a piece of lime and spices, wrapped in a leaf of *Piper betle* (betel pepper, see p.320), and chewed. Elaborately decorated cutters and repositories are used to prepare and store the betel quids. Betel nuts contain tannins and alkaloids, which stimulate saliva flow, accelerate heart and perspiration rates, and suppress hunger, while offering positive protection against intestinal worms. They also possess a pigment that turns the saliva red and blackens the teeth. Chewing the seeds is now discouraged since it is thought to be a possible cause of oral cancer.

CULTIVATION Moist, well-drained soil in sun, with high humidity.

PROPAGATION By seed sown in spring at 24–27°C (75–81°F).

Areca catechu

HARVEST Fruits are collected when ripe and dried for use in decoctions and liquid extracts, or as a powder.

■ *Areca catechu* (areca palm, betel nut palm, pinang)
Slender palm tree with a grey-green trunk and pinnate leaves, to 2m (6ft) long. Pale yellow flowers are produced in panicles about 60cm (24in) long, on trees aged six years or more, followed by yellow to orange or scarlet, egg-shaped fruits, containing one acorn-sized seed. Native to SE Asia. ‡20m (70ft), ↔ 4m (12ft).
HARDINESS Min. 16°C (61°F).
PARTS USED Fruit rind (*da fu pi*), seeds (*bing lang*).
PROPERTIES An astringent stimulant herb that relieves hunger, abdominal discomfort, and weariness. Kills intestinal parasites and other pathogens and has diuretic and laxative effects.
MEDICINAL USES Mainly in veterinary medicine to expel tapeworms. Internally, in traditional Chinese medicine, to destroy intestinal parasites, and for dysentery and malaria (seeds); as a laxative in constipation with flatulence and bloating, and as a diuretic in oedema (rind). Excess causes profuse salivation, vomiting, and stupor.
⚠ **WARNING** This herb is subject to legal restrictions in some countries.
▨ ▨ ▪ ▣

ARISAEMA
Jack-in-the-pulpit

Araceae

This genus contains about 170 species of tuberous or rhizomatous perennials that are widely distributed in Asia, from arid regions to the tropics and the Himalayas, and also in

N America and E Africa. These plants have unusual blooms, handsome foliage, and colourful fruits, making striking specimen plants for shady borders. In common with other members of the aroid family (Araceae), arisaemas contain crystals of calcium oxalate, which cause irritation to the mouth and throat if the plants are eaten raw, and to the eyes on accidental contact. In traditional Chinese medicine three different preparations are made from the corms of *A. consanguineum*: *tian nan xing* (sun-dried); *shi nan xing* (cooked with raw ginger); and *dan nan xing* (processed with ox bile). In China the term *nan xing* refers to the corms of several species, including those of *A. amurense* and *A. heterophyllum*, which have similar properties to *A. consanguineum*. The herb entered Chinese medicine at a late date, being first mentioned in 1765, during the Qing dynasty. Although poisonous when fresh, *A. triphyllum* was eaten by native N Americans, who destroyed the toxins by either roasting the tubers or pounding them with water before drying them to make flour. *Arisaema triphyllum* varies greatly in size and appearance, and some botanists regard the main variants as separate species, such as *A. atrorubens* and *A. stewardsonii*, or as subspecies.
CULTIVATION Moist, well-drained, humus-rich soil in dappled shade. Corms rot if too wet or cold. New foliage may be damaged by frosts.
PROPAGATION By seed sown in autumn or spring; by offset corms removed when dormant.
HARVEST Corms are lifted in autumn or in winter when plants are dormant, and dried for decoctions.
⚠ **WARNING** All parts are harmful if eaten. Irritant to skin, eyes, and mucous membranes.

■ *Arisaema consanguineum* (dragon plant)
Perennial with a rounded tuber, mottled stalk, and a solitary, compound leaf, composed of 11–20 leaflets, to 40cm (16in) long. The inflorescence consists of a white- and brown-

Arisaema consanguineum

Arisaema triphyllum

striped, green, hooded spathe, about 12cm (5in) long, and a green spadix, followed by a pendent cluster of scarlet fruits. Found from the E Himalayas to N Thailand, C China, and Taiwan. ‡1m (3ft), ↔ 30cm (12in).
HARDINESS Frost hardy.
PARTS USED Corms (*nan xing*).
PROPERTIES An acrid irritant herb that acts as an expectorant and relaxes convulsions. Research indicates possible anti-cancer effects.
MEDICINAL USES Internally for coughs with profuse phlegm, tumours, cervical cancer, epilepsy, tetanus, and complaints involving convulsions and spasmodic twitching.
▨ ▪

■ *Arisaema triphyllum* (Indian turnip, Jack-in-the-pulpit)
Perennial with globose tubers, blotched stalks, and 1–2 trifoliate leaves, composed of pointed ovate leaflets, 8–17cm (3–7in) long. A hooded, striped, green to purple spathe and spadix appear in spring, followed by red berries. Native to eastern N America. ‡↔ 15–60cm (6–12in).
HARDINESS Fully hardy.
PARTS USED Corms.
PROPERTIES An acrid antiseptic herb that has expectorant effects and increases perspiration.
MEDICINAL USES Internally, a traditional native N American remedy for asthma, whooping cough, and bronchitis. Externally for rheumatism, boils, and snake bite. Native people use dried aged roots, because these are less acrid but maintain their activity. The Pawnee and Hopi used dried powdered roots, taken in water, as a contraceptive, inducing permanent sterility by increasing the dose and water temperature.
CULINARY USES After slicing, drying, and storing to reduce acridity, corms yield a cocoa-flavoured flour for baking.
▨ ▪ ▨

A

ARISTOLOCHIA
Birthwort, Dutchman's pipe, snakeroot
Aristolochiaceae

This genus consists of some 300 species of poisonous, evergreen and deciduous, twining vines, shrubs, scramblers, and herbaceous perennials that occur in temperate and tropical regions in many parts of the world. Many of the climbing species are grown for their attractive foliage and intriguing, foul-smelling flowers. The name *Aristolochia* is derived from the Greek *aristos*, "best", and *lokhia*, "childbirth", referring to the main medicinal use for postpartum infections. As the common name "snakeroot" suggests, aristolochias are also used to treat snake bite. These uses may have originated in the medieval Doctrine of Signatures, which regarded the colour or shape of a herb as a sign of its purpose. The flowers of *Aristolochia* were seen to resemble a curved foetus or a snake. *Aristolochia clematitis* has a long history of use in childbirth, being recorded in ancient Egyptian times. It closely resembles *Asarum canadense* (see p.134) in its properties and uses. *Aristolochia debilis* was first mentioned in ancient Chinese medical texts in about AD600. *Aristolochia serpentaria* was valued by native N Americans as a remedy for snake bite. It was introduced into European medicine in the 17th century as a remedy for the bites of snakes and rabid dogs. Following modern research into its medicinal properties, it enjoyed a vogue during the 1970s and 1980s, resulting in over-collection from the wild. Various other species are used medicinally, including *A. indica* (Indian birthwort), an Ayurvedic herb, used to induce abortion; *A. fangchi* (*fang chi*, *guang fang ji*), a Chinese arthritis remedy; *A. bracteata* (*ukulwe*), used in both India and tropical Africa; the N American *A. longa*; and *A. rotunda*, a S European species. Aristolochia contains aristolochic acid, which can cause liver and kidney damage. In Chinese medicine, the same name may be used for several different plants, as it refers to the drug, not the species. Often, the drug is obtained from several quite different species. Following serious adverse reactions to a dieting preparation containing aristolochic acid, a ban was imposed by several countries in 2000 on the use of *Aristolochia* spp., together with various other species, such as *Akebia*, *Clematis*, *Cocculus*, and *Stephania*, that may be substituted for *Aristolochia* or contaminated with aristolochic acid.
CULTIVATION Well-drained soil in sun or partial shade. Thin out previous year's growths or cut back to two or three nodes in late winter. Aphids, whitefly, and spider mite may damage foliage of plants under cover.
PROPAGATION By seed sown in spring at 13–16°C (55–61°F); by semi-ripe cuttings in summer; by division in early spring or autumn; by layering in autumn.
HARVEST Roots are harvested in autumn, and fruits collected when ripe, and dried for liquid extracts, decoctions, powders, and tinctures. Oil is distilled from dried roots (*A. serpentaria*).
⚠ **WARNING** Toxic if eaten.

Aristolochia clematitis

◾ *Aristolochia clematitis* (birthwort, heartwort) Fetid perennial with a long creeping rhizome, upright stems, and heart-shaped leaves, 6–15cm (2½–6in) long. Clusters of 3–8 erect, tubular, yellow-green flowers appear in summer, followed by pear-shaped capsules. Native to C and S Europe. ‡↔ 20–85cm (8–34in).
HARDINESS Fully hardy.
PARTS USED Roots.
PROPERTIES An aromatic tonic herb that stimulates the uterus, reduces inflammation, controls bacterial infection, and promotes healing.
MEDICINAL USES Internally for gynaecological and obstetric disorders. A toxic herb, prescribed in small doses for short-term use only and not given during pregnancy. For use by qualified practitioners only. Externally for skin infections and diseases, and wounds (especially snake or insect bites).
⚠ **WARNING** This herb is subject to legal restrictions in some countries.
🔲 🔳

Aristolochia debilis (frail birthwort, long birthwort)
Scrambling perennial with branching, dark purple stems and narrowly ovate–triangular leaves, 4–7cm (1½–3in) long and 5cm (2in) wide. Solitary, slender, yellow-green flowers appear in the axils during summer, followed by globose capsules. Native to China and Japan. ‡↔ 1m (3ft).
HARDINESS Frost hardy.
PARTS USED Roots (*qing mu xiang*), fruits (*ma dou ling*).
PROPERTIES A herb with painkilling and anti-inflammatory effects (roots). It also lowers blood pressure, controls coughing, relaxes bronchial spasms, and acts as an expectorant (fruits).
MEDICINAL USES Internally for arthritis, purulent wounds, hypertension, snake and insect bites, and gastric disorders involving bloating

(roots); also for asthma, wet coughs, bronchitis, hypertension, and haemorrhoids (fruits). For use by qualified practitioners only.
⚠ **WARNING** This herb is subject to legal restrictions in some countries.
🔲 🔳 ▪

Aristolochia serpentaria (serpentary, Virginia snakeroot)
Perennial with upright zigzag stems and thin, heart-shaped leaves, 4–15cm (1½–6in) long. Solitary or clustered, brown-purple, S-shaped flowers, about 1cm (½in) long, appear at the base of the plant in early summer, followed by hard capsules, 1cm (½in) across. Native to E and S USA. ‡↔ 10–45cm (4–18in).
HARDINESS Frost hardy.
PARTS USED Roots, oil.
PROPERTIES A bitter, aromatic, tonic herb that induces perspiration, is anti-inflammatory, and acts as a diuretic.
MEDICINAL USES Internally for rheumatism, gout, arthritis owing to fevers, pneumonia, typhoid, and malaria. Externally for pleurisy, herpes, and slow-healing wounds. Included in proprietary tonics for the circulation, skin, and kidneys. For use by qualified practitioners only.
ECONOMIC USES Essential oil, similar to ginger and valerian in odour, is used to flavour alcoholic drinks.
⚠ **WARNING** Subject to legal restrictions in some countries.
🔲 🔳 ▪ ✎

ARMENIACA
Armeniaca mume. See *Prunus mume.*

ARMORACIA
Brassicaceae

Three species of tall, taprooted perennials make up this genus, found in Eurasia and E USA. *Armoracia rusticana* (horseradish) appears to have entered cultivation relatively recently, perhaps less than 2000 years ago. It was primarily a medicinal plant and did not become popular as a flavouring until the late 16th century. *Armoracia* is the original Latin name for the related wild radish. John Gerard (*The Herball, or Generall Historie of Plantes*, 1597) commented that "the Horse Radish stamped with a little vinegar put thereto, is commonly used among the Germans for sauce to eate fish with and such like meates as we do mustarde". By the mid-17th century both Britain and France had acquired the taste for horseradish sauce, which today is popular worldwide.
CULTIVATION Well-drained, rich soil, in sun or partial shade. Old plants are prone to mosaic virus and leafspot. Horseradish is difficult to eradicate when established because bits of root left in the ground grow into new plants. It may protect potatoes from Colorado beetles.
PROPAGATION By division in autumn or early spring; by seed sown *in situ* in spring and thinned to 30cm (12in) apart.
HARVEST Leaves are picked in spring and used

Armoracia rusticana

fresh. Roots are lifted in autumn and used fresh for culinary purposes and in poultices and syrups, or macerated in vinegar and honey for medicinal use. They store well in damp sand.

▣ **Armoracia rusticana** syn.
A. lapathifolia, Cochlearia armoracia (horseradish)
Upright stout perennial with a thick branched taproot and ovate to oblong, toothed leaves, 30–50cm (12–20in) long. Tiny white flowers are produced in terminal racemes in early summer. Native to SE Europe; widely naturalized in Europe, N America, and New Zealand. ‡30cm–1.2m (1–4ft), ↔ 60–90cm (24–36in). ▣ 'Variegata' has white-variegated leaves.
HARDINESS Fully hardy.

Armoracia rusticana 'Variegata'

PARTS USED Leaves, roots.
PROPERTIES A very pungent, stimulant herb that controls bacterial infection and lowers fever by increasing perspiration. It is diuretic and irritates the tissues, causing improved circulation locally.
MEDICINAL USES Internally for general debility, arthritis, gout, sciatica, respiratory and urinary infections, and fevers characterized by coldness. Excess causes vomiting and may provoke allergic responses. Not given to patients with stomach ulcers or thyroid problems. Externally as a poultice for infected wounds, pleurisy, arthritis, and pericarditis.
CULINARY USES Young fresh leaves have a mild pleasant flavour, and are excellent in salads and sandwiches. Fresh root is grated alone, or with apple, as a condiment for fish, or with vinegar and cream to accompany roast beef, cold chicken, or hard-boiled eggs. In E Europe, horseradish is often mixed with beets as a condiment. Horseradish sauces may be gently warmed, but cooking destroys the volatile oils responsible for the pungency.
▨ ▨ ▪ ◪

ARNICA

Asteraceae

About 30 species of rhizomatous perennials make up this genus, found mostly in subalpine zones of the northern hemisphere. *Arnica montana* is an alpine species and difficult to grow well at low elevations. It needs a cool climate and dislikes wet winters, so in areas that do not have winter snow cover, plants do better on ridges or in raised beds. American species, such as *A. chamissonis* and *A. cordifolia*, are easier to grow and equally effective. Arnica has long been a popular remedy in Germany and Austria, especially for bruises, sprains, and heart complaints; Goethe (1749–1832) apparently took arnica tea in old age for angina. Research has proved both its therapeutic effects and its toxicity. It remains widely used in Germany for heart conditions, but is restricted to external use in the UK and ruled unsafe in the USA. Wild-collection of *A. montana* is restricted by law in most countries, because of over-collection.
CULTIVATION Well-drained, humus-rich, acid soil in a sunny position.
PROPAGATION By seed sown in autumn (stratification is required in mild areas); by division in spring.
HARVEST Flowers are picked when fully open, and dried for use in creams, infusions, liniments, and tinctures.

▣ **Arnica montana** (arnica, leopard's bane, mountain tobacco)
Aromatic rhizomatous perennial with a basal rosette of ovate hairy leaves, 5–17cm (2–7in) long. Golden-yellow, daisy-like flowers, 5cm (2in) across, appear in summer. Native to W Asia and Europe. ‡10–60cm (4–24in), ↔ 15cm (6in).
HARDINESS Fully hardy.
PARTS USED Flowers.

Arnica montana

PROPERTIES An aromatic, bitter, astringent herb that stimulates the immune system and heart, relieves pain and inflammation, and clears fungal and bacterial infections.
MEDICINAL USES Internally for the short-term treatment of heart failure and coronary artery disease. For use by qualified practitioners only. Externally in liniments, and creams (often combined with *Hamamelis virginiana*, see p.230) for dislocations, sprains, bruises, chilblains, and varicose ulcers, and as a throat gargle. May cause contact dermatitis when used externally, and collapse when taken internally. These side-effects are not present in homeopathic preparations to help healing after accidents.
⚠ **WARNING** This herb is subject to legal restrictions in some countries.
▨ ▪

ARTEMISIA
Mugwort, sagebrush, wormwood

Asteraceae

This is a genus of about 300 species of annuals, biennials, perennials, or subshrubs that grow wild in northern temperate regions, western S America, and South Africa. Many artemisias are grown as ornamentals for their finely cut, aromatic, often silver foliage, which makes excellent background material for arrangements and posies. They are easily cultivated, even on poor dry soils. Several are attractive border plants, especially for white gardens. *Artemisia abrotanum, A. absinthium* 'Lambrook Silver', and *A. arborescens* may be grown as informal hedges. *Artemisia annua* is a large but neat plant with handsome fragrant foliage, useful for filling gaps in the back of a border or providing contrast to smaller, more colourful plants. Used as an anti-malarial for 2000 years in the East, its active ingredient, artemisinin (*qinghaosu*), was isolated in 1972. Synthetics derived from *A. annua* are now the most promising anti-malarials for drug-resistant strains of the disease. Populations of *A. annua* in Vietnam have the highest concentration of artemisinin. Various artemisias are used medicinally and include some of the most bitter herbs known. *Artemisia abrotanum* (southernwood) has been cultivated since antiquity to repel insects and contagion. It was popular in nosegays (posies carried to ward off infection and unpleasant smells); until the 19th century, a bunch of southernwood and rue was placed in court to protect against the spread of jail fever from the prisoner. Another traditional use was as a cure for baldness: "The ashes [of southernwood] mingled with old salad oil helps those that have their hair fallen and are bald, causing the hair to grow again, either on the head or the beard" (Culpeper, *The English Physician Enlarged*, 1653). *Artemisia absinthium* (wormwood) has been a household remedy since Biblical times, its bitterness becoming a metaphor for the consequences of sin: "for the lips of a strange woman drop as an honeycomb, And her mouth is smoother than oil: But her end is bitter as wormwood" (Proverbs 5:3–4). The word absinthium means "without sweetness", and refers to the intensely bitter taste. Essential oil of wormwood was an ingredient in absinthe, an alcoholic aperitif first made by Henri Pernod in 1797. Consumption of absinthe became a serious problem in the 19th century, both in Europe and the USA. The use of wormwood oil as a flavouring was banned in various countries, beginning in 1908 with Switzerland, after the discovery that the thujone content is addictive, and in excess causes hallucinations and damage to the central nervous system. Ironically, the common name "wormwood" comes from the German *wermut*, "preserver of the mind", as the herb was thought to enhance mental functions. Today's successors to absinthe – anisette and vermouth – do not contain thujone, although absinthe liqueurs are enjoying a revival in

France, Italy, and Spain. *Artemisia dracunculus* (tarragon) used to be known as a dragon herb, a cure for poisonous stings and bites, hence the species name. *Artemisia dracunculus* subsp. *dracunculoides* (Russian tarragon) is similar in appearance but hardier, with a pungent, less pleasant flavour. *Artemisia vulgaris* (mugwort) was important in Druidic and Anglo-Saxon times, being one of the nine herbs used to repel evil and poisons. The common name is from the Anglo-Saxon *mucgwrt*, "midge plant", because of its use in repelling insects. It was known as the "Mother of Herbs" and was associated with witchcraft (old goddess religions) and fertility rites. On the Isle of Man mugwort is worn on the national day, 5 July (midsummer day in the Old Calendar), and is known as "Bollan bane". The herb is mentioned frequently in 1st-century AD Greek and Roman writings and appears in Chinese medical literature dating back to c.AD500. It was reputedly planted beside roads by the Romans for soldiers to put in their sandals on long marches. Both the plant and its reputation for soothing sore feet persisted: "if a footman take mugwort and put it into his shoes in the morning he may goe forty miles before noon and not be weary ..." (William Coles, *The Art of Simpling*, 1656). Other wormwoods with medicinal and culinary uses include: *A. afra*, used in S Africa for digestive and menstrual problems, and feverish illnesses; *A. anomala*, used externally in China for burns and inflamed skin; *A. apiacea*, a fragrant, biennial, Asian species, used to lower fever, control bleeding, and improve appetite; *A. asiatica*, used to flavour and colour Japanese glutinous rice dumplings (*yomogi-mochi*); *A. cina* (Levant wormseed, santonica), one of the oldest and most reliable, though extremely toxic

anthelmintics, especially for roundworms in children; *A. frigida*, used by the Hopi tribe in N America to flavour corn; *A. genipi* (spiked wormwood), an Alpine species used to flavour *eau d'absinthe*; *A. glacialis*, from the SW Alps, used to flavour liqueurs and vermouth; *A. judaica* (*semen contra, graines à vers*), a Middle Eastern condiment and flavouring for liqueurs; *A. pallens* (davana), a fragrant Asian species, used in perfumery, food flavouring, and ritual; *A. princeps* (Japanese mugwort, *yomogi*), an important flavouring herb in Japanese and Korean cuisines; and *A. tilesii*, an Arctic species with properties similar to codeine.

CULTIVATION Well-drained, neutral to slightly alkaline soil in sun. *Artemisia absinthium*, *A. a.* 'Lambrook Silver', and *A. ludoviciana* tolerate drought. *Artemisia capillaris* thrives in moist soil and tolerates saline conditions. *Artemisia lactiflora* prefers moist, neutral to acid soil, and tolerates light shade. Hardiness varies with species; cover marginally hardy plants with loose straw or over-winter plants under cover. In spring, cut back shrubby species near ground level, or remove dead stems and trim to shape. Rust may attack foliage.

PROPAGATION By seed sown in spring (annuals, perennials, and *A. dracunculus* subsp. *dracunculoides*); by semi-ripe cuttings with a heel in summer (shrubby species); by division in autumn or spring (perennials).

HARVEST Whole plants are cut when flowering; leaves are picked before flowering. All parts are dried for decoctions, infusions, powders, tablets, and tinctures, or oil extraction. *Artemisia. vulgaris* is pressed into moxibustion sticks. Stems (*A. lactiflora*, *A. ludoviciana*) are cut for decorative use as flowers open. Young shoots are cut in spring, and used fresh or

Artemisia absinthium

Artemisia absinthium 'Lambrook Silver'

Artemisia abrotanum

Artemisia arborescens

Artemisia annua

A

dried in decoctions.

⚠ **WARNING** Artemisias, and extracts from them, such as cineole and santonin, are subject to legal restrictions in some countries.

▣ *Artemisia abrotanum* (lad's love, old man, southernwood)
Semi-evergreen subshrub with pungently aromatic, grey-green, pinnately divided leaves, about 5cm (2in) long. Tiny, dull yellow flowers are borne in dense panicles in late summer; flowering does not occur in cool summers. Native to S Europe. ↨↔ 1m (3ft).
HARDINESS Fully hardy.
PARTS USED Leaves.
PROPERTIES A strongly aromatic, bitter herb that improves digestion and liver function, encourages menstrual flow and stimulates the uterus, lowers fever, relaxes spasms, and destroys intestinal worms. It is reputed to stimulate hair growth.
MEDICINAL USES Internally for delayed or painful menstruation (often combined with *Chamaelirium luteum*, see p.164), poor appetite and digestion, threadworms in children, and hair loss. Not given to pregnant women. Externally for frostbite, extracting splinters, sciatic pains, swellings, and hair loss.
ECONOMIC USES Leaves are used in sachets and powders to repel moths and fleas.
▣ ▣ ▣

▣ *Artemisia absinthium* (wormwood)
Subshrub with grey-green, deeply dissected leaves, 6–10cm (2½–4in) long, with silky hairs on both sides. Insignificant, yellow, globose flowers are borne in panicles in summer. Native to Europe and temperate Asia. ↨ 1m (3ft), ↔ 60–90cm (24–36in). ▣ 'Lambrook Silver'

has luxuriant silver-grey foliage. ↨ 75cm (30in).
HARDINESS Fully hardy.
PARTS USED Whole plant, leaves.
PROPERTIES An aromatic, diuretic, bitter herb that has anti-inflammatory effects and acts as a tonic for the liver, digestive system, and nerves. It stimulates the uterus and expels intestinal worms.
MEDICINAL USES Internally for digestion, poor appetite, gall bladder complaints, and roundworms. Taken in small doses for short-term treatment only. Not given to children or pregnant women. Externally for bruises and bites.
▣ ▣ ▣

▣ *Artemisia annua* (sweet Annie, sweet wormwood)
Fast-growing, giant annual with upright, often red stems and bright green, pinnately divided, saw-toothed leaves. Tiny yellow flowers appear in loose panicles in summer. Found from SE Europe to Iran. ↨ 1.5m (5ft), ↔ 1–1.5m (3–5ft).
HARDINESS Hardy.
PARTS USED Whole plant (*qing hao*).
PROPERTIES An aromatic, anti-bacterial herb that destroys malarial parasites, lowers fevers, and checks bleeding.
MEDICINAL USES Internally in Chinese medicine for feverish illnesses, notably malaria and heat stroke. Externally for nosebleeds, bleeding rashes, and sores. Synthetic anti-malarials have been developed from *A. annua* for treating drug-resistant strains, such as *Plasmodium falciparum*.
▣ ▣

▣ *Artemisia arborescens*
(tree artemisia, tree wormwood)
Aromatic, upright, evergreen shrub with finely

divided, silver-grey leaves, to 10cm (4in) long. Small yellow flowers appear in panicles, 30cm (12in) long, in summer and in early autumn. Native to the Mediterranean region. ↨ 1m (3ft) ↔ 1.5m (5ft).
HARDINESS Fully hardy (borderline).
PARTS USED Leaves.
PROPERTIES An aromatic herb.
ECONOMIC USES Leaves are used fresh or dried in herbal posies.
▣ ▣

▣ *Artemisia capillaris* (fragrant wormwood)
A much-branched subshrub with purple stems and finely divided, bright green, highly aromatic, silky leaves. Panicles of minute, purple-brown flowers are borne in late summer. Native to China, Korea, Japan, and the Philippines. ↨↔ 30cm–1m (1–3ft).
HARDINESS Frost hardy.
PARTS USED Leaves, young shoots (*yin chen hao*, *Herba Artemisiae*).
PROPERTIES A bitter, aromatic, diuretic herb that acts as a tonic for the liver and gall bladder, and lowers fever.
MEDICINAL USES Internally for feverish illnesses, jaundice, hepatitis, and gall bladder complaints.
▣ ▣ ▣

▣ *Artemisia caucasica* syn. *A. assoana*, *A. lanata*, *A. pedemontana*
Tufted, mat-forming, evergreen or semi-evergreen shrublet with silky, finely cut, fern-like, silver-green leaves. Loose panicles of tiny, globose, yellow flowers appear in summer. Found from C Spain to S Ukraine. ↨↔ 15–30cm (6–12in).
HARDINESS Fully hardy.
PARTS USED Leaves.
PROPERTIES An aromatic herb.

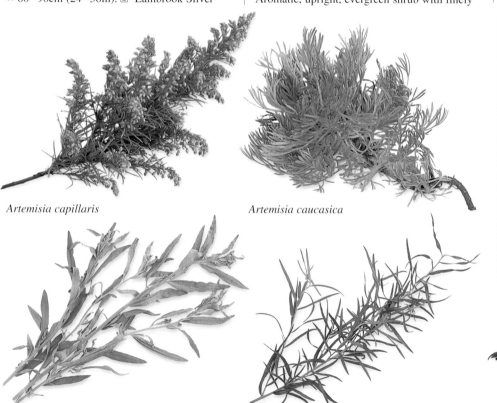

Artemisia capillaris

Artemisia caucasica

Artemisia dracunculus

Artemisia dracunculus subsp. *dracunculoides*

Artemisia lactiflora

ECONOMIC USES Leaves used fresh or dried in herbal posies.

■ *Artemisia dracunculus* (estragon, French tarragon, tarragon)

Aromatic perennial with upright branched stems and linear smooth leaves, 3–6cm (1¼–2½in) long, with a liquorice aroma. The tiny green flowers do not open or produce viable seed in cool summers. Native to SE Russia. ‡ 45cm–1m (1½–3ft), ↔ 30–38cm (12–15in). ■ subsp. *dracunculoides* (Russian tarragon) is hardier and more vigorous than the species, with narrower paler leaves. It sets seed more readily, and has a pungent, less pleasant flavour, said to improve in mature plants. ‡ 1.5m (5ft), ↔ 60cm (24in).
HARDINESS Fully hardy.
PARTS USED Leaves, oil.
PROPERTIES A bitter aromatic herb that stimulates the digestive system and uterus, and has diuretic, febrifugal, and anthelmintic effects.
MEDICINAL USES Internally for poor digestion, indigestion, and worms in children. Not given to pregnant women. Externally for rheumatism and toothache. In aromatherapy for digestive and menstrual problems.
CULINARY USES Leaves are used to flavour chicken, egg dishes, salad dressings, vinegar, mustard, and sauces, such as *béarnaise*, *béchamel*, and *tartare*. Popular in the form of a cordial, *tarhun*, in its native Georgia.
ECONOMIC USES Oil is used in commercial flavourings, perfumery, and detergents.

■ *Artemisia lactiflora* (white mugwort)

Vigorous, clump-forming perennial with pinnately divided, coarsely toothed, dark green leaves, 20–25cm (8–10in) long. Plumes of tiny, off-white flowers grow in late summer and autumn. Native to China. ‡ 1.2–1.5m (4–5ft), ↔ 60cm (24in). ■ Guizhou Group has white flowers, dark maroon stems, and young leaves. ‘Variegata’ has leaves variegated grey and green.
HARDINESS Fully hardy.
PARTS USED Leaves, flowering stems.
PROPERTIES A bitter, aromatic, tonic herb.
MEDICINAL USES A traditional Chinese remedy for menstrual and liver disorders.
ECONOMIC USES Leaves and flowering stems are used in herbal posies.

■ *Artemisia ludoviciana* syn. *A. palmeri*, *A. purshiana* (cudweed, Louisiana wormwood, western mugwort, white prairie sage)

Clump-forming, rhizomatous perennial with silver-green, lanceolate leaves, 10–12cm (4–5in) long, which are toothed or divided lower down the stem. Tiny, brownish-yellow flowers are borne in white-woolly panicles in summer and autumn. Native to western N America and Mexico. ‡ 60cm–1.2m (2–4ft), ↔ 60cm (24in). ■ ‘Silver Queen’ has larger leaves and flowers less freely. ‡ 75cm (30in). ‘Valerie Finnis’ has jagged, silver-grey leaves. ‡ 60cm (24in).
HARDINESS Fully hardy.
PARTS USED Leaves, flowering stems.
PROPERTIES An aromatic antiseptic herb.
MEDICINAL USES Internally in native N American medicine for tonsillitis and sore throats; externally for slow-healing sores, and as incense for ritual purification.
CULINARY USES Leaves and flower heads are used for tea and flavouring, especially in sauces, game, and pork.

■ *Artemisia pontica* (Roman wormwood, small absinthe)

Vigorous rhizomatous perennial with upright unbranched stems and finely cut, downy, grey-green leaves, about 4cm (1½in) long. Tiny, dull yellow flowers are produced in narrow panicles, 5–20cm (2–8in) long, in summer. Native to C and E Europe. ↔ 40–80cm (16–32in).
HARDINESS Fully hardy.
PARTS USED Leaves.
PROPERTIES Similar to *A. absinthium*, but milder.
ECONOMIC USES As a flavouring for wine (especially in Germany), bitters, cordials, and vermouth (notably Pontic vermouth).

■ *Artemisia* ‘Powis Castle’ syn. *A. arborescens* ‘Brass Band’

This dwarf, non-flowering, silver-leafed artemisia is possibly a hybrid between *A. absinthium* and *A. arborescens*. It is more compact than *A. absinthium* ‘Lambrook Silver’. ‡ 60cm (24in), ↔ 90cm (3ft).
HARDINESS Frost hardy.
PARTS USED Leaves.
PROPERTIES An aromatic herb.
ECONOMIC USES Leaves are used fresh or dried in herbal posies.

■ *Artemisia vulgaris* (Chinese moxa, felon herb, mugwort)

Aromatic perennial with red-purple stems and deeply cut, dark green leaves, 5–8cm (2–3in) long, with white undersides. Panicles of tiny, red-brown flowers appear in summer. Native to northern temperate regions. ‡ 60cm–1.7m

Artemisia lactiflora Guizhou Group

Artemisia pontica

Artemisia vulgaris

Artemisia ludoviciana

Artemisia ludoviciana ‘Silver Queen’

Artemisia ‘Powis Castle’

Artemisia vulgaris ‘Variegata’

(2–5½ft), ↔ 30cm–1m (1–3ft). 'Oriental Limelight' has yellow-variegated foliage. ■ 'Variegata' has white-flecked foliage.

HARDINESS Fully hardy.

PARTS USED Leaves (*ai ye*).

PROPERTIES A bitter, aromatic, tonic herb that acts as a digestive stimulant, diuretic, and nerve tonic, and increases perspiration. It stimulates the uterus and expels intestinal parasites.

MEDICINAL USES Internally for depression with loss of appetite, dyspepsia, threadworm and roundworm infestations, and menstrual complaints (in the West mainly to encourage menstruation; in the East to control uterine bleeding and threatened miscarriage). In traditional Chinese medicine the compressed dried leaf, known as *moxa*, is burned briefly on the skin to warm the acupuncture points in cases of internal cold. Used mainly in Ayurvedic medicine for the female reproductive system, nervous complaints, and as a wash for fungal infections. Not given internally to pregnant or lactating women.

CULINARY USES One of the more palatable wormwoods, used in traditional recipes (especially in the UK, Germany, and Spain) in dishes of eels or carp, and in stuffings for geese, duck, pork, and mutton. Used in China and Japan to flavour and colour rice cakes and dumplings. Dried leaves and flowering tops used for tea.

▨ ▪ ⊿

ASARUM
Wild ginger

Aristolochiaceae

Found widely through northern temperate zones, but centred on Japan, this genus consists of 70 or more rhizomatous, deciduous or evergreen perennials. Wild gingers are mostly woodland plants with a creeping habit and ginger-like smell. Their foliage resembles that of cyclamens; it is mainly for this feature that several species are popular in rock gardens and as ground cover. Several *Asarum* spp. are used medicinally as stimulating warming remedies. In addition to *A. canadense*, these include *A. europaeum* (asarabacca) from N and E Europe, which has expectorant, emetic, and purgative properties, and *A. sieboldii* (Chinese wild ginger), which is often combined with *Ephedra* (see p.201) for colds and chills. Characteristically, asarums contain aristolochic acid, which can cause liver and kidney damage (see *Aristolochia*, p.129), and asarone, a carcinogenic substance also found in *Acorus calamus* (see p.101). As a consequence, medicinal use of asarums is subject to legal restrictions in some countries.

CULTIVATION Well-drained, moist soil, enriched with leafmould, in a shady sheltered site.

PROPAGATION By seed sown when ripe; by division in early spring.

Asarum canadense

HARVEST Sections of rhizome are removed in autumn, and dried for powders, decoctions, liquid extracts, and tinctures.

■ *Asarum canadense* (wild ginger)
Evergreen prostrate perennial with a slender rhizome, smelling strongly of ginger, and dark green, hairy, heart-shaped leaves, 5–20cm (2–8in) across. Urn-shaped, purple-brown flowers on short stalks are borne near ground level in spring. Native to eastern N America. ↕ 8cm (3in), ↔ 60cm (24in).

HARDINESS Fully hardy.

PARTS USED Rhizomes.

PROPERTIES A bitter, pungent, aromatic, antibiotic herb that stimulates the digestive and respiratory systems and uterus, and increases perspiration. It acts as a diuretic, expectorant, and decongestant.

MEDICINAL USES Internally for coughs, asthma, chills, and rheumatic disorders. Women of the N American Pomo tribe take wild ginger as a contraceptive, and in Western medicine it is used to regulate menstruation and as a stimulant in difficult labour (but not in earlier stages of pregnancy). The Ojibwa tribe combined it with *Aralia racemosa* (see p.126) in poultices for fractures. Not given to pregnant women.

CULINARY USES Ginger-flavoured rhizomes are candied or made into a syrup.

▨ ▪ ⊿

ASCLEPIAS
Milkweed, silkweed

Asclepiadaceae

This genus of about 120 species of tuberous annuals, perennials, shrubs, and subshrubs, some evergreen, is found mainly in N America and Africa. Several species are grown as border plants for their colourful flowers, and for pods that split open to show the silk-tufted seeds. *Asclepias* is named after Asklepios, the Greek god of medicine. *Asclepias tuberosa* is widely regarded as one of the finest plant expectorants. The common name "pleurisy root" refers to its primary role in treating pleurisy. It was used by native N Americans for over 1000 years before entering European pharmacopoeias in

Asclepias tuberosa

the 18th century. In Ayurvedic medicine, the leaves of the related *Tylophora indica* syn. *T. asthmatica* have been well researched as a remedy for asthma and other respiratory disorders. The root is a good substitute for *Cephaelis ipecacuanha* (see p.163).

CULTIVATION Dry, sandy, neutral to acid soil in sun. May be attacked by cucumber mosaic virus. *Asclepias tuberosa* is sensitive to disturbance.

PROPAGATION By seed sown in spring; by root cuttings in autumn or spring; by basal cuttings in spring.

HARVEST Roots are lifted in autumn and used fresh in a syrup or dried for compresses, powders, decoctions, ointments, and tinctures.

■ *Asclepias tuberosa*
(butterfly weed, pleurisy root)
Perennial with large tuberous roots, erect hairy stems, and narrowly oval leaves, 10–14cm (4–5½in) long. Clusters of orange-red flowers appear in summer, followed by slender seed pods, to 15cm (6in) long. Native to eastern and southern N America. ↕ 60–90cm (12–24in), ↔ 23–45cm (9–18in).

HARDINESS Fully hardy.

PARTS USED Roots.

PROPERTIES A bitter, nutty-flavoured tonic herb that increases perspiration, relieves spasms, and acts as an expectorant.

MEDICINAL USES Internally for pleurisy, bronchitis, pneumonia, asthma, dry cough, gastritis, eruptive fevers, rheumatic fever, feverish stages of colds and influenza, and uterine disorders. Excess causes diarrhoea and vomiting. Not given to pregnant women. Externally for bruises, wounds, ulcers, and rheumatism.

▨ ▪

ASPALATHUS

Fabaceae

A large genus of 255 leguminous, mostly spiny shrubs, found only in South Africa. In the 19th century they were cultivated as greenhouse shrubs for their attractive flowers. *Aspalathus linearis*, native to the arid Cedarberg Mountains in W Cape Province, is the source of rooibos tea, first recorded in 1772 by Carl Thunberg, a Swedish botanist, as a beverage drunk by the Hottentots. It is one of the few wild species to be developed as a crop in the 20th century. Tea made from the dried fermented leaves of *A. linearis* tastes similar to *Camellia sinensis* (common tea, see p.151), but it is less astringent, due to the lower tannin content. It is caffeine-free but has a higher fluoride content than common tea, which may help protect against tooth decay. Japanese research in the 1980s showed that rooibos contains a substance similar to the enzyme superoxide dismutase (SOD), an antioxidant compound thought to retard ageing.

CULTIVATION Acid sand, in full sun. Pinch out to encourage bushy growth. Cut plants back hard to control growths from old wood.

PROPAGATION By seed sown in spring.

HARVEST Plants are cut 35cm (14in) above ground, fermented, and sun-dried for use in infusions, liquid extracts, and lotions.

■ *Aspalathus linearis* syn. *A. contaminatus*, *Psoralea linearis* (red bush, rooibos)
Variable, upright to weeping shrub with red-tinged branches and linear, bright green leaves, which turn red-brown when dried. Tiny, yellow, pea flowers are borne in summer. Native to South Africa. ‡↔ to 2m (6ft).

HARDINESS Frost hardy.

PARTS USED Leaves, stems.

PROPERTIES An aromatic, pleasant-tasting, mildly astringent herb that benefits the digestion and relaxes spasms. It relieves some allergic symptoms and skin conditions.

MEDICINAL USES Internally for allergies, especially eczema, hay fever, and asthma in infants. Externally for skin infections and irritations.

Aspalathus linearis

CULINARY USES As a low-tannin, caffeine-free substitute for China/India tea, marketed as rooibosch, kaffree, or redbush tea. Also as a basis for soups, sauces, fruit drinks, and in baking. Extract is used locally in liqueur (*buchenbosch*) and schnapps.

▨ ▨ ▨ ▨

ASPARAGUS

Asparagaceae

This genus has about 100 species, distributed in temperate and subtropical parts of Eurasia. It includes hardy and tender, usually tuberous, perennials, shrubs, and climbers, all with feathery foliage. *Asparagus* is from a Greek word, corrupted into such common names as "spearage" and "sparrow grass". Various *Asparagus* spp. are used medicinally in similar ways. Most contain asparagin, a diuretic that gives the urine a characteristic odour in those who lack the gene to break it down. *Asparagus cochinchinensis* was first mentioned in Chinese medical texts c.AD200. *Asparagus officinalis* has been cultivated for over 2000 years as a vegetable and also as a medicinal herb for its potent diuretic effects. In common with many popular medicinal plants, it was given the name *officinalis* to recognize its status as an "officinal" – a plant with a long commercial history as a medicinal herb. The common name of *A. racemosus*, *shatavari*, means "she who possesses a hundred husbands", and refers to the herb's rejuvenative effect on the female reproductive organs.

CULTIVATION Rich, light, well-drained soil, in a sunny position. *Asparagus officinalis* is often purchased as a dormant, one-year-old, male "crown" and renewed after ten years. *Asparagus racemosus* may be grown as an annual in cold areas; protect under cover in winter. Asparagus beetle may attack young shoots and foliage.

PROPAGATION By seed in spring, sown at 16°C (61°F), thinned to 30cm (12in) apart, then to 1m (3ft) apart; by division in early spring.

HARVEST Young "spears" (shoots) of *A. officinalis* are cut in late spring from established plants when about 23cm (9in) high, then eaten fresh or juiced for medicinal purposes. Rhizomes and tubers are lifted when dormant and boiled before drying for decoctions and powders; those of *A. racemosus* are used fresh to treat dysentery, and dried for decoctions, powders, and medicated oils.

⚠ **WARNING** Berries are harmful if eaten.

■ *Asparagus officinalis* (asparagus)
Perennial with creeping rhizomes and upright stems that appear in spring as stout fleshy shoots. Dense, soft, needle-like foliage consists of cladodes (flattened, leaf-like stems). Small, green-white, bell-shaped flowers appear in summer, followed by red berries. Found in coastal sands and cliffs in Europe. ‡ 1–1.5m (3–5ft), ↔ 45–90cm (18in–36in). 'Conover's Colossal' is a strong-growing, early19th-century American cultivar with thick fleshy spears. 'Purple Passion' is vigorous, with large purple shoots.

Asparagus officinalis

HARDINESS Fully hardy.

PARTS USED Young shoots, rhizomes.

PROPERTIES A bitter, restorative, cleansing herb that acts on the bowels, liver, and kidneys. It contains asparagusic acid, which is nematocidal.

MEDICINAL USES Internally for cystitis, pyelitis, kidney disease, rheumatism, gout, and oedema from heart failure. Asparagusic acid is used to treat schistosomiasis.

CULINARY USES Spears are steamed and served hot or cold as a vegetable, and puréed or finely chopped in soups.

▨ ▨ ▨ ▨

■ *Asparagus racemosus* (*shatavari*)
Climbing rhizomatous perennial with leaves that are hardened at the base into spines, and foliage of pointed cladodes, 1–3.5cm (½–1¼in) long. Fragrant white flowers, to 5mm (¼in) across, are produced in summer, followed by red berries. ‡ 7m (22ft). Found in S and E Africa to Asia and N Australia.

HARDINESS Half hardy.

PARTS USED Rhizomes.

PROPERTIES A soothing tonic herb that acts mainly on the circulatory, digestive, respiratory, and female reproductive organs.

MEDICINAL USES Internally for infertility, loss of libido, threatened miscarriage, menopausal problems, hyperacidity, stomach ulcers, dysentery, and bronchial infections. Externally for stiffness in joints and neck. The most important herb in Ayurvedic medicine for women, as *ashwagandha* (see *Withania*

Asparagus racemosus

somnifera, p.408) is for men. Used internally by Australian Aboriginals for digestive upsets, and externally for sores.

ASPERULA
Asperula odorata. See *Galium odoratum.*

ASPIDIUM
Aspidium filix-mas. See *Dryopteris filix-mas.*

ASPIDOSPERMA
Apocynaceae

There are 80 or so species of evergreen trees in this S American genus. They have fine timber and a milky sap containing alkaloids. Those contained in *A. quebracho-blanco* include the aphrodisiac quebrachine or yohimbine, also present in the unrelated *Pausinystalia yohimbe* (see p.304). The medicinal bark of *A. quebracho-blanco* first reached Europe in 1878, having long been used medicinally by native S Americans as a febrifuge. *Quebracho*, the Spanish for "axe breaks", refers to the hardness of the wood. *Blanco*, "white", distinguishes it from *Schinopsis quebracho-colorado* (red quebracho), which is used as a mild digestive stimulant.
CULTIVATION Well-drained to sandy soil in sun.
PROPAGATION By seed sown when ripe.
HARVEST Bark is removed as needed and dried for alkaloid extraction or use in liquid extracts.

Aspidosperma quebracho-blanco (*naawa*, quebracho, white quebracho)
Tender evergreen tree with thick corky bark, pendulous young twigs, and leathery, elliptic to lanceolate, spine-tipped leaves. Fragrant, yellow, funnel-shaped flowers are produced in short branched clusters, followed by woody capsules that split open to release numerous winged seeds. Native to S America (mainly Argentina). ‡ 30m (100ft), ↔ 5–12m (20–40ft).
HARDINESS Min. 15–18°C (59–64°F).
PARTS USED Bark.
PROPERTIES A bitter tonic herb that stimulates the circulatory, respiratory, and genito-urinary systems, lowers fever, and relaxes spasms.
MEDICINAL USES Internally for asthma, bronchitis, emphysema, and feverish illnesses. Excess causes nausea and vomiting.
⚠ **WARNING** This herb is subject to legal restrictions in some countries.

ASTER
Michaelmas daisy

Asteraceae

About 250 species of rhizomatous and fibrous-rooted perennials, a few annuals and biennials, are included in this genus, widely distributed in N America, Africa, and Eurasia. *Aster novae-angliae* (New England aster) and several other species commonly grown as ornamentals, such as *A. ericoides* and *A. lateriflorus*, were used medicinally by native N American tribes. The use of *A. novae-angliae*, both internally and externally, as a remedy for eruptive skin diseases, and rashes caused by poison ivy and poison oak, was first described by Constantine Rafinesque in *Medical Flora or Manual of Medical Botany of the United States* (1828, 1830). *Aster tataricus* is cultivated in China for medicinal use but is rarely used in the West. It was first mentioned in Chinese medical literature c.AD200. The common name "Michaelmas daisy" was given

to *A. novi-belgii*, another N American species, when the Gregorian calendar was introduced, which brought Michaelmas forward by 11 days (to 29 September), the time of flowering.
CULTIVATION Moist soil in sun or partial shade. May suffer from mildew in dry conditions.
PROPAGATION By seed sown in autumn or spring; by division in spring.
HARVEST Roots are lifted in autumn and used raw, or dried for decoctions.

Aster tataricus (Tatarian aster)
Tall perennial with a thickened stem base and long-stalked, elliptic, roughly hairy leaves, up to 40cm (16in) long, with strongly toothed margins. Flat-topped corymbs of purple to blue, daisy-like flowers, about 5cm (2in) across, open in summer and autumn. Native to Siberia, Mongolia, Korea, China, and Japan. ‡ 1.5–2m (5–6ft), ↔ 1–1.2m (3–4ft).
HARDINESS Fully hardy.
PARTS USED Roots (*zi wan*).
PROPERTIES A stimulant expectorant herb that helps clear infection from the bronchial system.
MEDICINAL USES Internally for chronic bronchitis and tuberculosis. Often taken raw with honey to increase the expectorant effect.

ASTRAGALUS
Milk vetch

Papilionaceae

This large genus of about 2000 species of annuals, perennials, and shrubs is distributed throughout northern temperate zones. Milk vetches of various kinds are used as food and fodder crops in many parts of the world and also as a source of gums to make gel-forming substances. Some accumulate minerals, and are used as indicators in prospecting. Those toxic to livestock are known as "locoweeds". About 100 species are cultivated for their colourful spikes of flowers. Gum tragacanth is collected from at least 20 species, mainly *A. gummifer*, which has been the principal source since ancient Greek times. The roots of *A. membranaceus* provide traditional Chinese medicine with a tonic on a par with ginseng. *Astragalus membranaceus* var. *mongholicus* is used interchangeably. It is similar in appearance but prefers damper habitats. Also important in Chinese medicine is *A. complanatus* (*sha yuan*), which has been used in China as a liver and kidney tonic since the 12th century.
CULTIVATION Well-drained soil in sun. *Astralagus membranaceus* prefers sandy, slightly alkaline soil.
PROPAGATION By seed in spring or autumn.
HARVEST Gum is collected from second-year plants of *A. gummifer* by incising the stem base; it is dried for use as a powder. Roots of *A. membranaceus* are lifted in autumn and dried for decoctions, powders, and tinctures.

Astragalus gummifer (gum tragacanth, tragacanth)
Low, evergreen or semi-evergreen, umbrella-shaped shrub with spiny-stalked, pinnate leaves

divided into 4–7 pairs of elliptic leaflets, to 1cm (½in) long. Small, downy, white, pea flowers are produced in the axils in summer. Native to Kurdistan (Middle East). ↔ 30cm (12in).
HARDINESS Frost hardy.
PARTS USED Gum.
PROPERTIES A mucilaginous herb that stimulates the immune system and suppresses tumours.
ECONOMIC USES Used as a stabilizing and thickening agent (E413) in the food and pharmaceutical industries, in products such as salad dressings, ice creams, desserts, sauces, processed cheese, confectionery, and toothpaste.

▣ *Astragalus membranaceus* (*huang qi*, milk vetch, *pak kei*)
Sprawling perennial with pale yellow roots and alternate, downy, light green leaves, 3–8cm (1½–3in) long, divided into 12–18 pairs of leaflets. Racemes of pale yellow, pea-like flowers, 2cm (¾in) long, appear in early summer, followed by papery pods, 2.5cm (1in) long, containing dark brown, kidney-shaped seeds. Native to E Asia. ↕ 40–60cm (16–24in), ↔ 30–45cm (12–18in).
HARDINESS Fully hardy.
PARTS USED Roots (*huang qi*).
PROPERTIES A sweet, tonic, adaptogenic herb that stimulates the immune system, spleen, lungs, liver, circulatory and urinary systems, lowers blood pressure and blood sugar levels, and increases stamina.
MEDICINAL USES An important ingredient in many traditional Chinese formulas; combined with *Angelica polymorpha* var. *sinensis* (see p.122) for sensitivity to cold, poor circulation, and low energy, and with *Atractylodes macrocephala* (see next column) and *Ledebouriella seseloides* for allergies and frequent colds. Also for diabetes, kidney problems, prolapsed organs, anaemia, and slow-healing skin eruptions. Improves recovery and longevity in cancer patients undergoing chemotherapy or radiation treatment.
CULINARY USES Roots are eaten in rice porridge (congee) and tonic soups, often with chicken, and combined with *Codonopsis*

pilosula and *Angelica polymorpha* var. *sinensis*. Also as an ingredient of tonic teas and wines.

ATRACTYLODES
Asteraceae

Seven species of rhizomatous perennials belong to this genus, which is E Asian in distribution. All seven species are used in traditional Chinese medicine, the most important being *A. macrocephala*, which was first recorded in AD659 in the *Tang Materia Medica*. It is not common in the wild and is now grown on a large scale to satisfy demand. Botanical gardens in China are also researching the cultivation requirements of other species used similarly, such as *A. lancea*. In addition to its tonic properties, *A. macrocephala* is reputed to calm a restless foetus. *Atractylodes chinensis* is also widely used, mainly as a digestive tonic, and for glaucoma and night blindness.
CULTIVATION Well-drained soil in sun or partial shade.
PROPAGATION By seed sown in spring.
HARVEST Rhizomes are lifted in autumn and baked for use in tonics.

▣ *Atractylodes macrocephala* (*bai zhu*, Chinese thistle daisy)
Erect perennial with thick warty rhizomes, branched, woody-based stems, and divided, pointed, toothed leaves. Purple, thistle-like flowers, 3.5cm (1¼in) across, are produced in summer, followed by bristly seeds. Native to China, Japan, and Korea. ↕ 30–60cm (12–24in), ↔ 45cm (18in).
HARDINESS Fully hardy.
PARTS USED Rhizomes (*bai zhu*).
PROPERTIES A bitter-sweet, tonic herb that acts mainly on the digestive system. It acts as a diuretic, lowers blood sugar levels, controls bacterial infections, and protects the liver.
MEDICINAL USES Internally for weak and disturbed digestion, often combined with *Codonopsis tangshen* (see p.174), *Glycyrrhiza uralensis* (see p.227), and *Wolfiporia cocos* (see p.408) in patent tonics, and with *Scutellaria baicalensis* (see p.364) to prevent miscarriage, and as a blood tonic in pregnancy.

CULINARY USES Rhizomes are eaten in tonic soups, rice dishes, and cakes, and are an ingredient of tonic teas.

ATRIPLEX
Orach

Chenopodiaceae

About 100 species of evergreen and semi-evergreen annuals, perennials, and shrubs make up this genus, which occurs worldwide in both temperate and warm regions. Orachs are closely related to goosefoots (*Chenopodium* spp., see p.166). They are unusual in being mostly salt-tolerant, which gives them potential in reclaiming saline soil. Most contain large amounts of saponins, which are toxic in excess. Various species are used: *Atriplex canescens* (fourwing saltbush) from southwestern N America, which has edible foliage and seeds and is burned to produce mineral-rich ashes that enhance the colour of blue corn products; *A. halimus* (sea orach, tree purslane), a S European shrub with silver-grey, edible leaves that are burned to produce an antacid powder. The Australian *A. nummularia* tolerates drought and saline soils and was used by early settlers as a soap substitute, vegetable, and cure for scurvy and blood diseases. The majority of orachs are pot-herbs, added to a dish to enhance its flavour or nutritional value but rarely eaten as a vegetable on their own. An exception is *A. patula* (European halberd-leafed saltbush, spearscale), which has edible, spinach-like, vitamin-rich leaves.
CULTIVATION Well-drained soil in sun; grows well in coastal locations.
PROPAGATION By seed sown in autumn. *A. hortensis* and *A. h.* 'Rubra' self-sow freely.
HARVEST Leaves are picked as required and used fresh.

▣ *Atriplex hortensis* (mountain spinach, orach)
Fast-growing annual with upright, often red-tinged stems and triangular to heart-shaped leaves, to 18cm (7in) long. Insignificant, yellow-green, red-flushed flowers appear in spike-like panicles, reaching 20cm (8in) long,

Astragalus membranaceus

Atractylodes macrocephala

Atriplex hortensis

A

Atriplex hortensis 'Rubra'

in summer. Native to Asia; widely naturalized in Europe and N America. ‡ 60cm–1.2m (2–4ft), ↔ 15–30cm (6–12in). 'Crimson Plume' has red-purple leaves that retain colour when cooked. 'Purple Savoyed' has thick, puckered, purple leaves. ▣ 'Rubra' (red mountain spinach, red orach) has beet-red foliage and flowers, and comes true from seed. 'Ruby' has vivid deep purple leaves and an excellent flavour. ‡ 1.2–2m (4–6ft). 'Yellow' has pale green-yellow leaves and a good flavour.

HARDINESS Half hardy.

PARTS USED Leaves.

PROPERTIES A mildly irritant herb that stimulates the metabolism.

MEDICINAL USES Internally to dispel sluggishness.

CULINARY USES Leaves are eaten raw or cooked, often mixed with other vegetables, notably with sorrel to reduce its acidity.

▨ ▮ ▨

ATROPA
Nightshade

Solanaceae

Four species of tall perennials make up this genus, occurring from W Europe to N Africa and the Himalayas. *Atropa* comes from the Greek *Atropos*, one of the Three Fates who snips the thread of life, and refers to the poisonous nature of these plants. The common name "dwale" is from a Nordic word for something that causes stupor. Legends tell of the use of deadly nightshade to subdue invaders, notably the Danish army by Macbeth (Buchanan, *History of Scotland*, 1582). *Atropa bella-donna* is of major importance in modern

medicine and is widely cultivated for the pharmaceutical industry, mainly in E Europe. It contains various alkaloids that have valuable medicinal applications and a macabre history of use by poisoners. The genus gives its name to one of these alkaloids, atropine, which dilates the pupil of the eye. Before the advent of modern anaesthetics, *A. bella-donna* was applied to the skin in a "sorcerer's pomade" to render the patient unconscious prior to surgery.

CULTIVATION Well-drained, moisture-retentive, alkaline soil in sun or partial shade. The alkaloid content of the plant is higher in a sunny position and in warm dry summers.

PROPAGATION By seed sown in spring; by division in spring.

HARVEST Whole plants are cut when flowering and dried for processing into dry and liquid extracts, tinctures, liniments, bandages, and glycerin preparations. Roots of two- to three-year-old plants are lifted in autumn and

Atropa bella-donna

processed using a similar method.

⚠ **WARNING** Toxic if eaten. Skin irritant and possible allergen.

▣ *Atropa bella-donna* (deadly nightshade, dwale) Tall perennial with erect branched stems and pointed ovate leaves, up to 20cm (8in) long. Purple-brown, bell-shaped flowers, about 2.5cm (1in) across, appear during summer, followed by shiny black berries, 1–2cm (½–¾in) across, with a persistent calyx. Native to W, C, and S Europe, W Asia, and N Africa. ‡ 1–1.5m (3–5ft), ↔ 60–90cm (24–36in). 'Lutea' has yellow-green flowers.

HARDINESS Fully hardy.

PARTS USED Whole plant, roots.

PROPERTIES A narcotic herb that relieves spasms and reduces secretions of the mouth, bronchi, and stomach.

MEDICINAL USES Internally for asthma, kidney stones and gallstones, Parkinson's disease, myocardial infarction, hypotension, hyperacidity, gastric ulcers, colic, motion sickness, and as a premedication before surgery. Excess causes dry mouth, loss of voice, enlarged pupils, aversion to light, confusion, respiratory failure, and death. Externally, in liniments and bandages, for rheumatic and muscular pain, and in eye drops for ophthalmic diagnosis and surgery. For use by qualified practitioners only. Important in homeopathy for sunstroke, painful menstruation, and infections or inflammations characterized by sudden onset, redness, and violent pain.

⚠ **WARNING** This herb and its alkaloids are subject to legal restrictions in some countries.

▨ ▨ ▨ ▮

AVENA
Oats

Poaceae

A genus of approximately 15 species of annual grasses, found wild in Eurasia and N Africa. The most important are *A. fatua* (wild oats), a S European species that reached northern parts during the Iron Age and became the main subsistence crop of Scotland; and *A. sativa* (cultivated oats), which was developed from wild oats. *Avena sativa* is commonly grown in northern temperate regions, as it needs more water and humidity than wheat and dislikes dry weather in early summer. *Avena sativa* is both a food and a herb, known to medical herbalists as a "tropho-restorative". It is a traditional food in Scotland and is widely grown as feed for livestock. In addition to protein, starch, and minerals, oats contain an alkaloid, glycosides, and fixed oils that are an important source of vitamin E.

CULTIVATION Well-drained, moist, fertile soil in sun.

PROPAGATION By seed sown in spring.

HARVEST Plants are cut in summer before fully ripe and threshed to separate the grains, which are then dehusked and rolled for use as cereals, and in liquid extracts, and tinctures. Dried stalks are sometimes included in tonics.

Avena sativa

▣ *Avena sativa* (oats, groats)
Erect annual grass with flat rough leaves and spreading panicles of large pendulous spikelets in summer. Seeds are spindle-shaped and pale gold. Not known in the wild; escapes from cultivation in temperate regions. ‡ 30cm–1m (1–3ft), ↔ 15–23cm (6–9in).
HARDINESS Hardy.
PARTS USED Seeds, stalks ("straw").
PROPERTIES A mealy nutritive herb that acts as a tonic to the heart, nerves, and thymus gland, and is externally emollient. Regular consumption of oat germ reduces cholesterol levels.
MEDICINAL USES Internally for depression, nervous exhaustion, shingles, herpes, menopausal symptoms, and debility following illness. Externally in preparations for eczema and dry skin. Often combined with *Cypripedium parviflorum* var. *pubescens* (see p.189) or *Scutellaria lateriflora* (see p.365) for depression.
CULINARY USES Seeds are milled as oatflakes, rolled oats, or flour. Flakes and rolled oats are popular for breakfast in the form of oatmeal and muesli. They are also ingredients of toasted cereal snacks, breads, biscuits, flapjacks, and speciality beers. Oat bran is added to breakfast cereals. Low-fat, lactose-free oat milk is used as a milk substitute. Seeds are sprouted for salads, dried for granola, or grown longer as seedlings then juiced or dried for food supplements.
▨ ▨ ▮ ▰

AZADIRACHTA

Meliaceae

There are two species of gum-secreting trees in this genus, which occurs in the tropics of Eurasia and Africa. *Azadirachta indica* (neem) is a fast-growing, long-lived tree that is popular in the tropics, where it is grown as an ornamental, for fuel, and for its workable but unpleasant-smelling timber. It is closely related to, and often confused with, *Melia azederach* (see p.274), which has similar properties and a more northerly distribution. The name is from the Persian *azaddhirakt*, "noble tree". Neem is one of the most important detoxicants in Ayurvedic medicine. It is a potent febrifuge, long used to treat intermittent fevers and shown to contain effective, anti-malarial compounds. The seeds yield margosa oil, a non-drying oil with insecticidal and antiseptic properties. The timber is highly prized for its insecticidal properties; in parts of Africa, it is grown in hedges to provide material for protection against insect-borne diseases.
CULTIVATION Well-drained soil in sun. Tolerates poor soils and prolonged drought.
PROPAGATION By seed sown as soon as ripe.
HARVEST Leaves, flowers, bark, and resin are collected as required and used fresh or dried in decoctions, infusions, medicated oils, powders, and pastes. Seeds are harvested when ripe for oil extraction.

▣ *Azadirachta indica* syn. *Melia azadirachta*, *M. indica* (*margosa*, neem, *nimba*)
Evergreen tree with pinnate leaves up to 30cm (12in) long. Small, yellow-white, fragrant flowers appear in panicles, to 30cm (12in) long, from spring to early winter, followed by yellow-green berries. Native to S Asia. ‡ 12–15m (40–50ft), ↔ 12m (40ft).
HARDINESS Min. 15–18°C (59–64°F).
PARTS USED Leaves, flowers, bark, seeds, oil.
PROPERTIES A bitter tonic herb that acts as an alterative clearing toxins, reducing inflammation, lowering fever, promoting

Azadirachta indica

healing, and improving all functions. It destroys a wide range of parasitic organisms and is also insecticidal and spermicidal.
MEDICINAL USES Internally for malaria, tuberculosis, rheumatism, arthritis, jaundice, intestinal worms, and skin diseases. Not given to the weak, old, or very young. Externally for ringworm, eczema, lice, fungal infections, and painful joints and muscles.
CULINARY USES Bitter leaves and flowers are added to appetizers, salads, and the Bengali dish *shukto*. Sap is fermented as an alcoholic drink. Neem honey is produced in parts of Asia.
ECONOMIC USES Leaves are used in libraries and herbaria to protect against insect damage. Oil is used in hair dressings and insecticides (especially to protect crops against locust attack). Resin is added to soap, toothpaste, and skin lotions.
▥ ▨ ▨ ▨ ▨ ▮ ▰ ▰ ▣

B

BACKHOUSIA

Myrtaceae

A genus of eight species of evergreen trees and shrubs that grow wild mainly in Australian rainforests, with one species in New Guinea. It was named after James Backhouse (1794–1869), a nurseryman of York, England. *Backhousia citriodora* is grown as an ornamental, both in pots and outdoors. It has a delightful lemon aroma, and in the 1990s became increasingly popular as a flavouring in the bushfood industry in Australia; there are now large plantations in NE New South Wales. *Backhousia anisata* (aniseed myrtle), from New South Wales, has anise-scented leaves, and *B. myrtifolia* (cinnamon myrtle), a shrub from cooler areas in S New South Wales, has a cinnamon or nutmeg aroma.
CULTIVATION Humus-rich, neutral to acid soil in sun or partial shade.
PROPAGATION By seed sown on the surface of compost in spring at 13–15°C (55–59°F); by semi-ripe cuttings, mainly in summer. Slow and difficult from cuttings.
HARVEST Leaves are picked as needed and used fresh or dried. Flowers are gathered in autumn, and seeds when ripe in late winter or spring.

▣ *Backhousia citriodora* (lemon ironwood, lemon myrtle, sweet verbena tree)
Large evergreen shrub or medium-sized tree with a short trunk, grey-brown bark, flaking to reveal orange new bark, reddish new shoots, and narrowly ovate, glossy, toothed leaves, 5–12cm (2–5in) long, which are strongly lemon-scented when crushed. Pale green to white, bell-shaped flowers, about 7mm (¼in) across, with long protruding stamens, are produced in clusters in the axils in autumn, followed by globose brown capsules. Native to Queensland and N New

B

Backhousia citriodora

South Wales (Australia). ↕ 3–20m (10–60ft), ↔ 2–10m (6–30ft).
HARDINESS Min. 5–7°C (41–45°F).
PARTS USED Leaves, flowers, seeds.
PROPERTIES An aromatic herb with a strong lemon aroma.
MEDICINAL USES Internally, in the form of an infusion, for colds.
CULINARY USES Fresh or dried leaves, flowers, and seeds are used to give a lemon flavour to vegetables, fish, seafood, and white meats, and as a substitute for lemon grass in SE Asian curries. Also in cakes, biscuits, sauces, and desserts. Makes a pleasant herb tea.
ECONOMIC USES Yields an essential oil, and is a source of citral, used in perfumery, soaps, and cleaning products.
⊠ ▱ ▨ ▣ ◹ ◿ ▣

BALLOTA

Lamiaceae

Native to Europe, the Mediterranean region, and W Asia, this genus contains about 35 species of perennials and subshrubs. Most species are rather weedy in appearance, but a few have velvety foliage that makes them worth growing as foliage plants. *Ballota nigra* (black horehound) is very attractive to bees, and, though of little ornamental merit in itself, it has one or two cultivars that make good border plants. Though widely grown in herb gardens, it is seldom used today by medical herbalists, who prefer the more effective and palatable *Marrubium vulgare* (see p.271). The oil extracted from *Ballota nigra* is used to adulterate that of *Marrubium vulgare*. *Ballota* was apparently named from the Greek *ballote*, "to reject", since livestock avoid the plants.

Ballota nigra

CULTIVATION Well-drained soil in sun or partial shade.
PROPAGATION By seed sown in spring; by division when dormant. *Ballota nigra* 'Archer's Variety' does not come true from seed. *Ballota nigra* self-sows readily.
HARVEST Whole plants are cut as flowering begins and dried for infusions, liquid extracts, and tinctures. Fresh herb may be used to make a syrup. Renew stocks of dried herb annually.

▣ *Ballota nigra* (black horehound)
Upright to lanky perennial with a pungent smell and round to ovate, hairy, toothed leaves, 2.5–5cm (1–2in) long. Dense whorls of purple, rarely white, 2-lipped, tubular flowers are produced throughout the summer. Native to Europe and Asia; naturalized in N America.
↕ 40cm–1m (16–36in), ↔ 24–60cm (10–24in).
▣ 'Archer's Variety' has white-marked foliage.
HARDINESS Fully hardy.
PARTS USED Whole plant.

PROPERTIES An unpleasant-tasting, expectorant herb that stimulates the uterus and calms spasms, especially in the digestive and bronchial systems. It is effective in controlling nausea and vomiting.
MEDICINAL USES Internally for nervous dyspepsia, motion sickness, morning sickness in pregnancy, menstrual disorders, and bronchial complaints.
▨ ▣

BALSAMITA

Balsamita major. See *Tanacetum balsamita*.

BAPTISIA
False indigo

Papilionaceae

A genus of 20 or more species of hardy N American perennials. One or two are grown as border plants for their yellow, white, or blue, lupin-like flowers. Charles Millspaugh (*Medicinal Plants*, 1892, republished as *American Medicinal Plants*, 1974) wrote of *B. tinctoria*, "young shoots of this plant resemble in form those of asparagus, and are used, especially in New England, in lieu of that herb for pottage". The name is derived from the Greek *bapto*, "to dye", since some species yield dyes. *Baptisia tinctoria* grows in dry woodlands and prairies from Massachusetts to Florida, and was well known to various native N American tribes before entering the *US Pharmacopoeia* (1831–42). The Mohicans and Meskwaki made a decoction of the roots as an antiseptic wash for wounds. Other species, such as *B. australis*, *B. bracteata* syn. *B. leucophaea*, and *B. lactea* syn. *B. leucantha* are also used medicinally.
CULTIVATION Well-drained, sandy soil in sun. Large roots resent disturbance.

Ballota nigra 'Archer's Variety'

PROPAGATION By seed sown when ripe; by division in early spring.

HARVEST Roots are lifted in autumn and dried for use in decoctions, liquid extracts, and tinctures. They can be kept for up to two years.

Baptisia tinctoria (indigoweed, rattleweed, wild indigo)
Erect, much-branched perennial with clover-like leaves, to 8cm (3in) across, and arching racemes, to 10cm (4in) long, of small, yellow, pea flowers in summer, followed by brown pods, 1cm (⅜in) long. Native to eastern N America.
‡ 1.2m (4ft), ↔ 60cm (24in).
HARDINESS Fully hardy.
PARTS USED Roots.
PROPERTIES An acrid, bitter, antiseptic herb that stimulates the immune system and is particularly effective against bacterial infections. It also lowers fever and has laxative and emetic effects.
MEDICINAL USES Internally for tonsillitis, pharyngitis, and upper respiratory tract infections; excess causes nausea and vomiting. Externally for boils, ulcers, gum disease, sore nipples, and vaginitis. Regarded in Ayurvedic medicine as a cooling alterative, which can have a deleterious effect if taken for too long or in excess. Combines well with cayenne pepper (see p.154), *Commiphora myrrha* (see p.177), and *Echinacea purpurea* (see p.199) for throat infections; with *Arctium lappa* (see p.127), *Phytolacca americana* (see p.314), and *Viola odorata* (see p.405) for boils and swollen lymph glands; and with *Cephaelis ipecacuanha* (see p.163) for aphthous ulcer. Used in homeopathy for influenza and sore throat associated with nervous exhaustion.
▩ ▪

BAROSMA

Barosma crenulata. See *Agathosma crenulata*.

BELAMCANDA

Iridaceae

Two species of perennials make up this genus, found in E Asia. *Belamcanda chinensis* is an unusual plant for the border, somewhere between an iris and a lily in appearance, with fans of iris-like leaves, colourful flowers, and three-chambered fruits that are a feature in autumn when they split open to reveal the jet-black fruits. Its common names, blackberry lily or leopard lily, refer respectively to the glossy black fruits and to the spotted flowers that last only a day. Widely used in traditional Chinese medicine, *B. chinensis* was first mentioned in the *Shen Nong Canon of Herbs* (AD25–220). It is valued in S China as a treatment for "rice field dermatitis", a fungal skin infection common among paddyfield workers.
CULTIVATION Well-drained, moist, sandy, humus-rich soil in sun or partial shade. May need protection in cold areas or during severe winters.
PROPAGATION By seed sown in spring; it takes

Belamcanda chinensis

about 15 days to germinate.
HARVEST Rhizomes are lifted in summer and autumn, and dried for use in decoctions.

▣ *Belamcanda chinensis* syn. *Ixia chinensis*, *Pardanthus chinensis* (blackberry lily, leopard lily)
Perennial with short rhizomes and a fan of grey-green, sword-shaped leaves, to 50cm (20in) long. Orange-red, dark-spotted flowers are borne in summer, followed by capsules containing shiny, round, black fruits. Native to E Asia, as far north as the Ussuri region of E Siberia.
‡ 60cm–1.2m (2–4ft), ↔ 15–25cm (6–10in).
'Hello Yellow' has unspotted yellow flowers.
HARDINESS Frost hardy.
PARTS USED Rhizomes (*she gan*).
PROPERTIES A bitter cooling herb that acts mainly on the lungs and liver, lowering fever and reducing inflammation. It is effective against a number of bacterial, fungal, and viral organisms.
MEDICINAL USES Internally for throat infections and for coughs characterized by profuse phlegm. Not given to pregnant women.
▩ ▪

BELLIS

Daisy

Asteraceae

This genus consists of seven species of hardy annuals and perennials, native to Europe and the Mediterranean. *Bellis perennis* is a very common and variable grassland species with many named cultivars that are mostly treated as biennials for spring bedding. They are easily grown and have a long flowering season. The name *Bellis* comes from the Latin *bellus*, "pretty". *Bellis perennis* has a long history as a healing herb. Gerard wrote

Bellis perennis

that "the daisies do mitigate all kinde of paines, but especially in the joints, and gout, if they be stamped with new butter unsalted, and applied upon the pained place …" (*The Herball, or Generall Historie of Plantes,* 1597). The flowers contain compounds that have been investigated for possible use in HIV therapy.
CULTIVATION Well-drained soil in sun or partial shade. Dead-head regularly to prolong flowering and avoid excessive self-sowing.
PROPAGATION By seed sown outdoors in early summer, or at 10–13°C (50–55°F) in early spring; by division in early spring, or after flowering. Double-flowered cultivars are usually sterile and cannot be raised from seed.
HARVEST Leaves are picked in spring and summer, and used fresh in decoctions, ointments, or poultices. Flowers are picked in spring and summer, and used fresh in infusions or ointments.

▣ *Bellis perennis* (common daisy)
Perennial with a basal rosette of obovate scalloped leaves. Numerous flowers, to 2.5cm (1in) across, with bright yellow discs and white, often pink-flushed, ray florets, appear from spring to autumn. Native to Europe and W Asia.
‡ 2.5–15cm (1–6in), ↔ 7–12cm (3–5in). ▣ 'Alba Plena' has pure white, double flowers. 'Dresden China' has small, double, shell-pink flowers.
▣ 'Prolifera' (hen-and-chickens daisy), known in Elizabethan times as the "childing daisy", has

Bellis perennis 'Alba Plena'

B

Bellis perennis 'Prolifera'

double white, often pink-flushed flowers that send out small ones from the main flower head. ‡ 10cm (4in). 'Rob Roy' dates from c.1818 and has crimson double flowers. ‡ 15cm (6in).

HARDINESS Fully hardy.

PARTS USED Leaves, flowers.

PROPERTIES An astringent, healing, expectorant herb that relaxes spasms.

MEDICINAL USES Internally for coughs and mucus. Externally for ruptures, varicose veins, minor wounds, and sore or watery eyes. A homeopathic remedy for deep bruising.

CULINARY USES Young leaves, flower buds, and petals have a pleasant sour flavour and may be added to salads. Flower buds can be pickled in vinegar as a substitute for capers.

▨ ▨ ▤ ◿

BENINCASA
Cucurbitaceae

A genus consisting of a single species of tender, climbing or trailing, annual vine, which is naturalized in many warm countries. It is exceptionally fast-growing, averaging 2.5cm (1in) per hour. Wax gourds are widely cultivated for their edible fruits, which store well, and are a source of wax (*petha*) for candles. Chinese medicinal uses were first recorded in the *Tang Materia Medica* (AD659). The fruits are eaten in China in reduction diets. Research has shown that they contain anti-cancer terpenes.

CULTIVATION Well-drained, humus-rich soil in sun, with ample water.

PROPAGATION By seed sown in spring at 18°C (64°F).

HARVEST Fruits are picked as required. Seeds and rind from ripe fruits are dried for decoctions.

▪ *Benincasa hispida* syn. *B. cerifera* (ash pumpkin, wax gourd, white gourd, winter melon) Climbing annual with hairy stems, forked tendrils, and palmately lobed, hairy leaves to 25cm (10in) long. Male and female flowers are borne separately on the same plant. They are bell-shaped and yellow: males are 5–17cm (2–7in) in length, on long stalks, and females are 2.5–4cm (1–1½in) long. Pollinated female flowers grow into dark green fruits, 25–40cm

Benincasa hispida

(10–16in) long, with white flesh. The skin is coated in wax, giving a white bloom. Native to tropical Asia and Africa. ‡ 6m (20ft).

HARDINESS Min. 16°C (61°F).

PARTS USED Fruit rind (*dong gua pi*), seeds (*dong gua zi* or *dong gua ren*).

PROPERTIES A cooling, pleasant-tasting herb that has diuretic effects (fruit rind), is anti-inflammatory and expectorant, and lowers fever (seeds).

MEDICINAL USES Internally, in Chinese medicine, for urinary dysfunction and summer fevers (rind); cough characterized by thick phlegm, internal abscesses, and vaginal discharge (seeds). Internally, in Ayurvedic medicine, for epilepsy, lung disease, asthma, coughs and hiccoughs, urine retention, internal haemorrhage (fruit); diabetes (rind), tapeworm (seeds); as an antidote to poisoning from mercury, alcohol, snake bite, and toxic plants (fresh juice).

CULINARY USES Mature fruits are eaten raw or cooked as a vegetable, especially in curries, or made into sweet pickles, preserves, and confectionery. They are the main ingredient in *tung kwa chung* (water melon pond), a classic Chinese dish in which the fruits are de-seeded and filled with soup before steaming. Immature fruits, young leaves, and flower buds are stir-fried or steamed. Ripe fruits are candied, often as an adulterant of citron. Seeds are eaten fried or roasted.

ECONOMIC USES Wax is scraped from the rind to make candles.

▨ ▨ ▤ ◿ ◿ ▨

BERBERIS
Barberry
Berberidaceae

Some 450 species of evergreen, semi-evergreen, and deciduous shrubs make up this genus, widely distributed in Eurasia, the Americas, and N Africa. Many species are grown for their scented flowers, brightly coloured fruits, and neat foliage, which, in the case of deciduous kinds, gives good autumn colour. The dense spiny habit makes barberries among the best shrubs for hedging or on steep banks. The medicinal uses of *Berberis* are an example of the Doctrine

of Signatures, in which the colour or structure of a plant was thought to be a divine indication of its healing properties. Many plants with mainly yellow coloration were thus used as liver remedies. Various species of *Berberis* are used medicinally in different parts of the world, including the Himalayan *B. aristata* and *B. asiatica*. In Ayurvedic medicine, these species are known generally as *daruharidra*, "wood turmeric", because they have similar properties to *Curcuma longa* (see p.186). They contain an important anti-bacterial alkaloid, known as berberine, which is used extensively in Japan and SE Asia to control tropical diarrhoea and certain eye diseases. The drug is obtained from the roots and rhizomes of various species of *Berberis* and the closely related *Mahonia* (see p.270). India produces up to 7 tonnes of the drug per year, extracted from 600–700 tonnes of roots. Similar alkaloids occur in *Coscinium fenestratum* (calumba wood), a vine belonging to the family Menispermaceae, which grows in SE Asian rainforests.

CULTIVATION Neutral to calcareous soil in sun or partial shade. Cut back old stems and straggly growths in late winter. May be attacked by honey fungus. As a host of wheat rust, *Berberis* may be illegal to grow in some areas.

PROPAGATION By seed sown when ripe; by softwood or semi-ripe cuttings in summer.

HARVEST Fruits are gathered in autumn and used fresh; stems and roots are collected in autumn and stripped of bark when fresh. Bark and roots are dried for use in decoctions and liquid extracts, and as powder.

⚠ **WARNING** All parts, except ripe berries, are harmful if eaten.

▪ *Berberis vulgaris* (common barberry) Deciduous shrub with yellow roots, grooved, yellow-grey stems, three-pronged spines, and obovate toothed leaves, to 6cm (2½in) long. Yellow flowers are produced in pendent racemes, to 6cm (2½in) long, in spring, followed by slender, oval, red fruits. Native to Europe. ‡ 2m (6ft), ↔ 1.2m (4ft).

Berberis vulgaris

HARDINESS Fully hardy.

PARTS USED Leaves, stem and root bark, roots, and fruits.

PROPERTIES A very bitter, sedative herb that is highly effective against many disease-causing organisms. It stimulates the liver, spleen, and uterus, lowers fever and blood pressure, controls bleeding, and reduces inflammation. Anti-cancer effects have been demonstrated.

MEDICINAL USES Internally for dysentery, leishmaniasis, malaria, hepatitis, liver tumour, gallstones, and hypertension, also to support cancer chemotherapy. Often combined with *Chionanthus virginicus* (see p.167) and/or *Veronicastrum virginicum* (see p.402) for gall bladder complaints. Highly regarded as a liver tonic and detoxicant in Ayurvedic medicine, and combined with *Curcuma longa* (see p.186) for liver complaints and diabetes. Not given to pregnant women.

CULINARY USES Ripe fruits are sour, with a high vitamin C content. They are made into jelly for lamb dishes, pickled, candied, and added to sauces and pies. The juice may be used like lemon juice in drinks and sorbets. Dried berries, known as *zereshk*, give a sour flavour to rice dishes, stuffings, and omelettes in Iranian cuisine. In France, fruits from the seedless form are made into jam, known as *confiture d'épine vinette*. Dried young leaves and tips are used for tea.

▣ ▨ ▧ ▩ ▤ ▪ ◿

BETONICA

Betonica officinale. See *Stachys officinalis.*

BETULA

Birch

Betulaceae

A genus of about 60 species of deciduous, mostly fast-growing trees and shrubs, distributed throughout the northern hemisphere. Birches are among the most common trees in most northern regions and are important in cultivation, being easily grown on most soils. They have a graceful habit, and the foliage of many species turns yellow in autumn. *Betula pendula* (silver birch) is highly regarded as a medicinal plant in Russia and Siberia, especially for treating arthritis. Large quantities of birch tar oil are produced in these regions. A number of different birches are used medicinally, including: the Eurasian *B. pubescens* (downy or white birch), which is used in identical ways to *B. pendula*; the N American *B. alleghaniensis* and *B. nigra* (river birch), used mainly for skin complaints and wounds; and *B. lenta* (black birch, cherry birch), the source of sweet birch oil, which contains large amounts of methyl salicylate and is used in perfumery and dental products. The wood is used for a wide range of purposes, including

charcoal, paper, spools for thread, toys, and fish smoking. The bark is used in the tanning industry, imparting a delicate fragrance to leather (notably *peau d'Espagne*). The slender flexible twigs are ideal for brooms – and for making "the birch", a rod or whip of birch twigs, which was used to flog offenders.

CULTIVATION Well-drained soil in sun or shade. *Betula pendula* prefers sandy soils below pH6.5 and dislikes shallow alkaline conditions, although it tolerates drier conditions than *B. pubescens*. Leaves may be damaged by aphids, caterpillars, leafminers, and weevils, and are also affected by rust. Trunk borers are a problem in many areas.

PROPAGATION By softwood cuttings in summer; by grafting in winter; by seed sown when ripe in a mixture of peat and sand. Seed does not store well, and germination is erratic.

HARVEST Leaf buds and young leaves are gathered in spring for use in infusions, poultices, and tinctures. Bark is stripped from felled trees as required for distillation of oil. Sap is tapped from mature trees for a week during early spring, at a rate of to 82 litres (18 gallons) per tree.

▣ *Betula pendula* syn. *B. alba*, *B. verrucosa* (silver birch)

Deciduous tree with drooping branches and silver-white, peeling bark. Catkins of male and female flowers are borne in spring on the same tree before new leaves appear; the males are pendent, females short and erect. They are followed by winged nutlets. Grows from Europe to W Siberia. ‡ 10–25m (30–80ft), ↔ 4–10m

(12–30ft). 'Fastigiata' has upright branches. ‡ 20m (70ft), ↔ 6m (20ft). ▣ 'Laciniata' syn. 'Dalecarlica' hort. (Swedish birch) has deeply cut leaves; this variant was found in the wild in Sweden in 1767. ‡ 6–9m (20–28ft), ↔ 4–5m (12–15ft). 'Purpurea' has purple-tinged bark and purple leaves. ‡10m (30ft), ↔3m (10ft). ▣ 'Tristis' has slender branches, a narrow symmetrical head, and drooping branches. ▣ 'Youngii' (Young's weeping birch) has a dome-shaped, weeping habit. ‡8m (25ft).

HARDINESS Fully hardy.

PARTS USED Leaves, bark, oil (occasionally buds, sap).

PROPERTIES A bitter, astringent, tonic herb that has diuretic and mild laxative effects, reduces inflammation, relieves pain, and increases perspiration.

MEDICINAL USES Internally for rheumatism, arthritis, gout, arteriosclerosis, water retention, cystitis, kidney stones, skin eruptions, and fevers. Some practitioners find that alternating *B. pendula* and *Urtica dioica* (see p.398) every three days is especially effective in conditions caused by chronic toxicity. Externally, in the form of birch tar oil, for psoriasis and eczema.

CULINARY USES Sap is fermented to make beer, wine, spirits, or vinegar.

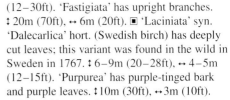

▣ ▨ ▢ ▪ ◿

Betula pendula 'Laciniata'

Betula pendula

Betula pendula 'Tristis'

Betula pendula 'Youngii'

BIDENS
Beggar ticks, bur marigold

Asteraceae

A genus of about 200 species of cosmopolitan, often weedy, annuals, perennials, and shrubs. A few are ornamental, notably *B. ferulifolia*, grown for its autumn display of golden daisies, and *B. atrosanguinea* (now *Cosmos atrosanguineus*), with its arching stems and deep maroon, chocolate-scented flowers. *Bidens* comes from the Latin *bis*, "twice", and *dens*, "tooth", and refers to the barbed fruits that adhere to fur and clothing. *Bidens tripartita* was once known as *Hepatorium* and used for "obstruction of the liver" and many other complaints, as well as being burned to repel insects. It is little used today. *Bidens bipinnata* (*ñachag*, Spanish needles) is a traditional N American herb for menstrual problems and infections of the throat and lungs. In Ecuador, it is regarded as a tranquillizer. *Bidens pilosa* (bur marigold, *picao preto*) is a cosmopolitan species, used for tea, as a pot-herb, and, in the Philippines, for flavouring rice wine.

CULTIVATION Damp to wet soil in sun.

PROPAGATION By seed sown in spring.

HARVEST Plants are cut as flowering begins and dried for use in infusions, liquid extracts, and tinctures.

■ *Bidens tripartita* (trifid bur marigold, water agrimony)
Waterside annual with four-angled, purple stems and toothed, lanceolate or divided leaves, to 11cm (4⅜in) long. Yellow-brown, button-like flowers, surrounded by leaf-like bracts, appear in summer. Native to temperate Eurasia. ↕ 15–60cm (6–24in), ↔ 10–30cm (4–12in).

HARDINESS Hardy.

PARTS USED Whole plant.

PROPERTIES A bitter, astringent, diuretic herb that controls bleeding.

MEDICINAL USES Internally for blood in the urine, uterine bleeding, ulcerative colitis, and peptic ulcer. Externally, in Russia, for alopecia. Combined with *Acorus calamus* (see p.101) or *Zingiber officinale* (see p.411) for digestive

Bidens tripartita

tract complaints, and with *Agrimonia eupatoria* (see p.107) to control haemorrhage.
🗎 ◨

BIOTA
Biota orientalis. See *Thuja orientalis.*

BIXA
Annatto

Bixaceae

This genus consists of one species of evergreen shrubby tree, found on rich soil along forest margins throughout the American tropics. *Bixa orellana*, known in Brazil as *urucú*, has an ancient history of use by the Mayas and Aztecs (Mexico), Incas (Peru), and native Amazonians as a red or orange body dye, which may have insect-repellent properties. It was first imported to Europe in the 16th century, and commercial cultivation began in India in 1787. The dye is reputedly an antidote to prussic acid poisoning, caused by eating *Manihot esculenta* (manioc) from which the toxin has not been completely removed. Its medicinal properties are poorly understood. Today, it is of great importance in world trade as a tasteless and harmless food colouring. The seeds contain 4–5 per cent orange and yellow carotenoids. It is also widely planted in the tropics as an ornamental and for hedges, especially along damp boundary ditches. The bright red, spiny capsules are very decorative; the flowers are a rich source of nectar for bees. There is a variety with yellow pods, and another with pink flowers and purple-brown pods, though these are little known outside the tropics.

CULTIVATION Well-drained, moist soil and high humidity. Prune hard if grown as a hedge. Trim specimen plants as required.

PROPAGATION By seed sown as soon as ripe in sand, at 19–24°C (66–75°F); by semi-ripe cuttings at 30°C (86°F). Seed-raised plants are slow to reach flowering size. Plants from cuttings of mature plants flower when small.

HARVEST Leaves are picked as required and dried for use in infusions. Seeds are collected as the fruits split open and are soaked in hot oil or lard, crushed in water, fermented, and made into cakes or ground up, depending on region and intended use.

■ *Bixa orellana* (*achiote*, annatto, lipstick tree, *roucou*)
Small tree with pointed, broadly ovate leaves to 20cm (8in) long. Panicles of pink or white, five-petalled flowers appear from late summer, followed by red spiny capsules, 5cm (2in) long, containing up to 50 red seeds. Native to tropical America and the West Indies. ↕ 7m (22ft), ↔ 3–4m (10–12ft).

HARDINESS Min. 16°C (61°F).

PARTS USED Leaves, fruits, seeds.

PROPERTIES A bitter, astringent, purgative herb that reputedly destroys intestinal worms, lowers fever, improves digestion, and has expectorant effects.

Bixa orellana

MEDICINAL USES Internally for mouth cancer (seed pulp, in Mexico), worms in children, dysentery, colic, and fevers (leaves, in the West Indies); fevers, especially in children and after childbirth (infusions of leaves, in Indo-China). Externally on burns to prevent blistering and scarring (ground seeds, in the Philippines).

CULINARY USES Seeds are used to colour and flavour rice, soups, chocolate, and dishes based on eggs, meat, fish, or vegetables.

ECONOMIC USES Fruit pulp yields colorant, used in foods (especially in margarine, cheese, soups, and smoked fish), in the cosmetics industry, and also to dye maggots for fish bait.
🗎 🗎 🗎 ◨ ✎ ✎ ▣

BLETIA
Bletia hyacinthina. See *Bletilla striata.*

BLETILLA

Orchidaceae

A genus of nine or ten species of terrestrial orchids, occurring in E Asia. *Bletilla striata* is an important wound herb in traditional Chinese medicine and was first described in medical literature in c.AD500. It is an attractive plant for shady borders in mild areas. Variegated forms are popular in the East. They are more tender, and are often grown in pots and given protection in winter. *Bletilla* is named after Don Louis Blet, a Spanish botanist.

CULTIVATION Well-drained, humus-rich soil, with added peat, or peat substitute, and leafmould, in shade or partial shade. Provide ample moisture in the growing season and keep on the dry side when dormant. Slugs may damage young leaves. Aphids and spider mite are often a problem under cover.

PROPAGATION By division or offsets of pseudobulbs in early spring.

HARVEST Pseudobulbs are lifted when dormant, and sliced and dried for use in decoctions and powder.

Bletilla striata

▣ **Bletilla striata** syn. *Bletia hyacinthina*
(bletilla)
Deciduous terrestrial orchid with flattened
underground pseudobulbs and pleated leaves,
to 50cm (20in) long. Loose spikes of magenta,
occasionally white, flowers, 3cm (1¼in) across,
appear in late spring. Native to China and Japan.
↕ 30–60cm (12–24in), ↔ 20–30cm (8–12in).
var. *japonica* f. *gebina* syn. f. *alba* has white
flowers. 'Variegata' has white-striped leaves.
HARDINESS Half hardy.
PARTS USED Pseudobulbs.
PROPERTIES A bitter, sweet, and sour herb that
checks bleeding, controls bacterial infection,
reduces swelling, and promotes healing.
MEDICINAL USES Internally for haemorrhage
of the lungs or stomach (e.g. in tuberculosis,
gastric ulcer), uterine bleeding, and nosebleeds.
Externally, often mixed with sesame oil, for
burns, bleeding injuries, abscesses, and sores.
▨ ▣

BOMBAX
Bombax pentandra. See *Ceiba pentandra*.

BORAGO
Borage

Boraginaceae

Three species of annuals and perennials make
up this genus, native to the Mediterranean
region and W Asia. *Borago* may be derived from
the Latin *burra*, "hairy garment", alluding to the
bristly foliage. Two species, *B. officinalis*
(borage) and *B. pygmaea*, are grown for their
clear blue flowers. Though often stocked by
herb nurseries, *B. pygmaea* cannot be used
as a substitute for culinary or medicinal uses
of borage. *Borago officinalis* was called
Euphrosinum by Pliny, because of its euphoric
effect, which was summarized by John Gerard
in *The Herball, or Generall Historie of Plantes*
(1597), "those of our time do use the floures in
sallads to exhilerate and make the minde glad.
There be also many things made of them, used
for the comfort of the heart, to drive away
sorrow, & increase the joy of the minde. The
leaves and floures of Borrage put into wine

make men and women glad and merry, driving
away all sadnesse, dulnesse, and melancholy,
as Dioscorides and Pliny affirme. Syrrup made
of the floures of Borrage comforteth the heart,
purgeth melancholy, and quieteth the phrenticke
or lunaticke person." The presence of
pyrrolizidine alkaloids in members of the borage
family now gives doubts about the safety of
borage as a culinary and medicinal herb where
regular or large amounts of foliage are consumed.
CULTIVATION Well-drained, moist soil in full
sun. Tolerates poor dry soil but makes a much
larger plant in better conditions. May develop
mildew in dry conditions or towards the end of
the growing season.
PROPAGATION By seed sown *in situ* in spring,
and thinned to 45cm (18in) apart.
HARVEST Leaves are gathered in spring and
summer, as the plant starts to flower, and are
used fresh, or dried for use in infusions and
liquid extracts. Flowers are picked as they open
and separated from the calyx before using fresh,
making into a syrup, or candying. Borage
develops a thick taproot and does not transplant
well. It is recommended in companion planting
to deter Japanese beetles and tomato hornworms;
also reputed to benefit strawberries. The flowers
attract bees. Properties deteriorate rapidly;
leaves and flowers must be processed promptly
and stocks of dried herb renewed annually.
Seeds are harvested when ripe for oil extraction.
⚠ **WARNING** Skin irritant and possible allergen.

▣ **Borago officinalis** (borage, starflower)
Bristly annual with upright hollow stems and
lanceolate leaves, to 15cm (6in) long. Blue,
five-petalled flowers, 1cm (⅜in) across, appear
in summer, followed by tiny, brown-black
seeds. Plants may appear with variegated
foliage. Native to Europe. ↕ 30cm–1m (1–3ft),
↔ 15–30cm (6–12in). ▣ 'Alba' has white flowers.

Borago officinalis

Borago officinalis 'Alba'

HARDINESS Half hardy.
PARTS USED Leaves, flowers, seeds, oil.
PROPERTIES A cooling, saline, diuretic herb that
soothes damaged or irritated tissues, increases
perspiration, and has mild sedative and anti-
depressant effects. Seeds are a rich source of
gamma-linolenic acid. Oil regulates hormonal
systems and lowers blood pressure. Plant (but not
oil) contains small amounts of pyrrolizidine
alkaloids (as found in *Symphytum officinale*,
see p.377) that may cause liver damage and
liver cancer.
MEDICINAL USES Internally for fevers, bronchial
infections (including pleurisy and tuberculosis),
mouth and throat infections, dry skin conditions,
cirrhosis, and chronic nephritis (leaves, flowers);
ringworm (juice); as an alternative to evening
primrose oil for skin conditions, rheumatic
complaints, and premenstrual syndrome (oil).
Externally in eyewashes, gargles, mouthwashes,
and poultices.
CULINARY USES Cucumber-flavoured leaves and
succulent leafstalks are traditionally added to
Pimms and wine-based drinks; they are also
chopped in salads and soft cheese, and in some
areas are cooked as a vegetable. Fresh flowers are
added to salad or used as a garnish but turn pink
on contact with acids, such as lemon juice or
vinegar. They are also made into a syrup, or
candied as cake decorations. Borage honey is
popular in New Zealand.
⚠ **WARNING** All parts of the herb, except the
seed oil, are subject to legal restrictions in some
countries.
▨ ◿ ▨ ▣ ▣ ◿

BOSWELLIA
Frankincense

Burseraceae

A genus of 25 species of evergreen shrubs or
small trees, native to tropical regions of Asia
and Africa. An oleo-gum resin, known as
frankincense, exudes naturally from the bark.
Exploited species include *B. frereana*,
B. papyrifera, *B. sacra*, and *B. serrata*.
Frankincense has been used for cosmetic and
medicinal purposes since earliest times, especially
as an ingredient in theriacs and panaceas. In one

tale, Adam was given gold, myrrh, and frankincense by God to console him for losing the garden of Eden. It was associated with longevity and memory in Classical times, and burned as incense to drive away evil spirits. Reliefs (c.1512–1482BC) on Queen Hatshepsut's temple at Luxor in Egypt show frankincense trees in pots, grown to make rejuvenating face masks.

CULTIVATION Well-drained to dry soil in full sun. Prune lightly in early spring.

PROPAGATION By semi-ripe cuttings in summer.

HARVEST Gum resin is collected all year, although quality is dependent on location and season, that from the driest areas in the hottest months being the finest; it is used fresh or dried for distillation, decoctions, or powders.

■ *Boswellia sacra* syn. *B. carteri* (frankincense, mastic tree, olibanum)
Resinous evergreen tree with papery peeling bark and clusters of pinnately divided leaves, 15–30cm (6–12in) long. Small, five-petalled, creamy white flowers appear in spring, followed by 3–5-angled, red-brown capsules. Native to Arabia and the Horn of Africa. ‡2–5m (6–15ft), ↔ 1–3m (3–10ft).

HARDINESS Min. 10–15°C (50–59°F).

PARTS USED Gum resin (*ru xiang*), oil.

PROPERTIES A bitter, pungent, warming herb that stimulates the circulation, calms the nerves, and has antiseptic, expectorant, and decongestant effects.

MEDICINAL USES Internally for bronchial and urinary infections. Not given to pregnant women (although traditionally used as a fumigant during and after childbirth in Oman). Externally as an inhalant for catarrh and a douche for vaginal infections. In Chinese medicine, internally for menstrual pain and externally for injuries, skin eruptions, and as a wash for gum, mouth, and throat complaints. Regarded as a rejuvenative in Ayurvedic medicine. Important in aromatherapy for relieving anxiety.

CULINARY USES Resin is chewed in countries of origin.

ECONOMIC USES Used in anti-wrinkle creams, incense, and perfumery. Essential oil used commercially to flavour

Boswellia sacra

confectionery, bakery produce, desserts, ice cream, and soft drinks.

BRASSICA
Cabbage, mustard

Brassicaceae

A genus of about 30 species of mainly annual or biennial herbs, distributed throughout Eurasia. Mustards have provided pungent flavourings, green vegetables, and medicinal compounds from very early times. Use as a condiment in the West dates back to at least 400BC, and medicinal uses were first mentioned in China in AD659. The Romans mixed ground seeds with grape juice; the word "mustard" derives from *mustum*, "grape must", and *ardens*, "burning". Pungency of mustard develops when cold water is added to the ground seed; an enzyme (myrosin) acts on a glycoside (sinigrin) to produce the sulphur compound, allyl isothiocyanate. The reaction takes 10–15 minutes. Mixing with hot water or vinegar, or adding salt, inhibits the enzyme, producing a mild bitter mustard. The three main kinds of commercially prepared mustard are: American, using *Sinapis alba* (white mustard, see p.369); English, using a mix of *S. alba* and *Brassica nigra* (black mustard) or *B. juncea* (brown mustard); and French, which is based on *B. nigra* or, more usually today, *B. juncea*. *Brassica juncea* has properties similar to other mustards but is used more for culinary than for medicinal purposes. It can be harvested mechanically, making it more commercially viable than *B. nigra*, though having only 70 per cent of its pungency. Other members of the genus include cultivars of *B. oleracea* (broccoli, Brussels sprouts, cabbages, kale), which have detoxicant effects and help prevent cancer when eaten regularly.

CULTIVATION Rich, well-drained, neutral to alkaline soil in full sun.

PROPAGATION By seed sown in early spring.

HARVEST Leaves and flowers are picked when young and used fresh. Pods are harvested as they begin to change colour, and dried to complete the ripening process; this prevents the seeds from being shed in the field. Seeds store indefinitely if kept dry. Volatile oil is distilled from seeds.

Brassica alba. See *Sinapis alba.*
Brassica hirta. See *Sinapis alba.*

■ *Brassica juncea* syn. *Sinapis juncea* (brown mustard, Chinese mustard, Indian mustard, mustard greens)
Annual with branched stems and glaucous, irregularly lobed leaves, 15–30cm (6–12in) long. Racemes of pale yellow flowers appear in summer, followed by beaked pods containing dark red-brown seeds. Native to Asia. ‡1–1.2m (3–4ft), ↔ 30cm (12in).

HARDINESS Hardy.

PARTS USED Leaves, seeds.

PROPERTIES A warming stimulant herb with antibiotic effects.

Brassica juncea

CULINARY USES Young leaves are eaten raw, pickled, or cooked as a vegetable. Pods are preserved in mustard-flavoured syrup (Italy). Seeds are ground and blended with other mustards or used alone as Russian, brown, or Sarrepta mustard, which has an especially strong flavour. They are used whole in curries and pickles, often heated in fat to destroy pungency and give a nutty flavour. Sprouted seeds are added to salads.

■ *Brassica nigra* syn. *Sinapis nigra* (black mustard)
Annual with a much-branched stem and lobed, roughly lyre-shaped leaves, to 16cm (6in) long. Bright yellow flowers are produced all summer, followed by small, erect, four-angled pods with dark brown seeds. Native to Eurasia. ‡90cm–3m (3–10ft) or more, ↔ 90cm–1.2m (3–4ft).

HARDINESS Hardy.

PARTS USED Leaves and flowers, seeds, oil.

PROPERTIES A pungent warming herb that stimulates the circulatory and digestive systems, and irritates the skin and mucous membranes. It is a potent emetic in large doses.

MEDICINAL USES Externally in poultices, mustard bandages, and baths for rheumatism, muscular pain, chilblains, and respiratory tract infections. A mustard footbath is a traditional

Brassica nigra

remedy for colds and headaches. Skin contact with mustard causes reddening, thus increasing blood flow and removal of toxins. Prolonged contact may result in blistering, especially in those with sensitive skin.

CULINARY USES Young leaves and flowers add pungency to salads. Seeds are ground to make mustard powder or dry mustard, mixed with vinegar as a relish, and used whole in curries, pickles, and sausages.

▨ ▧ ▢ ▨ ▪ ◪

BRUCEA

Simaroubaceae

Seven species of tender evergreen shrubs make up this genus, which occurs in tropical Asia, Africa, and Australia. All are extremely bitter. The berries are used to treat dysentery, and so well known for this purpose that one species is named *B. antidysenterica*. This species and *B. sumatrana* were listed in *The Illustrated Dictionary of Gardening* (ed. G. Nicholson, 1885), as "ornamental stove evergreen shrubs clothed with rufescent down". They are seldom seen in cultivation today, even in botanic gardens. *Brucea javanica* was first recorded in Chinese medicine c.AD720, and was described in a Vietnamese herbal in the 14th century. It is used in folk medicine to kill maggots and also internally for haemorrhoids. Research has shown that the seeds and seed oil are effective against warts and papillomas. *Brucea* is named after James Bruce (1730–94), author of *Travels to the Source of the Nile*, who in 1790 learned the use of *B. antidysenterica* from local people when suffering from dysentery in Abyssinia (now Ethiopia).

CULTIVATION Well-drained soil in sun or partial shade.

PROPAGATION By seed sown in spring; by ripewood cuttings in sand.

HARVEST Seeds are collected when ripe and the hard outer coating is removed.

▪ *Brucea javanica* (kusam seeds)
Shrub with downy branches and pinnately divided leaves, to 30cm (12in) long, with nine ovate pointed leaflets. Small, purple, four-petalled flowers are produced in axillary panicles in spring, followed by black berries, containing a single flat seed. ↕↔ 2–3m (6–10ft). Found from tropical E Asia to Australia.

HARDINESS Min. 15–18°C (59–64°F).

PARTS USED Seeds (*ya dan zi*).

PROPERTIES A bitter herb that lowers fever and is effective against a wide range of pathogens.

MEDICINAL USES Internally for malaria, amoebic dysentery, and vaginal thrush. Externally for warts and corns. Seeds are usually given whole, with dose and duration of treatment varying according to the complaint.

▨ ▪ ◪

BRUNFELSIA

Solanaceae

Some 40 species of evergreen shrubs and small trees belong to this tropical American genus. *Brunfelsia uniflora* is found in cloud forest and moist forest on the eastern slopes of the Andes. Several species are grown as ornamentals in warm regions, or under glass, for their large, often scented, five-lobed flowers, which in some species change colour as they age, giving rise to such common names as "yesterday, today, and tomorrow". The genus is named after Otto Brunfels (1489–1534), a monk and physician. Brunfelsias contain various alkaloids and a furocoumarin that is reputed to be anti-inflammatory. Several are used by native S Americans, both medicinally and as hallucinogens; they include *B. chiricaspi* and *B. grandiflora*, which characteristically produce a chilling tingling sensation. Several species appear to have anti-rheumatic effects. Leaves of *B. grandiflora* subsp. *schultesii* (*chiric sanango*, *chuchuwasha*, *moca pari*) are used to relieve rheumatism and arthritis.

CULTIVATION Rich, well-drained soil in partial shade and high humidity. Pinch out shoot tips in the growing season to encourage branching. Whitefly and mealybug may damage plants under cover.

PROPAGATION By softwood cuttings in spring and summer at 21°C (70°F).

HARVEST Roots are collected and dried for use in decoctions and liquid extracts.

▪ *Brunfelsia uniflora* syn. *B. hopeana* (*manaca*, *pohl*, vegetable mercury)
Shrub with pointed leaves, to 8cm (3in) long, and blue-violet, yellow-throated flowers, usually solitary but sometimes paired, measuring 2–3cm (¾–1¼in) across. Native to Brazil and Venezuela. ↕↔ 50cm (20in).

HARDINESS Min. 13°C (55°F).

PARTS USED Roots.

PROPERTIES Sweet, slightly aromatic herb with alterative, diuretic, and anti-rheumatic effects.

MEDICINAL USES Internally for syphilis, fevers, rheumatism, arthritis, and snake bite.

▨ ▪ ◪

BRYONIA

Cucurbitaceae

This genus of about ten species of tuberous climbing perennials occurs in Eurasia, N Africa, and the Canary Islands. *Bryonia dioica* is an easy, fast-growing climber for the wild garden or to cover eyesores, flowering from late spring to late summer. The red berries are poisonous. It is closely related to *B. alba*, differing mainly in having black, rather than red, berries. They are used in similar ways, although homeopathic remedies contain only *B. alba*. The name *Bryonia* comes from the Greek *bryo*, "to sprout", and refers to the annual growth from the tuber. The specific epithet *dioica* means "dioecious", that is, with male and female flowers on separate plants. The tuber of *B. dioica* was once known as "English mandrake" and traditionally hung in herb shops, often trimmed to a human-like shape to resemble the true mandrake *Mandragora officinarum* (see p.271). It can reach a great size: "the Queen's chief surgeon shewed me a root hereof that waied half an hundredweight, and of the bignes of a child of a yeare old" (Culpeper, *The English Physician Enlarged*, 1653). *Tamus communis* (black bryony) has similar uses. Though unrelated, it too is a climber and often occurs in the same areas as white bryony.

CULTIVATION Well-drained, neutral to alkaline soil in sun.

PROPAGATION By seed sown in autumn; by root cuttings or division of tuber in winter.

HARVEST Root is lifted in autumn, sliced, and dried for use in liquid extracts.

⚠ **WARNING** All parts are poisonous. Fresh root is a severe skin irritant.

▪ *Bryonia dioica* syn. *B. cretica* subsp. *dioica* (English mandrake, red bryony, white bryony)
Climbing herbaceous perennial with a large tuber, wiry stems, and palmate leaves to 7cm (3in) long. The five-petalled flowers are pale green – males long-stalked, females short-stalked, in umbels of two to five – followed by red berries. Native to Europe, except Scandinavia. ↕ 4m (12ft).

HARDINESS Fully hardy.

PARTS USED Roots.

PROPERTIES A bitter purgative herb that irritates the tissues, increasing blood supply to the area. It is known to have anti-tumour,

Brucea javanica

Brunfelsia uniflora

B

Bryonia dioica

anti-rheumatic, and anti-viral effects.
MEDICINAL USES Formerly used internally in small doses for bronchial complaints, asthma, intestinal ulcers, hypertension, and arthritis. Externally, as a rubefacient, in muscular and joint pains, and pleurisy. For use by qualified practitioners only. Not prescribed during pregnancy. Highly toxic in large doses.

BUPLEURUM
Thorow-wax

Apiaceae

There are about 100 species of annuals, perennials, and the occasional evergreen shrub in this genus, distributed through Europe, temperate Asia, and N America. A few species are grown for foliage and flowers. The common name "thorow-wax" is the Old English for "through grow", and refers to the perfoliate leaves that are characteristic of many species. *Bupleurum falcatum* was first mentioned in Chinese medical texts c.AD200, and is widely sold as a liver tonic in China and Japan.
CULTIVATION Well-drained soil in full sun.
PROPAGATION By seed sown in spring; by division in spring.
HARVEST Roots are lifted in autumn and used fresh, or dried for decoctions.

▣ *Bupleurum falcatum* syn. *B. chinense, B. scorzoneraefolium* (sickle-leaved hare's ear) Slender perennial with a woody rootstock, hollow stems, obovate basal leaves, and narrow stem leaves. Umbels of tiny yellow flowers are borne from midsummer to autumn. Native to S, C, and E Europe, and Asia. ‡ 30cm–1m (1–3ft), ↔ 30–60cm (12–24in).
HARDINESS Fully hardy.
PARTS USED Roots (*chai hu*).
PROPERTIES A bitter herb that acts as a tonic for the liver and circulatory system, lowers fevers, and has anti-inflammatory and anti-viral effects.
MEDICINAL USES Internally for blackwater fever, malaria, uterine and rectal prolapse, herpes simplex, haemorrhoids, sluggish liver associated with emotional instability, menstrual disorders, dizziness, and abdominal bloating. Often used

Bupleurum falcatum

raw with wine for feverish illnesses, with vinegar as a circulatory stimulant, with *Glycyrrhiza* spp. (see p.226) to improve liver function, or mixed with tortoise blood for malaria.

BURSERA
Torchwood

Burseraceae

This tropical American genus contains 40–50 species of deciduous trees and shrubs related to frankincense (*Boswellia*, see p.145) and myrrh (*Commiphora*, see p.177). The essential oils in various species were used as incense by the Mayas. Several species are sources of linalol, a sweetly scented liquid found in many essential oils, which is important in perfumes with floral notes. Linaloe oil, distilled from the wood (mainly in Mexico), is pale yellow, with a woody odour. Commonly used species in this genus are *Bursera delpechiana, B. fagaroides, B. glabrifolia* (76 per cent linalol), *B. penicillata* (Indian lavender), *B. simarda, B. simaruba* (gumbo-limbo, West Indian birch), and *B. spinosa. Bursera glabrifolia* was increasingly exploited after the Second World War, when production of linalol from *Aniba roseaodora* (see p.123) gave way to rubber plantations for the US military. Cayenne linaloe oil (*bois de rose femelle*) is distilled in French Guiana from *Protium altissimum* or from *Ocotea candata*. Scientific research has also shown interesting medicinal properties in burseras: anti-microbial in *B. delpechiana* and anti-tumour in *B. klugii* and *B. morelensis*.
CULTIVATION Well-drained to stony soil in sun or partial shade, with high humidity.
PROPAGATION By mallet cuttings in late summer at 15°C (59°F). In the tropics, by ripewood cuttings in the open ground.
HARVEST Wood is cut from trees at least 20 years old, and chipped and distilled for oil between December and June. Ripe fruits are collected in late summer for oil distillation.

Bursera glabrifolia
syn. *B. aloexylon* (linaloe, Mexican linaloe) Tender deciduous tree with pinnate leaves

arranged at the tips of branches. Clusters of white flowers, 1cm (⅜in) long, are produced at the start of the wet season, followed by ovoid, pea-sized, red berries. Native to C America. ‡ 5–6m (15–20ft), ↔ 3m (10ft).
HARDINESS Min. 12°C (54°F).
PARTS USED Wood, fruits, oil.
PROPERTIES A bitter, aromatic, antiseptic herb that reduces inflammation and controls convulsions.
MEDICINAL USES Internally for nervous tension. Externally for acne, wounds, and dermatitis.
ECONOMIC USES Oil is used in perfumery and in the food industry for its slightly bitter, lime-like flavour.

BUXUS
Box

Buxaceae

Found in W Europe, N and C America, E Asia, and the West Indies, this genus contains about 30 species of evergreen shrubs and small trees. Slow-growing, long-lived *B. sempervirens* has been used for topiary since Classical times: Pliny (AD23–79) described a terrace "adorned with the representation of divers animals in box". Box is extremely hard and heavy and gave its name to boxes; it was also used for printing blocks and mathematical, nautical, and musical instruments. *Buxus sempervirens* is reputedly comparable in effectiveness to quinine (*Cinchona* spp., see p.169) for treating malaria. However, it is rarely used today as a herb because of its toxicity.
CULTIVATION Well-drained, neutral to alkaline soil in sun or shade. Plant 20cm (8in) apart for hedges. Cut back hard in late spring to encourage new growth. Trim hedges and topiary specimens to shape in summer. *Buxus sempervirens* 'Elegantissima' tends to revert if pruned too hard or too often. Leaves may be affected by leafspot or rust. Young leaves may be attacked by box leaf suckers.
PROPAGATION By semi-ripe cuttings, with some hardened wood at the base, in a mixture of peat or peat substitute and sand, or directly into the ground in a shaded position. Cuttings can be taken at any time (best in autumn).
HARVEST Leaves are gathered in early spring, before flowering, and dried for infusions. Bark is stripped and dried for decoctions.
⚠ **WARNING** All parts are toxic if eaten. Possible skin irritant or allergen.

▣ *Buxus sempervirens* (common box) Evergreen shrub or small tree with grey-brown bark, and glossy, ovate to oblong leaves, 1–3cm (⅜–1¼in) long. Pale green, petal-less flowers, with a honey scent, appear in spring, followed by three-horned fruits containing black seeds. Native to Europe, N Africa, and Turkey. ‡ 2–5m (6–15ft), occasionally 10m (30ft), ↔ 1.2–2m (4–6ft) or more. ▣ 'Elegantissima' (silver box) is dense and slow-growing, with white-edged leaves, to 2cm (¾in) long. 'Handsworthensis' is dense and upright, with leaves to 4cm (1½in); good for hedging. ▣ 'Kingsville Dwarf' is very

C

slow-growing, increasing by only 1cm (⅜in) a year; ideal for bonsai. ↔ 1m (3ft). ◨ 'Latifolia Maculata' forms a dense, mound-shaped shrub, with leaves marbled dull yellow; new leaves are bright yellow in a sunny position. ↔ 1–2m (3–6ft). 'Marginata' syn. 'Aureomarginata' has yellow-margined leaves. ◨ 'Suffruticosa' (edging box) is compact, dwarf, and slow-growing; ideal for formal hedging or topiary. ↕ 1m (3ft), ↔ 1.5m (5ft).

HARDINESS Fully hardy.

PARTS USED Leaves, bark, wood.

PROPERTIES A strong-smelling, narcotic herb that lowers fever and may have anti-rheumatic effects. Destroys intestinal parasites.

MEDICINAL USES Internally for recurrent fevers (for example, malaria). Dosage is critical: excess causes vomiting, convulsions, and death. Also used in homeopathy for rheumatism.

ECONOMIC USES Included in preparations to stimulate hair growth. Wood used in engraving.

🖾 🗹 🗷 🗹

Buxus sempervirens

Buxus sempervirens
'Elegantissima'

Buxus sempervirens
'Kingsville Dwarf'

Buxus sempervirens
'Latifolia Maculata'

Buxus sempervirens
'Suffruticosa'

C

CALAMINTHA
Calamint

Lamiaceae

Eight or so species are included in this genus, ranging throughout Europe to C Asia. Several species are attractive and aromatic perennials for dry sunny borders or containers. In addition to those described below, the pink-flowered *C. grandiflora* (mint savory, showy calamint) and its cultivar 'Variegata' have mint-scented foliage that can be used for flavouring or teas. Calamints were important medicinally in medieval times, but are regarded as more ornamental than useful today. According to Culpeper (*The English Physician Enlarged*, 1653), calamint "hinders conception in women", and "works very violent upon the feminine part" – a view repeated in the *Irish Herbal* (1775), which recommends it "to expel dead child from womb". The active constituent is pulegone, as found in *Mentha pulegium* (see p.277), which is known to cause abortion.

CULTIVATION Well-drained to dry, neutral to alkaline soil in sun.

PROPAGATION By seed sown under cover in spring or autumn; by softwood cuttings in early summer; by division in spring.

HARVEST Flowering plants and leaves are cut in summer and used fresh, or dried for infusions.

Calamintha acinos. See *Acinos arvensis*.

◨ *Calamintha nepeta* syn. *C. nepetoides*, *Satureja nepeta* (lesser calamint, nepitella) Bushy perennial with a long creeping rhizome, upright branched stems, and peppermint-scented, ovate, toothed leaves, to 3.5cm (1⅜in) long. Loose clusters of tubular, pale lilac to white flowers, 6mm (¼in) long, appear in summer. Found in Europe, S Russia, N Africa, and Iran. ↕ 45cm (18in), ↔ 50–75cm (20–30in). ◨ subsp. *nepeta* is larger in all its parts.

Calamintha nepeta

Calamintha nepeta subsp. *nepeta*

↕ 45–60cm (18–24in), ↔ 60–90cm (24–36in). subsp. *nepeta* 'Blue Cloud' has blue flowers. ↕ 45–60cm (18–24in), ↔ 60–90cm (24–36in).

HARDINESS Fully hardy.

PARTS USED Whole plant.

PROPERTIES An aromatic herb that acts as a nerve tonic, increases perspiration, stimulates the uterus, and relieves indigestion.

MEDICINAL USES Internally for indigestion, nervous tension, depression, insomnia, feverish colds, and painful menstruation. Not given to pregnant women.

CULINARY USES Leaves can be used for flavouring; they are similar in aroma to those of common calamint, but more pungent.

🗹 🖾 🗷

◨ *Calamintha sylvatica* syn. *C. ascendens*, *C. officinalis* (common calamint) Rhizomatous perennial with mint-scented, slightly toothed leaves. Pale lilac, dark-spotted flowers from midsummer to early autumn. Native to Eurasia and the Middle East. ↔ 60cm (24in).

HARDINESS Fully hardy.

PARTS USED Whole plant, leaves.

PROPERTIES Like *C. nepeta*, but not as strong.

MEDICINAL USES As for *C. nepeta*.

CULINARY USES Leaves have a mint–marjoram flavour, used with roast meats and vegetables, such as courgettes and mushrooms.

🗷 🗹 🖾 🗷

Calamintha sylvatica

CALENDULA
Marigold, pot marigold

Asteraceae

There are 20–30 species of annuals, perennials, and evergreen subshrubs in this Mediterranean genus. The only species common in cultivation is *C. officinalis* (marigold), which is widely grown as an ornamental, as well as for culinary and medicinal uses. Marigold is a major herb in modern Western herbal medicine, having excellent healing, antiseptic, and detoxifying properties, combined with low toxicity. Double-flowered cultivars can be used in the same ways as single marigolds. *Calendula officinalis* was used in early Indian and Arabic cultures, and in ancient Greece and Rome, as a medicinal herb and as a colorant for fabrics, foods, and cosmetics. *Calendula arvensis* (field marigold), a common weed of fields and vineyards in Europe, has smaller flowers that can be used in similar ways to those of *C. officinalis*. The name *Calendula* comes from the Latin *kalendae*, "first day of the month" in the Roman calendar, perhaps because marigolds can be found in flower at the beginning of most months of the year. The common name "marigold" refers to its links with the Virgin Mary. Various plants are also called marigolds, notably *Tagetes* spp. (see p.379), which are used in different ways.

CULTIVATION Well-drained to poor soil in full sun. Remove dead flower heads to prolong flowering and prevent excessive self-sowing. Caterpillars, powdery mildew, rust, or cucumber mosaic virus may attack foliage.

PROPAGATION By seed sown *in situ* in spring or autumn. *Calendula officinalis* self-sows readily.

HARVEST Flowers are cut in dry conditions and used fresh or dried in infusions, liquid extracts, tinctures, and for culinary purposes; they are also macerated in oil for external use.

◾ *Calendula officinalis* (marigold, pot marigold)
Bushy aromatic annual with branched stems and lanceolate leaves, to 15cm (6in) long. Flowers are up to 7cm (3in) across, with yellow to orange ray florets, produced from spring to autumn where weather remains cool. Native to C Europe, and the Mediterranean. ↔ 50–70cm (20–28in). ◾ 'Fiesta Gitana' is dwarf, with double flowers in pastel shades. ◾ 'Lemon Queen' has double, lemon-yellow flowers. ↕45cm (18in). ◾ 'Orange King' has double, deep orange flowers. ↕ 45cm (18in). ◾ 'Prolifera' (hen-and-chickens marigold) is an old variety, in which the main flower head produces several smaller ones from its base. ↔ 40–50cm (16–20in).

HARDINESS Hardy.

PARTS USED Whole flower heads, petals.

PROPERTIES A bitter–sweet, salty herb that stimulates the liver, gall bladder, and uterus, soothes the digestive system, supports the heart, and clears infections. It benefits the skin especially, reducing inflammation, controlling bleeding, and healing damaged irritated tissues.

MEDICINAL USES Internally for gastric and duodenal ulcers (with *Geranium maculatum*, see p.223), colitis, diverticulitis, hepatitis, swollen glands, glandular fever, menstrual problems, pelvic inflammatory disease, disorders of the liver and gall bladder, and as a detoxicant in chronic skin disorders, such as eczema and acne. Externally for conjunctivitis, ringworm, eczema, athlete's foot, varicose veins (with *Hamamelis virginiana*, see p.230), leg ulcers, bedsores, cysts, minor injuries, surgical wounds, and skin problems, such as nappy rash and cradle cap in babies, and sore nipples in nursing mothers. As an antiseptic, *Calendula officinalis* is often combined with *Commiphora myrrha* (see p.177) and *Hydrastis canadensis* (see p.239). Used internally and externally in homeopathy for injuries where the skin is broken.

CULINARY USES Petals are used as a substitute for saffron in rice and soup, and infused to give colour to cheese, butter, milk desserts, and cakes; also added fresh to salads.

⊞ ◾ ◿

CALLUNA
Heather

Ericaceae

This genus consists of a single species of evergreen shrublet that is closely related to *Erica*. There are over 300 variants of *C. vulgaris*, grown for their year-round interest. Flowering heather dries well, retaining its colour for years, and white heather is considered lucky. *Calluna* comes from the Greek *kalluno*, "to sweep", as it was used in brooms. It was also gathered for fuel (the common name "ling" is from Anglo-Saxon *lig*, "fire"), and used in thatch. Heather is widely used as a medicinal plant in northern and upland Europe. Heather honey is an important product in these areas and also has reputed therapeutic properties. It has a pungent flavour, clear, dark amber colour, and thixotropic texture, which makes it difficult to extract, but it is excellent for cut honeycomb.

CULTIVATION Acid soil in an open sunny position. Tolerates wet conditions in winter. Trim after flowering to maintain shape.

PROPAGATION By semi-ripe cuttings in summer; by layering in spring.

HARVEST Flowering shoots are cut in summer and dried for use in infusions.

◾ *Calluna vulgaris* (heather, ling)
Dense evergreen shrublet with numerous, tortuous, rooting branches and very small, stalkless leaves. Loose racemes, 3–15cm (1¼–6in) long, of small, pink-purple, bell-shaped

Calluna vulgaris

Calluna vulgaris 'Alba Plena'

Calluna vulgaris 'Darkness'

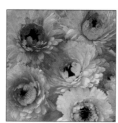

Calendula officinalis 'Fiesta Gitana'

Calendula officinalis 'Lemon Queen'

Calendula officinalis

Calendula officinalis 'Orange King'

Calendula officinalis 'Prolifera'

Calluna vulgaris 'Multicolor'

Calluna vulgaris 'Silver Queen'

flowers appear from late summer. Found from N and W Europe to Siberia, N Africa, and the Azores. ‡ 10–60cm (4–24in), ↔ 45–75 (18–30in). ▣ 'Alba Plena' has double white flowers. ↔ 30–45cm (12–18in). 'Beoley Gold' has yellow foliage and white flowers. ‡ 40cm (16in), ↔ 60cm (24in). ▣ 'Darkness' has deep rose-purple flowers and dark green foliage. ‡ 25cm (10in), ↔ 35cm (14in). ▣ 'Multicolor' is dwarf, with pink flowers and copper foliage, tinted orange, bronze, and yellow, and red all year. ‡ 10cm (4in), ↔ 25cm (10in). ▣ 'Silver Queen' has silver-grey foliage, lilac-pink flowers, and a spreading habit. ‡ 40cm (16in).
HARDINESS Fully hardy.
PARTS USED Flowering tips.
PROPERTIES An astringent, diuretic, mildly sedative herb that induces perspiration and has antiseptic effects, especially on the urinary system.
MEDICINAL USES Internally for coughs and colds, diarrhoea, kidney and urinary tract infections, arthritis, rheumatism, and nervous exhaustion. Used in homeopathy for arthritis, rheumatism, and insomnia.
CULINARY USES Dried flower heads are blended with other Scottish herbs, such as bramble, bilberry, wild thyme, and wild strawberry leaves, to make "Moorland tea". Heather honey is an ingredient of liqueurs, such as Drambuie and Irish Mist, and of Atholl Brose, a Scottish dessert made from oatmeal, raspberries, cream, and Scotch whisky.
▨ ▣ ✎

CAMELLIA

Theaceae

Over 250 species of evergreen shrubs and trees make up this Asian genus. Many species are grown as ornamentals for their handsome glossy foliage and fine flowers. The most important species commercially is *C. sinensis* (tea), native to China, which is cultivated on a vast scale and has over 350 cultivars. It was introduced to Europe in the 17th century. In addition to the various kinds of tea obtained from the leaves of *C. sinensis*, oil is extracted from the seeds, though the main source of tea seed oil is *C. sasanqua*, which yields higher amounts. Tea has been drunk in China for over 3000 years. The ritual tea ceremony began in China during the Sung dynasty (AD960–1279) and spread to Japan, where it remains close to the original. In legend, the origin of tea is given as Buddha's eyelids, which he cut off and hurled to the ground when he fell asleep while meditating. Where they fell, tea plants arose so that he would have tea to bestow alertness. Tea contains about 50mg of caffeine per cup (compared with 85mg per cup of coffee) and 10–24 per cent tannins, which are a possible cause of oesophageal cancer. Drinking tea with milk eliminates this risk because the tannins are neutralized. Tea contains antioxidants known as polyphenols, which help protect against heart disease, strokes, and cancer. Levels of polyphenols are probably higher in green tea, since they may be degraded during

Camellia sinensis

fermentation in black tea. Research has also shown that a chemical extracted from tea may help destroy antibiotic-resistant organisms. Camellia seeds are rich in oil. The quantity and quality varies from species to species, and is used according to grade in cooking, cosmetics, and paint. The main species prized for their oil are *C. crapnelliana*, *C. octopetala*, *C. oleifera*, *C. reticulata*, and *C. sasanqua*. *Camellia* is named after George Joseph Kamel (1661–1706), who wrote a history of Philippine plants.
CULTIVATION Rich moist soil in sun or partial shade. Bushes are normally pruned to 1m (3ft).
PROPAGATION By seed sown as soon as ripe, or in spring, at 15–18°C (59–64°F). Dried seeds need chipping. By semi-ripe cuttings in summer, at a minimum of 18°C (64°F).
HARVEST Leaves are picked during the year, from bushes over three years old, and dried for use in infusions or distilled for oil. Seeds are removed from capsules and pressed for oil, which is processed to remove saponins.

▣ *Camellia sinensis* syn. *Thea sinensis* (tea) Small, variable, evergreen shrub with leathery elliptic leaves, 5–9cm (2–3½in) long but to 13cm (5in) long in some varieties. White flowers, 2.5cm (1in) across, with a boss of yellow stamens, are borne in the axils in winter, followed by capsules, containing large oily seeds. Origin uncertain, but probably from W China. ‡ 1–6m (3–20ft), ↔ 60cm–4m (2–12ft).
HARDINESS Frost hardy.
PARTS USED Leaves (shoot tips only), essential oil (leaves), fixed oil (seeds).
PROPERTIES An aromatic, slightly bitter, astringent herb that stimulates the nervous system and has diuretic and bactericidal effects.
MEDICINAL USES Internally for diarrhoea, dysentery, hepatitis, and gastroenteritis. Excess causes constipation, indigestion, dizziness, palpitations, irritability, and insomnia. Externally for sore eyes, minor injuries, and insect bites. Regular consumption of green tea may protect against arteriosclerosis and dental cavities and may help lower blood pressure and cholesterol.

CULINARY USES Leaves are steamed and dried for green tea, or fermented and dried for black tea. Tea is occasionally used as a flavouring, notably for boiling eggs, or as a soaking liquid for dried fruits and ham. Leaf extracts are fermented to make *kombucha*, or "tea cider". Powdered green tea is an ingredient in Japanese confectionery. Oil is used in cooking.
ECONOMIC USES Essential oil is used in perfumes with a leathery note, and in commercial food flavouring. Fixed oil is used in manufacturing paint.
▨ ▣ ▦ ▪ ✎ ✎

CANANGA
Ylang-ylang

Annonaceae

A genus of two species of tender evergreen trees, native to tropical Asia and Australia. *Cananga odorata* (ylang-ylang), a night-scented species, is prized as an ornamental for the intense perfume of its pale flowers, which show up in the dark to attract pollinating moths. It is cultivated for the perfumery industry in Réunion, Indonesia, Madagascar, the Philippines, and the Comoro Islands. One tree produces approximately 120kg (265lb) flowers per year, yielding 350g (12oz) of essential oil. Ylang-ylang perfume is also produced from the flowers of the closely related *Artabotrys hexapetalus*. The use of ylang-ylang flowers in a coconut oil pomade in the Molucca Islands was recorded by Guibourt in *Natural History of Simple Drugs* (1866).
CULTIVATION Well-drained, moist soil in sun, with high humidity. Remove the terminal bud when the tree is 2m (6ft) tall, after about three years. Plants flower when young, and in cold areas may be grown in containers under glass, using soil-based potting compost.
PROPAGATION By seed sown when ripe at 21°C (70°F).
HARVEST Flowers are picked at night and dried for infusions, or distilled for oil.

▣ *Cananga odorata* syn. *Canangium odoratum* (ilang-ilang, Macassar oil tree, ylang-ylang) Open-headed, evergreen tree with drooping branches and ovate–oblong leaves, to 20cm

Cananga odorata

C

(8in) long. Intensely fragrant flowers, with six narrow, yellow-green petals, to 5cm (2in) long, appear all year, followed by green fruits. Grows in lowland forests from India to N Australia. ‡ 10–30m (30–90ft), ↔ 4–8m (12–25ft).
HARDINESS Min. 15–18°C (59–64°F).
PARTS USED Flowers.
PROPERTIES An antiseptic sedative herb that relieves tension, lowers blood pressure, and reduces fever. It is reputedly aphrodisiac.
MEDICINAL USES Internally for malaria and fevers. Externally for skin irritations, conjunctivitis, boils, and gout, and in baths for impotence and frigidity. Ylang-ylang is important in aromatherapy for treating tachycardia, rapid breathing, hypertension, gastrointestinal infections, and psycho-sexual complaints.
ECONOMIC USES Distilled oil (cananga oil) is used in perfumery and cosmetics, and with coconut oil in Macassar hair oil; also in the food industry, especially in peach and apricot flavourings.

CANANGIUM

Canangium odoratum. See *Cananga odorata*.

CANELLA

Canellaceae

One species of evergreen shrubby tree constitutes this genus, which occurs in the West Indies and Florida Keys (USA). The name is a diminutive of *canna*, "reed", referring to the quills of bark, produced for the pharmaceutical and food industries. It was grown as a "stove" (warm greenhouse) evergreen during Victorian times but is rarely seen today outside the tropics. The entire tree is aromatic, filling the air with fragrance when in flower. Canella or wild cinnamon is a familiar spice in the West Indies, and was long used by the native Carib people before the islands were colonized. It was introduced to Europe in the early 17th century, as a species of *Cinnamomum* (see p.169). The fruits are eaten by pigeons in Jamaica, which gives their flesh a spicy flavour. Dried flowers emit a musk-like scent when placed in warm water. *Canella winterana* is one of the 21 plants of the *Omiero*, the sacred elixir of Afro-Caribbean Santeria initiation.
CULTIVATION Well-drained, sandy soil in sun.
PROPAGATION By ripewood cuttings with a heel, in spring.
HARVEST Leaves are picked and used fresh or dried. Bark is dried in long quills for oil distillation or for use in condiments, decoctions, and tinctures, and as a powder with aloes.

▣ *Canella winterana* syn. *C. alba* (canella, white cinnamon, wild cinnamon)
Erect evergreen shrub or tree with aromatic bark and obovate leaves to 10cm (4in) long. Fragrant, violet to purple flowers in summer are followed by red to black berries. Native to the West Indies and USA (Florida Keys). ‡ 10–15m (30–50ft), ↔ 7–10m (22–30ft).

Canella winterana

HARDINESS Min. 7°C (45°F).
PARTS USED Leaves, bark, oil.
PROPERTIES A bitter aromatic herb that aids digestion and also has anti-microbial effects.
MEDICINAL USES Internally for poor digestion. Externally for rheumatic pains (Cuba). Combined with *Aloe vera* (aloe, see p.115) for constipation and menstrual problems (West Indies). An aromatic adjunct in prescriptions for treating digestive complaints.
CULINARY USES Bark and leaves are used in seasoning mixtures and added to tobacco (West Indies). Bark used in "clove vodka" (Russia).
ECONOMIC USES Bark used as fish poison (Puerto Rico). Oil used occasionally in perfumes with an Oriental bouquet.

CANNABIS

Hemp

Cannabidaceae

A genus containing a single species of tall coarse annual, found on most soils, especially as a weed of nitrogen-rich soils near human habitation. The Scythians, who lived north of the Black Sea 3000 years ago, produced intoxicating vapours by throwing cannabis on to hot stones. In Victorian gardening manuals it was listed as an elegant "dot plant" for summer borders. *Cannabis* is the Greek word for "hemp", from which the word "canvas" is derived, after the plant's fibrousness. Cannabis has been grown in Asia and the Middle East for over 4000 years, both as a fibre plant and as a drug. Therapeutic uses were described in Indian medical texts before 1000BC and in the Chinese herbal *Rh-ya* in the 5th century BC. Today its possession and use are illegal, or subject to strict controls, in most Western countries and in Australia and New Zealand, but legal and socially acceptable in many parts of Asia and the Middle East, where the dried plant or resin is commonly smoked or eaten. The various common names for *Cannabis* refer to specific preparations: *hasheesh* – resin from the female plant, usually smoked in water pipes; *bhang* – dried plant mixed into water, fruits, or candy; *charas* – resin smoked or eaten with spices; and *ganja* – dried tops of

the female plant. European herbals of the 16th century include the plant, which John Gerard called "Indian dreamer". *Cannabis* was listed in the pharmacopoeias of many countries, including the USA, until its restriction in the 1930s. It contains more than 60 kinds of cannabinoids, including delta 9-tetrahydrocannabinol (THC), which is largely responsible for the psychoactive effects. While modern research confirms the effectiveness of *Cannabis* for a wide range of conditions, its illegal status has suppressed therapeutic use in the West. However, *Cannabis* is still widely used in traditional Chinese medicine.
CULTIVATION Cultivation, harvesting, and processing of *Cannabis* plants are subject to legal restrictions in many countries. Approved varieties for fibre (hemp) production, with no to low narcotic content, are permitted by licence in producer countries. Subject to statutory control as a weed in some countries, notably in various parts of Australia.

▣ *Cannabis sativa* (*hasheesh*, hemp, marijuana) Strong-smelling, variable annual with a long taproot, erect branched stem, and palmate leaves. Panicles of small green flowers appear in summer – male and female on separate plants. Native to C Asia. ‡ 90cm–5m (3–15ft), ↔ 30cm–1.5m (1–5ft). subsp. *indica* (cannabis, marijuana) is rich in cannabinoids and essential oils. subsp. *sativa* (hemp) is hardier and lacks psychoactive compounds.
HARDINESS Hardy.
PARTS USED Whole plant, oil (subsp. *sativa*); flowering tops, seeds (subsp. *indica*).
PROPERTIES Subsp. *indica* has analgesic, anti-emetic, anti-inflammatory, and sedative properties; it is also a laxative and hypotensive.
MEDICINAL USES Internally for nausea and vomiting associated with cancer chemotherapy, to reduce ocular pressure in glaucoma, ease muscular stiffness and tremors in multiple sclerosis, and help AIDS patients gain weight (subsp. *indica*). Externally for corns, sores, and varicose ulcers (subsp. *indica*). Seeds (*huo ma ren*) are

Cannabis sativa

used in traditional Chinese medicine to treat constipation caused by debility or by fluid deficiency.
CULINARY USES Seeds are an ingredient in wholefood cuisine and beers, and used as a condiment in Japanese cuisine, notably in the spice mixture *shichimi*. Seed oil is used for culinary purposes. Dried herb is an ingredient of Moroccan candy (*majoun*) and is important as a flavouring in *Ital* (Rastafarian) cooking.
ECONOMIC USES Subsp. *sativa* is a source of fibres for rope-making. Oil pressed from seeds of subsp. *sativa* is added to cosmetics.
⚠ **WARNING** This herb is subject to legal restrictions in most countries.

CAPPARIS
Caper bush

Capparidaceae

This large genus of about 250 species of evergreen shrubs and small trees is native to tropical and subtropical regions. *Capparis spinosa* is a common coastal shrub in Mediterranean regions. It was described in *The Illustrated Dictionary of Gardening* (ed. G. Nicholson, 1885) as "an excellent greenhouse shrub perfectly hardy in the southern counties in England", though it is seldom seen in cultivation now. The Greek name *kapparis* is from the Persian *kabar*, "caper". *Capparis spinosa* is the only species of commercial importance in the genus, although several other species (notably *C. brevispina*, *C. decidua*, and *C. sepiaria*) are used for similar purposes. Pickled capers have been used as a condiment in S Europe for over 2000 years. Caper buds are both wild-collected and cultivated; plants grown in cultivation tend to be spineless. The unripe seeds of *Tropaeolum majus* (nasturtium, see p.394) make satisfactory substitutes; when pickled, they develop a similar taste, caused by capric acid. The Australian *C. mitchellii* (native pomegranate, wild orange) produces aromatic bittersweet fruits, used raw or cooked to flavour savoury dishes and desserts.
CULTIVATION Well-drained, sandy soil in sun.
PROPAGATION By seed sown in autumn or spring; by ripewood cuttings in summer at 19–24°C (66–75°F). Germination is erratic.
HARVEST Flower buds are picked in early morning and wilted before salting or pickling in salted white vinegar. Leaves and immature fruits are also pickled. Bark is stripped from roots lifted in autumn, and then dried.

▪ *Capparis spinosa* (caper)
Prostrate shrub with trailing stems, up to 1.5m (5ft) long, and ovate leaves, 6cm (2½in) long, with two spines at the base. Solitary, white to pink flowers, with four petals and long pink stamens, open from early summer to autumn, followed by olive-green fruits, to 5cm (2in) long. Native to the Mediterranean, Arabia, and C and W Asia. ‡1m (3ft), ↔1.5m (5ft); var. *inermis* lacks spines. 'Pantelleria' produces large flavourful capers.

Capparis spinosa

HARDINESS Frost hardy.
PARTS USED Root bark, flower buds, fruits ("caperberries").
PROPERTIES An astringent, diuretic, expectorant herb that is regarded as a stimulating tonic.
MEDICINAL USES Internally for gastrointestinal infections, diarrhoea, skin problems, fragile capillaries, internal bleeding, gout, rheumatism (root bark); for coughs (flower buds). Externally for eye infections (flower buds).
CULINARY USES Pickled or dry-salted caper buds are used in caper sauce for lamb, *tartare*, *ravigote*, *remoulade*, and *puttanesca* sauces, fish dishes, and hors d'oeuvres, especially *caponata*. Caperberries are used similarly, and to accompany smoked salmon.

CAPSELLA
Brassicaceae

A genus of five annual or biennial herbs, found throughout temperate and warm areas. The distinctive, heart-shaped seed pods of *C. bursa-pastoris* (shepherd's purse) have given rise to its specific name and various common names, such as witches' pouches and pick-pocket. This annual weed flourishes in a variety of situations, and became established in many countries (notably the USA) during European colonization. Shepherd's purse has been used as a food for thousands of years. Seeds were found in the stomach of Tollund man (c.500BC–AD400) and during excavation of the Catal Hüyük site, which dates back to 5950BC. According to Mrs Grieve (*A Modern Herbal*, 1931), the seeds are food for pet birds. In Japan, shepherd's purse is an important ingredient in the rice and barley porridge traditionally eaten on 7 January.
CULTIVATION Well-drained soil in sun or partial shade. Tolerates poor conditions.
PROPAGATION By seed sown in spring. It self-sows freely.
HARVEST Whole plants are cut from late spring to autumn and used fresh, or dried in bunches for infusions, decoctions, or liquid extracts. Leaves and seed pods are gathered as required for culinary use.

Capsella bursa-pastoris

▪ *Capsella bursa-pastoris* syn. *Thlaspi bursa-pastoris* (Chinese cress, *nazuna*, shepherd's purse)
Annual or biennial with a rosette of entire to pinnate basal leaves and a branched stem with smaller leaves. Tiny white flowers appear all year, followed by heart-shaped seed pods. Cosmopolitan. ‡3–40cm (1¼–16in), ↔3–15cm (1¼–6in).
HARDINESS Fully hardy.
PARTS USED Whole plant (*ji cai*), leaves, seed pods.
PROPERTIES An astringent diuretic herb that also acts as a urinary antiseptic and blood coagulant.
MEDICINAL USES Internally and externally to stop bleeding, especially in heavy menstruation, blood in urine, haemorrhoids, nosebleed, and wounds. Also internally for cystitis, and externally for varicose veins. In Chinese medicine, to cool the blood, with uses similar to the above; also for hypertension and postpartum bleeding.
CULINARY USES Leaves are rich in vitamins A, B, and C, and may be added to salads or cooked as a vegetable. Seed pods have a peppery flavour and may be used as seasoning.

CAPSICUM
Pepper

Solanaceae

About ten wild species and four or five domesticated species of shrubby annuals, biennials, and perennials are included in this tropical American genus. Capsicum peppers were first described in 1493 by Dr Chauca, a physician on Christopher Columbus's voyage, and were introduced from S America to India and Africa by the Portuguese. Today, peppers rank second in importance to *Piper nigrum* (black pepper) among the world's spices, and hundreds of different cultivars are grown in warm regions, and under cover in temperate parts. China and Turkey are the world's largest producers of chilli peppers, and most major producers (including C and S America, the West Indies, USA, Japan, Thailand, Hungary, and

C

Italy) have cultivars adapted to local growing conditions and cuisines. Fruiting plants are often ornamental, and a number of compact dwarf cultivars with upward-pointing fruits have been developed for the pot plant industry. *Capsicum* may be derived from the Latin *capsa*, "box", from the characteristically hollow fruits. Most cultivated capsicums belong to *C. annuum* and may be divided into five main groups: Cerasiforme (cherry); Conioides (cone); Fasciculatum (red cone); Grossum (bell pepper, pimento, sweet pepper); and Longum (cayenne, chilli). They are rich in vitamin C. Pungency is due to a bitter, acrid alkaloid, capsaicin, which is the main therapeutic and flavouring compound in hot peppers. Its presence depends on a single gene, and cultivars lacking the gene have sweet fruits. *Capsicum annuum* has both pungent and sweet cultivars, used respectively for cayenne or chilli powder, and paprika. Hot peppers are known as chillies in Europe, and chiles or chilis in N America.

CULTIVATION Rich, well-drained soil in sun. *Capsicum baccatum* var. *pendulum* and *C. pubescens* withstand cooler conditions. *Capsicum pubescens* may be espaliered or pruned. Plant bugs may damage growing points and leaves; plants under cover may be affected by spider mite, whitefly, and aphids.

PROPAGATION By seed sown in early spring.

HARVEST Unripe fruits are picked as required and used raw, pickled, or cooked. Ripe fruits are picked in summer and used fresh, pickled, or dried for condiments, decoctions, ointments, powders, tinctures, tablets, and oleo-resin.

⚠ **WARNING** Capsicum oleo-resin is subject to legal restrictions in some countries.

Capsicum annuum (bell pepper, chili pepper, chilli pepper, sweet pepper)
Tender variable annual or short-lived perennial with branched stems and simple, ovate–lanceolate leaves. Bell-shaped, white to green flowers appear in spring and summer, followed by hollow fruits, up to 15cm (6in) long, which ripen to varying colours. Native to tropical America. ‡1.5m (5ft), ↔50cm–2m (20in–6ft). ▣ 'Anaheim' is a New Mexican pod type, early, with tapering, pointed, mildly pungent, dark green fruits, 15–20cm (6–8in) long and up to 5cm (2in) wide, turning scarlet when ripe. Excellent for stuffing. Dried and ground into paprika when ripe. ‡60cm (24in), ↔38cm (15in). 'Ancho' has medium-hot, heart-shaped, thin-walled fruits, 8–15cm (3–6in) long and 7cm (3in) wide, known as poblanos; used in Mexican *mole* sauces and *chiles rellenos* (stuffed chillies). 'Cascabel' has moderately hot, thin-walled, rounded, shiny fruits that ripen brown with a fruity flavour. Dried whole and often used with seafood. 'Cayenne' is a pod type originating in Cayenne, French Guiana, with highly pungent, slender, often crescent-shaped pods, 13–25cm (5–10in) long, and 1–2.5cm (⅜–1in) wide, which may be green or yellow, ripening red. Commercially used for hot sauces and flaked chilli pepper. ‡75–90cm (2½–3ft). 'Chile Piquín'/'Chilpequín'/'Chiltepin' syn. *C. a.* var. *glabriusculum*, *C. a.* var. *minimum* (bird pepper) bears fiercely hot, bullet-shaped fruits, up to 2.5cm (1in) long and 1cm (⅜in) wide. Often harvested from the wild in Mexico. ‡2m (6ft), ↔1–1.2m (3–4ft). 'De Arbol' forms an erect, tree-like plant, bearing narrow fruits, 5–7cm (2–3in) long, with a

smoky flavour, which are usually ground into powder. 'Guajillo' has moderately hot, thin-walled, translucent, burgundy fruits, 13cm (5in) long, and tapering from 3.5cm (1⅜in) wide. Fruity flavour is ideal for red enchilada sauce. ‡90cm (3ft). ▣ 'Jalapeño' is a compact Mexican cultivar with usually very pungent, thick-walled, cylindrical, green fruits, 6–10cm (2½–4in) long, which ripen red and typically develop cracks or netting, called corkiness. A main ingredient in salsa. Mature red fruits are smoke-dried as *chipotle*. ‡60cm (24in), ↔ 45cm (18in). 'Mirasol' has a spreading, much-branched habit and ornamental clusters of erect, pointed, red fruits, 8–10cm (3–4in) long and 1–2cm (⅜–¾in) wide. Dried for chilli powder. ↔1.2m (4ft). 'Mulato' is a similar pod type to 'Ancho', with late-maturing, tapering, blunt-ended fruits, 10–15cm (4–6in) long and 7cm (3in) wide, which ripen brown and have a moderately hot, chocolate-like flavour. Used for stuffing when fresh, or dried for *mole* sauces. ‡90cm (3ft), ↔1.2m (4ft). 'Pasilla' is a vigorous, late-maturing type, with cylindrical, moderately hot, dark green pods, 15–30cm (6–12in) long and up to 2.5cm (1in) wide, which ripen brown and have a smoky, raisin-like flavour. Green fruits, known as *chilaca*, are eaten raw or cooked; mature fruits are dried for *mole* sauces. ▣ 'Purple Tiger' is compact, with foliage variegated white and purple, and small, extremely pungent, tear-shaped fruits that ripen through red to deep purple. ‡70cm (28in), ↔50cm (20in). 'Serrano' is an upland Mexican pod type with hairy leaves and cylindrical fruits, 5–13cm (2–5in) long, which ripen red, orange, yellow, or brown. Good for salsa known as *pico*

Capsicum annuum 'Anaheim'

Capsicum annuum 'Jalapeño'

Capsicum baccatum

Capsicum annuum 'Purple Tiger'

Capsicum chinense 'Habañero'

Capsicum frutescens

Capsicum frutescens 'Tabasco'

de gallo. ‡ 90cm (3ft), ↔ 45cm (18in). 'Thai Hot' is an Asian pod type, with a compact habit and prolific, highly pungent, cone-shaped fruits, 2.5–6cm (1–2½in) long, which ripen red and are used fresh or dried in Thai and other Asian dishes.

NOTE: Certain pod types have names that are not strictly cultivar names, but are often (as here) treated as such. Most pod types have a number of cultivars. For example, jalapeño is a pod type that originated in the town of Jalapa, Mexico. Cultivars of the jalapeño type include 'NuMex Primavera' and 'Jumbo Jalapeño'.
HARDINESS Min. 4–13°C (39–55°F), depending on cultivar.
PARTS USED Fruits.
PROPERTIES Pungent-fruited cultivars have tonic and antiseptic effects, stimulate the circulatory and digestive systems, and increase perspiration. They also irritate the tissues, increasing blood supply to the area, and reducing sensitivity to pain.
MEDICINAL USES Internally for the cold stage of fevers, debility in convalescence or old age, varicose veins, poor circulation, asthma, and digestive problems. Externally for sprains, arthritis, unbroken chilblains, neuralgia, lumbago, and pleurisy, and combined with *Commiphora myrrha* (see p.177) as a gargle for laryngitis. Pungent-fruited peppers are important as a gastrointestinal detoxicant and food preservative in the tropics.
CULINARY USES Both pungent-fruited and sweet-fruited cultivars are used ripe or unripe, fresh or dried, as vegetables (raw or cooked), stuffed, and in curries, pickles and chutneys, in many parts of the world, especially S and C America, Mexico, India, and SE Asia. Ripe fruits are dried to make cayenne, chilli powder, or paprika. Pungent-fruited peppers may cause painful inflammation in excess, or after accidental contact with eyes or broken skin.
🗷 🞉 ✍ ▣

■ *Capsicum baccatum* syn. *C. microcarpum* (*ají*)
Spreading shrubby perennial with white to yellow flowers, 1cm (⅜in) across, marked beige or green at the base, and spotted yellow to tan. Small red fruits are held erect and contain cream to yellow seeds. Native to Ecuador and Peru. ‡ 3m (10ft), ↔ 1.5–2m (5–6ft). var. *pendulum* syn. *C. pendulum* (Andean *ají*) is a cool-growing, late-maturing variety with medium to very hot fruits, to 13cm (5in) long. Common in S Andes and Ecuador. ‡ 45cm–2m (18in–6ft), ↔ 1.2m (4ft). 'Ají Amarillo' (yellow Peruvian pepper) has pungent, thin-walled, yellow to orange fruits, 13–18cm (3–7in) long. Typical of Peruvian cuisine, especially in ceviche (marinated raw fish). 'Christmas Bell' (orchid chilli) produces moderately pungent, well-flavoured, yellow fruits that are shaped like a crumpled bell and ripen red. Often dried for ornamental garlands.
HARDINESS Min. 4–13°C (39–55°F), depending on cultivar.
PARTS USED Fruits.

PROPERTIES As for pungent-fruited cultivars of *C. annuum*.
MEDICINAL USES As for pungent-fruited cultivars of *C. annuum*.
CULINARY USES As for pungent-fruited cultivars of *C. annuum*.
🗷 🞉 ✍ ▣

Capsicum chinense syn. *C. sinense*
Tender shrub with clusters of two or more white or green-tinged flowers. Fruits are pendulous, red-brown to cream. Native to West Indies, southern C America, and northern S America. ‡↔ 1.5m (5ft). ▣ 'Habañero' is a pod type from Belize and the Yucatán Peninsula (Mexico), with orange-red, lantern-shaped fruits, 6cm (2½in) long and 2.5cm (1in) wide. The hottest chilli, used fresh in salsas, in cooked dishes, and fermented for hot sauces. ‡ 1–1.2m (3–4ft), ↔ 60cm (24in). 'Rocotillo', from Puerto Rico, is a large-leafed cultivar with moderately hot, crumpled, beret-shaped fruits that mature red, orange, yellow, or white. ‡ 1.1m (3¼ft). Used in "jerk" seasoning. 'Scotch Bonnet' is similar to 'Rocotillo' but short-stalked and slightly hotter.
HARDINESS Min. 4–13°C (39–55°F), depending on cultivar.
PARTS USED Fruits.
PROPERTIES As for pungent-fruited cultivars of *C. annuum*.
MEDICINAL USES As for pungent-fruited cultivars of *C. annuum*.
CULINARY USES As for pungent-fruited cultivars of *C. annuum*.
🗷 🞉 ✍ ▣

■ *Capsicum frutescens* syn. *C. minimum* (hot pepper, spur pepper, tabasco pepper)
Bushy perennial with elliptic leaves up to 10cm (4in) long. Flowers are pale green to yellow, followed by green, very pungent fruits that turn red, orange, or yellow. Native to tropical America. Often called "bird pepper" in Africa and Asia. ‡ 45cm–1.5m (1½–5ft), ↔ 60cm (24in). ▣ 'Tabasco' has very pungent, erect, yellow to yellow-green fruits, 2.5–5cm (1–2in) long and 0.5cm (¼in) wide, which ripen red. Used in creole cooking and for tabasco sauce. ‡ 60–90cm (2–3ft), ↔ 60cm (2ft).
HARDINESS Min. 4–13°C (39–55°F), depending on cultivar.
PARTS USED Fruits.
PROPERTIES As for pungent-fruited cultivars of *C. annuum*.
MEDICINAL USES As for pungent-fruited cultivars of *C. annuum*.
CULINARY USES As for pungent-fruited cultivars of *C. annuum*.
🗷 🞉 ✍ ▣

Capsicum pubescens (caballo, canario, manzana, perón, rocoto, tree pepper)
Sprawling shrubby perennial with striped stems, purple nodes, and wrinkled, hairy, ovate leaves. Solitary, violet, white-eyed flowers are followed by pendent to erect, extremely pungent, juicy, apple- to pear-shaped, yellow, red, or brown fruits, containing black seeds. Found from the Andes of Peru to upland

Mexico. ‡ 3m (10ft), ↔ 2m (6ft).
HARDINESS Min. 4–13°C (39–55°F).
PARTS USED Fruits.
PROPERTIES As for pungent-fruited cultivars of *C. annuum*.
MEDICINAL USES As for pungent-fruited cultivars of *C. annuum*.
CULINARY USES As for pungent-fruited cultivars of *C. annuum*.
🗷 🞉 ✍ ▣

CARBENIA
Carbenia benedicta. See *Cnicus benedictus*.

CARDAMINE
Bitter cress

Brassicaceae

Some 130 annuals and perennials, found almost worldwide in temperate areas, comprise this genus. About a dozen species are grown as ornamentals in moist ground, including *C. pratensis*, which flowers as the cuckoos arrive in Europe, giving the common name of cuckoo flower. *Cardamine* is from the Greek *kardamon*, "cress", as many species resemble watercress in appearance and flavour. Like many genera of the cabbage family (Brassicaceae), *Cardamine* contains mustard oil glycosides. This gives the flavour a characteristic tang and endows the oil with medicinal properties similar to the true mustards: *Brassica juncea* (see p.146), *B. nigra* (see p.146), and *Sinapis alba* (see p.369). The leaves of *Cardamine amara* (large bitter cress) and *C. hirsuta* (hairy bitter cress) have the same culinary uses as *C. pratensis*.
CULTIVATION Moist soil in sun or partial shade.
PROPAGATION By seed in autumn or spring; by leaf-tip cuttings in midsummer; by division in spring or after flowering.
HARVEST Leaves are picked in spring and summer, and used fresh in infusions, or frozen.

Cardamine pratensis

C

Cardamine pratensis 'Flore Pleno'

▣ ***Cardamine pratensis*** (cuckoo flower, lady's smock, meadow cress)
Slender, clump-forming perennial with a basal rosette of long-stalked, pinnate leaves. Small, lilac to white, four-petalled flowers appear in late spring, followed by narrow erect pods. Native to N Asia, N America, and Europe. ↕ 30–45cm (12–18in), ↔ 30cm (12in). 'Edith' has pink buds and double flowers that fade to white. ↕ 20cm (8in). ▣ 'Flore Pleno' has double flowers. Forms clumps and offsets readily. First recorded in the mid-17th century. ↕ 20cm (8in).
HARDINESS Fully hardy.
PARTS USED Leaves.
PROPERTIES A tonic cleansing herb with a high level of vitamin C. It arrests spasms and encourages productive coughing.
MEDICINAL USES Internally for chronic skin complaints, asthma, and hysteria.
CULINARY USES Young leaves and flower buds are added to salads, sandwiches, and sauces.
▨ ▤ ▨

CARDUUS
Carduus benedictus. See *Cnicus benedictus*.
Carduus marianus. See *Silybum marianum*.

CARICA
Caricaceae

This S American genus has 22 species of trees and shrubs, characteristically with thick unbranched trunks. The best known is *C. papaya* (papaya), found in lowland tropical forest, which is grown for its pear-shaped fruits and as an ornamental. It has been cultivated since pre-Columbian times, reaching Europe in 1690 and Asia in the 18th century. Both male and female trees are normally needed for fruiting, but there are now cultivars with male and female flowers on the same plant, such as 'Solo'. The unripe fruits, leaves, sap, and seeds of *C. papaya* contain papain, an enzyme that breaks down protein. Fruits of *Asimina triloba* (American papaya, custard apple) have different properties, with edible flesh and unpleasant-smelling seeds that have an emetic effect.
CULTIVATION Rich moist soil in sun and high humidity. Red spider mite, aphid, and whitefly may damage plants under glass.
PROPAGATION By seed sown in spring at 24–30°C (75–86°F).
HARVEST Leaves are picked as required. Seeds are taken from ripe fruits and used fresh. Papain is extracted mainly from unripe fruits and from sap, which is collected from incisions in bark, and dried to a powder for medicinal and industrial uses.

▣ ***Carica papaya*** (papaya, pawpaw)
Evergreen tree with seven-lobed, palmate leaves, to 70cm (28in) across. Fruits are pear-shaped, 45cm (18in) long, with a leathery, yellow-green skin, apricot-coloured pulp, and a central cavity of round black seeds. Native to S America. ↕ 6m (20ft), ↔ 3m (10ft).
HARDINESS Min. 13–15°C (55–59°F).
PARTS USED Leaves, flowers, fruits, seeds, sap.
PROPERTIES An enzyme-rich herb that improves digestion of protein, reduces scarring, and expels intestinal worms.
MEDICINAL USES Internally for digestive disorders, and externally for deep or slow-healing wounds (papain). Internally, in countries of origin, to expel threadworms and roundworms (sap, seeds). Externally for wounds, boils, ulcers, warts, and skin tumours (sap). Papain is an ingredient of digestive supplements.

Carica papaya

CULINARY USES Ripe fruits are eaten raw in desserts and salads, candied, dried, and preserved. Unripe fruits are cooked as a vegetable, pickled, and made into relishes. Seeds have a peppery flavour, used as seasoning in countries of origin. Fresh leaves, unripe fruits, and fruit skins are used to tenderize meat. Flowers are added to cooked dishes or candied.
ECONOMIC USES Papain is used in the manufacture of chewing gum and sausage casings, in clarifying beer and modifying baking dough, in termite control, and the shrink-proofing of wool and silk.
▨ ▨ ▨ ▨ ▨ ▤ ▨ ▨ ▨

CARLINA
Carline thistle
Asteraceae

This genus of 28 species of annual, biennial, and perennial thistles is found in Europe, Mediterranean regions, and W Asia. *Carlina acaulis* grows in mountain pastures and has typical thistle fruits, with a plume to aid wind dispersal. It is grown as an ornamental for its flower heads, which have shiny papery bracts and dry well. *Carlina* was named after Charlemagne, who had a vision that the plant would ward off the plague. The carline thistle was an important herb in medieval times, classed as alexipharmic (antidote to poison). It is little used today since there are more effective thistles, such as *Cnicus benedictus* (see p.174) and *Silybum marianum* (see p.368).
CULTIVATION Well-drained, poor, neutral to alkaline soil in full sun. In fertile soil, the flowers develop stalks.
PROPAGATION By seed sown when ripe.
HARVEST Roots are dug in autumn and dried for decoctions, liquid extracts, and tinctures. Flowers and leaves are picked as required.

▣ ***Carlina acaulis*** (stemless carline thistle)
Low-growing biennial or perennial with a long taproot and a rosette of prickly leaves, 30cm (12in) long. Stemless, disc-shaped flowers, surrounded by silvery bracts, are produced in summer. Native to S and E Europe. ↕ 10cm (4in), ↔ 25cm (10in).

Carlina acaulis

HARDINESS Fully hardy.
PARTS USED Roots, flowers, leaves.
PROPERTIES A tonic cleansing herb that
benefits the liver and gall bladder, genito-urinary
system, and skin.
MEDICINAL USES Internally for fluid retention,
liver, gall bladder, and prostate problems,
bronchitis, and skin complaints, such as acne
and eczema (roots).
CULINARY USES Flower receptacles are eaten
as a substitute for artichoke hearts. Leaves can
be used to curdle milk.
⊞ ▨ ▥ ▦ ☑

CARTHAMUS

Asteraceae

Fourteen species, mostly annuals, with a few
perennials, belong to this thistle-like genus, native
to Asia and Mediterranean regions. *Carthamus
tinctorius* (safflower) was introduced into Europe
from Egypt in 1551. It is cultivated mainly for
the oil content of its seeds in Australia, China,
SE Asia, India, Africa, and Mediterranean
regions, and is increasingly popular as a
cutflower. The name *Carthamus* comes from the
Arabic *qurtom* or the Hebrew *qarthami*, "to
paint", because the flowers yield a pigment
(carthamin) that is yellow in water and red in
alcohol. It has been in great demand since ancient
times as a colouring agent for foods, fabrics,
feathers, and rouge; the robes of Buddhist
monks and nuns are traditionally dyed with
saffron thistle flowers. Found in Egyptian tombs
dating back to 3500BC, it was first described in
traditional Chinese medicine in AD1061.
CULTIVATION Light, well-drained soil in sun.
PROPAGATION By seed sown in spring at
10–15°C (50–59°F).
HARVEST Flower heads are harvested in
summer and used fresh or dried for infusions.
Alternatively, florets are carefully picked from
fully opened flowers, leaving ovaries to develop
into seeds for oil extraction.

■ *Carthamus tinctorius* (false saffron,
safflower, saffron thistle)
Tall annual with erect stem and spine-toothed
leaves, 3–9cm (1¼–3½in) long. Thistle-like
flower heads, to 4cm (1½in) across, with deep
yellow florets surrounded by leafy, spine-edged
bracts, appear in summer, followed by oblong
white seeds, 6mm (¼in) long. Native to
W Asia. ↕ 30–60cm (12–24in), ↔ 30cm (12in).
'Lasting White' has cream flowers. 'Orange
Ball' has orange flowers.
HARDINESS Hardy.
PARTS USED Flowers (*hong hua*), seeds, oil.
PROPERTIES A bitter aromatic herb that
stimulates the circulation, heart, and uterus,
reducing fevers and inflammation, relieving
pain, and lowering cholesterol levels.
MEDICINAL USES Internally for coronary artery
disease, menstrual and menopausal problems,
jaundice, and measles (flowers). Not given to
pregnant women. Externally for bruising,
sprains, skin inflammations, wounds, and
painful or paralyzed joints (flowers).

Carthamus tinctorius

CULINARY USES Oil is used in cooking and as
part of cholesterol-reducing diets.
ECONOMIC USES Flowers are a source of red
and yellow dyes used to colour dairy produce,
liqueurs, and confectionery. Seeds are edible
and can be used to coagulate milk. Oil is used
to make margarine.
⊞ ▢ ▥ ▦ ☑ ☑

CARUM

Apiaceae

Thirty species make up this genus of biennials
and perennials, which is found in Europe,
N Africa, and temperate Asia. The most
important herb in the genus is *C. carvi*
(caraway), which occurs in damp grassland and
disturbed ground. It was used in the Middle
East for 5000 years before reaching Europe in
the 13th century. The typical smell of caraway
is produced by carvone, which forms 40–63 per
cent of the volatile oil in the seeds. Various
herbs were once included in the genus *Carum*,
including *Petroselinum crispum* (see p.310),
formerly known as *C. petroselinum*, and
Trachyspermum ammi (see p.392), formerly
known as *Carum copticum*. *Carum
roxburghianum* (ajmud) is grown in parts of
Asia for its seeds, which are used in curries and
kecap (Indonesian soy sauce). *Carum* is named
after Caria, an ancient region of Asia Minor
that corresponds to present-day S Aydin and
W Mugla (Turkey).
CULTIVATION Well-drained, fertile soil in full
sun. Caraway tolerates heavy soils. Flowers
attract parasitic wasps, which prey on aphids.
PROPAGATION By seed sown *in situ* in spring
or early autumn. Does not transplant well. Self-
sows in suitable conditions.
HARVEST Leaves and roots are gathered to be
used fresh as vegetables. Seeds are gathered as
they ripen and are dried for use in infusions,
pills, and tinctures. Oil is distilled commercially
for flavouring and pharmaceutical products.

■ *Carum carvi* (caraway)
Erect biennial with a spindle-shaped taproot,
hollow stems, and deeply divided, fern-like
leaves, 8–15cm (3–6in) long. Tiny, white- to

Carum carvi

pink-rayed flowers are
produced in umbels, 4cm
(1½in) across, in summer,
followed by aromatic, five-
ribbed fruits, to 6mm (¼in)
long. Found from Europe to
W Asia. ↕ 60–90cm (2–3ft), ↔ 30cm (12in).
HARDINESS Fully hardy.
PARTS USED Leaves, roots, seeds, oil.
PROPERTIES A pungently aromatic, stimulant
herb that reduces gastrointestinal and uterine
spasms, and encourages productive coughing.
MEDICINAL USES Internally for indigestion,
wind, colic (especially in children), hiatus
hernia, stomach ulcer, diarrhoea, menstrual
cramps, and bronchitis. Externally as a gargle
for laryngitis. Added to laxatives to reduce
griping and to various products for digestive
problems. Seeds are chewed for relief of
indigestion.
CULINARY USES Leaves have a mild parsley–
dill flavour, pleasant in soups and salads. Roots
may be cooked as a vegetable. Seeds are
especially popular in Jewish cuisine and in the
cuisines of N and E Europe, flavouring cakes
and bread (notably rye bread), goulash,
cabbage, sauerkraut, sausages, cheese, cooked
apples, liqueur (such as kümmel), and spirits
(schnapps); also sugar-coated as "sugar plums".
ECONOMIC USES Oil is used in perfumery and
for flavouring ice cream, confectionery, pickles,
and soft drinks.
▨ ▢ ▥ ▦ ▩ ☑ ☑

Carum copticum. See *Trachyspermum ammi*.

CASSIA
Cassia angustifolia. See *Senna alexandrina*.
Cassia marilandica. See *Senna marilandica*.

CASTANEA
Chestnut

Fagaceae

This genus includes about 12 species of
deciduous trees and shrubs from warm
temperate parts of the northern hemisphere.
Castanea sativa has been planted since Roman

C

times. Cultivars vary in flavour, keeping qualities, and ease of peeling. Culpeper wrote in *The English Physician Enlarged* (1653) that chestnuts "provoke lust exceedingly" and are "an admirable remedy for the cough and spitting of blood". Leaves of *C. dentata* (American chestnut) are also used to relieve coughs. The genus is named after Castania (Greece), which was renowned for its chestnuts.

CULTIVATION Deep, well-drained, neutral to slightly acidic soil in sun or partial shade.
PROPAGATION By seed sown in autumn; by budding in summer; by grafting in late winter.
HARVEST Leaves are gathered in summer and dried for infusions and liquid extracts. Seeds are collected in autumn and cooked before use.

▣ *Castanea sativa* (Spanish chestnut, sweet chestnut)
Deciduous tree with spirally furrowed bark and oblong–lanceolate, toothed leaves, to 24cm (10in) long. Tiny, yellow-green, musky-smelling flowers appear in summer, followed by prickly fruits, containing 1–3 brown nuts. Native to S Europe, N Africa, and SW Asia; widely naturalized. ‡ 30m (100ft), ↔ 15m (50ft).
▣ 'Albomarginata' syn. 'Argenteomarginata' has white-margined leaves. 'Marron de Lyon' bears fruits with a single kernel, which is preferred for commercial production.
HARDINESS Fully hardy.
PARTS USED Leaves, seeds.
PROPERTIES An astringent herb that controls coughing and has anti-rheumatic effects.
MEDICINAL USES Internally for paroxysmal coughs, whooping cough, catarrh, diarrhoea, and rheumatism (leaves). Externally as a gargle for pharyngitis (leaves).
CULINARY USES Chestnuts are used in sauces, soups, stuffings, and desserts, and eaten roasted or boiled as a snack or vegetable. They are also

| *Castanea sativa*

Castanea sativa 'Albomarginata'

puréed (*purée de marrons*), crystallized (*marrons glacés*), ground into flour (*farine de châtaigne*) for breads and cakes (*castagnaccio*). Leaves are used to wrap cheeses in France. Chestnut honey is popular in Italy.

▨ ▩ ▣ ☑

CATHA
Celastraceae

This genus consists of a single species of tree, widely distributed in E Africa, from Ethiopia to the Horn of Africa and South Yemen. *Catha edulis* (*khat*, *qat*) is widely cultivated in Ethiopia, Somalia, Yemen, and Kenya for its leaves, which are chewed fresh as a stimulant locally, and air-freighted to Arab communities worldwide in countries where it has not been banned. Between a third and a half of cultivable land in Yemen is devoted to growing *khat*. It contains alkaloids similar in effect to amphetamine, and to ephedrine in *Ephedra* spp. (see p.201), including cathinone, which remains active for only 24 hours after harvesting, and cathine or norpseudoephedrine, which is used in geriatric medicine. *Khat* chewing is thought to have originated in the Harar region (Ethiopia), and is acceptable in the Koran as an alternative to alcohol and other stimulants. The use of *khat* is considered psychologically rather than physically addictive.
CULTIVATION Well-drained to dry soil in sun.
PROPAGATION By seed sown when ripe.
HARVEST Twigs are picked all year round and used fresh within 24 hours.

▣ *Catha edulis* (Arabian tea, bushman's tea, *khat*, *qat*)
Evergreen shrub or small tree with bright green, shiny, ovate, pointed leaves, to 8cm (3in) long, with evenly toothed margins and a characteristic drooping habit. Dense clusters of small white flowers appear along the twigs in summer, followed by dry capsules. Native to E Africa, the Horn of Africa, and South Yemen. ‡ 15m (50ft), ↔ 6m (20ft).
HARDINESS Min. 10°C (50°F).
PARTS USED Leaves.
PROPERTIES A bitter, astringent, stimulant

Catha edulis

herb that suppresses the appetite.
MEDICINAL USES Leaves are chewed or infused as a stimulant. Internally for malaria, coughs, asthma and other bronchial complaints, and to improve mental function in old age (Africa). Taken as an aid for weight reduction in Germany. Excess raises blood pressure and causes headache, arrhythmia, hyperthermia, or other side-effects; persistent use may result in aggressive behaviour and personality disorders.
CULINARY USES Leaves are brewed as tea, and are an ingredient of *tej*, an Arabic mead.
⚠ **WARNING** This herb is illegal in many countries, including Canada, France, Italy, Morocco, Norway, Sweden, Saudi Arabia, and USA.

▨ ▣ ☑ ▩

CATHARANTHUS
Apocynaceae

Eight species of Madagascan annuals and perennials are included in this genus. *Catharanthus roseus* has become a pantropical weed and is grown in temperate regions as an indoor plant or summer bedding plant for its attractive, periwinkle-like flowers. Extraction of alkaloids for medicinal uses was developed in the 1950s, after *C. roseus* was screened by an American pharmaceutical company for possible therapeutic properties. It contains more than 75 alkaloids, including vincristine and vinblastine, which have revolutionized cancer therapy, especially the treatment of acute leukaemia in children. Isolated alkaloids are highly toxic and quite different in effect from the leaves, which have long been used in folk medicine for other purposes.
CULTIVATION Moist, well-drained soil in sun. Cut back in spring to maintain compact shape. Low temperatures and wet conditions may cause fungal diseases.
PROPAGATION By seed sown in spring at 13–18°C (55–64°F); by softwood cuttings in late spring; by semi-ripe cuttings in summer.
HARVEST Leaves are picked before or during flowering and dried for infusions, liquid extracts, and tinctures; and for extraction of alkaloids.
⚠ **WARNING** Toxic if eaten.

Catharanthus roseus

■ **Catharanthus roseus** syn. *Vinca rosea*
(Cayenne jasmine, Madagascar periwinkle, old
maid, rosy periwinkle)
Small erect perennial with smooth, shiny,
oval leaves, up to 5cm (2in) long, and pink,
flat-petalled flowers, 4cm (1½in) across, with
darker pink centres. Native to Madagascar;
now pantropical. ‡↔ 30–60cm (12–24in).
var. *ocellatus* has red-eyed flowers. ■ Pacifica
Series has a vigorous, compact, bushy habit,
with large, lilac, pale pink, or white, often red-
eyed flowers. ‡↔ 30cm (12in).
HARDINESS Min. 13°C (55°F).
PARTS USED Leaves.
PROPERTIES An astringent herb that reduces
blood sugar levels, increases perspiration, and
stimulates the uterus.
MEDICINAL USES Internally for diabetes (West
Indies); diabetes, hypertension, chronic
constipation, and indigestion (Mauritius,
Surinam, Vietnam); asthma (Bahamas);
menstrual regulation (Africa, Philippines).

Catharanthus roseus Pacifica Series

Isolated alkaloids treat acute leukaemia
(especially in children), Hodgkin's disease, and
other cancers, with side-effects such as nausea,
alopecia, and bone marrow depression.

CAULOPHYLLUM
Berberidaceae

Two species of rhizomatous perennials belong
to this genus: one in E Asia, and the other,
C. thalictroides, in rich moist woods in eastern
N America. The name comes from the Greek
kaulon, "stem", and *phyllon*, "leaf", referring
to the way the stem of the plant forms a stalk for
the solitary compound leaf, which divides into
three deeply lobed leaflets. The flowers of
C. thalictroides arise from the base of the
uppermost leaflet in spring. The common name
"cohosh" is of Algonquin origin. *Caulophyllum
thalictroides* is one of the most important herbs
for women and was used by various native
American tribes to facilitate childbirth, giving
rise to names such as squaw root and papoose
root. Its popularity led to inclusion in the
US Pharmacopoeia (1882–1905). The Asian
species, *C. robustum*, once considered a variety
of *C. thalictroides*, may have similar properties,
and is known to be fungicidal. It is used in
Chinese folk medicine to heal injuries, including
fractures, rheumatism, digestive problems, and
menstrual disorders.
CULTIVATION Rich, moist, neutral to acid soil
in dappled or deep shade.
PROPAGATION By seed sown when ripe (slow
to germinate); by division in autumn.
HARVEST Rhizomes and roots are lifted in
autumn and dried for decoctions, liquid extracts,
powders, and tinctures.

■ **Caulophyllum thalictroides** (blue cohosh,
papoose root, squaw root)
Slow-growing, rhizomatous perennial with a
matted rootstock and glaucous compound leaf.
Yellow-green to purplish, star-shaped flowers,
1cm (⅜in) across, appear with new leaves,
followed by deep blue berries. Native to eastern
N America. ‡ 30–75cm (12–30in), ↔ indefinite.
HARDINESS Fully hardy.

Caulophyllum thalictroides

PARTS USED Rhizomes, roots.
PROPERTIES An acrid, bitter, warming herb that
stimulates the uterus, reduces inflammation,
relaxes spasms, expels intestinal worms, and
has diuretic effects.
MEDICINAL USES Internally for pelvic
inflammatory disease, endometriosis, slow
erratic menstruation and parturition, and
retained placenta. Taken in the last four weeks
of pregnancy, and during labour, to facilitate
contractions and cervical dilation. Also for
rheumatism, arthritis, and gout. Not given to
patients with hypertension and heart disease.
For use by qualified practitioners only.

CEANOTHUS
California lilac, redroot
Rhamnaceae

Some 50–60 species of evergreen and deciduous
shrubs or small trees belong to this N American
genus, which is mainly western in distribution.
Some species grow in arid places and live in
association with a soil fungus that provides the
roots with nitrogen. The blue-flowered species
are among the most popular garden shrubs for
mild areas. Less ornamental, but interesting for
its medicinal properties, is *C. americanus*, which
is found in eastern N America. It was used as a
substitute for tea during the American Revolution
and is a parent of many hybrids. The Cherokee
people of N America used *C. americanus*
externally to treat skin cancer and venereal
sores. Several other species are used
medicinally, including *C. cuneatus* (buckbrush),
C. integerrimus (deerbrush), and *C. velutinus*
(tobacco brush), which are interchangeable and
generally known as redroot. They benefit the
circulatory and lymphatic systems, control
bleeding, and are effective astringents for
inflammations of the throat and mouth.
CULTIVATION Well-drained soil in sun. Dislikes
alkaline conditions but tolerates poor dry soils.
Cut back to within 8–10cm (3–4in) of the
previous season's growth in spring. Scale
insects may attack stems. Dislikes disturbance.
PROPAGATION By seed sown in autumn; by
semi-ripe cuttings in summer.
HARVEST Roots are harvested from midsummer
to midwinter, and dried for use in decoctions,
liquid extracts, and tinctures. Leaves are gathered
during the flowering period and dried.

■ **Ceanothus americanus** (New Jersey tea,
redroot)
Small deciduous shrub with tough, dark red roots
and ovate leaves, to 10cm (4in) long. Dense,
long-stalked panicles of tiny, off-white flowers
appear in summer, followed by triangular seed
pods. Native to eastern C and SE USA and
S Canada. ‡ 1m (3ft), ↔ 45cm (18in).
HARDINESS Fully hardy.
PARTS USED Roots.
PROPERTIES A bitter, astringent, cleansing herb
that is expectorant, relaxes spasms, and has a
tonic effect on the circulatory and lymphatic
systems.

Ceanothus americanus

Cedronella canariensis

Cedrus atlantica

MEDICINAL USES Internally for colds, bronchitis, whooping cough, tonsillitis, diphtheria, sinusitis, enlarged spleen, abnormal uterine bleeding, nosebleeds, haemorrhoids, and depression. Contraindicated during pregnancy, and when suffering from blood disorders or taking medication that affects blood clotting.
CULINARY USES Leaves are used as a caffeine-free tea substitute.

⬛ ▣ ✎

CEDRONELLA

Lamiaceae

This genus contains a single species of perennial, endemic to the Canary Islands. *Cedronella canariensis* is an attractive fragrant plant, which is often seen in herb gardens. Though known as "balm of Gilead" because of its camphoraceous odour, it bears no resemblance to the balm of Gilead obtained from various *Populus* spp. (see p.327), nor to the original balm of Gilead (*Commiphora gileadensis*). Where marginally hardy, it may be grown in a large pot or in a sunny sheltered position, perhaps against a wall, and given protection from cold. *Cedronella* is a diminutive of *kedros*, "cedar", and refers to the cedar-like aroma given off by the plant's leaves.
CULTIVATION Well-drained soil in sun. Cut back in spring. Plants in the open ground may be cut down by cold but often re-emerge the following spring.
PROPAGATION By seed sown at 15–18°C (59–64°F); by division in spring; by softwood cuttings in spring.
HARVEST Leaves are picked before flowering and dried for infusions and scented articles.

⬛ *Cedronella canariensis* syn *C. triphylla* (balm of Gilead, Canary balm)
Shrubby, semi-evergreen perennial with a square stem, aromatic trifoliate leaves, up to 10cm (4in) long, and spikes of pink-violet to lilac, tubular, two-lipped flowers in summer. Native to the Canary Islands. ‡ 1.2–1.5m (4–5ft), ↔ 60–90cm (2–3ft).
HARDINESS Frost hardy.
PARTS USED Leaves.

PROPERTIES An aromatic herb with no known therapeutic uses.
CULINARY USES Leaves are infused for tea, known as *thé de Canaries*.
ECONOMIC USES Leaves are dried for potpourris with a musky woody scent.

▨ ✐ ✎

Cedronella mexicana. See *Agastache mexicana*.

CEDRUS

Cedar

Pinaceae

There are four species of true cedar, quite different from the many other trees that share the same common name. Native to W Asia and NW Africa, they have large spreading branches, which tend to form flat plates of foliage. Closely related to *Larix* spp. (larch, see p.251), cedars are among the most ornamental of conifers. The fragrant durable wood of *Cedrus atlantica* has always been prized for joinery and veneers, and the image of a cedar is depicted on the Lebanese flag. King Solomon is said to have felled most of the cedars on Mount Lebanon to build his temple. During the First World War, 60 per cent of remaining trees were felled to fuel the Damascus–Hejaz railway. Four small forests of mature trees, some over 1500 years old, still exist. *Cedrus atlantica* is rich in volatile oils that have medicinal properties. Cedar oil was used for embalming in ancient Egypt and is burned as temple incense by the Tibetans. Turkish carpet shops are often constructed or lined with cedar wood to deter moths. *Cedrus deodara* (deodar) and *C. libani* (cedar of Lebanon) are used in similar ways.
CULTIVATION Well-drained soil in sun. *Cedrus atlantica* tolerates chalky soils. To maintain a single leader, remove competing branches in autumn. Remove ageing lower branches flush with the bole in early spring. Honey fungus may attack trees.
PROPAGATION By seed sown in spring, after 21 days' moist chilling at 0–1°C (32–34°F); by grafting in late summer or winter. *Cedrus atlantica* f. *glauca* is usually grafted

commercially, but comes fairly true from seed.
HARVEST Branches are chipped for oil distillation or dried for use in decoctions.

⬛ *Cedrus atlantica* (Atlas cedar)
Large tree with ascending branches and needle-like, grey-green to blue-grey leaves in whorls of 30–40. Male cones, up to 5cm (2in) long, are borne mainly on lower branches; barrel-shaped female cones, 8cm (3in) long when mature, occur higher up, disintegrating after 2–3 winters. Native to Atlas Mountains of N Africa. ‡ 15–25m (50–80ft), ↔ 5–10m (15–30ft). 'Aurea' is slow-growing, with yellow foliage when young, becoming green in older specimens; f. *fastigiata* has an

Cedrus atlantica f. *glauca*

upright habit and blue-green leaves. ■ f. *glauca* (blue atlas cedar) has glaucous blue foliage.

HARDINESS Fully hardy.

PARTS USED Wood, oil.

PROPERTIES A good antiseptic and fungicide that stimulates the circulatory and respiratory systems, and calms the nerves. The odour repels insects.

MEDICINAL USES Externally for skin diseases, ulcers, and dandruff, and as an inhalation for bronchitis, tuberculosis, and nervous tension.

ECONOMIC USES Wood is used in joinery and for making insect-repellent articles for storing textiles. Oil is used in perfumery, notably in jasmine-scented soap.

CEIBA

Bombacaceae

A genus of four species of large deciduous trees, often with buttressed trunks, native to tropical America and Africa. *Ceiba pentandra* may have been introduced to Africa from S America, and it is widely cultivated and naturalized throughout the tropics for food, medicine, and raw materials, such as kapok. In Africa and the West Indies, it is venerated as the home of spirits. The flowers are pollinated by bats. Kapok fibre is a downy material that surrounds the seeds. It is eight times lighter than cotton, and absorbs sound. A single tree bears 300–400 pods a year, yielding up to 20kg (44lb) of kapok, from its fifth year until it is about 60 years old. *Ceiba pentandra* also yields a dark red-brown gum that resembles tragacanth (see *Astragalus gummifer*, p.136).

CULTIVATION Rich, deep, moisture-retentive but well-drained soil in sun. May be damaged by wind. Prune pot-grown plants to shape in spring.

PROPAGATION By seed sown when ripe at 21–24°C (70–75°F); by semi-ripe cuttings in summer. In the tropics, *Ceiba* is propagated by cutting branches, or "post cuttings", 1.2–2m (4–6ft) long, which are spaced 3m (10ft) apart in the open ground. They may also be inserted closer together and used as poles for the cultivation of *Piper* spp. (see p.219).

HARVEST Leaves are picked during the growing season and used fresh or dried in infusions and poultices. Buds, flowers, and stamens are collected as required and used fresh. Wood is cut in the dry season ("when spirits are absent") and bark removed for use in decoctions. Gum is collected from incisions into young trees, made as the sap is rising at the end of the dry season. Fruits are collected when ripe and are dried before removal of seeds, separation of fibre, and processing for kapok.

■ *Ceiba pentandra* syn. *Bombax pentandra* (kapok, silk cotton tree)
Deciduous or semi-evergreen tree with a spiny trunk and buttresses, wide-spreading branches, palmate leaves, 8–15cm (3–6in) long, and yellow, pink, or white, five-petalled flowers, 6cm (2½in) across, followed by spiny fruits, 10–30cm (4–12in) long, containing black seeds embedded in silky white fibres. Native to

Ceiba pentandra

W Africa; naturalized throughout the tropics.
‡ 25–70m (80–230ft),
↔ to 25m (80ft).

HARDINESS Min. 16°C (61°F).

PARTS USED Leaves, buds, flowers, stamens, bark, seeds, oil, gum.

PROPERTIES An astringent diuretic herb that lowers fever, relaxes spasms, and controls bleeding.

MEDICINAL USES Internally for abnormal uterine bleeding, dysentery, diarrhoea in children (gum), bronchial congestion (bark, leaves). Externally, in baths, for fevers and headaches (bark, leaves), and as a poultice for erysipelas, sprains (leaves) and wounds (bark).

CULINARY USES Mucilaginous leaves, buds, and immature fruits are cooked as vegetables. Seeds are sprouted and eaten raw, roasted as a flavouring, added to soups, or made into a sauce. They also yield a cooking oil. Flowers are blanched before eating. Stamens are used to colour soups and curries.

ECONOMIC USES Kapok is used in pillows, mattresses, acoustic insulation, and life jackets.

CENTAUREA
Knapweed

Asteraceae

There are some 450 species of annuals, biennials, perennials, and subshrubs in this genus, which occurs in Mediterranean regions, Eurasia, N America, and Australia. Various species are grown as ornamentals for their brightly coloured, thistle-like flowers. *Centaurea cyanus* (cornflower) is the best-known herb in the genus,

Centaurea cyanus

although *C. montana* (perennial cornflower), *C. nigra* (black knapweed), and *C. scabiosa* (greater knapweed) have similar properties. According to the Doctrine of Signatures (see p.15), the bright blue of cornflowers indicated that the flowers were good for eye problems. Cornflowers were common European cornfield weeds until the 1920s, but they have become increasingly scarce owing to modern farming practices. *Centaurea* is named after the legendary centaur, Chiron, known for his knowledge of herbs, who first revealed the healing properties of knapweeds.

CULTIVATION Well-drained soil in sun. Flowers may be affected by petal blight; leaves may be damaged by rust.

PROPAGATION By seed sown *in situ* in autumn or spring. Seedlings do not transplant well.

HARVEST Flowers are cut as they open and dried whole or as florets, according to use.

■ *Centaurea cyanus* (bachelor's buttons, bluebottle, cornflower)
Tall slender annual, sometimes over-wintering, with grey-green, lanceolate leaves. Bright blue, occasionally white, pink, or purple, flowers are borne in summer. Native to Europe and Mediterranean regions. ‡ 20cm–1m (8–36in), ↔ 15–30cm (6–12in). ■ 'Blue Diadem' has double blue flowers, to 6cm (2½in) across.

Centaurea cyanus 'Blue Diadem'

C

Centaurea cyanus Florence Series

↕ 75cm (30in). ▣ Florence Series has flowers in shades of blue, pink, carmine, and white. ↕ 35cm (14in).

HARDINESS Hardy.

PARTS USED Flowers.

PROPERTIES An astringent herb that reduces inflammation.

MEDICINAL USES Externally for corneal ulcers, conjunctivitis, minor wounds, or mouth ulcers.

CULINARY USES Florets may be used fresh in salads.

ECONOMIC USES Extracts of cornflower are added to hair shampoos and rinses. Florets may be dried for potpourris.

✤ ▣ ✎ ✎

CENTAURIUM
Centaury
Gentianaceae

A genus of about 40 species of annuals and biennials, occasionally perennials, found throughout temperate regions. One or two species are grown as ornamentals for their colourful flowers, and a few have medicinal properties. Best known is *C. erythraea*, which, in common with many members of the gentian family, is extremely bitter, prompting Nicholas Culpeper to comment, in *The English Physician Enlarged, or the Herbal* (1653), that "it is very wholesome, but not very toothsome". Its constituents include bitter glycosides that stimulate the liver and gall bladder, increasing bile flow and improving the appetite and digestion. Bitter compounds are also present in *C. chilensis* (canchalagua), a similar plant that grows on the west coast of N America. Bitters are at their most effective taken 30 minutes before eating.

CULTIVATION Sandy, neutral to alkaline soil in sun.

PROPAGATION By seed sown when ripe.

HARVEST Flowering plants are cut in summer and dried for infusions and liquid extracts.

▣ *Centaurium erythraea* syn. *Erythraea centaurium* (centaury, feverwort)
Variable annual or biennial with a basal rosette and elliptic veined leaves, to 5cm (2in) long. Five-petalled, pink flowers are borne in dense

Centaurium erythraea

clusters on long branched stalks in summer. Native to dry grassland and dunes in Europe and SW Asia; naturalized in N America. ↕ 15–24cm (6–10in), ↔ 7–15cm (3–6in).

HARDINESS Hardy.

PARTS USED Whole plant.

PROPERTIES A very bitter, dry herb that acts as a tonic for the digestive system and lowers fever.

MEDICINAL USES Internally for dyspepsia, liver and gall bladder complaints, hepatitis, jaundice, anorexia, chronic fatigue syndrome, poor appetite in convalescence, and feverish illnesses. Combined with *Althaea officinalis* (see p.117), *Chamaemelum nobile* (see p.165), and *Filipendula ulmaria* (see p.214) for dyspepsia, and with *Berberis vulgaris* (see p.142) and *Rumex crispus* (see p.351) for jaundice. Not given to pregnant women.

▣ ▣

CENTELLA
Apiaceae

About 20 species of low-growing perennials are included in this genus, which occurs in most parts of the tropics. Best known is *C. asiatica* (gotu kola), which resembles the related European marsh pennywort (*Hydrocotyle vulgaris*) in appearance. It is a variable species, thriving mainly in wet places along the margins of ponds and lakes, and in paddy fields. *Centella asiatica* is one of the most important herbs in Ayurvedic medicine. In recent years it has become popular worldwide and is now among the top 25 best-selling herbs in the USA. Known as *brahmi*, "bringing knowledge of Brahman [Supreme Reality]", it has long been used medicinally and to aid meditation in India. Traditionally used for leprosy in both India and Africa, for hypertension and cancer in Mauritius, and for fever and respiratory diseases in China, it entered the French pharmacopoeia via Madagascar. In China, "long-life tea" made from the leaves was taken regularly by Professor Li Chung Yon, who apparently reached the age of 265 and married 24 times. Recent research has shown that *C. asiatica*

contains substances that increase collagen production, speed healing and reduce scarring, improve circulation (in skin and lower limbs especially), and improve performance in those suffering from learning difficulties and mental confusion. In SE Asia several varieties of *C. asiatica* are recognized, including one with bright green, frilly leaves, preferred for salads.

CULTIVATION Moist to wet, humus-rich, sandy soil in sun or light shade. In temperate regions, *C. asiatica* is easily grown in containers under cover. It may lose its leaves in low temperatures but quickly re-sprouts in spring.

PROPAGATION By seed sown in spring; by separation of runners with at least one node during the growing season.

HARVEST Whole plants or leaves are gathered at any time and used fresh or dried in infusions, milk decoctions, powder, medicated ghee, or medicated oil.

⚠ **WARNING** May cause dermatitis or photosensitization in susceptible individuals.

▣ *Centella asiatica* syn. *Hydrocotyle asiatica* (gotu kola, Indian pennywort, *pegaga*)
Creeping evergreen perennial, rooting at nodes, with clusters of kidney-shaped leaves, up to 5cm (2in) across, with indented margins. Tiny pink flowers are borne beneath the foliage in summer. Pantropical. ↕ 15–20cm (6–8in), ↔ indefinite.

HARDINESS Min. 10°C (50°F).

PARTS USED Whole plant, leaves.

PROPERTIES A rejuvenating diuretic herb that clears toxins, reduces inflammation and fever, boosts healing and immunity, and has a balancing effect on the nervous system. It increases production of peripheral blood vessels and connective tissue, thus improving circulation and helping to retain or restore elasticity of the skin.

MEDICINAL USES Internally for wounds, chronic skin conditions (including leprosy), venereal diseases, malaria, varicose veins and ulcers, thread veins, night cramps, nervous disorders, mental retardation, and senility. Excess causes headaches and transient unconsciousness, or may interfere with hypoglycaemic therapy. It may also

Centella asiatica

C

increase serum-cholesterol levels. Gotu kola is contraindicated in pregancy and epilepsy. Externally for wounds (especially after surgery or burns), ulcers, eczema, haemorrhoids, and rheumatic joints.

CULINARY USES Leaves are eaten raw in salads, added to soups and curries in SE Asia, and steamed as a vegetable. Dried herb and juice are used in herbal teas and tonic drinks.

ECONOMIC USES Extracts are added to cosmetic masks and creams to increase collagen and firm the skin.

⚠ **WARNING** This herb is subject to legal restrictions in some countries.

🗎 🗎 🗎 🗎 🗎 🗎

CEPHAELIS
Ipecacuanha

Rubiaceae

Closely related to the genera *Psychotria* and *Palicourea*, the 180 or so species of *Cephaelis* are tender, mostly evergreen shrubs and small trees that occur in various parts of the tropics. The terminal clusters of trumpet-shaped flowers are produced in the rainy season. Many species are known to contain alkaloids, but only *C. ipecacuanha*, an understorey shrub of Brazilian rainforests, is in large-scale production, mainly in Singapore and Malaysia, where it is often grown under rubber trees. Ipecacuanha was known to native Brazilians for centuries before its introduction to Portugal by a monk in colonial times. A Parisian doctor confirmed its effectiveness against dysentery and in 1688 sold his patent medicine to the court of Louis XIV for 1000 *louis d'or*. *Cephaelis ipecacuanha* contains a potent emetic that as a side-effect stimulates mucus secretion in the lungs. It is an ingredient of most proprietary cough remedies.

CULTIVATION Well-drained, humus-rich soil in shade, with ample moisture and humidity. Difficult to cultivate outside its natural habitat.

PROPAGATION By greenwood cuttings in late spring, in sandy soil compost at 21–24°C (70–75°F); by root cuttings during harvesting.

HARVEST Roots are dug when the plants are in flower and dried for use by the pharmaceutical industry. Cultivated plants are replanted after partial removal of roots.

■ *Cephaelis ipecacuanha* (ipecac, ipecacuanha) Slender evergreen shrub with a creeping rootstock and glossy, pointed, ovate leaves, 8–16cm (3–6in). White flowers, 1cm (⅜in) long, are followed by blue-purple berries with two seeds. Native to Brazil and C America. ↔ 30–50cm (12–20in).

HARDINESS Min. 15–18°C (59–64°F).

PARTS USED Roots.

PROPERTIES A violent irritant that stimulates the gastric and bronchial systems, lowers fevers, and prevents cyst formation in amoebic dysentery.

MEDICINAL USES Internally for coughs, bronchitis, whooping cough, and amoebic dysentery. Also used in a syrup to induce vomiting in drug overdoses, and in children who have swallowed poisons, being preferable

Cephaelis ipecacuanha

to the use of a stomach pump for the very young. Excess causes severe vomiting and diarrhoea, and may prove fatal. Used in homeopathy for nausea. For use by qualified practitioners only. For use strictly according to instructions in proprietary medicines.

🗎 🗎 🗎

CETRARIA

Parmeliaceae

A genus of 40 species of lichens found worldwide, especially in Arctic regions. *Cetraria islandica* forms tufts on lichen-rich heaths, mostly in hilly and montane regions, and is ecologically important in northern areas as a food for reindeer. Lichens have been used since earliest times for medicines, dyes, and perfumes. They are exclusively gathered from the wild and are increasingly scarce, due to loss of habitat and pollution; many herbalists now use lichen-based remedies in serious cases only. Recent research has shown that lichen acids are effective against organisms such as *Mycobacterium tuberculosis*, *Salmonella* spp., and *Trichomonas vaginalis*.

CULTIVATION Lichens are not cultivated, though their growth can be encouraged. They thrive on bark of trees, and rocks on acid substrate, and must have clean air and water.

PROPAGATION There has apparently been no research into the possibility of growing lichens from spores.

HARVEST Whole plants are collected all year round and dried for use in decoctions, liquid extracts, powder, and tinctures.

■ *Cetraria islandica* (Iceland moss) Lichen with leathery, crinkled, grey-green to dark brown branches, which are profusely forked and have minute spiny projections along the margins. Native to Europe, Arctic regions, and Australasia. ↕ 2–6cm (¾–2½in), ↔ indefinite.

HARDINESS Fully hardy.

PARTS USED Whole plant.

PROPERTIES A bitter–sweet, cooling, strongly antibiotic herb that is expectorant, soothes irritated tissues, and controls vomiting.

MEDICINAL USES Internally for gastroenteritis, food poisoning, tuberculosis, and bronchitis.

Cetraria islandica

Externally for vaginal discharge, boils, and impetigo. Extracts are added to antiseptics and to throat pastilles for dry coughs and sore throats.

🗎 🗎

CHAENOMELES
Flowering quince, japonica

Rosaceae

A genus of three species of deciduous, sometimes spiny, shrubs and small trees, native to E Asia. All are widely cultivated as ornamentals, both in the open and as wall shrubs. *Chaenomeles speciosa* has many cultivars, with a variety of habits and colours, and single or double flowers, ranging from white to pink and crimson. These are among the loveliest and most easily grown of early spring-flowering plants, with the added interest of edible fruits. Medicinal use of *C. speciosa* was first mentioned in China c.AD470; it was introduced to Kew in 1796 by Sir Joseph Banks. Its popularity as a subject for bonsai has spread to the West from China and Japan.

CULTIVATION Well-drained soil in sun or partial shade, either in the open or trained against a wall. Fruiting is best in sun. Plants grown in the open need little pruning other than thinning out or shaping branches after flowering. Prune wall-trained specimens after flowering, reducing the previous year's growth to two or three buds and cutting back any outward-growing shoots. Plants may be affected by fireblight and may suffer from chlorosis on very alkaline soils.

PROPAGATION By seed sown in autumn and placed in a cold frame; by semi-ripe cuttings in summer; by layering long shoots in early autumn. Cultivars do not come true from seed.

HARVEST Fruits are gathered when ripe in the autumn and dried for use in decoctions, or consumed fresh.

■ *Chaenomeles speciosa* syn *C. lagenaria*, *Cydonia speciosa* (flowering quince, Japanese quince, japonica)
Deciduous spreading shrub with dense spiny twigs and ovate leaves, 4–9cm (1½–3½in) long. Scarlet, five-petalled flowers, to 4.5cm (1¾in) across, appear from late winter, followed

C

Chaenomeles speciosa

Chaenomeles speciosa
'Cameo'

Chaenomeles speciosa
'Moerloosei'

Chaenomeles speciosa 'Nivalis'

by aromatic speckled fruits, to 6cm (2½in) long. Native to woodland in China. ‡ 2.5m (8ft), ↔ 5m (15ft). ▣ 'Cameo' is a compact shrub with few thorns, producing semi-double, apricot-pink flowers and greenish-yellow fruits with a lemon-like aroma. ‡ 1–1.5m (3–5ft).
▣ 'Moerloosei' syn. 'Apple Blossom' has dense clusters of pink-flushed, white flowers that resemble apple blossoms. ▣ 'Nivalis' has pure white flowers. 'Simonii' has large, double, deep red flowers.

HARDINESS Fully hardy.

PARTS USED Fruits (*mu gua*).

PROPERTIES An anti-inflammatory and anti-spasmodic herb that acts mainly as a circulatory and digestive stimulant.

MEDICINAL USES Internally for rheumatism, arthritis, cramps (especially in the calf muscles), painful, weak, or swollen lower limbs, stomach cramps due to indigestion, diarrhoea, and vomiting.

CULINARY USES Fruits may be used as a substitute for *Cydonia oblonga* (quince) in jams and jellies, and for flavouring apples and other stewed or baked fruit.

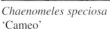

CHAMAELIRIUM

Melanthiaceae

There is only one species in this N American genus, which is closely related to *Helonias*. *Chamaelirium luteum* is an elusive plant that grows in damp woods and bogs, and is seldom seen in cultivation. *Chamaelirium* comes from the Greek *chamai*, "slow-growing", and *leirion*, "lily". The name *luteum* means "yellow", an inappropriate description for a white-flowered plant, which was given when the species was first described from a rather poor dried specimen. First used by native N Americans to prevent miscarriage, *C. luteum* won favour with settlers in the 18th and 19th centuries for depression and "derangements of women". According to John Bartram's appendix to *Medicina Britannica* (1751), it is "a great resister of fermenting poisons". *Chamaelirium luteum* was listed in the *US National Formulary* (1916–47) and is still regarded by medical herbalists (who often refer to it as "helonias") as invaluable for gynaecological problems. *Chamaelirium luteum* is also called "false unicorn root" to distinguish it from *Aletris farinosa* (true unicorn root, see p.110).

CULTIVATION Moist to wet, well-drained, humus-rich, neutral to acid soil in partial shade.

PROPAGATION By seed sown in autumn; by division in spring.

HARVEST Rhizomes with roots are lifted in autumn and dried for use in infusions, liquid extracts, tablets, and tinctures.

Chamaelirium luteum syn. *Helonias dioica* (devil's bit, fairy wand, false unicorn root, helonias)
Tuberous, summer-flowering perennial with a basal rosette of obovate to spoon-shaped leaves, to 20cm (8in) long. Flowering stem is erect, bearing smaller, linear–lanceolate leaves and a dense cylindrical raceme of tiny, white, star-shaped flowers, yellowing with age. Male and female flowers occur on different plants; female plants are leafier. Native to eastern N America. ‡ 30–90cm (1–3ft), ↔ 15–38cm (6–15in).

HARDINESS Fully hardy.

PARTS USED Rhizomes, roots.

PROPERTIES An astringent, bitter, diuretic herb that acts mainly as an ovarian and uterine tonic. It expels intestinal worms.

MEDICINAL USES Internally for menstrual and menopausal complaints, infertility, pelvic inflammatory disease, endometriosis, fibroids, threatened miscarriage, and morning sickness. Excess causes vomiting. Often combined with *Trillium erectum* (see p.394). Also as a tonic for digestive and genito-urinary complaints, and to expel intestinal parasites. For use by qualified practitioners only.
▣ ▪

CHAMAEMELUM

Chamomile

Asteraceae

Containing only four species of annuals and evergreen perennials, this small genus is native to Europe and Mediterranean regions and is closely related to *Anthemis*, *Chamomilla*, and *Matricaria*. The name of the genus comes from the Greek *chamaimelon*, which means "apple on the ground", referring to the strong apple scent of the foliage when stepped upon. "Chamomile" is the name given to several different, daisy-like plants, but only two species are important as herbs: *Chamaemelum nobile* (Roman chamomile) and *Matricaria recutita* (wild or German chamomile, see p.272). Both are used for similar purposes, although their odours and chemical analysis are slightly different. Essential oil of chamomile is blue, due to the presence of chamazulene, which forms during steam distillation of the oil and varies in quantity depending on origin and age of flowers. *Chamaemelum nobile* is a prostrate plant with a delightful aroma that is best appreciated when planted in paving, containers, or lawns. Chamomile tea is one of the most popular herb teas, immortalized in Beatrix Potter's *Tale of Peter Rabbit*. The cultivar 'Treneague' reputedly originated from chamomile lawns at Buckingham Palace, London, in 1932.

CULTIVATION Light, well-drained soil in full sun. Chamomile plants for lawns are planted 10cm (4in) apart and weeded regularly until established. Plants may deteriorate in very cold or wet winters, but usually recover. *Chamaemelum nobile* has been called "the plant's physician": ailing garden plants are supposedly cured by planting chamomile beside them, and cutflowers revive and last longer with the addition of chamomile tea to the water. An infusion is also said to prevent damping off.

PROPAGATION By seed sown in spring or autumn; by division in spring. Variants are sterile and can only be divided.

HARVEST Flowers are gathered in summer and distilled for oil, or dried for use in infusions, liquid extracts, and dermatological

creams. Dried flowers keep for one year only.
⚠ **WARNING** Handling chamomile may cause dermatitis.

■ *Chamaemelum nobile* syn. *Anthemis nobilis*
(chamomile, Roman chamomile)
Mat-forming, evergreen perennial with aromatic, finely divided leaves, to 5cm (2in) long. Long-stalked, solitary flowers, with yellow discs and creamy white ray florets, appear in summer. Native to W Europe, N America, and the Azores. ‡ 10–30cm (4–12in), ↔ 45cm (18in). ■ 'Flore Pleno' (double chamomile) has rather shaggy, creamy white, double flowers. ‡ 15cm (6in), ↔ 45cm (18in). ■ 'Treneague' (lawn chamomile) is a non-flowering cultivar that forms a mossy carpet. Tolerates acid soil. ‡ 10cm (4in), ‡ 45cm (18in).
HARDINESS Fully hardy.
PARTS USED Flowers, essential oil.
PROPERTIES A bitter, aromatic, anti-inflammatory herb with relaxant properties that acts mainly on the digestive system.
MEDICINAL USES Internally for digestive problems (including colic, diverticulitis, morning sickness, and stress-induced dyspepsia), painful menstruation, and insomnia, and for feverish illnesses, hyperactivity, and temper tantrums in children (flowers). Externally for irritated or sore skin (flowers); nappy rash (essential oil). Used in homeopathy for complaints caused by anger or too much caffeine. Essential oil is a uterine stimulant; it should not be taken internally, and not used externally in pregnancy. It is used in aromatherapy, and in inhalations for asthma and bronchial congestion.
CULINARY USES Flowers are used to

make tea and flavour *manzanilla* sherry. In small amounts, leaves can be finely chopped to flavour cream sauces.
ECONOMIC USES Oil is used in hair products to lighten and condition the hair.
⚠ **WARNING** This herb, in the form of essential oil, is subject to legal restrictions in some countries.
⊡ ⬠ ▪ ⁄ ⁄

CHAMOMILLA
Chamomilla recutita. See *Matricaria recutita*.

CHELIDONIUM
Celandine

Papaveraceae

A genus containing a single species of perennial that in general appearance resembles the closely related *Meconopsis* spp. (Himalayan poppies). *Chelidonium majus* (greater celandine) is found along banks, hedgerows, and walls, usually on wasteground near human habitation. Its foliage contains a distinctive, bright orange sap, containing enzymes that have proteolytic effects (cause the breakdown of proteins). It is dabbed on to the skin, directly from the plant, as a traditional treatment for warts and corns, and has a long history of use for eyesight problems, such as cataracts. According to Pliny (AD23–79), swallows used the orange sap to clear their eyes, hence the common name, swallow wort. On the other hand, the Doctrine of Signatures (see p.15) stated that, because the sap resembled bile in colour, the herb was a remedy for liver disorders.
CULTIVATION Almost any soil, including clay, in sun or shade.
PROPAGATION By seed sown in spring; by division in spring. *Chelidonium majus* and its variants self-sow readily.
HARVEST Flowering plants are cut in summer and used fresh in infusions or tinctures, or as juice. Sap is used fresh; the properties are largely lost on drying.
⚠ **WARNING** Orange sap produces yellow stains when handled.

■ *Chelidonium majus* (greater celandine, swallow wort, tetterwort)
Perennial with branched brittle stems and divided, slightly glaucous, pale green leaves, 10–25cm (4–10in) long, which exude orange sap when damaged. Four-petalled, yellow flowers, 2–2.5cm (³⁄₄–1in) across, appear from spring to autumn, followed by linear capsules, containing black seeds with a white crest. Native to temperate and subarctic Eurasia; naturalized in N America. ‡ 30–60cm (1–2ft), ↔ 20–45cm (8–18in). ■ 'Flore Pleno' has double flowers. var. *laciniatum* has deeply cut leaves. ■ 'Laciniatum Flore Pleno' is smaller than the species, with deeply cut leaves and small ragged flowers. First recorded at Heidelberg (Germany), c.1590. ‡ 25–38cm (10–15in), ↔ 15–38cm (6–15in).
HARDINESS Fully hardy.
PARTS USED Whole plant, sap.
PROPERTIES A cleansing, anti-inflammatory herb that improves bile flow, stimulates the uterus and circulatory system, and acts as an anti-spasmodic, diuretic, and laxative.
MEDICINAL USES Internally for inflammation of the gall bladder and bile duct, jaundice, hepatitis, gout, arthritis, and rheumatism; remittent fevers, spasmodic cough and bronchitis; skin eruptions, ulcers, and cancer (especially of skin and stomach). Excess causes sleepiness, skin irritation, irritant coughing, and difficulty in breathing. Not given to pregnant women. Externally for eye inflammations and cataract, bruises and sprains, warts, ringworm, psoriasis, eczema, and malignant tumours. Also used in Chinese medicine (as *bai qu cai*) and homeopathy for similar complaints. For use by qualified practitioners only.
⚠ **WARNING** This herb is subject to legal restrictions in some countries.
◨ ⬚ ▪

CHELONE
Turtlehead

Scrophulariaceae

This genus of N American perennials contains six species. *Chelone glabra* is one of several species grown as border plants in damp situations

Chamaemelum nobile

Chamaemelum nobile
'Flore Pleno'

Chamaemelum nobile
'Treneague'

Chelidonium majus

Chelidonium majus
'Flore Pleno'

Chelidonium majus
'Laciniatum Flore Pleno'

C

Chelone glabra

for their snapdragon-like flowers. *Chelone* is the Greek word for "tortoise", because the tubular flower, seen from the front, resembles a tortoise's head. This shape has also given rise to various common names for the plant, such as fishmouth, snakehead, and snakemouth, as well as turtlehead. *Chelone glabra* yields a digestive tonic that is increasingly favoured by herbalists, because the aerial parts of the plant are used rather than the roots, so causing less environmental damage when the herb is collected from the wild.

CULTIVATION Moist rich soil in sun or partial shade. Tolerates heavy and boggy soils.

PROPAGATION By seed sown in spring; by soft tip cuttings in spring or early summer; by division in autumn or spring.

HARVEST Plants are cut when in flower and dried for use in infusions, liquid extracts, powder, or tinctures.

■ *Chelone glabra* (balmony, turtlehead)
Upright perennial with ovate to lanceolate leaves, 5–15cm (2–6in) long, and clusters of white, sometimes pink-tinged, flowers, 2.5cm (1in) long, in which the upper lip forms a hood over the bearded lower lip. Native to eastern and southern N America. ‡60cm (24in), ↔45cm (18in).

HARDINESS Fully hardy.

PARTS USED Whole plant.

PROPERTIES A very bitter herb with a tea-like flavour that acts mainly as a tonic for the liver and digestive system. It also has anti-depressant and laxative effects.

MEDICINAL USES Internally for gallstones with jaundice, chronic liver disease, colic, constipation, anorexia, and poor digestion (especially in the elderly and during convalescence). Combines well with *Juglans cinerea* for constipation, and with *Gentiana lutea* (see p.223) and *Hydrastis canadensis* (see p.239) for jaundice.

CHENOPODIUM
Goosefoot, pigweed

Chenopodiaceae

A cosmopolitan genus of some 150 species of annuals, perennials, and subshrubs. *Chenopodium ambrosioides* (epazote), a pungent

tropical American weed, is much used in Mexican cooking but is almost unknown elsewhere. Though warm-growing, it is highly adaptable, often surviving mild winters in temperate areas. Several non-aromatic species have a long history of use as food plants. Seeds of *C. album* (fat hen, lamb's quarters, pigweed) were found in the stomach of Tollund man (c.500BC–AD400). It is still grown as a vegetable and pot-herb, as is *C. bonus-henricus* (good King Henry). Oil of chenopodium contains a broad-spectrum vermifuge, which is widely used in veterinary medicine. It is produced from both *C. ambrosioides* and *C. ambrosioides* var. *anthelminticum*, the latter having a higher content of the active constituent.

CULTIVATION Rich, well-drained soil in sun. Pinch out tips to encourage bushiness.

PROPAGATION By seed sown in spring. Self-sows freely, even in temperate regions.

HARVEST Plants are cut in autumn for oil, or dried for liquid extracts and powder. Leaves are picked as required and used fresh.

⚠ **WARNING** Skin allergen.

■ *Chenopodium ambrosioides* (epazote, Mexican tea, wormseed)
Strong-smelling, upright annual or short-lived perennial with oblanceolate, slightly toothed leaves, to 12cm (5in) long. Tiny green flowers appear in panicles in summer, followed by green-brown fruits, each containing a single black seed. Native to tropical and subtropical America; widely naturalized. ‡1.2m (4ft), ↔75cm (30in).

HARDINESS Frost hardy.

PARTS USED Whole plant, leaves, oil.

PROPERTIES An acrid, astringent, strongly aromatic herb that destroys intestinal parasites, increases perspiration, and relaxes spasms. It also has expectorant, anti-fungal, and insecticidal effects.

MEDICINAL USES Internally for roundworms, hookworms, small tapeworms, amoebic dysentery, asthma, and catarrh. Not given to pregnant women. Excess causes dizziness, vomiting, convulsions, and death. Externally for athlete's foot and insect bites.

Chenopodium ambrosioides

CULINARY USES Leaves flavour corn, beans, mushrooms, seafood, fish, soups, and sauces.

ECONOMIC USES Used as a fumigant against mosquitoes and in fertilizer to inhibit insect larvae.

⚠ **WARNING** This herb is subject to legal restrictions in some countries.

CHIMAPHILA
Prince's pine

Ericaceae

Six species of shrubby evergreen perennials make up this genus, distributed throughout N America, Europe, and E Asia. Several species are occasionally grown in rock gardens and peat beds for their neat, ground-covering foliage and waxy flowers. The name *Chimaphila* comes from the Greek *cheima*, "winter", and *phileo*, "love", because the plants remain green in winter. *Chimaphila umbellata* is found in acid woodland, often on sandy soils. It was an important herb among native N Americans, who used it for various problems, including rheumatism, and it became popular with settlers, especially Pennsylvania Germans, as a tonic and diuretic for kidney complaints and rheumatism. *Chimaphila umbellata* was listed as an astringent in the *US Pharmacopoeia* (1820–1916); it contains quinone glycosides, such as are found in *Arctostaphylos uva-ursi* (see p.127), but is less astringent and more diuretic, thus better for long-term use.

CULTIVATION Moist, well-drained, acid, sandy soil in shade or dappled shade. Difficult to establish.

PROPAGATION By seed sown in autumn; by division in spring.

HARVEST Whole plants are picked when in flower, and leaves during the growing season; both are dried for infusions and liquid extracts.

■ *Chimaphila umbellata* (ground holly, pipsissewa, prince's pine)
Evergreen shrubby perennial with a creeping rootstock, slender stems, and whorls of leathery, toothed, white-veined leaves, to 7cm (3in) long. Clusters of 3–10 white to pink, cup-shaped

Chimaphila umbellata

flowers, 1cm (³⁄₈in) across, appear on pendent
stalks in summer. Native to eastern N America,
N and C Europe, N Asia, and Japan. ↕ 10–25cm
(4–10in), ↕ 20cm (8in).

HARDINESS Fully hardy.

PARTS USED Whole plant, leaves.

PROPERTIES A bitter, astringent, diuretic herb
that has tonic effects on the kidneys and spleen.

MEDICINAL USES Internally for urinary
infections, prostatitis, urethritis, kidney stones,
arthritis, and rheumatism.

CULINARY USES A traditional ingredient of
root beer.

CHIONANTHUS
Fringe tree

Oleaceae

A genus of about 120 species of mostly tender,
deciduous trees and shrubs, found in tropical
and subtropical E Asia, Australia, and eastern
N America, with a few in Africa and Madagascar.
There are just two hardy species, the better
known being *C. virginicus*, which is widely
grown for its delightful display of white, fringe-
like blossoms. The name *Chionanthus* comes
from the Greek *chion*, "snow", and *anthos*,
"flower". *Chionanthus virginicus* is one of the
most reliable remedies for disorders of the liver
and gall bladder. The bark was used in native
N American medicine as a remedy for wounds,
toothache, and mouth and gum problems.

CULTIVATION Well-drained soil in sun. Slow-
growing in regions with cool summers. Flowers
best in areas with long hot summers.

PROPAGATION By seed sown in autumn, which
requires stratification; by softwood cuttings in
spring; by budding in summer. Germination
may take up to 18 months.

HARVEST Bark is peeled from roots, which are
removed as required, and dried for use in
infusions, liquid extracts, and tinctures.

■ *Chionanthus virginicus* (fringe tree)
Spreading deciduous shrub or small
tree with bright green, ovate leaves,
5–10cm (2–4in) long, which have pale
downy undersides. Loose panicles,

Chionanthus virginicus

10–20cm (4–8in) long, of fragrant, slender,
white flowers are borne on second-year wood,
followed by blue-purple berries. Native to
eastern N America. ↕ 8m (25ft), ↔ 5m (15ft).

HARDINESS Fully hardy.

PARTS USED Root bark.

PROPERTIES A bitter, tonic, alterative herb that
stimulates the liver and gall bladder, and has both
diuretic and laxative effects.

MEDICINAL USES Internally for jaundice,
cirrhosis, chronic hepatitis, pancreatitis,
gallstones, enlarged spleen, poor liver function,
bilious headache, and migraine. Also as a tonic
in chronic illness. Externally for cuts, bruises,
and scrapes.

CHONDRODENDRON

Menispermaceae

A genus of ten species of lianas, native to tropical
rainforests in C and S America. Several species
are key ingredients of curare, an arrow poison
used by native S Americans. The name comes
from the Greek *chondros*, "cartilage", and
dendron, "tree", and refers to the flexible, branch-
like stems. *Chondrodendron tomentosum*
contains alkaloids, notably *d*-tubocurarine, a
skeletal muscle relaxant that acts instantaneously
when injected but is unstable if taken orally.
Supplies are dependent on wild stocks because
the species is not cultivated, and attempts to
synthesize it have so far been unsuccessful. Stems
and roots are used by native S Americans to treat
various ailments, including dropsy, madness, and
bruising. The closely related *Cissampelos pareira*
is also an ingredient of curare and source of a
potent muscle relaxant, known as "cissampeline".

CULTIVATION Not cultivated.

PROPAGATION There is no information on
propagation requirements.

HARVEST Roots and stems are collected from
the wild as available and processed by the
pharmaceutical industry into liquid extracts.

Chondrodendron tomentosum (pareira, pareira
brava)
Large canopy liana with a hairy trunk, up to
10cm (4in) across at the base, and ovate to
rounded leaves, to 20cm (8in) long, which have
woolly stalks and undersides. Panicles of tiny,
green-white, male and female flowers are borne
on separate plants. Native to Panama, Brazil,
Bolivia, and Peru. ↕ 30m (100ft), ↔ indefinite.

HARDINESS Min. 15–18°C (59–64°F).

PARTS USED Stems, roots.

PROPERTIES A bitter–sweet, diuretic, laxative
herb that lowers fever and stimulates the uterus,
when taken orally.

MEDICINAL USES Mainly intravenously as a
source of *d*-tubocurarine, used to relax muscles
during surgery. Used in folk medicine to treat
inflammation of the urinary tract, and as a
remedy for snake bite.

⚠ **WARNING** This herb, especially in the form
of curare, is subject to legal restrictions in some
countries.

CHONDRUS

Gigartinaceae

A genus of around 15 species of marine algae.
Several species are collected from the wild for
their uses in various industries. *Chondrus
crispus* is an important edible seaweed on both
sides of the Atlantic. Plants are harvested by
boat, using a rake that causes minimal damage
to the holdfasts, and by hand from rocks.
Gel-forming polysaccharides, known as
carrageenans, are found in *C. crispus*. Various
grades are produced, those of high molecular
weight being used in the food industry, on the
grounds that they pass through the gut and are
therefore non-toxic. However, carrageenans are
suspected of being carcinogenic and a possible
cause of ulcerative colitis.

CULTIVATION Grows on rocks and stones in
pools and shallow saltwater. Plants are left
intact after harvesting to allow regeneration.

HARVEST Plants are cut in autumn and dried
whole, or processed for extraction of
polysaccharides.

Chondrus crispus (carragheen, Irish moss)
Red-purple to green, cartilaginous alga with a
disc-shaped holdfast. Basal growth is narrow,
expanding into branched fronds, often crimped
along the margin, with narrow and broader
forms occurring. Found in the lower littoral
zone of the Atlantic, English Channel, and
North Sea. ↔ 7–15cm (3–6in).

HARDINESS Not applicable.

PARTS USED Whole plant.

PROPERTIES A mucilaginous, sweet, salty herb
that has a softening soothing effect on tissues,
and is a mild laxative and expectorant.

MEDICINAL USES Internally for dry coughs, sore
throat, cystitis, bronchitis, gastritis, and dyspepsia
with nausea and heartburn; often combined with
Cinnamomum cassia (see p.169) and *Glycyrrhiza
glabra* (see p.226) for bronchitis, and with
Althaea officinalis (see p.117) and *Ballota nigra*
(see p.140) for dyspepsia. Externally, in lotions or
creams, for chapped skin and dermatitis. Not
given to patients on anti-coagulant medication,
because it thins the blood.

CULINARY USES Cooked in water or milk to
make jelly or blancmange. Blended with kelp
(*Laminaria saccharina*) to make a spread,
known as *pain d'algues* (France).

ECONOMIC USES Important in the food industry
as a stabilizer in dairy produce, desserts, salad
dressings, sauces, and in pharmaceutical products,
such as cod liver oil, cleansing creams, and
toothpaste. Also used in air-freshener gels and
for various processes in the textile, leather,
brewing, and paint industries.

CHRYSANTHEMUM

Asteraceae

This genus comprises 20 species of aromatic
perennials that grow wild in Europe and in
C and E Asia. Though now mostly attributed to

C

C

Chrysanthemum × morifolium

the genus *Dendranthema*, the popularity of chrysanthemums in cultivation has resulted in widespread retention of the former name in the gardening media. The genus includes the florists' chrysanthemum, *Chrysanthemum × morifolium* (correctly known as *Dendranthema × grandiflorum*), a complex hybrid group of perennials raised in China before 500BC from *D. indicum* and other species. Florists' chrysanthemums were introduced to the West from China in the 18th century and rapidly became popular as ornamentals. In the East they have been valued for medicinal and culinary purposes since at least the 1st century AD. Chrysanthemum flowers for cooking and tea in the East are yellow, double, and about 5cm (2in) in diameter. The edible chrysanthemum leaves (known as chop suey greens) that feature in Asian cooking are from *Chrysanthemum coronarium* (garland chrysanthemum, *shungiku*), which has spicy foliage and yellow flowers.
CULTIVATION Rich, well-drained, neutral to slightly acid soil in a sunny sheltered position. Protect plants from severe frost and winter wet. Pinch out plants when 15–20cm (6–8in) tall to encourage side shoots. Chrysanthemums are prone to a wide range of viruses, fungal diseases, and a wide range of pests.
PROPAGATION By seed sown in late winter or spring at 13–16°C (55–61°F); by basal cuttings in winter or spring; by division in autumn or early spring.
HARVEST Leaves are picked as required. Flowers are gathered when fully open and used fresh or dried for culinary purposes, or dried (often after being steamed first to reduce bitterness) for use in infusions and tinctures.
⚠ **WARNING** Skin allergen.

Chrysanthemum cinerariifolium. See *Tanecetum cinerariifolium*.

◾ ***Chrysanthemum × morifolium*** (florists' chrysanthemum, mulberry-leaved chrysanthemum)
Perennial with branched, erect, or spreading stems and strongly aromatic, pinnately lobed leaves, to 12cm (5in) long. Clusters of single or double flowers, 2.5–30cm (1–12in) across, with white, yellow, bronze, pink, or red ray florets,

are borne from late summer to late autumn. Garden origin. ↕ 30cm–2.2m (1–7ft), ↔ 30–90cm (1–3ft). Choose a small-flowered, double, yellow cultivar for culinary use.
HARDINESS Fully hardy (borderline) to frost tender, min. 10°C (50°F), depending on cultivar.
PARTS USED Leaves, flowers (*ju hua*), petals.
PROPERTIES A bitter aromatic herb that lowers fevers, soothes inflammation, dilates the coronary artery (increasing blood flow to the heart), and inhibits the growth of pathogens.
MEDICINAL USES Internally for hypertension, coronary artery disease, angina, feverish colds, and liver-related disorders.
CULINARY USES Leaves are used for tea, or made into fritters. Flowers are cooked or pickled in Oriental cuisine. Petals are used to make tea or to flavour China tea. Flowers and petals are added to soup.
▨ ▨ ▪ ▨ ▨

Chrysanthemum parthenium. See *Tanacetum parthenium*.
Chrysanthemum vulgare. See *Tanacetum vulgare*.

CICHORIUM
Chicory

Asteraceae

A genus of eight species of perennials and annuals, occurring in Europe, temperate Asia, and Ethiopia. *Cichorium intybus* (chicory) is related to *C. endivia* (endive); the words *intybus* and *endivia* both derive from the Arabic *hendibeh*. *Cichorium* is from an Egyptian word taken into many European languages, such as *chichorée* (French) and *cicoria* (Italian). Confusingly, in some countries curly endive is known as *chicorée* and Witloof chicory is called "endive". Chicory was grown as a vegetable in Roman times and remains an important crop throughout continental Europe. The leaves and roots have quite different uses. There are three main kinds of leaf chicory: bitter, loose-leafed cultivars, grown as a green winter vegetable, especially in S Italy; narrow-leafed, Witloof or Belgian kinds, with a compact elongate head (chicon), which is blanched for use in salads or cooked dishes; and broad-

leafed, red chicory or radicchio types, which form cabbage-like heads, eaten cooked or raw. Roots are harvested for coffee (especially in France) and medicinal preparations. In England, a law forbidding its use in coffee was passed in 1832 but repealed in 1840, provided that the ingredient appeared on the label. Young chicory roots give a slightly bitter, caramel flavour when roasted; roots over two years old are more bitter.
CULTIVATION Well-drained, neutral to alkaline soil in sun.
PROPAGATION By seed sown in autumn or spring, thinned to 25cm (10in) apart. May self-sow, becoming a weed in dry alkaline soil.
HARVEST Roots are lifted in early spring of the second year and sliced before roasting at 180°C (350°F) as a coffee additive, or drying for decoctions and liquid extracts. Chicons are produced by lifting roots in the autumn of the first year, cutting off leaves and packing in boxes kept in complete darkness at 10°C (50°F) for four weeks. Loose-leaf chicories are harvested when mature. Flowers and sap are collected in the summer.

◾ ***Cichorium intybus*** (chicory, succory)
Tall, clump-forming perennial with a thick taproot and oblanceolate toothed leaves, 7–30cm (3–12in) long. Clusters of sky-blue (occasionally pink or white) flowers, 3.5cm (1⅜in) across, resembling dandelions, appear in the upper axils throughout summer. Native to Europe, W Asia, and N Africa; naturalized in N America. ↕ 30cm–1.2m (1–4ft), ↔ 45–60cm (18–24in). ◾ 'Red Devil' is one of several radicchio-type cultivars that produce loose, deep red, white-veined, cabbage-like heads that mature in autumn and withstand early frosts. ↕ 15–20cm (6–8in), ↔ 7–10cm (3–4in).
HARDINESS Fully hardy.

Cichorium intybus

Cichorium intybus 'Red Devil'

PARTS USED Leaves, flowers, roots, sap.
PROPERTIES A bitter, diuretic, laxative herb that reduces inflammation and has a tonic effect on the liver and gall bladder.
MEDICINAL USES Internally for liver complaints, rheumatism, gout, and haemorrhoids. Regarded as a cooling alterative herb in Ayurvedic medicine.
CULINARY USES Loose-leaf chicories are boiled to remove bitterness and served with white or cheese sauce; heads of Witloof and radicchio chicories are eaten in salads or cooked as a vegetable. Roasted root is added to coffee. Flowers can be added to salads. Chewing gum (*da-sakizi*) is made from sap (Turkey).

CIMICIFUGA

Cimicifuga foetida. See *Actaea foetida*.
Cimicifuga racemosa. See *Actaea racemosa*.

CINCHONA
Quinine

Rubiaceae

This genus of about 40 species of tender evergreen trees and shrubs is found on warm moist slopes of the Andes, mostly at 1500–2500m (5000–8000ft). The species are difficult to tell apart; some authorities consider that there may be as few as 20. *Cinchona pubescens* is one of several cinchonas, including *C. calisaya*, *C. ledgeriana* (both known as yellow cinchona), and *C. officinalis*, from which the alkaloid quinine, a potent anti-malarial, is extracted. The story of cinchona's discovery by the eponymous Countess of Chinchon, wife of the Viceroy of Peru, after a bout of malaria, has been disproved by historians. It is certain, however, that Jesuits in the Lima area were familiar with its uses c.1630 (hence the name "Jesuit's bark"); it was first mentioned in medical literature by Herman van der Heyden (*Discours et advis sur les flus de ventre douloureux*, 1643). The use of quinine to give protection against malaria played a significant role in enabling Europeans to survive in the tropics and establish colonial empires. Made more palatable by the addition of gin, the daily

dose of quinine gave rise to "gin and tonic", the latter containing quinine to this day. By the early 19th century, populations of wild cinchona were severely depleted, leading to competition between the Dutch and English to establish plantations. The Dutch succeeded, cultivating *C. ledgeriana* in Java, which became the world centre for quinine production for many years. Cinchona is now grown in many tropical regions, some 8000–10,000 tonnes of bark producing 400–500 tonnes of alkaloids (mainly quinine) annually. Though largely replaced by synthetic drugs towards the end of the 20th century, *Cinchona* and other plants, such as *Artemisia annua* (see p.130), are increasingly important, as various strains of malaria become resistant to synthetics. Another alkaloid, quinidine, is also important as a cardiac depressant. Quinine is famous as the first substance that Samuel Hahnemann (1755–1843), founder of homeopathy, tested on himself, leading to the formulation of the Law of Similars (*similia similibus curentur*, "like cures like").
CULTIVATION Well-drained, moist soil, with high humidity, in sun or partial shade. In late winter, cut back specimen plants hard to encourage strong new growth. Commercial plantations are usually coppiced when about six years old.
PROPAGATION By nodal greenwood cuttings in late spring; by semi-ripe cuttings in summer at 15–18°C (59–64°F).
HARVEST Bark is collected from May until September, and dried for liquid extracts, tablets, or tinctures, or powder. It may be shaved off *in situ* or peeled from coppiced branches.

▣ *Cinchona pubescens* (Jesuit's bark, Peruvian bark, red cinchona)
Fast-growing, evergreen tree with ovate leaves, about 15cm (6in) long, sometimes flushed red on the undersides. Lilac-like panicles of small, tubular, pink flowers are followed by two-lobed capsules, 2cm (¾in) long. Native to Ecuador.
‡ 25m (80ft), ↔ variable.
HARDINESS Min. 15–18°C (59–64°F).
PARTS USED Stem and root bark.
PROPERTIES A bitter astringent herb that lowers fever, relaxes spasms, and is anti-malarial (quinine), and slows the heart (quinidine).
MEDICINAL USES Internally for malaria, acute

Cinchona pubescens

fevers, neuralgia, muscle cramps, cardiac fibrillation; an ingredient of most proprietary cold and influenza remedies. Excess causes cinchonism, a syndrome characterized by headache, rash, abdominal pain, deafness, and blindness. Not given to pregnant women unless suffering from malaria. Externally as a gargle for sore throat. Used in homeopathy (as *China officinalis*) for nervous exhaustion, anaemia, and convalescence.
CULINARY USES Quinine is used as a bitter flavouring in tonic water, soft drinks, and alcoholic drinks, such as Campari and Dubonnet.
⚠ **WARNING** This herb, especially in the form of quinine, is subject to legal restrictions in some countries.

CINNAMOMUM
Camphor tree

Lauraceae

Some 250 species of evergreen trees and shrubs belong to this genus, occurring in E and SE Asia, and in Australia. *Cinnamomum camphora*, *C. cassia*, and *C. verum* syn. *C. zeylanicum* provide three different commodities: camphor, cassia bark, and cinnamon, respectively. Camphor (often called camphorated oil) is an aromatic terpene ketone, familiar as mothballs, which is used medicinally and in the manufacture of celluloid. It is best known in the compound camphorated oil, in which camphor is blended with peanut oil. Similar compounds are extracted from *Blumea balsamifera* (Ngai camphor) and *Dryobalanops aromatica* (Borneo camphor, see p.197). Cassia and cinnamon are usually produced as bark quills, from which powdered cinnamon and essential oil are produced. They are of major importance in food flavouring and are ingredients in numerous medicinal formulas for their warming stimulant properties. *Cinnamomum cassia* is one of the oldest spices known, first recorded in China in 2700BC and in Egypt in 1600BC. Oil from *C. camphora* contains safrole (as in *Sassafras albidum*, see p.361), which can be extracted for flavouring but is now banned in many countries because it is potentially carcinogenic. *Cinnamomum verum* is a major world spice, which played a significant role in colonial expansion; the Portuguese invaded Ceylon in 1536 to obtain a monopoly of cinnamon; the Dutch began to cultivate it in 1770, and, thereafter, the Dutch East India Company dominated world trade in it from 1796 to 1833. Commercially less important species include: *C. burmanii* (Batavia cinnamon, Indonesian cassia, *korintje*), a good cinnamon substitute, also used in incense; *C. iners* (wild cinnamon), used in SE Asia for curries; *C. loureirii* (Saigon cassia/cinnamon), a sweet variety used for baking and made into a cordial; *C. massoia* (massoia bark) from New Guinea, which has a clove-like aroma, used for flavouring and perfumery; *C. oliveri* (black sassafras, Oliver bark), an Australian species with a pungent, clove–sassafras flavour; and

C

C. tamala (Indian bay/cassia, *tejpat*), with aromatic leaves and coarsely flavoured bark, used in Indian cuisine and to adulterate cinnamon.

CULTIVATION Moist, well-drained soil in sun or partial shade. Trees tolerate coppicing.

PROPAGATION By seed sown when ripe at 13–18°C (55–64°F); by semi-ripe cuttings in summer.

HARVEST Leaves of *C. camphora* are picked as required; wood is cut from trees over 50 years old and boiled to extract camphor, which is steam-distilled for oil or use in infusions, liniments, powder, and other medicated preparations. Bark of *C. cassia* is dried in quills without fermentation for use in infusions, powder, and tinctures; branches and leaves are distilled for oil. Unripe fruits of *C. cassia* are picked in summer and dried as cassia buds. Shoots of coppiced plants of *C. verum* are cut every second year during the rainy season, and stripped of leaves for distillation. The bark is left 24 hours to ferment; outer bark is then scraped away to expose inner bark, which is peeled and dried for use, whole or powdered, in infusions and tinctures, or distilled for oil.

■ *Cinnamomum camphora* syn. *Laurus camphora* (camphor)
Evergreen tree with pointed glossy leaves, up to 10cm (4in) long, which are red-flushed when young and camphor-scented. Small, pale yellow-green flowers are produced in clusters, 5–7cm (2–3in) across, in spring and summer, followed by black fruits, 6–10mm (¼–⅜in) in diameter. Native to Japan and tropical SE Asia. ‡ 12–30m (40–100ft), ↔ 5–12m (15–40ft).

HARDINESS Min. 10°C (50°F). Withstands an occasional fall in temperature to 0°C (32°F).

PARTS USED Wood and leaves (*zhang nao*), from which a crystalline camphor extract is prepared.

PROPERTIES A bitter, strongly aromatic herb that stimulates the circulatory and nervous systems, reduces inflammation, and relieves pain and spasms. It also benefits the digestion and destroys parasites.

MEDICINAL USES Externally in liniments, for joint and muscle pain, balms for chilblains, cold sores, chapped lips, and as an inhalant for nasal and bronchial congestion; in traditional Chinese medicine, for skin diseases, wounds, and as a stimulant in unconsciousness; in aromatherapy, for digestive complaints and depression. Internally, in Ayurvedic medicine, for bronchitis, asthma, sinusitis, eye complaints, epilepsy, painful menstruation, gout, rheumatism, and insomnia. Excess causes palpitations, vomiting, convulsions, and death; it may be absorbed through the skin, causing systemic poisoning.

⚠ **WARNING** This herb, especially in the form of camphorated oil, is subject to legal restrictions in some countries.

■ *Cinnamomum cassia* syn. *C. aromaticum* (cassia bark, Chinese cinnamon)
Evergreen tree with thick leathery leaves, to 20cm (8in) long. Yellow flowers appear in panicles, 8–18cm (3–7in) long, in summer, followed by single-seeded berries. Native to

China. ‡ 12–20m (40–70ft), ↔ 6–12m (20–40ft).

HARDINESS Min. 15°C (59°F).

PARTS USED Inner bark (*rou gui*), leafy twigs (*gou zhi*), fruits, oil.

PROPERTIES Inner bark is a pungent, sweet, hot herb that stimulates the circulatory system, improves digestion, relieves spasms and vomiting, and controls infections. Twigs increase perspiration and lower fever.

MEDICINAL USES Internally, in Western medicine, mainly in preparations for diarrhoea, flatulent dyspepsia and colic, and colds; in Chinese medicine, for diarrhoea, poor appetite, low vitality, kidney weakness (*yang* deficiency manifesting in oedema and light urination), rheumatism, and coldness (*rou gui*); and for colds, influenza, fevers, arthritic and rheumatic complaints, angina, palpitations, and digestive ailments related to cold and chills (*gou zhi*).

CULINARY USES Bark is used to flavour curries, baked foods, confectionery, soft drinks, chewing gum, and condiments. An ingredient of the Chinese "five spices", with anise, star anise, cloves, and fennel seeds. Fruits, known as "cassia buds", resemble cloves in appearance and are also widely used for flavouring.

ECONOMIC USES Cassia oil contains 80–90 per cent cinnamaldehyde, used mainly in medicines, baked foods, confectionery, and cosmetics.

■ *Cinnamomum verum*, syn. *C. zeylanicum* (Ceylon cinnamon, cinnamon)
Evergreen tree with light brown, papery bark and leathery leaves, to 18cm (7in) long. Small, yellow-white flowers appear in clusters, to 18cm (7in) long, in summer, followed by ovoid purple berries, 1cm (⅜in) long. Native to S India and Sri Lanka.

Cinnamomum camphora

Cinnamomum cassia

Cinnamomum verum

‡10–18m (30–60ft), ↔ 6–10m (20–30ft).

HARDINESS Min. 15°C (59°F).

PARTS USED Inner bark, leaves, oil.

PROPERTIES A pungent, sweet, warming herb that stimulates peripheral circulation, relieves spasms, lowers fever and blood pressure, controls bleeding and infections, and improves digestion.

MEDICINAL USES Internally for diarrhoea, nausea and vomiting, gastroenteritis, colds, influenza, hypertension, arthritis, rheumatism, and candidiasis; used especially for cold people. Not given to pregnant women.

CULINARY USES Ground bark is used to flavour curries, desserts, cakes, biscuits, breads, and pastries; also mixed with sugar as a topping for toast and drinks, such as cappuccino. Cinnamon sticks are used whole to flavour hot drinks, such as mulled wine. Leaves are used for flavouring, notably hominy, and jerked pork (Jamaica).

ECONOMIC USES Bark and bark oil, in which cinnamaldehyde predominates, are used in the food industry for flavouring baked foods, meat products, confectionery, pickles, cola-type soft drinks, ice cream, and liqueurs; also in oral hygiene products and cosmetics. Leaf oil, which is more delicate, containing 70–80 per cent eugenol, is used in carnation-type perfumes.

CISTUS
Rock rose, sun rose

Cistaceae

Native to S Europe and N Africa, this genus contains about 20 species of evergreen and semi-evergreen shrubs. Rock roses are attractive plants, popular in dry warm borders and coastal gardens for their short-lived but showy flowers. The name *Cistus* comes from the Greek *kiste*, "box", and refers to the shape of the capsules. Ladanum, or labdanum, is an oleo-resin made from several species of *Cistus*, including *C. albiflorus*, *C. creticus*, *C. ladanifer*, and *C. maculatus*. It is the best plant substitute for ambergris from sperm whales and is important in perfume manufacture. The sticky substance is collected in France and Spain by whipping the bushes, so that the exudate adheres to the leather thongs, or, in Crete, by combing it from the hides of sheep and goats with a leather rake, or *ladanisterion*.

CULTIVATION Well-drained, light to poor soil in sun. Cut out dead wood in spring. Rock roses dislike hard pruning and transplanting.

PROPAGATION By seed sown when ripe, or in spring; by softwood or greenwood cuttings in summer.

HARVEST Leaves and twigs are collected in late spring and early summer for use in infusions, and boiled to extract oleo-resin. Oil is steam-distilled commercially from the oleo-resin.

■ *Cistus ladanifer* (gum cistus)
Evergreen shrub with a stiff upright habit and sticky, aromatic, linear–lanceolate leaves, 10cm (4in) long. Solitary, five-petalled, white flowers, about 7cm (3in) across, with a maroon basal blotch on each petal, appear from early to late

Cistus ladanifer

summer. Grows from SW Europe to N Africa.
↕ 2–2.5m (6–8ft), ↔ 1.5m (5ft).
HARDINESS Frost hardy.
PARTS USED Leaves, oleo-resin, oil.
PROPERTIES An aromatic, stimulant, expectorant herb that controls bleeding and has antibiotic effects.
MEDICINAL USES Internally for catarrh and diarrhoea.
ECONOMIC USES Important as a fixative in lavender, fern, and *chypre* perfumes, and as a commercial food flavouring for baked foods, soft drinks, ice cream, and confectionery.

CITRUS
Rutaceae

Some 16 species of small evergreen trees and shrubs comprise this genus, native to SE Asia and E Pacific islands. Most citruses have been cultivated for so long that their origins are obscure. The species are very closely related, with numerous hybrids and cultivars. *Citrus* was unknown in Europe in Classical times, though *C. aurantium* and *C. bergamia* were first mentioned in Chinese medicine in the 1st century AD. The first citrus to arrive in Europe was *C. aurantium* (bitter orange), probably brought by the Portuguese from the East Indies. It was followed by *C. limon*, probably from China, somewhere between the 11th and 13th centuries. Medicinal uses of citruses are complex. Various parts of the tree are used, and also various parts of the fruit at different stages of ripeness. Commonly, the leaves, fruits, juice and bark are used, while in China several quite different drugs are prepared from the fruits alone – one of the most valuable being the peel of *C. reticulata*, which becomes more potent with age. The related *Poncirus trifoliata* (hardy orange, Japanese bitter orange) is used in identical ways to *C. aurantium*. Citruses are high in vitamin C, flavonoids, acids, and volatile oils. They also contain coumarins, such as bergapten, which sensitize the skin to sunlight. Bergapten may be added to tanning products but may cause dermatitis or allergic responses. Recent uses of citruses are as antioxidants and

chemical exfoliants in cosmetics.
CULTIVATION Well-drained, neutral to slightly acid soil in sun, with ample moisture during the growing season. Scale insects, mealybugs, and tortrix moth caterpillars may affect plants under cover. Citrus does not transplant well.
PROPAGATION By seed sown when ripe or in spring at 16°C (61°F); by semi-ripe cuttings in summer. Cultivars do not come true from seed.
HARVEST Flowers (*C. aurantium*, *C. bergamia*) are picked when first open and distilled for oil. Leaves (*C. aurantiifolia*, *C. hystrix*) are picked as required for flavouring and infusions. Oil is distilled from foliage, unripe fruits (*C. aurantium*), and ripe fruits (*C. bergamia*). Fruits are picked when unripe or ripe for culinary use, candying, or oil distillation, and either unripe or ripe (*C. aurantium*, *C. reticulata*) for use in Chinese medicine.

▣ ***Citrus aurantiifolia*** (lime)
Small tree with short spiny branches and light green, ovate leaves, 5–7.5cm (2–3in) long. Clusters of 2–7 white flowers appear in lax racemes in spring and summer, followed by ovoid green fruits, to 6cm (2½in) across, with a sour pulp. Native to tropical Asia; widely cultivated in the West Indies. ↕ 3–5m (10–15ft), ↔ 2–3m (6–10ft).
▣ *C. aurantiifolia* × *Fortunella japonica* (limequat) has fruits similar in appearance to kumquats but yellow-green and lime-flavoured. Easier to grow in cooler areas than the true lime. 'Mexican' (bartender's lime, key lime,

West Indian lime) is compact and thorny, with small, round, yellow-green fruits that have very thin skin. ▣ 'Tahiti' syn. 'Bearss' (Persian lime, Tahitian lime) has oval seedless fruits of excellent flavour.
HARDINESS Min. 13°C (55°F). Sometimes withstands short periods at 0°C (32°F).
PARTS USED Leaves, fruits, peel, oil.
PROPERTIES An aromatic, cooling, and astringent herb.
MEDICINAL USES Internally for minor complaints such as bilious headache (infusions of leaves); juice is added to medicinal preparations in SE Asia and Guyana, notably for diarrhoea.
CULINARY USES Fruits are used in preserves and pickles, and as a garnish. Dried fruits feature in Persian cuisine. Juice is used in drinks, and as a flavouring for fish, curries, and confectionery. Used in India to curdle milk for fresh cheese, such as *paneer*. Peel is used like lemon peel.
ECONOMIC USES Oil is used as a source of citral in perfumery.

▣ ***Citrus aurantium*** (bitter orange, Seville orange)
Rounded tree with slender, blunt-spined branches and ovate leaves, 7–10cm (3–4in) long. White fragrant flowers, 2cm (¾in) across, are borne during spring and summer, followed by orange fruits, 5–7cm (2–3in) across, with aromatic rind and acidic pulp. Native to SE Asia. ↕ 10m (30ft), ↔ 6m (20ft). ▣ 'Bouquet de Fleurs' has highly scented flowers that are distilled for oil of neroli. 'Bouquet de Nice' has double flowers and fruits embedded with a secondary fruit.
▣ var. *myrtifolia* (chinotto) has symmetrical

Citrus aurantiifolia   *Citrus aurantiifolia* × *Fortunella japonica*   *Citrus aurantiifolia* 'Tahiti'

Citrus aurantium

Citrus aurantium 'Bouquet de Fleurs'

Citrus aurantium var. *myrtifolia*

C

compact growth, very tiny leaves, numerous flowers, and small fruits ideal for crystallizing, preserving, or pickling whole.

HARDINESS Min. 7°C (45°F). Sometimes withstands short periods at 0°C (32°F).

PARTS USED Leaves, stems, flowers, ripe fruits with seeds and peel removed (*zhi ke*), whole unripe fruits (*zhi shi*), peel, oil.

PROPERTIES A bitter, aromatic, expectorant, diuretic herb that lowers blood pressure and improves digestion. It reduces inflammation and controls bacterial and fungal infections.

MEDICINAL USES Internally for flatulent indigestion and diarrhoea, stubborn coughs, colic in babies, and shock. Externally in aromatherapy for tension, depression, and skin problems.

CULINARY USES Fruits are used to make marmalade. Juice is used in drinks and sauces. Dried peel is used in *bouquet garni* and to flavour speciality beers. Essential oil flavours liqueurs, such as Cointreau, Grand Marnier, and Triple Sec. Flowers are used to scent tea. Orange-flower water is used in desserts.

ECONOMIC USES Neroli oil (from flowers) and petitgrain (from foliage/twigs) used in perfumery.

▣ *Citrus bergamia* syn. *C. aurantium* var. *bergamia* (bergamot orange)
Similar in appearance to *C. aurantium* but with broader leaves and more aromatic, yellow rind. Origin uncertain. ↕ 10m (30ft), ↔ 7m (22ft). 'Femminello' has highly aromatic, spherical, smooth fruits.

HARDINESS Min. 7°C (45°F). Sometimes withstands short periods at 0°C (32°F).

PARTS USED Flowers, ripe fruit peel, oil.

PROPERTIES A bitter aromatic herb that relieves tension, relaxes spasms, and improves digestion. Neroli oil (from flowers) is stimulant, and reputedly aphrodisiac; bergamot oil (from peel) is more sedative and healing.

MEDICINAL USES Internally for colic in babies (orange-flower water). Externally in douches and baths for vaginal infections (bergamot oil), and in aromatherapy for stress-related complaints and skin conditions (bergamot and neroli oils).

CULINARY USES Main source of orange-flower water for desserts (especially blancmange) and pastries. Fruits are used as a substitute for limes.

ECONOMIC USES Bergamot oil is used to flavour Earl Grey tea; neroli oil in perfumery.

▣ *Citrus hystrix* (kaffir lime, leech lime, makrut)
Small tree with dark green, broadly ovate, flat leaves with winged stalks almost as large as the leaf blades. Small white flowers are followed by small, dark green fruits with warty skins. Native to SE Asia. ↕ 3–5m (10–15ft), ↔ 2.5–3m (8–10ft).

HARDINESS Min. 7°C (45°F). Stands short periods of 0°C (32°F).

PARTS USED Leaves, fruits.

PROPERTIES A bitter aromatic herb.

CULINARY USES Fresh or dried leaves are used to flavour soups, such as *tom yam*, curries, and *kecap* (Indonesian soy sauce), especially in SE Asian cooking. Fruit rind is candied, or dried to flavour curry pastes.

▣ *Citrus limon* (lemon)
Small spiny tree or shrub with narrowly ovate, light green leaves, 5–10cm (2–4in)

long. Pale purple-budded, fragrant, white flowers, 4–5cm (1½–2in) across, appear in spring and summer, followed by ovoid yellow fruits, 7–15cm (3–6in) long, containing very sour pulp. Origin unknown (probably China); introduced to the Mediterranean AD1000–1200. ↕ 2–7m (6–22ft), ↔ 1.5–3m (5–10ft).

▣ 'Meyer' syn. *C.* × *meyeri* is compact, with prolific blossom and medium-sized, rounded fruits. Discovered in China in early 1900s.

▣ 'Variegata' has yellow-edged leaves and immature fruits striped yellow and green.

HARDINESS Min. 5°C (41°F). Sometimes withstands short periods at 0°C (32°F).

PARTS USED Fruits, juice, peel, oil.

PROPERTIES A bitter, aromatic, cooling herb that has diuretic and anti-inflammatory effects, and improves peripheral circulation.

MEDICINAL USES Internally for varicose veins, haemorrhoids, kidney stones, feverish minor illnesses, and bronchial congestion. Juice taken in hot water (with addition of honey, garlic, cinnamon, etc.) for colds and flu. Externally for eczema, chilblains, sunburn, and poisonous stings, and as a gargle for sore throats. Essential oil is used externally to treat mouth ulcers.

CULINARY USES Fruits and grated peel (zest) are ingredients in lemonade and other soft drinks, ice cream, sorbets, desserts, marmalades, salad dressings, and marinades. Juice is used as a coagulant in cheese-making, and to set jams. Sliced lemons are a garnish for drinks, fish, and seafood dishes. Preserved lemons feature in Moroccan

Citrus bergamia

Citrus hystrix

Citrus limon

Citrus limon 'Meyer'

Citrus limon 'Variegata'

Citrus medica

Citrus medica var. *digitata*

Citrus reticulata

C

cuisine. Lemons are pressed with olives to produce lemon olive oil, known as *limonato*.

ECONOMIC USES Inner peel and pulp are a source of pectin, used to set sugarless jams and jellies. Essential oil, known as *cedro oil*, is used as a flavouring in the food industry. Oil is also used to scent soaps, detergents, and perfumery. Peel is dried for potpourris.

▣ *Citrus medica* (citron)
Large shrub or small spiny tree with elliptic–ovate, toothed leaves, 10–18cm (4–7in) long. White, purple-flushed flowers, 4cm (1½in) wide, appear in spring and summer, followed by ovoid–oblong, yellow fruits, to 30cm (12in) long. Native to SW Asia. ‡ 3–5m (10–15ft), ↔ 2–3m (6–10ft). ▣ var. *digitata* syn. var. *sarcodactylis* (Buddha's hand/fingers) has strange fruits, wholly or partly divided into finger-like sections, lacking pulp and often seedless. Popular as an offering in Buddhist temples, for scenting rooms and clothing. 'Etrog' is smaller and less vigorous, with thick-skinned, highly aromatic fruits, 15–25cm (6–10in) long, excellent for candying.
HARDINESS Min. 3–5°C (37–41°F). At times withstands short periods at 0°C (32°F).
PARTS USED Fruits, peel.
PROPERTIES A highly aromatic herb.
CULINARY USES Fruits of 'Etrog' are eaten during the Jewish Feast of the Tabernacles. Peel is candied or used in making confectionery.

▣ *Citrus reticulata* (mandarin orange, tangerine)
Large shrub or small, spreading, often spiny tree with ovate to lanceolate leaves, 3–4cm (1¼–1½in) long. Fragrant white flowers, less than 2.5cm (1in) across, appear in spring and summer, followed by yellow- to red-orange fruits, to 8cm (3in) in diameter, with thin, easily removed peel and sweet pulp. Native to SE Asia. ‡ 2–8m (6–25ft), ↔ 1.5–3m (5–10ft). 'Clementine' is a N American cultivar of the Mandarin Group, with an upright bushy habit and early, sweet, orange-red fruit.
HARDINESS Min. 3–5°C (37–41°F). At times withstands short periods at 0°C (32°F).
PARTS USED Fruits, dried ripe peel (*chen pi*), unripe peel (*qing pi*), seeds (*ju he*).
PROPERTIES A bitter, spicy, warming herb that stimulates the digestion, lungs, and spleen (*chen pi*); acts mainly on the liver, gall bladder, and breasts (*qing piq*); an energy stimulant, it affects the liver and kidneys, and relieves pain (*ju he*).
MEDICINAL USES Internally for indigestion, vomiting, and wet coughs (*chen pi*); liver or gall bladder disorders, bronchial congestion, mastitis, breast cancer, and pain in liver, chest, and breasts (*qing pi*); lumbago, orchitis, mastitis (*ju he*).
CULINARY USES Fruits are eaten fresh, preserved whole in syrup, canned, or juiced. Peel is dried as a condiment (*kuo pei*) in China for a sweet spicy flavour and to reduce odours.
ECONOMIC USES Essential oil is used for flavouring in the food industry.

CLAVICEPS
Clavicipitaceae

This cosmopolitan genus has 35 species of fungi, parasitic on grasses and rushes. Outbreaks of poisoning by *C. purpurea* (ergot) have long been recorded. Rye flour contaminated with the fungus causes hallucinations, convulsions, and a burning sensation in the limbs, followed by gangrene as the blood supply is restricted. The syndrome, now known as "ergotism", was once believed to be a punishment for sin, when it was called "St Anthony's fire" or "holy fire". *Claviceps purpurea* has been used to strengthen contractions in childbirth since the 16th century. Rarely used in its crude state today, it is split into component alkaloids, such as ergometrine (a uterine stimulant) and ergotamine (a vasoconstrictor). *Ustilago zeae* (corn ergot), a fungus found on corn (maize), also contains alkaloids that stimulate the uterus. The chemistry of ergot is similar to that of lysergic acid diethylamide (LSD); supplies of the fungus are carefully monitored to prevent its use in the manufacture of the illicit drug.
PROPAGATION Propagate by spores raised in the laboratory and sprayed on a cereal crop (usually rye).
HARVEST Sclerotia are harvested mechanically, then processed commercially into liquid extracts and alkaloids.

▣ *Claviceps purpurea* (ergot)
Poisonous fungus with a hard, purple-black, spindle-shaped sclerotium, to 2.5cm (1in) long, parasitic on ovaries of cereal flowers in summer, and globose, brown-purple stroma (resting stage), 2mm (¹⁄₁₆in) across, on the ground in autumn and winter, followed by release of colourless, filiform spores in spring. Cosmopolitan.
HARDINESS Hardy.
PARTS USED Sclerotia.
PROPERTIES An unpleasant-smelling herb that stimulates the uterus, constricts blood vessels, and acts on the central nervous system, blocking release of adrenalin.
MEDICINAL USES Internally in childbirth (expulsion of placenta only), postpartum

Claviceps purpurea

haemorrhage (ergometrine), and migraine (ergotamine). For use only by qualified practitioners.
⚠ **WARNING** This herb, especially in the form of ergometrine and ergotamine, is subject to legal restrictions in some countries.

CLEMATIS
Ranunculaceae

Over 200 species of deciduous or evergreen climbers and woody perennials belong to this genus, which occurs in most temperate regions. Many species are grown as ornamentals for their fine flowers and often attractive foliage. Clematis are acrid plants, containing glycosides that have a burning taste and blistering effect. A few are used medicinally, including the European *C. recta* and *C. vitalba*, in homeopathic preparations for rheumatism and skin eruptions. The latter is known as *herbe aux gueux* ("beggar's weed") in France, having once been used by beggars to irritate the skin in order to simulate sores. *Clematis chinensis* was first described in Chinese medicinal formulas 1000 years ago. Other species used in traditional Chinese medicine include *C. armandii*, *C. montana*, and *C. uncinata*. An Australian species, *C. glycinoides*, is a traditional Aboriginal remedy for colds and headaches, the acrid smell of the foliage causing profuse watering of the eyes and nose when inhaled.
CULTIVATION Well-drained, neutral to alkaline soil in sun, with roots in shade. In spring, cut back shoots and dead stems after flowering. Plants may suffer from powdery mildew and clematis wilt.
PROPAGATION By seed sown when ripe; by softwood cuttings in spring; by semi-ripe cuttings in early summer.
HARVEST Roots are lifted in autumn and dried for use in decoctions.
⚠ **WARNING** Harmful if eaten. Mild skin irritant.

Clematis chinensis (Chinese clematis)
Deciduous climber or scrambler with ribbed stems and pinnately divided leaves, which have five ovate to heart-shaped leaflets, to 8cm (3in) long. Panicles of white flowers, 2cm (¾in) across, are produced in autumn. Native to C and W China. ‡↔ 8m (25ft).
HARDINESS Fully hardy.
PARTS USED Roots (*wei ling xian*).
PROPERTIES A pungent warming herb that has painkilling, sedative, and diuretic effects, lowering fever and relieving spasms.
MEDICINAL USES Internally for rheumatism and arthritis, usually taken in wine. A decoction in rice vinegar is a traditional remedy for dissolving fish bones lodged in the throat.

CLINOPODIUM
Clinopodium acinos. See *Acinos arvensis*.

173

CNICUS
Blessed thistle

Asteraceae

A genus containing a single species of thistle-like annual. Widely naturalized in dry parts of lowland Europe, having escaped from cultivation as a medicinal herb in the Middle Ages, *C. benedictus* is now grown mainly in C Europe for the pharmaceutical industry. The name *Cnicus* comes from the Greek *knekos*, "thistle", which in turn may be derived from *chnizein*, "to injure", referring to the plant's extreme prickliness. Blessed thistle, originally cultivated in monastery gardens, was once regarded as a cure-all, and in the 16th century was widely recommended for the plague.

CULTIVATION Well-drained soil in sun.
PROPAGATION By seed sown in spring.
HARVEST Plants are cut when flowering and dried for infusions, liquid extracts, and tablets.

■ *Cnicus benedictus* syn. *Carbenia benedicta*, *Carduus benedictus* (blessed thistle, holy thistle) Spiny annual with a cylindrical taproot, branched hairy stems, and pinnately lobed, sharply toothed, pale-veined leaves, 10–30cm (4–12in) long. Solitary flowers, to 4cm (1½in) across, with yellow florets and bristly bracts, are produced over many weeks in summer, followed by brown ribbed fruits, about 7mm (¼in) long, each bearing a pappus of yellow hairs. Native to Mediterranean regions.
‡ 24–65cm (10–26in), ↔ 30cm (12in).
HARDINESS Hardy.
PARTS USED Flowering tops.
PROPERTIES A very bitter, antiseptic, antibiotic herb that acts mainly as a digestive tonic. It is also a mild expectorant, checks bleeding, encourages healing, lowers fever, and stimulates lactation.
MEDICINAL USES Internally for anorexia, poor appetite associated with depression, dyspepsia, flatulent colic, diarrhoea, catarrh, and insufficient lactation.

174 | *Cnicus benedictus*

Excess causes vomiting. Externally for wounds and ulcers. Combines well with *Chelone glabra* (see p.165) and *Cola* spp. (see p.175) for anorexia, and with *Agrimonia eupatoria* (see p.107), *Filipendula ulmaria* (see p.214), and *Potentilla erecta* (see p.329) for diarrhoea.
⚠ **WARNING** This herb is subject to legal restrictions in some countries.
▣ ▪

COCHLEARIA
Cochlearia armoracia. See *Armoracia rusticana*.

CODONOPSIS
Bonnet bellflower

Campanulaceae

Thirty species of perennial climbers belong to this genus, which is distributed through the Himalayas to Japan. Most of the species are in cultivation, often grown on banks and trained over supports or larger plants, so that the intricately patterned insides of the flowers can be appreciated. The name is from the Greek *kodon*, "bell", and *opsis*, "resemblance", because the flowers are bell-shaped. *Codonopsis pilosula* is extensively cultivated in China as a medicinal plant. It is highly regarded in traditional Chinese medicine as a substitute for *Panax ginseng* (see p.299). Several other species are used interchangeably, including *C. tangshen* (*chuan dang*) and *C. tubulosa* (white *dang shen*). A famous Chinese energy tonic is the "soup of the four gentlemen", first described c.AD1200, which contains *Codonopsis pilosula*, *Atractylodes macrocephala* (see p.137), *Glycyrrhiza uralensis* (see p.227), and *Wolfiporia cocos* (see p.408).
CULTIVATION Light, well-drained, sandy, slightly acid soil in semi-shade.
PROPAGATION By seed sown under cover in spring or autumn; by cuttings of basal shoots in spring. Seedlings have delicate taproots, needing care when transplanting.
HARVEST Roots are lifted in autumn from plants at least three years old and used fresh, or dried for decoctions by threading on to strings and rubbing vigorously at intervals to distribute moisture until completely dry. Often used in the form of a tincture by Western herbalists.

■ *Codonopsis pilosula* (bastard ginseng, bellflower, *dang shen*)
Twining climber with slender stems and pale green, hairy, ovate leaves, to 4cm (1½in) long. Solitary, bell-shaped, pale green flowers, about 2.5cm (1in) long, appear on leafy lateral branches in summer. Native to NE Asia. ‡ 2m (6ft).
HARDINESS Fully hardy.
PARTS USED Roots (*dang shen*).
PROPERTIES A sweet, warm, soothing herb, taken as an energy tonic. It acts mainly on the spleen, lungs, and stomach, raising body-fluid secretions and blood sugar levels, lowering blood pressure, and stimulating the immune system.
MEDICINAL USES Internally for low energy,

Codonopsis pilosula

poor appetite and digestion, anaemia, shallow breathing, asthma, fatigue, and debility after illness. In Chinese folk medicine, used to stimulate milk production in nursing mothers. As a tonic food, often cooked with rice until glutinous.
CULINARY USES Roots are roasted with millet or eaten raw, baked, or pickled in miso. An ingredient of tonic teas and soups in China.
▣ ▪ ✏

COFFEA
Coffee

Rubiaceae

Forty or so species of mainly evergreen shrubs and small trees belong to this genus, which occurs in tropical Asia and Africa. *Coffea arabica* is the most widely cultivated species commercially and is occasionally grown as an ornamental for containers in cool climates. Coffee drinking began in Africa some thousand years ago and was first noted by Leonhart Rauwolf, a German traveller to the Middle East, in 1573. Europeans acquired the taste in the 17th century; since then, coffee has become a crop of global importance. The longer-lived and higher-yielding *C. canephora* (robusta coffee) is grown mainly in Africa. It produces beans with the highest caffeine of any species but is inferior in flavour and used mainly in cheaper blends and instant coffee. *Coffea liberica* (Liberian coffee) is cultivated for local consumption in Malaysia and Guyana; its flavour is inferior and plants need more warmth and humidity. *Coffea stenophylla* (highland coffee, Sierra Leone coffee) produces fine-flavoured coffee, comparable with mocha. Coffee contains up to 0.32 per cent caffeine when fresh. It also contains chlorogenic acid, a stimulant and diuretic, which remains after decaffeination and is a known allergen. Caffeine is used in many proprietary painkillers to potentiate aspirin and paracetamol, and in homeopathic remedies for hyperactivity and tension headaches.

CULTIVATION Well-drained, moisture-retentive soil in semi-shade. Trim container-grown plants in spring to maintain shape. Plants grown under cover may be damaged by scale insects and mealybugs.

PROPAGATION By seed sown when ripe, at 30°C (86°F); by tip cuttings at 30°C (86°F).

HARVEST Berries are picked when ripe and the seeds ("beans") are dried, fermented, or roasted for infusions and essence. Homeopathic tinctures are made from unroasted beans.

■ *Coffea arabica* (Arabian coffee, coffee)
Evergreen shrub with glossy, dark green, elliptic to ovate, pointed leaves, to 10cm (4in) long. Dense axillary clusters of fragrant white flowers in late summer and autumn, followed by rounded to ellipsoid fruits, about 1cm (⅜in) long, which ripen red and each contain two seeds. Native to NE tropical Africa. ‡ 7m (22ft), ↔ 2–3m (6–10ft). 'Kona' has very fragrant flowers and seeds that produce aromatic, finely flavoured coffee. 'Nana' is dwarf, with wavy edged leaves. Makes a good container plant.

HARDINESS Min. 10°C (50°F).

PARTS USED Seeds.

PROPERTIES A bitter, aromatic, stimulant herb that has diuretic effects and controls vomiting.

MEDICINAL USES Internally for nausea and vomiting, and collapse following narcotic poisoning. Unripe seeds used in Ayurvedic medicine for headaches. Externally for burns and scalds (powdered seeds), and as an enema to cleanse the large bowel (infusion).

CULINARY USES Coffee is the basis of many stimulant drinks, served hot, iced, spiced, fortified with various spirits and liqueurs, with or without milk or cream, and sweetening. Used to flavour cakes, desserts, and sweet sauces.

ECONOMIC USES Coffee extract is used in baked produce, desserts, ice cream, yogurt, confectionery, syrups, liqueurs (such as Kahlua and Tia Maria), and cola-type drinks, sometimes combined with chocolate to give mocha flavour. Roasted whole beans are chocolate-coated as a snack or confectionery.

▨ ▣ ✎ ✐ ▣

COIX
Poaceae

Five or six species of annual and perennial grasses make up this tropical Asian genus. *Coix lachryma-jobi* has been grown as an ornamental since antiquity. It is an interesting plant for summer bedding, though in cool areas the fruits may not ripen. Theophrastus gave the name *Coix* to a reed-like plant. *Coix lachryma-jobi* was first described in Chinese medicine c.AD200 and is widely used in Chinese patent remedies. The pearl-grey fruits are worn as necklaces in Colombia and Cuba to prevent tooth decay.

CULTIVATION Moist soil in sun. May be affected by powdery mildew.

PROPAGATION By seed sown in spring at 13–16°C (55–61°F).

HARVEST Fruits are collected when ripe in autumn, and the husks are removed before using fresh, roasted, or fermented.

■ *Coix lachryma-jobi* (Job's tears)
Robust upright annual grass with linear leaves, to 60cm (24in) long, and arching inflorescences with racemes of separate male and female spikelets in summer. Female flowers are enclosed in a hard, tear-shaped husk, green at first, turning grey or grey-mauve when ripe. Male flowers are borne in clusters at the end of the flower spike. Native to SE Asia. ‡ 45cm–1.5m (1½–5ft), ↔ 30cm (12in).

HARDINESS Half hardy.

PARTS USED Fruits (*yi yi ren*).

PROPERTIES A sweet cooling herb that reduces inflammation, relieves pain and spasms, lowers fever, and controls bacterial and fungal infections. It acts mainly as a spleen tonic and has sedative effects. Large doses lower blood sugar levels.

MEDICINAL USES Internally for arthritis (especially rheumatoid), urinary problems, lung abscesses, and diarrhoea associated with spleen weakness; liquor from fermented seeds is given for rheumatic pain. Not given to pregnant women.

CULINARY USES Seeds can be hulled and boiled like rice or ground as flour. Grains are also added to soups and desserts, or brewed into beer (India). Seeds used for making tea (Japan).

▨ ▣ ✎

COLA
Sterculiaceae

A genus of about 125 species of evergreen, tropical African trees. Cola has been used for centuries as a masticatory in Africa, being exported from the western tropics into arid regions via camel traders, who chewed the seeds to maintain alertness on long monotonous journeys. Though bitter at first, seeds have the after-effect of making other foods and drinks taste sweet. Cola nuts are important in social ceremony in Africa, S America, and Asia, and are often chewed before meals to aid digestion. Cola nuts contain up to 2.4 per cent caffeine (3.5 per cent in *C. nitida*), some theobromine, and "cola red", a pigment that dyes the mouth and teeth; obtained from various species, including *C. acuminata* (Abata cola), *C. anomala* (Bamenda cola), *C. nitida* (gbanja cola), and *C. verticillata* (Owé cola). Trees fruit at 12–15 years old, producing 10–16kg (22–35lb) annually until 70–100 years old, and are often planted as shade trees for cocoa. The name *Cola* probably comes from *kolo*, the Mandingo name for the plant. "Cola" is now a household name for cola-flavoured soft drinks.

CULTIVATION Rich, well-drained soil in sun.

PROPAGATION By seed sown when ripe at 20–24°C (68–75°F); by hardwood cuttings in sand at 21–24°C (70–75°F).

HARVEST Seeds are taken from ripe fruits and used fresh or dried for liquid extracts, powder, tablets, and tinctures.

Coffea arabica

Coix lachryma-jobi

Cola nitida

■ *Cola nitida* syn. *C. vera* (cola, gbanja cola, *goora* nut, kola)
Evergreen tree with glossy, pointed, oblanceolate leaves, 7–30cm (3–12in) long. Five-lobed, cream flowers, about 3cm (1¼in) across, usually with purple-red markings inside, are followed by compound fruits, to 17cm (7in) long, containing up to ten seeds ("nuts"), 4–5cm (1½–2in) long. Native to tropical W Africa. ‡ 20m (70ft), ↔ 10–17m (30–55ft).
HARDINESS Min. 13–15°C (55–59°F).
PARTS USED Seeds.
PROPERTIES An astringent, bitter–sweet, anti-depressant herb that has a stimulant effect, especially on the heart.
MEDICINAL USES Internally, in tonics, for low energy, exhaustion, and poor appetite; also for diarrhoea. Not given to patients with hypertension, palpitations, or peptic ulcers. Chewed fresh or made into a hot drink as an energy and digestive stimulant in countries of origin.
ECONOMIC USES Extracts added to soft drinks, baked produce, and liqueurs.
▨ ▯ ✎ ▣

COLCHICUM

Colchicaceae

In this genus, distributed throughout Europe, N Africa, and W Asia to W China, are 45 species of poisonous cormous perennials. *Colchicum* is named after Colchis, an area of Georgia near the Black Sea, where these plants abound. Despite their toxicity, colchicum is a popular garden plant for borders, rock gardens, moist grasslands, and under trees, with large colourful blooms in late summer and early autumn. The ancient Greeks took *C. autumnale* in tiny amounts for gout, asthma, dropsy, and kidney complaints. Therapeutic doses were evaluated by Anton von Stoerck in 1763, and used since as a standard treatment for gout. Colchicum contains colchicine, an alkaloid that affects cell division and is used in plant breeding and genetic engineering.
CULTIVATION Moisture-retentive soil in sun or semi-shade, allowing space for large leaves to develop in spring. Slugs may damage corms.
PROPAGATION By seed sown when ripe; by separation of corms or offsets in summer. Seeds may take 18 months to germinate.
HARVEST Corms are lifted in summer, and seeds collected in early summer; both are dried, for use in liquid and dry extracts, and tinctures.
⚠ **WARNING** All parts are highly toxic if eaten. Handling of corms may cause skin allergy.

■ *Colchicum autumnale* (autumn crocus, meadow saffron, naked ladies)
Perennial with ovoid corm, to 6cm (2½in) long, and 3–5 erect, linear to lanceolate leaves, 14–35cm (5½–14in) long. Up to six pale purple, goblet-shaped flowers, 4–6cm (1½–2½in) long, appear in late summer and autumn, followed by obovoid seed capsules. Found from Europe to Ukraine. ‡ 30cm (12in).
■ 'Alboplenum' has double white flowers.
■ 'Album' has white flowers. ■ 'Pleniflorum' syn. 'Roseum Plenum' has double flowers.

Colchicum autumnale

Colchicum autumnale 'Alboplenum'

Colchicum autumnale 'Album'

Colchicum autumnale 'Pleniflorum'

HARDINESS Fully hardy.
PARTS USED Corms, seeds.
PROPERTIES A bitter acrid herb that relieves pain and reduces inflammation.
MEDICINAL USES Internally for acute gout, Behÿet's syndrome, familial Mediterranean fever, and scleroderma. Externally for neuralgia. For use only by qualified practitioners. Excess causes gastric pain, diarrhoea, and renal damage. May cause foetal abnormalities; not given to pregnant women or patients with kidney disease. Prolonged use may cause hair loss, blood disorders, muscular pain and weakness, and tingling in hands and feet. Used in homeopathy for joint pains, diarrhoea, and nausea caused by wet weather.
⚠ **WARNING** This herb and its alkaloids are subject to legal restrictions in some countries.
▨ ▨ ▯

COLEUS

Coleus amboinicus. See *Plectranthus amboinicus*.
Coleus aromaticus. See *Plectranthus amboinicus*.

COLLINSONIA

Lamiaceae

This genus consists of five species of perennials from eastern N America, including *C. canadensis* (stone root) which, like many of the mint family, has strongly aromatic foliage. It is an unusual herb in that the root is well tolerated, but even small amounts of the fresh leaves may cause vomiting. Stone root is always used with other herbs, forming part of many herbal remedies for kidney complaints. The exact nature of its constituents is unknown. The common name "stone root" may refer to either the unusually hard roots or its use in treating kidney stones. The genus was named after Peter Collinson, an 18th-century English Quaker, who introduced many N American plants to the UK.
CULTIVATION Moist soil in partial shade.
PROPAGATION By seed sown in spring or autumn.
HARVEST Roots are lifted in autumn and used fresh or dried for decoctions, liquid extracts, and tinctures. Roots need long extraction and are better fresh or made into a syrup. Leaves are picked as required and used fresh.

■ *Collinsonia canadensis* (horse balm, richweed, stone root)
Tall, lemon-scented perennial with stout, very hard rhizomes and ovate leaves, 9–15cm (3½–6in) long. Loose spikes of pale yellow, tubular flowers are produced in summer. Native to E USA. ‡ 60cm–1.2m (2–4ft), ↔ 45–90cm (18–36in).
HARDINESS Fully hardy.
PARTS USED Roots, leaves.
PROPERTIES A bitter, astringent, unpleasant-tasting herb that has diuretic and anti-inflammatory effects, and acts as a tonic for the capillaries and digestive system.

Collinsonia canadensis

MEDICINAL USES Internally for kidney and urinary stones, cystitis, diarrhoea, gastroenteritis, irritable bowel syndrome, mucous colitis, haemorrhoids, and varicose veins (roots). Combines well with *Aphanes arvensis* (see p.124), *Eupatorium purpureum* (see p.209), and *Hydrangea arborescens* (see p.238). Externally for healing bruised or sore skin (leaf poultice).

COMMIPHORA

Burseraceae

About 180 species of small, deciduous, mostly thorny shrubs and trees belong to this genus, occurring in E and W Africa, Arabia, India, S America, and the West Indies. The genus was not discovered in the New World until the 1980s. Commiphora exudes an oleo-gum resin known as myrrh that varies slightly in composition from one species to another. It is obtained from several species, including *C. foliacea*, *C. gileadensis* (balm of Gilead, opalbalsamum), *C. habessinica*, and *C. wightii* syn. *C. mukul* (guggul). The term "bdellium" can refer to these trees collectively, or to the resin. Myrrh has been a standard medicament in the Middle East since biblical times for infected wounds, bronchial and digestive complaints, and is especially associated with women's health and purification rituals. Being a symbol of suffering, myrrh was one of the three gifts presented by the Magi to the infant Jesus and was used to embalm Christ's body after the crucifixion. According to the Gospel of St Mark, myrrh wine, *vinum murratum*, was offered by soldiers to Jesus before the crucifixion. Chinese medical texts first described myrrh c.AD600, and it has a long history of use in Ayurvedic medicine as a rejuvenative. Scientific research has shown that myrrh contains compounds that have a powerful painkilling effect. Guggul (the resin from *C. wightii*) is of great importance in Ayurvedic medicine as a rejuvenative and remedy for diseases of old age, and for conditions associated with bone, joint, or nerve pain. It is also combined with *triphala* (see p.384), to make a restorative formula known as *triphala guggula*. Guggul has recently been found to contain unique saponins, known as guggulipid, that lower cholesterol and have anti-inflammatory effects in arthritis. It also contains phytosterols that have a hormonal effect. Populations of *C. wightii* are decreasing due to over-collection and destructive harvesting.

CULTIVATION Well-drained soil in sun.
PROPAGATION By seed sown in spring; by hardwood cuttings at end of growing season.
HARVEST Resin is collected from cut branches and dried to a solid, which is distilled for oil, ground for powder, tablets and capsules, or dissolved in tinctures.

■ *Commiphora myrrha* syn. *C. molmol* (bola, myrrh)
Deciduous, aromatic, spiny shrub with trifoliate leaves that have obovate leaflets, the terminal leaflet about 1cm (⅜in) long. Yellow-red, four-

Commiphora myrrha

petalled flowers, with a persistent calyx, appear after the rains, often before the new leaves, followed by pointed ellipsoid fruits, to 7mm (¼in) long. Native to N Somalia, Arabia, and Yemen. ‡ to 5m (16ft), ↔ 1.5m (5ft).
HARDINESS Min. 10–15°C (50–59°F).
PARTS USED Gum resin (*mo yao*), oil.
PROPERTIES A pungent, astringent, aromatic herb that is strongly stimulant, antiseptic, and expectorant. It relieves spasms, inflammation, and digestive discomfort; encourages healing.
MEDICINAL USES Internally for dyspepsia, bronchial and ear infections, mononucleosis, tonsillitis, pharyngitis, gingivitis, and menstrual and circulatory problems. Not given during pregnancy. Externally for mouth ulcers, wounds, boils, and pressure sores. Added to oral hygiene preparations. Combined with *Hamamelis virginiana* (see p.230) for bruises; with *Cephaelis ipecacuanha* (see p.163) for mouth ulcers and gum infections; and with *Echinacea* spp. (see p.199) and *Baptisia tinctoria* (see p.141) for various throat infections. Oil is diluted in carrier oil for massage; not to be taken internally.

COMPTONIA

Myricaceae

This genus consists of one species of deciduous shrub, found in scrub on poor, dry, acid soils, mainly in coastal regions of eastern N America. *Comptonia peregrina* is an elegant plant but is seldom seen in cultivation. The leaves are aromatic, with a fragrance more noticeable in early morning and evening. They were used by native N Americans as a poultice for toothache and in a wash for poison-ivy rash. The herb was a popular household remedy for diarrhoea in the 19th century. *Comptonia* is named after Henry Compton (1632–1713), a bishop of London.
CULTIVATION Well-drained to dry, acid soil in sun or partial shade.
PROPAGATION By seed sown when ripe; by removal of rooted suckers in spring; by layering in spring. Difficult to transplant successfully.
HARVEST Leaves are cut in early summer and dried for use in infusions.

Comptonia peregrina

■ *Comptonia peregrina* (sweet fern)
Shrub with fern-like, narrowly lanceolate, regularly lobed leaves, to 12cm (5in) long, clad in rust-coloured hairs. Flowers appear in summer – males are catkin-like, females smaller and spherical – followed by small, shiny, brown nutlets. Native to E USA. ‡ 1–2m (3–6ft), ↔ 60cm–1.2m (2–4ft).
HARDINESS Fully hardy.
PARTS USED Leaves.
PROPERTIES An aromatic astringent herb that controls bleeding and discharges.
MEDICINAL USES Internally for diarrhoea, vaginal discharge, dysentery, and vomiting of blood. Externally for minor haemorrhage, rashes, and stings.
CULINARY USES Fresh or dried leaves make a pleasant herb tea.

CONIUM
Poison hemlock

Apiaceae

Two species of biennials make up this genus, which occurs in northern temperate regions. *Conium maculatum* (hemlock) is one of the most poisonous plants in these regions and is rarely used today. White-flowered members of the parsley family are notoriously difficult to tell apart. Some self-sow freely, so they should not be grown near culinary herbs or where children have access. Hemlock contains alkaloids, chiefly coniine, which paralyze the respiratory nerves, so that the victim dies of suffocation before the heart stops beating. The medicinal uses of hemlock date back to the 1st century AD, when Dioscorides used it externally to treat herpes and erysipelas. Death by hemlock poisoning was the method of execution adopted in ancient Athens – its most famous victim being the philosopher Socrates in 399BC. Under Jewish law, hemlock was also

C

Conium maculatum

administered to criminals who were crucified or stoned to death, in order to deaden the pain. Coniine was the first alkaloid to be synthesized, in 1886.

CULTIVATION Damp rich soil in sun or partial shade. Subject to statutory control as a weed in some countries, notably in parts of Australia.

PROPAGATION By seed sown in spring.

HARVEST Leaves are gathered in early summer, and the fruits slightly later, for industrial processing into ointments and oils.

⚠ **WARNING** All parts are extremely toxic if eaten. Skin irritant.

▣ *Conium maculatum* (poison hemlock, poison parsley)
Tall fetid biennial with purple-spotted stems and finely divided leaves, to 30cm (12in) long. Tiny white flowers are produced in umbels, to 5cm (2in) across, in summer, followed by tiny rounded fruits. Native to Europe and temperate Asia; naturalized in N America and Australia. ‡ 1.5–3m (5–10ft), ↔ 1–1.2m (3–4ft).

HARDINESS Fully hardy.

PARTS USED Leaves, fruits (young foliage and unripe seeds have the highest alkaloid content).

PROPERTIES A narcotic sedative herb that relieves pain.

MEDICINAL USES Formerly used internally for epilepsy, Parkinson's disease, mania, chorea, cramps, and asthma. Excess causes dilation of pupils, difficulty in breathing, paralysis (especially of hind legs in animals), stupor, and death. Externally, usually in ointments or oils, for mastitis, malignant tumours (especially breast cancer), anal fissure, and haemorrhoids. In homeopathy for dizziness, anxiety and

depression, and premenstrual tension. For use only by qualified practitioners.

⚠ **WARNING** This herb is subject to legal restrictions in some countries.

▨ ▧ ▩ ▪

CONVALLARIA
Lily of the valley

Convallariaceae

There are three species (or possibly variants of the same species) of rhizomatous perennials in this genus, which occurs in northern temperate regions. The name comes from the Latin *convallis*, "valley", and refers to the plant's natural habitat, while *majalis* signifies the flowering time, which is May. *Convallaria majalis* is more common in gardens than in the wild. Forced lilies of the valley were popular for winter decoration in Victorian times, and were exported (as "Berlin crowns") from Germany in great quantities. The use of *C. majalis* as a medicinal herb dates back to at least the 2nd century AD, when it was described in a herbal written by Apuleius. Research has revealed a range of constituents and effects on the heart that have increased its importance. *Convallaria majalis* is similar in action to *Digitalis* spp. (see p.193) but is less cumulative, therefore safer for elderly patients. It is used instead of *Digitalis* by most herbalists.

CULTIVATION Moist, humus-rich soil in shade or partial shade. Rhizomes may be attacked by caterpillars. Leaves have a tendency to develop *Botrytis* in wet conditions or develop leaf spotting on dry soils in sun.

PROPAGATION By seed sown when ripe; by division after flowering or in autumn. Cultivars do not come true from seed.

HARVEST Flowering plants are picked in spring and used fresh or dried in liquid extracts and tinctures. The glycoside content diminishes in the dried leaf. Flowers are collected in spring for extraction of volatile oil.

⚠ **WARNING** All parts, especially fruits and seeds, are toxic if eaten.

▣ *Convallaria majalis* (lily of the valley, may lily)
Creeping perennial with branched rhizomes and pairs of ovate to elliptic leaves, 4–20cm (1½–8in) long. Arching racemes of 5–13 white, fragrant, bell-shaped flowers, about 6mm (¼in) across and waxy in texture, appear in spring, followed by globose red berries. Native to Europe and NE Asia. ‡ 23cm (9in), ↔ 30cm (12in). ▣ 'Albostriata' has golden stripes down the leaves. Tends to revert if grown in deep shade. 'Flore Pleno' has double flowers. 'Fortin's Giant' is vigorous, with broad leaves and flowers to 1.5cm (½in) across. ‡ 30cm (12in). ▣ 'Hardwick Hall' has broad leaves with gold margins and flowers to 1cm (⅜in) across. Forces well. ‡ 25cm (10in). ▣ 'Prolificans' has dense spikes of double, often slightly malformed flowers. ▣ var. *rosea* has pale mauve-pink-spotted flowers.

HARDINESS Fully hardy.

PARTS USED Leaves, flowers, oil.

PROPERTIES A bitter diuretic herb that acts as a tonic for the heart and cardiovascular system.

MEDICINAL USES Internally for congestive heart failure, arteriosclerosis with angina, and arterial hypotension. Often combined with *Crataegus* spp. (see p.182). For use only by qualified practitioners.

ECONOMIC USES Volatile oil, rich in farnesol, is used for perfumery and snuff.

⚠ **WARNING** This herb is subject to legal restrictions in some countries.

▨ ▧ ▢ ▪ ▨

CONVOLVULUS
Convolvulus jalapa. See *Ipomoea purga.*

CONYZA

Asteraceae

Fifty or so annuals and perennials comprise this N American genus, which is widely naturalized in Europe, Asia, Australia, and various Pacific islands. *Conyza canadensis* is a common

Convallaria majalis

Convallaria majalis 'Albostriata'

Convallaria majalis 'Hardwick Hall'

Convallaria majalis 'Prolificans'

Convallaria majalis var. *rosea*

Conyza canadensis

American weed that reached N France in 1653, and England in 1690, spreading to all parts of Europe by the end of the 17th century. Having no ornamental merit, it was presumably first imported as a medicinal plant. *Conyza canadensis* was a native N American herb before entering the *US Pharmacopoeia* (1836–1916). It was used by various tribes to deter insects and cure diarrhoea, haemorrhage, and menstrual irregularities. *Conyza bonariensis*, originally from tropical America, is naturalized in N Africa, where it is used as a diuretic and anti-rheumatic.

CULTIVATION Light, sandy soil in sun. Tolerates most conditions, varying in size accordingly.
PROPAGATION By seed sown in spring.
HARVEST Plants are cut when in flower and are best used fresh for oil extraction and liquid extracts. They may also be frozen or made into syrup. Dried herb deteriorates within a year.

■ *Conyza canadensis* syn. *Erigeron canadensis* (Canadian fleabane, horseweed)
Tall annual with narrowly oblanceolate leaves, to 10cm (4in) long. Panicles of tiny, thistle-like flowers, with green-white to pale mauve ray florets and yellow discs, appear in late summer and early autumn. Found from tropical America and USA to S Canada; widely naturalized. ‡ to 1.5m (5ft), ↔ 45cm (18in).
HARDINESS Hardy.
PARTS USED Whole plant, oil.
PROPERTIES A slightly aromatic, bitter, tonic herb that acts as a diuretic, and checks bleeding.
MEDICINAL USES Internally for diarrhoea, haemorrhage, excessive menstruation, haemorrhoids, kidney disorders, and bronchial complaints. Externally for eczema and ringworm.
CULINARY USES Young leaves and plants are cooked as a vegetable.
ECONOMIC USES Essential oil is used for flavouring confectionery, condiments, and soft drinks.

COPAIFERA
Leguminosae

This genus consists of 35–40 species of evergreen trees, native to tropical America and

Africa. Copaiba balsam, one of the most plentiful natural perfumery ingredients, is an oleo-resin, collected from several species, including *C. guyanensis*, *C. martii*, *C. multijuga*, *C. officinalis*, and *C. reticulata*, as well as *C. lansdorffii*. The balsam varies considerably in colour, viscosity, and odour, according to the source; balsam from *C. reticulata* has an unpleasant smell and taste, while that from *C. multijuga* has a delightful coumarin-like odour. The balsam contains 30–90 per cent volatile oil, and unusual condensed tannins. It is tapped by drilling holes in the trunk, each tree yielding up to 55 litres (12 gallons). The name *Copaifera* comes from *copai*, the native N American Tupi word for the tree and its resin.
CULTIVATION Well-drained, sandy soil in shade and high humidity.
PROPAGATION By softwood cuttings in spring.
HARVEST Resin is tapped from trees at intervals (the hole is sealed afterwards) and used in infusions or distilled for oil.

Copaifera lansdorffii syn. *C. nitida*, *C. sellowii* (copaiba, copaiva)
Evergreen tree with aromatic bark and pinnate leaves, to 13cm (5in) long, which have 3–5 pairs of ovate leaflets. Very small, yellow flowers are followed by dehiscent, yellow-brown to dark red fruits with black seeds. Found mainly in Brazilian rainforest. ‡ 18–20m (60–70ft), ↔ 10–15m (30–50ft).
HARDINESS Min. 13–15°C (55–59°F).
PARTS USED Oleo-resin.
PROPERTIES An aromatic, antiseptic, stimulant herb with a bitter burning taste. It improves digestion, has diuretic and expectorant effects, and controls bacterial infections.
MEDICINAL USES Internally for cystitis, bronchitis, vaginal discharge, haemorrhoids, and diarrhoea. Externally for chilblains, sores, eczema, and psoriasis. Often combined with *Agathosma* spp. (see p.106), *Piper cubeba* (see p.320), and *Santalum album* (see p.359). Excess is purgative and may cause skin rashes and kidney damage.
ECONOMIC USES An important fixative in perfumes (especially those with violet, woody, and spicy notes) and a main source of copal, a resin used in varnishes and lacquers. Usable direct from the tree as a substitute for diesel oil.

COPTIS
Goldthread
Ranunculaceae

Ten species of low, moisture-loving perennials belong to this genus, distributed throughout northern temperate regions. A few are grown in rock gardens or in peat beds for their anemone-like flowers. The common name "goldthread" describes the fine yellow roots, which grow near the surface. Goldthreads contain alkaloids, notably berberine (as found in *Berberis vulgaris*, see p.142, and *Hydrastis canadensis*, see p.239). *Coptis chinensis* was first mentioned in Chinese medical texts c.AD200. It has

similar uses to *C. japonica* and *C. teeta*, with which it is sometimes adulterated. Other useful species include the N American *C. groenlandica* (canker root, goldthread, mouth root) and *C. trifolia* (Indian goldthread). The latter was a standard remedy among many native N American tribes for mouth ulcers and was listed as a treatment for mouth and eye inflammations in the *US Pharmacopoeia* (1820–82) and the *US National Formulary* (1916–36). *Coptis trifolia* has also been used to flavour and colour root beer made from *Sassafras* (see p.361) and Irish moss (*Chondrus crispus*, see p.167).
CULTIVATION Moist to wet, humus-rich, slightly acid soil in shade.
PROPAGATION By seed sown when ripe; by division in spring.
HARVEST Roots are lifted in autumn and used fresh or dried in decoctions.

Coptis chinensis (Chinese goldthread, mishmi bitter)
Rhizomatous delicate perennial with long-stalked, tripartite, finely divided leaves. Clusters of 3–4 yellow-white flowers appear in spring, consisting of 5–8 sepals, to 1cm (⅜in) long, and nectar-secreting petals half the size of the sepals. Native to China. ‡ 25cm (10in), ↔ 15cm (6in).
HARDINESS Fully hardy.
PARTS USED Roots (*huang lian*).
PROPERTIES A pungent, very bitter, cooling herb that controls bacterial and viral infections, relaxes spasms, lowers fever, and stimulates the circulation. It is locally analgesic and anaesthetic.
MEDICINAL USES Internally for "hot" conditions, such as dysentery, enteritis, high fever, inflamed mouth and tongue, middle ear infection, conjunctivitis, tuberculosis, and palpitations. Externally for inflamed mucous membranes in mouth and eyes, boils, abscesses, acne, and burns. An ingredient of the Chinese drug *san huang zhe she ye* ("injection of three yellow herbs"), given intra-muscularly for upper respiratory tract infections. For use only by qualified practitioners.

CORDYCEPS
Clavicipitaceae

A genus of 100 species of parasitic fungi, found worldwide. *Cordyceps sinensis* is parasitic on caterpillars of a rare Himalayan moth. It has been harvested by the Yung people in W China for thousands of years, a process aided by annual burning of the alpine meadows. The fungus is now produced more cheaply on wheat in California but may still be bought in China, in small bundles tied with red thread (symbol of good fortune), identical to those collected by 19th-century explorers. *Cordyceps sinensis* was first described in Chinese medical texts c.AD200. A later account, c.AD1600, compared this bizarre medicinal caterpillar-fungus to ginseng as a tonic. Traditionally, *dong chong xia cao* consists of both the parasitized larva and stroma

C

(spore-producing body) of the fungus, which protrudes from the head of the caterpillar. According to the *Chinese Materia Medica* (G.A. Stuart, 1911), "large fat larvae with yellow insides and short stromata are marks of good quality". It is, however, the fungus and not the caterpillar that possesses the medicinal properties, which explains why modern production techniques, cultivating the fungus on wheat, are equally effective. In China, *dong chong xia cao* is usually cooked with chicken to make a tonic broth, in early spring and early winter, to help the body adjust to seasonal changes. It is also a popular aphrodisiac for men, cooked with gin and soy sauce inside the head of a duck.

CULTIVATION Parasitic on moth larvae in the wild. May be cultivated on wheat.

PROPAGATION By spores on suitable host.

HARVEST Fungus is collected in early spring (as the snow melts) in the wild, or from a cultivated grain base, and dried for use as capsules, compressed slices, powder, or tinctures.

Cordyceps sinensis (Chinese caterpillar fungus) Fungus parasitic on the larvae of *Hepialus armoricanus*. Larva measures 3–6cm (1¼–2½in) long and up to 7mm (¼in) in diameter. Spores invade the host through the nostrils and consume the entire body contents to form a sclerotium that overwinters beneath the snow. The spring thaw triggers production of stromata (spore-producing bodies), which emerge from the carcass and infect the surrounding soil. The stromata are club-shaped, hollow in the centre, and brown to black-brown with white interior tissue. They are 4–8cm (1¼–3in) long and 3mm (⅛in) in diameter. Found only in the foothills of the eastern Himalayas in grassland above 3353m (11,000ft).

HARDINESS Hardy.

PARTS USED Whole fungus (*dong chong xia cao*).

PROPERTIES A sweet energy tonic for lungs and kidneys, and a tranquillizer and muscle relaxant, controlling coughs and having anti-bacterial and anti-cancer effects.

MEDICINAL USES Internally for coughs, tuberculosis, conditions associated with kidney weakness (impotence, back pains, night sweats), menopausal problems, convalescence, and nasopharyngeal cancer.

CULINARY USES Fungus cooked with meat or fish in tonic soups and stews, and in rice porridge (China). Also as an ingredient of ginseng elixir and other herbal tonics.

CORIANDRUM
Coriander

Apiaceae

Two species of slender upright annuals belong to this genus, which is native to SW Asia and N Africa. *Coriandrum sativum* (coriander) is a weed of cultivated and waste ground. One of the oldest known herbs, it has been cultivated for over 3000 years and mentioned in Sanskrit,

Coriandrum sativum

ancient Egyptian, Greek, and Latin texts, as well as in virtually all medieval herbals. Coriander was introduced to Chinese cooking and medicine c.AD600, since when it has been known as *hu*, "foreign". In *Chinese Materia Medica* (G.A. Stuart, 1911), it was recommended for certain types of non-pathogenic food poisoning caused by decaying matter. The fresh foliage and ripe seeds have quite different aromas and uses. *Coriandrum* comes from the Greek *koriannon*, a type of bed bug that apparently smells like coriander leaves. The characteristic scent of coriander foliage occurs in several unrelated species, including *Eryngium foetidum* (see p.205) and *Porophyllum ruderale* subsp. *macrocephalum* (see p.328), which are often grown as a substitute in tropical regions where coriander does not do well as a leaf crop.

CULTIVATION Well-drained, fertile soil in sun. Plants grown for leaves may be more productive in partial shade. Coriander tends to bolt if too dry or overcrowded at the seedling stage. Recommended in companion planting to improve germination in anise, and to repel aphids and carrot rust fly. An infusion may help reduce spider mite infestation. Coriander is thought to reduce seed yield in fennel if planted nearby.

PROPAGATION By seed sown *in situ* in spring.

HARVEST Leaves are gathered when young and used fresh. Seeds are harvested when ripe and are used whole or ground for culinary purposes. Medicinal preparations usually call for powdered seeds, liquid extracts, or distilled oil.

▣ *Coriandrum sativum* (Chinese parsley, cilantro, coriander)
Erect annual with pungently aromatic, pinnately divided, lobed leaves, becoming more finely divided higher up the flowering stem. White to mauve flowers are produced in umbels, to 3cm (1¼in) across, in summer, followed by globular, ribbed, pale brown fruits that have a fruity scent when ripe. Native to E Mediterranean; naturalized in N America. ↕ 15–70cm (6–28in), ↔ 10–30cm (4–12in). 'Leisure' has lush, rich green leaves and is bolt resistant, standing well, even in hot conditions. ↕ 60cm (2ft). 'Moroccan' is excellent for seed

production, being quick to bolt, with minimal leaf production. 'Santo' is fast-growing but extremely slow to bolt; good for leaf production in spring and summer. ↕ 38cm (15in).

HARDINESS Hardy.

PARTS USED Roots, leaves, seeds, oil.

PROPERTIES Both leaves and seeds are rich in volatile oils that act mainly on the digestive system, stimulating the appetite, and relieving irritation. They are also expectorant. Oil is fungicidal and bactericidal.

MEDICINAL USES Internally for minor digestive problems. Externally for haemorrhoids and painful joints (seeds). Seeds reduce griping in laxative preparations based on *Rheum officinale* and *Senna alexandrina* (see p.366).

CULINARY USES Roots are used in Thai cuisine. Leaves and leafstalks are used to flavour soups, salads, beans, and curries, especially in the Middle East, and SE Asia. Dried stems are used for smoking foods. Seeds are an ingredient of curries, curry powder, pickles, pickling spices, dishes *à la grecque*, baked foods, sausages, and sauces.

ECONOMIC USES Oil flavours gin, vermouth, liqueurs, and tobacco, and is prized in perfumery.

CORIDOTHYMUS
Coridothymus capitatus. See *Thymus capitatus*.

CORNUS
Dogwood

Cornaceae

Found mostly in temperate regions of the northern hemisphere, this is a genus of some 45 species of trees, shrubs, subshrubs, and perennials. Many dogwoods are ornamental and easily grown in mixed borders or as specimen plants, for their flowers, fruits, often interesting bark, and good autumn colour. The name *Cornus* comes from the Latin *cornu*, "horn", because the wood of some species is extremely hard, resembling animal horn. *Cornus officinalis* was first described in Chinese medicine c.AD200. Other species with therapeutic properties are: *C. florida* (American boxwood, flowering dogwood), used as a tonic for nervous exhaustion and tension headaches; *C. mas* (cornelian cherry) and *C. sanguinea* (common dogwood), which are both astringent fever remedies; and *C. stolonifera* syn. *C. sericea* (American red osier), a traditional remedy for indigestion, diarrhoea, and vomiting.

CULTIVATION Well-drained soil in sun or partial shade.

PROPAGATION By seed in autumn, or stratified and sown in spring; by greenwood cuttings in summer.

HARVEST Fruits are collected when ripe and dried for use in decoctions.

⚠ **WARNING** Skin allergen.

▣ *Cornus officinalis* (Japanese cornel, Japanese cornelian cherry)

Deciduous, large, spreading shrub or small tree with peeling bark and ovate to elliptic leaves, to 12cm (5in) long, turning red-purple in autumn. Clusters of tiny yellow flowers appear along the bare branches in late winter, followed by edible, bright red fruits, about 1cm (³⁄₈in) across. Native to China, Japan, and Korea. ↔ 5–10m (15–30ft).

HARDINESS Fully hardy.

PARTS USED Fruits (*shan zhu yu*).

PROPERTIES A sour, astringent, diuretic herb that acts mainly as an energy tonic for the liver and kidneys. It also checks bleeding, lowers blood pressure, and controls bacterial and fungal infections.

MEDICINAL USES Internally to reduce excessive secretions and discharges (such as profuse perspiration, frequent urination, or heavy menstruation), and for conditions associated with weak kidney and liver energy

Cornus officinalis

(such as urinary dysfunction and impotence). Often combined with *Rehmannia glutinosa* (see p.341) to suppress excretion of fluids. ⊠ ▣

CORYDALIS
Papaveraceae

About 300 species of annuals and perennials, commonly tuberous and often floppy in habit, make up this genus, widely distributed through northern temperate areas and in tropical montane regions. Although related to poppies, *Corydalis* spp. are quite different in appearance, with fern-like leaves and spurred tubular flowers. *Corydalis solida* and *C. cava* have both been known in horticulture as *C. bulbosa*. *Corydalis solida* is very similar to *C. cava*, the main differences being that the former has hollow, rather than solid, tubers and a more westerly distribution. It is likely that both species are wild-collected for medicinal purposes. *Corydalis solida* has been used as a painkiller in traditional Chinese medicine since at least the 8th century, when it was mentioned in the *Omissions from the Materia Medica* by Chen Cang-Zi. It contains alkaloids that have analgesic and sedative effects.

CULTIVATION Well-drained, humus-rich, moist soil in partial shade. Position of plants should be clearly marked because they die down completely in summer. All parts of *Corydalis* are very brittle and must be handled carefully. The tender foliage is prone to attack by slugs and snails.

PROPAGATION By seed sown when ripe; by division of tubers in autumn.

HARVEST Tubers are collected during dormancy and dried for use in decoctions.

▣ *Corydalis solida* syn. *C. halleri*, *C. transsylvanica* hort. (bulbous corydalis, fumewort)

Variable tuberous perennial with grey-green, segmented, fern-like leaves, to 8cm (3in) long. Dull purple to mauve-pink flowers, with a long, nearly straight spur, appear in terminal racemes in spring, followed by fruits containing black seeds. Grows from N Europe to W Asia. ↕ 10–25cm (4–10in), ↔ 10–20cm (4–8in).

Corydalis solida

HARDINESS Fully hardy.

PARTS USED Tubers (*yan hu suo*).

PROPERTIES A painkilling herb that stimulates the circulation, controls spasms and nausea, and has sedative and anti-bacterial properties. Research also suggests action on the thyroid and adrenal cortex.

MEDICINAL USES Internally for painful menstruation, abdominal pain (especially in appendicitis and peptic ulcer), traumatic injury, insomnia, and tremors in neurological disease. Not given to pregnant women. ⊠ ▣

CORYNANTHE
Corynanthe johimbe. See *Pausinystalia johimbe*.

COSTUS
Zingiberaceae

This genus includes over 90 species of clump-forming, rhizomatous perennials, found on forest floors in tropical regions of the Americas, Africa, Asia, and Australia. They have cane-like stems, spirally arranged leaves, and showy, tubular, three-petalled flowers. *Costus speciosus* is grown as an ornamental for its handsome foliage and large colourful flowers, either outdoors in the tropics or in containers for an exotic effect in summer. It has long been used in various parts of tropical Asia for medicinal purposes, and as an occasional or famine food. The rhizomes have a cucumber-like, gingery flavour and have been used to adulterate true ginger (from *Zingiber officinale*, see p.410). Research has shown that they contain steroidal saponins, including diosgenin and ß-sitosterol, which have anti-inflammatory and anti-arthritic properties.

CULTIVATION Moist, well-drained, humus-rich, neutral to acid soil in shade and high humidity.

PROPAGATION Sow seed as soon as ripe at 20°C (68°F); divide in spring.

HARVEST Leaves, young stems, and rhizomes are collected as required and used fresh, often in the form of juice. Rhizomes may also be cooked or dried.

Costus speciosus (crepe ginger)

Tall rhizomatous perennial with erect, cane-like stems and oblanceolate pointed leaves, 15–30cm (6–12in) long. White flowers, 4–8cm (1½–3in) across, with a yellow-centred lip and bright red bracts, are borne in dense terminal spikes at any time of the year, followed by red capsules containing numerous shiny black seeds. Native to SE Asia. ↕ 2–3m (6–10ft), ↔ 1m (3ft).

HARDINESS Min. 13°C (55°F).

PARTS USED Leaves, young stems, rhizomes.

PROPERTIES A bitter, astringent, stimulant herb that clears toxins, improves digestion, and reputedly has aphrodisiac effects. Fresh juice of rhizomes is purgative.

MEDICINAL USES Internally for eye and ear infections, diarrhoea (sap from leaves, young stems), colds, catarrh, coughs, dyspepsia, intestinal worms, and skin diseases (rhizome). Formerly used in Malaysia for smallpox.

▨ ▨ ▨ ▪ ▣

COUMAROUNA
Coumarouna odorata. See *Dipteryx odorata*.

CRATAEGUS
Hawthorn, thorn

Rosaceae

A genus of about 280 deciduous, often thorny, shrubs and trees, which occur throughout northern temperate regions. *Crataegus laevigata* and *C. monogyna* are very similar, the latter differing mainly in having more deeply lobed leaves, and fruits with one stony seed, rather than two. The former tends to grow farther north in Europe, while *C. monogyna* occurs throughout Europe as far as Afghanistan. Hybrids between *C. laevigata* and *C. monogyna*, known as *C. × media*, are common in the wild. Many species of *Crataegus* are very variable, which in the past has led to the naming of over 1000 different species, some of which are probably of hybrid origin. Taxonomic research has reduced this number considerably, but the numerous forms and hybrids continue to pose problems of identification. The common names of *C. laevigata* refer to different aspects of the plant: "may" from its time of flowering; "quickset" from its use as a "quick" or "living" hedge; and "bread-and-cheese" from the tasty young leaves, which were traditionally added to sandwiches in country areas. Many practices are associated with the hawthorn, notably the custom of going "a-Maying", and choosing a May queen, which pre-dates Christian times. In pagan times the king and queen of the May were killed at the end

of the growing season – hence the ambiguity today of hawthorn being both a symbol of hope and an omen of death. As a medicinal herb, hawthorn was traditionally used to treat kidney and bladder problems. Its use as a heart remedy began towards the end of the 19th century. *Crataegus laevigata*, *C. monogyna*, and their hybrids are now used interchangeably for medicinal purposes. Unlike most medicinal plants that act on the heart, hawthorn is relatively non-toxic, although its use for such serious conditions should be confined to qualified practitioners. *Crataegus pinnatifida* was first mentioned as a herb in the *Supplement to the Extension of the Materia Medica* by Zhu Zhen Heng (c.1347). Fruits of another Chinese species, *C. cuneata*, have a sour but pleasant taste and are used mainly to control diarrhoea.

CULTIVATION Moist soils, including alkaline, in sun or partial shade. *Crataegus laevigata* flowers and fruits better in an open sunny position. Trim to shape at any time from late summer to early spring, or in winter for shrubs in which autumn colour is a feature. Leaves may be attacked by caterpillars or affected by leafspot, powdery mildew, or rust. Honey fungus may cause rapid death. *Crataegus laevigata*, *C. monogyna*, and their hybrids are subject to plant controls in parts of Australia.

PROPAGATION By seed separated from ripe berries in autumn and sown in a seedbed or cold frame. Germination may take 18 months. Cultivars do not come true from seed, and are propagated by grafting in winter or budding in midsummer on to stocks of *C. monogyna*.

HARVEST Flowering sprigs (with leaves) are collected in spring and dried for infusions, decoctions, tinctures, and tablets. Fruits are collected when ripe and used raw or cooked, or dried whole for use in tinctures.

■ *Crataegus laevigata* syn. *C. oxyacantha* (hawthorn, may, quickset)
Deciduous, densely branched, spiny shrub or

small tree with shallowly lobed, obovate leaves, to 5cm (2in) long. Scented white flowers, 1cm (⅜in) across, are produced in clusters in late spring, followed by dark red, egg-shaped fruits, to 1.5cm (½in) long. Native to Europe, especially the north. ↔ 5–8m (15–25ft). 'Crimson Cloud' has large, deep pink flowers with white centres. ■ 'Paul's Scarlet' syn. 'Coccinea Plena' has double, deep pink flowers. It arose as a sport of *C. laevigata* 'Rosea Flore Pleno' (which has paler pink, double flowers) in a garden in Hertfordshire, England in 1858. ■ 'Plena' has double white flowers. It has been grown in gardens since c.1770.

HARDINESS Fully hardy.
PARTS USED Flower clusters (with leaves), fruits.
PROPERTIES An aromatic, sweet and sour, warming herb that improves peripheral circulation and regulates heart rate, blood pressure, and coronary blood flow. It is also diuretic and antioxidant.
MEDICINAL USES Internally for circulatory disorders and heart disease of all kinds, often combined with *Selenicereus grandiflorus* (see p.365), *Tilia* spp. (see p.391), *Viscum album* (see p.406), or *Scutellaria lateriflora* (see p.365). Also combined with *Ginkgo biloba* (see p.224) for poor memory.

▣ ▨ ▨ ▪

■ *Crataegus pinnatifida* (Chinese haw)
Deciduous small tree with short thorns and broadly triangular–ovate, deeply lobed leaves, 5–10cm (2–4in) long. White flowers, 1.5cm (½in) across, with pink anthers, are borne in spring, followed by red fruits, 1.5cm (½in) in diameter. Native to N China. ↔ to 6m (20ft).
HARDINESS Fully hardy.
PARTS USED Fruits (*shan zha*).
PROPERTIES A digestive, circulatory, and uterine stimulant that also has hypotensive and anti-bacterial properties.
MEDICINAL USES Internally for "food stagnation" (a term used in Chinese medicine to cover indigestion, bloating, irritable bowel syndrome, or gall bladder weakness), hypertension associated with coronary artery disease, failure to menstruate, and postpartum pain. Fruits are used raw for circulatory disorders and baked for digestive problems.

▨ ▪

CRATEVA
Garlic pear

Capparidaceae

A genus of nine species of evergreen or deciduous shrubs or small trees, found throughout the tropics. In common with other members of the caper family, which all produce mustard-oil compounds, *Crateva* spp. are unpleasant-smelling, with garlic-scented flowers and trifoliate leaves. *Crateva religiosa* grows wild near streams and is widely grown as an ornamental and sacred plant, especially around temples, in India and Bangladesh. It was first recorded in Ayurvedic medicine in the 8th

Crataegus laevigata

Crataegus laevigata 'Paul's Scarlet'

Crataegus pinnatifida

Crataegus laevigata 'Plena'

century BC. Research in the late 20th century showed that the bark has anti-inflammatory effects and helps both remove and prevent urinary stones. *Crateva roxburghii* syn. *C. religiosa* var. *roxburghii* has similar properties.

CULTIVATION Moist, humus-rich, neutral to acid soil in sun or partial shade.

PROPAGATION By seed sown when ripe at 18°C (64°F); by semi-ripe cuttings in summer.

HARVEST Young shoots, leaves, and flowers are picked as required and used fresh. Leaves are also dried for infusions. Bark is collected throughout the year and dried for decoctions, or ground into powder.

Crateva religiosa syn. *C. nurvala* (*barna*, garlic pear, three-leafed caper, *varuna*)
Deciduous spineless tree with white-marked bark, long-stalked leaves, divided into three leaflets, to 16cm (6in) long and 10cm (4in) wide. Cream to white flowers, 5–8cm (2–3in) across, sometimes yellow to orange, with long-clawed petals and dark red to purple stamens, are produced in terminal corymbs, followed by ovoid–globose berries. Found from Asia to Australia and Pacific islands. ‡ to 15m (50ft), ↔ 9m (30ft).

HARDINESS Min. 15°C (59°F).

PARTS USED Leaves, shoots, flowers, bark.

PROPERTIES A bitter pungent herb that has diuretic and rubefacient effects, improves digestion, and prevents and treats formation of stones in the kidneys and bladder.

MEDICINAL USES Internally for urinary tract infections, urinary problems associated with prostate enlargement, kidney and bladder stones, gastritis, poor appetite, fevers (bark); obesity, rheumatism (leaves). Externally for rheumatism (leaves).

CULINARY USES Leaves and young shoots are cooked as a vegetable. Flowers are pickled. Berries and seeds are also edible.
▨ ▨ ▨ ▨ ▨ ▨ ▨

CRITHMUM
Samphire

Apiaceae

This genus contains a single species that grows wild on coastal cliffs, rocks, and shores. *Crithmum* is from the Greek *krithe*, "barley", and refers to the ribbed ovate seeds. The common name "samphire" is derived from the French *sampière*, a contraction of *herbe de Saint Pierre* – St Peter having been a fisherman. Though known also as sea fennel, it bears little resemblance to true fennel (see *Foeniculum vulgare*, p.215), other than having flowers arranged in umbels. *Crithmum maritimum* has been gathered from coastal areas for pickling and salads since time immemorial. John Evelyn in *Acetaria* (1699) remarked on "its excellent Vertues and effects against the Spleen, Cleansing the Passages, sharpning Appetite, etc. so far preferrable to most of our hotter Herbs". This succulent coastal plant contains high levels of vitamin C. It has a powerful salty flavour, described by Tom Stobart in *Herbs, Spices and*

Crithmum maritimum

Flavourings (1970) as like "a mixture of celery and kerosene". *C. maritimum* (rock samphire) is sometimes confused with *Salicornia* spp. (marsh samphire), as both are commonly referred to as "samphire".

CULTIVATION Well-drained to dry soil in sun. Needs a warm sheltered position inland and protection in cold winters.

PROPAGATION By seed sown when ripe; by division in spring. Seeds lose viability rapidly.

HARVEST Whole plants are gathered in late spring and used fresh for infusions. Leaves and flowers are picked fresh for use as a vegetable.

■ *Crithmum maritimum* (rock samphire, samphire, sea fennel)
Fleshy spreading perennial with branched ridged stems and glaucous leaves with rounded, linear–lanceolate segments. Tiny, yellow-green flowers are produced in umbels in summer. Native to Black Sea, Mediterranean, English Channel, and Atlantic coasts of Europe. ↔ 15–45cm (6–18in).

HARDINESS Fully hardy.

PARTS USED Whole plant, leaves, flowers.

PROPERTIES A strongly aromatic, salty herb that has diuretic effects, cleanses toxins, and improves digestion. It has a reputation for encouraging weight loss.

MEDICINAL USES Internally for obesity, kidney complaints, and sluggishness.

CULINARY USES Leaves are eaten in salads, cooked in butter, or pickled in vinegar and used in similar ways to capers. Flowers are also eaten in salads.
▨ ▨ ▨ ▨ ▨

CROCUS

Iridaceae

A genus of about 80 species of corm-forming perennials that grow wild in the Mediterranean region, and north and east as far as western China. Almost every species is ornamental and many are grown as garden plants, or as specimens for the alpine house, for their show of flowers in autumn, winter, and spring. *Crocus sativus* is a sterile triploid not known in the wild, most

probably derived from *C. cartwrightianus*. The name *Crocus* is derived from the Greek *krokas* "thread" and alludes to the stigmas. Saffron, from the Arabic *za'fân*, "yellow", is the world's most costly spice, requiring some 150,000 flowers and 400 hours' work to produce 1kg (2.2lb) of dried saffron. The Chinese value saffron as a medicinal herb; it reached China in the Yuen dynasty (1280–1368) from Persia and India. This unusual herb, which consists solely of the branched styles of the flower, has been prized as a flavouring and colorant for over 4000 years. Following the early Crusades in the 11th century, it became widely cultivated in Europe and the Middle East. Centres of saffron cultivation included Valencia (Spain), Nuremberg (Germany), and Saffron Walden (UK). Today it is grown mainly in Azerbaijan, Iran, Kashmir, and Spain. Over the centuries the high price of saffron gave rise to a thriving trade in adulterants, such as dyed fibres from beef and pomegranates. The penalties were severe: a trader in 15th-century Nuremberg was buried alive with his adulterated product. Genuine saffron consists of red, thread-like fibres. The orange colouring matter dissolves readily in warm water, diluting to yellow. Powdered saffron is cheaper but commonly contains adulterants. As well as its role as a spice and medicinal herb, saffron was once important as a dye for hair, nails, and fine textiles. *Crocus nudiflorus*, from the Pyrenees, was once grown as a saffron substitute. It was introduced into the UK by the Knights of St John of Jerusalem, and is still found growing on properties belonging to the Order. *Crocus cartwrightianus* is harvested locally; it grows on volcanic ash on the Greek island of Santorini. *Crocus sativus* must not be confused with the highly toxic *Colchicum autumnale* (meadow saffron, see p.176), which cannot be used as a substitute for saffron.

CULTIVATION Well-drained, light, rich soil, pH7, in full sun. For optimum flowering, plant corms 15cm (6in) deep and 10cm (4in) apart. *Crocus sativus* grows, but fails to flower, in areas with wet cloudy summers.

PROPAGATION By offsets removed from the parent corm in late spring.

HARVEST Flowers are picked when open and the styles removed for drying. Saffron does not store well and should be used within a year of harvesting.

■ *Crocus sativus* (saffron crocus)
Perennial with corms, to 5cm (2in) in diameter, and 5–11 erect linear leaves that appear in autumn with 1–4 lilac-purple, veined flowers. Flowers are fragrant, with purplish filaments, yellow anthers, and a deep red style, divided into three branches, to about 3cm (1¼in) long, rarely followed by three-valved capsules. Not known in the wild. ↔ 10cm (4in).
'Cashmirianus' is a high-yielding strain from Kashmir, with large corms and violet-blue flowers with deep orange styles.

HARDINESS Fully hardy.

PARTS USED Styles (*fan hong hua*).

PROPERTIES A pungent, bitter–sweet herb that improves digestion, increases perspiration, stimulates the circulation and menstruation, and

C

Crocus sativus

Croton tiglium

Cryptotaenia japonica

reduces high blood pressure.
MEDICINAL USES Internally, in traditional Chinese medicine, for "stagnant liver energy", as in depression and menstrual disorders. Contraindicated during pregnancy.
CULINARY USES Used as a flavouring and colorant for cakes, biscuits, puddings, Eastern sweetmeats, and sauces; in rice dishes, such as *paella* (Spain), *risotto milanese* (Italy), and *biryani* (India); in fish stews, such as *zarzuela* (Spain) and *bouillabaisse* (France).
ECONOMIC USES A flavouring and colorant in liqueurs.
▨ ▤ ▧ ▨

CROTON
Euphorbiaceae

Some 750 shrubs, trees, and perennials are included in this genus, distributed worldwide in tropical and subtropical regions. The genus is extremely complex chemically and yields a number of highly toxic compounds. *Croton tiglium* is found in mixed forest in Asia; it is an unpleasant-smelling, very poisonous plant. *Croton* is from the Greek *kroton*, "a tick", which refers to the appearance of the ovoid, light brown seeds. The ornamental foliage plants that are commonly known as "crotons" belong to the genus *Codiaeum* and do not have the same properties as *Croton*. Many *Croton* spp. contain resins that are used in making varnishes, and have medicinal properties. Apart from *C. tiglium*, the only species with wide usage is the West Indian *C. eleuteria* (cascarilla), which has aromatic bark, used in remedies for digestive upsets and to flavour tobacco. Other species are used locally, including *C. gratissimus* (lavender croton, maquassie), which has a buchu-like perfume and is used in South Africa to make a substitute for lavender water. Medicinally, the bark is used to treat fevers and various other complaints, and leaf infusions are taken for coughs. In Australia, *C. insularis* (Queensland cascarilla, warrel) and *C. phleboides* (native cascarilla) are used as bitter tonics.

CULTIVATION Damp soil in partial shade. Cut back in early spring to control growth.

PROPAGATION By seed sown in spring.
HARVEST Seeds are collected when ripe and used whole or crushed for oil extraction or use in pills.

▣ *Croton tiglium* (croton)
Evergreen tree with ovate, pointed, metallic green to bronze leaves, to 17cm (7in) long. Tiny, yellow-green flowers appear in racemes in spring – males at the top and females at the base – followed by fruits containing a single large seed. Found from India to Malaysia. ↕ 5–20m (15–70ft), ↔ 12m (40ft).
HARDINESS Min. 15°C (59°F).
PARTS USED Seeds (*ba dou*), oil.
PROPERTIES A pungent, unpleasant-smelling herb that is exceedingly irritant and purgative. Croton oil is the strongest of all purgatives.
MEDICINAL USES Internally, in minute amounts, for constipation, dysentery, biliary colic, intestinal obstructions, food poisoning, malaria, and mastitis. Externally for warts, dermatitis, abscesses, and boils (seeds, often after oil extraction to reduce toxicity). Croton oil is carcinogenic; excess causes shock (1ml/0.035fl oz can be fatal) and skin contact with it should be avoided. Side-effects include blistering of skin and mucous membranes, oedema, hypotension, and abdominal pain.
⚠ **WARNING** Subject to legal restrictions in some countries.
▢ ▨ ▤ ▨

CRYPTOTAENIA
Apiaceae

A genus of four species of annuals and perennials, occurring in northern temperate regions and montane tropical Africa. Two of the species, *C. canadensis* and *C. japonica*, are very similar, differing mainly in their distribution (from Manitoba to Texas for the former, and in parts of Asia for the latter), and are possibly synonymous. Leaves, stems, and flowers of *C. canadensis* are eaten raw in salads

or cooked as a vegetable or soup ingredient; roots are cooked like carrots; and seeds are used as a spice in baking. *Cryptotaenia japonica* is cultivated as a vegetable and pot-herb in Japan, and by Japanese communities in other parts of the world. Its flavour has been described by Joy Larkcom (*Oriental Vegetables*, 1991) as "a unique blend of parsley, celery, and angelica, with angelica predominating". The bronze form is more ornamental and can be used in similar ways.
CULTIVATION Rich moist soil in shade or partial shade. May be grown as an annual or perennial for culinary use. Plants from spring sowings may be blanched in winter/early spring by mounding with soil or covering with straw.
PROPAGATION By seed sown successively, from early spring to midsummer; by division in spring or autumn.
HARVEST Seedlings and young leaves are cut as required and used fresh. Roots are harvested when young. Seed heads are collected when almost ripe and hung upside down to dry.

▣ *Cryptotaenia japonica* (Japanese honewort, Japanese wild chervil/parsley, *mitsuba*)
Upright perennial with hollow stalks and trifoliate toothed leaves, to 13cm (5in) long and 15cm (6in) wide, borne on sheathed stalks, to 14cm (5½in) long. Minute white flowers appear in umbels in summer. Found in temperate Asia, mainly in China, Japan, Korea, and Taiwan. ↕ 30–90cm (1–3ft), ↔ 30cm (1ft). f. *atropurpurea* has deep purple foliage. 'Kansai' is a popular variety for annual cultivation of "green" *mitsuba*. 'Kanto' has pale stalks, favoured for blanching and perennial cultivation.
HARDINESS Fully hardy.
PARTS USED Leaves, leafstalks, roots, seeds.
PROPERTIES An aromatic herb with an angelica-like flavour.
CULINARY USES In Japanese cuisine, young leaves and leafstalks are cooked as a green vegetable, often served cold with soy sauce. Green or blanched leafstalks are added to soups, salads, tempura, savoury custards, and dishes such as *sukiyaki*. Seedlings are eaten in salads, roots are cooked like parsnips, and seeds are used as seasoning.
▧ ▤ ▨ ▨

CUCUMIS
Cucurbitaceae

A genus of about 30 climbing or scrambling annuals and perennials, native to tropical Asia and Africa. *Cucumis sativus* (cucumber) has been cultivated in India since earliest times and was known to ancient Greeks and Romans. There are numerous cucumber variants worldwide, from self-fertile, female cultivars to hardier "ridge" cucumbers and small-fruited gherkins. Most are picked when immature for use as vegetables, although ripe fruits contain seeds that are rich in edible oils. Culpeper wrote of the cucumber in *The English Physician Enlarged* (1653): "there is not a better remedy for ulcers in the bladder" and "the face being washed with their juice, cleanses the skin". *Cucumis colocynthis* (bitter cucumber) is an important homeopathic remedy for colic, while *C. metuliferus* (African horned cucumber) is important as a rootstock and source of disease-resistant genes for cucumbers. It has spiny, orange-red skin and green flesh that is eaten raw, cooked, dried, or pickled.

CULTIVATION Rich, well-drained soil in sun or partial shade. Pinch out growing tips when plants have three leaves and again when lateral shoots have four or five leaves. Prone to various diseases, including mosaic virus, *Botrytis*, anthracnose, *Verticillium* wilt, powdery mildew, root rot, and *Sclerotinia*. Cucumbers may be grown on poles or trellis, or on the ground, according to variety.

PROPAGATION By seed sown in spring at 18°C (64°F).

HARVEST Fruits are picked unripe and used fresh, or as pulp or juice. Seeds are collected from ripe fruits and dried.

▪ *Cucumis sativus* (cucumber)
Trailing annual with triangular–ovate leaves, to 18cm (7in) long and across. Yellow, funnel-shaped flowers, 4cm (1½in) across, appear in spring and summer – males in the axils, females, larger and usually solitary – and are followed by ovoid to elongate fruits containing white ovate seeds. Native to India. ‡ 2m (6ft). 'Burpless Tasty Green' is a mildew-resistant, outdoor (ridge) variety that produces numerous fruits, best when 25cm (10in) long. 'Carmen' is an all-female, greenhouse variety, highly resistant to mildew, scab, and leafspot, producing 50–100 fruits per plant. 'Eureka' has high disease resistance, yielding uniform fruits for pickling.

HARDINESS Min. 10°C (50°F).
PARTS USED Leaves, fruits, seeds, oil.
PROPERTIES A cooling, diuretic, alterative herb that clears and softens the skin. Seeds expel intestinal parasites.
MEDICINAL USES Internally for blemished skin, heat rashes, and overheating in hot weather (fruit); tapeworm (ground seeds). Externally for sunburn, scalds, sore eyes, and conjunctivitis.
CULINARY USES Fruits are eaten fresh, cooked, or pickled, sliced as a garnish, or added to

Cucumis sativus

yogurt or sour cream to make *raita* (India) and *tzatziki* (Greece). Leaves are eaten as a pot-herb. Seed kernels are eaten raw or roasted, like pumpkin seeds, or pressed for oil, known as *huile de concombre*, used in French cooking as a substitute for olive oil.
ECONOMIC USES Used in cleansing and toning lotions for the face (fruits).

CUCURBITA
Pumpkin, squash
Cucurbitaceae

This genus includes 27 species of prostrate or climbing annuals and perennials, native to tropical and subtropical America. *Cucurbita maxima* was first grown in Peru and reached Europe after the Spanish conquest of 1532. Also known as pumpkins or squashes are *C. moschata*, which may have originated in Mexico, but was known in S and N America 5000 years ago, and *C. pepo*, which is Mexican in origin but has been grown in southern N America for over 8000 years. Pumpkins, marrows, and winter and summer squashes belong to several different species, with interchangeable common names and the same medicinal properties. Pumpkin seeds are rich in oil, vitamins, and minerals, especially zinc, which is useful in treating enlarged prostate gland. As a remedy for intestinal parasites they are less potent than *Dryopteris filix-mas* (see p.197), but safer for pregnant women, children, and debilitated patients. Use of pumpkin seeds in Chinese medicine was adopted in the 17th century.

CULTIVATION Rich, well-drained soil in sun. Pinch out tips to encourage growth of lateral shoots. May be affected by mosaic virus,

Cucurbita maxima

Botrytis, and powdery mildew. Growing on poles or supports protects fruits from slugs.
PROPAGATION By seed sown in spring at 16–18°C (61–64°F).
HARVEST Seeds are collected from ripe fruits in autumn and dried whole (not dehusked for medicinal use) before grinding.

▪ *Cucurbita maxima* (pumpkin, winter squash)
Variable trailing annual with five-angled stems and toothed leaves. Yellow flowers in summer are followed by fruits, which when ripe may be green, grey, yellow, orange, or red, filled with orange flesh and green, white-husked seeds. Native to S America. ‡ 1m (3ft). ↔ 2m (6ft). 'Buttercup' has grey-green fruits, weighing 1.5kg (3.3lb), with firm dense flesh, ideal for roasting, pies, preserves, and soups.
HARDINESS Half hardy.
PARTS USED Seeds (*nan gua zi*), fruits, pulp.
PROPERTIES A sweet, warming, nutty-flavoured herb that acts as a diuretic, soothes irritated tissues, and expels intestinal worms.
MEDICINAL USES Internally, often combined with *Echinacea purpurea* (see p.199) and *Serenoa repens* (see p.367) for prostatitis, and with *Senna alexandrina* (see p.366) for tapeworms and roundworms; also for motion sickness and early stages of schistosomiasis (seeds). Internally to soothe inflammation of the digestive tract (pulp). Externally as a poultice for burns (pulp).
CULINARY USES Dehusked seeds are eaten raw or roasted as a snack, or added to bread. Fruits are steamed, roasted, baked, fried, stuffed, or mashed, and used to make pumpkin pie and pumpkin filling. Also added to bread, cakes, and muffins. Leaves and flowers are edible, too.

Cuminum

Cumin

Apiaceae

Found wild from the Mediterranean to the Sudan and C Asia, this genus contains two species of slender annuals. Cumin was once a familiar spice in Europe, particularly in ancient Rome. In Greek culture, cumin symbolized avarice, and miserly people were said to have eaten it. Today, it is used mainly in Asia and the Middle East, as it has been since biblical times. Its pungent, aromatic, rather bitter flavour is essential to curries and spicy dishes. Many kinds of cumin are used in India, the most common being *safed* (white) and *kala* (black). The name *Cuminum* comes from a Greek word of Hebrew origin for a plant that resembles *Carum carvi* (caraway, see p.157), sometimes confused with it in Indian recipes. Although similar, they have distinctive aromas and flavours and cannot be used interchangeably.

CULTIVATION Well-drained, fertile soil in full sun. Seeds may not ripen in cold climates.

PROPAGATION By seed sown in spring at 13–18°C (55–64°F).

HARVEST Seeds are collected when ripe and stored whole. They are used whole or ground for culinary use, or distilled for oil.

■ *Cuminum cyminum* (*comino*, cumin, *jeera*) Slender annual with finely divided, ovate leaves, reaching 10cm (4in) long. Tiny, white to pale pink flowers are produced in umbels to 2.5cm (1in) across, followed by grey-green, ovoid–oblong fruits, 5mm (¼in) long, containing pale brown seeds. Native to E Mediterranean. ‡↔ 30cm (12in).

HARDINESS Half hardy.

PARTS USED Seeds, oil.

PROPERTIES An aromatic astringent herb that benefits the digestive system and acts as a stimulant to the sexual organs. The oil is anti-bacterial and larvicidal.

MEDICINAL USES Internally for minor digestive problems and

Cuminum cyminum

migraine of digestive origin. Externally, ground with onion juice for poisonous stings. Widely used in Ayurvedic medicine to promote the assimilation of other herbs and to improve liver function; also used in veterinary medicine.

CULINARY USES Seeds are used to flavour soups, sauces, pickles, chutneys, and bread; important in spice mixtures, such as *garam masala* (India), and in couscous and *falafel* (Middle East), and to give a characteristic flavour to Eastern dishes based on lamb, and to side-dishes of cucumber and yogurt.

ECONOMIC USES Oil is used commercially to flavour sauces and sausages.

⬚ ▦ ▢ ✎ ✎

Cunila

Lamiaceae

A genus of 15 species of aromatic perennials and shrubs, found from eastern N America to Uruguay. The only species common in cultivation is *C. origanoides*, which is popular in native N American herb gardens. It has an oregano-like aroma and contains thymol. In the 18th century, dittany was popular among settlers as a cure-all and insect repellent.

CULTIVATION Well-drained to dry, sandy, acid soil in partial shade.

PROPAGATION By seed or division in spring.

HARVEST Leaves are picked in late summer and used fresh or dried.

Cunila origanoides (American dittany, stone mint) Erect branched perennial with stalkless, ovate, pointed leaves, to 2.5cm (1in) long. Tiny, violet to white, tubular flowers appear in clusters above the leaf axils from summer to autumn. Native to E USA. ‡ 30–60cm (1–2ft).

HARDINESS Fully hardy.

PARTS USED Leaves.

PROPERTIES An aromatic antiseptic herb that increases perspiration and stimulates the uterus.

MEDICINAL USES Internally for fevers, colds, and headaches, and to induce menstruation and ease labour pains. Externally in folk medicine to treat snake bite.

CULINARY USES Leaves are used as a substitute for oregano, and made into herb tea.

✎ ▢ ✎

Curcuma

Zingiberaceae

Forty species of perennials belong to this genus, found in seasonally dry tropical forests of Asia and Australia. Most have aromatic rhizomes or tubers that yield spices, starch, and dyes, and cone-shaped inflorescences with often colourful bracts. *Curcuma longa* (turmeric) is a source of orange and yellow dyes for silk, cotton, and wool, and is a traditional colouring for the robes of Buddhist monks. The name comes from *kurkum*, the Arabic name for these plants. It is also one of the most common food flavourings and colourings in Asian cuisine. Many medicinal uses are recorded, especially in

Curcuma aromatica

China, India, and Indonesia. Research has shown significant anti-inflammatory and liver-protective effects. Both *C. aromatica* (wild turmeric) and *C. longa* were described in Chinese medicine in the 7th century. The term *yu jin* is applied to *C. aromatica* on its own and to a mixture of *C. aromatica*, *C. longa*, and *C. zedoaria* (zedoary). Several other species are used for food and flavouring, including *C. amada* (mango ginger), which has edible young shoots and mango-scented rhizomes used in cooking, and candied or pickled in India.

CULTIVATION Well-drained soil in sun or light shade, with ample humidity.

PROPAGATION By seed sown when ripe at 20°C (68°F); by division in early spring.

HARVEST Leaves are cut as required and used fresh. Rhizomes are lifted during the dormant period and steamed or boiled before drying and grinding for use in decoctions, tinctures, pills, poultices, and powders.

■ *Curcuma aromatica* (wild turmeric) Perennial with a large, yellow-fleshed rhizome and pointed oblong leaves, to 60cm (24in) long. Yellow-white, pink-tinged flowers, with pale green lower bracts and pink upper bracts, are produced in spring, in a dense inflorescence that arises from the base of the plant. Native to India. ‡1m (3ft), ↔ indefinite.

HARDINESS Min. 15–18°C (59–64°F).

PARTS USED Rhizomes (*yu jin*).

PROPERTIES A pungent, bitter, cooling herb that improves digestion and stimulates the gall bladder and circulatory system. It both checks bleeding and dissolves clots.

MEDICINAL USES Internally for jaundice, nosebleeds, internal haemorrhage, painful menstruation, shock, chest pains associated with low liver energy, and angina.

▦ ▢ ⬚

■ *Curcuma longa* syn. *C. domestica* (haridra, turmeric) Perennial with a large rhizome and pointed, oblong–elliptic leaves, up to 50cm (20in) long. Yellow flowers, accompanied by pale green lower bracts and pink upper bracts, are borne in a dense inflorescence in summer. Native to India. ‡ 1m (3ft), ↔ indefinite.

Curcuma longa

HARDINESS Min. 13°C (55°F).
PARTS USED Rhizomes (*jiang huang*).
PROPERTIES A pungent, bitter, astringent herb with a characteristic smell and deep yellow colour. It stimulates the uterus, the digestive, circulatory, and respiratory systems, normalizes energy flow, lowers cholesterol levels; has antibiotic, anti-inflammatory, and anti-coagulant effects.
MEDICINAL USES Internally for digestive and skin complaints, circulatory disorders, uterine tumours, jaundice, liver disease, and menstrual problems. Also as an anti-inflammatory for asthma and eczema, and to reduce risk of strokes and heart attacks. Often combined with *Berberis vulgaris* (see p.142) or *Mahonia aquifolium* (see p.270) for liver complaints and diabetes. Externally for injuries, sores, athlete's foot, and ringworm.
CULINARY USES An essential ingredient of

Curcuma zedoaria

curries and curry powder.
ECONOMIC USES Pigment curcumin is a natural food colouring; it cannot be substituted for saffron or annatto, because of its strong flavour, but is used in products such as piccalilli. Also important as a natural dye for fabrics.

■ *Curcuma zedoaria* (zedoary)
Perennial with a thick, pale-fleshed, camphor-scented rhizome and oblong–lanceolate, pointed leaves, to 60cm (2ft) long, which have an irregular maroon band down either side of the midrib. In summer, yellow to white, pink-flushed flowers emerge from an inflorescence, to 10cm (4in) long, composed of greenish lower bracts and deep pink to purple upper bracts. Native to India. ‡ 1m (3ft), ↔ indefinite.
HARDINESS Min. 13°C (55°).
PARTS USED Leaves, rhizomes.
PROPERTIES A bitter aromatic herb that improves digestion and has anti-cancer effects.
MEDICINAL USES Internally as a digestive tonic, and to relieve indigestion, nausea, wind, and bloating. Similar in effects to *C. longa* and *Zingiber officinale* (see p.410). Used successfully in China to treat cervical cancer and improve the effectiveness of radiation therapy and chemotherapy.
CULINARY USES Leaves, used in cooking fish, resemble lemon grass in flavour. Rhizomes yield starch similar to arrowroot. Young rhizomes are added to salads.
ECONOMIC USES Dried rhizomes are used to flavour liqueurs and bitters.

CUSCUTA
Dodder

Convolvulaceae

About 100 twining parasitic annuals belong to this genus, which occurs throughout temperate and warm regions. These unusual plants have no roots and no green parts – their leaves being

reduced to scales. They obtain nutrients from the host plant, which they penetrate with suckers. Several species are used medicinally, including *C. epithymum* (common dodder), once popular among European herbalists for "melancholy diseases" and disorders of the spleen, kidneys, and liver, and *C. reflexa*, used in Ayurvedic medicine as an alterative, purgative, carminative, and anthelmintic. Descriptions of *C. japonica* appeared in Chinese medical literature of the 1st century AD, based on texts going back to 1500BC.
CULTIVATION Grows only on suitable host plants. Some species are subject to certain plant controls in parts of Australia.
PROPAGATION By seed in autumn, lodged among stems of host plant.
HARVEST Seeds are collected when ripe in autumn. They are then dried for use in decoctions.

Cuscuta japonica syn. *C. systyla* (Japanese dodder)
Twining annual with thin, much-branched, yellow stems, which are striped or spotted red. Numerous pale yellow, bell-shaped flowers are produced in short spikes in late summer. Native to E Asia. ↔ 1m (3ft).
HARDINESS Hardy.
PARTS USED Seeds (*tu si zi*).
PROPERTIES A sweet pungent herb that acts mainly as a kidney and liver stimulant.
MEDICINAL USES Internally for diarrhoea, impotence, urinary frequency, vaginal discharge, and poor eyesight associated with liver and kidney energy weakness.

CYDONIA
Cydonia speciosa. See *Chaenomeles speciosa*.

CYMBOPOGON

Poaceae

This genus of 56 species of mostly perennial grasses occurs in tropical and warm temperate parts of Asia and Europe. Many are rich in essential oils, containing large amounts of citral and geraniol, which are lemon- and rose-scented respectively. The best-known species is *C. citratus* (lemon grass), which is grown on a large scale in India and Guatemala. Lemon grass oil consists chiefly of citral (75–85 per cent) and citronellal. It is used directly in aromatherapy, perfumery, and food flavouring, or for manufacturing other perfume ingredients. Several other species are cultivated for their oils. These include: *C. flexuosus* (East Indian/Cochin lemon grass), grown mainly in Kerala (India), for lemon grass oil, used for food flavouring; *C. martinii* (geranium grass, *palmarosa*, rosha) from India, source of Turkish geranium oil, used to adulterate rose oil and widely used in rose perfumes, soaps, and insect repellents; *C. martinii* var. *sofia* (ginger grass), which has a cruder scent; and *C. nardus* (citronella), grown in Sri Lanka and Java for

Cymbopogon citratus

citronella oil – similar in fragrance and properties to *Melissa officinalis* (see p.275). *Cymbopogon* is from the Greek *kymbe*, "boat", and *pogon*, "beard", referring to the appearance of the floral spikelets.

CULTIVATION Well-drained soil in sun with moderate humidity. Flowering is rare in plants grown in containers or under cover.

PROPAGATION By seed sown in spring at 13–18°C (55–64°F); by division in spring.

HARVEST Stems are cut at ground level and used fresh for oil extraction, dried for powder, and either fresh or dried for infusions. The leaf blades may be removed and the lower 7–10cm (3–4in) used as a fresh herb.

■ *Cymbopogon citratus* (lemon grass) Clump-forming perennial with robust, dense, often cane-like stems and arching, lemon-scented, linear leaves, to 90cm (3ft) long. Awnless spikelets appear in lax panicles, to 5cm (2in) long, in summer. Native to S India and Sri Lanka. ‡ 1.5m (5ft), ↔ 1m (3ft).

HARDINESS Min. 7°C (45°F).

PARTS USED Leaves, stems, oil.

PROPERTIES A bitter, aromatic, cooling herb that increases perspiration and relieves spasms. Also has sedative action and is effective against fungal and bacterial infections.

MEDICINAL USES Internally for digestive problems in children, and minor feverish illnesses. Externally for ringworm, lice, athlete's foot, arthritis, and scabies.

CULINARY USES Base of leaves is used fresh, or as *sereh* powder, in SE Asian cooking, especially with fish, meat, sauces, and curries. Leaves are infused for tea.

ECONOMIC USES Oil is used in soaps, hair oils, perfumes and cosmetics, and for flavouring in the food industry. Also important in the manufacture of vitamin A, and ionones (synthetic violet perfumes).

CYNARA

Asteraceae

This genus includes ten species of perennials, native to the Mediterranean region and N Africa. *Cynara cardunculus* subsp. *cardunculus* (cardoon, globe artichoke) is an architectural plant, suited to the back of a large border or as a feature in the herb garden. Cultivated varieties of globe artichokes are often referred to as Scolymus Group to differentiate them from cardoons. *Cynara* comes from the Greek *kuon*, "dog", referring to the supposed resemblance of the involucral spines (bracts of the flower head) to dogs' teeth. Both cardoons and globe artichokes were grown as vegetables by the ancient Greeks and Romans. During the 20th century, globe artichoke became important as a medicinal herb, following the discovery of cynarin, a compound found in the leaves that improves liver and gall bladder function and lowers cholesterol levels.

CULTIVATION Deep, rich, well-drained soil in sun. May need winter protection in very cold areas. Flower heads may be affected by petal blight. Foliage is susceptible to *Botrytis*. Seeds may not ripen in areas with cool summers.

PROPAGATION By seed sown when ripe; by suckers (side shoots) in spring or autumn; by division in spring; by root cuttings in winter.

HARVEST Leaves are cut just before flowering, and roots are harvested in winter, for use fresh or dried in liquid extracts, syrup, and tablets. Flower heads are cut before the bracts open.

■ *Cynara cardunculus* subsp. *cardunculus*, *C. scolymus* (cardoon, globe artichoke) Clump-forming perennial with downy, grey-green, deeply cut, leathery leaves, to 80cm (32in) long and 40cm (16in) across. Large, thistle-like flowers, 8–15cm (3–6in) across, with purple florets, are produced in summer. Native to S Europe and temperate Asia. ‡ 2m (6ft), ↔ 1.2m (4ft).

Cynara cardunculus subsp. *cardunculus*

HARDINESS Fully hardy.

PARTS USED Leaves, roots, flower heads.

PROPERTIES A bitter, slightly salty herb that detoxifies and regenerates liver tissues, stimulates the gall bladder, and reduces blood lipids, serum cholesterol, and blood sugar.

MEDICINAL USES Internally for chronic liver and gall bladder diseases, poor digestion, jaundice, hepatitis, arteriosclerosis, and diabetes.

CULINARY USES Unopened flower heads are boiled and the fleshy bases are eaten hot, with hollandaise sauce or melted butter, or cold, with vinaigrette. Hearts are baked, fried, or marinated. Baby artichokes (from side shoots) are eaten whole, pickled, or preserved in oil. Young leafstalks, known as artichoke chard, are blanched and eaten as a vegetable.

CYNOGLOSSUM
Houndstongue

Boraginaceae

A genus of about 55 species of biennials, with some annuals and perennials, widely distributed in temperate regions and tropical uplands. *Cynoglossum* is derived from the Greek *kunoglosson*, "dog's tongue", after the shape and texture of the leaves. The common name "rats-and-mice" refers to the odour of the foliage. *Cynoglossum officinale* is widely distributed in dry grassy places, especially near coasts. It contains pyrrolizidine alkaloids, similar to those in *Symphytum officinale* (see p.377). Research has shown that these substances may be carcinogenic. For this reason, internal use of *S. officinale* is banned in some countries, hence the safety of *Cynoglossum officinale* must be questioned, too. Also in common with *Symphytum officinale*, it

Cynoglossum officinale

contains allantoin, a highly effective healing substance; the leaves were traditionally used as a compress for insect bites and other minor injuries. Leaf extract of *Cynoglossum officinale* and root extract of *Symphytum officinale* are combined in a German preparation for the external treatment of leg ulcers.

CULTIVATION Moist, well-drained soil in sun or partial shade.

PROPAGATION By seed sown in spring or autumn.

HARVEST Flowering plants and leaves are collected in early summer and dried for use in infusions. Roots are lifted in autumn and dried for use in decoctions.

⚠ **WARNING** Skin irritant and allergen.

◪ *Cynoglossum officinale* (houndstongue, rats-and-mice)
Erect biennial with elliptic–oblong, hairy, grey-green leaves, 5–12cm (2–5in) long. Maroon, bell-shaped flowers, 6mm (¼in) across, appear in summer, followed by fruits covered in fine hooked spines. Native to C Europe, S and C Russia, and C Asia. ‡ 80cm–1m (32–36in), ↔ 30–50cm (12–20in).

HARDINESS Fully hardy.

PARTS USED Whole plant, leaves, roots.

PROPERTIES A painkilling herb that soothes inflamed tissues and speeds healing.

MEDICINAL USES Formerly used internally for coughs and diarrhoea. Now mostly externally for minor injuries, bites, and leg ulcers, and as a suppository for haemorrhoids. Not prescribed for children or women during lactation.

⚠ **WARNING** This herb is subject to legal restrictions in some countries.

▨ ▧ ▨ ▪

CYPERUS
Sedge

Cyperaceae

Some 500–600 species of rhizomatous, grass-like annuals and perennials belong to this genus, which occurs worldwide. It includes such plants as *C. esculentus* (chufa or tiger nut), *C. involucratus* (umbrella grass), a popular houseplant, and *C. papyrus* (Egyptian paper rush). Many sedges contain volatile oils and astringent substances, used in perfumery and as remedies for digestive problems. The black tubers of *C. articulatus* (adrue) have a lavender aroma and are useful in treating nausea and dyspepsia. *Cyperus longus* (sweet galingale) was once used as a spice and made into an aromatic tonic, but its uses are now limited to perfumery. *Cyperus rotundus*, a common weed of damp places in the tropics, is important in traditional Chinese and Ayurvedic medicine.

CULTIVATION Damp soil in sun. Subject to statutory control as a weed in some countries, notably in parts of Australia.

PROPAGATION By seed sown in wet soil in spring at 18–21°C (64–70°F); by division in spring.

HARVEST Rootstocks are lifted in summer or winter and dried for use in decoctions.

Cyperus rotundus

◪ *Cyperus rotundus* (coco grass, nut grass, sedge root)
Perennial with a slender scaly rhizome and linear leaves, to 60cm (24in) long and 1cm (⅜in) wide. An inflorescence of tiny flowers, with red-brown husks, in summer is followed by black, three-angled nuts. Cosmopolitan weed. ‡ 10–60cm (4–24in), ↔ indefinite.

HARDINESS Min. 13°C (55°F).

PARTS USED Rhizomes, roots and tubers (*xiang fu*).

PROPERTIES A pungent, bitter–sweet herb that relieves spasms and pain, acting mainly on the digestive system and uterus. Tubers have a strong camphoraceous aroma when fresh, less when dried.

MEDICINAL USES Internally for digestive problems related to blocked liver energy, and menstrual complaints. Often combined with *Angelica polymorpha* var. *sinensis* (see p.122) for irregular menstruation, and with *Atractylodes macrocephala* (see p.137) for nausea and vomiting.

▧ ▪ ▣

CYPRIPEDIUM
Lady's slipper orchid

Orchidaceae

A genus of 35 species of perennial terrestrial orchids, found in C and N America, Europe, and Asia, which are increasingly rare in the wild. They are choice plants for the rock garden or woodland border, but are slow-growing and often difficult to establish. Collecting slipper orchids from the wild for horticultural and medicinal purposes has been a major factor in their decline. *Cypripedium* is from the Greek *Kypris*, "Venus", and *pedilon*, "slipper", from the inflated shape of the flower lip. There are two kinds of yellow lady's slipper orchid in N America: *C. parviflorum* var. *parviflorum* syn. *C. calceolus* var. *parviflorum* (lesser yellow lady's slipper) and *C. parviflorum* var. *pubescens* (greater yellow lady's slipper). Both have similar uses. Claims that they are cultivated for medicinal use are mostly spurious, and stocks are largely wild-collected. They were used by native N Americans as

tranquillizers, and listed in the *US Pharmocopoeia* (1863–1916). Few medical herbalists now prescribe greater yellow lady's slipper, preferring herbs such as *Lavandula angustifolia* (see p.252) and *Scutellaria lateriflora* (see p.365), which have similar effects and are considerably cheaper.

CULTIVATION Humus-rich soil in an open shady situation.

PROPAGATION By division in spring; commercially, by seed sown under sterile laboratory conditions.

HARVEST Rhizomes are lifted in autumn and dried for infusions, liquid extracts, powder, and tinctures.

⚠ **WARNING** Handling lady's slipper orchids may cause an allergic reaction.

Cypripedium parviflorum var. *pubescens*
syn. *C. calceolus* var. *pubescens*, *C. pubescens* var. *pubescens* (American valerian, greater yellow lady's slipper, nerve root)
Rhizomatous perennial with 3–4 ovate–oblong leaves, to 20cm (8in) long. Solitary flowers, about 8cm (3in) long, with yellow-green, twisted petals and a yellow lip, appear in early summer. Native to N America. ‡ 30–60cm (12–24in), ↔ 23–40cm (9–16in).

HARDINESS Fully hardy.

PARTS USED Rhizomes.

PROPERTIES A pungent, bitter–sweet herb, with an unpleasant odour, similar to that of *Valeriana officinalis* (see p.399). It relieves spasms and has sedative and tonic effects on the nervous system.

MEDICINAL USES Internally for anxiety, nervous tension, insomnia, depression, and tension headaches. Often combined with *Avena sativa* (see p.138) and *Scutellaria lateriflora* (see p.365) for anxiety.

▧ ▪

CYTISUS
Broom

Papilionaceae

About 50 species of evergreen and deciduous shrubs and small trees belong to this genus, which is closely related to *Genista* (see p.222)

C

Cytisus scoparius

and occurs in N Africa, W Asia, and Europe. *Cytisus scoparius*, a native of European heaths, wasteground, and woods, is a familar plant in the wild and in cultivation. It contains alkaloids, notably sparteine, which affects the heart and nerves in similar ways to curare (see *Chondrodendron* spp., p.167, and *Strychnos* spp., p.376). Most of the brooms stocked by garden centres are hybrids not suitable for medicinal use. Medicinal uses of *C. scoparius* are listed in early European herbals under *Planta genista*, from which the British royal house of Plantagenet took its name.

CULTIVATION Well-drained soil in sun or partial shade. Cut back shoots by two-thirds after flowering. Cytisus does not transplant well. Subject to statutory control as a weed in some countries, notably in parts of Australia.

PROPAGATION By seed sown in spring or autumn; by ripewood cuttings in midsummer; by semi-ripe cuttings in late summer. Germination is erratic.

Cytisus scoparius subsp. *maritimus*

HARVEST Tops of shoots are cut as flowering begins and dried for use in decoctions, infusions, liquid extracts, and tinctures; stocks are renewed annually.

⚠ **WARNING** Toxic if eaten.

▣ *Cytisus scoparius* syn. *Sarothamnus scoparius* (broom, Scotch broom)
Erect shrub with slender, arching, green branches and mostly trifoliate leaves, 1–2cm (⅜–¾in) long. Bright yellow, pea flowers, 1.5–2.5cm (½–1in) long, appear in summer, followed by black pods, 2.5–4cm (1–1½in) long. Native to W Europe. ↔ 1.5–2m (5–6ft). f. *andreanus* has bicoloured, red and yellow flowers. ▣ subsp. *maritimus* syn. var. *prostratus* is low-growing, with arching overlapping stems and grey-green foliage. ‡ 20cm (8in), ↔ 1.5m (5ft).

HARDINESS Fully hardy.

PARTS USED Whole plant.

PROPERTIES A bitter narcotic herb that depresses respiration, regulates heart action, and has diuretic and purgative effects.

MEDICINAL USES Internally, mainly for heart complaints, especially with *Convallaria majalis* (see p.178) in heart failure. Excess causes respiratory collapse. Not given to pregnant women or patients with high blood pressure. For use only by qualified practitioners.

⚠ **WARNING** This herb is subject to legal restrictions in some countries.

▨ ▣

D

DAPHNE
Thymelaeaceae

Fifty or so species of deciduous, semi-evergreen, and evergreen shrubs belong to this genus, occurring in Europe, N Africa, and Asia. Daphnes are choice small shrubs for borders and containers, though certain species, such as the Chinese *D. genkwa*, are challenging to grow. *Daphne* is the Greek word for laurel, perhaps so called because some species have laurel-like leaves; in Greek legend, the nymph Daphne was saved from Apollo's advances by being changed into a laurel tree. Daphnes of various kinds have therapeutic properties. *Daphne mezereum* (mezereon) was once prescribed for rheumatism and indolent ulcers, but is seldom used today on account of its toxicity. It contains similar compounds to those in *D. gnidium* and *D. laureola* (spurge laurel), which have anti-leukaemic effects. *Daphne genkwa* was described in Chinese medical literature c.AD25–200, based on texts going back to 1500BC.

CULTIVATION Well-drained, humus-rich, neutral to alkaline soil in sun or partial shade. Remove weak and badly placed shoots in spring. Daphnes do not transplant successfully.

PROPAGATION By seed sown when ripe; by

Daphne genkwa

softwood cuttings in early and midsummer; by semi-ripe cuttings in mid- to late summer.

HARVEST Flower buds are picked in spring and dried for use in decoctions.

⚠ **WARNING** Toxic if eaten.

▣ *Daphne genkwa*
Upright, sparsely branched, deciduous shrub with light green, lanceolate to ovate leaves, 3–6cm (1¼–2½in) long. Slightly fragrant, lilac flowers are produced in clusters as the new leaves develop in spring. Native to W Hubei (China). ‡↔ 1m (3ft).

HARDINESS Fully hardy.

PARTS USED Flower buds (*yuan hua*).

PROPERTIES A bitter acrid herb that controls coughs and has germicidal, diuretic, expectorant, and laxative effects.

MEDICINAL USES Internally for bronchitis, constipation, oedema, and skin diseases (especially scabies); used in Chinese hospitals as an abortifacient. Externally for frostbite.

▨ ▣

DATURA
Thorn apple
Solanaceae

There are only eight species of tropical annuals or short-lived perennials in this genus, since the shrubby species are now included in *Brugmansia*. All daturas have a long local history of medicinal and ritual use, and several species are grown as ornamentals for their large, often scented, trumpet-shaped flowers. They are extremely poisonous, containing tropane alkaloids similar to those in *Atropa bella-donna* (see p.138) and *Hyoscyamus niger* (see p.239). Alkaloids are extracted from several species, including *Datura inoxia* syn. *D. meteloides* and *D. metel*. The name *Datura* derives from *dhât*, the Hindi word for these plants, which were used as a poison by *thuggi* (bands of robbers and assassins in India) to subdue their victims. *Datura stramonium* is commonly known as jimsonweed, a corruption of Jamestown weed, recalling an incident in Virginia in 1676 when soldiers became delirious for 11 days after cooking and eating the leaves as a vegetable. *Datura inoxia* (*toloache*, western jimsonweed) is a thornless

Datura stramonium

downy plant with similar
narcotic properties. It was
used as an anaesthetic during
surgery by medicine men of
various tribes, including the Zuñi and Navaho.
CULTIVATION Rich, light soil in sun. Subject to
statutory control as a weed in some countries.
PROPAGATION By seed sown in spring at 16°C
(61°F).
HARVEST Leaves and flowering tops are
collected in summer, and seeds in autumn, for
commercial extraction of alkaloids or use in
anti-asthmatic smoking mixtures, liquid
extracts, powders, and tinctures.
⚠ **WARNING** Toxic if eaten.

■ *Datura stramonium* syn. *D. inermis* (devil's
apple, jimsonweed, thorn apple)
Bushy annual with unpleasant-smelling, elliptic
to ovate leaves, to 18cm (7in) long. White,
funnel-shaped flowers, to 5cm (2in) wide,
appear in summer, followed by spiny ovoid
capsules containing black seeds. Native to
N and S America. ‡ 2m (6ft), ↔ 1.2m (4ft).
f. *inermis* has smooth thornless fruits.
HARDINESS Frost hardy.
PARTS USED Leaves, flowering tops, seeds.
PROPERTIES A bitter narcotic herb that relaxes
spasms, relieves pain, and encourages healing.
MEDICINAL USES Internally for asthma and
Parkinson's disease. Excess causes giddiness,
dry mouth, hallucinations, and coma. Externally
for fistulas, abscesses, and severe neuralgia. For
use only by professional practitioners.
⚠ **WARNING** This herb and its alkaloids are
subject to legal restrictions in some countries.
▨ ▨ ▨ ▪

DAUCUS
Carrot

Apiaceae

A genus of 22 species of hairy annuals and
biennials, distributed through temperate regions
in both hemispheres. Only *D. carota* is common
in cultivation, being grown as a vegetable,
medicinal herb, and fodder crop. It is a coastal
plant and relatively easy to identify, though care
should still be taken: white-flowered members

of the parsley family are notoriously difficult to
tell apart, and many are highly poisonous.
Daucus carota has been an important vegetable
crop in Europe, N Africa, and many parts of
Asia since at least Classical times, and its long
history of cultivation has led to the development
of the subspecies *sativus*. The familiar, orange-
fleshed carrot is eaten mainly in Europe, but
Asian varieties range from orange to yellow,
white, dark red, and purple, while fodder
varieties are mostly larger and yellow to white.
Carrots are versatile vegetables, easily digested
and nutritious; they contain large amounts of
sugar and carotene (a source of vitamin A).
Including carrots regularly in the diet improves
vision, especially at night.
CULTIVATION Well-drained, fertile, alkaline soil
in sun or partial shade. Carrot rust fly may
damage the roots. Virus disease may cause
chlorosis and twisting of the leafstalks.
PROPAGATION By seed sown in spring,
summer, or autumn.
HARVEST Whole plants (*D. carota*) are cut in
summer and dried for use in infusions and
liquid extracts. Seeds are collected when ripe
and dried for use in infusions or distilled for oil.
Roots of subsp. *sativus* are harvested when
young or mature.

■ *Daucus carota* (wild carrot)
Variable biennial with pinnately divided, fern-
like leaves. Tiny white flowers are borne in
umbels, to 7cm (3in) across, in summer,
characteristically purple-flushed towards the
centre, and subtended by conspicuous hairy
bracts. Fruits are ovoid, with spiny ridges.
Native to Europe, temperate Asia, and N Africa;
naturalized in N America and elsewhere.
‡ 30cm–1m (1–3ft), ↔ 15–60cm (6–24in).
■ subsp. *sativus* (carrot) has a large, succulent,
commonly orange taproot. There are
numerous cultivars worldwide.
HARDINESS Fully hardy.
PARTS USED Whole plant, roots,
seeds, oil.
PROPERTIES An aromatic herb
that acts as a diuretic, soothes
the digestive tract, and stimulates
the uterus (*D. carota*). Also a rich
source of antioxidant compounds,

Daucus carota

Daucus carota subsp. *sativus*

notably beta carotene (subsp. *sativa*).
MEDICINAL USES Internally for urinary stones,
cystitis, gout (whole plant); oedema, flatulent
indigestion, menstrual problems (seeds); and in
anti-cancer diets (e.g. Gerson diet), often in the
form of juice (subsp. *sativa*). Also as raw,
grated, or crushed root, for threadworms in
children (subsp. *sativa*). Remedies based on
seeds are not prescribed during pregnancy.
CULINARY USES Fresh carrots are used raw in
salads (especially coleslaw), crushed for juice,
or cooked as a vegetable.
ECONOMIC USES Oil (*D. carota*) has an orris-
like scent and is used in anti-wrinkle creams
and perfumery. Carrots (subsp. *sativa*) are
processed as a source of carotene for food
supplements.
▨ ▨ ▨ ▨ ▪ ▨ ▨

Daucus visnaga. See *Ammi visnaga*.

DELPHINIUM

Ranunculaceae

A genus of some 250 species of biennials and
perennials, found in northern temperate regions
and montane areas of C Africa. Delphiniums are
closely related to *Aconitum* spp. (monkshoods,
see p.100). Both are very poisonous but are
widely grown for their fine blue flowers.
Delphinium is from the Greek *delphis*,
"dolphin", because the spurred flowers of some
species are rather similar in shape. *Delphinium
staphisagria* (stavesacre) and the closely related
Consolida ajacis (larkspur) contain diterpene
alkaloids. Both are extremely toxic plants and
are rarely used by herbalists today. *Delphinium
staphisagria* was used as a parasiticide in Greek
and Roman times. It is a handsome plant that

Delphinium staphisagria

deserves to be more widely grown. The common name "stavesacre" is from *staphis*, "raisin", and *agria*, "wild", the reason for which is somewhat obscure.

CULTIVATION Well-drained soil in sun.

PROPAGATION By seed sown in spring at 13°C (55°F).

HARVEST Seeds are collected when ripe for use in lotions and ointments.

⚠ **WARNING** Toxic if eaten.

■ *Delphinium staphisagria* (stavesacre)
Hairy biennial with stout stems and glossy, downy, palmate leaves, to 15cm (6in) across. Dusky mauve-blue, short-spurred flowers, to 2.5cm (1in) across, appear in racemes in late spring and early summer. Native to the Mediterranean region. ‡1.5m (5ft), ↔ 45–75cm (18–30in).

HARDINESS Fully hardy.

PARTS USED Seeds.

PROPERTIES An acrid bitter herb with potent insecticidal and parasiticidal effects.

MEDICINAL USES Externally for head lice.

▨ ▤

DENDRANTHEMA

Dendranthema × *grandiflorum*. See *Chrysanthemum* × *morifolium*.

DENDROBIUM

Orchidaceae

Over 1000 species of orchids belong to this genus, found through E Asia to Australia. Most are epiphytic or lithophytic (rarely terrestrial) perennials. *Dendrobium* is from the Greek *dendron*, "tree", and bios, "life", referring to these orchids' tree-dwelling habit. *Dendrobium nobile* is grown worldwide for its lovely flowers, described as smelling of grass in the morning, honey at noon, and primroses in the evening. As a Chinese medicinal herb, it dates back to at least 2000BC, and features in Taoist longevity formulas. In the patent remedies market, it is often known by its Korean name, *suk gok*.

CULTIVATION Partial shade on a tree branch or in orchid compost, with ample water and

Dendrobium nobile

humidity during the growing season and a cool, dry, winter rest in a light position. Dendrobiums dislike disturbance and flower well in small containers. Flower buds and new growths may be damaged by aphids.

PROPAGATION By division in spring; grown commercially by seed or micropropagation in sterile laboratory conditions.

HARVEST Stems are cut before flowering and dried for use in decoctions and tinctures.

■ *Dendrobium nobile*
Semi-evergreen, epiphytic perennial with stout erect pseudobulbs, 30–50cm (12–20in) tall, and oppositely arranged, ovate–lanceolate leaves, 7–12cm (3–5in) long. Pale magenta, scented flowers, 6cm (2½in) across, with a maroon throat, appear in pairs in spring. Native to the Himalayas, S China, and Taiwan. ‡45cm (18in), ↔ 15cm (6in).

HARDINESS Min. 10°C (50°F).

PARTS USED Stems (*shi hu*).

PROPERTIES A mildly analgesic herb that lowers fever and acts as a tonic for the lungs and stomach. It also increases salivation and is reputedly aphrodisiac.

MEDICINAL USES Internally for fever with vomiting and abdominal pain, dry cough, and complaints with symptoms such as dry mouth and severe thirst. Combined with *Glycyrrhiza uralensis* (see p.227) in tonic formulae.

▨ ▤ ▣

DIANTHUS

Pink

Caryophyllaceae

A genus of about 300 species of evergreen annuals, biennials, perennials, and subshrubs, found from Eurasia to South Africa. Pinks have long been cultivated for their fragrant flowers, and both *D. caryophyllus* (wild carnation) and *D. chinensis* (Chinese/Indian pink) have numerous cultivars that make excellent plants for dry sunny positions. The word "carnation" has the same origin as "coronation"; pinks were used for celebratory garlands in ancient Greece. *Dianthus chinensis* was first mentioned in Chinese medical texts during the Han dynasty

(AD23–206) and is still important in traditional Chinese medicine. Seeds were first sent from China to Paris in 1705 under the name *Caryophyllus sinensis*. The closely related *Dianthus superbus* (fringed pink) is used interchangeably with *D. chinensis* as the drug *qu mai*. The Mediterranean *D. caryophyllus* has similar constituents but is little used in Western herbal medicine.

CULTIVATION Well-drained, neutral to alkaline soil in sun. May be affected by a number of diseases, especially when grown under cover, including *Botrytis, Fusarium,* and *Verticillium* wilts, powdery mildew, and leaf and stem rots.

PROPAGATION By seed sown in spring or autumn at 13°C (55°F); by cuttings of non-flowering shoots in summer. *Dianthus chinensis* is usually grown as an annual.

HARVEST Flowers of *D. caryophyllus* are picked after three hours' exposure to morning sunshine and used fresh for oil extraction and culinary use, or dried for potpourris. Plants of *D. chinensis* are cut just before the flower buds open and dried for use in decoctions, pills, powders, and poultices.

■ *Dianthus caryophyllus* (clove pink, gillyflower, wild carnation)
Tufted evergreen perennial with a woody base and grey-green, linear–lanceolate leaves, to 15cm (6in) long. Deep pink to purple, clove-scented flowers appear in a lax cyme on stiff stems, to 80cm (32in) tall, in summer. Native to S Europe and N Africa. ‡20–50cm (8–20in), ↔ 15–23cm (6–9in).

HARDINESS Fully hardy.

PARTS USED Flowers, oil.

PROPERTIES An aromatic stimulant herb that lowers fevers.

MEDICINAL USES Internally for nervous and coronary disorders. Once used in tonic cordials to treat fevers.

CULINARY USES Fresh petals, with the bitter white base removed, are added to salads, candied, pickled in vinegar, and made into a syrup.

ECONOMIC USES Flower heads are dried for potpourris; oil is extracted for use in perfumery.

▨ ▧ ▤ ▨ ▨

Dianthus caryophyllus

Dianthus chinensis

◨ *Dianthus chinensis* (Chinese/Indian pink, rainbow pink)

Bushy, slow-growing annual, biennial, or short-lived perennial with light green, pointed leaves, to 8cm (3in) long. Red, pink, or white flowers, about 2.5cm (1in) across, often intricately spotted and patterned, with blue stamens, appear in summer. ‡ 30–45cm (12–18in), ↔ 15–23cm (6–9in). ◨ 'Strawberry Parfait' is compact, with white, pink-flushed, red-centred flowers, 5cm (2in) across. ‡↔ 20cm (8in).

HARDINESS Fully hardy.

PARTS USED Whole plant (*qu mai*).

PROPERTIES A bitter, tonic, diuretic herb that stimulates the digestive and urinary systems, and bowels. It also lowers blood pressure, relieves fevers, and controls bacterial infections.

MEDICINAL USES Internally for acute urinary tract infections (especially cystitis), urinary stones, constipation, and failure to menstruate. Combined with *Salvia miltiorhiza* (see p.355)

Dianthus chinensis 'Strawberry Parfait'

to induce menstruation. Externally, for skin inflammations, swellings, and eczema.
🗹 🖾

DICTAMNUS
Dittany

Rutaceae

Six species of perennials were formerly included in this genus, but it is now regarded as monotypic. *Dictamnus albus*, a native of dry scrub and pine woods, is an attractive, long-lived plant for borders. Known also as the gas plant, *D. albus* is rich in volatile oils that in hot weather can be ignited as they evaporate, leaving the plant undamaged. This aromatic herb was first described in Chinese medical texts c.AD600 and remains important for dispelling pathogenic heat. *Dictamnus* is named after the similarly scented *Origanum dictamnus* (see p.295), which in turn is probably named after Mount Dikte in Crete. The common name "dittany" has a similar origin. American dittany is *Cunila origanoides* (see p.186).

CULTIVATION Well-drained, fertile, neutral to alkaline soil in sun or partial shade.

PROPAGATION By seed sown when ripe; by division in autumn or spring, though plants are slow to re-establish. Does not transplant well.

HARVEST Bark is peeled from roots lifted in autumn and dried for use in decoctions.

⚠ **WARNING** Skin irritant in sunlight. All parts are harmful if eaten.

◨ *Dictamnus albus* syn. *D. dasycarpus*, *D. fraxinella* (burning bush, dittany, gas plant) Aromatic, clump-forming perennial with pinnately divided, gland-dotted leaves, to 35cm (14in) long. White to pink or mauve, long-stamened flowers, to 2.5cm (1in) across, sometimes with darker markings, appear in summer, followed by five-lobed capsules containing hard black seeds. Found in SW Europe to China and Korea. ‡ 40–80cm (16–32in), ↔ 60cm (24in). ◨ var. *purpureus* has pink flowers, striped in darker pink.

Dictamnus albus

Dictamnus albus var. *purpureus*

More commonly seen in cultivation than the species. ‡ 40–80cm (16–32in), ↔ 24–45cm (10–18in).

HARDINESS Fully hardy.

PARTS USED Root bark (*bai xian pi*).

PROPERTIES A bitter, strong-smelling herb that lowers fever, stimulates the uterus, and controls bacterial and fungal infections.

MEDICINAL USES Internally and externally for skin diseases (especially scabies and eczema), German measles, arthritic pain, and jaundice. May be combined with *Sophora flavescens* (see p.372) as an external wash. Contraindicated during pregnancy. For use only by professional practitioners.
🛍 🖾 🖐

DIGITALIS
Foxglove

Scrophulariaceae

This genus of over 20 species of biennials and perennials occurs in Europe, N Africa, and W and C Asia. Although very poisonous, foxgloves are popular as garden plants for their elegant spires of flowers. *Digitalis* is from the Latin *digitus*, "finger", because the flowers fit neatly over the fingers. Foxgloves contain cardioactive glycosides, which vary from species to species, according to weather and site. Their use in the treatment of heart disease was developed by William Withering, an English physician, who in 1785 published his findings after analyzing a herbal mixture made by a Shropshire woman as a cure for dropsy (fluid retention due to heart failure). Both *D. purpurea* and *D. lanata* are grown commercially for the pharmaceutical industry, but the latter is an easier crop plant. It is a major

Digitalis lanata

source of digitoxin, digoxin, and gitoxin, while the glycosides in *D. purpurea* include digitoxin, gitoxin, and gitaloxin. *Digitalis grandiflora* and *D. lutea* have similar properties, but are seldom used. Digoxin is the most rapidly excreted and least cumulative. In pharmaceutical terms, "digitalis" refers to the powdered leaf of *D. purpurea*, used in the form of tablets or capsules for certain conditions. Leaves of *D. purpurea* are easily confused with those of *Symphytum officinale* (comfrey, see p.377) and have caused poisoning when accidentally included in herbal preparations. Digitalin is a standardized mixture of glycosides from *Digitalis purpurea*, formerly used in solution for injection. Isolated glycosides are now used in preference to the whole herb, so that the dose can be more accurately monitored.

CULTIVATION Well-drained, humus-rich, neutral to acid soil in partial shade. May develop crown rot and root rot in damp conditions.

PROPAGATION By seed sown in autumn or spring. Sow on the surface, because seed needs light to germinate.

HARVEST Leaves are picked before flowering and dried for commercial extraction of alkaloids.

⚠ **WARNING** All parts are toxic if eaten.

▣ *Digitalis lanata* (woolly foxglove)
Biennial or short-lived perennial with usually only one stem, and stalkless, oblong to lanceolate, toothed leaves, to 12cm (5in) long. Cream to beige, brown-veined flowers, 3cm (1¼in) long, are produced in dense leafy racemes in summer, followed by many-seeded capsules. Native to Italy, Balkans, Hungary, and Turkey. ↕ 1m (3ft), ↔ 30cm (12in).

HARDINESS Fully hardy.

PARTS USED Leaves.

PROPERTIES A very bitter, diuretic herb that strengthens heart contractions.

MEDICINAL USES Internally for heart failure and irregular heart beat. Excess causes nausea, vomiting, slow pulse, visual disturbance, anorexia, and fainting. For use only by professional practitioners.

⚠ **WARNING** This herb and *D. purpurea*, especially in the form of glycosides, are subject to legal restrictions in some countries.

DIOSCOREA
Yam

Dioscoreaceae

About 600 species make up this large genus of tuberous, deciduous or evergreen, twining climbers, which are widely distributed in the tropics and subtropics. A few are grown as ornamentals and many are cultivated as food crops in warm regions. Some of the edible yams produce very large tubers – those of *D. alata* (white yam) can reach 50kg (110lb). The common name "yam" is from a W African dialect word meaning "eat". Many species contain steroidal saponins, used in the preparation of steroids by the pharmaceutical industry. The discovery of hormones in yams was made in 1943 by Russell E. Marker, an eccentric American organic chemist who produced progesterone from Mexican yams in a pottery shop-cum-laboratory, and presented two jars of the hormone, then worth $160,000, to the pharmaceutical firm Laboratorios Hormona (later to become Syntex), thus initiating production of an affordable contraceptive pill. Until the hormone diosgenin was synthesized in 1970, *D. macrostachya* (Mexican yam) was the sole source for manufacture of contraceptive pills. A small Himalayan species, *D. deltoidea*, has proved the richest of all yams in steroidal saponins; it is now endangered from over-collection. *Dioscorea batatas*, the hardiest of the commercially cultivated yams, contains allantoin, a cell proliferant also found in *Symphytum officinale* (see p.377). Various yams are used in traditional medicine. *Dioscorea hypoglauca* and *D. nipponica* are used in similar ways to *D. batatas*, and the N American *D. quaternata* has similar uses to *D. villosa*. Known as *aluka*, yams are also used in Ayurvedic medicine for sexual and hormonal problems, and hysteria.

CULTIVATION Rich, well-drained soil in sun or partial shade. Tubers may rot in cool damp conditions when dormant.

PROPAGATION By seed sown in spring at 19–24°C (66–75°F); by division or sections of tubers in autumn or early spring; by bulbils planted in spring.

HARVEST Tubers, roots, and rhizomes are lifted in autumn. *Dioscorea batatas* is used raw or baked with flour or soil, according to diagnosis, and *D. villosa* is dried for use in liquid extracts or used fresh for homeopathic preparations.

▣ *Dioscorea batatas* syn. *D. opposita* (Chinese yam, cinnamon yam)
Perennial climber with vertical tubers, to 1m (3ft) long, and heart-shaped, pointed leaves, 4–8cm (1½–3in) long. Bulbils form in leaf axils. Tiny, white, cinnamon-scented flowers are produced in axillary spikes (male and female separate), followed by three-angled capsules. Native to China, Japan, Korea, and Taiwan. ↕ 3m (10ft).

HARDINESS Fully hardy (borderline).

PARTS USED Tubers (*shan yao*).

PROPERTIES A sweet soothing herb that

Dioscorea batatas

stimulates the stomach and spleen and has a tonic effect on the lungs and kidneys.

MEDICINAL USES Internally for poor appetite, chronic diarrhoea, asthma, dry coughs, frequent or uncontrollable urination, excessive thirst or sweating, diabetes, and emotional instability associated with *qi* deficiency. An ingredient of "The Pill of Eight Ingredients", a traditional Chinese remedy for diabetes, kidney problems, and underactive thyroid. Externally for boils and abscesses.

CULINARY USES Tubers yield starch, known as Guiana arrowroot, and are eaten boiled, baked, mashed, or fried. Often combined in tonic soups with *Lycium barbarum* (see p.267) and *Polygonatum odoratum* (see p.327).

▣ *Dioscorea villosa* (colic root, rheumatism root, wild yam)
Perennial climber with slender rhizomes and pointed, heart-shaped–ovate leaves, 5–10cm (2–4in) long. Minute, yellow-green flowers appear in drooping axillary spikes in summer, with male and female borne separately. Native to N America. ↕ 5m (15ft).

HARDINESS Fully hardy.

PARTS USED Roots, rhizomes.

PROPERTIES An acrid, anti-inflammatory herb that relaxes spasms, stimulates bile flow, and dilates blood vessels.

Dioscorea villosa

MEDICINAL USES Internally for arthritis, colitis, irritable bowel syndrome, diverticulitis, gastritis (especially in alcoholics), gall bladder complaints, Crohn's disease, morning sickness, painful menstruation, ovarian and labour pains, bronchitis, catarrh, asthma, whooping cough, and cramp. Used in homeopathy for colic (especially in babies).

DIOSMA

Diosma crenulata. See *Agathosma crenulata*.

DIOSPYROS

Persimmon

Ebenaceae

Some 475 species of evergreen and deciduous trees and shrubs belong to this mainly tropical genus, which occurs in N and S America, Africa, Asia, Australia, and S Europe. Some species are a source of valuable ebony timber. Others are grown for their fruit, including *D. lotus* (date plum) and *D. virginiana* (persimmon), which are also ornamental. Commercially, persimmons are from *D. kaki*, now grown on a large scale in S Europe. It normally needs both male and female trees for successful fruiting, though hermaphrodite and dwarf cultivars are available for confined spaces. *Diospyros kaki* was first recorded in Chinese medicine c.AD720. It is a renowned cure for hiccups, taken with *Syzygium aromaticum* (clove, see p.378) and *Zingiber officinale* (fresh ginger, see p.411). *Diospyros virginiana* was used as an astringent by native N Americans and was listed in the *US Pharmacopoeia* (1820–82).

CULTIVATION Fertile, well-drained soil in sun, with shelter from cold winds and late frosts. Remove crowded or badly placed growths and cut back leaders by one-third during dormancy. Plants grown outdoors may be damaged by thrips, mealybugs, scale insects, fruit flies, and fungal leafspots. Spider mites and whitefly may attack plants under cover. For successful fruiting, *D. kaki* requires one male tree to pollinate 8–10 female trees.

PROPAGATION By seed sown when ripe; by grafting in winter.

HARVEST Calyces are usually collected during flowering, and dried for decoctions. Fruits are gathered when unripe for juice, or ripe for using fresh, dried, or powdered as saccharum.

■ *Diospyros kaki* (Chinese persimmon, Japanese persimmon, kaki)
Deciduous tree with glossy ovate leaves, to 20cm (8in) long, turning orange-red and purple in autumn. Tiny, bell-shaped, pale yellow flowers, 1.5cm (½in) across, appear in summer – males in groups of 2–5, females solitary – followed by yellow to orange-red fruits, to 8cm (3in) across, which are very astringent when unripe. Native to China. ‡ 10–15m (30–50ft), ↔ 7m (22ft).

HARDINESS Frost hardy.

PARTS USED Calyces (*shi di*), fruits, juice, powder (“saccharum”).

Diospyros kaki

PROPERTIES An astringent expectorant herb that checks bleeding and lowers blood pressure.

MEDICINAL USES Internally for hiccups, internal bleeding (calyx), bronchial complaints (dried ripe fruits), dry coughs (saccharum), high blood pressure (juice of unripe fruit), constipation, haemorrhoids (raw ripe fruit), and diarrhoea (cooked ripe fruit).

CULINARY USES Ripe fruits are eaten fresh, dried, or cooked in desserts, and used in making jam. Dried fruits are used in Korean punch, *sujonggwa*. Peel is powdered as a sweetener.

DIPTERYX

Fabaceae

Ten species of evergreen trees make up this tropical American genus. The seeds of *D. odorata* and other species, such as *D. oppositifolia*, contain coumarin (1–3 per cent) and coumarin glycosides, which release the scent of sweet hay in the course of drying. *Dipteryx odorata* was grown in Victorian times to scent snuff, but the value of the species in perfumery has decreased since the discovery of synthetic coumarin in 1868. Medicinal uses are also largely discontinued following recent findings that coumarin may damage the heart and liver and cause cancer. The seeds are available dried for use in potpourris but cannot be germinated; like most rainforest seeds, they are viable for only a short time and have no dormant period. Most are collected from the wild in Venezuela, or from cultivated trees in Trinidad, which are grown both in plantations and as a windbreak for cocoa trees. *Dipteryx* is derived from the Greek *dis*, “double”, and *pteron*, “wing”, and refers to the wing-like, upper lobes of the calyx.

CULTIVATION Well-drained, gravelly or sandy, acid soil, with ample rainfall and humidity. Remove leading shoots of saplings when 2m (6ft) tall.

PROPAGATION By fresh seed sown *in situ*, which takes about six weeks to germinate. Seedlings do not transplant well.

Dipteryx odorata

HARVEST Fallen ripe fruits are collected and dried to remove seeds, which are then cured by soaking in rum for 2–3 days. This process causes the coumarin to crystallize on the surface, known as “frosting”.

■ *Dipteryx odorata* syn. *Coumarouna odorata* (tonka bean, tonquin bean)
Tender, compact, rainforest tree with a trunk to 1m (3ft) in diameter, smooth, pale grey bark, and leathery glossy leaves, divided into 3–6 elliptic leaflets, to 15cm (6in) long. Small, very fragrant, rose-violet, pea flowers are followed by fleshy, pale yellow-brown, oval fruits, to 10cm (4in) long, each containing a single, mahogany-coloured seed, 3–5cm (1¼–2in) long. Native to tropical S America, mainly Venezuela. ‡ 25–40m (80–130ft), ↔ 15–20m (50–70ft).

HARDINESS Min. 15–18°C (59–64°F).

PARTS USED Seeds.

PROPERTIES An aromatic herb that improves the lasting qualities of perfumes.

MEDICINAL USES Formerly used to treat whooping cough.

ECONOMIC USES Used as a vanilla substitute for flavouring confectionery, cocoa, liqueurs, and medicinal preparations, such as cod liver oil (banned in some countries, including the USA); perfume fixative in potpourris and scented goods; also used as an aromatic ingredient in tobaccos and snuff.

DODONAEA

Sapindaceae

Some 50–60 species of evergreen trees and shrubs make up this genus, occurring in the tropics and subtropics. *Dodonaea viscosa* and its colourful cultivar ‘Purpurea’ are popular garden shrubs, making good hedges for windy coastal sites in warm regions, and handsome foliage plants for containers under cover. *Dodonaea viscosa* is used medicinally in many different countries, including Peru, Burma, India, Taiwan, South Africa, and by Aboriginals in Australia. The leaves contain up to 18 per cent

Dodonaea viscosa

tannin, comparable with amounts in *Potentilla erecta* (see p.329). In cases of toothache, the leaves are apparently effective if chewed without swallowing the juice. *Dodonaea* is named after Rembert Dodoens (1517–85), a Flemish royal physician and professor of medicine at Leiden, who in 1554 published a herbal (*Cruÿdboeck*).

CULTIVATION Moist, well-drained soil in sun. Pinch out tips to encourage compact growth in container plants. Cut back in spring, and again in late summer if necessary, to maintain shape. Trim hedges lightly in spring.
PROPAGATION By seed sown in spring at 18°C (64°F); by semi-ripe cuttings in summer.
HARVEST Leaves are picked in summer and used fresh for gargles and poultices or dried for infusions.

▣ *Dodonaea viscosa* (native hops, sticky hop bush, switch sorrel)
Dense spreading shrub or small tree with sticky, yellow-green, elliptic leaves, 7–13cm (3–5in) long. Yellow-green flowers appear in summer, followed by round black seeds in three-winged, reddish to brown or yellow capsules. Found around the coastal areas in tropics and subtropics worldwide. ‡ 3m (10ft), ↔ 1.5m (5ft).
▣ 'Purpurea' has bronze-purple foliage and purple-red capsules.
HARDINESS Min. 3–5°C (37–41°F).
PARTS USED Leaves.
PROPERTIES A strongly astringent herb that lowers fever and relieves pain.
MEDICINAL USES Internally for fevers. Externally for toothache, sore throat, wounds, and stings.
CULINARY USES Capsules are used as a substitute for hops in brewing.

▨ ▣ ✎ ▣

DOREMA

Apiaceae

Sixteen species of short-lived, large-leafed perennials and subshrubs belong to this genus, occurring in C and SW Asia. All are monocarpic. *Dorema ammoniacum* is listed in Victorian gardening manuals as "of easy culture" and "increased readily by seed". This imposing member of the parsley family would make an interesting feature in the herb garden, but it seems to have disappeared from cultivation. *Dorema ammoniacum* was named after the temple of Ammon, because the gum resin was first extracted from plants in this area of Libya – its use being mentioned by Hippocrates in the 1st century AD. The gum resin exudes naturally from holes in the stems caused by beetles.
CULTIVATION Well-drained to dry, stony soil in sun.
PROPAGATION By seed sown in autumn or spring.
HARVEST Gum resin is collected from incisions in stems and leafstalks during the flowering and fruiting periods. It is solidified into "tears" or blocks before grinding into powder.

Dorema ammoniacum (ammoniac, gum ammoniac)
Giant perennial with branched hairy stems, woody at the base and 3–6cm (1¼–2½in) in diameter, and large divided leaves. Tiny white flowers are produced in umbels in spring and summer, followed by elliptic seeds, about 7mm (¼in) long. Grows from Iran to Afghanistan and Pakistan. ‡ 2–3m (6–10ft), ↔ 1–1.5m (3–5ft).
HARDINESS Frost hardy.
PARTS USED Gum resin.
PROPERTIES A strong-smelling, acrid, stimulant herb that has expectorant effects, relaxes spasms, and increases perspiration.
MEDICINAL USES Internally for chronic bronchitis (especially in the elderly), asthma, or catarrh. Externally for swollen joints and indolent tumours.
ECONOMIC USES Formerly used in perfumery and in porcelain cement.

▣ ▣ ✎

DRIMYS

Pepper tree

Winteraceae

This genus contains about 30 species of evergreen aromatic trees and shrubs, distributed from Mexico to southern S America, and from the Malay Peninsula to New Guinea, Australia, and New Zealand. *Drimys winteri* (Winter's bark) is the only species common in cultivation. The dwarf var. *andina*, which flowers when only 30cm (12in) high, is ideal for small gardens. Also grown is the closely related *Tasmannia lanceolata* (see p.383), formerly classified as *Drimys lanceolata*, an Australasian shrub with peppery edible leaves and berries. *Drimys winteri* was first described as a medicinal herb by Captain John Winter, on Sir Francis Drake's voyage round the world (1577–80); he introduced it to Europe from S America in 1578. It was apparently "very powerful against the scurvy", which was a common complaint on long voyages and caused by lack of vitamin C. The bark is no longer used for this, but is recognized as having similar effects on the digestive system to the more widely available *Canella winterana* (see p.152) and *Cinnamomum verum* (see p.170). Commercial supplies of Winter's bark may also include bark from *Cinnamodendron corticosum* (false Winter's bark) and *Drimys granadensis*.
CULTIVATION Moist, fertile, well-drained soil in sun or partial shade. In cold areas plants need the protection of a wall or other sheltered position.
PROPAGATION By seed sown in autumn; by semi-ripe cuttings in summer.
HARVEST Bark is removed from branches in autumn and winter, and dried for powders and infusions.

▣ *Drimys winteri* (Winter's bark)
Upright conical tree or shrub with oblong–elliptic to lanceolate, glossy, pointed leaves, to 20cm (8in) long. Fragrant, ivory-white flowers, 2.5cm (1in) across, with 5–7 (–11) lanceolate petals, are produced in large loose umbels in late spring and early summer. Native to Chile and Argentina. ‡ 15m (50ft), ↔ 10m (30ft).
HARDINESS Frost hardy.

Drimys winteri

Dodonaea viscosa 'Purpurea'

PARTS USED Bark.
PROPERTIES A pungent, bitter, tonic herb that relieves indigestion. It resembles *Acorus calamus* (see p.101) in aroma.
MEDICINAL USES Internally for indigestion and colic.

🏛 ▮

DROSERA
Sundew

Droseraceae

About 100 species of evergreen or herbaceous, insectivorous perennials belong to this diverse genus, which occurs in boggy areas worldwide. Many sundews are grown by collectors of carnivorous plants, and the more common species are sold as pot plants. The name comes from the Greek *drosos*, "dew", and refers to the sticky droplets of digestive enzymes on the leaf hairs, which trap and digest insects. *Drosera rotundifolia* has a long history of use in medicine. William Turner wrote in 1568 that "our Englishmen nowadays set very much faith by it, and hold it good for consumptions and swooning, and faintness of the harte" (*A New Herball*, 1551–68). A sundew liqueur, known as *Rosa Solis*, was popular in Britain, France, and Germany during the 17th century for its reputedly fortifying and aphrodisiac effects. One of the main constituents of *Drosera* spp. is plumbagin, which is active against a broad spectrum of pathogenic bacteria, fungi, and viruses, including organisms that cause tuberculosis. *Drosera rotundifolia* is collected mainly in Finland, where some 20–25 million plants are harvested from the wild annually. *Drosera anglica* is also used; both species can be cultivated for the herb trade. Larger Madagascan species, such as *D. ramantacea*, are also collected, despite their lower plumbagin content, and are becoming increasingly scarce as a result. Butterworts, such as *Pinguicula vulgaris* and *P. grandiflora*, which are also insectivorous (though belonging to a different family, the Lentibulariaceae), have similar properties to *Drosera*.

CULTIVATION Wet peat in sun.
PROPAGATION By seed sown when ripe at 10–13°C (50–55°F); by leaf cuttings from young, fully developed leaves, with base, in summer; by root cuttings when dormant.
HARVEST Plants are collected as flowering begins and dried for use in infusions, liquid extracts, and tinctures.

▪ **Drosera rotundifolia** (dewplant, *rosée du soleil*, round-leafed sundew)
Rosette-forming perennial, occasionally annual, with a rosette of long-stalked, red-green, sticky, spoon-shaped leaves. Small, white, five-petalled flowers are produced on long erect stalks in summer, followed by capsules of winged seeds. Native to temperate Eurasia and N America.
↕ 10–15cm (4–6in), ↔ 8cm (3in).
HARDINESS Fully hardy.
PARTS USED Whole plant.
PROPERTIES An acrid, warming, soothing herb that has diuretic and expectorant effects, relaxes

Drosera rotundifolia

spasms, and controls coughing. It contains pigments active against a range of pathogens.
MEDICINAL USES Internally for asthma, whooping cough, bronchitis, influenza, gastritis, and gastric ulcer. Combined with *Euphorbia hirta* (see p.210), *Grindelia camporum* (see p.229), and *Polygala senega* (see p.326) for asthma. In homeopathy for whooping cough, dry coughs, sore throat, and laryngitis. Imparts a dark colour to the urine.

▤ ▮

DRYOBALANOPS

Dipterocarpaceae

Seven species of SE Asian rainforest trees belong to this genus. *Dryobalanops aromatica* (Borneo camphor) has a long history of use in Eastern medicine. It was mentioned by Marco Polo as being exported from N Sumatra and Johore to the Middle East since at least the 6th century AD. Its uses include embalming; organic matter has been found preserved in borneol after 2000 years. Camphor is an aromatic crystalline substance that forms in cavities in the trunks of trees such as *D. aromatica* and *Cinnamomum camphora* (see p.170). Young trees produce a clear yellow liquid, known as "oil of camphor", which sometimes crystallizes in older specimens. The name, from the Greek *drys*, "tree", *balanos*, "acorn", and *opsis*, "look", refers to the fruits.

CULTIVATION Well-drained, moist, sandy soil in sun or partial shade, with high humidity.
PROPAGATION By seed sown when ripe at 21°C (70°F).
HARVEST Camphor crystals are collected from fissures in trunk; oil of camphor by tapping young trees or by distillation of wood. Both crystals and oil are used in capsules, infusions, lotions, pills, powders, and rubbing oils.

▪ **Dryobalanops aromatica** (Borneo camphor, borneol)
Tall evergreen tree with flaking bark and broadly ovate, leathery leaves, 4–6cm (1½–2½in) long. Small white flowers appear in panicles, to 7cm (3in) long, in summer every 3–4 years, followed by three-celled nuts. Native to

Dryobalanops aromatica

Malaysia, Sumatra, and Borneo. ↕ 40–50m (130–160ft), rarely to 60m (200ft), ↔ 15m (50ft).
HARDINESS Min. 15–18°C (59–64°F).
PARTS USED Camphor crystals, oil.
PROPERTIES A bitter, pungent, stimulant herb that relieves pain, lowers fever, relaxes spasms, reduces inflammation, and also has anti-bacterial effects.
MEDICINAL USES Internally for fainting, convulsions associated with high fever, cholera, and pneumonia. Externally for ringworm, rheumatism, abscesses, boils, cold sores, mouth ulcers, sore throat, chest infections, and conjunctivitis. Used in aromatherapy internally and externally as an antiseptic, sedative, and tonic for the heart and adrenal cortex, mainly in skin problems, rheumatism, infectious diseases, depression, and convalescence.
ECONOMIC USES Source of *d*-borneol, a volatile oil used in perfumes with a camphoraceous note. Timber is valued for its resistance to termites.

▣ ▮ ✎ ▣

DRYOPTERIS
Buckler fern

Dryopteridaceae

A genus of mostly deciduous, rhizomatous ferns containing some 200 species, found in woods, mountain rocks, and damp places in northern temperate regions. Many species are grown for their often vase-shaped crowns of fine foliage. Some are demanding in requirements, but several species, including *D. filix-mas*, are easily grown as garden plants, being very hardy and drought-resistant. *Dryopteris filix-mas* is very variable in size and frond shape and has numerous cultivars. A number of species contain phloroglucinol derivatives ("filicin"), which paralyze intestinal parasites. In addition to *D. filix-mas*, *D. cristata* (buckler fern, crested field fern), *D. oreades* (dwarf male fern), and *D. crassirhizoma* are used. Drugs derived from these ferns are used in conjunction with an effective purgative. *Dryopteris crassirhizoma* has been recorded in Chinese medicine since at least the later Han dynasty (AD25–220). Known as *guan zhong*, it reduces inflammation, controls bleeding, and lowers fever.

Dryopteris filix-mas

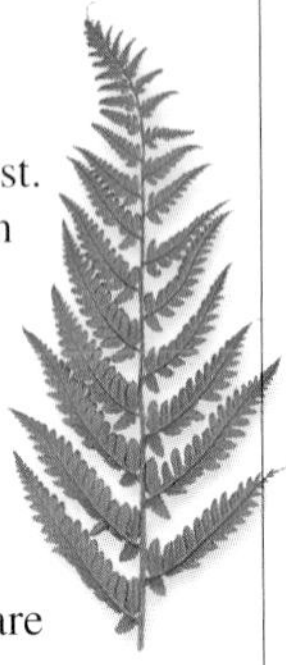

CULTIVATION Humus-rich soil in shade. Foliage may be affected by rust.
PROPAGATION By spores sown when ripe at 15°C (59°F); by division in autumn or spring. Variants do not come true from spores.
HARVEST Rhizomes are lifted in autumn, leaving bases of fronds but removing roots, and dried for use in liquid extracts and powders. Stocks are renewed annually.

▣ ***Dryopteris filix-mas*** syn. *Aspidium filix-mas* (male fern)
Deciduous fern with thick rhizomes and large clumps of broadly lanceolate fronds, to 1m (3ft) long. Spores are released from the undersides of the upper leaflets in summer. Native to Europe and N America. ↕↔ 1m (3ft). 'Barnesii' has long narrow fronds. ↕↔ 1.2m (4ft). ▣ 'Crispa Cristata' is smaller, with crested fronds and leaflets both crisped and crested. ↕ 60cm (2ft). ▣ 'Linearis' has narrower divisions, giving slender, more graceful fronds.
HARDINESS Fully hardy.
PARTS USED Rhizomes.
PROPERTIES A bitter, unpleasant-tasting, highly toxic herb that expels intestinal worms and has anti-bacterial and anti-viral effects. It also controls bleeding, relieves pain, reduces inflammation, and lowers fever.

Dryopteris filix-mas 'Crispa Cristata'

Dryopteris filix-mas 'Linearis'

MEDICINAL USES Internally for all intestinal parasites, liver flukes, internal haemorrhage, uterine bleeding, mumps, and feverish illnesses (including colds, influenza, measles, pneumonia, and meningitis). Doses for intestinal worms are critical; poisoning is prevented by combining with a saline purgative, such as magnesium sulphate, but not with castor oil, which increases absorption. Excess causes nausea and vomiting, delirium, breathing difficulties, blindness, and heart failure. Externally for abscesses, boils, carbuncles, and sores. For use only by qualified practitioners.
⚠ **WARNING** This herb is subject to legal restrictions in some countries.

DUBOISIA

Solanaceae

Three species of trees and shrubs belong to this genus, which occurs in Australasia. *Duboisia myoporoides* is found on sandy soils in open forest, rainforest margins, and coastal dunes. It is a major source of tropane alkaloids for the pharmaceutical industry. These include atropine, hyoscine, hyoscyamine, and scopolamine, which occur in other members of the nightshade family, such as *Atropa bella-donna* (see p.138), *Hyoscyamus niger* (see p.239), and *Scopolia carniolica* (see p.363). In Australia, hybrids of *Duboisia leichardtii* and *D. myoporoides* have been developed that yield over three per cent total alkaloids. *Duboisia* is named after Charles Du Bois (1656–1740), treasurer of the East India Company, who compiled a large herbarium.
CULTIVATION Sandy soil in sun with high humidity. Trim plants regularly to control size.
PROPAGATION By seed sown when ripe.

Duboisia myoporoides

HARVEST Leaves are collected during the flowering season and dried for processing.
⚠ **WARNING** All parts are toxic if eaten.

▣ ***Duboisia myoporoides*** (cork tree, corkwood, eyeplant)
Small tree or tall shrub with soft, spoon-shaped leaves. Tiny, white to pale lavender, bell-shaped flowers, 6mm (¼in) across, appear from late winter to spring, followed by small, juicy, black berries, 6mm (¼in) long, containing 6–12 seeds. Native to Queensland and New South Wales (Australia), New Caledonia, and New Guinea. ↕ 12m (40ft), ↔ 2–5m (6–15ft).
HARDINESS Min. 15–18°C (59–64°F).
PARTS USED Leaves.
PROPERTIES A bitter, hypnotic, sedative herb that dilates the pupils and stimulates respiration.
MEDICINAL USES In homeopathy for eye complaints. For use only by qualified practitioners.
ECONOMIC USES A source of pharmaceutical alkaloids.
⚠ **WARNING** This herb and *D. leichardtii* are subject to legal restrictions in some countries.

E

ECBALLIUM

Cucurbitaceae

Only one species of trailing perennial is included in this genus, which occurs in semi-arid and waste areas of the Mediterranean region and W Asia. *Ecballium elaterium* is often recommended as a novelty plant for the border or containers, on account of its explosive fruits. When the fruits are ripe, they eject their ripe seeds, together with an astringent mucilage, with considerable force up to 2m (6ft) or more. They are toxic, and their acrid contents may damage the eyes. *Ecballium elaterium* has been used medicinally since Classical times. Theophrastus mentioned the root as a cure for mange in sheep,

Ecballium elaterium

and the fruit extract was recommended as an emetic. It contains cucurbitacins.

CULTIVATION Well-drained soil in sun. Thrives in poor soil and dry conditions. Subject to statutory control as a weed in some countries.

PROPAGATION By seed sown in spring at 18°C (64°F).

HARVEST Fruits are picked under-ripe and left in containers until contents are expelled. Juice is then dried in flakes as the drug elaterium.

⚠ **WARNING** Toxic if eaten. Repeated handling of seeds and other parts may cause poisoning. Ripe fruits eject contents forcibly and may cause injuries, especially to the eyes.

▣ *Ecballium elaterium* syn. *Momordica elateria* (squirting cucumber)
Tuberous bushy perennial with stout hairy stems and grey-green, ovate–triangular, palmately lobed leaves, 5–15cm (2–6in) long. Pale yellow, five-petalled flowers, to 2.5cm (1in) across, are produced in summer – males in a raceme and females solitary – followed by grey-green, bristly, ovoid fruits, to 5cm (2in) long, which eject ripe seeds explosively. ‡ 50cm (20in), ↔ 1m (3ft).

HARDINESS Half hardy.

PARTS USED Fruits.

PROPERTIES A purgative herb that causes evacuation of water from the bowels.

MEDICINAL USES Internally for oedema associated with kidney complaints, rheumatism, paralysis, and shingles. Excess causes irritation to the stomach and bowels, and may be fatal. Externally for sinusitis and painful joints. For use only by qualified practitioners.

⚠ **WARNING** This herb is subject to legal restrictions in some countries.

▨ ▣

ECHINACEA
Coneflower

Asteraceae

Nine species of rhizomatous perennials make up this genus, which is native to E USA. Coneflowers give a colourful display in the border from midsummer to early autumn and are excellent for cutting. The generic name

Echinacea comes from the Greek *echinos*, "hedgehog", and refers to the prickly scales of the flowers' central cone. *Echinacea purpurea* is one of several species, including *E. angustifolia* and *E. pallida*, used by native N Americans, mainly to treat wounds. In particular, the Plains tribes regarded *E. angustifolia* as a cure-all. The three species have similar constituents and can be used interchangeably. Both *E. angustifolia* and *E. pallida* were listed in the *US National Formulary* (1916–50), and the former became important in homeopathy in Europe in the early 20th century. Cultivation of *E. purpurea* began in Europe when the seed of *E. angustifolia* was in short supply. The seed was imported in 1939 by the German herbal company Madaus, who pioneered research into this species. It proved an easier crop, hence its place as a market leader today. *Echinacea* is considered the most effective detoxicant in Western medicine for the circulatory, lymphatic, and respiratory systems. The chemistry of *Echinacea* is complex, and there appears to be no single constituent responsible for the detoxifying, immune-stimulating effects. Key constituents are: alkylamides, which are anti-bacterial, anti-fungal, immune-stimulating, and detoxifying and cause a tingling sensation on the tongue; echinosides, with anti-bacterial properties; polysaccharides, which are anti-inflammatory and stimulate production of interferon (a protein that inhibits virus replication); inulin (as in *Inula helenium* see p.243); flavonoids, which strengthen blood vessels and destroy free radicals; polyacetylenes, which are anti-bacterial and anti-fungal; caffeoyl derivatives that are strongly antioxidant, preventing skin photodamage; resins; and volatile oil. *Echinacea* products are standardized for echinosides and polysaccharides, though other constituents may be equally important in the overall effect.

CULTIVATION Rich, deep, well-drained, neutral to alkaline soil (ideally a sandy soil) in sun. Tolerates drought.

PROPAGATION By seed sown when ripe at 20°C (68°F); by root cuttings in late autumn to early winter; by division in autumn or spring. Fresh seed germinates in 5–20 days. Seed sown in spring may need stratifying for 28 days. Sow in deep pots, rather than seed trays, to allow root development.

HARVEST Roots and rhizomes are lifted in autumn and dried for use in decoctions, infusions, liquid extracts, powders, tablets, and tinctures.

▣ *Echinacea purpurea* syn. *Rudbeckia purpurea* (purple coneflower)
Tall rhizomatous perennial with hairy, ovate–lanceolate leaves, to 15cm (6in) long. Purple-pink, honey-scented, daisy-like flowers, to 12cm (5in) across, with conical, orange-brown centres, are produced in summer and early autumn. Native to E USA. ‡ 1.5m (5ft), ↔ 45cm (18in). 'Leuchstern' syn. 'Bright Star' has deep magenta flower heads, ‡ 80cm (32in).
▣ 'Magnus' has large flower heads, to 18cm (7in) across, with deep purple ray petals.
▣ 'Robert Bloom' has vivid, magenta-pink ray petals that open out wide. ▣ 'White Lustre' has

Echinacea purpurea

Echinacea purpurea 'Magnus'

Echinacea purpurea 'Robert Bloom'

Echinacea purpurea 'White Lustre'

Echinacea purpurea 'White Swan'

E

creamy white flower heads. ‡ 80cm (32in).
◨ 'White Swan' is dwarf, with white-rayed
flowers, to 11cm (4¼in) across. ‡ 60cm (24in).
HARDINESS Fully hardy.
PARTS USED Roots, rhizomes, above-ground
parts.
PROPERTIES A bitter, slightly aromatic,
alterative herb that stimulates the immune
system, promotes healing, and has anti-viral
and anti-bacterial effects.
MEDICINAL USES Internally for skin diseases,
fungal infections, septicaemia, boils, abscesses,
slow-healing wounds, chronic infections,
chronic fatigue syndrome (CFS), venereal
diseases, and early stages of coughs and colds;
excess causes throat irritation. Externally for
herpes, acne, psoriasis, and infected injuries,
also as a gargle for sore throat, and to prevent
premature ageing and UV damage to skin.
Often combined with *Arctium lappa* (see p.127)
for boils, with *Baptisia tinctoria* (see p.141) or
Commiphora myrrha (see p.177) for throat
infections, and with *Hypericum perforatum*
(see p.240) for herpes.
▨ ▰

ECLIPTA
Asteraceae

Four species of annuals and perennials are
included in this genus, native to warm parts
of N and S America and widely naturalized in
Eurasia. Originally from wet and muddy areas
of warm temperate and tropical America,
Eclipta prostrata spread as a weed into many
parts of Asia. It became important in Ayurvedic
medicine, and was first recorded in traditional
Chinese medicine in the *Tang Materia Medica*
(AD659). The Ayurvedic name, *bhringaraja*,
means "ruler of the hair", and refers to its use
in restoring and darkening hair. It is also widely
used as a rejuvenative. Traditional Chinese
medicine describes it as a good general tonic for
liver and kidney *yin*, for which purpose it is often
combined with *Centella asiatica* (see p.162).
Eclipta prostrata yields thiophene derivatives
that are used in preparations to destroy
nematodes. When damaged, the foliage exudes
white sap that turns black on contact with air.
CULTIVATION Damp to wet soil in shade.
PROPAGATION By seed sown in spring at 18°C
(68°F).
HARVEST Whole plants are cut when flowering
and dried for use in decoctions, infusions,
medicated oil, powders, and tinctures. Fresh
plant is sometimes used externally, crushed for
topical application.

◨ *Eclipta prostrata* syn. *E. alba* (*bhringaraja*,
false daisy)
Downy annual with stems often rooting at the
nodes, and lanceolate leaves, to 25cm (10in)
long. Tiny, white, daisy-like flowers are borne
in summer, followed by minute fruits, each with
a tuft of small teeth. Pantropical. ‡↔ 20–90cm
(8–35in).
HARDINESS Min. 10°C (50°F).
PARTS USED Whole plant (*han lian cao*).

Eclipta prostrata

PROPERTIES A bitter, sweet and sour, cooling
herb that has a tonic effect on the circulatory,
nervous, and digestive systems, and checks
bleeding.
MEDICINAL USES Internally for kidney and
liver weakness (manifesting as tinnitus, loss
and premature greying of hair, poor teeth and
eyesight, and nervous disorders), cirrhosis,
hepatitis, complaints involving bleeding
(especially postpartum and abnormal uterine
bleeding), anaemia, and diphtheria. Used in
Chinese folk medicine for eczema, athlete's
foot, dermatitis, and child malnutrition; in
Ayurvedic medicine, both internally and
externally as an oil, for hair loss. Externally,
combined with *Senna obtusifolia* in an oil for
ringworm (India, Burma).
ECONOMIC USES Source of a black dye used
as a hair dye and in tattooing.
▨ ▰ ✎ ▣

ELETTARIA
Zingiberaceae

Four species of rhizomatous perennials belong
to this genus, which occurs in India, Sri Lanka,
Sumatra, and Malaysia. *Elettaria cardamomum*
(cardamom) is a rainforest species that has been
exported from the East to Europe via caravan
routes since Classical times, mainly for use in
perfumery. It can be grown under cover in
temperate regions but rarely flowers or fruits.
Elettaria is derived from *elettari*, the name given
to the plant in SW India. There are several
varieties of cardamom and other *Elettaria* spp.
that produce similar fruits, all varying in flavour
and appearance. True cardamom seeds have a
eucalyptus-like aroma, which deteriorates
rapidly when ground, while substitutes often
have a more camphoraceous odour. *Elettaria
cardamomum* was first mentioned as a
medicinal plant in China c.AD720. Large white
fruits (*bai dou kou*) are considered better for the
lungs, while small green fruits (*sha ren*) are
regarded as a kidney tonic. In Ayurvedic
medicine, cardamom is known as *ela*.
CULTIVATION Rich, moist, well-drained soil in
sun or partial shade. Plants grown under cover
may suffer from spider mite. Prone to mosaic

Elettaria cardamomum

virus and thrips in the tropics.
PROPAGATION By seed sown when
ripe at 19–24°C (66–75°F); by division
in spring.
HARVEST Fruits are collected during the dry
season and dried whole; seeds are removed for
oil extraction or used in infusions, liquid
extracts, powders, and tinctures.

◨ *Elettaria cardamomum* (cardamom)
Evergreen perennial with thick rhizomes and
erect stems bearing linear–lanceolate, pointed
leaves, to 60cm (2ft) long. White flowers, 2cm
(¾in) long, each with a pink- to violet-striped
lip, are borne in a loose spike in summer,
followed by pale green to beige, three-celled
capsules, containing 15–20 aromatic seeds.
Native to India. ‡↔ 3m (10ft).
HARDINESS Min. 10°C (50°F).
PARTS USED Seeds, oil.
PROPERTIES A pungent, warm, aromatic herb
that has stimulating tonic effects, especially
on the lungs and kidneys. It relaxes spasms, is
expectorant, and improves digestion. Reputedly
aphrodisiac, it also detoxifies caffeine and
counteracts mucus-forming foods, such as
dairy produce.
MEDICINAL USES Internally for indigestion,
nausea and vomiting, enuresis, and pulmonary
disease with copious phlegm. Used in
Ayurvedic medicine for bronchial and digestive
complaints. Seeds are chewed to sweeten breath.
CULINARY USES Seeds are used to flavour baked
goods (especially in N Europe), coffee (Middle
East), curries, pickles, milk-based desserts, fruit
compotes, and mulled wine. An ingredient of
the Ethiopian hot spice blend *mit'mit'a*.
ECONOMIC USES Essential oil is important in
perfumery.
⚠ **WARNING** This herb, as a tincture, is subject
to legal restrictions in some countries.
▱ ▨ ▰ ✎ ✎ ▣

ELEUTHEROCOCCUS
Araliaceae

Thirty or so species of deciduous, often prickly,
shrubs and trees belong to this genus, which
occurs in S and E Asia. *Eleutherococcus*

senticosus is easy to grow but seldom seen in Western herb gardens. It does not appear in traditional Russian medicine, but was researched by the Russian scientists Brekhman and Dardymov from 1960 onwards, as part of an extensive study of adaptogenic herbs. Since then it has been widely publicized and marketed as a kind of ginseng. *Eleutherococcus senticosus* belongs to the same family as true ginsengs (*Panax* spp., see p.299) but differs in the form of its saponin glycosides, which are eleutherosides, rather than ginsenosides (or panaxosides). It is also a much larger plant and cheaper to produce. Several other species of *Eleutherococcus*, as well as *E. senticosus*, are known in Chinese medicine as *wu jia pi*. They have been used for rheumatic complaints, low vitality, and weak liver and kidney energy for 2000 years, and are regarded as less heating than *Panax ginseng* (see p.300).

CULTIVATION Well-drained, rich, moist soil in sun or partial shade.

PROPAGATION By seed sown in spring or autumn (needs stratification); by greenwood cuttings in early summer; by root cuttings in winter; by hardwood cuttings, 15–30cm (6–12in) long, in autumn; by suckers in winter or early spring.

HARVEST Roots are lifted in autumn and dried whole or decorticated. Both roots and root bark are used in decoctions, powders, tablets, teas, and tinctures.

■ *Eleutherococcus senticosus* syn. *Acanthopanax senticosus* (eleuthero, Siberian ginseng)
Deciduous suckering shrub, forming large thickets, with thick roots, spiny stems, and dark green, palmately divided leaves, to 15cm (6in) across. Tiny, star-shaped flowers appear in rounded umbels in summer – males lilac to purple, females green – followed by blue-black berries. Native to N Asia. ‡ 2.5–7m (8–22ft), ↔ indefinite.

HARDINESS Fully hardy.

PARTS USED Roots, root bark.

PROPERTIES A pungent, bitter–sweet, warming herb that stimulates the immune and circulatory systems, regulates blood pressure, lowers blood sugar, and

Eleutherococcus senticosus

reduces inflammation. It is adaptogenic, having a tonic effect on all organs.

MEDICINAL USES Internally for convalescence, menopausal complaints, geriatric debility, physical and mental stress, and insomnia caused by prolonged anxiety. Used in the background treatment of cancer and exposure to toxic chemicals and radiation, and to improve resistance to infection. Not given to children, or taken for longer than six weeks at a time. Contraindicated with caffeine.

CULINARY USES Young leaves are cooked as a pot-herb or dried for making tea.

ELYMUS
Poaceae

About 100 species make up this genus of perennial grasses common in northern temperate regions. Though a pernicious weed to gardeners, *E. repens* (couch grass) is an important medicinal plant that has appeared in herbals and pharmacopoeias since the time of Dioscorides (1st century AD). It is a gentle, well-tolerated remedy, included in many preparations for the treatment of prostatitis, with no side-effects. The name *Elymus* comes from the Greek *elymos*, "cereal".

CULTIVATION Most soils in sun or shade. Light sandy soils give highest yields of rhizomes. *Elymus repens* is extremely invasive and difficult to eradicate. It should be grown in containers and not allowed to seed.

PROPAGATION By division in autumn or spring.

HARVEST Rhizomes are dug in spring and used fresh in homeopathic preparations, or cut into 5cm (2in) sections, and dried below 30°C (86°F) for use in decoctions, liquid extracts, and tinctures.

■ *Elymus repens* syn. *Agropyron repens* (couch grass, quack grass, twitch)
Perennial with numerous rhizomes, to 3mm (⅛in) across, and dull green, linear leaves. Stiff erect flower spikes, with spikelets arranged in zigzag formation, are produced on long stalks in summer. Native to Europe, N Africa, Siberia, and N America. ‡ 30cm–1m (1–3ft), ↔ indefinite.

Elymus repens

HARDINESS Fully hardy.

PARTS USED Rhizomes.

PROPERTIES A soothing herb that improves excretion from kidneys and bowels, lowers cholesterol levels, and clears infection.

MEDICINAL USES Internally for kidney and bladder complaints (especially enlarged prostate and cystitis), gout, and rheumatism. Combines well with *Agathosma* spp. (see p.106) for cystitis and *Hydrangea arborescens* (see p.238) for prostatitis.

EMBLICA
Emblica officinalis. See *Phyllanthus emblica*.

EOPEPON
Eopepon vitifolius. See *Trichosanthes kirilowii*.

EPHEDRA
Joint fir

Ephedraceae

This genus of about 40 species of shrubs and climbers occurs in S Europe, N Africa, Asia, and subtropical America. Joint firs have green branches and scale-like, much-reduced leaves. A few species are cultivated, mainly as a ground cover for dry situations. Male and female plants must be grown together for fruits to be produced. *Ephedra* spp. contain alkaloids, notably ephedrine, which was first isolated by Nagai and Hamanashi in 1885. Extracts are included in many patent medicines for catarrh and asthma, and added to stimulant products aimed at young people and athletes, though the consumption of ephedrine in any form is banned in international sporting events. Various species are used medicinally, including *Ephedra equisetina*, *E. intermedia*, the Indian *E. gerardiana*, and *E. sinica* – the last usually having the highest alkaloid content. The pharmaceutical term *Ephedrae herba* and Chinese name *ma huang* are used for the drug sourced from any of these species. Research has shown anti-viral effects, notably against influenza. A similar stimulant to ephedrine, norpseudoephedrine, or cathine is found in *Catha edulis* (see p.158). American species of *Ephedra* are low in alkaloids and not considered a viable source commercially. Several are known as Mormon tea, being used as a substitute for tea and coffee, which are avoided by Mormons.

CULTIVATION Sharply drained to dry soil in sun. Tolerates poor soil.

PROPAGATION By seed sown in autumn; by division in autumn or spring.

HARVEST Stems are collected at any time and dried for use in powders, decoctions, tinctures, or liquid extracts.

■ *Ephedra distachya* (joint fir, *ma huang*, shrubby horsetail)
Dwarf evergreen shrub with upright to sprawling stems and minute leaves, reduced to scales at the nodes. Male inflorescence is cone-like; female

E

Ephedra distachya

Ephedra nevadensis

is solitary, appearing in early summer, followed by fleshy red fruits. Native to S and E Europe. ↔ 1m (3ft).

HARDINESS Fully hardy.

PARTS USED Stems.

PROPERTIES A pungent, bitter, warm, diuretic herb that dilates the bronchial vessels, stimulates the heart and central nervous system, and increases perspiration.

MEDICINAL USES Internally for asthma, hay fever, and allergic complaints. Often combined with *Hyssopus officinalis* (see p.240), *Marrubium vulgare* (see p.271), *Primula veris* (see p.330), or *Thymus vulgaris* (see p.390) for asthma or serious bronchial complaints, and with *Chamaemelum nobile* (see p.165) or *Urtica dioica* (see p.398) for allergic reactions. In traditional Chinese medicine, is often combined with *Rehmannia glutinosa* (see p.341) for kidney weakness, *Prunus dulcis* (see p.332) for asthma, *Cinnamomum cassia* (see p.170) for colds, or *Mentha arvensis* (see p.276) for allergies. Used in Ayurvedic medicine for arthritis and oedema. For use only by qualified practitioners. Not given to patients taking monoamine oxidase (MAO) inhibitors or suffering from high blood pressure, angina, glaucoma, prostate disease, or hyperthyroidism.

CULINARY USES Fruits are edible when ripe.

△ **WARNING** *Ephedra* spp. are subject to legal restrictions in some countries. Ephedrine-containing substances are listed as addictive by the International Olympic Committee and by the German Sports Association.

▨ ▨ ▨

■ *Ephedra nevadensis* (*canatillo*, desert tea, Mormon tea, *popatillo*)
Evergreen shrub with dense green, leafless stems and tiny green flowers in late winter or early spring, followed by red berries on female plants. Found from arid regions of Mexico and SW USA to North Dakota. ↔ to 1m (3ft).

HARDINESS Fully hardy.

PARTS USED Stems.

PROPERTIES An astringent, decongestant, diuretic herb with tonic effects.

MEDICINAL USES Internally for colds, hay fever, kidney problems, and peptic ulcers.

CULINARY USES Fresh or dried stems are used

to make a pleasant-tasting tea. Traditionally taken as a "blood purifier".

▨ ▨ ▨

EPIGAEA
Ericaceae

A genus of three species of creeping evergreen subshrubs, native to N America and Japan. *Epigaea repens* is a choice plant for lime-free soil in rock gardens, raised beds, and containers, combining well with dwarf rhododendrons and conifers. It does not transplant successfully from the wild and is a protected plant in some states. *Epigaea* comes from the Greek *epi*, "upon", and *gaia*, "the earth"; *repens* is the Latin word for "creeping". Native N Americans make a leaf tea from *E. repens* to treat kidney disorders and purify the blood. The Shakers use it for "gravel" (kidney stones), hence its name "gravel plant". It is prescribed by herbalists today in much the same way as *Agathosma* (see p.106) and *Arctostaphylos uva-ursi* spp. (see p.127).

CULTIVATION Moist, acid, humus-rich soil in shade. Tolerates deep shade.

PROPAGATION By seed sown on the soil surface when ripe at 10–13°C (55–61°F); by greenwood cuttings in early summer; by

Epigaea repens

separation of rooted sections in spring.

HARVEST Plants are cut in summer and dried for use in infusions, liquid extracts, and tinctures.

■ *Epigaea repens* (Mayflower, trailing arbutus)
Prostrate evergreen shrub with hairy stems, rooting at the nodes, and leathery, ovate–oblong, glossy leaves, to 8cm (3in) long. White, occasionally pink-flushed, spicily fragrant flowers, to 1.5cm (½in) long, appear in clusters in spring, followed by globose capsules filled with seeds. Native to central and eastern N America. ‡ 8–10cm (3–4in), ↔ 30cm (12in).

HARDINESS Fully hardy.

PARTS USED Whole plant.

PROPERTIES An astringent diuretic herb.

MEDICINAL USES Internally for cystitis, kidney stones, and kidney and urinary tract infections.

▨ ▨

EPIMEDIUM
Berberidaceae

There are 30–40 species of deciduous and evergreen, rhizomatous perennials in this genus, which occurs from Mediterranean regions to E Asia. Various species and hybrids are grown as ornamentals in shady borders, and with shrubs, mainly as a ground cover. The name comes from the Greek *epimedion*, which was Dioscorides's name for these plants (literally "akin to a plant growing in Media"). *Epimedium sagittatum* was first described as a medicinal herb in the *Shen Nong Canon of Herbs* (written AD25–220).

CULTIVATION Moist, humus-rich, well-drained soil in partial shade. Cut back before new growth appears in spring. Young shoots and flowers may be damaged by frost.

PROPAGATION By seed sown when ripe; by division after flowering, or in autumn; by rhizome sections in warmth in winter.

HARVEST Whole plants are cut in the growing season and dried for decoctions.

■ *Epimedium sagittatum* (barrenwort, horny goat weed)
Evergreen perennial with creeping rhizomes, trifoliate leathery leaves, and lanceolate–ovate,

Epimedium sagittatum

pointed leaflets, to 5cm (2in) long, which have spiny-toothed margins. Pale yellow flowers are borne in panicles of 20–60 in spring. Native to C China; naturalized in Japan. ↕ 25–50cm (10–20in), ↔ 30–45cm (12–18in).
HARDINESS Fully hardy.
PARTS USED Whole plant (*yin yang huo*).
PROPERTIES A warming, pleasant-tasting herb that acts mainly as an aphrodisiac and as a tonic to liver and kidneys. It dilates blood vessels, lowers blood pressure, controls coughing, and is expectorant.
MEDICINAL USES Internally for cold or numb extremities, asthma, bronchitis, arthritis, lumbago, impotence, involuntary and premature ejaculation, high blood pressure, and absent-mindedness. Excess causes vomiting, dizziness, thirst, and nosebleed.
ECONOMIC USES An ingredient of Chinese "spring wine".

EQUISETUM
Horsetail
Equisetaceae

A genus of 29 species of spore-bearing perennials that occurs worldwide (except Australasia) in cool damp places. Horsetails have barely changed since prehistoric times, when they formed a large part of the vegetation that decomposed to form coal seams. Some species are pernicious weeds. Once they have produced the cone-like heads from which the spores are shed, the fertile stems die and are replaced by sterile ones. Horsetails have an unusual chemistry, containing alkaloids (including nicotine) and various minerals. They are rich in silica, giving abrasive properties that were used from the Middle Ages until the 18th century for scouring pots and pans, especially pewter. *Equisetum hyemale* (Dutch rush) was once exported from the Netherlands, where it grows abundantly, for this purpose. Certain horsetails concentrate gold in their tissues (although not sufficient to warrant extraction) and are useful indicators for gold prospectors.
CULTIVATION Moist soil in sun or partial shade. Horsetails are invasive and difficult to eradicate. *Equisetum* spp. are subject to statutory control as a weed in parts of Australia.
PROPAGATION By division in early spring.
HARVEST Stems are cut at any time during the growing season and dried for use in decoctions, infusions, liquid extracts, and powders.

■ *Equisetum arvense* (bottlebrush, field horsetail, shave grass)
Herbaceous perennial with a hairy tuberous rhizome. Erect, often branched, sterile stems have black-toothed sheaths and whorls of spreading green branches. Spores ripen in spring. Found from Europe to C China, N America, and Greenland. ↕ 20–80cm (8–32in), ↔ indefinite.
HARDINESS Fully hardy.
PARTS USED Stems.
PROPERTIES An astringent healing herb that acts mainly on the genito-urinary system and

Equisetum arvense

controls both internal and external bleeding.
MEDICINAL USES Internally for prostatitis, incontinence, cystitis, and urethritis. Often used with *Hydrangea arborescens* (see p.238) for prostate problems. Internally and externally for haemorrhage. An irritant, best combined with demulcent herbs, and restricted to short-term use.

■ *Equisetum hyemale* (Dutch rush, rough horsetail)
Perennial with upright, glaucous, unbranched stems that remain green in winter. The swollen joints are banded and have tiny blunt teeth. Spore-producing "cones" ripen in summer. Found from Europe to N and C Asia and N America. ↕ 70cm–1m (28–36in), ↔ indefinite.
HARDINESS Fully hardy.

Equisetum hyemale

PARTS USED Stems (*mu zei*).
PROPERTIES A bitter–sweet, astringent herb that has diuretic and anti-inflammatory effects.
MEDICINAL USES Internally in traditional Chinese medicine for cataracts, conjunctivitis, and sore or watering eyes related to feverish colds. Often combined with *Chrysanthemum × morifolium* (see p.168) to treat eye problems associated with the liver meridian. Used internally in Ayurvedic medicine for kidney, gall bladder, or urinary problems, venereal diseases, and fractures.

ERIGERON
Erigeron canadensis. See *Conyza canadensis*.

ERIOBOTRYA
Rosaceae

This genus contains about 30 species of evergreen shrubs and trees, native to the Himalayas and E Asia. One or two species are grown for their handsome foliage and edible fruits. *Eriobotrya japonica* is widely cultivated in warm regions, or against walls and in containers in cold areas. Loquats are mostly self-infertile, needing other trees flowering at the same time in the same area for successful fruiting. *Eriobotrya* is from the Greek *erion*, "wool", and *botrys*, "a bunch of grapes", referring to the flower clusters. *Eriobotrya japonica* is the most popular cough remedy in the Far East and is used in many patent remedies.
CULTIVATION Fertile, well-drained soil in sun. Remove badly placed shoots in late winter to maintain an open, well-balanced crown.
PROPAGATION By seed sown in spring at 13–16°C (55–61°F); by semi-ripe cuttings in summer.
HARVEST Leaves are picked as required and, after hairs have been removed (to prevent irritation of the throat), used fresh or dried in decoctions, or made into jelly. Fruits are harvested in late spring when ripe.

■ *Eriobotrya japonica* (Japanese medlar, loquat, *nispero*)
Spreading tree with stout shoots and narrowly

Eriobotrya japonica

E

obovate, dark green, pointed leaves, to 25cm (10in) long, with corrugated, shiny upper surfaces and pale downy undersides. Fragrant white flowers are produced in erect panicles from autumn to winter, followed by globose, edible, yellow fruits, 4cm (1½in) long. Native to China and Japan. ↕ 8m (25ft). 'Advance' is dwarf and resistant to pear blight. It bears medium to large fruit, excellent in quality, and is a good pollinator for other cultivars. ↔ 1.5m (5ft).

HARDINESS Frost hardy.

PARTS USED Leaves (*pi pa ye*), fruits, seeds.

PROPERTIES A bitter expectorant herb that controls coughing and vomiting; it is effective against bacterial and viral infections (leaves).

MEDICINAL USES Internally for bronchitis, coughs with feverish colds, nausea, vomiting, hiccups, and persistent belching. Often taken in the form of loquat leaf jelly.

CULINARY USES Fruit is eaten raw, stewed, or made into jam, jellies, sauces, and drinks. Seeds are roasted as a substitute for coffee.

◨ ▨ ▨ ▣ ◭ ◪

ERIODICTYON

Hydrophyllaceae

Eight species of woolly or smooth, sticky, evergreen shrubs make up this genus, which occurs in southwestern N America and Mexico. *Eriodictyon* is from the Greek *erion*, "wool", and *dictyon*, "net", referring to the white hairs and network of veins on the leaf undersides. Though ornamental and aromatic, *Eriodictyon* spp. are difficult to grow and seldom seen in cultivation outside their native ranges. *Eriodictyon californicum* is most important in the traditional medicine of Mendocino County, California. Rich in flavonoids and resin, it was revered as a holy herb (*yerba santa*) and found in every household medicine chest. Spanish missionaries learned its uses from the native N Americans and it was listed in the *US Pharmacopoeia* (1894–1905; 1916–47), after which it entered the *US National Formulary* as an expectorant.

CULTIVATION Sandy, gravelly, or rocky soil in dry sunny conditions. Thrives on slopes in full sun. If required, trim to shape in spring or summer, cutting into new or one-year-old wood.

PROPAGATION By seed sown in spring or autumn; by semi-ripe cuttings of side shoots in summer.

HARVEST Leaves are picked in late spring; used fresh or dried for infusions and liquid extracts.

◨ *Eriodictyon californicum* (gum leaves, mountain balm, tar weed, wild balsam, *yerba santa*)

Evergreen shrub with lanceolate leaves, to 15cm (6in) long, which have smooth, resinous upper surfaces, white woolly undersides, and wavy or toothed margins. Lilac to white, five-lobed, funnel-shaped flowers, about 1cm (½in) long, appear in clusters in summer, followed by four-valved capsules. Native to California and Oregon. ↕ 2.5m (8ft), ↔ 2m (6ft).

HARDINESS Min. 5–7°C (41–45°F).

Eriodictyon californicum

PARTS USED Leaves.

PROPERTIES An aromatic, pleasant-tasting, tonic herb that reduces spasms, expels phlegm, and lowers fever.

MEDICINAL USES Internally for asthma, bronchitis, laryngitis, sinusitis, and hay fever. An ingredient in patent cough mixtures; added to bitter medicines to improve the taste. Smoked by native N Americans for asthma and chewed for mouth hygiene.

CULINARY USES Fresh or dried leaves make an aromatic, sweet, pleasant-tasting tea.

ECONOMIC USES Leaf extract is used to flavour baked goods, confectionery, ice cream, and soft drinks.

▨ ▣ ◪ ◪ ◨

ERUCA

Rocket

Brassicaceae

This genus includes five species of annuals and perennials that occur in Mediterranean regions. *Eruca vesicaria* subsp. *sativa* has such a long history of cultivation that cultivated plants are now classified as a subspecies, being larger all around than wild plants, and bearing paler flowers. It was a popular salad plant in Roman times, and is still sometimes called Roman rocket. Rocket was once used medicinally but is now known only as a salad herb. Dioscorides wrote in *De Materia Medica* (1st century AD) that "this being eaten raw in any great quantitie doth provoke Venery, and the seed of it also doth work ye like effect, being ureticall and digestive, and good for ye belly. They doe also use the seed of it in making Sawces."

CULTIVATION Moist fertile soil in sun or partial shade. Leaves from plants grown in cool, moist, rich soil are more tender and less pungent than those from plants in hot dry conditions. Leaves may be damaged by flea beetles.

PROPAGATION By seed sown from late winter to early summer. Usually self-sows.

HARVEST Leaves are picked before the flowering stem appears, when they are less pungent than those picked later. Flower buds and flowers are picked as required and used fresh. Seeds are collected when ripe and pressed for oil.

Eruca vesicaria subsp. *sativa*

◨ *Eruca vesicaria* subsp. *sativa* (arugula, rocket, rucola)

Upright, mustard-like annual with asymmetric, lyre-shaped to pinnately lobed and divided, toothed leaves. Cream, four-petalled flowers, to 2cm (¾in) across, veined purple, are produced from spring to autumn, followed by slender erect pods. Found in Mediterranean regions and E Asia; naturalized in parts of N America. ↕ 60cm–1m (24–36in), ↔ 15–20cm (6–8in).

HARDINESS Hardy.

PARTS USED Leaves, flower buds, flowers, seeds, oil.

PROPERTIES A bitter, pungent, tonic herb with a peppery flavour.

CULINARY USES Mainly as a salad herb, notably in *mesclun*, a traditional mixed salad of tiny leaves from the Nice area of France. May also be added to stir-fries, soups, and sauces, notably arugula sauce in Umbria (Italy). Flowers and flower buds are added to salads. Seeds yield edible oil, known as "jamba oil", and are used as a substitute for mustard, or sprouted for salads.

◨ ▨ ◪ ▨ ◪

ERYNGIUM

Apiaceae

A large genus of 230 biennials and perennials, occurring in temperate and subtropical regions, especially in S America. Many eryngium are grown for their handsome foliage and long-lasting flowers, which often have a metallic appearance and dry well. Several species are used medicinally in various parts of the world. The N American *E. aquaticum* (button snakeroot) and *E. yuccifolium* (rattlesnake master) are used mainly for disorders of the kidneys and sexual organs. *Eryngium planum*, from E Europe, is used in Transylvania for whooping cough, and the European *E. campestre* (field eryngo), which can be substituted for *E. maritimum*, is taken for urinary tract infections, skin complaints, and whooping cough. The roots of *E. maritimum* were collected on a large scale in England during the 17th and 18th centuries as an ingredient of "marrow-bone pie", and for candying as restorative, quasi-aphrodisiac pastilles, known as "eryngoes", which were mentioned in

E

Shakespeare's *The Merry Wives of Windsor*. Old records of Colchester in E England show that it was famous for "oysters and eringo root". *Eryngium foetidum* has a strong, cilantro-like aroma and is widely used as a substitute in regions that are too hot for growing *Coriandrum sativum* (cilantro, see p.180) as a leaf crop.
CULTIVATION Damp heavy soil in sun or shade with ample warmth and humidity all year round (*E. foetidum*); well-drained, sandy or stony soil in sun (*E. maritimum*).
PROPAGATION By seed sown when ripe; by root cuttings in late winter. By seed sown in spring after stratifying for four weeks (*E. maritimum*).
HARVEST Leaves (*E. foetidum*) are picked before flowering; roots of second-year plants are lifted in autumn and used fresh for flavouring, and fresh or dried in infusions and decoctions. Roots of *E. maritimum* are lifted in autumn and used fresh for conserve, or dried for use in powders, decoctions, and flavourings.

▣ *Eryngium foetidum* syn. *E. antihystericum* (chadon benni/shadow bennie, culantro, fitweed, perennial coriander)
Evergreen branched biennial with fibrous roots and lanceolate leaves, 5–25cm (2–10in) long, which have spiny-toothed margins. Numerous tiny, green-white flowers, with leafy bracts, appear in cylindrical umbels in summer. Native to seasonally dry grassland in the West Indies, C America, and Florida. ↕ 60cm (24in).
HARDINESS Min. 15–18°C (59–64°F).
PARTS USED Leaves, roots.
PROPERTIES A pungent aromatic herb that lowers fever, relaxes spasms, and benefits the digestion.
MEDICINAL USES Internally, in Carib medicine, as a cure-all and, specifically, for epilepsy, high blood pressure, and fevers, fits, and chills in children.
CULINARY USES Leaves and roots are important in Latin America and SE Asia in soups, curries, and rice and fish dishes. An ingredient of *sofrito*, a seasoning mix that also includes coriander/cilantro and chillies (usually *ajicitos*, small bonnet peppers from *Capsicum chinense*, see p.155).

Eryngium foetidum

Eryngium maritimum

▣ *Eryngium maritimum*
(eryngo, sea holly)
Perennial with stout fleshy roots and stiff, blue-green, very spiny leaves, 5–12cm (2–5in) across. Tiny, powder-blue flowers, surrounded by spiny, leaf-like bracts, are produced in umbels in summer. Found in coastal sands and gravel in Europe, N Africa, and SW Asia. ↕ 30–45cm (12–18in).
HARDINESS Fully hardy.
PARTS USED Roots.
PROPERTIES A sweet mucilaginous herb that is diuretic, anti-inflammatory, and expectorant.
MEDICINAL USES Internally for urinary infections, especially cystitis, urethritis, excessive urine production (as in diabetes), prostate complaints, and renal colic.
CULINARY USES Roots are boiled or roasted like parsnips. Once candied, they are made into a conserve and used to flavour jellies and toffee.

ERYSIMUM

Erysimum officinale. See *Sisymbrium officinale*.

ERYTHRAEA

Erythraea centaurium. See *Centaurium erythraea*.

ERYTHROXYLUM
Erythroxylaceae

A genus of some 250 species of tropical shrubs and small trees, found mainly in the Americas and Madagascar. *Erythroxylum coca* and several other species, such as *E. cataractacum* and *E. novogranatense*, contain tropane alkaloids. The most important is cocaine, first extracted in 1860, but this has now been largely replaced by synthetic derivatives. Coca extracts provided the basis for Coca-Cola until 1902, when cocaine was banned in the USA, and cocaine-free extracts were used instead. *Erythroxylum coca* has an ancient history of use as a medicinal, psychoactive, and ritual plant, featuring in the

origin myths of several S American tribes. The use of powdered dried leaves, mixed with the ashes of other plants as a stimulant, was first recorded c.AD500. Catuaba is one of the best-known herbs in Brazil, familiar as an ingredient of tonic wines, widely sold in supermarkets, and increasingly marketed in herbal remedies worldwide. Despite its popularity, the source of catuaba has caused confusion for almost a century. *Erythroxylum vaccinifolium* is one species identified as a source. It is harvested intensively in the Caatinga region of Brazil, especially in Piauí. Other species referred to as catuaba include *E. catuaba* (a non-existent species), *Anemopaegma arvense*, *A. mirandum* (Bignoniaceae), *Trichilia catuaba*, *T. catigua* (Meliaceae), *Tetragastris catuaba* (Burseraceae), which is almost extinct, and the non-existent *Juniperus brasiliensis* ('Brazilian juniper', Cupressaceae). One explanation for this confusion is that catuaba may refer to several different species that look alike or have similar properties, arising perhaps when Brazilians in the northeast dispersed to other areas and found substitutes for the herb of their homelands. Misidentification is also a possibility. It is also probable that the herb's true identity has at times been deliberately concealed to add to its mystique or to deter competitors in the herb trade. A full account of catuaba and the problems over its identity was given by Douglas C. Daly in the *Kew Bulletin* Vol. 45 (1990). The correct identification of any medicinal herb in commerce is of course essential for quality control, safety, and efficacy. Nevertheless, it is recognized that in Brazilian folk medicine catuaba may refer to different species in different areas, and possibly with different properties. The word catuaba is probably from the Tupi-Guarani *katu*, "good", and either *abá*, "person", *rába*, "leaf", or *íba*, "tree". The name *Erythroxylum* derives from the Greek *erythros*, "red", and *xylon*, "wood". It is frequently, although incorrectly, spelled *Erythroxylon*.
CULTIVATION AND HARVEST Cultivation, harvesting, and processing of coca are subject to legal restrictions in many countries. *Erythroxylum vaccinifolium* is wild-collected; no information has been found on the details.

Erythroxylum coca

E

■ *Erythroxylum coca* (coca)
Evergreen shrub with red-brown bark and
light green, elliptic leaves, to 7cm (3in) long.
Clusters of small white flowers appear in the
axils, followed by orange-red berries, about
5mm (¼in) long. Native to E Andes. ‡↔ to 2m
(6ft) in cultivation, 4–5m (12–15ft) in the wild.
HARDINESS Min. 10–15°C (50–59°F).
PARTS USED Leaves.
PROPERTIES A bitter, locally anaesthetic herb
that stimulates the central nervous system.
MEDICINAL USES Externally in preparations for
eczema, nettle rash, haemorrhoids, facial
neuralgia, and as a local anaesthetic in surgery
(cocaine). Combined with morphine (see
Papaver somniferum, p.301) as a "Brompton
cocktail" to relieve pain in the terminally ill; for
use by qualified practitioners only. Fresh or
dried powdered leaves are held in the mouth
(not chewed or swallowed) in countries of
origin to relieve fatigue and hunger. Excess or
persistent use of cocaine (but not coca) causes
tremors, loss of memory, convulsions,
delusions, hyperactivity, and emaciation.
CULINARY USES Coca extracts (usually
de-cocainized) are used to flavour cola-type
soft drinks, alcoholic drinks, and confectionery.
⚠**WARNING** This herb, especially in the form
of cocaine and coca leaf, is subject to legal
restrictions in most countries.
▨▣✎▣

Erythroxylum vaccinifolium (catuaba)
Erect, densely branched shrub with shiny, dark
green, obovate leaves, to 2.5cm (1in) long,
which have dull, pale brown undersides. Tiny
flowers are produced singly or in clusters of
2–4. Fruits are unrecorded. Native to the
mountains of E Brazil. ‡ 2.5m (8ft).
HARDINESS Min. 15°C (59°F).
PARTS USED Bark (possibly roots).
PROPERTIES A tonic stimulant herb that
acts mainly on the nervous system and has
aphrodisiac effects. Research shows that
catuaba extracts have anti-bacterial, anti-viral,
and anti-HIV activity.
MEDICINAL USES Internally for impotence,
exhaustion, chronic fatigue, neurasthenia, and
pain, agitation, or insomnia related to
conditions of the nervous system.
ECONOMIC USES An ingredient of tonic wines.
▥▨▣✎▣

ESCHSCHOLZIA
Californian poppy

Papaveraceae

A genus of 8–10 slender branched annuals and
perennials, native to western N America.
Eschscholzia californica is the state flower of
California and is among the most popular and
easily grown annuals for dry sunny places; a
wide range of cultivars is available with single,
double, or semi-double flowers in various
shades of orange, yellow, cream, pink, and red.
The poppy-like flowers close in dull or wet
weather, and the foliage contains a watery
sap that is mildly narcotic, used by native

Eschscholzia californica

N Americans to relieve toothache. *Eschscholzia
californica* is similar in effect to *Papaver
somniferum* (see p.301) but non-addictive, much
milder, and does not depress the central nervous
system.
CULTIVATION Well-drained to poor soil in full
sun.
PROPAGATION By seed sown *in situ* in early
autumn or from spring to early summer.
HARVEST Whole plants are cut when flowering
and dried for use in infusions and tinctures.

■ *Eschscholzia californica* (Californian poppy)
Annual with lanceolate, finely cut, blue-green
leaves, 15–20cm (6–8in) long. Yellow to
orange flowers, 5–7cm (2–3in) across, are
followed in summer by slender curved capsules,
7–10cm (3–4in) long. Native to southwestern
N America. ‡ 20–60cm (8–24in), ↔ 15–30cm
(6–12in). ■ 'Alba' has cream flowers; comes
true from seed. ↔ 35cm (14in). 'Inferno'
bears orange-scarlet flowers on bushy plants.
‡ 23–25cm (9–10in). ■ 'Mission Bells' has
double flowers in shades of orange, cream, and
pink. ↔ 38cm (15in). 'Purple Cap' has large
cerise flowers with cream centres. ↔ 20–25cm
(8–10in). 'Rose Chiffon' is compact, with fine,
blue-grey foliage and double, pink, cream-
centred flowers. ■ 'Thai Silk' has fluted, single
or semi-double, bronze-flushed flowers in red,
pink, or orange.
HARDINESS Hardy.
PARTS USED Whole plant.
PROPERTIES A bitter sedative herb that acts as
a diuretic, relieves pain, relaxes spasms, and
promotes perspiration.
MEDICINAL USES Internally for nervous tension,
anxiety, insomnia, and incontinence (especially
in children).
▨▣

Eschscholzia californica 'Alba'

Eschscholzia californica
'Mission Bells'

*Eschscholzia
californica* 'Thai Silk'

EUCALYPTUS
Gum tree

Myrtaceae

Over 600 species of evergreen aromatic trees
and shrubs belong to this genus, which occurs
mainly in Australia. They are among the world's
fastest-growing and tallest trees, recorded at
99m (326ft). Many species are grown for timber
and as ornamentals for their handsome foliage
and patterned bark. Gum trees are rich in
volatile oils, with over 40 different kinds
recorded. The most common oils are: cineole
(eucalyptol) with the typical eucalyptus scent;
citronellal (lemon-scented); piperitone
(peppermint-scented); and pinene, with a
turpentine-like odour. Eucalypts also exude an
oleo-resin, known as kino, containing tannins.
Australian Aboriginals use eucalyptus bark,
kino, and leaves in remedies. Bark decoctions
are used to bathe sores and treat dysentery, and
bark charcoal is considered antiseptic; water
solutions of kino (e.g. of *E. gummifera*) are
used against dysentery and bladder
inflammation. People in N Australia preferred
Melaleuca spp. (see p.273), since northern
eucalypts have relatively low oil contents. In
addition to those described below,
E. polybractea, *E. radiata* var. *australiana*, and
E. smithii are distilled for eucalyptus oil; others,
such as *E. gummifera*, *E. haemastoma*, and
E. racemosa, are sources of kino; the rutin
contained in *E. macrorhyncha* is used to
strengthen capillaries. Only two species yield
perfumery oils: *E. citriodora* is the richest
known source of citronellal; and *E. macarthurii*
is a source of geranyl acetate and eudesmol,
used in perfumery. The leaves of several
species, including *E. mannifera* and

E. viminalis, exude a sweet substance when damaged by insects. This "manna" has a mild laxative effect, as found in the exudate from *Fraxinus ornus* (see p.216). Commercial production of eucalyptus oils began in 1852 in Dandenong, Victoria (Australia), pioneered by Joseph Bosisto, an emigrant from Yorkshire (England). Production of oils from *E. polybractea* (blue mallee) has now increased, as this species has proved more adaptable than *E. dives* to coppice cultivation and mechanized harvesting. In common with all volatile oils, eucalyptus oils are toxic, requiring caution in handling, storage, and use. Oil derived from *E. smithii* may be less irritant to the skin and is often preferred by aromatherapists.

⚠ **WARNING** Subject to legal restrictions in some countries in the form of eucalyptus oil.

CULTIVATION Fertile, well-drained, neutral to acid soil in sun; *E. camaldulensis* thrives in moist to wet soil and shallow water. *Eucalyptus citriodora* and *E. globulus* may be grown as annuals for summer bedding or containers, but do not thrive long-term in pots. Prone to silver leaf, oedema, and psyllids.

PROPAGATION By seed sown in spring or summer at 13–18°C (55–64°F). Cut back in spring only to restrict size or to retain juvenile foliage.

HARVEST Leaves are cut as required and dried for decoctions and infusions, or distilled for oil. Kino is collected from bark incisions and dried for use in pastilles, powders, and tinctures.

⚠ **WARNING** Skin irritant.

▣ *Eucalyptus camaldulensis* (Murray red gum, red gum, red river gum)
Spreading tree with smooth, white to brown or red bark and ovate to broadly lanceolate, grey-green juvenile leaves becoming narrower and more pointed, to 30cm (12in) long, in mature trees. Umbels of 7–11 creamy white flowers appear mainly in summer. Grows near rivers in Australia (except Tasmania). ‡ 20–45m (70–150ft), ↔ 15–35m (50–120ft).

HARDINESS Half hardy.

PARTS USED Leaves, oil, resin (kino).

PROPERTIES An aromatic, astringent, tonic herb that sticks to the teeth and turns the saliva red.

MEDICINAL USES Internally for diarrhoea; externally for sore throats, colds, fevers, sores, and wounds.

▣◐▣

▣ *Eucalyptus citriodora* (lemon-scented gum)
Slender tree with powdery grey to pinkish, peeling bark and rough, green, broadly lanceolate, often peltate juvenile leaves, to 16cm (6in) long, becoming smoother, narrower, and longer in adult specimens. Foliage is strongly lemon-scented. Clusters of creamy white flowers, 2cm (¾in) across, are produced in winter and spring. Native to dry forests, plateaus, and ridges in coastal subtropical Queensland. ‡ 25–50m (80–160ft), ↔ to 25m (80ft).

HARDINESS Min. 5–7°C (41–45°F).

PARTS USED Leaves, oil, resin (kino).

PROPERTIES An aromatic astringent herb that is effective against some bacterial and fungal infections.

Eucalyptus camaldulensis

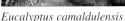

MEDICINAL USES Externally for athlete's foot, dandruff, herpes, candidiasis, infections caused by *Staphylococcus aureus* (such as boils, impetigo, and septicaemia), and as an inhalation for fevers, asthma, and laryngitis.

ECONOMIC USES Lemon-scented oil is used in perfumery, detergents, and insect repellents. Dried leaves are included in potpourris and linen sachets.

▣◐▣◢▣

▣ *Eucalyptus dives* (Australian peppermint, broad-leaved peppermint)
Short-trunked tree with stalkless, heart-shaped, blue-green juvenile leaves becoming thick, shiny, and broadly lanceolate, to 15cm (6in) long, in adult specimens. Small white flowers appear in the axils in summer. Native to open woodland in New South Wales and Victoria (Australia). ‡ 25m (80ft), ↔ 15–20m (50–70ft).

HARDINESS Frost hardy.

PARTS USED Leaves, oil. Volatile oil varies according to chemotype, with either piperitone, phellandrene, cineole (eucalyptol), or thymol predominating.

PROPERTIES An aromatic antiseptic herb that has anti-inflammatory and antiseptic effects. Plants containing mainly piperitone are the most widely used.

MEDICINAL USES Externally for bronchitis, mouth and throat infections, influenza, colds, neuralgia, sciatica, arthritis, and sprains.

ECONOMIC USES Source of phellandrene, and cineole, used in disinfectants, liquid soaps, and germicidal preparations, and piperitone, the base material for manufacture of synthetic menthol and thymol for oral hygiene preparations.

▣◐▣◢

▣ *Eucalyptus globulus* (blue gum, Tasmanian blue gum)
Spreading tree with smooth, creamy white bark, peeling in red flakes, and ovate, often perfoliate, silver-blue juvenile leaves becoming pendent,

Eucalyptus citriodora

Eucalyptus dives

Eucalyptus globulus

green, and lanceolate to sickle-shaped, to 25cm (10in) long, in adult specimens. Solitary, creamy white flowers appear from spring to summer. Native to moist valleys in uplands of New South Wales and Victoria (Australia). ‡ 15–45m (50–150ft), ↔ 10–25m (30–80ft).

HARDINESS Frost hardy

PARTS USED Leaves, oil.

PROPERTIES An aromatic, stimulant, decongestant herb that is expectorant, relaxes spasms, and lowers fever. It is effective against many bacteria, especially *Staphylococci*.

MEDICINAL USES Externally, in inhalations and vapour rubs, for catarrh, bronchitis, sinusitis, colds, and influenza; in liniments, for bruises, sprains, and muscular pains; in ointments, for wounds and abscesses. Excess causes headaches, convulsions, and delirium, and may prove fatal.

ECONOMIC USES Used as a flavouring in pharmaceutical products and in spot removers for oil and grease. An important timber species, used for the keels of ships in the 19th century. Widely planted to dry out swampy ground, notably in Italy and California (USA).

▣◐▣◢

EUCOMMIA
Eucommiaceae

A single species of deciduous tree makes up this Chinese genus. *Eucommia ulmoides* is often grown as an ornamental and curiosity. It is unique as the only hardy, rubber-producing tree and in having leaves that, if gently pulled apart, adhere together by the hair-like strands of latex exuding from the broken veins. The first European to collect *Eucommia* was Dr Augustine Henry, a British physician, who sent herbarium specimens to Kew in 1886. As a herb, it was first described

E

Eucommia ulmoides

in the *Shen Nong Ben Cao Jing* in the 1st
century AD, and is still used for the same
purposes in traditional Chinese medicine.
Research has shown that it contains a resinous
diglucoside with anti-hypertensive effects.
Eucommia is from the Greek *eu*, "good", and
kommi, "thread", referring to the useful rubbery
latex; *ulmoides* means "elm-like".
CULTIVATION Fertile, well-drained soil in sun
or partial shade.
PROPAGATION By seed sown in autumn; by
greenwood cuttings in summer.
HARVEST Bark is harvested in strips, from one
side of the trunk only, in April and May from
trees 15–20 years old, and fermented before
removing inner bark for drying or roasting.

◼ *Eucommia ulmoides* (gutta-percha tree,
hardy rubber tree)
Spreading tree with ovate to elliptic, pointed,
finely toothed leaves, 7–20cm (3–8in) long.
Minute, green, petal-less flowers – males and
females on separate plants – appear before or
with the new leaves in spring, followed on
female plants by one-seeded, winged fruits.
Native to C China. ‡ 12–20m (40–70ft),
↔ 8m (25ft).
HARDINESS Fully hardy.
PARTS USED Inner bark (*du zhong*).
PROPERTIES A diuretic, sedative, analgesic
herb that acts as a tonic for the liver and
kidneys, and lowers blood pressure.
MEDICINAL USES Internally for hypertension,
lumbago, rheumatism, frequent urination
owing to weak kidney energy; also to calm an
overactive foetus and control placental leakage.
CULINARY USES Bark and extracts are used in
tonic soups, wines, and elixirs, especially by
the Cantonese.
▥ ▤ ▧

EUGENIA

Eugenia caryophyllata. See *Syzygium
aromaticum*.

EUODIA

Euodia officinalis. See *Tetradenia ruticarpum*.
Euodia rutaecarpa. See *Tetradenia ruticarpum*.

Euonymus atropurpureus

EUONYMUS
Spindle

Celastraceae

A large and widespread genus of 177 species of
deciduous, semi-evergreen, and evergreen trees,
shrubs, and climbers, found in N America,
Eurasia, and Australia. Many spindles are
grown as ornamentals; some deciduous species
have spectacular autumn colour, with pink to
red foliage and fruits. Several species were
valued by native N Americans, the most
important being *E. atropurpureus*, used for
various ailments, from uterine discomfort to
sore eyes. In the 19th century it became popular
as a heart medicine, following reports of
digitalis-like effects. *Euonymus atropurpureus*
has also found its way into Ayurvedic medicine
as a diuretic, purgative, and anti-pyretic.
CULTIVATION Well-drained soil in sun or partial
shade. Thin out shoots in late winter to maintain
shape. *Euonymus europaeus* is prone to scale
insects and aphids.
PROPAGATION By seed sown when ripe; by
greenwood cuttings in summer. Seed needs
stratifying and is viable for two years.
HARVEST Bark is collected in autumn and dried
for use in decoctions, tablets, and tinctures.
⚠ **WARNING** All parts, especially fruits and
seeds, are harmful if eaten.

Euonymus europaeus

Euonymus europaeus 'Red Cascade'

◼ *Euonymus atropurpureus* (burning bush,
Indian arrow-wood, wahoo)
Deciduous shrubby tree with oblong–ovate,
pointed leaves, to 12cm (5in) long, which turn
yellow in autumn. Purple flowers, to 1cm (½in)
across, appear from spring to summer, followed
by purple-red capsules containing brown seeds
with a scarlet aril. Native to central and eastern
N America. ‡ 2–8m (6–25ft), ↔ 1.2–3m (4–10ft).
HARDINESS Fully hardy.
PARTS USED Bark of stems and roots.
PROPERTIES An acrid bitter herb that
stimulates the gall bladder and circulatory
system, has diuretic and laxative effects, and
acts as a mild cardiac tonic.
MEDICINAL USES Internally for constipation
and skin eruptions associated with liver and gall
bladder dysfunction. Often combined with
Berberis vulgaris (see p.142), *Chionanthus
virginicus* (see p.167), *Pulsatilla vulgaris* (see
p.337), and *Taraxacum officinale* (see p.382)
for liver and gall bladder disorders.
▥ ▨ ▧ ▣

◼ *Euonymus europaeus* (spindle tree)
Deciduous shrub or small tree with smooth
grey bark and ovate–lanceolate, pointed leaves,
3–13cm (1¼–5in) long. Small green flowers
appear in axillary clusters in spring and early
summer, followed by four-lobed, pink capsules
containing orange seeds. ‡ 2–8m (6–25ft),
↔ 1.2–3m (4–10ft). ◼ 'Red Cascade' has rich
autumn colour. ‡ 3m (10ft), ↔ 2.5m (8ft).
HARDINESS Fully hardy.
PARTS USED Bark, root bark.
PROPERTIES A bitter astringent herb that acts
as a diuretic and emetic, and stimulates bile flow.
MEDICINAL USES Internally for liver and gall
bladder complaints. Externally for chilblains,
abscesses, acne, and wounds.
▥ ▨ ▣

EUPATORIUM
Hemp agrimony

Asteraceae

This genus of 40 species of annuals, herbaceous
perennials, subshrubs, and evergreen shrubs
occurs in a wide range of habitats and climatic

zones in Europe, Asia, Africa, N and S America. Originally a large genus of near 1000 species, most have been reclassified in other genera, such as *Ageratina* and *Barlettina*. Hemp agrimonies have rayless, long-stamened flowers; some are ornamental, late-flowering plants for damp garden areas. *Eupatorium purpureum* is an imposing plant for the wild garden or large border. The common name "Joe Pye weed" refers to an Indian who apparently used the plant to cure typhus fever. *Eupatorium cannabinum* has been described in herbals since the 10th century, mainly as a spring tonic and detoxicant. Research has shown that it has immune-stimulant and anti-cancer properties. In the 18th and 19th centuries *E. perfoliatum* was the standard household remedy in N America for coughs and colds, and regarded as a cure-all. The common name "boneset" was given because the herb was also used to treat break-bone or dengue fever, which was once prevalent in southern states. Snake bite was another frequent hazard, for which *E. hyssopifolium* was used. The main species used in traditional Chinese medicine is *E. fortunei*. In addition, *E. lindleyanum* is used for bronchitis and dysentery, and *E. chinense* for colds, diphtheria, and rheumatoid arthritis.
CULTIVATION Moist soil in sun or partial shade. Cut stems almost to ground level in autumn after flowering. *Eupatorium purpureum* prefers alkaline soil. Some species are subject to statutory controls as weeds in parts of Australia.
PROPAGATION By seed sown in spring; by division in spring.
HARVEST Plants are cut when in bud, and dried for use in infusions, liquid extracts, and tinctures. Rhizomes and roots are lifted in autumn, and dried for use in decoctions or tinctures.

◾ *Eupatorium cannabinum* (hemp agrimony) Robust, clump-forming perennial with erect, reddish, downy stems and palmately lobed leaves, to 12cm (5in) across. Mauve-pink to purple or white flowers are borne in dense, flat-topped corymbs, to 10cm (4in) across, from summer to early autumn. Native to Europe. ↕ 30cm–1.5m (1–5ft), ↔ 1.2m (4ft).

Eupatorium cannabinum

Eupatorium cannabinum 'Flore Pleno'

◾ 'Flore Pleno' has double, long-lasting flowers.
HARDINESS Fully hardy.
PARTS USED Whole plant.
PROPERTIES A bitter–sweet, slightly aromatic herb that is diuretic and has a tonic effect, stimulating the immune system and arresting the growth of tumours. It contains pyrrolizidine alkaloids that are toxic to the liver.
MEDICINAL USES Internally for arthritis, rheumatism, feverish colds, and influenza. Excess is purgative and emetic. Combined with other herbs as a tonic for low energy with biliousness or constipation. Externally for ulcers, sores, and as an insect repellent for animals. Used in homeopathic tinctures for influenza.
▨ ▪

Eupatorium fortunei syn. *E. japonicum* var. *fortunei*, *E. stoechadasum* (thoroughwort) Clump-forming perennial with divided, sharply toothed, oppositely arranged leaves. White flowers are borne in corymbs in late summer. Native to Korea, China, and Japan. ↕ 1–1.5m (3–5ft), ↔ 30cm–1m (1–3ft).
HARDINESS Fully hardy.
PARTS USED Whole plant (*pei lan*).
PROPERTIES A tonic herb that acts mainly on the stomach and spleen; considered cooling and drying in traditional Chinese medicine.
MEDICINAL USES Internally for indigestion, nausea and vomiting, diarrhoea, heat stroke, and feverish summer colds. Excess is irritant to the stomach.
▨ ▪

◾ *Eupatorium perfoliatum* (boneset, thoroughwort, feverwort) Clump-forming perennial with erect stems and light green, lanceolate, perfoliate leaves, to 20cm (8in) long. White, often purple-tinged, flowers are borne in large corymbs in summer. Native to SE USA. ↕ 1.5m (5ft), ↔ 30cm–1m (1–3ft).
HARDINESS Fully hardy.
PARTS USED Whole plant.
PROPERTIES A bitter astringent herb that lowers fevers, relieves bronchial congestion and constipation, and stimulates the immune system.
MEDICINAL USES Internally for influenza, colds, acute bronchitis, catarrh, and skin

Eupatorium perfoliatum

diseases. Combined with *Achillea millefolium* (see p.99), *Asclepias tuberosa* (see p.134), *Sambucus nigra* (see p.357), *Zingiber officinale* (see p.411), and/or *Capsicum annuum* (see p.154) for influenza.
▨ ▪

◾ *Eupatorium purpureum* (gravel root, Joe Pye weed, queen of the meadow) Robust, clump-forming perennial with erect stems and whorls of finely toothed, ovate leaves, to 25cm (10in) long, vanilla-scented when crushed. Pink to purple-pink flowers are borne in domed corymbs, 10–15cm (4–6in) across, from summer to early autumn. Native to E USA. ↕ 1.2–3m (4–10ft), ↔ 1m (3ft). 'Album' has white flowers. 'Atropurpureum' has deep purple-pink flowers.
HARDINESS Fully hardy.
PARTS USED Rhizomes, roots.
PROPERTIES A slightly bitter, restorative, cleansing herb that acts especially on the genito-urinary organs and uterus.
MEDICINAL USES Internally for kidney and urinary disorders, including stones, cystitis, and urethritis; for prostate problems (combined with *Lamium album*, see p.250); and for painful menstruation or a history of miscarriage and difficult labour.
▨ ▪

Eupatorium purpureum

EUPHORBIA

Spurge

Euphorbiaceae

A large cosmopolitan genus of about 2000
annuals, biennials, perennials, deciduous and
evergreen shrubs and trees, many of which
are succulent. Many spurges are grown as
ornamentals. They include such familiar plants
as *E. pulcherrima* (poinsettia) and *E. lathyrus*
(caper spurge, mole plant), often seen in herb
gardens, but they are far too toxic for culinary
or medicinal use. Some species are weeds,
subject to statutory control in certain countries,
notably in parts of Australia. All spurges contain
white latex and most are poisonous, being
strongly purgative and containing carcinogenic,
highly irritant, diterpene esters. The Chinese
E. kansui (*gan sui*) is laxative, as is
E. pekinensis, which also has diuretic and anti-
bacterial effects. The Moroccan *E. resinifera*
(euphorbium) is another drastic purgative, now
more or less confined to veterinary medicine.
Euphorbia lathyrus contains a violently purgative
oil similar to croton oil (see *Croton tiglium*,
p.184). *Euphorbia hirta* is ester-free and
regarded as a safe effective herb. In Chinese
medicine the genus is considered incompatible
with liquorice (*Glycyrrhiza uralensis*, see p.227).
CULTIVATION Well-drained to dry, sandy soil
in sun.
PROPAGATION By seed sown in spring at
15–20°C (59–68°F).
HARVEST Plants are cut when flowering and
used fresh for juice, or dried for use in
infusions, liquid extracts, and tinctures.
⚠ **WARNING** All euphorbias are toxic if eaten.
The sap (latex) is a serious skin and eye irritant.

■ *Euphorbia hirta* syn. *E. pilulifera* (asthma
weed, pill-bearing spurge)
Erect or spreading annual with hairy stems and
ovate, oppositely arranged leaves, 2.5–4cm
(1–1½in) long. Insignificant flowers are borne in
dense globose clusters, followed by three-celled,
red-green capsules. Weed of tropics and subtropics.
↕ 20–40cm (8–16in), ↔ 20–30cm (8–12in).
HARDINESS Min. 10–15°C (50–59°F).
PARTS USED Whole plant, juice.

PROPERTIES An acrid, bitter, antiseptic herb
that expels phlegm and relieves spasms.
MEDICINAL USES Internally for asthma,
bronchitis, emphysema, nervous cough, catarrh,
hay fever, and amoebic dysentery. Externally
for burns and warts (juice). Combined with
Grindelia camporum (see p.229) or *Lobelia
inflata* (see p.265) for bronchitis and asthma.
▢ ▨ ▮ ▣

EUPHRASIA

Scrophulariaceae

This cosmopolitan genus includes some 450 semi-
parasitic species. Euphrasias are difficult to
cultivate because of this habit of growth. The
genus is generally considered to be a group of
similar species, sometimes given separate species
status. As a medicinal herb, eyebright may be
derived from *E. officinalis*, *E. brevipila*, or
E. rostkoviana. *Euphrasia officinalis*, a grassland
species, parasitic on *Trifolium pratense* (see
p.393) and *Plantago* spp. (see p.322), as well as
on grasses, is the best known. It was first
recorded as a medicinal herb for "all evils of
the eye" in the 14th century, gaining credibility
through the Doctrine of Signatures: "the purple
and yellow spots and stripes which are upon the
flowers of the eyebright doth very much resemble
the diseases of the eye, as bloodshot, etc., by
which signature it hath been found out that this
herb is effectual for the curing of the same." The
safety and effectiveness of eyebright for eye
problems has not been established. *Euphrasia* is
a translation of the Greek, meaning "good cheer".
CULTIVATION Grows in natural grassland, near
host plants. Tolerates a wide range of soils and
conditions.
PROPAGATION By seed, scattered around host
plants.
HARVEST Plants are cut when flowering and
dried for use in infusions, liquid extracts,
tinctures, and homeopathic preparations.

■ *Euphrasia officinalis* (eyebright)
Variable annual with upright stems and rounded
toothed leaves, usually less than 1cm (½in)
long. Small white flowers, often purple-veined,
with a yellow-marked throat and three-lobed

lower lip, appear in summer. Native to Europe.
↕ 5–30cm (2–12in).
HARDINESS Hardy.
PARTS USED Whole plant.
PROPERTIES A bitter astringent herb that
reduces inflammation and secretion of mucus.
MEDICINAL USES Internally for catarrh,
sinusitis, allergic rhinitis, hay fever, and upper
respiratory tract infections. Excess causes
symptoms such as mental confusion, redness,
itching, and swelling of eyes, dimming of vision,
and photophobia. Externally for conjunctivitis,
eye injuries, herpes, and weeping eczema.
▨ ▮

EURYALE

Euryalaceae/Nymphaeaceae

A genus containing a single species of giant
Asian tropical aquatic, found in deep, still or
slow-moving, fresh water. *Euryale ferox* is
grown as an ornamental in tropical pools, often
as an annual. It was first mentioned in Chinese
medical literature in c.AD1600, and it is also
used in Ayurvedic medicine, where it is known
as *makhanna*. The common name "foxnut"
refers to the edible floury seeds, for which it
has been cultivated in China for 3000 years.
Euryale is named after one of the Three
Gorgons, who had monstrous thorny hair.
CULTIVATION Rich mud in still water, at least
60cm (2ft) deep, in full sun. Seeds are rarely
produced when cultivated under cover.
PROPAGATION By seed sown singly in containers
of aquatic planting medium, submerged just
below the surface, at 21–24°C (70–75°F).
HARVEST Fruits are picked when ripe and used
fresh. Seeds are collected in autumn and used
fresh or dried for culinary purposes, and dried
for decoctions.

Euphorbia hirta

Euphrasia officinalis

Euryale ferox

■ *Euryale ferox* (foxnut, gorgon, *khee sat*, prickly water lily)
Perennial aquatic with a thick rhizome and circular peltate leaves, to 1.5m (5ft) across, puckered and spiny on the upper surface and purple-red beneath. Red or purple to lilac flowers are borne on or below the surface in summer, followed by prickly, berry-like fruits, 7cm (3in) across, containing numerous black seeds. Grows in N India, Bangladesh, China, Japan, and Taiwan. ↔ 3m (10ft) or more.
HARDINESS Min. 5°C (41°F).
PARTS USED Seeds (*qian shi*), fruits.
PROPERTIES A sweet and sour, astringent herb that acts as a spleen and kidney tonic.
MEDICINAL USES Internally for chronic diarrhoea, vaginal discharge, kidney weakness associated with frequent urination, impotence, premature and involuntary ejaculation, and nocturnal emissions.
CULINARY USES Glutinous pulp of fruits is eaten as a cooling tonic. Fresh or dried seeds are pickled, popped, roasted, added to curries and soups, and ground as a source of flour for baking (China).
◩ ▣ ▣ ✐ ▣

EUTREMA

Eutrema wasabi. See *Wasabia japonica*.

EVERNIA

Usneaceae

This cosmopolitan genus consists of about ten species of lichens. Common in areas with an unpolluted atmosphere, *E. prunastri* is an attractive, extremely slow-growing lichen that often occurs naturally in gardens but is difficult to cultivate. In ancient times, it was imported from Greece and Cyprus to Egypt for packing embalmed mummies, and as an ingredient in bread-making. Centuries later, in Europe, it was in great demand for powdering wigs and was described in the *Compendium Aromatorium* by Saladin of Askalon (1137–93). Approximately 9000 tonnes of *E. prunastri* are collected annually, mainly from cork oak and fruit trees in France, the Balkans, and Morocco. Volatile oils in the plant are extracted in benzene and evaporated to a viscous solid, known as oak moss resin or *mousse de chêne*. *Evernia prunastri* is often mixed with the related *Pseudoevernia furfuracea*, which is more aromatic but inferior when used as a perfume fixative. The related *Usnea* spp. (beard lichens) yield usnic acid, a yellow crystalline compound extracted by the pharmaceutical industry for use as an antibiotic.
CULTIVATION Grows mostly on trunks of deciduous trees, mainly oak, sycamore, willow, and alder; also on fences, walls, rocks, and soil. Prefers a neutral substrate. Plants are damaged by sulphur levels above 0.021 p.p.m.
PROPAGATION The ecology and reproductive biology of lichens are complex; little progress has been made in their propagation and cultivation.
HARVEST Plants are collected in dry winter weather for drying and oil extraction.

Evernia prunastri

■ *Evernia prunastri* (oak moss)
Lichen with soft, pendent, antler-shaped branches, which are grey-green above and have white cottony undersurfaces. Pink-brown, spore-producing discs are rare. ↔ 6cm (2½in).
HARDINESS Fully hardy.
PARTS USED Whole plant, oil.
PROPERTIES An aromatic antibiotic herb with lichen acids that inhibit the tuberculosis bacillus.
CULINARY USES Used as a leavening agent for bread, and as a hops substitute in beer.
ECONOMIC USES Mainly as a fixative in perfumes with a mossy note, such as *chypre*, *ambre*, and *fougère*. Extracts are also used for flavouring in the food and beverage industries.
◪ ▣ ✐ ✐

F

FAGARA

Fagara capensis. See *Zanthoxylum capense*.

FAGOPYRUM

Polygonaceae

This genus includes about six species of annuals, native to temperate Eurasia. *Fagopyrum esculentum* (buckwheat) was introduced into Europe from Asia by the Crusaders, hence the common names such as "Saracen corn", *sarrasin*, *grano saraceno*, and *trigo sarraceno*. It is cultivated in parts of Europe, N America, C Asia, and Japan, as a grain crop, food plant, and cover for game birds. The seeds mature over a long period, giving a relatively low yield; this is offset by the fact that buckwheat is fast-growing, even on poor acid soils, and is a useful grain crop in areas of subsistence farming. It is popular among organic gardeners as a green manure that enriches the soil and attracts hoverflies, whose larvae eat large quantities of aphids. The nutlets vary in colour according to the cultivar; they contain 11 per cent protein. All parts, especially the flowers (4 per cent), are rich

Fagopyrum esculentum

in rutin, a flavonoid glycoside also found in *Ruta graveolens* (see p.353) and *Citrus* spp. (see p.171), which has beneficial effects on the blood vessels. Buckwheat yields a dark brown, strongly flavoured honey. *Fagopyrum tataricum* (Tatarian buckwheat) produces small seeds that are ground to make a flour, used in France for buckwheat crepes, known as *ployes de boquite*.
CULTIVATION Well-drained, sandy soil in sun.
PROPAGATION By seed sown in spring.
HARVEST Leaves and flowers are collected as flowering begins and dried for infusions and tablets. Seeds are harvested when ripe and dried for use whole or ground. Buckwheat products are stored in the dark, because their properties deteriorate rapidly on exposure to light.

■ *Fagopyrum esculentum* (buckwheat, soba)
Slender annual with upright, often red-tinged stems and broadly triangular leaves, to 7cm (3in) long. Small, scented, pink to white flowers are produced in clusters in summer, followed by angular brown nutlets, about 6mm (¼in) long. ↕ 20–60cm (8–24in), ↔ 10–23cm (4–9 in). 'Kaneko' is a Japanese heirloom variety, prized for making noodles. ↕ 1m (3ft). 'Mancan' is a high-yielding, white-flowered Canadian cultivar that matures in 80 days.
HARDINESS Hardy.
PARTS USED Leaves, flowers, seeds.
PROPERTIES A bitter but pleasant-tasting herb that controls bleeding, dilates blood vessels, reduces capillary permeability, and lowers blood pressure.
MEDICINAL USES Internally for varicose veins, chilblains, spontaneous bruising, frostbite, radiation damage, retinal haemorrhage, and hypertension. Combined with vitamin C and/or *Equisetum arvense* (see p.203) to strengthen capillaries. May cause light-sensitive dermatitis.
CULINARY USES Hulled grain (groats) is eaten in breakfast cereals, made into *kasha* (Poland, Russia) and *polenta* (N Italy), and brewed into beer and spirits. Flour is used to make pancakes, noodles, and bread; also as a thickener for soups and gravy. Buckwheat honey is a traditional ingredient of Jewish honey wine, and gingerbread (*pains d'épice*) in France.
▣ ✐ ▣ ▣ ✐

F

FAGUS
Beech

Fagaceae

There are ten species of deciduous trees in this genus, which occurs widely in northern temperate regions. *Fagus sylvatica* is the most adaptable species in cultivation and has numerous cultivars, in various habits, leaf shapes, and colours. It is one of the most successful, large trees for alkaline soils; it thrives just as well in acidic conditions. When grown as a hedge, the leaves remain throughout the winter, but change colour from green to brown. Beech nuts, known as beech mast when fallen, were once an important food for pigs, forming part of the rights of pannage (the right to pasture pigs in a forest). They have been eaten in times of famine and roasted as a coffee substitute, but contain several toxins that make it inadvisable to consume large amounts. Beech wood is the main source of the creosote used for medicinal purposes, which is distilled from wood tar. Medicinal creosote is quite different from creosote made from coal tar, which is used to preserve wood. The active ingredient in beech creosote is guaiacol, which is also extracted from *Guaiacum officinale* (see p.229).
CULTIVATION Well-drained, moist to dry, acid to alkaline soil in sun or partial shade. For hedging, space 45–60cm (18–24in) apart. Specimen trees require no pruning. Hedges should have the top quarter removed after planting, and again in the first summer. Thereafter, trim to shape in summer. Trees may be attacked by various fungal diseases, beech scale, aphid, or weevils. Foliage may be damaged by late frosts and by scorching.
PROPAGATION By seed sown in autumn, or stratified and sown in spring (species only); by grafting in midwinter.
HARVEST Wood is cut and distilled for tar and creosote, from which guaiacol is then extracted. Seeds are collected when ripe, peeled, and pressed for oil, leaving a poisonous residue. Young leaves are gathered in spring.

■ *Fagus sylvatica* (European beech)
Large tree with smooth grey bark and elliptic–ovate, shiny, toothed leaves, to 10cm (4in) long,

Fagus sylvatica

Fagus sylvatica Atropurpurea Group

turning yellow and golden-brown in autumn. Inconspicuous flowers are borne in spring, followed by brown, four-valved, woody fruits, clad in blunt spines, which contain usually two shiny brown nuts. ↕25–40m (80–130ft), ↔15m (50ft). ▣Atropurpurea Group (copper beech) refers to purple-leaved beeches that arise from seed-raised plants. Outstanding seedlings have cultivar names such as 'Riversii', which has dark purple leaves, and 'Rohanii', with deeply cut, purple leaves. ▣'Dawyck' (Dawyck beech) has a neat columnar habit, good for confined spaces. Golden and purple Dawyck beeches are also available. ↕30m (100ft), ↔7m (22ft). ▣var. *heterophylla* 'Aspleniifolia' (fern-leafed beech) has slender leaves, cut into narrow lobes. 'Zlatia' has yellow new leaves, turning green in summer.
HARDINESS Fully hardy.
PARTS USED Creosote (from wood), oil (from seeds), young leaves.
PROPERTIES An antiseptic, stimulating,

Fagus sylvatica 'Dawyck'

Fagus sylvatica var. *heterophylla* 'Aspleniifolia'

expectorant herb with a burning taste and penetrating odour.
MEDICINAL USES Internally for chronic bronchitis and upper respiratory tract infections; externally for skin diseases (creosote).
CULINARY USES Oil is used in salads and cooking, and made into beechnut butter. Wood is used for smoking foods, notably Westphalian and Prague hams, and in ageing beers. Young leaves are eaten in salads and made into liqueur.
▨ ▨ ▨ ▨ ▨

FALLOPIA
Fo ti

Polygonaceae

A genus of about seven species of rhizomatous, climbing or scrambling perennials found in northern temperate regions. The best-known species is the rampant climber *F. baldschuanica* (Russian vine). *Fallopia multiflora* is similar in appearance but is less vigorous and less hardy; care should nevertheless be taken when siting it in the herb garden. It develops an extensive root system with tubers weighing up to 2.7kg (6lb). This species is a major Chinese tonic herb with a long history of use, first described in medical literature in AD713. One of its Chinese names, *he shou wu*, "black-haired mister", alludes to its fame as a hair restorative. It is also popular in Japan, where it is known as *kashuu*.
CULTIVATION Rich, moist, sandy soil in sun. Protect from severe or prolonged frost. Cut back to 30cm (12in) above ground level in spring. Aphids may attack new growth.
PROPAGATION By seed sown in spring; by softwood or semi-ripe cuttings in summer; by division of tubers in early spring. Roots easily in water.
HARVEST Tubers are collected from plants 3–4 years old in spring or autumn, and sometimes boiled before drying and slicing for use in decoctions; often decocted with black beans or yellow wine.

Fallopia multiflora syn. *Polygonum multiflorum* (Chinese cornbind, flowery knotweed)
Deciduous twining climber with tuberous

rhizomes, red stems when young, and light green, ovate leaves, to 10cm (4in) long. Small, white or pink-tinted flowers are produced in slender panicles, 20–24cm (8–10in) long, in autumn, followed by three-winged fruits. Native to China, Taiwan, Japan, and N Vietnam. ‡ 7–10m (22–30ft).

HARDINESS Fully hardy (borderline).

PARTS USED Roots (*he shou wu, fo ti*), stems (*shou wou teng*).

PROPERTIES A bitter–sweet, astringent, slightly warming herb that has a tonic rejuvenative effect on the liver and the reproductive, urinary, and circulatory systems. It also lowers blood sugar and cholesterol levels, clears toxins, and is effective against many bacterial infections.

MEDICINAL USES Internally for menstrual and menopausal complaints, weak kidney and liver energy, constipation in the elderly, swollen lymph glands, and high cholesterol (roots), insomnia, and neurasthenia (stems). Externally for bleeding wounds and sores (roots), and ringworm (roots and stems). Roots are combined, in Chinese medicine, with *Panax ginseng* (see p.300) and *Angelica polymorpha* var. *sinensis* (see p.122) as a tonic, known as *shou wu chih*. Excess may cause skin rash and numbness of the extremities.

CULINARY USES Roots are important in China as an ingredient of tonic soups, porridges, and wines.

▨ ▧ ▣ ◪

FERULA
Giant fennel

Apiaceae

This genus consists of 172 species of robust perennials, found from the Mediterranean to C Asia. Although known as giant fennels, because of their similarity in appearance to *Foeniculum* spp. (see p.214), many have an unpleasant smell. *Ferula assa-foetida* is probably the most foul-smelling of all herbs, with a sulphurous odour that surprisingly, in judicious quantities, gives a pleasant flavour to foods. Airtight storage is necessary to avoid contamination of surroundings. Both *F. assa-foetida* and *F. gummosa* have been important since ancient times for their gum resins; the former is also much used in Ayurvedic medicine. *Ferula assa-foetida* is also a very effective medicinal herb, much used in the Ayurvedic tradition. A similar gum resin is also collected from related species, such as *F. rubicaulis*. The pleasant-smelling *F. sumbul* (musk root) is used like *F. gummosa* in incense, and to treat hysteria. *Ferula communis*, which is widely grown as an ornamental, also yields a gum resin, used in N Africa to treat joint pains, skin diseases, and rheumatism.

CULTIVATION Rich, well-drained soil in sun.

PROPAGATION By seed sown in deep containers when ripe.

HARVEST *Ferula assa-foetida* is cut down as it begins to flower, and the gum resin is scraped from the top of the root. Slices are removed and scraped until the root is exhausted. Stems and roots of *F. gummosa* are incised to collect gum

Ferula assa-foetida

resin during the growing season. Resins are formed into lumps, which are processed into paste, pills, powders, or tinctures.

■ *Ferula assa-foetida* (asafoetida, devil's dung, food-of-the-gods)
Large perennial with a thick rootstock and large, finely divided leaves, to 35cm (14in) long, which have an unpleasant, garlic-like odour. Tiny yellow flowers are produced in a compact umbel in summer, usually in the fifth year, after which the plant dies. Native to coastal regions and rocky areas in Iran. ‡ 2m (6ft), ↔ 1.5m (5ft).

HARDINESS Frost hardy.

PARTS USED Gum resin (*e wei*).

PROPERTIES A pungent herb that acts mainly on the digestive system, strengthening and cleansing the gastrointestinal tract. It relieves pain and spasms, encourages productive coughing, and has hypotensive and anti-coagulant effects.

MEDICINAL USES Internally for indigestion, flatulence, colic, constipation, intestinal worms, dysentery, whooping cough, bronchitis, or convulsive illnesses. Externally for painful joints.

CULINARY USES Ground resin is used in minute amounts to flavour legume dishes, vegetables, sauces, and pickles, especially in Indian cuisine.

ECONOMIC USES An ingredient of Worcestershire sauce.

▣ ▣ ◪ ◪

Ferula gummosa syn. *F. galbaniflua* (galbanum)
Perennial with solid stems and divided, grey-green, hairy leaves, to 30cm (1ft) long, which smell like celery. Tiny yellow flowers are borne in umbels in spring, followed by thin flat seeds. Native to C Iran, Turkey, and S Russia. ↔ 1m (3ft).

HARDINESS Fully hardy.

PARTS USED Gum resin.

PROPERTIES A bitter, stimulant, antiseptic herb that is expectorant and anti-inflammatory, relieves indigestion, and reduces spasms.

MEDICINAL USES Internally for bronchitis, asthma, and minor digestive complaints. Externally for ulcers, boils, wounds, abscesses, and skin disorders.

ECONOMIC USES A perfume fixative and ingredient of incense.

▣ ▣ ◪

FICUS
Fig

Moraceae

A large genus of about 800 species of tropical and subtropical, mainly evergreen trees, shrubs, lianas, epiphytes, and hemi-epiphytes. Many are grown as ornamentals for their foliage, and a number have delicious fruits, though only *F. carica* is cultivated to any extent for this purpose. The flowers of figs are completely hidden within a round to pear-shaped, fleshy receptacle, with a tiny opening to the outside that admits pollinating wasps. *Ficus carica* has been cultivated since earliest times. It was a major crop in ancient Greece, and 29 cultivars were later described by Pliny (AD23–79), including 'Kadota', still grown today. Most figs are self-fertile, but Smyrna types require pollen from a "caprifig" tree, a process known as "caprification". The fig was sacred to the Romans, having sheltered the wolf that suckled Romulus and Remus. The fruits are important as food and medicine, containing laxative substances, flavonoids, sugars, vitamins A and C, acids, and enzymes.

CULTIVATION Well-drained, neutral to alkaline soil in sun. Figs thrive in containers. A mature tree needs only 1cu.m (1.3cu.yd) of soil, and in the open ground it will fruit better if confined in a pit lined with bricks or cement and the base filled with rubble. Shorten and thin out shoots in early spring to maintain an open compact bush. Harder pruning is needed in cool climates to encourage well-ripened shoots. Shoots may be damaged by coral spot and *Botrytis*. Ripening fruits are often attacked by birds and wasps. Plants under cover may be affected by scale insect, mealybug, and spider mite.

PROPAGATION Sow seed in spring at 15–21°C (59–70°F); by semi-ripe or leaf-bud cuttings in spring or summer; by rooted suckers in winter.

HARVEST Fruits are picked when ripe and used fresh or dried. For medicinal use, they are soaked or made into an elixir.

⚠ **WARNING** Skin irritant in sunlight. Skin allergen. Sap is a serious eye irritant.

Ficus carica

F

Ficus carica 'Brown Turkey'

▣ *Ficus carica* (fig)
Deciduous small tree or large spreading shrub
with palmately lobed leaves, to 20cm (8in) long,
and pear-shaped fruits, 5–8cm (2–3in) long,
which ripen green, purple, or brown. Native to
W Asia and E Mediterranean. ‡10m (30ft),
↔ 4m (12ft). ▣ 'Brown Turkey' is early and
prolific, with large brown fruits best eaten fresh.
'Calimyrna' is a Smyrna type that bears large
golden fruits, good for drying. It is an heirloom
Turkish cultivar, now grown commercially in
California. 'Ischia' syn. 'White Ischia' is dwarf,
with small, green-white, thin-skinned fruits,
good for preserves; ideal for pot culture. ‡↔ 5m
(15ft). 'Kadota' syn. 'Dottato' is a very ancient
cultivar with thick-skinned, golden-green,
almost seedless fruits, ideal for canning. 'Royal
Vineyard' syn. 'Drap d'Or' is a San Pedro type
that produces bronze fruits with few seeds, ideal
for crystallized and glacé fruits.
HARDINESS Fully hardy to frost hardy.
PARTS USED Fruits, leaves, sap.
PROPERTIES A sweet laxative herb that
soothes irritated tissues.
MEDICINAL USES Internally for constipation,
sore throat, cough, bronchial infections, and
inflammation of the trachea. Externally for
haemorrhoids, sore eyes, corns, and warts (sap).
CULINARY USES Fruits are eaten raw or stewed,
candied, made into jam, wine, and liqueurs, and
used to flavour coffee. Sap is used to coagulate
milk for making cheese.
▨ ▱ ▢ ▰ ▱

FILAGINELLA
Filaginella uliginosa. See *Gnaphalium
uliginosum*.

FILIPENDULA
Meadowsweet

Rosaceae

A genus of about ten species of rhizomatous
perennials, found mostly in moist or boggy soils
throughout northern temperate regions. Several
species are popular ornamentals, especially for
waterside planting. *Filipendula ulmaria*
(meadowsweet) has an aromatic rootstock and the

Filipendula ulmaria

foliage yields an aroma of wintergreen when
crushed. The common name derives from
"meadwort", meaning a herb ("wort") used to
flavour mead and beer, not from the plant's
habitat in meadows. Meadowsweet was one of
the three most sacred herbs of the Druids, the
others being *Mentha aquatica* (water mint, see
p.276) and *Verbena officinalis* (vervain, see
p.402). It was also important as a strewing herb
in medieval times. In common with many other
plants, meadowsweet contains salicylates,
aspirin-like compounds that reduce
inflammation and relieve pain. Unlike aspirin,
which is highly irritant to the lining of the
digestive tract, causing gastric ulceration, plant
salicylates are bound with other substances that
act together to protect and heal the tissues. This is
a good example of a synergistic effect, whereby
the whole herb has different properties from
isolated constituents. Formerly included in the
genus *Spiraea*, it was from *Filipendula ulmaria*,
and not from willow, as is often stated, that the
glycoside salicin was first isolated in 1838. This
substance was later (in 1899) synthesized as
acetylsalicylic acid, "aspirin", a name derived
from the plant's older name, *Spiraea ulmaria*.
CULTIVATION Rich, moisture-retentive to wet
soil in sun or partial shade. Dislikes acid soil;
prone to powdery mildew in dry conditions.
PROPAGATION By seed sown in autumn and
left to over-winter, or in spring at 10–13°C
(50–55°F); by division in autumn or spring; by
root cuttings from late winter to early spring.
HARVEST Plants are cut as flowering begins and
dried for use in tablets, infusions, decoctions,
liquid extracts, and tinctures. Flowers may be
gathered separately to make infusions.

▣ *Filipendula ulmaria* (meadowsweet, queen of
the meadow)
Clump-forming perennial with irregularly
pinnate, toothed, deeply veined leaves divided

Filipendula ulmaria 'Aurea'

Filipendula ulmaria
'Flore Pleno'

Filipendula ulmaria
'Variegata'

into 2–5 pairs of leaflets, to 8cm (3in) long.
Creamy white, almond-scented flowers are
borne in dense corymbs in summer. Native to
Europe and W Asia. ‡ 60cm–1.2m (2–4ft),
↔ 60cm (2ft). ▣ 'Aurea' has yellow new foliage.
‡ 30–45cm (12–18in), ↔ 30cm (12in). ▣ 'Flore
Pleno' has long-lasting, double flowers.
▣ 'Variegata' has leaves irregularly splashed
with yellow, fading to cream in summer.
HARDINESS Fully hardy.
PARTS USED Whole plant, flowers.
PROPERTIES An astringent, aromatic, antacid
herb that heals, soothes, and relieves pain,
especially in the joints and digestive tract. It is
effective against organisms causing diphtheria,
dysentery, and pneumonia.
MEDICINAL USES Internally for hyperacidity,
heartburn, gastritis, and peptic ulcers, for which
meadowsweet is among the most effective of
plant remedies. Also for diarrhoea in children,
dysentery, rheumatic and joint pains, influenza,
and cystitis. Combined with *Althaea officinalis*
(see p.117) and *Melissa officinalis* (see p.275)
for gastric complaints. Not given to patients
hypersensitive to salicylates (aspirin).
CULINARY USES Flowers are preserved as syrup
or used to flavour stewed fruits.
ECONOMIC USES Flowers and leaves are used
to flavour herbal beers and liqueurs and non-
alcoholic herbal drinks, such as Norfolk Punch.
▣ ▨ ▰ ▱ ▱

FOENICULUM
Fennel

Apiaceae

The single species of biennial or perennial in
this European genus is found on wasteland and
in dry sunny places, especially in coastal areas.
Fennel is an ornamental plant that has been
cultivated as a vegetable and a herb since

Classical times. Under Charlemagne (742–814) it spread into N and C Europe, being grown on the imperial farms. All parts are aromatic, with an anise-like scent and flavour, which is dependent on the proportions of its main constituents: anethole, which has a sweet anise aroma; and bitter-tasting fenchone and estragole. These vary according to strain and region; sweet, or Roman, fennel predominates in Mediterranean regions and the less pleasant bitter, or wild, fennel is most common in C Europe and Russia. The seeds were eaten in medieval times as a flavouring, and during Lent to allay hunger.

CULTIVATION Light, well-drained, neutral to alkaline soil in full sun. *Foeniculum vulgare* is not reliably hardy in areas with cold wet winters; var. *dulce* needs rich, light soil, a warm position, and ample moisture to produce compact "bulbs" that are earthed up as they develop. The flowers attract beneficial insects, such as hoverflies, parasitic wasps, and tachinid flies, which prey on garden pests. Fennel should not be planted near beans, kohlrabi, or tomatoes, as it is said to affect their growth adversely, and also that of *Coriandrum sativum* (see p.180). Fennel and *Anethum graveolens* (dill, see p.121) should not be grown close together since hybridization produces seedlings with an indeterminate flavour. Subject to statutory control as a weed in some countries, notably in parts of Australia.

PROPAGATION By seed sown in spring at 13–18°C (55–64°F); by division in early spring; var. *dulce* is grown as a half-hardy annual. 'Purpureum' comes true from seed. Fennel self-sows freely in light soils.

HARVEST Leaves are picked for use at any time during the growing season; leaf bases are most tender in spring. Stems for use in cooking are cut as required. Roots are lifted in autumn and dried for use in decoctions. Unripe seeds are collected in summer for using fresh. Ripe seeds are harvested before they fall by cutting the seed heads and upturning into a paper bag for drying; they are used whole, ground, or distilled for oil.

■ *Foeniculum vulgare* (fennel)
Tall, clump-forming biennial or perennial with deep roots, erect hollow stems, and glossy pinnate leaves, to 30cm (12in) long, divided into thread-like leaflets. Tiny, dull yellow flowers are produced in umbels in summer, followed by ovoid, grey-brown seeds, 6mm (¼in) long. Native to S Europe; naturalized in N Europe, N America, Australia, and elsewhere. ‡ 2m (6ft), ↔ 45cm (18in). ■ var. *dulce* syn. var. *azoricum* (finocchio, Florence fennel, sweet fennel) is a smaller plant with bulbous stalk bases. ‡ 60cm (24in), ↔ 45cm (18in). 'Mammoth' is a slow-bolting Florence fennel, best sown in autumn. 'Perfection' is a fast-growing Florence fennel, developed for northern climates. ■ 'Purpureum' (bronze fennel) has deep brown foliage and is slightly hardier than the species. ■ 'Smokey' is a superior bronze fennel with a sweet, liquorice-like flavour.

HARDINESS Fully hardy to half hardy.
PARTS USED Leaves, stems, roots, seeds, oil.
PROPERTIES A sweet, aromatic, diuretic herb that relieves digestive problems, increases milk

flow, relaxes spasms, and reduces inflammation.
MEDICINAL USES Internally for indigestion, wind, colic, and insufficient lactation (seeds), urinary disorders (root). Externally as a mouthwash or gargle for gum disease and sore throat. Combines with *Chamaemelum nobile* (see p.165), *Filipendula ulmaria* (see p.214), *Geranium maculatum* (see p.223), and *Mentha* × *piperita* (see p.277) for digestive problems, and with *Arctostaphylos uva-ursi* (see p.127) for cystitis. Oil is combined with oils of *Eucalyptus globulus* (see p.207) and *Thymus vulgaris* (see p.390), and diluted with vegetable oil as a rub for bronchial congestion; also added to laxative preparations to prevent griping and to "gripe water" for babies: not given to pregnant women.
CULINARY USES Leaves are eaten in salads and as a garnish and flavouring, especially with snails, olives, and fish dishes, such as *pasta con le sarde* (Sicily). Leaf bases, especially of var. *dulce*, are eaten raw in salads (as *cartucci* in Italy) or cooked as a vegetable. Whole, cracked, or ground seeds are used to flavour bread, biscuits, sausages (notably *finocchiona*, an Italian salami), and stuffings. Flower heads are used to flavour capers. Dried stems are used in barbecuing fish. Seeds or leaves are used to make herb tea.
ECONOMIC USES Fennel oil is used as a flavouring in the food industry, and in liqueurs, such as *Fenouillette* and *Sambuca*; also in toothpastes, soaps, air fresheners and perfumes.
⬛◻▨▧▨◼✎✎

Foeniculum vulgare

Foeniculum vulgare
var. *dulce*

Foeniculum vulgare
'Purpureum'

Foeniculum vulgare
'Smokey'

FORSYTHIA
Oleaceae

Seven species of mainly deciduous shrubs make up this genus, which occurs in E Asia, with a single species in SE Europe (Albania). Forsythia was introduced to cultivation in the 19th century and rapidly became popular for its spring display of yellow flowers. *Forsythia suspensa* was first described scientifically in 1784 as *Ligustrum suspensum*. It is a familiar garden shrub and a parent of *Forsythia* × *intermedia*, one of the most widely planted of all shrubs. This species also has an extremely long history as a medicinal herb, being mentioned in some of the very earliest Chinese medical texts, which date back to at least 2000BC. *Forsythia viridissima*, the other parent of *F.* × *intermedia*, is also used as a source of fruits for the drug *lian qiao*. *Forsythia* is named after William Forsyth (1737–1804), who was a gardener at Kensington Palace, London.

CULTIVATION Most soils in sun or partial shade. Remove old wood after flowering and trim vigorous shoots to shape. Cut back wall-trained plants of *F. suspensa* and its cultivars to within one or two buds of the old wood after flowering.
PROPAGATION By seed sown in spring after stratifying for 60 days; by greenwood cuttings in late spring or early summer; by semi-ripe cuttings in late summer.
HARVEST Unripe fruits ("green" forsythia or *qing lian qiao*) are collected in late August or early September, parboiled, and then sun-dried. Ripe fruits ("yellow/old" forsythia, *lian qiao*) are harvested when ripe and dried for use in decoctions.

■ *Forsythia suspensa* (golden bells, weeping forsythia)
Deciduous, upright or arching shrub with ovate, sometimes trilobed or trifoliate, toothed leaves, 5–10cm (2–4in) long. Bright yellow flowers, 2–3cm (1–1¼in) across, appear in axillary clusters in spring, followed by woody beaked fruits. Native to temperate regions of China. ‡↔ 2.5–3.5m (8–10ft). ■ f. *atrocaulis* has dark maroon young stems, purplish new leaves, and pale yellow flowers. 'Nymans' is a sport of f. *atrocaulis* with larger, more open flowers.

Forsythia suspensa

F

Forsythia suspensa f. *atrocaulis*

HARDINESS Fully hardy.
PARTS USED Fruits (*lian qiao*).
PROPERTIES A bitter astringent herb that
stimulates the nervous system, heart, and gall
bladder, and is diuretic and anti-inflammatory.
It also lowers fevers and clears bacterial
infections, especially those that cause pus. The
vitamin P content strengthens capillaries.
MEDICINAL USES Internally for acute
infectious diseases (such as mumps and
erysipelas), tonsillitis, urinary tract infection,
septic sores and abscesses, allergic rashes, and
retinal haemorrhage. Often combined with
Lonicera japonica (see p.266).

FRAGARIA
Strawberry

Rosaceae

This genus contains about 12 species of low-
growing, stoloniferous perennials, widely
distributed in grassy woods and hedgerows in
northern temperate regions and Chile. Alpine
strawberries are cultivars of *F. vesca*; they have
smaller, more aromatic fruits on bushier plants
than the species, and lack runners, making neat
plants that are good for edging and containers.
The garden strawberry *F.* × *ananassa* was
developed during the 18th century by crossing
the American species *F. chiloensis* and
F. virginiana. Strawberries of various kinds
have always been a popular source of household
remedies. Both roots and leaves contain tannins.
Culpeper regarded strawberries as a cooling
remedy for "wheals and other breakings forth
of hot and sharp humours in the face and hands
and to take away any redness in the face, or
spots, or other deformities in the skin, and to

make it clear and smooth" (*The English
Physician Enlarged*, 1653).
CULTIVATION Rich, neutral to alkaline soil in
sun or partial shade. Plants deteriorate after a
few years and need replacing.
PROPAGATION By seed sown in spring at
13–18°C (55–64°F); by separation of plantlets.
HARVEST Leaves are gathered in early summer
and dried for use in infusions. Roots are lifted
in autumn and dried for use in decoctions.
Fruits are picked in summer and used fresh.

▣ *Fragaria vesca* (wild strawberry)
Rosette-forming perennial with long runners,
rooting at the nodes, and trifoliate leaves with
ovate toothed leaflets, to 4cm (1½in) long. White,
five-petalled flowers, to 2cm (¾in) across, with
yellow centres, appear in spring and summer,
followed by bright red, ovoid fruits, 1cm (⅜in)
long, which have seeds embedded in the skin.
Native to Europe, W Asia, and N America.
‡ 25–30cm (10–12in), ↔ indefinite. 'Alexandria'
syn. 'Baron Solemacher Improved' is disease-
resistant and high-yielding, with large, richly
flavoured fruits. ‡ 20–25cm (8–10in). ▣ 'Fructu
Albo' has creamy white fruits that taste the
same as red-fruited varieties but are reputedly
less attractive to birds. ▣ 'Multiplex' has double
flowers, numerous runners, and small red fruits.
'Pineapple Crush' is compact and productive,
bearing large, pale yellow fruits with a pineapple-
strawberry flavour. 'Rügen' has deep red, richly
flavoured fruits over a long period. 'Variegata'
has cream-variegated, grey-green leaves.
HARDINESS Fully hardy.
PARTS USED Leaves, roots, fruits.
PROPERTIES A cooling, astringent, tonic herb,
with mild diuretic and laxative effects, that
improves digestive function and benefits skin.

Fragaria vesca

Fragaria vesca
'Fructu Albo'

Fragaria vesca
'Multiplex'

MEDICINAL USES Internally for diarrhoea,
digestive upsets, and gout (leaves, roots).
Externally for sunburn, skin blemishes, and
discoloured teeth (fruit juice).
CULINARY USES Leaves are included in
blended herb teas. Fruits are eaten fresh, added
to summer drinks, and made into desserts, juice,
jam, syrup, and wine.

FRANGULA
Frangula alnus. See *Rhamnus frangula*.

FRAXINUS
Ash

Oleaceae

About 65 species of mostly deciduous trees
make up this genus, occurring in woodland
throughout northern temperate regions. Most
ashes are fast-growing and tolerate a range of
conditions. They have pinnate leaves and
inconspicuous flowers, with the exception of the
so-called "flowering ashes". These include a
number of ornamental species, such as *F. ornus*
(manna ash), that produce panicles of showy
white flowers. The common name "manna ash"
refers to the sugary sap that oozes from the bark
when the tree is tapped, and granulates as
"manna". In Italy manna has been collected
from *F. ornus*, mainly grown in plantations in
Sicily, since the 15th century. The word
"manna" has been used since biblical times to
describe the sweet exudates of various plants,
but in 1927 an Italian law reserved the name
for the product of the manna ash and defined
its constituents. Other ashes with medicinal
properties include *F. excelsior* (common ash),
a laxative, anti-inflammatory herb, once taken
for rheumatism and arthritis, and *F. bungeana*
(northern ash), which is similarly anti-
inflammatory and also diuretic and analgesic,
controlling bacterial infections and coughs.
CULTIVATION Well-drained, moist, neutral to
alkaline soil, in an open position.
PROPAGATION By seed sown in autumn or
spring, stratified for 2–3 months over winter.
HARVEST Manna is obtained from trees aged
eight years or more, with trunks at least 7.5cm
(3in) across. A series of slanting incisions is
made on alternate sides of the trunk during
warm dry weather in summer and the exudate
scraped off the surface when solidified.
⚠ **WARNING** Contact may cause skin or
systemic allergic reactions.

▣ *Fraxinus ornus* (manna ash)
Small deciduous tree with a rounded crown,
smooth grey bark, and pinnately divided leaves,
to 20cm (8in) long. Creamy white, heavily
scented flowers are produced in large panicles
in late spring. Native to S Europe and SW Asia.
‡↔ 15–20m (50–60ft).
HARDINESS Fully hardy.
PARTS USED Sap.
PROPERTIES A sweet, mildly laxative herb that
soothes irritated tissues.

Fraxinus ornus

MEDICINAL USES Internally, dissolved in water, as a gentle laxative for children and pregnant women. Also added to other laxatives.
ECONOMIC USES A source of mannitol, used as a sweetener in sugar-free preparations and as an anti-caking agent.

FRITILLARIA
Fritillary

Liliaceae

A genus of about 100 species of bulbous perennials, found in a wide range of habitats throughout northern temperate zones. Most species flower in spring and become dormant during summer. They range in size from diminutive alpines to the rugged *F. imperialis* (crown imperial), a species from W Asia that reaches 1m (3ft) and has expectorant effects. Several species are used medicinally in China. Fritillary bulbs gathered from the wild or grown for medicinal use are referred to as *bei mu*. They include *F. cirrhosa* (*chuan bei mu*), which has similar properties to *F. thunbergii*, though the latter is used for more acute conditions. The genus name *Fritillaria* derives from the Latin *fritillus*, "dice box", referring to the squarish flowers and spotted markings.
CULTIVATION Well-drained, fertile soil in sun. Bulbs are best planted on their sides or surrounded by sand or grit.
PROPAGATION By seed sown when ripe, which germinates the following spring; by bulbils or offsets of mature bulbs when dormant.
HARVEST Bulbs are lifted in summer, and dried for decoctions and powder.
⚠ **WARNING** Most fritillaries are toxic if eaten.

◨ *Fritillaria thunbergii* syn. *F. verticillata* var. *thunbergii*
Bulbous perennial with opposite, alternate, or whorled, linear leaves, to 15cm (6in) long. Creamy white, bell-shaped, nodding flowers, to 3.5cm (1⅜in) long, faintly patterned green, appear in spring. Native to C China. ‡ 60cm (24in), ↔ 10–12cm (4–5in).
HARDINESS Fully hardy.

Fritillaria thunbergii

PARTS USED Bulbs (*zhe bei mu*).
PROPERTIES A sweet pungent herb that controls coughs, is expectorant, relaxes bronchial spasms, and lowers fever and blood pressure.
MEDICINAL USES Internally for coughs, bronchitis, tonsillitis, pneumonia, feverish and respiratory symptoms of acute infections, abscesses, tumours of the thyroid and lymph glands, breast, or lungs. Excess causes breathing difficulties and heart failure. For use only by qualified practitioners.

FUCUS
Wrack

Fucaceae

This genus of six species of marine algae is found widely in shallow waters and on shores in the northern hemisphere, where it often forms a distinct zone. *Fucus vesiculosus* (bladderwrack) has conspicuous air bladders, arranged in groups of two or three along the fronds to give buoyancy. The common name "wrack" is derived from the same source as "wreck", meaning something that has been washed ashore. Bladderwrack is an important seaweed manure, soil conditioner, and high-potash fertilizer, especially for potatoes. It also has a reputation for being a food supplement that improves the condition of skin and hair, and encourages weight loss by stimulating the thyroid gland. *Fucus serratus* (toothed wrack) is used similarly, and both are used to make kelp tablets. The discovery of iodine in the 19th century was made by distilling *Fucus*.
CULTIVATION Not cultivated. Found in the wild, on unpolluted shores.
HARVEST Plants are collected in summer, when the nutrient content is highest; washed-up plants

Fucus vesiculosus

are not suitable for medicinal use, having lost important nutrients. They are dried in thin layers, being turned regularly; when brittle, the blackish-brown strips are chopped and ground. As a fertilizer, it is spread, fresh or dried, directly on to the soil and dug in, rather than being composted. Small amounts are also added to compost heaps as an activator.

◨ *Fucus vesiculosus* (black-tang, bladderwrack)
Leathery, olive-brown seaweed with branched, strap-like fronds, which are forked at the tips and have air bladders, usually in pairs, on either side of the thick midrib. Found in the Atlantic, English Channel, North Sea, and Baltic. ‡ 15cm–1m (6–36in), ↔ 7.5–50cm (3–20in).
HARDINESS Not applicable.
PARTS USED Whole plant.
PROPERTIES A mucilaginous, salty, tonic herb that stimulates the thyroid, helps control weight, and has antibiotic effects.
MEDICINAL USES Internally for goitre and obesity that is associated with thyroid deficiency. Excess may over-stimulate the thyroid, leading to thyrotoxicosis. Contraindicated during pregnancy and lactation, and in over-active thyroid. Externally for rheumatic complaints.
CULINARY USES Plants are steamed or boiled in cheesecloth bags (removed before serving) with seafood or vegetables to give a sweet salty flavour, as in New England clambakes.
ECONOMIC USES Used for fertilizers, livestock feed, and mineral supplements, and as a source of iodine. Source of alginates for the food, textile, cosmetic, and pharmaceutical industries.

FUMARIA
Fumitory

Papaveraceae

A genus of 55 annuals, usually climbing or scrambling, that occur throughout Europe to C Asia, and in E African highlands. Fumitories are closely related to poppies and similarly contain alkaloids, although in smaller amounts. *Fumaria* is from the Latin *fumus*, "smoke",

F

Fumaria officinalis

referring either to a legend that the plant grew from earthly vapours, or to the irritating smoke it produces when it is burned. There are many old prescriptions containing *F. officinalis*, once used for a wide range of complaints. A syrup made from the juice of the herb, mixed with the syrup of damask roses, peach blossoms, or senna, was "a most singular thing against hypochondriack melancholy in any person whatsoever" (quoted without reference by Mrs Grieve in *A Modern Herbal*, 1931).

CULTIVATION Light, well-drained soil in sun.

PROPAGATION By seed sown in spring where the plants are to flower. Self-sows readily.

HARVEST Plants are collected as flowering begins and dried for use in infusions, liquid extracts, pills, and tinctures.

▣ *Fumaria officinalis* (earth smoke, fumitory, wax dolls)
Robust but weak-stemmed, sprawling or climbing annual with pinnately divided, grey-green leaves, 5–15cm (2–6in) long. Pink flowers, 7mm (¼in) long and tipped dark maroon, are borne in dense elongated racemes from midsummer to late autumn. Found from Europe to Iran; naturalized in N America and Australia. ↔ 30–40cm (12–16in).

HARDINESS Hardy.

PARTS USED Flowering plant.

PROPERTIES A bitter tonic herb with mild diuretic and laxative effects; improves liver and gall bladder function and reduces inflammation.

MEDICINAL USES Internally for biliary colic and migraine with digestive disturbances. Externally for conjunctivitis. Both internally and externally used for skin complaints, including eczema and dermatitis. Excess causes drowsiness.

CULINARY USES Flowering sprigs are added to sour milk to improve taste of curds and act as preservative.

G

GALEGA
Goat's rue

Papilionaceae

About six species of bushy perennials make up this genus, which occurs in C and S Europe, W Asia, and tropical E Africa. A few species are grown for their attractive pinnate leaves and spikes of pea flowers. The common name "goat's rue" arises from the foul smell of the foliage when bruised. *Galega* comes from the Greek *gala*, "milk", because these plants have a reputation for increasing lactation. This was validated by research in France, which in 1873 showed that, in cows given goat's rue, milk yields were increased by 35–50 per cent. *Galega officinalis* was once important in the treatment of plague, fevers, and infectious diseases, hence the German name of *Pestilenzkraut*.

CULTIVATION Moist, well-drained soil in sun or partial shade. May self-sow excessively in good conditions.

PROPAGATION By seed sown in spring; by division in autumn or spring.

HARVEST Plants are cut as flowering begins and dried for use in infusions, liquid extracts, powders, and tinctures.

▣ *Galega officinalis* (French lilac, goat's rue)
Vigorous, clump-forming perennial with pinnate leaves, to 15cm (6in) long, divided into 9–17 elliptic to lanceolate leaflets. Lavender to white or bicoloured flowers, 1cm (⅜in) long, are borne in racemes, to 18cm (7in) long, in summer. Native to C and S Europe and from Turkey to Pakistan.
↕ 1–1.5m (3–5ft), ↔ 60cm–1m (2–3ft). ▣ 'Alba' has white flowers.

HARDINESS Fully hardy.

PARTS USED Whole plant.

PROPERTIES A bitter, mildly diuretic herb that increases milk flow, lowers blood sugar levels, and improves digestion.

Galega officinalis

Galega officinalis 'Alba'

MEDICINAL USES Internally for insufficient lactation, late-onset diabetes, pancreatitis, and digestive problems, especially chronic constipation caused by lack of digestive enzymes. For use by professional practitioners only in the treatment of diabetes.

GALIPEA

Rutaceae

There are 8–10 species of evergreen trees and shrubs in this genus, which occurs in tropical C and S America. *Galipea officinalis* had a long history of use as a bitter tonic by native S Americans before its introduction to Europe in 1759. Angostura aromatic bitters were first made in Angostura (now Ciudad Bolívar), Venezuela, and the recipe (originally a medicine for fevers) was patented by Dr Johann Siegert in 1824. The recipe is a closely guarded secret, though it is known that *Gentiana lutea* (gentian, see p.223) is one of the other main ingredients. Production of Angostura bitters, best known as the ingredient of "pink gin", is now based in Trinidad. Angostura bark is obtained from both *Galipea officinalis* and the related *Angostura febrifuga*. When added to water courses, the active constituents of *Galipea officinalis* have the effect of stunning fish. Fishing by means of ichthyotoxic plants does not affect edibility or cause pollution, since the compounds break down rapidly. The skill has been developed by many tribes in S America, using various species of *Galipea*.

CULTIVATION Humus-rich soil in partial shade. This species does not appear to be cultivated; no information has been found about its needs.

HARVEST Bark is dried for use in concentrated infusions, liquid extracts, and powders.

Galipea officinalis syn. *G. cusparia* (angostura, cusparia bark)
Rainforest shrub or small tree with smooth grey bark and shiny, trifoliate, tobacco-scented leaves, to 30cm (12in) long. White, tubular, five-lobed flowers, with an unpleasant scent, are produced in panicles, to 8cm (3in) long, followed by five-celled capsules containing round black seeds.

Native to tropical S America. ↕15m (50ft),
↔ 10m (30ft).
HARDINESS Min. 15–18°C (59–64°F).
PARTS USED Bark.
PROPERTIES A bitter, musty-smelling, tonic
herb that stimulates the liver and gall bladder,
lowers fever, and relaxes spasms.
MEDICINAL USES Internally for dysentery,
bilious diarrhoea, poor appetite, and feverish
illnesses. Large doses are laxative and emetic.
ECONOMIC USES Extracts are used in the food
industry to flavour alcoholic and soft drinks,
confectionery, and baked produce; also as an
ingredient of bitters, such as Angostura.
🎐 ▣ ✎ ▣

GALIUM
Bedstraw

Rubiaceae

This cosmopolitan genus includes about 400
species of annuals and perennials. A few species
are grown as garden plants, notably *G. odoratum*,
which makes a good deciduous ground cover in
shady areas. Bedstraws contain asperuloside,
which produces coumarin, giving the sweet
smell of new-mown hay as the foliage dries.
Asperuloside can be converted to prostaglandins
(hormone-like compounds that stimulate the
uterus and affect the blood vessels), making
Galium spp. of great interest to the
pharmaceutical industry. Roots of some species
contain a red dye, similar to that produced by the
closely related *Rubia tinctorum* (see p.350). The
roots of *Galium verum* were once gathered on a
large scale in Scotland for dyeing tartans, a
practice banned in 1695 owing to extensive
erosion of sandy grasslands. In England, the
foliage was once used to colour cheese (notably
Cheshire cheese) and butter. *Galium* comes from
the Greek *gala*, "milk", because several species
are used to curdle milk in cheese-making. The
common name "bedstraw" refers to the former
use of these plants in stuffing mattresses.
CULTIVATION Moist, well-drained, neutral to
alkaline soil in shade. *G. verum* prefers drier
sunny conditions.
PROPAGATION By seed sown when ripe; by
division in autumn or early spring.
HARVEST Plants are cut when flowering and
dried for infusions, liquid extracts, and tablets.
Galium aparine is usually used fresh, either
juiced or in oil for external use. Seeds are
collected when ripe.

▣ *Galium aparine* (cleavers, goosegrass, sticky
Willie)
Scrambling annual, climbing by hooked
bristles, with four-angled, weak, bristly stems
with whorls of 6–9 elliptic leaves, about 2.5cm
(1in) long. Tiny white flowers appear in spring
and summer, followed by bristly, globose,
green-purple fruits. Native to Europe and
N and W Asia. ↕1.2m (4ft), ↔ to 3m (10ft).
HARDINESS Hardy.
PARTS USED Whole plant, seeds.
PROPERTIES A bitter, cooling, salty herb that
acts as a tonic for the lymphatic system and has

Galium aparine

mild laxative, diuretic, and astringent effects. It
lowers blood pressure, promotes healing, and is
alterative.
MEDICINAL USES Internally for glandular fever,
tonsillitis, chronic fatigue syndrome (CFS),
hepatitis, benign breast tumours and cysts,
cystitis, eczema, and psoriasis. Externally for
swollen lymph glands, breast lumps, ulcers,
skin inflammations, minor injuries, and
psoriasis. Combined with *Althaea officinalis*
(see p.117) for cystitis; with *Echinacea purpurea*
(see p.199) or *Hydrastis canadensis* (see p.239)
for throat infections; with *Trifolium pratense*
(see p.393), *Urtica dioica* (see p.398), and
Scrophularia nodosa (see p.364) for psoriasis.
CULINARY USES Eaten as a vegetable or added
to soups, with reputed slimming effects. Dried
seeds are roasted as coffee substitute.
▣ ▣ ▣ ✎

▣ *Galium odoratum* syn. *Asperula odorata*
(sweet woodruff)
Rhizomatous perennial with
four-angled stems and whorls of
lanceolate leaves, to 4cm (1½in)
long. Star-shaped, white, fragrant
flowers, to 6mm (¼in) across, are
produced in clusters in late
spring. Native to Europe, N Africa,
and Russia. ↕45cm (18in), ↔ indefinite.
HARDINESS Fully hardy.

Galium odoratum

Galium verum

PARTS USED Whole plant.
PROPERTIES An astringent, slightly bitter herb,
aromatic when dried, with tonic, diuretic, and
sedative effects. It improves liver function,
relaxes spasms, strengthens capillaries, and
reduces blood clotting.
MEDICINAL USES Internally for thrombo-
phlebitis, varicose veins, biliary obstruction,
hepatitis, jaundice, and insomnia in children. Used
in homeopathy for inflammation of the uterus.
CULINARY USES Sprigs are soaked in white
wine to make *Maitrank* or *Maibowle* (Alsace),
and added to fruit cups.
ECONOMIC USES Dried herb is an ingredient
of potpourris.
▣ ▣ ✎ ✎

▣ *Galium verum* (cheese rennet, lady's
bedstraw, yellow bedstraw)
Perennial with a slender creeping rootstock,
four-angled stems, and whorls of 8–12 linear
leaves, to 2.5cm (1in) long. Tiny, bright yellow,
honey-scented flowers are produced in panicles
in summer. Native to Europe, W Asia, and
N America. ↕ 15cm–1m (6–36in), ↔ indefinite.
HARDINESS Fully hardy.
PARTS USED Whole plant.
PROPERTIES An astringent, acidic, slightly
bitter herb that is alterative and diuretic, and
relaxes spasms.
MEDICINAL USES Internally for kidney,
bladder, and urinary complaints.
CULINARY USES Flowering tops are used to
curdle milk for making cheese.
▣ ▣ ✎

GANODERMA
Polyporaceae

A genus of 50 species of saprophytic bracket
fungi, which occur in most regions, especially
the tropics. They obtain their nutrients from
wood, growing either on dead trees or on living
specimens, causing serious heart rot. Wood-
decaying fungi play an important role in forest
ecosystems. *Ganoderma lucidum* grows at the
base of oaks and other deciduous trees, and is
cultivated in China for the herb trade. It is not
palatable as a vegetable but is one of the most

G

Ganoderma lucidum

Gardenia augusta

Gardenia augusta 'Veitchii'

important Taoist longevity herbs, much valued by early Chinese emperors, including the Yellow Emperor, legendary founder of traditional Chinese medicine, who lived c.2500BC. Scientific research has shown that it contains substances that may be of value in treating cancer, viral infections, and allergies; new drugs are being developed from the spores.

CULTIVATION On living or dead wood of deciduous trees, often *Quercus* spp. (see p.339), frequently near the base.

PROPAGATION By spores.

HARVEST Fungi are collected when mature and sun-dried for use in syrups, powders, tablets, and tinctures.

■ *Ganoderma lucidum* (lacquered bracket fungus, reishi)
Bracket fungus bearing a large, stalked, fan-shaped, fruiting body (toadstool) with a shiny upper surface, zoned yellow to dark red. Rust-coloured spores are released from the undersurface in summer. Native to warm and temperate regions. ↔ 15–30cm (6–12in).

HARDINESS Fully hardy.

PARTS USED Whole plant (*ling zhi*).

PROPERTIES A tonic sedative herb that is expectorant, lowers blood sugar and cholesterol levels, controls coughing, relieves pain, and stimulates the immune system. It improves heart and liver function, and has anti-allergenic, anti-viral, and anti-bacterial effects.

MEDICINAL USES Internally for bronchitis, asthma, liver disorders, rheumatoid arthritis, heart disease, palpitations, high blood pressure, high cholesterol levels, nervous disorders, insomnia, and debility.

CULINARY USES Extracts are made into a tonic candy.

▤ ▣ ✍

GARDENIA

Rubiaceae

Some 200 species of evergreen shrubs and trees are included in this genus, which occurs in tropical and warm regions of Africa and Asia. *Gardenia augusta* is widely grown for its handsome foliage and fragrant flowers. It was

first described in traditional Chinese medicine during the Han dynasty (AD25–220), and is an ingredient in several patent remedies for feverish colds or coughs. Known as the "happiness herb" in the East, it improves liver function, which in turn releases blocked emotions. Gardenia fruits contain yellow pigments, including crocin and crocetin, as in *Crocus* spp. (see p.183). *Gardenia* is named after Dr Alexander Garden (1730–91), a Scottish physician who corresponded with Linnaeus and lived in Charleston, South Carolina (USA). The common name "Cape jasmine" is a misnomer, caused by confusion about the origin and identity of the plant when it was first sent to England in the 1750s; it is not related to *Jasminum* (see p.245) and is not from South Africa.

CULTIVATION Well-drained, humus-rich, sandy, neutral to acid soil in light or partial shade. Plants in containers need lime-free (ericaceous) compost and should be kept evenly moist, using soft water.

Gardenia augusta 'Fortuniana'

Avoid sudden changes in temperature and cold draughts. Young plants flower more freely. Cut back after flowering to maintain a bushy habit. Plants under cover may be damaged by spider mites, aphids, whitefly, and mealybugs.

PROPAGATION By seed sown in spring at 19–24°C (66–75F°); by greenwood cuttings in late spring or early summer; by semi-ripe cuttings in late summer.

HARVEST Fruits are collected when ripe and dried for use in decoctions.

■ *Gardenia augusta* syn. *G. florida*, *G. jasminoides* (Cape jasmine, gardenia)
Evergreen shrub with glossy, ovate to elliptic leaves, about 10cm (4in) long. White, waxy, strongly fragrant flowers, to 8cm (3in) across, appear in summer, followed by oblong fruits, to 2.5cm (1in) long. Native to S China, Taiwan, Japan, and Vietnam. ↕ 2–12m (6–40ft), ↔ 1–3m (3–10ft) in cultivation. ■ 'Fortuniana' has double flowers. ■ 'Veitchii' syn. 'Veitchiana' produces double flowers in winter.

HARDINESS Min. 10°C (50°F).

PARTS USED Fruits (*zhi zi*), flowers.

PROPERTIES A bitter, cold, alterative herb that lowers fever and blood pressure, checks bleeding, stimulates bile flow, and promotes healing. It has anti-bacterial and anti-fungal effects. Flowers are haemostatic, sedative, and diuretic.

MEDICINAL USES Internally for feverish illness, hepatitis, jaundice, and haemorrhage. Externally for wounds, sprains, skin inflammations, and toothache. Flowers are used internally in traditional Vietnamese medicine to control bleeding, and externally for eye problems.

CULINARY USES Flowers are used to flavour tea in China. Fruits are edible and yield a yellow colouring, used as a substitute for saffron.

▦ ▨ ▣ ✍ ▨

GASTRODIA

Orchidaceae

A genus of 20 saprophytic species of orchids, found from E Asia to New Zealand. They are extremely difficult to cultivate because of their lack of green parts and complete dependence on a fungus for food. *Gastrodia elata* was first described in traditional Chinese medicine c.AD470. The literal translation of the Chinese name is "heavenly hemp". Because of its increasing rarity in the wild, techniques for cultivating this saprophytic orchid have now been devised in China.

CULTIVATION Damp, humus-rich soil in shade, in association with fungal partner.

PROPAGATION By seed sown when ripe in the natural habitat near existing colonies, or on to a bed of *Quercus* wood, inoculated with the fungus *Armillariella mellea*; by division of rhizomes during dormancy.

HARVEST Rhizomes are lifted in autumn and dried for use in decoctions.

Gastrodia elata

Perennial leafless saprophyte with an angular, horizontal, tuber-like rhizome, 10–15cm (4–6in) long and 5–6cm (2–2½in) wide, and brown stem clad in scale-like sheaths. Small, pale green-brown flowers appear in summer. Native to China, Japan, Korea, Tibet, and Siberia. ‡ 60cm–1m (2–3ft), ↔ 30cm (12in).

HARDINESS Fully hardy.

PARTS USED Rhizomes (*tian ma*).

PROPERTIES A sweet, acrid, sedative herb that lowers blood pressure, relieves pain, stimulates bile flow, and relaxes spasms.

MEDICINAL USES Internally for convulsive illnesses (such as epilepsy and tetanus), rheumatoid arthritis, vertigo, and numbness associated with liver disharmony.

▨ ▣

GAULTHERIA

Ericaceae

This genus includes some 170 species of evergreen shrubs, closely related to *Vaccinium* (see p.399), occurring mainly in the Andes but also in N America, E Asia, the Himalayas, and Australasia. Many are naturally dwarf, with a neat habit, waxy flowers, and colourful fruits, making good subjects for rock gardens and containers. *Gaultheria procumbens* (wintergreen) is a traditional, native N American remedy, used for aches and pains, and to help breathing while hunting or carrying heavy loads. Wintergreen leaves were listed in the *US Pharmacopoeia* (1820–94); oil of wintergreen is still listed. The oil was once a major source of methyl salicylate (an anti-inflammatory, similar in effect to aspirin), produced mainly in Monroe County, Pennsylvania; most methyl salicylate is now synthesized. *Gaultheria* was named after Jean François Gaulthier (1708–56), a physician and botanist who worked in Canada.

CULTIVATION Moist, peaty, neutral to acid soil in partial shade.

PROPAGATION By seed sown in autumn on soil surface; by semi-ripe cuttings in summer; by separation of rooted suckers in spring.

HARVEST Leaves are gathered from spring to early autumn and dried for use in infusions and liquid extracts. Oil is extracted from fresh leaves for use in rubbing oils, inhalants, liniments, and ointments. Fruits are picked when ripe.

Gaultheria procumbens

▣ *Gaultheria procumbens* (checkerberry, teaberry, wintergreen)
Dense, creeping, prostrate shrub with glossy, ovate-elliptic leaves, 2–5cm (¾–2in) long. White to pink, solitary, pendent flowers appear in spring and summer, followed by globose, red, aromatic fruits, to 1.5cm (½in) across, which remain all winter. Native to eastern N America. ‡ 7–15cm (3–6in), ↔ 1m (3ft) or more.

HARDINESS Fully hardy.

PARTS USED Leaves, oil, fruits.

PROPERTIES An astringent, aromatic, warming herb that is anti-inflammatory, diuretic, and expectorant. It is a good antiseptic and counter-irritant.

MEDICINAL USES Mainly externally for rheumatism, arthritis, sciatica, myalgia, sprains, neuralgia, and catarrh. Oil of wintergreen is toxic in excess, causing liver and kidney damage. Not given to patients hypersensitive to salicylates (aspirin).

CULINARY USES Leaves are used for tea, known as "mountain tea". Fruits are eaten raw or cooked in pies, or preserved as jam, jelly, or syrup.

ECONOMIC USES Oil is used to flavour root beer, chewing gum, and toothpaste; also in perfumery with woody notes.

▨ ▨ ▢ ▣ ▨ ▨

GELIDIUM

Gelidiaceae

A genus of about 20 species of red seaweeds, found mainly in waters off Spain, Portugal, W Scotland, Ireland, N, S, and W Africa, Madagascar, Japan, California, and Chile. They are collected with rakes from boats or by divers from deep water, and are now cultivated by the Japanese on poles in coastal waters. *Gelidium amansii* is a source of agar or *kanten*, a colloidal extract used in similar ways to gelatin. The earliest observations of the properties of *G. amansii* (tengusa) are attributed to a Japanese innkeeper, Minoya Tarozaemon, in 1660, though seaweed gels have been eaten in Japan for over 1200 years. Its use as agar, a culture medium for bacteria, was developed in the 1880s by Robert Koch, who thereby discovered the organisms that cause tuberculosis. Some 30 species of algae,

belonging to about ten different genera, are used worldwide for agar production; the main ones are *G. amansii* (Japan), *G. cartilagineum* (USA), *Gracilaria verrucosa* (Australia), and *Pterocladia pinnata* (New Zealand). The 20th century saw demand for *Gelidium* increase in many areas, including medicine, dentistry, forensic science, and the food industry. It is prepared as strips of solidified mucilaginous extract, which gels at 32°C (90°F) and melts at 85°C (185°F). The high melting point makes agar useful in foods that might otherwise melt in warm temperatures. In addition, its constituents are non-toxic and not absorbed from the gut.

CULTIVATION In shallow coastal water on poles.

PROPAGATION By spores, which spread naturally.

HARVEST Plants are collected during the growing season and sun-dried before processing into dried agar strips and powder.

Gelidium amansii (agar, agar-agar, Japanese isinglass, tengusa)

Perennial, tuft-forming seaweed with pinnately branched, rigid, cartilaginous fronds divided into thread-like segments. Found in intertidal and subtidal zones around China, Japan, Korea, and Pacific coasts of Russia. ↔ 10–30cm (4–12in).

HARDINESS Not applicable.

PARTS USED Whole plant.

PROPERTIES A nutritive, almost tasteless, gelatinous herb that acts as a bulk laxative.

MEDICINAL USES Internally for constipation.

CULINARY USES Powdered or flaked agar is used to set jellies. *Kanten* is a popular food in Japan, made into a firm jelly or into *tokoroten* (noodles).

ECONOMIC USES Used in invalid foods, and as a gelling and stabilizing agent in tinned meats, ice cream, sauces, desserts, and dairy produce.

▨ ▨ ▣ ▨

GELSEMIUM

Loganiaceae

There are three species of evergreen, twining, perennial climbers in this genus, which occurs in N and C America and SE Asia. *Gelsemium sempervirens* is widely grown as an ornamental in the open in warm regions, or under cover, and makes a fine specimen trained against a wall or trellis. It is the state flower of South Carolina (USA). The uses of *G. sempervirens* were discovered by a Mississippi planter, who drank an infusion made from the roots of the plant, mistaking it for another. He developed serious symptoms of poisoning, but recovered to find himself cured of his bilious fever. A physician who observed the case went on to develop a remedy from *Gelsemium*, known as "Electrical Febrifuge". *Gelsemium sempervirens* was listed in most pharmacopoeias in the mid-19th century. *Gelsemium*, from the Italian *gelsomino*, "jessamine", refers to the jasmine-like flowers.

CULTIVATION Moist, fertile, well-drained soil in sun. Thin out stems in spring or after flowering.

PROPAGATION By seed sown in spring at 13–18°C (55–64°F) (species only); by semi-ripe cuttings in summer.

G

Gelsemium sempervirens

HARVEST Roots and rhizomes are lifted in autumn and dried for decoctions and tinctures.
⚠ **WARNING** Toxic if eaten (one flower may be fatal to a child). Skin allergen. Contact may cause systemic poisoning.

◾ *Gelsemium sempervirens* (Carolina jasmine, yellow jessamine)
Evergreen climber with twining stems and shiny, ovate–lanceolate leaves, to 5cm (2in) long. Fragrant, funnel-shaped, yellow flowers, 3cm (1¼in) long, appear in clusters in spring and summer, followed by two-valved capsules that contain flattened seeds. Native to SE USA, Mexico, and Guatemala. ‡ 3–6m (10–20ft).
HARDINESS Half hardy (borderline).
PARTS USED Roots and rhizomes.
PROPERTIES A bitter, slightly aromatic, sedative herb that lowers fever, increases perspiration, relieves pain, and relaxes spasms.
MEDICINAL USES Internally for neuralgia, migraine, sciatica, toothache, severe pain (especially in terminal illness or accidents), and meningitis. May be combined with *Lavandula angustifolia* (see p.253), or *Rosmarinus officinalis* (see p.348) and *Piscidia piscipula* (see p.321), for migraine. Excess causes respiratory depression, giddiness, double vision, and death. Not given to patients with heart disease, hypotension, or myasthenia gravis. Also in homeopathy for feverish illnesses (including influenza and measles) and acute anxiety. For use only by qualified practitioners.
⚠ **WARNING** This herb and its alkaloids are subject to legal restrictions in some countries.
▨ ▲

GENISTA
Broom

Papilionaceae

This genus contains about 90 species of mainly deciduous, sometimes spiny shrubs, found in Europe, N Africa, and W Asia; it differs from *Cytisus* only in minute anatomical detail. *Genista tinctoria* was once widely used as a dye plant. All parts contain glycosides, notably luteolin glycosides, which produce a yellow dye that has been used since Roman times for

dyeing fabrics. When used with *Isatis tinctoria* (woad, see p.245) it produces Kendal green, the colour used to dye woollen cloth, and also Lincoln green, the colour worn by Robin Hood. Other constituents include alkaloids, some of which are similar to those found in the closely related *Cytisus scoparius* (see p.190). Comparatively little research has been done on *Genista*, but it should be treated with caution, given that the alkaloids in *Cytisus* are known to affect the heart and respiration. In the 14th century both *Genista tinctoria* and *Cytisus scoparius* were used to make *unguentum geneste*, an ointment for gouty limbs.
CULTIVATION Light, well-drained soil in sun. Tolerates dry, poor, or sandy soils. Established plants do not transplant well. No regular pruning is required, but shoots can be thinned and/or pinched out after flowering to improve shape. Some *Genista* spp. are subject to certain plant controls in parts of Australia.
PROPAGATION By seed sown in autumn or spring; by semi-ripe cuttings in summer.
HARVEST Leafy branches are cut before the plant sets seed, and dried for infusions. Dried herb should not be stored for more than a year.

◾ *Genista tinctoria* (dyer's greenweed, woad-waxen)
Variable, deciduous, usually non-spiny shrub with bright green, stalkless, lanceolate leaves,

Genista tinctoria

Genista tinctoria 'Flore Pleno'

to 5cm (2in) long. Yellow pea flowers, about 1cm (½in) long, appear in upright racemes, to 6cm (2½in) long, in summer. Native to Europe and W. Asia. ‡ 60–90cm (24–36in), ↔ 1m (3ft).
◾ 'Flore Pleno' syn. 'Plena' is dwarf, with double flowers. ‡ 35cm (14in). 'Royal Gold' is upright, with flowers in conical racemes, to 8cm (3in) long. ‡ 1m (3ft).
HARDINESS Fully hardy.
PARTS USED Flowering plant.
PROPERTIES A bitter, diuretic, purgative, emetic herb that acts as a weak cardiac stimulant and vasoconstrictor.
MEDICINAL USES Formerly used internally for gout, rheumatism, and dropsy; externally for fractures, sciatica, abscesses, and tumours.
CULINARY USES Flower buds can be pickled as a substitute for capers.
ECONOMIC USES Flowers yield natural yellow dyes for wool.
▨ ▲ ✎ ✎

GENTIANA
Gentian

Gentianaceae

A cosmopolitan genus of about 400 species of annuals, biennials, and deciduous or evergreen perennials. Gentians of many kinds are grown for their funnel-shaped flowers, which in some species are bright blue and in others may be purple, yellow, or white. Gentians contain some of the most bitter compounds known, against which the bitterness of other substances is scientifically measured. Bitter-tasting herbs benefit the digestive system, stimulating gastric secretions and improving digestion. *Gentiana lutea* is the classic bitter digestive, so much so that the taste can still be detected when diluted to 1 in 12,000 parts. Many different species are used similarly in different parts of the world – the choice being largely dependent on local availability. Wild collection of *Gentiana* spp. is subject to management measures in certain countries. *Gentiana* was named after king Gentius of Illyria (c.500BC), who is credited with discovering the medicinal uses of *G. lutea*.
CULTIVATION Moist, light, well-drained, humus-rich, neutral to acid soil in sun or partial shade. *Gentiana lutea* prefers alkaline soil. Plants may succumb to root rot in wet conditions.
PROPAGATION By seed sown when ripe; by division or offshoots in spring.
HARVEST Roots and rhizomes are lifted in autumn and dried for use in decoctions, tablets, and tinctures.

◾ *Gentiana burseri* var. *villarsii* syn. *G. macrophylla* (large-leafed gentian)
Erect perennial with a stout rootstock and pale green, pointed, lanceolate leaves, 20–40cm (8–16in) long. Violet-blue flowers appear in dense clusters in the upper axils in summer. Native to N Asia, China, and Mongolia.
‡ 40–70cm (16–28in), ↔ 60cm (24in).
HARDINESS Fully hardy.
PARTS USED Roots (*qin jiao*).

Gentiana burseri var. *villarsii*

PROPERTIES A bitter, pungent, sedative herb that has a tonic effect on the liver, gall bladder, and stomach, and increases blood sugar levels. It lowers fever, relieves pain, and reduces inflammation.
MEDICINAL USES Internally for rheumatism, arthritis, low-grade fevers associated with chronic disease, allergic inflammations, hepatitis, jaundice, and constipation-related liver complaints.

■ *Gentiana lutea* (bitterwort, yellow gentian) Clump-forming, herbaceous perennial with fleshy roots, stout hollow stems, and broadly ovate, pleated, basal leaves, to 30cm (12in) long. Yellow flowers, 2.5cm (1in) across, with short tubes and narrow petals, appear in whorled clusters in summer. Native to the Alps, Apennines, Pyrenees, and Carpathians. ‡ 1–2m (3–6ft), ↔ 60cm (24in).
HARDINESS Fully hardy.
PARTS USED Roots and rhizomes.
PROPERTIES An intensely bitter (though sweet at first) tonic herb that stimulates the liver, gall bladder, and digestive system. It reduces inflammation and lowers fever.
MEDICINAL USES Internally for liver complaints, indigestion, gastric infections, and anorexia. Not given to patients with gastric and duodenal ulcers.

Gentiana lutea

Gentiana scabra

ECONOMIC USES Used in making gentian liqueurs, brandy, and Enzian schnapps; a key ingredient of Angostura bitters (see p.218).

■ *Gentiana scabra* (Japanese gentian, *ryntem* root)
Perennial with leafy stems and paired, ovate to lanceolate, three-veined leaves, to 3.5cm (1⅜in) long. Deep blue, often spotted flowers appear in terminal clusters or axillary pairs, in summer. Native to N Asia and Japan. ‡ 30cm (12in), ↔ 20cm (8in).
HARDINESS Fully hardy.
PARTS USED Roots (*long dan cao*).
PROPERTIES A bitter, cooling, anti-inflammatory herb that stimulates the appetite and digestion, increases blood sugar levels, and potentiates the sedative and analgesic properties of other herbs.
MEDICINAL USES Internally for liver disorders, eye complaints related to liver disharmony (such as conjunctivitis), acute urinary infections, hypertension with dizziness or tinnitus, and tantrums in children. Included in many Chinese patent remedies for "liver heat".

GERANIUM
Cranesbill

Geraniaceae

A genus of some 300 species of herbaceous or evergreen, sometimes tuberous perennials, with a few annuals and biennials, widely distributed in temperate regions. Cranesbills are popular garden plants, with attractive leaves and small, delicately veined flowers, borne over a long period. The related *Pelargonium* (see p.304), also known as "geranium", has different uses. Cranesbills are high in tannins, providing astringent remedies important in traditional medicine for the emergency treatment of injuries and diarrhoea. *Geranium maculatum* was widely used by native N Americans, both as an astringent and as a remedy for venereal disease, before becoming popular with settlers in the 19th century; it was listed in the *US Pharmacopoeia* from 1820 to 1990. *Geranium*

dissectum (cut-leafed cranesbill), a European species, appears to have similar properties. The Chinese *G. wilfordii* is used for rheumatic pain and gastrointestinal infections with diarrhoea.
CULTIVATION Moist, humus-rich, well-drained soil in partial shade (*G. maculatum*); well-drained to dry soil in sun or shade (*G. robertianum*). Rust may attack foliage.
PROPAGATION By seed sown when ripe or in spring; by division in spring; by basal cuttings in spring. *Geranium robertianum* self-sows freely. Cultivars come true from seed.
HARVEST Plants are cut as flowering begins, roots (*G. maculatum*) are harvested in autumn; both are dried for use in decoctions, infusions, liquid extracts, powder, tablets, and tinctures. *Geranium robertianum* is often used fresh.

■ *Geranium maculatum* (alumroot, American cranesbill, spotted cranesbill)
Erect, clump-forming, herbaceous perennial with a compact rootstock and palmate toothed leaves, to 20cm (8in) across. Lilac-pink to pink, saucer-shaped flowers, 3cm (1¼in) across, appear in spring and early summer, followed by beaked fruits, 2.5cm (1in) long. Native to eastern N America. ‡ 60–75cm (24–30in), ↔ 45cm (18in). ■ f. *albiflorum* is less vigorous and has white flowers.
HARDINESS Fully hardy.
PARTS USED Whole plant, roots.
PROPERTIES A highly astringent, tonic herb that is antiseptic, checks bleeding, controls discharges, and promotes healing.
MEDICINAL USES Internally for diarrhoea (especially in children and the elderly), dysentery, cholera, gastroenteritis, colitis, peptic ulcer,

Geranium maculatum

Geranium maculatum f. *albiflorum*

Geranium robertianum

Geranium robertianum 'Album'

Geranium robertianum 'Celtic White'

haemorrhage, and excessive menstruation. Externally for purulent wounds, haemorrhoids, thrush, vaginal discharge, and inflammations of the mouth, gums, and throat. Combined with *Bidens tripartita* (see p.144) for haemorrhage in the digestive tract; with *Trillium erectum* (see p.394) as a douche for vaginal discharge; with *Geum urbanum* (see below), *Agrimonia eupatoria* (see p.107), and *Symphytum officinale* (see p.377) for peptic ulcer; with *Agrimonia eupatoria* (see p.107), *Althaea officinalis* (see p.117), *Chamaemelum nobile* (see p.165), or *Filipendula ulmaria* (see p.214) for digestive upsets. 🔲 🔲 🔲

🔲 **Geranium robertianum** (herb Robert) Rosette-forming, fetid annual or biennial with hairy, often red-tinged stems and deeply divided, palmate leaves, to 11cm (4¼in) wide. Pink flowers, 1cm (⅜in) across, are produced from early summer to late autumn. ↔ 50cm (20in). 🔲 'Album' has white flowers. 🔲 'Celtic White' is smaller and more compact, with bright green foliage, devoid of red tones. ‡ 10–40cm (4–16in), ↔ 30cm (12in).
HARDINESS Fully hardy.
PARTS USED Whole plant.
PROPERTIES A bitter, astringent, mildly diuretic herb that checks bleeding and mucus discharge, and promotes healing.
MEDICINAL USES Internally for diarrhoea, gastrointestinal infections, peptic ulcer, and haemorrhage. Externally for skin eruptions, wounds, inflamed gums and throat, and herpes. 🔲 🔲

GEUM
Avens
Rosaceae

There are about 50 species of mostly rhizomatous perennials in this genus, which occurs in temperate and cold regions. Geum is popular for the front of borders or in rock gardens, and has long-lasting flowers in shades of red, orange, and yellow. *Geum urbanum* has been used medicinally since Roman times. It was once known as *herba benedicta*, because its aromatic roots were thought to protect against evil and poisons: hence the common names "herb bennet" or "herb Benedict". The root contains eugenol, as found in *Syzygium aromaticum* (see p.378); *Geum rivale* (water avens) has similar but weaker properties.
CULTIVATION Rich moist soil in shade.
PROPAGATION By seed sown in autumn or spring. Self-sows freely.
HARVEST Plants are cut as flowering begins and dried for infusions and liquid extracts. Roots are lifted in spring and used fresh or dried for decoctions and liquid extracts.

🔲 **Geum urbanum** (avens, herb Benedict, herb bennet, wood avens)
Slender downy perennial with a clove-scented rhizome, upright stems, and pinnate leaves. Small, yellow, five-petalled flowers appear in

Geum urbanum

summer, followed by purple-tinged fruits covered in hooked bristles. Native to Europe, W Asia, and Mediterranean regions. ↔ 20–60cm (8–24in).
HARDINESS Fully hardy.
PARTS USED Whole plant, roots.
PROPERTIES An astringent antiseptic herb that reduces inflammation, checks bleeding and discharges, lowers fever, and has a tonic effect on the digestive system.
MEDICINAL USES Internally for diarrhoea, gastrointestinal infections, bowel disease, uterine haemorrhage, and intermittent fever. Externally for haemorrhoids, vaginal discharge, and inflammations of the mouth, gums, and throat. 🔲 🔲 🔲

GILLENIA
Rosaceae

Two closely related species of rhizomatous woodland perennials belong to this eastern N American genus. *Gillenia trifoliata* is widely grown as an ornamental for its elegant display of white flowers. *Gillenia stipulata*, similar in both properties and appearance, is found farther south in the wild. They are distinguished mainly by the number of leaflets: three in the case of *G. trifoliata* and five in the case of *G. stipulata* (the two extra ones are actually stipules). *Gillenia trifoliata* was known to many N American tribes and was adopted by the early colonists. It was listed in the *US Pharmacopoeia* (1820–82). The same common names are generally shared between *G. trifoliata* and *G. stipulata*.
CULTIVATION Moist, well-drained, neutral to acid soil in partial shade.
PROPAGATION By seed sown when ripe; by division in autumn or spring.
HARVEST Roots are lifted in early autumn and stripped of bark, which is dried for use in decoctions and powder.

🔲 **Gillenia trifoliata** syn. *Porteranthus trifoliatus* (American ipecac, Bowman's root, Indian physic)
Erect herbaceous perennial with branched, red-green stalks and trifoliate, deeply toothed and

Gillenia trifoliata

veined leaves, to 8cm (3in) long. White or pink-tinged flowers, 1–2cm (⅜–¾in) across, with narrow petals and red-green calyces, are borne in loose panicles in late spring and summer. Native to eastern N America. ‡ 1–1.2m (3–4ft), ↔ 60cm (24in).
HARDINESS Fully hardy.
PARTS USED Root bark.
PROPERTIES An emetic herb, similar in effects to *Cephaelis ipecacuanha* (see p.163). It also has purgative and expectorant effects. Small doses act as a stimulant.
MEDICINAL USES Internally, in small doses, for feverish illnesses, chronic diarrhoea, constipation, and bronchial and asthmatic complaints. 🔲 🔲 🔲

GINKGO
Maidenhair tree
Ginkgoaceae

A single species of deciduous tree makes up this genus, which is found wild in Zhejiang and Guizhou provinces (C China) and which has no close relatives. *Ginkgo biloba* is rare in the wild, but has long been grown as a sacred tree in China and Japan. Seeds reached Europe c.1727, and *Ginkgo* rapidly became popular in cultivation. Male and female flowers are borne on separate plants; fruiting occurs only when male and female trees are grown together, and in warm summers. *Ginkgo* is often referred to as a living fossil, because trees alive today are almost identical to those in fossil records that pre-date the evolution of mammals. It is classified in the same group as conifers and cycads, but is distinct from both. Seeds have long been used in traditional Chinese medicine, but Western research has concentrated on the leaves. Among

the plant's main constituents are ginkgolides, which are not known in any other plant species; these are PAF (platelet activating factor) blockers, which inhibit allergic responses. Ginkgo flavonoids appear to be particularly effective in improving the circulation to the brain, and the herb is increasingly used in geriatric medicine. *Ginkgo* comes from the Japanese words *gin*, "silver", and *kyo*, "apricot".
CULTIVATION Fertile, well-drained soil in sun. *Ginkgo* dies back if pruned.
PROPAGATION By seed sown when ripe (species only); by semi-ripe cuttings in summer; by side-veneer grafting in winter.
HARVEST Leaves are picked as they change colour in autumn, and are dried for use in distilled extracts, infusions, powders, tinctures, and tablets. Kernels from ripe fruits are cooked for use in decoctions.

■ *Ginkgo biloba* (ginkgo, maidenhair tree) Erect deciduous tree with a conical habit when young, furrowed grey bark, and fan-shaped leaves, to 12cm (5in) across, which turn yellow in autumn. Male flowers are borne in thick, yellow, pendulous catkins, 8cm (3in) long, while female flowers are round, solitary, on long stalks. They are followed by yellow-green, plum-like fruits, 3cm (1¼in) long, which smell unpleasant when ripe. Native to China. ‡ 40m (130ft), ↔ 20m (70ft). 'Mother Load' is a female clone that produces large crops of odour-free fruits. ■ Pendula Group has a weeping habit. ‡ 3m (10ft), ↔ 5m (15ft). 'Princeton Sentry' is a narrow, upright, male clone.
HARDINESS Fully hardy.
PARTS USED Leaves, seeds (*bai guo*), oil.
PROPERTIES A bitter–sweet, astringent herb that dilates bronchial tubes and blood vessels, controls allergic responses, and stimulates the circulation (leaves); has anti-fungal and anti-bacterial effects (seeds).
MEDICINAL USES Internally for asthma, allergic inflammatory responses, cerebral insufficiency in the elderly, senile dementia, circulatory complaints, such as Raynaud's disease, varicose veins, or irregular heartbeat (leaves); also for asthma, coughs with thick phlegm, and urinary incontinence (seeds). Combined with *Tilia* spp. (see p.391), and *Vinca major* (see p.404) or

Ginkgo biloba

Ginkgo biloba Pendula Group

Crataegus laevigata (see p.182), for circulatory disorders, and with *Melilotus officinalis* (see p.274) for venous complaints (leaves); with *Ephedra* spp. (see p.201), *Tussilago farfara* (see p.396), and leaves of *Morus alba* (see p.283) for asthma and coughs (seeds). Excess may cause dermatitis, headaches, diarrhoea, and vomiting.
CULINARY USES Seeds (nuts) are roasted as a snack or garnish, and canned or dried for use in soups, stir-fries, and stews. Seeds yield an edible oil.
🗎 🗆 🔲 🗎 ✎

GLECHOMA
Lamiaceae

About 12 species of creeping perennials make up this European genus. *Glechoma hederacea* is a common lawn and garden weed with a variegated cultivar ('Variegata') that is sometimes offered alongside bedding plants as a trailing plant for tubs, windowboxes, and hanging baskets. It is equally useful as ground cover beneath shrubs and hedges. *Glechoma hederacea* was important in brewing until about the 16th century, giving rise to its common name "alehoof" ("hoof" meant a herb); it was superseded by *Humulus lupulus* (hop, see p.237). *Glechoma* was also

Glechoma hederacea

Glechoma hederacea 'Variegata'

made into a cough medicine known as "gill tea", from the French *guiller*, "to ferment" (as in beer). *Glechoma* comes from the Greek *glechon*, "mint-like plant".
CULTIVATION Moist, well-drained soil in sun or shade. Invasive.
PROPAGATION By seed sown in spring (species only); by division in autumn or spring; by separation of rooted stolons at any time.
HARVEST Flowering plants are dried for infusions and liquid extracts.

■ *Glechoma hederacea* syn. *Nepeta glechoma, N. hederacea* (alehoof, ground ivy)
Creeping, stoloniferous, evergreen or semi-evergreen perennial with aromatic, kidney-shaped leaves, to 3cm (1¼in) across, which are often purple-tinged and have scalloped margins. Tubular, two-lipped, blue-mauve flowers are produced in spring and early summer. ‡ 15cm (6in), ↔ 2m (6ft). ■ 'Variegata' (nepeta, variegated ground ivy) has white-variegated leaves.
HARDINESS Fully hardy.
PARTS USED Whole plant.
PROPERTIES A bitter, aromatic, astringent herb; it has a tonic effect on the bronchial, digestive, and urinary systems, and is diuretic and expectorant.
MEDICINAL USES Internally for catarrh, sinusitis, ear infections, bronchitis, gastritis, and cystitis. Externally for inflammations of throat and mouth, and haemorrhoids.
CULINARY USES Fresh or dried leaves are used to make herb tea. Young leaves can be added to soups.
🗎 🗎 ✎

GLORIOSA
Glory lily
Colchicaceae

Several species of tuberous perennials were once included in this genus, now reduced to variants of a single, very variable species, occurring in tropical Africa and Asia, usually in savannah bush or teak forest, often near rivers. *Gloriosa superba* was introduced into cultivation in 1690 and soon became a favourite exotic ornamental.

Gloriosa superba 'Rothschildiana'

Gloriosa superba is a very poisonous plant; it contains alkaloids, including colchicine, as in *Colchicum* spp. (see p.176), which affect cell division. It is grown in India as a commercial source of this compound, which is used in medicine and genetic engineering.

CULTIVATION Rich, well-drained soil in sun. Over-watering causes discoloured foliage and premature leaf fall. Plants in pots should be left dry, cool, and undisturbed in the winter, and be repotted in early spring.

PROPAGATION By seed sown in spring at 21–24°C (70–75°F); by offsets in early spring, started into growth at 16–19°C (61–66°F).

HARVEST Tubers are lifted in autumn and dried for use in pastes and powder.

⚠ **WARNING** All parts, especially tubers, are extremely toxic if eaten. Repeated handling of tubers causes skin irritation.

Gloriosa superba (glory lily, Malabar glory lily, Mozambique lily)
Climbing perennial with brittle, finger-shaped tubers and sparsely branched stems bearing glossy, ovate–lanceolate leaves, 5–8cm (2–3in) long, which end in a tendril. Flowers may be yellow, orange, red, or bicoloured, with narrow, recurved, wavy-margined petals, to 10cm (4in) long, and long protruding stamens. Native to Africa and India. ‡ 2.5m (8ft), ↔ 30cm (12in). 'Citrina' has yellow flowers, flushed or striped purple-red. ◼ 'Rothschildiana' syn. *G. rothschildiana* has bright red flowers, yellow at the base and margins.

HARDINESS Min. 8–10°C (46–50°F).
PARTS USED Tubers.
PROPERTIES A bitter stimulant herb with anti-bacterial effects.
MEDICINAL USES Internally, use of fresh tuber causes abortion; it has been used to speed labour, soaked in milk to reduce toxicity. Mainly externally for lice, scabies, and leprosy. Excess causes numbness, nausea, spasms, and unconsciousness. For use only by qualified practitioners.
ECONOMIC USES Used in countries of origin for making arrow poison, and to poison vermin. A source of colchicine for the pharmaceutical and horticultural industries.

GLYCINE
Fabaceae

A genus of nine species of leguminous annuals, found from Asia to Australia. The most important species in cultivation is *Glycine max* (soya bean), which has been grown for at least 3000 years and is the main legume crop in China, Japan, Korea, and Malaysia. Large quantities are also produced in the USA. It does not exist in the wild and is thought to have appeared as a hybrid between two *Glycine* spp. in China. The first soya beans reached Europe in the 18th century, and the USA in the 19th century. Soya beans contain over 35 per cent protein, 20 per cent fixed oil, 22 amino acids, lecithin (which benefits nervous and circulatory systems), linoleic acid (a polyunsaturated fatty acid that is essential for hormone production), and coumestrol and isoflavones that closely resemble human oestrogen. They are immensely useful, yielding a wide range of foodstuffs and industrial materials. Though seldom recognized as a herb, the soya bean has a number of therapeutic applications, in addition to its high nutritional value. Fermented, salted black soya beans have been used medicinally in China since earliest times. *Glycine* is from the Greek *glykys*, "sweet", referring to the sweet-tasting roots and leaves of some species. The Australian *G. tabacina* (vanilla glycine) has liquorice-flavoured roots.

CULTIVATION Moist, rich, well-drained soil in sun.
PROPAGATION By seed sown in spring.
HARVEST Seeds are harvested when unripe and used fresh, or ripe and soaked or cooked before using whole, ground, fermented, or processed further.

Glycine max (soya, soya bean, soybean)
Erect bushy annual, clad in red-grey hairs, with trifoliate leaves, 4–10cm (1½–4in) long. Small, white or mauve, pea flowers appear in clusters of 3–15 in the axils in summer, followed by yellow-brown to grey, brown, or almost black pods, 3–7cm (1¼–3in) long, containing 1–5 yellow, green, brown, black, or mottled seeds, according to cultivar. Native to E Asia. ‡ 25cm–2m (10in–6ft), ↔ 15cm–1m (6in–3ft).
HARDINESS Half hardy.
PARTS USED Seeds (beans) (*dou chi*).
PROPERTIES A sweet, slightly bitter, cooling herb that in Chinese medicine is regarded as carminative, sedative, anti-spasmodic, diaphoretic, and anti-pyretic. It has hormonal effects and benefits the liver and circulation.
MEDICINAL USES Internally in Chinese medicine for fever, headache, insomnia, restlessness, and chest discomfort associated with colds, and measles. Internally, in the form of soy lecithin, to help lower serum cholesterol levels, and in the form of soy phospholipid enriched with 73–79 per cent (3-sn phosphatidyl)-choline for severe hypercholesterolemia, chronic liver disease, and chronic hepatitis.
CULINARY USES Unripe beans are cooked and eaten like peas. Dried beans are cooked in soups, stews and casseroles, roasted as a coffee substitute, liquidized with water to make soya milk, tofu (bean curd), sprouted for salads, or ground and fermented to make soy sauce, miso, and other sauces and pastes.
ECONOMIC USES Beans yield protein, processed as textured vegetable protein (TVP); flour; oil for salads and cooking; and lecithin, used as a food supplement, emulsifier, and substitute for eggs and animal fats in the food industry. Oil is further processed into margarine, and used in the manufacture of soap, paints, printing inks, and linoleum. Proteins are used in the manufacture of synthetic fibres, fire-fighting foam, and adhesives. Lecithin is used as a wetting and stabilizing agent in various industrial processes. Residue is an important component of livestock feed.

GLYCYRRHIZA
Papilionaceae

A genus of 20 species of perennials with sticky pinnate leaves, found in a variety of habitats in the Mediterranean, tropical Asia, Australia, and the Americas. *Glycyrrhiza glabra* was recorded in ancient Assyrian and Classical times, and was cultivated and processed into liquorice extract in Germany by the 11th century. Cultivation was well established in Italy in the 13th century, and in 1305 Edward I of England taxed liquorice imports to pay for the repair of London Bridge. Large-scale cultivation began in the late 1550s, notably in Pontefract, Yorkshire, to which it was introduced by Dominican friars, and which became famous for Pontefract cakes, or pomfrets (liquorice pastilles). Several different species and variants of liquorice are used medicinally, including *G. glabra* var. *typica* (Spanish or Italian liquorice), var. *violacea* (Persian or Turkish), and var. *glandulifera* (Russian). The main ingredient of *G. glabra* is *glycyrrhizin*, a substance 50 times sweeter than sucrose, with cortisone-like effects. *Glycyrrhiza echinata* (wild liquorice), from S Europe and Asia, is the main source of German and Russian liquorice. *Glycyrrhiza lepidota* (American liquorice) was used by native N Americans and by early settlers for problems with childbirth and menstruation. *Glycyrrhiza uralensis* is a key herb in traditional Chinese medicine, its use being associated with longevity. Two other species, *G. glabra* and *G. inflata*, are also used in Chinese medicine as *gan cao* (which means "sweet herb"). Research into Kampo (Sino-Japanese) herbal medicines has shown that liquorice reduces levels of immune complexes in auto-immune diseases, such as arthritis and systemic lupus erythematosus.

CULTIVATION Deep, rich, sandy soil in sun. Slightly alkaline, moisture-retentive conditions give the best results. Remove flower heads to encourage stronger roots and stolons, unless seed is required. Difficult to eradicate when well established.

Glycyrrhiza glabra

PROPAGATION By seed sown in spring; by division in autumn or spring; by stolon cuttings in spring. Seeds should be scarified or soaked overnight to speed germination. Seedlings are slow-growing.
HARVEST Roots and stolons are lifted in early autumn, 3–4 years after planting, and dried for decoctions, liquid extracts, pastilles, and powder, or crushed and boiled to produce juice, which is evaporated and rolled into sticks or cakes.

■ *Glycyrrhiza glabra* (liquorice)
Variable perennial with stoloniferous roots, downy stems, and pinnate leaves, 5–20cm (2–8in) long, which have 9–17 often sticky leaflets. Pale blue to violet, pea flowers are borne in loose spikes, 5–8cm (2–3in) long, followed by oblong pods, to 3cm (1¼in) long, containing 2–4 kidney-shaped seeds. Native to the Mediterranean and SW Asia. ‡ 1.5m (5ft), ↔ 1m (3ft). 'Pontefract' is a hardy, slow-growing clone. ‡ 1m (3ft). 'Poznan' is vigorous and free-flowering, with a high sugar content. ‡ 1.2m (4ft).
HARDINESS Fully hardy.
PARTS USED Roots, stolons. A very sweet, moist, soothing herb that is anti-inflammatory and expectorant, controls coughing, and has hormonal and laxative effects. It detoxifies and protects the liver.
MEDICINAL USES Internally for Addison's disease, asthma, bronchitis, coughs, peptic ulcer, arthritis, allergic complaints, and following steroid therapy. Not given to pregnant women or patients with anaemia, high blood pressure, kidney disease, or taking digoxin-based medication. Excess causes water retention and high blood pressure. Externally for eczema, herpes, and shingles. For use only by qualified practitioners.
CULINARY USES Roots ("liquorice sticks") are chewed as sweets.
ECONOMIC USES Liquorice extract and powder are used in confectionery and to flavour tobacco, beer, soft drinks, and pharmaceutical products (notably laxatives); also as an ingredient in herb teas, a foaming agent in beers and fire extinguishers, and colorant in stout.

Glycyrrhiza uralensis syn. *G. viscida* (Chinese liquorice, Manchurian liquorice)
Erect perennial with extensive branched rhizomes and pinnate leaves, 10–25cm (4–10in) long. Violet and white flowers appear in dense compact spikes, to 7cm (3in) long, followed by curved, linear–oblong pods, to 4cm (1½in) long. Native to C Asia, China, and Japan. ‡ 40cm–1m (16–36in), ↔ 30–60cm (12–24in).
HARDINESS Fully hardy.
PARTS USED Roots (*gan cao*).
PROPERTIES A sweet tonic herb that stimulates adrenocorticol hormones, relaxes spasms, reduces pain and inflammation, is expectorant, and laxative, and controls coughing. It also neutralizes toxins and balances blood sugar levels.
MEDICINAL USES Internally for Addison's disease, asthma, coughs, and peptic ulcer; externally for acne (combined with flowers of *Lonicera japonica*, see p.266), boils, and sore throat. Added to almost all formulas to harmonize and direct the effects of the various ingredients. Combined with *Panax ginseng* (see p.300) as an energy tonic. Precipitates many compounds, therefore considered incompatible with *Daphne genkwa* (see p.190), *Euphorbia kansui* (see p.210), *E. pekinensis*, and *Sargassum fusiforme* (see p.361); reduces effectiveness of *Coptis chinensis* (see p.179), *Corydalis solida* (see p.181), and *Tetradium ruticarpum* (see p.385); increases toxicity of salicylates, ephedrine, adrenaline, oral hypoglycaemics, and cortisone. Contraindicated in pregnancy, anaemia, hypertension, kidney disease, and for patients taking digoxin-based medication. Excess causes water retention and high blood pressure. Hormonal effects may cause impotence. For use only by qualified practitioners.

GNAPHALIUM
Asteraceae

About 150 species of annuals and perennials belong to this cosmopolitan genus, which is closely related to *Anaphalis*. Few have little to recommend them as garden plants, though some New Zealand species are sought after by alpine enthusiasts. According to Culpeper, "the juice of the herb taken with wine and milk, is, as Pliny saith, a sovereign remedy against the mumps and quinsey" (*The English Physician Enlarged*, 1653). The American *Gnaphalium obtusifolium* (sweet everlasting) was similarly used by the Creek people, who boiled the leaves in water, added lard, and then wrapped cloths soaked in the liquid around the swollen neck. Others include *G. polycephalum*, an Indian remedy for mouth ulcers, and *G. multiceps*, a Chinese cough cure. *Gnaphalium* comes from the Greek *gnaphalion*, "soft down", and refers to the woolly foliage.
CULTIVATION Moist to wet, acid soil in sun or partial shade.
PROPAGATION By seed sown in spring.
HARVEST Plants are cut when in flower and dried for infusions, liquid extracts, and tinctures.

Gnaphalium uliginosum

■ *Gnaphalium uliginosum* syn. *Filaginella uliginosa* (cottonweed, low cudweed, marsh cudweed)
Woolly annual with spreading stems and silver-grey, stalkless leaves, to 5cm (2in) long. Tiny, yellow-brown flowers are borne in dense terminal clusters in summer. Native to Europe, W Asia, and N America. ‡ 4–20cm (1½–8in), ↔ 20cm (8in).
HARDINESS Hardy.
PARTS USED Whole plant.
PROPERTIES An astringent, antiseptic, slightly aromatic herb that is diuretic, anti-inflammatory, resolves catarrh, and increases perspiration. May have anti-depressant and aphrodisiac effects.
MEDICINAL USES Internally and externally for laryngitis, upper respiratory catarrh, and tonsillitis. Combined with *Sambucus nigra* (see p.357), *Xanthium strumarium* (see p.409), or *Solidago virgaurea* (see p.372) for catarrh, and with *Echinacea purpurea* (see p.199) or *Galium aparine* (see p.219) for throat infections.

GOMPHRENA
Gomphrena paniculata. See *Pfaffia paniculatum.*

GOSSYPIUM
Malvaceae

There are 39 species of annuals, perennials, subshrubs, shrubs, and small trees in this genus, which is distributed throughout warm-temperate and tropical regions. *Gossypium* is closely related to *Hibiscus* (see p.235), but is less ornamental. The seeds are covered with long hairs, which can be spun into thread, and also short hairs, which are suitable for felt. Although perennial, cotton plants are usually grown as annuals in order to minimize the incidence of pests and diseases. *Gossypium herbaceum* was introduced from India to Egypt and China c.500BC and to the USA in 1774. Cotton is also produced from *G. arboreum* (short-staple American cotton), *G. barbadensis* (sea-island cotton), and *G. hirsutum* (upland cotton). Various parts of the cotton plant are also used in the traditional medicine of producer countries. Research into its potential as a male contraceptive began in the 1970s, following the use in China of cotton-seed oil for cooking, which caused infertility in men. The active constituent appears to be gossypol, a fraction of the oil that also stimulates the uterus in women.

CULTIVATION Rich, well-drained soil in sun. Pinch out tips in spring to encourage bushiness. Commercial crops are prone to numerous pests and diseases.

PROPAGATION By seed sown in spring at 24–30°C (75–85°F).

HARVEST Leaves are picked during the growing season for use in poultices or lotions. Roots are lifted in autumn, peeled and dried for decoctions, liquid extracts, and tinctures. Seed heads (bolls) are picked when ripe; seeds are separated from fibres for oil extraction and decoctions.

▣ *Gossypium herbaceum* (cotton, Levant cotton) Short-lived, shrubby perennial with lobed leaves, 15cm (6in) across, dotted with black oil glands. Yellow flowers, 5cm (2in) across, with purple centres, are followed by a brittle capsule, filled with lint-covered seeds. Native to Asia and Africa. ↕ 1.5m (5ft), ↔ 1m (3ft).

HARDINESS Min. 13–18°C (55–64°F).

PARTS USED Leaves, root bark, seeds.

PROPERTIES An astringent, slightly acidic, aromatic herb that causes uterine contractions, depresses sperm production, lowers fever, reduces inflammation, and soothes irritated tissues. It also has anti-bacterial and anti-viral effects.

MEDICINAL USES Internally for painful menstruation (root bark); dysentery, intermittent fever, and fibroids (seeds); gastroenteritis (leaves). Externally for thrush, scalds, bruises, and sores (leaves); herpes, scabies, wounds, and orchitis (seeds). For use only by qualified practitioners.

CULINARY USES Cotton-seed oil (with gossypol removed) is used as a salad and cooking oil, especially in Egyptian cuisine.

ECONOMIC USES Seed oil is used in making margarine, vegetable shortenings, soaps, and animal feeds. Seed fibres account for 56 per cent of all natural fibres used in fabrics, cordage, cotton wool, paper, and rayon. Other industrial uses include X-ray and photographic films and explosives.

▣ ◪ ▨ ▩ ◨ ◿ ◿ ▣

228 | *Gossypium herbaceum*

Gratiola officinalis

GRATIOLA
Scrophulariaceae

About 25 species of perennials belong to this genus, which occurs throughout temperate regions. *Gratiola officinalis* (hedge hyssop) is one of the few that has any merit as a garden plant, making a good subject for the margins of ponds and streams, or in damp areas of the wild garden. Hedge hyssop is an extremely poisonous plant and should not be confused with, or used as a substitute for, true hyssop (see *Hyssopus officinalis*, p.240). *Gratiola officinalis* was much used medicinally but is now obsolete on account of its toxicity; it contains cucurbitacins, which are poisonous to living cells, and glycosides similar in effect to those in *Digitalis* spp. (see p.193). Plants are still widely grown in herb gardens and sold as medicinal herbs by specialist nurseries. *Gratiola* comes from the Latin *gratia*, "grace" or "thanks", as it was once revered for its medicinal virtues.

CULTIVATION Rich, damp to wet, alkaline soil in sun.

PROPAGATION By seed sown in spring; by division in spring.

HARVEST Plants are cut when flowering and dried for use in infusions.

⚠ **WARNING** Toxic if eaten.

▣ *Gratiola officinalis* (hedge hyssop) Perennial with white scaly rhizomes and hollow stems bearing lanceolate leaves, to 2.5cm (1in) long. Small, solitary, yellow-white, tubular flowers, veined purple-red, appear in summer, followed by four-valved seed capsules. Native to Europe. ↕ 30–60cm (12–24in), ↔ 20–38cm (8–15in).

HARDINESS Fully hardy.

PARTS USED Whole plant.

PROPERTIES A bitter, acrid, diuretic herb that stimulates the heart and uterus and has purgative and emetic effects.

MEDICINAL USES Internally, formerly used for liver complaints, jaundice, dropsy, enlarged spleen, and intestinal worms. Excess causes abortion, kidney damage, and bowel haemorrhage.

◪ ▣

GRINDELIA
Gumplant
Asteraceae

Some 60 species of annuals, biennials, evergreen perennials, and subshrubs are included in this genus, distributed in dry sunny areas of southern, central, and western N America. A few are grown for their daisy-like, yellow flowers, which are protected when in bud by sticky white resin. *Grindelia* is unusual in containing up to 21 per cent resin – a substance more often associated with trees. Several species, including *G. lanceolata* and *G. squarrosa*, were used by native N Americans for bronchial complaints and poison-ivy rash. The latter use was observed by Dr Canfield of Monterey, California, in 1863, and *Grindelia* became an official drug, listed in the *US Pharmacopoeia* (1882–1926) and in the *US National Formulary* (1926–60). *Grindelia* is named after David Hieronymus Grindel (1776–1836), professor of chemistry and pharmacy in Dorpat (Estonia).

CULTIVATION Well-drained, poor soil in sun.

PROPAGATION By seed sown in spring at 16–19°C (61–66°F); by semi-ripe cuttings in summer.

HARVEST Plants are cut in full bloom and dried for use in infusions, liquid extracts, and tinctures, or used fresh in poultices. Flowers are preferred for tinctures.

Grindelia camporum

■ **Grindelia camporum**
syn. *G. robusta* var. *rigida*
(gumweed, rosinweed,
tarweed, *yerba del buey*)
Annual or short-lived,
aromatic perennial with
narrowly oblong, toothed, resinous
leaves, to 8cm (3in) long, and
yellow daisies, about 5cm (2in)
across, with resin-coated buds,
in summer. Native to California.
‡ 50cm−1.2m (20in−4ft), ↔ 75cm (30in).
HARDINESS Fully hardy.
PARTS USED Whole plant.
PROPERTIES A bitter, pungent, aromatic herb
that is anti-inflammatory and expectorant, relaxes
spasms, and has sedative effects.
MEDICINAL USES Internally for bronchitis,
asthma, whooping cough, and cystitis.
Externally for poison-ivy/oak rash, dermatitis,
eczema, and skin eruptions. Combined with
Euphorbia hirta (see p.210), *Glycyrrhiza glabra*
(see p.227), *Inula helenium* (see p.243), *Lobelia
inflata* (see p.265), or *Primula veris* (see p.330)
for bronchial complaints. Excess may irritate
the kidneys.
CULINARY USES The gum is chewed like
chewing gum.

GUAIACUM

Zygophyllaceae

Six species of evergreen shrubs and trees make
up this genus, which occurs in the West Indies
and warm parts of the Americas. *Guaiacum
officinale* grows in dry coastal areas but is
now rare in the wild, having been intensively
exploited for over four centuries. It is widely
cultivated for its magnificent blue flowers, and
it is the national flower of Jamaica. *Guaiacum*
is from the Spanish *guayaco*, originally a Taino
Indian word for the plant. The common name
"lignum vitae" is Latin in origin, meaning
"wood of life". The Spanish began exporting
G. officinale to Europe in 1503, monopolizing
the trade in its fine bicoloured wood and
medicinal byproducts. Exploitation was so
intensive that as long ago as 1701 Martinique

passed a law to protect lignum vitae trees.
Guaiacum officinale was used by native people
in S America to treat syphilis, which had been
introduced by the colonists; Europeans also
adopted this use for 200 years, until the advent
of modern drugs. The medicinal properties of
G. officinale were first described by Sir Hans
Sloane (1660−1753), who practised medicine
in Jamaica. The wood contains about 20 per
cent resin, which can be used as a chemical
reagent to detect bloodstains. *Guaiacum
sanctum* is also exploited as a source of lignum
vitae, as are the related *Bulnesia sarmienti*
(Paraguay lignum vitae) and *B. arborea*
(Maracaibo lignum vitae). Essential oil is also
extracted from *B. arborea* and *B. sarmienti* for
use as a fixative and fragrance in soaps,
cosmetics, and perfumery.
CULTIVATION Rich, sandy, fibrous soil.
Seedlings and saplings do not transplant well
from small pots and should be given relatively
large containers at each stage.
PROPAGATION By seed, sown with orange-
yellow pericarp intact, when ripe at 26°C
(79°F); by softwood cuttings in spring.
HARVEST Wood (preferably heartwood) is
cut as required and processed into chips and
shavings, which are heated to extract resin for
use in decoctions, liquid extracts, and tinctures.

■ **Guaiacum officinale** (guaiac, guaiacum,
lignum vitae)
Small tree with dark green, pinnate leaves,
about 9cm (3½in) long. Deep blue flowers, to
2.5cm (1in) across, are produced in abundance,
followed by orange-yellow capsules, for much
of the year. Native to southern C America to
northern S America and the West Indies.
‡ 5−9m (15−28ft), ↔ 7−8m (22−25ft).
HARDINESS Min. 15°C (59°F).
PARTS USED Wood, resin.
PROPERTIES A bitter aromatic herb that
stimulates the peripheral circulation, increases
perspiration rate, is diuretic, anti-inflammatory,
and expectorant, and clears toxins from the
tissues. A mild laxative.
MEDICINAL USES Internally for upper
respiratory tract infections. Internally and
externally for rheumatic and arthritic complaints,
and gout. Formerly used to treat syphilis.

Guaiacum officinale

ECONOMIC USES Resin is used to flavour
baked produce and chewing gum and is added
to edible oils to improve keeping qualities. The
wood is heavier than water and is used in the
propeller shafts of ships, as well as for bowling
balls and carving.
⚠ **WARNING** This herb is subject to legal
restrictions in some countries.

GYNOSTEMMA

Cucurbitaceae

This genus occurs in S and E Asia, and consists
of two species that climb by means of tendrils.
Gynostemma pentaphyllum was first described
in traditional Chinese medicine during the Ming
dynasty (1368−1644) as a folk remedy for
hepatitis, bronchitis, and peptic ulcers. A
better understanding of its properties was gained
in the 1980s, as part of a Japanese research
programme into herbs with possible anti-cancer
effects. It was rated among the ten most important
tonic herbs at the 1991 International Conference
on Traditional Medicine, in Beijing, China.
CULTIVATION Moist, well-drained soil in partial
shade.
PROPAGATION By seed sown in spring, soaked
for 24 hours before sowing.
HARVEST Plants are cut in summer and dried
for use in capsules, decoctions, extracts, tablets,
and teabags.

■ **Gynostemma pentaphyllum** (gospel herb,
sweet tea vine)
Annual or short-lived perennial climber with
palmate leaves, divided into 3−7 toothed
leaflets, terminal leaflet to 8cm (3in) long.
Small, yellow-green, star-shaped flowers are
produced in summer, in panicles, to 15cm (6in)
long, followed by smooth, dark green fruits, to
8cm (3in) across, marked with white lines.
Native to Japan. ‡ 8m (25ft).
HARDINESS Frost hardy.
PARTS USED Whole plant.
PROPERTIES A tonic herb that improves the
circulation, stimulates liver function,
strengthens the immune and nervous systems,
and reduces blood sugar and cholesterol levels.

G

Gynostemma pentaphyllum

It also has sedative effects, relaxing spasms and lowering blood pressure.

MEDICINAL USES Internally for nervous tension and exhaustion, peptic ulcer, asthma, bronchitis, diabetes, cardiovascular disease, and cancer.

ECONOMIC USES Used in anti-ageing tonics and cosmetics.

H

HAMAMELIS
Witch hazel

Hamamelidaceae

Five or six species of deciduous shrubs belong to this genus, which ranges across N America, Europe, and E Asia. *Hamamelis* spp. and hybrids are weather-tolerant shrubs that flower between autumn and spring. The common name "witch hazel" refers to occult powers attributed to these plants, whose hazel-like branches were used as divining rods for water and gold. Several native N American tribes knew the medicinal properties of *H. virginiana*; the Mohawk made a wash for bruised eyes by steeping the bark in water. The herb was adopted by settlers and listed in the *US Pharmacopoeia* (1862–1916) and in the *US National Formulary* (1916–55). Distilled witch hazel can be bought in a pharmacy for first aid or for making cosmetics but is less effective than the tincture for treating more serious conditions.

CULTIVATION Moist, humus-rich, neutral to acid soil in sun or partial shade. Cut back rangy growths after flowering.

PROPAGATION By seed sown when ripe; by suckers. Germination is slow and erratic and may take up to two years.

HARVEST Leaves are picked in summer for dry and liquid extracts and ointments. Branches are cut in spring and decorticated for use in tinctures. Twigs are cut in spring for use in distilled extracts.

■ *Hamamelis virginiana* (Virginian witch hazel) Shrub with broadly ovate to obovate leaves, to 15cm (6in) long, which turn yellow in autumn. Clusters of 2–4 scented flowers with crinkled, linear, yellow petals appear in autumn as the leaves fall, followed by dehiscent fruits. Native to eastern N America. ‡ 5m (15ft), ↔ 4m (12ft).

HARDINESS Fully hardy.

PARTS USED Leaves, branches, bark.

PROPERTIES An astringent, slightly aromatic herb that checks bleeding and mucus discharge, and reduces inflammation.

MEDICINAL USES Internally for diarrhoea, colitis, dysentery, haemorrhoids, vaginal discharge, excessive menstruation, haemorrhage in stomach or lungs, and prolapsed organs. Externally for varicose veins, sprains, bruises, burns, haemorrhoids, sore nipples, muscular aches, eye and skin inflammations, and sore throat. Combined with *Agrimonia eupatoria* (see p.107) and *Quercus robur* (see p.339) for

Hamamelis virginiana

diarrhoea; with *Plantago major* (see p.332) or *Ranunculus ficaria* (see p.340) for haemorrhoids; with *Aesculus hippocastanum* (see p.104) and *Calendula officinalis* (see p.150) for varicose veins.

ECONOMIC USES Distilled witch hazel is an important ingredient of eye drops, skin creams, ointments, and skin tonics.

HARPAGOPHYTUM

Pedaliaceae

Nine species of perennials make up this African genus. *Harpagophytum procumbens* (devil's claw) occurs in red sands of the Transvaal and is hazardous to animals that pick up the thorny fruits on their coats or feet; the fruits are apparently used as mouse traps in Madagascar. It has large colourful flowers but has proved impossible to cultivate outside its native habitat. Devil's claw was introduced to Western medicine by G. H. Mehnert, a South African farmer who observed local people using decoctions of the dried tubers to treat various ailments, notably digestive and rheumatic complaints. It contains bitter compounds, on a par with *Gentiana lutea* (see p.223), and harpagide, an iridoid glycoside, as found in the distantly related *Scrophularia nodosa* (see p.364). *Harpagophytum zeyheri* has similar properties and uses. In 1997 the German pharmaceutical company Sertürner Arznemittel succeeded in selecting, cultivating, and vegetatively propagating a high-quality chemotype of *H. procumbens* in Namibia.

CULTIVATION Sandy soil in sun.

PROPAGATION By seed sown in spring.

HARVEST Tubers are lifted when dormant and dried for use in decoctions, ointments, powders, and tinctures.

■ *Harpagophytum procumbens* (devil's claw, grapple plant)
Tender trailing perennial with tubers, up to 20cm (8in) long and 6cm (2½in) thick, and many stems bearing round to ovate, toothed to pinnately lobed leaves, about 7cm (3in) long, with white hairy undersides. Solitary, red to

Harpagophytum procumbens

purple, trumpet-shaped flowers, to 6cm (2½in) long, appear in spring, followed by dehiscent capsules, to 7cm (3in) long, armed with thorns, 2.5cm (1in) long. Native to South Africa. ‡ 40cm (16in), ↔ 1–1.5m (3–5ft).

HARDINESS Min. 5–10°C (41–50°F).

PARTS USED Tubers.

PROPERTIES A bitter, astringent, sedative, painkilling herb that reduces inflammation and stimulates the digestive and lymphatic systems.

MEDICINAL USES Internally for arthritis, rheumatoid arthritis, spondylosis, neuralgia, and digestive problems involving the gall bladder and pancreas. Externally for arthritic and rheumatic joints. Not given to patients with gastric or duodenal ulcers.

HEBANTHE
Hebanthe paniculata. See *Pfaffia paniculatum.*

HEDEOMA

Lamiaceae

There are 38 species of annuals and perennials in this N American genus. They have no great merit as garden plants, but *H. pulegioides* is often grown in herb gardens. Its neat habit and aromatic foliage make it especially suitable for containers and planting near seats and entrances. It had a long history of use by native N Americans for headaches, feverish colds, menstrual cramps, and abortion before becoming a household remedy among settlers for the same purposes, and a popular digestive herb tea. It has a similar chemistry to *Mentha pulegium* (see p.277), and was listed in the *US Pharmacopoeia* (1831–1916). *Hedeoma floribunda* (mapá, oregano) is used for flavouring and, in N Mexico, as a tea for indigestion. The closely related *Poliomintha bustamanta* (see p.326) is also used for flavouring. *Hedeoma* comes from the Greek *hedys*, "sweet", and *osme*, "scent", referring to the fragrant foliage.

CULTIVATION Rich sandy soil in sun or partial shade.

PROPAGATION By seed in autumn or spring.

Hedeoma pulegioides

Hedera helix

Hedera helix 'Buttercup'

Hedera helix 'Erecta'

Hedera helix 'Glacier'

Hedera helix 'Goldheart'

Hedera helix 'Pedata'

HARVEST Plants are cut when flowering and dried for use in infusions and liquid extracts, or distilled for oil.

■ *Hedeoma pulegioides* (American pennyroyal, squaw mint)
Bushy annual with ovate leaves, to 2.5cm (1in) long, which have a pungent, mint-like aroma. Tiny, pale lilac flowers appear in whorls in the upper leaf axils in summer. Native to eastern N America. ↕ 10–38cm (4–15in), ↔ 7–24cm (3–10in).
HARDINESS Hardy.
PARTS USED Whole plant, oil.
PROPERTIES A pungently aromatic herb that stimulates the uterus, induces perspiration, improves digestion, and is expectorant.
MEDICINAL USES Internally for colds, whooping cough, indigestion, wind, nausea, painful menstruation, and childbirth (plant). Essential oil is extremely toxic and may cause death if taken internally. For use only by qualified practitioners.
CULINARY USES Fresh or dried leaves can be used to make herb tea, or with discretion for flavouring.
ECONOMIC USES Oil is used in commercial food flavouring, insect repellents, and cleaning products.

HEDERA
Ivy

Araliaceae

This genus of 9–11 species of evergreen woody climbers and creepers occurs in Europe, Asia, N Africa, the Canary Islands, Madeira, and the Azores. There are over 300 cultivars of *H. helix* (common ivy), which are popular as ornamentals for ground cover, training on surfaces or as topiary, and for containers. Ivy was sacred to Dionysus (Bacchus), the god of wine; if bound to the brow, it was reputed to prevent intoxication. Wreaths of ivy symbolize fidelity and were part of the marriage ceremony in ancient Greece. They were banned by the early Christian church as a pagan custom. Ivy contains emetine, an amoebicidal alkaloid also found in *Cephaelis ipecacuanha* (see p.163),

and triterpene saponins, which are effective against liver flukes, molluscs, intestinal parasites, and fungal infections. *Hedera* is the original Latin name for ivy.
CULTIVATION Any soil or situation, except waterlogged. Tolerates heavy shade. Plant young climbers horizontally to encourage lateral climbing shoots. Variegated cultivars are often less hardy and need more light. Trim to shape in spring and summer to control new growth. Scale insects, spider mites, and leafspot may damage leaves.
PROPAGATION By separation of rooted sections; by semi-ripe cuttings in summer. Use juvenile growth for climbers, and mature growth for a bushy, non-climbing habit.
HARVEST Leaves are picked and used fresh for decoctions, liquid extracts, ointments, poultices, and tinctures, or macerated in vinegar.
⚠ **WARNING** All parts, especially young leaves and berries, are harmful if eaten. Severe skin irritant and allergen.

■ *Hedera helix* (common ivy)
Variable, self-clinging, evergreen climbing or carpet-forming perennial with stems clad in adventitious roots and dark green, broadly ovate to triangular, 3–5-lobed leaves, 4–6cm (1½–2½in) long. Small, yellow-green flowers, rich in nectar, appear in rounded umbels in autumn on mature plants, followed by globose black berries, 7mm (¼in) across. Native to Europe. ↕ 10–30m (30–100ft), ↔ 5m (15ft).
■ 'Buttercup' has bright yellow, five-lobed leaves (pale green when grown in shade), excellent for a sunny wall. ↕ 2m (6ft). ■ 'Erecta' is an upright, bushy, non-climbing ivy, with slightly rounded leaves. ↕ 1m (3ft), ↔ 1.2m (4ft). ■ 'Glacier' has small, grey-green leaves, marbled silver-grey and cream, popular as a houseplant. ↕ 3m (10ft), ↔ 2m (6ft). ■ 'Goldheart' syn. 'Jubiläum Goldherz', 'Oro di Bogliasco' has

three-lobed, dark green leaves with a yellow central blotch; excellent for walls. ↕ 8m (25ft), ↔ 3m (10ft). ■ 'Pedata' syn. 'Caenwoodiana' (bird's foot ivy) has grey-green, five-lobed leaves, each with an elongated central lobe and backward-pointing basal lobes. ↕ 4m (12ft). 'Sagittifolia Variegata' syn. 'Ingelise' has cream-variegated, medium-sized, five-lobed leaves. Good for walls. ↕ 2m (6ft). 'Spetchley' has tiny, dark green leaves, 5–15mm (¼–⅝in) long, usually with three lobes. Tends to revert. ↕ 1m (3ft).
HARDINESS Fully hardy to frost hardy.
PARTS USED Leaves.
PROPERTIES A bitter, aromatic, anti-bacterial herb with a nauseating taste. It lowers fever, relaxes spasms, is expectorant, and constricts veins.
MEDICINAL USES Internally for gout, rheumatic pain, whooping cough, and bronchitis. Excess destroys red blood cells and causes irritability, diarrhoea, and vomiting. Externally for burns, warts, impetigo, scabies, skin eruptions, swollen tissues, painful joints, neuralgia, toothache, and cellulitis. For use only by qualified practitioners.

HELIANTHUS
Sunflower

Asteraceae

A genus of 70–80 species of tall annuals and perennials. Native to N America, C America, Peru, and Chile. *Helianthus annuus* was grown by native peoples for 3000 years before its introduction to Spain in 1514. Cultivation as an oil seed crop began in Germany and Russia in the 18th century and spread into C Europe and the Mediterranean. Sunflower seeds, numbering up to 1000 per head, are usually striped black and white and arranged in concentric hyperbolic spirals. *Helianthus annuus* is a plant on the

Helianthus annuus

Helianthus annuus 'Elite Sun'

Helichrysum italicum

Helianthus annuus
'Italian White'

Helianthus annuus
Prado Series

Helianthus annuus
'Russian Giant'

Helianthus annuus
'Teddy Bear'

borderline between food and herb. It was, however, widely used for medicinal purposes in Russia; a treatment for malaria, involving the maceration of sunflower stems and heads in vodka to stimulate perspiration, was used successfully by a woman healer in Siberia and passed into the repertoire of folk remedies.

CULTIVATION Well-drained, neutral to alkaline soil in sun. Tolerates drought. Young plants are susceptible to slugs. Flower heads may be affected by *Botrytis* in cool damp conditions. Stems may collapse through *Sclerotinia* disease. Flowers attract beneficial insects, such as lacewings and parasitic wasps, which prey on garden pests, notably aphids.

PROPAGATION By seed sown in spring.

HARVEST Whole plants are cut as flowering begins and used fresh for liquid extracts or tinctures. Seeds are collected in autumn and used fresh, pressed for oil, or roasted.

▣ *Helianthus annuus* (sunflower)
Giant, summer-flowering annual with thick, erect, sometimes branched, hairy stems and broadly ovate, toothed, roughly hairy leaves, 10–40cm (4–16in) long. Large, daisy-like flower heads, to 30cm (12in) across, with brown disc florets and yellow ray florets, appear in summer. Found from the USA to C America. ‡ to 5m (15ft), ↔ 60cm (24in). ▣ 'Elite Sun' has large uniform flowers on comparatively short stems, ideal for cutting. ‡ 1.2m (4ft). ▣ 'Italian White' has small, black-centred, cream flowers on branched plants. ‡ 1.2m (4ft). ▣ Prado Series is well branched, producing up to 20 yellow or mahogany flowers that are almost pollen-free; ideal for cut flowers. ‡ 1.35–1.5m (4–5ft). ▣ 'Russian Giant' produces consistently tall plants with large flowers, to 25cm (10in) across.

‡ 3.5m (11ft). ▣ 'Teddy Bear' is dwarf, with fully double, yellow blooms. ‡ 45cm (18in), ↔ 30cm (12in).

HARDINESS Hardy.

PARTS USED Whole plant, seeds, oil.

PROPERTIES A nutritious herb that lowers cholesterol levels and soothes irritated tissues.

MEDICINAL USES Internally for bronchial infections (seeds), tuberculosis, and malaria (whole plant). Externally as a base for massage oils and liniments used for rheumatic complaints and muscular aches.

CULINARY USES Seeds are eaten fresh or roasted, salted, added to bread, biscuits, and confectionery, or ground for baking or making into sunflower butter or seed milk; also sprouted and fermented to make seed yogurt and cheese. Seedlings are eaten in salads. Oil is used for cooking and salads.

ECONOMIC USES Oil is used for manufacture of margarine. Residue is important in animal feeds.
▣ ▣ ▣ ▣ ✎ ✎

HELICHRYSUM
Everlasting flower

Asteraceae

This large genus of about 500 species of annuals, herbaceous or evergreen perennials, and evergreen shrubs and subshrubs occurs in Europe, Asia, Africa (especially South Africa), and Australasia, mostly in dry sunny places. Many species have aromatic grey foliage and papery "everlasting" flowers, making attractive plants for sunny borders. Though not particularly important as herbs, several species are grown in herb gardens for their scent and appearance. Some have minor uses: *H. orientale* (immortelle)

yields essential oil, used in perfume blending; *H. petiolare* syn. *H. petiolatum* hort. (liquorice plant, silver liquorice) has liquorice-flavoured roots; *H. serpyllifolium* (Hottentot tea) was popular as a tea in South Africa, until doubts were cast on its safety; and *H. stoechas* (eternal flower) is an obsolete medicinal herb, once used as an expectorant. Many helichrysum dry well for floral arrangements and potpourris. *Helichrysum* comes from the Greek *helios*, "sun", and *chrysos*, "golden", referring to the flower colour.

CULTIVATION Light, well-drained soil in sun. Dislikes excessively wet winters. Cut back to within 2.5cm (1in) of previous year's growth in spring.

PROPAGATION By seed sown at 13–16°C (55–61°F) in spring; by heel or semi-ripe cuttings in summer.

HARVEST Sprigs are picked in summer and used fresh for flavouring or extraction of essential oil.

▣ *Helichrysum italicum* syn. *H. angustifolium* Evergreen subshrub with aromatic, linear, silver-grey to yellow-green leaves, to 3cm (1¼in) long. Small, deep yellow, button-like flowers are borne in corymbs, to 8cm (3in) across, in summer and autumn. Native to S Europe. ‡ 60cm (24in), ↔ 1m (3ft). ▣ subsp. *serotinum* syn. *H. serotinum* (curry plant) is compact, with strongly aromatic leaves, to 4cm

Helichrysum italicum subsp. *serotinum*

(1½in) long. The whole plant smells strongly of curry, especially after rain. ‡ 40cm (16in), ↔ 75cm (30in).
HARDINESS Frost hardy.
PARTS USED Leaves, oil.
PROPERTIES An aromatic herb.
CULINARY USES Sprigs are added to rice, vegetables, and egg dishes to give a mild curry flavour; best cooked briefly.
ECONOMIC USES Oil and extract are used to enhance fruit flavours in foods and drinks.

HELLEBORUS
Hellebore

Ranunculaceae

A genus of 15 species of poisonous perennials, found mostly on alkaline soils from C, E, and S Europe to W Asia. Hellebores are popular garden plants, producing handsome foliage and a long-lasting display of bowl-shaped flowers in winter and spring. *Helleborus niger* (Christmas rose) is one of the earliest and most popular, often in flower during the coldest shortest days of winter. The species name *niger* and common name "black hellebore" refer to the colour of the roots. The word "hellebore" is Greek in origin and came to be used for any plant supposed to cure madness, as in *Veratrum viride* (American hellebore, see p.401) and *Adonis vernalis* (false hellebore, see p.103). In Classical times the plant was also known as "melampodium" after Melampus, a Greek shepherd who in c.1400BC reputedly discovered its use in treating nervous conditions after noticing its effect on goats. According to the Theory of Four Humours, black hellebore expelled black bile, which in excess was thought to cause mental disorders. It was an ingredient of Paracelsus's Elixir of Life and remained popular in medicine until the 18th century. Few herbalists now use it owing to its toxicity. One of its earlier uses was to destroy lice; it has caused abortion in pregnant women who used it for this purpose. The roots contain cardiac glycosides, similar in effects to those found in *Digitalis* spp. (see p.193).
CULTIVATION Moist, rich, neutral to alkaline soil in partial shade. Thrives in heavy soils.

Helleborus niger

Helleborus niger 'Potter's Wheel'

PROPAGATION By seed sown when ripe; by division after flowering or in late summer.
HARVEST Roots are collected in autumn for extraction of alkaloids.
⚠ **WARNING** All parts are extremely toxic if eaten. Prolonged handling may cause systemic poisoning.

◾ *Helleborus niger* (black hellebore, Christmas rose)
Clump-forming, semi-evergreen perennial with pedate, leathery, dark green leaves, 5–20cm (2–8in) long, divided into 7–9 narrowly ovate, toothed leaflets. White, often pink-flushed, five-petalled flowers, to 8cm (3in) across, ageing pink, are produced singly or in twos or threes from winter to spring. Native to Austria, Germany, Switzerland, Italy, and Slovenia.
‡ 15–30cm (6–12in), ↔ 45cm (18in). ◾ 'Potter's Wheel' has large, green-centred flowers.
HARDINESS Fully hardy.
PARTS USED Roots.
PROPERTIES A bitter, acrid, purgative herb that stimulates the heart and uterus, and has anthelmintic and insecticidal effects.
MEDICINAL USES Formerly used internally for nervous and mental disorders, amenorrhoea, dropsy, and intestinal parasites; externally to destroy lice. Used internally, in the form of alkaloids, to treat heart conditions in the elderly. For use only by professional practitioners. Excess causes abortion in pregnant women and may prove fatal.

HELONIAS
Helonias dioica. See *Chamaelirium luteum*.

HEPATICA
Ranunculaceae

Ten species of small perennials belong to this genus, which occurs throughout northern temperate regions. They are delightful plants for the rock garden or containers, with anemone-like flowers in early spring. *Hepatica* comes from the Greek *hepar*, "liver", and refers to the liver-like shape and colour of the leaves, which,

Hepatica nobilis

according to the Doctrine of Signatures (see p.15), indicate its use for liver complaints. *Hepatica nobilis* has a long history of use in traditional European medicine. Culpeper wrote that "it fortifies the liver exceedingly, and makes it impregnable" (*The English Physician Enlarged*, 1653). Early settlers in N America valued it for hepatitis and found that native tribes used the closely related *H. acutiloba* (sharplobe hepatica) in similar ways.
CULTIVATION Deep, moist, humus-rich, alkaline soil in shade. Thrives in heavy soils. Dislikes disturbance.
PROPAGATION By seed sown when ripe (species only); by division in spring.
HARVEST Plants are cut from late spring to midsummer and dried for use in infusions, liquid extracts, and tinctures.

◾ *Hepatica nobilis* syn. *H. triloba*, *Anemone hepatica* (kidneywort, liverwort, liverleaf)
Variable, semi-evergreen perennial with a thick rhizome and rounded to kidney-shaped, three-lobed leaves, 3–6cm (1¼–2½in) long, which have silky-haired, often purple undersides. Blue, blue-purple, pink, or white flowers, to 2.5cm (1in) across, appear in spring before or with the new leaves. Native to Europe.
‡ 8–10cm (3–4in), ↔ 15cm (6in). ◾ 'Rubra Plena' has double, deep purple-pink flowers. It is less vigorous than the species; needs careful

Hepatica nobilis 'Rubra Plena'

H

233

cultivation. ‡ 8cm (3in), ↔ 10–12cm (4–5in).
HARDINESS Fully hardy.
PARTS USED Whole plant.
PROPERTIES An astringent, diuretic, antibiotic herb that acts as a mild tonic for the liver and the digestive and bronchial systems. It also promotes healing.
MEDICINAL USES Internally for bronchial and digestive complaints, and liver and gall bladder disorders. Externally for minor injuries and ringworm. It is little used today.

HERACLEUM
Apiaceae

This genus of 70 species of annuals, biennials, and perennials is distributed in northern temperate regions and on tropical mountains. *Heracleum* comes from the Greek *herakleia*, "in honour of Hercules", and alludes to the great size of some species. Gerard's *Herball* (1597) recommended *H. sphondylium* for headaches, poor memory, melancholy, and agitation. It contains volatile oil and bergapten, a furanocoumarin that can cause photosensitivity. The fruits of the N American *H. lanatum* (cow parsnip) were used by Eclectic physicians in the 19th century to treat epilepsy, while various native N American tribes used the roots externally for healing and pain relief. *Heracleum maximum* (also known as "cow parsnip") was similarly used for rheumatic pain and palpitations, and internally for indigestion and asthma. The difficulty in identifying white-flowered members of the parsley family, many of which are toxic, makes it potentially dangerous to use these plants for food or medicine.
CULTIVATION Any soil in sun or partial shade. *Heracleum sphondylium* should not be confused with *H. mantegazzianum* (giant hogweed).
PROPAGATION By seed sown in spring.
HARVEST Plants are cut just before flowering for use fresh or dried in infusions.
Leaves are cut before flowering, and fruits are collected when ripe for use in infusions, liquid extracts, and tinctures.
⚠ **WARNING** Skin irritant in sunlight.

■ *Heracleum sphondylium* (cow parsnip, hogweed, keck)
Variable stout biennial with hollow stems and rough pinnate leaves, to 60cm (24in) long. White or pink flowers are produced in umbels, to 20cm (8in) across, in summer, followed by pale brown fruits. Native to Europe, Asia, and NW Africa. ‡ 2m (6ft), ↔ 1.2m (4ft).
HARDINESS Fully hardy.
PARTS USED Whole plant, leaves, leafstalks, fruits.
PROPERTIES An aromatic, sedative, mildly expectorant herb that has a tonic effect on the digestion, lowers blood pressure, and is reputedly aphrodisiac.
MEDICINAL USES Internally for laryngitis, bronchitis, and debility; little used today.
CULINARY USES Foliage and fruits are boiled and fermented to make a beer, known as *Parst*, or *Bartsch*; leafstalks are distilled either alone or with bilberries, as a spirit (E Europe). Leafstalks are tied in bundles and sun-dried until yellow, exuding a sugar substance eaten as a delicacy in Russia and Siberia. Young shoots are eaten raw or cooked like asparagus.

HERNIARIA
Caryophyllaceae

A genus of 15–20 species of low-growing annuals and perennials, found in Eurasia and Africa, especially in Mediterranean regions. The only species seen in cultivation is *H. glabra* (rupturewort), which makes good ground cover on poor soil but is mainly grown in herb gardens. Rupturewort first appeared in European herbals in the 16th century and was much used for "purifying the blood". Its therapeutic uses are not clinically proven. The N African *H. hirsuta* (*makir*, *mouker*), which occurs from Egypt to Morocco, is similarly used as a diuretic, astringent, depurative, and anti-spasmodic. *Herniaria* refers to its use in treating hernias.
CULTIVATION Well-drained, dry, sandy, neutral to alkaline soil in sun. Tolerates poor soil.
PROPAGATION By seed sown in spring.
HARVEST Plants are cut during the growing season and used fresh in infusions and poultices.

■ *Herniaria glabra* (rupturewort)
Prostrate annual or short-lived perennial with a taproot, branched stems, and tiny, bright green, elliptic to obovate leaves. Minute, green-white flowers appear in the axils in summer. Native to W, C, and S Europe, N Africa, and Asia. ‡ 4cm (1½in), ↔ 30cm (12in).
HARDINESS Fully hardy.
PARTS USED Whole plant.
PROPERTIES An astringent diuretic herb that has mild anti-spasmodic effects, especially on the kidneys.
MEDICINAL USES Internally for urinary and kidney problems, fluid retention, neuritis and neural catarrh, arthritis, and rheumatism. Externally to heal ulcers.

HEUCHERA
Coral flower
Saxifragaceae

There are about 55 species of evergreen and semi-evergreen perennials in this genus, which is N American and Mexican in distribution. Several species are grown as ornamentals, with handsome leaves and delicate flowers that are effective *en masse*. *Heuchera americana* was an important healing herb among native N Americans. It was adopted by settlers and listed briefly in the *US Pharmacopoeia* (1880–82). In the 18th century it had a reputation for curing cancer. *Heuchera* is named after Johann Heinrich von Heucher (1677–1747), professor of medicine at Wittenberg.
CULTIVATION Moist, well-drained, neutral soil in sun or partial shade. Shoots may be distorted by leafy gall; leaf eelworm may damage leaves.
PROPAGATION By seed sown in spring; by division in autumn.
HARVEST Roots are lifted in autumn and dried for decoctions and powders.

■ *Heuchera americana* (alumroot, American sanicle)
Clump-forming perennial with broadly ovate to heart-shaped, leathery leaves, 5–14cm (2–5½in) long, marbled and veined brown when young. Small, purple-green flowers appear in tall panicles during late spring and

Heracleum sphondylium

Herniaria glabra

Heuchera americana

early summer. Native to central and eastern N America. ‡ 45cm (18in), ↔ 30cm (12in).
HARDINESS Fully hardy.
PARTS USED Roots.
PROPERTIES A bitter astringent herb that controls bleeding and discharge, and promotes healing.
MEDICINAL USES Internally for diarrhoea, dysentery, and gastric ulcers. Excess irritates the stomach and causes kidney and liver failure. Externally for sores, wounds, sore throat, and vaginal discharge.
🔲 ▪

HIBISCUS

Malvaceae

Some 220 species of annuals, herbaceous perennials, and deciduous and evergreen shrubs and trees belong to this genus, which occurs in warm-temperate, subtropical, and tropical regions. The most widely cultivated species is *H. rosa-sinensis*, which has numerous cultivars in the tropics, though only red-flowered plants are suitable for the purposes described below. The distinctive flowers, with their projecting column of stamens and style, have become a symbol of exotic places such as Hawaii, and are important in Hindu devotional ceremonies, being sacred to Ganesh, the elephant god. *Hibiscus sabdariffa* was introduced to Jamaica in the 18th century and is now grown in many parts of Asia, Africa, C America, and in California and Florida (USA). It reached Europe in the late 19th century as "Sudanese tea", but was initially unpopular due to its blood-red colour. Today it is used to colour and flavour most fruit-based herb teas. *Hibiscus sabdariffa* var. *altissima* is widely grown for fibre; it has a taller narrower habit. *Hibiscus acetosella* (false roselle) has sour-tasting foliage, used in similar ways to *Rumex acetosa* (sorrel, see p.351). The related *Malvaviscus arboreus* (sleeping hibiscus, *tulipan del monte*) is used in C America and the Caribbean to stimulate hair growth and to promote sweating.
CULTIVATION Well-drained, moist, neutral to alkaline soil in sun. Hibiscus needs full sun and warm summers to flower well. Cut back hard in spring. Whitefly, aphids, and spider mite may attack plants under cover.
PROPAGATION By seed sown in spring (species only) at 13–18°C (55–64°F); by greenwood cuttings in late spring or semi-ripe cuttings in summer.
HARVEST Stems are cut for fibre. Leaves are picked when young and used fresh; flowers are cut and dried for infusions and powders. Calyces are collected when mature and used fresh or dried. Seeds for roasting are collected when ripe.

Hibiscus abelmoschus. See *Abelmoschus moschatus*.

🔲 *Hibiscus rosa-sinensis* (Chinese hibiscus, Hawaiian hibiscus, rose of China)
Dense evergreen shrub with broadly lanceolate to ovate, glossy, dark green leaves, to 15cm (6in) long. Solitary, bright crimson flowers,

Hibiscus rosa-sinensis

Hibiscus rosa-sinensis 'Scarlet Giant'

7–10cm (3–4in) across, with yellow-anthered, red stamens, appear in summer and autumn, or all year round in the tropics. Probably originated in tropical Asia. ‡↔ 1.5–3m (5–10ft). 🔲 'Cooperi' is compact, with lanceolate leaves, variegated white and often pink tinged. ‡↔ 1–2m (3–6ft). 🔲 'Scarlet Giant' has bright scarlet flowers, 12–17cm (5–7in) across.
HARDINESS Min. 10–13°C (50–55°F).
PARTS USED Flowers, juice from petals.
PROPERTIES A sweet, astringent, cooling herb that checks bleeding, soothes irritated tissues, and relaxes spasms.
MEDICINAL USES Internally for excessive and painful menstruation, cystitis, venereal diseases, feverish illnesses, coughs, and for hair growth.
CULINARY USES Flowers are eaten raw or steamed, and used for colouring foods, such as jellies and preserved fruits.
ECONOMIC USES Juice from petals is used in China to make shoe-blacking and mascara.
🔲 ▪ ✒ ✒ 🔲

🔲 *Hibiscus sabdariffa* (Jamaica sorrel, *karkadé*, roselle)
Woody-based perennial with prickly stems and palmately lobed leaves, to 15cm (6in) long. Pale yellow flowers, 8cm (3in) across, with dark purple centres, appear in summer followed by capsules, to 2.5cm (1in) long, each surrounded by an enlarged, fleshy, bright red calyx. Native to Old World Tropics. ‡ 2.5m (8ft), ↔ 2m (6ft).
HARDINESS Min. 10–13°C (50–55°F).
PARTS USED Leaves, stems, flower calyces, seeds.
PROPERTIES An aromatic, astringent, cooling herb that has diuretic effects, helps lower fever, and provides vitamin C.
MEDICINAL USES Internally as a tonic tea for

Hibiscus rosa-sinensis 'Cooperi'

Hibiscus sabdariffa

digestive and kidney functions.
CULINARY USES Leaves have a rhubarb-like flavour, eaten raw or cooked. Calyces are added to jams, curries, and chutneys, and made into cranberry-like sauces, drinks, and syrup. Seeds are eaten roasted, made into an oily sauce, or fermented into Sudanese meat substitute, *furundu*.
ECONOMIC USES Stems are a source of fibre (rosella hemp). Calyces are used to give colour and flavour to herb teas.
🔲 ✒ 🔲 🔲 ▪ ✒ ✒ 🔲

HIERACIUM
Hieracium pilosella. See *Pilosella officinarum*.

HIEROCHLOË
Holy grass

Poaceae

A genus of 15 species of fragrant perennial grasses, occurring mainly in temperate regions, and closely related to *Anthoxanthum* (see p.124), with which it shares the same characteristic scent of new-mown hay when dried. *Hierochloë odorata* (holy grass) is found in damp grassy places in colder parts of both hemispheres. It was held sacred to the Virgin, burned in New Mexico as incense, and used to scent clothes laid at church doors during festivals in C Europe. *Hierochloë odorata* contains glycosides, which on drying produce coumarin, a sweet-smelling, crystalline compound important in perfumery. Coumarin was synthesized from tar in 1868 but is still in demand from natural sources. More than 100 different coumarins are known.
CULTIVATION Well-drained, moisture-retentive

H

Hierochloë odorata

soil in sun.

PROPAGATION By division of rhizomes in spring and summer.

HARVEST Leaves are cut in summer, dried, and stored whole, or distilled for oil.

■ *Hierochloë odorata* syn. *H. borealis* (holy grass, sweet grass, vanilla grass, *zubrovka*)
Vigorous, tuft-forming, deciduous perennial with pointed, flat, linear leaves, 0.5cm (¼in) wide. Pyramidal panicles of ovate brown spikelets appear in spring. Circumboreal.
‡ 25–50cm (10–20in), ↔ 40–60cm (16–24in).

HARDINESS Fully hardy.

PARTS USED Leaves, oil.

PROPERTIES An aromatic herb, with a strong vanilla scent, that acts as an excitant in perfumes and as a fixative for other scents.

ECONOMIC USES Leaves are added to vodka as a flavouring (Poland). They are also in demand for basket weaving. Oil is used to flavour confectionery, soft drinks, and tobacco. Essential oil is used in perfumery.

HIPPOPHAE

Elaeagnaceae

This genus includes three species of deciduous Eurasian shrubs and trees. *Hippophae rhamnoides* is an ornamental resilient shrub for hedging, windbreaks, and soil stabilization, especially in coastal areas. The fruits last well into winter, though the flavour deteriorates in autumn; both male and female plants are needed for fruiting. Fruiting branches can be used in winter floral arrangements. Breeding of sea buckthorn has been carried out mainly in the former E Germany, and several high-yielding cultivars are available for commercial cultivation. The Himalayan *H. salicifolia* (willow-leafed sea buckthorn) is used for similar purposes.

CULTIVATION Well-drained, neutral to alkaline, sandy soil in sun. Plant one male for every eight females, spacing them 1.2–2m (4–6ft) apart. Prune to shape in late summer, if required.

PROPAGATION By seed sown in autumn or stratified for three months before sowing in spring; by semi-ripe cuttings in summer or

Hippophae rhamnoides

hardwood cuttings in late autumn.

HARVEST Fruits are picked when ripe and used whole, juiced, in decoctions, or for oil extraction.

■ *Hippophae rhamnoides* (sea buckthorn, *tsarap*)
Dense, deciduous, thorny shrub with linear, grey-green leaves, to 6cm (2½in) long. Tiny, yellow-green flowers are produced in racemes, to 2cm (¾in) long, in spring, followed on female plants by spherical orange berries, about 7mm (¼in) in diameter, speckled rusty brown. Native to Europe and Asia. ‡↔ 6m (20ft). 'Hergo' is upright, producing heavy crops of large, yellow-orange fruits that yield juice with an orange, passion-fruit flavour when sweetened. 'Leikora' is compact, bearing abundant, large, bright orange fruits. 'Pollmix' is male, selected for pollinating 'Leikora'.
‡ 1.2–1.5m (4–5ft), ↔ 1.5–2m (5–6ft).

HARDINESS Fully hardy.

PARTS USED Fruits, juice, oil.

PROPERTIES A sour astringent herb with a high vitamin A and C content.

MEDICINAL USES Internally as a tonic to increase resistance to infection. Externally for skin problems.

CULINARY USES Fruits are eaten with cheese in E Europe, and made into marmalade, jelly, syrup, and sauces.

ECONOMIC USES Fruits are used in making fruit-flavoured herb teas, liqueurs, and vitamin supplements. Oil is used in skin-care products.

HORDEUM

Barley

Poaceae

About 20 species of annual and perennial grasses belong to this genus, distributed in northern temperate regions and S America. *Hordeum vulgare* is found wild usually only as an escape from cultivation. Pliny referred to barley as the "oldest among human foods", a staple of bread- and beer-making. It is one of the hardiest grain crops, succeeding in parts of Lapland, Siberia, Alaska, and notably in Tibet, where it is the staple food. It was domesticated

in the Middle East c.10,000 years ago. Grains were found in ancient Egyptian and Swiss lake remains (c.2000BC). Barley was first grown in the USA in Massachusetts, in 1602. There are many cultigens, belonging to the two principal types (both included in *H. vulgare*): two-rowed barley (*H. distichum*) and six-rowed barley (*H. polystichum*). In addition, there are two main groups: Coeleste Group (hull-less barley), which sprouts more readily and is essential for making *miso*; and Cerinus–Coeleste Group (waxy hull-less barley), which is higher in soluble fibre and amylopectin (a kind of starch that rapidly converts to sugar). Medicinal uses of barley were featured in the *Ebers papyri* (c.1550BC), in recipes for laxatives, expelling intestinal parasites, and poultices for burns and fractures. Barley was first mentioned in traditional Chinese medicine in the 16th century. Both decorticated ("pearl" barley) and germinated, or sprouted ("malted" barley) seeds are used. Barley has a low gluten content and is unsuitable for leavened bread or baking.

CULTIVATION Well-drained soil in sun.

PROPAGATION By seed sown in autumn or spring.

HARVEST Seeds are collected in autumn and decorticated, flaked, ground into flour, or germinated for health foods and malt extracts.

■ *Hordeum vulgare* (barley)
Annual grass with pale green, linear leaves, about 1cm (⅜in) wide and 20–30cm (8–12in) long. Flowers are produced in 2, 4, or 6 rows, in a cylindrical spike, 7–10cm (3–4in) long, in summer, followed by golden to purple or black seeds, usually covered in a scale-like, membranous bract (hull). Native to the Middle East. ‡ 50–90cm (20–36in), ↔ 30cm (12in).

HARDINESS Hardy.

PARTS USED Seeds (*mai ya*), seedlings.

Hordeum vulgare

PROPERTIES A sweet warming herb that soothes irritated tissues, stimulates appetite, improves digestion, and suppresses lactation. Varieties high in beta-glucan fibre may help lower serum cholesterol and reduce the risk of bowel cancer.

MEDICINAL USES Internally for indigestion (especially in babies, or after eating cereals), *Candida albicans* infection, and in the management of diabetes. Also for excessive lactation, hepatitis, abdominal bloating (germinated seed); coughs, weak digestion (malt extract); poor appetite and digestion during convalescence (barley water). Not given to nursing mothers.

CULINARY USES Barley flour is a staple food, known as *tsampa* in Tibet and *gofio* in the Canary Islands. Pearl barley is cooked in soups and stews, and infused with lemon or orange as barley water.

ECONOMIC USES Source of maltose (barley sugar, malt sugar), used as a natural sweetener. Seeds are germinated and kiln-dried to produce "wort" for brewing beer, distilling whisky, and making malt extracts; also roasted as an ingredient of grain coffees, and made into a Korean tea, *poricha*. Flaked barley is an ingredient of breakfast cereals, and is used in brewing (especially stout). Seedlings are juiced for food supplements. Malted barley flour is used in baked produce. Fermented hull-less barley is an ingredient of *miso* (Japan).
■ ▣ ✎ ✎

HOUTTUYNIA
Saururaceae

This genus consists of a single species of perennial, found in damp shady places in woodland and marshes in E Asia. *Houttuynia cordata* is widely grown as an ornamental for wet soils and shallow water; it makes an excellent, if sometimes invasive, ground cover. The whole plant has an unusual, orange-cilantro aroma. There are two distinct chemotypes: one with an orange scent; and the other resembling cilantro leaves in aroma. *Houttuynia* is popular in the folk medicine of Japan and Vietnam. Survivors of the Hiroshima atom bomb who drank tea made from the plant apparently recuperated well from the effects of radioactivity and lived longer than expected. It is named after Maarten Houttuyn (1720–94), a celebrated Dutch physician and naturalist.

CULTIVATION Moist to wet, humus-rich soil, or shallow water, in sun or partial shade.

PROPAGATION By seed sown when ripe (species only); by division in spring; by softwood cuttings in late spring.

HARVEST Whole plants and leaves are cut in the growing season and used fresh for decoctions.

■ *Houttuynia cordata* (*doku-dami, giâp cá*)
Rhizomatous, deciduous, strongly aromatic perennial with erect branched stems and ovate to heart-shaped, pointed, dull green, often purple-flushed leaves, 3–9cm (1¼–3½in) long. Tiny, yellow-green flowers are borne in summer

Houttuynia cordata

Houttuynia cordata 'Chameleon'

Houttuynia cordata 'Flore Pleno'

in dense spikes, to 3cm (1¼in) long, surrounded at the base by 4–6 white, obovate, petal-like bracts. Native to China and Japan. ‡ 15–30cm (6–12in), ↔ indefinite. ■ 'Chameleon' syn. 'Tricolor' has leaves irregularly marked yellow and bright pink. ■ 'Flore Pleno' syn. 'Plena' has eight or more white bracts, giving the impression of double flowers.

HARDINESS Fully hardy.

PARTS USED Whole plant, leaves (*yu xing cao*).

PROPERTIES A pungent cooling herb that is aromatic and diuretic, clears fevers and toxins, and reduces swelling.

MEDICINAL USES Internally, in traditional Chinese medicine, for upper respiratory tract infections and for inflammation of the urinary tract. Externally for snake bite and skin disorders. In Vietnamese folk medicine, internally for kidney and urinary tract infections, mastitis, otitis media, haemorrhoids, and anal prolapse; externally (as crushed leaves) for urticaria, conjunctivitis, and abscesses.

CULINARY USES Leaves are used in Vietnamese cuisine as a garnish for fish stew and boiled duck eggs; also eaten raw in parts of China.
✎ ▣ ▣ ✎

HUMULUS
Hops
Cannabidaceae

Two species of climbing perennials make up this genus, distributed in northern temperate regions. The golden form of *H. lupulus* and the variegated form of *H. japonicus* are popular in cultivation as fast-growing, colourful climbers. *Humulus lupulus* 'Aureus' is among the finest, golden-leafed climbers, with little or no tendency

to scorch in sun. Male and female flowers are borne on separate plants; only females produce the decorative, cone-like inflorescences known as "hops". Most plants sold as ornamentals or for brewing are female. Beer was originally made using bitter herbs such as *Glechoma hederacea* (see p.225). From the 9th century, the use of hops in brewing beer gained popularity because of their preservative qualities, though acceptance of the new ingredient was slow. Regarded as an "unwholesome weed", the use of hops in beer was banned in Britain by Henry VI (1422–61) and again by Henry VIII (1509–47). Hops were used medicinally by several native N American tribes for insomnia and pain, and were well established in European medicine by the 17th century. Culpeper recommended them for skin infections, jaundice, headaches, and "heat of the liver and stomach" (*The English Physician Enlarged*, 1653). Extracts of hops were listed in the *US Pharmacopoeia* (1831–1916).

CULTIVATION Moist, well-drained, humus-rich soil in sun or partial shade. Remove previous season's growth during dormancy. Thin new shoots as required. Prone to *Verticillium* wilt and downy mildew.

PROPAGATION By seed sown in spring at 15–18°C (59–64°F); by softwood or greenwood cuttings in spring and by leaf-bud cuttings in summer (from female plants). Golden hops comes reasonably true from seed.

HARVEST Flowers are picked in autumn and used fresh or dried for infusions, liquid extracts, tinctures, tablets, and oil distillation. Young shoots are cut in spring for culinary use.

⚠ **WARNING** Skin irritant and allergen.

■ *Humulus lupulus* (hops)
Twining herbaceous climber with bristly stems and 3–5-lobed, coarsely toothed leaves, to 15cm (6in) long. Tiny green male flowers are produced in branched clusters; larger females appear in strobili ("hops") beneath soft, pale green, aromatic bracts, to 2.5cm (1in) long, in summer. Native to Europe, W Asia, and N America. ‡ 3–6m (10–20ft).
■ 'Aureus' (golden hop) has yellow foliage. 'Fuggle' is an early-maturing hop, regarded as the best for home brewing, especially dark beers.

Humulus lupulus

Humulus lupulus 'Aureus'

Hydnocarpus kurzii

Hydrangea arborescens

Thrives in cool climates; highly resistant to mildew. 'Wye Challenger' is a red-stemmed, free-flowering hop, resistant to mildew.

HARDINESS Fully hardy.

PARTS USED Leaves, shoots, female flowers (hops, strobili), oil.

PROPERTIES A bitter tonic herb that is aromatic and diuretic, relieves pain, and relaxes spasms. It is a potent sedative and has hormonal and anti-bacterial effects.

MEDICINAL USES Internally for insomnia, nervous tension, anxiety, irritability, nervous intestinal complaints (including irritable bowel syndrome), priapism, and premature ejaculation. Externally for skin infections, eczema, herpes, and leg ulcers. Combined with *Valeriana officinalis* (see p.400) as a sedative, and with *Chamaemelum nobile* (see p.165) or *Mentha* × *piperita* (see p.277) for nervous digestive problems. Contraindicated in depression.

CULINARY USES Young shoots are eaten raw or cooked like asparagus.

ECONOMIC USES Hops are the main flavouring in beers. Distilled oil and extracts are also used in food flavourings and soft drinks; also in perfumes of the *chypre* and *fougère* types. Dried hops are added to sleep pillows. Dried flowering stems ("bines") are used for decoration.

⊞ ▨ ◳ ⬓ ▣ ◿ ◿

HYDNOCARPUS

Flacourtiaceae

This genus of some 35 species of medium to large, evergreen trees occurs in the Indian subcontinent and Malaysia. *Hydnocarpus kurzii* is one of the few economically important species in the family. The common name "chaulmoogra", the Bengali word for the plant, also refers to *H. anthelmintica* and *H. wightiana*, used for similar purposes. Chaulmoogra was first mentioned in Chinese medical literature in 1347 as *da feng zi*, and spread worldwide as a treatment for serious skin diseases, especially leprosy. The brownish-yellow oil has a unique chemistry, containing acids unknown in any other oils.

CULTIVATION Rich, moist, well-drained soil in moderate humidity.

PROPAGATION By seeds sown when ripe at 18–21°C (64–70°F); by grafting in late spring or early summer.

HARVEST Seeds are separated from berries when ripe and used whole for decoctions, powdered for pills and pastes, or crushed for oil. Oil is given as an emulsion or by injection.

▣ *Hydnocarpus kurzii* syn. *Taraktogenos kurzii* (chaulmoogra)
Large tree with a trunk, to 1.2m (4ft) thick, and lanceolate leathery leaves, about 22cm (9in) long. Male and female flowers are borne separately in summer, followed by round berries containing 12–18 seeds in an oily pulp. Native to SE Asia.
↕ 20–30m (70–100ft), ↔ 15m (50ft).

HARDINESS Min. 12–14°C (54–57°F).

PARTS USED Seeds (*da feng zi*), oil.

PROPERTIES An acrid sedative herb, with an unpleasant smell, that lowers fever and expels intestinal worms. It is a potent antibiotic and alterative. In excess, it is a cardiovascular depressant.

MEDICINAL USES Internally for leprosy, scabies, eczema, psoriasis, scrofula, ringworm, and intestinal worms. May cause vomiting, dizziness, and breathing difficulties. Externally as a dressing for skin diseases and anal fissure, usually in the form of an ointment, 10 per cent oil to 90 per cent soft paraffin; also combined with walnut oil and pork lard for ringworm; with calomel and sesame oil for leprosy; or with sulphur and camphor for scabies. For use by qualified practitioners only.

◳ ▨ ▣ ◲

HYDRANGEA

Hydrangeaceae

There are about 80 species of deciduous and evergreen shrubs, small trees, and root climbers in this genus, which occurs in woodlands in E Asia and N and S America. Many hydrangeas are grown for their showy floral clusters. *Hydrangea arborescens* is not especially ornamental but it has some fine subspecies and cultivars. The uses of *H. arborescens* were known to native N Americans, notably the Cherokees, who used it to treat urinary stones.

It was adopted by settlers and much used by Physiomedical herbalists during the 19th century. *Hydrangea* comes from the Greek *hydor*, "water", and *angos*, "jar", referring to the cup-shaped fruits.

CULTIVATION Moist, well-drained, humus-rich soil in sun or partial shade, avoiding early morning sun in frosty areas. Cut back previous year's flowering shoots in early spring. Remove dead flower heads.

PROPAGATION By seed sown in spring; by softwood cuttings in summer; by hardwood cuttings in winter.

HARVEST Roots are lifted in autumn and dried for decoctions, liquid extracts, and tinctures.

▣ *Hydrangea arborescens* (seven barks, wild hydrangea)
Open deciduous shrub with long-stalked, broadly ovate leaves, to 18cm (7in) long. Off-white fertile flowers and creamy white sterile flowers are borne in corymbs, 5–15cm (2–6in)

Hydrangea arborescens 'Annabelle'

Hydrangea arborescens subsp. *discolor* 'Sterilis'

across, in summer. Native to E USA. ‡ 1–3m (3–10ft), ↔ 1.2–2.5m (4–8ft). ■ 'Annabelle' has spherical flower heads, 20cm (8in) across, and withstands wind and rain better than the other sterile forms. ■ subsp. *discolor* 'Sterilis' syn. 'Sterilis' has leaves with grey-green, hairy undersides and flower heads with large sterile flowers. 'Grandiflora' produces flower heads smaller than 'Annabelle', but the individual sterile flowers are larger.
HARDINESS Fully hardy.
PARTS USED Roots.
PROPERTIES A sweet pungent herb that is antiseptic and diuretic, soothes irritated tissues, and reduces formation of urinary stones.
MEDICINAL USES Internally for kidney and bladder stones, cystitis, urethritis, prostatitis, rheumatoid arthritis, gout, and oedema. Works well with *Aphanes arvensis* (see p.124), *Arctostaphylos uva-ursi* (see p.127), and *Eupatorium purpureum* (see p.209). Excess may cause dizziness and bronchial congestion.

HYDRASTIS
Ranunculaceae

Two species of rhizomatous perennials make up this genus, which occurs in northeastern N America and Japan. *Hydrastis canadensis* (goldenseal) shares the same habitats as *Panax quinquefolius* (American ginseng, see p.300); "seng" diggers therefore increased profits by also collecting "seal" plants. In 1909 "seal" fetched up to $3 per kg (2.2lb), when the rate for more common herbs was 2.5–5 cents. After centuries of exploitation, populations in the wild are now severely depleted; *Hydrastis canadensis* was listed as an endangered species and given international protection in 1997. Goldenseal was used for a variety of purposes by native N Americans. The Cherokees pounded the roots with bear fat as an insect-repellent unguent, and made decoctions for sore eyes and digestive problems. It became a popular home remedy among settlers and was listed in the *US Pharmacopoeia* at various times during the 19th and 20th centuries. The bright yellow roots contain isoquinoline alkaloids, including

berberine (as found in *Berberis vulgaris*, see p.142), suggesting that for some purposes *Berberis* spp. might be equally effective.
CULTIVATION Moist, humus-rich, well-drained soil, pH6.0–7.0, in shade.
PROPAGATION By seed sown when ripe; by division when dormant; by cuttings of roots or rhizomes in spring. Germination may be slow and erratic. Seedlings take 5–6 years to reach harvestable size; plants from cuttings take 3–4 years.
HARVEST Rhizomes are lifted in autumn, after foliage has died down, and dried for use in decoctions, liquid extracts, tablets, and tinctures.

■ *Hydrastis canadensis* (goldenseal, orangeroot, yellowroot)
Deciduous perennial with a yellow rhizome and roots, and palmate, deeply toothed leaves, 12–20cm (5–8in) long. Tiny flowers with green-white stamens appear in clusters in spring, followed by red inedible fruits. Native to northeastern N America. ‡ 20–38cm (8–15in), ↔ 15–30cm (6–12in) or more.
HARDINESS Fully hardy.
PARTS USED Rhizomes.
PROPERTIES A bitter, fetid, alterative herb that checks bleeding, reduces inflammation, stimulates bile flow and uterine contractions, and acts as a mild laxative. It also improves digestion, is decongestant, and effective against bacterial and amoebic infections.
MEDICINAL USES Internally for peptic ulcers, digestive disorders, catarrh, sinusitis, excessive and painful menstruation, postpartum haemorrhage, and pelvic inflammatory disease. Not given to pregnant women or patients with high blood pressure. Destroys beneficial intestinal organisms as well as pathogens, so it is prescribed for only limited periods (maximum three months). Externally for eczema, ear inflammations, conjunctivitis, vaginal infections, and gum disease. Combined with *Chamaemelum nobile* (see p.165) and *Filipendula ulmaria* (see p.214) for digestive problems; with *Trillium erectum* (see p.394) for uterine bleeding; and *Euphrasia officinalis* (see p.210) and *Hamamelis virginiana* (see p.230) for eye infections.

Hydrastis canadensis

HYDROCOTYLE
Hydrocotyle asiatica. See *Centella asiatica.*

HYOSCYAMUS
Henbane
Solanaceae

There are 15 species of taprooted, often unpleasant-smelling, hairy annuals, biennials, and perennials in this genus, which is distributed through W Europe, N Africa, and C and SW Asia. *Hyoscyamus niger* is found in bare sandy soil, often near the sea. Henbanes make interesting plants for dry slopes or walls, but are seldom cultivated. *Hyoscyamus niger* was recommended by Dioscorides in the 1st century AD as a soporific and painkiller, and long before that, in Babylonian times, it was smoked to relieve toothache. It contains tropane alkaloids (mainly hyoscyamine and hyoscine), as found in the related *Atropa bella-donna* (see p.138). Other species grown for alkaloid extraction include *Hyoscyamus muticus* (Egyptian henbane) and *H. albus* (Russian henbane). Henbane is notorious as a herb of sorcery, used to cause hallucinations and delirium. It has also been used by poisoners: Hamlet's father was dispatched by having henbane juice poured into his ear, and Dr Crippen murdered his wife with hyoscine. *Hyoscyamus* is from the Greek *hys*, "pig", and *kyamos*, "bean", perhaps because pigs can eat henbane without being poisoned.
CULTIVATION Light, well-drained, neutral to alkaline soil in sun.
PROPAGATION By seed sown in spring. Usually self-sows.
HARVEST Flowering tops and leaves are collected in summer for use in dry and liquid extracts, medicated oil, and tinctures.
⚠ **WARNING** All parts are extremely toxic if eaten. Possible skin irritant or allergen.

■ *Hyoscyamus niger* (henbane, hogbean)
Fetid annual or biennial with pale green, ovate leaves, to 30cm (12in) long, which are very hairy and sticky. Cream, purple-veined,

Hyoscyamus niger

H

five-lobed flowers, to 2.5cm (1in) across, appear from spring to autumn, followed by capsules, 1cm (⅜in) long. Native to Europe and W Asia. ↕ 60–90cm (2–3ft), ↔ 1m (3ft).

HARDINESS Fully hardy.

PARTS USED Whole plant, leaves.

PROPERTIES A narcotic sedative herb, with an unpleasant taste, that relaxes spasms, relieves pain, and dilates the pupils.

MEDICINAL USES Internally for asthma, whooping cough, motion sickness, Menière's syndrome, tremor in senility or paralysis, and as pre-operative medication. Excess causes impaired vision, convulsions, coma, and death from heart or respiratory failure. Externally for neuralgia and dental and rheumatic pain. Added to laxatives to prevent griping, and to anti-asthma and herbal cigarettes. For use only by qualified practitioners.

⚠ **WARNING** This herb is subject to legal restrictions in some countries.

HYPERICUM
St John's wort

Guttiferae

A genus of over 400 species of annuals, herbaceous perennials, and deciduous, semi-evergreen, and evergreen shrubs and trees, found mainly in temperate regions. This varied group provides many fine garden plants for most settings. *Hypericum perforatum* is a good subject for a wildflower meadow or woodland area. *Hypericum* may derive from the Greek *hyper*, "above", and *eikon*, "picture", as the flowers were placed above religious images to keep off evil at the northern Midsummer Day (24 June, St John's Day). The alleged magical properties of *H. perforatum* were partly due to hypericin, the fluorescent red pigment that oozes like blood from the crushed flowers. As a medicinal herb, St John's wort was traditionally used internally to treat nervous complaints and externally for healing, but fell into disuse in the 19th century. During the late 20th century, it underwent a revival following clinical trials that demonstrated its effectiveness in relieving mild to moderate depression and was described as "nature's Prozac". St John's wort contains hypericin and hyperforin, which have anti-depressant effects; adhyperforin, which promotes wound healing; and also proanthocyanidins that benefit circulation. Standardized herbal preparations are graded according to their hypericin content, though other constituents may have an important role to play in the overall effect. St John's wort is also a potent anti-viral and has potential in the development of drugs for treating human immuno-deficiency virus (HIV), viral hepatitis, and chronic fatigue syndrome (CFS). Synthetic hypericin is being developed as an anti-retroviral agent for blood transfusions.

CULTIVATION Well-drained to dry soil in sun or partial shade.

PROPAGATION By seed sown in autumn; by division in autumn or spring. Self-sows readily. Subject to statutory control as a weed in some countries, notably in Australia.

Hypericum perforatum

HARVEST Plants are cut as flowering begins and used fresh or dried in creams, infusions, liquid extracts, medicated oils, and tinctures.

⚠ **WARNING** Harmful if eaten. Skin allergen in sunlight.

◾ *Hypericum perforatum* (common St John's wort, perforate St John's wort)
Upright, clump-forming perennial, woody at the base, with blunt, oblong–elliptic to linear leaves, 3cm (1¼in) long. Yellow, five-petalled, gland-dotted flowers, 2cm (¾in) across, appear in large cymes in summer. Native to Europe and W Asia. ↕ 60cm–1m (2–3ft), ↔ 45–60cm (18–24in).

HARDINESS Fully hardy.

PARTS USED Whole plant.

PROPERTIES A bitter–sweet, cooling herb that is astringent, calms the nerves, reduces inflammation, and promotes healing. Locally antiseptic and analgesic.

MEDICINAL USES Internally for anxiety, mild to moderate depression, nervous tension, insomnia, enuresis (especially in children), menopausal disturbances, premenstrual syndrome, shingles, sciatica, and fibrositis. Not given to patients suffering from severe depression. Contraindicated with the following medications: warfarin; oral contraceptives; digoxin; anti-convulsants; theophylline; selective serotonin re-uptake inhibitors (SSRIs); triptans; cyclosporin; and with various anti-virals prescribed for HIV patients. Externally for burns, bruises, injuries (especially deep or painful wounds involving nerve damage), sores, sciatica, neuralgia, cramps, sprains, and tennis elbow. Works well with *Calendula officinalis* (see p.150) or *Hamamelis virginiana* (see p.230) for bruises. Used in homeopathy for pain and inflammation caused by nerve damage.

HYSSOPUS
Hyssop

Lamiaceae

Some five species of aromatic herbaceous perennials and evergreen or semi-evergreen shrubs are included in this genus, which occurs in dry, sandy or rocky areas from Mediterranean regions to C Asia. *Hyssopus officinalis* is an excellent plant for borders or informal hedging, with colourful flowers that attract bees and butterflies. *Hyssopus* is the name used by Hippocrates, derived from the Hebrew *ezob*, "holy herb". Hyssop is an ancient herb, mentioned several times in the Old Testament for purification, though these references may possibly be to *Origanum syriacum* (see p.296), rather than to *Hyssopus officinalis*. It contains a camphoraceous volatile oil, and compounds similar to those found in *Marrubium vulgare* (see p.271); hence its effectiveness for bronchial complaints, for which it has been used from ancient times.

CULTIVATION Well-drained to dry, neutral to alkaline soil in sun. Trim hedges and cut specimen plants back hard in spring.

PROPAGATION By seed sown in autumn; by softwood cuttings in summer. Variants may not come true from seed.

HARVEST Leaves and flowering tops are picked as the buds open, and dried for infusions, syrup, liquid extracts, and tinctures, or distilled for oil.

◾ *Hyssopus officinalis* (hyssop)
Semi-evergreen shrub with linear to narrowly lanceolate leaves, 2.5–5cm (1–2in) long. Dark blue (rarely pink or white), two-lipped flowers, 1.5cm (½in) long, are produced in dense spikes in late summer. Native to C and S Europe, W Asia, and N Africa. ↕ 45–60cm (18–24in), ↔ 60–90cm (24–36in). ◾ f. *albus* has pure white flowers. ◾ subsp. *aristatus* (rock hyssop) has a dense dwarf habit and smaller spikes of flowers in early autumn. ↕ 30cm (12in). ◾ f. *roseus* has pink flowers.

HARDINESS Fully hardy.

Hyssopus officinalis

Hyssopus officinalis f. *albus*

Hyssopus officinalis subsp. *aristatus*

Hyssopus officinalis f. *roseus*

PARTS USED Whole plant, leaves, flowers, oil.

PROPERTIES A bitter, aromatic, astringent herb that is expectorant, reduces inflammation, and lowers fever. It has a tonic effect on the digestive, urinary, nervous, and bronchial systems.

MEDICINAL USES Internally for bronchitis, upper respiratory tract infections and congestion, feverish illnesses and coughs in children, wind, and colic (flowering plant); coughs (flowering plant or flowers). Externally for cuts and bruises (flowering plant); bronchial infections (medicated oil); nervous exhaustion (bath oil). Combined with *Glycyrrhiza glabra* (see p.227) or *Verbascum thapsus* (see p.401) for persistent coughs, and with *Eucalyptus globulus* (see p.207) and *Thymus vulgaris* (see p.390) for bronchial congestion. Essential oil may cause epileptic fits.

CULINARY USES Leaves have a bitter, sage–mint flavour, used sparingly in soups, salads, pulses, and meat dishes. Flowers can be added to salads. Dried herb is used to make herb tea.

ECONOMIC USES Essential oil is used to flavour bitters and liqueurs, such as Chartreuse.

⚠ **WARNING** This herb, in the form of essential oil, is subject to legal restrictions in some countries.

🔲 🖾 🔲 🗷 🖺 ✏ ✎

I

IBOZA

Iboza riparia. See *Tetradenia riparia.*

ILEX

Holly

Aquifoliaceae

A genus of about 400 species of evergreen and deciduous trees and shrubs, occurring worldwide, especially in tropical and temperate parts of Asia and N and S America. *Ilex aquifolium* (common holly) is a variable species. Its role in Christmas decoration originated in pagan times, when the glossy evergreen foliage symbolized the continuation of life during winter dormancy. Various hollies are used medicinally. Some contain bitter compounds and stimulants, such as caffeine and theobromine, as found in tea, coffee, and cocoa. *Ilex paraguariensis* is more widely drunk in South America than either tea or coffee; it contains 0.2–2 per cent caffeine and 0.3–0.5 per cent theobromine. The N American *I. opaca* (American holly) has similar medicinal uses to common holly, and caffeine-free leaves that are roasted for making tea. *Ilex vomitoria* was important as the emetic "black drink" in native N American rituals; when roasted, the leaves can be made into tea or used for flavouring.

CULTIVATION Moist, well-drained soil in sun or shade. Variegated hollies need sun for optimum colour. *Ilex verticillata* tolerates wet conditions. Cut back or trim in spring; clip formal specimens

Ilex aquifolium

Ilex aquifolium 'Bacciflava'

Ilex aquifolium 'Ferox Argentea'

Ilex aquifolium 'Madame Briot'

Ilex aquifolium 'Pyramidalis'

Ilex aquifolium 'Silver Queen'

Ilex paraguariensis

Ilex verticillata

in summer. Prune *I. paraguariensis* into a low bush for ease of harvesting in the same way as *Camellia sinensis* (tea, see p.151). Leaves may be damaged by holly leaf miner or leafspot. Transplant or repot with the rootball intact.

PROPAGATION By seed sown in autumn (species only); by semi-ripe cuttings in late summer and autumn.

HARVEST Leaves are picked in early summer (*I. aquifolium*) and dried for infusions and liquid extracts. Leafy shoots (*I. paraguariensis*) may be picked at intervals throughout the year, in the same way as tea, and dried for infusions. Bark is peeled from twigs of *I. verticillata* in spring and dried for use in decoctions and liquid extracts.

⚠ **WARNING** Berries are harmful if eaten.

🔲 *Ilex aquifolium* (common holly, English holly)

Small evergreen tree or shrub with shiny, leathery, elliptic to ovate leaves, 5–10cm (2–4in) long, which have undulating spiny margins. Off-white, scented flowers are borne on older wood in summer, with male and female on separate plants. Females produce globose red berries, to 6mm (¼in) across. Native to W and S Europe, N Africa, and W Asia. ‡ 3–20m (10–70ft), ↔ 8m (25ft). 🔲 'Bacciflava' is female, with prickly leaves and yellow berries. ‡ 15m (50ft), ↔ 4m (12ft). 🔲 'Ferox Argentea' (silver hedgehog holly) is slower-growing and male, with purple twigs and small leaves, which have creamy white margins and spines over the entire upper surface. ‡ 6m (20ft), ↔ 4m (12ft). 🔲 'Madame Briot' is female, with purple-green twigs, scarlet berries, and large, stoutly spined leaves that have

irregular, bright yellow margins. ‡ 10m (30ft), ↔ 5m (15ft). 🔲 'Pyramidalis' is a narrowly conical, self-fertile female, with few or no spines and abundant red berries. 🔲 'Silver Queen' syn. 'Silver King' is a slow-growing male, with purple stems and broadly ovate, spiny, cream-margined leaves. ‡ 10m (30ft), ↔ 4m (12ft).

HARDINESS Fully hardy.

PARTS USED Leaves.

PROPERTIES A bitter, astringent, tonic herb that is diuretic and lowers fever.

MEDICINAL USES Internally for malaria, bronchial complaints, influenza, and rheumatism.

🖾 🖺

🔲 *Ilex paraguariensis* (maté, Paraguay tea, yerba maté)

Evergreen tree with elliptic–ovate leaves, to 12cm (5in) long and with scalloped margins. Small, green-white flowers appear in the axils of younger branches, followed by clusters of small, deep red berries. Native to Paraguay, Brazil, and Argentina. ‡ 15m (50ft), ↔ 10m (30ft).

HARDINESS Min. 7°C (45°F).

PARTS USED Leaves.

PROPERTIES A pleasant-tasting, slightly bitter, stimulant herb that is mildly analgesic and diuretic, relaxes spasms, and clears toxins. Reputed to reduce appetite.

MEDICINAL USES Internally for nervous tension headaches, migraine, neuralgia, mild depression, and rheumatic pain.

CULINARY USES Dried leaves are infused as a popular alternative to *Camellia sinensis* (tea, see p.151).

🖾 🖺 🗷 🔲

■ *Ilex verticillata* syn. *Prinos verticillatus*
(black alder, winterberry)
Large, deciduous, suckering shrub with elliptic
toothed leaves, to 7cm (3in) long. In early
summer, insignificant white flowers appear;
female plants bear bright red, poisonous berries.
Native to N America. ‡ 2–5m (6–15ft),
↔ 1.2–3m (4–10ft).
HARDINESS Fully hardy.
PARTS USED Bark.
PROPERTIES A bitter, astringent, antiseptic
herb that has tonic and laxative effects.
MEDICINAL USES Internally for fevers, hepatitis,
and jaundice. Externally for skin inflammations,
herpes, and gangrenous ulcers. Combined with
Ulmus rubra (see p.397) for skin problems.
🏛 ■

ILLICIUM
Anise tree

Illiciaceae

A genus of about 40 species of evergreen shrubs
and small trees, with aromatic bark and star-
shaped fruits, widely distributed in SE Asia and
the West Indies. The leathery leaves are
aniseed-scented, and in some species the
flowers are produced directly from the bark.
Illicium verum (star anise) should not be
confused with *I. anisatum*, which contains
sikimitoxin or anisatin and whose smaller
odourless fruits are used as fish poison and to
adulterate star anise. The two species are often
referred to by the same name – Chinese anise.
CULTIVATION Moist, well-drained, neutral to
acid soil in partial shade.
PROPAGATION By semi-ripe cuttings in summer.
HARVEST Fruits are collected unripe for
chewing, and ripe for oil distillation or use in
decoctions and powders.

■ *Illicium verum* (star anise, *badian*)
Evergreen tree with pointed elliptic leaves, to
15cm (6in) long. Solitary, yellow-white, magnolia-
like flowers, 1cm (³⁄₈in) across, often tinged red
to pink inside, appear in summer, followed by
eight-pointed, woody fruits with a single seed
in each segment. Native to S China and
N Vietnam. ‡ 18m (60ft), ↔ 7–12m (22–40ft).

HARDINESS Frost hardy.
PARTS USED Fruits (*ba jiao hui xiang*), oil.
PROPERTIES A warm stimulant herb that
benefits the digestion, relieves pain, and has
anti-fungal and anti-bacterial effects.
MEDICINAL USES Internally for abdominal
pain, digestive disturbances, and complaints
associated with cold conditions (such as
lumbago). Often included in remedies for
digestive disturbances and cough mixtures, and
as aniseed flavouring for medicines. Excess
causes trembling and convulsions, owing to the
high content of anethole (80–90 per cent) in
the essential oil.
CULINARY USES Ripe fruits are used to flavour
curries, tea, and pickles; also an ingredient of
"five spice powder" in Chinese and Vietnamese
cuisine. Unripe fruits are chewed after meals as
a digestive and breath sweetener in the East.
ECONOMIC USES Ripe fruits are used to flavour
coffee and confectionery. Essential oil is used to
flavour liqueurs, soft drinks, and bakery produce.
📶 🔲 ■ ✏ ✏

IMPATIENS
Jewelweed

Balsaminaceae

There are some 850 species of annuals,
evergreen perennials, and subshrubs in this
genus, which is widely distributed, especially in
damp habitats in tropical and subtropical parts
of Asia and Africa. Most have succulent stems,
orchid-like flowers, and five-valved capsules
that open explosively to release the seeds.
Jewelweeds have long been used by native
N Americans to relieve the pain and irritation
of rashes and eczema, particularly by the
Potawatomi, who applied the juice to poison-ivy
rash. One of the species used is *I. pallida*,
which grows wild mainly in limestone regions.
It is similar in appearance to the more common
I. capensis (orange balsam), but has more
glaucous foliage and paler, less spotted flowers.
In Asia, the species most used is *I. balsamina*,
which is popular as an ornamental in the West.
The leaves are used as a healing poultice and in
a decoction to encourage hair growth. In both
Chinese and Vietnamese medicine, the seeds are

Impatiens pallida

used to stimulate the uterus, and in Vietnam the
flowers are mixed with alum to dye the nails.
CULTIVATION Moist soil in sun or shade.
PROPAGATION By seed sown in spring at
16–18°C (61–64°F).
HARVEST Plants are cut when flowering and
used fresh for ointments and juice extraction.

■ *Impatiens pallida* (jewelweed, pale touch-
me-not)
Tall hairless annual with succulent stems and
grey-green, coarsely toothed leaves. Yellow
pendent flowers, occasionally spotted red-brown,
appear in summer. Native to eastern and central
N America. ‡ 60cm–1.5m (2–5ft), ↔ 30–60cm
(12–24in).
HARDINESS Hardy.
PARTS USED Whole plant, juice.
PROPERTIES An acrid herb that has diuretic,
purgative, and emetic effects if taken internally.
MEDICINAL USES Externally for rashes caused
by *Rhus* spp. (see p.344), corns, warts,
ringworm (juice), and haemorrhoids (ointment).
🔲 ☯ ■

IMPERATA

Poaceae

There are six species of rhizomatous perennial
grasses in this genus, which occurs in warm-
temperate and tropical areas of Japan, S China,
India, Sri Lanka, Indochina, and Africa. One or
two species, notably their red forms, are grown
as ornamentals. In parts of Asia, *I. cylindrica* is
a serious weed of abandoned fields and burned
forest; it is unpalatable to most domestic animals
but can be used for thatching and weaving. The
long, pale, flexible rhizomes contain various
sugars (18.8 per cent), acids, and two triterpene
methylethers (arundoin and cylindrin). Research
has shown anti-tumour effects.
CULTIVATION Moist, well-drained, humus-rich
soil in sun or dappled shade.
PROPAGATION By division in spring.
HARVEST Rhizomes and flowers are collected
as required and dried for decoctions.

Imperata cylindrica (*alang-alang*, *chigaya*,
cogon, *lalang*, white cottongrass, woolly grass)
Herbaceous perennial grass forming clumps of
flat linear leaves, to 50cm (20in) long. Fluffy,
silvery white spikelets, to 4.5cm (1³⁄₄in) long,
grow in narrow, spike-like panicles in summer.
Native to warm-temperate and tropical Asia.
‡ 40cm (16in), ↔ 30cm (12in) or more. ■ 'Rubra'
syn. 'Red Baron' (Japanese blood grass) has
red-flushed upper blades and deep red leaf tips.
HARDINESS Frost hardy.
PARTS USED Rhizomes, flowers (*bai mao gen*).
PROPERTIES A cooling, soothing, slightly
sweet herb that has tonic and diuretic effects.
It is strongly haemostatic, suppresses bruising,
and lowers fever.
MEDICINAL USES Internally for high fever with
thirst, urinary tract infections, acute kidney
infection, urine retention, haemorrhoids,
nosebleeds, injuries involving bleeding and
bruising, and for internal haemorrhage.

Impatiens pallida

Imperata cylindrica 'Rubra'

CULINARY USES Rhizomes are mixed with a purple form of *Saccharum officinale* (sugar cane), known as *miá lau*, to make a thirst-quenching drink. Immature flower heads are eaten as a pot-herb. Rhizomes yield edible manna, and a starch used in making beer.

INULA

Asteraceae

A genus of about 90 species of mainly perennials and subshrubs, which is distributed across warm and temperate parts of Europe, Asia, and Africa. Many are grown in rock gardens and borders for their showy, daisy-like flowers. Several species are used medicinally and as dye plants. *Inula helenium* is a giant, summer-flowering species that provides a focal point in the herb garden. Though long used in European herbal medicine, and widely naturalized in Europe and N America, *I. helenium* is Asian in origin. Known as *pushkaramula* in Ayurvedic medicine, it is highly regarded as a lung tonic and analgesic. *Inula helenium* contains up to 44 per cent inulin, a slightly sweet polysaccharide, which is of little food value but often recommended to diabetics as a sweetener. *Inula* is the Latin name used by Horace for the plant. The common name "elecampane" is thought to be a corruption of the medieval Latin *enula campana*, "Inula of the fields". Other species used include: the shrubby *I. cappa*, a popular remedy in S China for bronchial and rheumatic complaints, migraine, and skin infections; and the Himalayan *I. racemosa* (*poshkar*), whose aromatic roots protect fabrics from insect damage and have antiseptic, anthelmintic, expectorant, and diuretic properties. The fleshy leaves and shoots of *I. crithmoides* (golden samphire) are eaten locally in Europe as a substitute for *Crithmum maritimum* (rock samphire, see p.183).

CULTIVATION Moist, well-drained soil in sun.
PROPAGATION By seed sown in spring or autumn; by division in spring.
HARVEST Roots are lifted in autumn and distilled for oil, used fresh to make extracts and

syrup, or dried for decoctions, liquid extracts, powders, and tinctures. Flower heads are picked when fully open and dried whole for use in decoctions (prepared using a muslin bag to contain irritant fibres), infusions, and powders.

Inula britannica var. *chinensis* syn. *I. japonica* (Japanese elecampane, yellow starwort) Herbaceous perennial with stalkless, lanceolate to oblong leaves, to 10cm (4in) long, and yellow, daisy-like flowers, about 5cm (2in) across, in summer. Native to China, Japan, Manchuria, and Korea. ‡ 20–60cm (8–24in), ↔ 50cm (20in).
HARDINESS Fully hardy.
PARTS USED Flowers (*xuan fu hua*).
PROPERTIES A bitter, pungent, anti-bacterial herb that stimulates the digestive system, is expectorant, and controls vomiting.
MEDICINAL USES Internally for bronchial complaints with profuse phlegm, nausea and vomiting, hiccups, and flatulence. Combined with honey as an expectorant, and with *Glycyrrhiza glabra* (see p.227) and *Zingiber officinale* (see p.411) for digestive problems characterized by chronic catarrh.

◼ *Inula helenium* (elecampane, scabwort) Robust perennial with thick rhizomes, stout erect stems, and pointed toothed leaves, to 70cm (28in) long. Yellow, daisy-like flowers, to 7cm (3in) across, appear in summer. Native to Europe and W Asia. ‡ 3m (10ft), ↔ 1.5m (5ft).
HARDINESS Fully hardy.
PARTS USED Roots, flowers, oil.
PROPERTIES A bitter, pungent, aromatic herb that is expectorant and diuretic; it relaxes spasms, reduces inflammation, and increases perspiration. Effective against bacterial and fungal infections, it acts as an alterative, cleansing toxins and stimulating the immune and digestive systems.
MEDICINAL USES Internally for bronchitis, hay fever, irritant coughs, asthma, tuberculosis, pleurisy, catarrh, and weak digestion associated with mucus formation. Not given to pregnant women. Combines well with *Achillea*

Inula helenium

millefolium (see p.99), *Asclepias tuberosa* (see p.134), *Marrubium vulgare* (see p.271), and *Tussilago farfara* (see p.396). Sometimes recommended externally as a wash for skin inflammations and varicose ulcers, but may cause allergic reactions.
CULINARY USES Once popular as a flavouring for desserts and fish sauces. Root may be candied or made into a cordial.
ECONOMIC USES An ingredient of vermouth and absinthe. Camphor-scented oil is used in perfumery.

IPOMOEA
Morning glory

Convolvulaceae

This large genus consists of 450–500 species of annuals, perennials, small trees, and shrubs, many of which are climbers. Several different species, including *I. turpethum* (turpeth), now known as *Operculina turpethum*, and the closely related *Convolvulus arvensis*, contain gluco-resins that have a strong purgative effect. *Ipomoea arvensis* has been used for fevers and to control bleeding. *Ipomoea digitata* (*khoai xiêm*, Spanish woodbine, *vidari-kanda*) is used in Ayurvedic medicine as a diuretic, aphrodisiac, and rejuvenative tonic. In Vietnam and China, the seeds of *I. hederacea* syn. *Pharbitis hederacea*, a widely grown ornamental annual climber, are used for their diuretic and purgative properties and for their stimulating effect on the uterus. They contain pharbitin, a substance similar to the gluco-resins that occur in the tubers of perennial species.
CULTIVATION Well-drained, rich soil in sun. Cut back or thin out in spring. Whitefly, aphids, and spider mites may damage plants under cover.
PROPAGATION By seed sown in spring at 18°C (64°F); by softwood cuttings in spring or summer; by semi-ripe cuttings in summer. Soak seeds overnight in warm water, or nick seed coat to speed germination.
HARVEST Roots are lifted in autumn and dried for use in powders, resin extraction, and tinctures.
△ **WARNING** Seeds of many *Ipomoea* spp. are harmful if eaten.

Ipomoea purga syn. *I. jalapa*, *Convolvulus jalapa* (jalap)
Evergreen climber with a turnip-like tuber, purple-red, twining stems, and pointed, ovate to heart-shaped leaves. Purple-pink, funnel-shaped flowers, 12cm (5in) across, appear in autumn. Native to eastern slopes of Mexican Andes. ‡ to 3m (10ft).
HARDINESS Half hardy.
PARTS USED Tuber, resin.
PROPERTIES A resinous, acrid, purgative herb with an unpleasant taste.
MEDICINAL USES Internally for constipation, colic, and intestinal parasites. Added to laxative and carminative preparations to prevent griping.
△ **WARNING** This herb, in the form of jalap resin, is subject to legal restrictions in some countries.

I

IRESINE

Iresine erianthos. See *Pfaffia paniculatum.*

IRIS

Iridaceae

This large genus consists of about 300 species of perennials found mainly in northern temperate regions. Most species are in cultivation; they range from rock-garden plants to aquatics. Iris flowers are the origin of the sceptre and the fleur-de-lys; the three inner petals represent faith, wisdom, and valour. The genus is named after Iris, the Greek goddess of the rainbow. The use of dried iris root, known as "orris", was recorded in ancient Egypt, Greece, and Rome, and remains important in perfumery. Orris contains volatile oil, consisting partly of irone; the oil gives a violet scent that intensifies as the dried rhizome ages. Several different species are grown as sources of orris, including *I. pallida* (Dalmatian iris). Some authorities maintain that *I. germanica* var. *florentina*, which is common near Florence, is a separate species, *I. florentina*, while others regard it as the cultivar 'Florentina'. *Iris versicolor* (blue flag) was a major medicinal herb among native N Americans. It was listed in the *US Pharmacopoeia* (1820–95) as an emetic and purgative, but now has a far wider range of applications.

CULTIVATION Well-drained, neutral to alkaline soil in sun (*I. germanica* var. *florentina*); rich, moist to wet, acid soil or shallow water in sun (*I. versicolor*).

PROPAGATION By seed sown in autumn or spring; by division or offsets in summer. Cultivars may not come true from seed.

HARVEST Rhizomes are lifted in late summer and early autumn, and dried for use in decoctions, liquid extracts, and powders.

⚠ **WARNING** All parts of *Iris* spp., especially rhizomes, are potentially toxic if eaten. Skin irritant and allergen.

▣ *Iris germanica* var. *florentina* syn. *I. florentina* (orris)
Stout perennial with a rhizome, to 5cm (2in) thick, and fans of sword-shaped, grey-green

Iris germanica var. *florentina*

Iris versicolor

leaves, to 45cm (18in) long. White, violet-tinged flowers, 8–10cm (3–4in) across, appear on branched stems in early summer. Native to E Mediterranean. ‡ 60cm–1.2m (2–4ft), ↔ indefinite.

HARDINESS Fully hardy.

PARTS USED Rhizomes.

PROPERTIES A soothing aromatic herb that has diuretic and expectorant effects. It is both purgative and anti-diarrhoeal.

MEDICINAL USES Internally for coughs, catarrh, and diarrhoea. Externally for deep wounds.

ECONOMIC USES Added to dental preparations, breath fresheners, and dusting powders. Used as a fixative in perfumery and potpourris. Essential oil is used to flavour soft drinks, gin, and chewing gum, and to enhance fruit flavours.

▣ *Iris versicolor* (blue flag, wild iris)
Wetland perennial with a branched creeping rhizome and sword-shaped leaves, 35–60cm (14–24in) long. Purple to violet-blue, white-veined flowers, 6–8cm (2½–3in) across, bloom in groups of 4–6 in summer. Native to northeastern N America. ‡ 50cm–1m (20in–3ft), ↔ indefinite. ▣ 'Kermesina' has plum-coloured flowers.

HARDINESS Fully hardy.

PARTS USED Rhizomes.

Iris versicolor 'Kermesina'

PROPERTIES An acrid, slightly aromatic, alterative herb that stimulates the liver and gall bladder, reduces inflammation, increases rates of perspiration and salivation, and acts as a diuretic and laxative.

MEDICINAL USES Internally for psoriasis, acne, herpes, migraine due to liver dysfunction, arthritis, fibroids, swollen glands, pelvic inflammatory disease, and septicaemia. Fresh rhizome causes nausea and diarrhoea. Not given to pregnant women. Externally for skin diseases, rheumatism, and infected wounds. Combines well with *Phytolacca americana* (see p.314), *Rumex crispus* (see p.351), *Stillingia sylvatica* (see p.375), or *Trifolium pratense* (see p.393) for skin disease.

ISATIS

Brassicaceae

About 30 species of annuals, biennials, and perennials belong to this genus, which occurs through Europe to C Asia. *Isatis tinctoria* (woad), a species found mainly on chalky soils, is best known as a dye plant, containing a pigment similar to that of *Indigofera* spp. (indigo), but is important as a medicinal herb, too. It was a major crop in many parts of Europe during the Middle Ages, notably in S France whence the expression "Land of Cockaigne" arose, after the earthenware cups (*coques*) in which the dye paste was sold. Both Julius Caesar and Pliny described how the Britons painted their bodies with woad, the blue dye produced by fermenting the foliage. The process of fermentation gave off such a foul smell that it was banned by Queen Elizabeth I within 8km (5 miles) of any of her palaces. Woad remained a popular dye for fabrics until the 1630s, when it was superseded by indigo from the tropics. According to Mrs Grieve (*A Modern Herbal*, 1931), *Isatis tinctoria* "is so astringent that it is not fit to be given internally as a medicine, and has only been used medicinally as a plaster, applied to the region of the spleen, and as an ointment for ulcers, inflammation, and to staunch bleeding". It was first mentioned in traditional Chinese medicine in the 1590s and is often prescribed in large doses with apparently no ill-effects. In practice, high doses are recommended to maintain high levels of active ingredients. Scientific research suggests pronounced anti-viral effects. The Chinese drug *qing dai* (from the leaf pigment of *I. tinctoria*) is also prepared from *Indigofera suffruticosa* and *Persicaria tinctoria* syn. *Polygonum tinctorium.*

CULTIVATION Rich, well-drained, neutral to alkaline soil in sun.

PROPAGATION By seed sown in autumn or spring. Often self-sows readily, but does not thrive in the same soil for more than two years.

HARVEST Leaves are picked in summer for use fresh or dried in decoctions, or macerated for extraction of blue pigment, which is then dried as a powder. Roots are lifted in autumn and dried for use in decoctions.

Isatis tinctoria

◾ *Isatis tinctoria* (woad)
Biennial or short-lived perennial with a stout taproot and basal rosette of oblong–lanceolate, grey-green leaves, 4–10cm (1½–4in) long. Numerous small, yellow, four-petalled flowers are borne in branched panicles in summer, followed by pendent, fiddle-shaped, black seeds. Native to C and S Europe and W Asia.
↕ 50cm–1.2m (20in–4ft), ↔ 45cm (18in).
HARDINESS Fully hardy.
PARTS USED Leaves (*da qing ye*), roots (*ban lang gen*), pigment (*qing dai*).
PROPERTIES A bitter chilling herb that lowers fever and reduces inflammation. It controls a wide range of pathogenic organisms, including viruses, and reputedly has anti-cancer effects.
MEDICINAL USES Internally for meningitis, encephalitis, mumps, influenza, erysipelas, heat rash, sore throat, abscesses, and swellings (leaves, roots); convulsions and high fevers in children, coughing of blood, and as a detoxifier in infections such as mumps, erysipelas, and thrush (pigment).
▨ ▧ ◾

IXIA
Ixia chinensis. See *Belamcanda chinensis*.

J

JASMINUM
Jasmine

Oleaceae

A genus of about 200 species of deciduous and evergreen shrubs, climbers, and ramblers, distributed mainly in tropical Africa and Eurasia. Several species of jasmine have a long history of use in perfumery and medicine, and for flavouring tea. They are also popular as ornamentals for their exquisitely scented flowers. *Jasminum officinale* was introduced to Europe in the mid-16th century and is widely grown for the perfumery industry. The yellow-

flowered *J. odoratissimum* and *J. grandiflorum* are also used. Traditionally, essential oil of jasmine was made by *enfleurage*, a method in which the volatile scents are taken up by odourless oils. *Jasminum sambac*, especially in its double forms, is sacred to Vishnu and is used in Hindu ceremonies. It is the main species used for flavouring tea; *J. odoratissimum*, *J. officinale*, and *J. paniculatum* are also used. Good-quality jasmine tea does not necessarily contain jasmine flowers as it can be made by storing loose tea alongside the flowers for several weeks. *Jasminum sambac* 'Grand Duke of Tuscany' is a rare, double-flowered cultivar, first established in Europe in the garden of the Grand Duke, having been imported to Pisa from Goa c.1691. Medicinal jasmines include *J. angustifolium*, mixed with *Acorus calamus* (see p.101) in Ayurvedic medicine as a cure for ringworm, and *J. lanceolarium* stems, used in S China for rheumatic pains, injuries, boils, and abscesses. In Vietnam, the leaves of *J. subtriplinerve* are used after childbirth, and to treat breast abscesses, and the roots are a remedy for recurrent fever.
CULTIVATION Rich, well-drained soil in sun. Thin out shoots or cut back after flowering. Plants under cover may be affected by spider mite, aphids, whitefly, and mealybugs.
PROPAGATION By semi-ripe cuttings in summer; by layering in autumn.
HARVEST Roots are lifted in autumn and dried for use in decoctions (*J. sambac*). Leaves are picked as required and used fresh or dried. Flowers are picked soon after opening each morning and used fresh for oil extraction, or dried for infusions, medicated oil, pastes, and powders.

◾ *Jasminum grandiflorum* (Catalonian jasmine, jati, royal jasmine, Spanish jasmine)
Evergreen rambler with green stems and dark

green, pinnate leaves, to 10cm (4in) long, divided into 7–11 ovate leaflets, of which the terminal leaflet is often partially united with the upper pair. Highly scented, white, often purplish-tinged flowers, to 2.5 cm (1in) across, appear in terminal clusters from late spring to early autumn. Native to NW Himalayas (India).
↕ 5m (15ft).
HARDINESS Min. 7°C (45°F).
PARTS USED Leaves, flowers, oil.
PROPERTIES A bitter, astringent, cooling herb that calms the nerves, checks bleeding, and stimulates the uterus. Regarded as an aphrodisiac for women and an alterative, reputedly effective against various cancers and bacterial and viral infections.
MEDICINAL USES Internally, mainly in Ayurvedic medicine, for infectious illnesses with high fever, sunstroke, conjunctivitis, dermatitis, cancer (especially Hodgkin's disease and cancers of the bone, lymph nodes, and breast), emotional upsets, and headaches. Often combined with *Santalum album* (see p.359). Internally and externally for mouth ulcers (leaves). Externally for corns (leaf juice).
CULINARY USES Flowers are used to scent China tea.
ECONOMIC USES Essential oil is used in the perfumery industry.
▨ ▨ ◲ ◾ ▧ ▨ ◾

◾ *Jasminum officinale* (common jasmine, jessamine)
Vigorous, deciduous, twining climber with green stems and pinnate leaves, to 6cm (2½in) long, divided into 5–9 elliptic leaflets. Fragrant white flowers, 2cm (¾in) across, are borne in summer, followed by black berries. Native to Himalayas, N Iran, Afghanistan, and the Caucasus. ↕ 10m (30ft). ◾ f. *affine* syn. 'Grandiflorum' has larger flowers, with pink-

Jasminum grandiflorum

Jasminum officinale

Jasminum officinale 'Argenteovariegatum'

Jasminum officinale 'Aureum'

Jasminum officinale f. *affine*

Jasminum sambac

Jasminum sambac 'Grand Duke of Tuscany'

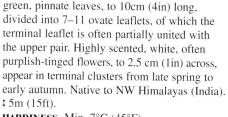

J

tinged buds. ◩ 'Argenteovariegatum' syn. 'Variegatum' has leaves variegated cream, and grey-green; new leaves are pink-flushed. ◩ 'Aureum' syn. 'Aureovariegatum' has yellow-variegated leaves. 'Frojas' syn. 'Fiona Sunrise' has yellow foliage.

HARDINESS Frost hardy.

PARTS USED Flowers, oil.

PROPERTIES An aromatic, tonic, euphoric herb that relieves spasms, increases milk flow, and stimulates the uterus. It also has aphrodisiac and antiseptic effects.

MEDICINAL USES Mainly in aromatherapy for depression, nervous tension, impotence, frigidity, menstrual disorders, respiratory disorders of nervous origin, and weak digestion.

ECONOMIC USES Essential oil is used in perfumes with a floral note, and in food flavourings (notably maraschino cherries).
◪ ◧ ▣ ▨ ◿

◼ *Jasminum sambac* (Arabian jasmine)
Sprawling evergreen shrub or scrambler with simple ovate leaves, to 8cm (3in) long. Tight clusters of three or more, fragrant, often double or semi-double, white flowers, to 2.5cm (1in) across, ageing to pink-purple, with 4–9 rounded lobes, are borne throughout the year, mainly at the tips of lateral shoots. Probably originated in tropical Asia. ‡ 1.5–2m (5–6ft). ◼ 'Grand Duke of Tuscany' syn. 'Trifoliatum' (*kudda-mulla*, Tuscan jasmine) is slow-growing, with leaves arranged in threes, and large, very double (occasionally fasciated) flowers. 'Maid of Orleans' syn. 'Flore Pleno' has double flowers.

HARDINESS Min. 13–15°C (55–59°F).

PARTS USED Roots, leaves, flowers.

PROPERTIES Similar to *J. officinale*. Shown experimentally to lower blood pressure and inhibit milk production.

MEDICINAL USES Externally for ear and eye infections, indolent ulcers, and as a poultice to reduce milk flow.

CULINARY USES Flowers are used to scent green (Hyson) tea (jasmine tea). Jasmine flower water is used to flavour desserts in SE Asia.

ECONOMIC USES Essential oil is used in commercial food flavouring and perfumery.
◪ ◿ ◪ ▣ ◿ ◿ ◨

JATEORHIZA

Menispermaceae

This genus of two species of herbaceous woody climbers occurs in tropical E Africa. *Jateorhiza palmata* (calumba) occurs in lowland rainforests and riparian forests. It was introduced to Europe in the 17th century by the Portuguese as an antidote to poisons but was not widely used until the end of the 18th century. It contains isoquinoline alkaloids, similar to those found in *Berberis vulgaris* (see p.142), and is one of the bitterest plants known. Unusual among bitter herbs, calumba contains no tannins and very little volatile oil – less than 1 per cent, which consists mainly of thymol. The closely related *Coscinium fenestratum* (calumba wood) also contains berberis-like alkaloids and is used as

a bitter tonic in Ayurvedic medicine. *Cocculus* and *Stephania*, two genera related to *Jateorhiza*, are much used in traditional Chinese medicine, and also in Ayurvedic, Japanese, and Korean herbal medicine. As they may be confused with *Aristolochia* spp. (see p.129), or may contain or be adulterated with aristolochic acid, they have been banned in a number of countries following cases of kidney failure.

CULTIVATION Moist, humus-rich soil in shade, with high humidity. Cut back stems in early spring or train on supports.

PROPAGATION By seed sown when ripe; by division in spring; by semi-ripe cuttings in summer.

HARVEST Roots are lifted in dry weather in spring and dried for use in concentrated infusions, liquid extracts, powders, and tinctures.

Jateorhiza palmata syn. *J. calumba*, *Menispermum palmatum* (calumba, colombo)
Perennial rhizomatous vine with fleshy roots and long-stalked, hairy, heart-shaped, palmately lobed leaves, to 40cm (16in) long. Small, green-white flowers are borne in axillary clusters – males in panicles, to 40cm (16in) long, and females in racemes, to 10cm (4in) long – followed by globose fruits, 2.5cm (1in) long. Native to E Africa. ‡ 15m (45ft).

HARDINESS Min. 15–18°C (59–64°F).

PARTS USED Roots.

PROPERTIES A very bitter, mucilaginous herb that acts mainly as a tonic for the digestive system. It also lowers blood pressure and has anti-fungal effects.

MEDICINAL USES Internally for morning sickness, loss of appetite, anorexia, indigestion, atonic dyspepsia with low stomach acid, diarrhoea, and dysentery. Combines well with *Senna alexandrina* (see p.366) and *Zingiber officinale* (see p.411). Contraindicated during pregnancy, except in small, carefully prescribed doses for morning sickness.
◪ ▣ ◪

JATROPHA

Euphorbiaceae

A genus of about 170 species of succulent perennials, evergreen shrubs, and occasionally trees, found in South Africa, Madagascar, tropical areas of the Americas, and the West Indies. They are closely related to *Manihot esculenta* (cassava, manioc, tapioca), which was once classified as *Jatropha manihot* and similarly contains a very acrid juice, and is toxic unless washed and dried before eating. *Jatropha curcas* (physic nut) was introduced by the Portuguese to the Old World tropics, where it soon became widely naturalized and used as a purgative. The seed oil contains a toxic irritant diterpenoid and an acid similar to the acids found in *Ricinus communis* (castor oil, see p.345) and croton oil (from *Croton tiglium*, see p.184). In spite of their toxicity, physic nuts taste pleasant and are often eaten by children, causing acute poisoning. The toxic effects are moderated by lime juice. *Jatropha multifida* and

J. podagrica, which are popular ornamentals, are also used medicinally: the former as a purgative, and the latter as a remedy for snake bite. *Jatropha* is from the Greek *iatros*, "physician", and *trophe*, "food", indicating that the seeds are tasty and also have medicinal properties.

CULTIVATION Sharply drained, rich soil in sun.

PROPAGATION By seed sown when ripe at 24°C (75°F); by stem-tip cuttings in spring and summer.

HARVEST Seeds are collected when ripe and used whole or pressed for oil. Leaves, roots, and bark are collected as required and used fresh in decoctions and poultices. Juice (latex) from stems is used fresh, or dried into a brittle brown substance.

⚠ **WARNING** All parts contain a milky latex that may irritate the skin and mucous membranes.

◼ *Jatropha curcas* (Barbados nut, physic nut, purging nut)
Deciduous shrub or small tree with hairless, heart-shaped, 3–7-lobed leaves, to 15cm (6in) across. Green-yellow, hairy male and female flowers are borne in clusters in spring and summer, followed by egg-shaped, dark brown to black fruits, which split into three when ripe, releasing three black seeds ("nuts"), to 2cm (¾in) long. Native to tropical America; widely naturalized. ‡ 6m (20ft).

HARDINESS Min. 10°C (50°F).

PARTS USED Seeds, oil, latex, leaves, roots.

PROPERTIES A strongly purgative, irritant, antiseptic herb that controls bleeding.

MEDICINAL USES Internally in carefully measured doses and externally, in the form of an enema or rubbing oil, as a purgative (seeds, leaves, bark). Internally for paralysis and intestinal worms. Externally for wounds, skin diseases, rheumatism, gum boils, and to control bleeding and produce an airtight film over

Jatropha curcas

broken or festering skin (latex); also as a poultice to increase lactation (leaves).
ECONOMIC USES Oil is used in the production of soaps and candles, and in oil lamps.

JUGLANS
Walnut

Juglandaceae

This genus consists of some 15 species of deciduous trees, distributed from Mediterranean regions to E Asia and through N America into the Andes. Several species are grown for their ash-like, often very large leaves, which in some species turn yellow in autumn. *Juglans regia* is often called "English" walnut, but it is not native to the British Isles and seldom crops well in cool climates. Cultivars of Carpathian origin are hardier than the Persian-type walnuts that are grown commercially in California. The walnut has been cultivated in France since at least Roman times for its nuts and oil. Walnut leaves and husks were the main source of brown hair dyes until the early 20th century, a use first described by Pliny (AD23–79). The N American *J. cinerea* (butternut) was much used medicinally and as a dye plant by Indian tribes; the Menominee dyed their deerskin shirts brown with juice from the husks. Its main medicinal use was for digestive disorders; it was listed in the *US Pharmacopoeia* (1820–1905) and was one of the most widely used laxatives in the 19th century. Although strongly purgative, it is considered safe during pregnancy. Among its constituents are naphthaquinones, which have a similar laxative effect to the anthraquinones found in *Rheum palmatum* (see p.344) and *Senna alexandrina* (see p.366). *Juglans nigra* (black walnut) is used in the same ways. Walnut wood and veneers come from various different species, including *J. regia*. *Juglans* comes from the Latin *Iupiter*, "Jupiter", and *glans*, "acorn".

CULTIVATION Deep, rich, well-drained soil in sun. For reliable crops of good quality nuts, plant self-fertile cultivars of *J. nigra*, rather than the wild species.

Juglans regia

Juglans regia 'Laciniata'

Remove badly placed and dead branches in winter. Leaves may be marked by bacterial leaf blotch and blight. Young shoots and flowers may be damaged by frost in cold sites.
PROPAGATION By seed sown when ripe, or in spring after stratifying (species only); by whip-and-tongue grafting; by chip-budding on to *J. nigra*.
HARVEST Leaves are picked during the growing season and dried for use in infusions and liquid extracts. Fruits are collected unripe, or when ripe in autumn, and separated into husks, shells, and kernels ("nuts"). Green rinds are used fresh for infusions; husks are infused for dye; and kernels pressed for oil. Inner bark is collected in autumn and dried for decoctions.

Juglans cinerea (butternut)
Vigorous, spreading, deciduous tree with pinnate leaves, to 50cm (20in) long, divided into 7–19 oblong–lanceolate, aromatic leaflets. Male flowers are produced in axillary catkins; females in terminal spikes, followed by clusters of 2–5 ovoid fruits, to 6cm (2½in) long. Native to eastern N America. ‡ 25m (80ft), ↔ 20m (70ft).
HARDINESS Fully hardy.
PARTS USED Inner bark.
PROPERTIES An astringent purgative herb that has a tonic effect on the liver, discourages intestinal parasites, lowers cholesterol levels, and has anti-microbial and anti-parasitic effects.
MEDICINAL USES Internally for constipation associated with dyspepsia, liver dysfunction, and skin eruptions; also for dysentery and intestinal parasites.
CULINARY USES Nuts are eaten raw or used in the same ways as walnuts. Unripe fruits are pickled. Seeds are pressed for oil used in cooking.

■ **Juglans regia** (common walnut)
Deciduous tree with pinnate aromatic leaves, 30cm (12in) long, divided into 5–9 ovate leaflets, which are bronze when young. Dark yellow male catkins and spikes of female flowers appear in late spring to early summer, followed by dark green fruits, to 5cm (2in) long, each containing a woody nut. Found from SE Europe to Himalayas, SW China, and

C Russia. ‡ 35m (120ft), ↔ 20m (70ft). 'Broadview' is very hardy; it produces large crops of easily cracked nuts at an early age. 'Hansen' is small and very hardy; produces round, thin-shelled nuts at an early age. ■ 'Laciniata' (cut-leafed walnut) has slightly pendent branches and deeply cut leaflets.
HARDINESS Fully hardy.
PARTS USED Leaves, bark, fruits (unripe rind), kernels (*hu tao ren*), oil.
PROPERTIES A bitter astringent herb that is expectorant and laxative, soothes irritated tissues, and dissolves kidney stones. It controls many disease-causing organisms and has anti-cancer properties.
MEDICINAL USES Internally for constipation, chronic coughs, asthma, and urinary stones (leaves); diarrhoea and anaemia (rind); and menstrual problems and dry skin conditions (oil). Externally for eczema, herpes, eruptive skin complaints, eye inflammations, and hair loss. Regarded in traditional Chinese medicine as a tonic for weak kidney energy.
CULINARY USES Walnuts are an important ingredient of cakes, biscuits, desserts, ice cream, and various savoury dishes and sauces, including Middle Eastern chicken dishes, Provençal *raito* (salt cod), and Italian *pesto* sauce for pasta. Walnut oil is a choice salad oil, used especially with fruit or herb-flavoured vinegars. Unripe fruits are pickled, preserved in syrup, and made into the French liqueur *brou de noix*. Leaves are used for tea and for wrapping cheeses.
ECONOMIC USES Leaves and husks yield brown dye, used in hair tints and conditioners for dark hair. Wood is used in furniture, veneers, and gunstocks. Oil is used for culinary purposes, and in cosmetics and artists' paints. Walnut meal is used as a thickening agent in the food industry.

JUNIPERUS
Juniper

Cupressaceae

About 50–60 species of coniferous trees and shrubs belong to this genus, which occurs throughout the northern hemisphere. Junipers

J

are popular ornamentals, with a great variety of size, habit, and colour. Most have two kinds of foliage: scale-like adult leaves and pointed juvenile leaves. *Juniperus communis* is a widely distributed and exceptionally variable species; it thrives on both acid and limestone soils. Many of its variants are propagated vegetatively from male plants and do not bear "berries". Juniper is perhaps best known as the principal flavouring of gin; the word "gin", a shortened form of the Dutch *genever*, is derived from the Latin *juniperus*. In medicinal terms, it is one of the most effective herbal remedies for cystitis. Various other junipers are used medicinally. Native N Americans treated a wide range of illnesses, from kidney complaints to dandruff and syphilis, with extracts of *J. scopulorum* (Rocky Mountain juniper). *Juniperus virginiana* (red cedar) was used for ailments such as coughs and colds, headaches, dysentery, and mumps. Red cedar oil is pleasantly aromatic but extremely toxic. Its use in inducing abortion carries considerable risk. *Juniperus sabina* (savin) is also considered too poisonous for internal use because it contains podophyllotoxin (as found in *Podophyllum peltatum*, see p.325), which destroys cells and has resulted in fatalities. *Juniperus oxycedrus* (prickly juniper) yields cade oil or juniper tar oil, a red-brown to black, oily liquid that controls itching and is used in topical preparations for eczema, psoriasis, and seborrhoea.

CULTIVATION Most soils in sun or light shade. Tolerates acid and alkaline conditions, dry and wet soils, and exposed positions. Plants may be damaged by various pests and diseases.

PROPAGATION By seed sown when ripe; by ripewood cuttings in early autumn. Germination may take up to five years.

HARVEST Fruits are gathered by shaking branches over a groundsheet; they are used fresh for oil distillation, or dried for infusions, liquid extracts, tablets, and tinctures.

⚠ **WARNING** Junipers may cause skin irritation and allergic responses.

Juniperus communis

Juniperus communis var. *depressa*

▣ *Juniperus communis* (common juniper)
Upright, spreading, or prostrate shrub with red-brown, papery bark and juvenile foliage only, consisting of whorls of three linear, sharply pointed, dark green to blue-green leaves, about 1cm (⅜in) long, which have a single white stripe on the inner surface. Tiny ovoid male cones and globose female cones are produced on separate plants, followed on females by spherical green fruits that ripen black with a grey bloom over three years. Found throughout the northern hemisphere. ‡ 0.5–6m (18in–20ft), occasionally to 12m (40ft), ↔ 1–6m (3–20ft).
▣ var. *depressa* is prostrate, with upturned shoot tips and leaves with very narrow, white bands. Native to N America. ‡ 60cm (2ft), ↔ 1.5m (5ft).
HARDINESS Fully hardy.
PARTS USED Fruits ("berries"), oil.
PROPERTIES A bitter aromatic herb that is antiseptic and diuretic, improves digestion, stimulates the uterus, and also reduces inflammation.
MEDICINAL USES Internally for cystitis, urethritis, kidney inflammation, rheumatism, gout, arthritis, and poor digestion with wind and colic. Externally for rheumatic pain and neuralgia. Combines well with *Aphanes arvensis* (see p.124) for cystitis. Juniper is an irritant, best combined with demulcent herbs, such as *Althaea officinalis* (see p.117) or *Zea mays* (see p.410). Contraindicated during pregnancy and in kidney disease or kidney infection.
CULINARY USES Juniper berries are used to flavour pickling brine, sauerkraut, stuffings, pâtés, game, ham, and pork.
ECONOMIC USES Juniper extracts and oil are used to flavour gin, beers (*genevrette*), liqueurs (*ginepro*), and meat products. Oil is also used in spicy fragrances.
▨ ▢ ▣ ▨ ▨

JUSTICIA
Water willow

Acanthaceae

This large genus consists of about 420 species of evergreen perennials, subshrubs, and shrubs occurring in tropical and subtropical parts of

Justicia adhatoda

both hemispheres. *Justicia adhatoda* (malabar nut) has long been important in India for treating a wide range of bronchial diseases. It was introduced to Europe in 1699. Research has shown that it contains various alkaloids, including vasicine (also known as peganine), which stimulates contraction of uterine muscles, thus inducing or accelerating labour. It is now important as a source of this clinically useful drug. Another substance found in *J. adhatoda* is adhatodic acid. According to Mrs Grieve (*A Modern Herbal*, 1931), adhatodic acid "exerts a strong poisoning influence upon the lower forms of animals and vegetable life, though non-poisonous to the higher animals". *Justicia* is named after James Justice, an 18th-century Scottish horticulturist.

CULTIVATION Well-drained soil in sun or partial shade, with high humidity. Cut back ornamental specimens hard in early spring, and pinch out regularly to encourage a bushy habit. Plants under cover may be attacked by whitefly.

PROPAGATION By seed sown at 16°C (61°F) in spring; by softwood cuttings in spring; by semi-ripe cuttings in summer.

HARVEST Leaves are collected in the growing season and dried for use in herbal smoking mixtures, liquid extracts, and tinctures.

▣ *Justicia adhatoda* syn. *Adhatoda vasica* (Malabar nut, *vasak*)
Erect, evergreen, sparsely branched shrub with ovate to lanceolate, prominently veined leaves, 10–20cm (4–8in) long. White, two-lipped flowers, 3cm (1¼in) long, with pink-veined lips, are borne in dense terminal spikes, 5cm (2in) long, mainly in summer. Native to India and Sri Lanka. ‡ 2–3m (6–10ft), ↔ 1–1.5m (3–5ft).
HARDINESS Min. 7°C (45°F).
PARTS USED Leaves.
PROPERTIES A bitter expectorant herb with a strong, tea-like odour. It relaxes spasms, lowers fever, and stimulates the uterus.
MEDICINAL USES Internally for tuberculosis, asthma, chronic bronchitis, and intermittent fever. Leaves are smoked to relieve asthma.
▨ ▣ ▣

Justicia paniculata. See *Andrographis paniculata.*

K

KAEMPFERIA
Zingiberaceae

A genus of about 70 species of rhizomatous aromatic perennials, found in tropical Africa and SE Asia. They have violet-like flowers, composed of three petals and a petal-like lip, and often variegated foliage, making attractive subjects for ground cover in warm areas, or as ornamentals for pots and shady greenhouse borders in temperate regions. *Kaempferia galanga* is used for flavouring in tropical Africa and Asia, as a hallucinogen in New Guinea, and is added to arrow poison in Malaysia. In the Middle Ages it was familiar in European cooking as galingale, perhaps because it resembled *Cyperus longus* (sweet galingale, see p.189) in flavour. The related *Kaempferia rotunda* (*kuntji puti*) and *Boesenbergia panduata* syn. *Kaempferia pandurata* are used for flavouring and as spicy vegetables in their countries of origin. In addition, *K. rotunda* is an ingredient of the Ayurvedic tonic *chyavanprash*. *Kaempferia* is named after Engelbert Kaempfer (1651–1716), a German physician who specialized in Japanese plants.

CULTIVATION Rich moist soil in shade, with high humidity. Kaempferias must be kept dry when dormant.

PROPAGATION By seed sown when ripe at 20°C (68°F); by division in spring.

HARVEST Rhizomes are lifted during dormancy, and used fresh as a vegetable, or dried for use in decoctions, poultices, and powders.

◼ *Kaempferia galanga* (resurrection lily)
Low-growing, stemless perennial with tuberous roots, 2–3 almost round, spreading leaves, 8–15cm (3–6in) across, and short-lived, white flowers, to 2.5cm (1in) across, marked purple on the lip. Native to India and China.

‡ 30cm (12in), ↔ 30–60cm (12–24in).
HARDINESS Min. 18°C (64°F).
PARTS USED Rhizomes.
PROPERTIES A bitter stimulant herb with a camphoraceous aroma. It is anti-bacterial, improves digestion, and has diuretic effects.
MEDICINAL USES Internally for bronchial complaints, dyspepsia, and headaches. Externally for wounds, dandruff, lice infestations, rheumatic joints, and as a gargle for sore throat. Combined with *Alpinia galanga* (see p.116), *Curcuma longa* (see p.186), and *Zingiber* spp. (see p.410) as *awas empas*, an Indonesian remedy for stiff joints, headaches, and urinary tract complaints.
CULINARY USES Fresh rhizomes and young shoots are pickled, eaten raw, or cooked as vegetables. Dried rhizomes are used to flavour rice and as a substitute for turmeric.
ECONOMIC USES Powdered rhizome is added to body powders and cosmetics; also used in linen sachets.
◼ ◼ ✎ ✐ ◼

KALMIA
Ericaceae

A genus of seven species of evergreen shrubs and small trees occurring in N America and Cuba. All have poisonous foliage. Most species are cultivated for their clusters of exquisite, saucer-shaped, pink to purple or white flowers. *Kalmia latifolia* is perhaps the most spectacular when in flower; it is the state flower of both Connecticut and Pennsylvania. The toxicity of *K. latifolia* is legendary: game birds and livestock may be poisonous to eat if they have ingested the leaves. According to Pehr Kalm (1715–79), after whom the genus is named, sheep are especially susceptible (hence the common name "lambkill"), whereas deer are unharmed (*Travels in North America*, Vol. 1, 1753). Though the flesh of affected animals is apparently not contaminated, the intestines will cause poisoning if fed to dogs, so that they "become quite stupid, and, as it were, intoxicated, and often fall so sick that they seem to be at the point of death" (Kalm). Symptoms of poisoning in humans include vertigo, headache, loss of sight, salivation, thirst, nausea, vomiting, palpitations, slow pulse, and difficulty in

Kalmia latifolia 'Clementine Churchill'

breathing. *Kalmia latifolia* contains arbutin (as in *Arctostaphylos uva-ursi*, see p.127), a urinary antiseptic, but this is of minor importance compared with the plant's narcotic effects.

CULTIVATION Acid soil in sun or partial shade. Remove dead flower heads.

PROPAGATION By seed sown in spring at 6–12°C (43–54°F) (species only); by greenwood cuttings in late spring; by semi-ripe cuttings in summer.

HARVEST Leaves are picked when plants are flowering and used fresh for infusions, tinctures, and ointments, or dried for powder.

⚠ **WARNING** All parts, including nectar, are harmful if eaten.

◼ *Kalmia latifolia* (calico bush, ivybush, mountain laurel)
Shrub or small tree with glossy, leathery, lanceolate leaves, to 5cm (2in) long. Pink to white flowers are borne in corymbs, 8–10cm (3–4in) across, in late spring and early summer. Native to eastern N America. ↕↔ 3m (10ft).
◼ 'Clementine Churchill' has deep pink buds and flowers. 'Elf' is dwarf, with tiny leaves, 3cm (1¼in) long, pale pink buds, and white flowers. ↕↔ 1m (3ft). f. *myrtifolia* is compact, with small leaves and pale pink flowers. ↕↔ 1.2m (4ft). 'Ostbo Red' has red buds and pale pink flowers; the first red-budded kalmia in cultivation, originating in the USA during the 1940s.

HARDINESS Fully hardy.
PARTS USED Leaves.
PROPERTIES An astringent, slightly bitter herb that acts as a cardiac sedative.
MEDICINAL USES Internally for syphilis, inflammatory fevers, diarrhoea, bowel haemorrhage, neuralgia, paralytic conditions, tinnitus, and angina. Externally for herpes, scalp conditions, and skin irritations. For use only by qualified practitioners; seldom used today.
✎ ◼

KRAMERIA
Krameriaceae

This genus is the only one in the family Krameriaceae; it contains 15–25 species of semi-parasitic trees, shrubs, and perennials,

Kaempferia galanga

Kalmia latifolia

occurring in desert areas of N and S America. Rhatany root is collected mainly from *K. lappacea* in Peru, where it is found in the wild. In other areas, such as the Colorado and Nevada deserts, the Mohave, and Baja California, *K. argentea*, *K. cistoidea*, *K. greyi* (*casahui*, *mezquitillo*), and *K. parvifolia* are exploited. *Krameria lappacea* was introduced to cultivation during the 19th century, but is no longer seen, presumably because it proved too difficult. Aqueous extracts of rhatany are red, like those from other tannin-rich herbs, such as *Agrimonia eupatoria* (see p.107) and *Potentilla erecta* (see p.329). Rhatany extracts contain 10–20 per cent condensed tannins, and also a red pigment, phlobaphene (rhatany red). They were widely used to improve the astringency, colour, and richness of red wine, and their source was a closely guarded secret among Portuguese and Spanish merchants during colonial times.

CULTIVATION Well-drained, sandy or stony soil in sun.

PROPAGATION This species does not appear to be in cultivation.

HARVEST Roots are lifted from wild plants and dried for use in tinctures and dry extracts.

Krameria lappacea, syn. *K. triandra* (*mapato*, *ratanhia*, rhatany)
Low-growing shrub with a wide-spreading, red-black rootstock, orange-red within, and procumbent stems bearing stalkless, ovate, hairy leaves, 1–2cm (⅜–¾in) long. Red flowers, with shiny pointed petals, appear in autumn, followed by rounded spiny fruits, 6mm (¼in) across. Native to Peru; found on western slopes of the Andes at 915–2785m (3000–9000ft). ↕ 50–90cm (20–36in), ↔ 60cm–1.2m (2–4ft).

HARDINESS Min. 5–10°C (41–50°F).

PARTS USED Roots.

PROPERTIES A strongly astringent herb that checks bleeding, controls discharges and diarrhoea, and encourages healing.

MEDICINAL USES Internally for diarrhoea, haemorrhage, and heavy menstruation. Externally for vaginal discharge, haemorrhoids, chilblains, wounds, gingivitis, and pharyngitis.

ECONOMIC USES Added to port wine to raise astringency, and also to oral hygiene products.

L

LACTUCA
Lettuce

Asteraceae

This genus contains about 100 species of annuals and perennials, which occur worldwide, especially in northern temperate regions. *Lactuca serriola* originated in Europe; it is more like sow thistle (*Sonchus* spp.) than garden lettuce (*Lactuca sativa*) and has little to recommend it as

Lactuca serriola

an ornamental or culinary plant. *Lactuca* spp. contain mildly narcotic compounds in the latex, known as *lactucarium* when dried. The active constituents increase during flowering and are relatively low in young plants. *Lactucarium* entered medical practice as a sedative in the 18th century. It was used to adulterate *Papaver somniferum* (opium, see p.301) and was known as "lettuce opium", because of its similar, but non-addictive, effects. In addition to *Lactuca serriola*, the main sources of *lactucarium* are *L. canadensis* (American wild lettuce) and *L. virosa* (wild or great lettuce). Centuries of breeding have reduced the amounts in *L. sativa*. *Lactuca* is from the Latin *lac*, "milk", and refers to the milky sap (latex), source of *lactucarium*.

CULTIVATION Well-drained to dry, alkaline soil in sun.

PROPAGATION By seed sown *in situ* in autumn.

HARVEST Latex is extracted from leaves and stems of flowering plants in summer and dried for use as *lactucarium* and in extracts, infusions, tablets, and tinctures.

■ *Lactuca serriola* (compass plant, prickly lettuce, wild lettuce)
Fetid hairless annual or biennial with prickly stems and prickly glaucous leaves, to 30cm (12in) long. Yellow flowers, resembling miniature dandelions, appear in panicles in summer. Cosmopolitan weed. ↕ 1–1.5m (3–5ft), ↔ 30cm–1m (12–36in).

HARDINESS Fully hardy.

PARTS USED Whole plant, leaves, latex.

PROPERTIES A very bitter, sedative, expectorant herb, with an unpleasant smell, that relieves pain and soothes irritated tissues.

MEDICINAL USES Internally for insomnia, anxiety, neuroses, hyperactivity in children, dry coughs, bronchitis, whooping cough, and rheumatic pain. Combined with *Cypripedium parviflorum* var. *pubescens* (see p.189), *Humulus lupulus* (see p.237), *Passiflora incarnata* (see p.303), *Scutellaria lateriflora* (see p.365), and *Valeriana officinalis* (see p.400) for insomnia. Causes drowsiness; excess causes restlessness.

CULINARY USES Young leaves are eaten raw in salads or cooked as a vegetable. Seeds yield edible Egyptian lettuce seed oil.

LAMIUM
Deadnettle

Lamiaceae

A genus consisting of about 50 species of annuals and usually rhizomatous perennials, occurring from Europe to Asia, especially in Mediterranean regions and N Africa. They resemble *Urtica dioica* (stinging nettles, see p.398) in appearance, and are known as deadnettles because they do not sting. Only a few species have any merit as garden plants. These include ornamental cultivars of *Lamium album*, which is otherwise a common weed; *L. album* has been used for gynaecological and obstetric problems since at least medieval times.

CULTIVATION Moist, well-drained soil in sun or partial shade.

PROPAGATION By seed sown in autumn or spring (species only); by division in autumn or early spring; by stem-tip cuttings of non-flowering shoots in summer.

HARVEST Whole plants are cut when in flower, or flowers are removed individually; both are dried for use in infusions and tinctures.

■ *Lamium album* (archangel, white deadnettle) Hairy perennial with creeping rhizomes, four-angled stems, and ovate, coarsely toothed leaves, 3–7cm (1¼–3in) long. Whorls of tubular, white, two-lipped flowers appear from spring to autumn. Native to Eurasia; naturalized in eastern N America. ↕ 15–60cm (6–24in), ↔ 60–90cm (24–36in). ■ 'Friday' has gold-centred leaves in two shades of green. ↕↔ 45–60cm (18–24in).

HARDINESS Fully hardy.

PARTS USED Whole plant, flowers.

PROPERTIES A slightly bitter, astringent, decongestant herb that checks bleeding and reduces inflammation.

MEDICINAL USES Internally for menstrual problems, bleeding after childbirth, vaginal discharge, and prostatitis. Externally as a douche for vaginal discharge. Combines well with *Achillea millefolium* (see p.99) for vaginal discharge, with *Vinca major* (see p.404) or *Geranium maculatum*

Lamium album

Lamium album 'Friday'

(see p.223) for heavy menstruation, and with *Elymus repens* (see p.201), *Hydrangea arborescens* (see p.238), or *Zea mays* (see p.410) for prostate problems.

CULINARY USES Flowers are used to make herb tea. Young leaves are cooked as a pot-herb and are mixed with *Rumex acetosa* (sorrel, see p.351) as an ingredient of the French eel dish *anguille au vert à la flamande*.

LARIX

Larch

Pinaceae

Nine species of large coniferous trees make up this genus, which abounds in cool parts of the northern hemisphere. Larches resemble *Cedrus* spp. (see p.160), except that the cones mature in a single year and the foliage is deciduous. Widely grown for timber, they are also popular as ornamentals. *Larix decidua* was introduced to the British Isles in 1639 and is so well established that it is now regarded as native. *Larix laricina* (American larch, *tamarac*) is also used medicinally. The bark can be used to treat rheumatism, jaundice, and skin complaints, and as a poultice for wounds. Resin from the bark was once collected as a chewing gum, which also relieved indigestion. *Larix occidentalis* (western larch) similarly exudes gum, which is used in the food industry as a substitute for gum arabic (from *Acacia senegal*, see p.98).

CULTIVATION Moist, well-drained soil in an open sunny position. Remove lower branches of specimen trees to give a clean trunk. To maintain a single leading shoot, remove secondary leaders. Larches may suffer from rust and honey fungus, adelgids, and sawfly.

Larix decidua

PROPAGATION By seed sown in early spring; by semi-ripe cuttings under mist in summer; by grafting in winter. Difficult to root from cuttings.

HARVEST Bark is stripped in late spring and dried for use in decoctions, powders, and tinctures. Tree is tapped for resin in autumn.

■ ***Larix decidua*** syn. *L. europaea* (common larch, European larch)

Deciduous conifer with grey scaly bark, drooping branches, and rosettes of soft, light green needles. Female cones, 2.5–4cm (1–1½in) long, are erect and pink (known as larch "roses"), ripening brown. Native to mountains of C Europe to N Russia and Siberia. ↕ 30m (100ft), ↔ 4–6m (12–20ft). 'Corley' is dwarf, with a rounded to spreading habit, suitable for rock gardens and containers. ↕↔ 1m (3ft). ■ 'Pendula' has a drooping, though often irregular, habit and is an attractive specimen when young.

HARDINESS Fully hardy.

PARTS USED Bark, resin.

PROPERTIES A bitter astringent herb with a turpentine-like smell. It relieves bronchial congestion, is diuretic, and promotes healing.

MEDICINAL USES Internally for bronchitis and urinary tract inflammation (bark); for tapeworm, diarrhoea, failure to menstruate, and as an antidote to phosphorus poisoning (resin). Not given to patients with kidney disease. Externally for infected wounds and skin problems, such as eczema and psoriasis (bark decoction, resin).

LARREA

Zygophyllaceae

A genus of five evergreen shrubs, found in deserts of S America and southwestern N America. These highly adapted plants are difficult to cultivate outside their native habitats. *Larrea tridentata* (chaparral) is a suckering shrub that forms large stands. In the Mohave Desert, some measure 7.8m (26ft) across and are estimated to be 11,700 years old. They are strongly aromatic, especially after rain, filling the air for miles with a creosote-like aroma and exuding substances that prevent the germination of the plant's own seeds, and the growth of other plants beneath its branches. *Larrea* spp. have a complex and unusual chemistry, containing nordihydroguaiaretic acid (NDGA), which is a potent antioxidant and parasiticide. They are also rich in resins and other substances that make the plants unpalatable to herbivores. NDGA was the main antioxidant used in the food industry to prevent rancidity of fats and oils until the late 1960s. Desert tribes have long used these plants medicinally, notably in the form of "chaparral tea", which was regarded as a cure-all. Colonists found *Larrea* useful for treating sexually transmitted diseases and malignant skin conditions. Eminent herbalists have described *Larrea* as "of low toxicity" (Thomas Bartram, *Encyclopedia of Herbal Medicine*, 1995), and as having "a strong and beneficial effect upon impaired liver metabolism" (Michael Moore, *Medicinal Plants of the Desert and Canyon West*, 1989). Nevertheless, medicinal use of *Larrea* has been banned in a number of countries following five cases of hepatitis that were apparently due to taking chaparral.

CULTIVATION AND PROPAGATION *Larrea* spp. do not appear to thrive outside their natural habitat.

HARVEST Young leafy twigs are cut and used fresh for teas and tinctures, or dried for tablets and ointment. The high resin content makes the twigs and foliage difficult to grind.

Larix decidua 'Pendula'

Larrea tridentata

■ *Larrea tridentata* (chaparral, creosote bush, grease bush)
Thorny, open, spreading shrub with smooth bark, slender branches, and small, bifurcated, dark olive-green leaves, covered in strong-smelling, sticky, varnish-like resin. Yellow, five-petalled flowers appear throughout the year after rain, but mainly from late winter to midspring, followed by fuzzy, pea-sized fruits. Native to deserts areas of Mexico and USA (California, Texas, Utah). ↔ 2–4m (6–12ft).
HARDINESS Fully hardy.
PARTS USED Leafy twigs.
PROPERTIES A strongly bitter, resinous, alterative herb that has potent antioxidant, antibiotic, anti-fungal, anti-inflammatory, and anti-tumour effects; also antiseptic, especially on the respiratory and urinary systems.
MEDICINAL USES Internally for kidney and gallstones, urinary tract infections, rheumatism and arthritis, diabetes, skin disorders, cancer (notably leukaemia), liver ailments, and tetanus. Externally for wounds, dry skin, brittle hair and nails, arthritic pain, and foot odour.
ECONOMIC USES Until synthetic antioxidants were developed, NDGA was important in the food industry for preventing rancidity in fats, oils, dairy produce, frozen meats and fish, and in pharmaceutical preparations containing vitamin A and reserpine (from *Rauvolfia serpentina*, see p.341).

LAUROCERASUS
Laurocerasus officinalis. See *Prunus laurocerasus.*

LAURUS
Bay laurel

Lauraceae

There are only two species of evergreen shrubs or small trees in this genus, which occurs in S Europe, the Canary Islands, and the Azores. Both are grown as ornamentals, but the popularity of *L. nobilis* (sweet bay) as a culinary

herb makes it far more common in cultivation than the more tender *L. azorica* (Canary Island laurel). The large, brittle, dried leaves of sweet bay are an important ingredient of both sweet and savoury dishes in European cuisines. Little use is made of *L. nobilis* medicinally, although it was long regarded as a potent antiseptic. Bay rum, an aromatic liquid used in hair dressings, cosmetics, and medicines, does not contain sweet bay leaves but is made by distilling the leaves of *Pimenta racemosa* (West Indian bay, see p.317) in rum. Other species known as bay include: *Magnolia virginiana* (sweet bay, see p.270); *Persea borbonia* (red bay, see p.308), which makes a very good substitute for *Laurus nobilis*; and *Umbellularia californica* (California bay, see p.397). *Laurus* is from the Latin *laus*, "praise", referring to the crown of bay leaves worn by victorious Romans.
CULTIVATION Well-drained soil in sun or partial shade. Trim to shape in summer, removing suckers from standards and topiaries as they appear. Prone to scale insect.
PROPAGATION By seed sown under cover in autumn; by semi-ripe cuttings in summer; by removal of suckers in summer; by layering in autumn.
HARVEST Leaves are collected in summer and dried whole, or as branches, for infusions, powders, and oil distillation. Dried leaves lose flavour after about a year.

Laurus camphora. See *Cinnamomum camphora.*

Laurus nobilis

Laurus nobilis
'Angustifolia'

Laurus nobilis
'Aurea'

■ *Laurus nobilis* (bay, bay laurel, sweet bay) Dense evergreen shrub or small tree with leathery pointed leaves. Clusters of small, cream-yellow flowers, with conspicuous stamens, appear in spring, followed by dark purple berries. Native to the Mediterranean. ↕ 3–15m (10–50ft), ↔ 10m (30ft). ■ 'Angustifolia' (willow-leaf bay) is an unusual cultivar with narrow, wavy-edged, pale green leaves, 3–7cm (1¼–3in) long. It is hardier than the species. ■ 'Aurea' (golden bay) has yellow-tinged leaves, which are at their best in winter and spring. Slightly hardier than the species.
HARDINESS Fully hardy (borderline).
PARTS USED Leaves, oil.
PROPERTIES A bitter, aromatic, stimulant herb that improves digestion and is locally antiseptic.
MEDICINAL USES Internally for indigestion, poor appetite, colic, and flatulence. Externally for dandruff, rheumatism, sprains, bruises, atonic ulcers, and scabies.
CULINARY USES Leaves are an important ingredient of bouquet garni and are commonly added to sauces, soups, stews, and desserts.
ECONOMIC USES Leaves are used in packing dried figs and liquorice in order to deter weevils. Essential oil is used to flavour commercial condiments, meat products, and liqueurs.

LAVANDULA
Lavender

Lamiaceae

A genus of about 25 aromatic evergreen perennials and shrubs that are found throughout Mediterranean regions, the Middle East, and India. Lavenders are among the most popular plants for herb gardens for their subtle colouring and delightful fragrance. The hardier lavenders make attractive hedges, while tender kinds may be grown under cover. Lavenders are all rich in volatile oils, and the resulting essential oils vary greatly in aroma, constituents, and quality. Due to their popularity and long history of cultivation, garden lavenders are mostly hybrids and cultivars, and accurate identification is often extremely difficult. The two most important lavenders with medicinal uses are *L. angustifolia* and *L. latifolia*. The former grows at high elevations, 600–1200m (2000–4000ft), in S Europe and therefore thrives and yields well in cool areas. Both are rich in essential oils but differ in constituents; *L. angustifolia* yields an exquisitely scented oil, known in France as *fine*, which is used in aromatherapy and high-quality perfumes; *L. latifolia*, a lowland species, yields much larger quantities of a rather harsh, camphoraceous oil, which is mainly used in cleaning products, and as insect-repellent. *Lavandula latifolia* is rarely seen as a garden plant but is grown in Spain for its oil. The hybrid lavender or lavandin, *L. × intermedia* (a cross between *L. angustifolia* and *L. latifolia* that appeared c.1900) is often preferred by the perfume industry, but it is not recommended for medicinal use. It is grown on a large scale for its

oil, and for its flowers, which are used in sachets, potpourri, and craft work. Lavandin combines the best properties of its parents, having a more pleasant perfume than *L. latifolia*, and yielding over four times as much oil as *L. angustifolia*. For many years lavender production centred on Provence (S France), but other countries, such as Japan, Australia, and New Zealand, increased production during the late 20th century. *Lavandula stoechas* was widely used as an antiseptic and toiletry herb in ancient times by the Greeks, Romans, and Arabs, but is little used today. It has a pungently scented volatile oil, containing 24–72 per cent camphor.
CULTIVATION Well-drained, neutral to alkaline soil in an open sunny position. *Lavandula stoechas* thrives in acid soil; *L. latifolia* tolerates slight acidity. Trim hedges and cut specimen plants back in spring to encourage bushiness. Dead-head and trim lightly after flowering. *Lavandula lanata* is very sensitive to over-watering and damp conditions. Lavenders are affected by grey mould, scab, leafspot, and honey fungus. Plants become woody with age and are best replaced every 3–4 years. *Lavandula stoechas* is subject to statutory control as a weed in parts of Australia.
PROPAGATION By seed sown on surface of compost in spring; by semi-ripe cuttings in summer. Seeds of *L. angustifolia* germinate more quickly if placed in the freezer for two hours before sowing. Cultivars do not come true from seed.
HARVEST Flowers of *L. angustifolia* and *L. × intermedia* are picked as they begin to open

and used fresh, distilled for oil, or (*L. angustifolia* only) dried for use in infusions, spirits, and tinctures. Flower heads and flowers of other lavenders are gathered as they open, for drying.

■ ***Lavandula × allardii*** (giant lavender)
A hybrid between *L. dentata* and *L. latifolia*, with broad, grey-green leaves, often scallop-edged towards the apex. Violet-blue flowers are produced in very large, narrowly conical spikes, 12–20cm (5–8in) long, throughout summer and autumn. ↕ 1.2–1.5m (4–5ft), ↔ 1.2m (4ft).
HARDINESS Half hardy.
PARTS USED Flowers, oil.
PROPERTIES An aromatic herb with a strong camphoraceous aroma.
ECONOMIC USES Oil is distilled from the flowers for the perfume industry in South Africa. Flowers are dried for potpourris and other scented articles.
✿ ❂ ✎

■ ***Lavandula angustifolia*** syn. *L. officinalis*, *L. spica* in part, *L. vera* in part (English lavender, lavender)
Small shrub with downy linear leaves, to 6cm (2½in) long, which are grey when young. Blue-violet flowers grow in compact or interrupted spikes, to 8cm (3in) long. ↕ 60–70cm (24–28in), ↔ 1m (3ft). ■ 'Blue Cushion' syn. 'Schola' is small and bushy, with midgreen leaves and violet-blue flowers in spikes, 4–7cm (1½–2¾in) long, borne on stems 15–18cm (6–7in) long; ideal for pots and low hedges. ↕ 50cm (20in). 'Bowles' Early' is upright and

bushy, with dense midgreen leaves and violet-blue flowers in cylindrical spikes, 2–3cm (¾–1¼in) long, borne on stems 14–18cm (5½–7in) long. ↕↔ 60cm (24in). 'Buena Vista' is a bushy, medium-sized plant, with green foliage and deep blue-purple flowers in evenly interrupted spikes 8–12cm (3–4¾in) long. Blooms into autumn; excellent for landscaping.
■ 'Cedar Blue' is small, with dense, grey-green foliage and violet-blue flowers in short spikes, to 3cm (1¼in) long, borne on stems 10–18cm (4–7in) long; good for containers and edging.
■ 'Folgate' is broad but compact in habit, with midgreen leaves and quite strongly scented, violet-blue flowers borne on stems 18–23cm (7–9in) long. 'Grey Lady' is vigorous, with large grey leaves. ↔ 1.2m (4ft). ■ 'Hidcote' is bushy, with dense, grey-green foliage and strongly scented, violet flowers in cylindrical, slightly interrupted spikes, 3–8cm (1¼–3in) long, on stems 12–23cm (4¾–9in) long. ↕ 60–70cm (24–28in), ↔ 75cm (30in).
■ 'Hidcote Pink' is bushy to spherical, with mauve-pink flowers on spikes 6–8cm (2½–3in) long, borne on stems 15–18cm (6–7in) long. ↕ 70cm (28in). ■ 'Imperial Gem' is bushy, with dense, grey-green leaves and deep violet, highly fragrant flowers in cylindrical, mostly interrupted spikes, 4–6cm (1½–2½in) long; good for hedging. ↕↔ 70cm (28in). ■ 'Jean Davis' is upright, with dense, grey-green foliage and mauve-pink flowers in spikes, 5–8cm (2–3in) long, borne on stems 12–25cm (4¾–10in) long. ■ 'Lady' syn. 'Atlee Burpee', 'Lavender Lady' is compact, with midgreen

L

Lavandula angustifolia

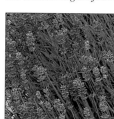

Lavandula × allardii

Lavandula angustifolia 'Blue Cushion'

Lavandula angustifolia 'Cedar Blue'

Lavandula angustifolia 'Folgate'

Lavandula angustifolia 'Hidcote'

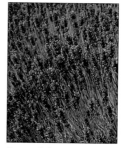

Lavandula angustifolia 'Hidcote Pink'

Lavandula angustifolia 'Imperial Gem'

Lavandula angustifolia 'Jean Davis'

Lavandula angustifolia 'Lady'

Lavandula angustifolia 'Loddon Blue'

Lavandula angustifolia 'Loddon Pink'

foliage and violet-blue flowers in globose to cylindrical spikes, 1–3cm (³⁄₈–1¼in) long, borne on stems 6–13cm (2½–5in) long. Usually grown from seed, therefore variable; often grown as an annual in cold areas. Needs hard pruning to prevent tendency to split open. ↕↔ 40–50cm (16–20in). ▣ 'Loddon Blue' is rounded, with dense, grey-green foliage and violet-blue flowers in spikes 4–7cm (1½–2¾in) long, borne on stems 14–18cm (5½–7in) long. ↕↔ 60cm (24in). ▣ 'Loddon Pink' is upright and bushy, with midgreen foliage and pink to mauve-pink flowers in spikes 6–10cm (2½–4in) long, borne on stems 18–28cm (7–11in) long. ↕↔ 50–60cm (20–24in). ▣ 'Miss Katherine' is relatively large and bushy, with dense, grey-green foliage and lilac-pink, very fragrant flowers in spikes 7–11cm (2¾–4¼in) long; excellent as a hedge or feature. ↕↔ 75cm (30in). ▣ 'Munstead' is compact, with dense, small, midgreen leaves and lavender-blue flowers in interrupted spikes, 6–13cm (2½–5in) long, on stems 14–23cm (5½–9in) long. Usually grown from seed, therefore variable. ↕ 45cm (18in), ↔ 60cm (24in). ▣ 'Nana Alba' is dwarf, compact, with silver-grey leaves and white flowers in spikes 4–5cm (1½–2in) long; the smallest, white-flowered cultivar, ideal for pots or edging. ↕↔ 30cm (12in). ▣ 'Okamurasaki' is bushy, with rather open, midgreen foliage and very large, violet-blue, pale-throated flowers in cylindrical interrupted spikes, 5–9cm (2–3½in) long, borne on stems 14–20cm (5½–8in) long. ↕ 70cm (28in).

▣ 'Princess Blue' is upright and bushy, with large, violet-blue flowers in spikes 6–10cm (2½–4in) long, borne on stems 13–23cm (5–9in) long. ↕ 70cm (28in). ▣ 'Rosea' is upright and bushy, with light green leaves and mauve-pink flowers in spikes 5–9cm (2–3½in) long, borne on stems 15–23cm (6–9in) long; the oldest pink lavender, introduced before 1937. ▣ 'Royal Purple' is a large cultivar that is good for hedging, with narrow, grey-green leaves and long spikes of deep purple flowers, which retain their colour well after drying. ↕↔ 80cm (32in). 'Royal Velvet' is small to medium and bushy, with grey-green foliage and vivid purple flowers in spikes, 7–9cm (2¾–3½in) long, borne on stems 30–35cm (12–14in) long. 'Sharon Roberts' is bushy, with midgreen to grey-green foliage and deep lavender-blue, very fragrant flowers in spikes, 6–10cm (2½–4in) long, borne on stout, dark-edged stems, 18–23cm (7–9in) long. Consistently blooms twice, in early summer and again in autumn. 'Tucker's Early Purple' is small and bushy, with rather open, grey-green foliage and early, long-blooming, violet-blue flowers in cylindrical interrupted spikes, 4–6cm (1½–2½in) long, borne on stems 8–23cm (3–9in) long. ▣ 'Twickel Purple' is tall and spherical, with open, midgreen to grey-green foliage and violet-blue flowers in cylindrical interrupted spikes, 8–18cm (3–7in) long, borne on strong stems, 25–35cm (10–14in) long; ideal for craft work. Needs pruning regularly to prevent excessive sprawling.

HARDINESS Fully hardy.

PARTS USED Flowers, oil.

PROPERTIES An aromatic tonic herb with a sweet scent. It relaxes spasms, benefits the digestion, stimulates the peripheral circulation and uterus, and lowers fevers. It has anti-depressant effects and is antiseptic.

MEDICINAL USES Internally for indigestion, depression, anxiety, exhaustion, irritability, tension headaches, migraine, and bronchial complaints (including tuberculosis). Externally for burns, sunburn, rheumatism, muscular pain, neuralgia, skin complaints, cold sores, insect and snake bites, head lice, halitosis, vaginal discharge, and anal fissure. Combines well with *Rosmarinus officinalis* (see p.348) for depression and tension headaches; with *Verbena officinalis* (see p.402) for migraine and nervous tension; and with *Filipendula ulmaria* (see p.214) and *Actaea racemosa* (see p.102) for rheumatism. Added to baths for patients suffering from debility, nervous tension, and insomnia.

CULINARY USES Fresh flowers are crystallized or added to salads, jams and jellies, ice cream, and vinegar. Leaves are used in salads, marinades, and for flavouring soups and stews. Flowers and leaves are used to make herb tea.

ECONOMIC USES Oil is used in perfumery and toiletries. Dried flowers are used in potpourris. ✿ ⬡ ▪ ✎ ✐

▣ *Lavandula dentata* (fringed lavender) Spreading bushy shrub with linear to narrowly oblong, green leaves, 2–4cm (¾–1½in) long, and slightly fragrant,

Lavandula angustifolia 'Okamurasaki'

Lavandula angustifolia 'Miss Katherine'

Lavandula angustifolia 'Munstead'

Lavandula angustifolia 'Nana Alba'

Lavandula angustifolia 'Princess Blue'

Lavandula angustifolia 'Rosea'

Lavandula angustifolia 'Royal Purple'

Lavandula angustifolia 'Twickel Purple'

Lavandula dentata

Lavandula dentata var. *candicans*

light blue-violet flowers in cylindrical spikes, 3–5cm (1¼–2in) long, borne on stems 10–20cm (4–8in) long. Native to Atlantic islands, W Mediterranean, and the Arabian Peninsula. ↔ 60–90cm (24–36in). ▪ var. *candicans* is upright and bushy, with silver-grey foliage and often longer flower stems, to 30cm (12in); long-flowering and hardier than the species. ‡ 1m (3ft), ↔ 1.5m (5ft).

HARDINESS Frost hardy to half hardy.
PARTS USED Flower spikes.
PROPERTIES An aromatic, diuretic, antiseptic herb with a rosemary-like scent.
MEDICINAL USES Internally, for urine retention and urinary stones (N Africa).
ECONOMIC USES Mainly grown as an aromatic ornamental, but flower heads are dried for potpourris.

▨ ▣ ✎

Lavandula 'Goodwin Creek Grey'

Wide-spreading bush with silver-grey, partly toothed leaves and bright violet-blue flowers in spikes, to 14cm (5½in) long, borne on woolly grey stems 18–35cm (7–14in) long. ‡ 45–80cm (18–32in), ↔ 75cm (30in). A hybrid between *L.* × *heterophylla* and *L. dentata* or *L. lanata*.

HARDINESS Frost hardy to half hardy.
PARTS USED Flower spikes.
PROPERTIES An aromatic herb.
ECONOMIC USES Mainly grown as an aromatic ornamental, but flower heads may be dried for potpourris.

▨ ✎

▪ *Lavandula* × *intermedia* (lavandin)
Robust variable hybrids between *L. angustifolia* and *L. latifolia*, with a rounded habit, branching stems, and oblong to lanceolate, grey-green leaves, 4–6cm (1½–2½in) long. Light blue-violet to violet, strongly fragrant flowers in spikes, 10–20cm (4–8in) long, are borne on long strong stems. ↔ very variable. 'Abrialii' syn. 'Abrial', 'Abrialis' has dense grey-green foliage and elegant spikes of violet-blue flowers. Grown in France since before 1935; oil is excellent for massage. ‡ 70–80cm (28–32in). ▪ 'Alba' is large, open, and bushy, with green to grey-green foliage and white flowers in spikes, 4–5cm (1½–2in) long, borne on upright stems, 25–33cm (10–13in) long. Known before 1880, this traditional cultivar is the largest, white-flowered lavender. ‡ 80cm (32in). ▪ Dutch Group syn. *L. vera* (hort.), 'Vera' is rounded and bushy, with large grey leaves and blue-violet flowers in narrowly conical spikes, 6–9cm (2½–3½in) long, borne on stout stems, 18–35cm (7–14in) long. ‡ 80cm (32in), ↔ 40cm (16in). 'Fred Boutin' has outstanding silver foliage, even in winter, and deep violet-blue flowers in spikes, to 8cm (3in) long, borne on stems 15–33cm (6–13in) long. ‡ 80cm (32in). ▪ 'Grappenhall' is robust and bushy, with narrowly oblong, green leaves, to 6cm (2½in) long, and slightly fragrant, lavender-violet flowers in narrowly conical, interrupted spikes, 5–9cm (2–3½in) long, borne on stout, more or less upright stems, 30–38cm (12–15in) long. ‡ 1m (3ft), ↔ 1.5m (5ft). ▪ 'Grosso' syn. 'Dilly Dilly', 'Wilson's Giant' is spherical, with

midgreen to grey, very dense foliage and violet-blue flowers in compact, broadly conical spikes, 5–9cm (2–3½in) long, borne on stout, dark-edged stems, 30–35cm (12–14in) long. One of the finest and most widely grown commercial lavandin cultivars, discovered in Vaucluse (France) in 1972; floriferous, high yielding, and disease-resistant. ▪ 'Hidcote Giant' is well branched and bushy, with grey-green foliage and violet-blue flowers in compact, very broad spikes, to 8cm (3in) long, borne on very stout, semi-upright to horizontal stems, 28–48cm (11–19in) long; excellent as a specimen plant. 'Lullingstone Castle' is large and bushy, with branched, dense, grey foliage and deep lavender-blue flowers in spikes, 8–11cm (3–4¼in) long, borne on grey-green, semi-upright stems, 28–35cm (11–13in) long. ‡ 90cm (36in); good for hedging. Old English Group is large and bushy to spherical, with lavender-violet flowers in narrowly conical spikes, 6–11cm (2½–4¼in) long, borne on upright green stems, 30–50cm (12–20in) long; excellent for hedging if well pruned. ▪ 'Seal' is robust, with green to grey-green foliage and pale violet, highly fragrant flowers in spikes, 5–8cm (2–3in) long, borne on branched, semi-upright, dark-edged stems, 40–50cm (16–20in) long; excellent for hedging and craft work, with a long-lasting fragrance. Introduced by The Herb Farm, Seal, Kent (UK) before 1935. ‡ 1.2–1.5m (4–5ft), ↔ 1.2m (4ft). 'Sumian' is large, with grey-green leaves, very long, dark-edged stems, to 38cm (15in), and violet flowers in spikes 5–8cm (2–3in) long. A French cultivar with good

L

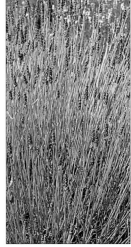

Lavandula × *intermedia*

Lavandula × *intermedia* 'Alba'

Lavandula × *intermedia* Dutch Group

Lavandula × *intermedia* 'Grappenhall'

Lavandula × *intermedia* 'Grosso'

Lavandula × *intermedia* 'Hidcote Giant'

Lavandula × *intermedia* 'Seal'

Lavandula × *intermedia* 'Walberton's Silver Edge'

Lavandula latifolia

Lavandula minutolii

Lavandula multifida

Lavandula pinnata

fragrance. ‡ 80cm (32in). 'Super' is a French cultivar, introduced c.1956, with grey-green foliage, strong lateral branching, stems to 45cm (18in) long, and violet-blue flowers. Several different strains are known. ■ 'Walberton's Silver Edge' is bushy and rather open in habit, with grey-green, cream-edged leaves and deep lavender-violet flowers in compact broad spikes, 2.5–4cm (1–1½in) long, borne on upright unbranched stems, 13–23cm (5–9in) long. 'Yuulong' is spherical, with dense, well-branched, green to grey-green foliage and deep lavender-violet flowers in short spikes, 3.5–5cm (1⅜–2in) long, borne on upright green stems, 33–40cm (13–16in) long; ideal for hedging and craft work. An Australian cultivar, named by the Royal Botanic Gardens, Melbourne, in 1986.
HARDINESS Fully hardy.
PARTS USED Flowers.
PROPERTIES An aromatic herb with a slightly camphoraceous, lavender scent.
CULINARY USES Fresh flowers are crystallized, or added to jams and vinegars.
ECONOMIC USES Essential oil is used in massage oils, perfumery, toiletries, and cleaning products. Dried flowers are added to herb pillows and potpourris.

Lavandula lanata (woolly lavender)
Small shrub with linear to oblong–lanceolate, white-woolly leaves, to 5cm (2in) long, and fragrant, deep purple flowers in spikes, to 10cm (4in) long, borne on stems 25–40cm (10–16in)

long in late summer. Native to S Spain. ‡ 75–80cm (28–30in), ↔ 90cm (36in).
HARDINESS Frost hardy.
PARTS USED Flowers.
PROPERTIES An aromatic herb with a balsam–lavender scent.
ECONOMIC USES Grown mainly as an aromatic ornamental. Flowers may be dried for potpourris.

■ *Lavandula latifolia* syn. *L. spica* in part (spike lavender)
Upright bushy shrub with linear to oblanceolate, grey-green leaves, to 8cm (3in) long, and fragrant, mauve-blue flowers in compact spikes, to 5cm (2in) long, or in interrupted spikes, 5–10cm (2–4in) long, borne on branched stems, 40–50cm (16–20in) long. Native to S Europe. ‡ 1m (3ft), ↔ 1.2m (4ft).
HARDINESS Frost hardy.
PARTS USED Flowers, oil.
PROPERTIES A bitter decongestant herb with a camphoraceous aroma. It has analgesic, anti-depressant, antiseptic, anti-viral, and insect-repellent effects.
MEDICINAL USES Mainly externally in aromatherapy for bronchial complaints, catarrh, sinusitis, muscular and rheumatic pain, stings and bites (oil). Contraindicated during pregnancy.
CULINARY USES As for *L. angustifolia*, but less pleasant in flavour.
ECONOMIC USES Oil, known as "oil of aspic", is used in cheaper perfumes, soaps, disinfectants, shampoos, varnishes, and ceramic paints.

■ *Lavandula minutolii*
Subshrub with pinnate green leaves and large, mauve-blue flowers in very slender spikes, usually branched at the base. Native to Gran Canaria. ‡ 80cm–1m (32–36in), ↔ 60cm (24in).
HARDINESS Half hardy.
PARTS USED Flowers.
PROPERTIES An aromatic herb with a camphor-like scent.
ECONOMIC USES As for *L. lanata*.

■ *Lavandula multifida* (branched lavender)
Subshrub with erect hairy stems and grey-green, feathery leaves. Blue-violet, large-lobed flowers are borne in slender branched spikes, to 8cm (3in) long. Native to W Mediterranean, Portugal, and N Africa. ‡ 50cm–1m (20in–3ft), ↔ 60–75cm (24–30in).
HARDINESS Min. 5°C (41°F).
PARTS USED Flowering branches.
PROPERTIES An aromatic herb with a camphoraceous scent.
MEDICINAL USES Internally for coughs (N Africa).
ECONOMIC USES As for *L. lanata*.

■ *Lavandula pinnata*
Shrub with branched stems, woolly, grey-green, pinnate leaves, to 8cm (3in) long, and fragrant, purple-blue flowers in spikes, 8–9cm (3–3½in) long, often branched at the base, borne on long stems for much of the year. Native to the Canary Islands and Madeira. ‡↔ 1m (3ft).

Lavandula stoechas

Lavandula 'Sawyers'

Lavandula stoechas 'Helmsdale'

Lavandula stoechas 'James Compton'

Lavandula stoechas 'Kew Red'

Lavandula stoechas f. *leucantha*

Lavandula stoechas 'Marshwood'

Lavandula stoechas subsp. *pedunculata*

Lavandula stoechas 'Pukehou'

Lavandula stoechas 'Willowvale'

Lavandula viridis

L

HARDINESS Frost hardy.
PARTS USED Flowers.
PROPERTIES An aromatic herb.
ECONOMIC USES As for *L. lanata*.

Lavandula 'Richard Grey'

A hybrid between *L. angustifolia* and *L. lanata*, with a low-growing, bushy habit, grey-green foliage, and violet flowers in short spikes, 3–4cm (1¼–1½in) long, borne on grey-green, more or less upright stems, 10–20cm (4–8in) long; excellent for containers or low hedging. Originated at the Royal Botanic Gardens, Kew (UK), in the 1980s.
HARDINESS Fully hardy.
PARTS USED Flowers.
PROPERTIES An aromatic herb.
ECONOMIC USES As for *L. lanata*.

Lavandula 'Sawyers'

A hybrid lavender between *L. angustifolia* and *L. lanata*, with a spherical habit, dense, grey-green foliage, and small, violet-blue flowers in tapering pubescent spikes, 6–11cm (2½–4¼in) long, borne on spreading, grey-green stems, 18–35cm (7–13in) long. ↕ 50–68cm (20–27in), ↔ 1.1m (3½ft).
HARDINESS Fully hardy.
PARTS USED Flowers.
PROPERTIES An aromatic herb with a balsam scent.
ECONOMIC USES Flowers may be dried for potpourris and other scented articles.

Lavandula stoechas (French lavender, Italian lavender, Spanish lavender)

Bushy shrub with linear to oblong–lanceolate, downy leaves, to 4cm (1½in) long, and flowering stems, 3–4cm (1¼–1½in) long, bearing dark purple flowers in dense short spikes, 2–3cm (¾–1¼in) long, topped by purple bracts. Native to the Mediterranean area, Portugal, N Africa, Madeira, and Tenerife, often on acid soil. ↕↔ 60cm (24in). ■ 'Helmsdale' has dense green foliage and deep burgundy bracts; excellent for hedging. ↕↔ 70–80cm (28–32in). ■ 'James Compton' syn. 'Butterfly', 'Fairy Wings' has narrow, undulating, bright red-violet bracts. ↕↔ 80cm (32in). ■ 'Kew Red' is dwarf, with very small spikes and bright magenta bracts. ■ f. *leucantha* syn. 'Snowman' is rounded, with dense, grey-green foliage, short flowering stems, to 3.5cm (1⅜in) long, and white flowers in globose–cylindrical spikes, to 3cm (1¼in) long, topped by small, green-veined bracts. Native to E Pyrenees. ↕↔ 40–50cm (16–20in). ■ 'Marshwood' has grey-green foliage and dusky grey-mauve bracts. ↕ 1m (3ft). ■ subsp. *pedunculata* syn. 'Papillon' (Spanish lavender) has narrower, lighter green leaves, deep purple-blue flowers in larger spikes, borne on longer stems, to 23cm (9in). Native to Atlantic islands, Spain, Portugal, N Africa, S Balkan peninsula, and Asia Minor, on calcareous soil. ↕↔ 75cm (30in). 'Pippa Pink' is compact, with bright green foliage, violet flowers, and pale pink

bracts. ↕ 60cm (24in). ■ 'Pukehou' has purple-edged flower stems, 10–18cm (4–7in) long, and strongly undulating, blue-purple bracts. ↕ 70cm (28in). 'Southern Lights' has grey-green foliage and very stout spikes, bearing cream to mauve-pink, double bracts. ↕ 70–80cm (28–32in). ■ 'Willowvale' has large purple bracts. Early and long-blooming. 'Wine' syn. 'Wine Red' has bright green foliage and mauve-violet bracts. ↕ 70–80cm (28–32in).
HARDINESS Fully hardy (borderline).
PARTS USED Flower spikes.
PROPERTIES An antiseptic, tonic, aromatic herb with a camphoraceous, balsam-like scent. It benefits the digestion, relaxes spasms, promotes healing, repels insects, has mild sedative effects on the nervous system, and stimulates the peripheral circulation.
MEDICINAL USES Internally for headaches, irritability, feverish colds, and nausea. Externally for wounds and rheumatic pain, and as insect-repellent.
ECONOMIC USES Dried flower spikes and leaves are added to potpourris and linen sachets for their perfume and moth-repellent properties.

Lavandula viridis (green lavender)

Upright shrub with oblong, bright green leaves, to 5cm (2in) long, and small, white to greenish-white flowers in dense, unbranched, cylindrical spikes, 2–3cm (¾–1¼in) long, topped by green bracts, borne on stems 5–8cm (2–3in) long. Native to SW Spain, S Portugal, and Madeira. ↕ 60cm–1m (24–36in), ↔ 75cm (30in). 'Silver Ghost' has white-variegated, slightly curly foliage, and white bracts. ↕ 60–70cm (24–28in).
HARDINESS Frost hardy.
PARTS USED Flowers.
PROPERTIES An aromatic herb with a pungent, lemon-like scent.
ECONOMIC USES Mainly grown as an unusual aromatic plant for the garden and containers, but flower spikes may be dried for potpourris.

LAWSONIA
Henna

Lythraceae

A single species of evergreen shrub makes up this genus, which occurs in N Africa, SW Asia, and Australia; naturalized in warm parts of America and Australia, and in the West Indies, where it is often referred to as "West Indian mignonette". Found on plains, low hills, and river banks, the species was traditionally planted as a windbreak for vineyards. Referred to as "camphire" in the Bible, *L. inermis* is now more familiar as "henna", from the Arabic name. Its religious significance is derived from its symbolization of fire and earth. In spite of its medicinal applications, *L. inermis* is mainly used as a dye plant. Henna has been important as an orange-red colorant for hair, skin, and nails in the Middle East since earliest times. Ancient Egyptian mummies were found with nails, fingertips, palms, and soles dyed with

Lawsonia inermis

henna. In addition to dyeing hair, it was also used to dye beards and moustaches, and the manes and tails of horses. Records show that as long ago as 3200BC, henna was mixed with indigo to make black hair dye. The flowers are valued for their fragrance, which is reminiscent of lilac. Henna was introduced to Europe at the end of the 19th century and is an important constituent of hair tints and conditioners to this day.
CULTIVATION Well-drained, sandy soil in sun. Remove dead wood and trim to shape in late spring. Trim hedges in early summer.
PROPAGATION By seed sown in spring at 18–21°C (64–70°F); by softwood cuttings in spring; by hardwood cuttings in autumn.
HARVEST Young leafy shoots, 20–25cm (8–10in) long, are picked during the growing season and dried for use in powders. Flowers are gathered in early morning and distilled for oil. Bark is stripped from cut branches as required.

Lawsonia inermis syn. *L. alba* (Egyptian privet, henna, mignonette tree)

Variable, often spiny shrub with dark green, pointed, elliptic to broadly lanceolate leaves, to 5cm (2in) long, which have a tea-like aroma. Small, white to pink, highly scented flowers are borne in pyramidal panicles, 20–40cm (8–16in) long, mainly in summer, followed by capsular fruits. Found from N Africa to SW Asia. ↕ 3–6m (10–20ft), ↔ 2–4m (6–12ft).
HARDINESS Min. 13°C (55°F).
PARTS USED Leaves, bark, flowers, oil.
PROPERTIES An astringent aromatic herb that controls bleeding and is antiseptic and anti-bacterial. Regarded as an alterative and nerve tonic in Ayurvedic medicine. Flowers are insecticidal.
MEDICINAL USES Internally for diarrhoea, amoebic dysentery (leaves); liver problems (bark). Externally for skin diseases (including leprosy), sore throat, wounds, burns, ulcers, acne, boils, and herpes. An ingredient of eye lotions and anti-rheumatic liniments in the Middle East.
ECONOMIC USES Dried powdered leaves are used for dyeing hair, feet, nails, and hands. Lilac-scented oil is used in perfumery.

LEDUM

Ericaceae

There are four species of low-growing, evergreen shrubs in this genus, occurring in wet moorland throughout cool northern temperate regions. All are in cultivation, making neat, rhododendron-like plants for pool edges and peat gardens. The dried foliage of *L. groenlandicum* makes a passable substitute for tea and was used as such during the American War of Independence. *Ledum* contains substances similar to those found in the related *Arctostaphylos uva-ursi* (see p.127). It is reputedly narcotic, causing "a peculiar delirium" when taken in excess. Said to deter insect pests and vermin, it was once placed among clothes and in grain storage. *Ledum palustre* (marsh tea, wild rosemary) has similar narcotic properties.

CULTIVATION Moist to wet, acid soil in sun or partial shade. Remove dead flower heads.

PROPAGATION By seed, surface-sown in autumn or spring; by semi-ripe cuttings in summer.

HARVEST Leaves and shoots are collected in late summer and autumn, and dried for infusions and tinctures. Spring and summer foliage can also be picked and used fresh for tinctures.

▣ *Ledum groenlandicum* syn. *L. latifolium* (Labrador tea)
Rounded evergreen shrub with rusty-woolly shoots and narrowly oval, dark green, aromatic leaves, 2–6cm (¾–2½in) long, which have red-brown undersides. Small, scented, white flowers appear in rounded corymbs, 5cm (2in) across, in late spring. Native to Greenland and N America (Alaska, Canada, N USA). ‡90cm (36in), ↔ 1.2m (4ft).

HARDINESS Fully hardy.

Ledum groenlandicum

PARTS USED Leaves, shoots.

PROPERTIES A bitter astringent herb with a camphoraceous aroma. It has expectorant, diuretic, and insecticidal effects.

MEDICINAL USES Internally for bronchial congestion, stomach upsets, and diarrhoea. Externally for dandruff, scabies, lice, chiggers, and fungal skin infections.

ECONOMIC USES Tincture used against bedbugs, mosquitoes, lice, fleas, and beetle larvae. Dried leaves deter pests in grain and fabrics.

LEONURUS

Motherwort

Lamiaceae

Approximately four species of upright biennials and perennials make up this genus, which is distributed throughout temperate Eurasia. They are widely grown in herb gardens and are attractive in spring, when the divided, deeply veined foliage is at its best. *Leonurus cardiaca* was prescribed in ancient Greece for anxiety in pregnant women; hence the name "motherwort". Research has proved that it is effective in calming the heart and reduces the risk of thrombosis. There has been much confusion over the identity of motherworts used in Chinese medicine. Studies by Shiu Ying Hu at Harvard University in the 1970s concluded that *L. heterophyllus* was the same plant as *Stachys artemisia*; the correct name therefore became a combination of the two: *Leonurus artemisia*. The differences between *L. artemisia* and *L. sibiricus* are small: the former has rather smaller flowers, with upper and lower lips about equal in length and undivided leaves on the upper part of the stem. However, some experts regard *L. heterophyllus* and *Stachys artemisia* as synonyms of *Leonurus sibiricus* – in other words, all three entities are the same species. For this reason, and the fact that all motherworts are thought to have similar properties, *L. artemisia* is not described separately here. *Leonurus artemisia* and its uses were described 2000 years ago in the *Shen Nong Ben Cao Jing*; *L. sibiricus* (as *L. heterophyllus*) was first mentioned in the *Illustrated Classic of the Materia Medica* by Su Song (AD1061). Motherwort is unusual among Chinese herbs in being often prescribed as a "simple" (that is, not mixed with other herbs).

CULTIVATION Well-drained, moist soil in sun or partial shade.

PROPAGATION By seed sown in spring; by division in spring or autumn (*L. cardiaca*).

HARVEST Plants are cut when flowering, but before the seeds are set, and dried for infusions, liquid extracts, and tinctures (*L. cardiaca*), or in decoctions, pills, powder, and poultices (*L. sibiricus*). Seeds (*L. sibiricus*) are collected when ripe in autumn by drying the whole plant, and threshing and sifting it to remove seeds.

▣ *Leonurus cardiaca* (motherwort)
Strong-smelling perennial with purple stems and palmate, deeply lobed leaves, to 7cm (3in) long. Mauve-pink to white, downy flowers, with

Leonurus cardiaca

purple-spotted lips, are produced in axillary whorls from midsummer to midautumn. Native to Europe, including S and C Russia.
‡ 1.2m (4ft), ↔ 60cm (24in).

HARDINESS Fully hardy.

PARTS USED Whole plant.

PROPERTIES A very bitter, diuretic herb that acts as a circulatory and uterine stimulant, lowers blood pressure, and relaxes spasms. It is a sedative and nerve tonic, and has anti-bacterial and anti-fungal effects.

MEDICINAL USES Internally for heart complaints (notably palpitations) and problems associated with menstruation, childbirth, and menopause, especially of nervous origin. Not given to pregnant women.

CULINARY USES Flowering tops are used to flavour beer and stout. Flowers are added to soups and made into tea.

▣ *Leonurus sibiricus* (Chinese motherwort)
Erect biennial with branched stems, square in cross-section, bearing deeply veined, pinnately divided leaves, to 10cm (4in) long, which have 3–5 lobes in the upper part. Small, two-lipped, pink to off-white flowers, with upper lips longer than lower lips, appear in axillary whorls in summer, followed by black nutlets. Native to

Leonurus sibiricus

Siberia, China, Korea, and Taiwan. ‡ 1m (3ft), ↔ 60cm (24in).

HARDINESS Fully hardy.

PARTS USED Whole plant (*yi mu cao*), seeds (*chong wei zu*).

PROPERTIES A bitter diuretic herb that stimulates the circulation and uterus, lowers blood pressure, regulates menstruation, and clears toxins. It is also effective against bacterial and fungal infections. Seeds are slightly sweet and have similar actions but are less effective as a diuretic and detoxicant.

MEDICINAL USES Internally for eye problems related to the liver meridian (seeds); painful and excessive menstruation, postpartum bleeding (whole plant, seeds); oedema, kidney complaints, kidney stones, eczema, and abscesses (whole plant). Not given to pregnant women.

CULINARY USES Young foliage is eaten as a vegetable. Roots are cooked with pork (China).

▨ ▧ ▣ ☑

LEPIDIUM
Pepperwort

Brassicaceae

A genus of about 150 species of annuals and perennials found worldwide, especially in temperate regions. Several species are wild-collected or cultivated for their edible, often peppery foliage or radish-like roots. Best known is *L. sativum* (cress), which is traditionally grown in baskets as "mustard and cress", though now largely replaced by salad rape (*Brassica napus*). Also used in similar ways are: *Lepidium campestre* (bastard cress, pepperwort); *L. fremontii* (desert pepperweed, mustard bite); *L. latifolium* (dittander), which was cultivated in ancient Greek times for flavouring; and *L. virginicum* (Virginia cress, wild peppergrass). The S American *L. meyenii* (*maca*) is grown for its white, yellow, or purplish, pear-shaped roots, which are made into an aromatic porridge, or used to flavour rum. Pepperworts have a piquant flavour, are easily grown, and are nutritious. They contain pungent mustard oils, similar to those found in *Sinapis alba* (mustard, see p.369).

CULTIVATION Well-drained soil in sun or partial shade.

PROPAGATION By seed sown from spring to early autumn in cool areas, from autumn to early spring in areas with hot dry summers or at any time under cover. When growing as "mustard and cress" for salads, sow four days earlier than mustard so that the cotyledons or seedlings are ready at the same time.

HARVEST Leaves are cut at seedling stage or when young and used fresh. Flowering tips are picked for salads. Seed pods are collected when unripe and used fresh or dried. Seeds are harvested when ripe and used whole or pressed for oil. Roots are dug in autumn and used fresh.

▣ *Lepidium sativum* (broad-leafed cress, cress) Fast-growing annual with deeply divided, three-lobed cotyledons and linear to pinnate or bipinnate mature leaves, 8–12cm (3–5in) long,

Lepidium sativum

borne on erect or sparsely branched stems. Tiny, white or purplish-white, four-petalled flowers appear in summer, followed by flattened rounded pods, to 7mm (¼in) long, notched at the apex. Native to W Asia; widely naturalized. ‡ 20–40cm (8–16in), ↔ 7–15cm (3–6in). 'Broad Leaved' has oval undivided leaves, to 5cm (2in) long. Ready in 10–40 days; good for soups. 'Curled' has finely divided leaves. Ready in 10–30 days; good for salads and garnishing. 'Greek' is fast-growing, with an excellent peppery flavour. Usually grown outdoors, sown in succession. 'Persian' (*barbeen*, *shahi*) has broad toothed leaves, 5–15cm (2–6in) long; popular in the Middle East as a garnish and pot-herb.

HARDINESS Fully hardy.

PARTS USED Cotyledons (seed leaves), young leaves, flowers, seed pods, seeds, roots.

PROPERTIES A strong-smelling herb with a pungent flavour. Leaves have tonic and diuretic effects. Seeds are stimulant, laxative, and diuretic, with carminative and expectorant effects; they stimulate the uterus and increase lactation.

MEDICINAL USES Internally, in Ayurvedic medicine, for skin diseases, hiccups, coughs, asthma, flatulence, indigestion, diarrhoea, debility (infusion of seeds), and externally for skin diseases, rheumatic pains, sprains, dislocations, and bruises. Not given during pregnancy.

CULINARY USES Fresh leaves give a piquant flavour to salads, sandwiches, soups, omelettes, and herb butters; also used as a garnish, like watercress. Flowers are added to salads. Fresh or dried pods are used as seasoning. Roots are used as a condiment, similar to horseradish.

▨ ▧ ▱ ▨ ▣ ☑

LEPTANDRA
Leptandra virginica. See *Veronicastrum virginicum*.

LEVISTICUM
Lovage

Apiaceae

A genus of a single species of perennial constitutes this genus. *Levisticum officinale* (lovage) is an especially useful plant as it

produces new shoots in early spring when few other fresh herbs are available. In medieval texts, lovage appears as *luvesche* (Old French) and *loveache*, associating the plant with love potions and aphrodisiacs. Lovage has a flavour resembling celery and yeast extract, yet is little used as a culinary herb. Medicinally, it resembles the Chinese *Angelica polymorpha* var. *sinensis* (see p.122), for which it has at times been substituted.

CULTIVATION Deep, rich, moist soil in sun or partial shade. Leaves may be damaged by leaf miners.

PROPAGATION By seed sown in autumn; by division in spring.

HARVEST Leaves are picked before flowering and distilled for oil or dried for use in infusions. Stems are cut in spring, when tender and succulent. Roots are lifted in the third year, and used fresh, or dried for decoctions, liquid extracts, tinctures, and oil distillation. Seeds are collected when ripe and dried for use in decoctions.

▣ *Levisticum officinale* syn. *Ligusticum levisticum* (lovage, love parsley) Large, celery-scented perennial with stout fleshy roots, hollow stems, and smooth, triangular- to diamond-shaped, divided leaves, to 70cm (28in) long. Tiny, yellow-green flowers are borne in umbels, about 8cm (3in) across, in summer, followed by ovoid green fruits. Native to E Mediterranean. ‡ 2m (6ft), ↔ 1m (3ft).

HARDINESS Fully hardy.

PARTS USED Leaves, stems, roots, seeds, oil.

PROPERTIES A bitter–sweet, sedative herb, pungently aromatic, that benefits the digestion, relaxes spasms, increases perspiration, and acts as a diuretic and expectorant. It is effective against many disease-causing organisms.

MEDICINAL USES Internally for indigestion, colic, flatulence, poor appetite, kidney stones, cystitis, painful menstruation, and slow labour. Externally for sore throat and aphthous ulcers.

CULINARY USES Young shoots and leafstalks are blanched and eaten as a vegetable; stalks are also candied like angelica. Seeds

Levisticum officinale

are added to soups, bread, and biscuits. Leaves are added to salads, soups, stews, and savoury dishes. Dried leaves are made into tea.

ECONOMIC USES Oil is used in commercial food flavouring, alcoholic drinks, and in perfumery.

▨ ◨ ▧ ▩ ◪ ▪ ◿ ◿

LIATRIS
Blazing star

Asteraceae

There are about 40 species of perennials in this genus, which occurs only in eastern N America. All grow from corms or flattened rootstocks. *Liatris spicata* (often called *L. callilepis* in horticulture) is found wild in damp places in rocky woodland, pine barrens, and grassland. It was introduced from N America to Europe in 1732, and has proved enduringly popular, both as a cutflower and as a garden plant for wet ground. Various blazing stars are used locally in N America: *L. scariosa* and *L. squarrosa* are interchangeable with *L. spicata* as diuretics and provide poultices for snake bites; root decoctions of *L. punctata* are applied as a wash for itching skin complaints; and *L. chapmannii* contains liatrin, which has anti-cancer properties. Blazing stars are known to contain coumarins, which were banned as flavourings in the USA in the early 1950s as a possible cause of liver damage and reduced blood clotting. The related *Trilisa odoratissima* (deer's tongue, vanilla leaf) is especially rich in coumarins, which crystallize on the tongue-shaped leaves.

CULTIVATION Moist to wet soil in an open sunny position. Dislikes heavy soil. Shoots may be damaged by slugs.

PROPAGATION By seed sown when ripe (species); by division in spring.

HARVEST Leaves are collected during summer,

Liatris spicata

Liatris spicata 'Alba'

and roots in autumn, and are used fresh in syrups or dried for use in decoctions.

▣ *Liatris spicata* (blazing star, button snakeroot, gay feather).
Stiffly upright perennial with linear leaves, to 40cm (16in) long. Bright purple flowers, like miniature thistles, are produced in spikes, 45–70cm (18–28in) long, opening from the top downwards, from late summer to autumn. Native to eastern USA. ↕ 1–1.5m (3–5ft), ↔ 45cm (18in). ▣ 'Alba' has white flowers. ▣ 'Kobold' syn. 'Goblin' is dwarf, with deep purple flowers. ↕ 40–50cm (16–20in).

HARDINESS Fully hardy.

PARTS USED Leaves, roots.

PROPERTIES A bitter aromatic herb that is tonic and astringent, and has anti-bacterial and diuretic effects.

MEDICINAL USES Internally for kidney disease and gonorrhoea. Externally for sore throat.

ECONOMIC USES Leaves and roots are added

Liatris spicata 'Kobold'

to insect-repellent mixtures made with herbs as well as to potpourris.

▨ ▧ ▪ ◿

LIGUSTICUM
Alpine lovage

Apiaceae

A genus of 25 species of perennials, occurring in northern temperate regions, closely related to *Levisticum officinale* (lovage, see p.259). Several different species of *Ligusticum* are used medicinally. They contain volatile and fixed oils, and a very bitter alkaloid, which has been shown to increase blood flow to coronary arteries and the brain. The Chinese drug *chuan-xiong* is a mixture of several herbs, the main ones being *L. sinense* and *Carthamus tinctorius* (see p.157). Plants grown in W Sichuan as *Ligusticum chuanxiong* are now regarded as a cultivar: *L. sinense* 'Chuanxiong'. *Ligusticum porteri* (oshá) was an important herb among Rocky Mountain tribes who, according to Navajo legend, learned its uses from brown bears – hence the common name "bear root". Apparently the bears chew the roots and rub the maceration into their fur – behaviour that may help protect them against parasites and infections. This highly effective herb has now been adopted by Chinese, Ayurvedic, and Western herbalists as superior to *L. sinense*. It is allegedly difficult to cultivate, being a montane species, rarely found below 3200m (10,000ft). Plants, roots, or seeds offered for sale as *L. porteri* are often *Conioselinum pacificum* (hemlock parsley) or the deadly poisonous *Conium maculatum* (poison hemlock, see p.178), and sometimes *Levisticum officinale* (lovage, see p.259); great care should therefore be taken over the identification of this species. *Oshá del campo* refers to *Angelica pinnata*, which apparently has similar properties. Other species with herbal uses include: *Ligusticum acutilobum*, used in China and Japan to facilitate childbirth; *L. canbyi* (Canby's lovage), used by the Flathead people of N America for colds; *L. hultenii* (sea lovage), with a celery-like flavour, used for culinary purposes in Alaska, especially with seal oil; *L. monnieri*, used in Vietnamese cuisine; and *L. scoticum* (Scots lovage), a celery-like plant, often grown as a pot-herb, but little used medicinally. *Ligusticum* comes from the Greek *ligustikas*, describing a plant that grows in the Italian region of Liguria.

CULTIVATION Well-drained to dry soil in sun. *Ligusticum sinense* tolerates damp conditions. *Ligusticum porteri* is challenging to cultivate at low elevations.

PROPAGATION By seed sown in spring; by division in autumn.

HARVEST Leaves and stems (*L. scoticum*) are cut in spring for use as a vegetable and at any time as a flavouring. Roots are lifted in autumn and used fresh or dried for oil extraction (*L. porteri*), decoctions, and tinctures. Seeds are collected when ripe and ground (*L. scoticum*) or distilled for oil (*L. porteri*). Roots are lifted in autumn and dried for decoctions (*L. sinense*).

L

Ligusticum levisticum. See *Levisticum officinale*.

Ligusticum porteri (bear root, Colorado cough root, Porter's lovage, oshá)
Perennial with a large, dark brown, hairy, celery-scented root, hollow stems, and dark green, divided leaves, to 60cm (24in) long, which have a celery–parsley aroma. Tiny white flowers are produced in umbels in summer, followed by seeds that taste like celery. Found in wet meadows and ravines at 3200–3600m (10,000–12,000ft) in the southern Rocky Mountains. ‡ 45–90cm (18–36in), ↔ 60cm (24in).
HARDINESS Fully hardy.
PARTS USED Roots, seeds, oil.
PROPERTIES A bitter, camphoraceous, warming herb that stimulates the circulation, kidneys, and uterus; it improves digestion, relieves spasms, is expectorant, and increases perspiration. Anti-bacterial and anti-viral effects are reported.
MEDICINAL USES Internally for eruptive fevers, virus infections, bronchial and digestive complaints, coughs, toothache, painful menstruation, and retained placenta. Externally for minor injuries and skin infections.
CULINARY USES Dried leaves and seeds have a flavour reminiscent of celery, parsley, and chervil.

▣ *Ligusticum scoticum* (Scots lovage, sea lovage)
Perennial with red-green stems and glossy leaves divided into three broad toothed leaflets. Green-white flowers are produced in summer, followed by tiny, oblong to ovoid seeds. Native to Europe, Greenland, and N America. ‡ 45–90cm (18–36in), ↔ 10–60cm (4–24in).
HARDINESS Fully hardy.
PARTS USED Leaves, stems, seeds.
PROPERTIES An aromatic diuretic herb that improves digestion and stimulates the circulation and uterus.
MEDICINAL USES Once used to treat digestive problems, uterine disorders, and rheumatism.
CULINARY USES Young leaves and stalks have a pungent, celery-like flavour, and are eaten raw (notably in the Hebrides, as *shunis*), cooked, or added to soups and stews.

ECONOMIC USES Seeds are ground as a condiment and used to improve the taste of medicines.

Ligusticum sinense syn. *L. chuanxiong*, *L. wallichii* (Chinese lovage, Szechuan lovage)
Perennial with a ribbed stem and compound toothed leaves, 15–20cm (6–8in) long and 10–15cm (4–6in) wide, which are deltoid–ovate in outline. Umbels of tiny white flowers are borne in summer, followed by oblong ribbed fruits, about 2mm ($^{1}/_{16}$in) long. Native to China (Nei Mongol, southern Yellow River basin). ‡ 1m (3ft), ↔ 45–60cm (18–24in).
HARDINESS Fully hardy.
PARTS USED Roots.
PROPERTIES An aromatic, anti-bacterial, sedative herb that stimulates the circulation, lowers blood pressure, relieves pain, and causes uterine contractions.
MEDICINAL USES Internally for menstrual problems, postpartum bleeding, coronary heart disease, poor circulation, headaches (especially those caused by concussion), and aches and pains caused by cold.

LIGUSTRUM
Privet

Oleaceae

A genus of about 50 species of deciduous and evergreen trees and shrubs, which are widely distributed in Europe, N Africa, E and SE Asia, and Australia. *Ligustrum lucidum* is similar in appearance to *L. vulgare* (common privet) but more attractive, making a fine specimen plant. It was first mentioned in traditional Chinese medicine in a text that was probably written before AD1000. In recent years *L. lucidum* has been increasingly used to prevent bone marrow loss in cancer chemotherapy patients, and also has potential in the treatment of acquired immune deficiency syndrome (AIDS). Chinese research has shown good results in the treatment of respiratory tract infections,

Ligustrum lucidum 'Excelsum Superbum'

hypertension, Parkinson's disease, and hepatitis. *Ligustrum* is the Latin word used by Pliny for privet, possibly derived from the Latin *ligare*, "to tie", referring to the use of the flexible twigs as cordage.
CULTIVATION Well-drained soil in sun or shade. Variegated cultivars are best in sun.
PROPAGATION By seed sown in winter (species only); by semi-ripe cuttings in summer; by hardwood cuttings in winter. Leafspot may damage leaves.
HARVEST Fruits are collected when ripe, and dried, then usually mixed with honey and steamed before further drying for use in decoctions, powders, and pills.
⚠**WARNING** Harmful if eaten.

▣ *Ligustrum lucidum* (Chinese privet, glossy privet)
Small evergreen tree or shrub with glossy, dark green, ovate leaves, to 15cm (6in) long. Tiny, creamy white, strongly scented flowers appear in panicles, to 20cm (8in) long, in late summer, followed by blue-black berries, which ripen in winter. Native to China, Japan, and Korea. ↔ 10m (30ft). ▣ 'Excelsum Superbum' has yellow-edged, bright green leaves with pale green markings. ▣ 'Tricolor' has narrow leaves, variegated grey-green, with white margins, pink-flushed when young.
HARDINESS Fully hardy.

Ligusticum scoticum

Ligustrum lucidum

Ligustrum lucidum 'Tricolor'

L

PARTS USED Fruits.
PROPERTIES A bitter, slightly sweet herb that acts as a tonic for the kidneys and liver. It has diuretic, anti-tumour, anti-bacterial, and possibly anti-viral effects.
MEDICINAL USES Internally for complaints associated with weak kidney and liver energy, such as menopausal problems (especially premature menopause), blurred vision, cataracts, tinnitus, greying of hair, rheumatic pains, palpitations, backache, and insomnia.

LILIUM
Lily
Liliaceae

This genus of about 100 species of bulbous perennials is found throughout temperate parts of the northern hemisphere. Most are grown as ornamentals, and *L. candidum* is one of the few species with medicinal uses. It was recorded by Pliny as a cure for foot complaints and skin problems, but is seldom used today because of its scarcity. *Lilium candidum* can be unpredictable in cultivation and will thrive only when conditions are exactly right. Its white flowers are a symbol of purity associated with the Virgin Mary; in pre-Christian times, it was sacred to Juno, consort of Jupiter and queen of heaven. Various lilies have edible bulbs and are important as vegetables in parts of China and Japan (where they are cultivated for the purpose), and among native N Americans. Several Chinese species, including *L. concolor*, are used in traditional medicine for bronchial complaints.
CULTIVATION Well-drained, alkaline

Lilium candidum

soil in sun, with the bulb just below the surface. Prone to *Botrytis* infection and viruses; resents disturbance.
PROPAGATION By seed sown when ripe; by scales and offsets when dormant in summer.
HARVEST Bulbs are lifted in late summer, and flowers picked as they open; they are used for juice, ointments, and tinctures.

■ *Lilium candidum* (Madonna lily)
Perennial with pale yellow, scaly bulbs and dark maroon stems bearing lanceolate leaves, to 3in (7cm) long. Up to 20 pure white, fragrant, trumpet-shaped flowers, yellow inside at the base, are borne in summer. Native to SE Europe and E Mediterranean. ‡ 1–1.8m (3–6ft).
HARDINESS Fully hardy.
PARTS USED Bulbs, flowers.
PROPERTIES An astringent mucilaginous herb that heals damaged or irritated tissues.
MEDICINAL USES Externally for burns, abscesses, chapped or inflamed skin, chilblains, ulcers, and hair loss.

LIMNOPHILA
Scrophulariaceae

There are some 40 species of aromatic, aquatic or marsh-dwelling annuals and perennials in this genus, which occurs in the Old World tropics. They creep when growing in boggy ground, growing erect when submerged. About a dozen species have finely divided, submerged foliage, making attractive specimens for aquaria. Several are used locally for medicinal or culinary purposes, but only one species, *L. aromatica*, is in more general circulation. It was introduced to N America during the 1970s by refugees from Vietnam, and is often stocked by Asian food stores. The distinctive flavour of *L. aromatica* is described as "floral". Other species used include *L. gratioloides*, which has a camphor–lemon aroma, and is given in India for dysentery, or made into a liniment with coconut oil to treat elephantiasis. *Limnophila* is derived from the Greek *limne*, "bog", and *philos*, "friend", referring to the marsh-loving nature of the genus.
CULTIVATION Damp to wet soil, or shallow water, in sun or partial shade.
PROPAGATION By seed sown when ripe; by stem-tip cuttings or division during the growing season.
HARVEST Sprigs of foliage are cut as required and used fresh for flavouring, poultices, and decoctions.

Limnophila chinensis subsp. *aromatica*
syn. *L. aromatica* (*berema, ngŏ om, rau ngŏ, rau om,* rice paddy herb, swamp leaf)
Aquatic annual with spongy, pale green stems, rooting from the nodes, and smooth, bluntly lanceolate leaves, to 2.5cm (1in) long, which have serrate margins. Small, pale violet-pink flowers appear singly or in short, leafy, axillary spikes, followed by two-valved capsules containing angular shiny seeds. Found from S Asia to Australia. ‡ 30cm (12in), ↔ indefinite.

HARDINESS Min. 20°C (68°F).
PARTS USED Leaves, stem tips.
PROPERTIES An aromatic herb with laxative, expectorant, and healing effects.
MEDICINAL USES Internally, in Sri Lanka, for fevers, and externally as a poultice for sores.
CULINARY USES Leafy stems are used to flavour soups, stews, curries, and sweet-and-sour dishes, especially in Vietnamese cuisine.

LINARIA
Toadflax
Scrophulariaceae

There are about 100 species of annuals and perennials in this genus, which is found in Europe and other northern temperate regions. *Linaria vulgaris*, found in grassland and hedgerows, is an easily grown, late-blooming plant. A peloric (monstrous) form occurs occasionally, which has five spurs instead of the normal one; the flowers then appear regular in shape, rather than having the usual irregular form. *Linaria vulgaris*, once highly regarded as a diuretic for oedema, has a long history of medicinal use but is seldom used today. *Linaria* is from the Greek *linon*, "flax", referring to the flax-like leaves of the plant.
CULTIVATION Well-drained, neutral to alkaline soil in sun or partial shade. Invasive.
PROPAGATION By seed sown in spring; by division in spring. Self-sows freely.
HARVEST Plants are cut when flowering and dried for use in infusions.

■ *Linaria vulgaris* (butter-and-eggs, toadflax)
Slender upright perennial with linear leaves, 6cm (2½in) long. Yellow, snapdragon-like flowers, marked orange at the mouth, with a 1cm (½in) long spur, are borne from summer to autumn. Native to Europe (except extreme north and Mediterranean). ‡ 15–90cm (6–36in), ↔ 30–45cm (12–18in).
HARDINESS Fully hardy.
PARTS USED Whole plant.
PROPERTIES A bitter, acrid, astringent herb that cleanses toxins from the tissues, and is diuretic and laxative. It acts mainly on the liver.

Linaria vulgaris

MEDICINAL USES Internally for skin diseases, enteritis, hepatitis, gall bladder complaints, and oedema. Not given to pregnant women. Externally for haemorrhoids, skin eruptions, sores, and malignant ulcers. For use only by qualified practitioners; dosage is critical.

🌿 ▣

LINDERA

Lauraceae

This genus of about 80 species of deciduous and evergreen, often aromatic trees and shrubs is closely related to *Laurus nobilis* (bay laurel, see p.252). Most occur in S and E Asia, with two species in N America. Some are grown as ornamentals for their aromatic foliage; the deciduous species are colourful in autumn. Male and female flowers are borne on separate plants, making it necessary to grow both for fruiting. *Lindera benzoin* was important to early settlers in N America as a source of medicines, food flavouring, and beverages. The powdered fruits were a good substitute for allspice (see *Pimenta dioica*, p.316) in the USA during the Revolutionary period in the 18th century, and the leaves made an acceptable tea. Several other species are valued for their aromatic properties, including: *Lindera communis*, used as a condiment and flavouring in China; *L. glauca*, used in the manufacture of incense and joss sticks, and for flavouring noodles and dumplings in Japanese cuisine; and *L. obtusifolia*, used as a tea substitute in Japan. *Lindera strychnifolia* is a warming remedy in Chinese medicine for menstrual pain, stomach chills, and urinary incontinence.

CULTIVATION Moist acid soil (pH4.5–6.0) in partial shade.

PROPAGATION By seed sown in autumn; by greenwood cuttings in early summer.

HARVEST Leaves are collected during the growing season, twigs in spring, bark as required, and berries in autumn; all are used fresh, or dried for decoctions and infusions.

▣ *Lindera benzoin* (feverbush, spice bush, wild allspice)
Aromatic deciduous shrub with obovate, bright

Lindera benzoin

green leaves, to 12cm (5in) long, which turn yellow in autumn. Tiny, star-shaped, green-yellow flowers appear in umbels in spring, followed by bright red berries on female plants. Native to SE Canada and E USA. ↔ 3m (10ft).

HARDINESS Fully hardy.

PARTS USED Leaves, twigs, bark, fruits.

PROPERTIES An aromatic, warming, tonic herb that improves the circulation, increases perspiration rate, and expels intestinal worms.

MEDICINAL USES Internally, formerly used as a household remedy for colds, dysentery, and intestinal parasites. CULINARY USES

CULINARY USES Flowering twigs and young leaves make an excellent herb tea. Dried powdered fruits are used as a substitute for allspice.

▥ ▨ ▨ ▨ ▣ ✔

LINUM

Flax

Linaceae

This large genus of some 200 species of annuals, biennials, perennials, and shrubs is found in northern temperate regions. Some are grown as ornamentals for their numerous, brightly coloured flowers, which are produced throughout the summer. *Linum usitatissimum* is one of the world's oldest crop plants, known in cultivation as a source of flax since 5000BC. In the 8th century, the Emperor Charlemagne decreed that flax seeds should be consumed in order to maintain good health. Though classified as a species, *L. usitatissimum* is probably an ancient cultigen, derived from *L. bienne*; it is not known in the wild. There are two distinct strains of *L. usitatissimum*: the taller flax, with fewer branches and flowers, which yields fibre; and the shorter, more floriferous and fruitful linseed, which is grown for oil and as a fodder crop. Seeds contain 30–40 per cent of a fixed oil, known as linseed oil, which consists of mainly linoleic and linolenic acids. In common with many members of the Linaceae, Rosaceae, and Caprifoliaceae families, they also contain cyanogenic glycosides, or prussic acid. In small amounts, these compounds stimulate respiration and improve digestion, but, in excess, cause respiratory failure and death. There is no indication that recommended doses of *L. usitatissimum* pose any threat. The related *L. catharticum* (mountain or purging flax) was once used as a laxative and anti-rheumatic.

CULTIVATION Well-drained to dry, sandy soil in sun. Dislikes being transplanted.

PROPAGATION By seed sown *in situ* in spring.

HARVEST Plants are cut when mature for fibre extraction. Seeds are collected when ripe, stored whole, or pressed for oil.

▣ *Linum usitatissimum* (flax, flaxseed, linseed)
Erect annual with narrow, grey-green leaves, to 2.5cm (1in) long. Sky-blue, saucer-shaped flowers, 3cm (1¼in) across, appear in summer, followed by spherical capsules, about 1cm (⅜in) in diameter, containing shiny, oval, flattened seeds. ↕ 80cm–1.2m (2½–4ft), ↔ 30–60cm (12–24in).

Linum usitatissimum

HARDINESS Fully hardy.

PARTS USED Whole plant, stems, seeds, oil.

PROPERTIES A sweet mucilaginous herb that is laxative and expectorant, soothes irritated tissues, controls coughing, and relieves pain.

MEDICINAL USES Internally as a bulk laxative for chronic constipation and diverticulitis (crushed seeds mixed with breakfast cereals and ample liquid), gastritis, pharyngitis (macerated seeds), chronic bronchial complaints, coughs, and sore throat; as a dietary supplement for eczema, menstrual problems, arteriosclerosis, and rheumatoid arthritis (oil). Externally for bronchitis, pleurisy, sore throat, burns, scalds, boils, abscesses, and ulcers. Crushed seeds are combined, as a poultice, with *Sinapis alba* (see p.369) for chest complaints, and with honey and lemon as a cough remedy.

CULINARY USES Seeds are added to breads, sprouted for salads, infused as tea, or roasted as a coffee substitute.

ECONOMIC USES Seeds are important as a source of linolenic acid (omega-3 oil) in food supplements; also as an egg substitute in baked produce for special diets. Fibres yield flax, used to make linen. Linseed oil is used in the manufacture of paints and flooring; seed residue is made into linseed cake for animal feed.

▥ ▨ ▨ ▨ ▣ ✔ ✔

LIPPIA

Verbenaceae

About 200 species of shrubs and small trees belong to this genus, which occurs in tropical Africa and the Americas. A dozen or more species are wild-collected or cultivated in

L

warmer parts of the world for their aromatic foliage, but are little known in northern temperate regions. They are used medicinally, or for food flavouring and teas. *Lippia* is closely related to *Aloysia*; *A. triphylla* (lemon verbena) was once classified as *Lippia citriodora*. Also closely related are *Phyla scaberrima* syn. *Lippia dulcis* (see p.312) and *Nashia inaguensis* (moujean tea, pineapple verbena), a fruit-scented herb that has a vanilla-like flavour when infused as tea. Medicinal or culinary *Lippia* spp. include: *L. graveolens* and *L. palmeri*, with oregano-scented leaves, which are exported from Mexico as dried oregano; the S American *L. micromera* (Dominican oregano, false thyme), used as a substitute for thyme; *L. adoensis*, an African species, and the Brazilian *L. pseudo-thea*, both infused for tea; *L. nodiflora*, a creeping annual from tropical Asia, used in folk medicine for bronchial infections, and as a diuretic; and *L. alba* syn. *Phyla alba* (anise verbena, liquorice verbena), which is used for tea, or as an anise-like flavouring.

CULTIVATION Light sandy soil in sun. Tolerates drought. Cut back and remove dead wood in late winter; pinch out stem tips, to encourage compact growth. Spider mites, whitefly, and aphids may attack plants under cover.

PROPAGATION By seed sown in spring; by softwood cuttings in summer.

HARVEST Leaves are picked in spring and summer, and dried for culinary use.

Lippia citriodora. See *Aloysia triphylla*.
Lippia dulcis. See *Phyla scaberrima*.

▣ *Lippia graveolens* (Mexican oregano, *té de pais*)
Upright aromatic shrub with elliptic to oblong, downy, crinkled leaves, to 6cm (2½ in) long. Tiny, yellow-white flowers, often with a yellow eye, are produced in axillary clusters from spring to winter. Native to C America and Texas. ↕ 2m (6ft), ↔ 30cm–1.5m (1–5ft).

HARDINESS Min. 5–10°C (41–50°F).

PARTS USED Leaves.

PROPERTIES An aromatic herb with an oregano scent.

CULINARY USES Leaves are used to flavour soups, stews, sausages, and bean dishes

Lippia graveolens

(especially in Mexican cuisine); also dishes based on tomatoes, aubergines, and squashes (especially of Italian origin).

ECONOMIC USES Leaves are a source of commercial dried oregano.

▨ ▨ ▨ ▣

LIQUIDAMBAR
Sweet gum

Hamamelidaceae

A genus of four species of deciduous trees found through N America and Eurasia into China, often in damp woodland. They have handsome, maple-like leaves and spectacular autumn colour. Species grown in cultivation are considerably smaller than wild specimens. *Liquidambar styraciflua* was widely used by native N Americans to heal wounds, and by settlers for skin complaints. It was first listed as an antiseptic in the *US Pharmacopoeia* in 1926. *Liquidambar orientalis* appeared in Chinese medicine c.AD500. *Liquidambar formosana* (Chinese/Formosan sweet gum) is also important medicinally. It has analgesic, anti-inflammatory, and anti-rheumatic properties. In China the leaves and roots are used to treat malignant growths. The fruits contain beturonic acid, a substance that appears to protect the liver from damage by extremely toxic, dry-cleaning chemicals, such as carbon tetrachloride. Traditionally, the fruits are used in Taiwan for liver problems and hepatitis, while the resin is applied to carbuncles. The light yellow, almost transparent resin obtained from

Liquidambar orientalis

Liquidambar styraciflua
'Lane Roberts'

Liquidambar styraciflua
'Variegata'

L. formosana contains cinnamic acid, which gives it a pleasant, cinnamon-like scent.

CULTIVATION Deep, rich, moist, neutral to slightly acid soil in sun or partial shade.

PROPAGATION By seed sown in autumn; by greenwood cuttings in summer.

HARVEST Balsam is collected as a natural exudate, or from cuts in the bark, and made into syrups and tinctures. It is also extracted from the bark, after beating the trees to increase flow.

▣ *Liquidambar orientalis* (Oriental sweet gum, storax)
Bushy deciduous tree with mostly five-lobed leaves, 7–10cm (3–4in) across, which have coarsely toothed margins; they turn yellow and orange in autumn. Inconspicuous flowers appear in spring, followed by small, spiny, ball-shaped fruits. Native to SW Asia. ↕ to 30m (100ft) in the wild, 6m (20ft) in cultivation, ↔ 4–20m (12–70ft).

HARDINESS Fully hardy (borderline).

PARTS USED Balsam (*su he xiang*).

PROPERTIES An aromatic stimulant herb that is antiseptic and anti-inflammatory, has expectorant effects, and promotes healing.

MEDICINAL USES Internally for strokes, infantile convulsions, coma, heart disease, and pruritus. Externally, mixed with olive oil, for scabies. (Leaves, fruits, and roots are also used in similar ways in folk medicine.)

▨ ▣

▣ *Liquidambar styraciflua* (American storax, sweet gum)
Deciduous conical tree with glossy 5–7-lobed

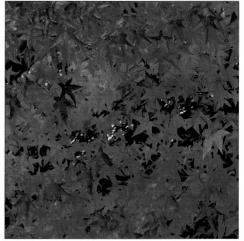
Liquidambar styraciflua

Liquidambar styraciflua
'Worplesdon'

leaves, to 15cm (6in) across, which turn orange, red, and burgundy in autumn. Inconspicuous flowers appear in spring as the fragrant new leaves open, followed by globose spiny fruits. Native to E USA and Mexico. ‡30m (100ft) in the wild, 25m (80ft) in cultivation, ↔12–20m (40–70ft). ▣‘Lane Roberts’ turns deep maroon in autumn. ▣‘Variegata’ syn. ‘Aurea’ has leaves striped and marbled yellow. ‡15m (50ft), ↔ 8m (25ft). ▣‘Worplesdon’ has long, narrowly lobed leaves, which turn purple, then yellow-orange in autumn.

HARDINESS Fully hardy.

PARTS USED Balsam.

PROPERTIES An aromatic stimulant herb that has antiseptic, anti-inflammatory, and expectorant effects.

MEDICINAL USES Internally for sore throats, coughs, colds, asthma, bronchitis, cystitis, and vaginal discharge. Externally for sores, haemorrhoids, ringworm, scabies, and frostbite. An ingredient of friar's balsam, a preparation based on benzoin (see *Styrax benzoin*, p.376), which relieves colds and skin problems.

ECONOMIC USES Used in commercial flavouring of foods and tobacco.

◨ ◨ ◨

LITHOSPERMUM
Gromwell

Boraginaceae

This genus consists of about 60 species of rhizomatous perennials, found in all temperate regions except Australasia. It once included several shrubby species, now reclassified in *Lithodora*, which are widely grown in rock gardens. Few of the perennial species have any merit as ornamentals. Little is known of the chemistry of this genus, but the effectiveness of several species as contraceptives and as depuratives for skin conditions warrants further investigation. *Lithospermum erythrorhizon* has an ancient history of use in Chinese medicine. *Lithospermum ruderale* (gromwell, puccoon) was one of several species used by native N Americans: by the Algonquin as dyes and body paints; and by the Shoshoni as a contraceptive, apparently causing permanent sterility after six months. *Lithospermum* is from the Greek *lithos*, "stone", and *spermum*, "seed", referring to the small hard nutlets.

CULTIVATION Well-drained, neutral to alkaline soil in sun or partial shade.

PROPAGATION By seed sown in autumn; by division in autumn.

HARVEST Whole plants are cut when flowering, and roots are lifted in autumn; all parts are dried for use in decoctions.

▣ *Lithospermum erythrorhizon* syn. *L. officinale* subsp. *erythrorhizon* (red-rooted gromwell)
Erect, coarsely hairy perennial with thick roots, which turn purple when dried, and lanceolate leaves. White flowers are borne in clusters in autumn, followed by grey-white nutlets. Native to E China, Korea, and Japan. ‡40–70cm

Lithospermum erythrorhizon

(16–28in), ↔ 30cm (12in).

HARDINESS Fully hardy.

PARTS USED Whole plant, roots (*zi cao*).

PROPERTIES A sweet, soothing, healing herb that lowers fever and clears toxins. It stimulates the liver, heart, and circulation, and has contraceptive and anti-cancer effects.

MEDICINAL USES Internally for irritant skin conditions, measles, chickenpox, boils, carbuncles, hepatitis, and skin cancer. Externally for eczema, nappy rash, burns, abscesses, poison oak or ivy rash, vaginal discharge, and herpes.

ECONOMIC USES Extracts are added to skin-care creams.

◨ ◨ ◨ ◨

LOBELIA

Campanulaceae

This large genus consists of about 370 species of annuals, perennials, deciduous and evergreen shrubs and small trees distributed throughout temperate and tropical zones, especially in the Americas. It provides a wide range of colourful, long-flowering plants for most garden situations, including moist soil and containers. A number of lobelias contain piperidine alkaloids, notably lobeline, which stimulate respiration and cause vomiting. These include the ornamental *L. cardinalis*; *L. tupa* (devil's tobacco), used to treat toothache and smoked as a narcotic by Chilean tribes; and *L. siphilitica* (great lobelia), used with *Podophyllum peltatum* (see p.325) as a remedy for venereal diseases. *Lobelia inflata* was used by native N Americans for bronchial complaints and was popularized by Samuel Thomson (1769–1843), a pioneer herbalist and founder of Physiomedicalism. He was prosecuted but found not guilty of its misuse in 1809. *Lobelia* is named after Matthias de l'Obel (1538–1616), physician to James I of England.

CULTIVATION Rich moist soil in sun or partial shade. *L. inflata* prefers slightly acid soil.

PROPAGATION By division in spring (perennials); by seed sown at 13–18°C (55–64°F): annuals in late winter, perennials as soon as ripe.

HARVEST Whole plants are cut when flowering (*L. inflata* when lower fruits are ripe); used fresh, or dried in decoctions (*L. chinensis*),

Lobelia chinensis

infusions, liquid extracts, and tinctures.

⚠ **WARNING** Harmful if eaten. Skin irritant and allergen.

▣ *Lobelia chinensis* syn. *L. radicans* (Chinese lobelia)
Slender creeping perennial, rooting at its nodes, with ascending branches and lanceolate leaves, to 2.5cm (1in) long. White to rose-purple flowers are borne singly or in pairs in summer. Native to E Asia. ‡20cm (8in), ↔ indefinite.

HARDINESS Min. 10°C (50°F).

PARTS USED Whole plant (*ban bian lian*).

PROPERTIES An acrid, anti-fungal herb that is diuretic, reduces inflammation, lowers fever, contracts tissues, and clears toxins. It acts mainly on the liver and kidneys.

MEDICINAL USES Internally for dysentery, gastroenteritis, cirrhosis, oedema, jaundice, schistosomiasis, stomach cancer, eczema, and snake bite with depressed respiration. Excess causes nausea, vomiting, drowsiness, and respiratory failure. For use only by qualified practitioners.

◨ ◨ ◨

▣ *Lobelia inflata* (asthma weed, Indian tobacco, pukeweed)
Spreading downy annual with ovate toothed leaves, 5–8cm (2–3in) long. Light blue, often pink-tinged flowers appear in summer, followed

Lobelia inflata

by inflated, two-valved capsules. Native to eastern and central N America. ‡ 20–60cm (8–24in), ↔ 10–30cm (4–12in).
HARDINESS Fully hardy.
PARTS USED Whole plant.
PROPERTIES An acrid emetic herb that stimulates respiration, increases perspiration rate, reduces inflammation, and is expectorant.
MEDICINAL USES Internally for asthma, bronchitis, whooping cough, and pleurisy. Excess causes nausea, vomiting, drowsiness, and respiratory failure. Not given to pregnant women or patients with heart complaints. Externally for pleurisy, rheumatism, tennis elbow, whiplash injuries, boils, and ulcers. For use by qualified practitioners only.
ECONOMIC USES An important ingredient of proprietary anti-smoking tobaccos (imitating effects of nicotine) and cough mixtures.
⚠ **WARNING** This herb and its alkaloids are subject to legal restrictions in some countries.
🗓 🔳 ✏

LONICERA
Honeysuckle
Caprifoliaceae

A genus of around 180 species of deciduous, occasionally evergreen shrubs and climbers, found throughout the northern hemisphere and in the Philippines. Many are grown as ornamentals, mainly for their flowers, one of the most popular being *L. japonica*. As a medicinal herb, *L. japonica* has played an important role in Chinese medicine since the time of the *Tang Materia Medica* (AD659). *Lonicera caprifolium* (Dutch honeysuckle, perfoliate honeysuckle) and *L. periclymenum* (honeysuckle, woodbine) are often listed as medicinal herbs, but are seldom used today. The former has laxative and expectorant effects; the latter is an expectorant, antiseptic, and diuretic that causes vomiting but, in small doses, is a useful addition to cough mixtures.
CULTIVATION Well-drained soil in sun or partial shade. Cut back or remove surplus stems after flowering. Aphids may attack flowers.
PROPAGATION By seed sown in autumn or spring (species only); by semi-ripe cuttings in

Lonicera japonica

Lonicera japonica 'Aureoreticulata'

summer or hardwood cuttings in late autumn; by layering in late autumn.
HARVEST Stems are cut in autumn and winter, and dried for decoctions, pills, poultices, powders, tinctures, and dry extracts. Flowers are collected in the early morning, before they open, and are dried for decoctions.

▪ *Lonicera japonica* (Japanese honeysuckle) Vigorous, twining, evergreen or semi-evergreen climber with hollow hairy stems and paired, ovate, dark green leaves, to 10cm (4in) long. Fragrant, white, often purple-flushed flowers, to 4cm (1½in) long, appear in summer and autumn, followed by poisonous, blue-black berries. Native to E Asia. ‡ to 10m (30ft).
▪ 'Aureoreticulata' has yellow-veined leaves and is slightly less hardy than the species. 'Dart's World' is very hardy and evergreen, with red-flushed, white flowers that age yellow.
▪ 'Halliana' is vigorous (to the point of noxious weediness in some areas), with white flowers

Lonicera japonica 'Halliana'

that age yellow; var. *repens* has purple-flushed foliage and purple-flushed, white flowers.
HARDINESS Fully hardy.
PARTS USED Stems (*jin yin teng*), flower buds (*jin yin hua*).
PROPERTIES A slightly sweet, cooling herb that is anti-bacterial, diuretic, lowers fever, reduces inflammation and blood pressure, relaxes spasms, and increases perspiration. Regarded as an alterative.
MEDICINAL USES Internally for acute rheumatoid arthritis, mumps, hepatitis (stems); upper respiratory tract infections, including pneumonia, and dysentery (flowers, stems); high fevers, conjunctivitis, throat inflammations, childhood infections (including measles and chickenpox), boils, nettle rash, infected wounds, gastroenteritis, food poisoning, urinary tract infections, mastitis, and breast cancer (flowers). Externally for skin inflammations, infectious rashes, and sores (flowers).
❎ 🔲 🔳

LUFFA
Loofa, loofah
Cucurbitaceae

Six species of unpleasant-smelling, climbing annuals related to cucumbers and melons belong to this genus, which occurs throughout the tropics. *Luffa cylindrica* may be grown outdoors in warm regions, or under cover in a cold climate. It is a surprisingly useful plant, producing edible leaves, flowers, fruits, seeds, oil, and fibrous materials. The large fruits contain a sponge-like network of fibres – the familiar bathroom loofah – which persist long after the flesh has decayed, being resistant to moulds, even when regularly wetted. Loofahs stimulate the skin and circulation and are especially popular for exfoliant treatments. Fibres of fully ripe loofah fruits have been used in traditional Chinese medicine since the 10th century AD. Pieces of loofah are boiled in water to make a strong decoction for internal use or gently heated in a sealed container until reduced to charcoal for external application. Before the Second World War, 60 per cent of the harvest in the USA was used to filter out oil from water in ships' boilers. Japan is now the main producer. *Luffa* and "loofah" are from the Arabic name for the plant.
CULTIVATION Rich sandy soil in sun. Pinch out side branches when the first fruit is set to encourage development. Shorten growths as necessary to train against a wall or trellis. Spider mites, whitefly, and aphids may attack plants under cover.
PROPAGATION By seed sown in spring.
HARVEST Leaves and flowers are cut as required and used fresh. Fruits are cut when 15cm (6in) long for culinary use or left on vine to dry, before skinning and retting to clean flesh from fibres. Seeds are pressed for oil.

▪ *Luffa cylindrica* syn. *L. aegyptica* (dishcloth gourd, loofah, sponge gourd, vine okra) Annual, tendril-bearing climber with large bristly leaves, to 20cm (8in) long. Male and female

Luffa cylindrica

flowers are yellow and strongly veined: males have shorter stalks than females. Cylindrical green fruits, to 50cm (20in) long, turn yellow when ripe. Native to tropical Africa and Asia. ↕ 15m (50ft).

HARDINESS Min. 10°C (50°F).
PARTS USED Fruits, fibres (*si gua luo*), seeds, oil.
PROPERTIES An astringent painkilling herb that controls bleeding, promotes healing, improves circulation, and increases milk flow. It acts mainly on the lungs, liver, and stomach.
MEDICINAL USES Internally for rheumatism, chest pains, backache, orchitis, haemorrhoids, internal haemorrhage, and insufficient lactation. Externally for shingles and boils. Dried fruit fibres are used as abrasive sponges in skin care to remove dead skin and stimulate the peripheral circulation.
CULINARY USES Young fruits are eaten raw like cucumbers, cooked like marrows, pickled, or dried. Young leaves, shoot tips, flower buds, and flowers are eaten lightly steamed. Seeds are roasted as a snack, made into a tofu-like product, or pressed for cooking oil.
ECONOMIC USES Ripe cleaned loofahs are used like bath sponges, and provide material for shock-absorbent helmets.

LYCIUM
Boxthorn

Solanaceae

This genus of about 100 species of deciduous and evergreen, often spiny shrubs occurs in most temperate and subtropical regions. *Lycium barbarum* is a useful, fast-growing shrub for hedging, especially in coastal sites or on unstable sandy banks. The fruits are attractive in autumn. In cultivation, it is often labelled *L. europaeum*. According to European folklore, boxthorn causes discord between husband and wife if planted near the home: hence the common name "matrimony vine". The root bark and fruits of both *L. barbarum* and *L. chinense* are used in identical ways in Chinese medicine; the bark was first mentioned c.AD500, and the fruits in texts dating 206BC–AD23 but based on much

earlier records. *Lycium chinense* differs from *L. barbarum* in being seldom spiny, and having slightly larger leaves, flowers, and fruits. The leaves of *L. chinense* have a minty aroma, so are used for flavouring and to make a tea known as Lord Macartney's tea; the fruits are sweet, with a liquorice-like flavour. Other species with similar properties, such as *L. dasystemum* and *L. turcomanicum*, are often used as substitutes for *L. barbarum* and *L. chinense*. In common with most members of the nightshade family (Solanaceae), *Lycium* spp. contain poisonous alkaloids. *Lycium* comes from the Greek *lykion*, the name given by Dioscorides to a thorny shrub from Lycia, in Asia Minor.
CULTIVATION Sandy, alkaline, moist but well-drained soil in sun. Remove dead wood in winter and cut back growth in spring. Prune plants grown for commercial use two or three times a year, to encourage a compact, well-branched shrub for heavier fruiting and easier harvesting.
PROPAGATION By seed sown in autumn; by softwood cuttings in summer; by hardwood cuttings in winter.
HARVEST Bark is stripped from roots in winter and dried for decoctions, pills, and powders. Fruits are collected in autumn and dried for decoctions.

▪ *Lycium barbarum* syn. *L. halimifolium* (boxthorn, Duke of Argyll's tea tree, matrimony vine, wolfberry)
Deciduous, arching, often spiny shrub with elliptic to ovate leaves, to 6cm (2½in) long. Small, purple, lilac, or pink, funnel-shaped flowers appear in summer, followed by ovoid, orange-red to yellow berries, to 2cm (¾in) long. Found from S Europe to China. ↕ 3.5m (11ft), ↔ 5m (15ft).
HARDINESS Fully hardy.
PARTS USED Root bark (*di gu pi*), fruits (*gou qi zi*).
PROPERTIES Fruits produce a sweet tonic decoction that lowers blood pressure and cholesterol levels, acting mainly on the liver and kidneys. The bitter, cooling, anti-bacterial root bark controls coughs and lowers fever, blood pressure, and cholesterol levels.
MEDICINAL USES Internally for high blood pressure, diabetes, poor eyesight, vertigo, lumbago, impotence, and menopausal complaints (fruits); chronic fevers, internal haemorrhage,

nosebleed, tuberculosis, coughs, asthma, verrucas, and childhood eczema (root bark). Externally for genital itching.
CULINARY USES Fruits are added to Chinese tonic soups. Leaves used for making tea, notably Essential Harmony, a classic Chinese herb tea.
ECONOMIC USES Fruit extracts are added to soft drinks.

LYCOPERDON
Puffball

Lycoperdaceae

A cosmopolitan genus of about 50 species of saprophytic fungi. All produce globose toadstools that release their spores in clouds when the ripe flesh is ruptured – hence the common name "puffball". The spores are very irritating to the lungs. Puffballs have long been used as food in many parts of the world; many *Lycoperdon* spp. are edible when young. However, the flesh changes texture and colour (from white to brown) as the spores develop, becoming unpalatable. Puffballs feature in both native N American and traditional Chinese medicine.
CULTIVATION Well-drained, moist, sandy soil.
PROPAGATION By spores sown when ripe on a suitable substrate.
HARVEST Whole fungi are collected in summer and used fresh for food, or in autumn and dried for use as pills and powders. Spores are collected in autumn and dried for powder.

▪ *Lycoperdon perlatum* syn. *L. gemmatum* (puffball)
Pear- to club-shaped fungus with a warted skin that is white at first, becoming yellow-brown. Skin becomes perforated at apex, releasing yellow-brown spores in autumn. Native to temperate regions. ↕ 2.5–9cm (1–3½in), ↔ 2.5–6cm (1–2½in).
HARDINESS Fully hardy.
PARTS USED Whole plant, spores (*ma bo*).
PROPERTIES An astringent herb that controls bleeding.
MEDICINAL USES Externally for bleeding wounds and haemorrhoids. In traditional Chinese medicine, spores are given internally,

Lycium barbarum

Lycoperdon perlatum

combined with honey or syrup, for inflammations of the respiratory tract, and used externally, as a powder, to stop bleeding.

CULINARY USES The firm white flesh of young puffballs is eaten as a delicacy, often batter-fried.

LYCOPODIUM
Clubmoss

Lycopodiaceae

This large cosmopolitan genus consists of about 450 species of rhizomatous, evergreen, perennial clubmosses, which may be terrestrial or epiphytic in habit. They are primitive plants, with small, scale- or needle-like leaves, reproducing by spores. Clubmoss spores are used in sound experiments, being so fine that they vibrate into patterns of sound waves, and also for stage effects and fireworks, since they are flammable. In ancient times the whole clubmoss plant was used as a diuretic and digestive. The use of the spores alone dates from the 17th century. According to Mrs Grieve (*A Modern Herbal*, 1931), "they have a strong repulsive power, that if the hand is powdered with them, it can be dipped in water without becoming wet". This property is put to use in coating pills, to seal in any unpleasant taste, and to prevent them from sticking together. *Lycopodium complanatum* (American ground pine) has similar properties to *L. clavatum* and is often combined with *Agrimonia eupatoria* (see p.107) and *Taraxacum officinale* (see p.382) for liver complaints. *Lycopodium cernuum* is decocted in water or sweet wine for internal use in Chinese medicine and crushed for topical treatment of aches, pains, and spasms in the arms or legs. The Chinese *L. serratum* syn. *Huperzia serrata* is also used medicinally. Wild-collection of *Lycopodium* spp. may be subject to restrictions in some areas.

CULTIVATION Damp acid soil in sun or shade.

PROPAGATION By spores sown on damp sphagnum moss; by layering at any time.

HARVEST Plants are cut all year round and used fresh, or dried for use in decoctions and infusions. Spores are shaken out into a sieve from plants cut in summer.

Lycopodium clavatum

■ *Lycopodium clavatum* (ground pine, stag's horn clubmoss)
Trailing perennial with erect forked branches and upward-pointing, lanceolate, tapered leaves. Yellow spores are shed from upright, forked, club-shaped branches, which appear in summer. Native to alpine and arctic zones of both hemispheres, and montane areas in temperate and tropical regions. ‡ 12cm (5in), ↔ 1m (3ft).

HARDINESS Fully hardy.

PARTS USED Whole plant (*shen jin cao*), spores.

PROPERTIES A sedative, anti-bacterial herb that is diuretic, lowers fever, benefits the digestion, and stimulates the uterus.

MEDICINAL USES Internally for urinary and kidney disorders, catarrhal cystitis, gastritis, and in Chinese medicine for rheumatoid arthritis and traumatic injury. Externally for skin diseases and irritation. Spores are the basis for a homeopathic preparation for dry coughs, rheumatic pains, mumps, and complaints that characteristically cause pain or discomfort on the right side of the body.

LYCOPUS
Bugleweed

Lamiaceae

A genus of four species of perennials, which occur in wet lowland habitats in northern temperate regions. They are similar to *Mentha* (see p.275), with stoloniferous rootstocks and angled stems, but are non-aromatic. None has great ornamental value, although *Lycopus virginicus* and *L. europaeus* (gipsywort) are sometimes grown in bog gardens. *Lycopus virginicus* was listed in the *US Pharmacopoeia* in the late 19th century as an effective anti-haemorrhagic. *Lycopus europaeus* and *L. americanus* (water horehound) have similar effects to *L. virginicus* and are often substituted. *Lycopus lucidus* has been used for over 2000 years in Chinese medicine for menstrual pain, painful injuries, and incontinence. *Lycopus* comes from the Greek *lykos*, "wolf", and *pous*, "foot".

CULTIVATION Moist to wet soil in sun or partial shade. Invasive.

PROPAGATION By seed sown in autumn or

Lycopus virginicus

spring; by division in autumn or spring.

HARVEST Plants are cut as flowering begins and dried for use in infusions, liquid extracts, and tinctures.

■ *Lycopus virginicus* (Virginia bugleweed)
Rhizomatous perennial with branched stems and purple-green, pointed, sharply toothed leaves, 6–9cm (2½–3½) long. Tiny white flowers, sometimes purple-marked, appear in summer, followed by three-angled nutlets. Native to SE USA. ‡ 20–80cm (8–32in), ↔ 50–60cm (20–24in).

HARDINESS Fully hardy.

PARTS USED Whole plant.

PROPERTIES A bitter, faintly aromatic herb that controls bleeding, suppresses coughs, and lowers blood sugar levels. It slows and strengthens heart contractions and inhibits thyroid-stimulating hormones.

MEDICINAL USES Internally for hyperthyroidism, nervous tachycardia, coughs (especially in patients with heart disease), tuberculosis, and excessive menstruation. Not given to pregnant women or patients with hypothyroidism. For use only by qualified practitioners.

LYTHRUM
Loosestrife

Lythraceae

There are 38 species of purple- or pink-flowered annuals, perennials, and small shrubs in this cosmopolitan genus. *Lythrum salicaria* (purple loosestrife) is an adaptable, long-lived species with a range of brightly coloured cultivars for damp rich soil. It has escaped from cultivation in many places, becoming an invasive weed in wetlands. *Lythrum salicaria* has a long history of use in European folk medicine. In *The English Physician Enlarged* (1653), Culpeper rated it as one of the best herbs for the eyes. It was popular in Ireland as a remedy for diarrhoea, and was widely used in cholera epidemics in England during the 19th century. Scientific research has shown it is effective against rickettsiae, very small bacteria, transmitted by lice, ticks, and rat fleas, that cause typhus and other feverish diseases. Its astringency is such that it was once used for tanning leather, but it apparently leaves mucous surfaces moist. The name *Lythrum* comes from the Greek *lythron*, "blood", which may refer to the plant's medicinal uses.

CULTIVATION Moist to wet, neutral to alkaline soil, or shallow water, in sun or partial shade. Import of plants and seeds is prohibited in parts of the USA and Canada.

PROPAGATION By seed sown at 13–18°C (55–63°F) in spring (species only); by division in spring; by basal cuttings in spring or early summer. Self-sows readily in damp conditions.

HARVEST Plants are cut when in flower and used fresh, or dried for use in decoctions and infusions.

■ Lythrum salicaria (purple loosestrife)
Upright perennial with four-angled stems and willow-like leaves, to 7cm (3in) long. Bright

Lythrum salicaria

Lythrum salicaria 'Feuerkerze'

Lythrum salicaria 'Happy'

Lythrum salicaria 'Lady Sackville'

Lythrum salicaria 'Robert'

pink-purple flowers are produced in whorled spikes from midsummer to midautumn. Native to Europe, Asia, and N Africa. ‡60cm–1.5m (2–5ft), ↔ 45cm–1.2m (1½–4ft). ▣ 'Feuerkerze' syn. 'Firecandle' has bright rose-pink flowers. ‡90cm (36in). ▣ 'Happy' is dwarf, with small leaves and deep pink flowers. ‡60cm (24in). ▣ 'Lady Sackville' has deep pink flowers. ‡90cm (36in). ▣ 'Robert' has a compact habit and bright pink flowers. ‡90cm (36in).
HARDINESS Fully hardy.
PARTS USED Whole plant.
PROPERTIES A highly astringent, anti-bacterial herb that is diuretic, soothes irritated tissues, and controls bleeding.
MEDICINAL USES Internally for diarrhoea, dysentery, cholera, typhoid, typhus, hepatitis, haemorrhage, excessive menstruation, and vaginal discharge. Externally for wounds, sores, impetigo, eczema, eye infections, and vaginal discharge. Combined with *Gnaphalium uliginosum* (see p.227) as a gargle for sore throat.

M

MAGNOLIA
Magnoliaceae

A genus consisting of about 125 species of deciduous and evergreen trees and shrubs, distributed through eastern N America to Venezuela, and from the Himalayas to E and SE Asia. Magnolias are widely grown as ornamentals for their fragrant exotic blooms, which resemble those of water lilies. Several species are used medicinally in N America, originally by native tribes. The active constituents of magnolia bark dissolve readily in alcohol, which gave rise to the use by N American settlers of bitter alcoholic extracts to prevent malaria. The non-astringent bark of *M. acuminata* (cucumber tree) and *M. tripetala* (umbrella tree), as well as of *M. virginiana*, were listed in the *US Pharmacopoeia* (1820–94), mainly for intermittent fevers and rheumatism. *Magnolia liliiflora* and *M. officinalis* have been important in traditional Chinese medicine for over 2000 years. *Magnolia officinalis* contains magnocurarine, which is similar to curare (a muscle relaxant obtained from various species of *Chondrodendron*, see p.167, and *Strychnos*, see p.376).
CULTIVATION Moist, neutral to acid, humus-rich soil in sun or partial shade, with shelter from cold winds and late frosts. *Magnolia virginiana* tolerates wet soils. Buds and open flowers turn brown when damaged by frost.
PROPAGATION By seed sown in autumn (species only); by greenwood cuttings in early summer, or semi-ripe cuttings in late summer (deciduous magnolias); by semi-ripe cuttings from late summer to early autumn (evergreen magnolias).

HARVEST Bark is collected in autumn and dried for use in decoctions, liquid extracts, powders, and tinctures. Its aromatic properties do not keep well and stocks are renewed annually. Flower buds and flowers are picked in spring (*M. liliiflora*) or when open in summer (*M. officinalis*), and are used fresh or dried in decoctions, or dried for powders.

▣ *Magnolia liliiflora* syn. *M. quinquepeta* (lily-flowered magnolia)
Spreading deciduous shrub with elliptic to obovate leaves, to 20cm (8in) long. Fragrant, white, purple-flushed flowers, to 7cm (3in) across, appear from spring to midsummer. Native to China. ‡3m (10ft), ↔ 4m (12ft). ▣ 'Nigra' is compact and flowers when young, bearing numerous, deep purple flowers intermittently from spring to autumn. ↔ 2.5m (8ft).
HARDINESS Fully hardy.
PARTS USED Flowers, flower buds (*xin yi*).
PROPERTIES A pungent, warming, sedative herb that constricts blood vessels in the nasal passages. It also lowers blood pressure, relieves pain, and has anti-fungal effects.
MEDICINAL USES Internally for sinusitis, allergic rhinitis, colds with catarrh or runny nose. Excess causes dizziness. Incompatible with *Astragalus membranaceus* (see p.137).

▣ *Magnolia officinalis* (magnolia)
Deciduous tree with peeling grey bark and obovate leaves, to 40cm (16in) long, which have pale downy undersides. Creamy white, strongly scented flowers appear in late spring and early summer. Native to W and C China. ‡20–22m (70–75ft), ↔ 10–15m (30–50ft).
HARDINESS Fully hardy.
PARTS USED Bark, flowers (*hou po hua*).
PROPERTIES A bitter, warming, relaxant herb that improves digestion, lowers blood pressure, and has anti-bacterial and anti-fungal effects. The

Magnolia officinalis

Magnolia liliiflora

Magnolia liliiflora 'Nigra'

Magnolia virginiana

flowers act mainly as an aromatic digestive tonic.

MEDICINAL USES Internally for abdominal distention, stomach pains, diarrhoea and vomiting associated with indigestion, asthma, coughs with profuse phlegm (bark); pressure and fullness in the abdomen and chest, and shortness of breath associated with disturbed stomach energy (flowers). Bark is often combined with *Zingiber officinale* (see p.411) and *Paeonia* spp. (see p.298).

⬜ 🔲 ⬛

■ *Magnolia virginiana* syn. *M. glauca* (beaver tree, sweet bay)
Deciduous or semi-evergreen shrub or small tree with glossy, elliptic to ovate leaves, 13–15cm (5–6in) long, which have blue-white undersides. Very fragrant, creamy white, globular flowers, to 6cm (2½in) across, appear in summer. Native to E USA. ‡ 9m (28ft), ↔ 6m (20ft).

HARDINESS Fully hardy.

PARTS USED Bark.

PROPERTIES A bitter, aromatic, tonic herb that increases perspiration and reduces inflammation.

MEDICINAL USES Internally for bronchial diseases, upper respiratory tract infections, malaria, rheumatism, and gout.

CULINARY USES Leaves are used to make tea, and to flavour meat dishes and sauces.

⬜ ⬛ ✅

MAHONIA
Berberidaceae

Some 70 evergreen shrubs and small trees belong to this genus, which grows wild in N and C America and E Asia. It is closely related to *Berberis* (see p.142), differing mainly in its pinnate leaves and spineless stems. Many mahonias have handsome foliage, scented yellow flowers, and bloom-covered berries, providing a long period of interest. Smaller species, such as *Mahonia aquifolium* (Oregon grape), make excellent ground cover. *Mahonia aquifolium* closely resembles *Berberis vulgaris* (see p.142) in its chemistry and is used in similar ways. One of the main differences is the lower content of the antiseptic, anti-inflammatory berberine, which makes it less effective for infectious diseases but rather better as a liver tonic. It has been called *yerba de la sangre* ("herb of the blood"), indicating its importance as a blood purifier or alterative. The smaller but otherwise similar *Mahonia repens* (creeping Oregon grape) is also used.

CULTIVATION Well-drained, humus-rich soil in sun or partial shade. *Mahonia aquifolium* colours better in winter when planted in full sun. Cut back groundcover plants and old straggly specimens hard in spring. Leafspot, powdery mildew, and rust may attack foliage.

PROPAGATION By seed sown in autumn (species only); by leaf-bud or semi-ripe cuttings from late summer to autumn.

HARVEST Roots and root bark are collected in late autumn or early spring, and dried for use in decoctions and liquid extracts. Fruits are collected when ripe and used fresh.

Mahonia aquifolium

■ *Mahonia aquifolium* (mountain grape, Oregon grape)
Suckering shrub with spiny, glossy, dark green leaves, to 30cm (12in) long, turning purple-red in winter. Fragrant yellow flowers are borne in terminal clusters, to 8cm (3in) long, in spring, followed by spherical, blue-black berries. Native to western N America. ‡ 1–1.5m (3–5ft), ↔ 1.5–2m (5–6ft). ■ 'Apollo' is vigorous, with a dense spreading habit, good for use as ground cover; its red-stalked, brown-tinged leaves turn bronze in winter; bears large clusters of bright yellow flowers. ‡ 60cm (24in). 'Compactum' has glossier leaves, which turn bronze in winter. ‡ 60–90cm (24–36in). 'Moseri' has red-orange, new foliage. ■ 'Smaragd' syn. 'Emerald' is compact, with large clusters of flowers. ‡ 60cm (24in), ↔ 1m (3ft).

HARDINESS Fully hardy.

PARTS USED Roots, root bark, fruits.

PROPERTIES A bitter, astringent, decongestant

Mahonia aquifolium 'Apollo'

Mahonia aquifolium 'Smaragd'

herb that stimulates bile flow and releases toxins.

MEDICINAL USES Internally for skin diseases (especially dry eczema), gall bladder complaints, chronic hepatitis B, catarrhal gastritis, and diarrhoea.

CULINARY USES Berries are added to fruit pies, jams, and jellies; they are also pressed for juice, which is added to fruit drinks or made into wine.

⬜ 🔲 ⬛ ⬛ ✅

MAJORANA
Majorana hortensis. See *Origanum majorana*.
Majorana onites. See *Origanum onites*.

MALVA
Mallow
Malvaceae

A genus of about 30 species of annuals, biennials, perennials, and subshrubs, distributed through Europe, Asia, and Africa, and widely naturalized in temperate and tropical regions. A few species make attractive border plants that are easily grown, even in poor soils. *Malva sylvestris* (common mallow) has been grown as a medicinal plant and pot-herb since Roman times. In the 16th century it was known as an omnimorbia, or cure-all. Several species have very similar constituents, and *M. sylvestris* is used interchangeably with the less potent *M. moschata* (musk mallow) and the stronger *M. neglecta* (dwarf mallow). All are regarded as inferior to the closely related *Althaea officinalis* (marsh mallow, see p.117). The Chinese *Malva verticillata* (farmer's tobacco, whorled mallow) is a soothing diuretic, used for urinary tract infections. The common name "mallow" is derived from the Old English *malwe*, "soft", referring to the soothing mucilage in certain species, which softens the skin.

CULTIVATION Well-drained to poor soil, in sun or partial shade. Prone to rust.

PROPAGATION By seed sown in early spring or summer; by basal cuttings in spring.

HARVEST Leaves and flowers are gathered in summer and used fresh for compresses or dried for infusions and liquid extracts. Fruits (seed capsules) are picked when green and used fresh.

Malva sylvestris

Malva sylvestris 'Brave Heart'

Malva sylvestris   *Malva sylvestris*
'Cottenham Blue'   'Primley Blue'

 Malva sylvestris (blue mallow, common mallow, high mallow)
Robust variable perennial with 3–7-lobed leaves, to 10cm (4in) long, each usually with a dark basal spot. Pale to purple-pink flowers, to 6cm (2½in) across, with purple-pink veins and notched petals, are borne from early summer to autumn. Native to Europe, N Africa, and SW Asia. ‡ 45–90cm (18–36in), ↔ 60cm (24in).
■ 'Brave Heart' has purple-pink, strongly veined flowers, to 8cm (3in) across. ‡ 90cm (36in).
■ 'Cottenham Blue' is early flowering, with pale blue-mauve flowers. ‡ 70cm (30in). ■ 'Primley Blue' is prostrate, with pale blue-mauve flowers. ‡ 20cm (8in), ↔ 30–60cm (12–24in).
HARDINESS Fully hardy.
PARTS USED Leaves, flowers, fruits.
PROPERTIES A mucilaginous, slightly astringent herb that is expectorant, soothes irritated tissues, and reduces inflammation.
MEDICINAL USES Internally for bronchitis, catarrh, coughs, throat infections, asthma, emphysema, and gastritis. Combines well with *Eucalyptus globulus* (see p.207) for bronchial infections. Large doses are laxative. Externally for weeping eczema, boils, abscesses, and insect bites.
CULINARY USES Young leaves and shoots are eaten raw in salads or cooked in vegetable dishes.

Unripe seed capsules, known as "cheeses" because of their shape, make an unusual addition to salads.
◨ ◪ ◧ ◼ ◿

MANDRAGORA
Mandrake
Solanaceae

Six species of short-stemmed, rosette-forming perennials belong to this genus, which is distributed through Mediterranean regions to the Himalayas. *Mandragora officinarum* is an interesting, early flowering plant for a dry sunny border. The mandrake is a strange plant, both in appearance and associations, with a forked root that resembles the human form and was once esteemed as an aphrodisiac and cure for sterility. Its narcotic hallucinogenic properties were exploited in witchcraft and magic ritual during ancient and medieval times. According to folklore, digging up a mandrake causes the plant to shriek, scaring the perpetrator to death: hence the tradition of tying a dog to the root for the final pull. Like the closely related *Atropa bella-donna* (deadly nightshade, see p.138) and *Hyoscyamus niger* (henbane, see p.239), *Mandragora officinarum* is poisonous, containing potent sedative and painkilling alkaloids. In sufficient quantities, these compounds induce unconsciousness, an effect utilized in early surgery. *Mandragora officinarum* became an official homeopathic preparation in 1877, and is rarely used for any other purpose today; *M. officinarum* should not be confused with *Podophyllum peltatum* (American mandrake, see p.325), a major medicinal herb, often loosely referred to as mandrake. *Mandragora autumnalis* (autumn mandrake) is slightly smaller with a different flowering time and distribution; it has similar properties. *Mandragora* is the plant's ancient Greek name and may be a corruption of the Assyrian *nam tar ira*, "male drug of Namtar", since the plant was reputed to cure sterility.
CULTIVATION Deep, light, well-drained soil, around pH7, in a sunny sheltered position. Resents root disturbance. Dislikes cold wet conditions in winter. Prone to damage by slugs and snails.
PROPAGATION By seed sown when ripe; by root cuttings in winter.
HARVEST Roots are collected during dormancy and grated fresh for extraction of juice, or dried for use in decoctions.
⚠ **WARNING** Toxic if eaten.

■ *Mandragora officinarum* (devil's apples, mandrake)
Stemless perennial with a fleshy taproot and spreading rosettes of broadly ovate, wavy-margined leaves, to 30cm (12in) long. Greenish-white to violet, upward-facing, bell-shaped flowers, to 2.5cm (1in) across, are borne at ground level in spring, as the new leaves emerge, followed by aromatic, spherical, yellow fruits, to 3cm (1¼in) across. Native to N Italy, W Balkans, Greece, and W Turkey. ‡ 30cm (12in), ↔ 60cm (24in).

Mandragora officinarum

HARDINESS Frost hardy.
PARTS USED Roots.
PROPERTIES A sedative painkilling herb that has purgative and emetic effects.
MEDICINAL USES Internally, used formerly as a painkiller, aphrodisiac, and treatment for nervous disorders. Externally for ulcers and rheumatic or arthritic pain. For use only by qualified practitioners.
⚠ **WARNING** This herb is subject to legal restrictions in some countries.
◪ ◼

MARRUBIUM
Horehound
Lamiaceae

This genus consists of 40 species of annuals and perennials, ranging through Europe and Mediterranean regions. Their main attraction as ornamentals is the white-haired, velvety or woolly foliage. *Marrubium vulgare* (horehound) contains the diterpene marrubiin, a potent expectorant, alkaloids, and volatile oil; it was first used as a cough remedy in ancient Egyptian times. A popular way of taking horehound is in the form of candy, which is sucked to relieve chest coughs and bronchitis. *Marrubium* may be derived from *Maria urbs*, an ancient town in Italy, or from the Hebrew *marrob*, "bitter juice", since horehound was one of the five bitter herbs traditionally eaten at the feast of the Passover (the others being horseradish, coriander, lettuce, and nettles).
CULTIVATION Well-drained to dry, neutral to alkaline, poor soil in sun. Cut back plants after flowering for a second crop of new leaves. Subject to statutory control as a weed in some countries, notably in parts of Australia.
PROPAGATION By seed sown in spring; by softwood cuttings in spring.
HARVEST Plants are cut when flowering and used fresh or dried in cough mixtures, candy, infusions, liquid extracts, powders, and syrups.

■ *Marrubium vulgare* (horehound, white horehound)
Aromatic woody perennial with downy stems and ovate, downy, grey-green leaves, to 5cm (2in)

M

271

M

Marrubium vulgare

long, which have toothed margins. Small, off-white, hairy flowers appear in summer. Native to Eurasia and N Africa. ↔ 20–60cm (8–24in).
HARDINESS Fully hardy.
PARTS USED Whole plant.
PROPERTIES A bitter aromatic herb that is antiseptic and expectorant, reduces inflammation, and relieves spasms. It increases perspiration rate, stimulates bile flow, and has a sedative effect on the heart.
MEDICINAL USES Internally for bronchitis, asthma, catarrh, chest coughs and colds, whooping cough, liver and gall bladder disorders, typhoid fever, and palpitations. Combines well with *Zingiber officinale* (see p.411) for whooping cough, with *Hyssopus officinalis* (see p.240) and *Tussilago farfara* (see p.396) for coughs, and with *Cephaelis ipecacuanha* (see p.163), *Lobelia inflata* (see p.265), and *Tussilago farfara* (see p.396) for bronchial congestion. Prolonged use may cause high blood pressure. Externally for minor injuries and skin eruptions.
CULINARY USES Leaves are used in making herbal beer (horehound ale) and also in flavouring liqueurs.

MARSDENIA

Asclepiadaceae

There are about 100 species of tender, evergreen or deciduous, woody climbers and shrubs in this genus, which occurs in tropical and warm parts of Africa, Eurasia, and the Americas. All contain poisonous white latex, which in some species is processed as rubber. Research has been carried out on several marsdenias since the 1970s. They are reported to contain unusual glycosides that may have potential in cancer treatment. *Marsdenia tinctoria* (Java indigo), which is grown as a dye plant, also has anti-fertility properties. Several species are known to be extremely toxic, with strychnine-like effects, and have been used to poison wild dogs.
CULTIVATION Sandy, humus-rich soil in partial shade. Cut back leading shoots after flowering to restrict growth and encourage production of laterals.

PROPAGATION By seed sown when ripe at 13–18°C (55–64°F); by semi-ripe cuttings with a heel in summer; by layering during the growing season.
HARVEST Bark is beaten from the stems after drying and stored as liquid extracts, powders, or quills.

Marsdenia cundurango syn. *M. reichenbachii* (condor vine, condurango, eagle vine)
Twining, evergreen, aromatic climber with oblong to rounded, pointed leaves. Waxy, off-white, bell- to funnel-shaped flowers are produced in summer, followed by fleshy fruits containing seeds that each have a tuft of hairs. Native to Colombia, Ecuador, and Peru. ↕ 9m (30ft).
HARDINESS Min. 15–18°C (59–64°F).
PARTS USED Bark.
PROPERTIES A bitter, slightly aromatic, acrid herb that improves appetite and digestion. It is regarded as an alterative and gastric sedative.
MEDICINAL USES Internally for anorexia, nervous dyspepsia, liver disorders, cancers of stomach and bowel. Combined with *Acorus calamus* (see p.101), *Chamaemelum nobile* (see p.165), *Chelone glabra* (see p.166), *Gentiana lutea* (see p.223), and *Humulus lupulus* (see p.237) for anorexia. Externally for warts.

MATRICARIA

Asteraceae

A genus of about five species of Eurasian annuals, which occasionally may live longer as biennials or short-lived perennials. The genus has undergone revision, and *Matricaria recutita* (German chamomile) is often listed under its synonyms in older literature. Easily raised from seed, it gives an attractive display of feathery foliage and daisy-like flowers in summer. It is not suitable for chamomile lawns. German chamomile is similar in effects to Roman chamomile (see *Chamaemelum nobile*, p.165) but has a less pronounced aroma. Some herbalists combine the flowers, using two parts German to one part Roman, while others prefer Roman chamomile, especially in its double variant, *C. nobile* 'Flore Pleno' (see p.165). German chamomile has a slightly higher proportion of volatile oil, containing an anti-inflammatory and analgesic that is particularly effective in healing burns and preventing ulceration and infection. It is less bitter than Roman chamomile as an ingredient of herb teas.
CULTIVATION Well-drained, moist to dry, neutral to slightly acid soil in sun.
PROPAGATION By seed sown in autumn or spring.
HARVEST Flowers are collected when first fully opened and used fresh, frozen, or dried in infusions, liquid extracts, and powders. For long-term storage, flowers are better used fresh or frozen, because they lose volatile oil rapidly when dried.

Matricaria parthenium. See *Tanacetum parthenium*.

Matricaria recutita

■ *Matricaria recutita* syn. *M. chamomilla*, *Chamomilla recutita* (German chamomile, scented mayweed)
Sweetly scented annual with much-branched stems and finely divided leaves, 4–7cm (1½–3in) long. Daisy-like flowers, to 2.5cm (1in) across, are produced from early summer to autumn. Found from Europe and W Asia to India. ↕ 15–60cm (6–24in), ↔ 10–38cm (4–15in).
HARDINESS Fully hardy.
PARTS USED Flowers.
PROPERTIES A bitter, aromatic, sedative herb that relaxes spasms, reduces inflammation, relieves pain, and promotes healing. It benefits the digestion and stimulates the immune system.
MEDICINAL USES Internally for nervous digestive upsets, irritable bowel syndrome, insomnia, motion sickness, and children's complaints, such as teething, colic, and infantile convulsions. Externally for wounds, sunburn, burns, haemorrhoids, mastitis, and leg ulcers. Contraindicated during pregnancy and lactation, with anti-coagulant medication, and in known hypersensitivity to members of the Asteraceae (daisy) family. Some practitioners do not recommend chamomile for infants.
ECONOMIC USES Added to cosmetics as an anti-allergenic agent and to hair preparations as a conditioner and lightener. Extracts used to flavour liqueurs, and to enhance fruit flavours in ice cream and confectionery.

MEDICAGO

Medick

Papilionaceae

A genus of 50–60 species of annuals, perennials, and small shrubs, widely distributed in Europe, Mediterranean regions, Ethiopia, South Africa, and Asia. The cultivated *M. sativa* is thought to have originated in C Asia. From there it was introduced to China 2000 years ago, to Greece in the 5th century BC, and into N Africa and Spain during the spread of the Ottoman Empire in the 8th century, where it became known by its Arabic name, *alfalfa*. *Medicago sativa* is of major importance as a fodder crop. It is a long-lived, deep-rooted plant that can be cut up to five times each season for hay or silage, transforming the agricultural potential of areas with poor pasture. Excellent honey is obtained from alfalfa fields. Less tolerant of competition than *Trifolium* spp. (clover, see p.392), *Medicago sativa* is usually grown on its own. It is rich in nutrients, including protein, minerals (notably calcium), pro-vitamin A, and vitamins of the B group, C, D, E, and K. While beneficial in moderation, consumption of alfalfa is known to trigger attacks in patients with systemic lupus erythematosus (SLE). It also contains porphyrins, which adversely affect liver function and other substances that, in excess, cause cellular damage.

CULTIVATION Light, well-drained to dry, neutral to alkaline soil in sun.

PROPAGATION By seed sown *in situ* in spring or autumn.

HARVEST Plants are cut before flowering and dried for infusions. Young leaves are used fresh. Seeds are germinated for 3–6 days for eating raw.

■ *Medicago sativa* (alfalfa, lucerne)
Slender bushy perennial with trifoliate, blue-green leaves, to 3cm (1¼in) long. Pale mauve to purple, pea flowers are produced in long-stalked racemes in summer and early autumn, followed by coiled or sickle-shaped pods containing shiny seeds. Crops often include the yellow-flowered subsp. *falcata* and hybrids between them. Native to Europe and W Asia.
↕ 30–80cm (12–32in), ↔ 80cm (32in).

HARDINESS Fully hardy.

PARTS USED Whole plant, leaves, seeds.

PROPERTIES A sweet, astringent, cooling herb that cleanses toxins from the tissues, controls bleeding, stimulates appetite, lowers cholesterol levels, and is diuretic. It acts mainly on the circulatory and urinary systems,

Medicago sativa

and influences hormones.

MEDICINAL USES Internally for debility in convalescence or anaemia, haemorrhage, menopausal complaints, premenstrual tension, fibroids, and other conditions indicating hormonal imbalance. Contraindicated in auto-immune diseases. Excess may cause photosensitization, and breakdown of red blood cells.

CULINARY USES Leaves are eaten raw or cooked as a vegetable. Seeds are sprouted for use in salads, giving a sweet, pea-like flavour.

ECONOMIC USES Leaves are a source of chlorophyll, carotene, and vitamin K, used in food supplements.

MELALEUCA
Myrtaceae

This large genus of some 150 species of evergreen trees and shrubs is distributed mainly in Australia. Closely related to *Callistemon* (bottlebrush), many are cultivated for their spiky, often brightly coloured flowers, though some species are difficult to tell apart. They may be grown outdoors in mild areas or under cover in cool-temperate regions. *Melaleuca* is rich in germicidal volatile oils, notably cineole (as found in *Eucalyptus*, see p.206), which can irritate skin and mucous membranes. The cineole content varies according to species, genetic constitution, and growing conditions. The best tea tree oil (from *M. alternifolia*) has a higher proportion of terpenes, notably terpinen-4-ol, which is an excellent, non-irritant antiseptic. Tea tree oil was used by Australian forces in the Second World War for dressing wounds. After the war, as synthetic pharmaceuticals gained favour, production almost ceased. Research during the 1990s revived interest in its antiseptic properties, which are effective against a wide range of pathogens, including antibiotic-resistant "superbugs". Cajuput oil was first exported from Malaysia in the 17th century – hence its name, which is derived from the Malaysian *kayu-puti*, "white wood". It is obtained mainly from *M. leucadendra* (sometimes spelled *leucadendron*) and the closely related *M. cajuputi*. *Melaleuca quinquenervia* as well as *M. viridiflora* yield a similar oil (niaouli) that is used in perfumery and has strong antiseptic properties, especially against thrush.

CULTIVATION Moisture-retentive to wet, neutral to acid soil in sun; *M. leucadendra* tolerates light and saline soils. Pinch out young, pot-grown plants, to induce bushiness.

PROPAGATION By seed sown in spring at 13–24°C (55–75°F); by semi-ripe cuttings in summer.

HARVEST Oil is distilled from leaves and twigs, used directly, or in spirits and ointments.

Melaleuca alternifolia (tea tree)
Shrub or small tree with papery bark, in several layers, and linear pointed leaves, to 3.5cm (1½in) long. Small, white, five-petalled flowers

Melaleuca leucadendra

are borne in dense spikes, to 5cm (2in) long, in spring, followed by tiny, cup-shaped to cylindrical, woody capsules. Native to N Australia, S New Guinea, and the Moluccas.
↕ 5–7m (15–22ft), ↔ 3–5m (10–15ft).

HARDINESS Half hardy.

PARTS USED Oil.

PROPERTIES An aromatic antiseptic herb that is expectorant, increases perspiration, and stimulates the immune system. It is effective against bacterial and fungal infections.

MEDICINAL USES Externally for thrush, vaginal infection, acne, athlete's foot, verrucas, warts, insect bites, cold sores, nits (eggs of head lice). May be applied directly to verrucas, warts, and nits, but dilute with a carrier oil (such as almond oil) for other uses.

ECONOMIC USES Oil used in deodorants, soaps, antiseptic creams, mouthwashes, and toilet waters.

■ *Melaleuca leucadendra* (cajuput, weeping paperbark, weeping tea tree)
Large tree with pale peeling bark, slender drooping branches, and narrow pointed leaves, to 23cm (9in) long. Slender, creamy white flower spikes, 6–15cm (2½–6in) long, appear mainly in summer and autumn. Found from Indonesia, Papua New Guinea, and the Moluccas to N and W Australia. ↕ 10m (30ft), ↔ variable.

HARDINESS Min. 15–18°C (59–64°F).

PARTS USED Oil.

PROPERTIES A stimulant antiseptic herb with a strong camphoraceous aroma. It is expectorant, relieves spasms, increases perspiration, and expels intestinal parasites.

MEDICINAL USES Internally for bronchitis, tuberculosis, colds, sinusitis, gastric infections, and roundworms. Contraindicated during pregnancy. Externally for rheumatism, gout, neuralgia, acne, nasal congestion, sinusitis, toothache, chilblains, and skin diseases. An antiseptic and painkiller in aromatherapy.

ECONOMIC USES Oil used in perfumery, detergents, soaps, and insect-repellents.

⚠ **WARNING** Subject to legal restrictions in some countries, in the form of cajuput oil.

M

MELIA

Meliaceae

There are three to five species of deciduous and semi-evergreen trees and shrubs in this genus, which occurs in Eurasia, tropical Africa, and Australia. *Melia azedarach* is widely grown for reforestation and as a street tree in warm parts of the world. It is fast-growing and drought-tolerant, with ornamental foliage, scented flowers, and abundant golden fruits, which are poisonous but used as beads in Asia. In parts of S USA it has become naturalized and weedy. As a medicinal herb, it was first described in Chinese medicine in AD1082. *Melia azedarach* is closely related to the more tender *Azadirachta indica* (see p.139), and the two are often confused.

CULTIVATION Well-drained to dry soil in sun. Tolerates very dry, coastal sites in warm areas.
PROPAGATION By seed sown at 13–18°C (55–64°F) in spring; softwood cuttings in summer.
HARVEST Leaves are collected during the growing season, bark and root bark at any time, and fruits in autumn; all parts are used fresh or dried in decoctions, ointments, and pills.

Melia azadirachta. See *Azadirachta indica*.

▪ *Melia azedarach* (bead tree, chinaberry, Persian lilac)
Fast-growing, deciduous tree with grey bark and pinnate or twice-pinnate leaves, to 80cm (32in) long, divided into ovate to elliptic, pointed leaflets, which have toothed or lobed margins. Fragrant lilac flowers, 2cm (¾in) across, are borne in loose panicles in summer, followed by broadly ovoid, yellow fruits, 1cm (⅜in) long. Native to N India and China. ‡ 12–15m (40–50ft), ↔ 12m (40ft). 'Umbraculifera' is a multi-stemmed, umbrella-like tree, less hardy than the species. It comes true from seed and is weedy in some areas. ‡ 6–8m (20–25ft).
HARDINESS Half hardy.
PARTS USED Leaves, bark, root bark, fruits.
PROPERTIES A bitter irritant herb that has anti-parasitic and anti-fungal effects.
MEDICINAL USES Internally for intestinal worms and candidiasis. Usually combined

with *Glycyrrhiza glabra* (see p.227) to reduce toxicity for internal use. Excess causes diarrhoea, vomiting, and symptoms of narcotic poisoning. Externally for vaginal infections and skin diseases. For use only by qualified practitioners.
▦ ▨ ▧ ▨ ▪

Melia indica. See *Azadirachta indica*.

MELILOTUS

Melilot

Papilionaceae

Some 20 species of annuals, biennials, and short-lived perennials belong to this genus, which spans Eurasia, N Africa, and Ethiopia. *Melilotus officinalis*, found in fields and on wasteground, is widely cultivated for hay, silage, and green manure, and makes an attractive addition to the wildflower meadow. It contains coumarins, which release the pleasant smell of new-mown hay when drying. Poorly dried or fermented melilot produces dicoumarol, a potent anti-coagulant, which is extremely poisonous; it is used in rat poison. Melilot effectively draws out toxins and reduces inflammation; melilot bandages were used from ancient Greek times until the 19th century for this purpose. *Melilotus* comes from the Greek *meli*, "honey", and *lotos*, "fodder" or "clover", because these plants are important sources of nectar and animal fodder.
CULTIVATION Well-drained to dry, neutral to alkaline soil in sun. *Melilotus officinalis* is drought-tolerant.
PROPAGATION By seed sown in autumn or spring.
HARVEST Plants are cut when flowering and dried for compresses, infusions, and tinctures.

▪ *Melilotus officinalis* syn. *M. arvensis* (ribbed melilot, yellow melilot, yellow sweet clover)
Upright or spreading biennial with ribbed stems and trifoliate toothed leaves, divided into oblong–elliptic leaflets, to 3cm (1¼in) long. Yellow, honey-scented flowers, to 7mm (¼in) long, appear in slender racemes in summer, followed by brown hairless pods. Native to Eurasia; naturalized in N America. ‡ 60cm–1.5m (2–5ft), ↔ 20–90cm (8in–3ft).

HARDINESS Fully hardy.
PARTS USED Whole plant.
PROPERTIES An aromatic sedative herb that is diuretic, relieves spasms and pain, clears congestion, reduces inflammation, and has anti-thrombotic effects.
MEDICINAL USES Internally for tension headaches, neuralgia, palpitations, insomnia, varicose veins, or painful congestive menstruation, and to prevent thrombosis. Contraindicated with anti-coagulant medication and in cases of poor clotting (low platelet count). Externally for eye inflammations, rheumatic pain, swollen joints, severe bruising, boils, and erysipelas.
CULINARY USES Leaves are used to flavour marinades, stews (especially of rabbit), and *sapsago* (Schabzieger) cheese. Dried herb can be used as a substitute for vanilla in desserts.
ECONOMIC USES Dried herb is added as flavouring to snuff and tobacco, and used as a moth-repellent.
▨ ▪ ▧ ▧

MELISSA

Lamiaceae

This is a genus of three species of perennials, which occurs throughout Europe to C Asia. *Melissa officinalis* has been cultivated for over 2000 years. It was originally grown as a bee plant, which probably gave rise to its name, as *Melissa* is the Greek word for "honey bee". Its therapeutic uses were promoted by Arab physicians in the 10th and 11th centuries. *Melissa officinalis* contains a lemon-scented, volatile oil that has anti-viral activity. Commercial sources of oil are often adulterated with oils of *Citrus limon* (see p.172) or *Cymbopogon citratus* (see p.188). Lemon balm is most popular as an ingredient of herb teas, having a pleasant flavour and calming effect. Paracelsus (1493–1541) called it "the elixir of life" and John Evelyn (1620–1706) described it as "sovereign for the brain, strengthening the memory, and powerfully chasing away melancholy". Scientific research has shown that *Melissa* is helpful in controlling an over-active thyroid and may be used in conjunction with conventional treatment. Clinical trials in the 1990s confirmed that topical applications of *Melissa* are effective in the treatment of herpes simplex infections if started in the early stages.
CULTIVATION Moist soil in sun or partial shade. Cut back plants after flowering to produce a fresh crop of leaves.
PROPAGATION By seed sown *in situ* in autumn or spring (species only); by division or stem cuttings in autumn or spring.
HARVEST Plants are cut as flowering begins and used fresh or dried in infusions, dry extracts, liquid extracts, ointments, and tinctures. Fresh foliage is distilled for oil.

▪ *Melissa officinalis* (balm, lemon balm, melissa)
Lemon-scented perennial with a four-angled stem and ovate toothed leaves, 3–7cm

Melia azedarach

Melilotus officinalis

M

Melissa officinalis

Melissa officinalis
'All Gold'

Melissa officinalis
'Aurea'

(1¼–3in) long. Insignificant, pale yellow flowers are produced in axillary clusters in summer. Native to S Europe, W Asia, and N Africa. ‡ 30–80cm (12–32in), ↔ 30–45cm (12–18in). ■ 'All Gold' has bright yellow foliage. Tends to scorch in full sun. ■ 'Aurea' syn. 'Variegata' has yellow-variegated leaves. 'Citronella' is compact, with a high oil content, to 0.4 per cent. Mildew resistant. ‡ 25–30cm (10–12in). 'Compacta' is dwarf and non-flowering. ‡ 15cm (6in), ↔ 30cm (12in). 'Quedlingburger Niederliegende' is tall and uniform, with an oil content of 0.2 per cent. Good as a field crop. ‡ 50–60cm (20–24in).

HARDINESS Fully hardy.

PARTS USED Whole plant, leaves, oil.

PROPERTIES An aromatic, cooling, sedative herb that lowers fever, improves digestion, relaxes spasms and peripheral blood vessels, and inhibits thyroid activity. It has anti-viral, anti-bacterial, and insect-repellent effects.

MEDICINAL USES Internally for nervous disorders, indigestion associated with nervous tension, excitability with digestive upsets in children, hyperthyroidism, depression, anxiety, palpitations, and tension headaches. Combines well with *Chamaemelum nobile* (see p.165), *Filipendula ulmaria* (see p.214), and *Humulus lupulus* (see p.237) for nervous indigestion. Externally for herpes (cold sores), sores, gout, insect bites, and as an insect-repellent. Oil is used in aromatherapy to relax and rejuvenate, especially in cases of depression and nervous tension.

CULINARY USES Fresh leaves give a lemon flavour to salads, soups, sauces, herb vinegars, game, and fish (especially in Spain), and are an ingredient in *eau de mélisse des Carmes* (melissa cordial), in liqueurs such as Benedictine and Chartreuse, and in wine cups.

Fresh or dried leaves are used to make tea.

ECONOMIC USES Dried leaves are added to potpourris and herb pillows.

MENISPERMUM

Menispermum palmatum. See *Jateorhiza palmata*.

MENTHA

Mint

Lamiaceae

This genus consists of 25 often variable species of aromatic perennials and a few annuals, occurring in temperate regions of Europe, Asia, and Africa. Most flower from summer to early autumn. Mints of various kinds have a place in every garden. The bright green *M. spicata* has been the indispensable culinary mint since Roman times. Variegated mints can be grown in a border, provided that they have dense or vigorous neighbours. *Mentha aquatica* and *M. cervina* thrive beside pools and in boggy areas. In the Middle Ages, *M. aquatica* was known as "menastrum", and used for strewing floors. The small-growing but strongly scented *M. diemenica*, *M. pulegium*, and *M. requienii* will grow between paving stones and at the edges of paths. The mints are a complex group, involving hybridization in both the wild and cultivation, which makes individual plants often difficult to identify. A few species, such as *M. pulegium* and *M. requienii*, do not hybridize with other mints. All mints are rich in volatile oils of variable composition. It is menthol that gives mints their typical smell and taste, which is simultaneously cool and warming. Menthol is an antiseptic, decongestant, analgesic compound that predominates in *M. arvensis* var. *piperascens* (Japanese mint) and *M. × piperita* (peppermint); it is also mildly anaesthetic, giving the cooling numbing sensation experienced when smelling or tasting

peppermint. The anaesthetic effect overwhelms more subtle flavours, which is why peppermint is best used with sweet foods, such as chocolate, ice cream, and confectionery. Japanese mint yields 75 per cent menthol and is the main commercial source of menthol. Spearmint and peppermint are among the world's most popular flavourings, and crops for leaf and oil production are grown on a large scale in Europe, USA, the Middle East, Brazil, Paraguay, Japan, and China. Less pleasant in aroma is pulegone, a toxic compound notorious for causing abortion, which is present in the oils of both *M. pulegium* and *Hedeoma pulegioides* (see p.231). The Australian *Mentha diemenica*, owing to its pulegone content, has been used as a substitute for *M. pulegium*, and *M. longifolia* contains the diuretic diosphenol, which predominates in *Agathosma* spp. (see p.106). Fruit-scented mints owe their aroma to a higher concentration of limonene. Some mints, notably *Mentha spicata*, have high concentrations of carvone, a compound that characterizes the aroma of *Carum carvi* (caraway, see p.157). Various other kinds of plants are mint-scented, such as species from the genera *Eucalyptus* (see p.206), *Micromeria* (see p.279), *Monardella*, *Prostanthera* (see p.330), *Pycnanthemum* (see p.338), and *Satureja* (see p.361).

CULTIVATION Rich moist soil in sun or partial shade. *Mentha aquatica* thrives in wet soil and *M. arvensis* tolerates dry conditions. *Mentha pulegium* prefers damp, sandy, acid soil, while *M. requienii* needs moist shady conditions. Foliage may be damaged by mildew and rust, though *M. × villosa* var. *alopecuroides* is resistant to rust. Most mints are invasive and are best grown in a confined space. *Mentha pulegium* is a protected species in parts of Europe, and subject to statutory control as a weed in some countries, notably in parts of Australia.

PROPAGATION By seed sown in spring (*M. pulegium*, *M. requienii*, *M. satureioides* only); by division in spring or autumn; by tip cuttings during the growing season, placed in moist compost or water (not *M. requienii*).

M

Mentha aquatica

Mentha arvensis

Mentha cervina

Mentha requienii usually self-sows.

HARVEST Whole plants are cut as flowering begins, and leaves are cut during the growing season, and used fresh or dried for use in concentrated waters, infusions, liquid extracts, powders, spirits, or oil distillation. *Mentha arvensis* is mainly decocted or powdered in Chinese remedies.

◼ *Mentha aquatica* syn. *M. hirsuta* (water mint)
Variable perennial with rhizomes on the soil surface, red-purple stems, and ovate, toothed, hairy leaves, to 6cm (2½in) long, which have a peppermint–pennyroyal aroma. Lilac flowers are borne in a terminal head, with smaller heads on side branches. Native to Eurasia. ‡15–90cm (6–36in), ↔ indefinite. var. *crispa* has curled leaves.
HARDINESS Fully hardy.
PARTS USED Whole plant, leaves.
PROPERTIES A strongly aromatic, astringent herb that stimulates bile flow, improves digestion, and relieves spasms.
MEDICINAL USES Internally for diarrhoea, gastroenteritis, colds, and painful menstruation. Excess causes vomiting.
CULINARY USES Leaves are used for flavouring and tea.
◪ ▣ ▪ ☑

◼ *Mentha arvensis* syn. *M. austriaca* (corn mint, field mint)
Variable hairy annual or perennial with white rhizomes below the surface and ovate–lanceolate, toothed leaves, to 6cm (2½in) long, which have a rather acrid smell. Lilac to pink flowers are borne in whorls with no terminal head. Found from Europe, N Asia, and the Himalayas to Japan. ‡10–60cm (4–24in), ↔ indefinite. 'Banana' is a French cultivar with a banana aroma. subsp. *haplocalyx* syn. *M. haplocalyx* (Chinese mint) has a sweet scent, likened to heliotrope. var. *piperascens* (*hakka*, Japanese mint) has ovate, gland-dotted leaves with a strong peppermint scent; var. *villosa* syn. *M. canadensis* (American mint) has lanceolate

hairy leaves, pink or white flowers, and pleasant aroma. ‡20–50cm (8–20in), ↔ indefinite.
HARDINESS Fully hardy.
PARTS USED Whole plant (*bo he*), leaves, oil.
PROPERTIES A pungently aromatic, stimulant, anti-bacterial herb that benefits the digestion, relaxes spasms, reduces inflammation, and increases perspiration rate. It also relieves pain and itching, and suppresses lactation. According to Chinese medicine, it acts mainly on the lung and liver energies.
MEDICINAL USES Internally for colds, sore throats, headaches, measles, and indigestion; for nausea (var. *villosa*) by native N Americans. Externally for skin irritations. Combined with *Chrysanthemum × morifolium* (see p.168) and *Schizonepeta tenuifolia* in a powder for sore throats, blown down the throat through a tube. May reduce milk flow if taken when breast-feeding.
CULINARY USES Leaves used for flavouring and tea; traditionally used to prevent milk curdling.
ECONOMIC USES Source of Japanese mint oil (var. *piperascens*), used as a substitute for, or adulterant of, peppermint oil.
◪ ▢ ▣ ▪ ☑ ✎

Mentha australis (Australian mint, river mint)
Erect perennial with purple-tinged stems and lanceolate, sometimes slightly toothed leaves, to 5cm (2in) long, which have a strong peppermint aroma. White flowers are produced in clusters in the uppermost leaf axils in spring. Native to Australia, inland in all states. ‡ 80cm (32in), ↔ 1m (3ft).
HARDINESS Fully hardy.
PARTS USED Whole plant, leaves.
PROPERTIES An aromatic decongestant herb with a peppermint aroma.
MEDICINAL USES Internally, in Aboriginal medicine, for coughs and colds, and as an abortifacient. Externally, crushed and inhaled for headaches.
CULINARY USES Leaves are used for flavouring.
◪ ▣ ▪ ☑

◼ *Mentha cervina* syn. *Preslia cervina* (Hart's pennyroyal, Holt's pennyroyal)
Low-growing perennial with above-ground rhizomes and smooth, linear–oblanceolate, sometimes slightly toothed leaves, to 2.5cm (1in) long. Lilac to white flowers are produced in dense rounded clusters in the leaf axils. Native to SW Europe. ‡ 10–40cm (4–16in), ↔ indefinite.
HARDINESS Frost hardy.
PARTS USED Leaves.
PROPERTIES An aromatic herb with a pennyroyal aroma.
CULINARY USES Leaves may be used as a substitute for pennyroyal.
◪ ✎

Mentha diemenica (slender mint)
Mat-forming perennial with underground rhizomes and stalkless elliptic leaves, to 2cm (¾in) long. White to pink flowers occur in clusters of 2–8 in the leaf axils in spring. Native to Australia (except Western Australia and Queensland). ‡60cm (24in), ↔ indefinite.
HARDINESS Frost hardy.
PARTS USED Leaves.
PROPERTIES A stimulant herb with a spearmint–peppermint scent, and effects similar to *M. pulegium*. It is diuretic and diaphoretic, and repels insects.
MEDICINAL USES Internally for digestive upsets, colic, cramps, and menstrual disorders.
CULINARY USES Leaves are used sparingly in bushfoods for flavouring savoury dishes and desserts.
◪ ▪ ☑

◼ *Mentha × gracilis* syn. *M. × cardiaca*, *M. × gentilis* (basil mint, cardiac mint, Scotch spearmint)
Variable, sweetly scented perennial with erect, often red-tinged stems and ovate–lanceolate, more or less smooth leaves, 3–7cm (1¼–3in) long. Lilac flowers are produced in distinct whorls. A hybrid between *M. arvensis* and *M. spicata*. ‡ 30–90cm (12–36in), ↔ indefinite. 'Madalene

Mentha × gracilis

Mentha × gracilis 'Variegata'

Mentha longifolia

Mentha × piperita

Mentha × piperita f. *citrata* 'Lemon'

M

Hill' (doublemint) is red stemmed, and has a spearmint–peppermint flavour. Good for teas.
■ 'Variegata' (ginger mint) has yellow-variegated leaves. ‡ 30–90cm (12–36in), ↔ indefinite.
HARDINESS Fully hardy.
PARTS USED Whole plant, leaves, oil.
PROPERTIES A stimulant herb with a sweet, basil–mint aroma; benefits digestion and relieves spasms. Essential oil has high limonene content.
CULINARY USES Leaves are used fresh as a flavouring, especially with melon, tomatoes, and fruit salads.
ECONOMIC USES Source of Scotch spearmint oil used in toothpastes, pharmaceutical products, and chewing gum.
🗎 🗍 🖉 ✎ ✏

■ *Mentha longifolia* syn. *M. incana*, *M. sylvestris* (horsemint)
Variable, tall, downy perennial with rhizomes below the surface and narrowly lanceolate, toothed, grey-green, stalkless leaves, 5–9cm (2–3½in) long. Lilac or white flowers are borne in tapering spikes, to 10cm (4in) long, in summer. Native to Europe, W Asia, C Russia, Caucasus, and South Africa. ‡ 40cm–1.2m (16in–4ft), ↔ indefinite. Buddleia Mint Group has silver-grey foliage. var. *capensis* (Cape spearmint) has linear–lanceolate, densely hairy leaves and a soft spearmint aroma. ‡ 60cm (2ft). 'Variegata' has velvety grey leaves, splashed pale yellow.
HARDINESS Fully hardy.
PARTS USED Whole plant, leaves, oil.
PROPERTIES A stimulant carminative herb with a spearmint-like scent.
MEDICINAL USES Internally as a tea to aid digestion. Externally for skin problems and dandruff.
CULINARY USES Mainly in Asian, Middle Eastern, and Greek cuisine, in similar ways to spearmint; also in Indian chutneys. Leaves are candied.
ECONOMIC USES A source of oil, used for flavouring, perfumery, and pharmaceuticals.
🗎 🗍 🖉 🖻 ✎ ✏

■ *Mentha* × *piperita* syn. *M. nigricans* (peppermint)
Vigorous, creeping, often purple-tinged perennial with smooth, lanceolate, toothed leaves, to 8cm (3in) long. Lilac-pink, sterile flowers are borne in oblong terminal spikes. A hybrid between *M. aquatica* and *M. spicata*. ‡ 30–90cm (12–36in), ↔ indefinite. f. *citrata* syn. 'Citrata' (bergamot mint, eau-de-cologne mint) has ovate, bronze-purple leaves and a lavender-like aroma; f. *citrata* 'Basil' has a distinctive basil aroma; f. *citrata* 'Chocolate' has a chocolate–peppermint scent. f. *citrata* 'Lavender' has grey-green leaves with purple undersides; dried leaves are distinctly lavender-scented. ■ f. *citrata* 'Lemon' syn. 'Lemon Bergamot' (lemon mint) has light green, lemon-scented leaves and pink flowers; f. *citrata* 'Lime' has rounded, dark green leaves with a lime-like aroma. f. *citrata* 'Orange' syn. 'Orange Bergamot' has purple-edged, dark green leaves with a strong, citrus-like scent; good for tea. 'Swiss Ricola' syn. 'Swiss' has a light, refreshing, peppermint flavour; extracts used in Swiss herbal confectionery. 'Variegata' has dark green leaves with irregular cream variegation.
HARDINESS Fully hardy.
PARTS USED Whole plant, leaves, oil.
PROPERTIES A decongestant, strongly aromatic, bitter herb. Relieves spasms, increases perspiration, improves digestion, and has antiseptic, mildly anaesthetic effects; acts mainly on the digestive system, especially on the lower bowel.
MEDICINAL USES Internally (*M.* × *piperita*) for nausea, morning sickness, indigestion, gastric ulcer, gastroenteritis, irritable bowel syndrome, colic, influenza (especially in the feverish stage), and colds. Externally for upper respiratory tract infections, sinusitis, catarrh, asthma, itching skin conditions, burns, ringworm, neuralgia, rheumatism, and as an insect-repellent. Excessive use of essential oil causes irritation to mucous membranes. May cause allergic reaction. Not given to infants in

any form. *Mentha* × *piperita* f. *citrata* has uses (such as for infertility, nervous exhaustion, and rapid heartbeat) more akin to *Lavandula angustifolia* (see p.253) than to peppermint.
CULINARY USES Leaves (*M.* × *piperita*) are used in teas, iced drinks, and salads.
ECONOMIC USES Oil (*M.* × *piperita*, *M.* × *piperita* f. *citrata*) is used in oral hygiene preparations, cold and influenza remedies, antacids, and toiletries; also in perfumery, and to flavour medicines, cigarettes, confectionery, ice cream, and liqueurs, including *crème de menthe*. *M.* × *piperita* f. *citrata* is a source of lavender oil for perfumery. Leaves are added to potpourris.
🗎 🗍 🖉 🖻 ✎ ✏

■ *Mentha pulegium* (pennyroyal, pudding grass)
Pungent, upright to decumbent, creeping perennial with stems, to 40cm (16in) long, and shiny, elliptic to ovate, entire or sparsely toothed leaves, to 3cm (1¼in) long. Lilac flowers are produced in distinct whorls in late summer and autumn. Native to SW and C Europe and the Mediterranean region to Iran. ‡ 10–20cm (4–8in), ↔ 50cm (20in). ■ 'Cunningham Mint' syn. 'Dwarf Pennyroyal' (creeping pennyroyal) is compact, with small, ovate, light green leaves. ‡ 5–10cm (2–4in).
HARDINESS Fully hardy.
PARTS USED Whole plant, leaves, oil.
PROPERTIES A pungently aromatic, bitter, astringent herb that improves digestion, increases perspiration, and stimulates the uterus.
MEDICINAL USES Internally for indigestion, colic, feverish colds, and menstrual complaints. Not given to pregnant women. Externally for skin irritations.
CULINARY USES Leaves are added to black pudding (N England) and sausages (Spain). Historically used to purify drinking water on sea voyages.
ECONOMIC USES Traditionally used to repel mice and insects. Oil is used in soaps and detergents. Leaves added to potpourris.
🗎 🗍 🖉 🖻 ✎ ✏

M

Mentha pulegium

Mentha pulegium 'Cunningham Mint'

Mentha requienii

Mentha × *smithiana*

Mentha spicata

■ **Mentha requienii** (Corsican mint)
Tiny, mat-forming perennial with very thin, prostrate, rooting stems and pungently scented, round to ovate leaves, to 7mm (¼in) long. Minute lilac flowers appear in late spring and summer. Native to Corsica and Sardinia. ‡1–2cm (⅜–¾in), ↔ indefinite.
HARDINESS Frost hardy.
PARTS USED Whole plant.
PROPERTIES An aromatic herb with a strong peppermint scent.
ECONOMIC USES Used to flavour liqueurs.

Mentha satureioides (Brisbane pennyroyal, native pennyroyal)
Erect or prostrate, creeping perennial with smooth, oblong, untoothed leaves, to 3.5cm (1⅜in) long. Small clusters of white flowers appear mainly in spring. Native to Australia (all states except Tasmania). ‡30cm (12in), ↔ indefinite.
HARDINESS Fully hardy.
PARTS USED Whole plant, leaves.
PROPERTIES A pungently aromatic, tonic, decongestant herb that improves the digestion, stimulates the uterus, and relieves spasms and pain; also insect-repellent. It has a pungent, peppermint–pennyroyal aroma, and similar properties to *M. pulegium*.
MEDICINAL USES Internally for colds, catarrh, indigestion, colic, and menstrual complaints. Used as a substitute for both *M. × piperita* and *M. pulegium*. Contraindicated during pregnancy.

■ **Mentha × smithiana** syn. *M. rubra* (red mint)
Tall creeping perennial with reddish stems and sweetly scented, ovate leaves, to 7cm (3in) long. Rosy purple, sterile flowers are borne in whorls in late summer and autumn. A hybrid between *M. aquatica*, *M. arvensis*, and *M. spicata*. Native to Europe; naturalized in USA. ‡50cm–1.5m (20in–5ft), ↔ indefinite. 'Red Raripila' syn. *M. rubra* var. *raripila* (pea mint, raripila mint) has red-veined leaves, with

a fine spearmint flavour; good with peas, salads, and drinks. ‡60cm (2ft).
HARDINESS Fully hardy.
PARTS USED Leaves.
PROPERTIES An aromatic herb with a spearmint-like flavour.
CULINARY USES As for *M. spicata*.

■ **Mentha spicata** syn. *M. crispa*, *M. viridis* (garden mint, lamb mint, spearmint)
Creeping, sweetly scented perennial with bright green, lanceolate to almost ovate, wrinkled leaves, 5–9cm (2–3½in) long. Lilac, pink, or white flowers are borne in terminal cylindrical spikes. Native to W and C Europe and the Mediterranean region. ‡30cm–1m (12–36in), ↔ indefinite. ■var. *crispa* syn. 'Crispa' (curly spearmint) has strongly crinkled leaves. 'Moroccan' has close-set, fine spearmint-flavoured leaves. ■'Tashkent' is vigorous, with a good spearmint flavour.
HARDINESS Fully hardy.
PARTS USED Whole plant, leaves, oil.
PROPERTIES An aromatic stimulant herb that improves digestion and relieves spasms. Oil is less pungent than peppermint oil and is non-irritant.
MEDICINAL USES Internally for colic, wind, indigestion, hiccups, and feverish childhood illnesses. Combined with *Ballota nigra* (see p.140) for upper respiratory tract infections.
CULINARY USES Leaves are widely used for flavouring, with peas and potatoes; for making mint sauce and jelly to accompany lamb (UK); and as an ingredient of herb teas and iced drinks, appetizers, such as *tzatziki* (E Europe), and salads, such as *tabbouleh* (Middle East); also for garnishing (notably *halloumi* cheese in Greece).
ECONOMIC USES Oil is used in commercial food flavouring (notably in chewing gum), oral hygiene preparations, and herb tea blends.

■ **Mentha suaveolens** syn. *M. insularis*, *M. macrostachya* (applemint, round-leafed mint, woolly mint)
Vigorous, erect, downy perennial with oblong–

ovate to rounded, wrinkled leaves, to 5cm (2in) long. Pink to white flowers are produced in dense, tapering, terminal spikes in autumn. Often misnamed *M. rotundifolia* in cultivation. Native to W and S Europe; widely naturalized. ‡40cm–1m (16–36in), ↔ indefinite.
■ 'Variegata' (pineapple mint) is less vigorous, with irregular, creamy white variegation and a sweet fruity fragrance. ‡40–60cm (16–24in).
HARDINESS Fully hardy.
PARTS USED Leaves.
PROPERTIES An aromatic herb with a fruity spearmint flavour.
CULINARY USES As for *M. spicata*; considered superior in flavour, but hairy leaves are less suitable for garnishing. Leaves may be candied.

■ **Mentha × villosa** (heart-leafed mint)
Extremely variable, sterile hybrid between *M. spicata* and *M. suaveolens*, with smooth or hairy, broadly ovate, toothed leaves and pink flowers. Native to Europe. ‡30cm–1m (12–36in), ↔ indefinite. ■ var. *alopecuroides* syn. *M. nemorosa* var. *alopecuroides* (Bowles' mint) is vigorous, with a fine spearmint aroma; considered the best for mint sauce. ‡1.2m (4ft).
HARDINESS Fully hardy.
PARTS USED Leaves.
PROPERTIES An aromatic herb with a spearmint flavour.
CULINARY USES As for *M. spicata*.

MENYANTHES
Bog bean

Menyanthaceae

A single species of creeping, deciduous, aquatic or marginal aquatic perennial belongs to this genus, which is widely distributed in northern temperate regions. *Menyanthes trifoliata* is a decorative plant for bog gardens and pool margins, having distinctive leaves, resembling those of the broad bean, and delicately fringed flowers. *Menyanthes* is closely related to *Gentiana* (see p.222) and contains similarly bitter glycosides. It is used as a substitute for *G. lutea* (see p.223) but may irritate the digestive system in patients with gastric inflammation or infection. The name *Menyanthes* comes from the Greek *menyanthos*, a name used by Theophrastus for a water plant.
CULTIVATION Shallow acid water or wet soil in sun.
PROPAGATION By seed sown in wet compost in winter; by sections of rhizome, 23–30cm (9–12in) long, pegged horizontally in mud or in baskets of aquatic compost in spring.
HARVEST Leaves are picked in summer and dried for use in infusions, liquid extracts, or tinctures.

■ **Menyanthes trifoliata** (bog bean, buckbean, marsh trefoil)
Upright perennial with a thick horizontal rhizome and long-stalked, trifoliate leaves divided into elliptic to obovate leaflets, to 10cm

Mentha spicata var. *crispa*

Mentha suaveolens

Mentha × villosa

Mentha spicata 'Tashkent'

Mentha suaveolens 'Variegata'

Mentha × villosa var. *alopecuroides*

M

Menyanthes trifoliata

(4in) long. White fringed flowers, to 2.5cm (1in) across, flushed pink on the outside, are borne in long spikes from late spring to summer. Native to Europe, N Asia, NW India, and N America. ‡ 20–30cm (8–12in), ↔ indefinite.
HARDINESS Fully hardy.
PARTS USED Leaves.
PROPERTIES A very bitter herb that is diuretic and laxative, stimulates the digestion, and improves lymphatic drainage.
MEDICINAL USES Internally for indigestion, anorexia, arthritis, rheumatism, muscular weakness in chronic fatigue syndrome (CFS), and chronic infections with debility and exhaustion. Often combined with *Apium graveolens* (see p.125) or *Actaea racemosa* (see p.102) to relieve joint and muscular pain. Excess causes vomiting. Not given to patients with diarrhoea, dysentery, or colitis.
CULINARY USES Dried leaves are made into tea, and used as a substitute for hops in brewing beer (Sweden).
🗆 🖿 🗹

MICROMERIA
Lamiaceae

There are about 70 species of aromatic annuals, perennials, and dwarf evergreen shrubs in this genus, which occurs in dry rocky regions of the Mediterranean, the Caucasus, SW China, and USA. Identification of *Micromeria* is often difficult; some species are now classified in the genus *Acinos* (see p.100), and others have been transferred to *Satureja* (see p.361). A few species are grown in herb gardens, and one or two are seen occasionally in rock gardens. *Micromeria brownei* (St John's mint) has a strong minty aroma, with a high proportion of pulegone (as in *Mentha pulegium*, see p.277) in its essential oil. It is locally used for flavouring and herb tea. There are three varieties: *Micromeria brownei* var. *brownei*, found only in Jamaica; var. *ludens* from Cuba; and var. *pilosiuscula*, which occurs from Mexico to Georgia. *Micromeria fruticosa* is a dwarf shrub with white flowers and silver, pennyroyal-scented leaves, used for tea in parts of Europe and W Asia where it occurs. Studies show that

M. thymifolia is effective against a wide range of bacteria and fungi, notably pathogenic organisms that cause skin diseases. The so-called "Emperor's mint", often sold in the UK as a species of *Micromeria*, appears to be *Calamintha nepeta* subsp. *glandulosa*.
CULTIVATION Well-drained soil in sun or partial shade. Dislikes excessive winter moisture.
PROPAGATION By seed sown in spring at 5°C (41°F); by division in spring (perennials); by softwood cuttings in early summer (shrubs). Germination is often erratic and slow.
HARVEST Leaves are picked in the growing season and used fresh.

Micromeria thymifolia syn. *Satureja thymifolia* (thyme-leaved savory)
Erect, evergreen, branched perennial with smooth, elliptic to ovate, midgreen leaves, to 2cm (¾in) long, and tubular, white and violet flowers in summer. Native to the W Balkan Peninsula, extending into Hungary and N Italy. ‡ 20–50cm (8–20in), ↔ 15–25cm (6–10in).
HARDINESS Half hardy.
PARTS USED Leaves.
PROPERTIES An anti-bacterial, anti-fungal herb with a mint–thyme aroma.
MEDICINAL USES *Micromeria thymifolia* seems to be little used medicinally, but may have potential in the treatment of skin infections.
CULINARY USES Leaves are used to make tea, and sparingly to flavour savoury dishes.
🗆 🖿 🗹

Micromeria viminea. See Satureja viminea.

MITCHELLA
Rubiaceae

Two species of trailing evergreen perennials make up this genus, which occurs in N America and Japan. *Mitchella repens* is a pretty plant for rock gardens and ground cover. In Victorian times it was grown beneath specimen plants in ferneries. *Mitchella repens* was first used by N American tribes, such as the Cherokee and Penobscot, to ease labour; hence the common name "squaw vine". Its uses were adopted by colonists and it was listed as an astringent, tonic, and diuretic in the *US National Formulary* (1926–47). *Mitchella* is named after John Mitchell (1711–68) of Virginia, a botanist, physician, and early correspondent of Linnaeus, the Swedish botanist.
CULTIVATION Moist, humus-rich, neutral to acid soil in shade.
PROPAGATION By seed sown in autumn; by division in spring. May be invasive.
HARVEST Plants are cut in summer and dried for infusions, liquid extracts, and tinctures.

■ *Mitchella repens* (partridge berry, running box, squaw vine)
Mat-forming, prostrate, evergreen perennial with rooting stems and glossy, ovate, white-veined leaves, to 2cm (¾in) long. White flowers, sometimes pink-tinged, appear in late spring and early summer, followed by scarlet

Mitchella repens

edible berries, to 1cm (⅜in) across. Native to N America. ‡ 5–30cm (2–12in), ↔ indefinite.
HARDINESS Fully hardy.
PARTS USED Whole plant.
PROPERTIES A bitter astringent herb that is diuretic, relaxes the uterus, strengthens uterine contractions, and calms the nerves.
MEDICINAL USES Internally for menstrual disorders, preparation for childbirth, labour pains, nervous exhaustion, and irritability. Not given during the first six months of pregnancy but may be given alone, or combined with *Rubus fruticosus* (see p.350) as a uterine tonic during the last two months.
🗆 🖿

MOMORDICA
Cucurbitaceae

There are 45 species of scrambling annuals and perennials in this genus, which occurs in tropical Africa and Asia, and is naturalized in the Americas. *Momordica charantia* was introduced to Europe in 1710 and recorded as a garden plant in France by Vilmorin in 1870. It may be grown against a wall or trellis, under cover in cool areas, for its intricate foliage and colourful knobby fruits, which are especially decorative when they split open to reveal the seeds. Bitter substances, known as cucurbitacins, are common in the family. In edible species they have been either largely bred out (as in cucumbers) or must be removed by careful soaking of the fruits before use. *Momordica charantia* is an important food plant in parts of the tropics and is used medicinally in most countries of origin. Other species with medicinal applications include the oriental *M. cochinchinensis*, whose poisonous seeds are used externally for skin eruptions and infections, haemorrhoids, mastitis, and enlarged lymph nodes, and *M. grosvenori*, an expectorant and lymphatic cleanser.
CULTIVATION Rich, well-drained soil in sun. Plants flower in 30–35 days, producing fruits 15–20 days later. Stop shoots after fruits have set. Plants under cover may be damaged by whitefly, spider mites, and aphids. Plants grown outdoors may be protected by individual paper

Momordica charantia

covers against insect damage.

PROPAGATION By seed sown in spring at
15–18°C (59–64°F).

HARVEST Leaves are collected during the
growing season and used fresh or dried in
infusions. Fruits are picked when young, and
used fresh as pulp or juice.

▣ *Momordica charantia* (balsam pear, bitter
gourd/melon, *karela*)
Annual tendril climber with palmately
5–7-lobed leaves, 5–10cm (2–4in) across.
Solitary yellow flowers, to 2.5cm (1in) across,
are produced in summer, followed by ovoid,
warty, orange fruits, 20–25cm (8–10in) long,
pointed at both ends, which split into three
segments when ripe, revealing seeds with red
arils. Native to tropical Africa and Asia. ‡ 5m
(15ft).

HARDINESS Min. 15–18°C (59–64°F).

PARTS USED Leaves, fruits.

PROPERTIES A laxative diuretic herb that
soothes irritated tissues, lowers fever, kills
parasites, and cleanses toxins from the system.
It is probably a uterine stimulant.

MEDICINAL USES Internally for colitis and
dysentery (fresh juice), intestinal worms,
jaundice, and fevers (leaves). Externally for
haemorrhoids, chapped skin, and burns (fruit).

CULINARY USES Unripe (green) fruits are
added to curries or eaten raw, boiled, or fried,
after parboiling or soaking in saltwater, to
remove bitterness. Young leaves and shoots are
cooked as a vegetable.
▨ ▨ ▣ ▨ ▣

Momordica elateria. See Ecballium elaterium.

MONARDA
Horsemint

Lamiaceae

This N American genus contains about 15 species
of annuals and clump-forming perennials, found
mainly in prairies, dry scrub, and woodland.
Monarda didyma and *M. fistulosa*, and their
hybrids, such as 'Cambridge Scarlet', are
deservedly popular as garden plants. The
brightly coloured flowers attract butterflies and,

Monarda citriodora   *Monarda fistulosa*

where present, hummingbirds; when dried,
individual florets make a colourful and fragrant
addition to potpourris. Monardas are also
known as bergamots, because their aroma
resembles that of bergamot orange (see *Citrus
bergamia*, p.172). *Monarda fistulosa* was
widely used by native N Americans for
bronchial complaints and as a seasoning for
meat, and *M. punctata* was listed in the *US
Pharmacopoeia* (1820–82) as a digestive and
anti-rheumatic. The volatile oil is rich in thymol
(as found in *Thymus vulgaris*, see p.390), a
potent antiseptic and expectorant; *Monarda
didyma* is famous as the source of "Oswego
tea", named after an area near Lake Ontario,
where it grew abundantly. Other species include
the mauve-flowered *M. austromontana*, with
oregano-flavoured leaves, used with meat dishes
in Mexico. Also oregano-like is *M. fistulosa*
var. *menthaefolia*, rich in geraniol, a compound
more commonly associated with *Pelargonium*
spp. (see p.304). *Monarda* is named after
Nicolas Monardes of Seville, a physician and
botanist who was author of the first European
book on American medicinal plants, translated
into English in 1577 as *Joyfull News out of the
newe founde Worlde*.

CULTIVATION Rich moist soil in sun
(*M. didyma*); sandy or rocky soil in sun
(*M. citriodora*); light, dry, alkaline soil in sun
(*M. fistulosa* and *M. punctata*). *Monarda
didyma* is prone to mildew in dry conditions.

PROPAGATION By seed sown in spring or
autumn; by division in spring; by softwood
cuttings in early summer.

HARVEST Plants are cut when flowering, and
leaves before flowering, and used fresh, or dried
for infusions.

Monarda punctata

Monarda 'Adam'

Monarda 'Balance'

▣ *Monarda citriodora* (lemon bergamot)
Annual with lanceolate to oblong leaves,
3–6cm (1¼–2½in) long, and white or pink,
purple-dotted flowers. Native to C and S USA
and N Mexico. ‡ 30–60cm (12–24in),
↔ 15–23cm (6–9in).

HARDINESS Half hardy.

PARTS USED Leaves.

PROPERTIES An aromatic herb with a lemon-
like aroma.

MEDICINAL USES Leaves contain citronellol,
effective as an insect-repellent when rubbed
on the skin.

CULINARY USES Traditionally used by Hopi tribe
to flavour wild game, such as hare; also for tea.
▨ ▣ ▨

Monarda didyma (bee balm, bergamot, Oswego
tea)
Aromatic perennial with erect, four-angled
stems and ovate toothed leaves, to 14cm
(5½in) long. Bright red, claw-shaped flowers,
to 4.5cm (1¾in) long, with red-green bracts,
are produced in terminal whorls in summer.
Native to eastern N America. ‡ 40cm–1.2m
(16–48in), ↔ 45cm (18in).

HARDINESS Fully hardy.

PARTS USED Whole plant, leaves, flowers.

PROPERTIES An aromatic, stimulant,
expectorant herb that lowers fever and benefits
the digestion.

MEDICINAL USES Internally for minor digestive
complaints.

CULINARY USES Fresh or dried leaves and
flower heads are infused as tea, and give an
Earl Grey flavour to China tea and iced drinks.
Flowers are added to salads.
▨ ▨ ▨ ▣ ▨

M

Monarda 'Beauty of Cobham'

Monarda 'Cambridge Scarlet'

Monarda 'Schneewitchen'

Monarda 'Blaustrumpf'

Monarda 'Loddon Crown'

Monarda 'Mahogany'

Monarda 'Scorpion'

Monarda 'Squaw'

■ **Monarda fistulosa** (horsemint, wild bergamot) Variable, pungent, hairy perennial with lanceolate, grey-green, tapering leaves, to 10cm (4in) long. Lilac to pink flowers, to 3cm (1¼in) long, with pink-tinted bracts, are produced in a terminal whorl from summer to autumn. Native to eastern N America. ‡ 1.2m (4ft), ↔ 45cm (18in). var. *menthaefolia* syn. *M. menthaefolia* (mint-leafed bergamot, mountain oregano, *oregano de la sierra*) has a sweet, oregano-like fragrance and lavender flowers.
HARDINESS Fully hardy.
PARTS USED Whole plant, leaves.
PROPERTIES An aromatic stimulant herb that improves the digestion and increases perspiration.
MEDICINAL USES Internally for colds, sore throats, catarrh, headaches, fevers, and gastric disorders. Externally for skin eruptions. Contraindicated during pregnancy.
CULINARY USES Leaves are used to flavour meat and beans; young shoots and leaves are infused for tea.

■ **Monarda punctata** (dotted monarda, horsemint, spotted monarda)
Aromatic annual, biennial, or perennial with lanceolate to narrowly elliptic leaves, to 9cm (3½in) long. Yellow, purple-spotted flowers are produced in dense whorls, surrounded by prominent, pink, lavender, or whitish bracts, in summer. Variable, with a number of subspecies. Native to USA. ‡ 30–90cm (12–36in), ↔ 30–45cm (12–18in).
HARDINESS Fully hardy.
PARTS USED Whole plant, leaves.
PROPERTIES A bitter, pungent, diuretic herb

with a mint–thyme aroma. It increases perspiration, benefits the digestion, and is rubefacient when applied topically.
MEDICINAL USES Internally for indigestion, colic, nausea and vomiting, diarrhoea, feverish chills, colds, and backache. Externally for neuralgia and rheumatism.
CULINARY USES Leaves made into "rignum" tea in South Carolina.

Monarda hybrids (bee balm, bergamot)
Erect perennial with ovate toothed leaves, to 14cm (5½in) long, and tubular, claw-shaped flowers, to 5cm (2in) long, produced in whorls, usually with red-tinged bracts, in summer. ‡ 90cm (36in), ↔ 45cm (18in). ■ 'Adam' has cherry-red flowers. 'Aquarius' has broad, light violet flowers and deep violet-tinged bracts. ■ 'Balance' syn. 'Libra' has bright pink flowers; highly resistant to mildew. ■ 'Beauty of Cobham' has purple-tinged foliage, pale pink flowers, and purple-pink bracts. ■ 'Blaustrumpf' syn. 'Blue Stocking' has deep violet-purple flowers and purple bracts. ■ 'Cambridge Scarlet' has bright red flowers and brown-red bracts. 'Croftway Pink' has clear pink flowers and pink-tinged bracts. 'Elsie's Lavender' has grey-green leaves, light lavender flowers, and light green bracts. 'Fishes' syn. 'Pisces' has bright green leaves, rose-white flowers, and green to white, sometimes pink-tinged bracts. ‡ 80cm (32in). ■ 'Loddon Crown' has dark red-purple flowers and purple-brown bracts. ■ 'Mahogany' has wine-red flowers and brown-red bracts. 'Ou Charm' has light rose-pink flowers and red-brown bracts. ‡ 80cm (32in). 'Pawnee' has soft lilac flowers and light green bracts; mildew resistant.

■ 'Schneewitchen' syn. 'Snow Witch' has pure white flowers and green bracts. ■ 'Scorpion' syn. 'Scorpio' is vigorous, with bright magenta flowers. 'Snow Queen' has very large heads of white flowers, and light green bracts. ■ 'Squaw' is similar to 'Cambridge Scarlet' but taller and more resistant to mildew. ‡ 1.2m (4ft).

MORINDA
Rubiaceae

This genus includes some 50–80 species of deciduous small trees, shrubs, and woody climbers, most of which occur in tropical Africa, Asia, and Australia. Most species have white, often scented flowers, and the roots yield a yellow dye, known as morindin, once used in Javanese batik. Recommended for greenhouse culture in the 19th century, they are rarely seen today. *Morinda officinalis* was first mentioned in Chinese medical literature during the Han dynasty (206BC–AD23) as a tonic warming herb that acts mainly on the kidney energy. The roots (*ba ji*) are combined with *Glycyrrhiza uralensis* to reduce toxicity. *Morinda tinctoria* (dyer's mulberry) is best known as a source of red dye, but both leaves and roots have astringent properties. *Morinda citrifolia* is the most widely cultivated species, being ornamental and useful for both culinary and medicinal purposes.
CULTIVATION Well-drained, sandy soil in sun. Tolerates saline conditions.
PROPAGATION By seed sown when ripe at 18–21°C (64–70°F); by semi-ripe cuttings in summer at 18°C (64°F).
HARVEST Roots are lifted as required, and used in decoctions. Leaves are collected during the

281

Morinda citrifolia

growing season for juice extraction, decoctions, or pastes. Fruits may be picked ripe or unripe, and are often charred and mixed with salt for medicinal use.

▪ *Morinda citrifolia* (awl tree, Indian mulberry) Small tree with ovate glossy leaves, 15–20cm (6–8in) long. Clusters of fragrant, white, tubular flowers appear all year, followed by irregularly ovoid, cream fruits, to 7.5cm (3in) long, which smell like blue cheese when ripe. Native to tropical Asia, Australia, and Polynesia. ‡ 3m (10ft), ↔ 2–2.5m (6–8ft).
HARDINESS Min. 15–18°C (59–64°F).
PARTS USED Roots (*ba ji*), leaves, fruits.
PROPERTIES An astringent purgative herb that reduces inflammation.
MEDICINAL USES Internally for dysentery, haemorrhage (fruits), constipation (roots), tuberculosis (leaves). Externally for gout (leaf juice), chronic ulcers, snake bite (leaves), and gum disease (fruits).
CULINARY USES Unripe fruits are eaten in curries and sambals. Juice of ripe fruits is used in sauces, dressings, and marinades in Australian bush cuisine. Young leaves are eaten raw, cooked as a vegetable, or used for wrapping in fish dishes.

MORINGA

Moringaceae

A genus of 14 species of deciduous succulent trees, which occur in Africa, Madagascar, India, and Arabia. *Moringa oleifera* is a fast-growing, decorative tree that resembles *Robinia* in appearance, and flowers and fruits all year. It is the most commonly grown species, with medicinal uses that date back to ancient Greek times. Nearly all parts of the tree are edible; the bark yields a reddish gum, called ben gum, used for flavouring, and ben oil, extracted from the seeds, is a useful ingredient in foods and pharmaceutical products, since it does not go rancid. The roots are similar to horseradish, and the foliage, which contains 7–10 per cent protein, is mustard-flavoured. *Moringa peregrina*, a graceful African tree, has edible,

potato-like roots and yields an oil that is used to treat infantile convulsions. *Moringa pterygosperma* is important in India; young leaves and unripe pods are eaten as vegetables, flowers are added to curries, and various parts of the tree have medicinal uses.
CULTIVATION Well-drained sandy soil in sun. Cut plants back hard when harvesting.
PROPAGATION By seed sown when ripe; by semi-ripe cuttings in summer.
HARVEST Leaves, flowers, and immature fruits are collected as available and used fresh. Seeds are removed from pods when ripe, and roasted for eating, or pressed for oil, which stores well. Bark, roots, and root bark are harvested as required for juice extraction, or used fresh or dried for decoctions. Gum is collected from bark for use in infusions and decoctions.

▪ *Moringa oleifera* (ben, horseradish tree) Deciduous tree with a pale grey to copper-coloured trunk, which stores water, and compound, pinnately divided leaves, 30–60cm (12–24in) long. Scented, cream, five-petalled flowers, 2.5cm (1in) across, are produced in loose panicles, to 15cm (6in) long, followed by pendulous, brown, bean-like capsules, to 50cm (20in) long. Native to Arabia and India.
‡ 8–15m (25–50ft), ↔ 6–10m (20–30ft).
HARDINESS Min. 15–18°C (59–64°F).
PARTS USED Leaves, bark, roots, flowers, fruits, seeds, oil, gum.
PROPERTIES A nutritious, diuretic, laxative herb that is expectorant, increases milk flow, controls bacterial infections, and is rubefacient when applied topically. It contains a potent antibiotic. Ben oil has no taste, smell, or colour, and is exceptionally resistant to oxidation. Gum has similar

Moringa oleifera

properties to tragacanth (see *Astragalus gummifera*, p.136).
MEDICINAL USES Internally for insufficient lactation (young leaves), tuberculosis, septicaemia (bark, gum); asthma, gout, rheumatism, enlarged spleen and liver, bladder and kidney stones, inflammatory conditions (juice of root). Externally for boils, ulcers, glandular swellings, infected wounds, skin diseases, dental infections, snake bite, and gout (seeds, bark, root, gum).
CULINARY USES Leaves, flowers, seedlings, and young pods are eaten as vegetables (leaves are often added to shellfish dishes to counteract any toxins). Roots make an acceptable substitute for horseradish. Seeds are roasted like nuts; immature seeds are eaten like peas. Gum is used for seasoning.
ECONOMIC USES Oil is used in salad dressings, lubricants, artists' paints, soaps, and ointments. Wood is used in the manufacture of rayon and cellophane; bark is used in tanning. Crushed seeds are used to purify drinking water.

MORUS
Mulberry

Moraceae

This genus of ten species of deciduous trees occurs in N and S America, Africa, and Asia, mainly in subtropical regions. Both *M. alba* and *M. nigra* have been cultivated for centuries and have an attractive, often gnarled appearance, edible, blackberry-like fruits, and medicinal properties. They have similar constituents and are interchangeable for medicinal purposes, though *M. nigra* is superior for fruit production. *Morus alba* has been used in traditional Chinese medicine since AD659. The leaves, root bark, branches, and fruits are still listed in the *Chinese Pharmacopoeia* (1985) but other parts, including sap and wood ash, are also widely used. All parts are prepared in a great variety of ways. Research has shown improvements in elephantiasis when treated with leaf extract injections, and in tetanus following oral doses of sap mixed with sugar. *Morus alba* is also the preferred food of silkworms and is widely cultivated for this purpose. In China the start of silk production using mulberry leaves is generally attributed to the Empress Si-Ling, who lived c.2960BC. *Morus* is the original Latin name for mulberry. It comes from *demorari*, "to delay", and refers to the tree's habit of forming buds only after the last frosts are past.
CULTIVATION Rich, deep, well-drained soil in sun. Mulberries have brittle roots and need careful handling when planting. Prune only when fully dormant in winter because mulberries bleed when cut. Ideally prune only badly placed branches and dead wood. Canker and die-back may damage young shoots.
PROPAGATION By seed sown in autumn (species only); by softwood cuttings in summer, or hardwood cuttings in autumn.
HARVEST For medicinal use, leaves are collected after frost in autumn, branches in late

Morus alba

spring or early summer, roots
in winter, and fruits when
nearly ripe. Leaves and root
bark are traditionally processed
with honey. Fresh leaves and fruits are
sometimes juiced but otherwise all parts are
dried, for use in decoctions or poultices. Fruits
may be steamed or blanched before drying to
improve storage qualities; for culinary use they
are harvested when ripe.

▣ *Morus alba* (white mulberry)
Deciduous tree with dull green, orange-tinged
bark and ovate toothed leaves, to 20cm (8in)
long. Female flowers are borne in erect
cylindrical catkins, followed by white to pink or
purple fruits, 2.5cm (1in) long; male flowers are
borne separately on the same plant. Native to
China. ‡ 20m (70ft), ↔ 10m (30ft). ▣ 'Pendula'
has a weeping habit. ‡ 3m (10ft), ↔ 5m (15ft).
HARDINESS Fully hardy.
PARTS USED Leaves (*sang ye*), branches (*sang zhi*), root bark (*sang bai pi*), fruits (*sang shen*).
PROPERTIES A pleasant-tasting, bitter or sweet
herb (depending on the part). It increases
perspiration rate and has anti-bacterial, cooling
effects (leaves), is anti-rheumatic (branches),
controls coughing, is expectorant and diuretic
(root bark), and has a tonic effect on kidney
energy (fruits). Both root bark and branches
reduce blood pressure.

Morus alba 'Pendula'

MEDICINAL USES Internally for colds,
influenza, eye infections, and nosebleeds
(leaves); rheumatic pains and hypertension
(branches); coughs, asthma, bronchitis, oedema,
hypertension, and diabetes (root bark); urinary
incontinence, tinnitus, premature greying of
hair, thirst, or constipation in the elderly (fruits).
CULINARY USES Fruits are dried, or eaten fresh
and made into jellies, jams, syrup, and wine.
ECONOMIC USES Leaves are fed to silkworms.
Wood is used in ageing balsamic vinegar, and in
the manufacture of sports equipment, such as
tennis rackets and bats, especially in India.

▣ ✕ ▨ ▨ ▨ ▣ ✎ ✎

MUCUNA
Velvet bean

Fabaceae

About 100 species of tropical and subtropical
woody lianas, climbers, and shrubs belong to
this leguminous genus. Some species are bat-
pollinated, and most contain alkaloids. A few
are grown as ornamentals, such as the scarlet-
flowered *M. bennettii*, which is among the
world's most spectacular climbers. *Mucuna
pruriens* (often given incorrectly as *M. prurita*)
is a species with several variants; the main one
is var. *utilis*, which is widely grown in the
tropics as a fodder crop. *Mucuna pruriens* var.
utilis is unusual among herbs in that among the
parts used are the bristly hairs on the pods. The
use of this species as an anthelmintic was first
recorded by Patrick Browne in his *Civil and
Natural History of Jamaica*, 1756. Ancient
Sanskrit texts indicate that it was used as an
aphrodisiac. Seeds of *M. pruriens* var. *utilis*
yield L-dopa, which revolutionized the
treatment of Parkinson's disease in the 1960s.
They also contain toxic hallucinogenic
compounds. Though poisonous, the seeds are a
common famine food, edible if boiled in several
changes of water.
CULTIVATION Well-drained, moist, humus-rich
soil in sun or partial shade. Remove crowded
branches in winter and cut back flowered shoots
to within 5–8cm (2–3in) of the base. Spider
mite and whitefly may attack plants indoors.
PROPAGATION By seed sown at 18–24°C
(64–75°F) in spring.
HARVEST Roots are lifted as required and dried
for decoctions and powders. Pods are collected
when ripe and scraped to remove hairs, which
are powdered and mixed with honey or added
to ointment. Seeds are removed from ripe pods,
cooked, and ground to a paste.
⚠ **WARNING** Pods, hairs, and powder are irritant
to skin, eyes, and mucous membranes.

Mucuna pruriens var. *utilis*
syn. *M. deeringiana*, *M. pruriens* Utilis Group,
M. utilis, *Stizolobium deeringianum* (benguk,
cowage, velvet bean)
Semi-woody, annual or short-lived perennial,
twining climber with trifoliate leaves, to 45cm
(18in) long, divided into elliptic pointed
leaflets, 8–15cm (3–6in) long. Clusters of dark
purple to lilac or white, pea-like flowers, to 4cm

(1½in) long, appear in summer, followed by
flattened hairy pods, to 9cm (3½in) long and
2cm (¾in) wide, with a pointed, often hooked,
apex. The pods contain 3–6 seeds, about 1cm
(⅜in) long, and are covered in orange or dark
brown, irritant bristles. Native to tropical Asia;
widely naturalized. ‡ 4m (12ft).
HARDINESS Min. 8°C (46°F).
PARTS USED Roots, pods, hairs from pods, seeds.
PROPERTIES An irritant, rubefacient herb that
destroys intestinal parasites (hairs), and acts
as a diuretic (roots), hallucinogen, and
aphrodisiac (seeds).
MEDICINAL USES Internally for nervous and
kidney complaints, and paralysis (roots),
roundworms (hairs); externally for elephantiasis
and fluid retention (roots). Internal use of the
hairs is highly irritant; excess may prove fatal.
Extracts are used internally to control
involuntary movements in Parkinsonism (seeds).
CULINARY USES Seeds are boiled in milk,
decorticated, fried, and made into a confection
with honey; also fermented in *miso* (Japan) and
in Indonesian foods, such as *tempeh benguk*.
Immature pods and young leaves are cooked
as vegetables.

▨ ▨ ▨ ▣ ✎ ▣

MURRAYA
Rutaceae

A genus of four species of evergreen trees and
shrubs, occuring in tropical Asia, Pacific islands,
and tropical and subtropical Australia. *Murraya
paniculata* (jasmine orange, orange jessamine)
is popular as a houseplant for its aromatic
foliage, fragrant white flowers, and edible red
berries; the leaves are added to curries, and the
flowers are used to scent tea. The fresh leaves
of *M. koenigii* are an indispensable ingredient
of curries in S India and Sri Lanka, where it is
sold fresh in food stores and markets. *Murraya*
is closely related to *Citrus* (see p.171); lemon
trees (*C. limon*) can be grafted on to the
rootstock of *Murraya koenigii*. The genus was
named after Johann Andreas Murray (1740–91),
a pupil of Linnaeus, and professor of botany
and medicine at Göttingen (Sweden).
CULTIVATION Moist, humus-rich, well-drained
soil in sun or partial shade. Remove excessive
growth in late winter.
PROPAGATION By seed sown in spring; by
semi-ripe cuttings in summer.
HARVEST Leaves are picked all year round, and
used fresh for juice, infusions, and poultices; also
dried and ground for flavouring. Bark and roots
are collected as required, and used fresh or dried
in decoctions. Oil is extracted from ripe seeds.

▣ *Murraya koenigii* (curry leaf)
Small evergreen tree with dark grey bark and
pinnate leaves, 15–25cm (6–10in) long, which
have a strong curry aroma when bruised. Clusters
of small, fragrant, white flowers are produced
in summer, followed by edible, spherical, black
berries, to 1cm (⅜in) across. Native to India,
Pakistan, Sri Lanka, and the Andaman Islands.
‡ 6m (20ft), ↔ 3–5m (10–15ft).

M

Murraya koenigii

HARDINESS Min. 15–18°C (59–64°F).
PARTS USED Leaves, bark, root, fruits, oil.
PROPERTIES A warming, strongly aromatic herb that improves appetite and digestion.
MEDICINAL USES Internally for digestive problems (leaves, roots, bark), constipation, colic, diarrhoea (leaves).
CULINARY USES Dried ground leaves are the basis for curry powder; fresh or dried leaves, fried in ghee or oil, are the basis for curries; also used in chutneys and marinades. Peppery fruits are used for seasoning.

M

MYRICA
Wax myrtle

Myricaceae

This cosmopolitan genus contains about 50 species of deciduous and evergreen shrubs and small trees. Several species have aromatic foliage and are able to thrive in difficult growing conditions. *Myrica cerifera* (wax myrtle) is especially adaptable, tolerating both poor sandy soils and swamps. *Myrica pensylvanica* (bayberry) is similar but hardier. The fruits of various species are boiled to produce wax for making candles, which are aromatic and smokeless. *Myrica cerifera* and *M. gale* (bog myrtle) contain tannins, resins, gums, and bactericidal substances. *Myrica gale* was once an important herb for tea and flavouring in some northern communities; it is the badge of the Campbells, the Scottish clan. *Myrica cerifera* is a key herb in the Thomsonian system of medicine, being the main astringent used for "any stomach or bowel derangement, particularly after fevers". *Myrica californica* is similarly used for gastrointestinal disorders and for infections.
CULTIVATION Well-drained to wet, acid, sandy soil in sun or partial shade. *Myrica gale* prefers permanently wet conditions.
PROPAGATION By seed sown when ripe; by layering in spring; by suckers (*M. gale*); by semi-ripe cuttings in summer.
HARVEST Whole plants or leaves are collected during the growing season; bark and root bark in late autumn or early spring. All parts are dried for decoctions, infusions, liquid extracts,

and powders. Fruits are gathered when ripe for wax extraction.

Myrica cerifera

◼ *Myrica cerifera* (bayberry, candleberry, wax myrtle)
Evergreen shrub or small tree with oblanceolate leaves, to 9cm (3½in) long. Male flowers are borne in scaly catkins, to 2cm (¾in) long; females in an ovoid cluster, followed by spherical, grey-white, waxy fruits, to 3mm (⅛in) across. Native to SE USA. ↕ 3–12m (10–40ft), ↔ 5m (15ft).
HARDINESS Frost hardy.
PARTS USED Bark, root bark, wax.
PROPERTIES A bitter, astringent, aromatic herb that stimulates the circulation, increases perspiration, and controls bacterial infections.
MEDICINAL USES Internally for fevers, colds, influenza, catarrh, diarrhoea, colitis, excessive menstruation, and vaginal discharge. Externally for sore throat, ulcers, sores, itching skin, dandruff, and hair loss. Combined with *Mentha × piperita* (see p.277) and *Sambucus nigra* (see p.357) for feverish illnesses; with *Capsicum annuum* (see p.154), *Syzygium aromaticum* (see p.378), and *Zingiber officinale* (see p.411) as a circulatory stimulant; and with *Lavandula* (see p.252) in hair preparations.
CULINARY USES Fruits are used with strongly flavoured meat dishes, such as game, in the same way as juniper berries (see Juniperus, p.247). Leaves are used for flavouring in the same way as bay leaves (see Laurus *nobilis*, p.252); also made into tea.
ECONOMIC USES Wax from fruits is used in making candles and soap.

◼ *Myrica gale* (bog myrtle, sweet gale)
Deciduous suckering shrub with red-brown twigs and narrowly oblanceolate leaves, to 6cm (2½in) long. Male and female catkins are borne on separate plants in spring, before the new leaves, followed by spherical, yellow-brown fruits, to 3mm (⅛in) across. Native to Europe, Asia, and N America. ↔ to 1.5m (5ft).
HARDINESS Fully hardy.
PARTS USED Whole plant, leaves, fruits.
PROPERTIES A bitter, astringent, antiseptic herb with a resinous, bay-like aroma.

Myrica gale

CULINARY USES Leaves are infused for tea; both leaves and berries are added to soups, stews, and meat dishes. Traditionally used in Yorkshire (England) as a substitute for hops to flavour ale, known as gale beer.
ECONOMIC USES Wax is used to make aromatic candles.

MYRISTICA
Nutmeg

Myristicaceae

This genus of about 100 large evergreen trees ranges through Asia and Australia. *Myristica fragrans* is an important crop in Indonesia, Sri Lanka, and the Caribbean island of Grenada. The golden fruits split open when ripe to reveal a single seed (nutmeg) in a woody brown shell, which in turn is clasped by a bright red aril (mace) that turns yellow when dried. Fruits of *M. fragrans* are rich in volatile oils, which differ in concentration (and hence flavour) in the seed (nutmeg) and aril (mace). These include safrole (as found in *Sassafras albidum*, see p.361), which in excess is carcinogenic, and myristicin, a hallucinogenic compound. Inferior fruits are obtained from *M. argentea* (Macassar nutmeg, Papua nutmeg), *M. fatua*, and *M. malabarica*. Nutmeg and mace probably reached Europe via Arab traders in the 1st century AD, and were mainly used for medicinal purposes. Although now used almost exclusively as a spice, *M. fragrans* was promoted as a tonic after the Portuguese took the Moluccas and obtained a monopoly on its production in 1512. The first recorded case of nutmeg poisoning came in 1576, when a "pregnant English lady" consumed 10–12 fruits and became "deliriously inebriated". *Myristica fragrans* has been listed as a Chinese medicinal herb since c.AD600.
CULTIVATION Well-drained, humus-rich, sandy soil, with high humidity.
PROPAGATION By seed sown when ripe; by hardwood cuttings at the end of the growing season. Dried nutmegs are prone to insect attack; they are usually limed, and stored in sealed containers.

HARVEST Seeds are removed from ripe fruits and separated from arils; both are dried for oil distillation or used in decoctions and powders.

▪ *Myristica fragrans* (*jatiphala*, nutmeg) Bushy evergreen tree with aromatic oblong leaves, to 12cm (5in) long, covered in silvery aromatic scales when young. Pale yellow flowers, 1cm (³⁄₈in) across, are produced in axillary clusters, followed by fleshy, yellow, rounded, pendent fruits, 6–9cm (2½–3½in) long, containing a lustrous brown, ovoid seed, to 4cm (1½in) long, encased in a hard thin shell and leathery, laciniate, scarlet aril. Native to Moluccas and Banda Islands. ↕10–20m (30–70ft), ↔ 8m (25ft).
HARDINESS Min. 15–18°C (59–64°F).
PARTS USED Seeds (*rou dou kou*), arils, oil.
PROPERTIES A bitter, astringent, spicy herb that acts as a warming digestive tonic. It controls vomiting and relaxes spasms. Topical application is anti-inflammatory.
MEDICINAL USES Internally for diarrhoea, dysentery, gastoenteritis, vomiting, abdominal distention, indigestion, and colic. Excess causes severe headache, nausea, dizziness, and delirium. Externally for toothache, eczema, and rheumatic and abdominal pains (including labour pains). Used in Ayurvedic medicine for poor digestion, insomnia, urinary incontinence, and premature ejaculation. Contraindicated during pregnancy.
CULINARY USES Ground or grated nutmeg gives flavour to bakery produce, puddings, drinks, meat dishes, vegetables (notably spinach and mushrooms), cheese dishes, sauces (such as onion, bread, and *béchamel*), and pasta stuffings. Powdered or whole mace gives a similar but less pungent flavour and is better suited to soufflés, fish, clear soups, and sauces, where nutmeg would spoil the appearance. Nutmeg and mace are key ingredients of the N African spice mixture *ras-el-hanout*. Flesh of nutmeg fruits is candied, pickled, and made into jellies and syrups.
ECONOMIC USES Fatty oil, known as "nutmeg butter", is used in the pharmaceutical industry, mainly in perfume, soap, and candle manufacture.

MYROXYLON
Bálsamo

Papilionaceae

Three closely related species of evergreen trees make up this tropical S American genus. They yield balsams with a cinnamon–vanilla aroma, which have long been used in medicine, perfumery, and food flavouring. *Myroxylon balsamum* is widely cultivated for these purposes. It is often planted as a windbreak or shade tree, and tolerates both moist and dry, alkaline conditions. Balsam trees were cultivated by the Incas. The first European to record their medicinal uses was Nicolas Monardes in 1565, who noted that balsam was collected by either cutting the bark or by boiling the branches in water. Following the Spanish conquest, balsam was exported to Europe for medicines and perfumery. It was also approved for use in anointing oils: papal bulls of 1562 and 1571 declared it sacrilege to destroy balsam trees. The resin extracted from *M. balsamum* is known as Tolu balsam, after Santiago de Tolu (Colombia). Tolu balsam differs only slightly in chemistry from balsam of Peru, an oily fluid produced by *M. balsamum* var. *pereirae*, which was originally shipped from Callao (Peru). Both contain benzoic acid, which is a common cause of allergic reactions. Tolu balsam is collected from V-shaped incisions in the tree bark and solidifies to a yellow-red or brown, crystalline consistency. For balsam of Peru, the bark is beaten, left a few days, then burned off; balsam exudes from the wounded areas and is soaked up by rags, which are boiled in water to separate the balsam into an oily layer. *Myroxylon* is from the Greek *myron*, "myrrh", and *xylon*, "wood".
CULTIVATION Well-drained soil with added sand and leafmould, in sun, with ample water when in growth; *M. balsamum* var. *pereirae* tolerates alkaline and poor soils. Balsam trees are resilient, tolerating heavy tapping and often reaching 100 years old.
PROPAGATION By seed sown when ripe; by semi-ripe cuttings in late summer.
HARVEST Oleo-resin is collected at any time of the year, but mostly during the dry season, by wounding the bark; it is used raw, or processed into extracts, oils, syrups, and tinctures. Oil is distilled from oleo-resin. Seed are collected when ripe, and used whole.

▪ *Myroxylon balsamum* syn. *M. toluiferum* (*bálsamo*, Tolu balsam)
Spreading evergreen tree with fragrant bark and glossy, leathery, pinnate leaves, to 15cm (6in) long, divided into 5–13 ovate pointed leaflets, which have undulating margins. The foliage has a balsam–citrus scent. Downy clusters of small white flowers are followed by leathery winged fruits, 11cm (4¼in) long, containing two seeds. Native to Mexico, Panama, and Peru; widely naturalized. ↕12–15m (40–50ft), ↔ 5–10m (15–30ft). var. *pereirae* syn. *M. pereirae* (balsam of Peru) has smaller leaflets.
HARDINESS Min. 15–18°C (59–64°F).
PARTS USED Seeds, oleo-resin, oil.
PROPERTIES A sweet, acid-tasting, aromatic herb that acts as an antiseptic and stimulating expectorant.
MEDICINAL USES Mainly as a pleasant-tasting ingredient in friar's balsam and cough mixtures; also as a base for pastilles (oleo-resin).
CULINARY USES Seeds of *M. balsamum* var. *pereirae* are added to *aguardiente* (Guatemala).
ECONOMIC USES Resin is used in commercial food flavouring (mainly for chewing gum, ice cream, confectionery, soft drinks, and bakery produce). Oil is used in perfumery.

MYRRHIS
Sweet Cicely

Apiaceae

A single species of aromatic perennial makes up this genus, which is native to Europe but widely naturalized elsewhere. *Myrrhis odorata* is found wild in cool damp areas, in grassland, and hedgerows. It is an excellent plant for rich moist soil, with its soft, anise-scented foliage and relatively large, shiny, black seeds. Its fern-like appearance complements other shade-tolerant herbs, such as *Chelidonium majus* (see p.165) and *Rheum palmatum* (see p.344). *Myrrhis odorata* contains a volatile oil, which includes anethole, as found in *Foeniculum vulgare* (see

M

Myristica fragrans

Myroxylon balsamum

Myrrhis odorata

p.215), *Illicium verum* (see p.242), and *Pimpinella anisum* (see p.317). This same constituent is also present in *Osmorhiza claytonii* (American sweet Cicely, see p.298).

CULTIVATION Moist, humus-rich soil in sun or shade.

PROPAGATION By seed sown when ripe; by division in autumn or spring. Seed may be slow to germinate. May self-sow prolifically in good conditions.

HARVEST Leaves are picked during the growing season and used fresh or frozen. Roots are lifted in autumn and used fresh, or dried for use in decoctions. Seeds are collected when green and used fresh.

■ *Myrrhis odorata* (garden myrrh, sweet chervil, sweet Cicely)
Large downy perennial with hollow stems and fern-like leaves, to 50cm (12in) long, which are often blotched white. Tiny white flowers appear in umbels from late spring, followed by ridged, brown-black fruits, to 2cm (¾in) long. Native to Europe. ↕ 1–2m (3–6ft), ↔ 60cm–1.2m (2–4ft).

HARDINESS Fully hardy.

PARTS USED Leaves, roots, seeds.

PROPERTIES A sweet, aromatic, expectorant herb that benefits the digestion.

MEDICINAL USES Internally for coughs, minor digestive complaints, and anaemia.

CULINARY USES Leaves are added to salads, soups, stews, and wine cups, and are used as a low-calorie sweetener and flavouring for stewed fruit, yogurt, and whipped cream. Roots are cooked as a vegetable and eaten cold in salads. Unripe seeds are eaten raw in salads.
▨ ▧ ▩ ▪ ◪

MYRTUS
Myrtle

Myrtaceae

Two species of aromatic evergreen shrubs belong to this genus, which occurs in Mediterranean regions. *Myrtus communis* makes a dense, wind-resistant hedge in mild areas. The dwarf subsp. *tarentina* is an ideal specimen and container plant. Variegated forms are less hardy. In ancient Greece, myrtle was sacred to Aphrodite, goddess of love and beauty. It is still carried today in wedding bouquets in the Middle East and elsewhere. The active compounds in *M. communis* are rapidly absorbed and give a violet-like scent

Myrtus communis

Myrtus communis 'Flore Pleno'

Myrtus communis subsp. *tarentina*

Myrtus communis 'Variegata'

to the urine within 15 minutes.

CULTIVATION Well-drained, neutral to alkaline soil in sun. Given sharply drained soil and protection from cold, *M. communis* may survive down to –10°C (14°F) outdoors. Even with optimum conditions, 'Variegata' rarely survives below –5°C (23°F). Trim plants in spring and remove damaged or dead shoots. Plants under cover may be damaged by whitefly and red spider mite.

PROPAGATION By seed sown in autumn (species only); by semi-ripe cuttings in late summer.

HARVEST Plants are cut with or without flowers and distilled for oil. Leaves are picked as required and used fresh, or dried for use in infusions. Flower buds are picked before opening and dried. Fruits are collected when ripe and dried for using whole or ground.

■ *Myrtus communis* (myrtle)
Erect shrub with lustrous, ovate–lanceolate leaves, to 5cm (2in) long, which have a juniper-like aroma when crushed. Fragrant white flowers, 3cm (1¼in) across, with golden stamens, appear in spring and summer, followed by blue-black berries, 1cm (⅜in) long. Native to Mediterranean and SW Europe. ↔ 3m (10ft). ■ 'Flore Pleno' has longer lasting, fully double, white flowers. ■ subsp. *tarentina* syn. 'Jenny Reitenbach', 'Microphylla', 'Nana' (Tarentum

myrtle) is a compact, free-flowering variant with narrowly elliptic leaves, to 2cm (¾in) long, smaller, pink-tinged flowers, and white fruits. ↔ 1.5m (5ft). subsp. *tarentina* 'Microphylla Variegata' has white-margined leaves. ■ 'Variegata' has leaves variegated grey-green and creamy white.

HARDINESS Fully hardy (borderline).

PARTS USED Whole plant, leaves, flower buds, fruits, oil.

PROPERTIES An aromatic astringent herb that is antiseptic and an effective decongestant.

MEDICINAL USES Internally for urinary infections (as a substitute for *Agathosma crenulata*, see p.106), vaginal discharge, bronchial congestion, sinusitis, and dry coughs. Externally for acne (oil), gum infections, and haemorrhoids.

CULINARY USES Leaves, flower buds, and fruits are used to flavour dishes of pork, lamb, and small birds, sauces, and liqueurs, such as *myrthe*, especially in Corsica and Sardinia. Fruits (known as mursins) are used as a spice in the Middle East.

ECONOMIC USES Oil is used in soaps, skin-care products, and perfumery; also as food flavouring.
▨ ▧ ▨ ▢ ▨ ▪ ◪ ◪

N

NARDOSTACHYS
Spikenard

Valerianaceae

A genus consisting of a single species of Asian perennial, found on rock ledges and undisturbed alpine slopes at 3000–5000m (1000–1600ft); it is closely related to *Valeriana* (see p.399). *Nardostachys grandiflora* is an attractive plant, rarely seen in cultivation today, but it was recommended for rock gardens in Victorian times. It is the spikenard of the Bible, mentioned in the Song of Solomon and source of the substance used to anoint the feet of Jesus at the Last Supper. The perfume extracted from the roots was a valuable commodity in the Roman Empire, worth 660 denarii per kg (300 denari per lb). (A denarius was a labourer's average daily wage.) It was used by the Moghul empress Nur Jahan to make rejuvenating cosmetics. The essential oil contains borneol acetate (similar to the main constituent of *Dryobalanops aromatica*, see p.197) and patchouli alcohol, as found in *Pogostemon cablin* (see p.325). As a herb, *Nardostachys* is regarded as similar but superior to *Valeriana officinalis* (see p.400) in Ayurvedic medicine, harmonizing the constitution and strengthening the mind. Habitat degradation and over-collection to satisfy increased international trade in the 1990s resulted in drastic reduction of wild populations. As a consequence, trade in *Nardostachys grandiflora* is now strictly regulated, and the species is fully protected throughout its range. In addition, a programme

Nardostachys grandiflora

Nasturtium officinale

of measures has been introduced to conserve and re-introduce the plant in its native habitats, and to encourage commercial cultivation.

CULTIVATION Well-drained, gritty, moisture-retentive soil in partial shade or shade from midday sun. Needs a cool root run. Dislikes rich soil. May be grown as an alpine in a deep clay pot.

PROPAGATION By seed sown when ripe; by division in spring; by cuttings of rhizomes in late winter. Requires light for germination.

HARVEST Roots are dried for oil distillation or use in decoctions.

■ *Nardostachys grandiflora* (*jatamansi*, nard, spikenard)
Small perennial with very fragrant, deep roots, stout aromatic rhizomes, clad in fibres from remains of previous leafstalks, and mostly basal, elliptic–lanceolate leaves, 15–20cm (6–8in) long. Small, pale rose-purple to pink flowers appear in panicles in summer. Native to the Himalayas, from Himachal Pradesh to Nepal, Sikkim, Bhutan, Tibet, and W China. ‡ 10–60cm (4–24in), ↔ 20–30cm (8–12in).

HARDINESS Fully hardy.

PARTS USED Roots, oil.

PROPERTIES A bitter, astringent, aromatic herb that improves digestion, calms the nerves, relaxes spasms, and lowers blood pressure.

MEDICINAL USES Internally for nervous indigestion, insomnia, depression, and tension headaches. Externally for rashes and as a deodorant.

ECONOMIC USES Oil is used in perfumery.

NASTURTIUM
Watercress

Brassicaceae

A genus of six species of perennials, distributed through Europe to C Asia. The plant commonly known as nasturtium is *Tropaeolum majus* (see p.394). Commercial cultivation of *Nasturtium officinale* (watercress) began in the 19th century; it is now grown in most parts of Europe. In some countries, such as New Zealand, it has become a serious weed of waterways.

Nasturtium officinale contains a volatile mustard oil and compounds similar to those in *Raphanus sativus* (see p.340), with a characteristic burning taste. It is also rich in vitamins and minerals, including iron, iodine, and calcium. Many watercress beds are stocked with mild-flavoured hybrids of *Nasturtium officinale*, which grow through the winter, allowing up to ten crops a year. *Nasturtium* comes from the Latin *nasus tortus*, "twisted nose", referring to the pungent taste of these plants.

CULTIVATION Shallow, flowing, slightly alkaline water, in sun, at about 10°C (50°F). May be grown in pots, using rich compost and standing the pots in a dish of water, changing the water daily. Three or four cuttings are sufficient for a 15–20cm (6–8in) pot. Pinch out to encourage bushiness and delay flowering.

PROPAGATION By root cuttings in water during the growing season.

HARVEST Leaves are cut as required and used whole or liquefied. Gathering from the wild is not recommended in view of the frequent occurrence in watercourses of pollutants and pathogenic organisms.

■ *Nasturtium officinale* syn. *Rorippa nasturtium-aquaticum* (watercress)
Aquatic evergreen perennial with floating, freely rooting stems and dark green, pungent-tasting, pinnate leaves divided into 3–5 pairs of elliptic to ovate leaflets and a broadly heart-shaped terminal leaflet. Tiny, four-petalled, white flowers are produced throughout summer, followed by upward-pointing, narrow pods, about 1cm (⅜in) long. ‡ 10–65cm (4–26in), ↔ indefinite.

HARDINESS Fully hardy.

PARTS USED Leaves, shoots.

PROPERTIES A bitter, pungent, stimulant herb that clears toxins, benefits the digestion, and has diuretic and expectorant effects.

MEDICINAL USES Internally for oedema, catarrh, bronchitis, wet coughs, skin eruptions, rheumatism, anaemia, debility associated with chronic disease, and gall bladder complaints.

CULINARY USES Traditionally eaten as a spring tonic. Leaves are added to salads, blended with

butter as a spread, made into soup, and sauce for fish. They are also used as a garnish, especially for cold salmon.

NELUMBIUM
Nelumbium speciosum. See *Nelumbo nucifera*.

NELUMBO
Lotus

Nelumbonaceae

This genus of two species of aquatic perennials occurs in eastern N America and warm parts of Asia to Australia. *Nelumbo nucifera* is grown worldwide in tropical pools for its large circular leaves and exquisite, chalice-shaped flowers. It is revered in ancient Indian, Chinese, Tibetan, and Egyptian cultures. To Hindus, it is sacred to Brahma as the jewel in the lotus (*om mani padma hum*). In Buddhist mythology, Buddha first appeared floating on a lotus and is traditionally depicted on a lotus throne. Specific parts of it are used in traditional Chinese medicine, where the earliest mention in medical texts, c.AD500, is of the seeds. *Nelumbo* is the Sinhalese name for these plants.

CULTIVATION Sunny position in rich heavy soil in still or slow-moving water, at least 60cm (24in) deep, or in large pots of rich wet compost under cover. May be invasive in good conditions outdoors.

PROPAGATION By seed sown at 25°C (77°F) covered by 5cm (2in) of water; by division in spring.

HARVEST Leaves and leafstalks are collected in summer and autumn; rhizomes in autumn and winter; stamens from early to midsummer; seeds and flower stalks with receptacles from mid- to late summer. All parts are dried for use in decoctions and powders. (Plumule and radicle are separated from seeds before drying.)

■ *Nelumbo nucifera* syn. *Nelumbium speciosum* (*padma*, sacred lotus)
Aquatic perennial with thick rhizomes and glaucous peltate leaves, to 80cm (32in) in diameter. Large, fragrant, pink to white flowers,

Nelumbo nucifera

Nelumbo nucifera 'Alba Grandiflora'

30cm (12in) across, are followed by "showerhead" receptacles, containing hard nuts. Native to Asia, from Iran to Japan, and N Australia. ‡ 2.5m (8ft) above water, ↔ indefinite; less in cultivation. ▣ 'Alba Grandiflora' has pure white flowers, 22–25cm (9–10in) across. ‡ 1.2–1.8m (4–6ft), ↔ 60–90cm (24–36in). 'Charles Thomas' has deep lavender-pink flowers, 15–20cm (6–8in) across. ‡ 60–90cm (2–3ft). 'Momo Botan' has deep pink flowers, 15cm (6in) across, shading to yellow in the centre. ‡ 60cm–1.2m (2–4ft). ▣ 'Rosea Plena' has double pink flowers, 25–35cm (10–14in) across. ‡ 1.2–1.5m (4–5ft).
HARDINESS Min. 1–7°C (34–45°F).
PARTS USED Leaves (*he ye*), stems i.e. leafstalk (*lian geng*) or flower stalk with receptacle attached (*lian fang*), rhizomes (*ou jie*), flower stamens (*lian xu*), seed plumule and radicle (*lian zi xin*), seeds (*lian zi*).
PROPERTIES An astringent cooling herb that controls bleeding, lowers blood pressure and fever, sedates the heart energy, and acts as a tonic for the spleen and kidney energies.
MEDICINAL USES Internally for haemorrhage, nosebleed, heavy menstruation (rhizome);

Nelumbo nucifera 'Rosea Plena'

hypertension, insomnia, restlessness (plumule and radicle); diarrhoea, poor digestion, insomnia, palpitations (seeds); urinary frequency, premature ejaculation (stamens); bleeding gastric ulcer, heavy menstruation, postpartum haemorrhage (flower stalk). In Ayurvedic medicine, mainly as cooling remedies for bleeding disorders, and tonics for the heart and reproductive centres (rhizome and seeds).
CULINARY USES Rhizomes are cooked as vegetables, pickled, or conserved; also a source of edible starch. Seeds are eaten raw, roasted, pickled, candied, puffed (*makhana*), or used as a garnish. Young leaves are eaten raw or lightly stir-fried. Dried whole leaves are used as a wrapping for *dim sum* and other foods. Stamens and pollen are used to scent tea.

⊠ ⊿ ▩ ⊞ ▪ ⊿ ⊡

NEPETA
Lamiaceae

There are about 250 species of perennials, and a few annuals, in this genus, occurring in a variety of habitats in all but tropical regions of the northern hemisphere. *Nepeta cataria* (catmint) is a medicinal herb with little merit as a garden plant, though widely grown in herb gardens. Its names refer to the stimulant effect it has on most cats, which eat and roll in the plant with obvious pleasure. The constituent responsible for this effect is thought to be actinidine, an iridoid glycoside, similar to that found in *Valeriana officinalis* (see p.400). Some cats do not respond to catmint, perhaps because their reaction may be genetically determined. The hybrid *Nepeta × faassenii*, also commonly known as "catmint", is a popular ornamental but has less effect on some cats and no medicinal properties. *Nepeta cataria* contains citronellol (as found in *Melissa officinalis*, see p.274), pulegone (as found in *Mentha pulegium*, see p.277), and thymol (as found in *Thymus vulgaris*, see p.390). The closely related *Schizonepeta tenuifolia* (Japanese catnip, *jing jie*) is used in Chinese medicine for haemorrhages, especially postnatal bleeding and heavy menstruation, colds, measles, and nettle rash. It is an attractive plant with lobed divided leaves and dense spikes of light purple flowers; the foliage is aromatic, with a pennyroyal-like fragrance. Research has shown that Japanese catnip increases surface blood flow.
CULTIVATION Moist, well-drained soil in sun. Seedlings reach flowering size in the first year. Cut back hard for a second harvest. Powdery mildew may damage leaves. *Nepeta cataria* is said to repel cabbage pests, aphids (including peach aphids), flea beetles, cucumber beetles, squash bugs, and ants, if planted among garden plants and vegetables.
PROPAGATION By seed sown in autumn; by division in spring or autumn; by stem-tip or softwood cuttings in early summer.
HARVEST Plants are cut when in bud and dried for use in infusions. Leaves are picked when young for culinary purposes and used fresh or dried.

Nepeta cataria

▣ *Nepeta cataria* (catmint, catnip) Pungent hairy perennial with erect branched stems and grey-green, ovate, toothed leaves, to 7cm (3in) long. White, purple-spotted, tubular flowers are borne in whorls in summer. Native to Europe and SW and C Asia. ‡ 30cm–1.5m (1–5ft), ↔ 23–90cm (9–36in). 'Citriodora' is shorter and lemon-scented. Often preferred for tea; is less attractive to cats. ‡ 30cm–1m (1–3ft), ↔ 23–60cm (9–24in).
HARDINESS Fully hardy.
PARTS USED Whole plant, leaves.
PROPERTIES A bitter, astringent, cooling herb with a camphoraceous, pennyroyal–thyme aroma. It lowers fever, relaxes spasms, increases perspiration, and has carminative and sedative effects.
MEDICINAL USES Internally for feverish illnesses (especially colds, and influenza), insomnia, excitability, palpitations, nervous indigestion, diarrhoea, stomach upsets, colic, and digestion-related headaches. May be combined with *Achillea millefolium* (see p.99) and *Sambucus nigra* (see p.357) for feverish stages of colds and influenza, and with *Glechoma hederacea* (see p.225) for congestive stages. Externally for haemorrhoids, and as a rub for rheumatism and arthritis.
CULINARY USES Leaves are infused for a mint-like tea (lemon-scented in the case of 'Citriodora'), and added to salads, sauces, and stews.
ECONOMIC USES Dried catnip is used to stuff cat toys.

⊿ ▨ ▪ ⊿ ⊿

Nepeta glechoma. See *Glechoma hederacea*.
Nepeta hederacea. See *Glechoma hederacea*.

NIGELLA
Ranunculaceae

Twenty species of annuals belong to this Eurasian genus, which occurs mainly on rocky ground, wasteland, and fallow fields. Several are grown as ornamentals and for dried floral arrangements. Most important as a herb is *N. sativa* (black cumin, *kalaunji*), which in the Old Testament is referred to as "fitches", from

the Hebrew *ketzah*, "vetch". Black cumin is a popular spice in India, Turkey, Greece, and the Middle East (especially in Egypt and Tunisia). The seeds have a spicy fruity taste and were important as a seasoning before the introduction of pepper (see *Piper nigrum*, p.321) to Europe from SE Asia in the 5th century AD. As a medicinal herb it has a long history of use in Islamic medicine, and is especially important in Unani medicine. According to the Prophet Mohammed, black cumin is a cure for all diseases except old age. *Nigella sativa* should not be confused with *N. damascena* (love-in-a-mist), the familiar garden annual. The two species look similar but have no uses in common. Essential oil is distilled from *N. damascena* for lipsticks and perfumery. *Nigella* is the diminutive of the Latin *niger*, "black", referring to the black seeds.
CULTIVATION Well-drained soil in sun.
PROPAGATION By seed sown *in situ* in autumn or spring.
HARVEST Seeds are collected when ripe and dried for oil extraction; used whole or ground, or in infusions.

◼ *Nigella sativa* (black cumin, fennel flower, *kalaunji*, *kammum aswad*)
Erect branched annual with pinnately divided leaves, 2–3cm (¾–1¼in) long. Small, white, blue-tinged flowers, to 4.5cm (1¾in) across, appear in summer, followed by inflated fruits with horn-like styles, containing aromatic black seeds. Native to SW Asia. ‡ 30cm (12in), ↔ 23cm (9in).
HARDINESS Fully hardy.
PARTS USED Seeds, oil.
PROPERTIES An aromatic laxative herb that stimulates the uterus, increases lactation, benefits the digestion, reduces inflammation, and expels intestinal worms.
MEDICINAL USES
Internally for painful menstruation, postpartum contractions, insufficient lactation, poor appetite, fevers (especially intermittent), and worms (especially in children). Externally for abscesses,

Nigella sativa

haemorrhoids, skin diseases, and orchitis. Contraindicated during pregnancy.
CULINARY USES Seeds flavour bread, pastries, curries, meat, chutneys, sauces, vegetable dishes, Middle Eastern fermented foods, and cheeses.
▢ ▨ ▪ ☑

NYMPHAEA
Water lily

Nymphaeaceae

A cosmopolitan genus of 50 species of aquatic perennials with floating leaves. Ten species and many hybrids are grown as ornamentals, including tropical and hardy kinds, in a great variety of colours and sizes. These include the European *N. alba* and American *N. tuberosa*, which resemble *N. odorata* in appearance and are used interchangeably for medicinal purposes. *Nymphaea odorata* has a long history of medicinal use among native N Americans. In the 19th century the powdered rhizome was widely sold by apothecaries for making poultices. Research has shown that the flowers of *N. alba* are anaphrodisiac, confirming its reputation for depressing sexual function. *Nymphaea lotus* (white lotus) was one of the most important plants in ancient Egyptian art, ritual, food, and medicine. The flowers were a common ingredient of oils, ointments, poultices, and enemas; the leaves appear in remedies for liver disease; the roots were eaten raw or cooked; the seeds were added to bread. White lotus flowers are still used by Egyptian herbalists for their cooling calming effects; *N. caerulea* (blue lotus) was similarly venerated and used medicinally. It is found in tropical and N Africa, where it is used internally for kidney or bladder complaints, and externally as a soothing antiseptic remedy for sunburn, heat rashes, and skin inflammations. *Nymphaea* is from the Greek *nymphaia*, "water nymph".
CULTIVATION Rich soil in still water, to 45cm (18in) deep (*N. odorata*); rich soil in still water, at least 30cm (12in) deep (*N. lotus*). Both species need full sun. Dormant tubers of *N. lotus* may be stored in moist sand. Aphids may attack plants. Water lily beetles and caterpillars may eat leaves. Deep water and over-rich soil inhibit flowering.
PROPAGATION By seed sown when ripe at 10–13°C (50–55°F) for hardy species and 23–27°C (73–81°F) for tender species; by offsets or division of rhizomes in spring or early summer. Sow seed on surface of wet compost, covering with 2.5cm (1in) of water.
HARVEST Flowers are cut when open and used fresh for infusions. Rootstocks are lifted when dormant and used fresh or dried for decoctions (*N. lotus*). Fruits and seeds are harvested when ripe and used fresh. Rhizomes are lifted in autumn, after the leaves have died down, and are dried for decoctions, liquid extracts, and powders (*N. odorata*).

◼ *Nymphaea lotus* (Egyptian lotus, white lotus)
Aquatic perennial with a tuberous rootstock and rounded, toothed, dark green leaves, to 50cm (20in) across, which have wavy margins. White, sometimes pink-tinged, slightly fragrant flowers,

Nymphaea lotus

to 25cm (10in) across, are held above the surface, opening at night or during the day. Globose fruits containing numerous ribbed seeds ripen under water. Grows from Egypt to tropical and SE Africa. ↔ 2–3m (6–10ft).
HARDINESS Min. 10°C (50°F).
PARTS USED Rootstock, flowers, fruits, seeds.
PROPERTIES A soothing astringent herb that has diuretic and tranquillizing effects, and is reputedly detoxicant and aphrodisiac.
MEDICINAL USES Internally in Ayurvedic medicine for dyspepsia, enteritis, diarrhoea, fevers, haemorrhoids, urinary problems, and insomnia (rootstock); palpitations (flowers); blood in urine from snake bite (juice of fruits mixed with *Setaria italica*, or foxtail millet, and salt). Seeds, crushed in water, are a traditional remedy for diabetes.
CULINARY USES Rootstock is boiled as a starchy vegetable, and ground into flour in parts of India, Sri Lanka, and China. Unripe fruits are eaten raw. Seeds are roasted, fried, pickled, added to curries, or ground and mixed with flour for baking.
▨ ▨ ▨ ▨ ▪ ☑ ▣

◼ *Nymphaea odorata* (fragrant water lily, white pond lily)
Aquatic perennial with stout rhizomes and ovate to rounded, leathery, glossy leaves, 15–30cm (6–12in) across, which are cleft at the base and often have purple-green undersides. Fragrant

Nymphaea odorata

N

Nymphaea odorata var. *rosea*

white flowers, 10–22cm (4–9in) across, with yellow stamens, appear in summer. Native to NE USA. ↔ 1.2–1.8m (4–6ft). ▣ var. *rosea* has deep pink, strongly scented flowers, to 10cm (4in) across. Native to E USA.

HARDINESS Fully hardy.

PARTS USED Rhizomes.

PROPERTIES A soothing, astringent, antiseptic herb; relieves pain and has alterative effects.

MEDICINAL USES Internally for tuberculosis, chronic bronchial complaints, diarrhoea, dysentery, gastrointestinal inflammation, gonorrhoea, vaginal discharge, cystitis, prostatitis, uterine infections, and uterine cancer. Externally for boils, abscesses, conjunctivitis, sore throat, and vaginitis. Combined with *Prunus serotina* (see p.334) for bronchial complaints, and with *Linum usitatissimum* (see p.263) and *Ulmus rubra* (see p.397) for boils.

CULINARY USES Leaves are added to soups and stews. Flower buds are pickled or cooked as a vegetable.

▨ ▩ ✎

O

OCIMUM
Basil

Lamiaceae

About 35 species of aromatic annuals, evergreen perennials and shrubs belong to this genus, which occurs in most warm and tropical regions, especially Africa. All basils need ample warmth and light, and do not thrive outdoors in areas with cool summers. The most widely grown basil is *O. basilicum*, a highly variable species in terms of appearance and aroma. Purple-leafed variants, such as 'Dark Opal' and 'Purple Ruffles', are ornamental and can be grown as container or bedding plants; they are also used for giving a purple tint to basil vinegar. Basils are rich in volatile oils, which often vary considerably within the same species and according to growing conditions. Some 20 or more constituents have been isolated, the main ones being methyl chavicol (anise), methyl cinnamate (cinnamon), eugenol (clove), citral (lemon), geraniol (rose), linalol (lilac/orange blossom), thymol (thyme), and camphor. Variants in which certain constituents predominate are known as chemotypes; *O. americanum* has three distinct chemotypes: floral-lemony, camphoraceous, and spicy. Its essential oil characteristically contains 70–88 per cent methyl chavicol, an anise-scented compound, which in excess may be carcinogenic. The Mexican *O. selloi* (sometimes incorrectly given as *O. sellowii*) has an unusual scent resembling green peppers. In green peppers this characteristic aroma is due to pyrazines, which are difficult to detect in essential oil. Analysis of *O. selloi* shows that elemicin, methyl eugenol, alpha-copaene, and beta-caryophyllene predominate. The composition of oils in a particular plant affects its aroma, flavour, and uses, though it may not differ in appearance from other plants of the same species. Mediterranean types of *O. basilicum* contain mainly linalol and methyl chavicol, with little or no camphor, which give the typical, sweet, basil flavour; E European types are characterized by methyl cinnamate; SE Asian types contain a high proportion of clove-scented eugenol; and, in Réunion or African types, camphor and methyl chavicol predominate. Hybridization in cultivation further complicates the picture. The most widely grown basils for commercial drying and oil extraction go under many different names,

not necessarily recognized by botanists as distinct cultivars. Though mainly grown for their aromatic leaves, most basils also have seeds that are high in mucilage and have different uses from the foliage. Some basils are important in folklore and religion. The common name "basil" may be associated with the basilisk (a mythical, serpent-like creature whose glance and breath were fatal), as it was believed that basil could turn into a scorpion. *Ocimum tenuiflorum*, regarded in India as the most sacred plant after *Nelumbo nucifera* (lotus, p.287), is grown in most Hindu homes and around temples, for its protective influence; holding basil root protects against thunder, and wearing a string of beads made from basil stems wards off infection and "induces religious tendency and longevity" (*Indian Materia Medica*, 1976). The tropical American *Ocimum campechianum* syn. *O. micranthum* (duppy basil, mosquito bush/plant, Peruvian basil) is crushed and hung in homes to repel mosquitoes; "duppy" is a word used in the Caribbean for a ghost or a mosquito. It also goes by the name "married man pork" and is used to flavour soups and stews. *Ocimum* is from the Greek *okimon*, used by Theophrastus for basil.

CULTIVATION Rich, light, well-drained to dry soil, pH5–8, in sun. Pinch out growing tips to encourage bushiness and delay flowering. *Ocimum* × *citriodorum* dislikes transplanting so is best sown *in situ*. Slugs, aphids, whitefly, red spider mite, and *Botrytis* may attack plants. Basil is often used in companion planting because it is said to repel aphids, asparagus beetles, mites, and tomato hornworms, and to slow the growth of milkweed bugs.

PROPAGATION By seed sown in spring at 13°C (55°F); by softwood cuttings in spring (perennials and shrubs).

HARVEST Whole plants (*O. americanum*, *O. basilicum*, *O. gratissimum*, *O. tenuiflorum*) are cut just before flowering begins and dried or distilled for oil. Leaves are picked during the

Ocimum basilicum

Ocimum basilicum 'Cinnamon'

Ocimum 'African Blue'

Ocimum basilicum 'Dark Opal'

Ocimum basilicum 'Genovese'

growing season and used fresh or juiced, or dried for infusions and decoctions. *Ocimum tenuiflorum* is prepared as powder and medicated ghee. Seeds (*O. americanum*, *O. basilicum*, *O. tenuiflorum*) are collected when ripe and dried for decoctions. Roots are harvested and dried for decoctions.

◼ *Ocimum* 'African Blue'

(*O. kilimandscharicum* × *O. basilicum* 'Dark Opal')
Perennial with purple stems and dark green, purple-veined leaves, to 5cm (2in) long, which have a sweet camphoraceous aroma. Small purple flowers are produced in purple-flushed spikes. Sterile hybrid. ‡ 60cm–1.5m (2–5ft), ↔ 30cm–1m (1–3ft).
HARDINESS Min. 10–15°C (50–59°F).
PARTS USED Leaves.
PROPERTIES An aromatic herb with a balsam–camphor scent.
CULINARY USES Usable but inferior for flavouring or tea.

Ocimum americanum syn. *O. canum*,

O. 'Maeng Lak'/'Meng Luk' (hairy basil, hoary basil)
Annual or short-lived, much-branched perennial, woody at the base, with hairy stems and narrowly ovate to elliptic, entire to shallowly toothed leaves, 5–8cm (2–3in) long. White or pale mauve flowers are produced in whorls, to 1cm (½in) apart. Native to tropical and southern Africa, Madagascar, Sri Lanka, India, China. ‡ 15–70cm (6–28in), ↔ 8–38cm (3–15in). 'Spice' has heart-shaped, hairy, strongly veined leaves, 5–6cm (2–2½in) long, with toothed margins, and pale violet flowers on hairy stems, 13–15cm (5–6in) long. Has a spicy, camphor-like aroma. ‡ 50cm (20in), ↔ 30cm (12in).
HARDINESS Min. 10°C (50°F).
PARTS USED Leaves, seeds, oil.

PROPERTIES An aromatic tonic herb that lowers fever and has expectorant effects. May have a cinnamon, camphor, or citrus-like scent.
MEDICINAL USES Internally for fever, dysentery, catarrh, and malaria.
CULINARY USES Leaves are used to flavour curries, soups, salads, meat dishes, and stuffings. Seeds, soaked in water, are mixed with coconut milk and sugar as a cooling drink.
ECONOMIC USES Oil is used in perfumery, soaps, and dental products.

◼ *Ocimum basilicum* (basil, sweet basil)
Erect, much-branched, aromatic annual or short-lived perennial, woody at the base, with narrowly ovate to elliptic, entire or toothed, bright green leaves, to 5cm (2in) long. Small, white, tubular flowers are borne in whorls, to 2cm (¾in) apart. Native to tropical Asia. ‡ 30–60cm (12–24in), ↔ 15–30cm (6–15in). ◼ 'Cinnamon' has purple-veined leaves, lavender-pink flowers, and a cinnamon-like aroma. A hardier Mexican cultivar. ‡ 60cm (24in). 'Cuban' is vigorous, columnar, and hardier than the species, with small, light green leaves and a spicy flavour. ◼ 'Dark Opal' has purple-black leaves, 5–7cm (2–3in) long, cerise-pink flowers, and a delicate aroma. ‡ 60cm (24in), ↔ 30cm (12in). ◼ 'Genovese' syn. 'Perfume Basil' has a tall uniform habit, slightly wrinkled leaves, and is slow to bolt. An Italian strain, widely regarded as the best for pesto. ‡ 45–50cm (18–20in). 'Green Bouquet' is a rounded bushy plant with small leaves, to 1.5cm (½in) long, and white flowers. It has a floral, spicy, clove-like flavour. ‡ 25–45cm (10–18in). 'Green Globe' forms a dense ball of tiny leaves, with a spicy flavour. ‡↔ 50–70cm (20–28in). ◼ 'Green Ruffles' has large, light green, crinkled, deeply toothed leaves. 'Horapha' syn. 'Anise', 'Glycyrrhiza', 'Licorice', 'Thai' has purple-flushed leaves, pink flowers with purple bracts, and a sweet, anise–liquorice aroma. Much used in SE Asian

cuisines. ‡ 60cm–1m (2–3ft) ↔ 30–45cm (12–18in). 'Mammoth' syn. 'Monstruoso' has very large leaves, 15cm (6in) long, with a fine flavour. Dries well and is good for wrapping foods. ◼ 'Napolitano' syn. var. *crispum*, var. *difforme*, 'Italian', 'Lettuce Leaf', 'Neopolitano' (curly basil) has large, light green, crinkled leaves with a sweet flavour. Originally from Naples (Italy); much used for pesto. ‡ 45cm (18in). 'New Guinea' has very narrow, purple-flushed leaves, small, pale violet flowers, and a strong liquorice–cinnamon aroma. 'Nufar' is a Genovese-type basil with high resistance to *Fusarium* wilt. 'Osmin' has very dark purple leaves. ‡ 50cm (20in). ◼ 'Purple Ruffles' has large, dark purple, crinkled leaves, with deeply toothed margins, and pink flowers. May partially revert to green. ‡ 45–60cm (18–24in). var. *purpurascens* has purple-flushed or splashed leaves. ◼ 'Rubin' syn. 'Red Rubin' has bronze-purple leaves and a fine flavour. ◼ 'Siam Queen' has red-purple stems, large leaves, 8–10cm (3–4in) long, 4–5cm (1½–2in) wide, and purple flowers. Similar in flavour to 'Horapha'. ‡ 75cm–1m (30–36in). 'Spicy Globe' forms a compact mound of tiny, very fragrant leaves. ‡ 25cm (10in), ↔ 30–45cm (12–18in). 'Sweet Dani' has a strong lemon aroma. ‡ 65cm (26in). ◼ 'Well-Sweep Miniature Purple' syn. 'Mini Purpurascens Well-Sweep' is compact, with small, purple-flushed leaves and a spicy flavour. ‡ 20cm (8in), ↔ 15cm (6in).
HARDINESS Min. 10°C (50°F).
PARTS USED Whole plant, leaves, seeds, oil.
PROPERTIES A restorative, warming, aromatic herb that relaxes spasms, lowers fever, improves digestion, and is effective against bacterial infections and intestinal parasites. It has a mild sedative action.
MEDICINAL USES Internally for feverish illnesses (especially colds and influenza), poor digestion, nausea, abdominal cramps, gastro-enteritis, migraine, insomnia, low spirits, anxiety,

O

Ocimum basilicum 'Green Ruffles'

Ocimum basilicum 'Napolitano'

Ocimum basilicum 'Purple Ruffles'

Ocimum basilicum 'Rubin'

Ocimum basilicum 'Siam Queen'

Ocimum basilicum 'Well-Sweep Miniature Purple'

and exhaustion. Externally for acne, loss of smell, insect stings, snake bite, and skin infections.

CULINARY USES Leaves are added to salads, and used to flavour tomatoes and tomato-based dishes, pasta sauces (notably pesto), vegetables (especially beans, peppers, and aubergines), soups (*soupe au pistou*), and herb oils and vinegars. Seeds soaked in water make a refreshing drink.

ECONOMIC USES Oil is used in perfumery, aromatherapy, and commercial food flavouring; also in dental products and insect-repellents.

▨ ▣ ▩ ▩ ▣ ▨ ▨

■ *Ocimum × citriodorum* (*kemangi*, lemon basil)
Bushy annual with thin, narrowly ovate, slightly grey-green, citrus-scented leaves. Small white flowers are followed by lemon-scented seeds. Natural hybrid between *O. americanum* and *O. basilicum* that back-crosses to *O. basilicum*, producing further hybrids. Grows from SE Asia to NE Africa. ‡ 30–45cm (12–18in), ↔ 25cm (10in). 'Lesbos' syn. 'Aussie Sweetie', 'Greek Column' has a narrowly upright, columnar habit and small leaves with a typical, sweet basil flavour; seldom blooms. ‡ 90cm (36in). ■ 'Mrs Burns' Lemon' is robust, with large, lemon-scented leaves and white to pink flowers. An old New Mexican cultivar. ‡ 1m (39in).

HARDINESS Min. 10°C (50°F).

PARTS USED Leaves, seeds.

PROPERTIES An aromatic herb with a strong, lemon–basil flavour.

CULINARY USES Leaves are used with fish and chicken, and in herb vinegars. Seeds are soaked in water to make a tonic drink.

▨ ▩ ▨ ▣

■ *Ocimum gratissimum* syn. *O. suave*, *O. viride* (clove basil, East Indian basil, fever plant, shrubby basil, tree basil)
Shrubby, much-branched perennial, woody at the base, with purple stems and velvety, lanceolate, pointed, downy leaves, to 15cm (6in) long, which have toothed margins and a sweet, clove-like or lemon scent, according to chemotype. Cream to pale green-yellow flowers, with short purplish hairs and pointed green bracts, are borne in spikes, 12–15cm (5–6in) long. Native to India, Sri Lanka, Java, and tropical Africa and America. ‡ 1.3–2m (4½–6ft), ↔ 60cm–1m (2–3ft). var. *viride* (green basil, tea bush, West African basil) has a thyme aroma, containing 32–65 per cent thymol.

HARDINESS Min. 10°C (50°F).

PARTS USED Leaves, seeds, oil.

PROPERTIES An aromatic, stimulant, antiseptic herb that improves digestion, relieves spasms, expels intestinal parasites, and lowers fever. It is diuretic and expectorant, and also insect-repellent. Aroma depends on chemotype – predominantly thymol (thyme-scented) or eugenol (clove-scented).

MEDICINAL USES Internally for urinary disorders (seeds), fevers, headache, impotence, diarrhoea, dysentery, postpartum problems, and worms in children (leaves, leaf juice). Externally in baths for rheumatism and lumbago, and chewed for toothache.

CULINARY USES Leaves are infused for tea, and are used for flavouring; var. *viride* is a substitute for thyme in stuffings for poultry.

ECONOMIC USES Plants are grown to repel mosquitoes. Oil is used in perfumery and insect-repellents.

▨ ▣ ▩ ▩ ▨ ▨ ▣

Ocimum kilimandscharicum (camphor basil, feverplant)
Perennial shrub with downy branches and oblong to ovate, pointed, tapering leaves, 3–5cm (1¼–2in) long, which are hairy on both sides and sharply toothed. Creamy white flowers, with exserted stamens, are produced in long racemes. Native to E Africa. ‡ 1–1.2m (3–4ft), ↔ 60cm (2ft).

HARDINESS Min. 5°C (41°F).

PARTS USED Leaves, seeds.

PROPERTIES An aromatic herb that lowers fever and repels insects.

MEDICINAL USES Internally for malaria and other feverish infections. Leaves and seeds used to repel insects, especially mosquitoes.

ECONOMIC USES A commercial source of camphor.

▨ ▩ ▩ ▨ ▣

■ *Ocimum minimum* syn. *O. basilicum* var. *minimum* (bush basil, Greek basil)
Compact annual with very small, strongly scented leaves, less than 1cm (½in) long. Tiny white flowers occur in whorls or in terminal spikes. Native to India and Sri Lanka. ↔ 15–30cm (6–12in).

HARDINESS Min. 10°C (50°F).

PARTS USED Leaves.

PROPERTIES As for *O. basilicum*.

CULINARY USES As for *O. basilicum*.

▨ ▨ ▣

■ *Ocimum tenuiflorum* syn. *O. sanctum* (holy basil, sacred basil, *tulsi*)
Much-branched, softly hairy perennial with woody-based, often purplish stems and downy, toothed, often purple-veined and purple-flushed, ovate leaves, to 3.5cm (1½in) long, which have a spicy pungent aroma. Very small, purple-pink flowers are borne in slender racemes in summer. Native to India, Sri Lanka, and Malaysia. ‡ 30cm–60cm (12–24in), ↔ 15–30cm (6–12in). 'Purple' syn. 'Krishna Tulsi' has pronounced purple coloration and a sweet, clove-like flavour.

HARDINESS Min. 10°C (50°F).

PARTS USED Whole plant, roots, leaves, stems, seeds, oil.

PROPERTIES A pungently aromatic, warming, antiseptic herb that lowers fever, reduces

Ocimum × citriodorum

Ocimum × citriodorum 'Mrs Burns' Lemon'

Ocimum gratissimum

Ocimum minimum

Ocimum tenuiflorum

O

inflammation, relaxes spasms, clears bacterial infections, strengthens the immune and nervous systems, and benefits the digestive respiratory systems. It is considered tonic and adaptogenic, and lowers blood pressure and blood sugar levels.

MEDICINAL USES Internally for gonorrhoea (leaves and roots), malaria (roots), feverish illnesses, and gastric problems (especially in children), colds, coughs, influenza, bronchitis, pleurisy, asthma, sinusitis, headaches, rheumatism, arthritis, abdominal distension and cramps, diabetes, low libido, and negativity. In Ayurvedic medicine, often mixed with *Piper nigrum* (see p.321), *Zingiber officinale* (see p.411), and honey to lower fever or prevent infection. Externally for skin and ear infections, mouth ulcers, stings, and bites.

CULINARY USES Fresh leaves are added to salads and used to flavour fruit dishes, jellies, preserves, and sweet breads. Dried leaves are an ingredient of Ethiopian spice mixtures. Seeds are soaked in water to make a cooling drink.

ECONOMIC USES Stems are cut into beads for rosaries and amulets. Seeds are made into tonics. Oil is used as an insect-repellent and antibiotic.

OENANTHE

Apiaceae

Some 30 species of creeping perennials from wet places in the northern hemisphere, South Africa, and Australia belong to this genus. It includes several extremely poisonous plants, such as *O. crocata* (hemlock water dropwort), so great care must be taken over identification of wild specimens. The only species common in cultivation is *O. javanica*, plus its cultivar 'Flamingo', which is a colourful plant for waterside plantings or boggy ground. *Oenanthe javanica* is edible and widely grown as a pot-herb in Asian countries, where it often occurs as a weed of paddy fields. It is also used in traditional Chinese medicine, and in folk medicine in Vietnam.

CULTIVATION Damp to wet soil in sun or partial shade. Invasive.

PROPAGATION By division or stem-tip cuttings

Oenanthe javanica

Oenanthe javanica 'Flamingo'

in spring. Roots readily in water.

HARVEST Young shoots are picked for culinary use from autumn to spring in warm areas, and from spring to summer in areas with cold winters. Whole plant, leaves, and fruits are collected later in the growing season for medicinal use, usually in the form of decoctions.

◉ ***Oenanthe javanica*** syn. *O. japonica*, *O. stolonifera* (Korean watercress, *seri*, Vietnamese celery, water dropwort) Creeping aromatic perennial with triangular pinnate leaves, 7–15cm (3–6in) long, divided into narrowly ovate, toothed segments. Tiny white flowers are produced in umbels in summer, then four-angled fruits, 4mm (⅛in) long. Found from India to Japan, also in Taiwan, Malaysia, and N Australia (Queensland). ‡ 20–80cm (8–32in), ↔ 90cm (36in). ◉ 'Flamingo' has pink, white, and cream variegation. ‡ 15–20cm (6–8in).

HARDINESS Frost hardy.

PARTS USED Whole plant, leaves, young shoots, fruits.

PROPERTIES A pleasant-tasting, aromatic herb with cleansing, diuretic, and carminative effects. It lowers fever and controls bleeding.

MEDICINAL USES Internally for fever in influenza, blood in urine, and heavy menstruation. Externally as a poultice for poisonous bites, abscesses, and malignant swellings.

CULINARY USES Young shoots are eaten raw, steamed, stir-fried, or added to other dishes; also as flavouring for soups. Traditionally eaten with six other herbs in Japan during festivals on 7 and 15 January.

OENOTHERA

Evening primrose

Onagraceae

About 125 species of annuals, biennials, and perennials belong to this N American genus, many of which are widely naturalized in other parts of the world. They are related to *Epilobium* spp. (willow herb), but not to *Primula* spp. (primrose, see p.330). *Oenothera biennis* is a tall plant with scented flowers, which thrives in very poor soil; it naturalizes

well in sandy coastal gardens, steep banks, and gravel. According to Mrs Grieve (*A Modern Herbal*, 1931), a drug was made from the leaves and stem peelings of *O. biennis* to treat asthma, gastrointestinal disorders, whooping cough, and "certain female complaints, such as pelvic fullness". The medicinal uses of evening primrose oil are a recent discovery, following scientific research in the 1980s that demonstrated its effectiveness for a wide range of intractable complaints. The oil contains gammalinolenic acid (GLA), an unsaturated fatty acid that functions as a precursor in the production of hormone-like substances. Through deficiencies in the diet or digestion, this fatty acid may be absent or blocked, causing disorders that affect uterine muscles, blood vessels, nervous system, and metabolism. Evening primrose oil is also produced from *O. glazioviana* and *O. parviflora*. GLA is also found in the seeds of *Borago officinalis* (see p.145) and *Ribes nigrum* (see p.345). A drug produced from GLA has shown promising results in the treatment of various cancers, notably pancreatic cancer. *Oenothera* may derive from the Greek *oinos*, "wine", and *thera*, "hunt", from a name given by Theophrastus to a plant whose roots were eaten to arouse desire for wine.

CULTIVATION Well-drained to dry soil, including sandy and stony soils, in sun. Plants may succumb to root rot in wet conditions. Powdery mildew may attack leaves. Self-sows freely in optimum conditions.

PROPAGATION By seed sown in autumn.

HARVEST Leaves, stem bark, flowers, and immature pods are collected in summer and used fresh. Seeds are collected when ripe and pressed for oil, which is combined with vitamin E to prevent oxidation.

◉ ***Oenothera biennis*** (evening primrose) Erect annual or biennial with a rosette of oblanceolate basal leaves, 20cm (8in) long. Yellow, bowl-shaped flowers, to 5cm (2in) across, open in the evening throughout summer and autumn, followed by downy pods containing tiny seeds. Native to eastern N America; widely naturalized. ‡ 1–1.5m (3–5ft), ↔ 22–30cm (9–12in).

HARDINESS Fully hardy.

Oenothera biennis

PARTS USED Leaves, stem bark, flowers, pods, oil.

PROPERTIES An astringent soothing herb. Oil is alterative, regulating hormonal systems.

MEDICINAL USES Internally for whooping cough, asthma, and digestive problems (leaves, stem bark, flowers). Externally for rheumatic pain (leaves, stem bark, flowers). Internally for premenstrual and menopausal syndromes, circulatory problems (such as intermittent claudication), eczema, acne, brittle nails, hyperactivity in children, rheumatoid arthritis, coronary artery disease, complications of diabetes, alcohol-related liver damage, and multiple sclerosis (oil). Contraindicated in schizophrenia, and with phenothiazine drugs in the management of epilepsy. Excess may have laxative effects and cause abdominal pain. Externally for dry skin, scaly and itchy skin disorders, and brittle nails (oil).

CULINARY USES Young leaves are added to salads or cooked as a pot-herb. Flowers are edible. Parsnip-like roots are cooked as vegetables or added to soups and stews. Immature pods are steamed or stir-fried.

ECONOMIC USES Oil is added to food supplements, skin products, and cosmetics.

OLDENLANDIA

Rubiaceae

This large genus, consisting of about 300 species of annuals, perennials, and shrubs, occurs through the tropics and subtropics. Few are ornamental or have practical uses, though *O. umbellata* (chay, Indian madder) yields a dye used for turbans. *Oldenlandia diffusa* is a weed of moist ground and fields. It has a long history in Chinese folk medicine, and has come to prominence in recent years following pharmacological research. In traditional Chinese medicine it is renowned as a remedy for snake bite, especially of pit vipers. *Oldenlandia hedyotidea* is used in some parts of China for similar purposes. Leaves and roots have expectorant properties, and the root is a specific for snake bite. In Vietnam, *O. capitellata* is used for mouth ulcers and peptic ulcers, and *O. corymbosa* is known in folk medicine as a febrifuge; the latter is also used in India and the Philippines.

CULTIVATION Damp soil in partial shade.

PROPAGATION By seed sown in spring.

HARVEST Plants are cut in summer and dried for use in decoctions and syrups.

Oldenlandia diffusa (snake-needle grass)
Densely branched, prostrate annual with linear leaves, about 3cm (1¼in) long. Tiny, purple-white flowers are produced in axillary pairs all year, mainly in late summer. Native to China.
‡ 20–30cm (8–12in), ↔ 30cm (12in).

HARDINESS Frost hardy.

PARTS USED Whole plant (*bai hua zhe she cao*).

PROPERTIES A pleasant-tasting, cooling, alterative herb that lowers fever, reduces inflammation, relieves pain, and is diuretic as well as anti-bacterial. It acts mainly on the liver and stimulates the immune system.

MEDICINAL USES Internally for fever, coughs, asthma, jaundice, urinary tract infections, and cancers of the digestive tract. Externally for snake bite, boils, abscesses, and severe bruising.

OLEA

Olive

Oleaceae

This genus of 20 species of evergreen trees and shrubs occurs throughout the tropics and warm-temperate regions of Africa and Eurasia. *Olea europaea* thrives successfully outdoors in the Mediterranean area and similar climates. The tradition of the olive branch as a symbol of peace began with the biblical account of the dove returning to Noah's Ark with an olive branch after the flood waters had abated. Olive trees have been cultivated since prehistoric times, providing the oil and fruits that characterize the cuisines of most Mediterranean countries and, in the days before electricity, as a source of oil for lamps. Trees begin fruiting in their seventh year, reaching their prime at about 35 years, and continuing until at least 150 years old, though living very much longer; trees some 1000 years old are known. Olives and olive oil vary greatly in flavour, depending on variety, time of harvesting, and processing techniques. Green olives are unripe, and are usually preserved in brine; all olives turn black, soft, and oily when ripe. However, green olives are often blackened by first soaking in caustic soda and then washing in ferrous gluconate to produce a firm (though poorly flavoured) olive for bottling or canning, which is also easier to stone and slice. Blackened olives cannot be used instead of ripe black olives in recipes that depend on them for flavour (such as *tapenade*), though they are fine for garnishing. The finest oil (extra virgin) often comes from unpalatable varieties and is pressed without using heat or chemical solvents. It has the lowest percentage (about one per cent) of acidity and therefore the best flavour. In addition, extra virgin oil from different regions has a characteristic flavour. Spanish oils are fruity, and Italian are peppery, while those from France are sweet, and Greek oils have a leafy aroma. The culinary uses of the olive are well known; less familiar are the medicinal applications, which involve leaves as well as the oil. Olive oil is mono-unsaturated; it reduces gastric secretions, which is of benefit to patients suffering from hyperacidity. Regular consumption of olive oil is thought to reduce the risk of circulatory disease. *Olea* (Greek *elaio*) is the Latin word for "olive" or "oil".

CULTIVATION Well-drained soil in sun. Remove leading shoot when the plant reaches 1.5m (5ft). Remove old branches to encourage new growths, as fruits are produced mostly on one-year-old wood. Trees may be damaged by scale insects, root-knot eelworm, and *Verticillium* wilt. Plants under cover may suffer from whitefly, thrips, and spider mites. Subject to statutory controls as a weed in parts of Australia.

PROPAGATION By seed sown at 13–15°C

Olea europaea

(55–59°F) in spring; by semi-ripe cuttings in summer.

HARVEST Bark is removed as required and used fresh in infusions. Leaves are collected as required and dried for infusions, liquid extracts, or tinctures. Fruits are harvested in autumn and winter; the oil pressed from them is stored in cool dark conditions.

■ *Olea europaea* (olive)
Rugged evergreen tree with grey fissured bark and grey-green, leathery, elliptic to lanceolate leaves, to 8cm (3in) long, which have silvery, scurfy undersides. Fragrant cream flowers are borne in panicles in late spring and early summer, followed by ovoid, egg-shaped, green fruits, to 4cm (1½in) long, which ripen black in winter. Native to the Mediterranean region.
‡10–15m (30–45ft), ↔10m (30ft). 'Aglandau' is self-fertile, and reputedly the hardiest olive. 'El Greco' is a heavy cropping New Zealand olive with good oil content. Bears well when young. 'Frantoio' is vigorous and early ripening, bearing small oblong fruits that yield excellent oil. 'Kalamata' produces medium-sized, pointed fruits that turn purple when cured in brine and red wine vinegar. Originated in the Greek town of Kalamata. 'Lucques' is a vigorous French olive, yielding superbly flavoured fruits and oil. 'Manzanillo' is vigorous, early, and prolific, producing large rounded fruits, excellent for pickling and oil. Originated in Spain. 'Niçoise' produces small, fine-flavoured fruits, difficult to stone; often flavoured with *herbes de Provence* and traditionally used in *salade Niçoise*. 'Picholine' bears small elongated fruits with firm succulent flesh, often picked green for stuffing.

HARDINESS Frost hardy.

PARTS USED Leaves, fruits, oil, bark.

PROPERTIES An antiseptic astringent herb that lowers fever and blood pressure, improves kidney functions, and has a calming effect. It is also a laxative and emollient.

MEDICINAL USES Internally for colic (bark), minor feverish illnesses, nervous tension, and hypertension, diabetes (leaves); constipation and peptic ulcers (oil). Oil is combined with lemon juice for gallstones. Externally for abrasions, sore eyes, sore throats (leaves); dry skin and hair, dandruff (oil).

CULINARY USES Olives feature in *hors d'oeuvres*, salads, spreads (such as *tapenade*), pasta sauces, tomato and aubergine dishes, pizzas, and breads; also for garnishing. Olive oil is important as a cooking oil, also used in salad dressings, mayonnaise, sauces, and as a dip for bread in Mediterranean regions.

ECONOMIC USES Oil is an ingredient of liniments, ointments, skin and hair preparations, and soap.

OPHELIA

Ophelia chirata. See *Swertia chirata*.

OPHIOPOGON

Japanese hyacinth, lilyturf

Convallariaceae

About 40 species of evergreen, tuft-forming perennials make up this genus, which occurs in woodland in E Asia, especially in China and Japan. Several species are grown for their grass-like foliage, violet to white flowers, and mostly blue or black fruits. *Ophiopogon japonicus* is especially attractive as ground cover and edging. It is widely used in landscaping in Australia and Hawaii. As a herb, *Ophiopogon japonicus* contains substances that "replenish vital essence and promote secretion of body fluids". It has been used in traditional Chinese medicine as a *yin* tonic since the 1st century AD.

CULTIVATION Rich, moist but well-drained soil in sun or partial shade.

PROPAGATION By seed sown when ripe; by division in spring.

HARVEST Tubers are lifted in spring and dried for use in decoctions.

▪ *Ophiopogon japonicus* (lilyturf, mondo grass) Evergreen perennial with large underground stolons, tuberous roots, and linear arching leaves, 20–40cm (8–16in) long. Small, white to pale lilac, bell-shaped flowers appear in racemes, 5–8cm (2–3in) long, in summer, followed by blue berries. Native to Japan. ‡ 20–30cm (8–12in), ↔ 30cm (12in).

Ophiopogon japonicus

'Compactus' is dense and dwarf. ‡ 5cm (2in). 'Minor' is compact, with black-green, curled leaves. ‡ 8cm (3in).

HARDINESS Fully hardy.

PARTS USED Tubers (*mai men dong*).

PROPERTIES A sweet, soothing, sedative herb that controls coughs and lubricates the digestive and bronchial tracts.

MEDICINAL USES Internally for dry coughs, fevers, thirst, dry constipation, insomnia, anxiety, and palpitations. Often mixed with cinnabar (mercuric sulphide) to increase sedation.

ORIGANUM

Marjoram

Lamiaceae

There are 20 species of perennials and subshrubs in this genus, which is distributed through Eurasia, with various species found in S Europe, Crete, and N Africa. Most are grown as ornamentals for their attractive aromatic foliage and purple-pink to white flowers, which in certain species are surrounded by conspicuous bracts. They vary in habit and cultural requirements. Some are bushy perennials suitable for the border; others are arching to prostrate subshrubs, which are best grown on an elevation or in containers. All dislike winter wet and poor air circulation; *Origanum dictamnus* is especially sensitive, and in areas with wet winters is usually grown in the alpine house. Marjorams are mainly used as culinary herbs, but are rich in flavonoids and volatile oils, notably carvacrol and thymol, which have medicinal applications. *Origanum dictamnus* was a revered herb in ancient times and is mentioned in many Classical texts as a miraculous healing herb and ingredient of Mithridates's antidote to poisons. Theophrastus (370–285BC) wrote, in his *Enquiry into Plants*, that *O. dictamnus* "is marvellous in virtue and is useful for many purposes, but especially for women in childbirth". It is no longer widely used medicinally, perhaps because it is rare in the wild and not as easy to cultivate as most other origanums. Wild plants are protected but there are commercial plantations in Crete, and dittany tea remains popular on the island, especially after meals. *Origanum vulgare* is extremely variable in both appearance and chemical composition. In addition, plants in warm dry regions have a more pungent flavour than those that grow in cooler northern parts. To complicate the picture, *O. vulgare* hybridizes readily in cultivation, giving rise to plants that often cause confusion over identification and naming. According to the International Code of Botanical Nomenclature, hybrids between *O. majorana* and *O. vulgare* must be called *O. × majoricum*. However, they are often incorrectly given as *O. × applii*. Confusion also occurs over the name *O. heracleoticum*, which is technically two different names, having been attributed to different authors. Thus *O. heracleoticum* Auct. is synonymous with *O. vulgare* subsp. *hirtum*, and *O. heracleoticum* L. is a synonym of *O. vulgare* subsp. *viride*. It should also be noted that the

---

common name "winter marjoram" is applied to *O. onites* in the USA and to *O. vulgare* subsp. *hirtum* in the UK. Overall, *O. vulgare* contains a higher proportion of thymol than *O. majorana*, which gives it a more thyme-like aroma. Although several species of *Origanum* are known as "oregano", commercial dried oregano is produced from several different unrelated plants. Sources include *Lippia graveolens* (Mexican oregano, see p.264) and *L. palmeri*, *Origanum vulgare* subsp. *hirtum* (winter marjoram) from Greece and Turkey, and the Middle Eastern *O. syriacum*, as well as from *O. vulgare* itself. Much commercial oregano oil is from *Thymus capitatus* (conehead thyme, see p.388). The Arabic word for oregano is *za'atar*. This term is also used for a spice mixture containing the ground berries of *Rhus coriaria* (sumach), roasted sesame seeds, salt, and *za'atar* leaves of some kind, which may be from *Origanum syriacum*, *Satureja thymbra*, *Thymbra spicata*, or *Thymus capitatus*. Za'atar is often mixed with olive oil and spread on bread. The word *origanum* comes from the Greek *origanon*, meaning "bitter herb".

CULTIVATION Well-drained to dry, neutral to alkaline soil in sun. *Origanum dictamnus* needs sharp drainage and protection from wet winters. *Origanum majorana*, *O. × majoricum*, and *O. onites* may be slightly hardier in a sheltered, sharply drained situation.

PROPAGATION By seed sown in autumn or at 10–13°C (50–55°F) in spring (species only); by basal cuttings in late spring; by division in spring.

HARVEST Plants are collected as flowering begins, and leaves during the growing season, and used fresh, distilled for oil, or dried for infusions.

▪ *Origanum dictamnus* (dittany of Crete, hop marjoram)
Dwarf evergreen subshrub with arching stems and almost round, woolly, grey-white leaves, to 2.5cm (1in) long. Tiny, tubular pink flowers, enclosed by hop-like, purple-pink bracts, are

Origanum dictamnus

O

produced in dense pendent whorls, to 2cm (¾in) long, in summer. Native to Crete. ‡ 12–15cm (5–6in), ↔ 40cm (16in).

HARDINESS Frost hardy.

PARTS USED Leaves, flowers.

PROPERTIES An aromatic tonic herb that benefits the digestion.

MEDICINAL USES Internally for stomach ache, chest complaints, and rheumatism. Externally for snake bite, sciatica, and wounds caused by metal.

CULINARY USES Leaves are added to salads and sauces. Flowering tops are infused for tea.

ECONOMIC USES Extracts are used to flavour vermouth.

Origanum × hybridinum syn. *O. × hybridum*, *O. pulchellum* (showy marjoram)
Perennial subshrub with sprawling stems and downy, ovate, grey-green leaves, to 2.5cm (1in) long. Pink flowers in pendent, hop-like clusters of bracts, appear from late summer to autumn. Natural hybrid between *O. dictamnus* and *O. sipyleum*. Native to Lebanon, Syria, and Israel. ‡ 25–45cm (10–18in), ↔ 25–30cm (10–12in).

HARDINESS Frost hardy.

PARTS USED Leaves.

PROPERTIES An aromatic herb with an oregano-like flavour.

CULINARY USES Leaves are used in similar ways to *O. vulgare*.

▪ *Origanum majorana* syn. *Majorana hortensis* (knotted marjoram, sweet marjoram)
Perennial evergreen subshrub, often grown as an annual, with wiry, more or less upright, red-brown stems and downy, grey-green, ovate leaves, to 3cm (1¼in) long. Tiny, white to pink flowers, with grey-green bracts, are produced in dense rounded spikes in summer. Native to S Europe, N Africa, and Turkey. ‡ 60cm (24in), ↔ 45cm (18in).

HARDINESS Frost hardy.

PARTS USED Whole plant, leaves, flowering heads, seeds, oil.

PROPERTIES A warming, relaxing, restorative herb that relieves spasms, stimulates the uterus and circulation, and improves digestion, and has expectorant effects. It has a sweet, floral, thyme-like aroma.

MEDICINAL USES Internally for bronchial complaints, tension headaches, insomnia, anxiety, minor digestive upsets, and painful menstruation. Contraindicated during pregnancy. Externally for bronchial congestion, muscular pain, arthritis, sprains, and stiff joints; also infused in warm olive oil for ear infections.

CULINARY USES *Origanum majorana* has a more delicate flavour than *O. vulgare* and is best used fresh towards the end of cooking. Leaves and flowering sprigs are popular in Italian and Greek cooking, with meat dishes, soups, stuffings, tomato sauces, and pasta, and to flavour oil and vinegar.

ECONOMIC USES Seeds are added to condiments and meat products. Oil is used in food flavouring, liqueurs, perfumery, soaps, and hair products.

Origanum × majoricum (hardy marjoram, Italian oregano)
Perennial resembling *O. majorana* in appearance and aroma, but rather hardier. Sterile hybrid, probably between *O. majorana* and the yellow-bracted *O. vulgare* subsp. *virens*. ‡ 45–60cm (18–24in), ↔ 45cm (18in).

HARDINESS Fully hardy (borderline).

PARTS USED Leaves.

PROPERTIES Similar to *O. majorana*.

CULINARY USES May be substituted for *O. majorana* in cooking.

▪ *Origanum* 'Norton Gold'
Perennial with reddish stems and small, rounded-ovate, aromatic, lime-green leaves, which are yellow-green in spring. Pink flowers, resembling

those of *O. laevigatum*, are produced in summer. Probably a hybrid between *O. laevigatum* and *O. vulgare* 'Aureum'. ↔ 45cm (18in).

HARDINESS Fully hardy.

PARTS USED Leaves, flower heads.

PROPERTIES An aromatic herb with a pleasant, marjoram-like scent.

CULINARY USES Leaves can be used in salads, and for flavouring.

▪ *Origanum onites* syn. *Majorana onites* (Greek oregano, pot marjoram, *rhigani*, Turkish oregano)
Small, semi-evergreen subshrub with reddish hairy stems and ovate to elliptic, pointed, bright green leaves, to 2cm (¾in) long, which have heart-shaped bases. White flowers, with green bracts, are borne in dense whorls in late summer. Native to the Mediterranean region. ‡ 60cm (24in), ↔ 30cm (12in).

HARDINESS Frost hardy.

PARTS USED Leaves, flowers.

PROPERTIES A slightly bitter, aromatic herb with a peppery, thyme-like aroma.

CULINARY USES As a culinary substitute for *O. majorana* or *O. vulgare*, but inferior in flavour. Best with strongly flavoured meats.

ECONOMIC USES Leaves and flowering sprigs are added to potpourris and scented articles.

Origanum syriacum syn. *O. maru* (bible hyssop, Syrian oregano, *za'ater*)
Subshrub with stiff, erect, hairy stems and blunt ovate leaves, to 3.5cm (1¼in) long. Oblong spikes of purple-pink flowers, with woolly bracts, are produced in panicles from late spring to autumn. Native to Syria. ‡ 45–90cm (18–36in), ↔ 30–45cm (12–18in).

HARDINESS Frost hardy.

PARTS USED Leaves, flowering tops.

PROPERTIES An aromatic herb with a thyme–oregano flavour.

Origanum majorana

Origanum 'Norton Gold'

Origanum onites

Origanum vulgare

Origanum vulgare 'Acorn Bank'

Origanum vulgare var. *album*

Origanum vulgare 'Aureum'

Origanum vulgare 'Aureum Crispum'

Origanum vulgare 'Compactum'

Origanum vulgare 'Country Cream'

Origanum vulgare 'Gold Tip'

CULINARY USES An important ingredient of *za'ater* (see *Origanum* introduction).

Origanum vulgare (oregano, wild marjoram) Variable, bushy, rhizomatous perennial with woody-based, upright to spreading, purple-brown stems and broadly ovate leaves, to 4cm (1½in) long. Purple-pink (occasionally pink or white) flowers appear in loose panicles in summer. Native to Europe. ↔ 30–90cm (12–36in). ■ 'Acorn Bank' has distinctly pointed leaves, 2.5cm (1in) long, with inward-curling margins, and white flowers (creamy pink in bud) with pink stamens. ↔ 50cm (20in). ■ var. *album* is small and bushy, with light green leaves and white flowers. ↔ 25cm (10in). ■ 'Aureum' (golden marjoram) has small, bright yellow-green leaves and lavender-pink flowers. ↕ 75cm (30in), ↔ 30cm (12in). ■ 'Aureum Crispum' has rounded, wrinkled, yellow-green leaves, to 1cm (½in) long, which are at their best in spring. Scorches in full sun and is less vigorous, and more tender, than 'Aureum'. ↕ 30cm (12in), ↔ 45cm (18in). ■ 'Compactum' (compact marjoram) is dwarf and mound-forming, with rounded, dark green leaves, to 2cm (¾in) long, and numerous, pink-violet flowers. ↕ 15cm (6in), ↔ 30cm (12in). ■ 'Country Cream' has white-variegated leaves and pink flowers. ↔ 30cm (12in). ■ 'Gold Tip' syn. 'Variegatum' has yellow-tipped leaves, brightest in spring. ↕ 40cm (16in), ↔ 45cm (18in). subsp. *gracile* syn. *O. tyttanthum* (Kyrgyz/Russian/Turkestan oregano) has a slender habit, non-hairy stems, and smooth, gland-dotted leaves that have an excellent mild flavour. Native to C Asia. subsp. *hirtum* syn. *O. heracleoticum* (oregano, winter marjoram) is compact, with pungently scented, hairy, pointed leaves, hairy, green, sometimes purple-tinged bracts, and white flowers from late spring to winter. Native to E Mediterranean. ↕ 30–70cm (12–28in), ↔ 20–45cm (8–18in). subsp. *hirtum* 'Greek' has

Origanum vulgare 'Nanum'

Origanum vulgare 'Thumble's Variety'

bright green leaves and white flowers; excellent culinary herb, often dried as oregano. ↕ 45–60cm (18–24in). ■ 'Nanum' is neat and small-growing. ↕ 20cm (8in), ↔ 25cm (10in). ■ 'Polyphant' is a white-variegated, white-flowered cultivar, found as a sport of 'Aureum Crispum' at the Polyphant Herb Nursery in Cornwall (UK) in the 1980s. Scorches in full sun. ↔ 30cm (12in). ■ 'Thumble's Variety' is strong-growing, with mild-flavoured, rounded, yellow-green leaves and white flowers. ↔ 30cm (12in). subsp. *viride* usually has yellow-green bracts and white flowers. ■ 'White Anniversary' has bright green, white-margined leaves. ↕ 20cm (8in), ↔ 15–20cm (6–8in).

HARDINESS Fully hardy.

PARTS USED Whole plant, leaves, oil.

PROPERTIES A pungently aromatic, antiseptic, warming herb that relaxes spasms, increases perspiration, benefits the digestion, stimulates the uterus, and acts as a mild expectorant.

MEDICINAL USES Internally for colds, influenza, minor feverish illnesses, indigestion, flatulence, stomach upsets, and painful menstruation. Contraindicated during pregnancy. Externally for bronchitis, asthma, arthritis, and muscular pain. Oil used in aromatherapy for similar conditions and, externally, to kill lice; it may cause skin irritation.

CULINARY USES An important herb in Italian, Greek, and Mexican cooking, often used dried rather than fresh, in strongly flavoured dishes in which ingredients such as chilli, garlic, tomatoes, onions, olives, and wine predominate. Leaves and flowering tops are infused for tea.

ECONOMIC USES Oil is used in commercial food flavouring, toiletries, and men's perfumes. Leaves and flowers are added to potpourris.

ORYZA

Rice

Poaceae

There are about 20 species of annual and perennial grasses in this tropical Asian genus. Rice is now grown in parts of Europe and the USA, as well as in its native Asia. Wild rice comes from another species, *Zizania aquatica*, a grass native to E Canada and NE USA. Pots of rice plants, easily raised from untreated, long-grained brown rice, make an ornamental feature for tropical pools. Rice has been cultivated in India and China for at least 4000 years, and is the staple food of over half the world's population. It was introduced to SE Asia from India in the 1st century AD and to Spain by the Arabs in the 8th or 9th century. *Oryza sativa* was first mentioned in traditional Chinese medicine in the 7th century, as a sprouted grain used in diet therapy. It is often prescribed with germinated barley (see *Hordeum vulgare*, p.236), notably in *yi tang*, a digestive tonic and cough remedy. Rice water is used in the East for stomach upsets in the same way as barley water is used in the West. Rice syrup has similar properties to (barley) malt extract, strengthening the bronchial and digestive systems, especially

Origanum vulgare 'Polyphant'

Origanum vulgare 'White Anniversary'

in children. Rice paper is not made from rice, but from the pith of *Tetrapanax papyrifera* (Araliaceae). *Oryza sativa* has two main subspecies: subsp. *indica*, which produces long grains suitable for "dry" dishes, such as pilaf; and the hardier, short-grained subsp. *japonica*, which is more suitable for "wet" dishes, such as risotto, paella, and rice pudding. Indica-type cultivars include 'Basmati' and 'Jasmine', while japonica types include Italian risotto rices 'Arborio' and 'Carnaroli', and Japanese sushi rice 'Koshihikari'. Glutinous rice (Glutinosa Group) is high in amylopectin, a waxy starch that causes the steamed grains to form a sticky sweetish mass, popular for desserts in Asian cuisines. Unprocessed rice grains may be brown to pink, red, or black, depending on variety. *Oryza* may be from the Greek *orusso*, meaning "to dig a trench", referring to the method of rice cultivation.

CULTIVATION Inundated soil in sun. Optimum average growing temperatures for subsp. *indica* are 25–30°C (77–86°F), and 18°C (64°F) for subsp. *japonica*. The latter stops growing below 5°C (41°F) but may survive frost.

PROPAGATION By seed sown on surface in late winter at 19–24°C (66–75°F) in pots or trays of compost standing in water, and transplanted in clumps of 2–6 seedlings. Seed viability of subsp. *japonica* is poor after a cold summer.

HARVEST Rhizomes are lifted in autumn and dried for use in decoctions. Seeds are collected when ripe and germinated as required, or dried for use in decoctions and powders.

Oryza sativa (rice)
Annual, rhizomatous, wetland grass with thick, upright, arching stems and upright narrow leaves, 1.5m (5ft) long. Panicles of spikelets, each containing a single flower, are followed by hard, pale brown seeds. Native to tropical Asia. ↕ 50cm–1.7m (20in–5ft), ↔ 20cm–1m (8in–3ft).

HARDINESS Min. 15–18°C (59–64°F) for subsp. *indica* and 10–12°C (50–54°F) for subsp. *japonica*.

PARTS USED Rhizomes (*nuo dao gen xu*), seeds (*jing mi*), germinated seeds (*gu ya*).

Oryza sativa

PROPERTIES A nutritive, soothing, tonic herb that is diuretic, reduces lactation, improves the digestion, and controls sweating.
MEDICINAL USES Internally for urinary dysfunction (seeds); excessive lactation (seeds, germinated seeds); poor appetite, indigestion, and abdominal discomfort and bloating (germinated seeds); night sweats, especially in tuberculosis and chronic pneumonia (rhizomes). In Chinese medicine, grains are often cooked with herbs to make a medicinal gruel.
CULINARY USES Rice is eaten boiled or steamed, and may be fried before or after boiling; it is an essential accompaniment of curries and Far Eastern dishes and a key ingredient of paella (Spain), pilaf (Turkey, Middle East, India), risotto (Italy), and sushi (Japan); also used in milk desserts (such as rice pudding) and glutinous rice cakes or desserts.
ECONOMIC USES Rice grains are "popped" as breakfast cereals and granola-type products, and in Japan are added to tea after roasting; also fermented to make *saki* (Japanese rice wine), *miso*, and vinegar, and pressed to make rice "milk". Rice flour and rice bran are used in baking; brown rice malt syrup (*mizuame*) is a natural sweetener.

OSMORHIZA
Sweet Cicely

Apiaceae

This small genus includes ten species of aromatic perennials with thick fleshy roots, occurring in the Americas and Asia. Though commonly known as sweet Cicely, they should not be confused with the European sweet Cicely (see *Myrrhis odorata*, p.286). One or two species are occasionally cultivated in herb gardens, especially those devoted to native N American herbs. According to the Meskwaki tribe in Wisconsin, *Osmorhiza longistylis* is "a good medicine for everything". The plants are also a favourite food for livestock, and the roots are used by several tribes to entice or reward horses. *Osmorhiza claytonii* may have been used by settlers as a substitute for chervil (see *Anthriscus cerefolium*, see p.124), hence the common name "jarvil". Little is known about the chemistry and properties of *Osmorhiza* spp. Their characteristic anise aroma is due to anethole, a constituent of the volatile oil. *Osmorhiza occidentalis* is known to contain falcarindiol, a potent anti-fungal.
CULTIVATION Moist, well-drained soil in partial shade.
PROPAGATION By seed sown when ripe.
HARVEST Leaves are picked when young and used fresh or dried. Unripe and ripe fruits are collected when ready, for use as flavourings. Roots are harvested from late summer to midautumn, after the plant has set seed, and used fresh as a vegetable, or dried for use in decoctions and tinctures.

▪ *Osmorhiza claytonii* (anise sweet Cicely, sweet jarvil, woolly sweet Cicely)
Upright hairy perennial with compound downy

Osmorhiza claytonii

leaves divided into ovate to lanceolate, toothed segments, 3–7cm (1¼–3in) long. Tiny white flowers are borne in umbels, to 8cm (3in) wide, in summer, followed by narrow, angular, brown fruits, about 3mm (⅛in) long. Native to eastern N America. ‡ 1m (3ft), ↔ 23–30cm (9–12in).
HARDINESS Fully hardy.
PARTS USED Fruits, roots.
PROPERTIES An aromatic herb with soothing carminative effects and an anise-like scent. Possibly anti-fungal. May stimulate the uterus.
MEDICINAL USES Internally to aid childbirth (roots). Externally, in the form of powder, for ulcerated skin and sores, and either chewed or as a decoction for sore throat (root).
CULINARY USES Anise-flavoured roots and unripe seeds are edible.

Osmorhiza longistylis (aniseroot, smooth sweet Cicely, sweet jarvil, sweet myrrh, wild chervil)
Upright perennial with compound leaves, 8–25cm (3–10in) long, deeply divided into ovate toothed segments, to 10cm (4in) long (less deeply cut than in *O. claytonii*). Tiny white flowers are produced in umbels, to 8cm (3in) across, in summer, followed by narrow, angular, brown fruits that have longer points, to 4mm (⅛in), than *O. claytonii*.
HARDINESS Fully hardy.
PARTS USED Leaves, seeds, roots.
PROPERTIES An aromatic herb with soothing carminative effects and an anise-like scent. Possibly anti-fungal. May stimulate the uterus.
MEDICINAL USES Internally for sore throat, coughs, digestive complaints, flatulence, debility, kidney problems, and to aid childbirth (roots). Externally for eye problems, ulcers, boils, wounds, and sores.
CULINARY USES Leaves and green fruits are eaten raw in salads. Roots are used for flavouring and made into tea. Ripe fruits are used to flavour cakes, confectionery, and liqueurs.

Osmorhiza occidentalis (mountain sweet Cicely, sweet root, western sweet Cicely)
Upright, strongly aromatic perennial with dark brown-grey roots and liquorice-scented, compound leaves, 10–20cm (4–8in) long,

divided into ovate to oblong–lanceolate, finely toothed segments, to 10cm (4in) long. Tiny, yellow to yellow-green flowers are produced in umbels, to 13cm (5in) across, in spring, followed by long, thin, angular, brown fruits. Native to western N America. ‡ 60cm–1.2m (2–4ft), ↔ 30–60cm (12–24in).
HARDINESS Fully hardy.
PARTS USED Leaves, seeds, roots.
PROPERTIES An aromatic herb that is carminative, laxative, and anti-fungal, and helps to lower blood sugar. It has anise-scented fruits, and roots with an aroma resembling anise or root beer.
MEDICINAL USES Internally for gastrointestinal infections and constipation. Combined with *Aralia nudicaulis* (see p.126) or *Smilax* spp. (see p.370), and *Glycyrrhiza glabra* (see p.227) for hyperglycaemia. Externally as a douche for candidiasis, and a wash for ringworm, athlete's foot, and other fungal infections.
CULINARY USES Leaves are added to salad dressings and marinades. Dried ground roots and fruits are used as a substitute for anise in baking. Leaves and roots are used to make tea.

P

PACKERA
Packera aurea. See *Senecio aureus.*

PAEONIA
Peony

Paeoniaceae

There are 30 or so species of perennials and small deciduous shrubs in this genus, found from Europe to E Asia and western N America. Peonies have a long history of cultivation: *P. lactiflora* has been grown in the East since 900BC, and *P. suffruticosa* was the favourite flower of Chinese emperors for over 1000 years. *Paeonia officinalis* was a popular medicinal herb in Europe until the 16th century, but is seldom used today. Culpeper distinguished two variants: the male peony, with purple-red flowers, barely divided leaves, and both black and crimson seeds; and the female peony, with leafier, more divided foliage, smaller, scented, darker purple flowers, and black seeds. They were used for male and female complaints respectively. The uses of *P. lactiflora* date back to at least AD500. *Paeonia suffruticosa* was first mentioned in Chinese medicine in *Pouch of Pearls*, a 12th-century work by Zhang Yuan-Su. Regardless of flower or root colour, the roots of cultivated and wild plants are considered to be different drugs by Chinese herbalists. Cultivated ("white peony") *P. lactiflora* is a *yin* tonic for the liver and circulation, known as *bai shao*; wild-collected plants are termed "red peony" (*chi shao*) and

O

considered mainly as a remedy for cooling the blood. The roots of both *P. lactiflora* and *P. veitchii* are harvested from the wild as the drug *chi shao*, which was used successfully to treat eczema at the Great Ormond Street Children's Hospital, London (UK). *Paeonia* is named after Paeon, physician to the Greek gods.

CULTIVATION Rich, well-drained soil in sun or partial shade, avoiding early morning sun, which may cause damage after frost. Remove dead wood from *P. suffruticosa* in early spring. Shoots and buds may be damaged by peony wilt (grey mould blight). Foliage may be damaged by leafspot and virus diseases. Buds and stem bases may be affected by *Botrytis*. Susceptible to honey fungus, eelworms, and swift moth larvae.

PROPAGATION By seed sown in autumn (species only); by division in autumn or early spring; by root cuttings in winter (*P. lactiflora* and *P. officinalis*); by layering or semi-ripe cuttings in spring (*P. suffruticosa*); by grafting in winter (*P. suffruticosa*). Seed may take 2–3 years to germinate.

HARVEST Roots (*P. lactiflora*) are lifted from cultivated plants 4–5 years old, in late summer to midautumn, and boiled and dried for use in decoctions, pills, and powders; wild plants are lifted in spring or (preferably) autumn and sun-dried. Roots (*P. officinalis*) are lifted from two-year-old plants and dried for decoctions. Root bark (*P. suffruticosa*) is stripped from roots in autumn and used raw or dried in decoctions.

■ *Paeonia lactiflora* syn. *P. albiflora* (Chinese peony)
Perennial with fleshy roots, red-marked stems, and dark green leaves divided into elliptic to lanceolate, tapering leaflets, which have rough margins. Fragrant, single, white flowers, 7–10cm (3–4in) across, with pale yellow

Paeonia lactiflora

stamens, appear in late spring and early summer. Found from Tibet to N and W China, Mongolia, and E Siberia. ↔ 50–70cm (20–28in).
HARDINESS Fully hardy.
PARTS USED Roots (*bai shao*, white peony; *chi shao*, red peony).
PROPERTIES A bitter, cooling, astringent herb that reduces inflammation, relaxes spasms, and lowers fever and blood pressure. It is sour-tasting, with analgesic, tranquillizing, and anti-bacterial effects.
MEDICINAL USES Internally for menstrual complaints, injuries, and skin conditions associated with heat excess, such as eczema (*chi shao*), hypertension, premenstrual syndrome, and liver disorders (*bai shao*). Combined with *Angelica polymorpha* var. *sinensis* (see p.122), *chuan xiong* (see p.260), and *Rehmannia glutinosa* (see p.341) as "Four Things Soup", a Chinese herbal tonic for women. Contraindicated during pregnancy. For use only by qualified practitioners.

■ *Paeonia officinalis* (common peony)
Perennial with thick, knotted, dark brown roots, erect stems, and midgreen leaves divided into nine narrowly elliptic to oblong segments, to 11cm (4¼in) long. Single, crimson, occasionally pink to white, eight-petalled flowers, to 13cm (5in) across, appear in late spring and early summer. Native to Europe. ↔ 60–70cm (24–28in). 'Alba Plena' has large, double, white flowers, sometimes flushed pink. 'Rubra Plena' has dark green leaves, divided into broadly ovate segments, and large, double, crimson flowers, with satiny petals. ↔ 70–75cm (28–30in).
HARDINESS Fully hardy.
PARTS USED Roots.
PROPERTIES A diuretic, sedative, cleansing

Paeonia officinalis

Paeonia suffruticosa

herb that relaxes spasms, stimulates the uterus, and constricts blood vessels.
MEDICINAL USES Formerly used internally for epilepsy, convulsions, whooping cough, kidney and gallstones, haemorrhoids, intestinal spasms, menstrual and postpartum problems, and varicose veins. For use only by qualified practitioners.

■ *Paeonia suffruticosa* syn. *P. moutan* (moutan peony, tree peony)
Upright, sparsely branched, deciduous shrub with dark green, dissected leaves, divided into nine main, elliptic to ovate leaflets, to 10cm (4in) long. Single, sometimes scented, white to pink flowers, to 15cm (6in) across, stained purple in the centre, appear in spring and early summer. Native to China. ↔ 2.2m (7ft). 'Hana-daijin' syn. 'Magnificent Flower' has double violet flowers. 'Renkaku' syn. 'Flight of Cranes' has double white flowers with deep yellow stamens. 'Yae-zakura' syn. 'Double Cherry' has double, pale pink flowers.
HARDINESS Fully hardy.
PARTS USED Root bark (*mu dan pi*).
PROPERTIES A pungent, bitter, analgesic herb that cools the blood, lowers blood pressure, and has anti-allergenic, anti-bacterial, and tranquillizing effects.
MEDICINAL USES Internally for fevers, boils, menstrual disorders, nosebleed, ulcers, irritability, and gastrointestinal infections. Used raw for blood heat, stir-baked for stagnant circulation, and carbonized to control bleeding. For use only by qualified practitioners.

PANAX
Ginseng

Araliaceae

The number of species in this genus of perennials is disputed and may be three or six, depending on whether *P. pseudoginseng* is regarded as a single species with variants or four separate species. They are distributed in S and E Asia and N America. *Panax ginseng* is an ancient Taoist tonic herb, which has been used as a *qi* (vital essence) tonic in Chinese medicine for about 5000 years. It was introduced to Europe several times from the 9th century onwards but assumed no importance in Western medicine until studies by Soviet scientists in the early 1950s established it as an "adaptogen". To increase availability of the drug, they also searched for similar properties in related native species and discovered *Eleutherococcus senticosus* (Siberian ginseng, see p.201). *Panax pseudoginseng* var. *notoginseng* was first mentioned in Chinese medical texts in the 16th century. It is primarily a healing herb and was used extensively by the Vietcong during the Vietnam war to improve recovery from gunshot wounds. *Panax quinquefolius* was discovered in the 18th century by Jesuit colleagues of Père Jartoux, who deduced that similar plants might exist in N America. It was first collected for export to China by backwoodsmen ("seng diggers"), and was first described in Chinese medicine c.1765. Regarded as more *yin* than *P. ginseng*, *P. quinquefolius* is given to children and young people, for whom *P. ginseng* might not be appropriate. In appearance as well as uses, the two species are very similar. *Panax japonicus* (bamboo ginseng, Japanese ginseng) is important in Japan, and in macrobiotic diets, often as an ingredient of tonic teas and liqueurs. The main medicinal species are now rare in the wild, and are cultivated commercially in Korea, China, Russia, and the USA (mainly Wisconsin). An unrelated species, *Pfaffia paniculata* (see p.311), is known as Brazilian ginseng.

CULTIVATION Moist, well-drained, rich soil in shade, with ample warmth and humidity during the growing season.

PROPAGATION By seed sown 2.5cm (1in) deep when ripe. Keep seed in damp moss before sowing; do not allow to dry out. Germination is slow and erratic.

HARVEST Roots are lifted from 6–7-year-old plants in autumn and used fresh or dried in decoctions, liquid extracts, pills, and powders. Processing of *P. ginseng* varies according to product and quality. Red ginseng is steamed, heat-dried, then sun-dried; white ginseng is peeled and dried for chewing. Flowers are picked in spring and summer for decoctions.

■ *Panax ginseng* (ginseng)
Perennial with a branched, carrot-shaped, aromatic rootstock and upright stems bearing a whorl of 2–5, long-stalked leaves divided into five elliptic to ovate leaflets, to 15cm (6in) long, which have finely toothed margins. Small, yellow-green, five-petalled flowers are produced in an umbel in spring, followed by red berries, each containing two seeds. Native to Korea and NE China. ‡ 60cm (24in), ↔ 45cm (18in).

HARDINESS Fully hardy.

PARTS USED Roots (*ren shen*), processed to produce red or white ginseng as required.

PROPERTIES A sweet tonic herb that both

Panax ginseng

relaxes and stimulates the nervous system, encourages secretion of hormones, improves stamina, lowers blood sugar and cholesterol levels, and increases resistance to disease.

MEDICINAL USES Internally for debility associated with old age or illness, lack of appetite, insomnia, stress, shock, and chronic illness. An ingredient in many important Chinese formulas; also taken as a "simple" (that is, not mixed with other herbs), often as a *yang* tonic before winter or a period of great stress. Not usually prescribed for pregnant women or patients under 40 years old, or with depression, anxiety, or acute inflammatory disease. Use is normally restricted to six weeks. Excess may cause headaches, restlessness, high blood pressure, and other side-effects, especially if taken with caffeine, alcohol, turnips, and bitter or spicy foods.

CULINARY USES Fresh roots can be eaten raw, fried, candied, or added to stuffings, soups, and other dishes in the same way as carrots. Whole, good-quality roots are aged in bottles of spirits or liqueurs to make tonic elixirs. Ground dried roots are made into tea.

ECONOMIC USES Ginseng extracts are added to food supplements, soft drinks, herb teas, and drinks, and chewing gum; also to skin and hair products.

▨ ▮ ◿ ◿

Panax pseudoginseng var. *notoginseng*
syn. *P. notoginseng* (*san qi/sanchi* ginseng, *tienchi* ginseng)
Perennial with thick roots, long thick rhizomes, and long-stalked, palmate leaves divided into 3–7 ovate, abruptly pointed leaflets, 7–17cm (3–7in) long. Small flowers appear in a solitary dense umbel in spring or summer, followed by cocoon-shaped berries. Native to mountain woodlands in S China (Yunnan). ‡ 90cm (3ft), ↔ 75cm (30in).

HARDINESS Fully hardy.

PARTS USED Roots (occasionally flowers).

PROPERTIES A bitter–sweet warming herb that controls bleeding, reduces inflammation, relieves pain, improves circulation and function of adrenal glands, and has anti-bacterial effects.

MEDICINAL USES Internally for coronary heart disease and angina (roots), dizziness, and vertigo (flowers). Internally and externally for nosebleed, and haemorrhage from lungs, digestive tract, uterus, or injuries (roots). Contraindicated during pregnancy.

CULINARY USES Roots are added to tonic soups.

▨ ▨ ▮ ◿

■ *Panax quinquefolius* (American ginseng)
Perennial with an aromatic branched rootstock and short-stalked leaves divided into 3–7 toothed leaflets, to 15cm (6in) long, which have coarsely toothed margins. Small, green-white flowers appear in an umbel in spring, followed by red berries. Native to eastern N America. ‡ 30–50cm (12–20in), ↔ 45–60cm (18–24in).

HARDINESS Fully hardy.

PARTS USED Roots (*xi yang shen*).

PROPERTIES A bittersweet tonic herb with similar properties to *P. ginseng*.

Panax quinquefolius

MEDICINAL USES Similar to *P. ginseng*, but mainly prescribed for younger patients with *yin* deficiency.

CULINARY USES Roots are slightly more bitter than those of *P. ginseng*, but can be used in the same ways.

ECONOMIC USES As for *P. ginseng*.

▨ ▮ ◿ ◿

PANDANUS
Screw pine

Pandanaceae

This large genus includes about 250 species of evergreen trees, shrubs, and scramblers, which occur in tropical Africa, India, Asia, Australasia, and Pacific islands. Various species are grown for their architectural appearance, either as landscape plants or as ornamentals under cover. They resemble *Ananas* plants (pineapple, see p.120) and are known as screw pines, because the strap-shaped leaves are arranged spirally. *Pandanus tectorius* is widely grown in the tropics, often to prevent erosion; the non-spiny var. *laevis* is preferred for weaving and thatching. The essential oil in the fragrant male inflorescences of both *P. fascicularis* and *P. tectorius* is extracted, using sesame oil to produce *kewda* or *kevda otto*, and distilled to make a water or essence. These products are used locally as perfumes, flavourings, and medicines. *Pandanus amaryllifolius* is a characteristic herb of SE Asia cuisines, though seldom seen elsewhere. Synthetic pandan essence is available in Malaysia.

CULTIVATION Well-drained soil in sun or partial shade, with moderate to high humidity. Plants take 3–4 years to flower.

PROPAGATION By seed sown when ripe at 18°C (64°F), soaking for 24 hours before sowing; or by removal of suckers or offsets in spring.

HARVEST All parts are collected as required and used fresh.

■ *Pandanus amaryllifolius* syn. *P. odorus* (pandan, *pandan wangi*)
Shrub with a stout stem, usually branched low down, and aromatic, linear, pointed leaves, about 80cm (32in) long and 5cm (2in) wide.

Pandanus amaryllifolius

Flowers and fruits are unknown. Native to the Malay Peninsula. ‡ 1.2–1.5m (4–5ft), ↔ 60–90cm (24–36in).
HARDINESS Min. 13°C (55°F).
PARTS USED Leaves, juice.
PROPERTIES An aromatic herb with a musky aroma, likened to new-mown hay or newly harvested rice.
CULINARY USES Leaves are added to rice before cooking or to cooking oil before adding other ingredients; also to give flavour and colour to Malaysian and Indonesian desserts, often in the form of pounded leaves or juice from liquidized leaves. Whole leaves are made into containers for wrapping food before frying (Thailand).
◨ ◪ ◩ ◪

■ *Pandanus tectorius* syn. *P. odoratissimus* (*ketaki*, screw pine)
Upright, small, much-branched tree with a stout trunk and prop roots, and stiff, leathery, blue-green leaves, 1–1.5m (3–5ft) long, which have spiny margins and a lower midrib. Male and female flowers appear separately: males in a spike, 20–30cm (8–12in) long, enclosed by a fragrant white spathe; and females solitary, to 5cm (2in) across, followed by rounded, red-flushed, yellow to light green fruits, 15–25cm (6–10in) long. Found from West India to C Moluccas. ‡ 3–10m (10–30ft), ↔ 2–4m (6–12ft). var. *laevis* has spineless leaves.
HARDINESS Min. 13°C (55°F).

Pandanus tectorius

PARTS USED Aerial roots, leaf bud ("cabbage"), flowers, fruits, seeds, oil.
PROPERTIES A stimulant diuretic herb (roots and leaf bud) with a hyacinth–ylang-ylang scent (flowers). It relaxes spasms and lowers fever.
MEDICINAL USES Internally in folk medicine as a diuretic, depurative, and tonic (roots), for headache and rheumatism (oil, otto), and to treat sterility and threatened miscarriage (root). Externally as a poultice for boils (leaf bud), earache (oil), epilepsy (powdered anthers and bracts, taken as snuff).
CULINARY USES Fruits are eaten by Pacific Islanders; seeds are a staple food in parts of New Guinea. Otto (attar) is used to flavour betel nuts (see *Areca catechu*, p.128). *Kewra* water and essence are used to flavour syrups, soft drinks, and Indian dishes, such as *biryani* and *rasgoola*.
ECONOMIC USES Oil is added to sandalwood oil for perfumery, and used in skin-care products.
◨ ◪ ◩ ◧ ◪ ◪ ▣ ◢ ◪ ◪

PAPAVER
Poppy

Papaveraceae

There are 70 species of annuals and perennials in this genus, which occur in a wide range of habitats in S and C Europe and temperate Asia, with a few species in South Africa, Australia, and western N America. *Papaver rhoeas* is the Flanders poppy, which appeared in vast numbers on the battlefields around Ypres and the Somme following the First World War, and is the origin of the poppies worn on Remembrance Day (11 November) in the UK. Coincidentally, it has been a symbol of blood and new life since ancient Egyptian times. In horticultural terms, *P. rhoeas* is renowned as the parent of the ornamental Shirley poppies, raised in Shirley, Warwickshire (UK), in the 19th century by the Reverend William Wilks, who found a pale-centred specimen in his garden in the summer of 1879 or 1880. All poppies contain bitter latex and have showy, short-lived, four-petalled flowers, followed by pepperpot capsules, which at every stage make attractive annuals for borders and wildflower gardens. Cultivars of *P. somniferum* (opium poppy) are popular ornamentals, too, though it is illegal to grow this species in some countries. Medicinal uses of opium were first described on clay tablets by the Sumerians, who dominated SW Asia in the 4th millennium BC. *Papaver somniferum* is now cultivated on a large scale as the source of major analgesics and the illicit drug heroin (diamorphine). It contains 26 alkaloids, the most important being morphine and codeine. Morphine is an extremely potent painkiller but is addictive and therefore normally reserved for patients with severely painful, terminal illnesses. Alkaloids are separated for specific uses or given as a total extract, known as "papaveretum", which is widely used as a

pre-operative analgesic and relaxant. Two main kinds of opium poppy are grown commercially: subsp. *somniferum* and subsp. *hortense*, for opium production and for seeds for culinary use, respectively. The seeds of both *P. rhoeas* and *P. somniferum* are alkaloid-free and safe for culinary purposes. They are used in Ayurvedic medicine, mainly for digestive problems. *Papaver rhoeas* contains different, less potent alkaloids and a red pigment. *Argemone mexicana* (Mexican poppy) contains alkaloids similar to those in *Papaver somniferum* and a milky latex that is used in parts of S America to treat warts, cold sores, and cataracts.
CULTIVATION Well-drained soil in sun. Leaves may be damaged by downy mildew. *Papaver somniferum* is subject to statutory control as an illicit plant or weed in some countries, notably in the USA and parts of Australia.
PROPAGATION By seed sown in autumn or spring. *Papaver rhoeas*, *P. somniferum*, and their cultivars self-sow freely, but cultivars tend to revert. Poppies resent disturbance and rarely transplant successfully.
HARVEST Petals are collected as flowers open, and dried for use whole, or in infusions and syrups (*P. rhoeas*). Seeds are harvested from ripe capsules and dried for use whole, ground, or in infusions. Oil is pressed from ripe seeds (mostly from *P. somniferum*). Latex (raw opium) and various alkaloids are extracted from green capsules after petal fall (*P. somniferum*).
⚠ **WARNING** All parts of *Papaver* spp., except the seeds, are toxic if eaten. Cultivation of *P. somniferum* is subject to legal restrictions in some countries.

■ *Papaver rhoeas* (corn poppy, field poppy)
Annual with upright hairy stems and hairy, light green leaves, to 15cm (6in) long, divided into lanceolate segments. Solitary, bowl-shaped, four-petalled, bright red flowers, 5–10cm (2–4in) across, sometimes marked black in the centre, are borne on long stems in summer. Native to Eurasia and N Africa; widely naturalized. ‡ 20–90cm (8–36in), ↔ 10–45cm (4–18in). ▣ 'Mother of Pearl' has single and semi-double flowers in pastel shades of dusky pink, mauve, grey, and pink-flushed white, often speckled and sometimes bicoloured. ‡ 25–35cm (10–14in). ▣ Shirley Series has single, semi-double, and double flowers in shades of pink, rose, salmon, crimson, and white, always with a pale centre. ‡ 60cm (24in), ↔ 30cm (12in).
HARDINESS Fully hardy.
PARTS USED Flowers, seeds.
PROPERTIES A sweet, astringent, sedative herb that relieves pain, relaxes spasms, is expectorant, and improves digestion.
MEDICINAL USES Internally for irritating coughs, asthma, insomnia, poor digestion, nervous digestive disorders, and minor painful conditions (petals).
CULINARY USES Seeds are used, whole or ground, in similar ways to those of *P. somniferum*.

Papaver rhoeas

Papaver rhoeas 'Mother of Pearl'

P

Papaver rhoeas
Shirley Series

Papaver somniferum

Papaver somniferum
'Danebrog'

Papaver somniferum
'Peony-flowered Mixed'

ECONOMIC USES Petals of red-flowered plants are used to colour medicines and wine.

■ *Papaver somniferum* (opium poppy)
Robust annual with grey-green, waxy, deeply toothed leaves, to 25cm (10in) long. Mauve or white flowers, 8–18cm (3–7in) across, with blue anthers, appear in summer, followed by capsules, 3–9cm (1¼–3½in) long, containing numerous, grey, black, or white seeds. Probably native to W and C Mediterranean; widely naturalized.
‡ 30cm–1.5m (1–5ft), ↔ 23–45cm (9–18in).
■ 'Danebrog' syn. 'Danish Flag' is a 19th-century cultivar with bright red, often fringed petals, which have large, white, basal blotches. ‡ 75cm (30in), ↔ 30cm (12in). 'Hen and Chickens' has pale pink flowers and very large pods, surrounded by a cluster of smaller pods. ■ 'Peony-flowered Mixed' has large double flowers, in shades of lilac, pink, purple, red, maroon, and white.
HARDINESS Fully hardy.
PARTS USED Fruits, seeds, latex, oil.
PROPERTIES A bitter, narcotic, sedative herb that relieves pain, relaxes spasms, controls coughing and diarrhoea, and increases perspiration.
MEDICINAL USES Internally, in commercial formulas, for painful conditions, coughs, and diarrhoea. In homeopathy for shock, torpor, apathy, alcohol poisoning, and breathing difficulties.
CULINARY USES Seeds, sometimes known as "maw seed", are used whole, or ground and sweetened as a filling, in breads, biscuits, pastries; also in spiced meat dishes, curries, salad dressings, and as a garnish. Cold-pressed, almond-flavoured oil (*huile d'oeillette* or *olivette*) is used for salad dressings.
ECONOMIC USES Lower grades of oil are used in paints, soaps, and ointments.
⚠ **WARNING** This herb, especially in the form of opium and its alkaloids, is subject to legal restrictions in most countries.

PARDANTHUS

Pardanthus chinensis. See *Belamcanda chinensis*.

PARIETARIA
Pellitory

Urticaceae

There are about 20 species of annuals and perennials in this almost cosmopolitan genus, which is especially common in temperate regions. *Parietaria judaica* is seldom cultivated but makes a picturesque sight on old roofs and walls. It begins to grow early in the year and has fresh green foliage when most other deciduous plants are still bare. *Parietaria judaica* was once known as *P. officinalis*, indicating that it was formerly widely used medicinally. It is still a respected, non-irritating treatment for chronic urinary complaints. *Parietaria* is from the Latin *parietarius*, "belonging to walls".
CULTIVATION Well-drained to dry, alkaline soil in sun or partial shade. Subject to statutory control as a weed in parts of Australia.
PROPAGATION By seed sown in autumn or spring.
HARVEST Plants are cut when flowering and used mainly fresh for infusions, decoctions,

Parietaria judaica

compresses, liquid extracts, and tinctures. Fresh extracts are more effective. Decoctions may be frozen for later use.

■ *Parietaria judaica* syn. *P. diffusa* (pellitory-of-the-wall)
Softly hairy perennial with red-green, spreading stems and ovate to lanceolate leaves, to 7cm (3in) long. Tiny green flowers are borne in forked clusters in summer. Found from W and C Europe to N Africa. ↔ 40cm (16in).
HARDINESS Fully hardy.
PARTS USED Whole plant.
PROPERTIES An acrid, soothing, cooling herb that has diuretic, anti-lithic, and anti-inflammatory effects.
MEDICINAL USES Internally for cystitis, pyelitis, urinary stones, and oedema associated with kidney complaints. Combines well with *Agathosma crenulata* (see p.106), *Aphanes arvensis* (see p.124), *Apium graveolens* (see p.125), *Arctostaphylos uva-ursi* (see p.127), *Juniperus communis* (see p.248), and *Petroselinum crispum* (see p.310) to control infection; and with *Elymus repens* (see p.201) and *Zea mays* (see p.410) to relieve pain and inflammation. Not given to patients with hay fever or other allergic conditions.

PARTHENIUM

Asteraceae

There are 15 aromatic perennials and shrubs in this genus, which occurs in tropical and subtropical America and the West Indies. The best-known species is *P. argentatum* (guayule), which contains 20 per cent rubber and was cultivated for emergency supplies in the USA during the Second World War. *Parthenium integrifolium* (prairie dock, wild quinine) is little used medicinally today but is notorious as an adulterant of *Echinacea* roots. German research into *E. angustifolia* (see p.199) found that some samples contained 80 per cent prairie dock roots. The leaves of prairie dock were placed on burns by the Catawba Indians, and *Parthenium hysterophorum* (bastard feverfew, wild wormwood) was used by black Americans

Parthenium integrifolium

to heal ulcers on legs.
CULTIVATION Moist, well-drained soil in sun or partial shade.
PROPAGATION By seed sown when ripe; by division in spring.
HARVEST Leaves are picked during the growing season, and used fresh or dried in infusions.

■ *Parthenium integrifolium* (American feverfew, Missouri snakeroot, prairie dock, wild quinine)
Perennial with upright stems and lanceolate–elliptic to broadly ovate leaves, to 20cm (8in) long. Tiny, off-white flowers are produced in small, dense, cauliflower-like heads, to 1cm (³⁄₈in) across, in summer, with several heads borne in a flat-topped corymb. Native to E USA.
‡ 45–90cm (18–36in), ↔ 30cm (12in).
HARDINESS Fully hardy.
PARTS USED Leaves, roots.
PROPERTIES An aromatic, anti-inflammatory herb that lowers fever and stimulates the uterus. Research shows immune stimulating effects.
MEDICINAL USES Internally for urinary and kidney inflammations, and amenorrhoea; also as a substitute for quinine in lowering fever. Externally for burns and ulcers (leaves).

PASSIFLORA
Passionflower

Passifloraceae

There are over 400 species in this large genus, which occurs in tropical America, Asia, Australia, New Zealand, and Pacific islands. It consists mainly of tendril climbers and climbing shrubs, with some perennials, small trees, and shrubs. Many of the climbing species are grown as ornamentals for their unique flowers, and often edible fruits. Spanish missionaries in S America regarded the flowers as symbols of Christ's passion – the three stigmas representing the nails, the five anthers the wounds, and the ten sepals the apostles (Peter and Judas Iscariot being absent). Passionflowers may be grown outdoors where the climate permits, or in pots, trained on a trellis or frame, under glass. The American *P. incarnata* is one of the hardiest

species, and deserves a place in the herb garden for its handsome foliage, flowers, and fruits, as well as for its importance as a medicinal plant. It was used in native N American medicine, notably by the Houma tribe, who added it to drinking water as a tonic. *Passiflora incarnata* was first described by a visiting European doctor in 1783 as a remedy for epilepsy; it became a popular treatment for insomnia in the 19th century, and later entered the *US National Formulary* (1916–36). The herb contains alkaloids, glycosides, and flavonoids, which are effective, non-addictive sedatives; in prescribed doses it does not cause drowsiness. One flavonoid, apigenin, is an anti-spasmodic and anti-inflammatory, and occurs in various unrelated plants, notably *Apium graveolens* (see p.125).
CULTIVATION Well-drained, sandy, slightly acid soil in sun. Cut back in early spring. Cucumber mosaic virus may attack leaves.
PROPAGATION By seed sown in spring, at 18–21°C (64–70°F); by semi-ripe cuttings in summer; by layering in spring. Germination is slow and erratic.
HARVEST Plants are cut when fruiting and dried for use in infusions, liquid extracts, tablets, and tinctures. Fruits for culinary use are picked when ripe in autumn and used fresh or cooked.

■ *Passiflora incarnata* (apricot vine, maypops, wild passionflower)
Perennial climber, deciduous in cold areas, with deeply 3–5-lobed, finely toothed leaves, to 15cm (6in) long. Fragrant, lavender to white flowers, to 7cm (3in) across, appear in summer, followed by ovoid yellow fruits, to 5cm (2in) long. Native to E USA. ‡ 2–8m (6–25ft).
HARDINESS Fully hardy.
PARTS USED Whole plant, fruits.
PROPERTIES A bitter, sedative, cooling herb that relieves pain, relaxes spasms, and lowers blood pressure.
MEDICINAL USES Internally for nervous tension, anxiety, insomnia, irritability, tension headache, asthma, irritable bowel syndrome, premenstrual tension, nervous tachycardia, hypertension, and shingles; also to assist withdrawal from addictive drugs, including benzodiazepine and Valium. Combines well with *Chamaemelum nobile* (see

Passiflora incarnata

p.165), *Humulus lupulus* (see p.237), and *Valeriana officinalis* (see p.400) for insomnia; and with *Avena sativa* (see p.138), *Humulus lupulus* (see p.237), and *Valeriana officinalis* (see p.400) for drug addiction. High doses are contraindicated during pregnancy.
CULINARY USES Ripe fruits are eaten raw, and made into jams, jellies, wines, and fruit-based drinks. Flowers are made into syrup.

PAULLINIA
Sapindaceae

This genus of about 180 species of evergreen woody lianas and climbing shrubs occurs mainly in tropical America. The fruits of *Paullinia cupana* var. *sorbilis*, a rainforest climber, are made into a stimulant drink known as *guaraná*, which is as important to tribes in central Amazonian Brazil as tea and coffee are elsewhere in the world. This use was first noted by João Felipe Betendorf, a Jesuit missionary, in 1669. By the 18th century, the use of *guaraná* as an aphrodisiac, and as protection against malaria and amoebic dysentery, had spread widely in Brazil. Commercial plantations were established in the 1970s, and it is now a major cash crop, often grown with manioc to prevent scrub regeneration once the manioc is harvested. Seeds of *P. cupana* are dried, powdered, pressed into a dough with water, and rolled into sticks, 12–20cm (5–8in) long, which are then dried. The sticks are grated into hot water to make *guaraná*. Unlike tea and coffee, which are highly water soluble, *guaraná* does not readily dissolve, owing to its high content of fats, oils, and resins, leaving a nutritious film and sediment, which is thought to slow the absorption of stimulant compounds. Traditional techniques of hand-processing *guaraná* by the Saterê-Mawé Indians gives a superior product to mechanized processing, since it avoids oxidation of compounds, which results in a dark bitter drink that irritates the digestive tract. *Guaraná* contains 2.7–5.8 per cent (dry weight) of a compound that was first isolated in 1826 as guaranine. This compound is now known to be tetramethylxanthine, a xanthine derivative almost identical to caffeine, and often referred to as such. Also present in *guaraná* are alkaloids, such as theobromine, as found in *Theobroma cacao* (see p.386), tannins (5–6 per cent), and saponins. Though the identity of plants grown as *guaraná* is usually given as the typical species, *Paullinia cupana*, this is rare in the wild and not in cultivation. Cultivated plants are in fact var. *sorbilis*; they adopt a shrubby habit when grown in the open. Stems of the closely related *P. yoco* (yoco) are used by native people in Colombia, Ecuador, and N Peru to make a similar drink, and medicinally to lower fever and relieve biliousness following malaria.
CULTIVATION Moist, humus-rich soil in partial shade.
PROPAGATION By seed sown when ripe; by ripewood cuttings at the end of the growing season.

P

Paullinia cupana var. *sorbilis*

HARVEST Seeds are collected when ripe, then roasted, ground, and stored as dried paste or powder.

■ *Paullinia cupana* var. **sorbilis** syn. *P. sorbilis* (Brazilian cocoa, *guaraná*, zoom)
Woody evergreen liana with angular stems and glossy pinnate leaves divided into five ovate pointed leaflets, 20–25cm (8–10in) long, which have toothed margins and deep-set veins. Yellow, four-petalled flowers are produced in spike-like panicles, to 10cm (4in) long, followed by obovate, segmented, orange-red capsules, which split open when ripe to reveal 1–3 shiny, purple-brown seeds. Native to Brazil, Uruguay, and Venezuela. ‡10m (30ft).
HARDINESS Min. 18°C (65°F).
PARTS USED Seeds.
PROPERTIES A slightly bitter, stimulant, tonic herb that lowers fever and has astringent and diuretic effects. It is reputedly aphrodisiac.
MEDICINAL USES Internally to relieve fatigue, aid concentration, and lift the spirits; also for diarrhoea, leucorrhoea, migraine, and headache. May cause sleeplessness. Contraindicated in cardiovascular disease and hypertension.
CULINARY USES Seeds are roasted, ground, and pressed into paste (*pasta guaraná*), which is dried into sticks and grated into water as a coffee-like drink; also fermented to make an alcoholic drink.
ECONOMIC USES A source of caffeine and flavourings for the food and beverage industries. Extracts are added to diet and tonic foods. Sweetened paste, or "Brazilian chocolate", is used in soft drinks, confectionery, and liqueurs.
▨ ▲ ▨ ▨ ▣

PAUSINYSTALIA
Rubiaceae

This W African genus consists of 13 species of large trees, characterized by panicles of tubular flowers with conspicuous appendages. *Pausinystalia johimbe* and the related *P. macroceras* and *P. tillesii* contain indole alkaloids, the principal one being johimbine, which blocks the nerve-transmitting hormone noradrenaline, and constricts the genital blood

vessels, thus acting as a sexual stimulant. Johimbe has a long history of use as a stimulant among Bantu people. Medicinal use of johimbe bark appears to have reached Europe in the 1890s. In Africa, *P. lane-poolei* (*igbepo*, *pamprana*) is also used medicinally; dressings of ground bark are applied to yaws and itching skin.
CULTIVATION/PROPAGATION *Pausinystalia johimbe* does not appear to be in cultivation, and no information has been found on its requirements.
HARVEST Bark is collected from trunks and branches at any time of the year and dried in strips for pills, liquid extracts, and extraction of johimbine.

■ *Pausinystalia johimbe* syn. *Corynanthe johimbe* (*endone*, *johimbe*)
Evergreen tree with red to yellow-ochre wood and glossy, oblanceolate, dark green leaves, to 35cm (14in) long. Umbel-like clusters of white or yellowish to pink, tubular flowers are produced in panicles, to 18cm (7in) long, from late autumn to midwinter, followed by capsules containing winged seeds, 6mm (¼in) long. Native to S Nigeria, Cameroon, Gabon, and Zaire. ‡27m (90ft), ↔ 12m (40ft).
HARDINESS Min. 15–18°C (59–64°F).
PARTS USED Bark.
PROPERTIES A bitter, warming, anti-diuretic herb with reputedly aphrodisiac effects. It has a stimulant effect on the heart, increases heart rate and blood pressure, and is locally anaesthetic.
MEDICINAL USES Internally for impotence, frigidity, exhaustion, and debility. Excess causes nervousness, anxiety, sleeplessness, high blood pressure, tachycardia, nausea, and vomiting. Contraindicated in hypertension, renal and hepatic disease; interacts with certain anti-hypertension drugs, such as clonidine.
⚠ **WARNING** This herb is subject to legal restrictions in some countries.
▥ ▲ ▣

PEGANUM
Zygophyllaceae

A genus of five or six species of branched perennials, distributed in dry parts of the tropics and subtropics of both hemispheres, especially from Mediterranean regions to C and E Asia. The aromatic *P. harmala* is a desert plant that adapts well to cultivation. Revered in many parts of Asia as a hallucinogen, research indicates that it may form the intoxicating drink *soma*, or *huoma*, of ancient India and Persia. *Peganum harmala* is much used in Arabic medicine and is mentioned in early Muslim medical literature. It contains hallucinogenic alkaloids and has a history of use in folk medicine.
CULTIVATION Well-drained to dry, poor soil in sun.
PROPAGATION By seed sown in late spring; by division in late spring. Subject to statutory control as a weed in parts of Australia.
HARVEST Whole plants and roots are collected as required for decoctions and inhalations. Fruits and seeds are collected when ripe. Fruits

Peganum harmala

are pressed for dye. Seeds are pressed for oil, dried, and used whole or powdered in infusions, embrocations, and ointments.

■ *Peganum harmala* (*harmal/harmel*, Syrian rue)
Shrubby perennial with grey-green, waxy leaves, 5–8cm (2–3in) long, divided into linear lobes. White, green-veined flowers, to 2.5cm (1in) across, appear in spring and summer, followed by dry capsules containing numerous, dark brown seeds. Native to S Europe, N Africa, and subtropical Asia. ‡50–90cm (20–36in), ↔ 45–60cm (18–24in).
HARDINESS Fully hardy (borderline).
PARTS USED Whole plant, roots, fruits, seeds, oil.
PROPERTIES A bitter, spicy, diuretic herb that stimulates the uterus and digestive system, relieves pain, expels intestinal parasites, and is reputedly aphrodisiac and purifying. In large quantities, is emetic.
MEDICINAL USES Locally, internally for stomach complaints, urinary and sexual disorders, epilepsy, menstrual problems, nervous and mental illnesses. Excess causes hallucinations and vomiting. Externally for haemorrhoids, rheumatism, skin diseases, and baldness; also burned and inhaled for headaches (whole plant), and smoked for toothache (roots and seeds).
CULINARY USES Seeds are used as a spice (Turkey).
ECONOMIC USES Fruits yield a red dye.
▨ ▢ ▨ ▨ ▨ ▲ ▨

PELARGONIUM
Geranium
Geraniaceae

This genus contains about 230 species of mainly evergreen perennials, succulents, subshrubs, and shrubs, which occur mostly in South Africa. Pelargoniums are commonly known as geraniums, confusing them with members of the related genus *Geranium* (see p.223). Scented-leafed pelargoniums have been cultivated in Europe since the 17th century for their intensely aromatic foliage and subtle colours. They are quite different in appearance and uses from the zonal, regal, and ivy-leafed pelargoniums, which are commonly grown for summer display. Most flower all summer and intermittently through the year. In the late 20th century, many new scented-leafed pelargonium hybrids and cultivars were introduced. Few of these have specific culinary or medicinal uses but may be added to potpourris and enjoyed for their fragrance, which is released when the leaves are touched or brushed past. Depending on the aroma, any scented-leafed pelargonium can be used with discretion for flavouring. They contain very complex volatile oils; over 2000 components have been found, including those with discernible similarities to orange, lemon, peppermint, rose, nutmeg, and eucalyptus. Most species are easily propagated and hybridized, and the feasibility of producing aromas for the food and perfumery industries from plant cells grown in vitro has been examined. Rose-scented species, such as *P. capitatum*, and cultivars 'Graveolens', 'Radula', and 'Attar of Roses', yield geranium oil, which is a fragrance in its own right and is often used as an adulterant of attar of roses. Geranium oil is produced in parts of France, Italy, India, Egypt, Algeria, and the former Soviet Union. The finest, known as "Bourbon oil", comes from the island of Réunion. Many species are used medicinally in South Africa, mainly for digestive, bronchial, and skin problems. *Pelargonium betulinum* (birch-leaf geranium, camphor geranium) and *P. cucullatum* are ingredients of "Umckaloabo", a German medicine popular in South Africa for treating bronchitis in children. They have decongestant effects, and are also used externally for soothing and healing wounds. A number of species, known generally as *rabas*, *rabassam*, or *rooirabas*, have tuberous roots that are chewed, taken in the form of infusions or decoctions (sometimes in milk), or powdered and mixed with food to control diarrhoea. These include

P. rapaceum, *P. reniforme*, *P. sidoides*, *P. triste*, and the aptly named *P. antidysentericum* (dysentery pelargonium), which is often infused and taken with lemon juice for gastrointestinal complaints. The leaves of *P. acetosum* (sorrel leaf) have an acidic taste, and may be eaten raw in salads, or added to soups and stews. *Pelargonium* comes from the Greek *pelargos*, "stork"; it refers to the shape of the fruit, which resembles a stork's beak.

CULTIVATION Well-drained, neutral to alkaline soil in sun. *Pelargonium crispum*, *P. odoratissimum*, and *P. tomentosum* tolerate partial shade. Plants may be cut back in early spring. If grown outdoors in cool climates, they may also be cut back before bringing in for the winter. Leafhoppers, aphid, red spider mite, and whitefly may attack plants under cover.

PROPAGATION By softwood cuttings in spring, late summer, or early autumn.

HARVEST Plants are cut in late summer and distilled for oil. Leaves are picked as required.

■ *Pelargonium capitatum* (rose-scented geranium, wild rose geranium)
Low, spreading, evergreen perennial with velvety, crinkled, 3–5-lobed, rose-scented leaves, 2–8cm (¾–3¼in) across, and clusters of 10–20 mauve-pink flowers, to 2cm (¾in) across. Native to South Africa. ‡ 30–90cm (12–36in), ↔ 45–1.5m (1½–5ft).
HARDINESS Min. 2°C (36°F).
PARTS USED Whole plant, leaves, oil.
PROPERTIES An aromatic, soothing, emollient herb with a rose-like aroma. Oil is fungicidal, antioxidant, and insect-repellent.
MEDICINAL USES Internally as a traditional Cape remedy for minor digestive ailments, and kidney and bladder disorders. Externally for rashes, and calloused and cracked skin. Oil is a major component of geranium oil, used in aromatherapy.
ECONOMIC USES Oil is used in perfumery

and skin-care products. Leaves are dried for potpourris.

■ *Pelargonium citronellum*
Upright bushy subshrub with deeply veined, strongly lemon-scented leaves, about 6cm (2½in) long and 8cm (3½in) wide, and clusters of 5–8 purple-pink flowers with dark purple markings. Native to South Africa (S Cape). ‡ 1.2–2m (4–6ft), ↔ 1m (3ft).
HARDINESS Min. 2°C (36°F).
PARTS USED Leaves.
PROPERTIES An aromatic, lemon-scented herb.
CULINARY USES Leaves may be infused to make tea, and used fresh to flavour desserts, punch, and vinegar.
ECONOMIC USES Leaves are dried for potpourris and herb pillows.

■ *Pelargonium crispum* (lemon geranium)
Stiffly upright subshrub with numerous, rough, crinkled, kidney-shaped leaves, 1cm (½in) long, which are strongly lemon-scented, and pink flowers, 2cm (¾in) across. Native to South Africa. ‡ 60–70cm (24–28in), ↔ 30–45cm (12–18in). ■ 'Major' (fingerbowl geranium) has larger leaves, to 2.5cm (1in) long. Ideal for finger bowls instead of lemon slices. 'Minor' has a stiff compact habit. ■ 'Peach Cream' has a fruity scent and irregular, creamy white variegation, with some leaves entirely cream or overlaid with cream. ■ 'Variegatum' has crinkled, cream-edged leaves. Suitable for training as a standard, reaching 1m (3ft).
HARDINESS Min. 2°C (36°F).
PARTS USED Leaves.
PROPERTIES An aromatic herb with a lemon aroma.
CULINARY USES Leaves may be infused to make tea, and used fresh to give a lemon flavour to fish, poultry, soups, sauces, sorbets,

Pelargonium capitatum

Pelargonium citronellum

Pelargonium crispum

Pelargonium crispum 'Major'

Pelargonium crispum 'Peach Cream'

Pelargonium crispum 'Variegatum'

Pelargonium Fragrans Group

Pelargonium Fragrans Group 'Creamy Nutmeg'

Pelargonium Fragrans Group 'Fragrans Variegatum'

Pelargonium 'Graveolens'

P

ice cream, fruit punch, and vinegar; also placed at bottom of cake tins to infuse batter with lemon flavour.

ECONOMIC USES Leaves are dried for potpourris and herb pillows.

▨ ◪ ◪ ◻

▣ *Pelargonium* **Fragrans Group** syn.
P. 'Fragrans', *P.* × *fragrans* (nutmeg geranium)
Bushy subshrub with small, pine-scented, grey-green, ovate–cordate leaves, which have a silky texture and three lobes. Clusters of 4–8 white flowers, about 1cm (½in) across, marked with two red lines, appear in spring and summer. Probably a cross between *P. exstipulatum* and *P. odoratissimum* but considered a true species by some botanists. ↔ 30–40cm (12–16in).
▣ 'Creamy Nutmeg' has a low habit and small leaves with broad cream margins. ▣ 'Fragrans Variegatum' syn. 'Snowy Nutmeg' has cream to chartreuse variegation.

HARDINESS Min. 2°C (36°F).
PARTS USED Leaves.
PROPERTIES An aromatic herb with a spicy, pine-like scent.
MEDICINAL USES Externally as a rub for aching feet or legs (fresh leaves).
CULINARY USES Leaves give flavour to pâté, jellies, desserts, cakes, punches, and coffee.
ECONOMIC USES Dried leaves are added to potpourris.

▨ ▣ ◪ ◪ ◻

▣ *Pelargonium* **'Graveolens'** (rose geranium)
Vigorous erect subshrub with midgreen, rose-scented, triangular, toothed leaves, to 6cm (2½in) long, which have a slightly rough texture. Pale pink flowers, with two purple spots, are borne in spring and summer. Possibly derived from *P. capitatum*, *P. graveolens*, and *P. radens*. Dates back to the 1790s. ↕ 1–1.5m (3–5ft), ↔ 60cm–1.5m (2–5ft).

HARDINESS Min. 2°C (36°F).
PARTS USED Leaves, oil.
PROPERTIES An aromatic herb that has relaxant, anti-depressant, and antiseptic effects, reduces inflammation, and controls bleeding. It has a strong, lemon–rose scent. Oil is anti-fungal, antioxidant, and insect-repellent.
MEDICINAL USES Internally for premenstrual and menopausal problems, nausea, tonsillitis, and poor circulation. Externally for acne, eczema, haemorrhoids, bruises, ringworm, and lice.
CULINARY USES Fresh leaves are infused for tea and used to flavour fruit drinks, punches, jellies, desserts, creams and custards, confectionery, pastries, and baked fruits.
ECONOMIC USES Oil is the main constituent of geranium oil, used in skin-care products, perfumery, aromatherapy, and food flavouring. Dried leaves are added to potpourris.

▨ ▣ ▣ ◪ ◪ ◻

▣ *Pelargonium* **odoratissimum** (apple geranium)
Low-growing, bushy, evergreen perennial with light green, rounded, wavy-edged leaves, 4–5cm (1½–2in) across, which have a pronounced apple aroma. Clusters of 3–10 white, red-veined flowers, about 1cm (⅜in) across, are borne on trailing flower stems. Native to South Africa (KwaZulu/Natal, N Transvaal, E and W Cape). ↕ 20–30cm (8–12in), ↔ 45–60cm (18–24in).

HARDINESS Min. 2°C (36°F).
PARTS USED Whole plant, leaves, oil.
PROPERTIES An aromatic herb with a fruity scent. It has astringent, tonic, and antiseptic effects, controls bleeding, promotes healing, and repels insects.
MEDICINAL USES Internally for debility, gastroenteritis, and haemorrhage. Externally for skin complaints, injuries, neuralgia, and throat infections. Oil used in aromatherapy for burns,

Pelargonium odoratissimum

sores, and shingles.
CULINARY USES Leaves are used to flavour desserts, syrups, sauces, fruit drinks, and punches.
ECONOMIC USES Leaves are dried for potpourris.

▨ ▣ ▣ ▣ ◪ ◪ ◻

▣ *Pelargonium* **radens** (rasp-leafed pelargonium)
Upright, bushy, evergreen subshrub with rough, triangular, grey-green leaves, to 6cm (2½in) long, deeply divided into oblong segments, which have a strong lemon scent and margins rolled under. Clusters of star-shaped, pale to purple-pink flowers, to 1.5cm (½in) across, appear in late spring and summer. Native to South Africa (E and W Cape). ↔ 1–1.5m (3–5ft).

HARDINESS Min. 2°C (36°F).
PARTS USED Leaves.
PROPERTIES An aromatic herb with a lemon scent.
MEDICINAL USES Externally as a rub for aching feet or legs (fresh leaves).

Pelargonium radens

Pelargonium tomentosum

Pelargonium 'Chocolate Peppermint'

Pelargonium 'Clorinda'

Pelargonium 'Fair Ellen'

Pelargonium 'Galway Star'

Pelargonium 'Grey Lady Plymouth'

Pelargonium 'Lady Plymouth'

P

CULINARY USES Leaves are used to flavour cakes, tea, and foods requiring a lemon flavour.
ECONOMIC USES Dried leaves are added to insect-repellent sachets and act as a fixative for other perfumes in potpourris.

◪ ▣ ◿ ◿ ▣

■ *Pelargonium tomentosum* (peppermint geranium)
Spreading, evergreen, shrubby perennial with midgreen, heart-shaped, lobed, velvety leaves, 10–12cm (4–5in) across, which are strongly peppermint scented. Clusters of 5–15 narrow-petalled, white flowers, 1.5cm (½in) across, with purple markings, appear in spring and summer. South Africa (W Cape). ‡ 30–50cm (12–20in), ↔ 1–1.2m (3–4ft).
HARDINESS Min. 2°C (36°F).
PARTS USED Leaves.
PROPERTIES Aromatic herb with peppermint scent.
MEDICINAL USES As a poultice for bruises and sprains.
CULINARY USES Fresh leaves are used to flavour tea, desserts, jellies, and chocolate cakes.
ECONOMIC USES Dried leaves are added to potpourris.

◪ ▣ ◿ ◿ ▣

Pelargonium hybrids (scented-leafed pelargoniums): 'Attar of Roses' has an upright habit, with rough, strongly rose-scented, three-lobed leaves and mauve flowers, to 3cm (1¼in) across. ‡ 50–60cm (20–24in), ↔ 25–30cm (10–12in). ■ 'Chocolate Peppermint' syn. 'Chocolate' has leaves with a dark brown central blotch. ‡ 30–50cm (12–20in), ↔ 1–1.2m (3–4ft). ■ 'Clorinda' is vigorous, with bright green, three-lobed, cedar-scented leaves, about 6cm (2½in) long, and clusters of rose-pink flowers, 4cm (1½in) across. ‡↔ 1.2m (4ft). ■ 'Fair Ellen' is compact, with divided,

Pelargonium 'Radula Rosea'

balsam-scented leaves, which have a dark mark along the midrib, and pale mauve-pink flowers with deep pink markings and toothed petals. ‡ 30–60cm (12–24in), ↔ 60–90cm (24–36in). ■ 'Galway Star' has cream-edged, crinkled, lemon-scented leaves and pale pink flowers with cerise and purple markings. Possibly derived from *P. crispum*. ‡ 45–60cm (18–24in), ↔ 30–45cm (12–18in). ■ 'Grey Lady Plymouth' has grey-green foliage. ‡ 1–1.5m (3–5ft), ↔ 60cm–1.5m (2–5ft). ■ 'Lady Plymouth' has irregular cream margins, and a minty, rose–lemon scent. First recorded c.1800. ‡ 1–1.5m (3–5ft), ↔ 60cm–1.5m (2–5ft). 'Mabel Grey' is robust, with rough-textured, 5–7-lobed leaves, which have an intense lemon scent. Excellent for culinary use. ‡ 1.2–2m (4–6ft), ↔ 1m (3ft). ■ 'Old Spice' has a compact habit and crinkled leaves. ‡ 60–70cm (24–28in), ↔ 30–45cm (12–18in). ■ 'Prince of Orange' has a compact habit and fan-shaped, orange-scented leaves. Derived from *P. crispum* before 1880. ‡ 25–60cm (10–24in), ↔ 15–60cm (6–24in). ■ 'Radula' has deeply cut leaves,

10cm (4in) across, with a camphoraceous, rose–lemon scent, and small, pink-purple flowers. Suitable for linen sachets. ‡ 1–1.5m (3–5ft), ↔ 60cm–1.5m (2–5ft). ■ 'Radula Rosea' is similar to 'Radula' but has deep rose-pink flowers. ■ 'Rober's Lemon Rose' is vigorous, with soft, grey-green, unevenly lobed leaves, about 5cm (2in) long, with a lemon–rose scent. ‡ 1–1.5m (3–5ft), ↔ 60cm–1.5m (2–5ft). ■ 'Royal Oak' is vigorous, with slightly sticky, shiny, balsam-scented leaves, 5–7cm (2–3in) long, which resemble oak leaves in shape and have dark central markings. Pink-purple flowers with darker spots are borne in clusters to 3cm (1¼in) across. ‡ 60cm–1.5m (2–5ft), ↔ 60cm–1.2m (2–4ft). ■ 'Sweet Mimosa' has bright green, round-lobed leaves, about 9cm (3½in) across, with a sweet fruit scent, and shell-pink flowers, 2.5cm (1in) across. ‡↔ 1–1.2m (3–4ft).

PERILLA
Lamiaceae

A genus of six species of aromatic annuals, with erect, four-angled stems, which occurs from India to Japan. *Perilla frutescens* is widely grown as a culinary herb in E Asia and is increasingly popular as an ornamental for summer bedding. It is similar in appearance to *Solenostemon* spp. (coleus). Plants with curly leaves were once described as a separate species, *Perilla crispa*, but are now regarded as a cultivated variety. Volatile oil in the leaves of *P. frutescens* contains perillaldehyde, which is 2000 times sweeter than sugar and up to eight times sweeter than saccharin. The seed oil is high in linolenic acid. *Perilla* has been used medicinally in China since c.AD500. Both green- and purple-leafed forms (sometimes referred to as green *shiso* and red *shiso*) of *P. frutescens* are used for culinary purposes, but seeds of purple-leafed variants are preferred for all uses.
CULTIVATION Well-drained, moist, fertile soil in sun or partial shade. Pinch out growing tips, to encourage bushiness.
PROPAGATION By seed sown at 13–18°C (55–64°F) in spring.
HARVEST Leaves are cut in summer and used fresh or pickled, or dried for decoctions. Stems are cut when young in summer, or after the plant has gone to seed. Ripe seeds are collected in autumn and dried for decoctions.
⚠ **WARNING** Prolonged skin contact with perilla may cause dermatitis.

■ *Perilla frutescens* syn. *P. ocimoides* (beefsteak plant, *shiso*)
Vigorous, strongly aromatic, branched annual with broadly ovate, pointed, midgreen, sometimes purple-flecked or -flushed leaves, to 12cm (5in) long, which have toothed margins and distinct veins. Tiny, white to violet-pink flowers appear in spikes, to 10cm (4in) long, in summer, followed by pale brown nutlets. Found from Himalayas to Japan; naturalized in parts of N America. ‡ 60cm–1.2m (2–4ft), ↔ 30–60cm

Pelargonium 'Old Spice'

Pelargonium 'Prince of Orange'

Pelargonium 'Radula'

Pelargonium 'Rober's Lemon Rose'

Pelargonium 'Royal Oak'

Pelargonium 'Sweet Mimosa'

Perilla frutescens

(12–24in). ■ var. *crispa* syn. var. *nankinensis* has deeply cut, crinkled, bronze-purple leaves and pink flowers. Very variable. 'Green' syn. 'Ao Shiso' has bright green, ginger-flavoured leaves and a cinnamon aroma. Preferred for salads and garnishing. 'Green Cumin' has green, cumin-flavoured leaves and a cinnamon aroma. Used fresh or dried. 'Hojiso' has green, red-backed leaves and compact flower spikes, harvested before flowering when 7cm (3in) long. 'Kkaennip' is a Korean cultivar with large green leaves, to 15cm (6in) long, lacking the cinnamon aroma of Japanese varieties. Eaten raw, cooked, or used for wrapping meat before cooking. 'Purple Cumin' is like 'Green Cumin' but with ruffled purple leaves. 'Red' syn. 'Aka Shiso' has strongly flavoured, red-purple leaves, used to flavour and colour pickles.

HARDINESS Hardy.

PARTS USED Leaves (*zi su ye*), stems (*su gen, zi su geng*), seeds (*su zi, zi su zi*), flower spikes (*hojiso*), oil.

PROPERTIES A pungent, aromatic, warming herb that relaxes spasms, increases perspiration, and is effective against bacterial infections. It is also laxative, expectorant, and controls coughing.

MEDICINAL USES Internally for colds and chills, coughs, rheumatism, bronchitis, asthma, constipation, nausea, abdominal pain, food poisoning, and allergic reactions, especially from seafood (seeds). Stems are a traditional Chinese remedy for morning sickness.

CULINARY USES Fresh leaves are eaten in salads

Perilla frutescens var. *crispa*

and used for garnishing or wrapping meats prior to cooking. Pickled leaves are used as a garnish or condiment. Red (purple) leaves are used to colour and flavour pickled *umeboshi* plums, ginger, and Chinese artichokes. Seeds are sprouted for salads or salted as a condiment for Japanese raw fish, bean curd, tempura, and pickles. Immature flower spikes are used raw for garnishing, or fried as a vegetable.

ECONOMIC USES Oil from foliage is used in sauces, tobacco, confectionery, and dental products. Oil from seeds (*yegoma*) is used in waterproofing and in the paper, printing, and paint industries.

⊞ ▱ ▤ ▨ ▧ ▪ ⁄ ⁄

PERSEA
Lauraceae

A genus of about 150 species of evergreen trees and shrubs, found in tropical and subtropical America, Macaronesia, and SE Asia. Avocado is a major crop in many warm regions worldwide for its nutritious fruits, which are rich in oil, vitamin A, B1, and B2, and have the highest protein content of any fruit (about 25 per cent). Including avocados regularly in the diet helps lower cholesterol levels. There are three main kinds of avocado: Guatemalan, which are common in Florida and Australia, with thick granular skins, which peel easily, and a high oil content (18–27 per cent); Mexican cultivars, with aromatic, anise-scented foliage and thin skins, which cling to the flesh; and West Indian varieties, which have very large fruits, weighing up to 2kg (5lb), with pliable leathery skin and a low oil content. *Persea borbonia*, *P. humilis*, and *P. palustris* (all known as "red bay") have aromatic leaves that are reminiscent of sweet bay (see *Laurus nobilis*, p.252) and can be used as a substitute. They are characteristic of Creole cuisine. Similarly, *Litsea glaucescens* (Mexican bay), which also belongs to the family Lauraceae, is used to give a bay-like flavour in Mexican cuisine.

CULTIVATION Well-drained, medium soil, pH5.5–6.5, in full sun, between 20–28°C (68–82°F), with humidity above 60 per cent (avocados); some Mexican and Guatemalan cultivars withstand low temperatures but do not usually flower or fruit well as a result. Avocados are prone to root rot, fungal leafspot, and, under glass, to whitefly, red spider mite, and mealybugs. Rich, moist, slightly acidic soil in sun or partial shade (*Persea borbonia*).

PROPAGATION By seed sown when ripe in sandy compost, with upper half above surface, at 20–28°C (68–82°F) (avocado). Soak seed in hot water for 30 minutes, then cut off 1cm (⅜in) from tip of seed, before sowing. By seed sown when ripe, chilled for seven days before sowing (*P. borbonia*).

HARVEST Fruits are picked when ripe and used fresh or pressed for oil. Leaves are collected during the growing season and dried for infusions. Bark is removed from young branches after pruning for use in decoctions.

Persea americana

■ *Persea americana* (alligator pear, avocado) Spreading, much-branched, evergreen tree with ovate–elliptic, pointed, dark green leaves, 10–25cm (4–10in) long, which have paler undersides and a slightly leathery to papery texture. Small greenish flowers are followed by oblong–ovoid, globose, or pear-shaped, yellow-green to maroon, brown, or dark purple-green fruits, to 12cm (5in) long, containing lime-green to yellow flesh and a single large seed. Native to C America. ↔ 10–15m (30–45ft). 'Hass' is a prolific Guatemalan × Mexican variety, bearing medium-sized, pear-shaped to ovoid, dark purple to black fruits. 'Pollock' is a West Indian avocado with few but very large, oblong to pear-shaped, glossy fruits, to 2kg (5lb). 'Wurtz' syn. 'Little Cado' is a slow-growing Guatemalan cultivar, with a small weeping habit and small to medium, green fruits. Suitable for containers and greenhouse cultivation. ↔ 2.5–3m (8–10ft).

HARDINESS Min. 10°C (50°F).

PARTS USED Fruits, seeds, leaves, bark, oil.

PROPERTIES A nutritious, emollient (fruits), astringent (seeds, bark) herb that is diuretic, carminative, and lowers blood pressure (leaves). Leaves and bark stimulate the uterus.

MEDICINAL USES Internally for high blood pressure (leaves), coughs and colds, fever, diarrhoea, digestive and bronchial complaints (bark, leaves), dysentery, intestinal obstructions (seeds). Externally for headaches, rheumatism, and sprains (poultice of leaves), dry skin, scalp, and hair, and to stimulate hair growth (fruits, oil).

CULINARY USES Fruits are eaten raw in salads, sandwiches, and spreads (*guacamole*); also used to make ice cream, desserts, and iced drinks. Oil is used in salad dressings. Leaves are made into tea or toasted as a flavouring for bean stews.

▣ ▨ ▱ ▤ ▧ ▪ ⁄ ⊡

Persea borbonia (red bay, tisswood) Small evergreen tree with ascending, red-brown branches and lustrous, lanceolate, tapering leaves, to 15cm (6in) long. Creamy white to yellow, bell-shaped flowers, 1–2cm (⅜–¾in) long, are produced in clusters in the axils in spring, followed by blue-black fruits, 5mm (¼in) across, with a powdery or waxy coating and persistent calyx. Native to SE USA. ↕ 10–12m (30–40ft), ↔ 5m (15ft).

HARDINESS Min. 10°C (50°F).
PARTS USED Leaves.
PROPERTIES An aromatic herb with insect-repellent effects. Leaves have an aroma similar to *Laurus nobilis* (bay, see p.252) but more camphoraceous.
CULINARY USES Fresh or dried leaves are used to flavour Creole dishes, and as a substitute for bay leaves; also infused for tea.
ECONOMIC USES Foliage is used to repel insects from dried foods in pantries and cupboards.

PERSICARIA
Knotweed
Polygonaceae

This cosmopolitan genus of annuals, perennials, and deciduous shrubby climbers numbers about 150 species, mainly distributed in temperate regions. Many are weeds and often invasive as garden plants. *Persicaria bistorta* (bistort) is grown in herb gardens, but its variants are much better for borders and ground cover, making a better show of colour. *Persicaria bistorta* was once known as "serpentaria", because of its contorted, snake-like rhizomes. A number of other species are used medicinally, including *P. aviculare* (knotgrass), an astringent diuretic herb traditionally used in both Western and Chinese herbal medicine to expel intestinal parasites and control diarrhoea, bleeding, and discharges. Research has shown that it is an effective remedy for bacillary dysentery. *Persicaria hydropiper* (smartweed, water pepper) is also used medicinally, mainly for failure to menstruate. Similar in appearance to *P. hydropiper* is the tender, moisture-loving *P. odorata*, used as a medicinal and culinary herb in SE Asia. The young leaves have a pungent, coriander-like aroma and develop a biting hot taste as they age. Very similar in aroma and appearance to *P. odorata* is the smaller-leafed *P. minus* (*kesum*), which is used in Malaysian cuisine to give a coriander-like flavour to dishes such as *laksa*. It is also used medicinally for indigestion, and after childbirth. The essential oil is rich in aldehydes, which have potential in commercial food flavouring and perfumery.
CULTIVATION Rich moist soil in sun or partial shade.
PROPAGATION By seed sown in autumn or spring; by division in autumn or spring; by semi-ripe cuttings in summer, which root easily in soil or water.
HARVEST Rhizomes are lifted in autumn and dried for decoctions, infusions, liquid extracts, powders, and tinctures. Young leaves are picked as required and used fresh.

◾ *Persicaria bistorta* syn. *Polygonum bistorta* (bistort, English serpentary, snakeweed)
Erect perennial with a stout contorted rhizome and broadly ovate basal leaves, to 15cm (6in) long. Tiny, pale pink flowers appear in dense spikes, 5–7cm (2–3in) long, in summer, followed by hard nutlets. Native to Europe and

Persicaria bistorta

N and W Asia. ‡ 25–50cm (10–20in), ↔ 45–90cm (18–36in). ◾ 'Superba' is larger all round and more floriferous than the species. ‡ 90cm (36in).
HARDINESS Fully hardy.
PARTS USED Rhizomes.
PROPERTIES An astringent, soothing, cooling herb that reduces inflammation, controls diarrhoea and bleeding, and promotes healing.
MEDICINAL USES Internally for diarrhoea (especially in babies), cholera, dysentery, catarrh, cystitis, mucous colitis, and heavy menstruation. Externally for pharyngitis, stomatitis, vaginal discharge, anal fissure, purulent wounds, haemorrhoids, mouth ulcers, and gum disease. Combines well with *Agrimonia eupatoria* (see p.107), *Geranium maculatum* (see p.223), or *Quercus robur* (see p.339) for diarrhoea.
CULINARY USES Young leaves and shoots are the main ingredient of a traditional savoury herb pudding, known as Easter ledger/ledges, or Easter mangiant (often abbreviated to "Easter

Persicaria bistorta 'Superba'

giant") in N England. Roots are edible after soaking in water to reduce astringency.

Persicaria odorata syn. *Polygonum odoratum* (Asian mint, hot mint, laksa plant/leaves, *rau răm*, Vietnamese coriander)
Sprawling perennial, rooting at nodes, with jointed stems and lanceolate leaves, to 5–10cm (2–4in) long, often with a dark maroon, heart-shaped patch near the centre of the blade. Tiny pink flowers are produced in spikes. Native to SE Asia. ‡ 45cm (18in), ↔ 1.2m (4ft).
HARDINESS Min. 7°C (45°F).
PARTS USED Leaves.
PROPERTIES A strongly aromatic herb that aids digestion and has anaphrodisiac effects.
MEDICINAL USES Internally to improve digestion and depress sexual appetite. Externally for ringworm.
CULINARY USES Coriander-flavoured young leaves are added to salads, meat dishes (especially fowl), duck eggs, and the sauerkraut-like *du'a cân* in Vietnamese cuisine.

PETIVERIA
Phytolaccaceae

A single species of perennial belongs to this genus, which occurs in tropical and warm parts of America and is naturalized in parts of tropical Asia and Africa. It is related to *Phytolacca* (pokeweed, see p.314). *Petiveria alliacea* is not in general cultivation but may occasionally be seen in botanic gardens. Being widely used as a ritual and magic plant in S and C America and the Caribbean, the plant has innumerable common names in many languages. The strong, garlic-like smell of *P. alliacea* is caused by the presence of a compound containing sulphur. This pungent odour may account for its popularity as a medicinal herb. No information is available on its efficacy; it is apparently always used in conjunction with other herbs.
CULTIVATION Rich moist soil in partial shade.
PROPAGATION By seed sown when ripe; by semi-ripe cuttings during the growing season.
HARVEST Whole plants, leaves, and roots are collected for use in decoctions. Fresh leaves are bound around the head for headaches or juiced for direct application for earache.

◾ *Petiveria alliacea* (conga root, Guinea hen weed, strong man's weed)
Perennial, woody at the base, with a thick taproot, slender stems, and elliptic to obovate, pointed leaves, 10–15cm (4–6in) long. All parts exude a strong garlic odour when crushed. Tiny, white to green-white, star-like flowers are borne in sparse slender racemes, 15–40cm (6–16in) long, all year round, followed by hooked fruits. Found from S USA to Argentina and the West Indies. ‡ 1m (3ft), ↔ 30–60cm (1–2ft).
HARDINESS Min. 10°C (50°F).
PARTS USED Whole plant, leaves, roots.
PROPERTIES A pungent, diuretic, antiseptic herb that reputedly calms the nerves, controls

Petiveria alliacea

diarrhoea, lowers fever, stimulates the uterus, and relaxes spasms.

MEDICINAL USES Internally for nervous spasms, paralysis, hysteria, asthma, whooping cough, pneumonia, bronchitis, hoarseness, fevers, headaches, influenza, cystitis, venereal disease, and menstrual complaints; also to induce abortion. Combined with *Eryngium foetidum* (see p.205) for fevers. Steeped in rum as an aphrodisiac (Caribbean). Externally for earache, fever, skin eruptions, toothache, and headache.

PETROSELINUM

Apiaceae

Three species of biennials belong to this European genus. *Petroselinum crispum* (parsley) is the most widely cultivated herb in Europe, usually grown as an annual year-round by sowing at intervals from early spring to early autumn. It became popular in Roman times; a curly variant was first mentioned in AD42 and rapidly gained favour for its appearance. Curly parsleys are neat attractive plants that may be grown as edging or in containers. Plain or flat-leafed parsleys have a stronger flavour than curly-leafed cultivars; leaves of var. *tuberosum* (Hamburg parsley) are inferior for flavouring purposes. Parsley is rich in iron and vitamins A, C, and E; it also contains apigenin, a flavonoid that reduces allergic responses and acts as an antioxidant. The composition of volatile oils differs between the leaves and seeds. Although quite safe in the amounts given in recipes, parsley is toxic in excess, especially in the form of essential oil. Hamburg parsley has been grown for its edible roots since the 16th century. As the name suggests, it is most popular in Germany, where there are a number of cultivars that produce larger, better-quality roots.

CULTIVATION Rich, well-drained, neutral to alkaline soil in sun or partial shade. Plants may be damaged by leafspot, virus disease, and larvae of carrot fly and celery fly. Winter crops may need protection in frost-prone areas.

PROPAGATION By seed sown from spring to late summer. Parsley seed takes 3–6 weeks to germinate but will do so sooner if seeds are soaked overnight in warm water.

HARVEST Leaves are picked before flowering and used fresh, frozen, juiced, or dried. Roots are lifted in late autumn of first year, or spring of second year, and dried for decoctions and liquid extracts. Seeds are collected when ripe and dried for infusions and liquid extracts. Oil is distilled from leaves and seeds.

■ *Petroselinum crispum* (parsley)
Clump-forming biennial with a white taproot and bright green, triangular, pinnate leaves, divided into ovate toothed segments, to 3cm (1¼in) long, which have variably curled margins. Tiny, yellow-green flowers are produced in flat-topped umbels, to 4cm (1½in) across, in summer, followed by tiny, ribbed, ovoid fruits. Native to SE Europe and W Asia. ‡ 30–80cm (12–32in), ↔ 30–45cm (12–18in). ■ 'Afro' has strong stems and tightly curled leaves. ‡ 20–30cm (8–12in). 'Clivi' is compact and dwarf. Ideal for containers. ‡ 20cm (8in), ↔ 30cm (12in); ■ var. *neapolitanum* syn. 'Italian' (French parsley, Italian parsley) has large, dark green leaves, with flat segments, and a stronger flavour. Hardier and more weather-resistant. ‡ 90cm (36in), ↔ 60cm (24in). ■ var. *tuberosum* (Hamburg parsley, turnip-rooted parsley) has parsnip-like roots and non-curly foliage, with a parsley–celery flavour. ‡ 35cm (14in), ↔ 30cm (12in).

HARDINESS Fully hardy.
PARTS USED Leaves, roots, seeds, oil.

Petroselinum crispum

Petroselinum crispum 'Afro'

Petroselinum crispum var. *neapolitanum*

Petroselinum crispum var. *tuberosum*

PROPERTIES A bitter, aromatic, diuretic herb that relaxes spasms, reduces inflammation, and clears toxins. It stimulates the digestion and uterus.

MEDICINAL USES Internally for menstrual complaints, oedema, cystitis, prostatitis, kidney stones, indigestion, colic, anorexia, anaemia, arthritis, and rheumatism (roots, seeds); after delivery, for promoting lactation and contracting the uterus (roots, seeds). Excess causes abortion, liver and kidney damage, nerve inflammation, and gastrointestinal haemorrhage. Contraindicated in pregnancy and kidney disease (seeds).

CULINARY USES Leaves are used as garnish and to flavour sauces, butter, dressings, stuffings, and savoury dishes. An essential ingredient of *salsa verde* (Mexico), *tabouleh* (Middle East), and *chimichurri* (Argentina); also of sautéed herb and garlic garnishes *persillade* (France) and *gremolata* (Italy).

ECONOMIC USES Oil is used in commercial food flavouring and perfumes for men. Juice is added to blended vegetable juices.

PEUCEDANUM

Peucedanum graveolens. See *Anethum graveolens*.

PEUMUS

Monimiaceae

This genus consists of a single species of evergreen shrub or small tree, which is found only in Chile. It belongs to the family Monimiaceae, which has an unusually high number of single-species genera, most of which yield aromatic oils. *Peumus boldus* is economically important in Chile, yielding hardwood, tannins, and dye from the bark, edible fruits, and medicinal compounds. It is seldom seen in cultivation. The foliage has a lemon–camphor aroma. *Peumus boldus* was first investigated by a French physician in 1869. It contains a volatile oil that destroys internal parasites, and alkaloids that stimulate the liver. Alkaloids extracted from the bark are more effective than leaf-based preparations.

CULTIVATION Well-drained, sandy, acid soil in sun.

PROPAGATION By seed sown in spring; by semi-ripe cuttings in summer.

HARVEST Leaves are picked during the growing season and dried for infusions, liquid extracts, and tinctures. Alkaloids are extracted commercially from the bark.

■ *Peumus boldus* (boldo)
Shrubby tree with smooth brown bark and ovate, leathery, aromatic leaves, to 7cm (3in) long. Pale yellow-green, scented flowers, to 1cm (⅜in) across, appear in clusters in autumn, male and female flowers on separate plants; females bear edible, pale yellow fruits, to 7mm (¼in) long. Native to Chile. ‡ 7m (22ft), ↔ 5m (15ft).

HARDINESS Frost hardy.

P

Peumus boldus

PARTS USED Leaves, bark.

PROPERTIES A bitter aromatic herb that improves liver and gall bladder function, and expels worms. It is diuretic and a mild urinary antiseptic.

MEDICINAL USES Internally for liver disease, gallstones, urinary tract infections, intestinal parasites, and rheumatism. Formerly given as a substitute for quinine. Often added to weight-reduction formulas. Combines well with *Berberis vulgaris* (see p.142) and *Chionanthus virginicus* (see p.167) for liver and gall bladder complaints. Contraindicated during pregnancy.

CULINARY USES Aromatic leaves and bark are used locally for flavouring.

⚠ **WARNING** This herb is subject to legal restrictions in some countries.

🏠 🗎 🖈 ✎

PFAFFIA

Amaranthaceae

There are about 50 mostly shrubby species in this genus, which occurs in warmer parts of C and S America. Best known is *Pfaffia paniculata*, which grows in the Upper Amazon rainforest and is known locally as *paratudo*, "for everything", a cure-all. The roots have been used by native Brazilians as a tonic, aphrodisiac, and healing herb for at least 300 years. They contain 11 per cent saponins, known as pfaffosides, including pfaffic acid and derivatives that have been patented as anti-tumour drugs. Other constituents include ecdysone, which has analgesic and anti-diabetic effects, and trace elements, such as germanium, and allantoin, a healing substance also found in *Symphytum officinale* (see p.377). The ground root is popular as a tonic during convalescence and menopause. As an immune stimulant and adaptogen, it is considered on a par with *Panax* spp. (ginseng, see p.299), though with hormonal effects better suited to women.

CULTIVATION AND PROPAGATION Pfaffia appears to be wild-collected, as no references have been found on its cultivation.

HARVEST Roots are collected from mature plants, about seven years old, and dried for decoctions, powder, and tablets.

Pfaffia paniculata syn. *Gomphrena paniculata*, *Hebanthe paniculata*, *Iresine erianthos* (Brazilian ginseng, *corang-acu*, *paratudo*, pfaffia, suma)
Scrambling shrubby vine with a large rootstock, lustrous woody stems, hairy young branches, and smooth, elliptic to oblong–elliptic, pointed leaves, 10–13cm (4–5in) long, which have shallowly toothed or scalloped margins. Tiny, greenish-white flowers, surrounded by a tuft of whitish hairs, are produced in branched panicles. Found in rainforest in Brazil, Ecuador, Paraguay, and Peru; also in Panama, possibly introduced rather than native. ↕ 2–3m (6–10ft).

HARDINESS Min. 15°C (59°F).

PARTS USED Roots.

PROPERTIES A tonic, sedative, analgesic herb that lowers blood sugar and cholesterol levels, and has hormonal, tissue-healing, and anti-inflammatory effects. It is an adaptogen and immune stimulant, and is reputedly aphrodisiac.

MEDICINAL USES Internally for stress, chronic fatigue, debility, poor appetite, Epstein-Barr disease, glandular fever, infertility, impotence, menstrual and menopausal problems, diabetes, pancreas dysfunction, ulcers, rheumatism, osteomyelitis, hypertension, cardiovascular disease, nervous disorders, chronic degenerative diseases, and various kinds of cancer. Also to improve resistance to infection and increase stamina. Internally and externally for wounds and fractures.

ECONOMIC USES Extracts are added to food supplements and herbal tonics.

🗺 🗎 🖈 🏠

PHELLODENDRON

Rutaceae

Ten species of deciduous trees belong to this genus, which is E Asian in distribution. They resemble *Ailanthus* spp. (see p.107) in appearance, with a graceful spreading habit. *Phellodendron amurense* is grown as an ornamental for its attractive bark and aromatic leaves, which turn yellow in autumn. It has a long history of use in traditional Chinese medicine. *Phellodendron chinense*, a smaller tree from C China, is used for similar purposes. Both contain alkaloids, such as berberine (as found in *Berberis vulgaris*, see p.142), sesquiterpene lactones, and plant sterols. *Phellodendron* is from the Greek *phellos*, "cork", and *dendron*, "tree", an allusion to the bark of these trees.

CULTIVATION Rich, well-drained, neutral to alkaline soil in sun. Young growth may be damaged by late frosts in cold areas.

PROPAGATION By seed sown in autumn; by heeled semi-ripe cuttings in summer.

HARVEST Bark is stripped in winter and dried for use in decoctions.

▪ *Phellodendron amurense* (Amur cork tree)
Spreading deciduous tree with thick, corky, pale grey-brown bark and glossy, dark green, pinnate leaves, to 35cm (14in) long, divided

Phellodendron amurense

into 9–13 ovate leaflets, 5–10cm (2–4in) long. Small, yellow-green flowers are produced in downy panicles, to 8cm (3in) long, in early summer – males and females on separate plants – followed on females by black fruits, 1cm (⅜in) across, with a turpentine aroma. Native to NE Asia. ↕ 12–15m (40–50ft), ↔ 15m (50ft).

HARDINESS Fully hardy.

PARTS USED Bark (*huang bai*).

PROPERTIES A bitter, diuretic, cooling herb that stimulates the liver and gall bladder, lowers fever, reduces blood pressure and blood sugar levels, and is strongly anti-bacterial. It acts mainly on the kidneys and is traditionally regarded as a detoxicant for hot damp conditions.

MEDICINAL USES Internally for diarrhoea, dysentery, jaundice, meningitis, acute urinary tract infections, enteritis, boils, abscesses, night sweats, conjunctivitis, and skin diseases. An ingredient of the Chinese drug *san huang zhe she ye* ("injection of three yellow herbs"), the others being *Coptis chinensis* (see p.179) and *Scutellaria baicalensis* (see p.364). The drug is given intramuscularly for upper respiratory tract infections.

🏠 🗎

P

PHRAGMITES

Poaceae

About four species of perennial reed grasses make up this cosmopolitan genus, which occurs in both temperate and tropical regions. *Phragmites australis* (common reed) is extremely fast-growing and adaptable, forming large stands in wetlands throughout the world. It is used in flood control and is a major source of raw materials, including stems for thatching and matting, fibres for the textile and paper industries, fuel, alcohol, and fertilizer. Roots, shoots, and seeds are edible, and stems contain a sweet gum that was used as a source of sugar by native N Americans. The flower heads are excellent for dried flower arrangements. As a medicinal herb it was first recorded in the *Collection of Commentaries of the Classic*

Phragmites australis

Materia Medica, by Tao Hong-Jing, c.AD500. It contains asparagine, a diuretic, as found in *Asparagus officinalis* (see p.135). *Phragmites* is from the Greek *phragma*, "fence" or "screen", an abbreviation of the description *kalamos phragmata*, "reed of hedges".

CULTIVATION Deep, moist to wet soil or shallow water in sun. Invasive.

PROPAGATION By division from early spring to early summer.

HARVEST Rhizomes are lifted in autumn and juiced, or dried for use in decoctions.

■ *Phragmites australis* syn. *P. communis* (*carrizo*, common reed, wild broomcorn) Vigorous rhizomatous reed with robust stems and arching, pointed, linear leaves, to 60cm (24in) long, turning golden-brown in autumn. Purple-brown spikelets are produced in erect to pendent panicles, to 45cm (18in) long, in late summer and autumn, persisting into winter. Found in temperate and tropical regions worldwide. ‡ 3.5m (11ft), ↔ indefinite. 'Variegatus' has yellow-striped leaves and is less invasive.

HARDINESS Fully hardy.

PARTS USED Rhizomes (*lu gen*).

PROPERTIES A sweet, cooling, sedative herb that is diuretic, controls coughing and vomiting, relieves pain, and lowers fever.

MEDICINAL USES Internally for fevers, vomiting, coughs with thick dark phlegm, lung abscesses, urinary tract infections, and food poisoning (especially from seafood). Externally, combined with gypsum, for halitosis and toothache.

CULINARY USES Young shoots and leaves are eaten as pot-herbs. Starchy rhizomes are cooked as a vegetable. Sugary gum in stems is used to make sweetmeats.

▨ ▣ ☑

PHYLA
Verbenaceae

A genus of about 15 species of creeping or prostrate, sometimes woody-based perennials, occurring in C and S America. It is closely related to *Lippia* and *Verbena*, and several species now belonging to *Phyla* were once classified in one or other of these other genera. A few species are in cultivation, the best known being *P. nodiflora* (capeweed, matgrass, Turkey tangle), which makes good ground cover in warm areas. *Phyla scaberrima* was known as *tzonpelic xihuitl*, "sweet herb", by the Aztecs, and is mentioned (as *tzopelicacoc*) in the earliest Aztec herbal, which was translated into Latin in 1552 by Juannes Badianus as *Libellus de Medicinalibus Indorum Herbis*. In Mexico, Aztec sweet herb is used medicinally in various ways. In the 19th century, it was an ingredient in a pharmaceutical tincture to treat coughs and bronchitis. The essential oil contains 53 per cent camphor, which probably accounts for the expectorant effect, though in excess it is toxic, especially for children. Another chemical constituent of Aztec sweet herb is hernadulcin, a compound about three times as sweet as sucrose but with a bitter note and rather unpleasant aftertaste.

CULTIVATION Well-drained soil in sun or light shade.

PROPAGATION By semi-ripe cuttings in spring and summer.

HARVEST Leaves and plants are picked as required and used fresh or dried.

■ *Phyla scaberrima* syn. *Lippia dulcis* (Aztec sweet herb, *yerba dulce*) Upright to sprawling, evergreen perennial, often woody-based, with aromatic, ovate to rhombic leaves, to 5cm (2in) long, which have indented margins. Tiny white flowers are produced in cone-like clusters almost year round. Native to Mexico, C America, and the Caribbean. ‡↔ 60cm (24in).

Phyla scaberrima

HARDINESS Half hardy.

PARTS USED Leaves, whole plant.

PROPERTIES A very sweet, slightly bitter herb with a camphoraceous aroma. It has an expectorant effect and stimulates the uterus. Reputedly abortifacient.

MEDICINAL USES Internally for coughs and bronchitis, and to induce menstruation. Contraindicated for small children and during pregnancy.

CULINARY USES Leaves may be used with discretion for flavouring and sweetening, especially herb teas.

▨ ▣ ▪ ☑

PHYLLANTHUS
Euphorbiaceae

This large genus includes 650–700 species of trees, shrubs, annuals, and perennials, found widely in tropical and warm-temperate regions. In many species the new growth is flushed red, and the foliage has an interesting structure, often with flattened, leaf-like stems (cladophylls) that give the appearance of pinnate leaves. As is characteristic of the family Euphorbiaceae, the foliage exudes an irritant milky sap when damaged. A number of species are medicinally used in Asia and are important in Ayurvedic and Chinese medicine. Two very different species are particularly important: *P. emblica*, a tree with small, gooseberry-like fruits, and *P. niruri*, a common annual weed in many parts of tropical Asia. The former is known in Hindi as *amalaki* ("nurse"), because it heals so many ailments. Emblic fruits, which are among the highest known sources of vitamin C (3000mg per fruit), are used in many different preparations in Ayurvedic medicine; when unripe they are exceedingly sour. The fruits are a key ingredient of *chyavanprash*, the most important Ayurvedic restorative, which is also applied as a paste to the head for mental disorders. They are also an ingredient of the *triphala* ("three fruits"), another rejuvenative tonic that also includes *Terminalia chebula* (myrobalan, see p.384) and *T. belerica* (bastard myrobalan). Other species include *Phyllanthus urinaria*, a potent diuretic, used for liver and kidney diseases and urinary tract infections; it is strongly anti-bacterial, and a useful remedy also for dysentery, eye infections, and boils. *Phyllanthus reticulatus* is also diuretic and astringent, and is used to heal burns and sores, and to treat diarrhoea in children, dysentery, and asthma. Among the constituents in *Phyllanthus* spp. is phyllanthin, which acts as a fish poison. *Phyllanthus* is from the Greek *phyllon*, "leaf", and *anthos*, "flower", referring to the fact that in some species the flowers are produced on the edges of the leaf-like stems.

CULTIVATION Well-drained soil in sun with high humidity.

PROPAGATION By seeds sown when ripe.

HARVEST Whole plants are collected during summer and autumn and used fresh or dried in decoctions, or pounded with roots as a poultice. Fruits are collected when unripe or

Phyllanthus emblica

ripe for decoctions, powder, and confectionery. Roots and bark are collected as required for decoctions.

■ *Phyllanthus emblica* syn. *Emblica officinalis* (*amalaki, amla, aonla,* emblic myrobalan)
Slender, spreading, much-branched tree with a crooked trunk, thin grey bark, and linear–oblong leaves bearing two ranks of leaflet-like cladophylls, 1–2cm (⅜–¾in) long. Tiny, yellow-green flowers are followed by globose, edible, pale green to yellow fruits, about 2cm (¾in) across, with very sour flesh. Native to tropical Asia. ‡ 10–15m (30–45ft), ↔ 5–8m (15–25ft).
HARDINESS Min. 15°C (59°F).
PARTS USED Fruits, leaves, bark, roots.
PROPERTIES A cooling, astringent, tonic herb that controls bleeding, improves digestion, and has laxative effects. It is considered rejuvenative and aphrodisiac.
MEDICINAL USES Internally for debility, anaemia, poor appetite, fever, diabetes, nausea and vomiting, constipation, gastritis, colitis, hepatitis, jaundice, haemorrhage, haemorrhoids, and diarrhoea. Externally for sores, eye infections, and pruritus.
CULINARY USES Acid fruits are eaten raw or used in pickles, chutneys, sweetmeats, and preserves; also as a sour flavouring, like lemon juice, and dried as fruit chips, which are eaten as snacks after fasting.
ECONOMIC USES Extracts are a common ingredient in Ayurvedic tonics.

Phyllanthus niruri syn. *P. debilis* (*dukung anak, jaramla, niruri*)
Erect slender annual, branched at the base, with oblong to elliptic leaves, to 8cm (3in) long, composed of two ranks of dark green, leaflet-like cladophylls. Minute flowers are borne in

the axils, followed by tiny globose fruits. Native to tropical Asia. ‡ 40–50cm (16–20in), ↔ 15–25cm (6–10in).
HARDINESS Min. 15°C (59°F).
PARTS USED Whole plant.
PROPERTIES A cooling, bitter, astringent herb that relaxes spasms, improves digestion, and has potent diuretic effects; also lowers blood sugar.
MEDICINAL USES Internally for urinary tract infections, urinary stones, diarrhoea, gonorrhea, jaundice, yellow fever, and diabetes. Externally for sores, ulcers, wounds, bruises, scabies, ringworm, and eye infections.

PHYLLOSTACHYS

Poaceae

This genus of about 80 species of medium to large bamboos occurs in India, China, and Burma. It includes some of the most ornamental bamboos for gardens and large containers, with graceful foliage and rather zigzag canes, which are often beautifully coloured and patterned. Less invasive than most, they may be planted as focal points in lawns or large borders. Bamboos are of great economic and cultural importance in Asia, with a wide range of uses, from furniture and utensils, paper, and musical instruments to scaffolding, fishing rods, and drainpipes. The stems are particularly strong, due to their high silica content. Young shoots of many species, notably *P. pubescens*, are edible, and large quantities are canned for export. Various species are used medicinally in China, apparently interchangeably, as *zhu*. The first mention in medical texts of bamboo sap (*zhu li*) and stem shavings (*zhu ru*) was made c.AD500. A siliceous substance, known as *tabasher* or *tabashir* (*tian zhu huang*), is used in similar ways to the dried sap. It occurs in fragile angular concretions, up to the size of a hen's egg, inside the lower internodes.
CULTIVATION Moist, well-drained, humus-rich soil in sun or dappled shade, with shelter from cold drying winds. Remove dead stems at any time. Clumps may be thinned in spring to leave only the strongest stems.
PROPAGATION By division in spring during wet weather; by cuttings of young rhizomes in late winter. Divisions from open ground do not transplant well and should be nurtured in pots under cover until late spring. Small divisions are more successful than large clumps.
HARVEST Leaves are collected during the growing season, young stems are cut for shavings in summer, and roots are lifted in winter; all are dried for use in decoctions. Sap is pressed from young stems and evaporated.

Phyllostachys nigra (black bamboo, *kuro-chiku*)
Evergreen, rhizomatous, clump-forming bamboo with arching slender stems, turning from green-brown to black in the second or third year, and narrowly lanceolate leaves, to 13cm (5in) long. Native to E and C China. ‡ 3–10m (10–30ft), ↔ indefinite. 'Boryana' has green to yellow-

green canes, with purple-brown streaks. var. *henonis* syn. 'Henonis' has bright green stems, which age yellow-green, and glossy foliage.
HARDINESS Fully hardy.
PARTS USED Leaves, stem shavings, roots, sap.
PROPERTIES A sweet, cooling, diuretic and expectorant herb that lowers fever, controls vomiting, checks bleeding, and is effective against bacterial infections.
MEDICINAL USES Internally for lung infections with cough and phlegm (stem, sap); vomiting, nosebleed (leaves, stem); fevers, especially infantile convulsions (leaves, roots); rabies (roots).

PHYSALIS

Solanaceae

A cosmopolitan genus of around 80 species of occasionally rhizomatous, upright or sprawling annuals and perennials. All produce numerous seeds in a globose berry, enclosed in an inflated calyx. *Physalis alkekengi* is popular as an ornamental for the papery orange calyces surrounding the ripe fruits, and may be grown as an annual. It should not to be confused with *Solanum capsicastrum*, which is also called "winter cherry". According to Dioscorides, the fruits of *Physalis alkekengi* are a cure for epilepsy. In European folk medicine the fruits were taken to relieve scarlet fever, and the foliage was used in tonics for anaemia and malaria. In common with many species belonging to the nightshade family (Solanaceae), *P. alkekengi* has an interesting chemistry but is rarely used in medicine today. The fruits, though edible, are less palatable than those of its relatives: *P. ixocarpa* (Mexican ground cherry, tomatillo), whose fruits are one of the main ingredients in *salsa verde*; *P. philadelphica* (purple ground cherry, wild tomatillo), used in C American chilli sauces; and *P. peruviana* (Cape gooseberry), which is grown commercially as a dessert fruit.
CULTIVATION Well-drained soil in sun or light shade.
PROPAGATION By seed sown in spring; by division in spring.
HARVEST Fruits are harvested when ripe and used fresh, as juice, or dried. For medicinal use, the calyx is removed. Leaves are picked in summer and used fresh as a poultice.
⚠ **WARNING** Foliage and unripe fruits are harmful if eaten.

■ *Physalis alkekengi* (bladder cherry, Chinese lantern, winter cherry)
Rhizomatous perennial with broadly ovate to diamond-shaped, pointed leaves, to 9cm (3½in) long. Pendent, five-lobed, cream flowers appear in summer, followed by edible, orange to red berries surrounded by a papery calyx, to 5cm (2in) across. Found in C and S Europe, and from W Asia to Japan. ‡ 60–75cm (24–30in), ↔ 90cm (36in) or more.
HARDINESS Fully hardy.

P

Physalis alkekengi

PARTS USED Fruits, fruit juice.
PROPERTIES A bitter–sweet, diuretic, laxative herb that lowers fever and reduces inflammation.
MEDICINAL USES Internally for intermittent fevers, urinary disorders, kidney and bladder stones, arthritis, rheumatism, and gout. Leaves formerly used externally for skin inflammations. Used in homeopathy for arthritic, rheumatic, and urinary disorders, and jaundice.

PHYSOSTIGMA
Fabaceae

Four species of perennial climbers belong to this W African genus, which is placed in the family Papilionaceae by some botanists. Before its adoption by Western medicine, *P. venenosum* was notorious as the plant used in the "ordeal by poison" in the Calabar Province of Nigeria. In this ritual, an accused person drinks a solution of poisonous beans, dying if guilty and apparently surviving if innocent. The success of the method may be based on the probability that innocent people will tend to gulp the entire drink, causing vomiting and expulsion of toxins, while the guilty are perhaps more likely to sip cautiously and thereby ingest more poison. *Physostigma venenosum* contains alkaloids, of which the most important is physostigmine (eserine), which influences the parasympathetic nervous system. It is mainly used in eye drops to reduce pressure on the eyeball, and as an antidote to atropine (see *Atropa bella-donna*, p.138). Another alkaloid, calabarine, has opposite effects. Extracts of whole seeds differ in effects from isolated alkaloids.
CULTIVATION Rich, well-drained soil in sun.
PROPAGATION By seed sown when ripe.
HARVEST Seeds are collected when ripe, mainly in the rainy season, and dried for use in decoctions and for extraction of alkaloids.

Physostigma venenosum (Calabar bean, esere bean, ordeal bean)
Evergreen climber with trifoliate, ovate, pointed leaves, 15cm (6in) long and 10cm (4in) wide. Pink-purple, pea flowers, about 2.5cm (1in) long, are produced in spring, followed by pods, to 15cm (6in) long, containing 2–3 brown-black seeds, 3cm (1¼in) long. Native to tropical W Africa. ‡ 15m (50ft), ↔ indefinite.
HARDINESS Min. 15–18°C (59–64°F).
PARTS USED Seeds (with outer coat removed).
PROPERTIES A narcotic herb that depresses the central nervous system, mimics the parasympathetic nervous system, contracts the pupil of the eye, raises blood pressure, and stimulates peristalsis.
MEDICINAL USES As physostigmine, internally for neuromuscular diseases (notably myasthenia gravis), and post-operative constipation; externally as eye drops (especially for glaucoma). Formerly used in the treatment of tetanus, epilepsy, and rheumatism. Excess causes muscular weakness, respiratory failure, and cardiac arrest. For use only by qualified practitioners.

PHYTOLACCA
Phytolaccaceae

A genus of about 25 species of perennials, shrubs, and trees, distributed in both warm and temperate regions of Africa, Asia, and the Americas. *Phytolacca americana* is one of several species cultivated for its imposing habit and ornamental but poisonous berries. *Phytolacca* has an unusual chemistry, containing potent, anti-inflammatory agents, anti-viral proteins, and substances (referred to collectively as "pokeweed mitogens") that affect cell division. These compounds are toxic to many disease-causing organisms, including the water snails that cause schistosomiasis, and may have potential in the treatment of AIDS. *Phytolacca acinosa* was first recorded in Chinese medicine during the Han dynasty (206BC–AD23). Occasionally the roots are mistakenly sold as ginseng (see *Panax*, p.299) in Oriental markets, causing outbreaks of poisoning. *Phytolacca americana* was used by native N Americans as an emetic and anti-rheumatic, and was listed as an analgesic and anti-inflammatory in the *US Pharmacopoeia* (1820–1916). Although most parts of these plants are poisonous, the shoots and young leaves are eaten in various countries after boiling in several changes of water. The deep red juice from the berries has been used to colour wine. *Phytolacca* comes from the Greek *phyton*, "plant", and the Hindi *lakh*, a dye extracted from the lac insect, the colour of which resembles that found in the berries.
CULTIVATION Rich, moist, well-drained soil in sun or partial shade.
PROPAGATION By seed sown at 13–18°C (55–64°F) in early spring.
HARVEST Roots and fruits are collected in autumn and dried for decoctions, liquid

Phytolacca acinosa

extracts, powder, poultices, and tinctures.
⚠ **WARNING** All parts, notably leaves and berries, are toxic if eaten. Sap is irritant to skin and eyes.

■ *Phytolacca acinosa* (Indian poke)
Robust perennial with succulent stems and lanceolate pointed leaves, to 25cm (10in) long. Small, green-white flowers appear in more or less erect racemes in summer, followed by stout spikes, 10–20cm (4–8in) long, of dark purple berries. Found from Kashmir to SW China. ‡↔ 90cm –1.5m (3–5ft).
HARDINESS Frost hardy.
PARTS USED Roots (*shang lu*).
PROPERTIES A bitter, pungent, cooling herb that has diuretic and expectorant effects, and controls coughing. It is effective against various bacterial and fungal infections.
MEDICINAL USES Internally for urinary disorders, nephritis, oedema, and abdominal distension. Externally for boils, carbuncles, and sores.

■ *Phytolacca americana* syn. *P. decandra* (pokeberry, pokeroot, pokeweed, red-ink plant)
Upright fetid perennial with red-flushed, succulent stems and ovate to lanceolate, pointed leaves, to 30cm (12in) long. Small, pink-white flowers appear in erect racemes, to 20cm (8in) long, in summer, followed by thick spikes of fleshy, purple-black berries. Found from eastern N America to Mexico. ‡ 2–4m (6–12ft), ↔ 1.2–2.5m (4–8ft).
HARDINESS Fully hardy.
PARTS USED Roots, fruits (berries).
PROPERTIES A bitter, pungent, alterative herb that reduces inflammation, stimulates the immune and lymphatic systems, and clears toxins. It is effective against many bacterial, viral, fungal, and parasitic organisms.
MEDICINAL USES Internally for auto-immune diseases (especially rheumatoid arthritis), tonsillitis, mumps, swollen glands (including glandular fever), chronic catarrh, bronchitis, mastitis, skin diseases, and inflammations. Excess causes diarrhoea and vomiting. Contraindicated during pregnancy. Externally for skin complaints (including fungal infections), joint inflammation, haemorrhoids,

Phytolacca americana

mastitis, breast abscesses, and varicose ulcers. Berries are milder than roots. Combines well with *Guaiacum officinale* (see p.229) and *Zanthoxylum* spp. (see p.409) for rheumatic conditions; with *Galium aparine* (see p.219) and *Iris versicolor* (see p.244) for swollen glands. For use only by qualified practitioners. Used in homeopathic preparations for breast complaints, swollen tonsils, mumps, teething, halitosis, and shooting pains.
CULINARY USES Young leaves are cooked as a vegetable. Young shoots are steamed like asparagus or pickled, and may be blanched for winter use.
🗷 🗷 🖢 ✐

PICRAENIA

Picraenia excelsa. See *Picrasma excelsa*.

PICRASMA

Simaroubaceae

This genus has eight species of deciduous trees, which occur in forests in tropical America, the West Indies, and E and SE Asia. *Picrasma quassioides* (Japanese quassia) is sometimes grown as an ornamental for its autumn colour. *Picrasma excelsa* (Jamaica quassia) has slightly different constituents from *P. quassioides* and the related *Quassia amara* (Surinam quassia), but they are often used interchangeably. Quassia first reached Europe from Surinam in 1756 and entered the *London Pharmacopoeia* in 1788. The term "quassia" refers to a bitter compound extracted from the bark and wood of *Picrasma excelsa* or *Quassia amara*. It was apparently named after a healer named Quassi, from whom European colonists learned of its uses.
CULTIVATION Moist, sandy, humus-rich soil in

Picrasma excelsa

sun or partial shade, with moderate to high humidity. Trim plants to shape before new growth begins.
PROPAGATION By seed sown when ripe; by semi-ripe cuttings in summer.
HARVEST Wood is chipped and dried for use in concentrated infusions, powders, and tinctures.

■ *Picrasma excelsa* syn. *Picraenia excelsa* (bitter ash, Jamaica quassia)
Deciduous tree with pinnate, coarsely toothed leaves, to 30cm (12in) long. Small, green-white flowers are produced in branched panicles in autumn, followed by black, shiny, globose berries, which ripen in winter. Native to the West Indies. ‡ 25m (80ft), ↔ 15m (50ft).
HARDINESS Min. 15–18°C (59–64°F).
PARTS USED Wood.
PROPERTIES An intensely bitter, non-astringent, odourless herb that lowers fever, stimulates appetite, and improves digestion. It is an effective insecticide and parasiticide, and is reputedly anti-leukaemic.
MEDICINAL USES Internally for convalescent debility, poor appetite, malaria, and nematode worms. Excess causes gastric irritation and vomiting. Externally as a lotion for parasites, such as lice, and an enema for threadworms.
ECONOMIC USES Quassia extract is used to give a bitter flavour to beer, soft drinks, liqueurs, and aperitifs; also in insecticides against flies, red spider mite, aphid, and woolly aphid.
🗷 🖢 ✐ ▣

PICRORHIZA

Scrophulariaceae

This genus consists of a single species of perennial, found in the W Himalayas. *Picrorhiza kurrooa* grows wild on rocky slopes of the Himalayas, between 3300 and 4300m (10,000–13,000ft). The genus was once considered to have two species, the other being *P. scrophulariiflora*, a rare species now known as *Neopicrorhiza scrophulariiflora*, which is used as a febrifuge, and often interchangeably with *Picrorhiza kurrooa*. Both have a long history of medicinal use in the region. *P. kurrooa* is especially important as a bitter

tonic in both Ayurvedic and Unani medicine; the roots are also used as an adulterant of or substitute for *Gentiana kurroo* (Indian gentian). During the 1990s, in response to growing demand worldwide for medicinal herbs, plants were over-collected, leading to environmental damage and a loss of over 60 per cent of the wild population. As a consequence, *Picrorhiza kurrooa* was banned from international trade in 1997 and is now a protected species.
CULTIVATION Moist, well-drained soil in sun or partial shade.
PROPAGATION By seed sown when ripe; by division of rhizomes in early spring.
HARVEST Rhizomes are collected in autumn and dried for use in decoctions and tinctures, or ground as powder.

■ *Picrorhiza kurrooa* (*kuru, kutki*)
Rhizomatous perennial, rooting at nodes, with rootstock, to 5mm (¼in) in diameter, covered in withered leaf bases, and dark green, narrowly elliptic to spathulate, coarsely toothed leaves, 5–15cm (2–6in) long. Pale blue or purplish-blue flowers, with long extruding stamens, are produced in a compact spike in summer, followed by an ovoid capsule enclosed in the calyx, containing many seeds. Native to the Himalayas (Bhutan, India, and Nepal).
‡ 15–23in (6–9in), ↔ 30cm (12in).
HARDINESS Fully hardy.
PARTS USED Rhizomes.
PROPERTIES A very bitter, tonic, laxative herb that lowers fever, improves liver function, increases gastric secretions, expels intestinal parasites, and in larger doses is cathartic and emetic, and stimulates the uterus. Reported to have anti-inflammatory, liver-protecting, and immune stimulating effects, and to be effective against the organism that causes leishmaniasis.
MEDICINAL USES Internally for bilious fever, constipation, dyspepsia, jaundice, liver complaints, chronic diarrhoea, dysentery, intestinal parasites in children, psoriasis, vitiligo, epilepsy, asthma, and gout; also as an antidote in snake bite and dog bite. Externally for skin diseases, burns, ringworm, scabies, and haemorrhoids. Contraindicated during pregnancy.
🗷 🖢

P

Picrorhiza kurrooa

PILOCARPUS
Jaborandi

Rutaceae

About 20 species of shrubs and small trees belong to this genus, which occurs mainly in rainforests in tropical America and the West Indies. Jaborandi is the source of an important alkaloid, pilocarpine, which is obtained from several species, including *P. jaborandi* (Pernambuco jaborandi), *P. microphyllus* (Maranham jaborandi), *P. pinnatifolius* (Paraguay jaborandi), and *P. trachylophus* (Ceara jaborandi). Medicinal uses of jaborandi were introduced to Europe in 1873 by Symphronio Coutinho (1832–87), a Brazilian physician who observed that chewing the leaves causes excessive salivation – an effect then thought to be of value in treating dropsy (oedema or fluid retention). The alkaloid pilocarpine was isolated in 1875 and became the standard treatment for oedema until potent diuretics were introduced in the 1920s. Pilocarpine stimulates the parasympathetic nervous system and is now used mainly in ophthalmology to constrict the pupil of the eye and reduce intra-ocular pressure. Supplies of foliage are still collected mainly from the wild, though plantations have been established in Brazil.

CULTIVATION Rich, well-drained soil in partial shade and high humidity.

PROPAGATION By seed sown when ripe; by ripewood cuttings with leaves intact during the growing season.

HARVEST Leaves and leafy twigs are picked as required, and dried for extraction of alkaloids and for use in liquid extracts and tinctures.

Pilocarpus microphyllus (jaborandi, Maranham jaborandi)
Evergreen shrub with smooth grey bark and dull yellow-green, pinnate leaves. Small, red-purple flowers are produced in lax racemes, followed by two-valved fruits consisting of 1–5 nearly separate, one-seeded carpels. Native to Brazil. ‡ 1.2–1.5m (4–5ft), ↔ 1m (3ft).

HARDINESS Min. 15–18°C (59–64°F).

PARTS USED Leaves, leafy twigs.

PROPERTIES A bitter, slightly aromatic herb that stimulates the heart, causes copious perspiration and salivation, contracts the pupils, and reputedly increases hair growth.

MEDICINAL USES Internally for psoriasis, itching of the skin, syphilis, chronic catarrh, and dropsy (leaf extracts). Internally and externally for glaucoma and as an antidote to atropine (pilocarpine); externally for hair loss (leaf extracts). Excess causes profuse perspiration and salivation, rapid pulse, contracted pupils, diarrhoea, and vomiting, and may be fatal.

⚠ **WARNING** This herb, especially in the form of pilocarpine and leaf extracts, is subject to legal restrictions in some countries. Use of jaborandi in cosmetics is prohibited in many countries.

316

PILOSELLA
Mouse-ear hawkweed

Asteraceae

This complex genus consists of about 250–260 species, which are distributed throughout the northern hemisphere. In many cases the species are groups of micro-species, able to produce viable seed without fertilization. They are also highly variable. Most hawkweeds are weedy, but a few species are grown as ornamentals for their downy foliage and yellow flowers. *Pilosella officinarum* (mouse-ear hawkweed) has been a popular herb since at least medieval times. It is recommended by Culpeper in *The English Physician Enlarged* (1653) as a "cooling, somewhat drying and binding" herb, for a wide range of ailments.

CULTIVATION Well-drained to dry, poor soil in sun.

PROPAGATION By seed sown in autumn or spring; by division in spring.

HARVEST Plants are cut in summer and used fresh or dried in infusions, liquid extracts, syrups, and tinctures. Preparations are made fresh each year.

Pilosella officinarum syn. *Hieracium pilosella* (mouse-ear hawkweed)
Rosette-forming, hairy perennial with long stolons and obovate–oblong, blunt leaves, about 7cm (3in) long, which have white felted undersides. Solitary, lemon-yellow flowers, 3cm (1¼in) across, appear from late spring to autumn. Native to Europe. ‡ 15–30cm (6–12in), ↔ indefinite.

HARDINESS Fully hardy.

PARTS USED Whole plant.

PROPERTIES A bitter antibiotic herb that is diuretic and expectorant, promotes healing, relaxes spasms, reduces inflammation, and increases salivation.

MEDICINAL USES Internally for asthma, bronchitis, catarrh, whooping cough, bronchial infections with haemorrhage, heavy menstruation, influenza, cystitis, inflammation of the kidney, kidney stones, diarrhoea, and brucellosis. Externally for wounds, fractures, hernia, and nosebleed. Combined with *Marrubium vulgare* (see p.271), *Verbascum thapsus* (see p.401), and *Tussilago farfara* (see p.396) for whooping cough; with *Drosera rotundifolia* (see p.197), *Grindelia camporum* (see p.229), *Euphorbia hirta* (see p.210), or *Polygala senega* (see p.326) for asthma.

PIMENTA
Myrtaceae

About four species of aromatic evergreen trees belong to this tropical American genus. The fruits of *Pimenta dioica* were first imported to Europe by the Spanish in the 16th century and given the name "allspice" by John Ray (1627–1705), an English botanist, who likened their flavour to a combination of cloves, cinnamon, and nutmeg. Allspice is an important crop in Jamaica; trees are grown in plantations, known as "pimento walks", which fill the air with their fragrance during the flowering season. *Pimenta dioica* is rich in volatile oil, which consists mainly of eugenol (as found in *Syzygium aromaticum*, p.378). The related West Indian *Pimenta racemosa* was once important as the source of bay rum, an aromatic liquid used in hair dressings, which was distilled from the leaves and is now synthesized. This species has five varieties that differ in distribution and in the chemical composition of their essential oils. The most widespread and commercially important is *P. racemosa* var. *racemosa*, which is cultivated, notably in the Dominican Republic, as a source of bay oil or West Indian bay oil; it has a pleasant spicy aroma and also contains eugenol.

CULTIVATION Rich, well-drained, sandy soil in sun.

PROPAGATION By seed sown when ripe; by semi-ripe cuttings in summer. Remove weak branches in spring.

HARVEST Leaves are picked as required and used fresh for infusions. Fruits are collected when fully grown but unripe and green, and distilled for oil, or dried for liquid extracts and powders; they turn black when dried. Bark is removed from prunings, dried and ground.

■ *Pimenta dioica* (allspice, Jamaica pepper, pimento)
Evergreen tree with an often crooked trunk, smooth, shiny, silvery bark, slender branches, and aromatic, elliptic to oblong, thinly leathery leaves, 6–20cm (2½–8in) long. Small, white, scented flowers are borne in panicles, 4–12cm (1½–5in) long, in spring and summer, followed by strongly aromatic, red-brown, globose berries, about 6mm (¼in) in diameter. Native to Mexico, C America, and Cuba. ‡ 10–15m (30–50ft), ↔ 5m (15ft).

HARDINESS Min. 15–18°C (59–64°F).

PARTS USED Leaves, fruits (berries), oil.

PROPERTIES A pungent, warming, aromatic herb with a clove-like aroma.

Pimenta dioica

It improves the digestion, has a tonic effect on the nervous system, and is locally antiseptic and anaesthetic. Oil of pimento is carminative and antioxidant.

MEDICINAL USES Internally for indigestion, flatulence, diarrhoea, and nervous exhaustion. Externally for chest infections, and muscular aches and pains.

CULINARY USES Dried fruits are used whole in pickling spices, marinades, and mulled wine; also steeped in rum to make *pimento dram*, a Jamaican liqueur, and ground for flavouring cakes, biscuits, desserts, sauces, ketchups, and chutneys. An essential ingredient of Jamaican *jerk* dishes (pork or chicken marinated in spices and barbecued). Leaves are infused for tea.

ECONOMIC USES Powdered berries are added to medicines to disguise the flavour, and to liniments and bandages. Oil is used in commercial food flavouring; also in perfumery, notably Asian fragrances, and aftershave lotions.

■ *Pimenta racemosa* syn. *P. acris* (bay rum tree, West Indian bay)
Evergreen, often shrubby tree with grey to light brown, peeling bark and elliptic to obovate, stiffly leathery leaves, to 10cm (4in) long, which have rounded tips and revolute margins. Fragrant white flowers, 1cm (⅜in) across, are produced in branched clusters in spring and summer, followed by fleshy black berries, about 1cm (⅜in) across. Native to the West Indies, Venezuela, and the Guianas. ‡ 14m (42ft), ↔ 5m (15ft).
HARDINESS Min. 15–18°C (59–64°F).
PARTS USED Bark, fruits, leaves, oil.
PROPERTIES An astringent, antiseptic, aromatic herb with rubefacient effects when applied externally.
MEDICINAL USES Internally, as a tea for chills. Externally for muscular aches and pains, rheumatism, neuralgia, greasy hair, dandruff, and hair loss.
CULINARY USES Bark and fruits are used for flavouring in the Caribbean, notably in *blaff* (fish broth).
ECONOMIC USES Oil and extracts are used for flavouring in the food industry.

Pimenta racemosa

PIMPINELLA
Apiaceae

This genus of about 150 species of annuals, biennials, and perennials ranges through Eurasia and N Africa. *Pimpinella anisum* was first cultivated as a spice by the ancient Egyptians and later by the Greeks, Romans, and Arabs. It needs a hot summer to thrive and for seed to ripen, and it is seldom successful outdoors in northern temperate regions. Though widely grown commercially, it has declined in recent years through competition with cheaper anise flavourings, such as *Illicium verum* (see p.242), and synthetic anethole. The essential oil consists of 70–90 per cent anethole, which has oestrogenic effects. *Pimpinella saxifraga* is mainly used for medicinal purposes. It has a large proportion of coumarins in the roots, and is used interchangeably with the larger-rooted var. *nigra* (black caraway) and the closely related *P. major* (greater burnet saxifrage, greater pimpernel). Neither *P. major* nor *P. saxifraga* is particularly ornamental, though *P. major* 'Rosea' is an attractive, pink-flowered cultivar. *Pimpinella* may be from the Latin *bipinnula*, referring to the twice-pinnately divided leaves, or from "pimpernel" (Latin *piper*, "pepper") perhaps referring to the spicy flavour.
CULTIVATION Rich, well-drained, sandy soil, pH6.0–7.5, in sun (*P. anisum*). Dry alkaline soil in sun or light shade (*P. saxifraga*). *Pimpinella anisum* is recommended in companion planting to repel aphids and cabbage worms; the flowers attract parasitic wasps that prey on a number of garden pests.
PROPAGATION By seed sown when ripe. Prick out seedlings into deep containers to allow development of taproots.
HARVEST Plants and leaves are cut in summer and used fresh; roots are lifted in autumn and dried for use in decoctions or distilled for oil (*P. saxifraga*). Seeds are collected as they ripen and distilled for oil, or dried for use whole, ground, or distilled in water, infusions, and spirits (*P. anisum*).
⚠ **WARNING** All white-flowered umbellifers (members of the family Apiaceae) must be accurately identified before use, because many look alike and a number are extremely poisonous.

■ *Pimpinella anisum* (anise, aniseed)
Aromatic downy annual with kidney-shaped to ovate, pinnate leaves, to 5cm (2in) long, divided into linear segments. Tiny, off-white flowers are produced in umbels, to 4cm (1½in) across, in summer, followed by ribbed seeds, about 5mm (¼in) long. Found in C and S Europe, Russia, Cyprus, Syria, and Egypt. ‡ 50cm (20in), ↔ 24–45cm (10–18in).
HARDINESS Half hardy.
PARTS USED Leaves, seeds, oil.
PROPERTIES A sweet, warming, stimulant herb that improves digestion, benefits the liver and circulation, and has expectorant and oestrogenic effects. Traditionally regarded as an aphrodisiac.
MEDICINAL USES Internally for dry coughs, whooping cough, bronchitis, tracheitis,

Pimpinella anisum

bronchial asthma, indigestion, flatulence, colic, and insufficient lactation. Externally for lice, scabies, and as a chest rub for bronchial complaints. Combines well with *Mentha × piperita* (see p.277) for colic; *Prunus serotina* (see p.334) for tracheitis; *Lactuca* spp. (see p.250) for dry coughs; and with *Lobelia inflata* (see p.265), *Marrubium vulgare* (see p.271), *Symplocarpus foetidus* (see p.378), and *Tussilago farfara* (see p.396) for bronchial complaints. Oil is often mixed with oil of *Sassafras albidum* (see p.361) for skin parasites, and with oil of *Eucalyptus globulus* (see p.207) as a chest rub.
CULINARY USES Fresh leaves are added to salads, vegetables, soups, and various cooked dishes in countries of origin. Seeds are used to flavour confectionery (especially aniseed balls), dried figs, cakes, bread, and curries.
ECONOMIC USES Seeds and oil form the basis of anise-flavoured drinks, such as *pastis*, *ouzo*, *raki*, and *arak*, which turn milky when diluted with water, and liqueurs, such as *anisette*. Oil is also used in perfumery, tobacco, and pharmaceutical products.

■ *Pimpinella saxifraga* (burnet saxifrage, small pimpernel)
Perennial with fetid taproot, slightly ridged stems, and pinnate leaves divided into ovate to lanceolate, toothed to divided segments, to 2.5cm (1in) long. Tiny white flowers, occasionally tinged pink or purple, appear in umbels, about 3cm (1¼in) across, in summer. Native to Europe. ‡ to 90cm (36in), ↔ 30–75cm (12–30in).
HARDINESS Fully hardy.
PARTS USED Whole plant, leaves, roots, oil.
PROPERTIES A bitter, pungent, diuretic herb that is expectorant, improves digestion, relieves spasms, and increases lactation. It is antiseptic and promotes healing.

317

Pimpinella saxifraga

MEDICINAL USES Internally for infections of the throat and upper respiratory tract, catarrh, measles, heartburn, cystitis, urinary stones, gout, and insufficient lactation. Externally for sore throats, inflamed gums, and wounds.

CULINARY USES Cucumber-flavoured, young leaves are added to salads and as a garnish for summer drinks. Traditionally, bundles of young shoots were suspended in casks of beer and wine, to improve flavour.

ECONOMIC USES Oil gives a bitter flavour to liqueurs and pharmaceutical products.

PINELLIA

Araceae

A genus of six species of small tuberous perennials, occurring in E Asia. *Pinellia ternata* is an eye-catching plant for the rock garden or shady corner, thriving beneath trees and shrubs. It was first recorded in Chinese medicine in the *Shen Nong Canon of Herbs*, which was completed during the later Han dynasty (AD25–220). Like most members of the aroid family, it is extremely acrid when fresh, containing toxins that are neutralized by drying, or by soaking in tea or vinegar. Among the constituents are alkaloids, which are thought to resemble coniine (as found in *Conium maculatum*, see p.178) and ephedrine (as found in *Ephedra* spp., see p.201). Its reputation for controlling nausea and vomiting has been scientifically validated; it is part of a successful Chinese prescription for removing gallstones without surgery, a process causing severe nausea. *Pinellia ternata* is also a key ingredient of classic expectorant formulae, such as Qing Qi Hua Tan Wan (Clean Air Tea). *Pinellia* is named after Giovanni Pinelli (1535–1601), owner of a botanic garden in Naples (Italy).

CULTIVATION Rich soil in dappled shade.

PROPAGATION By seed sown when ripe; by offsets in autumn or early spring; by bulbils in late summer. Invasive in good conditions.

HARVEST Tubers are lifted in summer and dried for use in decoctions.

⚠ **WARNING** Harmful if eaten. Irritant to skin, eyes, and mucous membranes.

Pinellia ternata

▣ ***Pinellia ternata*** (pinellia)
Slender perennial with a tuber, to 2cm (¾in) across, bulbil-bearing stalks, and three-palmate, adult leaves divided into ovate–elliptic to oblong leaflets, to 12cm (5in) long. A long-stalked inflorescence, with a green spathe, to 7cm (3in) long, and an erect protruding spadix, to 10cm (4in) long, appears in summer, followed by a cluster of green berries. Native to China, Japan, and Korea. ↕60cm (24in), ↔30cm (12in).

HARDINESS Fully hardy.

PARTS USED Tubers (*ban xia*).

PROPERTIES A pungent, slightly bitter, warming herb that controls coughing and has expectorant and anti-catarrhal effects. It is a potent anti-emetic.

MEDICINAL USES Internally for coughs with thin, watery phlegm, gastritis, nausea, and vomiting. Often combined with *Zingiber officinale* (see p.411) to control vomiting; with *Citrus reticulata* (*chen pi*, see p.173), *Coptis chinensis* (see p.179), or *Scutellaria baicalensis* (see p.364) for coughs; with *Glycyrrhiza uralensis* (see p.227), calcium carbonate, and alum as an expectorant. Usually prescribed with *Glycyrrhiza uralensis* (see p.227) or *Zingiber officinale* (see p.411) to reduce toxicity.

PINUS

Pine

Pinaceae

This genus includes about 120 species of evergreen coniferous trees and shrubs, which occur throughout northern temperate regions, C America, N Africa, and SE Asia. Pines of all kinds are grown as ornamentals for their long, needle-like leaves. Several species have dwarf variants, which are suitable for small spaces. Most pines dislike shade and polluted air, but some tolerate very poor soils and coastal sites, and make excellent windbreaks. Various pines have been used medicinally from earliest times. All are rich in resins and camphoraceous volatile oils, including pinene, which are strongly antiseptic and stimulant. Pine oil is extracted from the needles and branch tips of *P. mugo*, *P. nigra*, *P. pinaster*, and *P. sylvatica*;

it is widely used in massage oils for muscular stiffness, sciatica, and rheumatism, and in vapour rubs for bronchial congestion. The N American *P. strobus* (white pine) has expectorant effects; extracts of the inner bark (usually in the form of a syrup) are a common ingredient of cough and cold remedies. In traditional Chinese medicine, the main species used are *P. massoniana* (horsetail pine, Masson pine) and *P. tabuliformis* (Chinese red pine). Knotty pine wood (*song jie*) usually refers to the latter and was first mentioned in Chinese medical literature c.AD500 as an anti-arthritic and analgesic. Various parts of *P. massoniana* are used: the needles for influenza and rheumatoid arthritis; resin for eczema and burns; and pollen, given internally for peptic ulcers, dizziness, and facial oedema, and externally for boils and sores. Fossilized pine resin (amber, *hu po*) from *P. succinifera* (now extinct) is obtained from buried trees and used to treat urinary tract infections, urinary stones, heart disease, and infantile convulsions. A viscous oleo-resin, known as turpentine, is tapped from various species, including *P. palustris* and *P. pinaster* (maritime pine). It is distilled to produce oil of turpentine or spirits of turpentine; this should not be confused with petroleum-based turpentine substitute or white spirit. Rosin, or colophony, is a brittle translucent substance produced in the distillation of turpentine. Resin is tapped from *P. halepensis* (Aleppo pine) in Greece, to flavour retsina. A number of pines produce large edible seeds, known as "pine kernels", which are added to salads, cooked vegetables, and rice, and ground for sauces, such as pesto.

CULTIVATION Well-drained, neutral to acid soil in sun. *Pinus sylvestris* thrives in both acid and alkaline soils. *Pinus palustris* tolerates drought and poor soil but needs warmth and humidity. Remove dead branches in winter. Restrict the leading shoots. Foliage may be damaged by adelgids, caterpillars of the pine-shoot moth, sawfly larvae, canker, die-back, *Botrytis*, and rust. Trees may be killed by honey fungus.

PROPAGATION By seed sown in spring (species and varieties only); by layering (*P. mugo* Pumilio Group); by grafting in late winter (cultivars).

HARVEST Leaves and young shoots are collected during the growing season and usually used fresh for decoctions and syrups (*P. sylvestris*). Resin is tapped by cutting vertical grooves in the bark and collecting the exudate; oil is distilled or solvent extracted from wood and bark (*P. palustris*). Oil is distilled from leaves (*P. mugo* Pumilio Group). Oils are processed into ointments, gels, emulsions, inhalants, and rubbing oils. Tar is distilled from roots (*P. sylvestris*).

Pinus mugo (dwarf mountain pine, mugo pine) Shrub or rounded to spreading tree with scaly grey bark, thick ascending or spreading branches, very resinous buds, paired

needles, to 8cm (3in) long, and ovoid brown cones, to 6cm (2½) long. Native to C European Alps. ‡ 3.5m (11ft), ↔ 5m (15ft). ▣ 'Mops' is slow-growing, dense, and rounded. ‡ 1.5m (5ft). ▣ Pumilio Group syn. var. *pumilio* is shrubby, with erect branches.
HARDINESS Fully hardy.
PARTS USED Oil (pumilio pine oil).
PROPERTIES An aromatic, stimulant, antiseptic herb that is expectorant; relieves bronchial and nasal congestion; improves blood flow locally.
MEDICINAL USES Internally and externally for upper respiratory tract infections, whooping cough, chronic bronchitis, catarrh, and asthma. Externally for rheumatism and muscular stiffness; also as decongestant inhalation. May cause allergic reactions in susceptible individuals.
ECONOMIC USES Oil is used in commercial food flavouring, and in woody perfumes.
⚠ **WARNING** This herb, in the form of pumilio pine oil, is subject to legal restrictions in some countries.
🔲 ▪ ✎

▣ *Pinus palustris* (longleaf pine, pitch pine, southern yellow pine)
Large tree with an ovoid–conic crown, orange-brown, scaly bark, white, fire-resistant buds, and needles, to 45cm (18in) long, arranged in threes. Red-brown, cylindric cones are 15–25cm (6–10in) long. Native to SE USA.

‡ 30m (100ft), ↔ 5m (15ft).
HARDINESS Frost hardy.
PARTS USED Oil (turpentine), resin (colophony, rosin).
PROPERTIES An aromatic antiseptic herb that improves blood flow locally.
MEDICINAL USES Externally for boils, ulcers, bronchitis, and ringworm (resin), rheumatism and muscular stiffness (oil, resin).
ECONOMIC USES Oil is used as a solvent. Resin is used in varnishes, printing inks, sealing waxes, and for treating horsehair on stringed-instrument bows. Oil is used in perfumery.
🔲 ▪ ✎

▣ *Pinus sylvestris* (Scots pine)
Upright tree with a rounded crown in older specimens, orange-brown to purple-grey bark, twisted, blue-green, paired needles, 3–10cm (1¼–4in) long, and grey-brown cones, about 5cm (2in) long. Native to Europe (excluding far north) and temperate Asia. ‡ 15–30m (50–100ft), ↔ 6–9m (20–28ft). ▣ Aurea Group syn. 'Aurea' (golden Scots pine) is slow-growing, with bright yellow foliage in winter. ‡ 10–15m (30–50ft). ▣ 'Fastigiata' is narrow and upright, with ascending branches. ‡ 8m (25ft), ↔ 1–3m (3–10ft).
HARDINESS Fully hardy.
PARTS USED Leaves, young shoots and buds, tar, oil.

PROPERTIES A bitter, aromatic, warming herb that acts as a diuretic and expectorant, improves blood flow locally, and has a tonic effect on the nerves. It is strongly antiseptic.
MEDICINAL USES Internally for urinary and respiratory tract infections, and gall bladder complaints. Externally for arthritis, rheumatism, sciatica, poor circulation, bronchitis, catarrh, sinusitis, asthma, pneumonia, neuralgia, acne, fatigue, and nervous exhaustion. Oil is used in aromatherapy for similar complaints. Contraindicated in allergic skin conditions.
ECONOMIC USES Oil and tar are added to disinfectants, bath preparations, detergents, and preparations to stimulate hair growth.
🔲 🔲 🔲 🔲 ▪ ✎

PIPER
Pepper

Piperaceae

This pantropical genus includes over 1000 species of evergreen, pungent-smelling climbers, shrubs, and small trees. *Piper nigrum* (pepper) is one of the oldest known spices, and was the main commodity traded along caravan routes of the East. It was the inspiration for early European exploration of sea routes, which created the wealth of cities such as Venice. Pepper has always been one of the most valuable spices: Attila the Hun demanded a huge quantity of it as ransom during the siege of Rome (AD408), and its use as currency gave rise to the term "peppercorn rent". It accounts now for a quarter of the spice trade, India being the main producer. Most peppers are grown for their fruits, which are rich in volatile oil and pungent piperidine alkaloids. *Piper guineense* (Ashanti pepper, West African pepper) produces mild-flavoured peppercorns, and leaves that are used as a substitute for *P. betle* in betel quids. *Piper methysticum* (kava kava) is unusual among peppers in being a root crop; the roots may weigh 5.5–7.3kg (12–16lb). It is an important ritual plant in Oceania, used in social and religious gatherings. Research has shown that kava kava is as effective as benzodiazepene in relieving anxiety. *Piper auritum* (*hoja santa*) and *P. angustifolia* (*matico*) are tropical American species, grown for their leaves. Those of the former resemble spinach, and are used for flavouring in Mexican and Guatemalan cooking; the latter is an astringent styptic herb with a tea-like aroma, used in S America for wound healing, gastrointestinal complaints, and internal haemorrhage. *Piper auritum* is often grown as an ornamental shrub or small tree. The leaves contain large amounts of safrole (as in *Sassafras albidum*, see p.361), which is carcinogenic; they are traditionally fed to fish in Panama to flavour the flesh. In SE Asia, the leaves of *Piper sarmentosum* (*cha phloo*) are used as a vegetable and wrapping for savoury snacks; similarly *P. lolot* (*lá lót*) is used as a pleasant-flavoured wrapping in Vietnamese cuisine, and in folk medicine for arthritis and rheumatism. Numerous species other than *P. nigrum* are grown for their fruits, but only

Pinus mugo 'Mops'

Pinus mugo Pumilio Group

Pinus palustris

Pinus sylvestris

Pinus sylvestris Aurea Group

Pinus sylvestris 'Fastigiata'

P

P. longum and *P. retrofractum* (Javanese long pepper) are sufficiently similar in flavour to use as substitutes. Pink peppercorns come from an unrelated S American tree, *Schinus terebinthifolius*; they may be mixed with green, black, and white peppercorns for decoration, but they have a resinous flavour so cannot be used as a substitute. Red and chilli peppers are the fruits of *Capsicum* spp. (see p.153).

CULTIVATION Rich, well-drained soil in light shade and high humidity (*P. longum*, *P. nigrum*). Deep rich soil, including heavy clay, ample moisture, and shade (*P. betle*, *P. cubeba*). *P. auritum* thrives in full sun. Well-drained, stony soil, with ample water and humidity, in sun (*P. methysticum*). Plants are usually grown on frames. Remove weak or congested stems in late winter or early spring, before new growth begins. For optimum fruiting (*P. nigrum*), cut back young plants to 30cm (12in) several times a year, to stimulate growth of shoots, retaining the ten strongest and tying in at each node. Mature vines are pruned regularly, to 4m (12ft). Susceptible to fungal root rot, pepper weevil, and pepper flea beetle.

PROPAGATION By seed sown at 20–24°C (68–75°F); by semi-ripe cuttings in summer.

HARVEST Leaves are picked as required (*P. auritum*), blanched in the dark, often pressed together, and dried for extracts or to use whole (*P. betle*). Roots are lifted as required, usually from plants about 2m (6ft) tall, and used fresh, or dried for use in decoctions, liquid extracts, powders, and tablets (*P. methysticum*). Fruits are picked unripe and distilled for oleo-resin and oil, or dried for use in liquid extracts, powders, and tinctures (*P. cubeba*). Fruit clusters are picked unripe and dried for use whole, ground, or in decoctions (*P. longum*). Fruits of *P. nigrum* are picked unripe and used fresh, pickled (green peppercorns), and dried (green and black peppercorns); or ripe, and retted for eight days before drying (white peppercorns); black peppercorns are ground or decocted for medicinal use.

■ *Piper auritum* (hoja santa, makulan, yerba santa acuyo)
Shrubby tree with ovate, pointed, heart-shaped leaves, to 25cm (10in) long, which have slightly downy upper surfaces and are densely pubescent beneath. Minute flowers are borne in erect white spikes in summer and autumn. Native to Mexico. ↔ 4m (12ft).
HARDINESS Min. 10°C (50°F).
PARTS USED Leaves.
PROPERTIES An aromatic herb with a sarsaparilla-like flavour. It contains safrole, and aporphine-type alkaloids, whose effects are unknown.
MEDICINAL USES Externally as a poultice to relieve headaches.
CULINARY USES Leaves are used in C America as a flavouring in many different dishes, including *tamales*.
▨ ▪ ✎ ▣

■ *Piper betle* (betel pepper)
Shrubby vine with semi-woody stems and glossy, aromatic, pointed leaves, to 15cm (6in) long. Yellow-green, male and female flowers are borne on separate plants – males in 15cm (6in) long spikes, females slightly shorter – followed by fleshy red fruits. Found from India to the Malay Peninsula. ↕ 5m (15ft).
HARDINESS Min. 15–18°C (59–64°F).
PARTS USED Leaves, oil.
PROPERTIES An aromatic, anti-bacterial, stimulant herb with a clove-like flavour. It increases salivation and may protect against intestinal parasites and fungal infections.
MEDICINAL USES Externally in folk medicine for coughs, catarrh, diphtheria, headaches, pruritis, wounds, and boils (oil); and in Indonesia as a pessary after childbirth.
CULINARY USES Leaves are wrapped around betel nuts (seeds of *Areca catechu*, see p.128), in conjunction with lime and cutch (see *Acacia catechu*, p.98), together with various spices, to make a betel quid for chewing.
▨ ▢ ▪ ✎ ▣

■ *Piper cubeba* (cubeb, tailed pepper)
Shrubby vine with flexuous stems and tapering, ovate–elliptic, leathery leaves, 7–15cm (3–6in) long. Insignificant flowers are produced in spikes, to 10cm (4in) long; females bear rounded, 6mm (¼in), green fruits, which ripen to orange-brown. Native to SE Asia. ↕ 6m (20ft).

Piper cubeba

HARDINESS Min. 15–18°C (59–64°F).
PARTS USED Fruits, oil.
PROPERTIES A bitter, antiseptic, stimulant herb with a pungent, turpentine–allspice aroma. It has expectorant and diuretic effects, and improves digestion.
MEDICINAL USES Internally for coughs, bronchitis, sinusitis, throat and genito-urinary infections, poor digestion, and amoebic dysentery.
CULINARY USES Dried unripe fruits (cubeb berries) are used for seasoning; also as an ingredient of the Moroccan spice blend, *ras-el-hanout*.
ECONOMIC USES Oil is used in commercial flavouring of pickles, sauces, bitters, and tobacco, and in perfumery and toiletries.
▨ ▢ ▪ ✎ ✎ ▣

■ *Piper longum* (Indian long pepper, jaborandi pepper, *pippali*)
Slender shrub with much-branched, ascending or prostrate stems and ovate–cordate, pointed leaves, about 7cm (3in) long. Male flowers are borne in a lax spike, about 5cm (2in) long; females in a dense spike, elongating to 3.5cm (1½in) as the fused mass of small, red-brown fruits develops. Native to S and E India. ↕ 3m (10ft), ↔ 5–6m (15–20ft).
HARDINESS Min. 15–18°C (59–64°F).
PARTS USED Fruits (*bi ba*).

Piper auritum

Piper betle

Piper longum

Piper nigrum

PROPERTIES An aromatic, hot, stimulant herb that improves digestion and has decongestant, anti-bacterial, anti-fungal, and analgesic effects.
MEDICINAL USES Internally, in traditional Chinese medicine, for stomach chills, vomiting, acid regurgitation, headache, and rhinitis; and, in Ayurvedic medicine, for colds, asthma, bronchitis, arthritis, rheumatism, lumbago, sciatica, epilepsy, indigestion, and flatulence. Externally, in traditional Chinese medicine, for toothache. Combined with *P. nigrum* and *Zingiber officinale* (see p.411) in *trikatu*, an Ayurvedic remedy for cold conditions, and in *chyavanprash*, a rejuvenative tonic.
CULINARY USES Dried unripe fruits are used in curries and pickles; also to adulterate black pepper, and as an ingredient of the Moroccan spice blend *ras-el-hanout*.
☒ ☀ ✎ ▣

Piper methysticum (kava kava)
Robust, erect, slightly succulent, evergreen shrub with stout rhizomes, fleshy stems, and rounded, heart-shaped leaves, to 15cm (6in) long. Small flowers are produced in spikes, 7.5cm (3in) long. Native to islands of Oceania.
↕ 3–6m (9–18ft), ↔ 2–5m (6–15ft).
HARDINESS Min. 15–18°C (59–64°F).
PARTS USED Roots.
PROPERTIES A bitter, very pungent, warming herb with a lilac aroma. It acts as a diuretic, increases perspiration, relieves pain, relaxes spasms, has relaxant and locally anaesthetic effects, and is reputedly aphrodisiac.
MEDICINAL USES Internally for anxiety, tension, insomnia, genito-urinary infections, gall bladder complaints, gonorrhoea, arthritis and rheumatism; externally for joint pains, toothache, and mouth ulcers. Contraindicated during pregnancy and lactation, and in endogenous depression. Excess causes stupor; prolonged use may cause temporary yellowing of skin, hair, and nails. May cause drowsiness. Taken in conjunction with alcohol or barbiturates may potentiate inebriation.
CULINARY USES Chewed fermented roots are the basis of a ritual Polynesian drink that has a calming effect, but promotes mental awareness.
☒ ☀ ✎ ▣

■ *Piper nigrum* (pepper)
Shrubby vine with ovate leaves, 12–18cm (5–7in) long and heart-shaped at the bases. Tiny white flowers are borne on pendulous spikes, about 7cm (3in) long, with males and females usually on separate plants, followed by globose red berries, 6mm (¼in) across. Native to S and E India. ↕ 4m (12ft).
HARDINESS Min. 15–18°C (59–64°F).
PARTS USED Fruits (*hu jiao*).
PROPERTIES A pungent, aromatic, warming herb that lowers fever and improves digestion. It is regarded as a stimulating expectorant in Western and Ayurvedic medicine, and as tranquillizing and anti-emetic in Chinese practice.
MEDICINAL USES Internally, in Western medicine, for indigestion and flatulence; in Chinese medicine, for stomach chills, food poisoning (from fish, meat, crab, or fungi), cholera, dysentery, diarrhoea and vomiting caused by cold. Externally, in Ayurvedic medicine, mixed with ghee, for nasal congestion, sinusitis, epilepsy, and skin inflammations.
CULINARY USES Black and white peppercorns are, respectively, the dried unripe and ripe berries; they give flavour and piquancy to most savoury dishes, meat products, sauces, dressings, pickles, and coatings for fish, meat, and cheese. Ground white pepper is less aromatic. Mignonette pepper (also called "shot pepper", or *poivre gris*) is a blend of ground white and black peppercorns. Green (fresh, unripe) peppercorns are used in creamy sauces, to flavour duck, pickled for pâtés, butters, and sauces, and dried for stock, soup, and casseroles.
☒ ☀ ✎ ▣

PISCIDIA

Fabaceae

This genus includes eight or so species of trees, occurring in C America, the West Indies, and Florida. *Piscidia piscipula* is an important honey plant in the Yucatán, where the finest honey in Mexico is produced. It was introduced to Europe in 1690 and grown in greenhouses during the 19th century, but is seldom seen today. *Piscidia* is closely related, and similar in appearance, to *Lonchocarpus*, a much larger genus that is known for its fish poisons. Both genera contain rotenoids, which stun fish but leave the flesh untainted and edible. One of these compounds is rotenone, a powerful insecticide, which is extracted from the E Indian *Derris elliptica* for commercial purposes. Although known as Jamaica dogwood, *Piscidia* is not related to *Cornus* (dogwood, see p.180) and differs in appearance. *Piscidia* is from the Latin *piscis*, "fish", and *caedere*, "to kill", and refers to the use of crushed leaves and twigs by native N Americans to stupefy fish, so that they float to the surface and are easily caught.
CULTIVATION Deep, well-drained soil in sun with high humidity. Cut back hard after flowering to control size.
PROPAGATION By seed sown in spring; by semi-ripe cuttings in summer.

HARVEST Bark is collected as required, often after trees are felled for their timber, and dried for use in decoctions, liquid extracts, and tinctures.

Piscidia piscipula syn. *P. erythrina* (fish poison tree, Jamaica dogwood)
Deciduous tree with pinnate leaves, to 25cm (10in) long, divided into elliptic–ovate leaflets, to 10cm (4in) long. Blue-purple to white, red-striped flowers, about 1cm (⅜in) long, appear in panicles in spring before the new leaves, followed by winged pods, 7cm (3in) long. Native to Mexico, USA (S Florida), and the West Indies. ↕ 15m (50ft), ↔ 10m (30ft).
HARDINESS Min. 16–18°C (61–64°F).
PARTS USED Bark of stems and roots.
PROPERTIES A bitter, acrid, sedative herb with an opium-like aroma. It relaxes spasms, controls coughing, and relieves pain.
MEDICINAL USES Internally for whooping cough, asthma, neuralgia, migraine, nervous exhaustion, toothache, insomnia, painful menstruation, and postpartum pain. Combined with *Viburnum prunifolium* (see p.404) for gynaecological problems; with *Humulus lupulus* (see p.237), *Passiflora incarnata* (see p.303), or *Valeriana officinalis* (see p.400) for severe symptoms of nervous tension, such as palpitations and panic attacks. Contraindicated during pregnancy, and in cardiac insufficiency. For use only by qualified practitioners.
▣ ▨ ☀ ▣

PISTACIA
Pistachio

Anacardiaceae

A genus of about 11 species of trees and shrubs, found in Mediterranean areas, Asia, C America, and S USA. *Pistacia lentiscus* has been valued since Classical times for its resin, known as mastic, which is used as a temporary filling for teeth and to sweeten the breath. It contains pinene, a strongly antiseptic volatile oil,

Pistacia lentiscus

Pistacia terebinthus

commonly found in *Pinus* spp. (see p.318). Trees are tapped for 5–6 weeks by making incisions, about 2cm (¾in) long, in the bark and numbering 200–300 per plant. The main producer is the Greek island of Chios, where harvesting is restricted by law to between 15 July and 15 October. *Pistacia terebinthus* was described by Theophrastus in the 1st century BC as the source of turpentine, a viscous oleo-resin, which is also obtained from various conifers, such as *Pinus palustris* (see p.319). Essence of turpentine, used in aromatherapy, is made by distilling turpentine. Fioravanti's balm is a compound spirit of turpentine, made by distilling alcohol with turpentine and various other anti-rheumatic substances. Turpentine and mastic were among the 17 ingredients of *kyphi*, an Egyptian incense. *Pistacia* is from the Greek *pistake*, "pistachio tree", referring to the closely related *P. vera*.

CULTIVATION Well-drained to dry, sandy or stony, alkaline soil in sun. Trim plants in spring to restrict size.

PROPAGATION By seed sown at 25°C (77°F) in early spring; by greenwood cuttings in late spring or early summer; by semi-ripe cuttings in summer.

HARVEST Resin is obtained from incisions in bark from midsummer to midautumn, and dried for powder (*P. lentiscus*) or distilled for oil and essence (*P. lentiscus*, *P. terebinthus*). Seeds are pressed for oil when ripe.

■ *Pistacia lentiscus* (lentisc, mastic tree)
Large evergreen shrub or small tree with leathery, pungently scented, pinnate leaves, to 10cm (4in) long, divided into 2–7 pairs of narrowly oblong to ovate, glossy leaflets, which have winged stalks and no terminal leaflet. Dense clusters of red-green flowers appear from spring to early summer, followed by globose, fleshy, red fruits, ripening to black. Native to the Mediterranean. ↔ 1–4m (3–12ft).

HARDINESS Half hardy.

PARTS USED Resin, oil.

PROPERTIES An aromatic, stimulant, antiseptic herb with a pine-like aroma. It has diuretic and expectorant effects, and controls bleeding.

MEDICINAL USES Externally for boils, ulcers,

bronchitis, ringworm, and muscular stiffness.

CULINARY USES Liquorice-flavoured resin is chewed like chewing gum, and used to flavour cakes, desserts, and confectionery. Oil from seeds, known as *shina* oil, is used for cooking.

ECONOMIC USES Resin and oil are used as fixatives in perfumery and also in the Greek confectionery *masticha* and in the liqueur *mastiche*. Resin is used in varnishes, lacquers, and for sealing edges of microscope mounts.

◻ ▪ ✎ ✎

■ *Pistacia terebinthus* (Cyprus turpentine, terebinth tree)
Rounded deciduous tree or shrub with aromatic, dark green, pinnate leaves, 10–20cm (4–8in) long, divided into 3–6 pairs of ovate leaflets, which have a terminal leaflet. Small, red-green flowers appear in panicles in spring and early summer, followed by edible, red to purple-brown fruits, to 7mm (¼in) long. Native to the Mediterranean. ↕ 6m (20ft), ↔ 2–6m (6–20ft).

HARDINESS Half hardy.

PARTS USED Resin, essence.

PROPERTIES A bitter, aromatic, antiseptic herb that is expectorant, relaxes spasms, controls bleeding, promotes healing, and is effective against various parasitic organisms.

MEDICINAL USES Internally for chronic bronchial infections, streptococcal, urinary, and renal infections, haemorrhage, gallstones, tapeworm, and rheumatism. Externally for arthritis, gout, sciatica, scabies, and lice.

CULINARY USES Seeds and seed oil are edible. Resin is chewed as chewing gum. Immature fruit clusters are pickled as a condiment.

◻ ▪ ▪ ✎

PLANTAGO
Plantain

Plantaginaceae

This large cosmopolitan genus includes about 200 species of often weedy, invasive annuals, biennials, and perennials, found in a wide range of habitats. *Plantago major* (greater plantain) is a common weed of lawns and paths but has several variants that are grown in borders as ornamentals.

In many parts of the world, plantain is known as "white man's foot", alluding to the way that it was spread worldwide during colonial times in the trouser turn-ups of Europeans. A number of different plantains are used medicinally, some for their leaves and others for their seeds. The main constituents in the foliage are tannins and iridoid glycosides, notably aucubin, which stimulates uric acid secretion from the kidneys. *Plantago lanceolata* (ribwort plantain) is similar to *P. major* in chemistry and used interchangeably. The Chinese *P. asiatica* is very similar both in appearance and chemistry to *P. major*. It was first recorded in Chinese medicine during the Han dynasty (206BC–AD23). Plantain seeds, notably from *P. psyllium*, contain up to 30 per cent mucilage, which swells in the gut, acting as a bulk laxative and soothing irritated membranes. The husks, rather than whole seeds, are used in certain preparations. The common name "fleaseed" refers to the flea-like appearance of the seeds. *Plantago ovata* (blond psyllium, ispaghula) has pink- or grey-brown seeds, used interchangeably with those of *P. psyllium*. Other species, such as *P. indica* (black psyllium) and *P. arenaria* (golden psyllium), are also used.

CULTIVATION Well-drained soil in sun (*P. asiatica*, *P. psyllium*); moist soil in sun or partial shade (*P. major*). *Plantago major* is prone to powdery mildew in dry conditions.

PROPAGATION By seed sown in autumn or spring. *Plantago major* and variants self-sow freely and spread from borders into lawns and paths. Variants come reasonably true from seed.

HARVEST Plants are cut during the growing season and used fresh, as juice, or dried for decoctions (*P. asiatica*). Leaves are cut before flowering and dried for infusions, liquid extracts, and tinctures (*P. major*). Ripe seeds are dried for decoctions and powders.

■ *Plantago asiatica* syn. *P. major* var. *asiatica* (Asian plantain)
Evergreen perennial with a basal rosette of long-stalked, ovate, deeply veined leaves, to 15cm (6in) long. Minute green flowers are borne in spikes, to 50cm (20in) long, in summer, followed by capsules containing 4–9 dark brown seeds. Native to China. ↕ 20–60cm (8–24in), ↔ 15–30cm (6–12in). ■ 'Variegata' has irregular white variegation.

HARDINESS Fully hardy.

PARTS USED Whole plant (*che qian cao*), seeds (*che qian zi*).

PROPERTIES A cooling herb that is diuretic and expectorant, reduces inflammation, stops bleeding, and controls coughing.

MEDICINAL USES Internally for complaints associated with "overheating", such as acute infections of the lungs and urinary tract, hepatitis, and boils (whole plant); diarrhoea, urinary complaints, coughs with profuse phlegm, conjunctivitis, and vertigo (seeds).

▨ ▨ ▪

■ *Plantago major* (common plantain, greater plantain, rat-tail plantain)
Evergreen perennial with a basal rosette of long-stalked, ovate to elliptic leaves, to 15cm (6in)

P

Plantago asiatica

Plantago asiatica 'Variegata'

Plantago major

Platycodon grandiflorus

Plantago major 'Rosularis'

Plantago major 'Rubrifolia'

Plantago psyllium

long. Minute, yellow-green flowers are produced in cylindrical spikes, to 20cm (8in) long, in summer. Native to Europe and temperate Asia; widely naturalized. ↔ 40cm (16in). ▣ 'Rosularis' (rose plantain) has a leafy flower spike, resembling a green rose. ▣ 'Rubrifolia' has maroon leaves.
HARDINESS Fully hardy.
PARTS USED Leaves.
PROPERTIES An astringent herb that is diuretic, expectorant, and catarrhal, promotes healing, controls bleeding, and is effective against bacterial infections.
MEDICINAL USES Internally for diarrhoea, haemorrhage, haemorrhoids, cystitis, bronchitis, catarrh, sinusitis, asthma, hay fever, ear infections, dry coughs, gastritis, diarrhoea, gastric ulcers, and irritable bowel syndrome. Externally for wounds, bruises, insect bites, ulcers, eye inflammations, shingles, haemorrhoids, and varicose ulcers. Often used to moderate the irritant effect of herbs containing volatile oils.
CULINARY USES Young leaves are edible, though the midrib and veins are fibrous. Dried leaves are used to make tea. Seeds are edible.
▨ ▣ ▨

▣ *Plantago psyllium* (fleaseed, fleawort, Spanish psyllium)
Annual with linear, grey-green, downy leaves, mostly arranged in whorls of 3–6. Globose flower spikes appear in the axils in summer, followed

by tiny glossy seeds. Native to the Mediterranean. ↕ 60cm (24in), ↔ 30cm (12in).
HARDINESS Fully hardy.
PARTS USED Seeds.
PROPERTIES A sweet, astringent, cooling herb that moistens membranes, soothes irritation, and absorbs digestive toxins.
MEDICINAL USES Internally for constipation, diarrhoea, acid indigestion, gastric and duodenal ulcers, bowel problems, haemorrhoids, and urethritis. Used in Ayurvedic medicine with buttermilk for diarrhoea and with warm milk for constipation. Externally for skin irritation, boils, abscesses, whitlows, and inflamed eyelids. Combined with *Calendula officinalis* (see p.150) as a poultice for drawing out toxins.
CULINARY USES Seeds are sprouted for salads.
ECONOMIC USES Seeds or husks are an ingredient of face masks. Mucilage from seeds is used as a fabric dressing, and as a thickener and stabilizer in dairy-based desserts.
▨ ▣ ▨ ▨

PLATYCLADUS
Platycladus orientalis. See *Thuja orientalis*.

PLATYCODON
Campanulaceae

This genus contains a single species of perennial that occurs in E Asia. It is closely related to *Campanula*. *Platycodon grandiflorus*

is an easily grown border plant with double-flowered cultivars in shades of pink and white, and dwarf variants that are popular for rock gardens and containers. The first plants to reach the West were sent by Robert Fortune to England in 1844. *Platycodon* has a long history of use in traditional Chinese medicine, being first mentioned in the *Shen Nong Ben Cao Jing* during the Han dynasty (206BC–AD23). It is widely used in patent remedies, notably *platycodi* cough tablets. *Platycodon* is from the Greek *platys*, "broad", and *kodon*, "bell", referring to the wide, bell-shaped flowers.
CULTIVATION Rich, moist, well-drained, sandy soil in sun. Seedlings are very fragile and best planted out when dormant.
PROPAGATION By seed sown in spring; by division in summer; by separating rooted basal shoots in early summer.
HARVEST Roots are lifted in spring or autumn from plants 2–3 years old, peeled, and used fresh, or dried for decoctions and powders.

▣ *Platycodon grandiflorus* (balloon flower, Chinese bellflower)
Erect, clump-forming perennial with thick roots and blue-green, ovate, toothed leaves, to 5cm (2in) long. Large inflated buds open into five-petalled, bell-shaped, usually blue flowers, 5cm (2in) across, in summer. Native to N China, Japan, Korea, and Russia (E Siberia). ↕ 40–90cm (16–36in), ↔ 30cm (12in). ▣ var. *albus* has white flowers. ▣ 'Apoyama' syn.

P

Platycodon grandiflorus var. *albus*

Platycodon grandiflorus 'Apoyama'

var. *apoyama* is dwarf, with larger, deeper blue flowers. ↕ 20cm (8in). 'Perlmutterschale' syn. 'Mother of Pearl' has pale pink flowers.

HARDINESS Fully hardy.
PARTS USED Roots (*jie geng*).
PROPERTIES A bitter, pungent, warming herb that dilates the bronchial vessels; it is expectorant and effective against a number of disease-causing organisms.
MEDICINAL USES Internally for coughs with profuse phlegm, colds, bronchitis, pleurisy, pulmonary abscess, and throat infections. Combined with *Glycyrrhiza uralensis* (see p.227) for throat infections.
CULINARY USES Roots are eaten raw in salads, added to tonic soups, pickled, or preserved in sugar; also as one of seven herbs used to flavour Japanese *sake*.

PLECTRANTHUS

Lamiaceae

This genus of about 350 species of evergreen perennials and subshrubs occurs in warm and tropical parts of Africa, Asia, and Australia. Several species are cultivated as ornamentals. *Plectranthus amboinicus* deserves to be more widely grown, making an especially attractive, easily grown houseplant in its variegated forms. The foliage is highly aromatic and variously described as resembling thyme, sage, or oregano. This interesting and widely used herb is not known in the wild but is thought to have originated in Africa or India, from where it spread to the E Indies. The name *amboinicus* indicates that its origin was thought to be Ambon, one of the Molucca Islands in E Indonesia. Apparently introduced to America from Spain (hence "Spanish thyme"), today it is a popular culinary herb in many parts of the world, giving rise to common names such as "Indian borage" and "Cuban oregano". In India it is likened in taste and odour to *ajowan* (see *Trachyspermum ammi*, p.392). *Plectranthus barbatus* syn. *Coleus barbatus, C. forskohlii* is similar in appearance to *Plectranthus amboinicus*. It has a camphoraceous aroma and contains forskolin, which has been researched

for its potential in treating congestive heart disease, glaucoma, and chronic bronchial disease.

CULTIVATION Light, rich, well-drained soil in sun. Provide ample moisture during the growing season but keep on the dry side in winter. Pinch out tips during the growing season to encourage bushy growth. Cut back straggly plants in spring.
PROPAGATION By seed sown at 19–24°C (66–75°F) when ripe; by stem-tip cuttings at any time, avoiding excessively damp conditions.
HARVEST Leaves are picked as required and used fresh.

■ *Plectranthus amboinicus* syn. *Coleus amboinicus, C. aromaticus* (Cuban oregano, Indian borage, Spanish thyme)
Sprawling evergreen perennial with succulent, velvety, light green leaves, 4–8cm (1½–3in) long, which have finely scalloped margins. Small lavender flowers are borne in spikes, to 40cm (16in) long, in spring and summer. Unknown in the wild; possibly from Africa or India originally. ↔ 30–90cm (12–36in). 'Variegated' has white-variegated leaves. ■ 'Well-Sweep Wedgewood' has pale green leaves with darker green margins.
HARDINESS Min. 10–15°C (50–59°F).
PARTS USED Leaves.
PROPERTIES A strongly aromatic, healing herb with an oregano-like flavour. It relaxes spasms, reduces inflammation, benefits the digestion, and

Plectranthus amboinicus

Plectranthus amboinicus 'Well-Sweep Wedgewood'

has laxative, expectorant, and antibiotic effects.
MEDICINAL USES Internally for coughs, bronchitis, asthma, colic, dyspepsia, and postpartum pain. Externally for headache, sores, burns, and insect bites.
CULINARY USES Leaves are used to flavour beans, salads, and strong-smelling meat and fish; also infused as tea. An ingredient of Vietnamese sour soup *canh chua* and the Indian salad *bajeh*.

PODOPHYLLUM

Berberidaceae

A genus of about nine species of perennials, distributed throughout N America and the Himalayas. *Podophyllum peltatum* is a handsome plant for the woodland garden, with umbrella-shaped leaves, anemone-like flowers, and edible, lemon-flavoured fruits. It was used in various ways by native N Americans: in minute doses as a purgative, emetic, vermifuge, and liver tonic, and externally for removing warts. The Menominee made a decoction of the plant as an insecticide for potato crops. It was also used as a means of suicide. *Podophyllum* contains a resin, podophyllin, which consists of lignan glycosides, the most important being podophyllotoxin. These substances are highly toxic to cells, causing foetal death if ingested by pregnant women. Podophyllin resin was introduced as a purgative by John King, a young physican from Ohio, and it became popular worldwide for this purpose. It is no longer considered safe for internal use. In the 1970s, research by the pharmaceutical laboratory Sandoz led to the development of the semi-synthetic drug etoposide, a potent anti-tumour agent. The Himalayan *P. hexandrum* syn. *P. emodi* is especially rich in podophyllotoxin and is now a protected species, after serious depletion in the wild through over-collection for the pharmaceutical industry. *Podophyllum* comes from the Greek *pous*, "foot", and *phyllon*, "leaf", describing the leaf shape.
CULTIVATION Humus-rich, moist soil, pH4.0–7.0, in sheltered semi-shade. Young

P

Podophyllum peltatum

leaves may be damaged by frost in cold areas.
PROPAGATION By seed sown when ripe at 20°C (68°F); by division in spring or late summer.
HARVEST Rhizomes are lifted in autumn, and dried for use in tinctures and for commercial extraction of resin.
⚠ **WARNING** All parts, except ripe fruits, may be fatally toxic if eaten. Handling may cause systemic poisoning.

◼ *Podophyllum peltatum* (American mandrake, may apple, wild lemon)
Perennial with a red-brown rhizome, to 2m (6ft) long, and upright stems bearing drooping, 5–9-lobed, toothed leaves, to 30cm (12in) long. Solitary, semi-pendent, bowl-shaped, white flowers, 5cm (2in) across, are followed by yellow fruits, to 5cm (2in) long. Native to NE America. ‡ 30–45cm (12–18in), ↔ 1.2m (4ft).
HARDINESS Fully hardy.
PARTS USED Rhizomes, resin.
PROPERTIES An acrid caustic herb with an unpleasant smell. It has anti-cancer and anti-viral effects, and is a drastic purgative.
MEDICINAL USES Internally for certain cancers. Externally for venereal warts and verrucas. Contraindicated during pregnancy.
⚠ **WARNING** This herb is subject to legal restrictions in most countries.
◻ ▨ ◼

POGOSTEMON

Lamiaceae

A genus of about 70 species of perennials and subshrubs, occurring in India and Malaysia. *Pogostemon cablin* and various other species are widely cultivated in India and the Far East for patchouli, a heavy, long-lasting, mint–sandalwood fragrance, once used to distinguish fabrics of Indian origin. Fashionable in Europe during the 1860s, patchouli regained popularity through the hippie movement during the 1960s. In the East, patchouli oil is thought to prevent the spread of infection and is widely used for this purpose. It is produced from various different and, in some cases, unrelated species. *Pogostemon heyneanus* yields an inferior oil, known as Java or Indian patchouli. Other

sources include *P. plectranthoides* (*rudilo, thekkali*), *Microtoena insuavis* syn. *Gomphostemma insuave* (Chinese patchouli, *guan chun hua*, khasia patchouli), and *Plectranthus patchouli*. Several species of *Pogostemon* are used medicinally in India, notably *P. parviflorus*, which is a specific remedy for snake bite. *Pogostemon* is from the Greek *pogon*, "beard", and *stemon*, "stamen", referring to the bearded filaments.
CULTIVATION Rich moist soil with high humidity. Pinch out or cut back plants in spring, to encourage bushy growth.
PROPAGATION By seed sown when ripe (plants rarely set seed); by greenwood cuttings (most usual method) with a heel in late spring; by division in spring or autumn.
HARVEST Leaves are cut two or three times a year and dried, mainly for oil distillation.

◼ *Pogostemon cablin* syn. *P. patchouli* (patchouli)
Upright, bushy, evergreen perennial with aromatic, velvety, ovate to triangular leaves, to 12cm (5in) long. White, violet-marked flowers, with violet filaments, are produced in spikes, to 14cm (5½in) long. Native to India and Malaysia. ↔ 1m (3ft).
HARDINESS Min. 10–15°C (50–59°F).
PARTS USED Leaves, oil.
PROPERTIES An astringent, antiseptic, warming herb with a pervasive aroma. It acts as a diuretic, lowers fever, improves digestion, controls vomiting, has both a tonic and sedative effect on the nervous system, and is reputedly aphrodisiac.
MEDICINAL USES Internally for colds, headaches, fever, nausea, vomiting, abdominal pain, and diarrhoea (leaves). Externally for halitosis, snake bite, fungal skin infections, weeping eczema, acne, chapped skin, varicose veins, haemorrhoids, and impetigo (leaves, oil). Oil is used in aromatherapy for nervous exhaustion, depression, stress-related complaints, low libido, and frigidity.
ECONOMIC USES Oil is of major importance in perfumery; also in toiletries, cosmetics, breath fresheners, incense, insecticides and disinfectants, and in commercial food flavouring. Leaves are added to potpourris.
▨ ◻ ▣ ✎ ▨

Pogostemon cablin

POLEMONIUM
Jacob's ladder

Polemoniaceae

A genus of 25 species of rhizomatous and clump-forming perennials, and spreading annuals, often with unpleasant-smelling foliage. They occur in temperate regions of the northern hemisphere, mainly in N America, but also in southern S America and Asia. Most have blue or white, saucer-shaped flowers. *Polemonium caeruleum* is a variable species, widely grown in borders and wildflower meadows. The less vigorous *P. reptans* is also popular as a border perennial, with cultivars in shades of blue and pink. Both *P. caeruleum* and *P. reptans* are often called "Greek valerian", though they are not related to *Valeriana officinalis* (valerian, see p.400) and have quite different medicinal properties. The plants do, however, attract cats, which roll in them with evident pleasure. In ancient Greek times, *P. caeruleum* was prescribed in wine for dysentery, toothache, and poisonous bites. It passed into various European pharmacopoeias as *herba valerianae graeca*, and was used mainly for rabies and syphilis. Being ornamental and easily grown, *P. caeruleum* and *P. reptans* are often planted in herb gardens, though they are seldom used for medicinal purposes today.

Polemonium caeruleum

Polemonium caeruleum 'Blanjou'

CULTIVATION Moist soil in sun or partial shade. *P. caeruleum* tolerates alkaline conditions, while *P. reptans* prefers humus-rich soil. Cut back flower stems to base after flowering, unless seed is required.

PROPAGATION By seed sown in autumn or spring; by division in spring. Cultivars may not come true from seed. *P. caeruleum* may self-sow excessively in optimum conditions.

HARVEST Plants (*P. caeruleum*) are cut in summer for infusions. Rhizomes (*P. reptans*) are lifted in winter and dried for decoctions and tinctures.

◾ *Polemonium caeruleum* (charity, Greek valerian, Jacob's ladder)
Upright, clump-forming perennial with arching pinnate leaves, to 12cm (5in) long, divided into 19–27 oblanceolate leaflets, to 4cm (1½in) long. Blue (rarely white) flowers, to 2.5cm (1in) across, are produced in lax clusters in late spring and summer. Native to N and C Europe and N Asia. ↕ 30–90cm (12–36in), ↔ 30cm (12in). f. *album* syn. 'Album' has white flowers. ◾ 'Blanjou' syn. 'Brise d'Anjou' has white-variegated leaves.
HARDINESS Fully hardy.
PARTS USED Whole plant.
PROPERTIES A slightly bitter, odourless, astringent herb that increases perspiration.
MEDICINAL USES Formerly used internally for a range of conditions, from headaches to fevers and epilepsy.

◾ *Polemonium reptans* (abscess root, Greek valerian)
Spreading to upright perennial with a creeping rhizome and pinnate leaves, consisting of 7–19 elliptic to oblong, pointed leaflets. Clusters of small blue flowers, to 2cm (¾in) across, are borne in spring and early summer. Native to E USA. ↕ 15–30cm (6–12in), ↔ 38cm (15in). 'Pink Dawn' has pale pink flowers. 'Virginia White' syn. 'Album' has white flowers.
HARDINESS Fully hardy.
PARTS USED Rhizomes.
PROPERTIES A slightly bitter, acrid, astringent herb that increases perspiration, and has expectorant and alterative effects.
MEDICINAL USES Internally for coughs, colds,

Polemonium reptans

bronchitis, laryngitis, tuberculosis, feverish and inflammatory conditions, including skin diseases and poisonous bites. Rarely used today.

POLIOMINTHA
Lamiaceae

A genus of four species of shrubs and subshrubs, found in arid regions of SW USA and N Mexico. They have small simple leaves and tubular flowers. One or two species are cultivated for their aromatic foliage and attractive flowers. *Poliomintha bustamanta*, the most widely grown species, has a similar scent to *Origanum* spp. (oregano, see p.295). *Poliomintha incana* syn. *Hedeoma incana* (frosted mint, rosemary mint) is also used for flavouring.
CULTIVATION Well-drained, sandy soil in sun.
PROPAGATION By semi-ripe cuttings in summer.
HARVEST Leaves are picked as required for flavouring.

Poliomintha bustamanta syn. *P. longiflora*, *Hedeoma longiflora* (Mexican oregano)
Robust, semi-evergreen or deciduous shrub or subshrub with well-spaced, ovate to elliptic leaves, 7–15mm (¼–½in) long. Pale pink to violet, tubular flowers, to 3.5cm (1⅜in) long, are borne in the axils of upper leaves in summer. Native to Mexico and southwestern N America. ↔ 30cm – 1.2m (1–5ft).
HARDINESS Frost hardy in dry conditions.
PARTS USED Leaves.
PROPERTIES An aromatic herb with an oregano-like flavour.
CULINARY USES Fresh or dried leaves are used as a substitute for oregano in Mexico and Texas.

POLYGALA
Milkwort
Polygalaceae

This large genus includes about 500 species of annuals, perennials, shrubs, and trees, which are found almost worldwide. A few are grown as ornamentals for their pea-like flowers, but the medicinal species have little merit as garden plants. *Polygala senega* was named after the N American Seneca people, who used it as a remedy for rattlesnake bite. Its present uses were discovered c.1735 by John Tennent, a Scottish physician, who observed that the symptoms of snake bite were similar to those of pleurisy and the later stages of pneumonia. Experiments in using it for respiratory diseases were so successful that by 1740 the plant was being cultivated and used in Europe for this purpose. *Polygala tenuifolia* was first recorded in traditional Chinese medicine during the earlier Han dynasty (206BC–AD23). Both *P. senega* and *P. tenuifolia* contain similar compounds but are used differently in European and Chinese herbal medicine. The European *P. vulgaris* (common milkwort) has similar properties but is less potent. The bitter-tasting *P. amarella* (dwarf

milkwort) is also used. Contrary to traditional belief, their use does not increase lactation.
CULTIVATION Well-drained, moisture-retentive soil in sun or partial shade.
PROPAGATION By seed sown in autumn.
HARVEST Roots are lifted in autumn and dried for use in decoctions, concentrated infusions, liquid extracts, powders, and tinctures.

Polygala senega (rattlesnake root, Seneca snakeroot)
Perennial with a thick root and linear–lanceolate leaves, to 5cm (2in) long. Tiny, white to green-white flowers are produced in terminal racemes in summer. Native to N America. ↕ 45cm (18in).
HARDINESS Fully hardy.
PARTS USED Roots.
PROPERTIES A bitter, acrid, warming herb that has expectorant effects, and increases salivation and perspiration.
MEDICINAL USES Internally for bronchitis, catarrh, asthma, and croup. Excess causes diarrhoea and vomiting. Externally for pharyngitis and snake bite.

Polygala tenuifolia (Siberian milkwort)
Perennial with thin stems and linear leaves, to 3cm (1¼in) long. Pale violet to blue flowers are produced in lateral branches, followed by capsules, 5mm (¼in) in diameter. Native to Siberia, Mongolia, and China. ↕ 25cm (10in).
HARDINESS Fully hardy.
PARTS USED Roots (*yuan zhi*).
PROPERTIES A pungent, bitter, warming herb that lowers blood pressure and has expectorant, anti-bacterial, and tranquillizing effects. It acts mainly as a tonic for heart and kidney energies.
MEDICINAL USES Internally for coughs with profuse phlegm, bronchitis, insomnia, palpitations, poor memory, anxiety, depression, and nervous tension. Externally for boils and carbuncles. Combined with *Glycyrrhiza uralensis* (see p.227) for coughs in heavy smokers.

POLYGONATUM
Solomon's seal
Convallariaceae

A genus of about 50 species of rhizomatous perennials, found in Europe, Asia, and N USA. *Polygonatum odoratum* (Solomon's seal) is one of several, rather similar species, grown as an ornamental for its arching stems and pendent tubular flowers. Care should be taken not to confuse the names *Polygonatum multiflorum* and *Polygonum multiflorum*; the latter name is a synonym for *Fallopia multiflora* (see p.212). Several sources list *Polygonatum multiflorum*, rather than *P. odoratum*, as the species used medicinally. Both are quite rare in the wild. Most plants in cultivation are hybrids between *P. multiflorum* and *P. odoratum*, and there is probably little difference in

Polygonatum odoratum

their constituents. Solomon's seal was described as a medicinal herb in Classical times, and in China its uses go back to the 1st century AD. In N America, the native Solomon's seals – *P. biflorum* and *P. pubescens* – were used. In parts of S USA, the roots are known as John-the-Conqueror, and are important in voodoo. *Polygonatum* is from the Greek *polys*, "many", and *gonu*, "knee joint", referring to the jointed rhizomes.

CULTIVATION Well-drained, moist, rich soil in partial shade, or in sun with a cool root run. Leaves may be damaged by sawfly caterpillars.

PROPAGATION By seed sown in autumn; by division in early spring.

HARVEST Rhizomes are lifted in autumn and used fresh in tinctures and ointments, or dried for use in decoctions and powders.

⚠ **WARNING** All parts, especially the berries, are harmful if eaten.

▣ *Polygonatum odoratum* syn. *P. officinale* (angled Solomon's seal)
Rhizomatous perennial with angled arching stems and stalkless, ovate, pointed leaves, to 10cm (4in) long. Fragrant, white, green-tipped flowers, about 2cm (¾in) long, appear in early summer, followed by blue-black berries, 6mm (¼in) long. Native to Europe and Asia. ‡ 85cm (34in), ↔ 45cm (18in). 'Flore Pleno' has double flowers. 'Gilt Edge' has yellow-margined leaves.

Polygonatum odoratum 'Variegatum'

▣ 'Variegatum' has white-margined leaves.
HARDINESS Fully hardy.
PARTS USED Rhizomes (*yu zhu*).
PROPERTIES A bitter–sweet, astringent, tonic herb that acts as an expectorant, soothes irritated or damaged tissues, reduces inflammation, and clears toxins.
MEDICINAL USES Internally, in Chinese medicine, for heart disease, tuberculosis, dry cough, dry throat in diabetes, and to encourage secretion of body fluids. In Western herbalism, internally for coughs and gastric irritation; externally for bruises, broken nose, haemorrhoids, rupture, and dislocations. Internally, in Ayurvedic medicine, as a rejuvenative and aphrodisiac; one of eight root herbs (mostly belonging to the lily family) known as *ashtavarga*, used for infertility, insufficient lactation, chronic wasting diseases, or bleeding disorders related to kidney weakness. Given with warm milk and ghee as a tonic.
▣ ▣

POLYGONUM
Polygonum bistorta. See *Persicaria bistorta*.
Polygonum multiflorum. See *Fallopia multiflora*.
Polygonum odoratum. See *Persicaria odorata*.

POLYPODIUM
Polypody

Polypodiaceae

A genus of about 75 species of mostly evergreen, often epiphytic ferns with fleshy creeping rhizomes, occurring mainly in northern temperate regions. Polypodies make good ground cover for damp shady areas beneath trees, and in the wild often grow on trees. *Polypodium vulgare* has numerous cultivars, grown as ornamentals for their elegant fronds. It has an ancient history as a herb, being recommended by Dioscorides for chapped or dislocated hands, and by Culpeper as a laxative. The rhizome is rich in mucilage, containing sladin, a sweet-tasting saponin. This sweetness is very noticeable in *P. glycyrrhiza* (liquorice fern), used by native N Americans to treat measles and coughs. *Polypodium* is from the Greek *polys*, "many", and *pous*, "foot",

Polypodium vulgare

Polypodium vulgare 'Cornubiense'

referring to the much-branched rhizomes.
CULTIVATION Moist, well-drained, humus-rich soil in partial shade. Leaves may be damaged by rust fungi.
PROPAGATION By spores sown when ripe at 15–16°C (59–61°F); by division in spring or early summer.
HARVEST Rhizomes are lifted in autumn and used, usually fresh, in decoctions, liquid extracts, syrups, and tinctures.

▣ *Polypodium vulgare* (polypody)
Evergreen, creeping, often epiphytic fern with rhizomes, about 1cm (⅜in) thick, which are densely clad in red-brown scales when young. Fronds, up to 40cm (16in) long, are pinnately lobed, almost to the midrib, into 20–40 lanceolate segments. Native to Europe, Africa, and E Asia, mostly in northern or upland areas. ‡ 30cm (12in), ↔ indefinite. ▣ 'Cornubiense' has finely cut, light green fronds, which may be tripinnate or quadripinnate. Pinnate fronds, resembling those of the species, should be removed.
HARDINESS Fully hardy.
PARTS USED Rhizomes.
PROPERTIES A very sweet, slightly acrid, warming herb that acts as an expectorant and diuretic, increases bile flow, promotes healing, improves digestion and liver function, and kills intestinal worms. It also has anti-rheumatic, alterative, and mild purgative effects.
MEDICINAL USES Internally for dry cough, bronchial catarrh, chest infections, pleurisy, arthritis, indigestion, poor appetite, hepatitis, jaundice, constipation (especially in children), and intestinal parasites (especially tapeworm). Combined with *Althaea officinalis* (see p.117) for bronchial complaints. Externally for wounds. May cause a rash, which is harmless.
▣ ▣

POPULUS
Poplar

Salicaceae

There are about 35 species of fast-growing, deciduous trees in this genus, which occurs throughout northern temperate regions. Poplars grow in a wide range of situations, tolerating wet soils, coastal conditions, and urban pollution; they make excellent screens, avenues, and windbreaks. The new leaves of some species are scented in spring, and many have ornamental variants. Poplars are closely related to *Salix* spp. (willow, see p.352) and similarly contain salicin, which reduces inflammation and relieves pain. Salicylates provided the basis for aspirin, which was synthesized in the 19th century. Many poplars are very similar in chemistry and are used interchangeably for medicinal purposes. Poplar bark comes mainly from *P. alba*, but *P. nigra* (black poplar), *P. tremuloides* (American aspen), and other species are also used. *Populus alba* was listed in the *US Pharmacopoeia* (1895–1936) as a remedy for fevers and menstrual pain. Poplar buds are collected mainly from *P. × jackii*, but other sources include *P. balsamifera* (balsam poplar) and *P. nigra*. Poplar buds were listed in the *US Pharmacopoeia* (1916–65) as an expectorant and stimulant. The sticky bud resin is chemically similar to propolis, the resinous substance used by bees for sealing honeycombs and gaps in the hive, which has known antibiotic properties. *Populus × jackii* is often confused with other plants known as "balm of Gilead", such as *Abies balsamea* (see p.97) and *Cedronella canariensis* (see p.160). *Populus* may be derived from *arbor populi*, "the people's tree", since poplars have long been planted along town streets.

CULTIVATION Deep, moist, well-drained soil in sun. Poplars have extensive root systems and should not be planted close to buildings or drainage systems. Prone to bacterial canker and fungal diseases. Aphids, poplar beetle larvae, and caterpillars may attack leaves. *Populus alba* tolerates drier conditions than most poplars. Prune *P. × jackii* 'Aurora' hard in late winter to encourage vigorous shoots and colourful new leaves.

PROPAGATION By hardwood cuttings in winter; by removing suckers in autumn or winter.
HARVEST Buds are collected in spring before opening (*P. × jackii*), and dried for infusions, liquid extracts, and tinctures. Bark is stripped from side branches or coppiced trees, and dried for decoctions, liquid extracts, and powders.

◘ ***Populus alba*** (abele, white poplar)
Robust suckering tree with deciduous, broadly ovate, maple-like leaves, to 9cm (3½in) long, which have white downy undersides. Male and female flowers are borne on separate plants in spring: males bear red catkins, 7cm (3in) long; female catkins are shorter and green, and followed by capsules containing cottony seeds. Native to N Africa, C and W Asia, and Europe. ‡ 25m (80ft), ↔ 5–8m (15–25ft). ◘ 'Richardii' is shorter, with golden-yellow leaves. ‡ 15m (50ft), ↔ 12m (40ft).
HARDINESS Fully hardy.
PARTS USED Bark.
PROPERTIES An astringent, diuretic, cooling herb that reduces inflammation, relieves pain, and acts as a bitter tonic and alterative.
MEDICINAL USES Internally for rheumatoid arthritis, gout, fevers, lower back pain, urinary complaints, digestive and liver disorders, debility, and anorexia. Externally for chilblains, haemorrhoids, infected wounds, and sprains. Combined with *Actaea racemosa* (see p.102) and *Menyanthes trifoliata* (see p.278) for rheumatoid arthritis; and with *Chelone glabra* (see p.166) and *Mahonia aquifolium* (see p.270) for anorexia. Not given to patients allergic to aspirin.
▣ ▤

◘ ***Populus × jackii*** syn. *P. × candicans*, *P. × gileadensis* (balm of Gilead, Canadian poplar, Ontario poplar)
Fast-growing, conical tree with shiny buds and heart-shaped leaves, to 15cm (6in) long, which are balsam-scented when young. Male trees are not known; females produce catkins, 3–5cm

(1¼–2in) long, reaching 15cm (6in) long when in fruit. ‡ 15–25m (50–80ft), ↔ 6m (20ft).
◘ 'Aurora' has conspicuous new leaves, irregularly variegated creamy white, and often pink-flushed, which age to green.
HARDINESS Fully hardy.
PARTS USED Leaf buds.
PROPERTIES An antiseptic, anti-inflammatory, expectorant herb that lowers fever, stimulates the circulation, and has anti-bacterial and anti-fungal effects. Applied topically, it relieves pain and improves blood flow to the area.
MEDICINAL USES Internally for bronchitis and upper respiratory tract infections. Not given to patients sensitive to aspirin. Externally for colds, sinusitis, arthritis, rheumatism, muscular pain, psoriasis, and dry skin conditions. Widely used in cough mixtures, often with *Pinus strobus* (see p.318) and *Prunus serotina* (see p.334). Not prescribed to nursing mothers, or patients allergic to aspirin.
ECONOMIC USES Dried buds are added to potpourris.
▤ ▤ ▨

PORIA

Poria cocos. See *Wolfiporia cocos*.

POROPHYLLUM

Asteraceae

A genus of about 30 species of annuals and perennials, native to warm parts of the Americas. Some species are very strong smelling, with an aroma similar to *Coriandrum sativum* (see p.180), for which they are used as substitutes. The presence of conspicuous oil glands on the leaves gives them the name *Porophyllum*, which means "poreleaf". The common name "*papaloquelite*" is from *papalotl*, the Nahuatl word for "butterfly", perhaps because the flowers attract butterflies. The main culinary species is *P. ruderale*, which was first described by Linnaeus in 1753. It has two subspecies (*ruderale* and *macrocephalum*), which have slightly different but overlapping ranges in S and C America and Caribbean islands. Another species, *P. coloratum* (broadleaf, *hoja ancho*), likewise has two subspecies (the annual *coloratum* and the perennial *obtusifolium*) and

Populus alba 'Richardii'

Populus × jackii

Porophyllum ruderale

Populus alba

Populus × jackii 'Aurora'

has rounder, more scalloped leaves and even larger oil glands but is otherwise similar in flavour. These substitutes for coriander are much easier to grow in their homelands than *Coriandrum sativum*, which bolts quickly in hot climates. They are also much larger plants and therefore more productive.

CULTIVATION Well-drained soil in sun. Self-sows freely in suitable conditions.
PROPAGATION By seed sown in spring at 21°C (70°F).
HARVEST Leaves are picked as required and used fresh.

■ *Porophyllum ruderale* (papalo, *papaloquelite*, poreleaf)
Robust annual or short-lived perennial with blue-green, glaucous, oval leaves, to 7cm (3in) long, which have scalloped margins and conspicuous oil glands. Bronze, green, or purple flower heads, about 2.5cm (1in) long, are produced over a long period on mature plants, followed by seed heads resembling those of dandelions. Native to S and C America and the Caribbean islands. ‡ 1.5–2m (5–6ft).
HARDINESS Frost hardy.
PARTS USED Leaves.
PROPERTIES A bitter, strongly aromatic herb with a coriander-like flavour.
CULINARY USES Chopped leaves are added to salads, salsas, guacamole, and other Mexican dishes; also as a substitute for coriander in any recipe.
🗌 ✔

PORTERANTHUS
Porteranthus trifoliatus. See *Gillenia trifoliata*.

PORTULACA
Purslane

Portulacaceae

A genus of 100 species of fleshy trailing annuals, with a few perennials, found widely in dry sandy soils in warm-temperate and tropical regions. *Portulaca oleracea* is grown as a vegetable in many parts of the world. It was known to the ancient Egyptians and has also been grown for thousands of years in India and China. France is now the main European producer and consumer. Cultivated purslane is sometimes treated as a distinct variety (var. *sativa*). Research has shown that *P. oleracea* is a rich source of omega-3 fatty acids, which are thought to be important in preventing heart attacks and strengthening the immune system. *Portulaca oleracea* was first described in Chinese medical literature c.AD500. In Coptic medicine it was used for sore eyes, skin inflammations, and "anything swollen", as it is in Egypt today. *Portulaca grandiflora* (rose moss, sun plant) is also used, mainly in the form of fresh juice, for hepatitis or as a lotion for snake and insect bites, burns, scalds, and eczema. *Portulaca* is the original Latin name, used by Pliny.

Portulaca oleracea

CULTIVATION Rich, moist, well-drained soil in sun. Plants may be damaged by aphids and slugs.
PROPAGATION By seed sown *in situ* in spring.
HARVEST Plants are cut in summer, usually before flowering, and used fresh, or dried for use in decoctions. Leaves and young shoots are picked before flowering and used fresh.

■ *Portulaca oleracea* (purslane)
Annual with thick, soft, trailing stems and thick, fleshy, spoon-shaped leaves, to 3cm (1¼in) long. Small yellow flowers, with 4–6 petals, are produced in summer, then many-seeded capsules. Cosmopolitan weed, probably from India.
‡ 20–45cm (8–18in), ↔ 45–60cm (18–24in).
■ var. *aurea* (golden purslane) has golden leaves.
HARDINESS Half hardy.
PARTS USED Whole plant (*ma chi xian*), leaves.
PROPERTIES A sour, diuretic, cooling herb that lowers fever and clears toxins. It is effective against many bacterial infections.
MEDICINAL USES Internally for dysentery, acute enteritis, appendicitis, mastitis, haemorrhoids, and postpartum bleeding. Not given to pregnant women or to patients with digestive problems. Externally for boils, snake bite, bee stings, and eczema.
CULINARY USES Leaves are eaten raw in salads (especially the Middle Eastern bread salad *fattoush*), cooked as a vegetable, added to sauces and fillings, and pickled in vinegar. Like okra, they have a mucilaginous texture when cooked.
🗌 🗌 🗌 ✔

Portulaca oleracea var. *aurea*

POTENTILLA
Cinquefoil

Rosaceae

There are about 500 species in this large genus, which is distributed throughout the northern hemisphere. Most are perennials or shrubs, with some annuals and biennials, and many are found on heaths and in woodland. Several species are used medicinally for their high tannin content, which in *P. erecta* approaches 20 per cent. These include *P. anserina* (silverweed) and *P. reptans* (creeping cinquefoil, fiveleaf grass), which contain less tannin but are still useful astringents. *Potentilla* means "powerful", from the Latin *potens*, alluding to the plant's curative powers.
CULTIVATION Moist or dry, acid soil in sun or light shade. Invasive.
PROPAGATION By seed sown in autumn or spring; by division in autumn or spring.
HARVEST Roots are lifted in autumn or spring and dried for use in infusions, liquid extracts, powders, and tinctures. Whole plants are cut in summer and dried for use in infusions, lotions, and ointments.

■ *Potentilla erecta* syn. *P. tormentilla* (bloodroot, tormentil)
Perennial with a thick woody rootstock, red inside, and slender branched stems bearing three-lobed basal leaves and five-lobed stem leaves. Small, bright yellow, four-petalled flowers are borne from early summer. Native to N Europe, W Asia, and Siberia. ‡ 50cm (20in), ↔ 20–30cm (8–12in).
HARDINESS Fully hardy.
PARTS USED Roots, whole plant.
PROPERTIES A bitter, astringent, cooling herb that controls bleeding, reduces inflammation, and promotes healing.
MEDICINAL USES Internally for diarrhoea, enteritis, Crohn's disease, mucous colitis, ulcerative colitis, gastritis, diverticulitis, peptic ulcer, and inflammation of the colon. Externally for haemorrhoids, vaginal discharge, sore throat, mouth ulcers, cuts, sores, ulcers, burns, sunburn, frostbite, and shingles. Care is needed in topical application of strong tannins, which can cause scarring.
🗌 🗌 🗌

Potentilla erecta

P

POTERIUM

Poterium officinalis. See *Sanguisorba officinalis*.

PRESLIA

Preslia cervina. See *Mentha cervina*.

PRIMULA

Primulaceae

This genus includes about 400 species of perennials, occurring mostly in temperate and mountainous areas of the northern hemisphere. Many are grown as ornamentals in a wide range of situations, including rock gardens and watersides. Primroses and cowslips are enduringly popular as garden plants, and naturalize well in grass. They should be planted well apart to avoid hybridization. Both species have a long history of use as medicinal herbs. *Primula vulgaris* was recommended by Pliny for paralysis, gout, and rheumatism, and by Culpeper for healing wounds. *Primula veris* was once known as *herba paralysis*, *radix arthritica*, and "palsywort", due to its widespread use, dating back to at least medieval times, for conditions involving spasms, cramps, paralysis, and rheumatic pain. Culpeper also prescribed the flowers, mixed with nutmeg, for "all infirmities of the head", and referred to the use of the leaves "by our city dames" in cosmetics, to enhance beauty and to treat "spots and wrinkles of the skin, sun-burning, and freckles". Until cowslips became quite rare in the 20th century, through habitat loss and modern farming practices, the flowers were collected each spring to make wine, which was taken largely as a sedative and nervine. Both species have similar constituents that may be used interchangeably; these include saponins, which have an expectorant effect, and salicylates (as in aspirin). *Primula veris* is now the more widely used.

CULTIVATION Dry, neutral to alkaline soil in sun or partial shade (*P. veris*). Moist, well-drained soil in sun or shade (*P. vulgaris*). Regular division is necessary to ensure

330 | *Primula veris*

Primula vulgaris

Primula vulgaris 'Alba Plena'

Primula vulgaris 'Jack in the Green'

vigour. Plants may be affected by rust, *Botrytis*, leafspot, and other fungal and viral diseases. Aphids, caterpillars, cutworms, and vine weevils may damage leaves.

PROPAGATION By seed sown in late summer (species only); by division in late spring or early autumn.

HARVEST Flowers (including calyx) are picked in spring and used fresh, or dried for use in infusions, ointments, and tinctures. Whole plant (*P. vulgaris*) is cut when flowering, and dried for use in infusions. Roots are lifted in spring (*P. veris*), or autumn of second year (*P. vulgaris*), and dried for decoctions and tinctures.

⚠ **WARNING** Skin irritant and allergen.

■ *Primula veris* (cowslip, paigle)
Small, clump-forming perennial with a short stout rhizome, long thin roots, and ovate–oblong leaves, 5–20cm (2–8in) long. Small, deep yellow, fragrant, orange-marked flowers, with cylindrical pale green calyces, are borne in clusters in spring. Native to Europe and W Asia. ‡↔ 15–20cm (6–8in).
HARDINESS Fully hardy.
PARTS USED Roots, flowers.
PROPERTIES A sedative expectorant herb that relaxes spasms and reduces inflammation.
MEDICINAL USES Internally for bronchitis, catarrh, dry cough, whooping cough, asthma, arthritis, insomnia, headache, and restlessness (especially in children). Not given during pregnancy, or to patients sensitive to aspirin or taking anti-coagulant drugs (e.g. warfarin). Externally for facial neuralgia, arthritic pain, skin blemishes, sunburn, and migraine.
CULINARY USES Young leaves and flowers are added to salads; flowers are also candied and used for making country wines and tea.
⊞ ▨ ▣ ▪ ⬚

■ *Primula vulgaris* (primrose)
Small, clump-forming perennial with a short thick rhizome and oblanceolate leaves, 5–25cm (2–10in) long. Solitary, pale yellow flowers, 3–4cm (1¼–1½in) across, with notched petals, appear in late winter and spring. Found from Europe and N Asia to the Caucasus. ‡ 15cm (6in), ↔ 25cm (10in). ■ 'Alba Plena' syn. 'Double White' has double white flowers. 'Double Sulphur' has double, pale yellow flowers.

■ 'Jack in the Green' has single, pale yellow flowers, each backed by small, bract-like leaves.
HARDINESS Fully hardy.
PARTS USED Whole plant, leaves, roots, flowers.
PROPERTIES An expectorant, anti-inflammatory herb that relieves pain, relaxes spasms, and promotes healing.
MEDICINAL USES Internally for bronchitis, respiratory tract infections, insomnia, anxiety, rheumatic disorders, and gout. Not given during pregnancy, or to patients sensitive to aspirin or taking anti-coagulant drugs (e.g. warfarin). Externally for minor wounds, and nerve and joint pain. May be used as a substitute for *P. veris*, although generally considered less effective.
CULINARY USES Flowers and young leaves are added to salads. Flowers are used to make desserts, such as primrose pottage, based on ground rice flavoured with saffron, honey, and almonds.
⊞ ▨ ▣ ▣ ▪ ⬚

PRINOS

Prinos verticillatus. See *Ilex verticillata*.

PROSTANTHERA

Mint bush

Lamiaceae

A genus of about 50 species of evergreen shrubs and small trees from a variety of habitats in Australia. Most have a strong, mint-like aroma. Several species are grown as ornamentals for their neat fragrant foliage and profuse flowering, both outdoors in warm climates, and under glass in colder regions. Mint bushes are rich in volatile oils, including menthol and cineole (as found in *Mentha* spp., see p.275), which have bactericidal and fungicidal properties. Several species, including *Prostanthera cineolifera*, were used by Australian Aboriginals in infusions to relieve headaches and colds. *Prostanthera* is from the Greek *prosthema*, "addition", and *anthos*, "growth", as the anthers have spur-like appendages.

CULTIVATION Well-drained soil in sun. Prone to spider mites and whitefly when grown under glass.

PROPAGATION By seed sown in spring at

Prostanthera rotundifolia

13–18°C (55–64°F); by semi-ripe cuttings in summer. Prune lightly immediately after flowering. *Prostanthera* dislikes hard pruning.

HARVEST Leaves are picked as required for infusions, and dried for potpourris.

▣ *Prostanthera rotundifolia* (round-leaved mint bush)
Large bushy shrub with rounded to obovate leaves, 1cm (½in) long. Lilac to mauve, occasionally pink, broadly bell-shaped flowers, 1cm (½in) across, are produced in racemes, to 7cm (3in) long, in spring. Native to SE and S Australia. ‡2–4m (6–12ft), ↔1–3m (3–10ft).

HARDINESS Half hardy.

PARTS USED Leaves.

PROPERTIES An aromatic decongestant herb with a strong, peppery, mint-like flavour. It has anti-bacterial and anti-fungal effects.

MEDICINAL USES Externally for colds and headaches.

CULINARY USES Fresh or dried leaves are used to flavour meat and sauces; also to make tea.

ECONOMIC USES Leaves are used in potpourris.

▨ ▩ ▧ ▧

PRUNELLA
Selfheal

Lamiaceae

A genus of seven species of perennials, occurring in northern temperate regions and NW Africa. *Prunella vulgaris* (selfheal) is rather invasive as a garden plant but is well worth including in a wildflower meadow. It has a long history of use in herbal medicine. Culpeper explained that it is called selfheal because "when you are hurt, you may heal yourself". John Gerard, the 16th-century English herbalist, wrote "there is not a better wounde herbe in the world". Though European herbalists have always regarded it primarily as a wound herb, in Chinese medicine it is used mainly for complaints associated with disturbed liver energy. The first mention of selfheal in Chinese medical literature was in the *Shen Nong* herbal during the Han dynasty (206BC–AD23). *Prunella* is an alternative spelling of *Brunella*, from the German *bräune*, "quinsy" (a throat infection), for which *P. vulgaris* was a standard treatment.

CULTIVATION Moist, well-drained soil in sun or light shade. Invasive.

PROPAGATION By seed sown in autumn or spring; by division in spring.

HARVEST Plants are cut in summer when flowering and dried for use in infusions, ointments, and tinctures. Flower spikes are cut in autumn and dried for use in decoctions.

▣ *Prunella vulgaris* (heal-all, selfheal)
Creeping aromatic perennial with four-angled stems and oblong–ovate, toothed leaves, 4–5cm (1½–2in) long. Purple, two-lipped flowers are produced in compact spikes from summer to autumn. Native to Europe, temperate Asia, and N Africa. ‡50cm (20in), ↔indefinite. f. *alba* has white flowers.

HARDINESS Fully hardy.

Prunella vulgaris

PARTS USED Whole plant, flowers (*xia ku cao*).

PROPERTIES An astringent, slightly bitter, saline herb that lowers fever and blood pressure, stimulates the liver and gall bladder, and promotes healing. It has diuretic, anti-bacterial, and alterative effects.

MEDICINAL USES Internally, in Western medicine, for haemorrhage and excessive menstruation (whole plant); in Chinese medicine, often combined with *Chrysanthemum × morifolium* (see p.168), for fevers, headaches, high blood pressure, mumps, mastitis, conjunctivitis, and hyperactivity in children related to liver energy problems (flowers). Externally, in Western medicine, for minor injuries, sores, burns, bruises, sore throat, mouth inflammations, and haemorrhoids (whole plant).

▣ ▨ ▩

PRUNUS
Almond, apricot, cherry, peach, plum

Rosaceae

There are over 200 species of deciduous or evergreen trees and shrubs in this genus, which occurs throughout northern temperate regions, the Andes of S America, and SE Asia. It includes many economically important fruit and nut trees, and numerous ornamentals that are grown mainly for their blossom. Both *P. armeniaca* and *P. persica* are probably Chinese in origin; the former reached Italy in Roman times and the latter, which has been cultivated in China for over 2500 years, was recorded in Greece as early as the 4th century BC. *Prunus dulcis* is the world's most widely grown nut tree. Prunes are dried plums from cultivars of *P. domestica* subsp. *domestica*; they have large, oval, black-skinned fruits, a rich flavour, and a high sugar and fibre content that allows drying without fermentation or loss of flavour. Prunes were apparently brought to France by crusaders returning from Syria; in 1856 they were taken to California, where 70 per cent of the world's crop is now produced. *Prunus laurocerasus*, a shade-tolerant species,

is extensively grown for hedging and screening. Its many cultivars include low spreading variants that make excellent ground cover. *Prunus mume* is the classic winter-flowering "plum blossom", used for Japanese bonsai. Many species are used medicinally, yielding a range of therapeutic products, from emollient oils to cough cures and laxatives. The Chinese species have a particularly long history of use: *P. armeniaca* and *P. mume* were first mentioned in medical literature c.AD500, and references to *P. japonica* date back to the Han dynasty (206BC–AD23). Most of the medicinal properties result from the presence of amygdalin and prunasin, which break down in water to form hydrocyanic acid (cyanide). In small amounts, this exceedingly poisonous compound stimulates respiration, improves digestion, and gives a sense of well being. Also present is benzaldehyde, which gives the typical almond scent. This is now synthesized as a substitute for bitter almond oil in food flavouring. *Prunus africana* (African cherry, red stinkwood), a montane forest species, entered international trade in the 1960s, when it was found to contain a liposoluble complex, which has proved effective in treating prostate gland enlargement. The bark has long been used by traditional healers, but large-scale demand and destructive harvesting have led to serious depletion of wild populations, especially in Cameroon. *Prunus africana* received international protection as an endangered species in 1997; plantations have been established in Kenya to provide material for the pharmaceutical industry, and the propagation technique of marcotting has been used successfully to increase stocks. The fruit stalks of *P. avium* (gean, wild cherry) and *P. cerasus* (sour cherry) are infused to make a diuretic astringent remedy for cystitis, oedema, and diarrhoea. *Prunus serotina* was used by the Cherokee people to relieve labour pains, and first listed in the *US Pharmacopoeia* in 1820 as a sedative and anti-tussive. It is still used, in the form of wild cherry syrup, in cough remedies.

CULTIVATION Well-drained, neutral to alkaline soil in sun. *Prunus laurocerasus* tolerates shade. *Prunus spinosa* (blackthorn) is a useful plant for hedging in cold, exposed, or coastal areas. Prune fruiting specimens in summer to restrict growth and encourage formation of fruit buds. Trim *P. laurocerasus* in spring. Leaves and young shoots are often attacked by aphids and caterpillars. Likely diseases and disorders include peach leaf curl, bacterial canker, witches' broom, chlorosis, and honey fungus; *P. laurocerasus* may be affected by leafspot and powdery mildew. Many *Prunus* spp. are relatively short-lived, and most are shallow-rooted and will sucker if roots are damaged. Early-flowering species are prone to frost damage.

PROPAGATION By seed sown in autumn (species only); by greenwood cuttings in early summer (deciduous species); by semi-ripe cuttings in summer (*P. laurocerasus*). Cultivars are budded in summer or grafted in early spring.

HARVEST Leaves (*P. persica*) are picked in summer and dried for infusions, or

P

(*P. laurocerasus*) distilled for aqueous extract (cherry laurel water). Bark (*P. africana*, *P. persica*, *P. serotina*) is stripped in autumn and winter, and dried for infusions, liquid extracts, powders, syrups, and tinctures; bark of *P. africana* is also processed for pharmaceutical extracts. Flowers (*P. persica*) are gathered in spring, and unripe fruits (*P. armeniaca*, *P. domestica*, *P. mume*, *P. persica*) in summer, and dried for decoctions. Fruits are picked ripe or unripe, depending on use; prunes (cultivars of *P. domestica*) are often left on the trees to dry. Seeds from ripe fruits are dried for decoctions (*P. japonica*) or crushed for oil (*P. armeniaca*, *P. dulcis*, *P. persica*).
△ **WARNING** All parts of *P. laurocerasus*, notably the leaves and seeds, are harmful if eaten. Bitter-tasting kernels of *Prunus* spp. may be fatally toxic in excess.

Prunus africana syn. *Pygeum africanum* (African cherry, pygeum, red stinkwood)
Large spreading tree with coarse, dark brown bark and glossy, ovate, pointed leaves, about 8cm (3in) long, which have finely toothed margins and smell of almonds when crushed. Small white flowers are produced in elongated clusters in spring, followed by red-brown fruits, about 1cm (³⁄₈in) in diameter. Native to Afro-montane forests, mostly above 1500–2000m (5000–6500ft), in Africa, Madagascar, and islands of Grand Comore, São Tomé, and Fernando Po. ↕ 30m (100ft), ↔ 20m (70ft).
HARDINESS Min. 10°C (50°F).
PARTS USED Bark.
PROPERTIES A bitter herb with hormonal effects.
MEDICINAL USES Internally, for chest pain, prostate disorders, and prostatitis.

Prunus armeniaca syn. *Armeniaca vulgaris* (apricot)
Deciduous tree with ovate to rounded leaves, to 12cm (5in) long. White single flowers, about 4cm (1½in) across, appear in spring, followed by globose, white to orange-red or yellow fruits, to 5cm (2in) in diameter. Native to N China. ↕ 10m (30ft), ↔ 5–7m (15–22ft). ■ 'Hemskirke' bears yellow, red-flushed fruits with excellent flavour; early ripening. ■ 'Moorpark' has golden-yellow skin and sweet orange flesh.
HARDINESS Fully hardy.
PARTS USED Fruits, kernels (*xing ren*), oil.
PROPERTIES A bitter–sweet, warming, lubricant herb that is expectorant and controls coughing. Extracted laetrile has been used in cancer therapy.
MEDICINAL USES Internally for dry coughs, bronchitis, asthma, emphysema, and dry constipation. Excess causes central nervous system depression and respiratory failure. Toxicity of amygdalin is reduced by stir-baking or steaming, and may be neutralized by a decoction of the outer bark.
CULINARY USES Fruits are eaten fresh, stewed, dried, or preserved, and used to make juice, jams, confectionery, paste, and fruit leather. Ripe and unripe fruits are added to savoury dishes, such as pilafs. Kernels are used in similar ways to almonds. Seed (kernel) oil can be a substitute for olive oil.
ECONOMIC USES Oil is used in cosmetics.

Prunus domestica (plum)
Variable, sometimes spiny, deciduous tree with elliptic to oblong leaves, to 10cm (4in) long. Clusters of white flowers, to 2.5cm (1in) across, appear in spring, followed by ovoid to rounded, yellow, red, purple, or blue-black fruits, with yellow or green flesh. Possibly originated as a

cross between *P. spinosa* and *P. cerasifera*. Native to Eurasia. ↕ 10–12m (30–40ft), ↔ 8–10m (25–30ft). 'Mirabelle' bears yellow, pit-free fruits with a bloomed skin and sweet, firm, pale yellow flesh; ideal for conserves, spirits, and prunes. ■ 'Prune d'Agen' bears long, ovoid, dark purple fruits with very sweet, aromatic flesh; good for desserts and drying as prunes.
HARDINESS Fully hardy.
PARTS USED Dried fruits (prunes).
PROPERTIES A cooling, lubricant, laxative herb.
MEDICINAL USES Internally for constipation. Often added to laxative preparations.
CULINARY USES Prunes are eaten dried, soaked, or cooked, preserved in brandy or vinegar, and made into liqueurs and spirits, such as *slobovitz*; also added to sauces and stews (especially the Middle Eastern *tadjub ahmar*), stuffings, desserts, and cakes.
ECONOMIC USES Due to their moisture-holding properties, prunes are used in commercial fat and egg substitutes for baked produce.

Prunus dulcis syn. *Amygdalus communis*, *P. amygdalus* (almond)
Deciduous tree with lanceolate, tapering, finely toothed leaves, to 13cm (5in) long. Pink or almost white, solitary or paired flowers, to 5cm (2in) across, appear before the new leaves, followed by pale green, ovoid, velvety fruits, 4–6cm (1½–2½in) long, containing a single seed. Native from Syria to N Africa. ↕↔ 8m (25ft). 'All-in-One' is vigorous but small growing, with white flowers late in the season, and heavy crops of good-quality nuts. Self-fertile. 'Amara' (bitter almond) has bitter poisonous seeds (nuts), which are detoxified for culinary use. 'Macrocarpa' has pale pink flowers and large fruits, to 8cm (3in) long.

Prunus armeniaca   *Prunus armeniaca* 'Hemskirke'

Prunus armeniaca 'Moorpark'

Prunus domestica

Prunus laurocerasus

Prunus laurocerasus 'Castlewellan'

Prunus domestica 'Prune d'Agen'   *Prunus dulcis*

HARDINESS Fully hardy.
PARTS USED Seeds, oil.
PROPERTIES A soothing laxative herb that relaxes spasms.
MEDICINAL USES Internally for kidney stones, gallstones, and constipation. Externally for dry skin conditions.
CULINARY USES Seeds (nuts) are eaten raw, roasted, salted, and ground into paste (marzipan); also ground and diluted with water to make almond milk, and pressed for oil, which is made into almond butter. Almonds are an ingredient of many sweet and savoury dishes, especially pilafs, cakes, pastries, biscuits, and confectionery.
ECONOMIC USES Sweet almond oil is used in the manufacture of emulsions for medicines, massage oils, skin-care products, and cosmetics. Detoxified bitter almond oil is used in commercial food flavouring, especially in cakes, biscuits, confectionery, ice cream, maraschino cherries, liqueurs, and marzipan.
◻ ▨ ▪ ✎ ✎

Prunus japonica (Chinese plum, oriental bush cherry)
Deciduous shrub with wiry branches and ovate, pointed, toothed leaves, to 7cm (3in) long. Small, white or pale pink flowers are produced in spring, followed by dark red fruits, about 1cm (½in) in diameter. Found from C China to Korea and Japan. ‡↔ 1.5m (5ft).
HARDINESS Fully hardy.
PARTS USED Seeds (*yu li ren*).
PROPERTIES A bitter–sweet, pungent, laxative herb that is diuretic and lowers blood pressure.
MEDICINAL USES Internally for dry constipation and oedema, and in folk medicine for insomnia following trauma. Often combined with *Cannabis sativa* (see p.152) for chronic constipation.
▨ ▪

◼ *Prunus laurocerasus* syn. *Laurocerasus officinalis* (cherry bay, cherry laurel, English laurel)
Evergreen shrub or spreading tree with oblong, shiny, pointed leaves, to 15cm (6in) long, which are almond-scented when crushed. Fragrant white flowers are produced in dense cylindrical racemes, to 10cm (4in) long, in spring, followed by purple-black fruits. Native to E Europe and SW Asia. ‡ 6–8m (20–25ft), ↔ 10m (30ft).
◼ 'Castlewellan' syn. 'Marbled White' is slow-growing and narrow, with white-speckled leaves. ↔ 5m (15ft). ◼ 'Otto Luyken' is compact and free-flowering, with narrow leaves. Often flowers again in autumn. ‡ 1m (3ft), ↔ 1.5m (5ft). ◼ 'Schipkaensis' has a low spreading habit, narrow leaves, and flowers profusely. Found near the Schipka Pass (Bulgaria) in 1888. ‡ 2m (6ft), ↔ 3m (10ft).
HARDINESS Fully hardy.
PARTS USED Distilled extract (cherry laurel water).
PROPERTIES A very poisonous, sedative herb that relaxes spasms, improves digestion, and controls coughing.
MEDICINAL USES Internally for nausea and vomiting. Externally for eye infections.
ECONOMIC USES Almond-flavoured cherry laurel water is occasionally used in commercial food flavouring.
◻ ▪ ✎

◼ *Prunus mume* syn. *Armeniaca mume* (Japanese apricot, *ume*)
Spreading deciduous tree with green shoots and broadly ovate to rounded, toothed leaves, to 10cm (4in) long. White to dark pink, solitary or paired, almond-scented flowers, 2.5cm (1in) across, appear along the bare branches in late winter, followed by globose, slightly downy,

yellow fruits, 3cm (1¼in) in diameter. Native to China, Japan, and Korea. ‡↔ 9m (28ft). ◼ 'Beni-chidori' syn. 'Benishidore' is shrubby, with deep pink flowers. ‡↔ 2.5m (8ft). 'Microcarpa' (*ko-ume*) has small fruits, pickled as *ko-umeboshi* (tiny salt "plums"). 'Peggy Clarke' has double, deep pink flowers. Heavy cropping.
HARDINESS Fully hardy.
PARTS USED Unripe fruits (*wu mei*).
PROPERTIES An astringent sour herb that expels intestinal parasites and stimulates bile flow. It is effective against many bacterial and fungal infections.
MEDICINAL USES Internally for chronic coughs, chronic diarrhoea, and roundworms. Externally for fungal skin infections, corns, and warts.
CULINARY USES Fruits are eaten raw, candied, preserved, or pickled, notably as *umeboshi* or salt "plums", which are coloured using red *shiso* (see *Perilla*, p.307); also made into a liqueur, sour jam (*ume-bishio*), and "plum" sauce.
▨ ▪ ✎

◼ *Prunus persica* (peach)
Small, bushy, deciduous tree or large shrub with lanceolate tapering leaves, to 15cm (6in) long. Pale pink to white, solitary or paired flowers, to 3.5cm (1⅜in) across, appear before the leaves in spring, followed by globose, velvety, red-flushed, yellow or white fruits, which have very juicy flesh. Native to China. ‡↔ 8m (25ft). Compressa Group (doughnut peach, flat peach, *ping tzu-t'ao*) bears flattened, very sweet, white-fleshed fruits, often with a slight bitter, almond flavour. 'O'Henry' syn. 'Merrill O'Henry' has large showy flowers and medium to large, pit-free fruits.
HARDINESS Fully hardy.
PARTS USED Leaves, bark, fruits, flowers, seeds (*tao ren*), oil.

P

Prunus laurocerasus
'Otto Luyken'

Prunus laurocerasus 'Schipkaensis'

Prunus mume

Prunus mume 'Beni-chidori'

Prunus persica

Prunus serotina

Prunus spinosa

Prunus spinosa 'Purpurea'

PROPERTIES A bitter–sweet, soothing, laxative herb that controls coughing, stimulates the uterus and circulatory system, lowers fever, and is diuretic, sedative, and expectorant.
MEDICINAL USES Internally, in Western medicine, for gastritis, coughs, whooping cough, and bronchitis (bark, leaves); in Chinese medicine, for malaria, boils, haemorrhoids, and eczema (leaves); constipation and oedema (flowers); constipation in the elderly, coughs, asthma, and menstrual disorders (seeds). Contraindicated during pregnancy.
CULINARY USES Fruits are eaten fresh, cooked, candied, and preserved (often in brandy); also made into jam and juice. Leaves are infused in brandy to make a cordial. Flowers are used to make tea.
ECONOMIC USES Kernels are a source of bitter almond oil, used in food flavouring. Oil is used in skin-care products. Fruits are used to flavour confectionery, ice cream, Bourbon whiskey (Southern Comfort). Flowers are distilled as a spirit.

▣ *Prunus serotina* (rum cherry, wild black cherry)
Deciduous tree with shiny, narrowly ovate, finely toothed leaves, about 8cm (3in) long, which turn yellow or red in autumn. Fragrant white flowers, 1.5cm (½in) across, are borne in racemes, to 15cm (6in) long, in late spring and early summer, followed by small black fruits, 1cm (⅜in) in diameter. Native to N America. ↕ 18–30m (60–100ft), ↔ 10–25m (30–80ft).
HARDINESS Fully hardy.
PARTS USED Bark, fruits.
PROPERTIES A bitter, astringent, warming herb that controls coughing, increases perspiration rate, improves digestion, and has sedative, anti-bacterial, and anti-viral effects.
MEDICINAL USES Internally for chronic and dry coughs, whooping cough, bronchitis, nervous dyspepsia, poor digestion, gastritis, diarrhoea, and convalescent debility.
CULINARY USES Fruits are eaten fresh or stewed, made into pies and jellies, and used to flavour spirits and liqueurs.
ECONOMIC USES Bark extract is used in commercial food flavouring.

▣ *Prunus spinosa* (blackthorn)
Dense, spiny, deciduous shrub or small tree with elliptic leaves, to 5cm (2in) long. Numerous, fragile, white flowers, 1.5cm (½in) across, appear before the leaves in late winter and early spring, followed by spherical, blue-black fruits, 1.5cm (½in) in diameter. Found from Europe to Russia (W Siberia). ↕ 5m (15ft), ↔ 4m (12ft). ▣ 'Purpurea' has dark purple leaves and pink flowers.
HARDINESS Fully hardy.
PARTS USED Flowers, fruits.
PROPERTIES An astringent, tonic, depurative herb that relaxes spasms, and has diuretic, laxative, and diaphoretic effects.
MEDICINAL USES Internally for upper respiratory tract infections, dyspepsia, colic, bloating, fluid retention, kidney and bladder problems, and rashes associated with constipation (flowers). Externally, as a mouth rinse for minor mouth and throat inflammations (fruits).
CULINARY USES The highly astringent fruits, known as sloes, are used to flavour sloe gin and other liqueurs. They are also made into jellies, syrups, conserves, and pickles.

PSIDIUM
Guava

Myrtaceae

There are some 100 species of evergreen trees and shrubs in this genus, which has its origin in the Americas. The most widely cultivated species is *P. guajava*, the common guava. Other species with commercial importance include: *P. guineense* (Brazilian guava), which has been crossed with *P. guajava* to produce smaller, hardier, more productive trees; *P. littorale* var. *littorale* (yellow strawberry guava), which bears relatively large, sweet, yellow fruits; and *P. littorale* var. *longipes* (red strawberry guava), which has purple-red fruits, similar to strawberries in flavour. Guavas of various kinds have acid aromatic fruits that are rich in vitamin C and in great demand in the tropics for making drinks and preserves. They are now naturalized in many parts of the tropics; though harvested for both culinary and medicinal purposes, they are a weed in some areas.
CULTIVATION Well-drained soil, pH4.8–8, in sun, with humidity to 70 per cent. Aphids and scale insects may damage foliage; under glass, whitefly and thrips may be a problem.
PROPAGATION By seed sown when ripe; by semi-ripe cuttings, 12–15cm (5–6in) long during the growing season. Seedlings are prone to damping off.
HARVEST Fruits are picked when ripe for culinary uses; unripe fruits are harvested for infusions. Leaves are collected as required for use in infusions.

▣ *Psidium guajava* (apple guava, guava, yellow guava)
Evergreen shrub or small tree with peeling bark, four-angled branchlets, and ovate to oblong–

Psidium guajava

elliptic, prominently veined leaves, to 15cm (6in) long. White flowers, about 2.5cm (1in) across, with numerous stamens, appear in early summer, followed by rounded to pear-shaped, yellow fruits, to 10cm (4in) long, containing white or pink flesh and numerous seeds. Native to tropical America; widely naturalized. ↕ 8m (25ft), ↔ 7m (22ft). 'Beaumont' has large, round, pink-fleshed fruits with a mildly acid flavour. Originated in Hawaii (Oahu). 'Red Indian' has very aromatic, yellow, often pink-flushed fruits with sweet red flesh. Originated in USA (Florida) in 1946.
HARDINESS Min. 18°C (64°F).
PARTS USED Leaves, fruits (occasionally bark or roots).
PROPERTIES An astringent, antioxidant herb that has antibiotic effects. It controls bleeding and lowers blood sugar levels. Anti-carcinogenic and anti-HIV properties have been reported.
MEDICINAL USES Internally for diarrhoea, dysentery, diabetes, feverish illnesses (notably malaria), and coughs. Externally for wounds, boils, and ulcers. Leaf infusions, occasionally decoctions of unripe fruits, bark or roots, are used for various complaints.
CULINARY USES Ripe fruits are eaten raw, cooked, dried, and made into preserves (notably guava cheese), jellies, and chutneys; also juiced for drinks.

PSORALEA
Scurf pea

Papilionaceae

About 130 species of perennials and subshrubs belong to this genus, which ranges through N and S America, South Africa, and Asia. A number of the Cape species were grown as ornamentals during the 19th century; the most common in cultivation today is *P. pinnata* (blue pea). Some species, including the N American *P. esculenta* (Indian breadroot) have edible tubers. *Psoralea* seeds are used medicinally in both Ayurvedic and Chinese medicine; they were first described in Chinese medical literature c.AD470. The use of *P. corylifolia* in Ayurvedic medicine to treat leucoderma or vitiligo (loss of pigment from skin, causing white patches) has prompted a good deal of research into the properties of this herb. Among its constituents are furanocoumarins, notably psoralen, which affects pigment production. Extracts of the seeds have also shown pronounced activity against a wide range of pathogenic bacteria and fungi, including a number that are resistant to most conventional antibiotics.
CULTIVATION Well-drained soil in sun.
PROPAGATION By seed sown in spring, soaked in hot water to speed germination.
HARVEST Seeds are collected when ripe and dried for use in decoctions.

Psoralea corylifolia (babchi, Malay tea, scurf pea)
Erect annual with simple, broadly ovate, toothed leaves, to 8cm (3in) long, dotted with blackish glands. Yellow, clover-like flowers

appear in dense, long-stalked, axillary clusters from spring to summer, followed by short black pods, to 5mm (¼in) long, containing a single, compressed, oval, yellow-black seed. Found on arable land in Asia (mainly in India and Iran). ‡ 90cm (3ft), ↔ 10–20cm (4–8in).
HARDINESS Min. 10–15°C (50–59°F).
PARTS USED Seeds (*bu gu zhi*).
PROPERTIES A bitter, astringent, warming herb that stimulates kidney (*yang*) energy, and has diuretic and anti-bacterial effects.
MEDICINAL USES Internally, in Chinese medicine, for disorders related to kidney weakness, such as early-morning diarrhoea, urinary complaints, impotence, asthma, and baldness. May be mixed with salt to increase action on kidneys. Injection of psoralea extract has been used with considerable success in Chinese research to treat hair loss. Internally and externally, in Ayurvedic medicine, for skin diseases and hair loss.
▨ ▣ ▣

Psoralea linearis. See *Aspalathus linearis*.

PTELEA
Rutaceae

There are three or more shrubs and small trees in this N American genus. Most have musky-smelling leaves. They occur in moist rich woods, thickets, and rocky slopes. *Ptelea trifoliata* is widely cultivated for its scented foliage and attractive clusters of fruits; the cultivar 'Aurea' is an outstanding golden tree for small gardens. *Ptelea trifoliata* was sacred to the Menominee people of N America, who regarded it as a panacea and added its root bark to other medicines to increase their effectiveness. The herb was first described in *Medical Flora* by Constantine Rafinesque (2 vols, 1828–30); it was adopted as a home remedy by colonists, and by Eclectic practitioners. *Ptelea* is the ancient Greek name for the elm, given to this genus because its fruits appear similar to those of the true elm.
CULTIVATION Moist, well-drained soil in sun or lightly dappled shade.

Ptelea trifoliata

PROPAGATION By seed sown in autumn or spring (species only); by greenwood cuttings in early summer.
HARVEST Roots are lifted in autumn and peeled for bark, which is dried for use in infusions and powders.

▣ *Ptelea trifoliata* (hop tree, wafer ash)
Upright deciduous tree or large shrub with aromatic bark and trifoliate leaves, divided into ovate to elliptic leaflets, to 12cm (5in) long. Pale green-white, star-shaped, scented flowers are borne in branched clusters in early summer, followed by round, flattened, pale green, winged fruits, to 2.5cm (1in) across. Native to N America (Ontario to Florida, Texas, and N Mexico). ‡ 7m (25ft), ↔ 4m (12ft). ▣ 'Aurea' has yellow-green leaves that turn yellow in autumn. ‡ 5m (15ft).
HARDINESS Fully hardy.
PARTS USED Root bark.
PROPERTIES A bitter, pungent, tonic herb that lowers fever and improves digestion; it expels intestinal parasites and has anti-bacterial effects.
MEDICINAL USES Internally for fevers (especially intermittent), heartburn, poor digestion, roundworms, and pinworms. Externally for wounds.
▥ ▨ ▣

PTEROCARPUS
Papilionaceae

Twenty species of leguminous trees and woody climbers belong to this genus, which occurs throughout the tropics. *Pterocarpus marsupium* was cultivated under glass in the 19th century, but is seldom seen today outside the tropics. It yields a very astringent sap, known as "kino", that hardens into brittle, shiny, red-black pieces; when chewed, kino turns the saliva red. Kino resembles *Acacia catechu* (see p.98) in its chemistry, containing compounds similar to those extracted from other *Pterocarpus* spp. and from the unrelated *Coccoloba uvifera* (Jamaica kino, West Indian kino) and *Butea frondosa* (Bengal kino). *Pterocarpus santalinus* is valued for its purple-red wood, which has anti-diabetic properties and is used as a

Ptelea trifoliata 'Aurea'

Pterocarpus marsupium

colouring agent in medicines. In Cambodia, the red sap of *P. cambodianus* is used to fill teeth. *Pterocarpus* comes from the Greek *pteron*, "wing", and *karpos*, "fruit", referring to the winged pods.
CULTIVATION Well-drained soil in sun.
PROPAGATION By seed sown when ripe.
HARVEST Sap is tapped from incisions in the trunk and dried for use in powders and tinctures. Bark is collected as required and used in the form of powder and decoctions. Leaves are picked during the growing season and crushed for poultices.

▣ *Pterocarpus marsupium* (bastard teak, kino, Malabar kino)
Large deciduous tree with grey bark, red gum, and leathery leaves. Pale yellow flowers appear in lax clusters in late spring, followed by conspicuous pods, encircled by a broad wing, to 5cm (2in) across, and containing kidney-shaped seeds. Native to S and C India and Sri Lanka. ‡ 18m (60ft), ↔ 10cm (30ft).
HARDINESS Min. 15–18°C (59–64°F).
PARTS USED Sap, occasionally bark and leaves.
PROPERTIES A very astringent herb that controls diarrhoea and discharges, promotes healing, and has anti-diabetic effects.
MEDICINAL USES Internally for diarrhoea, dysentery, and diabetes. Externally for sore throats, boils, sores, skin diseases, and vaginal discharge.
▥ ▨ ▣ ▣ ▣

PTYCHOPETALUM
Olacaceae

Thirteen species of tropical trees and shrubs belong to this S American genus. Little is known about *P. olacoides*, although it has a long history of use in the Amazonian region. It has been popular in modern herbal medicine since the 1920s. *Ptychopetalum uncinatum* and *Dulacia inopiflora* syn. *Liriosma ovata* are used in similar ways. The active constituents are reported to include long-chain fatty acids, alkaloids, sterols, essential oils, and coumarin.
CULTIVATION AND PROPAGATION Moist soil in

P

shade. *Ptychopetalum olacoides* does not appear
to be in cultivation.
HARVEST Roots, bark, wood, and balsam are
collected for liquid extracts.

Ptychopetalum olacoides (marapuama, muira
puama, potency wood)
Rainforest understorey tree with grey fissured
trunk and oblong, rather leathery, dark brown
leaves, 6–8cm (2½–3in) long. Tiny, white,
jasmine-scented flowers are followed by
orange to yellow fruits. Native to Amazonian
Colombia, Venezuela, Peru, and Brazil. ↕5–15m
(15–50ft), ↔ 3–5m (10–15ft).
HARDINESS Min. 15–18°C (60–65°F).
PARTS USED Roots, bark, wood, balsam.
PROPERTIES A spicy, warming, astringent herb
that has aphrodisiac and stimulant effects,
probably acting mainly on the kidney energy.
MEDICINAL USES Internally for impotence,
infertility, paralysis and other central nervous
system disorders, menstrual problems,
rheumatism, and dysentery.

PUERARIA
Papilionaceae

There are 17 species of evergreen or deciduous,
twining climbers in this genus, which is
distributed in SE Asia and Japan. *Pueraria
lobata* was introduced to the USA in the 1870s
and widely planted in 1933 in the southeast for
erosion control. Within ten years it had become
an invasive weed, spreading over 200,000
hectares (500,000 acres). In warm areas it can
grow 18m (60ft) in a single season; the flowers,
although attractive, are largely hidden beneath
the luxuriant foliage. The first mention of
P. lobata in Chinese medicine was in the *Shen
Nong Canon of Herbs*, begun during the Han
dynasty (206BC–AD23). The plant has long
been used in Chinese medicine to treat alcohol
abuse, and has been publicized as a potentially
safe and effective treatment; in both roots and
flowers it contains chemicals (daidzin and
daidzein) that suppress the appetite for alcohol.
(Existing drugs interfere with the way alcohol is
metabolized and can cause a buildup of toxins.)
It is also planted in the East to prevent soil

erosion and as a fodder crop, and is an
important ingredient in Japanese cuisine.
Pueraria is named after Marc Puerari
(1766–1845), born in Geneva, who was a
professor of botany in Copenhagen.
CULTIVATION Moist, well-drained soil in sun
or partial shade. Train and prune regularly, to
control growth. May be grown as an annual.
Remove all pieces of root when harvesting to
avoid unwanted regrowth. Extremely invasive
weed in warm areas.
PROPAGATION By seed sown in spring at
13–18°C (55–64°F); by division in spring;
by layering during the growing season. Seeds
germinate more quickly if soaked before sowing.
HARVEST Roots are lifted from autumn to
spring and used fresh as juice, or dried for use
in decoctions and powders. Flowers are picked
before fully open and dried for use in decoctions.

Pueraria lobata syn. *P. thunbergiana*
(Japanese arrowroot, kudzu vine)
Vigorous, deciduous, twining climber with a
massive tuber, hairy stems, and palmate leaves
divided into three ovate to diamond-shaped,
lobed leaflets, to 18cm (7in) long. Fragrant
purple flowers, 2cm (¾in) long, are produced in
erect racemes, to 25cm (10in) long, in summer,
followed by flat hairy fruits that split open
when ripe. Native to China, Japan, and Pacific
islands. ↕20m (70ft).
HARDINESS Frost hardy.
PARTS USED Roots (*ge gen*), flowers (*ge hua*).
PROPERTIES A sweet, cooling, tonic herb that
increases perspiration, relieves pain, relaxes
spasms, lowers blood pressure, and soothes the
digestive system.
MEDICINAL USES Internally for colds,
influenza, feverish illnesses, thirst in diabetes,
and muscular tension in neck and shoulders;
also for acute conditions, such as stiff neck and
sudden deafness (roots), gastritis, nausea and
vomiting, alcohol poisoning, and abdominal
bloating (flowers). Often combined with the
flowers of *Chrysanthemum × morifolium* (see
p.168) for alcoholism, hangovers, and alcohol
poisoning. Externally for snake bite (roots).
Ground root is widely used in remedies for
colds, influenza, and minor digestive problems.
CULINARY USES Root yields very fine
arrowroot, used in Japanese cuisine to thicken
sauces and soups, make noodles and coatings
for tempura, and as a gelling agent. Popular
in macrobiotic and vegetarian cooking.

PULMONARIA
Lungwort
Boraginaceae

This genus of about 14 species of deciduous or
evergreen, low-growing, rhizomatous perennials
occurs in woodland areas of Europe, Asia, and
western N America. Many are grown for their
spotted leaves and early flowers. In some species
the flowers are bicoloured, giving rise to
common names such as "Joseph and Mary" and
"soldiers and sailors" – the latter referring to the

red and blue uniforms that once characterized
the British army and navy. Lungworts are an
interesting and much-quoted example of the
Doctrine of Signatures, which dominated
European medical thinking in the 16th and 17th
centuries. This held that herbs were given by God
to heal human ills and that the appearance of a
plant indicated its appropriate use: thus the
mottled ovate leaves of lungwort suggested
diseased lungs and could be used to treat them.
This theory is fully described in *The Art of
Simpling* (William Coles, 1656). In fact, many
herbs are used to this day for the purposes
described – if not for the reasons given.
Pulmonaria officinalis should not be confused
with *Lobaria pulmonaria*, also known as
"lungwort". The genus *Pulmonaria* is closely
related to *Symphytum* (see p.377), and is
suspected of similar toxicity, due to pyrrolizidine
alkaloids that may cause liver damage.
Pulmonaria is derived from the Latin *pulmo*,
"lung", because the plants were used for treating
bronchial diseases.
CULTIVATION Moist soil, including clay, in sun
or shade. Sawfly larvae, slugs, and snails may
attack foliage. Prone to powdery mildew in dry
conditions.
PROPAGATION By seed sown when ripe; by
division in spring immediately after flowering,
or in autumn; by root cuttings in midwinter.
Germination may be slow.
HARVEST Plants are cut in early summer, and
dried for infusions and extracts.
⚠ **WARNING** Skin irritant and allergen.

Pulmonaria officinalis (Jerusalem cowslip,
lungwort, soldiers and sailors)
Clump-forming, rhizomatous perennial with
hairy stems and white-spotted, ovate leaves,
10–13cm (4–5in) long, covered in bristly hairs.
Funnel-shaped flowers appear in spring, opening
pink and turning blue. Native to Europe. ↕25cm
(10in), ↔45cm (18in). ▣ Cambridge Blue Group
has eggshell-blue flowers, opening from pink
buds. ↕30cm (12in). ▣ 'White Wings' has pink-
centred, white flowers in late spring.
HARDINESS Fully hardy.
PARTS USED Leaves.
PROPERTIES A soothing, astringent,
expectorant herb.
MEDICINAL USES Internally for coughs,

Pueraria lobata

Pulmonaria officinalis

Pulmonaria officinalis Cambridge Blue Group

Pulmonaria officinalis 'White Wings'

bronchitis, asthma, catarrh, haemorrhoids, and diarrhoea. Combines well with *Marrubium vulgare* (see p.271) and *Tussilago farfara* (see p.396) for coughs in tuberculosis, and with *Ephedra* spp. (see p.201) for obstructed airways. Externally for wounds and as an eyewash.
CULINARY USES Young leaves are added to salads and soups.
ECONOMIC USES Extract is an ingredient of vermouth.
⚠ **WARNING** This herb is subject to legal restrictions in some countries.

PULSATILLA
Pasque flower

Ranunculaceae

This genus consists of 30 species of clump-forming perennials that occur mainly in short grassland and alpine meadows in temperate Eurasia and N Africa. *Pulsatilla vulgaris* is now rare in the wild through over-collection and loss of habitat. Its common name, "pasque flower", was given by John Gerard, the 16th-century herbalist, who wrote, "They floure for the most part about Easter, which has moved mee to name it *Pasque-Floure*, or Easter floure". The flowers yield a green dye once used to colour eggs at Easter. A number of different species are used medicinally in various parts of the world.

Pulsatilla chinensis (Chinese anemone) is an anti-inflammatory, astringent, anti-bacterial herb, first recorded during the Han dynasty (206BC–AD23). The dried root, known as *bai tou weng*, is used to treat gastrointestinal infections, especially amoebic dysentery. *Pulsatilla patens* was known to the Thompson people of British Columbia as "bleeding nose plant". It was listed in the *US Pharmacopoeia* (1882–1905) as a diuretic, expectorant, and uterine stimulant. *Pulsatilla pratensis* (small pasque flower) is used in homeopathy for a range of conditions.
CULTIVATION Sharply drained, neutral to alkaline soil in sun.
PROPAGATION By seed sown when ripe; by division after flowering; by root cuttings in winter. *Pulsatilla vulgaris* does not transplant well.
HARVEST Plants are cut when flowering for use fresh in elixirs, liquid extracts, and tinctures; these must be used within a year.
⚠ **WARNING** Harmful if eaten. Repeated handling may cause skin irritation.

▣ *Pulsatilla vulgaris* syn. *Anemone pulsatilla* (pasque flower)
Small, hairy, clump-forming perennial with pinnate leaves, 8–20cm (3–8in) long, which are finely divided into linear lobes and very hairy when young. Blue-violet, nodding, bell-shaped flowers, about 3cm (1¼in) long, appear in spring with the new leaves, followed by silky feathery seed heads on elongated stalks.
‡ 10–20cm (4–8in), reaching 40cm (16in) when fruiting, ↔ 20cm (8in). Native to Europe and W Asia. ▣ 'Alba' has white flowers. 'Eva Constance' is vigorous, with deep red flowers. ▣ var. *rubra* has ruby-red to brick-red or purple-red flowers.
HARDINESS Fully hardy.
PARTS USED Flowering plant.
PROPERTIES A bitter, cooling, alterative herb that relaxes spasms, relieves pain, and calms the nerves.
MEDICINAL USES Internally for premenstrual syndrome, inflammations of the reproductive organs, tension headache, neuralgia, insomnia, hyperactivity, bacterial skin infections, septicaemia, spasmodic coughs in asthma, whooping cough, and bronchitis. Not given to

patients with colds. Excess causes diarrhoea and vomiting, and convulsions. For use only by qualified practitioners.

PUNICA
Punicaceae

Two species of deciduous shrubs or small trees belong to this genus, distributed from E Mediterranean regions to the Himalayas. *Punica granatum*, which is evergreen in the subtropics and deciduous in temperate regions, has been cultivated since earliest times. The apocryphal apple that tempted Adam and Eve in the Garden of Eden may have been a pomegranate. Five pomegranate trees were planted in the garden belonging to Ineni, chief builder to the pharoah Tuthmosis I (1528–1510BC), in Thebes, and pomegranates feature in ancient Egyptian tomb paintings. The pomegranate reached China from Kabul, capital of Afghanistan, in 126BC, and soon became popular for ceremonies, because of its auspicious red colour. In Classical times the pomegranate was a symbol of fertility, and was eaten by childless women. It was first mentioned as a cure for tapeworms in the Ebers papyri (c.1500BC), and as a Chinese medicinal herb around AD470. Pomegranate rind and bark contain unusual and very toxic alkaloids, known as pelletierines, that paralyze tapeworms. When given in a carefully measured dose, followed promptly by a purgative, the worms are easily expelled. Roundworms and pinworms are similarly affected. Interestingly, though known about in Classical times, this use of pomegranate was neglected in Western medicine until it was investigated by the British in India after an Englishman was cured of tapeworms by an Indian practitioner. *Punica* is a contraction of the Latin *punicum malum*, "Carthaginian apple".
CULTIVATION Well-drained soil in sun. Remove suckers as they appear unless required for propagation. *Punica granatum* and varieties tolerate short periods just below freezing, especially when older. Successful fruiting requires long hot summers followed by autumn temperatures of 13–16°C (55–61°F).
PROPAGATION By seed sown in spring at 22°C (72°F); by semi-ripe cuttings in summer; by root suckers in autumn.
HARVEST Roots are lifted in autumn; the bark is peeled and dried for use in decoctions and liquid extracts. Fruits are picked when ripe in autumn, and the rind removed and dried for use in decoctions and powders; seeds and pulp are separated from the bitter pith and eaten fresh or pressed for juice.

▣ *Punica granatum* (pomegranate)
Dense, twiggy, sometimes spiny shrub or small tree with light green, shiny, oblong leaves, to 8cm (3in) long. Orange-red, funnel-shaped, five-petalled flowers, to 4cm (1½in) across, are followed by spherical, yellow-brown, leathery-skinned fruits, to 12cm (5in) in diameter, which contain numerous seeds in a pink juicy pulp.

P

Pulsatilla vulgaris

Pulsatilla vulgaris 'Alba'

Pulsatilla vulgaris var. *rubra*

Punica granatum

‡ 6m (20ft), ↔ 5m (15ft). 'Daru' is very hardy, bearing small, yellow-green, acidic fruits, traditionally sun-dried as a souring agent. Native to the W Himalayas. ◼ var. *nana* is dwarf, with narrower leaves, smaller flowers, and fruits about the size of a nutmeg. ↔ 1m (3ft). ◼ f. *plena* has double flowers. ◼ 'Wonderful' bears large, purple-red fruits with deep pink flesh. Makes excellent juice. Originated in USA (California) in 1896 and is now a major commercial variety.

HARDINESS Frost hardy.

PARTS USED Root bark, fruit rind (*shi liu pi*) and juice, seeds.

PROPERTIES A bitter–sweet, astringent, warming herb that destroys intestinal parasites. It is also anti-viral and controls diarrhoea.

MEDICINAL USES Internally for chronic diarrhoea, amoebic dysentery, and intestinal worms. For use only by qualified practitioners. Externally for vaginal discharge, mouth sores, and throat infections.

CULINARY USES Fruits are eaten fresh, especially in fruit salads and desserts. Juice is made into sauces, jellies, and syrup; also into a thick paste or molasses (*dibs rumman*), used in Middle Eastern cuisine, and the cordial grenadine, a flavouring for drinks (especially cocktails), fruit salad, sorbet, and ice cream. Dried fruits of the variety 'Daru' are used as a souring agent, and as a condiment known as *anardana*.

⚠ **WARNING** This herb, especially in the form of bark extracts, is subject to legal restrictions in some countries.

◫ ▨ ◘ ▧ ▨ ▪ ◿

Punica granatum var. *nana*

Punica granatum
f. *plena*

Punica granatum
'Wonderful'

PYCNANTHEMUM
Mountain mint

Lamiaceae

Some 17–21 species of mint-scented perennials found in N America belong to this genus. Several species are grown in herb gardens and wildflower plantings in the USA but are seldom seen elsewhere. *Pycnanthemum virginianum* is a traditional N American seasoning for soups and meat, and is one of several species, including *P. incanum* (hoary mountain mint), *P. muticum*, and *P. pilosum*, that can be used as a mint substitute in the kitchen. The Fox and Chippewa tribes are known to have used *P. virginianum* medicinally; *P. flexuosum* and *P. incanum* were used by the Cherokee, Choctaw, and Koasati as a general tonic, and to treat stomach upsets, bowel problems, fevers, colds, and sinus headaches. *Pycnanthemum* comes from the Greek *pyknos*, "dense", and *anthos*, "flower", and refers to the crowded flower heads.

CULTIVATION Rich soil in sun or partial shade.

PROPAGATION By seed sown in spring or autumn; by division when dormant.

HARVEST Whole plants, leaves, and flowers are collected as flowering begins and used fresh for seasoning, or dried for use in infusions.

◼ *Pycnanthemum virginianum* (prairie hyssop, Virginia mountain mint, wild basil)
Aromatic branched perennial with square stems and whorls of pointed, linear–lanceolate leaves. White to lilac flowers are borne in dense, flat-topped heads in late summer. Native to N America (Quebec to North Dakota and southwards). ‡ 70–90cm (28–36in), ↔ 20–60cm (8–24in).

HARDINESS Fully hardy.

PARTS USED Whole plant, leaves, flowers, buds.

PROPERTIES An aromatic, tonic, stimulant herb that increases perspiration, relaxes spasms, and improves digestion.

MEDICINAL USES Internally for indigestion, colic, chills, coughs, and fevers.

CULINARY USES Leaves, flowering tops, and flower buds are used to flavour soups and savoury dishes, and make an excellent mint-like tea.

▨ ◿ ▨ ▪ ◿

Pycnanthemum virginianum

PYRETHRUM

Pyrethrum cinerariifolium. See *Tanecetum cinerariifolium.*

QUASSIA

Simaroubaceae

This genus consists of 35 species of deciduous trees and shrubs, found in tropical Africa, SE Asia, and Australia. *Quassia amara* occurs in forests and beside rivers, often in marshy places. It was introduced to Europe in 1756 and entered the *London Pharmacopoeia* in 1788. The wood contains alkaloids and very bitter substances known as quassinoids. Two other species, *Q. excelsa* (now *Picrasma excelsa*, see p.315) and *Quassia ailanthoides*, have similar properties. The former replaced *Q. amara* in the *London Pharmacopoeia* in 1809, though in a number of other pharmacopoeias, including those of the Netherlands and Germany, *Q. amara* remains to this day as the official source of quassia. A traditional way of taking quassia was by "bitter cups" made from quassia wood, which were filled with water and left overnight, producing a weak decoction that was taken the following morning. *Quassia* was named after a Guyanan slave called Quassi, who used the wood to treat fevers – a remedy he may have learned from Mayan Indians.

CULTIVATION Moist, rich, sandy soil in partial shade. Prefers high humidity.

PROPAGATION By ripewood cuttings in autumn.

HARVEST Wood is cut as required and chipped for use in decoctions.

Quassia amara (bitter wood, Surinam quassia)
Upright shrub with winged leafstalks and pinnate leaves divided into 3–5 elliptic, abruptly pointed leaflets, which are purple-red when young. Bright red, tubular flowers, to 4.5cm (1¾in) long, are borne on red-stalked racemes, to 25cm (10in) long, towards the end of the rainy season or early in the dry season, followed by purple-black fruits. Found from C America to Brazil. ‡ 3m (10ft), ↔ 1.5m (5ft).

HARDINESS Min. 10°C (50°F).

PARTS USED Wood.

PROPERTIES An odourless, bitter, tonic herb that lowers fever, stimulates the digestive system, and expels intestinal parasites.

MEDICINAL USES Internally for poor appetite and digestion, anorexia, alcoholism, feverish illnesses (especially malaria), and roundworms. Externally as an enema for threadworms, as a lotion for skin parasites, and in rinses for dandruff and head lice; also in preparations to stop nail biting. Excess causes gastric irritation and vomiting.

CULINARY USES Extracts are added to beer, spirits, and soft drinks.

P

ECONOMIC USES Quassia chips are used to make an insecticide for insect pests, such as aphid and red spider mite; also as a fly killer.
🖾 🔲 ✂ ✦ ◉

Quassia cedron. See *Simaba cedron.*

QUERCUS
Oak

Fagaceae

A genus of about 600 species of evergreen, semi-evergreen, and deciduous trees and a few shrubs, distributed throughout the northern hemisphere and in some montane regions of the southern hemisphere. Various species of oak are of particular importance in the timber and tanning industries, and have a long history of use in shipbuilding. They are long-lived, and many are planted in parks and open spaces. The rigidly narrow *Q. robur* f. *fastigiata* is particularly useful for confined areas. In ancient times the oak was dedicated to Thor, the god of thunder. This gave rise to the belief that an oak tree could never be struck by lightning; hence the acorn-shaped wooden pulls attached to blind cords are thought to protect a house. The bark, galls, and acorns of various oaks are a major source of tannic acid. They contain up to 20 per cent tannin, reaching 36–58 per cent in *Q. infectoria*, an eastern Mediterranean species widely exploited by the pharmaceutical industry. *Quercus alba* (white oak) was important in native N American medicine as a remedy for diarrhoea, wounds, and haemorrhoids. The Menominee and Potawatomi made syringes, using an animal bladder and hollow bone of a bird, for the injection of oak-bark infusion into the rectum. *Quercus alba* was adopted by settlers as a substitute for the common oak, and was listed as an astringent, tonic, and antiseptic in the *US Pharmacopoeia* (1820–1916). Boiled in milk and water with the root of *Verbena urticifolia* (white vervain), it makes a useful antidote to *Rhus radicans* (poison ivy).
CULTIVATION Deep, well-drained soil in sun or partial shade. Remove lateral branches in late winter, to maintain a clean trunk. Foliage may be damaged by mildew, oak phylloxera, chafer beetles, and caterpillars, particularly those of gypsy moth. Gall wasps cause the formation of galls on various parts of the tree, most commonly occurring on the leaves. Trees may be infected by honey fungus and various species of bracket fungus. Oak wilt is a major, usually lethal fungal disease in some areas.
PROPAGATION By seed sown when ripe; by grafting in midautumn or late winter.
HARVEST Bark is removed in spring from trees 10–25 years old and dried for use in decoctions and liquid extracts.

■ *Quercus robur* (common oak, English oak, pedunculate oak)
Large deciduous tree with a broad crown, fissured bark, and very short-stalked, ovate–oblong leaves, to 14cm (5½in) long, which have lobed margins. Male flowers are borne in

Quercus robur

catkins; females in spikes of 1–5 in spring, followed by ovoid acorns, 4cm (1½in) long. ‡ 25–35m (80–120ft), ↔ 25m (80ft). Native from Europe to W Russia. ■ 'Atropurpurea' is slow-growing, with red-purple young leaves, which mature to grey-purple. ‡↔ 10m (30ft). ■ 'Concordia' (golden oak) is slow-growing and rounded, with golden young foliage that becomes yellow-green in summer. Originated in Ghent in 1843. ‡↔ 10m (30ft). ■ f. *fastigiata* (cypress oak) is very narrow, with upright branches. ‡ 25m (80ft), ↔ 5m (15ft).
HARDINESS Fully hardy.
PARTS USED Bark.
PROPERTIES A bitter, astringent, antiseptic herb that reduces inflammation and controls bleeding.
MEDICINAL USES Internally for diarrhoea, dysentery, haemorrhage, and prolapsed uterus or anus. Not taken for longer than four weeks at a time. Externally for haemorrhoids, vaginal discharge, sore throat, bleeding gums, minor injuries, dermatitis, weeping eczema, ringworm,

Quercus robur
'Atropurpurea'

Quercus robur
'Concordia'

Quercus robur
f. *fastigiata*

ulcers, and varicose veins.
CULINARY USES Acorns can be ground into flour and roasted as a coffee substitute.
ECONOMIC USES Wood is traditionally used for making oak barrels, which give a distinctive flavour to wine. Bark and galls are used in tanning, and also in dyeing, the colour produced being dependent on the mordant.
🖾 🔲 ✂ ✦

QUILLAJA
Soapbark tree

Rosaceae

Three or four species of evergreen trees and shrubs belong to this genus, which occurs in temperate parts of S America. *Quillaja saponaria* is grown for its attractive glossy foliage, large flowers, and curious soapy bark. It succeeds outdoors in northern regions if given a sheltered position, and is cultivated commercially in California (USA) and India. Nine per cent of the bark of *Q. saponaria* is made up of complex saponins, known collectively as "quillajasaponin", together with calcium oxalate and tannins. It is now used mainly in pharmaceutical and cosmetic preparations, since research has shown that internal use may have unpleasant side-effects. *Quillaja* is from the Chilean term *quillai*, "to wash", and refers to the soap-like properties of the genus.
CULTIVATION Fertile, well-drained soil, sited in a sheltered position in cold areas.
PROPAGATION By ripe cuttings at the end of the growing season.
HARVEST Bark is dried for use in liquid extracts, powders, and tinctures.

■ *Quillaja saponaria* (halava wood, Panama bark, quillai, soapbark tree)
Large evergreen tree with smooth, shiny, ovate leaves, to 5cm (2in) long. White to green-yellow, purple-centred flowers, about 1.5cm (½in) across, appear in spring and early summer, followed by star-shaped fruits containing 10–18 oblong seeds, 1cm (½in) long. Native to Chile and Peru. ‡ 15–18m (50–60ft), ↔ 6–7m (20–22ft).

Quillaja saponaria

Q

HARDINESS Frost hardy to half hardy.
PARTS USED Inner bark, bark.
PROPERTIES An acrid, astringent, cleansing herb that reduces inflammation and has expectorant effects.
MEDICINAL USES Internally for bronchial congestion. May cause irritation and inflammation of the digestive tract, and is no longer considered safe. Externally for skin ulcers and eruptions, and dandruff. Powdered bark causes violent sneezing.
CULINARY USES Powdered dried bark is mixed with citrus-flavoured syrup to make Middle Eastern cream or mousse, *natef* or *natife*, served with pastries.
ECONOMIC USES Bark extracts are used to flavour baked produce, confectionery, soft drinks, and ice cream; also as a foaming agent in beers and fire extinguishers. Cleansing properties are utilized in anti-dandruff shampoos and exfoliant cleansers.

R

RANUNCULUS
Buttercup

Ranunculaceae

Distributed throughout temperate, far northern, and tropical montane regions, this genus contains about 400 species of mainly deciduous annuals, biennials, and perennials. Although *R. ficaria* (wild celandine) is very invasive as a garden plant, it has numerous variants with attractive foliage and colourful, often double flowers that are better behaved. Most members of the buttercup family contain acrid compounds that are too irritant for internal use. *Ranunculus ficaria* is an exception and is often taken in tablet form for haemorrhoids (piles). The traditional use of this herb for treating piles gave rise to the common name "pilewort". Its suitability for this purpose was in accordance with the Doctrine of Signatures (according to which a plant's appearance indicated its use), because the clustered tuberous roots of pilewort were thought to resemble piles. *Ranunculus* is the diminutive of the Latin *rana*, "frog", as many species are aquatic or grow in wet places.
CULTIVATION Moist, neutral to alkaline soil in sun or shade. *Ranunculus ficaria* is particularly invasive when grown in shade, which encourages formation of bulbils at leaf bases.
PROPAGATION By seed sown when ripe (species only); by division in spring or autumn.
HARVEST Plants are lifted after flowering, complete with roots, and used fresh for ointments and suppositories, or dried for use in infusions, liquid extracts, and tablets.
⚠ **WARNING** Harmful if eaten. Skin irritant.

◼ *Ranunculus ficaria* (lesser celandine, pilewort)
Mat-forming, very variable, tuberous perennial with heart-shaped leaves, to 4cm (1½in) long, often forming bulbils at the leaf bases. Bright yellow, solitary flowers, 2–3cm (¾–1¼in) across, with glossy petals, appear in early spring. Native to Europe, W Asia, and NW Africa. ‡5–15cm (2–6in), ↔30cm (12in).
◼ var. *albus* has bronze-marked leaves and pale cream flowers, fading to white.

◼ var. *aurantiacus* syn. 'Cupreus' has silver-green leaves, with a central bronze mark, and copper-coloured flowers. ◼ 'Brazen Hussy' has dark brown foliage and yellow flowers, with bronze undersides. ◼ f. *flore pleno* has double flowers.
HARDINESS Fully hardy.
PARTS USED Whole plant, including roots.
PROPERTIES An astringent, slightly bitter herb that is specifically anti-haemorrhoidal.
MEDICINAL USES Externally for haemorrhoids, and for perineal damage after childbirth. Often combined with *Hamamelis virginiana* (see p.230) in creams and ointments, and with *Calendula officinalis* (see p.150), *Hamamelis virginiana* (see p.230), or *Plantago major* (see p.322) in suppositories.

RAPHANUS
Radish

Brassicaceae

Eight species of annuals and perennials belong to this genus, which ranges through W and C Europe to C Asia. *Raphanus sativus* was cultivated 4500 years ago in Egypt and at least 2000 years ago in China. Black radishes probably originated in Spain during the Middle Ages. Radishes reached Britain in 1548, and four varieties were recorded by John Gerard in 1597. Nicholas Culpeper recommended radishes for urinary problems but condemned them as food. "Garden radishes are in wantonness by the gentry eaten as a sallad, but they breed scurvy humours in the stomach, and corrupt the blood" (*The English Physician Enlarged*, 1653). *Raphanus sativus*, which contains the antibiotic raphinin, is less pungent than *R. raphanistrum* (wild radish), which is closer in chemistry to *Sinapis alba* (white mustard, see p.369). Radishes were first mentioned in Chinese medical literature during the 14th century. Those of Asian origin, sometimes classed as *Raphanus sativus* var. *macropodus*, have much larger roots, weighing up to 20kg (44lb). They include the white-rooted *mooli*, or *daikon*, which is harvested in autumn and stored for winter use. Black radishes, which are favoured for homeopathic remedies, differ in having a pronounced effect on the liver. In China they are taken in the form of juice as a laxative and digestive tonic.
CULTIVATION Rich, moist, well-drained soil in sun. Roots may be damaged by scab and slugs, and leaves by flea beetles. Radishes are said to repel cucumber beetles, if planted around the base of cucumber plants, and to deter vine borers, which attack marrows and courgettes.
PROPAGATION By seed sown in spring as a seed crop; by seed sown in succession from late winter to late summer for roots.
HARVEST Leaves are picked when young and used fresh. Roots are lifted as required and used fresh. Seeds are collected when ripe and dried for use in decoctions and pills. Seed pods and flower clusters are picked when immature and used fresh.

Ranunculus ficaria

Ranunculus ficaria var. *albus*

Ranunculus ficaria var. *aurantiacus*

Ranunculus ficaria 'Brazen Hussy'

Ranunculus ficaria f. *flore pleno*

Raphanus sativus

■ *Raphanus sativus* (radish)
Bristly annual or biennial with lyre-shaped, lobed leaves and a turnip- or spindle-shaped, white-fleshed taproot, which may have white, red, green, yellow, purple, or black skin. Small, white or lilac, four-petalled flowers appear in summer, followed by inflated beaked fruits containing 6–12 seeds. Unknown in the wild; probably derived from *R. raphanistrum*.
‡ 20–90cm (8–36in), ↔ 20–38cm (8–15in).
'Cherry Belle' has small, globose, bright red roots and a mild flavour. Fast-maturing and slow to go woody. 'Full House' has long smooth leaves, ideal for winter and spring salad crops. 'Long Black Spanish' has cylindrical, black-skinned roots, 18–25cm (7–10in) long, with dense pungent flesh. Stores well. 'Tokinashi' is a *mooli*-type radish with tapering, white-skinned roots and crisp pungent flesh. Tolerates extreme temperatures and is slow to bolt.
HARDINESS Fully hardy.
PARTS USED Leaves, roots, seeds (*lai fu zi*), pods, flower buds.
PROPERTIES A sweet, slightly pungent, tonic herb that improves digestion, acts as an expectorant, and is effective against many bacterial and fungal infections.
MEDICINAL USES Internally for indigestion, abdominal bloating, flatulence, acid regurgitation, diarrhoea caused by "food stagnation", and bronchitis. Roots are usually "dry-fried" or toasted for bronchial complaints.
CULINARY USES Whole or sliced young roots are eaten in salads and as an appetizer, or used as garnishing. Shredded or grated roots are eaten raw, cooked, or pickled; also used to tenderize octopus. Immature seed pods are eaten raw in salads, or pickled. Young leaves are eaten in salads or briefly cooked as a vegetable. Seeds are sprouted for salads. Unopened flower clusters are eaten in salads or steamed as a vegetable.
▣ ▨ ▨ ▧ ▨ ▪ ✓

RAUVOLFIA
Apocynaceae

Over 100 species of evergreen and deciduous shrubs and small trees make up this genus, occurring in most tropical and subtropical regions. A few species are occasionally seen in botanic gardens today, but none is common as an ornamental. *Rauvolfia serpentina* was introduced to cultivation in Europe in 1690 and was recommended for pots under glass during the 19th century. Known as *sarpagandha* in Sanskrit, it was mentioned in Hindu texts c.600BC. A tea made from the whole plant has been used for centuries in India for treating madness, hysteria, and restlessness. Mahatma Gandhi is said to have drunk it regularly for its calming effect. It contains about 25 alkaloids, the most important of which is reserpine, a potent hypotensive. Demand for *R. serpentina* has led to over-collecting; it became a protected species in 1997. Other useful species include *R. verticillata*, which contains similar alkaloids to those found in *R. serpentina*, and *R. vomitoria* (African serpentwood), which is even richer in alkaloids, notably ajmaline, which has largely superseded reserpine because it has fewer side-effects. Roots of *R. vomitoria* have long been used in traditional African medicine for calming mentally disturbed patients. It is collected mainly from Zaïre, Rwanda, and Mozambique for processing in Europe. *Rauvolfia caffra* (quinine tree), found in eastern South Africa and E Africa, is used to treat fevers, malaria, insomnia, and hysteria. It too is rich in indole alkaloids. The unrelated *Bacopa monnieri*, a SE Asian member of the foxglove family, Scrophulariaceae, contains saponins (notably hersaponin) that are similar in effect to reserpine. *Rauvolfia* is named after Leonhart Rauwolf, a 16th-century German physician.
CULTIVATION Well-drained soil in sun or partial shade, with an almost dry, winter resting period.
PROPAGATION By seed sown at 24°C (75°F) in spring; by stem cuttings in spring and summer; by root cuttings in winter. Seeds have a low germination rate.
HARVEST Roots, 1cm (½in) in diameter, are lifted in winter, from plants at least 15 months old, and dried for use in decoctions and powders, or for commercial extraction of alkaloids. Bark and inner root may be separated before drying.

■ *Rauvolfia serpentina* (Indian snakeroot, rauwolfia, serpentwood)
Small, understorey, evergreen shrub with a long, vertical, rather tuberous, nodular rootstock and lanceolate tapering leaves, 5–13cm (2–5in) long, borne in whorls of three. Tiny, pale pink,

Rauvolfia serpentina

tubular flowers, about 2cm (¾in) long, with five white to red lobes, appear in spring, followed by glossy, black-purple, ovoid fruits, to 7mm (¼in) long. Native to India, Sri Lanka, Burma (Myanmar), Andaman Islands, and Java.
‡↔ 30–60cm (1–2ft).
HARDINESS Min. 10–13°C (50–55°F).
PARTS USED Roots.
PROPERTIES A tranquillizing sedative herb that lowers blood pressure and slows heartbeat.
MEDICINAL USES Internally for mild hypertension, rapid heartbeat, and nervous and mental disorders. Contraindicated during pregnancy and lactation, and in depression. Side-effects include dry mouth, nasal congestion, depression, fatigue, and slowed heartbeat. Interacts with a number of prescription drugs, including *Digitalis* glycosides, barbiturates, cough and cold medications, and appetite suppressants. In folk medicine, internally for fever, cholera, high blood pressure, snake bite, intestinal worms, and to increase contractions in childbirth; externally for eye problems.
⚠ **WARNING** This herb is subject to legal restrictions in some countries.
▨ ▪ ▧

REHMANNIA
Chinese foxglove

Scrophulariaceae

A genus of eight or nine species of perennials that occur in E Asia. A few species are cultivated for their large, foxglove-like flowers; they tend to deteriorate after the first year and are therefore often grown as biennials. *Rehmannia glutinosa* was the first species of the genus to be cultivated in the West. It has been superseded by *R. elata* as an ornamental. However, due to its long cultivation for medicinal purposes, many variants of *R. glutinosa* are available in China, differing in size, habit, and root flavour. *Rehmannia glutinosa* is one of the most popular tonic herbs in Chinese medicine and among the 50 most important Chinese herbs. The fresh or dried roots (*sheng di huang*) were first mentioned in Chinese medical literature during the Han dynasty (206BC–AD23). Roots steamed in rice wine, known as *shu di huang*, were described in the *Illustrated Classic of the Materia Medica* by Su Song (AD1061). *Rehmannia* was named after Joseph Rehmann (1799–1831), a German physician.
CULTIVATION Light, moist, well-drained, humus-rich, neutral to acid, sandy soil in sun. Plants are prone to fungal infections, especially in damp conditions.
PROPAGATION By seed sown in late winter at 13–16°C (55–61°F); by root cuttings in late autumn; by softwood cuttings of basal shoots in spring.
HARVEST Roots are lifted in autumn and early winter (cultivated crops), or early spring (wild plants), and used fresh or dried (*sheng di huang*) for use in decoctions, extracts, pills, powders, and tinctures, or steamed in rice wine (*shu di huang*).

R

Rehmannia glutinosa

■ *Rehmannia glutinosa* (Chinese foxglove)
Purple-hairy, sticky perennial with slender,
tuberous, orange roots and a basal rosette of
ovate scalloped leaves, to 10cm (4in) long,
which often have reddish undersides. Red-
brown to dull yellow, purple-streaked, pendent,
tubular flowers, to 5cm (2in) long, with flared
lobed mouths, appear from spring to summer,
followed by ovoid seed capsules. Native to
N China. ‡ 15–30cm (6–12in), ↔ 30cm (12in).
HARDINESS Fully hardy.
PARTS USED Roots (*di huang*).
PROPERTIES A sweet, cooling (*sheng di
huang*) to slightly warming (*shu di huang*) herb
that controls bleeding, lowers fever, reduces
blood sugar, and has diuretic and anti-bacterial
effects (*sheng di huang*). It acts as a tonic for
the heart, blood, and kidney energy, regulates
menstruation, and strengthens women after
childbirth (*shu di huang*).
MEDICINAL USES Internally for thirst associated
with feverish illnesses, heat rash, haemorrhage
of all kinds, excessive menstruation, and
diabetes (*sheng di huang*); anaemia, night
sweats, menopausal problems, weakness
following childbirth, and involuntary ejaculation
(*shu di huang*). Not given to patients with
digestive problems. Often combined with
Angelica polymorpha var. *sinensis* (see p.122),
the peel of *Citrus reticulata* (see p.173), and
Ziziphus jujuba (see p.411).

RESEDA
Mignonette
Resedaceae

This genus consists of 55–60 species of annuals
and perennials from stony hillsides, scrub, and
field margins, mainly in Mediterranean regions
and SW Asia. *Reseda luteola* (weld) has an
ancient history as a dye plant. It was used to
dye wedding garments and the robes of vestal
virgins in Roman times, and in England was
mixed with *Genista tinctoria* (see p.222) and
Isatis tinctoria (see p.245) or *Indigofera
tinctoria* (indigo) to make the colour Kendal or
Lincoln green, as worn by Robin Hood and his
men. Weld is unusual among natural dyes in

producing very good, permanent yellows
and greens; examples can be seen in textiles
hundreds of years old. Though little used
medicinally, weld contains the flavones luteolin
and apigenin. The former is an interesting
pigment, not found in other species of *Reseda*;
the latter is an important constituent of
Petroselinum crispum (see p.310) and is known
to have antioxidant and anti-allergic properties.
Reseda odorata is a common weed in N Africa;
it was introduced to France by Napoleon, who
sent seeds from Egypt to the Empress
Josephine. During the 19th century, it was a
popular container plant for balconies and other
positions where its fragrance would be most
appreciated. The French named it *mignonette*,
meaning "little darling". Mignonette was once
cultivated in the south of France for the
perfumery industry; the flowers were picked
in early to midspring. Their perfume has been
described as resembling that of violet leaves
and basil. Traditionally the essential oil was
extracted by enfleurage. In Britain the plant
was first grown at the Chelsea Physic Garden
in London from seed sent from Leiden in 1752.
Modern varieties, with more deeply coloured
flowers, are less fragrant; the original species
has a long-lasting fragrance, even when dried.
CULTIVATION Well-drained to dry, alkaline soil
in sun.
PROPAGATION By seed sown in late winter at
13°C (55°F) or *in situ* in early spring or autumn.
HARVEST Flowers are picked as they open
(*R. odorata*). Whole plants are cut in summer
for infusions.

■ *Reseda luteola* (weld, yellow weed)
Annual or perennial with a basal rosette of dark
green, linear to ovate, wavy-margined leaves, to
12cm (5in) long. Tiny, pale yellow-green flowers,
with numerous stamens, are produced in dense,
sometimes branched spikes. Found from Europe
to C Asia. ‡ 1.5m (5ft), ↔ 50cm (20in).
HARDINESS Fully hardy.
PARTS USED Whole plant (except roots).
PROPERTIES A bitter astringent herb that
may have antioxidant and anti-allergic
effects.
MEDICINAL USES Internally for
stomach ache and diarrhoea
(N Africa).

Reseda luteola

Reseda odorata

ECONOMIC USES Yields natural dye in shades
of yellow, orange, and olive.

■ *Reseda odorata* (mignonette)
Erect to spreading annual with ribbed stems
and bright green, elliptic to spoon-shaped,
sometimes three-lobed leaves, to 10cm (4in)
long. Very fragrant, white or buff flowers, 7mm
(¼in) across, tinted yellow-green to red-green,
and with orange stamens, are borne in conical
heads from summer to early autumn. Native to
N Africa; widely naturalized. ‡ 30–60cm
(12–24in), ↔ 23in (9in).
HARDINESS Fully hardy.
PARTS USED Flowers.
PROPERTIES An aromatic herb.
CULINARY USES Flowers are used to flavour
salt in Turkish cuisine; also used to garnish
white wine cups.

RHAMNUS
Rhamnaceae

A genus of 125 species of deciduous and
evergreen, often thorny trees and shrubs that
occur mainly in northern temperate regions.
Rhamnus frangula and *R. cathartica* are ideal
for hedges in a wild or woodland garden. The
former, which grows wild in damp peaty
ground, has good autumn colour, and its flowers
are especially attractive to bees. It was once
grown to make charcoal for small-arms
gunpowder. *Rhamnus purshiana*, which is
native to coastal redwood and mixed evergreen
forests, is particularly noticeable in winter,
forming groups of upright, silver-grey stems.
The bark of *Rhamnus* spp. contains
anthraquinone glycosides, which have a strong
purgative effect and cause severe griping pains,
nausea, and vomiting unless stored for at least a
year after drying. *Rhamnus cathartica* has been
used as a purgative since at least the 9th century
and was included in the *British Pharmacopoeia*
in 1650. Its effect is so drastic that it is no
longer prescribed, although buckthorn syrup,
made from the berries, is used in veterinary
practice. *Rhamnus frangula* and *R. purshiana*

R

have superseded *R. cathartica* in medicine, having a gentler effect; the latter is mild enough for treating children and the elderly. *Rhamnus purshiana* was first listed in the *US Pharmacopoeia* in 1890. Indiscriminate stripping of bark, leading to the destruction of some 100,000 trees a year, was reported as early as 1909, and shortages led to the exploitation of the much smaller *R. alnifolia* (alderleaf buckthorn), which is similar in chemistry. Anthraquinones are pigments, so plants that contain them are almost always used for dyeing – a purpose that usually pre-dates their importance in medicine. *Rhamnus infectoria* (Avignon berry) was once an important source of yellow dye; *R. davurica* and *R. utilis* were sources of the pigment known as "Chinese green indigo", used in dyeing silk. Fruits of *R. cathartica*, known as "Rhine berries", also yield an artist's pigment.

CULTIVATION Well-drained soil in sun or partial shade. *Rhamnus cathartica* prefers alkaline soil, *R. frangula* neutral to acid soil. Shorten or thin out branches, and remove dead wood, in late winter or early spring.

PROPAGATION By seed sown when ripe; by greenwood cuttings in early summer; by layering in autumn or early spring.

HARVEST Bark is stripped from young plants during spring and early summer, and it is dried for one to two years before being used in decoctions, liquid extracts, powders, and tablets. Bark from two-year-old plants is preferred in the case of *R. frangula*. Fruits (*R. cathartica*) are collected when ripe and made into syrup.

⚠ **WARNING** All parts, especially the berries, are harmful if eaten. Sap and berries are skin irritants.

■ *Rhamnus cathartica* (buckthorn)
Dense, thicket-forming, deciduous shrub or small tree with grey-brown bark and ovate to elliptic leaves, to 6cm (2½in) long, which turn yellow in autumn. Tiny, yellow-green, four-petalled flowers are produced in axillary clusters in late spring, followed by globose red berries, about 6mm (¼in) across. Native to Europe, NW Africa, and Asia. ‡ 6m (20ft), ↔ 5m (15ft).
HARDINESS Fully hardy.
PARTS USED Bark, fruits.

Rhamnus catharticus

PROPERTIES A bitter, cooling, purgative herb that cleanses toxins from tissues and has diuretic effects.
MEDICINAL USES Internally for constipation. Small amounts are occasionally used in alterative formulas to treat skin diseases, intestinal parasites, and gallstones.
ECONOMIC USES Bark and fruits yield a yellow dye, once used to colour paper and maps. Fruits are mixed with gum arabic and limewater to make a green pigment used in watercolour painting.
🖾 ⬚ ⬛ ✎

■ *Rhamnus frangula* syn. *Frangula alnus* (alder buckthorn)
Deciduous thornless shrub or small tree with ovate leaves, to 7cm (3in) long, turning yellow and brown in autumn. Tiny green flowers appear in axillary clusters in late spring, followed by red berries, 1cm (½in) across, ripening to black. Native to Europe, N Africa, and Russia. ‡ 5m (15ft), ↔ 3–5m (10–15ft).
HARDINESS Fully hardy.
PARTS USED Inner bark.
PROPERTIES A bitter, astringent, antiseptic herb that stimulates the liver and gall bladder, and acts as a purgative.
MEDICINAL USES Internally for chronic, atonic constipation, abdominal bloating, hepatitis, cirrhosis, jaundice, and liver and gall bladder complaints. Externally for gum disease and scalp infestations.
🖾 ⬛

Rhamnus purshianus (cascara sagrada)
Lax evergreen shrub or tree with obovate, irregularly toothed, deeply veined leaves, to 15cm (6in) long. Umbels of small flowers appear in late spring, followed by toxic black berries, 1cm (½in) in diameter. Native to western N America. ‡ 3–12m (10–40ft), ↔ 3–10m (10–30ft).
HARDINESS Fully hardy.
PARTS USED Bark.
PROPERTIES A bitter, astringent, cooling herb that has a tonic effect on the liver and digestive system, and acts as a laxative.
MEDICINAL USES Internally for chronic constipation, colitis,

Rhamnus frangula

digestive complaints, haemorrhoids, liver problems, and jaundice. Fruits taken in excess cause diarrhoea and vomiting. Contraindicated during pregnancy and lactation, and for intestinal obstruction. Externally to deter nail biting.
ECONOMIC USES Bark extracts, with bitterness removed, are used for flavouring in the food and soft drinks industries.
🖾 ⬛ ✎

RHEUM
Rhubarb

Polygonaceae

Some 50 species of stout perennials make up this genus, which is Eurasian in distribution. The two main medicinal species of rhubarb are *R. palmatum*, which reached Europe in 1762, and *R. officinale*, introduced in 1867. Both have laxative effects. Purgatives were historically of much greater importance than they are in medicine today. Various rhubarbs have been cultivated in China as medicinal herbs for over 2000 years and were recorded as imports by the ancient Greeks. For centuries, trade was controlled by the Chinese and Russians through the Kiakhta Rhubarb Commission, or Rhubarb Office, on the border between Siberia and Mongolia. This was abolished in 1782 after Europeans succeeded in obtaining live plants and cultivating domestic supplies. The cultivation of *R. palmatum* was given high priority in the 18th century. A map, dated 1777, of the Royal Botanic Garden Edinburgh (originally a physic garden) indicates a very large area devoted to its cultivation. *Rheum palmatum*, one of the most widely used Chinese herbs, was first mentioned in the *Shen Nong Canon of Herbs*, which dates back to the Han dynasty (206BC–AD23). Many common names exist, such as "Turkey rhubarb" and "Dutch rhubarb", which usually refer to a trade source rather than the origin of the wild plant. Rhubarbs contain anthraquinone glycosides (as found in *Rhamnus* spp., see p.342), which act as strong laxatives. Several other species are used medicinally, including *R. australe* (Himalayan rhubarb, Indian rhubarb) and the hybrid *R. palmatum* × *R. coreanum* (Japanese rhubarb). These rhubarbs vary slightly in chemistry but are used interchangeably. Only the roots are used; the leaves are poisonous. The familiar edible rhubarb was derived from *R. rhabarbarum* syn. *R. rhaponticum*, developed through hybridization during the 19th century. The roots of edible rhubarbs are not used for medicinal purposes.
CULTIVATION Well-drained, moist, humus-rich soil in sun.
PROPAGATION By seed sown in autumn (species and varieties only); by division in early spring.
HARVEST Rhizomes are lifted in autumn from plants at least three years old and dried for use in decoctions, dry extracts, powders, tinctures, and tablets.
⚠ **WARNING** Leaves are harmful if eaten.

R

Rheum palmatum

■ *Rheum palmatum* (Chinese rhubarb, *chinghai* rhubarb) Robust perennial with a thick rhizome, thick succulent leafstalks, and rounded, palmately lobed, jagged-toothed leaves, to 90cm (36in) long, with maroon undersides. Tiny, star-shaped, buff-green to deep red flowers are produced in a spire-like panicle in summer, followed by three-winged fruits. Native to NW China and NE Tibet. ‡ 2.5m (8ft), ↔ 1.8m (6ft).

■ 'Atrosanguineum' syn. 'Atropurpureum' has bright red buds, red-purple young leaves, and cherry-red flowers followed by pink fruits. var. *tanguticum* has jagged leaves, red-green when young, and white, pink, or red flowers. ‡ 2m (6ft).

HARDINESS Fully hardy.

PARTS USED Rhizomes (*da huang*).

PROPERTIES A bitter, astringent, cooling herb that improves digestion, stimulates the uterus, promotes healing, and has a laxative effect.

MEDICINAL USES Internally for chronic constipation, diarrhoea, liver and gall bladder complaints, haemorrhoids, menstrual problems, heat-related symptoms (such as nosebleed), and skin eruptions owing to the accumulation of toxins. Contraindicated during pregnancy and lactation, and for intestinal obstruction. Externally for burns. Used in homeopathy for irritability and teething in children.

RHUS syn. *Toxicodendron*
Sumach

Anacardiaceae

A genus of about 200 species of mostly hardy, deciduous, or evergreen trees, shrubs, and scrambling climbers, widely distributed in temperate and subtropical regions. *Rhus glabra* is an excellent subject for mass planting, providing vivid autumn colour and, in female plants, upright clusters of scarlet fruits. The common name "sumach" comes from the Arabic *summaq*, a preparation used for tanning and dyeing. Various sumachs have a high tannin content and are valued for their astringent properties. These include the N American *R. aromatica*, used mainly for urinary incontinence, and *R. coriaria* (Sicilian or tanner's sumach). The latter also has acidic fruits, which are made into a condiment and sour drink in the Middle East. Similarly, the N American *R. ovata* (lemonade berry, sugar bush) has sherbet-tasting fruits, which are sucked for refreshment or used to flavour drinks. Sumachs commonly bear galls, caused by parasitic insects. Those of *R. chinensis* (Chinese sumach) contain up to 70 per cent tannins, and were first described in traditional Chinese medicine c.AD720 for coughs, diarrhoea, haemorrhage, injuries, mouth ulcers, and haemorrhoids. *Rhus radicans* (poison ivy) differs from most species in containing toxins that cause severe contact dermatitis.

CULTIVATION Moist, well-drained soil in sun. Cut back to the ground in early spring to encourage vigorous new growth and large leaves. Plants may be damaged by die-back and various fungal diseases. Sumachs are short-lived and brittle, especially as single-stemmed specimens. Growing them as coppiced shrubs prolongs life and minimizes damage from wind and snow.

PROPAGATION By seed sown in autumn (species only); by semi-ripe cuttings in summer; by root cuttings in winter. Separate suckers in autumn.

HARVEST Roots are lifted as required, bark is peeled and dried for use in decoctions and liquid extracts. Fruits are collected when ripe and dried for use in decoctions, liquid extracts, and powders.

Rhus glabra

■ *Rhus glabra* (scarlet sumach, smooth sumach) Suckering deciduous shrub with smooth, wax-coated branches and glossy pinnate leaves, to 45cm (18in) long, divided into 15–31 oblanceolate toothed leaflets, which turn red in autumn. Green flowers are borne in dense conical panicles in summer; males and females on separate plants, followed on female plants by globose, downy, scarlet fruits. Native to NE USA and S Canada. ‡ 3m (10ft), ↔ 2.5m (8ft).

HARDINESS Fully hardy.

PARTS USED Root bark, fruits.

PROPERTIES An astringent, antiseptic, mucilaginous herb with tonic effects. The bark is regarded as an alterative; the fruits are cooling and diuretic.

MEDICINAL USES Internally for diarrhoea and dysentery (root bark), feverish illnesses and urinary complaints (fruits). Externally for skin irritations, sores, ulcers, vaginal discharge, and haemorrhoids (root bark).

RIBES
Currant

Grossulariaceae

A genus of about 150 species of small to medium-sized, mainly deciduous shrubs, widely distributed in northern temperate regions. *Ribes nigrum* is the most widely grown and economically important member of the genus in Europe; it is less common in the USA because it hosts *Cronartium ribicola* (pine blister rust), which can devastate forests. The distinctive flavour of blackcurrants was not as popular in the past as it is now. John Gerard, in his *Generall Historie of Plantes* (1597), described them as "of a stinking and somewhat loathing savour". The fruits were also thought to breed worms in the stomach. Blackcurrant leaves were once important as a substitute for Indian and China tea. At various times during the 18th and 19th centuries in the UK, shortages and high prices of tea led to the widespread practice of making substitute blends. "A serviceable English 'tea' may be made with hawthorn for bulk, and sage, lemon balm, woodruff (the plant), and blackcurrant leaves for flavour if currant and

Rheum palmatum 'Atrosanguineum'

sage predominate, the tea will somewhat favour Ceylon" (Dorothy Hartley, *Food in England*, 1954). Dried blackcurrant leaves were also added to Indian blends to make them go further. Commercial breeding of blackcurrants is a recent phenomenon, and for centuries cultivated plants differed little from the wild species. Most present-day cultivars were developed by growers and research institutes after the Second World War, when food shortages stimulated an interest in the nutritional value of the species. The medicinal properties of *R. nigrum* were first described in 1614 by Peter Forestus, who used the leaves to treat urinary retention and bladder stones. The leaves contain tannins, and the fruits are high in vitamin C, 120mg per 100g (0.12 per cent by weight) of fresh fruit. The common name, "quinsy berry", refers to its effectiveness in treating quinsy, a severe throat inflammation. The seeds are a source of oil, rich in gamma-linolenic acid, an unsaturated fatty acid found in evening primrose (see *Oenothera biennis*, p.293).

CULTIVATION Well-drained, fertile, preferably clay soil in sun or partial shade, with protection from cold winds and late frosts. Remove weak growths and one-third of older (grey or black) shoots in autumn. Bushes tend to lose vigour with age and are usually replaced every ten years or so. Buds may be damaged by birds, aphid, and blackcurrant ("big bud") gall mites.

PROPAGATION By hardwood cuttings in winter.

HARVEST Leaves are gathered during the growing season and used fresh, or dried for use in infusions; essential oil is extracted from buds. Fruits are picked when ripe; fixed oil is extracted from ripe seeds.

■ *Ribes nigrum* (blackcurrant, quinsy berry) Aromatic shrub with yellow-brown shoots and five-lobed leaves, to 10cm (4in) long. Tiny, green-white flowers are borne in pendent clusters of 4–10 in spring, followed by globose, many-seeded, black berries, 1cm (½in) in diameter. Found from Europe to C Asia and the Himalayas. ↨ 2m (6ft). 'Ben Sarek' is a compact, very high-yielding, midseason variety, producing large, high-quality fruits. 'Ben Tirran' produces large, well-flavoured

Ribes nigrum

fruits that ripen late; high-yielding and disease-resistant. 'Goliath' is upright, with very large, superbly flavoured, midseason berries. Originated before 1847.

HARDINESS Fully hardy.

PARTS USED Leaves, fruits, seeds, buds.

PROPERTIES A sweet–sour, astringent, tonic herb that reduces inflammation, strengthens capillaries, and controls bacterial infections.

MEDICINAL USES Internally for colds, capillary fragility, and mouth and throat infections. Externally for sore throat.

CULINARY USES Fruits are eaten raw or cooked, and made into jams, jellies, syrup, and cordials; also used to flavour wine vinegar. Dried leaves are used to make tea.

ECONOMIC USES Fruit extracts are used in herb teas, cordials, and to make liqueur, known as *crème de cassis*. Fixed oil is used in cosmetics and food supplements; pungent musky essential oil, known as cassis, is used in perfumery. Dried leaves are used in blended herb teas.

⊠ ⊠ ⊡ ⊞ ▣ ✎ ✐

RICINUS
Castor oil plant

Euphorbiaceae

This genus of a single species of evergreen shrub is found wild throughout W Asia and NE Africa, and is naturalized in many parts of the tropics. It reaches tree-like proportions in warm regions, and thrives as a half-hardy annual in temperate areas. The large luxuriant leaves are effective as a focal point or background in subtropical bedding. *Ricinus communis* has been cultivated for over 6000 years and was a source of oil for lamps and cosmetics in ancient Egypt. All parts of the plant are poisonous; the seeds contain ricin, an exceedingly toxic protein. The toxicity of the plant was well publicized in 1978 following a political assassination in London that was carried out using an umbrella tipped with seed extract. Necklaces are sometimes made from the attractive seeds, though as few as two may prove fatal if swallowed. Greek physicians of the 1st century AD regarded the oil as suitable only for external application. This view persisted until the 1780s, when castor oil was listed in many pharmacopoeias as a purgative, following a report of its use for this purpose in the West Indies. *Ricinus* is the Latin word for a tick, as the mottled seeds of the plant are similar in shape to these parasites.

CULTIVATION Well-drained, humus-rich soil in sun. Starved or pot-bound plants tend to flower, rather than producing handsome foliage. Subject to statutory control as a weed in some countries, notably in parts of Australia.

PROPAGATION By seed sown in spring at 21°C (70°F). Germination is quicker if seeds are soaked in water for 24 hours prior to sowing.

HARVEST Ripe seeds are collected and pressed for oil.

⚠ **WARNING** All parts, especially seeds, are extremely toxic if eaten. Repeated handling of foliage or seeds may cause skin irritation or allergic reactions.

Ricinus communis

Ricinus communis 'Carmencita'

Ricinus communis 'Impala'

Ricinus communis 'Zanzibarensis'

■ *Ricinus communis* (castor oil plant, palma-christi)
Upright, fast-growing shrub with dark red stems and long-stalked, palmately lobed, toothed leaves, to 60cm (24in) across. Yellow-green female flowers, to 2.5cm (1in) across, each with a conspicuous red stigma, are borne above the males in ovoid spikes, to 15cm (6in) long, in summer; females are followed by red-brown, spiny capsules, to 2.5cm (1in) in diameter, containing three oblong, mottled, grey-brown seeds. Native to NE Africa and W Asia. ↕ 1.8m (6ft), ↔ 1–1.2m (3–4ft) as an annual; ↕ 10–12m (30–40ft), ↔ 4m (12ft) as an evergreen shrub. Heights for cultivars are for annual growth.
■ 'Carmencita' has bronze leaves, bright red female flowers, and red capsules. ↕ 2–3m (6–10ft), ↔ 1m (3ft). ■ 'Impala' is compact, with maroon foliage, creamy yellow flowers, and maroon capsules. ↕ 1.2m (4ft), ↔ 60–90cm (24–36in). ■ 'Zanzibarensis' has white-veined, green leaves, 50cm (20in) long. ↕ 2–3m (6–10ft).

HARDINESS Half hardy.

PARTS USED Oil.

PROPERTIES A purgative emollient herb with an unpleasant taste.

MEDICINAL USES Internally for constipation and acute diarrhoea due to food poisoning. Excess causes severe colic, vomiting, and purgation. Externally as an enema in severe constipation, and for irritating skin and eye conditions. Used in Ayurvedic medicine for

R

disorders of the nervous system.

CULINARY USES Castor oil is used to coat grains and legumes in India.

ECONOMIC USES Oil is added to soaps, cosmetics, and ophthalmic products, and is used in the making of candles, crayons, varnishes, lubricating oils, high-performance fuels, carbon paper, polyamide fibre, leather preservatives, fabric waterproofing, and dyes for cotton; also in the food industry to give nutty or buttery flavours. Castor oil repels insects, notably cockroaches. Seed residue is used in fertilizers, and in fibre and board manufacture.

RORIPPA

Rorippa nasturtium-aquaticum. See *Nasturtium officinale.*

ROSA
Rose

Rosaceae

A genus consisting of about 150 species of deciduous and semi-evergreen shrubs and climbers, widespread in northern temperate regions. The cultivation of roses dates back thousands of years. In many cases, the origins and correct names of roses are extremely difficult to elucidate. It is thought that *R. gallica* var. *officinalis* is descended from the S European *R. rubra*, and was named in the 13th century when it spread into Gaul (present-day France). In the 14th century, *R. × damascena* (known as *R.* 'Summer Damask' in the USA) was brought from Persia by knights returning from the Crusades. *Rosa rugosa* and *R. laevigata* are both of Asian origin. Roses have been important since earliest times in ritual, cosmetics, perfumes, and medicines. Various kinds were used medicinally by the ancient Greeks, Romans, and Persians; in AD77 Pliny recorded 32 different disorders that responded well to treatment by rose preparations. *Rosa gallica* var. *officinalis* and *R. × damascena* were widely grown in medieval times for medicinal purposes. *Rosa laevigata* was first mentioned in Chinese medical literature about AD470, and probably reached the USA via the East India Company in 1759; as the Cherokee rose it later became the state flower of Georgia. *Rosa rugosa* is used to a lesser extent in Chinese medicine and is fairly recent, being first mentioned in *Food as Materia Medica* during the Ming dynasty (AD1368–1644); it reached Europe, the USA, and Australia during the 19th century from its homelands in Japan and N China. Red rose petals were listed in the *British Pharmacopoeia* until the 1930s as an astringent and flavouring for medicines. Rose oil, or attar (otto) of roses, is a steam-distilled, clear essential oil consisting mainly of beta-damascenone, which gives the typical rose fragrance; its constituents include citronellol, an insecticidal, anti-rheumatic compound that is isolated commercially (but mainly from *Pelargonium* spp., see p.304) for use in rose-scented perfumes, cosmetics, and soap. The essential oil was originally extracted by macerating rose petals in oil or molten fat. In the 16th century, Persian chemists produced a superior oil by distillation. Genuine rose oil is a costly commodity, taking 0.98 tonnes of petals to produce 300g (11oz) of oil; for this reason, it is now largely synthesized. Rose absolute is a solvent-extracted, yellow-orange essential oil, widely used in perfumery. Rose leaf oil is also used. Some 96 per cent of women's perfumes and 42 per cent of men's fragrances contain rose oil, putting it on a par with jasmine in popularity. Rose oil also predominates in the anointing oil used in the coronation of British monarchs. Rosewater was first produced by a Persian physician, Avicenna, in the 1st century AD. "Cold cream" was originally known as "ointment of rosewater", because it contained rosewater and rose oil. Several different roses are traditionally grown for essential oil and rosewater, including *R. × centifolia* (cabbage rose, Provence rose, *rose de Mai*), *R. × damascena, R. gallica*, and variants of *R. × alba*, though any strongly scented rose can be used. Bulgarian rose attar is mainly from *R. × alba* and *R. × damascena*. *Rosa × damascena* 'Trigintipetala' (Kazanlik rose) is outstandingly fragrant but the true cultivar is rarely seen; *R.* 'Professeur Emile Perrot' is very similar and widely cultivated. Rosehips contain large amounts of vitamins, notably vitamin C; one cup of rosehip pulp contains as much vitamin C as 40 oranges. Towards the end of the Second World War, when citrus fruits were unavailable, 120–450 tonnes of rosehips were harvested from the wild in Britain each year to make rosehip syrup as a vitamin C supplement for children.

CULTIVATION Well-drained, moist, humus-rich, neutral to slightly

acid soil (including clay) in sun. *Rosa rubiginosa* enjoys dry calcareous conditions; *R. laevigata* thrives in poor soils; *R. rugosa* tolerates dry, sandy or coastal conditions. Remove dead and damaged wood, and prune lightly in early winter, removing weak growths. Most species and old roses flower on the previous year's growth and should not be cut back hard. Rosehips, especially of *R. rugosa*, may be damaged by birds. Leaves may be damaged by blackspot, downy mildew, rust, viruses, and sawfly. Buds and flowers are prone to attack by aphid.

PROPAGATION By seed sown in autumn (species only); by budding in summer; by hardwood cuttings in autumn.

HARVEST Petals are collected when flowers first open and distilled for oil and rosewater, used fresh for syrups, crushed into paste, or dried for use in decoctions. Fruits are picked when ripe and used fresh or dried in decoctions, or made into syrups and confectionery. Seeds (*R. rubiginosa*) from ripe fruits are processed commercially for oil extraction.

⚠ **WARNING** Hips and seeds contain irritant hairs. *R. canina* and *R. rubiginosa* are subject to statutory control as weeds in some countries, notably in parts of Australia and the USA.

■ *Rosa canina* (dog rose)
Variable deciduous shrub with arching stems, curved prickles, and pinnate leaves, to 5cm (2in) long, divided into 5–7 ovate leaflets. Scented, pale pink or white, five-petalled flowers, to 5cm (2in) across, are produced in clusters of 1–4 from early to midsummer, followed by ovoid scarlet hips, to 3cm (1¼in) long. Native to Europe, W Asia, and N Africa; naturalized in N America. ↨ 3m (10ft).

HARDINESS Fully hardy.

PARTS USED Fruits (hips), with seeds and irritant hairs removed.

Rosa canina

Rosa gallica

Rosa gallica var. *officinalis*

Rosa gallica 'Versicolor'

Rosa laevigata

PROPERTIES An acidic, astringent, tonic herb, rich in vitamins A, B1, B2, B3, C, and K, flavonoids, tannins, plant sugars and acids, pectin, carotenoids, and volatile oil.
MEDICINAL USES Internally for colds, influenza, minor infectious diseases, scurvy, and gastritis; also to control diarrhoea.
CULINARY USES Rosehips are used in making wine, vinegar, jams, jellies, syrup, soup, and tea.
ECONOMIC USES Fruits are made into syrup as a nutritional supplement, especially for babies. Syrup is also added to cough mixtures and used to flavour medicines. Extracts are added to vitamin C tablets, food supplements, herbal remedies, and herb teas.

Rosa × *damascena* (damask rose)
Vigorous, arching, deciduous shrub with grey-green leaves, divided into five, rarely seven, ovate to elliptic leaflets, to 6cm (2½in) long. Fragrant, semi-double, pale pink to white flowers, to 8cm (3in) across, are borne in clusters of up to 12 in summer, followed by bristly, red, cone-shaped fruits, to 2.5cm (1in) long. Native to the Middle East. ‡ 2m (6ft), ↔ 1.5m (5ft). 'Trigintipetala' syn. 'Kazanlik' (Kazanlik rose) has very fragrant, semi-double, red flowers. var. *versicolor* (York and Lancaster rose) bears loosely double flowers, to 6cm (2½in) across, marbled pale pink and deep pink.
HARDINESS Fully hardy.
PARTS USED Flower buds, petals.
PROPERTIES An aromatic, relaxing, tonic herb.
CULINARY USES Petals, with bitter "heel" removed, are added to salads, crystallized, made into jams, jellies, and syrups; used to scent tea.
ECONOMIC USES Petals are used to make rose oil, rose absolute, and rosewater, used in perfumery, and in bath and skin-care products. Rosewater is used to flavour confectionery

(notably Turkish Delight), desserts, sorbets, mousses, jams, syrups, and jellies. Petals are crystallized for decorating cakes and chocolates. Dried petals and flower buds are important ingredients of the N African spice mixture *ras-el-hanout*; also used in potpourris.

Rosa gallica (French rose, Provins rose)
Erect, suckering, deciduous shrub with bristly stems and leathery leaves divided into 3–5, occasionally seven, broadly elliptic to rounded, dark green leaflets. Fragrant, single or semi-double, rose-pink to crimson flowers, 4–8cm (1½–3in) across, are produced in summer, followed by almost spherical, brick-red, bristly hips. Found from S and C Europe to the Caucasus. ‡ 50cm–2m (20in–6ft), ↔ 1m (3ft).
var. *officinalis* (apothecary's rose) bears very fragrant, semi-double, crimson flowers. ‡ 80cm (32in), ↔ 1m (3ft). 'Versicolor' (*rosa mundi*) bears semi-double, deep pink flowers, 7–9cm (3–3½in) across, irregularly striped pale pink to white.
HARDINESS Fully hardy.
PARTS USED Flower buds, petals.
PROPERTIES An aromatic, astringent, tonic herb that controls bacterial infections, promotes healing, and improves morale.
MEDICINAL USES Internally for colds, bronchial infections, gastritis, diarrhoea, depression, and lethargy; externally for sore throat, eye irritations, minor injuries, and skin problems. Internally in Ayurvedic medicine, for inflammations, circulatory congestion, sore throat, mouth sores, and menstrual complaints. Combined with *Asparagus racemosus* (see p.135) as a tonic, and with *Hibiscus rosa-sinensis* (see p.235) or *Carthamus tinctorius* (see p.157) for menstrual irregularity. Used in aromatherapy to counter depression, anxiety, grief, and negative feelings.

CULINARY USES As for *R.* × *damascena*.
ECONOMIC USES As for *R.* × *damascena*.

■ *Rosa laevigata* (Cherokee rose)
Vigorous, evergreen, climbing shrub with stout prickles and glossy, dark green leaves divided into three, rarely five, lanceolate to ovate leaflets. Solitary, white, single, fragrant flowers 5–10cm (2–4in) across, with persistent bristly sepals, appear in early summer, followed by pear-shaped, bristly, orange-red hips, to 4cm (1½in) long. Native to E and S China, Taiwan, and SE Asia; naturalized in S USA. ↔ 2–6m (6–20ft).
HARDINESS Frost hardy.
PARTS USED Fruits (*jing ying zi*).
PROPERTIES An acidic astringent herb that regulates kidney energy, stimulates the digestion, and is effective against many bacterial and viral infections.
MEDICINAL USES Internally for urinary dysfunction, infertility, and chronic diarrhoea.
ECONOMIC USES Major source of rosehips for the food and herbal products industries.

■ *Rosa rubiginosa* syn. *R. eglanteria* (eglantine, sweet briar)
Dense, arching to upright, deciduous shrub with hooked thorns and pinnate leaves divided into 5–9 ovate to rounded, apple-scented leaflets that bear rust-coloured, sticky hairs on the undersides. Fragrant, pale to bright pink flowers, to 5cm (2in) across, appear in summer, followed by scarlet, round to ovoid hips, to 2.5cm (1in) long. Native to Europe, W Asia, and N Africa; naturalized in N America. ↔ 2.5m (8ft).
HARDINESS Fully hardy.
PARTS USED Oil (seeds).
PROPERTIES A healing herb that promotes tissue regeneration.
MEDICINAL USES Externally for burns, scars, and wrinkles.

■ *Rosa rugosa* (hedgehog rose, Japanese rose, Ramanas rose, tomato rose)
Vigorous, dense, deciduous shrub with very prickly stems and deeply veined leaves divided into 7–9, rarely 11, narrowly oblong leaflets, 2.5–5cm (1–2in) long. Single, fragrant, magenta-pink flowers, 8cm (3in) across, appear in summer, followed by globose, tomato-like, red hips, to 2.5cm (1in) long, which have a conspicuous crown of sepals. Native to E Russia, N China, Japan, and Korea. ↔ 1–2.5m (3–8ft).
■ 'Alba' has single white flowers, 9cm (3½in) across, opening from pink-flushed buds.
■ 'Rubra' has purple-pink flowers.
HARDINESS Fully hardy.
PARTS USED Flowers (*mei gui hua*), petals, fruits.
PROPERTIES An aromatic tonic herb that stimulates the liver, improves circulation, and acts as an antidote in antimony poisoning (flowers).
MEDICINAL USES Internally for poor appetite and digestion, and menstrual complaints arising from constrained liver energy (flowers). Combined with *Leonurus cardiaca* (see p.258)

Rosa rugosa

Rosa rubiginosa

Rosa rugosa 'Alba'

Rosa rugosa 'Rubra'

or *L. sibiricus* (see p.258) for heavy menstruation.
CULINARY USES Petals are crystallized, made into jam, syrup, and spirit (*mei kuei lu*), and used to make rose congou tea. Fruits are made into purée, jam, jelly, wine, soup, and tea.
ECONOMIC USES Fruits are an important source of vitamin C and flavonoids for food supplements, especially in the USA.

ROSMARINUS
Rosemary

Lamiaceae

This genus contains two species of evergreen shrubs, native to dry rocky woodland and scrub, often in coastal areas around the Mediterranean. *Rosmarinus officinalis* is very variable and has a wide distribution in Mediterranean regions. The other species, *R. eriocalyx* (also known as *R. lavandulaceus* and *R. officinalis* var. *prostratus*), is usually prostrate and has a much more restricted distribution on calcareous rocks in S Spain and N Africa. Opinion differs on the number of species in the genus; some authorities regard *R. officinalis* as the only species. The situation is complicated by the fact that plants in cultivation as *R. lavandulaceus* may be prostrate forms of *R. officinalis* rather than true *R. eriocalyx. Rosmarinus officinalis* and its many variants are popular worldwide as garden and container plants. Low-growing variants make attractive specimens for pots, steep banks, or the tops of walls. Rosemary is a symbol of friendship, loyalty, and remembrance in many parts of the world; it is traditionally carried by mourners at funerals and by the bride at her wedding. Greek scholars wore garlands of rosemary when they were taking examinations to improve their memory and concentration. In the 14th century, Queen Izabella of Hungary claimed that, at the age of 72 years, when crippled with gout and rheumatism, she had so regained her strength and beauty by using Hungary water (rosemary tops macerated in alcohol) that the King of Poland proposed to her. Rosemary contains volatile oil, flavonoids, and phenolic acids, which are strongly antiseptic and anti-inflammatory. Other constituents include: tannins, which are astringent; rosmaricine, which has stimulant and painkilling effects; and rosmarinic acid, an anti-inflammatory that has potential in the treatment of toxic shock syndrome. The flavonoid diosmin is reputedly more effective than rutin (see *Ruta graveolens*, p.352) in reducing capillary fragility. Essential oil of rosemary may vary considerably in constituents, depending on the plant's genetics and growing conditions; oil with a high camphor content is good for medicinal purposes but less pleasant in flavour for cooking. The strong flavour and tough foliage of rosemary need care when used in food. Tender tips, chopped finely, are best. Alternatively, add a sprig that can be removed at the end of cooking. *Rosmarinus* is from the Latin for "dew of the sea", referring to the dew-like appearance of its pale blue flowers from a distance.
CULTIVATION Well-drained, ideally neutral to alkaline soil, in full sun, with shelter in cold areas. Tolerates soil pH 5–8. Remove dead stems and straggly shoots in spring. Prune after flowering to encourage bushy growth. Rosemary dislikes cold wet winters, and rarely survives prolonged freezing. Affected plants rot at the roots, often remaining green above ground until late spring. They seldom recover, but cuttings can usually be rooted successfully before the plant dies.
PROPAGATION By seed sown in spring (species only); by semi-ripe cuttings in summer.
HARVEST Leaves and flowering tops are collected in spring and early summer, and distilled for oil, or dried for infusions, decoctions, extracts, spirits, and tinctures.

▣ *Rosmarinus officinalis* (rosemary)
Variable, aromatic, evergreen shrub with upright to sprawling branches and tough, blunt-ended, needle-like leaves, to 2.5cm (1in) long. Pale to dark blue, rarely pink or white, tubular, two-lipped flowers appear in spring. Native to the Mediterranean region. ‡2m (6ft), ↔ 1.5–2m (5–6ft). ▣ var. *albiflorus* has white flowers. ▣ ‘Arp’ is exceptionally hardy, with an open habit and thick, resinous, grey-green, lemon-scented leaves. Found at Arp, Texas (USA), in 1972. Good flavour for cooking. ▣ ‘Aureus’ (gilded rosemary) has irregular yellow variegation. ▣ ‘Benenden Blue’ syn. ‘Collingwood Ingram’ is small-growing, with a dense cascading habit, very narrow, dark green, glossy foliage, and large, sky-blue flowers. Good for containers. ‘Blue Boy’ is dwarf, compact, and free-flowering, with very small leaves. ‡60cm (24in), ↔ 30cm (12in). ▣ ‘Fota Blue’ is semi-prostrate and free-flowering, with very dark blue flowers. Rather tender. ‡30–45cm (12–18in), ↔ 60–90cm (24–36in). ‘Gorizia’ has stout upright stems, very large leaves, and medium-blue flowers. Good flavour for cooking. Originated in Gorizia, on the border between Italy and Slovenia. ‘Joyce de Baggio’ syn. ‘Golden Rain’ is compact, with golden, green-centred leaves and dark blue flowers. ▣ ‘Majorca Pink’ has a columnar arching habit, small, dull green leaves, and mauve-pink flowers. ‡1.2m (4ft), ↔ 30–60cm (12–24in). ▣ ‘McConnell's Blue’ is a spreading prostrate rosemary, with broad leaves and clear blue flowers. ‡30–40cm (12–16in), ↔ 1m (3ft). ▣ ‘Miss Jessopp's Upright’ syn. ‘Pyramidalis’ is vigorous, with a columnar upright habit and pale blue flowers. ▣ ‘Pinkie’ has short, grey-green leaves and pink flowers. ‡1.2m (4ft), ↔ 1m (3ft). ▣ ‘Primley Blue’ has an upright habit and clear blue flowers. ‡1m (3ft), ↔ 60cm (24in). ▣ Prostratus Group syn. *R. lavandulaceus* hort. (creeping rosemary) has an arching to prostrate habit. Good for pots, hanging baskets, banks, walls, rock gardens, and bonsai. ‡15–30cm (6–12in), ↔ 60–90cm (24–36in). ▣ ‘Roseus’ has pink flowers. ‘Santa Barbara’ syn. ‘Lockwood de Forest’ has a

Rosmarinus officinalis

R. officinalis var. *albiflorus*

R. officinalis ‘Arp’

R. officinalis ‘Aureus’

R. officinalis ‘Benenden Blue’

R. officinalis ‘Fota Blue’

R. officinalis ‘Majorca Pink’

R. officinalis ‘McConnell's Blue’

R. officinalis ‘Miss Jessopp's Upright’

R. officinalis ‘Pinkie’

mounding habit, with very dark green, shiny foliage and clear blue flowers. ▣ 'Severn Sea' has a spreading arching habit, narrow leaves, and violet-blue flowers. ↨→ 1m (3ft). ▣ 'Silver Spires' has white-variegated foliage. Tends to revert. ▣ 'Sissinghurst Blue' is exceptionally free-flowering and relatively hardy, with an upright habit. ↕ 1–1.2m (3–4ft), ↔ 1m (3ft). ▣ 'Sudbury Blue' has dense, blue-green foliage, an upright habit, and midblue flowers. ↕ 1.5–2m (5–6ft), ↔ 1.2–1.5m (4–5ft). ▣ 'Tuscan Blue' is fast-growing, with an upright habit, slightly glossy leaves, and dark blue flowers. Good flavour for cooking. ↨→ 1–2m (3–6ft).

HARDINESS Fully hardy (borderline).

PARTS USED Leaves, flowering tops, oil.

PROPERTIES An aromatic restorative herb that relaxes spasms, relieves pain, and increases perspiration rate. It also stimulates the liver and gall bladder, improves digestion and circulation, and controls many pathogenic organisms.

MEDICINAL USES Internally for depression, apathy, nervous exhaustion, headaches and migraines associated with nervous tension or feeling cold, poor circulation, and digestive problems associated with anxiety. Excess causes abortion in pregnant women and convulsions. Externally for rheumatism, arthritis, neuralgia, muscular injuries, wounds, dandruff, scurf, and hair loss. May be combined with *Avena sativa* (see p.138), *Scutellaria lateriflora* (see p.365), or *Verbena officinalis* (see p.402) for depression.

CULINARY USES Fresh or dried leaves are used to flavour meat (especially lamb and goat), sausages, stuffings, soups, and stews; also to make tea. Very small amounts, often ground or powdered, are added to biscuits and jams. Fresh sprigs are steeped whole in vinegar, wine, or olive oil, to give a rosemary flavour to sauces and dressings. Flowers can be added to salads.

ECONOMIC USES Extracts are used in hair, skin-care, and bath products.

▣ ▣ ▣ ▣ ▣ ▣

ROUPELLIA
Roupellia grata. See *Strophanthus gratus*.

ROXBURGHIA
Roxburghia gloriosa. See *Stemona tuberosa*.

RUBIA
Madder

Rubiaceae

A genus of about 60 species of perennials and subshrubs, occurring in Europe, Asia, and Africa. Various species contain pigments, which include alizarin (madder red), purpurin (madder purple), rubiacin (madder orange), and xanthine (madder yellow). These compounds are similar to those in the related *Galium aparine* (see p.219) and *G. verum* (see p.219). *Rubia tinctorum* yields a permanent red dye, known as "Turkey red", traditionally used to colour Turkish fezzes, soldiers' uniforms, and hunting jackets, which was originally exported from Turkey for cultivation in the main textile centres of N Europe. The main pigment, alizarin, was synthesized in 1868, reducing demand for the cultivated plant. Though best known as a dye plant, *R. tinctorum* is used medicinally too; it was mentioned by Pliny (AD23–79) as a cure for jaundice. *Rubia cordifolia* was first described in Chinese medicine in the *Shen Nong Canon of Herbs*, during the Han dynasty (206BC–AD23). It also has a long history of use in Ayurvedic medicine. The whole plant is used to dye fabrics reds or pinks. Mixed with indigo, it produces "Egyptian purple"; Coptic textiles, c.AD500, were dyed using *R. cordifolia*. It contains munjistin, an anthraquinone, and pigments purpurin, pseudopurpurin, and purpuroxanthin, which are also found in *R. tinctorum*; it does not contain alizarin. *Rubia* is from the Latin *ruber*, "red", referring to the red dye yielded by these plants.

Rubia cordifolia

CULTIVATION Well-drained soil in sun or partial shade. *Rubia tinctorum* prefers light dry soil, and thrives in alkaline conditions.

PROPAGATION By seed sown when ripe; by division in spring.

HARVEST Rhizomes and roots are lifted in autumn from plants at least three years old, and peeled and dried for decoctions and powders. Chinese herbalists also lift roots in spring. Whole plants, including roots, are lifted from two-year-old plants in spring and autumn for dye production.

⚠ **WARNING** Internal use of madders stains urine, milk, and bones red.

▣ *Rubia cordifolia* syn. *R. manjith* (Indian madder, *manjishta*, *munjeet*)
Perennial climber or scrambler with long red roots, weak, four-angled stems, and whorls of four slender, long-pointed, heart-shaped leaves, to 8cm (3in) long. The whole plant is covered in minute hooked bristles. Tiny, red-brown to yellow-green flowers appear in loose clusters from summer to autumn, followed by globose, fleshy, black fruits, to 8mm (⅜in) across, containing red juice. Native to mountainous regions of Asia, from the Himalayas to Japan, extending into SE Asia and tropical Africa. ↕ 6m (20ft).

HARDINESS Frost hardy.

PARTS USED Whole plant, roots (*qian cao gen*).

PROPERTIES A bitter–sweet, cooling herb that is diuretic and expectorant, checks bleeding, controls coughing, reduces inflammation, and has anti-bacterial effects (Chinese medicine). It also stimulates the circulation, dissolves and inhibits formation of kidney stones, and has alterative effects (Ayurvedic medicine).

MEDICINAL USES Internally for abnormal uterine bleeding, internal and external haemorrhage, bronchitis, and rheumatism (Chinese medicine); menstrual and menopausal complaints, jaundice, hepatitis, kidney stones, bladder stones and gallstones, herpes, skin complaints, and dysentery (Ayurvedic medicine). Externally, combined with honey for skin inflammations and with *Glycyrrhiza glabra* (see p.227) for burns and injuries (Ayurvedic medicine).

ECONOMIC USES Source of natural red dyes.

▣ ▣ ▣ ▣

R. officinalis
'Primley Blue'

R. officinalis
Prostratus Group

R. officinalis
'Roseus'

R. officinalis
'Severn Sea'

R. officinalis
'Silver Spires'

R. officinalis
'Sissinghurst Blue'

R. officinalis
'Sudbury Blue'

R. officinalis
'Tuscan Blue'

R

Rubia tinctorum

■ ***Rubia tinctorum*** (madder)
Perennial climber or scrambler with a red branched rhizome and whorls of rough, lanceolate to ovate, stalkless leaves, to 10cm (4in) long. Tiny, pale yellow-green to cream flowers are borne in loose clusters in summer and autumn, followed by fleshy, red-brown to black berries, 6mm (¼in) in diameter. Native to SE Europe and W and C Asia.
‡ 25cm–1m (10–36in).
HARDINESS Fully hardy.
PARTS USED Roots.
PROPERTIES An antiseptic, diuretic, laxative herb that stimulates the liver and uterus, and relaxes spasms.
MEDICINAL USES Internally for kidney and bladder stones. Used in N African folk medicine for anaemia and blood diseases, and as an aphrodisiac; also as a tonic, appetizer, and expectorant. Externally for wounds, ulcers, and sciatica.
ECONOMIC USES Dried roots are used as a source of natural red, pink, orange, apricot, and purple dyes. Alizarin is used in making dyes, and yields pigments for inks and paints.
▨ ▣ ◢

R

RUBUS
Bramble

Rosaceae

A cosmopolitan genus of about 250 species of deciduous, semi-evergreen, and evergreen shrubs, scramblers, climbers, and trailers, found worldwide in a variety of habitats, from woodland and scrub to coastal dunes and uplands. Most species produce edible fruits, though some are rather tasteless. *Rubus idaeus* (raspberry) has been cultivated in England since the mid-16th century. The western N American *R. ursinus* (dewberry) was cultivated in the early 19th century; many hybrids were developed using this species, notably the loganberry, which is a dewberry–raspberry cross. *Rubus fruticosus* (blackberry) remained a wild-collected food until well into the 20th century, although hybridization began in the 19th century. Fossil evidence shows that raspberries and blackberries have formed part of the human diet

from very early times. The raspberry was mentioned by the Roman poet Propertius (c.50–16BC), and the blackberry by Greek dramatist Aeschylus (c.525–456BC) and physician Hippocrates (c.460–357BC). The roots and foliage of most *Rubus* spp. contain tannins and flavonoids, while the fruits are rich in vitamins A, B1, and C, organic acids, sugars, and pectin. *Rubus fruticosus* was used by the ancient Greeks to treat gout, and by the Romans for sore mouths and inflammation of the bowel. Various species were used by native N Americans to cure diarrhoea and dysentery, including *R. hispidus* (swamp dewberry), *R. laciniatus* (cut-leafed bramble), *R. odoratus* (purple-flowered raspberry, thimbleberry), *R. parviflorus* (thimbleberry), *R. procumbens* (creeping blackberry), and *R. villosus* (American blackberry), which entered the *US Pharmacopoeia* in 1820 as an astringent tonic. *Rubus idaeus* was used by N American colonists, but it proved less successful than native species such as *R. occidentalis* (black raspberry, thimbleberry), with which it was crossed to give black-red or purple raspberries. *Rubus coreanus* was first mentioned in Chinese medical literature c.AD500. It is one of several Asian species known as "ghost brambles" or "white-washed brambles", because of their stems, which are coated in a grey-white wax. It is used interchangeably with *R. chingii*. The red-fruited *R. parvifolius* (Japanese bramble) is also used; leaves and roots are decocted for skin problems, and unripe dried fruits are regarded as tonic and aphrodisiac.
CULTIVATION Moist, well-drained soil in sun or partial shade. *Rubus fruticosus* may be trained on wires or solid surfaces to make harvesting easier. Remove old stems after fruiting. In spring, lightly prune plants grown for fruit. Plants may be damaged by aphid, plant bugs, raspberry beetle, crown gall, *Rubus* stunt, *Botrytis*, and virus disease. *Rubus fruticosus* is subject to statutory control as a weed in some countries, notably in parts of Australia.

PROPAGATION By seed sown in spring (species only); by softwood cuttings in summer; by leaf-bud cuttings in late summer; by hardwood cuttings in winter; by tip layering in summer (*R. fruticosus*); by root cuttings and suckers during dormancy (*R. idaeus*); by division in early spring or autumn.
HARVEST Leaves are picked before flowering and dried for use in infusions, liquid extracts, and tablets. Roots are lifted in summer and dried for use in decoctions. Fruits are harvested when ripe and dried for use in decoctions (*R. coreanus*), or used fresh or frozen for juice, syrups, and culinary purposes.

■ ***Rubus coreanus*** (Chinese raspberry)
Deciduous suckering shrub with dark, wax-coated, erect or arching stems, bearing stout prickles, and leaves divided into 5–7 oval toothed leaflets, to 7cm (3in) long, which have white woolly undersides. Small pink flowers appear in clusters in summer, followed by small, red to black fruits. Native to Korea, Japan, and China. ‡ 4m (12ft), ↔ indefinite.
HARDINESS Fully hardy.
PARTS USED Fruits (*fu pen zi*).
PROPERTIES An astringent herb that acts as a kidney and liver tonic.
MEDICINAL USES Internally for complaints associated with disturbed liver and kidney functions, such as urinary dysfunction, premature greying, blurred vision, infertility, impotence, and premature ejaculation.
▨ ▣

■ ***Rubus fruticosus*** (blackberry, bramble)
Very variable, semi-evergreen shrub with prickly stems and divided leaves, about 15cm (6in) long. Clusters of white to pink flowers are borne in summer, followed by juicy black fruits, 1–2cm (½–¾in) long. Native to Europe. ‡↔ 4m (12ft). 'Loch Ness' is a thornless, mid- to late-season blackberry with very large fruits.
HARDINESS Fully hardy.
PARTS USED Leaves, roots, root bark, fruits.
PROPERTIES An astringent, tonic, mildly diuretic herb.

Rubus coreanus

Rubus fruticosus

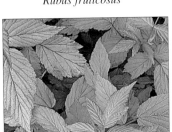

Rubus idaeus 'Aureus'

Rubus idaeus 'Autumn Bliss'

Rubus idaeus

MEDICINAL USES Internally for diarrhoea, dysentery, haemorrhoids, and cystitis. Externally for sore throat, mouth ulcers, and gum inflammations (leaves, roots, and root bark).
CULINARY USES Dried leaves are made into tea. Fruits are eaten raw or cooked, and made into syrups, cordials, jams, jellies, and wine; also used to flavour vinegar and colour red wine.
ECONOMIC USES Dried leaves are an ingredient of herb tea blends.

■ *Rubus idaeus* (raspberry)
Suckering deciduous shrub with bristly stems and pinnate leaves divided into 3–7 ovate toothed leaflets, which have white woolly undersides. White flowers, about 1cm (½in) across, are produced in drooping clusters in summer, followed by aromatic, juicy, red fruits. Native to Europe and temperate Asia; naturalized in N America. ↕1–1.7m (3–5½ft), ↔1–2m (3–6ft). ■'Aureus' has bright golden leaves. Makes good ground cover in semi-shade. ↕1–1.2m (3–4ft), ↔60–90cm (24–36in). ■'Autumn Bliss' bears well-flavoured berries from late summer to early autumn. Midseason 'Glen Ample' is non-bristly and heavy cropping.
HARDINESS Fully hardy.
PARTS USED Leaves, fruits.
PROPERTIES An astringent herb that tones the uterine muscles during pregnancy.
MEDICINAL USES Internally for diarrhoea and as a preparation for childbirth (leaves). Given to pregnant women in the last three months and during labour, but not in early pregnancy. Externally for tonsillitis, mouth inflammation, sores, conjunctivitis, minor wounds, burns, and varicose ulcers (leaves). Combines well with *Agrimonia eupatoria* (see p.107) and *Geum urbanum* (see p.224) for diarrhoea; with *Euphrasia officinalis* (see p.210) as an eye lotion; and with *Salvia officinalis* (see p.355) as a mouthwash and gargle.
CULINARY USES Fruits are eaten raw, cooked or made into jam, jelly, juice, syrup, compote, coulis, wine, and liqueur; also to flavour vinegar and beer. Leaves are used to make tea.
ECONOMIC USES Raspberry products and flavours are important in the food, drink, and confectionery industries; extracts are used to flavour medicines; essence is added to shampoos and bath products.

RUDBECKIA
Rudbeckia purpurea. See *Echinacea purpurea.*

RUMEX
Dock, sorrel
Polygonaceae

Some 200 species of annuals, biennials, and perennials make up this genus, which ranges throughout northern temperate regions. *Rumex scutatus* is one of the few species with any merit as an ornamental, though it may be difficult to eradicate when well established.

Rumex crispus (curled dock) and *R. obtusifolius* (broad-leaved dock, lapathum), long used to treat skin complaints, are similar in constituents, containing laxative anthraquinones; they stimulate bile flow and trigger the excretion of toxins. *Rumex crispus* gained ascendancy among 19th-century American Physiomedicalists and predominates in modern practice. The roots of *R. aquatica* (water dock) are powdered as a dentifrice and used internally in similar ways to *R. crispus.* According to Pliny, Julius Caesar's soldiers were cured of scurvy by the use of *herba britannica* (since identified as *R. aquatica*). *Rumex acetosella* (sheep's sorrel) is best known as an ingredient of "essiac", a native N American, anti-cancer remedy that also includes *Arctium lappa* (see p.127), *Rheum palmatum* (see p.344), and *Ulmus rubra* (see p.397). Most species contain oxalates, similar to those found in spinach and rhubarb. Oxalates are poisonous in excess, especially for those with a tendency to rheumatism, arthritis, gout, kidney stones, and hyperacidity. They are also acidic, which may affect sensitive teeth. In the past, young leaves of several species of *Rumex* were picked as pot-herbs. Culpeper regarded docks as "exceeding strengthening to the liver and as wholesome a pot-herb as any" (*The English Physician Enlarged*, 1653). Most people today would find docks unpalatable, but sorrels remain popular.
CULTIVATION Moist soil in sun or partial shade. *Rumex crispus* has deep roots and may be difficult to eradicate when established. It is subject to statutory control as a weed in some countries, notably in parts of Australia.
PROPAGATION By seed sown in spring (species only); by division in autumn or spring.
HARVEST Leaves are picked when young and used fresh. Roots are lifted in autumn and dried for use in decoctions, liquid extracts, and tinctures.

■ *Rumex acetosa* (sheep's sorrel)
Clump-forming perennial with pale green stems and sagittate leaves, to 15cm (6in) long. Red-brown flowers are borne in slender loose spikes from early summer, followed by tiny hard fruits. Native to northern temperate and arctic regions. ↕50cm–1.2m (20–48in), ↔25–45cm (10–18in). 'Profusion' is non-flowering and produces new leaves throughout the growing season.
HARDINESS Fully hardy.
PARTS USED Leaves.
PROPERTIES An acidic, astringent, cooling herb with diuretic effects.
CULINARY USES Fresh young leaves are added to salads, sauces, soups, soft cheese, and egg dishes; also puréed as a stuffing for fish, or to add colour and acidity to mayonnaise and pancake batter.
ECONOMIC USES Juice is used to remove rust, mould, and ink stains from linen, wood, silver, and wicker.

■ *Rumex crispus* (curled dock, yellow dock)
Variable erect perennial with a stout rootstock and lanceolate leaves, to 30cm (12in) long, which

Rumex acetosa

have noticeably wavy margins. Very small, green flowers are produced in simple or little-branched whorls in summer, followed by tiny woody fruits. Native to Europe and Africa; naturalized in most temperate regions. ↕30cm–1.5m (1–5ft), ↔45–90cm (18–36in).
HARDINESS Fully hardy.
PARTS USED Roots.
PROPERTIES A bitter, astringent, cooling herb that stimulates the liver and gall bladder, cleanses toxins, and has a laxative effect.
MEDICINAL USES Internally for chronic skin diseases, jaundice, constipation (especially associated with skin eruptions), liver disorders, and anaemia. Excess may cause nausea and dermatitis. Combined with *Arctium lappa* (see p.127), *Taraxacum officinale* (see p.382), or *Smilax* spp. (see p.370) for skin conditions, and with molasses as a blood tonic. Used for dry cough, sore throat, and laryngitis in homeopathy.

■ *Rumex scutatus* (buckler-leaf sorrel, French sorrel)
Low-growing, mat-forming perennial with cordate to hastate leaves, to 5cm (2in) long. Red-green flowers appear in loose, sparely branched panicles in summer, turning pale

Rumex crispus

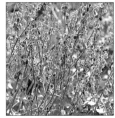
Rumex scutatus

Rumex scutatus 'Silver Shield'

brown as fruits ripen. Native to Europe, W Asia, and N Africa. ‡15–50cm (6–20in), ↔ 1.2m (4ft).
◨ 'Silver Shield' has silver-green leaves.
HARDINESS Fully hardy.
PARTS USED Leaves.
CULINARY USES Leaves are used in the same ways as those of *R. acetosa* but are more acidic.
▨ ☑

RUSCUS
Ruscaceae

Six species of evergreen, rhizomatous, clump-forming subshrubs belong to this genus, which occurs in the Azores, N Africa, and through W Europe to the Caspian Sea. They are unusual in having flattened, leaf-like branches, the true leaves being reduced to scales. *Ruscus aculeatus* makes excellent ground cover beneath trees; it is an attractive plant with disproportionately large fruits. Most plants are male or female, though hermaphrodite clones are known and are available from some nurseries. The common name "butcher's broom" refers to its traditional use in bundles to clean the floors of butchers' shops. *Ruscus aculeatus* contains saponins similar to those found in *Dioscorea* spp. (see p.194); they cause blood vessels to contract and reduce vascular permeability. Dioscorides (1st century AD) mentioned it as a remedy for kidney stones. Exploitation and wild-collection of *Ruscus* spp. may be subject to management measures.
CULTIVATION Well-drained to dry soil in sun or shade. Remove dead shoots in spring. For fruiting, plant hermaphrodite specimens, or set male and female plants in groups of several females to each male.
PROPAGATION By seed sown in autumn; by division in spring or autumn. Seeds may take 18 months to germinate.
HARVEST Plants are cut in late spring, and roots lifted in autumn, and dried for use in decoctions, ointments, and suppositories. Young shoots are gathered in spring for culinary use.

Ruscus aculeatus (box holly, butcher's broom, Jew's myrtle)
Small, clump-forming subshrub with erect shoots bearing stiff, ovate, leaf-like cladophylls, to 2.5cm (1in) long, tipped with spines. Tiny green flowers appear in late winter and spring on the upper side of the cladophylls, followed on female or hermaphrodite plants by globose red fruits, 8mm (⅜in) in diameter. Native to Europe, N Turkey, N Africa, and the Azores.
‡ 75cm–1.2m (2½–4ft), ↔ 1m (3ft).
HARDINESS Fully hardy.
PARTS USED Whole plant, young shoots, roots.
PROPERTIES An aromatic, diuretic, mildly laxative herb that reduces inflammation, increases perspiration, and constricts the veins.
MEDICINAL USES Internally for jaundice, gout, and kidney and bladder stones; also for venous insufficiency and haemorrhoids. Contraindicated for hypertension.

Externally for haemorrhoids.
CULINARY USES Young shoots are eaten like asparagus.
▨ ▨ ▨ ◨ ☑

RUTA
Rue

Rutaceae

A genus of eight species of strong-smelling, evergreen or semi-evergreen subshrubs, found in dry rocky places in Mediterranean regions, the Canary Islands, NE Africa, and SW Asia. In spite of its widespread use as a medicinal herb in the past, rue is little used for medicinal or culinary purposes today. Nevertheless, rue is an enduringly popular garden plant; it is one of the finest, grey-leafed evergreens, and remains neat and attractive all year. The common name, "herb of grace", refers to the tradition of using a sprig of rue to sprinkle holy water during Mass. *Ruta graveolens* contains flavonoids (notably rutin) that reduce capillary fragility (which may explain why rue is a traditional remedy for failing eyesight), together with a pungent volatile oil, furanocoumarins (including bergapten which sensitizes the skin to sunlight), and alkaloids. The potent chemistry of rue has always been regarded as protective: it was an ingredient of Mithridates's antidotes, and of "four thieves' vinegar", which protected from contagion a band of thieves who plundered the bodies of plague victims; posies of rue and *Artemisia abrotanum* (southernwood, see p.132) were once placed in courtrooms to ward off jail fever. Rue is also mentioned a number of times in the Bible, though this is more likely to refer to *R. chalepensis* (Egyptian rue, fringed rue), which has a more southerly distribution. Egyptian rue is used for flavouring in N Africa, especially in sausages known as *merguez*.
CULTIVATION Well-drained, neutral to alkaline soil in sun. Cut back hard (but not into main stem) in spring. May suffer from root rot in damp conditions.
PROPAGATION By seed (except 'Jackman's Blue') sown in spring; by semi-ripe cuttings in summer. 'Variegata' is unusual among variegated cultivars in coming true from seed.
HARVEST Leaves are picked in spring and summer, and dried for use in infusions, liquid extracts, and powders.
⚠ **WARNING** Serious skin irritant in sunlight, causing severe blistering.

◨ *Ruta graveolens* (herb of grace, herbygrass, rue)
Small, evergreen or semi-evergreen subshrub with glaucous, grey-green leaves, to 15cm (6in) long, deeply divided into numerous obovate lobes. Mustard-yellow, fringed, four-petalled flowers, to 1cm (½in) across, appear in summer, followed by four-lobed capsules. Native to SE Europe.
‡ 60cm (24in), ↔ 30–45cm (12 –18in). ◨ 'Jackman's Blue' has blue-grey leaves. ◨ 'Variegata' has

Ruta graveolens

Ruta graveolens 'Jackman's Blue'

Ruta graveolens 'Variegata'

irregular creamy white marks.
HARDINESS Fully hardy.
PARTS USED Leaves.
PROPERTIES A bitter, pungent, warming herb that stimulates the uterus, relaxes spasms, improves digestion, increases perspiration, and strengthens capillaries.
MEDICINAL USES Internally for menstrual problems, colic, epilepsy, palsy, and rheumatic pain. Excess affects central nervous system and may prove fatal. Contraindicated during pregnancy. Externally for sore eyes, earache, skin diseases, neuralgia, and rheumatism. Used in homeopathy for sprains, bruising over bones, tennis elbow, backache, weak eyesight, and eye strain.
CULINARY USES The pungent bitter leaves can be used to flavour vinegar. Seeds are used to flavour palm wine (N Africa), and are ground as an ingredient of Ethiopian spice mixtures.
ECONOMIC USES Leaves are used to flavour Italian grape spirit (*grappa*), and were an ingredient of sack (mead).
▨ ◨ ☑ ☑

S

SALIX
Osier, willow

Salicaceae

In this genus there are about 300 species of deciduous trees and shrubs, which occur worldwide, except in Australia. *Salix alba* (white willow) is a common tree in wetlands and near watercourses. It is less often planted in gardens than its varieties, which have colourful bare stems in winter. Though sometimes labelled *S. alba* 'Tristis', the familiar golden weeping

R

willow is a hybrid, more correctly known as *S.* × *sepulchralis* var. *chrysocoma*. The willow was also once regarded as a symbol of grief: garlands of the leaves were worn by those deserted by their loves. In parts of England, sprays of willow are woven into crosses at Easter. Willow bark was described by Dioscorides (1st century AD) as a remedy for relieving pain and lowering fever, and long before this it is mentioned on clay tablets of the Sumerian period (4th millennium BC) as an anti-rheumatic. It contains salicylic acid, which was first synthesized in 1838 and provides the basis of aspirin. Various other species, including *S. cinerea* (grey willow), *S. fragilis* (crack willow), the American *S. nigra* (black willow), *S. pentandra* (bay willow), and *S. purpurea* (purple osier), are used interchangeably with *S. alba* for medicinal purposes. Several other species were used by native N Americans, who drank strong, willow-bark tea to induce sweating as a cure for fever. In South Africa, *S. mucronata* is similarly used to relieve fever and rheumatism.

CULTIVATION Moist to wet, deep soil in sun. Willows are susceptible to aphid, caterpillars, scale insects, sawfly, leaf beetles, willow heart rot, rust, and watermark disease. Plants grown for winter colour are cut back to ground level in spring at least once every three years.

PROPAGATION By greenwood cuttings in early summer; by hardwood cuttings in winter.

HARVEST Leaves are collected during the growing season and used fresh or dried for infusions. Bark is removed throughout the summer and dried for use in decoctions, liquid extracts, powders, tablets, and tinctures.

■ *Salix alba* (white willow)
Large tree with deeply fissured, grey-brown bark, ascending branches, and lanceolate tapering leaves, to 10cm (4in) long. Flowers appear as yellow male catkins, to 5cm (2in) long, and

Salix alba

Salix alba subsp. *vitellina*

Salix alba subsp. *vitellina* 'Britzensis'

stalkless, yellow-green female catkins, 3cm (1¼in) long, with the new leaves in spring. Native to Europe, N Africa, and C Asia. ‡25m (80ft), ↔ 10m (30ft). ■ subsp. *vitellina* (golden willow) has yellow to orange young stems. ■ subsp. *vitellina* 'Britzensis' (scarlet willow) has bright orange-red young stems.

HARDINESS Fully hardy.

PARTS USED Leaves, bark.

PROPERTIES A bitter, astringent, cooling herb that relieves pain, lowers fever, and reduces inflammation.

MEDICINAL USES Internally for minor feverish illnesses and colic (leaves), rheumatism, arthritis, gout, inflammatory stages of auto-immune diseases, diarrhoea and dysentery, feverish illnesses, neuralgia, and headache (bark). Combined with *Actaea racemosa* (see p.102), *Apium graveolens* (see p.125), and *Guaiacum officinale* (see p.229) for rheumatoid arthritis; and with *Hypericum perforatum* (see p.240) and *Viburnum opulus* (see p.403) for muscular aches and pains. Not given to patients hypersensitive to salicylates (aspirin).

Ⓜ ▨ ▪

SALVADORA
Salvadoraceae

Four or five species of evergreen, salt-tolerant trees and shrubs make up this genus, known in drier areas of Africa, the Middle East, India, and China. *Salvadora persica* is found in seasonally flooded areas. The seeds of *Salvadora* spp. are rich in volatile mustard oils, which are similar in effect to those found in true mustards (see *Brassica juncea* and *B. nigra*, p.146, and *Sinapis alba*, p.369). Research suggests that *Salvadora persica*, which was first found in Persia, is the plant described in the parable of the mustard seed (Matthew 13: 31–2), "which indeed is the least of all seeds: but when it is grown, it is the greatest among herbs, and becometh a tree". All parts of *S. persica* are used locally for medicinal and veterinary purposes. Toothbrushes are made from sections of root by removing the bark from one end and fraying the inner wood, which is then chewed and applied to teeth and gums. The roots contain substances that are excellent for oral hygiene. *Salvadora* was named after Juan Salvador y Bosca (1598–1681), an apothecary in Barcelona.

CULTIVATION Well-drained, seasonally moist to wet soil in sun.

PROPAGATION By semi-ripe cuttings in summer, rooted in sand, at 18°C (64°F).

HARVEST Leaves are picked as required for use fresh, or dried and powdered. Both leaves and wood are burned to a fine ash for external veterinary applications. Bark and wood are dried and powdered. Twigs and roots are cut as required for use fresh. Fruits are collected when ripe for use fresh, cooked, or dried. Seeds may be removed for use whole or crushed in oil.

■ *Salvadora persica* (mustard tree, salt bush, toothbrush tree)
Evergreen shrub or small tree with grey

Salvadora persica

pendulous branches and bright green, elliptic leaves, to 6cm (2½in) long. Tiny, green-white, bell-shaped flowers are produced in panicles, to 10cm (4in) long, throughout the year, followed by globose, red to purple, aromatic fruits. Native to Africa, Arabia, and India. ‡2–6m (6–20ft), ↔ 5m (15ft).

HARDINESS Min. 10–13°C (50–55°F).

PARTS USED Leaves, twigs, wood, root bark, fruits, seeds.

PROPERTIES An astringent stimulant herb that is diuretic and expectorant, and cleanses toxins (leaves), destroys parasites (leaves, bark), promotes healing (wood), improves appetite and bowel function, lowers fever, regulates the menstrual cycle (fruits), and stimulates the circulation (fruits, seeds).

MEDICINAL USES Internally for colds, skin complaints, urinary problems, gonorrhoea, syphilis, and intestinal parasites; constipation, enlarged spleen, poor appetite, and menstrual problems; rheumatism, and arthritis. Externally for abscesses and swellings (leaves), poisonous bites, bruises, and oral hygiene.

CULINARY USES Young leaves are added to salads and made into a sauce. Fruits are eaten fresh or dried; can be used as a substitute for mustard seeds.

ECONOMIC USES Leaves are burned as a source of salt. Extracts are used to make chewing gum.

Ⓜ ▨ ▨ ▨ ▨ ▨ ▪ ╱ ╱ ▨

SALVIA
Sage

Lamiaceae

A genus of some 900 species of mostly aromatic annuals, biennials, perennials, and mainly evergreen shrubs and subshrubs, found worldwide in temperate, subtropical, and dry tropical areas. They favour dry, stony or rocky hillsides, scrub, and meadows, almost always in open sunny places. Sages have interesting and diverse aromas, textures, and colours, and their flowers secrete abundant nectar, making them locally important as bee plants. Over 100 species and many variants are available as ornamentals, some of which have medicinal and culinary uses. They are rewarding plants to grow, since they have a long flowering period and combine well with many other kinds of garden plants. Few make good cutflowers, the exceptions being *S. sclarea* and *S. viridis*, which are excellent both fresh and dried. The hardiest and most widely used species is *S. officinalis*

S

353

(common sage), which has been cultivated in N Europe since medieval times, and was introduced to N America in the 17th century. The Romans used it to increase fertility, and its medicinal uses were mentioned by Dioscorides, Theophrastus, and Pliny. Known as *S. salvatrix* ("sage the saviour"), its reputation for promoting longevity began in Classical times, giving rise to sayings such as "he that would live for aye [ever], must eat sage in May". The name of the genus also reflects this, being from the Latin *salvere*, "to be well". Sages are rich in volatile oils, which vary greatly from species to species. *Salvia officinalis* contains a camphoraceous oil, consisting of about 50 per cent thujone. In excess, this compound is hallucinogenic, addictive, and toxic. *Salvia fruticosa* has less thujone and *S. lavandulifolia* has none. *Salvia officinalis* also contains rosmarinic acid, which has the effect of stopping perspiration within about two hours of the correct dose being given. Dried sage is popular in the kitchen, and commercial dried sage may include leaves of *S. fruticosa*, *S. lavandulifolia*, and *S. pomifera*, as well as *S. officinalis*. *Salvia pratensis* (meadow sage) has also been used as a substitute for common sage, and as a flavouring for beer and wine. Sages are numerous in western N America and C America, and many are used locally for flavouring. Many species have bright red or yellow flowers that are pollinated by hummingbirds. Several species are valued for their seeds, which when soaked in water form a gelatinous mass that forms the basis for refreshing drinks. Examples are: *S. columbariae* (golden *chia*) and *S. tiliifolia* (lindenleaf sage, Tarahumara *chia*), whose nutritious seeds are also used for sprouting, or ground as a baking ingredient, while the aromatic foliage is used for flavouring and teas. Other interesting American sages include: *S. apiana* (white sage), a pungently aromatic species that was used in smudging ceremonies by native tribes, and has nutritious *chia*-type seeds; *S. lyrata* (cancerweed, lyre-leafed sage), which is used in folk medicine for colds, coughs, asthma, and cancer, and as a dressing for warts, wounds,

and sores; *S. mellifera* (black sage), used by settlers for tea and flavouring; and *S. microphylla* syn. *S. grahamii* (Graham's sage, red bush), whose flowers and minty leaves are infused to treat fevers. South Africa has a number of sages that have long been used for their disinfectant, healing, and aromatic properties. *Salvia africana* syn. *S. africana-caerulea* (*blousalie*, blue sage) was found by Dutch settlers to be a good substitute for common sage, in terms of home remedies and teas. *Salvia repens* (creeping or small sage) has little to recommend it for cooking, but is much used locally as a tea for bronchial infections and digestive problems, or a wash for infected wounds or sores. It is also burned to disinfect homes after illness, and to deter insect pests in the home. Similar medicinal uses are recorded for *S. aurea* (brown sage, dune sage), *S. disermas* (*groot salie*, Transvaal sage), *S. stenophylla* (*fynblaar salie*, narrow-leaf sage), and *S. verbenaca* (Free State sage, vervain sage, *vrystaat salie*). In China, the main species used is *S. miltiorhiza*, known as *dan shen*, redroot sage, or red sage because of its red roots; it was recorded as an important medicinal herb in 206BC. Two other species are used as sources of the drug *dan shen* – *S. bowleyana* (southern *dan shen*) and *S. przewalskii* (Gansu *dan shen*) – while various other species are used in folk medicine as "folk *dan shen*".

CULTIVATION Well-drained to dry, neutral to alkaline soil in sun. *Salvia miltiorhiza* needs moist, sandy soil; tolerates partial shade. Most sages dislike damp conditions and low light in winter; they are often hardier in dry sunny positions. Sages grown in a greenhouse are prone to red spider mite, aphid, and whitefly. Many sages become woody and sparse with age and should be replaced every 4–7 years.

PROPAGATION By seed sown in spring (species and annuals only); by basal or softwood cuttings in spring and summer; by semi-ripe cuttings in late summer and early autumn; by division (*S. miltiorhiza*). *Salvia lyrata*, *S. sclarea*, and *S. viridis* may self-sow freely. *Salvia greggii* is grown as an annual in areas with cold winters.

HARVEST Leaves are picked for immediate use,

or before flowers open for oil distillation and drying; dried leaves are used in infusions, liquid extracts, and tinctures. Roots are lifted in late autumn and winter, and dried for pills, decoctions, and tinctures. Ripe seeds are dried for use in macerations, or pressed for oil. Flower spikes are cut in summer. Galls (*S. pomifera*) are picked in spring, and candied.

▣ *Salvia clevelandii* (blue sage, Cleveland sage) Evergreen shrub with strongly aromatic, ovate to lanceolate, toothed leaves, to 2.5cm (1in) long. Lavender-blue, rarely violet or white flowers are produced in widely spaced whorls from late spring to midsummer. Native to USA (California). ‡ 1.2m (4ft). ↔ 1.2–1.5m (4–5ft).
HARDINESS Frost hardy.
PARTS USED Leaves.
PROPERTIES An aromatic herb with a strong resinous flavour. The volatile oil contains thujone.
CULINARY USES Fresh or dried leaves are used as a substitute for *S. officinalis* with strongly flavoured or rich foods, such as pork, duck, goose, game, sausages, and cheese dishes.
ECONOMIC USES Dried leaves may be added to potpourris.
▨ ▨ ✎

▣ *Salvia dorisiana* (fruit-scented sage) Shrubby evergreen perennial with velvety, cordate, light green, fruit-scented leaves, to 18cm (7in) long. Bright rose-pink, hairy flowers, 5cm (2in) long, are borne in spikes, to 15cm (6in) long, in winter. Native to the Honduras. ‡↔1–1.5m (3–5ft).
HARDINESS Min. 7°C (45°F).
PARTS USED Leaves.
PROPERTIES An aromatic herb with a fresh fruity scent.
CULINARY USES Leaves are used in salads and salad dressings; also to make tea.
ECONOMIC USES Leaves are dried for potpourris.
▨ ▨ ✎ ▣

▣ *Salvia elegans* (pineapple sage) Evergreen shrubby perennial with bright green, ovate, pointed leaves, to 10cm (4in) long, which

Salvia clevelandii

Salvia elegans

Salvia elegans 'Scarlet Pineapple'

Salvia fruticosa

Salvia greggii

Salvia greggii 'Peach'

Salvia dorisiana

S

have a pineapple-like scent. Whorls of slender scarlet flowers, 2.5cm (1in) long, appear in racemes, to 15cm (6in) long, in winter. Native to Mexico and Guatemala. ‡2m (6ft), ↔ 1.2m (4ft). 'Frieda Dixon' (peach pineapple sage) has salmon-pink flowers in autumn. ▣ 'Scarlet Pineapple' syn. *S. rutilans* has hairier stems, a stronger pineapple scent, and larger flowers, to 3.5cm (1½in) long. ‡90cm (36in), ↔ 60cm (24in). 'Tangerine' has more rounded leaves that have a light citrus scent.

HARDINESS Min. 5°C (41°F).

PARTS USED Leaves.

PROPERTIES An aromatic herb with pineapple scent.

CULINARY USES Sprigs are added to cold drinks and fruit salads. Fresh or dried leaves are used to make tea, or to give a sage-like aroma to pork dishes.

▨ ▧ ▣

▣ *Salvia fruticosa* syn. *S. triloba* (Greek sage)
Evergreen shrub with lavender-scented, ovate to oblong, simple or pinnately divided, grey-green leaves, to 5cm (2in) long, often with 1–2 pairs of small leaflets at the base. Mauve to pink, occasionally white flowers, to 2.5cm (1in) long, appear in racemes, to 20cm (8in) long, in spring and summer. Native to the Mediterranean. ‡1.2m (4ft), ↔ 1m (3ft).

HARDINESS Frost hardy.

PARTS USED Leaves, oil.

PROPERTIES Similar to *S. lavandulifolia*.

MEDICINAL USES Internally for influenza, coughs, and rheumatic pains.

CULINARY USES Leaves are infused for tea, known as *chanomilia* (Cyprus) and mixed with those of *S. pomifera* for *faskómelo* tea (Greece).

ECONOMIC USES Dried leaves make up 50–95 per cent of commercial sage. Oil is used to adulterate spike lavender oil (from *Lavandula latifolia*).

▨ ▣ ▪ ▧ ▧

▣ *Salvia greggii* (autumn sage, San Antone oregano)
Variable evergreen subshrub with leathery, ovate to oblong or linear leaves, to 2.5cm (1in) long.

Pairs of usually red, occasionally rose, white, or violet flowers, about 2cm (¾in) long, with a large lower lip, are produced in racemes from summer to autumn. Native to USA (SW Texas) and Mexico. ‡30cm–1.2m (1–4ft). 'Alba' has white flowers. 'Furman's Red' bears numerous deep red flowers. ▣ 'Peach' has salmon-pink flowers.

HARDINESS Frost hardy.

PARTS USED Leaves.

PROPERTIES A strongly aromatic herb with an oregano-like flavour. The volatile oil contains carvacrol.

CULINARY USES Leaves are used to flavour beans and stews made with strong-flavoured meats.

▨ ▧

▣ *Salvia hispanica* (Mexican *chia*)
Erect branched annual with bright green, ovate, pointed leaves, to 8cm (3in) long. Pale blue flowers are produced in dense racemes, to 15cm (6in) long, in summer. Found from Mexico to Peru; widely naturalized, especially in the West Indies. ‡60–90cm (24–36in), ↔ 30–45cm (12–18in).

HARDINESS Min. 5°C (41°F).

PARTS USED Seeds, oil.

PROPERTIES An aromatic herb with nutritious seeds.

CULINARY USES Mucilaginous seeds are soaked in water and diluted with water, lemon juice, and sugar to make the refreshing drink known as *chia*. Gelled seeds can also be eaten as a porridge or used to make desserts. Sprouted seeds are eaten in salads. Dried seeds are ground into meal for baking or pressed for oil, which is high in essential fatty acids (EFAs), used in food supplements.

▣ ▨ ▧ ▣

▣ *Salvia lavandulifolia* (Spanish sage)
Evergreen, woody-based perennial with grey-green, downy, lanceolate leaves, to 5cm (2in) long. Pale lavender-blue flowers, to 2.5cm (1in) long, are produced in widely spaced whorls in summer. Native to C, S, and E Spain and S France. ‡45cm (18in), ↔ 60cm (24in).

HARDINESS Fully hardy (borderline).

PARTS USED Leaves, oil.

PROPERTIES An antiseptic, astringent, tonic herb with a lavender–rosemary aroma. It improves digestion, lowers fever, strengthens the immune and nervous systems, cleanses toxins, stimulates the uterus, and has expectorant and oestrogenic effects.

MEDICINAL USES Internally for digestive and respiratory complaints, menstrual problems, infertility, nervous tension, and depression. Contraindicated during pregnancy.

CULINARY USES Leaves are used as a substitute for *S. officinalis* in cooking; also made into tea.

ECONOMIC USES Oil is used for flavouring in the food, drink, and confectionery industries; also in perfumery, soaps, and cosmetics.

▨ ▣ ▪ ▧ ▧

▣ *Salvia miltiorhiza* (Chinese sage, red sage)
Perennial with cylindrical red roots and dark green, oddly pinnate leaves divided into 3–7 ovate to rounded, toothed leaflets, to 5cm (2in) long. Whorls of deep blue-purple flowers, about 2.5cm (1in) long, are produced in racemes in summer. Native to NE China. ‡30–80cm (12–32in), ↔ 23–30cm (9–12in).

HARDINESS Fully hardy.

PARTS USED Roots (*dan shen*).

PROPERTIES A bitter, sedative, cooling herb that controls bleeding, stimulates the circulatory and immune systems, lowers cholesterol levels, promotes healing, and inhibits many disease-causing organisms. It acts mainly on the heart energy, removing excess heat and clearing stagnation.

MEDICINAL USES Internally for coronary heart disease, poor circulation, palpitations, irritability, insomnia, breast abscesses, mastitis, ulcers, boils, sores, bruises, menstrual problems, and postpartum pains. Often combined with *Angelica polymorpha* var. *sinensis* (see p.122) for suppressed menstruation.

▨ ▪

▣ *Salvia officinalis* (common sage)
Shrubby evergreen perennial with much-branched stems and wrinkled, velvety, pale grey-

Salvia hispanica

Salvia lavandulifolia   *Salvia miltiorhiza*

Salvia officinalis

Salvia officinalis 'Albiflora'

Salvia officinalis 'Aurea'

Salvia officinalis 'Berggarten'

Salvia officinalis 'Icterina'

Salvia officinalis 'Kew Gold'

Salvia officinalis 'Purpurascens'

S

purple flowers, 1.5cm (½in) long, are produced in racemes in summer. Native to the Mediterranean and N Africa. ↕60–80cm (24–32in), ↔1m (3ft). ▣ 'Albiflora' syn. 'Alba' has white flowers. ▣ 'Aurea' has chartreuse-yellow leaves, green along the veins. ↕45cm (18in), ↔60cm (2ft). ▣ 'Berggarten' has a dense compact habit and large broad leaves. ↕45cm (18in). 'Compacta' syn. 'Dwarf', 'Nana' has small leaves and a dwarf compact habit. ↕20–25cm (8–10in), ↔60cm (24in). 'Crispa' has crinkled leaves with crisped margins. 'Holt's Mammoth' is vigorous, with large leaves and a fine flavour; rarely flowers. ↕1m (3ft). ▣ 'Icterina' has yellow-variegated leaves. ▣ 'Kew Gold' has a compact dwarf habit and yellow leaves. ↕30cm (12in), ↔45cm (18in). ▣ 'Purpurascens' (purple sage) has purple-grey foliage. 'Purpurascens Variegata' has purple-grey leaves with irregular pink variegation. 'Tricolor' has irregular, pink and ivory variegation. Tends to be less vigorous and hardy than the species. 'White Dalmation' has small, very pale grey-green leaves and a superior, less bitter flavour.
HARDINESS Fully hardy.
PARTS USED Leaves, oil.
PROPERTIES An astringent, antiseptic, tonic herb with a camphoraceous aroma. It relaxes spasms, suppresses perspiration and lactation, improves liver function and digestion, and has anti-inflammatory, anti-depressant, and oestrogenic effects. Many herbalists regard 'Purpurascens' as more potent than the species.
MEDICINAL USES Internally for indigestion, flatulence, liver complaints, excessive lactation, night sweats, excessive salivation (as in Parkinson's disease), profuse perspiration (as in tuberculosis), anxiety, depression, female sterility, and menopausal problems. Toxic in excess or over long periods. Contraindicated during pregnancy and for epilepsy. Externally for insect bites, throat, mouth, gum, and skin infections, and vaginal discharge. Combined with *Potentilla erecta* (see p.329) as a gargle; and with *Chamaemelum nobile* (see p.165) and *Filipendula ulmaria* (see p.214) for digestive problems.

CULINARY USES Leaves are used to flavour meat dishes (especially pork), liver, goose, soups, stews, sauces, sausages, *saltimbocca* (an Italian dish of veal and ham), eels, and stuffings for pork and poultry; also as an ingredient of sage Derby cheese (England) and American sage cheese. Fresh or dried leaves are made into tea.
ECONOMIC USES Oil is used as a fixative for perfumes; also added to toothpastes and cosmetics.
▨▢▣▮✎✐

▣ *Salvia pomifera* syn. *S. calycina* (apple-bearing sage)
Evergreen, much-branched shrub often bearing fleshy galls, produced by gall wasps in the wild. Wrinkled, velvety, light green leaves are to 8cm (3in) long. Whorls of violet-blue flowers are borne in branched spikes in spring and summer. Native to Greece and Crete. ↕↔1m (3ft).
HARDINESS Half hardy.
PARTS USED Leaves, galls.
PROPERTIES Similar to *S. officinalis* but stronger.
CULINARY USES Leaves are used like *S. officinalis* for flavouring, and blended with *S. fruticosa* as *faskómelo* tea (Greece). Galls are made into a conserve and medicinal candy (Greece).
▨✎

▣ *Salvia sclarea* (clary sage, cleareye, muscatel sage)
Hairy perennial or biennial with strongly aromatic, light green, deeply veined, broadly ovate leaves, to 23cm (9in) long, which have indented margins. Whorls of bicoloured, cream and lilac to pink or blue flowers, to 3cm (1¼in) long, with conspicuous lilac bracts, appear in spring and summer. Found from SW and C Europe to C Asia. ↕1m (3ft), ↔60cm (24in). ▣ var. *turkestanica* has pink to white bracts, and pale blue and white flowers.
HARDINESS Fully hardy.
PARTS USED Leaves, flowers, seeds, oil.
PROPERTIES A bitter, astringent, warming herb with mucilaginous seeds and a vanilla–balsam aroma. It relaxes spasms, aids digestion,

stimulates the uterus and oestrogen production, calms nerves, controls vomiting, and is reputedly aphrodisiac.
MEDICINAL USES Internally for vomiting, poor appetite, and menstrual complaints. Contraindicated during pregnancy. Externally for foreign bodies in the eye or skin (seeds), minor injuries, and ulcers.
CULINARY USES Fresh young leaves are made into fritters. Flowers can be added to salads and made into tea.
ECONOMIC USES Young leaves are infused with elderflowers to give a muscatel bouquet to Rhine wines; also used to flavour vermouth, beers, and liqueurs. "Muscatel oil" has an ambergris aroma and is used in soaps and cosmetics, and as a fixative in perfumery.
▨▨▣▨▮✎✐

▣ *Salvia viridis* syn. *S. horminum* (annual clary, bluebeard, Joseph sage, painted sage)
Bushy erect annual with ovate to oblong, hairy, toothed leaves, 5cm (2in) long. Whorls of tiny, white to purple flowers, enclosed by conspicuous, green to purple bracts, with darker veins, are produced in spikes in summer. Native to the Mediterranean. ↕45–50cm (18–20in), ↔23cm (9in). ▣ 'Claryssa' has a compact branched habit and blue-purple, pink, and green-veined, white bracts. ↕40cm (16in).
HARDINESS Fully hardy.
PARTS USED Leaves, flowering spikes, seeds, oil.
PROPERTIES An aromatic antiseptic herb.
MEDICINAL USES Externally for sore gums and as snuff.
CULINARY USES Seeds and leaves are used to flavour food.
ECONOMIC USES Oil is used to flavour wine and beer.
▨▨▣▨▮✎✐

SAMBUCUS
Elder

Caprifoliaceae

This genus of about 25 species of small deciduous trees, shrubs, and perennials occurs in most temperate and subtropical regions. *Sambucus nigra* (common elder) is a useful attractive shrub for woodland and hedgerows but is seldom grown in borders, having been superseded by cultivars with more interesting foliage that can be used in the same ways. Elder has been called "the medicine chest of the people", providing remedies for most common complaints. It is revered by gypsies, associated with the Jewish cabbala, and is steeped in superstition and folklore. Traditionally, the cutting of elder required an apology to the Elder Mother, and her permission. All parts of *S. nigra* are used medicinally but modern usage favours the flowers. They contain many complex substances, such as flavonoids (including rutin, as found in *Ruta graveolens*, see p.352), tannins, volatile oil, and phenolic acids. The berries are also rich in flavonoids, and vitamins A and C. The leaves contain toxic cyanogenic glycosides

Salvia pomifera

Salvia sclarea

Salvia sclarea var. *turkestanica*

Salvia viridis

Salvia viridis 'Claryssa'

S

Sambucus nigra

Sambucus nigra
'Aurea'

Sambucus nigra
'Aureomarginata'

Sambucus nigra
'Marginata'

Sambucus nigra
'Pulverulenta'

Sambucus nigra
'Guincho Purple'

Sambucus nigra
f. laciniata

ECONOMIC USES Flowers are used in skin lotions (elderflower water, or *Aqua Sambuci*), oils, and ointments; also commercially to make white wine, cordial, and sparkling elderflower drinks. Leaves are boiled and strained to make a natural insecticidal spray.

SANGUINARIA
Bloodroot

Papaveraceae

A single species of perennial makes up this genus of the poppy family (Papaveraceae), which occurs in eastern N American woodlands. *Sanguinaria canadensis* is a choice plant for woodland borders, raised beds, and shady areas of the rock garden. It is at its best in spring, producing exquisite flowers and scalloped new leaves simultaneously. In common with most members of the poppy family, *S. canadensis* contains a number of opium-like alkaloids. This toxic herb was used by various native N American peoples to dye skin and implements red, and to induce therapeutic vomiting. It was also used to treat sore throats, ringworm, and rheumatism, and appeared in the *US Pharmacopoeia* (1820–1926) as a stimulating expectorant. It is now important as a source of anti-bacterial alkaloids, one of which (sanguinarine) is used as a dental plaque inhibitor. *Sanguinaria* comes from the Latin *sanguis*, "blood", referring to the red sap in the rhizomes.

CULTIVATION Well-drained, humus-rich soil in sun or partial shade.

PROPAGATION By seed sown in autumn (species only); by cuttings or division of rhizomes in late summer or early autumn. Rhizomes are brittle and should be handled carefully.

HARVEST Rhizomes are lifted in autumn and dried for liquid extracts, ointments, and tinctures.

■ *Sanguinaria canadensis* (bloodroot, Red Indian paint, red puccoon) Rhizomatous perennial with kidney-shaped, scalloped, grey-green leaves, 15–30cm (6–12in) across. Solitary, short-lived, white flowers, about 8cm (3in) across, sometimes pink-tinged, appear in spring as the

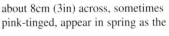

(as found in *Prunus* spp., see p.331). *Sambucus* is from the Greek *sambuke*, "a musical pipe", for which the hollowed-out shoots of elder bushes were traditionally used.
CULTIVATION Rich, moist, neutral to alkaline soil in sun or partial shade. Cut back almost to ground level during the winter to ensure large colourful leaves in ornamental varieties. Do not prune hard if flowers and fruit are required. Elders are prone to blackfly in poor conditions.
PROPAGATION By seed sown in autumn (species only); by greenwood cuttings in early summer; by hardwood cuttings in winter.
HARVEST Leaves are picked in summer and used fresh. Bark is stripped in late winter, before new leaves appear, or in autumn before leaves change colour, and dried for decoctions. Fully open flower heads are collected and dried whole; flowers are then stripped off for infusions, floral water, liquid extracts, ointment, and tinctures. Fruits are harvested when ripe, separated from stalks, and used fresh or as juice, or dried for use in decoctions, syrups, and tinctures.
⚠ **WARNING** Leaves and raw berries are harmful if eaten.

■ *Sambucus nigra* (common elder)
Large deciduous shrub with corky, grey-brown bark and pinnate leaves, to 25cm (10in) long, divided into five ovate toothed leaflets, to 9cm (3½in) long. The foliage has an unpleasant smell when crushed. Tiny, scented, cream flowers are borne in flat-topped clusters, 10–20cm (4–8in) across, in early summer, followed by globose black berries, about 7mm (¼in) in diameter. Native to Europe, W Asia, and N Africa. ‡6–10m (20–30ft), ↔3–6m (10–20ft). ■ 'Aurea' (golden elder) has bright yellow-green young leaves, becoming lime-green in summer. ↔6m (20ft). ■ 'Aureomarginata' has yellow-margined leaves.

'Black Beauty' has very dark purple leaves and pink flowers. ■ 'Guincho Purple' syn. 'Purpurea' (bronze elder) has dark purple-bronze foliage and pink-stamened flowers. ↔6m (20ft). ■ f. *laciniata* (fern-leafed elder, parsley-leafed elder) has deeply dissected leaves. ■ 'Marginata' syn. 'Albovariegata', 'Argenteomarginata' has cream-edged leaves. ■ 'Pulverulenta' has white-spotted foliage.
HARDINESS Fully hardy.
PARTS USED Leaves, bark, flowers, fruits.
PROPERTIES A bitter, pungent, cooling herb that lowers fever, reduces inflammation, soothes irritation, and has diuretic, alterative, and anti-catarrhal effects (flowers, fruits); leaves are insecticidal, antiseptic, and healing.
MEDICINAL USES Internally for influenza, colds, catarrh, sinusitis, and feverish illnesses (flowers, fruits), rheumatic complaints (fruits), and constipation and arthritic conditions (bark). Externally for minor burns and chilblains (leaves, bark); sore eyes, irritated or inflamed skin, mouth ulcers, and minor injuries (flowers). Combined with *Achillea millefolium* (see p.99), *Hyssopus officinalis* (see p.240), *Mentha* × *piperita* (see p.277), or *Tilia cordata* (see p.391) for upper respiratory tract infections (flowers, fruits); and with *Menyanthes trifoliata* (see p.278) or *Salix alba* (see p.353) for rheumatism (fruits).
CULINARY USES Flower heads are fried in batter (elderflower fritters). Flowers are made into cordials, summer drinks, and "champagne"; also used to give a muscatel flavour to stewed fruit, jellies, and jam (especially gooseberry). Dried flowers are made into tea. Fruits are made into sauces, jams, jellies, wine, chutneys, and ketchups; also used to flavour and colour stewed fruit and jellies (dried fruits are less bitter). Juice is boiled with sugar to make a cordial (elderberry rob), flavoured with ginger and cloves.

Sanguinaria canadensis

Sanguinaria canadensis 'Plena'

new leaves emerge, followed by an oblong capsule containing many seeds. Native to eastern N America. ‡ 15–60cm (6–24in), ↔ 30–45cm (12–18in). ▣ 'Plena' syn. 'Flore Pleno', 'Multiplex' has longer-lasting, double, white flowers.

HARDINESS Fully hardy.

PARTS USED Rhizomes.

PROPERTIES A bitter, acrid, warming herb that has expectorant and diuretic effects, lowers fever, relaxes spasms, and slows the heart rate. It is locally anaesthetic and effective against many pathogenic organisms.

MEDICINAL USES Internally for bronchial, respiratory tract, and throat infections, and poor peripheral circulation. Excess depresses the central nervous system, causes nausea and vomiting, and may prove fatal. Contraindicated during pregnancy and lactation. For use only by qualified practitioners. Externally for skin diseases, warts, nasal polyps, benign skin tumours, sore throat, and chilblains. Combined with *Lobelia inflata* (see p.265) for bronchial asthma; with *Capsicum annuum* (see p.154) and *Salvia officinalis* (p.355) as a gargle for pharyngitis; with *Myrica cerifera* (see p.284) in snuff for nasal polyps; and with *Chelidonium majus* (see p.165) to remove warts. Used in homeopathy for migraine.

ECONOMIC USES Extracts are added to toothpaste and mouthwash as an anti-plaque agent.

▨ ▣ ☑

SANGUISORBA

Rosaceae

There are about 18 species of rhizomatous perennials in this genus, which occurs throughout northern temperate regions. *Sanguisorba officinalis* is grown as a border plant for its elegant foliage and small bottlebrush flowers. It contains unique tannins, glycosides (sanguisorbins), and gum. Use of the roots was first recorded in Chinese medicine in the *Shen Nong Canon of Herbs* during the Han dynasty (206BC–AD23). Western medicine favours the leafy parts. Culpeper described its astringent qualities graphically: "to staunch bleeding inward or outward, lasks, scourings,

the bloody flux, women's too abundant flux of courses, the whites, and the choleric belchings and castings of the stomach, and is a wound-herb for all sorts of wounds, both of the head and body either inward or outward, for all old sores, running cankers, and moist sores." *Sanguisorba* comes from the Latin *sanguis*, "blood", and *sorbere*, "to soak up", and refers to the use of these plants to control bleeding.

CULTIVATION Moist, well-drained soil in sun or partial shade.

PROPAGATION Propagate by seed sown in autumn or spring; by division in autumn or spring.

HARVEST Leafy parts are cut before flowers open and dried for use in infusions, liquid extracts, and tinctures. Roots are lifted in autumn and dried for decoctions.

▣ *Sanguisorba minor* (salad burnet)
Erect, clump-forming perennial with pinnate leaves, to 15cm (6in) long, divided into 4–12 pairs of rounded–elliptic, toothed leaflets, about 2cm (¾in) long. Tiny green flowers, with maroon stamens, are produced in rounded spikes, to 2.5cm (1in) long, from late spring to late summer. Native to S, W, and C Europe, N Africa, Canary Islands, and W and C Asia. ‡↔ 40–75cm (16–30in).

HARDINESS Fully hardy.

PARTS USED Leaves.

PROPERTIES A cooling herb with a cucumber flavour.

CULINARY USES Young leaves and leaflets are added to salads, sandwiches, soups, soft cheeses, and summer drinks; also used as garnish. Dried leaves are made into tea.

▨ ☑

▣ *Sanguisorba officinalis* syn. *Poterium officinalis* (greater burnet)
Erect, clump-forming perennial with a stout woody rootstock and a basal rosette of pinnate leaves, 50cm (20in) long, divided into 3–7 pairs of oblong–elliptic, toothed leaflets. Tiny maroon flowers are produced in dense oblong spikes, to 3cm (1¼in) long, from summer to midautumn. Found from Europe to China and Japan; naturalized in parts of N America. ‡ 30cm–1.1m (1–3½ft), ↔ 23–60cm (9–24in).

HARDINESS Fully hardy.

PARTS USED Leaves, roots (*di yu*).

Sanguisorba minor

Sanguisorba officinalis

PROPERTIES A bitter, astringent, cooling herb that controls bleeding, reduces inflammation, promotes healing, and destroys many pathogenic organisms.

MEDICINAL USES Internally for diarrhoea, dysentery, ulcerative colitis, haemorrhoids, haemorrhage, and abnormal uterine bleeding. Externally for burns, scalds, sores, and skin diseases. An ingredient in Chinese formulas to treat cervical erosion and uterine and gastrointestinal haemorrhages, and in a dentifrice for peridontal disease. Roots are often stir-baked or charred to increase astringency.

CULINARY USES Young leaves, leaflets, and unopened flower heads are added to salads, stir-fries, and soups. Dried leaves are made into tea.

▨ ▧ ▣ ☑

SANICULA

Sanicle

Apiaceae

About 40 species make up this genus of biennials and perennials, which occurs worldwide, except in Australasia. *Sanicula europaea* is a woodland species, found mainly on alkaline soils. It is a charming, if unobtrusive plant for shady borders and banks, and thrives beneath trees and shrubs. The first description of sanicle as a medicinal herb was made by St Hildegaard of Bingen (1098–1179). Though little used by herbalists today, it was especially popular from the 15th to 17th centuries, when it was held on a par with *Prunella vulgaris* (see p.331) and *Symphytum officinale* (see p.377). Among its constituents are allantoin (as in *S. officinale*), tannins, saponins, volatile oil, and rosmarinic acid, as in *Rosmarinus* (see p.348) and *Salvia* (see p.353). Several N American species, including *Sanicula canadensis* (Canada sanicle), *S. gregaria* (clustered snakeroot), and *S. marilandica* (black snakeroot), are used for similar purposes. The snakeroot sanicles were important to native tribes as first aid for rattlesnake bites. *Sanicula* is probably from the Latin *sanus*, "healthy".

CULTIVATION Moist, well-drained, humus-rich soil in shade or partial shade.

PROPAGATION By seed sown when ripe; by division in autumn or spring.

Sanicula europaea

HARVEST Whole plants are picked while they are flowering so they can be made into infusions and liquid extracts.

 *Sanicula europaea* (sanicle)
Clump-forming perennial with shiny, palmately 3–5-lobed basal leaves, to 6cm (2½in) long. Tiny, green-white to pale pink flowers are produced in clusters of small dense umbels from late spring to midsummer. Native to Eurasia. ‡ 60cm (24in), ↔ 15–30cm (6–12in).
HARDINESS Fully hardy.
PARTS USED Whole plant.
PROPERTIES A cleansing, astringent, anti-inflammatory herb that controls bleeding and discharges, and speeds healing.
MEDICINAL USES Internally for diarrhoea, dysentery, catarrh, dry cough, bronchitis, internal haemorrhage, nosebleeds, and skin problems. Externally for minor injuries, bleeding wounds, burns, haemorrhoids, skin inflammations, chilblains, sore throat, gum infections, and ulcers.

SANTALUM
Sandalwood

Santalaceae

Nine species of evergreen trees and shrubs belong to this genus, which occurs in SE Asia, Australia, and the Pacific islands. Sandalwoods are semi-parasitic, deriving some food from photosynthesis but relying on a host plant, via sucker roots, for water and minerals. It was reported in a 19th-century gardening manual that *S. album* was being grown successfully at the Royal Botanic Gardens, Kew (UK), in "very sandy loam", but trees are now seldom seen outside the tropics. Various species have a long history of exploitation for their fragrant wood; *S. fernandezianum*, a native of the Juan Fernandez Islands in the S Pacific, was recorded as rare by 1740 and extinct by 1916. Sandalwood has been used as medicine, incense, and perfume in the East for 4000 years, with especial importance in Hindu devotional practices. Traditionally, the wood is burned at Buddhist funerals and is ground to make Hindu caste marks. Sandalwood reached Europe in the 1880s and soon became popular in perfumery. It takes at least 20–40 years for sandalwood trees to develop sufficient heartwood for oil extraction. They are now cultivated in a semi-wild state alongside the natural host. All parts are rich in volatile oil: 6 per cent of the root, 4 per cent of leaves, 5 per cent of heartwood, and 2 per cent of bark. The oil contains at least 90 per cent sesquiterpene alcohols, known as "santalols". Dry rocky areas give high yields and quality. Sandalwood oil is often adulterated with castor oil and oil of cedar; oil may also be substituted from the related *S. spicatum* (West Australian sandalwood) or from *Amyris balsamifera* (West Indian sandalwood), a member of the Rutaceae family. Various parts of *Santalum lanceolatum* (plumbush), a small tree or shrub common on rocky ground in most of Australia, are used in Aboriginal medicine for sores, boils, itching, gonorrhoea, constipation, and rheumatism; the tree contains a bactericidal volatile oil.
CULTIVATION Well-drained, moist, fertile soil in partial shade.
PROPAGATION By seed sown when ripe, pre-soaked in a 1:9 solution of bleach, sown in vermiculite at 15–21°C (59–70°F). Seedlings are planted alongside host when roots reach 4cm (1½in) long.
HARVEST Trees over 50 years old are felled for heartwood. Wood is dried for use in decoctions, liquid extracts, powders, and tinctures. Oil is pressed or extracted from heartwood and roots.

 *Santalum album* (Indian sandalwood, white sandalwood)
Small graceful tree with fragrant wood and ovate to lanceolate leaves, to 8cm (3in) long. Panicles of dull yellow to maroon flowers are followed by fleshy, dark red to black fruits, 1cm (½in) long. Probably native to coastal Malaysia and Indonesia. ‡ 5–10m (15–30ft), ↔ 3m (10ft).
HARDINESS Min. 15°C (59°F).
PARTS USED Heartwood, roots, oil.
PROPERTIES An aromatic, bitter–sweet, astringent herb that cools the body, calms the mind, relieves spasms, and improves digestion. It has diuretic, analgesic, and antiseptic effects.
MEDICINAL USES Internally for genito-urinary disorders, fever, sunstroke, digestive problems, and abdominal pain. Externally for skin complaints.

CULINARY USES Essence is used to flavour syrups and Indian milk desserts.
ECONOMIC USES Sapwood is used for carved objects. Ground wood provides a Hindu caste-mark pigment. Oil is used in perfumery, soaps, body oils, food flavouring, and incense.

SANTOLINA
Cotton lavender

Asteraceae

A genus of 18 species of small, aromatic, evergreen shrubs, found in dry stony places in Mediterranean regions. *Santolina chamaecyparissus* was grown in Classical times; it became popular for knot garden hedges in northern regions in the 16th century, having neat, silver-grey foliage that contrasts well with darker hedging plants, such as *Buxus sempervirens* 'Suffruticosa' (edging box, see p.149). Culpeper described *Santolina chamaecyparissus*, in *The English Physician Enlarged* (1653), as a remedy for poisonous bites, intestinal worms, and skin irritations. Although seldom used today, research in the 1980s showed it to be an effective anti-inflammatory. *Santolina* comes from the Latin *sanctum linum*, "holy flax".
CULTIVATION Light, well-drained to dry soil in sun. Tolerates sandy and poor, alkaline soils. Cut back hard in spring. Remove dead flower heads and trim in autumn.
PROPAGATION By seed sown in autumn or spring; by semi-ripe cuttings in late summer.
HARVEST Leaves are picked in the growing season, flowering stems in summer; both are dried for use in infusions and powders.

 Santolina chamaecyparissus (cotton lavender, lavender cotton)
Dense, strongly aromatic shrub with white-woolly, linear leaves, to 4cm (1½in) long, divided into closely packed, blunt segments. Solitary globose heads, to 1cm (½in) across, of deep yellow, tubular flowers are produced in summer. Native to W and C Mediterranean. ‡ 20–50cm (8–20in), ↔ 60–90cm (24–36in). ■ 'Lambrook Silver' has silver-grey leaves. ■ 'Lemon Queen' is compact, with cream flowers and grey-green leaves that have a slightly sweeter aroma than the species. ‡↔ 60cm (24in). ■ var. *nana* is the

Santalum album

Santolina chamaecyparissus

Santolina chamaecyparissus 'Lambrook Silver'

S

Santolina chamaecyparissus 'Lemon Queen'

Santolina chamaecyparissus var. *nana*

Saponaria officinalis

Saponaria officinalis 'Alba Plena'

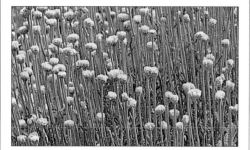

Santolina chamaecyparissus 'Pretty Carol'

Saponaria officinalis 'Dazzler'

Saponaria officinalis 'Rosea Plena'

Saponaria officinalis 'Rubra Plena'

smallest santolina. Ideal for alpine troughs. ↔ 15cm (6in). ▣ 'Pretty Carol' is compact, with silver foliage and bright yellow flowers. ↕ 25–50cm (10–20in), ↔ 60cm (24in). 'Small-Ness' is dwarf. Suitable for containers or a miniature hedge. ↕ 20cm (8in).

HARDINESS Fully hardy.

PARTS USED Leaves, flowering stems.

PROPERTIES A bitter stimulant herb with a strong, chamomile-like aroma. It reduces inflammation, improves digestion, stimulates the uterus and liver, and expels intestinal parasites.

MEDICINAL USES Internally for digestive and menstrual problems, worms in children, and jaundice. Externally for stings, bites, minor wounds, and skin inflammations.

CULINARY USES Leaves are used to flavour meat and fish dishes, grains, soups, and sauces.

ECONOMIC USES Dried leaves are blended with *Chamaemelum nobile* (see p.165) and *Tussilago farfara* (see p.396) in herbal tobacco. Dried leaves are added to potpourris.

▨ ▧ ▨ ▤ ▧ ▨

SAPONARIA
Soapwort

Caryophyllaceae

A genus of about 20 species of annuals and perennials, mostly from mountainous regions of S Europe but found throughout temperate Eurasia. *Saponaria officinalis* is a long-lived, late-flowering perennial for the border. It was used as a soap by the Assyrians in the 8th century BC, and is still used in the Middle East and by museums for cleaning furniture, tapestries, and pictures. In England, plants can often be found on the sites of old woollen mills, where it was grown for cleaning cloth before the commercial production of soap in the 1800s. In *The English Physician Enlarged* (1653), Culpeper described *S. officinalis* as "an absolute

cure in the French pox [syphilis]". Its use in treating these symptoms, and other venereal diseases, was also recommended by Mrs Grieve (*A Modern Herbal*, 1931), especially where the treatment with mercury (standard for nearly 400 years) had failed. *Saponaria* comes from the Latin *sapo*, "soap", referring to the use of these plants for washing.

CULTIVATION Well-drained, moist, neutral to alkaline soil in sun or partial shade. May be invasive. Poisonous to fish; roots or foliage should not contact pond water.

PROPAGATION By seed sown in autumn or spring (species only); by division in autumn or spring.

HARVEST Leafy stems are collected in summer, rhizomes in late autumn; both are dried for decoctions.

▣ *Saponaria officinalis* (bouncing Bet, soapwort)
Rhizomatous perennial with narrowly ovate, pointed leaves, 5–10cm (2–4in) long. Pale pink, scented flowers, 2cm (¾in) across, resembling miniature pinks, are borne in clusters from midsummer to midautumn. Native to Europe; naturalized in North America. ↕ 30–90cm (12–36in), ↔ 60cm (24in). ▣ 'Alba Plena' has double white flowers. ▣ 'Dazzler' syn. 'Taff's Dazzler', 'Variegata' has irregularly cream-variegated leaves and single pink flowers. Tends to revert. ▣ 'Rosea Plena' has double, pale pink flowers. ▣ 'Rubra Plena' has double, deep pink flowers.

HARDINESS Fully hardy.

PARTS USED Leafy stems, rhizomes.

PROPERTIES A diuretic, laxative, expectorant herb that clears toxins, and stimulates the liver.

MEDICINAL USES Internally for gout and skin diseases, bronchial congestion, and jaundice. Rarely used today, due to its irritant effect on

the digestive system. Excess destroys red blood cells and causes paralysis of the vasomotor centre. Externally for skin diseases.

ECONOMIC USES Extract is used as an emulsifier in Middle Eastern confectionery known as *halva*, based on sesame seeds; also in Ukraine to a similar product made from sunflower seeds. Dried herb is used as a soap substitute for delicate materials, and as an ingredient of natural shampoos.

⚠ **WARNING** Soapwort solutions are irritant to eyes.

▨ ▧ ▨ ▤ ▧

SARGASSUM
Gulfweed

Sargassaceae

A genus of 150 species of brown algae, found in warm seas, mainly from Australia north to Japan in the Pacific, and as far north as Cape Cod in the Atlantic. *Sargassum fusiforme*, first mentioned in the *Shen Nong Canon of Herbs* during the later Han dynasty (AD25–220), contains 0.2 per cent iodine and is effective in treating iodine deficiencies. In the 1940s, Japanese research showed anti-coagulant action similar to that of heparin. It also contains alginic acid, which is combined with calcium in plasters to stop bleeding in major trauma. *Sargaçao* was a description given by Portuguese navigators to floating seaweed, hence the names Sargasso Sea and *Sargassum*.

CULTIVATION Grows on partly submerged rocks between high tide and low tide zones.

PROPAGATION By holdfasts being left to regenerate.

HARVEST Whole plants are collected in winter and spring, and dried for decoctions and powders.

Sargassum fusiforme (gulfweed, *moku*)
Yellow-brown seaweed with a broad cylindrical holdfast and thick, fleshy, leaf-like branches with midribs, toothed to lobed margins, and axillary, spindle-shaped air sacs. Plants are attached to rocks when young and later become free-floating. Found off the coasts of China, Japan, and Korea. ↔ 20–50cm (8–20in).
PARTS USED Whole plant (*hai zao*).
PROPERTIES A bitter, saline, cooling herb that is expectorant and diuretic, controls bleeding, lowers blood pressure and lipid levels, softens hard swellings, acts on the thyroid, and suppresses appetite.
MEDICINAL USES Internally for goitre, oedema, bronchitis, tuberculosis of lymph nodes, cysts, and hydrocele. Externally for haemorrhage.

SAROTHAMNUS

Sarothamnus scoparius. See *Cytisus scoparius*.

SASSAFRAS

Lauraceae

A genus of three species of aromatic deciduous trees, occurring in eastern N America and E Asia. *Sassafras albidum*, found in thickets and disturbed woods, is grown for its scented, distinctively shaped foliage, which colours well in autumn. It is said that the scent of sassafras trees played a part in the discovery of the New World by Christopher Colombus, who detected their fragrance from afar and was thus guided to land. Sassafras was probably the first N American medicinal herb to reach Europe and, after tobacco, was the most important. Discovered in Florida by the Spanish, it was used medicinally in Spain by c.1560, mainly for venereal diseases. For thousands of years before this, it was used by tribes within its range, almost as a cure-all. *Sassafras albidum* contains alkaloids, lignans, tannins, resin, and a volatile oil that consists of 80–90 per cent safrole. This constituent of the essential oil is a common substance in plants; it is commercially important as an ingredient of insecticides, and in the synthesis of heliotropin for the perfumery industry. The main sources are *Ocotea pretiosa* (Brazilian sassafras) and *Cinnamomum* spp. (see p.169). Safrole is carcinogenic in laboratory animals. As a consequence, sassafras root was banned in the USA in 1960, and in Europe in 1974. Many countries no longer use the oil as a food flavouring; safrole-free bark extracts may be used instead, although their flavour is inferior.
CULTIVATION Deep, rich, neutral to acid soil in sun or shade, sheltered from late spring frosts.
PROPAGATION Propagate by seed sown when ripe; by suckers in autumn; by root cuttings in winter. Seed may take two years to germinate.
HARVEST Leaves are picked in spring and used fresh or dried for powder. Roots are lifted in autumn and dried for decoctions, liquid extracts, powders, and tinctures. Root bark is distilled for oil. Root pith is dried for macerations.

Sassafras albidum

■ **Sassafras albidum** (sassafras)
Suckering deciduous tree with deeply fissured bark and aromatic, roughly ovate leaves, to 15cm (6in) long, which are mostly cut into three equal lobes, or sometimes into only one lateral lobe. Yellow-green flowers, 1cm (½in) across, appear in clusters as the new leaves unfold in spring, followed by red-stalked, deep blue, ovoid fruits, 1cm (½in) long. Native to eastern N America. ↕ 20m (70ft), ↔ 12–15m (40–50ft).
HARDINESS Fully hardy.
PARTS USED Leaves, roots (bark, pith, oil).
PROPERTIES A sweet warming herb with a fennel-like aroma. It increases perspiration, relieves pain, improves digestion, and has anti-rheumatic, antiseptic, diuretic, and alterative effects.
MEDICINAL USES Internally for gastrointestinal complaints, colic, menstrual pain, skin diseases, acne, syphilis, gonorrhoea, arthritis, and rheumatism (root bark). Excess causes vomiting, dilated pupils, stupor, collapse, and kidney and liver damage. Essential oil is extremely toxic; a few drops might kill a child, and one teaspoonful might prove fatal to an adult. Externally for sore eyes (root pith), lice, and insect bites (oil), though oil may irritate skin. Combined with *Guaiacum officinale* (see p.229) and *Smilax glabra* (see p.370) in a tea to induce therapeutic sweating in feverish illnesses.
CULINARY USES Leaves are dried and powdered to make filet or *filé*, used in Cajun cooking as a thickener for soup known as gumbo (Louisiana). Roots are made into tea with maple syrup, which is also set as a jelly. Sassafras wood is used for smoking hams in S USA.
ECONOMIC USES Extracts are used for flavouring in food and drink industries (especially in root beer); also in oral hygiene products.
⚠ **WARNING** This herb, especially in the form of oil and safrole, is subject to legal restrictions in some countries.

SATUREJA
Savory

Lamiaceae

This genus of about 30 species of annuals, semi-evergreen perennials, and subshrubs occurs widely in the northern hemisphere, especially in dry sunny places. Savories are grown mainly for their culinary uses. They are unassuming plants but fulfil a number of niches in the herb garden: *S. douglasii* is ideal as ground cover or as a trailing plant for the front of windowboxes and hanging baskets in semi-shade, while the annual *S. hortensis* (summer savory) thrives alongside other short-lived, warmth-loving herbs, such as *Ocimum* (basil, see p.290), *Perilla* (see p.307), and *Portulaca* (purslane, see p.329). Shrubby *Satureja montana* can be planted as a dwarf hedge or edging, and creeping *S. spicigera* makes a good, late-flowering companion for *Thymus* (thyme, see p.387). European savories have been used as herbs for over 2000 years; they are similar in flavour to thymes and *Origanum* (marjoram, see p.295). Though they undoubtedly contain therapeutic volatile oil and other constituents that benefit the digestion, savories are little used for medicinal purposes. *Satureja thymbra* is one of several oregano-flavoured herbs used in the Middle Eastern spice mixture known as *za'atar*. Others include *Origanum syriacum* (see p.296), *Thymus capitatus* (see p.388), and *Thymbra spicata* (donkey hyssop). American savories tend to have minty aromas; *Satureja viminea* has a high pulegone content, as in *Mentha pulegium* (see p.277) and should therefore be used with discretion. *Satureja douglasii* was named after David Douglas, the Scottish plant collector who explored the American West in the early 19th century. Its common name, *yerba buena*, was adopted by the Mexican village that later became San Francisco. This species grows in redwood forests and was much used by tribes in the Pacific Northwest. *Satureja* is probably derived from the Greek *saturos*, "satyr", a lustful woodland god, referring to the supposed aphrodisiac effects of savories.
CULTIVATION Well-drained to dry, neutral to alkaline soil in sun. *Satureja douglasii* needs moist, sandy, slightly acid loam and partial shade. Pinch out new shoots in spring, to encourage bushiness. Cut back perennials in early spring. Winter crops of *S. hortensis* may be grown in pots in greenhouses at 7–10°C (45–50°F) or from seed sown in early

Satureja hortensis

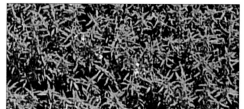

Satureja montana

Satureja spicigera

Satureja thymbra

autumn; it may deter Mexican bean beetle if planted along rows of legumes.

PROPAGATION By seed sown in spring at 13–16°C (55–61°F); by division in autumn or spring (perennials); by greenwood cuttings in summer (shrubby species).

HARVEST Leaves are harvested during the growing season. Flowering tops are picked in summer. Both are used fresh, or dried for infusions and oil extraction.

Satureja acinos. See *Acinos arvensis*.

Satureja douglasii syn. *Micromeria chamissonis* (*yerba buena*)
Creeping evergreen perennial with wiry stems, rooting at nodes, and pairs of aromatic, broadly ovate to rounded, toothed leaves, to 2cm (¾in) long. Tiny, white or purplish-white, two-lipped, tubular flowers are produced in the axils from spring to late summer. Native to western N America. ‡ 5cm (2in), ↔ indefinite.
HARDINESS Fully hardy.
PARTS USED Leaves (with flowers if present when stripped from stems).
PROPERTIES A tonic aromatic herb with diaphoretic, anti-arthritic, and carminative effects. It has a mint-like flavour.
MEDICINAL USES Internally for mild feverish illnesses and stomach upsets. Externally for toothache, rashes, and prickly heat.
CULINARY USES Dried leaves are used for tea, either alone, or blended with other herbs.
◻ ◻ ▪ ◿

■ *Satureja hortensis* (summer savory)
Bushy annual with linear–oblanceolate leaves, to 3cm (1¼in) long. Whorls of lilac to white or purple flowers appear in summer. Native to SE Europe. ‡ 10–35cm (4–14in), ↔ 30cm (12in). ‘Aromata’ is compact, with a stronger superior flavour. Originated in E Germany, where it is used for flavouring sausages.
HARDINESS Fully hardy.
PARTS USED Leaves, flowering tops.
PROPERTIES An antiseptic, astringent, warming, expectorant herb with a peppery flavour and high carvacrol content. It improves digestion, increases perspiration, stimulates the uterus and

nervous system, and is reputedly aphrodisiac.
MEDICINAL USES Internally for indigestion, nausea, colic, diarrhoea, bronchial congestion, sore throat, and menstrual disorders. Contraindicated during pregnancy. Externally for sore throat and insect stings.
CULINARY USES Leaves are used to flavour legumes, sausages, meat dishes, stuffings, and marinades (especially for olives). An ingredient of *herbes de Provence* (with *Rosmarinus officinalis*, see p.348, *Thymus vulgaris*, see p.387, and *Origanum* spp., see p.295).
⊞ ◻ ▪ ◿

■ *Satureja montana* (winter savory)
Small subshrub with leathery, linear–lanceolate, pointed leaves, to 3cm (1¼in) long. Whorls of pink-white to mauve or purple flowers appear in summer. Native to S Europe. ‡ 10–40cm (4–16in), ↔ 20cm (8in). var. *citriodora* (lemon savory) is small and spreading, with a lemon-like flavour. ‡ 15cm (6in). ‘Purple Mountain’ is compact, with a good flavour and bright purple flowers. ‡ 23cm (9in).
HARDINESS Fully hardy.
PARTS USED Leaves, shoots.
PROPERTIES As for *S. hortensis* but with a higher proportion of thymol.
MEDICINAL USES As for *S. hortensis*.
CULINARY USES Is used in the same ways as *S. hortensis*, but has a more pungent flavour.
◻ ⊞ ▪ ◿

Satureja nepeta. See *Calamintha nepeta*.

■ *Satureja spicigera* syn. *S. repandra* (creeping savory)
Prostrate shrublet with linear–oblanceolate leaves, to 2cm (¾in) long. White flowers, about 6mm (¼in) long, are produced in late summer and early autumn. Native to Turkey, Iran, and the Caucasus. ‡ 6cm (2½in), ↔ 30cm (12in).
HARDINESS Fully hardy.
PARTS USED Leaves.
PROPERTIES Similar to *S. hortensis* but more strongly flavoured.
MEDICINAL USES As for *S. hortensis*.
CULINARY USES As for *S. hortensis*.
◻ ▪ ◿

■ *Satureja thymbra* (pink savory, Roman hyssop, thyme-leaved savory, *za'atar rumi*)
Dense, much-branched shrublet with stiff, linear–oblong, almost bristly leaves, about 1cm (½in) long, and pink flowers in spring and summer. Found from E Mediterranean to the Balkans. ‡ 40cm (16in), ↔ 30–40cm (12–16in).
HARDINESS Frost hardy.
PARTS USED Leaves.
PROPERTIES A pungent aromatic herb that improves digestion, and has bactericidal and expectorant effects. It has a thyme-like flavour.
MEDICINAL USES Internally, in folk medicine as a tea to relieve minor digestive discomfort and bronchial congestion.
CULINARY USES Leaves are used to flavour meat dishes, grilled or barbecued meat, roasted vegetable dishes; also in a marinade for olives. An ingredient of the Middle Eastern spice mixture *za'atar*. Dried leaves are used to make tea. Strong infusion is used to clean wine barrels in Crete.
ECONOMIC USES Oil, rich in carvacrol and thymol, is distilled from the leaves for the pharmaceutical industry.
◻ ▪ ◿ ◿

Satureja viminea syn. *Micromeria viminea* (Costa Rican mint bush, Jamaican peppermint)
Upright, spreading, well-branched shrub with obovate leaves, to 1cm (½in) long. Tiny, tubular, white flowers appear in early summer. Native to the West Indies. ‡ 1.5m (5ft), ↔ 1m (3ft).
HARDINESS Min. 7°C (45°F).
PARTS USED Leaves.
PROPERTIES An aromatic herb that improves digestion. It has a pennyroyal-like scent.
MEDICINAL USES Leaves mixed with ginger as a remedy for colic (Costa Rica).
CULINARY USES Leaves are used to flavour meat (Trinidad).
◻ ▪ ◿ ⊞

SAUSSUREA

Asteraceae

This genus of some 300 species of perennials is found in mountains of Europe, Asia, and N America. One or two species are occasionally seen in cultivation, but most of these thistle-like plants have no ornamental value. *Saussurea costus* (costus, *kuth*) has been used in both Chinese and Ayurvedic medicine for thousands of years. The roots have a pervasive scent, as indicated by the Chinese name, *mu xiang*, which means "wood fragrance"; the scent has been described as "reminiscent of violet, orris, and vetiver". Crops of costus are grown in China (mainly in Guangdong province) for the herb trade, and in N India as a source of oil for perfumery. Wild plants have been seriously over-collected; *S. costus* was placed under international protection as an endangered species in 1997. *Saussurea* was named after the Swiss philosopher and botanist Horace Benedict de Saussure (1740–99).
CULTIVATION Moist soil in sun or partial shade.
PROPAGATION By seed sown when ripe; by division in spring.

Saussurea costus

HARVEST Roots are lifted in autumn and spring, and dried for use in decoctions, liquid extracts, and powders, or processed for oil extraction.

■ *Saussurea costus* syn. *S. lappa* (costus, *kuth*)
Perennial with a thick tapering root, lyre-shaped, pinnate lower leaves, 30–40cm (12–16in) long and about 30cm (12in) wide, and irregularly toothed upper leaves, which clasp the stem. Purple, burdock-like flower heads, to 3.5cm (1½in) across, are produced in dense clusters of 2–3 in summer. Native to the E Himalayas. ‡ 2–3m (6–10ft), ↔ 1m (3ft).
HARDINESS Fully hardy.
PARTS USED Roots (*mu xiang*), oil.
PROPERTIES A bitter, pungent, warming herb that relaxes spasms, lowers blood pressure, relieves pain, and has anti-bacterial effects. It regulates spleen and stomach energy.
MEDICINAL USES Internally for abdominal distension and pain, chest pains owing to liver problems and jaundice, gall bladder pain, constipation associated with energy stagnation, and asthma. Used in Ayurvedic medicine for digestive problems, coughs, asthma, cholera, and as an alterative in skin diseases and rheumatism.
CULINARY USES Roots are sometimes used for flavouring.
ECONOMIC USES Oil is used in commercial food flavouring; also used in perfumery.

SCHISANDRA
Schisandraceae

This genus of some 25 species of deciduous and evergreen climbers occurs in woodland in E Asia, with one species in SE USA. *Schisandra chinensis* was introduced to Western botanical gardens in the late 1850s. It is a large handsome climber with scented flowers and brightly coloured berries on female plants. It was first mentioned in Chinese medical texts during the later Han dynasty (AD25–220). Different schisandras are used in N and S China; these were first differentiated in 1596 by Li Shi Zhen in his *Compendium of Materia Medica*. *Schisandra chinensis* is used by both men and

women as a tonic for sexual energy, and is popular with women because of its reputation for improving the complexion. The Chinese name means "five flavour fruit", because it has sweet and sour flavours in the peel and pulp, and acrid, bitter, and salty flavours in the seeds. The red-flowered *S. sphenanthera* (southern schisandra), which grows farther south and west, is used in the same ways as *S. chinensis* but is seldom exported. *Schisandra* is from the Greek *schizo*, "to divide", and *andreios*, "male", and refers to the split anther cells.
CULTIVATION Rich, well-drained, moist soil in sun or partial shade. Both male and female plants must be grown for successful fruiting. Leaves and young growths may be damaged by aphid. Remove unwanted shoots in late winter from plants trained against a wall or fence.
PROPAGATION By seed sown when ripe, or in spring after soaking overnight; by greenwood or semi-ripe cuttings in summer.
HARVEST Fruits are collected after the first frosts and sun-dried for use in decoctions, powders, and tinctures.

■ *Schisandra chinensis* (schisandra)
Deciduous woody climber with red shoots and glossy, elliptic to obovate, pointed leaves, 6–14cm (2½–5½in) long. Solitary, cream to pink, fragrant flowers, 2cm (¾in) across, are borne in late spring, followed on female plants by pendent clusters, 10–15cm (4–6in) long, of fleshy scarlet fruits. Native to NE China and Japan. ‡ 8m (25ft).
HARDINESS Fully hardy.
PARTS USED Fruits (*wu wei zi*).
PROPERTIES A sweet and sour, astringent, warming herb that regulates secretion of body fluids, controls coughing, and moistens dry and irritated tissues. It acts as a tonic for the nervous system, and kidney and heart energies.
MEDICINAL USES Internally for dry coughs, asthma, night sweats, urinary disorders, involuntary ejaculation, chronic and early morning diarrhoea (associated with kidney weakness), palpitations, insomnia, poor memory, hyperacidity, hepatitis, and diabetes. Externally for irritating and allergic skin conditions. Combined with *Ophiopogon japonicus* (see p.295) and *Panax ginseng* (see p.300) as an injectable drug for shock.

SCLEROTIUM
Sclerotium cocos. See *Wolfiporia cocos*.

SCOPOLIA
Solanaceae

This genus of five species of rhizomatous perennials is found from S and C Europe, and N Russia (Siberia) to the Himalayas, China, and Japan. *Scopolia carniolica* is grown as an ornamental for its large, deeply veined leaves and bell-shaped flowers. It is a very poisonous plant, closely related to *Atropa bella-donna* (deadly nightshade, see p.138), and should be sited with care. The distribution of these two species overlaps in C Europe, and they have similar histories of medicinal uses. *Scopolia carniolica* contains hyoscine and hyoscyamine. It became popular in the USA during the 19th century as a substitute for *Atropa bella-donna*. In 1900 an alkaloid from *Scopolia carniolica* was combined with morphine from *Papaver somniferum* (see p.302) to produce "twilight sleep", a compound used as a pre-anaesthetic prior to the administration of chloroform or ether. *Scopolia* resembles both *Atropa* (see p.138) and *Hyoscyamus* (see p.239) in chemistry. Four of the five species – *Scopolia carniolica*, *S. lurida*, *S. physaloides*, and *S. tangutica* – are major sources of tropane alkaloids for the pharmaceutical industry. The Chinese *S. tangutica* yields hyoscyamine, anisodamine, and anisodine. *Scopolia* was named after Giovanni Antonio Scopoli (1723–88), polymath, author of botanical works, physician, and professor of natural history.
CULTIVATION Well-drained, moist, humus-rich, neutral to slightly alkaline soil in shade.
PROPAGATION By seed sown in autumn; by division in spring.
HARVEST Rhizomes are lifted in autumn and processed for extraction of alkaloids.
⚠ **WARNING** Toxic if eaten.

■ *Scopolia carniolica* syn. *S. atropoides* (Japanese belladonna, scopolia)
Clump-forming perennial with fleshy rhizomes and ovate to ovate–oblong, pointed, deeply veined leaves, to 20cm (8in) long. Solitary, pendent, brown-purple, bell-shaped flowers, 2.5cm (1in)

S

Schisandra chinensis

Scopolia carniolica

long, with yellowish-green inner surfaces, appear in spring and early summer. Native to C and SE Europe and the Caucasus. ↕ 60cm (24in).
HARDINESS Fully hardy.
PARTS USED Rhizomes.
PROPERTIES A narcotic warming herb that dilates the pupils, relaxes spasms, and relieves pain.
MEDICINAL USES Internally for spasms of the gastrointestinal tract, bile ducts, and urinary tract. Contraindicated for children under six, and for a number of clinical conditions. Also, in Chinese medicine, for chronic diarrhoea, dysentery, stomach ache, and manic-depressive states. For internal use only by qualified practitioners. Mainly as a source of hyoscine, and sometimes as a substitute for *Atropa bella-donna* (see p.138), notably in the manufacture of belladonna plasters, and for *Hyoscyamus niger* (see p.239).
⚠ **WARNING** This herb and its alkaloids are subject to legal restrictions in some countries.
🞖 ▣

SCROPHULARIA
Figwort

Scrophulariaceae

This genus contains about 200 species of annuals, perennials, and occasionally subshrubs, found in temperate regions and on mountains in the tropics. Few are ornamental, though the variegated form of *Scrophularia auriculata* (water figwort) is widely grown as a marginal aquatic. In France, *S. nodosa* is known as *herbe du siège* since the tubers were eaten by Cardinal Richelieu's starving troops during the siege of La Rochelle (1627–8). *Scrophularia nodosa* is an example of the Doctrine of Signatures (see p.44), the nodular roots revealing it as a remedy for swollen glands and tumours. Culpeper wrote that "a better remedy cannot be found for the king's evil" (*The English Physician Enlarged*, 1653). "King's evil" was a term used for scrofula (tuberculosis of the lymphatic glands), hence the name *Scrophularia*. Its constituents include aucubin, a mild laxative that increases excretion of uric acid from the kidneys, and anti-arthritic compounds harpagoside and harpagide, as in *Harpagophytum* (see p.230). *Scrophularia auriculata*, from

W Europe, and the American *S. marilandica* have similar properties. The use of *S. ningpoensis* in Chinese medicine dates back to the later Han dynasty (AD25–220).
CULTIVATION Moist to wet soil in sun or partial shade. Plants may be damaged by larvae of the figwort weevil.
PROPAGATION By seed sown in autumn or spring; by division in spring; by basal cuttings in spring; by softwood cuttings in summer.
HARVEST Roots (*S. ningpoensis*) are lifted in autumn and dried for use in decoctions. Plants (*S. nodosa*) are cut when flowering and dried for use in infusions, liquid extracts, ointments, poultices, and tinctures.

▣ *Scrophularia ningpoensis* (black figwort, Ningpo figwort)
Perennial with four-angled stems and ovate leaves, to 15cm (6in) long. Small, brown-red, two-lipped flowers are borne in panicles on thread-like stalks in spring, followed by ovoid capsules. Native to China. ↕ 60cm–1.2m (2–4ft), ↔ 30–45cm (12–18in).
HARDINESS Fully hardy.
PARTS USED Roots (*xuan shen*).
PROPERTIES A bitter, saline, cooling herb that lowers fever, blood pressure, and blood sugar, and has anti-bacterial effects. Small doses act as a heart tonic; large doses depress cardiac function.
MEDICINAL USES Internally for feverish illnesses with symptoms such as rashes, delirium, and insomnia (associated with excess heat), dry cough, throat infections, abscesses, and carbuncles.
🞖 ▣

▣ *Scrophularia nodosa* (common figwort)
Perennial with tuberous rhizomes and ovate, pointed, toothed leaves, to 12cm (5in) long. Small, green-brown flowers are borne in panicles in summer, followed by ovoid capsules. Native to Europe. ↕ 40cm–1.2m (16–48in), ↔ 15–38cm (6–15in).
HARDINESS Fully hardy.
PARTS USED Whole plant.
PROPERTIES A diuretic, alterative herb that is mildly laxative, relieves pain, and stimulates the liver, heart, and circulation.

MEDICINAL USES Internally for chronic skin diseases (such as eczema, psoriasis, pruritus), mastitis, swollen lymph nodes, and poor circulation. Contraindicated for heart conditions. Externally for skin diseases (including fungal infections), wounds, burns, ulcers, and skin inflammations. Combines well with *Rumex crispus* (see p.341) for skin diseases.
🞖 ▣

SCUTELLARIA
Skullcap

Lamiaceae

This is a cosmopolitan genus of about 300 species of annuals and perennials. *Scutellaria baicalensis* is an attractive small perennial for borders. Its first mention as a medicinal herb is in the *Shen Nong Canon of Herbs*, which dates back to the later Han dynasty (AD25–220). It has been well researched in China and found to contain flavonoids that improve liver function and have anti-inflammatory and anti-allergenic effects. The Himalayan *S. barbata* (barbed skullcap) is also used, mainly as a detoxicant for certain kinds of cancer, liver diseases, poisonous bites, and pharyngitis. *Scutellaria lateriflora* (Virginian skullcap) is widely grown in herb gardens and nurseries, although many plants labelled as such are in fact *S. altissima*, a larger plant with showier flowers; care should be taken to check the identity of plants grown for medicinal use. Virginian skullcap was used by native tribes, such as the Cherokee, for menstrual problems, but rose to fame in the 18th century after a Dr Vandesveer began using it as a cure for rabies, hence its common name, "mad dog skullcap". The plant was first listed as a sedative and anti-spasmodic in the *US Pharmacopoeia* in 1863 and was widely used by the Physiomedicalists (followers of Samuel Thomson) (see p.44) as a remedy for convulsions, epilepsy, and schizophrenia. The European *S. galericulata* appears to have similar constituents to *S. baicalensis*, and is used as a substitute for *S. lateriflora*. *Scutellaria* is from the Latin *scutella*, "a small dish", referring to the pouch-like appearance of the fruit's calyx.
CULTIVATION Light, well-drained soil in sun or partial shade. *Scutellaria lateriflora* enjoys damp conditions. *Scutellaria baicalensis* needs sharp drainage and tolerates drought. Cut back to within 7–10cm (3–4in) of the base in early spring and pinch out in spring, to encourage bushy growth.
PROPAGATION By seed sown in autumn; by division in autumn or spring; by basal or semi-ripe cuttings in spring or summer.
HARVEST Roots (*S. baicalensis*) are lifted in autumn or spring from plants 3–4 years old, and dried for decoctions. Plants (*S. lateriflora*) are cut when flowering for use in infusions, liquid extracts, and tinctures, or dried for tablets.

▣ *Scutellaria baicalensis* (Baikal skullcap)
Bushy spreading perennial with lanceolate leaves, to 4cm (1½in) long. Dense, one-sided racemes of hairy, tubular, blue-purple flowers,

Scrophularia ningpoensis

Scrophularia nodosa

Scutellaria baicalensis

2.5cm (1in) long, are produced in summer. Native to Mongolia, China, and Japan.
↕ 30–38cm (12–15in), ↔ 20–30cm (8–12in).
HARDINESS Fully hardy.
PARTS USED Roots (*huang qin*).
PROPERTIES A bitter, sedative, cooling herb that lowers fever, blood pressure, and cholesterol levels, relaxes spasms, stimulates the liver, improves digestion, controls bleeding, and has diuretic, anti-bacterial, and anti-toxic effects. It reputedly calms the foetus in pregnant women.
MEDICINAL USES Internally for enteritis, dysentery, diarrhoea, jaundice, chronic hepatitis, urinary tract infections, hypertension, threatened miscarriage, nosebleed, and haemorrhage from lungs or bowel. It is an ingredient of the Chinese drug *san huang zhe she ye* ("injection of three yellow herbs"), the others being *Coptis chinensis* (see p.179) and *Phellodendron amurense* (see p.311).

▣ *Scutellaria lateriflora* (mad dog skullcap, Virginian skullcap)
Perennial with slender rhizomes and thin, ovate–lanceolate, toothed leaves, to 8cm (3in) long. Blue, occasionally pink or white flowers are produced in one-sided, mostly axillary racemes in summer. Native to N America, especially northern and western. ↕ 15–75cm (6–30in), ↔ to 45cm (18in).
HARDINESS Fully hardy.
PARTS USED Whole plant.

PROPERTIES A bitter sedative herb that relaxes spasms, lowers fever, and stimulates the kidneys.
MEDICINAL USES Internally for nervous and convulsive complaints, insomnia, tension headaches, nervous exhaustion, irritability, delirium tremens, neuralgia, and withdrawal from barbiturates and tranquillizers. Excess causes giddiness, stupor, confusion, and twitching. Contraindicated during pregnancy.

SELENICEREUS
Cactaceae

This genus contains about 20 species of climbing or semi-pendent, epiphytic or lithophytic cacti, found in Texas, Mexico, C America, Colombia, and the West Indies. *Selenicereus grandiflorus* is one of several species grown for its exquisite blooms, which open in the evening and close at dawn. It was introduced from the West Indies to Britain in 1700 as a greenhouse ornamental, though its unappealing spiny stems were often trained out of sight along the eaves. A rapturous description in *The Illustrated Dictionary of Gardening* (ed. George Nicholson, 1885) concluded that "there is hardly any flower of greater beauty". *Selenicereus grandiflorus* contains cactine, an alkaloid that has a tonic effect on the heart, comparable to *Digitalis* (see p.193). It is cultivated in Florida and Mexico for the medicinal herb trade. *Selenicereus* is from the Greek *selene*, "moon" and *Cereus*, another genus of cacti.
CULTIVATION As an epiphytic climber, or in epiphytic compost, pH6 or lower, in sun or partial shade, with high humidity. Keep on the dry side in winter. Plants in greenhouses may be damaged by mealybugs and scale insects.
PROPAGATION By seed or stem cuttings sown in spring or summer at 16–19°C (61–66°F).
HARVEST Young stems and flowers are cut in summer, and dried for infusions, liquid extracts, and tinctures.

▣ *Selenicereus grandiflorus* (night-blooming cereus, queen-of-the-night)
Perennial, climbing, epiphytic cactus with 5–8-ribbed stems, 1–2.5cm (½–1in) thick, clad in tufts of yellow to grey spines. Fragrant white flowers, to 30cm (12in) across, with yellow-

brown outer segments and numerous stamens, open overnight in summer, followed by fleshy, globose to ovoid, red fruits, to 8cm (3in) long. Native to Mexico and the West Indies. ↕ 3–5m (10–15ft).
HARDINESS Min. 10–15°C (50–59°F).
PARTS USED Young stems, flowers.
PROPERTIES A diuretic, sedative, tonic herb that stimulates the heart.
MEDICINAL USES Internally for palpitations, angina, oedema, rheumatism, kidney congestion, and nervous headaches; in folk medicine for rheumatism and to expel intestinal parasites. Excess causes gastric irritation, confusion, and hallucinations. For use only by qualified practitioners.

SEMPERVIVUM
Hens and chicks, houseleek
Crassulaceae

This genus of about 40 evergreen species of mat-forming, evergreen, succulent perennials occurs in mountains of Europe, and W Asia. Known as "houseleeks", from the Anglo-Saxon *leac*, "a plant", they were grown in ornamental pots in front of houses during Roman times, and remain popular as trouble-free, drought-tolerant subjects for containers and walls. The Emperor Charlemagne decreed that his subjects should grow houseleeks on their roofs to ward off lightning; they are still traditionally planted for this purpose. *Sempervivum tectorum* contains tannins and mucilage, which soothe and heal damaged tissues; the leaves were traditionally halved and applied directly to the affected part. *Sempervivum* comes from the Latin *semper*, "always", and *vivus*, "alive", referring to the resilience of these plants.
CULTIVATION Well-drained, gritty or stony soil in sun. May also be planted in crevices of roofing tiles, thatch, walls, and paving. Individual rosettes die after flowering, having produced numerous offsets. Leaves may be damaged by rust (*Endophyllum sempervivi*). Houseleeks will survive without water for long periods.
PROPAGATION By seed sown in spring; by division; by offsets in spring or summer.
HARVEST Leaves are collected as required and used fresh in infusions, poultices, and tinctures.

S

Scutellaria lateriflora

Selenicereus grandiflorus

Sempervivum tectorum

■ **Sempervivum tectorum** (hens and chicks, houseleek)
Mat-forming succulent with rosettes, to 10cm (4in) across, and thick, fleshy, obovate, spine-tipped leaves, to 4cm (1½in) long, which are often purple-flushed, especially in hot dry conditions. Clusters of dull pink, star-shaped flowers are borne on erect leafy stems in summer. Native to S Europe. ‡30cm (when flowering), ↔ 50cm (20in). 'Nigrum' has purple-tipped leaves. 'Red Flush' has red-green leaves. 'Sunset' has orange-red leaves.
HARDINESS Fully hardy.
PARTS USED Leaves.
PROPERTIES An astringent, acidic, saline herb that is diuretic and has cooling, soothing, and healing effects.
MEDICINAL USES Internally, once used for shingles, skin complaints, and haemorrhoids. Excess is emetic and purgative. Externally for stings, bites, warts, burns, sunburn, inflamed or itching skin conditions, and corns.
▨ ▧ ▤

SENECIO

Asteraceae

This large cosmopolitan genus contains over 1000 species of annuals, biennials, perennials, and evergreen shrubs, trees, and climbers. They contain toxic pyrrolizidine alkaloids, similar to those found in *Symphytum officinale* (see p.377), which are associated with liver damage. Various species are grown as ornamentals but many others are weeds; those common in pasture cause serious poisoning and ill health in livestock. *Senecio aureus* (liferoot) is a classic herbal "female regulator", used by several native N American tribes to ease childbirth and treat complaints of the female reproductive system. It was also mentioned by Dr Charles Millspaugh (*American Medicinal Plants*, 1892) as a substitute for *Claviceps purpurea* (ergot, see p.173) to control pulmonary haemorrhage. Although declared a "completely safe aid in gynaecological disorders" (Hutchens, *Indian Herbology of North America*, 1973), it is no longer considered safe for internal use because of its alkaloids. *Senecio vulgaris* (groundsel) has similar uses but is also

Senecio aureus

no longer regarded as safe. *Senecio jacobaea* (ragwort) is used externally, often combined with *Gaultheria procumbens* (see p.221) and *Lobelia inflata* (see p.265) in lotions to relieve arthritis, rheumatism, muscular pain, and sciatica. *Senecio* is from the Latin *senex*, "old man", referring to the white-haired seeds.
CULTIVATION Damp to wet soil in sun or partial shade.
PROPAGATION By seed sown in autumn or spring; by division in autumn or spring.
HARVEST Plants are cut before flowering and dried for use in infusions and liquid extracts. Roots are lifted in autumn and dried for powder.

■ **Senecio aureus** syn. *Packera aurea* (golden ragwort, liferoot, squaw weed)
Perennial with heart-shaped, blunt, toothed basal leaves, to 15cm (6in) long, and narrow pinnate upper leaves. Yellow, daisy-like flowers are borne in branched terminal clusters in spring and early summer. Found from eastern N America to E USA (Texas). ‡15–75cm (6–30in), ↔15–60cm (6–24in).
HARDINESS Fully hardy.
PARTS USED Whole plant, rhizomes.
PROPERTIES A bitter astringent herb that is diuretic, stimulates the uterus, and controls bleeding.
MEDICINAL USES Internally for failure to menstruate, menopausal symptoms, prolonged labour, and pulmonary haemorrhage. Contraindicated during pregnancy. No longer considered safe for internal use. Externally for vaginal discharge.
⚠ **WARNING** This herb is subject to legal restrictions in some countries.
▨ ▧ ▤

SENNA

Caesalpiniaceae

This genus of about 260 species of perennials, shrubs, and trees occurs mainly in the tropics and subtropics. It is often included in *Cassia*. A few species are grown as ornamentals in warm regions or in greenhouses in temperate regions. *Senna marilandica* is one of the hardiest, but needs a sheltered situation outdoors in cold areas. The roots were used as a laxative by the Cherokee, and also to relieve fever, cramps, and heart problems. The use of *S. alexandrina* as a laxative was introduced to Europe by Arab physicians in the 9th and 10th centuries. *Senna alexandrina* is the main ingredient of most laxative preparations, but various other species also contain laxative anthraquinone glycosides (sennosides). The pods of *S. fistula* (pudding pipe tree) are up to 50cm (20in) long and contain a black pulp, which is used as a mild substitute for *S. alexandrina*. *Senna* is useful for a wide range of other complaints, ranging from ringworm (*S. alata*, *S. obtusifolia*, and *S. sophera*) to venereal disease (*S. sieberiana* and *S. surattensis*). *Senna reticulata* yields the antibiotic Rhein-cassic acid, which is effective against various bacterial and fungal infections. *Senna obtusifolia* (sickle senna) was recorded in

Senna alexandrina

Chinese medicine during the later Han dynasty (AD25–220). It is used in patent medicines and to treat hypertension, high cholesterol levels, constipation, skin diseases, and eye disorders. The seeds of *S. laevigata*, *S. obtusifolia*, *S. occidentalis*, and *S. sericea* are used as a coffee substitute in various parts of the world.
CULTIVATION Well-drained soil in sun. *Senna marilandica* needs rich, moist, sandy soil. Pot-grown plants are prone to root mealybugs.
PROPAGATION By seed sown in spring at 18–24°C (64–75°F); by semi-ripe cuttings in summer. Prune to shape and remove dead or badly placed growths in early spring.
HARVEST Leaves are picked before and during flowering; pods are collected in autumn when ripe. Both are dried for use in infusions, powders, tablets, and tinctures.
⚠ **WARNING** Leaves may cause contact dermatitis.

■ **Senna alexandrina** syn. *Cassia angustifolia*, *C. senna* (Alexandrian senna, Tinnevelly senna)
Shrubby perennial with pale green, pinnate leaves, 5–15cm (2–6in) long, divided into 3–8 pairs of pointed lanceolate leaflets. Yellow to tawny-yellow flowers, about 1cm (½in) across, are borne in axillary racemes, to 20cm (8in) long, in spring and summer, followed by straight pods, to 7cm (3in) long. Native to Arabia, Djibouti, and Somalia. ‡1m (3ft), ↔ 50–60cm (20–24in).
HARDINESS Min. 5°C (41°F).
PARTS USED Leaves (*fan xie ye*), pods.
PROPERTIES A sweet, cooling, laxative herb with a tea-like aroma and anti-bacterial effects.
MEDICINAL USES Internally for constipation. Usually prescribed with carminatives (such as *Coriandrum sativum*, see p.180, or *Zingiber officinale*, see p.411) to reduce griping. Excess or frequent usage may cause nausea, vomiting, abdominal pain, inflammation of the gastrointestinal tract, and deterioration in bowel function (laxative dependency). Contraindicated during pregnancy, and for colitis or spastic constipation.
▨ ▧ ▤ ▨

■ **Senna marilandica** (wild senna)
Perennial with erect to sprawling stems and dull yellow-green, pinnate leaves, to 28cm (11in) long, divided into 5–9 pairs of tapering elliptic leaflets. Yellow flowers appear in racemes in

Senna marilandica

summer, followed by stiff hairy pods, to 11cm (4½in) long. Native to Midwest and SE USA.
‡ 60cm–2m (2–6ft), ↔ 15cm–1.2m (6in–4ft).
HARDINESS Fully hardy (borderline).
PARTS USED Leaves, pods.
PROPERTIES A laxative herb with a milder slower effect than *S. alexandrina*.
MEDICINAL USES Internally for constipation.

SERENOA

Arecaceae

A single species of evergreen palm belongs to this genus. *Serenoa repens* (saw palmetto) is grown as an ornamental for its shrub-like habit and clumps of fan-shaped leaves. It occurs mainly in coastal areas, forming dense thickets as an understorey in swampy areas, such as the Everglades. Its sweet,

Serenoa repens

olive-shaped fruits, which are produced in abundance, provided food for native tribes, who also recognized their sedative and tonic properties. Settlers who regularly ate the fruits noticed improved digestion and increased strength and weight. They made a soft drink, known as "metto", from the juice. Animals fed on saw palmetto were similarly renowned for their health and vigour. The fruits contain hormonal substances that have anabolic and oestrogenic effects. Though best known as a remedy for prostate problems, saw palmetto is a useful herb for women, and for urinary complaints in either sex. Supplies of fruits for the herb trade are wild-collected, mainly in Florida (USA). *Serenoa* is named after Sereno Watson (1826–92), an eminent Harvard botanist who described many new plant species during pioneering expeditions.
CULTIVATION Moist to wet soil in sun or dappled shade. Plants grown under glass may be attacked by red spider mite and scale insects.
PROPAGATION By seed sown in spring; by separation of suckers in spring. Divided clumps are difficult to re-establish.
HARVEST Fruits are collected when ripe, partly dried for elixirs, infusions, liquid extracts, and tinctures, or dried and powdered for use in tablets.

■ *Serenoa repens* syn. *S. serrulata* (saw palmetto)
Clump-forming, rhizomatous palm with fan-shaped, blue-green to yellow-green leaves, 45cm–1m (18–36in) wide. Tiny, fragrant, cream flowers are borne in summer, followed by ovoid, oily, blue-black fruits, about 2.5cm (1in) long. Native to SE USA (South Carolina to Florida Keys and west to Alabama and Missouri). ‡ 2–4m (6–12ft), ↔ indefinite.
HARDINESS Min. 7°C (45°F).
PARTS USED Fruits.
PROPERTIES A sedative, warming, tonic herb with a soapy taste and pungent, vanilla-like aroma. It affects the endocrine system, is a urinary antiseptic, diuretic, and expectorant, and is reputedly aphrodisiac.
MEDICINAL USES Internally for impotence, low sex drive, debility in elderly men, prostate conditions, cystitis, bronchial complaints associated with coldness, and wasting diseases; also to encourage breast enlargement in women. May be combined with *Equisetum arvense* (see p.203) and *Hydrangea arborescens* (see p.238) for enlarged prostate.
CULINARY USES Fruits and seeds are edible.

SESAMUM

Pedaliaceae

This genus of 15 species of annuals and perennials occurs in tropical Asia and southern Africa. *Sesamum indicum* (sesame) is African in origin and has been cultivated in India and the Near East for thousands of years. A plant named *semsent*, mentioned in the Egyptian Ebers papyri (c.1500BC), is probably the earliest record of *S. indicum*. It was also grown in ancient Egypt, and in Babylonia (2200–538BC). A site

excavated near Yerevan (Armenia) revealed jars of sesame seeds from c.900–600BC, and elaborate equipment for oil extraction. In ancient Greece, Theophrastus (c.370–c.287BC) recorded it as one of the main summer crops, and Dioscorides (1st century AD) described the custom of sprinkling the seeds on bread. Today the main producers are India, China, Myanmar (Burma), the Sudan, and Nigeria. Sesame plants have attractive flowers and, given sufficient warmth and humidity, are easily raised from seed bought for culinary purposes. Plants that produce black seeds were previously described as *S. orientale* but are now classed as a cultivar of *S. indicum*. Sesame has been used in Chinese medicine since the 16th century, and it is an important rejuvenative tonic in Ayurvedic medicine. In Africa the seeds are stewed whole; in India they are ground into meal; and in the Middle East, India, and China, they are made into sweetmeats. Sesame oil is widely used in Japan; it is an excellent culinary oil as it keeps for a long time without becoming rancid. Sesame seeds are rich in protein, unsaturated oil, vitamins B3, E, folic acid, and minerals, notably calcium. There are indications that the calcium is well absorbed, providing an excellent dietary source of this mineral. The word "sesame" was immortalized in the *Arabian Nights* when Ali Baba discovered the magic formula "Open Sesame!", which opened a cave where 40 thieves had hidden their treasure. It is a Greek word that may be derived from the Arabic *simsim*.
CULTIVATION Well-drained, sandy soil in sun.
PROPAGATION By seed sown in spring at 18–24°C (65–75°F).
HARVEST Leaves are picked during the growing season for use in infusions. Seeds are collected when ripe and stored whole for decoctions, pressed for oil, or ground into paste.

■ *Sesamum indicum* (benne, gingili, sesame)
Strong-smelling annual or short-lived perennial, clad in sticky hairs, with trifoliate lower leaves, to 20cm (8in) long, and lanceolate to oblong upper leaves. White, tubular, bell-shaped flowers, to 3cm (1¼in) long, often pink-tinged and spotted, are followed by oblong, four-grooved capsules containing yellowish-white seeds. Native to South Africa;

S

Sesamum indicum

widely naturalized and cultivated. ↕1–2m (3–6ft), ↔ 45–90cm (18–36in). 'Afghani' is dwarf and early, with abundant golden-brown seeds. ↕1m (3ft). 'Black Thai' has pink-white flowers and black, richly flavoured seeds.

HARDINESS Min. 15°C (59°F).

PARTS USED Leaves, seeds (*hei zhi ma*), oil.

PROPERTIES A sweet, warming, soothing herb that strengthens bones and teeth, lubricates dry tissues, relaxes spasms, and has a tonic effect on the liver and kidneys. It is a mild laxative and lowers blood sugar levels.

MEDICINAL USES Internally for premature hair loss and greying, convalescence, chronic dry constipation, dental caries, osteoporosis, stiff joints, dry cough, and symptoms such as tinnitus, poor vision, dizziness, headache associated with weak liver and kidney energy (seeds); infantile cholera, diarrhoea, dysentery, catarrh, and cystitis (leaves); dry constipation in the elderly (oil). Seeds and oil are high in calories, and may not be advisable in the treatment of obese patients. Externally for haemorrhoids (seeds), and burns, boils, and ulcers (oil mixed with limewater).

CULINARY USES Dry, roasted, or toasted seeds are used in breads, cakes, biscuits (such as *benne* wafers), and pastries; also as a garnishing and flavouring for vegetables. Ground seeds are made into a paste (*tahini*), dip *hummus* (Middle East), mixed with honey as *halva* (Middle East, India), or salt (*gomashio*); also to thicken sauces, soups, and stews. Sesame oil (also known as *benne/bene* oil or *gingili*) is used in cooking and salad dressings, especially in Japanese cuisine. Leaves are eaten in salads or cooked as a vegetable.

ECONOMIC USES Seeds are added to bakery produce. Sesame oil is used in the manufacture of margarine, lubricants, soaps, and pharmaceutical drugs. Residue is used in livestock feeds.

▨ ◳ ⊠ ▪ ◪ ◪ ⊡

SIDERITIS
Lamiaceae

S

There are about 100 species of annuals, perennials, and evergreen subshrubs and shrubs in this genus, which occurs in coastal parts of the Mediterranean. A few species are grown for their attractive, white-woolly leaves. Though little known outside its homelands, *S. syriaca* makes one of the finest herb teas. It is also quite easy to cultivate in northern regions, given sharp drainage.

CULTIVATION Well-drained, gritty or stony soil in full sun. Provide a dry position or mulch with grit in winter, to prevent excessive moisture and mud splashing.

PROPAGATION By seed sown in spring; by semi-ripe cuttings in summer; by division in spring.

HARVEST Leaves are collected in spring, flowering tops as the first flowers open, and dried for infusions.

■ *Sideritis syriaca* (Greek mountain tea, *tsai*, *tsailopita*)
Perennial with white-woolly, lanceolate to ovate leaves, to 6cm (2½in) long. Whorls of primrose-

Sideritis syriaca

yellow, tubular flowers are produced in woolly spikes, about 8cm (3in) long, in summer. Native to S Greece and Crete. ↔ 50cm (20in).

HARDINESS Fully hardy (borderline).

PARTS USED Leaves, flowering tops.

PROPERTIES An aromatic digestive herb.

CULINARY USES Dried leaves and flowering tops are made into tea.

⊡ ▨ ◪

SILYBUM
Milk thistle

Asteraceae

This genus of two species of robust annuals or biennials is found throughout Europe and Mediterranean regions to C Asia, and parts of W and E Africa. *Silybum marianum* (milk thistle) was once cultivated as a vegetable, but today is more popular as an ornamental and as a medicinal plant. According to legend, its handsome variegation was caused by the Virgin Mary's milk as it ran down the leaves, hence the plant's specific name, *marianum*. Milk thistle contains unique flavolignans, collectively referred to as "silymarin", which protects the liver against toxins. Silymarin is apparently so effective that animals given it are unaffected by *Amanita phalloides* (death cap), a fungus that often causes irreversible liver damage. Historically, milk thistle was used to treat depression, associated with poor liver function. John Gerard considered it "the best remedy that grows against all melancholy diseases" (*The Herball or Generall Historie of Plants*, 1597). *Silybum* is from the Greek *silybon*, a term used by Dioscorides for thistle-like plants.

CULTIVATION Well-drained, neutral to alkaline soil in sun. Slugs and snails may damage leaves. Subject to control as a weed in some countries, notably in parts of Australia.

PROPAGATION By seed sown in summer or early autumn.

HARVEST For medicinal use, plants are cut when flowering and seeds are collected when ripe. All parts are dried for use in infusions and tinctures, or for extraction of silymarin. As a vegetable, young leaves, flower buds, and roots are harvested when tender and used fresh.

Silybum marianum

■ *Silybum marianum* syn. *Carduus marianus* (blessed thistle, milk thistle) Stout annual or biennial with a basal rosette of white-marbled, deeply lobed, obovate leaves, to 60cm (24in) long, which have spiny margins. Purple, thistle-like flower heads, 5cm (2in) across, supported by spiny bracts, are produced in summer, followed by black seeds, each bearing a tuft of white hairs. Found from SW Europe to S Russia and N Africa. ↕ 1.2–1.5m (4–5ft), ↔ 60–90cm (24–36in).

HARDINESS Fully hardy.

PARTS USED Whole plant, seeds, leaves, flower buds, roots.

PROPERTIES A bitter, diuretic, tonic herb that regenerates liver cells, stimulates bile flow, increases milk production, and relaxes spasms.

MEDICINAL USES Internally for liver and gall bladder diseases, jaundice, hepatitis, liver damage, cirrhosis, and poisoning (especially by *Amanita phalloides*, alcohol, drugs, and chemicals); also to minimize side-effects from cancer chemotherapy.

CULINARY USES Young leaves, with spines removed, are eaten raw or cooked as a spinach-like vegetable. Flower buds can be eaten like mini-artichokes. Tender roots of first-year plants are similar to salsify.

⊡ ▨ ⊠ ⊠ ▨ ▪ ◪

SIMABA
Simaroubaceae

A genus of 14 species of deciduous and evergreen trees and shrubs, native to S and C America. *Simaba cedron* occurs in dry plains and along paths and hedges. It was first imported for medicinal use in Europe in the 1890s. The seeds contain anti-malarial quassinoids, as found in *Picrasma excelsa* (see p.315) and *Quassia amara* (see p.338), which belong to the same family.

CULTIVATION Well-drained soil in sun.

PROPAGATION By seed sown when ripe; by hardwood cuttings at the end of the growing season.

HARVEST Seeds are collected when ripe and powdered for use in infusions.

Simaba cedron syn. *Quassia cedron* (cedron)
Small tree with a slender trunk and pinnate
leaves, to 1m (3ft) long, divided into 20 or more
narrowly elliptic leaflets. Dark yellow, slightly
fragrant, five-petalled flowers, with brown hairy
petals and purplish stamens, are borne in panicles,
to 25cm (10in) long, in summer, followed by
ovoid fruits, to 4cm (1½in) long, each containing
one seed. Found from C America to N Brazil.
‡ 5–15m (15–50ft), ↔ 3–10m (10–30ft).
HARDINESS Min. 15–18°C (59–64°F).
PARTS USED Seeds.
PROPERTIES An exceedingly bitter, tonic herb
with a coconut-like aroma. It lowers fevers,
reduces inflammation, and relaxes spasms.
MEDICINAL USES Internally for malaria or
fevers; internally and externally for snake bite.
▨ ▣ ◪

SIMMONDSIA
Jojoba

Simmondsiaceae

A single species of evergreen shrub makes up
this genus, which is native to SW USA and
N Mexico. *Simmondsia chinensis* is cultivated
on a large scale in Arizona (USA), Mexico,
Israel, Argentina, and Australia for its seeds,
which yield up to 55 per cent jojoba oil. Seeds
are borne only on female plants, and it takes
three years from seed before male and female
bushes reach flowering size and can be told
apart. Though deep-rooted and slow-growing,
jojoba tolerates saline conditions and severe
drought, making a lucrative crop where little
else will succeed. Jojoba oil has long been used
by native N Americans for cosmetic purposes
and leather softening. It is unusual in being a
liquid wax and has exceptional lubricant
qualities that have many different applications
in the engineering, pharmaceutical, and cosmetics
industries. Cultivation of jojoba increased
greatly following scientific research in the
1970s that showed jojoba oil is an excellent
substitute for sperm whale oil. Tissue culture
of female plants further increased production.
Jojoba plants are also useful for erosion control
and desert reclamation. *Simmondsia* is named
after T.W. Simmonds (d.1805), a botanist;
jojoba (pronounced "hohoba") is the Mexican–
Spanish word for the plant.
CULTIVATION Deep, well-drained to dry, sandy
or gravelly, slightly acid soil in full sun.
Tolerates drought.
PROPAGATION By seed sown in spring; by nodal
cuttings in spring; by heel cuttings in autumn.
HARVEST Seeds are collected when ripe and
crushed to extract oil.

▣ *Simmondsia chinensis* syn. *S. californica*
(goat nut, jojoba)
Multi-stemmed shrub with leathery, grey-green,
oblong–ovate leaves, to 4cm (1½in) long. Small,
petal-less flowers appear in spring – males
yellow, in clusters; females green, solitary,
pendent, followed by ovoid capsules, usually
containing a single seed, about 1cm (½in) long.
Native to the Sonoran Desert (SW USA and

Simmondsia chinensis

NW Mexico). ‡ 2m (6ft), ↔ 1–2m (3–6ft).
HARDINESS Half hardy.
PARTS USED Oil (from seeds).
PROPERTIES An odourless soothing herb with
exceptional, skin-softening effects.
MEDICINAL USES Externally for dry skin and
hair, psoriasis, acne, and sunburn.
ECONOMIC USES Oil is added to shampoos,
conditioners, moisturizers, soaps, massage oils,
sunscreens, pharmaceutical creams; in coatings
for confectionery, food, and tablets. Jojoba oil has
numerous industrial applications as a lubricant,
surfactant, stabilizer, emulsifier, and solubilizer.
▢ ▨ ▣ ◪

SINAPIS

Brassicaceae

This genus of ten species of annuals is native to
Europe and Mediterranean regions. *Sinapis alba*
is widely cultivated for mustard production and as
a forage and green manure crop. Mustard was
popular among the Romans, and its use spread
through their influence to Gaul, then a region
of W Europe. Mustard seeds were traditionally
sown in punnets of "mustard and cress", but have
now been replaced by the hardier *Brassica
napus* (rape). The flavour of mustard depends
on the kind of seeds used and the method of
preparation, which may be with water,
unfermented wine, vinegar, or verjuice. The seeds
of *Sinapis alba* are larger than those of *Brassica
nigra* (black mustard, see p.146) and are pale
brown, with a mild flavour. They are the main
ingredient in American mustard and are blended
with seeds of *B. nigra* to make English mustard;
they are not used in French mustards. In *The
English Physician Enlarged* (1653), Culpeper
recommends mustard for all kinds of complaints,
from weak stomachs and cold diseases to
toothache, joint pains, skin problems, and a crick
in the neck. John Evelyn described mustard as
"exceeding hot and mordicant, not only in Seed
but Leaf also of incomparable effect to quicken
and revive the Spirits; strengthening the Memory,
expelling heaviness, preventing the Vertiginous
Palsie [giddiness] and is a laudable Cephalic"
(*Acetaria, a Discourse on Sallets*, 1699). *Sinapis*
comes from the Greek *sinapi*, "mustard".

CULTIVATION Most soils in sun.
PROPAGATION By seed sown in spring.
HARVEST Seeds are harvested as they ripen, dried,
and stored whole, ground, or crushed for oil.

▣ *Sinapis alba* syn. *Brassica alba*, *B. hirta*
(white mustard)
Annual with rough hairy leaves, to 15cm (6in)
long, which are deeply and irregularly cut, with
a large terminal lobe. Yellow, vanilla-scented
flowers are produced in summer, followed by
beaked pods, to 4.5cm (1¾in) long, containing
up to eight seeds. Native to the Mediterranean
and Near East; widely naturalized. ‡ 60–80cm
(24–32in), ↔ 30cm (12in).
HARDINESS Fully hardy.
PARTS USED Seeds (*bai jie zi*), oil.
PROPERTIES A pungent, stimulant, warming
herb that improves digestion and circulation,
relieves pain, and is expectorant, diuretic, and
antibiotic.
MEDICINAL USES Externally (usually in
mustard bandages, baths, or poultices) for
respiratory infections, arthritic joints, chilblains,
and skin eruptions. In traditional Chinese
medicine, for complaints characterized by cold
and torpor: internally for bronchial congestion,
coughs, and joint pains; externally for painful
extremities, neuralgia, sprains, sores, boils, and
bruises. Like other mustards, seeds of *S. alba*
contain substances that are extremely irritant to
the skin and mucous membranes. For use only
by qualified practitioners.
CULINARY USES Ground seeds provide the
basis for mustards to accompany meats. Whole
seeds are an important component of pickles.
Seeds are sprouted with those of *Lepidium
sativum* (see p.259) as "mustard and cress"; the
mustard seeds grow more quickly than the
cress, so are sown three days later.
▢ ▨ ▣ ◪

Sinapis juncea. See *Brassica juncea*.
Sinapis nigra. See *Brassica nigra*.

Sinapis alba

S

369

SISYMBRIUM
Brassicaceae

This genus of 80 species of annuals and perennials is widespread in Eurasia, N America, the Andes, and N and S Africa. *Sisymbrium officinale* (hedge mustard) is a weedy plant that grows on wasteground, against walls, and beside paths. Dioscorides, who knew it as *erysimon*, prescribed it with honey as an antidote to poisons and infections. It then became known as *herba erysimi*, hence its former species name, *Erysimum officinale*. One of its common names is "singer's plant", because it was used to remedy loss of voice. *Sisymbrium* contains glucosinolates, as found in the true mustards (*Brassica nigra*, see p.146, *B. juncea*, see p.146, and *Sinapis alba*, see p.369), and a glycoside similar to digitalin.
CULTIVATION Moist to dry, acid to alkaline soil in sun or light shade. Self-sows readily.
PROPAGATION By seed sown in autumn or spring.
HARVEST Plants and flowering tops are cut in summer for infusions and liquid extracts. Leaves are picked in spring and used fresh.

Sisymbrium alliaria. See *Alliaria petiolata*.

◾ *Sisymbrium officinale* syn. *Erysimum officinale* (hedge mustard)
Stiffly upright, bristly annual, sometimes over-wintering, with a basal rosette of pinnate leaves, 5–9cm (2–3½in) long. Tiny, pale yellow flowers appear through summer, followed by erect pods, about 1cm (½in) long, containing orange-brown seeds. Native to Europe, N Africa, and the Near East. ↕ 30–90cm (12–36in), ↔ 15–60cm (6–24in).
HARDINESS Fully hardy.
PARTS USED Whole plant, leaves, flowering tops.
PROPERTIES A tonic herb with a mustard-like aroma. It has laxative, diuretic, and expectorant effects, and benefits the digestion.
MEDICINAL USES Internally for bronchitis, pharyngitis, coughs, laryngitis, and bronchial catarrh. Excess may affect the heart.
CULINARY USES Young leaves can be added to salads, soups, sauces, and omelettes.
🔲 ✒ 🔲 ♠ ✏

Sisymbrium officinale

SMILAX
Greenbrier, Sarsaparilla
Smilacaceae

This genus includes about 200 species of deciduous and evergreen, climbing or scrambling vines, ranging throughout temperate and tropical regions, mainly in the Americas and Asia. The roots of various different species are a source of sarsaparilla. Several species were brought from C America by the Spanish in the 1530s and widely used as a remedy for syphilis. The three main species used were *S. aristolochiaefolia* (Mexican sarsaparilla), *S. febrifuga* (Ecuadorian sarsaparilla), and *S. regelii* (Honduran sarsaparilla), which are still listed in the pharmacopoeias of many countries. Sarsaparilla was popular among settlers in N America as an ingredient of patent medicines and as the flavouring of root beer. Native N American tribes made tea from sarsaparilla roots to cure kidney problems, and ground the dried roots to a flour mixed with water and honey as a jelly to accompany roast meat or fish. The roots contain steroidal saponins and antibiotic compounds that provide the basis for sarsaponin tablets, which are effective in many cases of eczema and psoriasis. Clinical tests have also shown that sarsaparilla is effective in treating leprosy and syphilis. The saponins have hormonal effects that affect both men and women; sarsaparilla may build muscle and help impotence in males, and may increase fertility in women with ovarian dysfunction. Other constituents have a diuretic effect, increasing the excretion of uric acid, a toxin implicated in gout and joint disease. Sarsaparillas are also part of the Chinese pharmacopoeia; *S. glabra*, first mentioned in the *Materia Medica of South Yunnan* during the Qing dynasty (1644–1911), is used internally to clear toxins, and to treat rheumatoid arthritis, syphilis, urinary tract infections, jaundice, skin ulcers, boils, and mercury poisoning. The leaves of *S. glyciphylla*, an Australian species, have been used medicinally, and as a substitute for S American sarsaparillas in soft drinks. German sarsaparilla, used for skin complaints and to prevent gout and arthritis, is from an unrelated species, *Carex arenaria*, and member of the sedge family, Cyperaceae.
CULTIVATION Well-drained soil in sun or partial shade.
PROPAGATION By seed sown in autumn; by division in autumn or spring; by separation of suckers in spring.
HARVEST Roots and rhizomes are lifted by severing larger roots near the crown, leaving smaller roots to increase. They are dried for use in decoctions, elixirs, liquid extracts, and powders. Leaves are picked during the growing season and used fresh or dried.

◾ *Smilax china* (China root)
Woody deciduous climber with a large fleshy root, sparsely prickly stems, and leathery, broadly ovate, tapering leaves, to 8cm (3in) long. Small umbels of tiny, yellow-green flowers appear in early summer – females

Smilax china

followed by globose red berries, 9mm (³⁄₈in) in diameter. Male and female flowers are borne on separate plants. Native to Japan, China, and Korea. ↕ 5m (15ft), ↔ indefinite.
HARDINESS Frost hardy.
PARTS USED Tuberous rhizomes.
PROPERTIES A cooling, slightly bitter, alterative herb that has antibiotic, anti-inflammatory, diuretic, and anti-rheumatic properties.
MEDICINAL USES Internally for rheumatoid arthritis, gout, syphilis, skin disorders (including psoriasis), enteritis, urinary tract infections, jaundice, skin ulcers, boils, abscesses, and various kinds of cancer.
CULINARY USES Leaves, young shoots, and roots are eaten as a vegetable. Leaves can be used for tea.
🔲 ♠ ✏

Smilax regelii syn. *S. officinalis*, *S. ornata* (Honduran sarsaparilla)
Variable evergreen climber with four-angled, spiny stems and ovate to oblong, glossy lower leaves, to 30cm (12in) long, and smaller, tapering, lanceolate upper leaves, which are often grey-variegated. White to pale green-yellow, six-petalled flowers appear in summer – male flowers are solitary or in clusters, to 6cm (2½in) long; females ones are solitary, on stalks, to 10cm (4in) long, followed by black berries, 1cm (½in) across. Native to C America. ↕↔ 1.5m (5ft).
HARDINESS Min. 12°C (54°F).
PARTS USED Roots, rhizomes.
PROPERTIES A sweet, acrid, alterative herb that reduces inflammation, controls itching, improves digestion and elimination, and is antiseptic.
MEDICINAL USES Internally for skin diseases, liver disorders, venereal diseases, herpes, and vaginal discharge. May be combined with other alteratives, such as *Arctium lappa* (see p.127), *Rumex crispus* (see p.351), *Taraxacum officinale* (see p.382), and *Trifolium pratense* (see p.393). Sarsaparilla may interact with various pharmaceutical drugs, including digitalis glycosides and bismuth.
ECONOMIC USES Root extracts are used to flavour soft drinks (especially root beer), ice cream, confectionery, and bakery produce.
🔲 ♠ ✏ 🔲

S

SMYRNIUM

Apiaceae

This genus of seven or eight species of biennials and short-lived perennials occurs in W Europe and Mediterranean regions. *Smyrnium olusatrum*, a coastal species, is a celery-like plant that was known to Theophrastus in 322BC and described as a pot-herb by Pliny in the 1st century AD. Its main asset as a garden plant is that it comes into growth early in the year, and bears attractive black seed heads in summer. The name, *olus*, "pot-herb", and *atrum*, "black" (referring to the black seeds), is derived from this use. *Smyrnium olusatrum* is still primarily a pot-herb. Now obsolete as a medicinal plant, it was once used for asthma, menstrual problems, and wounds. *Smyrnium* is from the Greek *smyrna*, "myrrh", referring to the aroma of these plants.

CULTIVATION Moist, rich, sandy soil in sun.
PROPAGATION By seed sown in late summer or early spring.
HARVEST Leaves, young stems and shoots, and flower buds are picked in spring and early summer. Roots are lifted in autumn. All parts are used fresh. Seeds are collected when ripe and stored whole or ground.

■ *Smyrnium olusatrum* (alexanders, black lovage)
Stout perennial with solid furrowed stems and shiny, deeply divided leaves, to 30cm (12in) long. Umbels of tiny, yellow-green flowers appear in spring, followed by aromatic black fruits, about 7mm (¼in) long. Native to Europe, SW Asia, and N Africa. ‡ 50cm–1.5m (20in–5ft), ↔ 30–90cm (12–36in).
HARDINESS Fully hardy.
PARTS USED Leaves, young stems and shoots, roots, flowers, seeds.
PROPERTIES A bitter diuretic herb, with a celery-like flavour, that benefits the digestion.
MEDICINAL USES Medicinal uses are obsolete.
CULINARY USES Leaves, young leafstalks, shoots, and roots are cooked as vegetables, and added to soups and stews. Flower buds make a pleasant addition to salads. Spicy seeds may be ground as a condiment.
▣ ▨ ▨ ▨ ▨ ▨ ▨   **CULINARY USES** Leaves,

Smyrnium olusatrum

SOLANUM

Nightshade

Solanaceae

This cosmopolitan genus is one of the largest in the world, consisting of some 1400 species of annuals, biennials, perennials, shrubs, trees, and climbers. Most solanums contain toxic alkaloids. In some species, certain parts are edible while other parts of the same plant are very poisonous. This is true of the main species grown as fruits and vegetables, such as potatoes, tomatoes, aubergines, and peppers. All solanums are regarded as poisonous by proponents of macrobiotics. *Solanum dulcamara* bears poisonous berries that have a bitter, then sweet taste. It has a long history of use for skin diseases, warts, tumours, and felons (inflammations of finger-end joints), hence another of its common names, "felonwort". Dried fruits of *S. dulcamara* were found threaded on a collarette in Tutankhamun's third coffin, though whether they were used medicinally is not known. The variegated form of *S. dulcamara* is widely grown as an ornamental climber for its colourful foliage, flowers, and fruits, which make an eye-catching display in summer and autumn. The N American *S. carolinense* (horsenettle), which also contains alkaloids, has a similarly bitter–sweet taste. Its effects are anti-bacterial, anti-spasmodic, and sedative. In Ayurvedic medicine, *S. xanthocarpum* (*kantakari*, thorny nightshade, yellow-berried nightshade) is used to treat various ailments; stems, flowers, and fruits are bitter and carminative; and seeds and roots are expectorant. A decoction of the plant "promotes conception in the female" (*Indian Materia Medica* by K.M. Nadkarni, 1976).
CULTIVATION Dry to wet, neutral to alkaline soil in sun or shade. Thin out or cut back in spring. Subject to statutory control as a weed in parts of Australia.
PROPAGATION By seed sown in spring (species only); by semi-ripe cuttings in summer.
HARVEST Stems 2–3 years old are cut in spring, or after the leaves have fallen in autumn. Roots are lifted in autumn and peeled. Both are dried for use in infusions, liquid extracts, and ointments.
⚠ **WARNING** All parts, especially leaves and unripe berries, are toxic if eaten.

Solanum dulcamara

Solanum dulcamara 'Variegatum'

■ *Solanum dulcamara* (bittersweet, woody nightshade)
Shrubby, often climbing or trailing perennial with green stems and ovate pointed leaves, to 12cm (5in) long. Purple flowers, with yellow centres, are borne in clusters in summer, followed by ovoid, bright red berries, to 1cm (½in) long. Native to Eurasia; naturalized in N America. ‡ 4m (12ft), ↔ indefinite.
■ 'Variegatum' has creamy white-variegated foliage.
HARDINESS Fully hardy.
PARTS USED Stems, root bark.
PROPERTIES An astringent cooling herb with a bitter, then sweet taste. It lowers fever, and has diuretic, expectorant, sedative, alterative, and anti-rheumatic effects.
MEDICINAL USES Internally for skin diseases, bronchial congestion, rheumatism, jaundice, and ulcerative colitis. Excess paralyzes the central nervous system, slows heart and respiration, and lowers temperature, causing vertigo, delirium, convulsions, and death. Externally for skin eruptions, ulcers, rheumatism, and cellulite. For use only by qualified practitioners.
▣ ▨ ▨ ▨

SOLIDAGO

Golden rod

Asteraceae

There are about 100 species of perennials in this genus, which is scattered throughout the northern hemisphere, but mainly in N America, where they have had a long history in native medicine. Many species and numerous hybrids and variants are grown in borders for their show of colour from midsummer to autumn. They also naturalize well in meadows and wildflower areas. The constituents of *Solidago virgaurea* include saponins (similar to those found in *Polygala* spp., see p.326), which are anti-fungal, rutin (as found in *Ruta graveolens*, see p.352), and phenolic glycosides, which are anti-inflammatory. Among the species recorded in native N American medicine are: *Solidago canadensis* (Canada golden rod), the flowers of which were chewed for sore throats; *S. odora* (sweet golden rod), listed as a stimulant and diaphoretic in the *US Pharmacopoeia* (1820–82); and *S. rigida* (stiff golden rod), which was made into a lotion for bee stings. Several species are used to make tea, including *S. canadensis*, *S. graminifolia* (fragrant golden rod), and *S. missouriensis* (Missouri golden rod). Best known is Blue Mountain tea, made from the dried leaves and flowers of *S. odora*. This species is further distinguished as the official state flower of Nebraska and Kentucky, and the state herb of Delaware. *Solidago* is from the Latin *solidare*, "to join" or "to make whole", and refers to the healing powers of these plants.

CULTIVATION Well-drained, sandy to poor soil in sun. Leaves may be damaged by powdery mildew. The flowers of *Solidago* attract many different beneficial insects, such as lacewing and ladybird, which are effective in controlling pests, especially aphid.

PROPAGATION By seed sown in spring; by division in autumn or spring.

HARVEST Leaves and flowering tops are picked before flowers are fully opened and dried for use in infusions, liquid extracts, ointments, powders, and tinctures.

▣ *Solidago virgaurea* (golden rod)
Variable perennial with a knotted rhizome, upright stems, and oblanceolate, finely toothed, pointed leaves, to 10cm (4in) long. Yellow flowers are borne in elongated, one-sided racemes in late summer, followed by brown fruits with a tuft of short white hairs. Native to Europe. ↕ 80cm (32in), ↔ 45–60cm (18–24in). ▣ subsp. *minuta* needs moist soil. ↕↔ 20cm (8in).

HARDINESS Fully hardy.

PARTS USED Leaves, flowering tops.

PROPERTIES A bitter, astringent, relaxant herb that reduces inflammation, stimulates the liver and kidneys, and is also a good urinary antiseptic. It is also expectorant, improves digestion, promotes healing, and has anti-fungal effects.

MEDICINAL USES Internally for kidney and bladder stones, urinary infections, chronic catarrh and skin diseases, influenza, whooping cough, flatulent dyspepsia associated with nervous tension, gastric infections in children, and fungal infections (such as *Candida*). Externally for wounds, insect bites, ulcers, sore throat, vaginal and oral thrush. Combines well with *Gnaphalium uliginosum* (see p.227) for nasal catarrh.

⊠ ▨ ▣

Solidago virgaurea

SOPHORA
Papilionaceae

This cosmopolitan genus has about 50 species of perennials and deciduous and evergreen trees and shrubs, which have handsome pinnate leaves and attractive, pea-like flowers and pods. *Sophora japonica* is widely grown as a landscape tree, especially in Japan and the Mediterranean. It needs hot summers to flower well. *Sophora* spp. contain the alkaloid cytisine, which resembles nicotine and is similarly toxic. The red seeds of the N American *S. secundiflora* (coral bean, mescal bean) were important in initiation rites of tribes in SW USA and Mexico, and were used to treat earache. *Sophora flavescens* was first mentioned during the later Han dynasty (AD25–220) and uses of *S. japonica* can be dated back to c.AD600. *Sophora subprostrata* (pigeon pea) was first recorded in Chinese medicine c.AD973, as an anti-inflammatory and detoxicant for mouth and throat infections, and for snake bite. Research suggests use in the treatment of various cancers. *Sophora* is from the Arabic *sophero*, a name given to various trees with pea-like flowers.

CULTIVATION Well-drained soil in sun.

PROPAGATION By seed sown when ripe (species only); by grafting in late winter (cultivars of *S. japonica*).

HARVEST Roots (*S. flavescens*) are lifted in autumn. Flowers and flower buds (*S. japonica*) are picked in late summer. Fruits are collected in autumn. All parts are dried for use in decoctions.

Sophora flavescens (yellow pagoda tree)
Deciduous shrub with upright downy stems and pinnate leaves, to 25cm (10in) long, divided into 15–40 narrowly oblong to lanceolate leaflets. Pale green-yellow, rarely purple flowers are produced in erect racemes in summer, followed by leathery pods, about 8cm (3in) long, constricted between the seeds. Native to Japan, China, Siberia, and Korea. ↕ 1.5m (5ft), ↔ 2m (6ft).

HARDINESS Fully hardy.

PARTS USED Roots (*ku shen*).

PROPERTIES A bitter, cooling, diuretic herb that controls itching and has anti-bacterial, anti-fungal, and anti-tumour effects.

Sophora japonica

Sophora japonica 'Pendula'

MEDICINAL USES Internally for jaundice, dysentery, diarrhoea, and urinary infections. Internally and externally for vaginitis, eczema, pruritus, ringworm, leprosy, syphilis, scabies, and itching allergic reactions.
⊠ ▣

▣ *Sophora japonica* (Japanese pagoda tree) Deciduous tree with dark green, shiny, pinnate leaves, to 25cm (10in) long, divided into 7–17 ovate leaflets, which have downy or glaucous undersides. Creamy white, fragrant flowers, 1cm (½in) long, are produced in panicles, to 25cm (10in) long, in summer, followed by pods, to 8cm (3in) long, constricted between the seeds. Native to China and Korea. ↕ 25m (80ft), ↔ 20m (70ft). ▣ 'Pendula' has weeping branches and rarely flowers. ↕↔ 3m (10ft). 'Violacea' has lilac-tinged flowers.

HARDINESS Fully hardy.

PARTS USED Flowers (including buds, *huai hua*), fruits (*huai jiao*).

PROPERTIES A bitter, cooling, anti-bacterial herb that controls bleeding. It also lowers blood pressure and cholesterol levels, strengthens capillaries, reduces inflammation, and relaxes spasms (flowers); soothes irritated and damaged tissues, increases blood sugar levels, expels intestinal parasites, and improves liver function (fruits).

MEDICINAL USES Internally for internal haemorrhage; hypertension and poor peripheral circulation; intestinal worms, liver energy imbalance with symptoms such as tight chest, dizziness, headache, red eyes, and hypertension. Contraindicated during pregnancy.
⊠ ⊠ ▣

SPHAGNUM
Peat moss

Sphagnaceae

This genus consists of about 100 species of bog mosses, found in wet bogs from tropical to Arctic and sub-Antarctic regions. The absorbent, sponge-like tissues are important in regulating water loss from various habitats. Decomposed sphagnum is a major component of peat, known for its preservative properties, which has been exploited as a soil conditioner and basis for

S

Sphagnum cymbilifolium

potting composts by the horticultural industry. Bog mosses have a long history of use by Eskimos, Lapps, Kashmiris, and Gaelic peoples for absorbent and antiseptic purposes, such as for menstruation, babies' nappies, and as stable litter. Sphagnum dressings have also been widely used in military field hospitals. *Sphagnum japonicum* is used internally in a Chinese formula to treat epidemic dysentery. Extracts of decomposed peat moss, such as peat tar and sphagnol, are cheap and effective astringent, antibiotic, and anti-pruritic treatments for skin diseases and irritations.

CULTIVATION Wet acid soil in sun or partial shade.

PROPAGATION By stem cuttings or division during the growing season.

HARVEST Plants are collected as required and dried whole.

⚠ **WARNING** Exploitation and wild-collection of *Sphagnum* spp. is subject to management measures in some areas.

▣ *Sphagnum cymbilifolium* (bog moss, sphagnum moss)
Dense, clump-forming moss with pale yellow-green foliage, often tinged bright green or salmon-pink. Dark brown fruit capsules are produced in summer. Native to NW Europe. ‡↔ 30cm (12in).
HARDINESS Fully hardy.
PARTS USED Whole plant.
PROPERTIES An astringent, antiseptic, absorbent herb.
MEDICINAL USES Externally for wounds and to absorb discharges.
ECONOMIC USES Dried sphagnum is added to orchid composts and used to line hanging baskets.
▨ ▣ ✎

SPIGELIA
Loganiaceae

There are about 50 species of annuals, perennials, and subshrubs in this genus, which occurs in tropical and N America. A few species are grown as ornamentals for their brightly coloured flowers, though they are by no means common in cultivation. *Spigelia anthelmia*

(horse poison, pinkroot of Demerara, worm grass) was one of the main herbs used by native N Americans to destroy intestinal parasites, which "it does in so extraordinary a manner, that no other simple can be of equal efficacy" (*The Civil and Natural History of Jamaica* by P. Browne, 1756). It is an annual found from Mexico to Brazil and the West Indies, and now naturalized in parts of Africa and Indonesia because of its medicinal uses. In addition to its use as a worming remedy, it contains alkaloids that are useful in treating heart disease. A warm decoction of the root is also used as a tranquillizing cooling bath for children. *Spigelia marilandica*, which grows farther north, was also originally an Indian remedy that became popular with settlers and was exported to Europe in the 18th and 19th centuries, where it was considered almost without equal as an anthelmintic. It contains alkaloids (mainly spigeleine), volatile oil, resin, and tannin.

CULTIVATION Rich, moist, well-drained soil in shade or partial shade.

PROPAGATION By seed sown in autumn or spring; by division in spring.

HARVEST Leaves are picked as required and whole plants are cut when in full bloom, and dried for infusions. Roots are collected in the autumn and dried for decoctions.

▣ *Spigelia marilandica* (pinkroot, worm grass)
Clump-forming perennial with opposite, ovate–lanceolate, pointed leaves, to 10cm (4in) long. Bright red, waxy, tubular flowers, 4cm (1½in) long, ending in five petal-like lobes, which are bright yellow inside, appear in loose clusters in spring. Native to SE USA (Maryland to Texas). ‡↔ 60cm (24in).
HARDINESS Frost hardy.
PARTS USED Leaves, whole plant, roots.
PROPERTIES A pungent, bitter–sweet, irritant herb that destroys intestinal parasites. In small doses, it improves digestion and lowers fever.
MEDICINAL USES Internally for fevers, malaria, and poor digestion (leaves, whole plant). Taken in conjunction with laxative herbs, such as *Senna alexandrina* (see. p.366), to expel tapeworms and roundworms (root). Excess causes vomiting, spasms, and convulsions, and may prove fatal. For use only by qualified practitioners.
▨ ▧ ▨ ▣

Spigelia marilandica

SPILANTHES
Asteraceae

A genus of about 60 species of mostly creeping or spreading annuals and perennials, widely distributed in the tropics and subtropics. Several species are used medicinally. They have an interesting chemistry, containing flavonoids, sterols, sesquiterpene lactones, and amides, notably spilanthol, which has anaesthetic effects; chewing a leaf is sufficient to numb the lips and tongue. Spilanthol is also a potent insecticide, able to kill mosquito larvae when diluted 1/100,000. *Spilanthes acmella* is the only species common in cultivation. In areas with cool summers it can be grown as a novelty pot plant, or as a half-hardy annual. Its use as a local anaesthetic for toothache and headaches is known in India, Sri Lanka, Indochina, Malaysia, Indonesia, and W Africa. In Sri Lanka the mature leaves are infused in sesame (*gingili*) oil as a dressing for burns and scalds. Other S American species with similar uses include: *S. alba*, used to relieve toothache; *S. ocymifolia*, used for toothache and painful eye conditions; and *S. mutisii* (*botoncillo*), chewed as a dentifrice and made into an ointment for skin diseases.
CULTIVATION Well-drained soil in sun.
PROPAGATION By seed sown in spring.
HARVEST Leaves, flowering plant, and flower heads are picked as required and used fresh.

▣ *Spilanthes acmella* syn. *S. paniculata* (toothache plant)
Sprawling to prostrate, much-branched annual with olive-green, ovate leaves, 3–7cm (1¼–3in) long. Minute flowers are borne in cone-shaped, yellowish-maroon heads, which are produced almost continuously. Native to S America; now pantropical in distribution. ‡↔ 40–70cm (16–28in). var. *oleracea* syn. 'Oleracea' (*brède mafane*, *jambú*, Pará cress) has larger, milder, purple-flushed leaves.
HARDINESS Half hardy.
PARTS USED Leaves, flower heads.
PROPERTIES An aromatic, pungent, expectorant herb that improves digestion and has anaesthetic and insecticidal effects. It stimulates the salivary glands, increasing salivation.
MEDICINAL USES Internally for dyspepsia and bronchitis (flowering plant). Externally for

S

Spilanthes acmella

toothache, sore mouth and gums, burns, scalds, headaches, migraine, itching skin conditions; also in India as a popular remedy for stammering in children (flower heads).

CULINARY USES Leaves (especially of var. *oleracea*) are added to salads or cooked in coconut milk. An important ingredient of Amazonian soups *pato no tucupi* and *tacacá*, and main ingredient of Malagasy national dish, *roumazave*.

STACHYS
Lamiaceae

This genus of about 300 species of annuals and perennials occurs in a wide range of habitats in northern temperate regions. Various species are grown as ornamentals, including *S. palustris*, which is an attractive plant for bog gardens and the margins of ponds. *Stachys officinalis* (betony) naturalizes well in European wildflower meadows, and has several cultivars that make excellent border plants. In Anglo-Saxon times, betony was an important medicinal and magical herb, and well known as a cure for headaches. According to Culpeper, "Antonius Musa, physician to the Emperor Augustus Caesar, wrote a peculiar book of the virtues of this herb; and among other virtues saith of it, that it preserves the liver and bodies of men from the danger of epidemical diseases, and from witchcraft also" (*The English Physician Enlarged*, 1653). A total of 47 different complaints were listed that betony would apparently cure. Both *S. officinalis* and *S. palustris* contain tannins and alkaloids; in addition, *S. palustris* contains allantoin, as in *Symphytum officinale* (see p.377). *Stachys*, "ear of corn" or "spike", refers to the arrangement of flowers on the stem.

CULTIVATION Well-drained soil in sun or partial shade. *Stachys palustris* needs damp to wet soil, or water to 8cm (3in) deep.

PROPAGATION By seed sown in autumn or spring; by division in spring.

HARVEST Flowering plants are cut in summer and dried for infusions, liquid extracts, and tinctures.

Stachys foeniculum. See *Agastache foeniculum*.

■ *Stachys officinalis* syn. *S. betonica*, *Betonica officinale* (betony, bishopswort)
Erect perennial with oblong, deeply veined, scallop-edged leaves, to 7cm (3in) long. Bright magenta (rarely pink or white) flowers are produced in oblong spikes in summer. Native to Europe. ‡ 15–60cm (6–24in), ↔ 30–45cm (12–18in). 'Alba' has white flowers. ■ 'Rosea' has pink flowers. ■ 'Rosea Superba' is robust, with large spikes of pink flowers.

HARDINESS Fully hardy.
PARTS USED Whole plant.
PROPERTIES A bitter, astringent, sedative herb that improves digestion and cerebral circulation.
MEDICINAL USES Internally for headaches associated with debility and nervous tension, and for anxiety, neuralgia, sinusitis, upper respiratory tract catarrh, gastritis, poor digestion, hypertension, and menopausal problems. Excess causes diarrhoea and vomiting. Contraindicated during pregnancy. Externally for wounds (especially if infected), bruises, ulcers, sore throat, and gum inflammation. Combines well with *Hypericum perforatum* (see p.240), *Lavandula angustifolia* (see p.253), *Scutellaria lateriflora* (see p.365), or *Verbena officinalis* (see p.402) for tension headaches.
CULINARY USES Leaves and flower spikes are used to make tea.
ECONOMIC USES Dried leaves are included in herbal tobacco and snuff.

■ *Stachys palustris* (marsh woundwort)
Rhizomatous perennial with tuberous roots and faintly aromatic, lanceolate, hairy leaves, to 7cm (3in) long. Pale lilac flowers with darker markings are borne in whorled spikes in summer. Native to Europe. ‡ 1m (3ft), ↔ 30–45cm (12–18in).
HARDINESS Fully hardy.
PARTS USED Whole plant.
PROPERTIES An astringent antiseptic herb with an unpleasant smell. It relaxes spasms, controls bleeding, and promotes healing.
MEDICINAL USES Internally for gout, cramp, vertigo, and haemorrhage. Externally for minor injuries.

Stellaria media

STELLARIA
Caryophyllaceae

There are some 120 species of annuals and perennials in this cosmopolitan genus. *Stellaria media* (chickweed) is an extremely prolific weed, providing an abundant source of edible and medicinal foliage, even in winter in milder areas. It has been used as a healing herb for centuries, and was also valued in many countries as a food for birds and domestic fowl, hence the name "chickweed". The leaves are readily infused in oil as a simple remedy for dry itchy skin; Culpeper's recommendation was to "Boil a handful of Chickweed, and a handful of red rose leaves (petals) dried, in a quart of muscadine, until a fourth part be consumed; then put to them a pint of oil of trotters of sheep's feet; let them boil a good while, still stirring them well; which being strained, anoint the grieved place therewith, warm against the fire, rubbing it well with one hand" (*The English Physician Enlarged*, 1653). *Stellaria* comes from the Latin *stella*, "star", referring to the star-shaped flowers.
CULTIVATION Moist soil in sun or shade.
PROPAGATION By seed sown at any time.
HARVEST Plants are cut and used fresh as juice or poultices, and fresh or dried in infusions, liquid extracts, medicated oils, ointments, creams, and tinctures.

■ *Stellaria media* (chickweed)
Spreading annual, often over-wintering, with a slender taproot, diffusely branched, brittle stems, and ovate leaves, to 2.5cm (1in) long. White, star-shaped flowers, 5mm (¼in) across, with deeply notched petals, appear at any time of the year. Cosmopolitan weed of temperate regions. ↔ 5–40cm (2–16in).
HARDINESS Frost hardy.
PARTS USED Whole plant.
PROPERTIES A soothing, cooling, slightly saline herb that relieves

Stachys officinalis

Stachys officinalis 'Rosea'

Stachys officinalis 'Rosea Superba'

Stachys palustris

S

itching, promotes healing, and has alterative, anti-rheumatic effects.
MEDICINAL USES Internally for rheumatism and chest infections. Excess causes diarrhoea and vomiting. Contraindicated during pregnancy. Externally for itching skin conditions, eczema, psoriasis, vaginitis, urticaria, ulcers, boils, and abscesses. Often blended with *Althaea officinalis* (see p.117) or *Ulmus rubra* (see p.397) in anti-pruritic prescriptions.
CULINARY USES Sprigs are added to salads and cooked as a vegetable; also liquidized with other herbs and vegetables as a tonic juice.

STEMONA
Stemonaceae

This genus of 25 species of perennial climbers occurs throughout Indo-Malaysia to E Asia and tropical Australia. Most species contain alkaloids, and a number are effective insecticides. According to a 19th-century gardening manual, *S. tuberosa* was introduced in 1803 from the East Indies; it has large, attractive but fetid flowers and is seldom seen in cultivation today. *Stemona tuberosa* was first mentioned in Chinese medical literature in the *Collection of Commentaries on the Classic of Materia Medica* (*Ben Cao Jing Ji Zhu*) by Tao Hong-Jing in AD500. *Stemona japonica* and *S. sessilifolia* are used interchangeably as the drug *bai bu*. In Cambodia, the tubers are used to make insecticidal sprays for pepper plantations.
CULTIVATION Light, well-drained soil in sun or partial shade. Cut back in early spring, to restrict growth.
PROPAGATION By seed sown in autumn; by semi-ripe cuttings in spring; by division when dormant.
HARVEST Tubers are lifted during dormancy, scalded in boiling water, and sun-dried for decoctions.

Stemona tuberosa syn. *Roxburghia gloriosa* (stemona)
Slender, evergreen, climbing perennial with a cluster of spindle-shaped, tuberous roots and pointed, ovate–cordate leaves, 10–15cm (4–6in) long, which have conspicuous veins. Bell-shaped, light purple flowers are produced singly or in pairs in the axils in spring, followed by capsules, 2.5cm (1in) long, containing four seeds. Native to India, China, Indochina, and northern mainland Malaysia. ‡ 5–10m (15–30ft).
HARDINESS Min. 15–18°C (59–64°F).
PARTS USED Tubers (*bai bu*).
PROPERTIES A bitter–sweet, cooling herb that lubricates the lungs, controls coughing, destroys parasites, and is anti-bacterial and anti-fungal.
MEDICINAL USES Internally for bronchitis, dry cough, tuberculosis, whooping cough, amoebic dysentery, and pinworms. Baked with honey for coughs. Externally for lice, fleas, and ringworm. Used fresh to make insecticidal washes and sprays.

STEVIA
Asteraceae

This genus includes some 280 species of shrubs and perennials, found in tropical and subtropical parts of N and S America. *Stevia rebaudiana* is widely cultivated for its leaves, which are used as a sweetener. It is uncertain how many members of the genus contain the same or similarly sweet substances, but at least one other, *S. serrata* (*roninowa*, sweet leaf) is used as a sugar substitute. In Paraguay the plant is called *caa'-ehe*, "sweet herb", by indigenous people, who have used it for generations as a sweetener, especially in maté tea. *Stevia rebaudiana* was first described scientifically in 1887; the sweet-tasting glycoside known as stevioside was isolated in the 1930s. Stevioside is 300 times sweeter than sucrose, and about a fifth as sweet as saccharine. It has been used by the Japanese food industry since the 1970s following the development of an extraction technique that removed the colour and bitterness. Dried leaves, and powder made from the dried leaves, are 10–15 times sweeter than sugar.
CULTIVATION Moist, sandy, acid soil in sun.
PROPAGATION By semi-ripe cuttings in summer. Seed is often infertile.
HARVEST Leaves are picked as flowering begins and dried whole, ground as powder, or processed into extracts.
⚠ **WARNING** *Stevia* and extracts are not permitted to be sold as sweeteners in some countries.

Stevia rebaudiana (*caa'-ehe*, stevia, sugar leaf, sweet herb of Paraguay)
Evergreen shrubby perennial with soft green, spathulate, deeply veined leaves, to 5cm (2in) long. Tiny, white, groundsel-like flowers are produced in clusters in winter. Native to Brazil, Argentina, and Paraguay. ‡↔ 60–90cm (24–36in).
HARDINESS Min. 7°C (45°F).
PARTS USED Leaves.
PROPERTIES A very sweet herb.
MEDICINAL USES Internally in folk medicine as a contraceptive, and to lower blood sugar levels.
CULINARY USES Leaves are used as a sugar substitute in food and drinks. The sweetening agent, stevioside, is stable when heated and does not precipitate in acids or cause fermentation.

STILLINGIA
Euphorbiaceae

This genus includes about 30 species of perennials and evergreen or deciduous shrubs, which range throughout tropical and warm parts of the Americas, to Madagascar and E Malaysia. It is doubtful whether any species are in cultivation. In common with most members of the family Euphorbiaceae, *Stillingia* spp. contain an irritant milky sap. In *S. sylvatica* the irritant properties are similar to those of *Daphne* spp. (see p.190) but are mostly lost in preparations of the dried root. The boiled mashed roots of *Stillingia sylvatica* were eaten by native N American women after childbirth and used by settlers as an external treatment for menstrual irregularity. The herb was popular in S USA as a cure for constipation and by 1828 was used to relieve pain and ulceration after treatment for syphilis. The acrid fresh root was chewed for bronchial complaints, and a tincture was made with *Drosera rotundifolia* (see p.197) and *Passiflora incarnata* (see p.303) to treat the early stages of tuberculosis.
CULTIVATION Dry, sandy, acid soil in sun or partial shade.
PROPAGATION By seed sown in autumn or spring; by division in spring.
HARVEST Roots are lifted in late summer and early autumn, and dried for use in decoctions, elixirs, liquid extracts, tablets, and tinctures. They should be processed as soon as possible after harvesting because their properties deteriorate rapidly. Dried roots should be discarded after two years.

Stillingia sylvatica (queen's delight, yaw root)
Perennial with leathery ovate leaves, to 8cm (3in) long. Small, green-yellow, male and female flowers, without petals, are borne separately in erect spikes, 5–10cm (2–4in) long, in summer, followed by three-seeded capsules. Native to eastern N America. ‡ 60cm–1.2m (2–4ft), ↔ 60–90cm (24–36in).
HARDINESS Half hardy.
PARTS USED Roots.
PROPERTIES A bitter, acrid, tonic herb with an unpleasant odour. It is alterative, diuretic, expectorant, and laxative.
MEDICINAL USES Internally for syphilis, and for liver, genito-urinary, and bronchial complaints. Combined with other depurative or alterative herbs, e.g. *Trifolium pratense* (see p.393), in tonic and "blood purifying" formulas. Excess causes diarrhoea and vomiting. For use only by qualified practitioners.

STIZOLOBIUM
Stizolobium deeringianum. See *Mucana pruriens* var. *utilis.*

STROPHANTHUS
Apocynaceae

This genus of 38 species of evergreen or deciduous shrubs, climbers, and small trees occurs in tropical Africa and Eurasia. Several species were cultivated under glass in the 19th century for their interesting flowers, which have long, ribbon-like petals. A few are occasionally seen today in botanical gardens. *Strophanthus gratus* contains cardiac glycosides, including ouabain, and strophanthin; the latter was first isolated in 1885. These compounds are poorly absorbed when taken orally and are usually given by injection. Unlike digitalis (see *Digitalis*, p.193), they are not cumulative. Similar glycosides are found in *Strophanthus hispidus*, *S. intermedius*, and *S. kombe*. Locally,

S

Strophanthus gratus

Strychnos nux-vomica

STYRAX

Styracaceae

This genus includes some 100 species of deciduous and evergreen shrubs and small trees, widely distributed in the Americas, Asia, and Europe. Several species are rich in resins that have medicinal properties. *Styrax benzoin* was first described by Ibn Batuta, an Arab who explored Sumatra between 1325 and 1349. He referred to it as *luban jawi*, "frankincense of Java", which over time became "Benjamin" and "benzoin". *Styrax benzoin* yields benzoin, a gum resin widely used in over-the-counter remedies for bronchial complaints. The resin became popular in Europe towards the end of the 16th century and was subject to tax at Worms (W Germany), under the name *asa dulcis*. It also entered Chinese medicine about this time, being first mentioned in Li Shi Zhen's herbal of 1596. *Styrax tonkinensis* (Siam benzoin) and *S. hypoglauca* are alternative sources of benzoin. The term "storax" refers to a vanilla-scented, solid resin obtained from the Eurasian species *S. officinalis* and used in incense, perfumery, and medicine. The liquid aromatic balsam from *Liquidambar* spp. (see p.264) is also called storax.

CULTIVATION Moist to wet soil in sun or partial shade.
PROPAGATION By seed sown when ripe; by greenwood cuttings in summer.
HARVEST Gum is collected from deep incisions made in the trunks of trees at least seven years old. Hardened gum is stored in pieces ("tears"), compressed into a solid mass, or made into tinctures.

◨ *Styrax benzoin* (benzoin, gum Benjamin) Evergreen tree with grey resinous bark and ovate, minutely toothed leaves, to 14cm (5½in) long, which have downy grey undersides. Clusters of 10–20 fragrant, cup-shaped, white flowers, about 3cm (1¼in) across, appear in spring and summer. Native to Indonesia (Sumatra). ‡ 8m (25ft), ↔ 5–6m (15–20ft).
HARDINESS Min. 15–18°C (59–64°F).
PARTS USED Gum resin (*an xi xiang*).
PROPERTIES An astringent, expectorant, and

these plants are used in the preparation of arrow and fish poisons. The seeds are soaked in water to obtain a highly toxic liquid that is mixed with adhesive and applied to the tips of weapons. The effects of *S. kombe* were noted by David Livingstone, the explorer, in 1861.
CULTIVATION Moist, well-drained, humus-rich soil in sun, with high humidity.
PROPAGATION By seed sown when ripe; by ripewood cuttings in early spring. Plants take three years to reach flowering size when grown from seed; maximum fruit production occurs after 6–10 years. Many flowers do not set seeds.
HARVEST Seeds are collected when ripe and processed for the extraction of glycosides.
⚠ **WARNING** Seeds are extremely toxic if eaten.

◨ *Strophanthus gratus* syn. *Roupellia grata* (climbing oleander, *sawai*, smooth strophanthus) Robust evergreen climber with purple-stalked, leathery, oblong–elliptic, pointed leaves, to 18cm (7in) long. Purple buds expand into night-scented, bell-shaped flowers, 6cm (2½in) across, which are purple-pink outside and white to pink inside, with five pairs of purple appendages. Forked fruits, to 40cm (16in) long, containing green-brown seeds with long silky plumes, develop over 12 months. Native to W Africa. ‡ 9m (28ft).
HARDINESS Min. 16°C (61°F).
PARTS USED Seeds.
PROPERTIES An extremely poisonous, diuretic, tonic herb that stimulates the heart.
MEDICINAL USES Internally, usually by injection, for heart failure, angina, hypertension, pulmonary oedema, and hypotension during anaesthesia and surgery. Excess causes cardiac arrest. For use only by qualified practitioners.
⚠ **WARNING** This herb is subject to legal restrictions in many countries.
▨ ▣ ▣

STRYCHNOS

Loganiaceae

Approximately 200 species of mainly evergreen trees, shrubs, and climbers belong to this genus, which is pantropical in distribution. The genus is rich in alkaloids, such as strychnine. A dozen or more species are used in making curare, a

black resinous arrow poison used by native American tribes, which causes instantaneous muscular paralysis but leaves the flesh of animals untainted. The preparation of curare was first observed by Alexander von Humboldt and Aimé Bonpland during their explorations in C and S America (1799–1804). Extracts of *S. nux-vomica* and *S. ignatii* (St Ignatius' bean) are used in minute amounts in tonic and restorative preparations. Both species are also used in homeopathy.
CULTIVATION Well-drained, humus-rich soil in sun or partial shade.
PROPAGATION By seed sown in spring; by semi-ripe cuttings in summer.
HARVEST Seeds are collected when ripe, and dried for elixirs, liquid extracts, pills, or tinctures, and for commercial extraction of alkaloids.
⚠ **WARNING** All parts are toxic: handle with care.

◨ *Strychnos nux-vomica* (nux-vomica, poison nut, strychnine)
Evergreen tree with leathery ovate leaves, to 15cm (6in) long. Numerous, white, green-tinged, tubular flowers, about 1cm (½in) long, opening into 4–5 lobes, are produced in terminal clusters in spring, followed by globose juicy fruits, to 6cm (2½in) in diameter, containing four disc-shaped seeds. Native to India and Burma (Myanmar). ‡ 20m (70ft), ↔ 15m (50ft).
HARDINESS Min. 15°C (59°F).
PARTS USED Seeds.
PROPERTIES A very bitter, tonic herb that stimulates the nervous system and improves appetite.
MEDICINAL USES Internally, in minute amounts, for nervous exhaustion, debility, and poor appetite (especially in the elderly and children). It is also used as a central nervous system stimulant in chloroform or chloral poisoning, surgical shock, and cardiac arrest. Excess causes paralysis (notably *risus sardonicus*, a fixed grin), convulsions, respiratory failure, and death. Used (as nux-vomica) in homeopathic preparations. For use only by qualified practitioners.
ECONOMIC USES Strychnine is extracted commercially for use in vermin poisons.
⚠ **WARNING** This herb and strychnine are subject to legal restrictions in most countries.
▨ ▣ ▨ ▣

Styrax benzoin

antiseptic herb with a cinnamon–camphor aroma. It is regarded as a circulatory stimulant in Chinese medicine and as a sedative in aromatherapy.

MEDICINAL USES In Western medicine, internally for coughs, colds, bronchitis, sore throat, wounds, ulcers, and mouth ulcers; externally for wounds and ulcers. An ingredient of cough and cold remedies, such as Friar's Balsam. In Chinese medicine, internally for chest and abdominal pains. In aromatherapy for influenza, chills, and itching skin conditions.

ECONOMIC USES Used as an antioxidant in cosmetics, a fixative in perfumes, and as a flavouring in the food industry.

⬛⬛✏️⬛

SWERTIA

Gentianaceae

Fifty species of mostly annuals and perennials belong to this genus, which occurs in montane regions of N America, Eurasia, and Africa. About half a dozen species, mainly of Indian annuals, were listed in 19th-century gardening manuals, but few are seen today outside botanical gardens. Chirata or chiretta is the common name for bitter, gentian-like plants sold in Indian bazaars. *Swertia chirata* reached Great Britain in 1829 and was listed in the *Edinburgh Pharmacopoeia* in 1839. It has an interesting chemistry, containing alkaloids and iridoids similar to those of *Gentiana lutea* (see p.223), and xanthones that are reputedly effective against malaria and tuberculosis. The iridoid amarogentin appears to protect the liver against carbon tetrachloride poisoning. Bitter compounds are also found in other species; *Swertia japonica* is cultivated in China as a source of bitterness agents. Green chiretta, a fever remedy, is obtained from the unrelated *Andrographis paniculata* (see p.120).

CULTIVATION Moist, well-drained soil in sun or partial shade.

PROPAGATION By seed sown in autumn or spring.

HARVEST Plants are cut towards the end of flowering and dried for use in infusions, liquid extracts, and powder.

Swertia chirata syn. *Ophelia chirata* (brown chirata, chiretta, Indian balmony) Robust erect annual with pointed, conspicuously veined, broadly lanceolate leaves, to 10cm (4in) long. Pale green, purple-striped, four-lobed flowers, about 1cm (½in) across, are produced in leafy panicles in autumn, followed by tiny, two-valved capsules. Native to the Himalayas (Kashmir, Bhutan and Khasi Hills). ‡ 1.5m (5ft), ↔ 60cm (2ft).

HARDINESS Fully hardy.

PARTS USED Whole plant.

PROPERTIES An extremely bitter, tonic herb that lowers fever and improves digestion.

MEDICINAL USES Internally for liver and gall bladder complaints, dyspepsia, constipation, malaria, hiccups, and convalescent debility.

⬛⬛

SYMPHYTUM
Comfrey

Boraginaceae

A genus of 25–35 species of bristly or hairy, rhizomatous perennials, ranging through Europe, from the Mediterranean to the Caucasus. *Symphytum officinale* and *S.* × *uplandicum* are grown as perennial fodder crops, and as a source of high nitrogen mulches, compost material, and fertilizer for organic cultivation. The variegated *S.* × *uplandicum* is popular as an ornamental for borders and bog gardens. *Symphytum officinale* was known to the Romans as *conferva* ("join together") from which the common name "comfrey" is derived. Another common name, "knitbone", also refers to the use of these plants in healing fractures. Comfrey contains allantoin, which promotes cell proliferation and is now synthesized for use in healing creams, and pyrrolizidine alkaloids (in higher quantities in the roots than in the foliage). The alkaloids have been shown to cause liver damage and tumours in laboratory animals. As a result, *S. officinale* is now banned in the form of tablets and capsules (made from roots or leaves) in several countries. Comfrey teas, tinctures, and preparations for external use are considered safe. Culpeper wrote that comfrey is "special good for ruptures and broken bones; yea it is said to be so powerful to consolidate and knit together, that if they be boiled with dissevered pieces of flesh in a pot, it will join them together again" (*The English Physician Enlarged*, 1653). He also used it for haemorrhoids and sore breasts, for which synthetic allantoin is now specifically used in pharmaceutical products.

CULTIVATION Moist to wet soil in sun

Symphytum officinale   *Symphytum* × *uplandicum*

Symphytum × *uplandicum* 'Variegatum'

or partial shade. Comfrey is invasive and deep-rooted, and difficult to eradicate when established. Plants may be affected by rust.

PROPAGATION By seed sown in autumn or spring (species only); by division in spring or autumn.

HARVEST Leaves are picked in early summer before flowering and dried for infusions, liquid extracts, and poultices. Roots are lifted during dormancy and dried for decoctions, liquid extracts, and ointments.

⚠ **WARNING** Bristly foliage is a skin irritant.

⬛ *Symphytum officinale* (comfrey, knitbone) Stout, bristly-haired perennial with mucilaginous thick roots and large, tapering, ovate–lanceolate leaves, 25cm (10in) long. Purple to pink or white, funnel-shaped flowers, to 2cm (¾in) long, are borne in summer. Native to Europe and W Asia. ‡ 60cm–1.2m (2–4ft), ↔ 30–60cm (12–24in).

HARDINESS Fully hardy.

PARTS USED Leaves, roots.

PROPERTIES A sweet, mucilaginous, cooling herb with expectorant, astringent, soothing, and healing effects. It reduces inflammation, and controls bleeding.

MEDICINAL USES Internally for gastric and duodenal ulcers, chronic bronchial diseases, colitis, irritable bowel syndrome, and rheumatism (leaves). Externally for psoriasis, eczema, sores, varicose veins and ulcers, arthritis, sprains, bunions, haemorrhoids, sore breasts during lactation, and injuries, including fractures.

CULINARY USES Fresh young leaves are added to salads, made into fritters, or cooked as a vegetable in similar ways to spinach. Dried leaves are used to make tea.

⚠ **WARNING** This herb, especially in the form of tablets and capsules of the roots or leaves, is subject to legal restrictions in some countries.

⬛⬛⬛✏️

⬛ *Symphytum* × *uplandicum* syn. *S. peregrinum* (Russian comfrey) Hybrid between *S. officinale* and *S. asperum*, similar in appearance to the former. It is extremely vigorous, with a thick rhizome and pink flowers that tend to turn blue as they age. ‡ 2m (6ft), ↔ 1.2m (4ft). 'Bocking 4' has violet flowers and a non-bitter taste. ⬛ 'Variegatum' has irregular ivory variegation. Tends to scorch in full sun. ‡ 1m (3ft), ↔ 60cm (24in).

HARDINESS Fully hardy.

PARTS USED Leaves, roots.

PROPERTIES As for *S. officinale*.

MEDICINAL USES As for *S. officinale*.

CULINARY USES 'Bocking 4' is popular for liquidizing as an ingredient of tonic drinks.

ECONOMIC USES Russian comfrey is preferred to *S. officinale* for livestock fodder.

⬛⬛⬛✏️✏️

SYMPLOCARPUS
Skunk cabbage

Araceae

This genus includes three species of rhizomatous perennials, occurring in northeastern N America and NE Asia. *Symplocarpus foetidus* is an unusual and interesting plant for the banks of streams and ponds. It is extremely hardy, tolerating −35°C (−31°F). The strange inflorescences appear at ground level early in the year, and produce their own internal heat to melt the surrounding snow and attract pollinators. The roots of *S. foetidus* are known to contain volatile oil, resins, and a slightly narcotic alkaloid, 5-hydroxytryptamine, but the pharmacology is poorly understood. Its uses among native N Americans include an inhalation of crushed leaves for headaches and a decoction of root hairs to treat external bleeding. *Symplocarpus* is from the Greek *symploke*, "union", and *karpos*, "fruit", and refers to the coalescence of the ovaries into a single fruit.

CULTIVATION Deep, humus-rich, moist to wet, lime-free soil in sun or shade. Does not transplant easily.

PROPAGATION By seed kept wet until sown in autumn or spring; by division of large clumps during dormancy. Seedlings are slow-growing and dislike disturbance.

HARVEST Rhizomes and roots are lifted during dormancy and dried for decoctions, infusions, liquid extracts, powders, and tinctures.

◉ **Symplocarpus foetidus** (polecat weed, skunk cabbage)
Large perennial with a stout vertical rhizome and ovate to heart-shaped leaves, to 50cm (20in) long, which emit a musky smell when bruised. Inflorescences, borne at ground level in winter, consist of a fleshy, incurved, maroon spathe, to 15cm (6in) long, and a rotund, black-maroon spadix, 3cm (1¼in) across. Native to northeastern N America. ↔ 75cm (30in).

HARDINESS Fully hardy.

PARTS USED Rhizomes, roots.

PROPERTIES A pungent, warming, anti-spasmodic, sedative herb with a fetid odour. It acts as an expectorant and diuretic, and increases perspiration.

MEDICINAL USES Internally for bronchitis, asthma, whooping cough, catarrh, hay fever, and irritating coughs. Combines well with *Grindelia camporum* (see p.229) and *Euphorbia hirta* (see p.210) for bronchitis and asthma. Excess causes vomiting.
▨ ▟

Symplocarpus foetidus

SYZYGIUM
Myrtaceae

There are 400–500 species of evergreen aromatic trees and shrubs in this genus, which occurs through tropical regions. The dried flower buds of *S. aromaticum* are known as "cloves". They are pink when fresh, turning brown as they dry and exuding oil when squeezed. The volatile oil contains eugenol, which gives the characteristic aroma, and methyl salicylate. According to ancient texts, cloves reached China, India, and the Roman Empire about 2000 years ago. In China, it was customary to hold a clove in the mouth as a breath-sweetener while addressing the Emperor; medicinal uses of cloves were recorded in Chinese medicine c.AD600. Cloves were a major item in the spice trade that sparked competition between colonial nations during the 16th century. Main producing countries today include Madagascar, Tanzania (Zanzibar), Indonesia, and the Comoro Islands. A number of *Syzygium* spp. have edible fruits that are enjoyed in the countries of origin. One or two others are used for flavouring. These include: *S. luehmannii* (clove lilli pilly, riberry), an Australian species that is popular in the bushfoods industry for its clove-flavoured fruits; and *S. polyanthum* (*daun salam*, Indonesian bay), which has aromatic leaves used in soups, sauces, and marinades. *Syzygium cumini* is one of the main herbal remedies for the early stages of diabetes. *Syzygium* comes from the Greek *syzygos*, "joined", and refers to the paired foliage of a Jamaican species.

CULTIVATION Well-drained, fertile soil in sun.

PROPAGATION By seed sown when ripe or in spring at 27°C (81°F); by greenwood cuttings in early summer; by semi-ripe cuttings in summer.

HARVEST Unopened flower buds (*S. aromaticum*) are picked as they develop and sun-dried for use in infusions and powders, and for oil extraction. Bark (*S. cumini*) is removed from prunings as required and dried for decoctions. Fruits (*S. cumini*) are collected when ripe and dried whole, or seeds are removed and dried separately for decoctions and tinctures.

◉ **Syzygium aromaticum** syn. *Eugenia caryophyllata* (clove)
Small, bushy, evergreen tree with ascending branches and shiny, leathery, aromatic, ovate–lanceolate leaves, 8–13cm (3–5in) long, which are salmon-pink when young. Fragrant, pink-white flowers, to 2cm (¾in) long, with petals that fall on opening, and a tuft of yellow stamens, are produced in late summer, followed by aromatic purple berries, 8mm (³⁄₈in) long. Native to the Spice Islands (Moluccas). ↕ 15–20m (50–70ft), ↔ 3–5m (10–15ft).

HARDINESS Min. 15–18°C (59–64°F).

PARTS USED Flower buds (*ding xiang*), oil.

PROPERTIES A spicy, warming, stimulant herb that relieves pain, controls nausea and vomiting, improves digestion, protects against intestinal parasites, and causes uterine contractions. It is

Syzygium aromaticum

strongly antiseptic. Regarded mainly as a kidney tonic in Chinese medicine.

MEDICINAL USES Internally for gastroenteritis and intestinal parasites. Externally for toothache and insect bites. In Chinese medicine, internally for nausea, vomiting, hiccups, stomach chills, and impotence.

CULINARY USES Whole or ground cloves are used to flavour pickles, preserves, ham, cooked apples, mincemeat, and cakes.

ECONOMIC USES Whole or ground cloves, and oil, are used as flavourings in the food and drinks industries, especially in vermouth; also as a flavouring in Indian and Indonesian cigarettes. Oil is used in perfumery and toothpaste. Whole cloves are used in potpourris and pomanders.
▨ ▨ ▟ ▨ ▨ ▨ ▨

Syzygium cumini (jambolan, jambul, Java plum)
Large evergreen tree with bright green, oval to oblong–oval, tapering leaves, about 8cm (3in) long. White, honey-scented flowers, with petals that fall on opening, and numerous stamens, appear in loose clusters in summer, followed by ovoid, purple-black fruits, about 1cm (½in) long. Native to India, Sri Lanka, and Java; widely cultivated in the tropics. ↕ 20m (60ft), ↔ 10m (30ft).

HARDINESS Min. 15–18°C (59–64°F).

PARTS USED Bark, fruits, seeds.

PROPERTIES A bitter, strongly astringent, aromatic herb that has diuretic effects. It improves digestion and significantly lowers blood sugar levels.

MEDICINAL USES Internally for indigestion, flatulence, colic, diabetes (fruits, seeds), diarrhoea, dysentery (bark, seeds). Externally for gum disease and ulcers (bark).

CULINARY USES Astringent fruits are used to make jam, jelly, preserves, and vinegar. Powdered bark is an ingredient of *basi*, a wine based on sugar cane juice (Philippines).
▨ ▨ ▨ ▟ ▨ ▨

T

TABEBUIA
Bignoniaceae

About 100 species of deciduous and evergreen, mainly spring-flowering trees and shrubs make up this genus, which occurs in C and S America and the West Indies. Some species yield very durable hardwoods, known to last hundreds of years in tropical climates; local tribes once made arrows from the wood, as indicated by the name *pau d'arco*, meaning "bow stick". Several species are grown as ornamentals, producing a fine display of blossoms before the new leaves appear; *T. serratifolia* (yellow poui), the national flower of Brazil, is especially popular. The heartwood of *T. impetiginosa* contains lapachol, a naphthoquinone that has antibiotic and anti-tumour effects. Known as *ipê*, a number of species have long been used medicinally by native S Americans. Some have a reputation for curing cancer; these include *T. impetiginosa* and *T. incana*, used by the Campas in Peru, *T. rosea* (pink poui) by the Mayas in Mexico (and to treat rabies in Guatemala), and *T. serratifolia* in Colombia. In addition, *T. insignis* var. *monophylla* and *T. neochrysantha* are used to treat stomach ulcers. *Tabebuia heptaphylla*, an important wood species, is reputedly effective against syphilis.

CULTIVATION Moist, well-drained, fertile soil in sun. Tabebuias can be grown in containers in cool areas but seldom flower. Young plants may be trimmed in autumn.
PROPAGATION By seed sown when ripe at 16°C (61°F); by air layering in spring; by semi-ripe cuttings in summer.
HARVEST Wood and inner bark are dried for decoctions, powder, tablets, and extraction of active constituents.

■ *Tabebuia impetiginosa* syn. *T. avellanedae* (*ipê-roxa*, *lapacho*, *pau d'arco*)
Large tree with smooth grey bark and grey-green, papery leaves, divided into 5–7 ovate pointed leaflets, to 20cm (8in) long. Rose-pink to deep purple flowers, to 7cm (3in) long, each with a yellow throat, appear in spring, followed by cylindrical capsules, to 55cm (22in) long. Found from N Mexico to Argentina. ‡ 30m (100ft), ↔ 15m (50ft).
HARDINESS Min. 10–15°C (50–59°F).
PARTS USED Wood, inner bark.
PROPERTIES A bitter, pungent, cooling herb that lowers fever, and reduces inflammation. It inhibits many pathogenic organisms, and has anti-cancer effects.
MEDICINAL USES Internally for inflammatory diseases, chronic degenerative diseases, cancers, tumours, ulcers, cysts, venereal, rheumatic, skin diseases (notably eczema, herpes, and scabies), and fungal infections (especially *Candida*). Combined with other alterative herbs, such as

Tabebuia impetiginosa

Echinacea purpurea (see p.199), *Panax ginseng* (see p.300), and *Trifolium pratense* (see p.393), in formulas to clear toxins, resolve congestion, and strengthen the immune system. Excess may cause nausea, vomiting, dizziness, and diarrhoea.
CULINARY USES Inner bark is made into a tonic tea, reputedly taken regularly by Mahatma Gandhi.
ECONOMIC USES Wood, known as *lapacho*, is valued for cabinet-making.

TAGETES
Marigold

Asteraceae

This is a genus of about 50 species of annuals and perennials, distributed mainly in tropical and warm parts of the Americas. Marigolds grown as bedding plants mostly come from two Mexican species: *Tagetes erecta* (African or Aztec marigold, *cempazuchil*) and *T. patula* (French marigold). Both have similar medicinal and culinary uses and feature in religious rituals in both Mexico and India; the association of *T. patula* with All Saints' Day and All Souls' Day in Mexico dates back to pre-Columbian ceremonies. *Tagetes lucida* was used to flavour *chocólatl*, the foaming, cocoa-

based drink of the Aztecs. It is one of several *Tagetes* spp. that have a tarragon-like flavour, including *T. anisatum* (anise marigold) and *T. filifolia* (*hierba anis*, Irish lace marigold). Other species with culinary uses have quite different aromas; *T. lemmonii* (Copper Canyon daisy) has a lemon–mint scent; and in *T. tenuifolia* (signet marigold) the leaves and flowers smell like lemons. *Tagetes minuta* is grown mainly for medicinal purposes but also has unusual importance in horticulture, because of its root extracts, known as thiophenes; these sulphur compounds inhibit the growth of nematodes (eelworms), which cause extensive damage to a wide range of cultivated plants. Thiophenes may also inhibit the growth of other plants – an effect that has been put to good use in the control of invasive weeds. *Tagetes* marigolds should not be confused with the pot or common marigold (see *Calendula officinalis*, p.150), which has quite different properties. *Tagetes* is named after Tages, an Etruscan deity, who sprang from the earth as it was ploughed, and revealed the art of divination.

CULTIVATION Well-drained, fertile soil in sun. Dead-head plants to prolong flowering. *Botrytis* and foot rot may affect plants. *Tagetes minuta* and, to a lesser extent, *T. patula* are widely used in companion planting; the former has an irritant sap that may cause dermatitis; the latter is often used to repel soil nematodes, slugs, and whitefly from tomatoes, though cultivars vary in effectiveness.
PROPAGATION By seed sown in spring, at 21°C (70°F).
HARVEST Plants are cut when flowering and distilled for oil, or dried for infusions. *Tagetes lucida* and *T. minuta* are used in ointments for external use. Leaves (*T. lucida*, *T. patula*) and flowers (*T. patula*) are picked in summer for use either fresh or dried in infusions.

■ *Tagetes lucida* (*anisillo*, Mexican tarragon, *pericón*, sweet mace, sweet marigold)
Woody-based perennial with aromatic, narrowly lanceolate, sharply toothed leaves, to 10cm (4in) long. Yellow flowers, 1cm (½in) across, are borne in flat-topped clusters in late summer. Native to Mexico and Guatemala. ‡ 30–80cm (12–32in), ↔ 45cm (18in).

Tagetes lucida

Tagetes minuta

Tagetes patula

'Sweetie' has a compact bushy habit and a strong, tarragon-like flavour.

HARDINESS Frost hardy.

PARTS USED Whole plant, leaves.

PROPERTIES A stimulant, diuretic, anise-scented herb that reduces fever, lowers blood pressure, and improves digestion. It depresses the central nervous system; is reputedly hallucinogenic and anaesthetic; and may help lower blood pressure.

MEDICINAL USES Internally for diarrhoea, indigestion, nausea, colic, hiccups, malaria, and feverish illnesses. Externally for scorpion bites and to remove ticks.

CULINARY USES Dried leaves and flowering tops make a popular tea in Latin America. Leaves are used as a substitute for *Artemisia dracunculus* (tarragon, see p.133).

ECONOMIC USES Dried plant is burned as incense and to repel insects.

■ *Tagetes minuta* (khaki weed, muster-John-Henry, stinking Roger)

Tall annual with leafy branched stems and strongly aromatic leaves, divided into 11–17 narrowly lanceolate segments, to 15cm (6in) long. Pale yellow flowers, 5mm (¼in) across, are produced in dense clusters in autumn. Native to C and S America; widely naturalized. ‡ 30cm–1m (1–3ft), ↔ 10–75cm (4–30in).

HARDINESS Half hardy.

PARTS USED Whole plant, oil.

PROPERTIES A strongly aromatic, diuretic, purgative herb that relaxes spasms, improves digestion, destroys intestinal parasites, and is effective against many pathogenic organisms. It is an effective insecticide.

MEDICINAL USES Internally for gastritis, indigestion, and intestinal worms. Externally for haemorrhoids and skin infections.

CULINARY USES Dried leaves give an apple-like aroma to soups, meat dishes, and vegetables.

ECONOMIC USES Plants are grown to protect crops against nematodes and slugs, and to suppress perennial weeds, such as *Aegopodium podagraria* (ground elder, see p.104), *Calystegia sepium* (bindweed), and *Elymus repens* (couch grass, see p.201). Dried plants are hung indoors or added to bedding to deter insects (Africa). Oil is used in perfumery, commercial food flavouring, and tobacco.

■ *Tagetes patula* (French marigold)

Bushy annual with aromatic, deeply divided, sharply toothed leaves, 5–10cm (2–4in) long. Yellow to orange or brown-red, or particoloured flowers, 2.5–5cm (1–2in) across, are borne from early summer to autumn. Native to Mexico. ‡↔ 20–50cm (8–20in). ■ 'Favourite Mixed' is compact and floriferous, with single blooms in various colours and combinations. ‡↔ 50cm (20in).

HARDINESS Half hardy.

PARTS USED Whole plant, leaves, flowers, oil.

PROPERTIES An aromatic, diuretic, calming herb that improves digestion. It is reputedly effective against a number of garden pests.

Tagetes patula 'Favourite Mixed'

MEDICINAL USES Internally for indigestion. Externally for sore eyes and rheumatism.

CULINARY USES Dried flowers are used for flavouring in Georgia, especially in beef soup (*kharcho*), and in sauces based on walnuts and vinegar, to prevent nuts from turning black; also to colour butter and cheese.

ECONOMIC USES Oil is blended with sandalwood oil in India to produce *attar genda* perfume. Dried flowers occur as adulterant of saffron (see *Crocus sativus*, p.183). Flower extracts give colour to dairy produce, poultry feed, and textiles. Oil is used in food flavouring but is inferior to that of *Tagetes minuta*.

TALINUM
Fameflower

Portulacaceae

This genus consists of 50 species of annuals, biennials, and often succulent and woody-based, usually deciduous perennials, found in dry grassland and scrub in subtropical and tropical regions of C and N America, and Africa. A few species are grown for their edible leaves, and as ornamentals for their showy, short-lived but freely produced flowers. Two rather similar tropical American species, *T. paniculatum* and *T. triangulare* (leaf ginseng, Surinam spinach, waterleaf), are widely cultivated and naturalized in tropical Asia, and in some areas are regarded as a substitute for ginseng. As a pot-herb and salad vegetable, they are similar to purslane (see *Portulaca oleracea*, p.329).

CULTIVATION Well-drained soil in sun. Tolerates poor soil and drought.

PROPAGATION By seed sown when ripe or in spring at 15–18°C (59–64°F).

HARVEST Young leaves and stems are picked during the growing season and used fresh. Roots are collected during dormancy and dried for decoctions.

Talinum paniculatum syn. *T. patens* (*carurú*, fameflower, jewels of Opar)

Deciduous perennial with tuberous roots, erect, usually unbranched stems, and smooth, elliptic to obovate leaves, to 10cm (4in) long. Bowl-shaped, red to yellow flowers, 1–2.5cm

(½–1in) across, are produced in terminal panicles in summer. Found from S USA to C America; widely naturalized in China and Indochina. ‡ 1m (3ft), ↔ 60cm (24in).

HARDINESS Min. 15°C (59°F).

PARTS USED Roots, leaves, stems.

PROPERTIES A slightly sour, mucilaginous herb that reputedly has ginseng-like effects.

MEDICINAL USES Root is used in folk medicine in parts of SE Asia as a substitute for ginseng (see *Panax ginseng*, p.300).

CULINARY USES Young leaves and stems are eaten fresh in salads, added to soups, or cooked briefly as a vegetable.

TAMARINDUS
Tamarind

Caesalpiniaceae

This genus contains a single species of evergreen tree, which may have originated in Africa but is now widespread throughout the tropics. *Tamarindus indica* has been cultivated in India for centuries, and was taken by the Spanish to the West Indies and Mexico in the 17th century. It is now widely grown in the tropics as an ornamental for shade. Tamarind fruits are usually sold compressed into a block. They contain sugars, plant acids, and a complex volatile oil that includes elements characteristic of lemons (limonene), rose geranium (geraniol), sassafras (safrole), cinnamon (cinnamaldehyde), mint (menthol), and wintergreen (methyl salicylate). Certain varieties of tamarind lack the tart element and are eaten locally like dates or raisins. Since its introduction in the 17th century, *T. indica* has become important in the cuisines of the West Indies, Thailand, and Mexico. *Tamarindus* comes from the Arabic *tamar-i-Hind*, "date of India", referring to the date-like pulp inside the pods.

CULTIVATION Light, well-drained soil in sun.

PROPAGATION By seed sown when ripe at 21°C (70°F); by greenwood cuttings in spring or summer; by air layering in spring; by grafting in spring.

HARVEST Fruits are picked when ripe and used fresh, or dried for use in concentrates and decoctions.

Tamarindus indica

■ **Tamarindus indica** (Indian date, tamarind) Evergreen tree with spreading branches, rough, grey-black bark, and pinnate leaves, 5–10cm (2–4in) long, divided into narrow oblong leaflets, to 3cm (1¼in) long. Creamy yellow, red-veined flowers are produced in racemes, to 15cm (6in) long, in summer, followed by brown pods, 3–15cm (1¼–6in) long, containing kidney-shaped seeds in sticky brown pulp. Native to tropical Africa; widely naturalized. ‡↔ 25m (80ft).
HARDINESS Min. 15–18°C (59–64°F).
PARTS USED Fruits.
PROPERTIES A sweet and sour, astringent, stimulant herb with a pleasant aroma. It lowers fever, improves digestion, and has antiseptic and laxative effects.
MEDICINAL USES Internally for fevers, jaundice, asthma, dysentery, and nausea in pregnancy. Externally for sore eyes, ulcers, and rheumatism. Combined with *Senna alexandrina* (see p.366) in laxative preparations.
CULINARY USES Fresh or dried fruits act as a souring agent, similar to lemon juice, in curries, fish dishes, chutneys, sauces (notably Worcestershire sauce), SE Asian satay, and sweet and sour dishes. Sweet varieties are eaten fresh or made into confectionery or desserts. Immature pods are eaten fresh, pickled, or added to soups, stews, and sauces.

TANACETUM
Tansy

Asteraceae

There are about 70 species of mostly aromatic annuals, perennials, and subshrubs in this genus, which ranges throughout northern temperate regions. It includes members of the daisy family, formerly classified in *Balsamita*, *Chrysanthemum*, *Matricaria*, and *Pyrethrum*. Many are aromatic, containing pungent volatile oils and insecticidal compounds that may cause unpleasant reactions if handled, or consumed in excess. Most are invasive and need vigilant control in the garden. These members of the daisy family are rich in volatile oils, bitters, and sesquiterpene lactones, which inhibit allergic inflammatory responses, and are insecticidal. They are extremely pungent, potent herbs and should be used with caution. *Tanacetum balsamita* is an attractive plant for the silver or white garden. Its leaves were once used as fragrant bookmarks, hence the obsolete common name, "bibleleaf". The word "cost" in its more widely used common names "alecost" and "costmary" is from the Sanskrit *kustha*, "an aromatic plant", while "ale" recalls its role in brewing, and "mary" refers to the Virgin Mary, to whom the plant was dedicated. *Tanacetum parthenium* (feverfew) was described in old herbals as a remedy for headaches but forgotten until the 1970s when Mrs Anne Jenkins, a doctor's wife in Cardiff (Wales), found that it cured her migraine and reported its effectiveness. Clinical trials in the 1980s supported evidence that it is

indeed an effective and relatively safe remedy in many cases of migraine. Insecticides based on pyrethrins were first made from the flowers of *T. coccineum* syn. *Chrysanthemum coccineum*, *Pyrethrum roseum* (red pyrethrum), and were known as Persian insect powder. The flowers of *Tanacetum cinerariifolium* were later found to be more effective. Dried flowers and powder retain their insecticidal properties almost indefinitely. Pyrethrins are non-toxic to mammals. *Tanacetum vulgare* was important as a strewing herb in the 16th century. It contains thujone, an insecticidal substance also found in *Artemisia absinthium* (see p.130), which is highly toxic in excess. Tansy featured in a number of Easter rituals in the British Isles, as a cleansing herb after the Lenten fast, and symbol of the bitter Passover herbs. Tansy cakes, a kind of omelette, were traditionally eaten at this time, and awarded to the victor in a handball game played in parishes between clergy and congregation. *Tanacetum* is from the Greek *athanasia*, "immortality", possibly referring to the long-lived flowers of certain species, or to the practice of packing corpses with tansy leaves to preserve them and deter insects until burial.
CULTIVATION Well-drained to dry, stony soil in sun. Remove dead flower heads of *T. parthenium* to prevent excessive self-sowing. *Tanacetum vulgare* is invasive.
PROPAGATION By seed sown at 10–13°C (50–55°F) in spring (species and some variants only); by division in spring or autumn; by basal cuttings in spring; by semi-ripe cuttings in summer.
HARVEST Whole plants (*T. parthenium*, *T. vulgare*) are cut when flowering, and leaves are picked as required, and used fresh or dried in infusions, liquid extracts, powders, and tinctures. *Tanacetum vulgare* is distilled for oil. Leaves (*T. parthenium*) are sometimes eaten fresh, or dried for use in tablets to treat migraine, rheumatism, and arthritis. Flowers (*T. cinerariifolium*) are picked as they open and are dried for powder.

■ **Tanacetum balsamita** syn. *Balsamita major*, *Chrysanthemum balsamita* (alecost, costmary) Rhizomatous perennial with oblong, silver-green, mint-scented leaves, to 30cm (12in) long. Clusters of daisy-like flowers, about 1cm (½in) across, are borne on long stalks in late summer. Found from Europe to C Asia. ‡90cm (36in), ↔ 60cm (24in). ■ subsp. *balsametoides* syn. var. *tomentosum* (camphor plant) has camphor-scented foliage. ‡↔ 1m (3ft).
HARDINESS Fully hardy.
PARTS USED Leaves.
PROPERTIES A bitter, astringent, laxative herb with a balsam–mint aroma. It improves digestion and liver function.
MEDICINAL USES Now obsolete medicinally, but once used internally as a liver and gall bladder remedy, and externally for insect stings.
CULINARY USES Fresh leaves may be added with discretion to salads, dressings, meat and vegetable dishes; dried leaves are infused as tea.
ECONOMIC USES Dried leaves added to potpourris. Leaves used in brewing beer.

■ **Tanacetum cinerariifolium** syn. *Chrysanthemum cinerariifolium*, *Pyrethrum cinerariifolium* (Dalmatian pellitory, pyrethrum) Perennial with slender stems and grey-green, lanceolate to oblong, deeply divided leaves, 10–20cm (4–8in) long. Solitary flowers, about 3cm (1¼in) across, with white ray petals and yellow disc florets, appear from early summer to early autumn. Native to the Balkans and Albania. ‡ 30–75cm (12–30in), ↔ 30cm (12in).
HARDINESS Fully hardy.
PARTS USED Flowers.
PROPERTIES An aromatic herb with strong insecticidal effects.
ECONOMIC USES Dried flowers are used in insecticides and fumigants, especially in sprays to control pests and insect-borne diseases in aircraft.

Tanacetum balsamita

Tanacetum balsamita subsp. *balsametoides*

Tanacetum cinerariifolium

Tanacetum parthenium

Tanacetum parthenium 'Aureum'

Tanacetum parthenium 'Golden Ball'

Tanacetum parthenium 'Golden Moss'

Tanacetum parthenium 'Plenum'

T

Tanacetum parthenium
'Snowball'

Tanacetum parthenium
'Tom Thumb White Stars'

Tanacetum parthenium 'White Bonnet'

Tanacetum vulgare

Tanacetum vulgare
var. crispum

Tanacetum vulgare
'Isla Gold'

Tanacetum vulgare
'Silver Lace'

◼ **Tanacetum parthenium** syn. *Chrysanthemum parthenium*, *Matricaria parthenium* (feverfew) Strong-smelling, short-lived perennial with yellow-green, ovate, pinnately lobed leaves, to 8cm (3in) long. Clusters of daisy-like flowers, to 2.5cm (1in) across, appear in summer. Native to Europe and the Caucasus. ‡ 45–60cm (18–24in), ↔ 30–45cm (12–18in). ◼ 'Aureum' has bright golden foliage. Comes true from seed. ◼ 'Golden Ball' is compact, with golden-yellow, button-like flowers. ‡↔ 23cm (9in). ◼ 'Golden Moss' is dwarf, with moss-like, golden foliage; ideal for edging and containers. ‡ 10cm (4in). ◼ 'Plenum' syn. 'Flore Pleno' has double white flowers; excellent for cutting. Produces a high percentage of double-flowered plants from seed. ‡ 35cm (14in). ◼ 'Snowball' has ivory, double, pompon-like flowers. ‡ 30cm (12in), ↔ 15cm (6in). ◼ 'Tom Thumb White Stars' has double, white, pompon-like flowers; excellent for containers and edging. ‡↔ 23cm (9in). ◼ 'White Bonnet' bears double, white, green-flecked flowers. ‡ 60cm (24in), ↔ 45cm (18in).
HARDINESS Fully hardy.
PARTS USED Whole plant, leaves.
PROPERTIES A bitter, tonic, cooling herb with a pungent odour and nauseating taste. It relieves pain, relaxes spasms, dilates blood vessels, lowers fever, improves digestion, stimulates the uterus, and has laxative effects.
MEDICINAL USES Internally for migraine, headache, rheumatic and arthritic complaints, minor feverish illnesses, and digestive and menstrual problems. Externally for insect bites and bruising. Contraindicated during pregnancy. Handling leaves may cause dermatitis; eating leaves may cause mouth ulcers.
◪ ◈ ▮

◼ **Tanacetum vulgare** syn. *Chrysanthemum vulgare* (tansy)
Strongly aromatic, erect, rhizomatous perennial with dark green, pinnate leaves, to 15cm (6in) long, divided into 7–10 pairs of lanceolate, pinnately lobed or toothed leaflets. Clusters of yellow, button-like flowers, to 1cm (½in) across, are borne in late summer and autumn. Native to Europe. ‡ 60cm–1.2m (2–4ft), ↔ indefinite. ◼ var. *crispum* (fern-leafed tansy) has finely cut leaves; less invasive than the species. ◼ 'Isla Gold' has golden foliage that withstands full sun. Originated at West Acre Gardens, Norfolk (England). ◼ 'Silver Lace' has white-variegated leaves.
HARDINESS Fully hardy.
PARTS USED Whole plant, oil.
PROPERTIES A bitter, acrid, warming herb with a pungent aroma. It expels intestinal parasites, benefits the digestion, and stimulates the uterus.
MEDICINAL USES Mainly used as a enema for expelling round and threadworms in children, and topically in lotions for scabies, lice, and fleas. The herb is possibly unsafe for internal use, especially in pregnancy, although sometimes recommended for nausea and failure to menstruate. Excess causes abortion, venous congestion of abdominal organs, and convulsions. Tansy oil is highly toxic for both internal and external use, and very small amounts may prove fatal.
CULINARY USES Leaves are used with discretion for flavouring; traditionally added to a kind of custard known as a tansy, and to tansy cakes and puddings.
⚠ **WARNING** This herb, especially as tansy oil, is subject to legal restrictions in some countries.
◪ ◈ ▮ ◿

TARAKTOGENOS
Taraktogenos kurzii. See *Hydnocarpus kurzii*.

TARAXACUM
Dandelion

Asteraceae

This genus of about 60 species of perennials is found in northern temperate regions and temperate parts of S America. The best-known member of the genus is *T. officinale* (dandelion), which is a potent diuretic, hence the French name, *pissenlit*, "wet-the-bed". It contains high levels of potassium salts; this is an advantage in a strong diuretic because large amounts are lost in urine. It was first described in Chinese medicine c.AD659 and in European medicine in 1485, although there are possible mentions dating back to Pliny (AD23–79). Promoted by Arab physicians in the 11th century, and mentioned by the physicians of Myddfai (Wales) in the 13th century, it became an "officinal" drug by the 16th century. The dandelion is grown as a vegetable, particularly in France, where improved forms were selected during the 19th century. Like chicory, it is very bitter but may be blanched or soaked in water for an hour or so before use. *Taraxacum* comes from the medieval Latin, which in turn was derived from the Arabic *tarakhshaqún*, "wild chicory" or "bitter herb".
CULTIVATION Moist to dry, neutral to alkaline soil in sun. Dandelion crops should be dead-headed to prevent seeding. Regenerates from its taproot, and is difficult to eradicate once established. Leaves are prone to powdery mildew; roots may be damaged by lettuce root aphid and root rot.
PROPAGATION By seed sown in spring.
HARVEST Plants are cut in early summer and dried for use in decoctions (Chinese medicine only). Leaves are picked in late spring, before flowering occurs, and juiced, or dried for use in infusions, liquid extracts, and tinctures. When used fresh as a vegetable, young leaves or blanched leaves are picked as required. Roots are best lifted in autumn from two-year-old plants for highest (40 per cent) inulin content and least bitterness; they are pressed for juice, roasted for coffee, or dried for decoctions, infusions, liquid extracts, and tinctures. Harvesting of roots can also be carried out in spring when inulin content is closer to 2 per cent. Stocks of preserved leaves and roots are replaced annually. Flowers for wine-making are picked in spring and all green parts removed.

◼ **Taraxacum officinale** (dandelion)
Variable perennial with a thick taproot, white latex, and a basal rosette of entire, saw-toothed or pinnately lobed leaves, to 25cm (10in) long. Solitary, bright yellow flowers, to 6cm (2½in) across, appear from spring to autumn, followed by ribbed fruits, bearing a tuft of fine white hairs. Cosmopolitan weed. ‡ 30cm (12in), ↔ 45cm (18in). 'Improved Full Heart' syn. '*Amélioré à Coeur Plein*' forms a dense clump of foliage; blanches easily. 'Thick Leaved' syn. 'Broad Leaved', 'Cabbage Leaved' has large, deeply lobed leaves in a semi-erect rosette; blanches well. ↔ 45–60cm (18–24in).
HARDINESS Fully hardy.
PARTS USED Whole plant (*pu gong ying*), leaves, roots, flowers.
PROPERTIES A bitter–sweet, cooling herb that has diuretic, laxative, and anti-rheumatic effects, stimulates liver function, improves digestion, and reduces swelling and inflammation.
MEDICINAL USES Internally for gall bladder and urinary disorders, gallstones, jaundice, cirrhosis, dyspepsia with constipation, oedema

T

Taraxacum officinale

associated with high blood pressure and heart weakness, chronic joint and skin complaints, gout, eczema, psoriasis, and acne. Internally in Chinese medicine for breast and lung tumours, mastitis, and abscesses, jaundice, hepatitis, and urinary tract infections; externally for snake bite. Combines well with *Berberis vulgaris* (see p.142), *Chelone glabra* (see p.166), and *Veronicastrum virginicum* (see p.402) for gall bladder complaints.
CULINARY USES Fresh leaves, usually blanched, are eaten in salads or cooked as a vegetable. Flowers are made into wine and jelly. Roots are roasted and ground as a caffeine-free substitute for coffee.
ECONOMIC USES Leaves and roots are used to flavour herbal cordials, beers, and soft drinks, such as dandelion and burdock.

TASMANNIA
Pepperberries

Winteraceae

A genus of about 25 species of evergreen trees and shrubs, found in Australasia and formerly classified as *Drimys* (see p.196). Male and female flowers are borne on different plants. Pepperberries contain a highly pungent substance known as polygodial, which is unique to the genus. Polygodial is present in both leaves and berries, which equal or surpass pepper (see *Piper nigrum*, p.321) and chillis (see *Capsicum* spp., p.153) in pungency. The main species cultivated is *Tasmannia lanceolata*, a species of wet mountain gullies, which is an attractive plant for hedging or understorey use in mild regions. It is also grown for the bushfood industry. Both leaves and berries are used commercially, though the flower buds have a hot spicy flavour, too. In the 19th century, the bark was harvested as a substitute for or adulterant of Winter's bark, from the closely related *Drimys lanceolata* (see p.196).
CULTIVATION Moist, well-drained soil in sun or partial shade.
PROPAGATION By seed sown when ripe; by semi-ripe cuttings in summer.

HARVEST Leaves are picked at any time and used fresh, dried whole, or dried and ground. Berries are collected when ripe and dried, frozen, pickled in brine, or packed in salt. Flower buds are collected in spring and used fresh. Bark is stripped from prunings and dried.

Tasmannia lanceolata syn. *T. aromatica*, *Drimys aromatica* (mountain pepper, native pepper)
Dense shrub or tree with crimson young stems and branches, and elliptic, dark green, leathery leaves, to 8cm (3in) long. Clusters of 7–18 white flowers, 1.5cm (½in) across, appear in spring, followed by glossy, black, fleshy fruits, about 7mm (¼in) across, containing black seeds. Australia (Tasmania, Victoria, New South Wales). ‡ 4m (12ft), ↔ 2.5m (8ft).
HARDINESS Frost hardy.
PARTS USED Leaves, fruits, flower buds, bark.
PROPERTIES An aromatic stimulant herb with a pungent peppery flavour.
MEDICINAL USES Bark has similar properties to *Drimys winteri* (Winter's bark, see p.196).
CULINARY USES Flower buds can be used to flavour salads. Ground, dried leaves and berries are used in the same way as pepper. Bark is made into tea.

TAXUS
Yew

Taxaceae

This genus includes 5–10 species of evergreen coniferous trees and shrubs, occurring throughout northern temperate zones and into SE Asia and C America. Male and female flowers are usually borne on separate plants. Yew trees are widely planted as specimen trees, hedges, and topiary, in spite of the fact that all parts, except the aril, are extremely poisonous. Eating the leaves of yews is a common cause of death among livestock, which succumb so quickly that the foliage of the plant is often found still in the mouth of the animal. *Taxus baccata* (common yew) is renowned for its longevity. Reliable records date some British trees to at least 1500 years old, and the Fortingall yew in Perthshire (Scotland) is estimated to be over 8000 years old, though the trunk is hollow, so precise dating is not possible. Yew trees were sacred to the Druids, who built their temples nearby – an association continued by the Christian practice of planting yew trees around churches. In the 1960s, *T. brevifolia* (Pacific yew) was found to contain paclitaxel or taxol, which was first isolated in 1971 and, after clinical trials that began in 1983, was hailed as one of the most promising drugs for treating ovarian and other cancers. In the form of tamoxifen, the drug reduces rates of death from breast cancer by 30 per cent. At the outset, an enormous number of trees were needed to supply Pacific yew bark for the drug; in order to provide sufficient taxol to treat a cancer patient, the bark of six trees is required. The resulting increase in exploitation of *T. brevifolia* in the USA led to the Pacific

Yew Act (1992), which provides for the management of trees on federal lands, covering both harvesting and conservation. Subsequent research, reported in 1996, found that taxol exists in a fungus, *Pestalotiopsis*, that grows symbiotically in other species of yew, and in other trees species, enabling taxol to be produced more cheaply and easily, and without further endangering the Pacific yew. In particular, *Taxus wallichiana* (Himalayan yew) yields far higher quantities of taxol. *Taxus baccata* also contains taxol; it has been utilized in the UK through a programme to collect prunings from properties where there are significant plantings of yew hedges. The bark and twigs of *T. canadensis* (Canadian yew) have been used by several native N American tribes in a tea to treat influenza.
CULTIVATION Well-drained soil in sun or shade. Trim hedges and topiary in summer and early autumn. Withstands hard remedial pruning.
PROPAGATION By seed sown in autumn; by semi-ripe cuttings in late summer or early autumn. Seeds may take two years or more to germinate.
HARVEST Leaves are picked in early autumn or in spring, and bark is collected from autumn to spring, for commercial extraction of taxol.
⚠ **WARNING** All parts, except aril, are extremely toxic if eaten.

Taxus baccata (common yew)
Domed, spreading, evergreen tree with scaly, purple-brown bark and dark green, linear leaves, to 3cm (1¼in) long, arranged in two ranks on either side of the twigs. Pale yellow flowers appear in spring; females are followed by single green seeds, surrounded by a fleshy red aril, 1cm (½in) across. Found from Europe to N Africa and Iran. ‡ 10–20m (30–70ft), ↔ 8–10m (25–30ft). ▣ 'Dovastonii Aurea' is a small female tree with spreading branches, pendent branchlets, yellow shoots, and yellow-margined leaves. ‡ 3–5m (10–15ft), ↔ 2m (6ft).

Taxus baccata 'Dovastonii Aurea'

Taxus baccata 'Repandens'

Taxus brevifolia

T

'Fastigiata' syn. 'Hibernica' (Irish yew) is a female tree with a narrow upright habit and leaves arranged radially. ‡ 10m (30ft), ↔ 6m (20ft). ▣ 'Repandens' is a female shrub with a prostrate, mound-forming habit. ‡ 60cm (24in), ↔ 5m (15ft).

HARDINESS Fully hardy.

PARTS USED Leaves, leaf extract (paclitaxel).

PROPERTIES A bitter, astringent, purgative herb that contains extremely poisonous alkaloids and anti-cancer paclitaxel (taxol).

MEDICINAL USES Internally, in the form of paclitaxel, for breast and ovarian cancers. For use only by qualified practitioners. Also, in the form of a homeopathic tincture only, for bronchial and urinary problems, arthritis, gout, and pustular skin diseases. No longer used in herbal medicine because of its toxicity.

▧ ▣

▣ *Taxus brevifolia* (Pacific yew)
Small tree with slender drooping branches, scaly, red-purple bark, and linear leathery leaves, to 2.5cm (1in) long. Small cream flowers appear in spring; female flowers are followed by green-brown seeds, surrounded by a fleshy red aril. Native to western N America (from SE British Columbia to N Idaho). ‡ 15m (50ft), ↔ 10m (30ft).

HARDINESS Fully hardy.

PARTS USED Extracts of leaves, bark (paclitaxel).

PROPERTIES A toxic herb that contains anti-cancer paclitaxel (taxol).

MEDICINAL USES Internally for breast and ovarian cancers. For use only by qualified practitioners.

▣ ▧ ▣

TERMINALIA
Myrobalan

Combretaceae

A genus of about 200 species of evergreen and deciduous, often buttressed trees that occur in most tropical regions. They characteristically have their foliage arranged in tiers at the tips of branches, hence the generic name, *Terminalia*, from the Latin *terminus*, "end". A number of species are important as sources of timber, gums, dyes, and tannin. The dried fruits of several species are sold in markets in SE Asia as "myrobalans". *Terminalia chebula* is widely grown in the tropics as a shade tree and ornamental; it is sacred to Shiva, and of central importance in Ayurvedic medicine. The *triphala* ("three fruits"), a laxative tonic, is based on *T. belerica* (bastard myrobalan, beleric myrobalan, *bibhitaki*), *T. chebula*, and *Phyllanthus emblica* (see p.313). *Terminalia chebula* was first mentioned in Chinese medicine in 1061. In Tibetan medicine it is known as "king of medicines" and, with *T. arjuna* and *T. belerica*, features in most formulas. The tropical Asian *T. catappa* (Indian almond) has highly astringent bark and leaves, which are important in folk medicine for treating diarrhoea and dysentery. It yields

Terminalia chebula

almond-flavoured seeds, surrounded by juicy edible flesh; the seeds are used in exactly the same ways as almonds; they can likewise be pressed for oil. In Cambodia and Vietnam, *T. nigrovenulosa* (*preah phnau*) is used in the form of bark decoctions to treat chronic diarrhoea, and the S African *T. sericea* is used internally for diarrhoea, pneumonia, and diabetes, and externally for wounds and eye complaints. The Australian *T. ferdinandiana* (Kakadu plum) produces small, gooseberry-like fruits that are one of the richest known sources of vitamin C, containing 50 times as much as oranges.

CULTIVATION Fertile sandy soil in sun.

PROPAGATION By seed sown when ripe at 18–24°C (64–75°F); by layering in spring.

HARVEST Fruits are collected when ripe and sun-dried for use in decoctions, pastes, and powders.

▣ *Terminalia chebula* (black chebulic, *haritaki*, myrobalan)
Evergreen tree with leathery, ovate, pointed leaves, to 12cm (5in) long, which have woolly undersides. Tiny, odoriferous, cream flowers are borne in spikes, to 8cm (3in) long, in summer, followed by ovoid–oblong, yellow-brown fruits, about 4cm (1½in) long. Native to Sri Lanka, India, Burma (Myanmar), and Nepal. ‡ 15–25m (50–80ft), ↔ 20m (70ft).

HARDINESS Min. 16–18°C (61–64°F).

PARTS USED Fruits (*he zi*).

PROPERTIES A sweet, astringent, warming herb with an unpleasant taste; it regulates colon function, improves digestion, is expectorant, controls bleeding and discharges, and destroys intestinal parasites. It also has a tonic, rejuvenative effect, especially on the digestive, respiratory, and nervous systems.

MEDICINAL USES Internally for constipation, digestive and nervous disorders, diarrhoea, dysentery, intestinal worms, haemorrhoids, rectal prolapse, abnormal uterine bleeding and inflammation, vaginal discharge, involuntary ejaculation, coughs, night sweats, and asthma.

Not given to pregnant women or patients with severe exhaustion or dehydration. Externally for ulcers, wounds, mouth inflammation, and gum disease.

CULINARY USES Sour fruits are eaten fresh in salads, pickled in brine, or fried; also used to make "black salt", which is an essential ingredient of a spice blend known as *chat masala*.

ECONOMIC USES Dried fruits are used in tanning and inks.

▧ ▣ ▧ ▧ ▣

TETRADENIA
Lamiaceae

A genus of five species of semi-succulent, aromatic shrubs or small trees, native to Africa and Madagascar. *Tetradenia riparia* is quite common in damp places, often beside streams, in E South Africa. It deserves to be more widely grown for its neat, highly aromatic foliage and profuse feathery flower spikes. In cool areas it makes an excellent container plant that is easily pruned to shape and propagated; the flowers last well in water. The leaves are widely used medicinally by African tribes, and in some areas were once regarded as a cure for malaria.

CULTIVATION Moist, well-drained soil in sun or partial shade.

PROPAGATION By seed sown when ripe; by semi-ripe cuttings in summer.

HARVEST Leaves are picked during the growing season and used fresh or dried in infusions, or crushed when fresh as an inhalation.

▣ *Tetradenia riparia* syn. *Iboza riparia* (ginger bush, *iboza*, *watersalie*)
Densely branched, deciduous shrub or small tree with succulent stems, clad in glandular hairs, and light green, rounded to cordate, velvety leaves, to 8cm (3in) long, which have white downy undersides and neatly scalloped margins. Tiny, white to mauve, tubular flowers are borne in spikes, to 8cm (3in) long, in early spring, with male and female flowers on separate plants. Found from E South Africa to Namibia, Angola, and Ethiopia.

HARDINESS Min. 10°C (50°F).

PARTS USED Leaves.

Tetradenia riparia

T

PROPERTIES A bitter aromatic herb that lowers fever, relaxes spasms, and is expectorant and antibiotic.

MEDICINAL USES Internally for colds and flu, bronchitis, stomach upsets, flatulence, mouth ulcers, diarrhoea, and fevers (especially malarial). Externally, as an inhalation, for headaches.

ECONOMIC USES Dried leaves are good in potpourri.

TETRADIUM

Rutaceae

This genus of nine species of evergreen and deciduous trees and shrubs occurs in the Himalayas and S and E Asia. It is closely related to *Euodia* and *Ravensara*, and resembles *Phellodendron* (see p.311) in appearance. Several species are grown for their attractive leaves and large clusters of fruits. *Tetradium ruticarpum* was first recorded in Chinese medicine before AD200, during the later Han dynasty. In contrast to its unpleasant-tasting, poisonous fruits, those of Madagascan *Ravensara aromatica*, to which *Tetradium* is closely related, are clove-scented and used in food flavouring. *Tetradium* is from the Greek *tetradeion*, "quaternion", as the floral parts are in fours.

CULTIVATION Well-drained soil in sun or partial shade. Remove dead or congested growths in early spring.

PROPAGATION By seed sown in autumn; by root cuttings in midwinter.

HARVEST Fruits are collected when ripe and dried for use in decoctions.

⚠ **WARNING** Fruits are poisonous.

▪ *Tetradium ruticarpum* syn. *Euodia officinalis*, *E. rutaecarpa*
Deciduous shrub or small tree with papery, gland-dotted, pinnate leaves, to 40cm (16in) long, divided into 7–15 ovate leaflets, to 17cm (7in) long. Small, white to yellow or green flowers are produced in clusters, to 18cm (7in) long, in spring and summer, followed by conspicuous, warty, rust red fruits containing glossy black seeds. Native to China and

Tetradium ruticarpum

Taiwan. ‡9m (28ft), ↔ 5m (15ft).
HARDINESS Half hardy.
PARTS USED Fruits (*wu zhu yu*).
PROPERTIES A pungent, bitter, very warming herb that relieves pain, destroys intestinal parasites, stimulates the uterus, controls vomiting, and is anti-bacterial. It increases both body temperature and blood pressure.
MEDICINAL USES Internally for stomach chills and pains, vomiting and acid regurgitation, diarrhoea (especially in early morning), painful menstruation, and threadworm infestations. Usually combined with *Glycyrrhiza glabra* (see p.227) to reduce toxicity and with *Zingiber officinale* (see p.411) for abdominal chills. Excess causes diarrhoea, dyspepsia, and delirium.

TEUCRIUM
Germander

Lamiaceae

This cosmopolitan genus of about 300 species of perennials and small, evergreen and deciduous shrubs is centred on the Mediterranean region. *Teucrium chamaedrys* is a useful small evergreen for steep banks, walls, containers, and edging. In cultivation it is often confused with the hybrid *T. × lucidrys* (*T. chamaedrys × T. lucidum*), which is not used medicinally. Plants in herb nurseries are often wrongly labelled, so it is important to check identification when purchasing for medicinal use. *Teucrium × lucidrys* is taller than *T. chamaedrys*, and more upright, with glossier, more leathery, darker green leaves. It is often planted as a dwarf hedge in knot gardens, for which purpose the smaller, more spreading *T. chamaedrys* is unsuitable. *Teucrium chamaedrys* has been used medicinally since ancient Greek times, when Dioscorides recommended it for coughs and asthma. The Holy Roman Emperor Charles V (1500–1558) was apparently cured of gout by taking decoctions of the herb for 60 days. Culpeper considered it "good against diseases of the brain, as continual headache, falling sickness [epilepsy], melancholy, drowsiness, and dullness of spirits, convulsions and palsies" (*The English Physician Enlarged*, 1653). Following several cases of liver damage caused by diet formulas containing *T. chamaedrys*, a voluntary ban was imposed by French herbal practitioners, and many other herbalists no longer prescribe it. *Teucrium marum* (cat thyme) is used to treat gall bladder and stomach complaints, and has a similar effect on cats to *Nepeta cataria* (see p.288). In N Africa, *Teucrium polium* (*ja'adah*, mountain germander) is taken as an infusion for gastrointestinal complaints, and used as a depurative in steam baths for colds and fevers; it is also used to flavour drinks. *Teucrium scorodonia* (sage-leafed germander, wood sage) has very bitter, hop-scented leaves that have similar medicinal properties to those of *T. chamaedrys*, and were once used in brewing.

Teucrium chamaedrys

CULTIVATION Light, well-drained, neutral to alkaline soil in dry or stony soil in sun. Cut off dead flower spikes to encourage bushy new growth.
PROPAGATION By seed sown when ripe; by division in spring; by softwood or semi-ripe cuttings in summer.
HARVEST Plants are cut when flowering, and dried for use in infusions and liquid extracts.

▪ *Teucrium chamaedrys* (wall germander)
Shrubby aromatic perennial with a creeping rootstock, upright to spreading stems, and ovate, deeply veined, lobed leaves, about 3cm (1¼in) long, resembling small oak leaves. Small, pink to magenta, two-lipped, tubular flowers appear in summer and autumn. Native to Europe and SW Asia. ‡↔ 10–25cm (4–10in).
HARDINESS Fully hardy.
PARTS USED Whole plant, leaves.
PROPERTIES A bitter, astringent, anti-rheumatic herb that reduces inflammation, stimulates the digestion, and lowers fever. It has antiseptic, diuretic, and decongestant effects.
MEDICINAL USES Internally for loss of appetite, gall bladder and digestive disorders, summer diarrhoea in children, gout, rheumatoid arthritis, nasal catarrh, and bronchitis; also to encourage weight loss. Externally for gum disease, skin eruptions, and injuries (including snake bite). Combined with *Apium graveolens* (see p.125), *Filipendula ulmaria* (see p.214), and *Guaiacum officinale* (see p.229) for rheumatoid arthritis; with *Achillea millefolium* (see p.99) and *Apium graveolens* for gout; and with *Lobelia inflata* (see p.265) and *Marrubium vulgare* (see p.271) for bronchitis. May cause liver damage and is subject to a voluntary ban by practitioners in some countries, notably in France.
ECONOMIC USES Leaves are used to flavour liqueurs, vermouths, and tonic wines.

THEA
Thea sinensis. See *Camellia sinensis*.

T

THEOBROMA

Sterculiaceae

This is a genus of 20 species of evergreen trees, native to lowland tropical America. They are unusual in bearing flowers directly from the trunk or branches, a habit known as "cauliflory". The fermented, dried, and roasted seeds of *T. cacao* produce cocoa butter and cocoa powder, used in a range of medicinal ways, and for preparing cocoa beverages and chocolate. Cocoa was the basis of the Aztec drink *chocólatl* and was held in such high esteem by the Incas, Mayas, and Aztecs that the seeds were used as currency. In Mayan times, it was consumed by the nobility as a foaming drink, coloured red with annatto (see *Bixa orellana*, p.144) and flavoured with vanilla and chilli. Christopher Columbus (1451–1506) first brought cocoa pods from S America to Spain, but the taste for cocoa did not develop in Europe until the 17th century, at which time 450g (1lb) of chocolate cost the equivalent of £500 today. Africa began cocoa cultivation in the 19th century and now produces over half of all cocoa beans. Cocoa contains over 300 chemicals, including the stimulants caffeine and theobromine, and substances known as tetrahydro-beta-carbolines that may be the cause of chocoholism. It also contains phenyl-ethylamine, similar to amphetamine, which raises blood pressure and blood sugar levels, giving a sense of well being and alertness. Cocoa powder and paste are bitter, and are usually sweetened when used as a food or flavouring. Chocolate varies greatly in flavour depending on the type of bean, and the methods of processing and manufacture: dark chocolate has the highest percentage of cocoa solids and lowest sugar content; milk chocolate contains dried or condensed milk; and white chocolate is cocoa butter with milk and sugar added. *Theobroma* is from Greek words meaning "food of the gods".

CULTIVATION Fertile, moist, well-drained soil in shade, with high humidity and shelter from wind. Cut back to required shape in early spring, to control growth.

PROPAGATION By seed sown when ripe; by air layering in spring or summer; by semi-ripe cuttings in summer. All methods require a minimum temperature of 26°C (79°F).

HARVEST Fruits are cut all year, especially from early summer to early winter; seeds are removed to be fermented, dried, roasted, and ground as paste (cocoa mass). Cocoa butter is extracted from cocoa mass, leaving cocoa powder.

■ *Theobroma cacao* (cacao, chocolate tree, cocoa)
Small evergreen tree with oblong, thinly leathery, glossy leaves, to 40cm (16in) long, which are pink when young. Clusters of small, pale yellow flowers appear directly from the trunk and branches, followed by yellow, brown, or purple, ribbed pods, 12–30cm (5–12in) long, containing numerous seeds in a white mucilaginous pulp. Native to C and S America. ‡ 8m (25ft), ↔ 5–6m (15–20ft).
HARDINESS Min. 16°C (61°F).
PARTS USED Fruits, seeds, fat, butter.
PROPERTIES A bitter, stimulant, diuretic herb that lowers blood pressure and dilates the coronary arteries. Cocoa powder and butter are nutritive; the latter also softens and soothes damaged skin.
MEDICINAL USES Internally for angina and high blood pressure (cocoa powder). Contra-indicated in irritable bowel syndrome. Externally for chapped skin and burns (cocoa butter). Cocoa products may cause allergies or migraine.
CULINARY USES Chocolate is used to flavour game, sauces (especially with chilli in Mexican *mole*), ice cream, cakes, biscuits, pastries, confectionery, and milk drinks; also as a food and ingredient in its own right.
ECONOMIC USES Chocolate is used to flavour liqueurs, such as Bailey's Irish Cream. Cocoa butter is used in cosmetics, skin creams, and as a base for pessaries and suppositories. By-products from cocoa processing include fertilizer, fodder, fuel (husks), jelly, alcohol, and vinegar (pulp).
🞖 🞐 🞖 🞐 🖉 🖉 🞖

THLASPI

Thlaspi bursa-pastoris. See *Capsella bursa-pastoris*.

THUJA

Arbor-vitae

Cupressaceae

This genus of six species of evergreen coniferous trees occurs in E Asia and N America. *Thuja occidentalis* and *T. orientalis* are widely grown as ornamentals; both have numerous cultivars, varying in size, habit, and colour, making them some of the most versatile conifers for garden use. Thujas have aromatic foliage, rich in volatile oil, which consists mainly of thujone, a toxic compound also found in *Artemisia absinthium* (see p.132). *Thuja occidentalis* has long been used by native N Americans, providing materials for bows, canoes, baskets, cordage, and roofing, and medicines to treat menstrual problems,

Thuja occidentalis   *Thuja occidentalis* ‘Rheingold’

Thuja occidentalis ‘Holmstrup’

headache, and heart disease. It was made into an anti-rheumatic tea by loggers in the wetland forests where it grows wild, and listed in the *US Pharmacopoeia* (1882–94) as a uterine stimulant and diuretic. *Thuja orientalis* was first described in Chinese medicine in the *Tang Materia Medica* (c.AD659). Some botanists now classify this species as *Platycladus orientalis*.

CULTIVATION Deep, moist, well-drained soil in sun. Dislikes cold drying winds when young. Trim hedges in spring and late summer. Trees may be damaged by scale insects, aphid, canker, and *Keithia* disease.
PROPAGATION By seed sown in late winter (species only); by semi-ripe cuttings in late summer.
HARVEST Foliage and bark are removed as required and dried for use in decoctions, liquid extracts, and tinctures. Seeds (*T. orientalis*) are collected from ripe cones in autumn and dried for use in decoctions, powders, and tinctures.
⚠ **WARNING** Leaves are toxic if eaten. Skin allergen.

■ *Thuja occidentalis* (American arbor-vitae, white cedar)
Slow-growing, narrow conifer with orange-brown bark and tiny, scale-like leaves, which turn bronze in winter and have an apple scent when crushed. Flowers consist of minute black male cones and erect, yellow-green,

Theobroma cacao

Thuja orientalis

Thuja orientalis 'Aurea Nana'

ovoid female cones, 1cm (½in) long, which turn brown and pendulous when ripe. Native to eastern N America. ‡ 10–20m (30–70ft), ↔ 3–5m (10–15ft). ▣ 'Holmstrup' is dense and conical, with rich green foliage, held vertically. ‡ 3–4m (10–12ft). ▣ 'Rheingold' has old-gold foliage, pinkish when young, which bronzes in winter. ‡ 1–2m (3–6ft). 'Smaragd' is compact and dwarf, with bright green foliage. ‡ 1m (3ft), ↔ 80cm (32in).
HARDINESS Fully hardy.
PARTS USED Foliage, bark.
PROPERTIES A bitter, astringent, cooling herb with a camphoraceous fruity aroma. It stimulates the heart, uterus, and nerves, reduces inflammation, clears toxins, and is diuretic, expectorant, anti-fungal, and anti-viral.
MEDICINAL USES Internally in cancer therapy and for bronchial complaints (especially associated with congestive heart failure), urinary infections (including cystitis), bed-wetting in children, psoriasis, eczema, failure to menstruate. Once used to treat side-effects of smallpox vaccinations. Contraindicated during pregnancy and in dry irritant coughs. Externally for vaginal infections, warts, muscular aches, and rheumatism. Combined with *Hamamelis virginiana* (see p.230) as a lotion for exudative eczema. For use only by qualified practitioners.
🖻 🗆 ▪

▣ **Thuja orientalis** syn. *Biota orientalis*, *Platycladus orientalis* (Chinese arbor-vitae) Pyramidal or conical, small tree with red-

brown, fibrous bark and vertical sprays of very small, scale-like leaves, which usually turn bronze or brown in winter. Upright, grey-bloomed cones, 2cm (¾in) long, are flask-shaped. Native to China and Iran. ‡ 15m (50ft), ↔ 6m (20ft). ▣ 'Aurea Nana' is dwarf, with yellow-green foliage that bronzes in winter. ‡↔ 60cm (24in).
HARDINESS Fully hardy.
PARTS USED Foliage (*ce bai ye*), seeds (*bai zi ren*).
PROPERTIES A bitter, astringent, cooling herb that controls bleeding and coughing, stimulates the uterus, encourages hair growth, and is expectorant and anti-bacterial (foliage); a sweet, sedative, mildly laxative herb (seeds).
MEDICINAL USES Internally for coughs, asthma, haemorrhage, excessive menstruation, bronchitis, skin infections, mumps, bacterial dysentery, arthritic pain, or premature baldness (foliage); and for palpitations, insomnia, nervous disorders, and constipation in the elderly (seeds). Preparations of leaves are contraindicated during pregnancy.
🗆 🗷 ▪

THYMUS
Thyme

Lamiaceae

Some 350 species of small, evergreen, aromatic, mostly woody-based perennials and subshrubs belong to this Eurasian genus, which occurs mainly on dry grassland and calcareous soils. Many species are good garden plants, having a neat habit, fragrant foliage, and colourful flowers; their small size is ideally suited to crevices in paving, rock gardens, walls, and containers. Although tiny, the numerous flowers produce copious nectar, making thymes important as bee plants. Thymes hybridize freely in cultivation, making the taxonomy of *Thymus* complex, with numerous synonyms and invalid names. In common with many pleasant-smelling plants, thyme came to symbolize death, because the souls of the dead were thought to rest in the flowers; the smell of thyme has apparently been detected at several haunted sites. It is also associated with various rituals once carried out by young women to reveal their true love. Thymes vary in aroma but the majority can be used to flavour food. Most widely used are *T. vulgaris*, *T. × citriodorus*, and their cultivars. The main medicinal thymes are *T. serpyllum* and *T. vulgaris*. Much of the dried thyme and essential oil of thyme in international trade comes from Spain, where there are 37 different species of *Thymus*, including 24 endemic species. The main species collected are *T. praecox* and *T. pulegioides* ("*tomillos serpoles*"), and *T. baeticus*, *T. capitatus*, *T. hyemalis*, *T. mastichina*, *T. orospedanus*, *T. serpilloides* subsp. *gadorensis*, *T. vulgaris*, *T. zygis* subsp. *gracilis*, and *T. zygis* subsp. *zygis* ("*tomillos*"). There is concern that the harvesting of some of the rarer thymes – and even rarer ones that are collected in error – is not sustainable. In addition, the practice of uprooting whole plants causes soil erosion in fragile arid ecosystems.

All thymes are rich in volatile oil, which consists mainly of thymol, a powerful antiseptic. The oil varies considerably in composition between species and from plant to plant. Commercial thyme oil is largely derived from *T. zygis* (Spanish sauce thyme), a white-flowered species found only in Spain and Portugal. Oil from *T. serpyllum* (sometimes known as serpolet oil) differs from *T. vulgaris* in being lower in carvacrol and higher in linalol and cymol, and thus having a sedative effect. Red and white thyme oil refer to the colour of the oil, which turns red when oxidized by contact with metal, but remains clear otherwise. *Thymus* is the original Greek name, which was used by Theophrastus for both thyme and savory (*Satureja*, see p.361).
CULTIVATION Well-drained soil in sun. Most thymes prefer neutral to alkaline soil and thrive in stony or rocky situations. Thymes dislike wet winters, and benefit from a layer of gravel to protect the foliage from contact with wet soil. In autumn, remove fallen leaves that settle on thyme plants as these may cause rotting. Trim lightly after flowering and remove dead flower heads to encourage bushiness. Remove green shoots of variegated cultivars to maintain variegation. In areas with cold damp winters, *T. camphoratus* is best grown in an alpine house. *Thymus vulgaris* is used in companion planting to control flea beetle, cabbage white butterfly, and other cabbage pests.
PROPAGATION By seed sown in spring (species only); by softwood or semi-ripe cuttings in summer; by division in spring.
HARVEST Whole plants and flowering tops are collected in summer, as flowering begins, and distilled for oil, or dried for elixirs, liquid extracts, and infusions. Sprigs are picked during the growing season and used fresh, or dried for infusions.

Thymus caespititius syn. *T. azoricus*, *T. micans* (Azores thyme)
Hummock-forming subshrub with upright flowering stems and narrow, slightly sticky leaves, about 6mm (¼in) long, which have a resinous aroma. Pink, lilac, or white flowers, with bracts similar to leaves, appear in small clusters, close to the mat, from late spring to summer. Native to Azores, NW Spain, and Portugal. ‡15cm (6in), ↔ 45cm (18in). ▣ 'Aureus' is slow-growing, with narrow, pale golden-green leaves and pink flowers. 'Celery' (celery thyme) forms small compact mounds, with celery-scented leaves and pale pink flowers. ‡ 8cm (3in).
HARDINESS Fully hardy.
PARTS USED Leaves.
PROPERTIES An aromatic herb with a tangerine–pine scent.
CULINARY USES As a substitute for *T. × citriodorus* in cooking, and as a flavouring in custards.
🗆 🗹

▣ **Thymus camphoratus** (camphor thyme) Small shrub with narrowly ovate to rounded–triangular, woolly leaves that are strongly camphor-scented. Green-white flowers,

Thymus caespititius 'Aureus'

Thymus camphoratus

Thymus capitatus

Thymus cilicicus

Thymus × citriodorus

Thymus × citriodorus 'Golden King'

Thymus × citriodorus 'Silver Queen'

Thymus herba-barona

accompanied by large, ovate, purple-green bracts, are produced in globose heads, about 1cm (½in) across, in summer. Native to Portugal. ↔ 40cm (16in).
HARDINESS Fully hardy.
PARTS USED Leaves and flowering tops.
PROPERTIES An aromatic herb with a camphor-like scent.
CULINARY USES May be used with discretion in cooking, perhaps with strong-flavoured meats.
ECONOMIC USES Leaves and flowering tops are used in potpourris and moth-repellent sachets.
⊠ ▨ ✓ ✓

■ **Thymus capitatus** syn. *Coridothymus capitatus* (conehead thyme)
Compact subshrub with grey, almost spiny stems and clusters of linear fleshy leaves, to 1cm (½in) long. Pink flowers, with red-tinged bracts, are produced in terminal conical clusters in summer. Native to Mediterranean Europe and Turkey. ↔ 25cm (10in).
HARDINESS Fully hardy.
PARTS USED Whole plant, leaves, flowering tops, oil.
PROPERTIES Similar to *T. vulgaris*.
CULINARY USES Leaves used to flavour roasted or grilled meat; also pickled and made into tea.
ECONOMIC USES Mainly as a source of essential oil, known as Spanish oregano oil, used in commercial food flavouring, soaps, and men's toiletries. Oil is irritant to mucous membranes and should not be used in aromatherapy. Source of Greek Hymettus honey.
⊠ ▨ ◻ ▤ ✓ ✓

■ **Thymus cilicicus** (Cilician thyme)
Compact bushy subshrub with deep green, prominently veined, linear leaves. Dense rounded clusters of mauve to lilac flowers appear in

midsummer. Native to Turkey. ‡ 10–15cm (4–6in), ↔ 45cm (18in).
HARDINESS Frost hardy.
PARTS USED Leaves.
PROPERTIES An aromatic herb with a lemon-like scent.
CULINARY USES Leaves may be used for flavouring.
▨ ✓

■ **Thymus × citriodorus** (lemon thyme)
Variable hybrid between *T. pulegioides* and *T. vulgaris*, with lemon-scented, ovate to lanceolate or diamond-shaped leaves, to 1cm (½in) long. Pale lilac flowers, with leaf-like bracts, appear in interrupted whorls in summer. Garden origin. ‡ 25–30cm (10–12in), ↔ 60cm (24in). ■ 'Golden King' is upright and bushy, with yellow-margined leaves. Tends to revert. ‡ 23cm (9in), ↔ 30cm (12in). 'Golden Queen' has an open habit, pale green, yellow-variegated leaves, and mauve flowers. 'Nyewoods' has yellow-green leaves with a central green zone. ■ 'Silver Queen' has silver-green to cream-marbled leaves. Differs in appearance from *T. vulgaris* 'Silver Posie' in having more variable variegation and pink-tinged tips in winter; also is less hardy and more liable to revert. ‡ 23cm (9in), ↔ 30–40cm (12–16in).
HARDINESS Fully hardy.
PARTS USED Whole plant, leaves, flowering tops, oil.
PROPERTIES An aromatic, decongestant, relaxant herb with a strong lemon scent.
MEDICINAL USES Oil is considered less irritant than other thyme oils, and is used in aromatherapy for asthma and other respiratory complaints, notably in children.
CULINARY USES Leaves are used to flavour savoury dishes, especially fish, stuffings for

poultry, and vegetables; also made into tea.
ECONOMIC USES Dried leaves are added to potpourris and herb pillows.
⊠ ▨ ◻ ▤ ▣ ✓ ✓

■ **Thymus herba-barona** (caraway thyme)
Wiry carpeting subshrub with long, slightly arching stems and dark green, ovate–lanceolate, caraway-scented leaves, to 7mm (¼in) long. Loose clusters of pink to mauve flowers appear in midsummer. Native to Corsica and Sardinia. ‡ 5–10cm (2–4in), ↔ 60cm (24in). 'Lemon-scented' syn. f. *citrata*, 'Lemon Caraway' has lemon-scented leaves and mauve flowers. 'Nutmeg' has nutmeg-scented leaves and darker pink flowers in late summer.
HARDINESS Fully hardy.
PARTS USED Leaves.
PROPERTIES An aromatic herb with a caraway scent.
CULINARY USES Leaves are traditionally used to flavour a baron of beef; also to flavour soups, game and meat dishes in which wine and garlic predominate.
▨ ✓

Thymus hyemalis (winter-flowering thyme)
Small shrub with dense clusters of linear, grey-green leaves, to 8mm (⅜in) long and 1mm (1/16in) wide. Mauve flowers appear in winter and spring. Native to SE Spain. ‡ 15–30cm (6–12in), ↔ 40cm (16in).
HARDINESS Fully hardy.
PARTS USED Leaves, flowering tops.
PROPERTIES An aromatic herb with a thyme-like scent.
CULINARY USES As for *T. vulgaris*.
ECONOMIC USES Source of commercial dried thyme and essential oil of thyme.
⊠ ▨ ✓ ✓

Thymus pseudolanuginosus

Thymus pulegioides

Thymus pulegioides 'Archer's Gold'

Thymus pulegioides 'Aureus'

Thymus pulegioides 'Bertram Anderson'

Thymus serpyllum

Thymus serpyllum 'Annie Hall'

Thymus serpyllum var. coccineus

Thymus mastichina (mastic thyme, Spanish marjoram)
Erect shrub with clusters of ovate to elliptic–lanceolate, wavy-edged, downy leaves, to 1.5cm (½in) long, which have a pungent, camphor-like aroma. Small, off-white flowers are borne in almost spherical heads in summer. Native to Spain and Portugal. ‡ 20–30cm (8–12in), ↔ 60–75cm (24–30in). 'Didi' has pink flowers.
HARDINESS Fully hardy.
PARTS USED Whole plant, leaves, flowering tops, oil.
PROPERTIES A pungent, bitter–sweet, aromatic herb with a eucalyptus-like scent.
CULINARY USES Leaves may be added to strong-flavoured meat dishes.
ECONOMIC USES Oil, known as "oil of wild marjoram", is used in commercial food flavouring, especially in meat sauces and soups.

Thymus polytrichus (creeping thyme, wild thyme)
Variable, mat-forming, creeping subshrub with prostrate, woody, branching stems and narrowly obovate, hair-fringed leaves, to 8mm (⅜in) long. Mauve to purple, rarely off-white flowers, with purple, leaf-like bracts, are borne in terminal heads in summer. Native to S Europe. ‡ 5cm (2in), ↔ 45cm (18in). subsp. *britannicus* syn. *T. praecox* subsp. *arcticus* has hairy stems and purple flowers. Native to W Europe.
HARDINESS Fully hardy.
PARTS USED Leaves.
PROPERTIES An aromatic herb with a typical thyme scent. May have similar properties to *T. serpyllum*.
CULINARY USES Leaves can be used for flavouring.

ECONOMIC USES Source of commercial dried thyme and essential oil of thyme.

■ **Thymus pseudolanuginosus** syn. *T. lanuginosus*, *T. serpyllum* subsp. *lanuginosus* (woolly thyme)
Prostrate subshrub with four-sided, hairy stems and tiny, elliptic, grey-green, woolly leaves. Pale pink flowers appear sparsely in the leaf axils in midsummer. Origin unknown. ‡ 2.5–7cm (1–3in), ↔ 1m (3ft).
HARDINESS Fully hardy.
PARTS USED Leaves.
PROPERTIES An aromatic herb with thyme scent.
CULINARY USES Leaves may be used for flavouring.

■ **Thymus pulegioides** (broad-leafed thyme, greater wild thyme, large thyme)
Spreading subshrub with four-angled stems and strongly aromatic, ovate–elliptic leaves, to 1cm (½in) long. Pink to purple flowers, with leaf-like bracts, appear in interrupted whorls in summer. Native to Europe. ‡ 20–25cm (8–10in), ↔ 40–45cm (16–18in). ■ 'Archer's Gold' is compact, with bright yellow, lemon-scented foliage and pale purple flowers; named after Bill Archer, who discovered it in Somerset (England). ‡ 15–23cm (6–9in), ↔ 45cm (18in). ■ 'Aureus' (golden lemon thyme) is a small, upright to spreading subshrub, with gold-splashed leaves. Tends to revert. ‡ 10–15cm (4–6in), ↔ 60cm (24in). ■ 'Bertram Anderson' syn. 'Anderson's Gold', 'E.B. Anderson' is low-growing, with red-flushed new growths and golden foliage. ‡ 15–23cm (6–9in), ↔ 30–60cm (12–24in). 'Oregano-scented' has an oregano-like aroma. Used as a substitute for

oregano. 'Pennsylvania Dutch Tea' has large, bright green leaves and a mild pleasant flavour; excellent for tea. ‡ 12–18cm (5–7in).
HARDINESS Fully hardy.
PARTS USED Leaves.
PROPERTIES An aromatic herb with a thyme-like scent.
CULINARY USES Used as a substitute for *T. vulgaris*.
ECONOMIC USES Source of commercial dried thyme and essential oil of thyme.

Thymus quinquecostatus syn. *T serpyllum* subsp. *quinquecostatus* (ibuki-jakô-sô, Japanese thyme)
Creeping subshrub with red wiry stems and ovate, shiny, bright green leaves, to 7mm (¼in) long, which are red-flushed when young. Deep pink flowers are produced in summer. Native to China, Japan, and the Himalayas. ‡ 10cm (4in), ↔ 50cm (20in).
HARDINESS Fully hardy.
PARTS USED Leaves.
PROPERTIES An aromatic herb with a thyme-like scent.
MEDICINAL USES Internally in Japanese folk medicine to lower fever and relieve flatulence.
CULINARY USES May be used for flavouring in similar ways to *T. vulgaris*.
ECONOMIC USES Source of an essential oil used in commercial food flavouring.

■ **Thymus serpyllum** (creeping thyme, mother of thyme, wild thyme)
Variable, prostrate, mat-forming subshrub with slender creeping stems and elliptic–ovate, hairy leaves, 4–8mm (⅛–⅜in) long. Rounded clusters of pink to purple flowers appear in summer.

389

Thymus serpyllum 'Elfin'

Thymus serpyllum 'Pink Chintz'

Thymus serpyllum 'Rainbow Falls'

Thymus serpyllum 'Russetings'

Thymus serpyllum 'Vey'

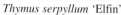

Thymus vulgaris

Thymus vulgaris 'Erectus'

Thymus vulgaris 'Silver Posie'

Native to N Europe. ↕ 1–7cm (½–3in), ↔ 1m (3ft). var. *albus* has white flowers. ▣ 'Annie Hall' has light green leaves and pale pink flowers. ▣ var. *coccineus* (red-flowered thyme) has bright magenta flowers. ▣ 'Elfin' forms a hummock of minute, glossy, rounded leaves, and has magenta-pink flowers. Shy-flowering. ↕ 5cm (2in), ↔ 10–20cm (4–8in). 'Goldstream' is vigorous, with variegated, gold and light green leaves and lilac flowers. 'Lemon Curd' has lemon-scented leaves and mauve-pink flowers. 'Minimus' is compact, with lanceolate leaves, to 4mm (⅛in) long, and pink flowers. ↕ 5cm (2in), ↔ 10cm (4in). 'Minor' syn. 'Minus' is slow-growing and compact, with tiny leaves and pink flowers. ↕ 1cm (½in), ↔ 60cm (24in). ▣ 'Pink Chintz' is vigorous, with grey-green, hairy leaves and flesh-pink flowers. Discovered as a seedling at The Royal Horticultural Society's garden, Wisley (England) in 1939. ↕ 1–7cm (½–3in), ↔ 60cm (24in). ▣ 'Rainbow Falls' forms a loose mat, with long stems, gold-variegated, red-flushed leaves, and mauve flowers. ▣ 'Russetings' has dark green, bronze-tinted foliage and deep pink flowers. 'Snowdrift' has pale green leaves and numerous, pure white flowers. ▣ 'Vey' is compact, with upright heads of dark-budded, salmon-pink flowers. ↕ 1–7cm (½–3in), ↔ 45cm (18in).
HARDINESS Fully hardy.
PARTS USED Whole plant, leaves, oil.
PROPERTIES An aromatic sedative herb that is diuretic and expectorant, reduces spasms, and improves digestion. It is strongly antiseptic and promotes healing.
MEDICINAL USES Internally for bronchitis, catarrh, sinusitis, whooping cough, laryngitis, flatulent indigestion, painful menstruation, colic, and hangovers. Effective in treating alcoholism. Contraindicated during pregnancy. Externally

for minor injuries, mastitis, sciatica, rheumatism, and mouth, gum, and throat infections. Combined with *Marrubium vulgare* (see p.271) and *Prunus serotina* (see p.334) for whooping cough; and with astringent herbs, such as *Commiphora myrrha* (see p.177) and *Rubus idaeus* (see p.351), for throat infections. Source of serpolet oil, which has similar effects to thyme oil (from *Thymus vulgaris*), used in aromatherapy for stress-related conditions, but may cause allergic reactions.
CULINARY USES Leaves may be used as for *T. vulgaris* in cooking.

▨ ▢ ▧ ▪ ✍

▣ *Thymus vulgaris* (common thyme)
Variable shrub with linear to elliptic, hairy, grey-green leaves, to 8mm (⅜in) long and 2.5mm (1/16in) wide. White to pale purple flowers, with grey-green, leaf-like bracts, are borne in whorls in summer. Found from W Mediterranean to S Italy. ↕ 15–30cm (6–12in), ↔ 40cm (16in). ▣ 'Erectus' has a strongly upright habit, grey-green, camphor-scented leaves, and white flowers. ↕ 15–23cm (6–9in), ↔ 10–15cm (4–6in). 'German Winter' has a compact spreading habit and is very hardy, with a good flavour. ↔ 20cm (8in). 'Lucy' has very pale pink flowers. ▣ 'Silver Posie' has white-variegated leaves and pale mauve-pink flowers.
HARDINESS Fully hardy.
PARTS USED Whole plant, leaves, flowering tops, oil.
PROPERTIES An aromatic, warming, astringent herb that is expectorant, improves digestion, relaxes spasms, and controls coughing. It is strongly antiseptic and anti-fungal.
MEDICINAL USES Internally for dry coughs, whooping cough, bronchitis, bronchial catarrh, asthma, laryngitis, indigestion, gastritis, and diarrhoea and enuresis in children. Externally

for tonsillitis, gum disease, rheumatism, arthritis, and fungal infections. Combined with *Lobelia inflata* (see p.265) and *Ephedra* spp. (see p.201) for asthma; and with *Marrubium vulgare* (see p.271), *Prunus serotina* (see p.334), and *Urginea maritima* (see p.398) for whooping cough. Oil is used in aromatherapy for aches and pains, exhaustion, depression, upper respiratory tract infections, and skin and scalp complaints. Herb and oil are contraindicated during pregnancy. Oil may cause irritation to skin and mucous membranes, and allergic reactions.
CULINARY USES Fresh or dried leaves and flowering tops are used to flavour soups, fish, meat, sausages, marinades (especially for olives), vinegar, stuffings, and baked or sautéed vegetables (especially mushrooms and courgettes); retains its flavour well in slowly cooked dishes. Thyme is an essential ingredient of *bouquet garni*, *herbes de Provence*, and many classic French dishes.
ECONOMIC USES Dried leaves are added to potpourris and moth-repellent sachets. Source of commercial dried thyme and essential oil of thyme. Thymol, from thyme oil, is an important ingredient of toothpastes, mouthwashes, and topical, anti-rheumatic preparations.

▨ ▨ ▢ ▧ ▪ ✍ ✎

Thymus zygis (Spanish sauce thyme)
Upright to spreading shrub with pale stems and linear, hairy, grey-green leaves, to 1cm (½in) long, which have in-rolled margins. Off-white flowers are borne in interrupted spikes, to 10cm (4in) long, in summer. Native to Spain and Portugal. ↔ 30cm (12in).
HARDINESS Fully hardy.
PARTS USED Whole plant, leaves.
PROPERTIES A strongly aromatic herb with a

T

Thymus 'Doone Valley'

Thymus 'Hartington Silver'

Thymus 'Pink Ripple'

thyme-like scent.
CULINARY USES Fresh or dried leaves are used for flavouring in the same ways as *T. vulgaris*.
ECONOMIC USES Source of commercial dried thyme and essential oil of thyme, reported to account for over 80 per cent of world production.

Thymus hybrids: ▣ 'Doone Valley' is mat-forming, with lanceolate, dark green leaves, irregularly yellow-splashed, and rounded heads of mauve-pink flowers opening from red-tinged buds. ‡ 12cm (5in), ↔ 35cm (14in). 'Fragrantissimus' (orange thyme) has an upright habit, grey-green, ovate leaves with an orange-balsam scent, and pale lilac flowers. ▣ 'Hartington Silver' syn. 'Highland Cream', *T. serpyllum* 'Variegatus' has a mat-forming habit, white-margined leaves, and pale pink flowers. 'Peter Davis' has fine, grey-green foliage and pink flowers. ‡ 12cm (5in). ▣ 'Pink Ripple' has relatively large, bright green leaves and pink flowers with dark purple bracts. Forms a large mat. ‡ 12cm (5in). 'Porlock' is robust and bushy, with dark green, ovate leaves and mauve-pink flowers. Has a classic thyme aroma, good for cooking. ‡ 30cm (12in).

TILIA
Lime, linden

Tiliaceae

A genus of 20–45 species of deciduous trees, found throughout northern temperate regions. Most species are in cultivation and hybridize readily. Limes tolerate most conditions and withstand hard pruning, which makes them good subjects for street planting and pleaching. They do, however, tend to sucker and become

infested with aphid in summer, dropping sticky honeydew on to surfaces below. *Tilia cordata* is non-suckering and resistant to aphid, and is therefore a better subject for gardens than *T. × europaea* (common lime) or *T. platyphyllos* (broad-leafed lime). The wood from various limes is prized for its pale colour, light weight, and suitability for carving, turning, and musical instruments. In folklore, lime flowers were thought to cure epilepsy if the sufferer sat under the tree. Lime flowers are collected from various species and hybrids, including *T. americana* (basswood), *T. cordata*, *T. platyphyllos*, and *T. × europaea*. Lime flower honey and linden or lime flower tea are important products in areas where trees are abundant.
CULTIVATION Moist, well-drained, preferably neutral to alkaline soil in sun or partial shade. Remove suckers from base and trunk as they appear. Aphid, caterpillars, gall mite, and leafspot may attack leaves. Shoots may be affected by die-back and canker.
PROPAGATION By seed sown when ripe, or in spring after stratifying for 3–5 months; by suckers in spring; by budding in late summer on to stock of *T. platyphyllos* or *T. tomentosa* (silver lime). Seed saved from garden trees may produce hybrid seedlings.
HARVEST Flowers are picked in summer; dried for use in infusions, liquid extracts, and tinctures. Lime flowers develop narcotic properties as they age and should only be collected when first opened.

▣ *Tilia cordata* syn. *T. parvifolia* (small-leafed lime)
Medium to large, columnar tree with dark green, shiny, heart-shaped leaves, to 8cm (3in) long, which have blue-green undersides and turn yellow in autumn. Pendulous clusters of fragrant, yellow-white flowers, 2cm (³⁄₄in) across, with stalks fused to narrow, papery, pale green bracts, appear in midsummer, followed by round green fruits, 6mm (¹⁄₄in) in diameter. Native to C and E Europe. ‡ 20–40m (70–130ft), ↔ 10–30m (30–100ft). 'Greenspire' is vigorous, with a narrow conical crown and orange shoots. ‡ 15m (50ft), ↔ 7m (22ft). ▣ 'Rancho' has an open, well-branched habit

Tilia cordata

Tilia cordata 'Rancho'

when young, becoming narrowly conical. ‡ 15m (50ft), ↔ 8m (25ft).
HARDINESS Fully hardy.
PARTS USED Flowers.
PROPERTIES An aromatic mucilaginous herb that is diuretic and expectorant, calms the nerves, lowers blood pressure, increases perspiration rate, relaxes spasms, and improves digestion.
MEDICINAL USES Internally for hypertension, arteriosclerosis, cardiovascular and digestive complaints associated with anxiety, urinary infections, feverish colds, influenza, respiratory catarrh, migraine, and headaches. Combines well with *Crataegus laevigata* (see p.182) for high blood pressure, with *Ginkgo biloba* (see p.225) for arteriosclerosis, with *Humulus lupulus* (see p.237) for nervous tension, and with *Sambucus nigra* (see p.357) for colds and influenza. Externally for itching skin.

TOXICODENDRON
Toxicodendron. See *Rhus.*

TRACHYSPERMUM

Apiaceae

Twenty species of aromatic annuals belong to this genus, distributed throughout N Africa to C Asia, India, and W China. All have umbels of white flowers and white-haired, ovoid fruits. *Trachyspermum ammi* (ajowan) is found in damp places, such as stream banks and ditches. It is an important crop in India for culinary, medicinal, and industrial purposes. The foliage and seeds are rich in volatile oil, particularly thymol, as found in *Thymus* spp. (see p.387). Prior to the First World War, some 1200 tonnes per year of essential oil was exported from India to Germany for extraction of thymol; thereafter, processing was developed in Calcutta. The aroma of ajowan seeds has been likened to a mixture of anise, oregano, and black pepper, while the oil is sweeter than oil of thyme (*Cornucopia II*, Stephen Facciola, 1998).
CULTIVATION Moist soil in sun.
PROPAGATION By seed sown in autumn or spring.
HARVEST Whole plants are cut when flowering

for extraction of oil. Seeds are collected when ripe and distilled for oil, or dried for use in infusions and powders.

Trachyspermum ammi syn. *T. copticum, Ammi copticum, Carum copticum* (ajowan, *ajwain*) Tender annual with stems branching from the base, and finely divided, pinnate leaves, 15–23cm (6–9in) long. Tiny white flowers, hairy outside, appear in long-stalked, dense umbels in summer, followed by tiny, pungently aromatic, ovoid fruits, about 2cm (¾in) long. Native to Asia. ‡ 30–90cm (1–3ft), ↔ 30–45cm (12–18in).
HARDINESS Min. 10–15°C (50–59°F).
PARTS USED Whole plant, fruits (seeds), oil.
PROPERTIES A bitter, aromatic, warming herb with a thyme-like aroma and tonic, diuretic, and expectorant effects. It relaxes spasms, improves digestion, increases perspiration, and is strongly antiseptic.
MEDICINAL USES Internally for colds, coughs, influenza, asthma, diarrhoea, cholera, colic, indigestion, flatulence, oedema, arthritis, and rheumatism (fruits). Contraindicated in hyperacidity. Externally for vaginal discharge and rheumatism (fruits). Used mainly in Ayurvedic medicine as a stimulating decongestant for the respiratory and digestive systems. Oil is given to expel hookworms.
CULINARY USES Seeds are used to flavour savoury dishes, including curries, legumes, breads (*naan, pakora, paratha*), and pastry snacks, especially in India, Iran, Ethiopia, and Afghanistan. An ingredient of a spice mix known as *chat masala*. Not suitable as a substitute for thyme in Western cooking.
ECONOMIC USES Seed extracts are added to cough medicines, soaps, and epoxy derivatives.
🖼 🔲 ▨ 🛡 🔋 ◩ ✎ 🔲

TRIBULUS
Zygophyllaceae

A genus of about 25 annuals, perennials and subshrubs, found throughout tropical and subtropical regions. They bear flattened, five-angled fruits that split into five spiny nutlets when ripe, catching on the fur and feet of passing animals. The fruits have a high nitrate content. *Tribulus terrestris* has a long history of use as a diuretic in Chinese and Ayurvedic medicine. In the 1990s, research showed that it has hormonal effects in men, prolonging erection and improving sperm counts. Cultivation of *T. terrestris* should be undertaken with caution; it is a noxious weed in certain regions, and causes liver damage, photosensitization, and swelling of the head in livestock. When herbicides failed to control its spread in California in the 1960s, weevils were introduced from India to feed on the plants. *Tribulus* is derived from the Latin word *tribulum*, a threshing board with a surface of sharp points.
CULTIVATION Moist sandy soil in sun.
PROPAGATION By seed sown in spring.
HARVEST Fruits are collected when ripe and dried for decoctions.
⚠ **WARNING** Subject to statutory control as a weed in certain areas.

Tribulus terrestris (caltrop, goatshead, puncturevine)
Sprawling to prostrate, hairy annual with much-branched stems and pinnate leaves, to 4cm (1½in) long, divided into 5–8 pairs of elliptic to oblanceolate, pointed leaflets. Solitary, short-lived, five-petalled, yellow flowers, to 1cm (½in) across, appear in summer, followed by yellow-brown, very hard, spiny fruits, about 1cm (½in) across, containing numerous seeds. Widespread in tropical and subtropical regions. ↔ 15–90cm (6–36in).
HARDINESS Min. 10°C (50°F).
PARTS USED Fruits.
PROPERTIES A bitter–sweet, warming, diuretic herb that controls bleeding, has a tonic effect on the liver and kidneys, and stimulates the circulation. It is reputedly aphrodisiac.
MEDICINAL USES Internally for impotence, premature ejaculation, spermatorrhoea, frequent urination, kidney complaints, blurred vision owing to deficient liver energy, lumbago, and nosebleeds; also to strengthen contractions during prolonged or difficult labour.
CULINARY USES Young leaves and shoots are cooked as a vegetable. Fruits are infused to make tea.
ECONOMIC USES Extracts are added to bodybuilding formulas as an alternative to anabolic steroids.
▨ 🔋 ◩ ✎ 🔲

TRICHOSANTHES
Cucurbitaceae

This genus of 15 species of annual and perennial, tendril climbers ranges from Indonesia and Malaysia to the Pacific Islands. *Trichosanthes kirilowii* is probably the hardiest species in the genus and is cultivated as a medicinal herb in S China, male plants being preferred for root production. It was first described in Chinese medicine in the *Shen Nong Canon of Herbs* during the later Han dynasty (AD25–220). Though best known in China for inducing abortion, research has shown it is a possible remedy for AIDS. The active constituent is trichosanthin, a protein investigated as "Compound Q". Chinese medicine also uses *T. japonica* and *T. rosthornii*, as well as *T. kirilowii*, and other species occur as adulterants. The dried fruits of *T. cucumeroides* are rich in saponins and used as a soap substitute. The related *Cucurbita foetidissima* (buffalo gourd) also has a high saponin content; native N Americans and early settlers crushed the plant in water for use as a washing agent. *Trichosanthes* is from the Greek *thrix*, "hair", and *anthos*, "flower", and refers to the fringed flowers.
CULTIVATION Moist, well-drained soil in partial shade. Thin out overcrowded branches to allow air to circulate around developing fruits. Prone to attack by red spider mite and whitefly when grown in a greenhouse.
PROPAGATION By seed sown at 20°C (68°F) in spring, soaked for 24 hours before sowing; by softwood cuttings in summer.

Trichosanthes kirilowii

HARVEST Tubers and fruits are harvested in autumn and dried for use in decoctions, pills, and powders.

■ ***Trichosanthes kirilowii*** syn. *Eopepon vitifolius* (Chinese cucumber, snake gourd)
Perennial, tuberous, tendril climber with annual stems and deeply lobed leaves, to 12cm (5in) across. White tubular flowers, about 4cm (1½in) across, with five deeply fringed lobes, appear in summer. Male and female flowers appear on separate plants: males in few-flowered clusters; females solitary, followed by smooth-skinned, ovoid to oblong, orange-red, fleshy fruits, to 10cm (4in) long, containing numerous pale brown seeds. Native to Mongolia, China, and Vietnam. ‡ 6–9m (20–28ft).
HARDINESS Half hardy.
PARTS USED Tubers (*gua lou gen, tian hua fen*), fruit peel (*gua lou pi*), seeds (*gua lou zi*).
PROPERTIES A bitter–sweet, anti-inflammatory, cooling herb that lowers fever, promotes secretions (notably lactation), and stimulates the uterus (tubers). A sweet, expectorant, laxative herb that stimulates the circulation, dilates the bronchial vessels, moistens dry tissues, and is anti-bacterial and anti-fungal (fruits).
MEDICINAL USES Internally for diabetes, dry coughs, abscesses, childbirth (second stage of labour), and abortion (tubers); bronchial infections with thick phlegm, chest pain and tightness, dry constipation, and lung and breast tumours (fruits). Contraindicated during pregnancy. Fruits are traditionally prepared as a winter soup to ward off colds and influenza.
🖼 ▨ ▨ 🔋

TRIFOLIUM
Clover

Papilionaceae

This large genus of about 240 species of annuals, biennials, and perennials is found through temperate and subtropical regions of the northern hemisphere, and is naturalized in Australasia. *Trifolium pratense* (red clover) has been important as a deep-rooted forage crop in mainland Europe since the Middle Ages, and was introduced to Britain from Flanders in the

17th century for this purpose. The roots fix nitrogen, enhancing the nutrient value of meadows. Red clover is also grown as a green manure crop to enrich and protect the soil. Culpeper describes *T. repens* (white clover) as a remedy for "hard swellings and imposthumes" but this species is seldom used today, having been superseded by red clover. During the 1930s, red clover had a reputation for curing cancer; in the 1990s, it became popular as an ingredient in herbal supplements for relieving menopausal symptoms. The leaves are rich in oestrogenic substances. *Trifolium* is from the Latin *tri*, "three", and *folium*, "leaf", referring to the three-lobed leaves which have long been regarded as symbols of the Holy Trinity. Apparently St Patrick used a leaf of this kind to teach this aspect of Christian theology, giving rise to the shamrock as emblem of Ireland. No one knows exactly which plant is the true shamrock; red clover is one of perhaps a dozen possibilities.

CULTIVATION Moist, well-drained, neutral soil in sun. 'Susan Smith' may be grown as a trailing plant in containers.

PROPAGATION By seed sown in spring; by division in spring. Leaves may be affected by powdery mildew in dry conditions.

HARVEST Flower heads with upper leaves are picked in summer as they open, and dried for infusions, liquid extracts, ointments, and tinctures.

■ *Trifolium pratense* (purple clover, red clover) Erect to sprawling, short-lived perennial with long-stalked, trifoliate leaves, divided into three obovate leaflets, to 3cm (1¼in) long. Purple-pink, sometimes cream, tubular flowers are borne in globose heads in late spring and summer. Native to Europe, except extreme north and south. ‡20–60cm (8–24in), ↔ 60cm (24in). ■ 'Susan Smith' syn. 'Dolly North', 'Goldnet' has yellow-veined leaves. ‡15cm (6in), ↔ 45cm (18in).

HARDINESS Fully hardy.

PARTS USED Flowering tops.

PROPERTIES A sweet, cooling, alterative herb that relaxes spasms, and has diuretic, hormonal, and expectorant effects.

MEDICINAL USES Internally for skin complaints, cancers of the breast, ovaries,

Trifolium pratense

Trifolium pratense 'Susan Smith'

and lymphatic system, chronic degenerative diseases, gout, whooping cough, and dry cough. Also as a source of oestrogen-like isoflavones during the menopause. Combined with *Larrea divaricata* in cancer therapy and with *Rumex crispus* (see p.351) for skin disease.
⬚ ▪

TRIGONELLA

Papilionaceae

This genus of 80 species of annuals extends from the Mediterranean to southern Africa and Australia. *Trigonella foenum-graecum* (fenugreek) is grown as a fodder crop in S and C Europe, and as a spice in most Mediterranean countries, the Middle East, Russia, the Balkans, W Asia, and China. Fenugreek has been used since the Early Bronze Age; it was cultivated in Assyria (7th century BC) and remains found in Iraq have been reliably dated to 4000BC. In the Ebers papyrus (c.1500BC) it is mentioned as a herb to induce childbirth. Dried plants are sold as *hilba* in Egypt as a remedy for painful menstruation. It was first mentioned in Chinese medicine in the 11th century and has a long tradition as a tonic herb in both Chinese and Ayurvedic medicine. Western interest in the herb centres on one of its constituent alkaloids, trigonelline, which has potential in treating cervical and liver cancer, and its saponins, which are extracted for use in oral contraceptives and other pharmaceutical products. *Trigonella* is from *trigonus*, "triangular", referring to the flower shape. *Foenum-graecum* means "Greek hay", because the plant was once grown as a fodder crop in Greece.

CULTIVATION Well-drained, fertile soil in sun.

PROPAGATION By seed sown in spring.

HARVEST Leaves are picked in summer and used fresh or dried in infusions, or as a vegetable. Seeds are collected when ripe and dried for decoctions, pastes, and powders, or commercially processed for extracts.

■ *Trigonella foenum-graecum* (fenugreek) Erect aromatic annual with trifoliate leaves divided into obovate to oblong, toothed leaflets, to 5cm (2in) long. Solitary or paired, yellow-

white flowers, about 1cm (½in) long, tinged violet at the base, appear in spring and summer, followed by beaked pods, to 11cm (4½in) long, containing 10–20 yellow-brown, rectangular seeds. Native to S Europe and W Asia; widely naturalized. ‡60cm (24in), ↔ 30–45cm (12–18in).

HARDINESS Frost hardy.

PARTS USED Leaves, seeds (*hu lu ba*).

PROPERTIES A bitter, pungent, warming herb that increases milk flow, stimulates the uterus, soothes irritated tissues, lowers fever, reduces blood sugar, improves digestion, promotes healing, and has laxative, expectorant, diuretic, anti-parasitic, and anti-tumour effects.

MEDICINAL USES Internally for late-onset diabetes, poor digestion, gastric inflammation, digestive disorders, tuberculosis, painful menstruation, labour pains, and insufficient lactation. Contraindicated during pregnancy and in hypoglycaemic therapy. Externally for skin inflammations and cellulitis. In Chinese medicine mainly for kidney-related disorders, such as back pain, premature ejaculation, loss of libido, oedema of the legs, or hernia; also for painful menstruation and as a pessary for cervical cancer. Regarded as a rejuvenative and aphrodisiac in Ayurvedic medicine, and used to treat digestive and bronchial complaints, debility, allergies, neurasthenia, gout, and arthritis.

CULINARY USES Dried leaves (*methi*) are used to flavour root vegetables in Indian and Middle Eastern dishes; fresh leaves are cooked as a vegetable curry (India). Seeds are lightly roasted to reduce bitterness, and ground as an ingredient of curry powder, pickles, and Ethiopian spice mixes; also as a flavouring for bread (Egypt, Ethiopia), stews, and fried foods. Seeds are sprouted as a salad vegetable, which is also eaten as a tonic for the liver, kidneys, and male sexual organs. *Helba* (N Yemen) is made from boiled seeds, served as a purée with a garnish of fried onion and meat.

ECONOMIC USES Seed extracts are used in synthetic maple syrup, or maple, vanilla, caramel, and butterscotch flavours for the food industry.
⬚ ▦ ▪ ◿ ◿

Trigonella foenum-graecum

Trillium erectum

Trillium erectum f. *albiflorum*

TRILLIUM

Liliaceae/Trilliaceae

There are about 30 species of rhizomatous perennials in this genus, occurring in N America and NE Asia. *Trillium erectum* is grown as an ornamental in the woodland garden or shady border for its attractive triangular foliage and flowers, which appear early in the year. It was introduced to herbal medicine by Constantine Rafinesque in his *Medical Flora* (2 vols, 1828–30) and listed in the *US National Formulary* (1916–47). The rhizomes contain steroidal saponins that have hormonal effects; hence their use in gynaecological and obstetric medicine. The white-flowered variety was preferred by native N Americans for treating sore nipples, inducing labour, and controlling postpartum haemorrhage, vaginal discharge, and heavy menstruation. The related Asiatic species (*T. kamtschaticum* and *T. tschonoskii*) have similar properties. *Trillium* comes from the Latin *trilix*, "triple", because all parts of these plants are tripartite.
CULTIVATION Moist, well-drained, neutral to slightly acid, humus-rich soil in partial shade. Leaves are prone to damage by slugs and snails.
PROPAGATION By seed sown in a cold frame in spring; by division during dormancy. Seeds take up to three years to germinate, and plants seldom flower until 5–7 years old.
HARVEST Rhizomes are lifted after leaves have died back in late summer, and dried for use in decoctions, liquid extracts, and tinctures.

■ *Trillium erectum* (bethroot, birthroot, wake robin)
Variable perennial with a short thick rootstock, erect stem, and three broadly ovate leaves, to 20cm (8in) long. A solitary, nodding, fetid flower, with three pale green, maroon-tinged sepals and three maroon (occasionally white or yellow) petals, to 5cm (2in) long, appears in the centre of the leaves in spring. Native to eastern N America. ‡ 30–50cm (12–20in), ↔ 30cm (12in). ■ f. *albiflorum* has white flowers. f. *luteum* has yellow flowers.
HARDINESS Fully hardy.
PARTS USED Rhizomes.
PROPERTIES A sweet–sour, astringent, warming herb that is expectorant, controls bleeding, and benefits the female reproductive system.
MEDICINAL USES Internally for haemorrhage from uterus, urinary tract and lungs, and excessive menstruation. Externally for vaginal discharge, ulcers (especially varicose), skin complaints, insect bites and stings. Combined with *Geranium maculatum* (see p.223) or *Vinca major* (see p.404) for heavy menstruation; with *Bidens tripartita* (see p.144) for blood in the urine; and with *Lobelia inflata* (see p.265) and *Ulmus rubra* (see p.397) for ulcers.
▨ ▣

TROPAEOLUM

Tropaeolaceae

This genus of 80–90 species of mostly climbing annuals and herbaceous perennials is native to C and S America. Nasturtiums are among the most easily grown hardy annuals. Climbing cultivars cover a fence or bank within a few weeks of germination, and more compact kinds are ideal for summer bedding and containers. *Tropaeolum majus* was introduced to Europe from Peru in the 16th century by the conquistadors, and was first known as *Nasturtium indicum*, "Indian cress", due to its pungent, watercress-like flavour. The species is seldom seen now, having been superseded by a wide range of cultivars. *Tropaeolum majus* has several properties that make it a useful medicinal and culinary herb. It contains large amounts of sulphur, which reputedly retards baldness, and a glycoside that reacts with water to produce an antibiotic. In addition, the pickled unripe seeds are the only acceptable substitute for capers; they develop capric acid, which gives the characteristic goaty flavour. *Tropaeolum minus* (dwarf nasturtium) and cultivars of *T. majus* can be used in the same ways as *T. majus*. *Tropaeolum* is from the Greek *tropaion*, "trophy", since the leaves are shaped like round shields, above which are the helmet-like flowers.
CULTIVATION Well-drained, moist, average to poor soil in sun. Self-sows freely in some gardens and may be invasive. Rich soil promotes leafy growth at the expense of flowers. Often used in companion planting to deter cucumber beetle and whitefly but it is susceptible to aphid, especially blackfly. Nasturtiums are reputed to deter woolly aphid if plants are grown at the base of apple trees. Prone to viral diseases. Over-winter sterile cultivars in sunny, frost-free conditions.
PROPAGATION By seed sown in early spring at 13–16°C (55–61°F); by basal or stem-tip cuttings in spring and summer (sterile cultivars).
HARVEST All parts are picked in summer and used fresh for infusions and tinctures. Plants are also cut for juice extraction.

■ *Tropaeolum majus* (garden nasturtium, Indian cress)
Fast-growing, trailing annual with almost circular, peltate leaves, to 6cm (2½in) across. Yellow to orange, long-spurred, slightly scented flowers, 5–6cm (2–2½in) across, sometimes red-blotched, appear from early summer, followed by globose fruits. Native to S America (Colombia to Bolivia). ‡ 3m (10ft), ↔ 1.5–2m (5–6ft).
■ 'Alaska' is dwarf and bushy, with leaves that

Tropaeolum majus

Tropaeolum majus 'Empress of India'

Tropaeolum majus 'Alaska'

Tropaeolum majus 'Hermine Grashoff'

Tropaeolum majus 'Peach Melba'

are irregularly marbled with creamy white, and yellow, cream, red, orange-red, and mahogany flowers. ‡ 30cm (12in), ↔ 45cm (18in).
■ 'Empress of India' is dwarf and bushy, with purple-green leaves and scented, semi-double, crimson flowers. Dates back to the 19th century. ‡ 30cm (12in), ↔ 45cm (18in). ■ 'Hermine Grashoff' is another 19th-century cultivar. It bears double, orange-scarlet flowers and is sterile. ‡ 20cm (8in), ↔ 45–60cm (18–24in).
■ 'Peach Melba' is compact and floriferous, with creamy yellow, single flowers, blotched with scarlet in the throat. ‡ 23–30cm (9–12in), ↔ 45cm (18in). Whirlybird Series is dwarf and compact, with single to semi-double, spur-less, upward-facing blooms, borne well above the foliage, in cream, orange, salmon, yellow, mahogany, scarlet, and cherry-red. Produces clean flowers for culinary purposes. ‡ 25cm (10in), ↔ 35cm (14in).
HARDINESS Half hardy to tender, min. 3°C (37°F).
PARTS USED Whole plant, leaves, flowers, buds, fruits.
PROPERTIES A bitter, antiseptic, tonic herb that has diuretic and expectorant effects, and controls fungal and bacterial infections.
MEDICINAL USES Internally for genito-urinary and respiratory infections, scurvy, and poor skin or hair conditions. Externally for baldness, minor injuries, and skin eruptions.
CULINARY USES Leaves, flowers, flower buds, nectar spurs are eaten in salads and sandwiches. Chopped fresh leaves give a peppery flavour to soft cheese or egg dishes. Flowers are used to make vinegar. Unripe fruits are pickled. Ripe seeds are roasted and ground as a seasoning.
ECONOMIC USES Combined with *Buxus sempervirens* (see p.148), *Quercus robur* (see p.339), and *Urtica dioica* (see p.398), in hair lotion.
🔯 🔀 ▨ 🗇 🔲 ▮ ✎ ✔

TULBAGHIA
Alliaceae

There are some 24 species of clump-forming, deciduous or semi-evergreen, rhizomatous or bulbous perennials in this genus, native to temperate regions of southern Africa. A number of species are grown as ornamentals for their pretty, often fragrant flowers and linear foliage, which smells like garlic or onions; they have a long flowering period and are effective as edging or in containers. Known in South Africa as wild garlics, tulbaghias are important for flavouring and are used medicinally by various tribes. They may have similar properties to *Allium sativum* (see p.113). *Tulbaghia alliacea* (flat-leaf chives, garlic chives, wild garlic) is used in much the same way as *T. violacea*, a traditional Cape remedy for fever. It is a smaller plant with fragrant, greenish-white flowers, with an orange-brown corona, resembling miniature narcissi. *Tulbaghia simmleri* syn. *T. fragrans* is also used instead of *T. violacea*. *Tulbaghia* is named after Rijk Tulbagh (1699–1771), Governor of the Cape of Good Hope during

Tulbaghia violacea

Dutch colonial times.
CULTIVATION Well-drained, humus-rich soil in sun or partial shade. Frost-hardy plants usually survive outdoors in cold areas if given a sheltered position and mulched in winter.
PROPAGATION By seed sown when ripe or in spring; by division in spring. Seeds germinate quickly and seedlings soon reach flowering size.
HARVEST Leaves and bulbs are harvested as required and used fresh.

■ *Tulbaghia violacea* (*isihaqa*, society garlic, *wilde knoffel*, wild garlic)
Clump-forming, semi-evergreen, bulbous perennial with narrowly linear, grey-green leaves, 30cm (12in) long. Fragrant, lilac-pink flowers, 2cm (¾in) long, are borne in long-stalked, terminal umbels, almost all year in mild areas. Native to South Africa (Eastern Cape, S KwaZulu/Natal). ‡ 45–60cm (18–24in), ↔ 25cm (10in). 'Silver Lace' syn. 'Variegata' has white-striped leaves and larger flowers, 2–4cm (¾–1½in) long.
HARDINESS Frost hardy.
PARTS USED Leaves, flowers, bulbs.
PROPERTIES An antiseptic expectorant herb that lowers fever and has laxative effects.
MEDICINAL USES Internally in folk medicine for colds, coughs, flu, asthma, tuberculosis, fevers, and cancer of the oesophagus. Externally as a bath or wash for rheumatism, paralysis, and feverish illnesses, and as an enema for digestive problems.
CULINARY USES Leaves and flowers are used in the same way as *Allium schoenoprasum* (chives, see p.114). Bulbs are used like spring onions.
🔯 ▨ ▨ 🔀 ▮ ✔

TURNERA
Turneraceae

Sixty species of shrubs and short-lived perennials and small shrubs belong to this genus, which occurs mainly in C and S America, with one species in SW Africa. *Turnera diffusa* is found in dry, sandy, or rocky places. Though renowned as an aphrodisiac, there is no clinical evidence for such an effect, though anti-depressant properties have been reported. The closely related *T. ulmifolia* (sage rose, West Indian holly) has

similar uses; it is common as an ornamental, having more attractive foliage and larger, hibiscus-like flowers.
CULTIVATION Dry soil in sun. Cut back in early spring.
PROPAGATION By seed sown in spring; by division in spring or autumn; by semi-ripe cuttings in summer.
HARVEST Plants are cut when flowering, and dried for use in compound mixtures, infusions, liquid extracts, and tablets.

Turnera diffusa syn. *T. diffusa* var. *aphrodisiaca* (damiana)
Aromatic shrubby perennial with light green, obovate, toothed leaves, to 2.5cm (1in) long. Yellow-orange, five-petalled flowers, about 1cm (½in) long, are borne in summer, followed by globose, aromatic, three-valved fruits, 2cm (¾in) across, with numerous, tiny, pear-shaped seeds. Native to tropical America. ‡ 1m (3ft), ↔ 60cm (2ft).
HARDINESS Half hardy.
PARTS USED Whole plant, leaves.
PROPERTIES A bitter, pungent, warming herb with a fig-like flavour. It improves digestion, lifts the spirits, calms the nerves, regulates hormone function, stimulates the genito-urinary tract, and rejuvenates kidney energy.
MEDICINAL USES Internally for nervous exhaustion, anxiety, depression, debility in convalescence, impotence, premature ejaculation, prostate complaints, urinary infections, frigidity, vaginal discharge, painful menstruation, poor appetite, menopausal problems, digestion, and atonic constipation. Combines well with *Serenoa repens* (see p.367) as a tonic for sexual neurosis: with *Avena sativa* (see p.138) for depression, and with *Scutellaria lateriflora* (see p.365) or *Stachys officinalis* (see p.374) for anxiety states.
CULINARY USES Dried leaves are used for tea. Extract is used to make the liqueur *Damiana*, which is popular in Mexico as a substitute for Cointreau, or added to hot cinnamon tea.
▨ ▨ ▮ ✔

TUSSILAGO
Coltsfoot
Asteraceae

This genus of 15 species of rhizomatous perennials ranges throughout northern temperate regions. *Tussilago farfara* (coltsfoot) is too invasive for general garden use, but can be grown in the wild garden or where its spread can be contained. A variegated cultivar was known in the 19th century but is now lost to cultivation. Pliny (AD23–79) recommended that coltsfoot leaves and roots were burned over cypress charcoal, and the smoke swallowed rather than inhaled to relieve coughs. Coltsfoot has similar applications in Chinese medicine but only the flower buds and flowers are used. The herb contains pyrrolizidine alkaloids, as in *Symphytum officinale* (see p.377) but these are largely broken down when the herb is boiled to make a decoction. *Tussilago* is from the Latin *tussis*, "cough", referring to the anti-tussive effects of *T. farfara*.

T

Tussilago farfara

CULTIVATION Moist, neutral to alkaline soil in sun or partial shade. Invasive.
PROPAGATION By seed sown in spring; by division in spring or autumn.
HARVEST Leaves are cut when fully grown and used fresh, or dried for smoking mixtures, liquid and solid extracts, and tinctures. Flowers are picked when they first open and are used fresh or dried in decoctions (in Chinese medicine), liquid extracts, syrups, and tinctures.

▣ *Tussilago farfara* (coltsfoot)
Robust creeping perennial with large, heart-shaped to rounded, toothed leaves, to 30cm (12in) across, which have a cobweb-like covering. Solitary, yellow, dandelion-like flowers bloom on woolly scaly stalks before the leaves in early spring. Native to Europe, W Asia, and N Africa. ‡ 30cm (12in), ↔ indefinite.
HARDINESS Fully hardy.
PARTS USED Leaves, flowers.
PROPERTIES A bitter–sweet, astringent, expectorant herb. It relaxes spasms, controls coughing, soothes sore tissues, reduces inflammation, and stimulates the immune system.
MEDICINAL USES Internally for coughs, asthma, whooping cough, catarrh, bronchitis, and laryngitis. Externally for ulcers, sores, eczema, insect bites, and skin inflammations. Combined with *Marrubium vulgare* (see p.271) and *Verbascum thapsus* (see p.401) for irritating coughs. Contraindicated during pregnancy and lactation. Remedies containing leaves are usually restricted to a 3–4-week course of treatment. Flowers contain higher amounts of pyrrolizidine alkaloids and are no longer recommended by Western herbalists.
CULINARY USES Young leaves, flower buds, and newly opened flowers were traditionally eaten raw in spring salads, added to soups, and made into tea. Flowers are used to make country wine.
ECONOMIC USES Dried leaves are an ingredient of herbal tobaccos and are used in curing pipe tobaccos.
⚠ **WARNING** This herb is subject to legal restrictions in some countries.

▣ ▨ ▣ ◪ ◪

TYPHA
Bulrush

Typhaceae

A cosmopolitan aquatic genus of 10–15 species of stout, rhizomatous, reed-like perennials. *Typha latifolia* and its variegated cultivar are grown as ornamentals in ponds and lakes for their imposing foliage and decorative brown seed heads, which are dried for floral arrangements. Although commonly known as "bulrush", *T. latifolia* is quite different from the plant referred to by this name in the Bible, which was *Cyperus papyrus*. *Typha angustifolia*, *T. bungeana*, *T. davidiana*, *T. minima*, and *T. orientalis* are used interchangeably with *T. latifolia* as the Chinese drug *pu huang*. Unusually, the drug consists of the pollen, which contains flavonoids, volatile oil, and hormonal compounds, known as ecdysteroids, that can be metabolized to either oestrogenic or androgenic substances. In South Africa, the rhizomes of *T. capensis* syn. *T. latifolia* subsp. *capensis* are used for reproductive problems in both men and women, suggesting that hormonal substances are present elsewhere in the plant. *Typha* is the original Greek name for this plant, used by Theophrastus.
CULTIVATION Wet soil or shallow water in sun or shade. Subject to statutory control as a weed in parts of Australia.
PROPAGATION By seed sown in spring (species only); by division in spring.
HARVEST Pollen is gently shaken from flower spikes when blooming, and dried for use in decoctions, pastes, powders, and suppositories.

▣ *Typha latifolia* (cat-tail, great reedmace)
Giant perennial with a branched long rhizome and linear leaves, to 2m (6ft) long. Minute beige flowers appear in a long-stalked, cylindrical spike, with males above the females, followed by dark brown seed heads that persist through winter, breaking up to release wind-dispersed seeds in spring. Native to Europe, Asia, N Africa, and N America. ‡ 2.5m (8ft), ↔ indefinite. ▣ 'Variegata' has white-striped leaves. ↔ 90cm–1.2m (3–4ft).
HARDINESS Fully hardy.
PARTS USED Pollen (*pu huang*).

Typha latifolia

Typha latifolia 'Variegata'

PROPERTIES A sweet acrid herb that is diuretic, controls bleeding, improves the circulation, promotes healing, and stimulates the uterus. Dried pollen is anti-coagulant; roasted with charcoal, it becomes haemostatic.
MEDICINAL USES Internally for haemorrhage, painful menstruation, abnormal uterine bleeding, postpartum pains, angina, and cancer of the lymphatic system. Contraindicated during pregnancy. Externally for tapeworms, diarrhoea, and injuries. May be combined with honey for abscesses and with powdered cuttlefish bone for bleeding injuries.
CULINARY USES Unripe flower spikes can be cooked as a vegetable. Pollen may be used to enrich flour for baking. Young shoots and inner stems, known as "Cossack asparagus", are eaten raw or cooked.
ECONOMIC USES Pollen is highly flammable and was used in the manufacture of fireworks.
▣ ▣ ◪ ◪

U

ULMUS
Elm

Ulmaceae

Some 45 species of mostly deciduous trees (rarely shrubs) belong to this genus, distributed in northern temperate regions. *Ulmus rubra* (slippery elm) is one of the most distinctive elms with its woolly buds and large velvety leaves. It was once planted as a street tree in the USA, but is rarely cultivated elsewhere. Both wild and cultivated slippery elm trees have been severely depleted by over-exploitation and Dutch elm disease. The outer bark was traditionally made into a healing salve, and decoctions to ease childbirth and relieve sore throats by native N Americans. It was also used as a mechanical irritant to abort mixed-race foetuses. Its use as an abortifacient became so widespread that it is now banned in many countries, though the powdered inner bark, which is useless for that purpose, is

Ulmus rubra

available commercially for
other medicinal applications.
When mixed with water,
the powdered inner elm bark
forms a pale pink-brown
gruel, which may be flavoured
with honey and spices; it is often taken internally
in this form. *Ulmus americana* (American white
elm) is used in similar ways. The unrelated
Fremontodendron californicum (California
slippery elm), which is widely grown as an
ornamental, also has similar properties. Chopped
leafy branches are made into a tea for sore
throats, stomach ulcers, and bronchial
congestion, or into a poultice for removing
foreign bodies and toxins. Various European
elms have also been used as soothing remedies
over the centuries, but are of little importance
now, especially since the demise of most English
elms (*Ulmus procera*) from Dutch elm disease.
CULTIVATION Deep moist soil in sun. Plants
may be damaged by aphid, caterpillars, gall
mite, fungal infections, and Dutch elm disease.
PROPAGATION By seed sown in autumn; by
greenwood cuttings in summer; by removing
rooted suckers in autumn; by grafting in winter.
HARVEST Inner bark is stripped from trunks
and larger branches in spring, dried and
powdered for use in decoctions, liquid extracts,
ointments, poultices, powders, and tablets. Fine
powder is used internally; coarse powder is
used for poultices.

■ *Ulmus rubra* syn. *U. fulva* (red elm, slippery
elm)
Medium to large tree with a broad crown,
downy shoots, and dark green, oblong, pointed,
toothed leaves, to 20cm (8in) long, which
have rough upper surfaces and paler downy
undersides. Inconspicuous flowers appear in
early summer, followed by rounded, red-brown,
winged fruits, to 2cm (¾in) long, consisting of
a single seed. Found from S Canada to
C America. ‡ 20m (70ft), ↔ 18m (60ft).
HARDINESS Fully hardy.
PARTS USED Inner bark.
PROPERTIES A sweet, mucilaginous, laxative
herb with a fenugreek-like odour. It soothes and
lubricates tissues, draws out toxins, and
promotes healing.

MEDICINAL USES Internally for gastric and
duodenal ulcers, gastritis, colitis, irritable bowel
syndrome, diverticulitis, gastric infections, acid
indigestion, digestive problems in infants, and
bronchial infections. Externally for sore throat,
coughs, wounds, burns, boils, abscesses, and
chilblains. Often added as a soothing element to
cough mixtures. Combines well with *Althaea
officinalis* (see p.117) for digestive disorders
and with *Linum usitatissimum* (see p.263) or
Calendula officinalis (see p.150) in poultices
for skin inflammations.
⚠**WARNING** This herb, especially as whole bark,
is subject to legal restrictions in some countries.

UMBELLULARIA
Lauraceae

This N American genus consists of a single
species of evergreen tree. *Umbellularia
californica* is a bay-like, shrubby tree, which
needs a sheltered position in cold areas to prevent
frost damage to new growths. It is generally
found in canyon bottoms and flood plains, below
1500m (5000ft). The leaves are so pungently
aromatic that inhaling their scent may cause a
headache. The herb is nevertheless a traditional
remedy for headaches, and may be taken as an
infusion, or the leaves bound to the forehead,
for this purpose. Native Californians also used
the leaves as insect-repellent. *Umbellularia* is
from the Latin *umbella*, "umbel", referring to
the shape of the inflorescence.
CULTIVATION Well-drained soil in sun. May
require winter protection when young.
PROPAGATION By seed sown in autumn; by
semi-ripe cuttings in summer.
HARVEST Leaves are picked as required and
used fresh, or dried whole for use in infusions.

■ *Umbellularia californica* (California
bay/laurel/pepper, headache tree)
Evergreen tree with dark green,
flat, elliptic to oblong, glossy
leaves, 10cm (4in) long, which
have a strong acrid aroma. Tiny,
pale green flowers appear in
umbels in spring, followed by
pear-shaped, purple-brown

Umbellularia californica

fruits, 2.5cm (1in) long. Native to USA
(S Oregon and N California). ‡ 18–25m
(60–80ft), ↔ 12m (40ft).
HARDINESS Fully hardy.
PARTS USED Leaves.
PROPERTIES A pungent analgesic herb with
a camphoraceous aroma.
MEDICINAL USES Internally for headache,
neuralgia, intestinal cramps, and gastroenteritis.
Externally for headache, fainting, fungal
infections, and joint pains.
CULINARY USES Leaves may be used sparingly
in soups, stews, and meat dishes as a substitute
for bay leaves (see *Laurus nobilis*, p.252).

UNCARIA
Rubiaceae

This pantropical genus includes about 60 species
of climbing shrubs and lianas that climb by
means of hook-like thorns. A number of species
are rich in alkaloids and tannins, and are used
locally for medicinal purposes. The most
important is *Uncaria tomentosa* (cat's claw),
from the Amazon rainforest, which has been
used by tribes in Peru for over 2000 years.
It entered international trade in the 1980s
following research that showed significant anti-
cancer and immune-stimulant effects. Reports
have also shown potential in the treatment of
AIDS. Traditionally, cat's claw is used in
Peruvian medicine as a contraceptive and
abortifacient, and to treat gastric ulcers and
tumours, intestinal disorders, rheumatism,
inflammations, arthritis, gonorrhoea, dysentery,
and cancers of the urinary tract. It has a
complex chemistry, including oxindole
alkaloids, plant sterols, antioxidants, and anti-
inflammatory glycosides. *Uncaria guaianensis*
is used interchangeably with *U. tomentosa*. The
Asian *U. gambir* (gambier, pale catechu) lowers
blood pressure and protects the liver, and is
traditionally used in India as a remedy for
diarrhoea, dysentery, sore throat, mouth ulcers,
and sores. In common with other species of
Uncaria, it contains catechin tannins, which
are strongly astringent. Stems and thorns of
U. rhyncophylla have been used in Chinese
medicine since at least AD500. Known as *gou
teng*, they have sedative and anti-spasmodic
effects, relieving tremors, seizures, convulsions,
and headaches.
CULTIVATION Rich, moist, well-drained soil
in shade and high humidity.
PROPAGATION By seed sown when ripe; by
semi-ripe cuttings of stem sections, 20cm (8in)
long, in summer.
HARVEST Bark and roots are collected in
summer – during the long dry season – from
vines in which the inner bark is 4–5cm
(1½–2in) thick; roots are partially harvested;
stems are cut about 20cm (8in) above ground
to allow regeneration.

Uncaria tomentosa (cat's claw, *uña de gato*)
Giant woody liana with downward-pointing
thorns, 2.5cm (1in) long, and ovate–oblong,

U

397

pointed leaves, 25cm (10in) long, which have
8–10 pairs of lateral veins. Small, yellow-white
flowers are produced in spherical clusters
towards the top of the vine. Native to C and
S America. ‡ 20–30m (65–100ft), ↔ indefinite.
HARDINESS Min. 15°C (59°F).
PARTS USED Bark, roots, leaves.
PROPERTIES A diuretic depurative herb that
has anti-inflammatory, anti-bacterial, anti-viral,
as well as anti-cancer effects. It lowers blood
pressure and stimulates the immune system.
MEDICINAL USES Internally for inflammatory
conditions of the digestive tract, chronic
inflammatory disorders, viral diseases, allergic
conditions, arthritic and rheumatic disorders, and
as part of anti-cancer and anti-AIDS therapies.
May cause diarrhoea during first ten days of use.
Contraindicated during pregnancy and lactation,
and for children three years old or younger.
Interacts with a number of drugs and therapeutic
regimes. For use only by qualified practitioners.

URGINEA
Hyacinthaceae

There are about 100 species of bulbous perennials
in this genus, found mainly in dry, often sandy,
coastal or grassland areas of tropical Africa, with
a few species in Mediterranean regions and
Portugal. *Urginea maritima* is grown as an
ornamental for its flower spikes, which resemble
those of *Eremurus* spp. (foxtail lily). Although
easily grown in warm sunny positions, it can be
shy-flowering in northern regions. This ancient
medicinal herb was mentioned in the Ebers
papyrus (c.1500BC) and is still cultivated for
medicinal purposes in Egypt and other
Mediterranean countries. Bulbs are harvested
after six years, with a yield of about 25,000 bulbs
per hectare (10,000 per acre). *Urginea maritima*
contains cardiac glycosides, notably scillarin,
which affect the heart in similar ways to *Digitalis*
spp. (see p.193) but are less cumulative. It is
known in the trade as "white squill" or "red
squill", depending on the colour of the bulb,
which varies across the area of distribution.
Although similar in constituents, only red bulbs
contain the rat poison scilliroside, which poisons
only rodents, while other animals vomit. *Urginea
indica* syn. *Drimia indica* (Indian squill) is
another source of scillarin. Squill is often given
as "squill vinegar", a preparation described by
Dioscorides. *Urginea maritima* should not be
confused with *Ornithogalum longibracteatum*
syn. *O. caudatum* (false sea onion), which it
superficially resembles. The false sea onion is
quite different in chemistry; it is used in South
African folk medicine to heal burns.
CULTIVATION Free-draining, sandy or stony soil
in full sun, with bulb partly or wholly above
surface. Protect from winter wet.
PROPAGATION By seed sown when ripe at
13–18°C (55–64°F); by offsets in summer
when bulbs are dormant.
HARVEST Bulbs are lifted in late autumn, sliced
transversely, and dried for use in infusions,
liquid extracts, squill vinegar, and tinctures.

Urginea maritima

■ *Urginea maritima* syn. *Drimia maritima*
(sea onion, squill)
Robust perennial with a globose bulb, to 15cm
(6in) across, composed of overlapping tunic
scales, and narrowly lanceolate, glaucous leaves,
30cm–1m (1–3ft) long. Small, star-shaped,
white flowers are produced in a dense spike
in late summer and early autumn, followed
by new leaves. Native to the Mediterranean.
‡ 1.5m (5ft), ↔ 30cm (12in).
HARDINESS Frost hardy.
PARTS USED Bulbs.
PROPERTIES A bitter, acrid, very poisonous
herb that has diuretic and expectorant effects,
stimulates the heart, and acts as a scalp tonic.
MEDICINAL USES Internally for bronchitis,
bronchial asthma, whooping cough, and
oedema. Large doses are emetic. For use only
by qualified practitioners. Externally for
dandruff and seborrhoea.
ECONOMIC USES Extracts are added to cough
mixtures and hair tonics. Used in rat poison.

URTICA
Nettle
Urticaceae

This genus includes about 50 species of annuals
and perennials, widespread in temperate regions.
Urtica dioica is a familiar weed of human
habitation, thriving in the nitrogen-rich soil of
cultivated land; as Culpeper wrote, stinging
nettles "need no description; they may be found
by feeling, in the darkest night" (*The English
Physician Enlarged*, 1653). The nettle is a
fibrous plant and was used in cloth manufacture
from the Bronze Age to the early 20th century.
It is rich in vitamins, notably A and C, and
minerals, especially iron; it also contains
amines (mainly histamine and serotonin), plant
sterols, and large amounts of chlorophyll. *Urtica
urens* (annual nettle) and *U. pilulifera* (Roman
nettle) have properties similar to *U. dioica*. *Urtica*
is the original Latin name, used by Horace and
Pliny, for the plant. It comes from *urere*, "to burn",
and refers to the stinging hairs, which in some
species are so virulent that stings may be fatal.
CULTIVATION Moist, nitrogen-rich soil in sun
or dappled shade. Cut stands of nettles to the

ground in summer to provide a second crop
of new leaves. Nettles are invasive but easily
controlled by pulling out dormant rhizomes.
They provide food for the caterpillars of various
butterflies, such as red admirals.
PROPAGATION By seed sown in spring; by
division in spring.
HARVEST Whole plants for medicinal use are
cut as flowering begins in summer and dried
for use in infusions, liquid extracts, ointments,
powders, and tinctures. For culinary use, pick
young leaf tips from plants less than 10cm (4in)
high, before they develop oxalate crystals.

■ *Urtica dioica* (nettle, stinging nettle)
Coarse perennial with creeping yellow roots and
ovate, pointed, deeply toothed leaves, to 8cm
(3in) long, which are covered with bristly
stinging hairs. Minute green flowers, with males
and females on separate plants, are borne in
pendulous clusters, to 10cm (4in) long, in
summer. Native to Eurasia. ‡ 1.5m (5ft),
↔ indefinite.
HARDINESS Fully hardy.
PARTS USED Whole plant, leaves, roots.
PROPERTIES An astringent, diuretic, tonic
herb that controls bleeding, clears toxins, and
slightly reduces blood pressure and blood sugar
levels (leaves). The root has similar properties
and in addition reduces prostate enlargement.
MEDICINAL USES Internally for anaemia
(leaves), haemorrhage (especially of the uterus),
heavy menstrual bleeding, haemorrhoids,
arthritis, rheumatism, gout, skin complaints
(especially eczema), and allergies (leaves,
roots); prostate enlargement (roots). Combines
well with *Arctium lappa* (see p.127) for eczema.
Externally for arthritic pain, gout, sciatica,
neuralgia, haemorrhoids, scalp and hair
problems, burns, insect bites, and nosebleed.
CULINARY USES Young leaves are cooked as a
spinach-like vegetable, made into soup, added
to meat, egg, and vegetable
dishes; also as an ingredient of
herbal beer, and as a wrapping
for cheese (notably Cornish yarg).
Raw leaves are highly irritant, and
recommendations for eating raw
in salads and soft cheeses should
be disregarded. Older leaves
contain crystals of calcium oxalate,

Urtica dioica

which give a gritty texture, even after cooking. Leaves are dried for tea, which is bland and non-aromatic; it may be added to Indian tea as a tonic.

ECONOMIC USES Plants are processed commercially for extraction of chlorophyll, which is used as a colouring agent in foods and medicines.

V

VACCINIUM

Ericaceae

This large genus includes some 450 species of evergreen, semi-evergreen, or deciduous, often stoloniferous shrubs and trees that occur in a wide range of habitats from the tropics to the Arctic. The most important species medicinally are cranberries (American *Vaccinium macrocarpon* and European *V. oxycoccus*), bilberries (European *V. myrtillus*), and blueberries (mainly from the American *V. corymbosum*). Cranberries were an important item in the winter diet of native N Americans, being an essential ingredient of pemmican, made from crushed dried berries, meat, and fat. They were first cultivated in 1816 and now constitute a major agricultural crop in areas of sandy marshes and wet coastal meadows in Massachusetts, New Jersey, Oregon, Washington, and Wisconsin. The medicinal use of cranberries to treat urinary tract disorders was first investigated scientifically in the 19th century, and early observations concluded that the therapeutic effects depended on their high acidity. It is now thought that cranberry juice contains a polymer that prevents bacterial colonization of tissues in the urinary tract. Pure cranberry juice is about as sour as lemon juice; it is sweetened mainly with corn syrup, blended with sweeter fruits, or processed into powder for capsules. Research into the beneficial effects of bilberry and blueberry fruits is focused on their high content of anthocyanosides, which in commercial preparations is standardized at 25–36 per cent. These substances have potent antioxidant effects, improving blood flow to skin, eyes, and nervous system, and thus preventing microcirculatory deterioration that results in mental and physical ageing. In addition, the leaves of *V. myrtillus* contain glucoquinones, which reduce blood sugar levels. *Vaccinium myrtillus* is seldom cultivated but bilberries are commonly harvested from the wild in Europe. Highbush blueberries, derived from *V. corymbosum*, are grown on a large scale in the USA, Australia, and New Zealand; there are numerous cultivars. Arbutin, which acts as a urinary antiseptic, is present in most *Vaccinium* spp., and in other members of the heather family, such as *Arctostaphylos uva-ursi* (see p.127). Leaves of *Vaccinium vitis-idaea*

(cowberry), which contain up to 7 per cent arbutin, are used to treat urinary tract infections, cystitis, diabetes, and diarrhoea.
CULTIVATION Moist, peaty or sandy, lime-free soil in sun or partial shade. Trim in spring, to encourage bushy growth.
PROPAGATION By seed sown in autumn (species only); by greenwood cuttings of deciduous species in early summer; by semi-ripe cuttings of evergreen species in mid- to late summer; by layering in late summer.
HARVEST Leaves are picked in spring and dried for decoctions. Fruits are collected in late summer and juiced, or dried for decoctions, and liquid extracts. Juice is further processed into concentrate powders.

Vaccinium macrocarpon (cranberry)
Prostrate, mat-forming, evergreen shrub with dark green, elliptic–oblong leaves, to 2cm (³⁄₄in) long, which turn bronze in winter. Pendent, bell-shaped, pink flowers, 1cm (¹⁄₂in) across, appear in summer, followed by spherical red fruits, to 2cm (³⁄₄in) across. Native to eastern N America. ‡ 15cm (6in), ↔ indefinite. 'Early Black' bears small to medium fruits that turn red-black when ripe. Adaptable plants, ripening simultaneously and colouring well when picked green. 'Franklin' is early, bearing medium to large, dark red fruits that store well.
HARDINESS Fully hardy.
PARTS USED Fruits.
PROPERTIES An acidic, anti-bacterial herb that acidifies and deodorizes the urine, and protects against urinary infections and formation of stones.
MEDICINAL USES Internally for urinary tract infections (notably recurrent cystitis), urinary stones, and incontinence.
CULINARY USES Fresh fruits are made into sauces, drinks, jellies, syrups, ice cream, and desserts. Dried sweetened fruits, known as "craisins", are used in baking and added to breakfast cereals.
ECONOMIC USES Fruit pulp is used as a commercial food colorant.

◼ *Vaccinium myrtillus* (bilberry, huckleberry, whortleberry)
Deciduous shrub with creeping rhizomes, erect green stems, and glossy, ovate–elliptic, bright green leaves, 1–3cm (¹⁄₂–1¹⁄₄in) long. Pendent, bell-shaped, greenish-pink flowers, 6mm (¹⁄₄in) long, appear in late spring and early summer, followed by spherical, blue-black fruits, 6–10mm (¹⁄₄–¹⁄₂in) across. Found from Europe to N Asia. ‡ 30–60cm (12–24in), ↔ indefinite.
HARDINESS Fully hardy.
PARTS USED Leaves, fruits.
PROPERTIES A bitter–sweet, astringent, cooling herb that acts as a diuretic, lowers blood sugar levels, and is antioxidant and vasoprotective, improving blood supply to veins and capillaries. Fresh fruits are laxative; dried fruits are anti-diarrhoeal.
MEDICINAL USES Internally for diabetes (leaves), oedema, anaemia, diarrhoea, dysentery, and urinary complaints, varicose veins, thread

Vaccinium myrtillus

veins, haemorrhoids, poor circulation, and eye conditions. Externally for gum and mouth inflammations, haemorrhoids, skin complaints, and burns (fruits).
CULINARY USES Fresh fruits are added to salads and muffins, and made into jams, syrups, tart and pie fillings, compotes, and desserts. Dried fruits are used in baking and added to breakfast cereals. Leaves are used to make tea.
ECONOMIC USES Fruits are made into wine or used to colour wines; extracts are used to flavour liqueurs.

VALERIANA
Valerian

Valerianaceae

This genus of about 200 species of annuals, perennials, semi-evergreen subshrubs, and evergreen shrubs occurs worldwide, except in Australia. *Valeriana officinalis* (valerian) is an attractive plant for the back of borders and woodland gardens. It should not be confused with *Centranthus ruber* (red valerian), a popular ornamental with no medicinal uses. The scent of dried valerian roots attracts cats; some cats find the smell of valerian-based herb teas quite irresistible and will search out discarded tea bags. *Valeriana officinalis* was used by Hippocrates in the 4th century BC, and appears in Anglo-Saxon herbals. In the Middle Ages, it was known as an all-heal and regarded as a cure for epilepsy. Valerian tincture was widely used in the First World War to treat shell shock (loss of memory and other functions owing to prolonged psychological strain). Today valerian is recognized as a safe effective sedative that does not react with alcohol, and does not cause dependency. The active constituents are complex; no single compound or group of compounds has been isolated as responsible for the sedative effect. The roots contain iridoids, known as "valepotriates", that appear to regulate the functioning of the nervous system. Some authorities claim that the valepotriates are not present in the root itself, or in preparations derived from it, but actually develop during processing. Similar constituents are found in other species, including *V. jatamansi* syn.

V

V. *wallichii* (Indian valerian) and *V. capensis* (Cape valerian); both have a long history of use for nervous disorders, insomnia, epilepsy, and hysteria.

CULTIVATION Moist soil in sun or shade. Remove flowers to encourage rhizome growth.

PROPAGATION By seed sown in spring; by basal cuttings in spring; by division in spring or autumn.

HARVEST Rhizomes and roots are lifted in the second year after the leaves have died off, and used fresh, dried for use in decoctions, infusions, liquid extracts, tablets, and tinctures, or distilled for oil.

◻ *Valeriana officinalis* (common valerian, garden heliotrope)
Variable, clump-forming perennial with short rhizomes and aromatic pinnate leaves, to 20cm (8in) long, irregularly divided into 7–10 pairs of lanceolate, entire or toothed leaflets. Small, tubular, pink or white flowers are borne in clusters in summer, followed by tiny seeds with a tuft of white hairs. Native to W Europe.
‡ 1.5m (5ft), ↔ 1.2m (4ft).

HARDINESS Fully hardy.

PARTS USED Rhizomes, roots, oil.

PROPERTIES A bitter, sedative, warming herb with a musky aroma. It calms the nerves, relaxes spasms, improves digestion, relieves pain, and lowers blood pressure.

MEDICINAL USES Internally for insomnia, hysteria, hyperactivity, anxiety, cramps, muscular tension and spasms, migraine, indigestion of nervous origin, hypertension, and painful menstruation. May cause drowsiness. Contraindicated with other sedative drugs and/or anti-depressants. Externally for eczema, ulcers, and minor injuries (especially splinters). Combined with *Scutellaria lateriflora* (see p.365) and *Viscum album* (see p.406) for hysteria; with *Humulus lupulus* (see p.237) and *Passiflora incarnata* (see p.303) for insomnia; with *Caulophyllum thalictroides* (see p.159), *Dioscorea villosa* (see p.194), and *Pulsatilla vulgaris* (see p.337) for painful menstruation.

ECONOMIC USES Oil is used in "mossy" perfumes. An ingredient of relaxant herb tea

400 | *Valeriana officinalis*

blends. Extracts are used to flavour ice cream, bakery produce, condiments, soft drinks, liqueurs, beers, and tobacco, and are especially important in apple flavours; also used in bait for trapping wild cats and rodents.
⬒ ▨ ▣ ◿

VANILLA
Orchidaceae

There are about 100 species of climbing, evergreen perennials in this genus, which occurs through the tropics and subtropics. *Vanilla planifolia* is the only member of the vast orchid family that is cultivated for a commercial product rather than as an ornamental. Orchid growers often train a vanilla vine on a greenhouse wall, and *V. planifolia* 'Variegata' is particularly attractive for this purpose. Vanilla is one of the world's most important flavourings; it was introduced to Europe in the 16th century by the Spanish, who found it used by the Aztecs as a flavouring for chocolate. Vanilla is often intercropped with sugar cane; production is now concentrated in Madagascar, Réunion, Tahiti, Java, and the Seychelles. Vanilla flowers are short-lived and have specific pollinators. In cultivation they must be pollinated by hand to produce fruits (vanilla pods), which take five to seven months to ripen. The aromatic compounds are developed during fermentation of the unripe pods. *Vanilla planifolia* fruits contain about 3.5 per cent vanillin, which is present in many natural balsams and resins. There is a large market for synthetic vanilla, which occurs as a by-product of paper manufacture and is extracted from both *Ferula assa-foetida* (see p.213) and the eugenol fraction in oil of cloves (*Syzygium aromaticum*, see p.378). The flavour does not compare in richness with that of natural vanilla, which contains some 35 other aromatic compounds. *Vanilla tahitensis* (Tahitian vanilla) and *V. pompona* (West Indian vanilla) are alternative, though inferior, sources of natural vanilla.

CULTIVATION Well-drained, moist, humus-rich soil with high humidity and daily temperatures between 26°C (79°F) and 30°C (86°F). For optimum fruiting, plants are trained in loops, rather than allowed to climb upwards. This encourages both formation of new shoots and, where the loop touches the ground, of adventitious roots that help feed the plant. Plants may be damaged by scale insects, mildew, vanilla root rot, and snails.

PROPAGATION By cuttings 1.5–2m (5–6ft) long at any time (but best towards the end of the dry season), kept loosely coiled in a dry shady place for 2–3 weeks before insertion in open soil.

HARVEST Fruits are picked when fully ripe, but before they split open, and scalded before undergoing various stages of fermentation and drying, which can take six months. Cured pods are stored whole, or processed commercially for solvent extractions (vanilla resinoid), and alcoholic tinctures (vanilla essence).

Vanilla planifolia

Vanilla planifolia 'Variegata'

◻ *Vanilla planifolia* (vanilla)
Stout climbing orchid with green zigzag stems, 1–2cm (½–¾in) in diameter, and fleshy, oblong, pointed leaves, 8–25cm (3–10in) long. Pale yellow-green flowers, 5cm (2in) across, with a yellow-haired lip, are produced in axillary racemes in spring, followed by elongated pendent capsules, 10–25cm (4–10in) long, containing minute seeds. Native to S America, West Indies, and USA (Florida). ‡ 6m (20ft). ◻ 'Variegata' has irregularly yellow-striped leaves.

HARDINESS Min. 16°C (61°F).

PARTS USED Fruits (pods).

PROPERTIES An aromatic herb that improves digestion.

CULINARY USES Vanilla is used to flavour ice cream, yogurt, milk- and cream-based desserts, and cakes; often combined with chocolate. Whole pods (vanilla beans) are stored in sugar, which is used to sweeten and give a vanilla flavour to desserts, fruit, and cakes.

ECONOMIC USES Extracts are used in perfumery, incense, potpourri, candles, and other room fragrances. Also used to flavour ice creams, yogurts, syrups, chocolate, bakery produce, confectionery, breakfast cereals, soft drinks, liqueurs (notably Galliano), and tobacco.
▨ ◿ ◿ ▣

VERATRUM
Melanthiaceae

A genus of about 45 species of perennials, found throughout the northern hemisphere. They have poisonous black rhizomes, handsome pleated foliage, and branched spires of star-shaped flowers. Several species are grown as ornamentals for shady borders, acid beds, or woodland areas. The two main species used medicinally are the American *V. viride* (green hellebore) and the European *V. album* (white hellebore). Native N Americans cured wounds with the powdered roots of *V. viride*, having first smeared the injury with animal fat, and eased muscular aches and pains by abrading and greasing the skin first before applying the powder. They also used the powder to relieve toothache. Settlers used crushed fresh roots, mixed with lard, to soothe itching, and as a decoction to remove head lice. Boiled with corn, they made an effective poison for crows. *Veratrum album* was once used as a remedy for mania and epilepsy, and a substitute for *Colchicum autumnale* (see p.176) as a cure for gout. Taken internally, *Veratrum* root is a drastic purgative and causes violent sneezing. Even moderate amounts cause serious poisoning. According to Mrs Grieve (*A Modern Herbal*, 1931), *V. viride* has a different chemistry from *V. album* and is less likely to cause intestinal distress. Both contain alkaloids that have been used in the treatment of hypertension but have been superseded by drugs that have fewer and less serious side-effects. They have also been used as insecticides and parasiticides. The name "hellebore", an Old English word for a herb used to cure madness, is also used for unrelated plants, such as false hellebore (see *Adonis vernalis*, p.103) and black hellebore (see *Helleborus niger*, p.233).

CULTIVATION Rich, moist, well-drained soil in partial shade.

PROPAGATION By seed sown when ripe; by division in autumn or early spring.

HARVEST Roots are collected in autumn and dried for fluid extracts and powder, and also for the extraction of alkaloids.

⚠ **WARNING** All parts are highly toxic if ingested. Contact with foliage may cause skin irritation; prolonged handling may cause systemic poisoning.

■ *Veratrum viride* (American hellebore, green hellebore, Indian poke)
Rhizomatous perennial with ovate to broadly elliptic, pleated leaves, to 30cm (12in) long. Green to yellow-green, star-shaped flowers, to 2cm (¾in) across, are borne in branched spikes in summer. Native to eastern N America. ‡ 2m (6ft), ↔ 60cm (24in).

HARDINESS Fully hardy.

PARTS USED Roots and rhizomes.

PROPERTIES An emetic cathartic herb that causes sneezing and lowers blood pressure. It is insecticidal.

MEDICINAL USES Formerly used internally for pneumonia, peritonitis, arteriosclerosis, and hypertension associated with toxaemia in pregnancy. Externally as a parasiticide for head lice; also in veterinary medicine to destroy parasites. Rarely used now. Excess causes diarrhoea and vomiting with severe retching, shallow breathing, pallor, perspiration, and potentially fatal collapse. For use only by qualified practitioners.

Veratrum viride

VERBASCUM
Mullein

Scrophulariaceae

This large genus of some 360 species of annuals, biennials, perennials, and subshrubs is distributed throughout Europe, N Africa, and W and C Asia. *Verbascum thapsus* is a stately plant, with woolly foliage and tall spires of yellow flowers. It tolerates a wide range of conditions, including dry stony soils, and is equally at home in borders, banks, walls, or gravel areas. *Verbascum* has been used medicinally for respiratory complaints since Classical times, but none is well researched. *Verbascum densiflorum* (large-flowered mullein) contains iridoid glycosides, similar to those found in *Plantago major* (see p.322), that stimulate the secretion of uric acid from the kidneys. Several species, including *Verbascum densiflorum*, *V. nigrum* (dark mullein), and the rare *V. phlomoides* (orange mullein), are used in similar ways to *V. thapsus*.

Verbascum thapsus

CULTIVATION Well-drained to poor dry soil in sun. *Verbascum thapsus* self-sows freely in suitable conditions. Foliage is highly susceptible to caterpillars of the mullein moth. Subject to statutory control as a weed in some countries, notably in parts of Australia.

PROPAGATION By seed sown in late spring or early summer; by root cuttings in late winter. May also be grown as an annual by sowing in early spring at 13–18°C (55–64°F).

HARVEST Leaves and flowers are collected in summer and dried for use in infusions, liquid extracts, and tinctures. Flowers may also be used fresh, or frozen for use in infusions, medicated oil, and syrup.

■ *Verbascum thapsus* (Aaron's rod, great mullein)
Robust biennial with obovate–oblong, grey-green, woolly leaves, to 50cm (20in) long, forming a basal rosette in the first year. Yellow, five-petalled flowers, to 3cm (1¼in) across, are borne in summer in a dense terminal spike. Native to W Europe; naturalized in N America. ‡ 2m (6ft), ↔ 1m (3ft).

HARDINESS Fully hardy.

PARTS USED Leaves, flowers.

PROPERTIES A bitter, cooling, mucilaginous herb that soothes and lubricates tissues, promotes healing, and has diuretic, analgesic, expectorant, and antiseptic effects.

MEDICINAL USES Internally for coughs, whooping cough, bronchitis, laryngitis, tonsillitis, tracheitis, asthma, influenza, respiratory catarrh, tuberculosis, urinary tract infections, nervous tension, and insomnia. Externally for earache (flowers in olive oil), sores, wounds, boils, rheumatic pain, haemorrhoids, and chilblains. Combines well with *Marrubium vulgare* (see p.271), *Lobelia inflata* (see p.265), and *Tussilago farfara* (see p.396) for bronchitis; and with *Thymus vulgaris* (see p.387) for coughs.

ECONOMIC USES Leaves are smoked alone, or with *Eriodictyon californicum* (see p.204) and *Tussilago farfara* (see p.396), as a substitute for tobacco.

VERBENA
Vervain

Verbenaceae

This genus of about 250 species of annuals, perennials, and subshrubs is distributed mainly in tropical and temperate parts of the Americas, with two European species. European *V. officinalis* (vervain) cannot compare in ornamental value with its S American relatives but is often grown in herb gardens and makes a good foil for bolder shapes. Vervain was revered in Celtic and Germanic cultures, and held sacred by both the Druids and the Romans; it had magical associations and was often carried as a talisman – a practice dismissed by the 16th-century herbalist John Gerard as "vaine and superstitious". Today *V. officinalis* is used mainly for nervous complaints in Western medicine, and for conditions associated with disturbances of the

Verbena officinalis

liver, spleen, and bladder meridians in Chinese medicine. The N American *V. hastata* (blue vervain) has similar constituents but is considered more alterative, acting mainly on the liver and lungs. It is used for liver disorders, respiratory, and menstrual complaints.

CULTIVATION Well-drained, moist soil in sun.

PROPAGATION By seed sown in spring or autumn; by division in spring; by stem cuttings in late summer. Self-sows freely.

HARVEST Plants are cut as flowering begins, and dried for use in decoctions (Chinese medicine), infusions, liquid extracts, ointments, and tinctures.

■ *Verbena officinalis* (vervain)
Perennial with a woody base, four-angled, branched stems, and ovate, often pinnate leaves, to 6cm (2½in) long. Tiny, pale lilac flowers are borne in slender terminal spikes in summer. Native to Europe, W Asia, and N Africa. ‡80cm (32in), ↔ 60cm (24in).

HARDINESS Fully hardy.

PARTS USED Whole plant (*ma bian cao*).

PROPERTIES A bitter, aromatic, cooling herb that is diuretic, calms the nerves, improves digestion, increases perspiration and lactation, reduces inflammation, and relieves pain; it controls bleeding, improves liver and gall bladder function, and stimulates the uterus. Regarded as anti-malarial in Chinese medicine.

MEDICINAL USES Internally for nervous exhaustion, depression, convalescent debility, asthma, migraine, jaundice, gall bladder problems, and insufficient lactation. Excess causes nausea and vomiting. Not recommended during pregnancy, but may facilitate contractions during labour. Externally for minor injuries, eczema, sores, neuralgia, and gum disease; also as a dentifrice. In Chinese medicine, for malaria, menstrual complaints, influenza, feverish illnesses, gum disease, abscesses, urinary disorders, and schistosomiasis. Combines well with *Avena sativa* (see p.138), *Cypripedium parviflorum* var. *pubescens* (see p.189), and *Scutellaria lateriflora* (see p.365) for depression.

CULINARY USES Flowers are used to flavour salt in Turkey, and may be added to salads or used as a garnish. Dried leaves are made into tea.

ECONOMIC USES Extract is used to flavour French liqueur *Verveine du Velay*.

VERONICA
Speedwell

Scrophulariaceae

This genus includes about 250 species of mostly blue-flowered annuals, perennials, and mostly deciduous subshrubs, which occur in Europe and Asia. Those in cultivation range from elegant border plants and aquatics, to mat-forming plants suitable for the rock garden; many have variants with pink, white, or purple flowers. The names "common speedwell" and "speedwell" are applied to several different species; for medicinal purposes care should be taken to identify the correct plant. *Veronica officinalis* was a popular healing herb in Europe during the Middle Ages, under the name *herba Veronica majoris*. In 1690 it was the subject of a 300-page treatise, *Polchresta Herba Veronica*, by Johannes Francus. By the 19th century it was used mostly as a tea substitute, known in France as *thé d'Europe*. It is regarded as obsolete by herbalists today. *Veronica* may be named after St Veronica. The common name "speedwell" (goodbye) refers to the rapid fall of the corollas if the flower spikes are picked.

CULTIVATION Dry, slightly acid soil in sun or partial shade. Prone to downy and powdery mildews.

PROPAGATION By seed sown in autumn; by division in spring or autumn; by semi-ripe cuttings in summer.

HARVEST Plants are cut when flowering and dried for infusions.

■ *Veronica officinalis* (common speedwell, fluellen, gypsyweed, heath speedwell)
Creeping, mat-forming, hairy perennial with ovate–elliptic, toothed leaves, to 6cm (2½in) long, and racemes of lilac-blue, veined flowers from late spring to early summer. Native to Europe. ‡10–50cm (4–20in), ↔ indefinite.

HARDINESS Fully hardy.

PARTS USED Whole plant.

PROPERTIES A bitter, astringent, alterative herb with a tea-like odour when dried. It has weak diuretic and expectorant effects.

MEDICINAL USES Formerly, internally for bronchial, arthritic, rheumatic, and skin complaints, nervous exhaustion, and stomach upsets; externally for minor injuries.

Veronica officinalis

CULINARY USES Dried herb may be added to tea blends.

Veronica virginica. See *Veronicastrum virginicum*.

VERONICASTRUM
Blackroot

Scrophulariaceae

There is one, or possibly two, perennial species in this genus, depending on whether the Siberian blackroot is regarded as a subspecies (*Veronicastrum virginicum* subsp. *sibiricum*) or as a separate species (*V. sibiricum*). The N American *V. virginicum* is a tall graceful plant for borders and the wild garden. It is a powerful purgative and emetic with a long history of use among native N Americans. The common names "Culver's root" and "Culver's physic" (and "Brinton's root") were first recorded in 1716; the first settler to use this herb was a Dr Culver (or possibly Brinton) though no other references have been found. The name *Veronicastrum* is a combination of *Veronica*, named after St Veronica, and *astrum*, "star", referring to the star-shaped arrangement of the leaves around the stem.

CULTIVATION Well-drained, moist, humus-rich soil in sun or partial shade. May need staking.

PROPAGATION By seed sown in autumn; by division in spring.

HARVEST Rhizomes and roots are lifted in autumn, and dried for use in decoctions, liquid extracts, powders, tablets, and tinctures.

■ *Veronicastrum virginicum* syn. *Leptandra virginica*, *Veronica virginica* (blackroot, Brinton's root, Culver's physic/root, physic root)
Upright perennial with horizontal black rhizomes, unbranched stems, and whorls of 3–7 oblanceolate, pointed, finely toothed leaves, to 15cm (6in) long. Tubular, white or pink flowers, 7mm (¼in) long, with protruding stamens, are borne in summer. Native to N America (Ontario to Texas). ‡2m (6ft), ↔ 45cm (18in). f. *album* has white flowers. ■ var. *incarnatum* syn. f. *roseum* has pale pink flowers.

HARDINESS Fully hardy.

PARTS USED Rhizomes and roots.

Veronicastrum virginicum

Veronicastrum virginicum var. *incarnatum*

PROPERTIES A bitter, laxative, tonic herb that increases perspiration, relaxes spasms, and stimulates the liver and gall bladder.

MEDICINAL USES Internally for chronic constipation and indigestion associated with liver disorders, and gall bladder inflammation. Combined with *Berberis vulgaris* (see p.142) and *Taraxacum officinale* (see p.382) for liver complaints; and with *Acorus calamus* (see p.101) and *Hydrastis canadensis* (see p.239) for constipation with flatulence and bloating. Fresh roots, or dried roots taken to excess, cause vomiting and severe diarrhoea with bleeding.
▨ ▮

VETIVERIA
Vetiver

Poaceae

Ten species of perennial grasses make up this genus, distributed throughout tropical Asia. *Vetiveria zizanioides* is an extremely useful, large, coarse grass. It is grown mainly in Haiti, India, Indonesia, Malaysia, Réunion, and Vietnam for essential oil, and in many parts of the world to control erosion, as the aromatic roots grow straight down for 3m (10ft). In India the grass is traditionally woven into screens, which are hung in doorways and windows and sprayed with water to keep rooms cool and free from insects. Vetiver roots are rich in volatile oil, known as "oil of tranquillity" in India and Sri Lanka. It has a heavy earthy aroma, and is strongly repellent to flies, cockroaches, bedbugs, and clothes moths. The name *Vetiveria* is derived from *vettiveri*, the word for the plant in S India, which in turn came from the Dravidian *ver*, "root".

CULTIVATION Wet to dry soil in sun. Trim plants grown as a hedge to encourage dense growth; burn over to destroy crop-pest larvae. Plants may be damaged by fungal diseases and termites.

PROPAGATION By division, or "slips", and layering at the start of the growing season; commercially by tissue culture.

Vetiveria zizanioides

HARVEST Roots are lifted as required and distilled for oil, or processed for solvent extraction.

▣ *Vetiveria zizanioides* (cuscus, *khus khus*, vetiver)
Robust giant grass with fibrous spongy roots and rigid linear leaves, 1–2m (3–6ft) long. Tiny, brown to purple flowers are produced in long-stalked spikes, to 1.5m (5ft) long, in summer. Native to tropical Asia. ‡ 2–3m (6–10ft), ↔ indefinite.
HARDINESS Min. 10°C (50°F).
PARTS USED Roots, oil.
PROPERTIES An aromatic, sedative, antiseptic herb that increases production of red blood corpuscles.
MEDICINAL USES Internally for nervous and circulatory problems. Externally for lice, and as a tonic bath.
CULINARY USES Roots are used to make *khus* essence and *khus* water to flavour confectionery and drinks (India).
ECONOMIC USES Oil is an ingredient in oriental "woody" perfumes. Extracts are used in hair care. Dried roots are woven into scented mats, screens, and fans; also used as insect-repellent. Oil is used in soaps and cosmetics, and as a fragrance fixative. Extracts are used to flavour tinned asparagus and Indian fruit drinks.
◨ ▨ ▮ ◿ ◿ ▨

VIBURNUM
Caprifoliaceae

This genus of about 150 species of evergreen, semi-evergreen, and deciduous shrubs and small trees is distributed widely in most temperate and warm areas, especially Asia and N America. *Viburnum opulus* is an excellent garden shrub with delightful flowers and early-ripening, brightly coloured fruits. *Viburnum prunifolium* has the largest fruits of any viburnum and brilliant autumn colour. It may be grown as a small garden tree if restricted to a single trunk.

Common to *V. opulus* and *V. prunifolium* is scopoletin, a coumarin that has a sedative effect on the uterus. *Viburnum prunifolium* also contains salicin, an analgesic that occurs in *Salix alba* (see p.353). The two viburnums are prescribed alternately or together; *V. opulus* is thought to be weaker in action, and *V. prunifolium* appears to act more strongly on the uterus. In parts of E USA, the fruits of *V. prunifolium* have been used for preserves and larger-fruited, palatable clones are grown for fruit production. The fruits of *V. opulus* and the N American *V. trilobum* can be used for making preserves and wine.

CULTIVATION Deep moist soil in sun or partial shade. Remove dead wood and older stems after flowering. Plants may be damaged by aphid and viburnum beetle, and are prone to honey fungus and leafspot.

PROPAGATION By seed sown in autumn (species only); by greenwood cuttings in summer.

HARVEST Bark is stripped before leaves change colour in autumn, or before leaf buds open in spring, and dried for decoctions, liquid extracts, and tinctures (*V. opulus*, *V. prunifolium*), creams (*V. opulus*), and infusions, elixirs, and powders (*V. prunifolium*). Fruits are picked when ripe in summer for culinary use.

⚠ **WARNING** Fruits of *V. opulus* may cause mild stomach upsets if eaten raw.

▣ *Viburnum opulus* (crampbark, guelder rose)
Vigorous deciduous shrub with three- or sometimes five-lobed, toothed leaves, to 10cm (4in) long. Flat-topped clusters of tiny flowers, surrounded by conspicuous, white, sterile flowers, to 2cm (¾in) across, appear in summer, followed by clusters of glossy, scarlet, almost spherical fruits, 8mm (⅜in) across. Native to Europe, N Africa, and C Asia. ‡ 5m (15ft), ↔ 4m (12ft). ▣ 'Aureum' has a compact habit and bright golden leaves, which tend to scorch in full sun. 'Compactum' is slow-growing, dense, and free-flowering. ‡ 2.5m (8ft), ↔ 1.5m (5ft). 'Fructu Luteo' has yellow, pink-flushed fruits. 'Nanum' is dwarf and rarely flowers, with good autumn colour and thin, upright, reddish winter stems. ‡ 1–1.2m (3–4ft), ↔ 60cm (24in). 'Nottcutt's Variety' is vigorous, bearing large clusters of fruit. ▣ 'Roseum' syn. 'Sterile' (snowball bush) bears conspicuous, creamy white, ball-shaped flower heads, composed entirely of sterile flowers. ▣ 'Xanthocarpum' has yellow fruits.
HARDINESS Fully hardy.
PARTS USED Bark, fruits.
PROPERTIES A bitter, astringent, sedative herb that relaxes spasms and regulates uterine function.
MEDICINAL USES Internally for painful menstruation, postpartum and ovarian pain, threatened miscarriage, hypertension, nervous constipation, irritable bowel syndrome, muscular tension, and cramps. Externally for muscular cramp and aching muscles. Combines well with *Dioscorea villosa* (see p.194) and *Zanthoxylum americanum* (see p.409) for cramp; and with *V. prunifolium* and *Chamaelirium luteum* (see p.164) for uterine pain and threatened miscarriage.

Viburnum opulus

Viburnum opulus 'Aureum'

Viburnum opulus 'Roseum'

Viburnum opulus 'Xanthocarpum'

CULINARY USES Fruits are made into preserves, sauces, and wine. Do not eat fruits when raw.

Viburnum prunifolium (black haw, stagbush)
Deciduous shrub or bushy tree with red-tinged shoots and shiny ovate leaves, to 8cm (3in) long, which turn red in autumn. White flowers, 8mm (³⁄₈in) across, are produced in flat clusters, to 10cm (4in) across, in late spring and early summer, followed by blue-black, oval fruits, almost 2cm (³⁄₄in) long. Native to E and eastern C USA. ‡ 5–9m (15–28ft), ↔ 1–6m (3–20ft).
HARDINESS Fully hardy.
PARTS USED Stem bark, root bark, fruits.
PROPERTIES A bitter, astringent, sedative herb that relaxes spasms, relieves pain, calms nerves, lowers blood pressure, and regulates the uterus.
MEDICINAL USES Internally for painful menstruation, threatened miscarriage, convulsive disorders, hysteria, colic, spasmodic pain in the gall bladder, urinary or digestive tracts, muscular cramps, asthma, and palpitations of nervous origin. Combined with *Chamaelirium luteum* (see p.164) and *Hydrastis canadensis* (see p.239) for threatened miscarriage. Contraindicated for anyone sensitive or allergic to aspirin.
CULINARY USES Fruits are eaten raw or made into preserves, sauces, and drinks.

404

VINCA
Periwinkle

Apocynaceae

This genus of seven species of low evergreen subshrubs and herbaceous perennials ranges throughout Europe, N Africa, and C Asia. *Vinca major* (greater periwinkle) and *V. minor* (lesser periwinkle), and their many cultivars, are excellent for ground cover, providing glossy, often variegated leaves and large colourful flowers. They thrive in shade but flower more freely in a sunny position. Periwinkles have been used medicinally, and as magical herbs, since at least Classical times. One medieval spell recommends periwinkle mashed with earthworms and *Sempervivum tectorum* (hens and chicks, see p.366) as a love potion for married couples. Culpeper recommended a periwinkle conserve to prevent nightmares; more realistically, both he and William Coles (*Adam in Eden*, 1657) regarded periwinkle as a useful anti-inflammatory and styptic. Both species are sources of the alkaloid vincamine, used by the pharmaceutical industry as a cerebral stimulant and vasodilator. They do not contain the anti-cancer alkaloids found in the related *Catharanthus roseus* (see p.159). *Vinca major* also contains reserpine, as found in *Rauvolfia serpentina* (see p.341), which lowers high blood pressure. *Vinca* is from *pervinca*, the Latin for "periwinkle", derived from *vincire*, "to bind", because the long trailing shoots were used to make wreaths.
CULTIVATION Moist soil in sun or partial shade. Invasive. Cut back plants in autumn or winter to control spread. Remove excess shoots in summer to restrict spread before rooting at nodes takes place. Leaves may be damaged by rust.

PROPAGATION By division from autumn to spring; by semi-ripe cuttings in summer.
HARVEST Plants are cut when flowering and processed commercially for alkaloid extraction, or dried for use in infusions, liquid extracts, powders, and tinctures.
⚠ **WARNING** Toxic if eaten.

■ *Vinca major* (greater periwinkle)
Arching to prostrate or trailing, evergreen subshrub with stems rooting at the tips and ovate, pointed, glossy leaves, to 9cm (3½ in) long. Blue, propeller-shaped flowers, 4cm (1½in) across, appear in the axils of short erect flowering stems in spring. Native to W Mediterranean. ‡ 45cm (18in), ↔ indefinite. var. *alba* has white flowers. ■ 'Maculata' has leaves with yellow-green centres. var. *oxyloba* syn. 'Dartington Star', 'Hidcote Purple' bears deep violet-blue flowers with pointed lobes. ■ 'Reticulata' has yellow-veined leaves. ■ 'Variegata' syn. 'Elegantissima' has leaves with irregular cream variegation.
HARDINESS Fully hardy.
PARTS USED Whole plant.
PROPERTIES An acrid, slightly bitter, astringent herb that controls bleeding.
MEDICINAL USES Internally for heavy menstruation and enuresis. Externally as a douche for vaginal discharge.

Vinca minor (lesser periwinkle)
Arching to prostrate or trailing, evergreen subshrub with stems rooting at the tips and elliptic to lanceolate or ovate, dark green leaves, to 5cm (2in) long. Purple-blue, mauve, or white, propeller-shaped flowers, 2.5–3cm (1–1¼in) across, appear from spring to autumn. Native to Europe, S Russia, and the N Caucasus.

Vinca major

Vinca major 'Maculata'

Vinca major 'Reticulata'

Vinca major 'Variegata'

Vinca minor 'Atropurpurea'

Vinca minor 'Gertrude Jekyll'

⬍ 10–20cm (4–8in), ↔ indefinite. 'Alba Variegata' syn. 'Alba Aureavariegata' has white flowers and yellow-margined leaves. 'Argenteovariegata' syn. 'Variegata' has pale violet-blue flowers and cream-margined leaves. ▣ 'Atropurpurea' syn. 'Purpurea', 'Rubra' has purple flowers. 'Azurea Flore Pleno' syn. 'Caerulea Plena' has double blue flowers. ▣ 'Gertrude Jekyll' is compact, with numerous white flowers. 'La Grave' syn. 'Bowles' Blue', 'Bowles' Variety' bears large, lavender-blue flowers. 'Multiplex' syn. 'Double Burgundy' bears double purple flowers.

HARDINESS Fully hardy.

PARTS USED Leaves.

PROPERTIES A bitter astringent herb that controls bleeding and discharges, and improves blood flow to the brain.

MEDICINAL USES Internally for heavy menstruation, internal haemorrhage, nosebleed, arteriosclerosis, and dementia caused by reduced blood flow to the brain. Contraindicated during pregnancy. Externally for sore throat, gum inflammation, and mouth ulcers. Combined with *Trillium erectum* (see p.394) for heavy menstruation and with *Ginkgo biloba* (see p.225) for hardening of the cerebral arteries.

▨ ▣

Vinca rosea. See *Catharanthus roseus*.

VIOLA
Violet

Violaceae

This large genus of some 500 species of mostly annuals, biennials, and perennials is found throughout temperate regions. *Viola odorata* (sweet violet) was grown commercially in Greece as early as 400BC for sale in the market in Athens. It was extolled by Muslims in the saying "the excellence of the violet is as the excellence of Islam above all other religions". The Romans drank violet-flavoured wine and were criticized by Horace (65–8BC) for spending more time growing violets than olives. Violets were the favourite flowers of Napoleon, who was nicknamed *Caporal Violette* and died wearing a locket of violets taken from Josephine's grave. During the reign of Queen Victoria (1837–1901), violets reached cult status and were grown on a vast scale for cutflowers and perfumery. Ionene, the main aromatic element in *V. odorata*, was synthesized in 1893, leading to a decline in the cultivation of violets for perfumery. The downward trend continued as a result of the First and Second World Wars and, by the mid-20th century, most of the highly scented, 19th-century cultivars were very scarce or extinct. Violets of various kinds are regarded as cleansing herbs and have been used in the background treatment of cancer. *Viola canina* (dog violet) has similar medicinal properties to *V. odorata* but has unscented flowers. *Viola yezoensis* has featured in trials for treating childhood eczema at the Great Ormond Street Children's Hospital in London (UK). *Viola striata* is also used medicinally and has anti-tumour effects. Chinese herbals feature a number of other species, including *V. diffusa*, *V. inconspicua*, and *V. patrinii*. High doses of violets cause nausea and vomiting, because of the irritant effect of the saponins on the digestive system.

CULTIVATION Well-drained, moist, humus-rich soil in sun or partial shade. Remove dead flowers promptly in order to prolong flowering. Plants may be damaged by slugs, snails, and viral and fungal diseases (notably pansy sickness). *Viola tricolor* self-sows freely.

PROPAGATION By seed sown when ripe or in spring; by stem-tip cuttings in spring or late summer; by division in autumn or spring.

HARVEST Whole plants, leaves, and flowers are collected during the flowering season, and dried for use in decoctions (*V. yezoensis*), infusions, and liquid extracts. Roots are collected in autumn and dried for decoctions. Leaves of *V. odorata* are often used fresh, and flowers may also be picked in spring for extraction of essential oil. *V. tricolor* is often powdered when dried and used in skin creams.

▣ *Viola odorata* (sweet violet, violet)
Semi-evergreen, rhizomatous perennial with slender stolons and tufts of ovate to heart-shaped leaves, to 6cm (2½in) long. Dark purple or white, occasionally yellow, sweetly scented flowers, about 2cm (¾in) across, appear from late winter to late spring, followed by globose, three-lobed capsules. Native to W and S Europe; widely naturalized. ⬍ 15cm (6in), ↔ 30cm (12in). ▣ 'Alba' has white flowers.
HARDINESS Fully hardy.

Viola odorata

Viola odorata 'Alba'

Viola tricolor

PARTS USED Leaves, flowers, root, essential oil.

PROPERTIES A bitter–sweet, mucilaginous, cooling herb that cleanses toxins, and has expectorant, antiseptic, and anti-cancer effects.

MEDICINAL USES Internally for bronchitis, catarrh, coughs, asthma, and cancer of the breast, stomach, lungs, or digestive tract. Excess (especially of root) causes vomiting. Externally for mouth and throat infections; in aromatherapy, for bronchial complaints, exhaustion, and skin problems (oil).

CULINARY USES Flowers and young leaves are added to salads or made into tea. Flowers are used as a garnish for desserts, candied, or added to vinegars, ices, and syrups.

ECONOMIC USES Essential oil is used in perfumery. Extracts are used in commercial food flavouring.

▣ ▨ ◪ ▧ ▣ ✎ ✎

▣ *Viola tricolor* (heartsease, wild pansy)
Annual, biennial, or short-lived perennial with upright to spreading stems and ovate to heart-shaped, toothed to lobed leaves, to 3cm (1¼in) long. Pansy-like flowers, about 2.5cm (1in) across, in various combinations of purple, lilac, white, and yellow, are produced in spring and summer. ↔ 38cm (15in).

HARDINESS Fully hardy.

PARTS USED Whole plant.

PROPERTIES A bitter–sweet, cooling herb that is laxative and diuretic, lowers fever, cleanses toxins, and reduces inflammation. It is also expectorant, relieves pain, and promotes healing.

MEDICINAL USES Internally for bronchitis, whooping cough, rheumatism, skin complaints (especially weeping eczema), urinary complaints, capillary fragility, and auto-immune disease involving several of these symptoms. Externally for itching skin complaints and varicose ulcers. Combines well with *Galium aparine* (see p.219), *Rumex crispus* (see p.351), *Trifolium pratense* (see p.393), and *Urtica dioica* (see p.398) for eczema; with *Agathosma crenulata* (see p.106), *Elymus repens* (see p.201), and *Eupatorium purpureum* (see p.209) for cystitis; and with *Tussilago farfara* (see p.396) or *Urginea maritima* (see p.398) for whooping cough.

CULINARY USES Flowers are added to salads, used as a garnish, or frozen in ice cubes for summer drinks.

▣ ▣ ✎

Viola yezoensis (Chinese violet)
Perennial with slender rhizomes and ovate–heart-shaped, toothed leaves, to 6cm (2½in) long. White, purple-striped flowers, about 3cm (1¼in) long, are produced in spring, followed by three-lobed capsules. Native to Japan. ↔ 20cm (8in).

HARDINESS Fully hardy.

PARTS USED Whole plant (*zi hua di ding*).

PROPERTIES A bitter, pungent, cooling herb that clears toxins, reduces inflammation, and is anti-bacterial.

MEDICINAL USES Internally for boils, snake bite, carbuncles, skin disorders (especially erysipelas), mumps, and "hot" disorders with inflammation of the eyes, throat, or ears.

▣ ▣

VISCUM
Mistletoe

Viscaceae

Occurring throughout temperate regions, this genus includes about 70 species of parasitic evergreen shrubs. *Viscum album* (mistletoe) is a rewarding plant to grow if a suitable host is available, such as an apple tree. Orchards are often used for commercial crops, thereby yielding a return in winter when the trees are dormant. The tradition of kissing under the mistletoe was popularized in Victorian England. It may have originated in Scandinavian legend, according to which Balder, the god of peace, was killed by an arrow made from mistletoe and was resurrected by the other deities. Mistletoe was then entrusted to the goddess of love, who established it as a symbol of love, with the custom that anyone passing beneath it should receive a kiss. Mistletoe was also an important Druidic herb, associated with welcoming the New Year. It was cut only from oak trees at a particular phase of the moon, using a golden sickle. The constituents of *V. album* appear to vary according to the host plant, which may explain why the Druids regarded mistletoe on oak as superior. These include compounds that affect protein synthesis, the immune and circulatory systems, and heart. *Viscum album* is sometimes used in Chinese medicine but more commonly used are *V. coloratum*, which grows farther east and has yellow to orange-red fruits, and *Loranthus europaeus* (mulberry mistletoe), a parasite on plants of the beech family (Fagaceae). *Viscum capense* (Cape mistletoe) is a traditional South African remedy for asthma, bronchitis, diarrhoea, and menstrual problems. The Moroccan *V. cruciatum* is used internally for asthma, epilepsy, and hysteria, and externally for bruises, sprains, and fractures. *Viscum* is the original Latin name, meaning both "mistletoe" and "birdlime". In certain countries, sale and use of *V. album* for therapeutic purposes are restricted.
CULTIVATION On young upper branches of a host tree, such as oak, apple, willow, hawthorn, lime, poplar, or rowan, at least 15 years old.
PROPAGATION By crushing fruit into crevices of bark, protected from birds, in spring. Best results are obtained by sowing into the same host tree as the fruit was harvested from. Seedlings are very slow-growing.
HARVEST Leafy stems and fruits are collected in autumn and dried for use in infusions, liquid extracts, tablets, and tinctures.
⚠ **WARNING** All parts, especially the berries, are toxic if eaten.

■ *Viscum album* (mistletoe)
Evergreen parasitic shrub with symmetrically branched stems and leathery, obovate, yellow-green leaves, to 5cm (2in) long. Clusters of inconspicuous yellow flowers appear in spring, with males and females on separate plants; females are followed by spherical, sticky, white fruits, about 1cm (½in) across. Native to Europe, east to the Caucasus. ↔ 1m (3ft).
HARDINESS Fully hardy.

Viscum album

PARTS USED Leafy stems, fruits.
PROPERTIES A pungent, bitter–sweet, warming herb that lowers blood pressure, stimulates the immune system, slows heartbeat, relaxes spasms, and has sedative, diuretic, and anti-cancer effects.
MEDICINAL USES Internally for arteriosclerosis, mild hypertension, nervous tachycardia, nervous tension, insomnia, panic attacks, tinnitus, epilepsy, St Vitus's dance, and cancer (especially of lungs and ovaries). Externally for rheumatism, arthritis, chilblains, leg ulcers, and varicose veins. Combines well with *Crataegus laevigata* (see p.182) and *Melissa officinalis* (see p.275) for mild hypertension; and with *Ginkgo biloba* (see p.225) or *Vinca major* (see p.404) for arteriosclerosis. For use only by qualified practitioners.

VITEX

Lamiaceae/Verbenaceae

This genus includes about 250 species of deciduous and evergreen trees and shrubs, occurring mainly in tropical and subtropical regions. Both *V. agnus-castus* and *V. negundo* are fine ornamental shrubs for warm-temperate regions or sheltered positions in colder parts. They have elegant compound leaves and spikes of mauve flowers. *Vitex agnus-castus* has long been associated with chastity – white-flowered plants in particular being a traditional symbol of virtue in S Europe. Ground seeds were used in monasteries as a condiment to suppress libido, hence the common names "monk's pepper" and "chaste tree". The fruits have hormonal effects on both men and women, inhibiting male androgens and increasing female progesterone, although it is not clear exactly which constituents are responsible for these effects. *Vitex negundo* is a very variable species, with seven or more recognized variants. The hemp-leafed variety, var. *cannabifolia*, is listed in the *Chinese Pharmacopoeia* (1985) as a different drug, *mu jing*, which has expectorant, anti-tussive, anti-asthmatic, sedative, anti-spasmodic, and anti-bacterial effects. The cut-leafed variety, var. *incisa*, also has specific uses in Chinese medicine. *Vitex canescens* and *V. quinata* are used as a substitute for *V. negundo* in Tibet. Chinese herbalists also use *V. trifolia* and

V. rotundifolia, which are both known as *man jing zi*.
CULTIVATION Well-drained to dry, poor soil in sun. Cut back the previous year's growths to 2.5–5cm (1–2in) in spring.
PROPAGATION By seed sown when ripe or in spring; by semi-ripe cuttings in summer.
HARVEST Leaves are picked in early summer, and used fresh as juice, or in infusions and poultices, or dried for use in decoctions. Stems are cut in late summer or autumn and dried for use in decoctions and charcoal powder. Roots are lifted in late summer or autumn, and dried for use in decoctions. Fruits are collected in autumn, and used fresh or dried in decoctions or powder. Oil is extracted mainly from *V. negundo* var. *cannabifolia*.

■ *Vitex agnus-castus* (agnus castus, chaste tree, monk's pepper)
Open deciduous shrub with aromatic palmate leaves, divided into five or seven elliptic pointed leaflets, to 10cm (4in) long. Small, tubular, lilac, scented flowers are borne in upright spikes, 13–18cm (5–7in) long, in summer, followed by red-black fruits, 2mm (¹⁄₁₆in) in diameter. Found from the Mediterranean to C Asia. ↔ 2–8m (6–25ft). var. *latifolia* is vigorous, with broader leaflets.
HARDINESS Frost hardy.
PARTS USED Fruits.
PROPERTIES A pungent, bitter–sweet, slightly astringent, relaxant herb that regulates hormonal functions, promotes lactation, and relieves spasms and pain.
MEDICINAL USES Internally for menstrual and menopausal complaints, infertility, insufficient lactation, and involuntary ejaculation. Combines well with *Hydrastis canadensis* for menopausal problems. Excess causes nerve disorder known as formication (sensation of insects crawling under the skin).
CULINARY USES Fruits are used as a substitute for pepper, and in Middle Eastern spice mixes.

Vitex agnus-castus

Vitex negundo

Vitex negundo var. *incisa*

V

■ ***Vitex negundo*** (Chinese chaste tree)
Deciduous bushy shrub with four-angled stems and palmate leaves divided into 3–5 lanceolate pointed leaflets, to 10cm (4in) long. Small, tubular, lavender flowers are borne in upright spikes, to 22cm (9in) long, in late summer and early autumn, followed by small fleshy fruits. Native to E Africa and E Asia. ↕↔ 3–5m (10–15ft). var. *cannabifolia* (hemp-leafed chaste tree) has leaves resembling those of *Cannabis sativa* (see p.152). ■ var. *incisa* syn. *V. incisa*, *V. negundo* var. *heterophylla* (cut-leafed chaste tree) has leaflets with deeply toothed margins, which in some plants are almost divided into segments.
HARDINESS Frost hardy.
PARTS USED Leaves, stems, roots, fruits (*huang jing zi*), oil.
PROPERTIES A sedative, cooling, detoxifying herb that lowers fever, relieves pain, improves digestion, and is expectorant and anti-bacterial.
MEDICINAL USES Internally for poisonous bites, malaria, arthritis, and breast cancer. Not given to patients with heart disease or hypertension. Externally for ringworm (leaves), rheumatic and arthritic pain, toothache, and sore throat (stems), colds and coughs (all parts); asthma and digestive disturbances (leaves, roots, fruits), bronchitis (roots, fruits, oil), haemorrhoids, migraine, and eye problems (fruits). In Ayurvedic medicine, internally for headache, catarrh, and gonorrhoea (leaves), fevers and bronchial congestion (roots); externally for ulcers (juice of leaves), and sores (medicated oil).
ECONOMIC USES Fresh leaves are burned with grass as a fumigant against mosquitoes.

VITIS

Vitaceae

This genus of some 65 species of sprawling deciduous vines and shrubs occurs throughout northern temperate regions. The most widely grown species is *V. vinifera* (grape vine), which originated in NW Asia. It has hundreds of cultivars, adapted to various climatic and pruning regimes, and is grown specifically for use as dessert grapes, currants, raisins, sultanas, and red or white wines. Some are suited to greenhouse culture in colder areas and make an attractive feature in conservatories. The grape vine is central to Jewish and Christian rituals, and is an integral part of most European cultures and cuisines, especially those of Mediterranean regions, where it has contributed to agriculture and trade since the Early Bronze Age. Grape vines were cultivated in Egypt over 4000 years ago; they were introduced to present-day wine-growing regions, such as Burgundy and the Rhineland, by the Romans. In the 19th century the aphid *Phylloxera vastatrix* devastated European vineyards. American species proved resistant, enabling European varieties to be grafted on to American rootstocks, and vineyards to be replanted. Various parts of the grape vine have long-established medicinal uses, mainly to relieve conditions associated with chronic congestion and excess heat. Grape fasts have long been a feature of therapeutic regimes, aimed at improved liver function and detoxification. Research in the 1990s showed that drinking one or two glasses of red wine a day improves cardiovascular health. Resveratrol, a flavonoid found in grape skins, has anti-cancer properties and is extracted for use in dietary supplements. Grape seeds contain polyphenols that are potent antioxidants. Extracts are taken to counteract damage from free radicals, thus retarding the ageing process.
CULTIVATION Deep, moist, humus-rich, neutral to alkaline soil in sun. Prune young plants to within 23–30cm (9–12in) of the ground in winter. In older vines, thin out old growths and shorten young growths in late summer. Plants may be damaged by powdery mildew, scale insects, mealybug, aphid, weevils, and caterpillars. Cultivars grown for fruit are prone to magnesium deficiency, grey mould, shanking, and various physiological disorders in unfavourable conditions.
PROPAGATION By seed sown in autumn or spring (species only); by hardwood cuttings in late winter; by "vine eye" cuttings, with a single bud, in early spring.
HARVEST Leaves and stems are collected in early summer and used fresh, preserved, or dried for decoctions, liquid extracts, and tinctures. Stems yield drops of liquid that are used directly as an eyewash and diuretic. Ripe fruits are used fresh for medicinal purposes, or processed to extract constituents.

Vitis vinifera (grape vine)
Deciduous tendril climber with fibrous bark, a twisted trunk, and palmately lobed leaves, 15cm (6in) long. Small, pale green flowers are borne in summer, followed by clusters of ovoid to rounded, green to purple-black fruits. Native to S and C Europe and NW Asia. ↕ 35m (120ft), pruned to 1–3m (3–9ft) in cultivation. ■ 'Ciotat' syn. 'Apiifolia', 'Laciniosa' (parsley-leafed grape) has finely cut leaves and small, sweet, pale green fruits. ↕ 6m (20ft). 'Incana' (dusty miller grape) has grey-green, unlobed or three-lobed leaves, which have a white, cobweb-like covering on the upper surface, and black fruits. ↕ 4–5m (12–15ft). ■ 'Müller Thurgau' is vigorous and late-flowering but early ripening, yielding medium-sized, aromatic, green fruits that produce Moselle-type wine. Suitable for regions with cool summers. ■ 'Purpurea' (Teinturier grape) has purple leaves, with a grey bloom when young, and small, unpalatable, shiny, black fruits. ↕ 7m (22ft). 'Schiava Grossa' syn. 'Black Hamburgh' produces large bunches of medium to large, purple-black, heavily bloomed dessert grapes, ripening midseason. Does well in pots.
HARDINESS Fully hardy.
PARTS USED Leaves, stems, fruits.
PROPERTIES A sour, astringent, cooling diuretic herb, reduces inflammation, controls bleeding, improves circulation, and clears toxins. Extracts have antioxidant and anti-cancer properties.
MEDICINAL USES Internally for varicose veins, heavy menstruation, menopausal syndrome, haemorrhage, urinary complaints, hypertension, high cholesterol, and skin rashes. Internally and externally for inflammations of the mouth, gums, throat, or eyes. Fruits are the basis of a cure for poor liver function.
CULINARY USES Blanched fresh leaves, or leaves preserved in brine, are used to parcel fillings, such as minced meat, fish, and rice (*dolmades*). Fruits are eaten raw, juiced, or made into jellies, sauces, wines, and vinegars. Grape seeds are used to coat cheeses, and are pressed for oil.
ECONOMIC USES Fruits are used fresh to make juices, wines, fortified and sparkling wines, sherry, liqueurs, spirits, and vinegars, and dried fruits as currants, raisins, or sultanas, according to the variety. Seeds yield a polyunsaturated oil, suitable for mayonnaise and cooking, especially frying. Cream of tartar or potassium bitartrate, a crystalline salt, is extracted from the residue or "marc" of pressed grapes and the sediment of wine barrels; it is used in baking powders, laxatives, and soldering fluxes. Grape skin extracts are used as colorants in the drinks industry; also in food supplements.

Vitis vinifera 'Ciotat'

Vitis vinifera 'Müller Thurgau'

Vitis vinifera 'Purpurea'

W

WASABIA

Wasabi

Brassicaceae

Only two species of perennials occur in this genus, which is endemic to Japan and is generally found beside mountain streams. *Wasabia japonica* is the oriental equivalent of horseradish (see *Armoracia rusticana*, p.130). Both belong

Wasabia japonica

to the same family as radish (see *Raphanus*, p.340), mustard (see *Brassica*, p.146), and *Sinapis* (see p.369); all contain pungent sulphur glycosides that give the characteristic burning taste. Wasabi is widely grown in Japan as a flavouring and condiment for raw fish (*sashimi*), but is exported to the West as powder.

CULTIVATION Moist to wet soil, ideally in clear running spring water, in partial shade, at 10–15°C (50–59°F) in the growing season.

PROPAGATION By seed sown in spring and kept constantly moist; by division in spring or autumn (most easily done when harvesting).

HARVEST Roots are lifted in spring or autumn, 15–24 months after planting, and used fresh, or dried and ground. Leaves and flowers are picked as flowering begins and used fresh.

■ *Wasabia japonica* syn. *Eutrema wasabi* (wasabi)
Perennial with stout creeping rhizomes, upright stems, and long-stalked, kidney-shaped basal leaves, to 15cm (6in) across. Racemes of small, white, four-petalled flowers are produced in spring, followed by linear–oblong, twisted pods containing a few large seeds. ‡ 20–40cm (8–16in), ↔ 30cm (12in).

HARDINESS Fully hardy.

PARTS USED Roots, leaves, and flowers.

PROPERTIES A pungent warming herb that stimulates the digestion.

MEDICINAL USES Internally as an antidote to fish poisoning.

CULINARY USES Fresh root is served grated or as a paste with *sashimi* (Japanese raw fish); powdered root is made into a paste to flavour meat and fish dishes, or blended with other ingredients as a dip. Leaves and flowers are made into a Japanese pickle known as *wasabi-zuke*.

WITHANIA
Solanaceae

About ten species of mostly evergreen shrubs belong to this genus, which is distributed mainly in Asia and Africa, with two species in Europe. Like most other members of the nightshade family (Solanaceae), they are rich in alkaloids and all parts should be regarded as poisonous. *Withania somnifera* occurs in stony places up to 1700m (5500ft), and as a weed

near habitation. It holds an important place in Ayurvedic medicine, similar to that of *Panax ginseng* (see p.300) in Chinese medicine, and is also widely used in the Middle East. In Oman and S Yemen, *Withania somnifera* and *W. qaraitica* (*gen-geneh*) are used interchangeably to treat a wide range of conditions. The plants are toxic to livestock, which ignore them, but are used in veterinary medicine to relieve mastitis.

CULTIVATION Dry stony soil in sun or partial shade. Cut back plants in early spring.

PROPAGATION By seed sown in spring; by greenwood cuttings with a heel in late spring.

HARVEST Roots are dried for use in medicated ghee, medicated oil, pastes, and powders.

⚠ **WARNING** Toxic if eaten.

■ *Withania somnifera* (ashwagandha, winter cherry)
Upright evergreen shrub with mealy stems and ovate leaves, 5–10cm (2–4in) long. Green to yellow, inconspicuous flowers grow in clusters in the leaf axils all year, followed by globose, orange-red berries, 6mm (¼in) across, enclosed in a papery inflated calyx. Found from the Mediterranean and Middle East to India and Sri Lanka. ‡ 60cm–2m (2–6ft), ↔ 30cm–1m (1–3ft).

HARDINESS Frost hardy.

PARTS USED Roots, fruits, leaves.

PROPERTIES A bitter–sweet, astringent, warming herb with a horse-like smell. It acts mainly on the reproductive and nervous systems, stimulates the uterus, and has sedative, rejuvenative, and aphrodisiac effects.

MEDICINAL USES Internally for debility, convalescence, nervous exhaustion, insomnia, geriatric complaints, wasting diseases, failure to thrive in children, impotence, infertility, joint and nerve pains, epilepsy, rheumatic pains, or multiple sclerosis (roots); also to induce contractions in prolonged labour or retained placenta (fruits, leaves). Usually given as a milk decoction in Ayurvedic medicine, often with raw sugar, honey, rice, or *Piper longum* (see p.320). Externally as a poultice for swellings, wounds, burns, stings, carbuncles, scorpion and snake bites (leaves).

CULINARY USES Seeds are used to coagulate milk.

ECONOMIC USES Powdered roots are an ingredient of various Ayurvedic tonic formulas and *Raja's Cup* coffee substitute.

Withania somnifera

WOLFIPORIA
Polyporaceae

A genus of 250 species of fungi, which live on tree roots and wood in Asia and temperate N America. *Wolfiporia cocos* is unusual in being distributed in both regions, which has resulted in a long history of use in both Chinese and native N American medicine. Fruiting bodies can be wild-collected from the base of hardwood or coniferous trees (often pines), providing expert identification is available. The fungus favours sandy loam.

CULTIVATION AND PROPAGATION Information is not available on cultivation techniques.

HARVEST Fungi are collected in winter and dried for decoctions and tinctures.

Wolfiporia cocos syn. *Poria cocos*, *Sclerotium cocos* (Indian bread, tuckahoe)
Subterranean fungus with large, globose to elliptic, tuber-like bodies, which have a hard, wrinkled, dark brown surface and a granular, pale pink interior. Found on the roots of hardwoods and conifers, often up to 60cm (24in) below the surface. ‡ 5–15cm (2–6in), ↔ 10–30cm (4–12in).

HARDINESS Fully hardy.

PARTS USED Whole plant (*fu ling*).

PROPERTIES A sweet sedative herb that is diuretic, regulates fluid metabolism, and calms the heart energy.

MEDICINAL USES Internally for palpitations, insomnia, emotional disturbances, abdominal bloating, urinary dysfunction, and diarrhoea. Used in many classic Chinese formulas, such as *si jun zi tang* ("soup of four noble things"), combining *W. cocos* with *Atractylodes macrocephala* (see p.137), *Glycyrrhiza uralensis* (see p.227), and *Panax ginseng* (see p.300).

X

XANTHIUM
Burweed
Asteraceae

Cosmopolitan in distribution, this genus consists of two species of large branched annuals. *Xanthium strumarium* is an invasive weed in many parts of the world, including Australia. It resembles *Arctium lappa* (burdock, see p.127) in appearance, with similar spiny burs that cling to clothing and passing animals. The name *strumarium* derives from the Latin *struma*, "swollen gland", and refers to the swelling fruits. The use of *Xanthium strumarium* was first mentioned in Chinese medicine during the Tang dynasty (AD618–907), in the *Thousand Ducat Prescriptions*. It is a common ingredient of Chinese patent remedies and is used to adulterate *Datura stramonium*.

Xanthium strumarium

CULTIVATION Poor dry soil in sun. Subject to statutory control as a weed in some countries, notably in parts of Australia.
PROPAGATION By seed sown in autumn or spring.
HARVEST Fruits are collected when ripe and dried for use in decoctions.

▣ *Xanthium strumarium* syn. *X. sibiricum* (cocklebur)
Stout annual with ovate–triangular, shallowly three-lobed, coarsely toothed leaves, to 15cm (6in) long. Pale green male and female flowers are borne separately in clusters in the leaf axils, followed by oblong spiny fruits, about 1cm (½in) long. Grows from Europe to E Asia; widely naturalized. ‡ 20cm–1m (8–36in), ↔ 10–60cm (4–24in).
HARDINESS Frost hardy.
PARTS USED Fruits (*cang er zi*).
PROPERTIES A pleasant-tasting, warming herb that relieves pain, relaxes spasms, and has anti-bacterial, anti-fungal, and anti-rheumatic effects.
MEDICINAL USES Internally for allergic rhinitis, sinusitis, catarrh, rheumatism, rheumatoid arthritis, lumbago, leprosy, and pruritus. Externally for pruritus.
▨ ▣

Z

ZANTHOXYLUM
Prickly ash

Rutaceae

This genus of about 250 species of spiny, deciduous or evergreen trees and shrubs occurs worldwide in warm-temperate and subtropical regions. Many species are cultivated in various parts of the world for wood, and for medicinal and culinary purposes. Most prickly ashes contain benzophenanthridine alkaloids, such as chelerythrine, an effective anti-microbial, and sanguinarine, an anti-inflammatory and dental plaque inhibitor that also occurs in *Sanguinaria canadensis* (see p.359). *Zanthoxylum americanum* is a traditional native N American remedy for toothache and was introduced into mainstream medicine in 1894 by John Nash, an Eclectic physician, who used it to treat typhus and cholera epidemics. In the C and S USA it is replaced by *Z. clavaherculis* (southern prickly ash). Many other prickly ashes have medicinal and culinary uses. Fruits of *Z. acanthopodium* are sold as a spice in Sikkim. Various parts of *Z. armatum* (winged prickly ash), which grows from Kashmir to SE Asia, are used to clean teeth and relieve toothache, and for poisoning fish; the seeds and young leaves are used as seasonings in China and India. *Zanthoxylum planispinum* (Chinese pepper, winged prickly ash) has similarly diverse uses. *Zanthoxylum schinifolium* and *Z. simulans* are used interchangeably with *Z. piperitum* as *hua jiao* in Chinese medicine. *Zanthoxylum* is from the Greek *xanthos*, "yellow", and *xylon*, "wood", referring to the yellow wood of certain species.
CULTIVATION Fertile soil in sun or shade. Remove dead wood (which is prone to coral spot fungus) and cut back in late winter or early spring.
PROPAGATION By seed sown in autumn; by root cuttings in late winter.
HARVEST Leaves (*Z. piperitum*) are picked during the growing season and used fresh. Bark is stripped in spring and dried for use in decoctions, liquid extracts, and tinctures. Fruits are collected in summer and dried for use in decoctions and liquid extracts.

▣ *Zanthoxylum americanum* (northern prickly ash, toothache tree)
Deciduous shrub or small tree with spiny branches and pinnately divided leaves. Small, yellow-green flowers appear before the new leaves in spring, followed by clusters of tiny black fruits. ‡ 4–8m (12–25ft), ↔ 6m (20ft).
HARDINESS Fully hardy.
PARTS USED Bark, fruits.
PROPERTIES A spicy, warming, stimulant herb that relieves pain, lowers fever, stimulates the circulation, improves digestion, controls diarrhoea, and is anti-rheumatic.
MEDICINAL USES Internally for rheumatic and arthritic complaints, lumbago, toothache, fevers, peripheral circulatory problems, abdominal chills, diarrhoea, indigestion, and chronic skin conditions. Externally for chronic joint pain and rheumatism. Combined with *Myrica cerifera* (see p.284) and *Zingiber officinale* (see p.411) for circulatory insufficiency; with *Actaea racemosa* for tinnitus; and with *Capsicum annuum* (see p.154), *Guaiacum officinale* (see p.229), and *Menyanthes trifoliata* (see p.278) for rheumatic complaints.
▥ ▨ ▣

Zanthoxylum capense syn. *Fagara capensis* (*kleinperdepram*, small knobwood, *umnungwana*)
Small, multi-branched tree with grey knobby bark, stout thorns, and sweetly aromatic, pinnate leaves, divided into 9–17 ovate, bluntly toothed leaflets, 2–4cm (¾–1½in) long, which have translucent oil glands along the margins. Clusters of inconspicuous, pale green, scented flowers appear in summer, followed by red-brown fruits, 5mm (¼in) across, which split open when ripe to reveal shiny black seeds. Native to E and N South Africa. ↔ 5–10m (15–30ft).
HARDINESS Frost hardy.
PARTS USED Bark, leaves, fruits.
PROPERTIES A warming, aromatic, antiseptic herb that reduces inflammation, lowers fever, relieves indigestion, and has painkilling effects.
MEDICINAL USES Internally for stomach upsets, diarrhoea, flatulence, colic, cramps, intestinal parasites, tuberculosis, bronchitis, paralysis, epilepsy, and snake bites. Externally for minor injuries, infected sores, insect bites, muscular aches and pains, lumbago, sciatica, toothache, and as a mouthwash for oral hygiene and dental or gum and mouth inflammations. Also used to treat anthrax in cattle, and to make anthrax-infected meat safe for consumption.
ECONOMIC USES Leaves added to potpourris.
▥ ▨ ▣ ▣ ◪

▣ *Zanthoxylum piperitum* (Japanese pepper, *sansho*)
Deciduous spiny shrub or small tree with pungent bark and shiny, aromatic, pinnate leaves, to 15cm (6in) long, divided into 11–23 ovate toothed leaflets, to 3.5cm (1½in) long. Clusters of small, yellow-green flowers appear in spring, followed by purple-red fruits containing black seeds. Native to China, Korea, Japan, and Taiwan. ↔ 2.5m (8ft). f. *inerme* lacks spines.
HARDINESS Fully hardy.
PARTS USED Leaves, bark, fruits, fruit pericarp or hull (*hua jiao*).
PROPERTIES A spicy, warming, stimulant herb that acts mainly on the spleen and stomach. It lowers blood pressure, has diuretic, anti-bacterial and anti-fungal effects, and is locally anaesthetic.

Zanthoxylum americanum

Zanthoxylum piperitum

MEDICINAL USES Internally for fever (bark), digestive complaints associated with cold (fruits), skin disorders, intestinal parasites. Externally for stings and bites (sap of young leaves).

CULINARY USES An important herb in Japanese cuisine. Young leaves and shoots (*kinome*) are used as garnish, and to flavour soups and salads. Fruit hulls are ground to flavour soups, noodles, and rice, and mixed with salt as a seasoning; also as an ingredient of Chinese five-spice powder, and a Japanese spice mixture known as *shichimi*. Seeds are simmered with soy sauce and rice wine to make *tsukudani*. Immature fruits are pickled.

🏠 ☒ ▱ 🛆 ✓

Zanthoxylum simulans syn. *Z. bungei* (Chinese pepper, *fagara*, Sichuan/Szechuan pepper) Spreading shrub or small tree with flattened spines and pinnate leaves, about 12cm (5in) long, divided into 7–11 ovate–oblong, toothed to scalloped leaflets, to 5cm (2in) long, which have prickly midribs. Small, yellow-green flowers are produced in clusters, to 6cm (2½in) across, in early summer, followed by small reddish fruits. Native to China and Taiwan. ‡↔ 3m (10ft).
HARDINESS Fully hardy.
PARTS USED Fruits.
PROPERTIES A pungent, warming, stimulant herb.
CULINARY USES Dry roasted fruits are used whole or ground as a condiment in Chinese cuisine, notably in Chinese five-spice powder.

☒ ✓

ZEA
Maize

Poaceae

This genus of four species of usually annual grasses is native to C America. *Zea mays* (maize) has been cultivated for over 5500 years – possibly as long as 7000 years – in the Americas, from Chile to Canada. Following the Spanish conquest of Mexico and Peru in the 16th century, maize was taken to Africa, and spread worldwide. It tolerates a range of climates and is now a major crop in many parts of the world. Maize makes exotic feature plants; varieties with variegated leaves and multi-coloured ears have been grown in containers and borders since at least the 19th century. The culinary uses of maize are well known. There are five principal kinds: dent maize (mostly white to yellow grains); flint maize (which shrinks on drying, and may have white, yellow, red, purple, or blue-black grains, often striped or mottled); popcorn (a primitive strain with hard grains, specifically grown for popcorn); sweet corn (with a higher sugar content and best as a vegetable); and waxy maize (containing starch with a waxy appearance). Dent and flint maize are widely grown for oil, cereals, flour, and animal fodder. Waxy maize yields a tapioca-like starch, used mainly in the Far East. Less familiar is the role of maize as a medicinal herb. The female flowers (cornsilk) were once used in spells and divination; they contain allantoin (as found in *Symphytum officinale*, see p.377), alkaloids, and large amounts of potassium that compensate for

the loss in urine, owing to the herb's diuretic effect. Aztec herbals mention the plant, which was apparently used to clear heat from the heart. It was also used in Mayan and Incan medicine. *Zea mays* reached China from N America after Li Shi Zhen's time (1518–93) and was first mentioned as a herb in the *Sichuan Journal of Chinese Herbal Medicine* in the 20th century. Its most recent use is in the form of a gel, extracted from corn bran, which is used as a medical dressing for leg ulcers, pressure sores, and other slow-healing skin conditions.

CULTIVATION Rich, well-drained soil in sun. *Zea mays* is wind-pollinated and fruits better if grown in a block. Birds may damage the ears.
PROPAGATION By seed sown in spring at 18°C (64°F).
HARVEST Cornsilk is collected in summer before the strands wither and is dried for use in decoctions, infusions, liquid extracts, and syrup. Ears are cut when immature for use as a vegetable, and when ripe for processing as cereals, flour, oil, and syrup.

■ *Zea mays* (corn, maize)
Robust upright annual with arching, pointed, lanceolate leaves, 30cm–1.5m (1–5ft) long. Male and female flowers are borne separately on the same plant in early summer; males in a tassel, to 40cm (16in) long, at the top of the stem; females in a cluster in the leaf axils, terminating in long filaments (cornsilk) and enclosed by overlapping, leaf-like sheaths that form a husk. Female flowers are followed by an ear, about 20cm (8in) long, consisting of close-set rows of angular seeds, about 5mm (¼in) long. Native to Mexico. ‡ 2–3m (6–10ft), ↔ 45–60cm (18–24in). 'Black Aztec' produces white unripe seeds that turn blue-black when ripe. A pre-Columbian cultivar, reportedly grown for 2000 years. 'Strawberry Corn' bears rounded ears, 5cm (2in) long, of mahogany-red seeds, enclosed in yellow-green husks. Suitable for popping. ‡ 1–1.2m (3–4ft), ↔ 45cm (18in). 'Variegata' has yellow-seeded ears and creamy white-striped foliage. ‡ 90cm (36in), ↔ 30–45cm (12–18in).
HARDINESS Half hardy.
PARTS USED Stigmas and styles of female flowers (cornsilk, *yu mi xu*), fruits (ears), seeds, oil.
PROPERTIES A sweet, cooling, soothing

Zea mays

herb that is diuretic, lowers blood sugar levels, stimulates bile flow, and prevents formation of urinary stones.
MEDICINAL USES Internally for cystitis, urinary stones, urethritis, prostatitis, and enuresis in children. Combines well with *Elymus repens* (see p.201) and *Arctostaphylos uva-ursi* (see p.127), or *Agathosma* spp. (see p.106) for cystitis; with *Agrimonia eupatoria* (see p.107) and *Equisetum arvense* (see p.203) for enuresis; and with *Aphanes arvensis* (see p.124) and *Eupatorium purpureum* (see p.209) for urinary stones. Used similarly in Chinese medicine for urinary problems, also for gallstones, jaundice, hepatitis, and cirrhosis. Externally, in the form of a poultice made from cornmeal, for sores or boils.
CULINARY USES Immature ears are eaten whole as a vegetable. Fresh unripe seeds are cooked as a vegetable, or roasted and dried for soups, stews, and chilli sauces. Cornmeal is used to make polenta, tortillas, tacos, tamales, and enchiladas, and in breads and cakes. Ripe seeds are heated to make popcorn. Fresh leaves and husks are used for wrapping foods, especially tamales.
ECONOMIC USES Dried ripe seeds are processed as cereals and flour (cornstarch, grits, cornmeal, cornflakes), fermented to make alcoholic drinks, such as *chicha* (beer), or pressed for oil. Corn syrup is extracted from fresh maize and may be blended with molasses.

☒ ☒ ▱ ☒ 🛆 ✓ ✓

ZINGIBER
Ginger

Zingiberaceae

A genus of about 100 species of perennials, native to tropical Asia. All have reed-like stems and aromatic rhizomes. Gingers of various kinds are grown commercially in all warm regions, notably in Jamaica, which produces some of the finest plants. Fresh rhizomes, bought for flavouring, may be grown in containers as exotic foliage plants, yielding a further supply of rhizomes when the canes die down in winter. *Zingiber officinale* has been cultivated for medicinal and culinary purposes since earliest times. It was listed as a taxable commodity by the Romans in AD200, and first mentioned in Chinese medical literature during the later Han dynasty (AD25–220). In Ayurvedic medicine *Z. officinale* is known as *vishwabhesaj*, "universal medicine", and in both Ayurvedic and Chinese medicine occurs in about half of all prescriptions. Ginger is rich in volatile oil, gingerols, and shogaols. Shogaols, which are a breakdown product of gingerols, produced only on drying, are twice as pungent as gingerols; thus dried ginger is hotter than fresh and is used for different purposes in Chinese medicine. *Zingiber officinale* is of worldwide importance as a flavouring. Other species, such as the SE Asian *Z. cassumar* (cassumar ginger), are used in the countries of origin. The shoots and aromatic flowers of *Z. mioga* (Japanese ginger, mioga ginger) are important in Japanese cuisine, either fresh or pickled as a flavouring. The leaves of *Z. zerumbet* (bitter ginger, wild ginger) are used for flavouring and wrapping foods; the rhizomes contain zerumbone, a cytotoxic compound used to treat cancer in China. *Zingiber* comes from the Greek *zingiberis*, "ginger".

CULTIVATION Well-drained, humus-rich, neutral to alkaline soil, in sun or partial shade, with high humidity. Ginger is treated as an annual or biennial crop; plants need a ten-month growing season for optimum rhizome production. Oldest growths may be removed when new shoots appear. Ginger is prone to bacterial wilt in parts of India, China, and Australia (Queensland).

PROPAGATION By division in late spring as growth begins.

HARVEST Rhizomes are lifted during the growing season for uses where lack of fibrousness is important, or when dormant for drying. Young fresh rhizomes bought for cooking will keep for 2–3 months in a cool dry place; they are soaked in brine and vinegar before processing in sugar syrup as crystallized ginger. Sliced fresh rhizomes are made into infusions and cordials for medicinal use. Mature rhizomes are peeled ("white ginger"), limed ("bleached"), or left unpeeled ("coated") before storing whole, or ground for use in infusions, decoctions, tinctures, and powders. Oil is distilled from unpeeled, dried, ground rhizomes.

■ *Zingiber officinale* (ginger)
Deciduous perennial with thick branching rhizomes, stout upright stems, and pointed lanceolate leaves, to 15cm (6in) long, arranged in two ranks on either side of the stem. Yellow-green flowers, with a deep purple, yellow-marked lip, are produced in dense ovoid spikes, 5cm (2in) long, consisting of overlapping, pale green to ochre bracts, and followed by three-valved, fleshy capsules. Native to tropical Asia. ↕ 1.5m (5ft), ↔ indefinite.

HARDINESS Min. 10°C (50°F).

PARTS USED Rhizomes (*jiang*), oil.

PROPERTIES A sweet, pungent, aromatic, warming herb that is expectorant, increases perspiration, improves digestion and liver function, controls nausea, vomiting, and coughing, stimulates the circulation, relaxes spasms, and relieves pain.

MEDICINAL USES Internally for motion sickness, nausea, morning sickness, indigestion, colic, abdominal chills, colds, coughs, influenza, and peripheral circulatory problems. Not given to patients with inflammatory skin complaints, ulcers of the digestive tract, or high fever. Externally for spasmodic pain, rheumatism, lumbago, menstrual cramps, and sprains. Often combined with *Gentiana lutea* (see p.223) and *Rheum palmatum* (see p.344) for digestive complaints. In Chinese medicine, internally, for coughs, cold, diarrhoea, vomiting, and abdominal pain associated with cold (fresh rhizome); uterine bleeding and blood in the urine (fresh carbonized rhizome); abdominal fullness and oedema (rhizome peel); coldness associated with shock, digestive disturbances arising from deficient spleen energy, and chronic bronchitis (dried rhizome).

Zingiber officinale

CULINARY USES Fresh young rhizomes (green ginger) are juiced, eaten raw, preserved in syrup, and candied; also used in marinades, soups, curries, chutneys, pickles, meat and fish dishes, and SE Asian stir-fried dishes. Pickled ginger (*gari*) is used in Japanese cooking, especially to flavour *sushi*. Dried ground ginger is used to flavour cakes, biscuits, curries, chutneys, and sauces.

ECONOMIC USES Oil is used in perfumery. Dried ground ginger and essential oil are used in commercial food flavouring, especially in confectionery, soft drinks, and condiments. Extracts are added to herb teas, cordials and soft drinks (notably ginger beer and ginger ale).

▢ ▨ ▤ ▧ ▨ ▣

ZIZIPHUS

Rhamnaceae

A cosmopolitan genus of about 85 species of deciduous and evergreen trees, shrubs, and subshrubs, found in tropical and subtropical regions. *Ziziphus jujuba* (jujube) has long been cultivated in China for its fruits, known in China as *da zao*, "big date", which are "to the Chinese what apples are to Americans" (*Herbal Emissaries*, 1992). Plants were introduced from China to W Asia some 3000 years ago, and have been used in Chinese medicine since at least the later Han dynasty (AD25–220). Jujubes were also grown by the ancient Greeks and Romans, who introduced the plant to Spain, where it became naturalized. By the 17th century there were 43 cultivars: now there are hundreds. Jujube fruits are sweet and nutritious, containing vitamins A, B2, and C, calcium, phosphorus, and iron, together with saponins, flavonoids, and mucilage. Research has shown that they improve liver function, and increase stamina and immunity. They moderate the actions of other herbs and make prescriptions more palatable. The fruits of *Z. mauritiana* (Indian jujube) are used for flavouring and made into preserves, chutneys, sauces, and drinks. *Ziziphus* is from the Persian *zizfum*, or *zizafun*, the name for *Z. lotus* (African lotus, jujube lotus), mentioned in many ancient texts, including the Greek myth about the lotus-eaters.

CULTIVATION Well-drained, moist to dry soil in sun. Cut back in winter to encourage the new growth, on which fruits are borne. *Ziziphus*

jujuba tolerates a wide range of growing conditions but needs a hot dry summer to fruit well. *Ziziphus* spp. are subject to certain plant controls as a weed in parts of Australia.

PROPAGATION By seed sown when ripe in sandy soil; by suckers in spring; by hardwood cuttings in autumn and winter; by root cuttings in late winter at 5–10°C (41–50°F).

HARVEST Fruits are collected in early autumn when ripe, then parboiled, and sun-dried. Seeds are removed from the ripe fruits and dried. Both are used in decoctions.

■ *Ziziphus jujuba* syn. *Z. sativa*, *Z. vulgaris* (Chinese date, jujube)
Deciduous tree or large shrub with spiny twigs, and ovate–elliptic, leathery leaves, to 6cm (2½in) long. Small, yellow, five-petalled flowers are borne in clusters in the axils in spring and summer, followed by oblong–ovoid, red-brown, fleshy fruits with one or two seeds. Native to temperate Asia. ↕ 9m (28ft), ↔ 7m (22ft). 'Lang' produces large, oblong to pear-shaped, mahogany-red fruits that dry well. 'Li' bears rounded to ovoid, brown fruits, to 5cm (2in) long; excellent when fresh.

HARDINESS Frost hardy.

PARTS USED Fruits (*da zao*), seeds (*suan zao ren*).

PROPERTIES A mucilaginous, nutritive, sedative herb with a sweet and sour taste; it controls allergic responses, relieves coughing, soothes irritated or damaged tissues, protects the liver, prevents stress ulcer formation, and has a tonic effect on spleen and stomach energies. It also strengthens the immune system.

MEDICINAL USES Internally for chronic fatigue, loss of appetite, diarrhoea, anaemia, irritability, and hysteria (fruits); palpitations, insomnia, nervous exhaustion, night sweats, and excessive perspiration (seeds). Often combined with *Angelica polymorpha* var. *sinensis* (see p.122) or *Panax ginseng* (see p.300), and added to tonic prescriptions as a buffer to improve synergy and minimize side-effects. Long-term use reputedly improves the complexion. Fruits are also used to sweeten and flavour medicines.

CULINARY USES Fruits are eaten fresh, semi-dried or dried, stewed, pickled, fermented, or preserved in syrup or honey. Jujube flour is an ingredient of the fermented Korean paste known as *kochujang*.

▨ ▨ ▤ ▧

Ziziphus jujuba

GLOSSARY OF TERMS

BOTANICAL

ACID [of soil]. With a pH value of less than 7.

ADVENTITIOUS [of roots]. Arising directly from a stem or leaf.

AERIAL ROOT. *See* root.

AGGREGATE SPECIES. A group of closely related species or microspecies that are often regarded as a single species.

AIR-LAYERING. A method of propagation by which a portion of stem is induced to root by enclosing it in a suitable medium while still attached to the parent plant.

ALKALINE [of soil]. With a pH value of more than 7.

ALPINE. A plant that is native or suited to montane conditions, or that grows above the tree line in mountainous regions; loosely applied to rock garden plants that may be grown at relatively low altitudes.

ALTERNATE [of leaves]. Borne singly at each node, on either side of a stem.

ANNUAL. A plant that completes its life cycle in one year.

ANTHER. The part of a stamen that produces pollen; it is usually borne on a filament.

APEX. The tip or growing point of an organ such as a leaf or shoot.

AQUATIC. A plant that grows in water.

ARCHITECTURAL. A term used in horticulture to describe plants that have strong, often spectacular shapes.

ARIL. A fleshy or hairy, often brightly coloured covering around a seed, as in nutmeg (*Myristica fragrans*).

AWN. A stiff, bristle-like projection commonly found on grass seeds and spikelets.

AXIL. The upper angle between a leafstalk and the stem, or (in trees) between a branch and the trunk.

AXILLARY. Growing in the axil.

BASAL. Growing at the base.

BEAKED. Having a beak-shaped part or projection.

BEDDING PLANT. A plant that is usually planted in quantity to provide a temporary display.

BIENNIAL. A plant that flowers and dies in the second season after germination, producing only stems, roots, and leaves in the first season.

BIPINNATE. A pinnate leaf in which the leaflets are further subdivided pinnately.

BLOOM. 1. A flower or blossom. 2. A fine, waxy, whitish or bluish-white coating on stems, leaves, or fruits.

BOLE. The trunk of a tree from ground level to the first major branch.

BOLT. To produce flowers and seed prematurely.

BRACT. A modified leaf at the base of a flower or flower cluster. Bracts vary greatly in size and form; they may be reduced and scale-like, large and brightly coloured, or leaf-like.

BUD. A rudimentary or condensed shoot containing embryonic leaves or flowers.

BUDDING (bud grafting). A method of grafting in which a bud (the scion), together with a small piece of bark, is removed from the desired variety, and inserted into a slit made in the bark of the chosen rootstock (the stock).

BULB. A storage organ consisting mainly of fleshy scales and swollen modified leaf-bases on a much reduced stem. Bulbs usually, but not always, grow underground.

BULBIL. A small, bulb-like organ, usually borne in a leaf axil or flower head, that detaches and grows into a new plant.

BULBLET. A small bulb produced at the base of a mature one.

BULBOUS. 1. Growing from or bearing bulbs. 2. Shaped like a bulb.

BUR. 1. A prickly or spiny fruit, or aggregate of fruits. 2. A woody outgrowth on the stems of certain trees.

CALCAREOUS. Alkaline, chalky.

CALYX (pl. calcyces). The outer part of a flower, usually small and green but sometimes showy and brightly coloured, that is formed from the sepals and encloses the petals in bud.

CAPSULE A dry fruit that splits open when ripe to release its seeds.

CATKIN. A flower cluster, normally pendulous, in which the flowers lack petals, are often stalkless, and surrounded by scale-like bracts. They are usually unisexual.

CHEMOTYPE. A population of plants within a species that differs consistently in certain chemical constituents.

CHICON. The blanched compact shoots of chicory (*Cichoricum intybus*).

CHLOROPHYLL. The green pigment in plants that absorbs light, providing the energy for photosynthesis.

CLADODE. A flattened, leaf-like stem.

CLIMBER. A plant that climbs using other plants or objects as a support: a leafstalk climber by coiling its leafstalks around supports; a root climber by producing aerial supporting roots; a self-clinging climber by means of suckering pads; a twining climber by coiling stems. Also referred to as a vine.

CLOUD FOREST. A mountain forest that is constantly covered in mist, creating stunted trees and abundant epiphytes.

COMPOUND LEAF. Divided into two or more leaflets.

CONE. The reproductive or woody, seed-bearing structure of a conifer.

COPPICE. To cut back to near ground level periodically in order to produce vigorous shoots for ornamental or practical purposes.

CORM. A bulb-like, underground storage organ consisting mainly of a swollen stem base and often surrounded by a papery tunic.

COROLLA. The often showy and coloured part of a flower formed by the petals.

CORONA (crown). A cup-shaped or trumpet-shaped, petal-like outgrowth borne in the centre of some flowers.

CORYMB. A flower cluster in which the inner flower stalks are shorter than the outer, resulting in a rounded or flat-topped head.

CREEPER. A plant that grows close to the ground, usually rooting as it spreads.

CRESTED. Shaped like a crest or ridge.

CRISPED. Minutely wavy-edged.

CROP. A cultivated plant that is grown on a field scale.

CROWN. 1. The part of the plant at or just below the soil surface from which new shoots are produced and to which they die back in autumn. 2. The upper branched or spreading part of a tree or other plant. 3. A corona.

CULTIVAR. A plant variety produced in cultivation, often by selective breeding. A cultivar is indicated by enclosing its name in single quotation marks, e.g. *Lavandula angustifolia* 'Hidcote'.

CUTTING. A section of a plant that is removed and used for propagation.

CYME. A flower cluster in which the first flower is the terminal bud of the main stem, and subsequent flowers develop as terminal buds of lateral stems.

DEAD-HEAD. To remove fading or dead flower heads in order to promote further growth or flowering, prevent seeding, or improve appearance.

DECIDUOUS. Describing a tree or shrub that sheds its leaves annually at the end of the growing season; semi-deciduous plants lose only some leaves.

DEHISCENT. Splitting open along predetermined lines to release contents.

DELTOID–OVATE [of leaves]. Midway between triangular and egg-shaped.

DIE-BACK. Death of the tips of shoots owing, for example, to frost or disease.

DISC FLORET OR DISC FLOWER. One of several or many small, tubular, usually fertile, and often individually inconspicuous flowers that form the central portion ("disc") of a composite flower head, such as in a daisy (*Bellis perennis*).

DIVISION. A method of propagation in which a perennial plant is split into several parts, one or more of which are replanted separately.

DORMANT. Alive but inactive.

ELLIPTIC [of leaves]. Broadest at the centre and narrowing towards each end.

ENTIRE [of leaves]. With untoothed margins.

EPIPHYTE. A plant that in nature grows on the surface of another without being parasitic.

ERICACEOUS. 1. Plants of the family Ericaceae, which mostly require lime-free soils of pH6.5 or less. 2. Compost with a suitable pH for growing lime-hating plants.

ESCAPE. A non-native plant originally cultivated in an area but now found growing in the wild.

ESPALIER. A plant trained with the main stem vertical, and branches horizontally on either side in a single plane.

EVERGREEN. Describing a plant that retains its foliage all year round and sheds older leaves at intervals throughout the year. Semi-evergreen plants retain only some leaves or lose older leaves only when the new growth is produced.

F1 HYBRID. The first generation derived from crossing two distinct individuals of pure bred lines. Offspring are vigorous, but seed from F1 hybrids does not come true to type.

FILAMENT. The slender, stalk-like part of the stamen that bears the anther.

FLEXUOUS. Bending or curving readily.

FLORET. A single flower in a head of many flowers.

FLOWER. The basic reproductive unit of an angiosperm (flowering plant). The basic flower forms are: *single*, with one row of usually 4–6 petals; *semi-double*, with more petals, usually in two rows; *double*, with many petals in several rows and few or no stamens; *fully double*, usually rounded in shape, with densely packed petals and with the stamens obscured.

FLOWER HEAD. A mass of small flowers or florets that together appear as one flower.

FORCE. To induce early growth, flowering, or fruiting in a plant.

FREE-FLOWERING. Flowering more easily or more generously than usual.

FROND. The compound leaf of a fern. Some ferns produce both barren and fertile fronds, the fertile fronds bearing spores.

FROST HARDY. Withstanding temperatures down to -5°C (23°F).

FRUIT. The structure in plants that bears one or more seeds, e.g. a berry or nut.

GENUS. A group of related species, denoted by the first part of the scientific name, e.g. *Acacia*.

GLAND-DOTTED. Marked with small, round, secretory cells.

GLAUCOUS. Covered with a waxy or powdery bloom.

GLOBOSE. Spherical.

GRAFTING. A method of propagation by which a section of stem (scion) of one plant is united with the rootstock of a different plant.

HABIT. The characteristic growth or general appearance of a plant.

HALF HARDY. Not tolerating frost, but withstanding temperatures down to 0°C (32°F).

HARDY. Tolerating year-round climatic conditions in temperate regions, including frost, without protection.

HEARTWOOD. The central core of wood in a tree trunk, consisting of non-functioning tissues that have become blocked with resins, tannins, gums, and oils.

HEEL. The small portion of old wood that is retained at the base of a cutting when it is manually detached from the stem.

HERBACEOUS. Describing a perennial that dies down at the end of the growing season but remains alive.

HIPS. The characteristic fruits of the genus *Rosa*. Also called roseships.

HOLDFAST. A structure found at the base of many algae in flowing or tidal water, which serves to attach the plant to a support.

HOST. A plant or animal that supports and nourishes a parasite.

HUMUS. The soft, moist, dark brown to black content of soil, derived from decaying plant and animal matter.

HYBRID. The offspring of genetically different parents, usually produced accidentally or artificially in cultivation, but occasionally arising in the wild.

INFLORESCENCE. A cluster of flowers with a distinct arrangement, e.g. corymb, cyme, panicle, raceme, spike, umbel.

INTERTIDAL. The zone of the shore between high- and low-water marks.

KINO. A dark red resin, used as an astringent and in tanning, which is obtained mainly from *Eucalyptus* spp. and from *Pterocarpus marsupium*.

LANCEOLATE [of leaves]. Narrow and tapering at both ends.

LATERAL. A side growth that arises from a shoot or root.

LATEX. A fluid produced by many plants, containing substances such as starch, alkaloids, mineral salts, and sugars; often white in appearance.

LAX. Loose, or with loosely arranged parts.

LAYERING. Propagation method by which a stem pegged down into the soil will produce roots and shoots while still attached to the parent plant.

LEADER. The dominant shoot at the apex of a tree or shrub.

LEAFLET. A subdivision of a compound leaf.

LEGUME. 1. A plant of the pea family Leguminosae, or of one of its three sub-families: Caesalpiniaceae, Mimosaceae, and Papilionaceae. 2. A one-celled, dehiscent fruit, splitting into two when mature, belonging to the family Leguminosae, as above.

LIANA. A woody climbing plant, found in tropical forests, often with very large stems that loop around and between trees.

LICHEN. An organism formed by the symbiotic association of a fungus and an alga.

LIFT. To take out of the ground for transplanting or harvesting.

LIME. Compounds of calcium; the amount of lime in soil determines whether it is alkaline, neutral, or acid.

LINEAR [of leaves]. Very narrow with parallel sides.

LIP or LABIUM [of a flower]. A lobe comprising two or more flat or sometimes pouched perianth segments.

LITHOPHYTE. A plant that in the wild grows on bare rock or stone.

LOAM. Well-structured, fertile soil that is moisture-retentive but free-draining.

LOBE. A rounded projection, forming part of a larger structure.

MICROPROPAGATION. Propagation of plants by tissue culture.

MIDRIB. The main central vein of a leaf, or the central stalk to which the leaflets of a pinnate leaf are attached.

MINERAL SALTS. Inorganic substances in plants, such as potassium, silicon, calcium, and selenium, that can supplement mineral shortages in the body.

MONOCARPIC. Flowering and fruiting only once before dying. Such plants may take several years to reach flowering size.

MONOTYPIC. A division that has only one subdivision, e.g. a family with just one genus; a genus with a single species.

MONTANE. Inhabiting mountainous regions.

MOUND-LAYERING. A method of propagation, suitable for small shrubs and subshrubs, by which sandy soil is mounded up round the crown of the plant, encouraging upper shoots to develop roots.

MULCH A layer of (usually) organic matter applied to the soil over or around a plant to conserve moisture, protect the roots from temperature fluctuations, reduce weed growth, and enrich the soil.

NATURALIZE. To establish and grow as if in the wild.

NECTAR. A sweet sugary liquid secreted by a nectary gland, usually found in the flower (floral), but sometimes on the leaves or stem (extra-floral).

NEUTRAL [of soil]. With a pH value of 7, the point at which soil is neither acid nor alkaline.

NODE. The point on a stem from which a leaf or leaves arise.

NOTCH. A V-shaped indentation.

NUTLET. A one-seeded portion of a fruit that fragments when mature.

OBLANCEOLATE [of leaves]. Having a broad rounded apex and a tapering base.

OBOVATE [of leaves]. Egg-shaped in outline, with the narrower end at the base.

OFFSET. A small plant that arises by natural vegetative reproduction, usually at the base of the mother plant.

OPPOSITE [of leaves]. Borne two to each node, one opposite the other.

ORNAMENTAL. A plant grown for decorative purposes.

OVARY. The swollen base of the female part of the flower. It is hollow, containing one or more ovules (embryonic seeds). After fertilization, the ovary wall forms the outer layer of the fruit.

OVATE [of leaves]. Egg-shaped in outline, with the broader end at the base, becoming more pointed at the tip.

PALMATE [of leaves]. Having four or more leaflets arising from a single point, as in horse chestnut (*Aesculus hippocastanum*).

PANICLE. A compound branched raceme in which the flowers develop on stalks (peduncles) arising from the main stem.

PANTROPICAL. Tropical regions in all parts of the world.

PARASITE. A plant that lives in or on another (the host), from which it obtains nourishment.

PEA-LIKE [of flowers]. Of the same structure as a pea flower.

PELTATE [of leaves]. Shield-shaped to circular, with the stalk inserted towards or at the centre of the underside, rather than at the edge.

413

PERENNIAL. Describing a plant that lives for at least three seasons.

PERFOLIATE [of leaves]. Having leaf bases that completely encircle the stem.

PERIANTH. The outer part of a flower, consisting of the calyx (sepals) and corolla (petals).

PETAL [of a flower]. A segment of the corolla.

PH. The scale by which the acidity of soil is measured, in which 7 is neutral, lower values are more acid, and higher values are more alkaline.

PHOTOSYNTHESIS. The process in green plants by which carbohydrates are produced from carbon dioxide and water, using light energy absorbed by chlorophyll, and generating oxygen as a byproduct.

PINCH OUT. To remove the growing tips of a plant to induce the production of side shoots.

PINNATE [of leaves]. Describing a compound leaf in which the leaflets grow in two rows on each side of the midrib.

PISTIL. The female part of a flower, comprising the ovary, stigma, and style.

PLUMULE. The embryonic shoot of a seed-bearing plant.

POLLINATION. The transfer of pollen from the anthers to the stigma of the same or different flowers, usually resulting in the fertilization of the embryonic seeds in the ovary.

PROSTRATE. With stems growing along the ground. Also called procumbent.

PSEUDOBULB. A swelling at the base of the stem in which epiphytic orchids store water and nutrients.

RACEME. An unbranched flower cluster with individual flowers produced on short equal stalks, evenly spaced along a central stem, those at the base developing before those farther up.

RADICLE. The embryonic root, normally the first organ to emerge from a seed on germination.

RAY FLORET. One of the flowers, usually with strap-shaped petals, in the outer ring of a composite flower head, such as a daisy (*Bellis perennis*).

RAY PETAL. The petal or fused petals, often showy, of a ray floret.

RECEPTACLE. The enlarged tip of the flower stalk that carries the parts of the flower.

RECURVED. Curved backwards.

RESIN. A solid or semi-solid compound, insoluble in water, occurring with varying amounts of oil and/or gum, which exudes from certain trees and other plants.

RETTING. The process of soaking cut stems, usually of fibre-producing plants, in order to promote bacterial action that helps separate fibrous tissues.

REVERT. Describing a plant that has returned to its original state, as when a plain green shoot is produced on a variegated plant, or a double-flowered hybrid produces single-flowered offspring.

REVOLUTE. Rolled backwards and downwards at the margin.

RHIZOME. An underground stem that grows horizontally, branching at intervals and bearing roots and leafy shoots.

ROOT. The part of a plant, normally underground, that functions as anchorage, and through which water and nutrients are absorbed. An aerial root emerges from the stem at some distance above the soil level.

ROOTBALL. The roots and accompanying soil or compost visible when a plant is lifted.

ROOTSTOCK (stock). A plant on to which another variety, species, or genus is grafted.

ROSETTE. A rose-like cluster of parts, as in a group of leaves radiating from a central point, often at the base of a low-growing plant.

RUNNER. A horizontally spreading, usually slender shoot that grows from the base of a plant along the ground, producing plantlets along its length; often confused with stolon.

SAPROPHYTIC. Lives and feeds on dead organic matter.

SCARIFY. To scar the coat of a seed by abrasion in order to ease water intake and speed germination.

SCLEROPHYLL. A woody plant with small, leathery, evergreen leaves, characteristic of hot dry areas.

SCLEROTIUM. The compact dormant phase of certain fungi, which gives rise to new growth or spore-producing structures.

SCREE. 1. An accumulation of rock fragments on a hillside.
2. A deep layer of stone chippings mixed with a small amount of loam. It provides extremely sharp drainage for plants that cannot tolerate moisture at their base.

SEED HEAD. Any usually dry fruit that contains ripe seeds.

SELF-FERTILE. Producing viable seed when fertilized with its own pollen.

SELF-SOW OR SELF-SEED. To produce seedlings around the parent plant.

SEPAL. Part of the calyx of a flower, typically green and leaf-like.

SERIES. The name applied to a group of similar but not identical plants, usually annual cultivars, linked by one or more common features, e.g. *Tropaeolum majus* Whirlybird Series.

SHEATH. A cylindrical structure that surrounds or encircles, partially or fully, another plant organ such as a stem.

SHOOT. The aerial part of a plant that bears the leaves, buds, and reproductive parts. A side shoot arises from the side of a main shoot.

SHRUB. A woody plant with several main stems arising from or near the base.

SHRUBLET. A miniature shrub.

SIMPLE [of leaves]. Not divided into leaflets.

SOILLESS COMPOST. A lightweight potting compost, based on peat, coir (coconut fibre), or other fibrous materials. Also called loamless compost.

SORI (sing. sorus). Clusters of spore-producing structures on the undersurface of fertile fern fronds.

SPADIX (pl. spadices). A spike-like flower cluster that is usually fleshy and bears numerous small flowers. Characteristic of the aroid family (Araceae), e.g. *Arisaema*.

SPATHE. A large bract, frequently coloured and showy, that encloses a flower cluster, especially the spadix of aroids (as above).

SPHAGNUM. 1. Bog or peat mosses, characteristic of waterlogged acid areas, that decompose to form peat. 2. A genus of moss (see p.372). The moisture-retentive character of sphagnum makes it an ideal component of some growing media.

SPECIES. Individuals that are alike and naturally breed with each other, denoted by the second part of the scientific name.

SPIKE. A flower cluster composed of stalkless flowers attached to a long central stem.

SPIKELET. 1. The flowering unit of grasses comprising one or several flowers with basal bracts. 2. A small spike, part of a branched flower cluster.

SPORE. The minute reproductive structure of flowerless plants, e.g. ferns, fungi, and mosses.

SPORT. A mutation, caused by an accidental or induced change in the genetic make-up of a plant, which gives rise to a shoot with different characteristics from those of the parent plant.

SPUR. 1. A hollow projection from a petal, often producing nectar, as in *Corydalis*. 2. A short stem bearing a group of flower buds, such as is found on fruit trees.

STAMEN. The male part of a flower, typically consisting of a filament, bearing an anther that produces pollen.

STANDARD. 1. A tree or shrub with a clear length of bare stem below the first branches. Certain shrubs, e.g. roses and bay, may be trained to form standards. 2. One of the three inner and often erect segments of an iris flower. 3. The larger, usually upright back petal of a flower belonging to a plant of the family Papilionaceae.

STERILE. Infertile, not bearing spores, pollen, seeds, etc.

STIGMA. The female part of the flower, borne at the tip of the style, that receives pollen.

STOCK. *See* rootstock.

STOLON. An arching or spreading stem that is unable to bear its own weight, bending down to the ground and rooting at its tip, or from a node, to produce a new plant.

STOP. To remove certain growing points of a plant so as to control growth or the size and number of flowers.

STRAP-SHAPED [of leaves]. Long and narrow.

STRATIFY. To break the dormancy of some seeds by exposing them to a period of cold.

STROBILUS OR STROBILE (pl. strobili or strobiles). A cone or cone-like structure.

STYLE. Part of the female organ in a flower, consisting of a narrow, often elongated extension of the ovary, on which the stigma is borne.

SUBALPINE Describing a plant that grows below the treeline in mountainous regions.

SUBSHRUB. A small, shrub-like plant, woody only at the base.

SUCCULENT. A plant with fleshy, water-storing leaves or stems, adapted to growing where water is either in short supply or where it is saline (salty).

SUCKER. A shoot that arises from the root of a plant, often emerging at some distance from the parent plant.

TAPROOT. A stout main root, sometimes swollen to store nutrients.

TENDER. Vulnerable to low temperatures. Tender plants are often categorized as: cool-growing, which means that they can usually withstand a minimum temperature of 10°C (50°F); intermediate, a minimum of 13°C (55°F); or warm-growing, a minimum of 18°C (64°F).

TENDRIL. A thread-like appendage used by climbing plants to twine round a support.

TEPAL. A segment of the outer whorl in a flower that has no distinct calyx and corolla, as in *Crocus*.

TERMINAL. At the tip of a stem or branch.

THROAT. The inner part of a tubular or bell-shaped flower.

TILTH. The fine, crumbly, surface layer of soil produced by cultivation.

TIP LAYERING. A method of propagation for shrubs and climbers in which the tip of a

shoot is pegged to the ground to encourage rooting.

TISSUE CULTURE. The growth of small pieces of plant tissue under sterile conditions in artificial media.

TOOTH. A small, marginal, often pointed lobe on a leaf, calyx, or corolla.

TOPIARY. The practice of trimming or training trees or shrubs into ornamental shapes, often geometric or resembling animals or birds.

TRANSPIRATION. Loss of water by evaporation from a plant surface.

TRIFOLIATE. Having three leaflets arising from the same point, as in clover (*Trifolium*).

TRILOBED. Having three lobes.

TRIM. To prune lightly by clipping.

TRUE [of seedlings]. Retaining the distinctive characteristics of the parent plant when raised from seed.

TUBER. A thickened, usually underground, storage organ derived from a stem or root.

UMBEL. A usually flat-topped or rounded flower cluster in which the individual flower stalks arise from a central point. In a compound umbel, each primary stalk ends in an umbel. Characteristic of the parsley family, Apiaceae, whose members are often referred to as "umbellifers".

UNDERSTOREY. A lower tier of shrubs and small trees beneath the main canopy of a forest.

UPRIGHT [of habit]. With vertical or semi-vertical main branches.

VALVE. A section of dry dehiscent fruit, especially of a capsule.

VARIEGATED [of leaves or petals]. Marked with patches or streaks of different-coloured tissues.

VEGETATIVE PROPAGATION. Any method of reproduction in plants, other than by seed.

VERMICULITE. A lightweight, mica-like mineral that is added to potting composts to improve moisture retention and aeration.

WEEPING. With slender branches that hang down.

WHORL. An arrangement of three or more leaves, branches, or flowers arising from the stem at the same level, encircling it. Characteristic of the family Rubiaceae, as in *Galium*.

WILD-COLLECTED. Harvested from the wild. Also referred to as wild-crafted (especially in the USA).

WINGED [of stems, seeds, or fruits]. Having a marginal flange or membrane.

WOODY-STEMMED. With a stem composed of woody fibres and therefore persistent, as opposed to soft-stemmed and herbaceous. A semi-woody stem contains some softer tissue.

x. The sign used to denote a hybrid plant derived from the crossing of two or more genetically distinct plants, as in *Lavandula* × *intermedia*, which is a cross between two distinct species, *L. angustifolia* and *L. latifolia*.

MEDICAL

ABORTIFACIENT. Causes abortion.

ACRID. Unpleasantly pungent or caustic.

ADAPTOGENIC. Improving resistance to stress.

ADRENAL CORTEX. Part of the adrenal gland that produces corticosteroid hormones.

ADRENALINE. A hormone secreted by the inner tissue of the endocrine glands, which prepares the body for "flight or fight" in response to stress.

ADRENOCORTICAL. Relating to the adrenal cortex.

ALEXIPHARMIC. Acting as an antidote.

ALKALOID. A nitrogen-containing compound produced by plants, which has a potent effect on body function.

ALLERGEN. Any substance that produces an allergic reaction.

ALTERATIVE. Increases vitality, mainly through improving the breakdown and excretion of waste products.

AMINO ACIDS. The basic structural units of proteins.

AMOEBIC DYSENTERY. Inflammation of the intestines caused by a parasitic amoeba.

ANAESTHETIC. Causes local or general loss of sensation.

ANALGESIC. Relieves pain.

ANETHOLE. A volatile oil with an aniseed odour, extracted mainly from *Pimpinella anisum* and *Illicium verum*, which has carminative and mildly expectorant effects.

ANODYNE. Soothes pain.

ANTHELMINTIC. Another word for vermifuge.

ANTI-BACTERIAL. Destroys or inhibits the growth of bacteria.

ANTIBIOTIC. Destroys or inhibits the growth of micro-organisms.

ANTI-COAGULANT. Prevents or slows clotting of the blood.

ANTI-INFLAMMATORY. Reduces inflammation.

ANTIOXIDANT. Prevents or slows the deterioration of cells by oxidation.

ANTI-PYRETIC. Relieves fever.

ANTI-RHEUMATIC. Mitigates the symptoms of rheumatism.

ANTISEPTIC. Prevents or controls infection.

ANTI-SPASMODIC. Reduces spasm or tension, especially of involuntary muscle.

APERIENT. A mild laxative.

APHRODISIAC. A substance that stimulates sexual excitement.

ASTRINGENT. Precipitates proteins from the surfaces of cells, causing contraction of tissues; forms a protective coating, and reduces bleeding and discharges.

BACILLUS. Any rod-shaped bacterium.

BACTERICIDAL. Destroys bacteria.

BALSAM. An aromatic oleo-resin obtained from various woody plants, and used as a base for medicines, perfume, and ritual ointments.

BETA-CAROTENE. The most important form of carotene, the orange-yellow plant pigment, which is converted in the body to vitamin A.

BILE. A thick bitter fluid secreted by the liver and stored in the gall bladder; aids digestion of fats.

BITTER. Stimulates secretion of digestive juices, improving appetite.

BITTER–SWEET. A flavour that combines bitter-tasting and sweet.

BLOOD COAGULANT. A substance that aids blood clotting.

BLOOD CLOTTING. The process in which blood protein is changed by

an enzyme from a liquid to a solid, in order to arrest bleeding.

BLOOD SUGAR. The concentration of glucose in the blood.

BORNEOL. A volatile oil with a camphoraceous aroma, extracted mainly from *Dryobalanops aromatica*.

BORNEOL ACETATE. A volatile fragrant liquid made from borneol, which is used in perfumery.

BRONCHIAL. Relating to the air passages in the lungs.

CAMPHORACEOUS. Having a camphor-like aroma.

CAPILLARY PERMEABILITY. The exchange of oxygen, carbon dioxide, water, salts, etc. between blood in the capillaries (fine blood vessels) and the tissues.

CARCINOGENIC. A substance that causes cancer.

CARDIAC FIBRILLATION. Rapid and irregular beating of heart muscles.

CARDIOVASCULAR SYSTEM. The heart and blood vessels that circulate blood around the body, transporting oxygen and nutrients to the tissues, and removing waste products.

CARMINATIVE. Relieves flatulence, colic, and digestive discomfort.

CARVACROL. A volatile oil, found in various herbs (notably in *Thymus* spp.), which stimulates secretions from mucous membranes.

CARVONE. A volatile oil with a caraway aroma and carminative effects, found mainly in *Carum carvi*.

CATARRH. Inflammation of the mucous membranes with increased production of mucus.

CAUSTIC. Capable of burning or corroding through chemical action.

CHOLESTEROL. A fat-like material, present in the blood and in most tissues, which is an important constituent of cell membranes, steroid hormones, and bile salts, but in high concentrations may cause atherosclerosis (hardening of the arteries).

CINEOLE. A volatile oil with a camphoraceous aroma, extracted mainly from *Eucalyptus* spp. and *Melaleuca leucadendra*, which has rubefacient and antiseptic effects. Also known as eucalyptol.

CIRCULATORY STIMULANT. Dilates the blood vessels and increases blood flow.

CITRONELLAL. A volatile oil with a lemon aroma, extracted mainly from *Cymbopogon nardus*, which is used in flavourings, perfumery, and insect-repellent.

CITRONELLOL. A volatile oil with a rose-like aroma, extracted mainly from *Pelargonium* spp., and used in perfumery and cosmetics.

CLEANSING HERB. A herb that improves excretion of waste products from the body.

COLONIC IRRIGATION. Washing out the contents of the large bowel by introducing copious amounts of water, often with soap or herb extracts, high into the colon.

COOLING. A remedy, often based on bitter or relaxant herbs, that reduces internal "heat" or physiological hyperactivity, mainly by clearing toxins.

COUMARIN. A vanilla-scented plant constituent, used in perfumes and flavourings, and in remedies to encourage blood clotting.

COUNTER-IRRITANT. Causes superficial irritation of the skin, increasing blood flow to the area, speeding removal of toxins, and thereby relieving inflammation of deeper tissues.

CUCURBITACINS. Toxic compounds, found especially in pumpkin seeds and *Bryonia dioica*, which have anthelmintic and anti-tumour effects.

DECONGESTANT. Relieves congestion (especially nasal).

DEMULCENT. Soothes and softens damaged, irritated, or inflamed tissues.

DEPRESSANT. Reduces nervous or functional activity.

DEPURATIVE. Promotes the elimination of waste products from the body.

DETOXICANT. Removes poisons (especially waste products) from the body.

DIAPHORETIC. Causes sweating, thus eliminating toxins and lowering fever.

DIOSPHENOL. A volatile oil, common in *Agathosma* spp., which has diuretic effects.

DIURETIC. Raises volume of urine.

EMETIC. Causes vomiting.

EMOLLIENT. Softens or soothes the skin.

ENZYME. A complex protein produced by cells, which acts as a catalyst, speeding biological reactions without itself being used up in the reaction.

EPIGASTRIC. Relating to the epigastrium (upper central region of the abdomen, above the navel and below the breast).

ESSENTIAL OIL. Volatile oil extracted from a plant, having the characteristic aroma or flavour of the plant.

EUGENOL. A volatile oil with a clove aroma, which has carminative and local anaesthetic effects; extracted mainly from *Syzygium aromaticum*.

EUPHORIC. Causing an increased sense of well being.

EXCITANT. Causing stimulation.

EXPECTORANT. Encourages the expulsion of phlegm from the respiratory tract.

FEBRIFUGE. Reduces fever.

FIXATIVE. A substance added to a perfume to make it less volatile and longer lasting.

FLAVONOIDS. Glycosides found widely in flowers, fruits, and leaves, which improve the circulation and have diuretic, anti-spasmodic, and anti-inflammatory effects.

FUNGAL. Caused by a fungus.

FUNGICIDE. A substance that destroys fungi.

FURANOCOUMARIN. A type of coumarin, found widely in plants, that has anti-spasmodic effects, but may cause photosensitivity.

GALACTOGOGUE. Increases milk flow.

GAMMA-LINOLENIC ACID (GLA). An unsaturated fatty acid, essential for growth and repair of cells, and for production of hormone-like substances. It is normally produced in the body, but in cases of deficit may be supplemented by the GLA component in oils of various plants.

GENITO-URINARY. Relating to both the reproductive and excretory systems.

GERMICIDAL. Destroys germs.

GLYCOSIDE. A constituent of certain plants, such as digitoxin in *Digitalis* spp., containing a sugar part or glycone, and a non-sugar part or aglycone.

GYNAECOLOGICAL. Relating to the branch of medicine that concerns diseases affecting the female reproductive system.

HAEMORRHAGE. Bleeding.

HAEMOSTATIC. Stops bleeding.

HORMONE. A chemical substance produced in the endocrine glands and transported in the blood to a certain tissue on which it exerts a specific effect.

HYPERACIDITY. Excess acidity of the digestive tract (especially of the stomach), producing a burning sensation.

HYPERTENSION. High blood pressure.

HYPOGLYCAEMIA. A deficiency of sugar in the blood, causing muscular weakness, mental confusion, and sweating.

HYPOTENSION. Low blood pressure.

HYSTERIA. A disorder characterized by emotional outbursts and instability.

IMMUNE SYSTEM. The body's defence mechanisms against infectious organisms and other foreign materials, such as allergens.

INDOLENT. Slow to heal (usually applied to painless ulcers of the skin or mucous membranes).

INSECTICIDAL. Destroys insects.

LACTATION. Secretion of milk by the mammary glands, which usually begins at the end of pregnancy.

LARVICIDAL. Destroys larvae (immature forms) of certain animals.

LAXATIVE. Encourages bowel movements.

LICHEN ACIDS. Bitter constituents of lichens, with antibiotic effects.

LINALOL OR LINALOOL. A fragrant liquid, found in many volatile oils, which has antiseptic effects, and is also used in perfumery.

LIPIDS. Fat-like substances, such as cholesterol, which are important structural materials in the body, and present in most tissues (especially the blood).

LUBRICANT. Reduces friction.

LYMPHATIC DRAINAGE. The return of lymph (fluid containing white blood cells) from the tissues of the body to the bloodstream via the lymphatic vessels.

MENSTRUATION. The "period" in the menstrual cycle, occurring at approximately monthly intervals, in which the lining of the womb breaks down and is discharged as blood and debris.

MENTHOL. A volatile oil with a peppermint aroma, extracted mainly from *Mentha* spp., which has antiseptic, carminative, and decongestant effects and a mild local anaesthetic action.

METABOLISM. The total chemical processes that occur in the body, resulting in growth, production of energy, elimination of wastes, etc.

MUCILAGE. A complex sticky carbohydrate, secreted by certain plants, such as comfrey (*Symphytum officinale*).

NARCOTIC. A drug that causes stupor and insensibility, and relieves pain; in legal terms, usually applied to an addictive drug that is subject to illegal use.

NASOPHARYNGEAL. Relating to the part of the pharynx that lies above and behind the soft palate.

NEMATOCIDAL. Destroys nematodes (unsegmented worms), some of which are disease-causing parasites, e.g. hookworm.

NERVE TONIC. A remedy that supports the proper functioning of the nervous system. Also called nervine.

NUTRITIVE. A herb that also provides nourishment as a food.

OAT GERM. The vitamin-rich embryo of the oat kernel.

OEDEMA. Excessive accumulation of fluid in the tissues.

OESTROGENIC. Similar in effects to the hormone oestrogen, which plays an important role in the development and functioning of female sexual organs.

OFFICINAL. A plant with pharmacological properties, available in medicinal form; origin of specific name of many herbs, such as *Salvia officinalis*.

OVARIAN. Relating to the ovary, the main female reproductive organ that produces ova (eggs) and secretes oestrogen hormones.

PAROXYSMAL. Convulsive.

PATHOGEN. A micro-organism that causes disease.

PERIPHERAL. Near the surface of the body.

PERISTALSIS. Waves of involuntary muscle contraction in the digestive tract, which push the contents along.

PHLEGM. Thick mucus, secreted by the walls of the respiratory tract.

PHOTODERMATITIS. A condition in which the skin becomes sensitized to a certain substance that, when exposed to sunlight, causes dermatitis.

PHOTOSENSITIVITY. Sensitivity to light.

PIGMENTATION. Coloration responsible for normal skin colour, produced in the body by pigments, such as melanin.

PIMENTO OIL. Essential oil extracted from allspice (*Pimenta dioica*), which has carminative and antioxidant effects.

PIPERITONE. A constituent of the volatile oil of peppermint (*Mentha × piperita*).

PORPHYRINS. Pigments found widely in living things, which are constituents of blood and of chlorophyll, in animals and plants respectively.

POSTPARTUM. Following childbirth.

POTASSIUM SALTS. A form of potassium given to maintain potassium levels in the body, which have been depleted through excessive fluid loss (e.g. through diarrhoea, burns, or use of diuretics).

PRODUCTIVE COUGHING. Resulting in expulsion of phlegm.

PROTEIN. A compound that forms the main structural material of muscles, tissues, and organs, synthesized in the body from amino acids.

PULEGONE. A volatile oil with a pennyroyal aroma, found mainly in *Mentha pulegium*, which has abortifacient and insect-repellent effects.

PUNGENT. Having an acrid smell or strong bitter flavour.

PURGATIVE. A strong laxative.

PYRROLIZIDINE ALKALOIDS. A group of alkaloids, found in herbs such as comfrey (*Symphytum officinale*), borage (*Borago officinalis*), and coltsfoot (*Tussilago farfara*), which in excess are associated with liver damage.

REJUVENATIVE. Restores vitality.

RELAXANT. Relaxes tense overactive tissues.

RESTORATIVE. Revives health or strength.

RUBEFACIENT. Causes reddening of the skin, thus increasing blood flow and cleansing the tissues of toxins.

SAFROLE. A volatile oil, extracted mainly from *Sassafras albidum*, and widely used in flavourings and toiletries; subject to restrictions as a possible cause of cancer and liver damage.

SALINE. Containing common salt.

SALIVATION. Secretion of saliva by the salivary glands in the mouth.

SAPONINS. A group of soap-like glycosides, found widely in plants, that have complex effects in herbal remedies; some resemble steroidal hormones.

SECRETION. A substance released from a cell (especially a glandular cell), which is synthesized in the cell from constituents of the blood or tissue fluids.

SEDATIVE. Reduces anxiety and tension.

SERUM. 1. The fluid that separates from clotted blood or blood plasma when it is allowed to stand. **2.** Anti-toxin obtained from the blood serum of immunized animals.

SIMPLE. A herb used as a remedy on its own.

SOPORIFIC. Inducing drowsiness or sleep.

SPERMICIDAL. Destroys sperm, thus acting as a contraceptive.

STAPHYLOCOCCI. Bacteria of the genus *Staphylococcus* that cause boils, infection in wounds, and septicaemia.

STEROIDS. Compounds containing a characteristic chemical ring structure, notably the sex hormones, hormones of the adrenal cortex, and vitamin D.

STEROL. A waxy steroid alcohol, such as cholesterol.

STIMULANT. Increases physiological activity.

SYNTHESIS. The process of producing a compound by chemical reaction from simpler materials.

THERAPEUTIC. Beneficial to health.

THIXOTROPIC. A gel that becomes less viscous when stirred.

THROMBOTIC. Forming a clot of coagulated blood in a blood vessel or in the heart, which remains at the site of formation, impeding blood flow.

THUJONE. A volatile oil, found mainly in *Salvia officinalis* and *Artemisia absinthium*, which produces carminative and antiseptic effects.

THYMOL. A constituent of the volatile oil of certain herbs, notably of thymes (*Thymus* spp.), which has antiseptic, fungicidal, and vermifugal effects.

THYROID. Relating to the thyroid gland, near the base of the neck, which controls metabolism and growth.

TONE. To strengthen or restore.

TONIC. Improves physiological functions and sense of well being.

TOPICAL. Applied to the body surface.

TOXIC. Harmful or poisonous.

TOXICITY. The degree of strength of a toxic substance.

TOXIN. A poisonous substance.

TRANQUILLIZING. Calming, without affecting clarity of consciousness.

TROPHO-RESTORATIVE. Nutritious and strengthening.

UTERUS. Womb.

VASOCONSTRICTOR. Causes narrowing of the walls of blood vessels.

VENEREAL. Relating to diseases transmitted by sexual intercourse.

VERMIFUGE. Destroys or expels intestinal worms.

VIRAL. Caused by a virus.

VIRUS. A disease-causing organism, capable of replication only within the cells of an animal or plant.

VOLATILE OILS. Complex aromatic plant constituents that may be extracted to produce essential oils, such as oil of geranium (from *Pelargonium* spp.), or isolated constituents, such as linalol.

WARMING. A remedy, often based on spicy pungent herbs, that dispels internal "coldness" or hypo-activity, and increases vitality, mainly by stimulating the digestion and circulation.

YIN AND YANG. The two complementary principles of Chinese philosophy, whose interaction maintains the harmony of the universe, and influences all qualities and activity. Yin is the female energy: dark, negative, damp, cold, descending, and interior. Yang is the male aspect: bright, positive, dry, hot, ascending, and exterior.

BOOKS FOR FURTHER READING

Akerele, O., Heywood, V., and Synge, H. (eds.), *The Conservation of Medicinal Plants* (Cambridge, 1991)

Bensky, D. and Gamble, A., *Chinese Materia Medica* (Seattle, Washington, 1993)

Bown, D., *Fine Herbs* (London, 1988; as *Ornamental Herbs for Your Garden*, London, 1993)

Bown, D., *Herbal* (London, 2001)

Bown, D., *RHS Plant Guides: Garden Herbs* (London, 1998)

Bremness, L., *Eyewitness Handbooks: Herbs* (London, 1994)

Chevallier, A., *The Encyclopedia of Medicinal Plants* (London, 1996, 2001)

Culpeper's *Complete Herbal* (Ware, 1995)

Davidow, J., *Infusions of Healing* (New York, 1999)

Duke, J., *A Handbook of Northeastern Indian Medicinal Plants* (Lincoln, Massachusetts, 1986)

Duke, J., *The Green Pharmacy* (Emmaus, Pennsylvania, 1997)

Duke, J. and Vasquez, R., *Amazonian Ethnobotanical Dictionary* (Boca Raton, Florida, 1994)

Evans, W. C., *Trease and Evans' Pharmacognosy* (London, 13th ed., 1989)

Facciola, S., *Cornucopia II – A Source Book of Edible Plants* (Vista, California, 1998)

Foster, S. and Duke, J., *Field Guide to Eastern/Central Medicinal Plants* (Boston, Massachusetts, 1990)

Foster, S. and Yue, C., *Herbal Emissaries* (Rochester, Vermont, 1992)

Frawley, D. and Lad, V., *The Yoga of Herbs: An Ayurvedic Guide to Herbal Medicine* (Santa Fe, New Mexico, 1986)

Genders, R., *Scented Flora of the World* (St Albans, 1978)

Grieve, M., *A Modern Herbal* (London, 1931; ed. C. F. Leyel, London, 1976, 1988)

Griggs, B., *New Green Pharmacy* (London, 1981, 1997)

Iwu, M., *A Handbook of African Medicinal Plants* (Boca Raton, Florida, 1990)

Krochmal, A. and C., *A Field Guide to Medicinal Plants* (New York, 1973)

Lassak, E.V. and McCarthy, T., *Australian Medicinal Plants* (Kew, Victoria, 1997)

Lehane, B., *The Power of Plants* (London, 1977)

Mabberley, D.J., *The Plant-Book* (Cambridge, 1997)

Miller, A.G. and Morris, M., *Plants of Dhofar* (Diwan of the Royal Court Sultanate of Oman, 1988)

Moore, M., *Medicinal Plants of the Desert and Canyon West* (Santa Fe, New Mexico, 1989)

Moore, M., *Medicinal Plants of the Pacific West* (Santa Fe, New Mexico, 1993)

Morton, J.F., *Herbs and Spices* (New York, 1976)

Murray, M.T., *The Healing Power of Herbs* (Rocklin, California, 1992, 1995)

Nadkarni, K.M., *Indian Materia Medica* (Bombay, 1908, 1996)

Ody, P., *The Herb Society's Complete Medicinal Herbal* (London, 1993)

Ortiz, E.L., *The Encyclopedia of Herbs, Spices, and Flavourings* (London, 1992)

Phillips, R. and Foy, N., *Herbs* (London, 1990)

Roberts, M., *Indigenous Healing Plants* (Johannesburg, 1990)

Rohde, E.S., *The Old English Herbals* (New York, 1971)

Schultes, R.E. and Raffauf, R.F., *The Healing Forest* (Portland, Oregon, 1990)

Stobart, T., *Herbs, Spices and Flavourings* (London, 1970)

Taylor, L., *Herbal Secrets of the Rainforest* (Rocklin, California, 1998)

The Revolutionary Health Committee of Hunan Province, *A Barefoot Doctor's Manual* (London, 1978)

Tierra, M., *Planetary Herbology* (Santa Fe, New Mexico, 1988)

Tyler, V.E., *Herbs of Choice* (Binghamton, New York, 1994)

Tyler, V.E., *The Honest Herbal* (Binghamton, New York, 1993)

Van Wyk, B-E., van Oudtshoorn, B., and Gericke, N., *Medicinal Plants of South Africa* (Pretoria, 1997)

Woodward, M. (ed.), *Gerard's Herbal* (London, 1994)

Wren, R.C., *Potter's New Cyclopedia of Botanical Drugs and Preparations* (Saffron Walden, 1988)

ALSO RECOMMENDED:

HerbalGram. Published quarterly by the American Botanical Council and the Herb Research Foundation, P.O. Box 144345, Austin, TX 78714-4345, USA (www.herbalgram.org)

Herbs, Journal of The Herb Society. Published quarterly by The Herb Society, Sulgrave Manor, Sulgrave, Banbury, Oxon OX17 2SD (01295 768899; www.herbsociety.org)

HERB GARDENS TO VISIT

NATIONAL COLLECTIONS

The National Council for the Conservation of Plants & Gardens (NCCPG) organizes a National Collections Scheme by genera or groups of associated plants. The following National Collections are of particular interest to those who grow and use herbs. Collections are not necessarily open to the public; contact Collection Holders for details. For genera not listed below, contact the NCCPG, The Stable Courtyard, The Royal Horticultural Society's Garden, Wisley, Woking, Surrey (01483 211465; www.nccpg.org.uk)

Acorus Mrs E. Honnor, 14 Homefield Close, Creech St Michael, Taunton, Somerset (01823 442507)

Artemisia Dr D. Twibell, 31 Smith St, Elsworth, Cambridge (01954 267414)

Buxus R. Kew, c/o Greenholm Nurseries Ltd., Lampley Rd, Kingston Seymour, North Somerset (01934 833350)

Citrus T. Read, Reads Nursery, Hales Hall, Lodden, Norfolk (01508 548395)

Digitalis Mrs N. Jardine, 64 Newbold Terrace East, Leamington Spa, Warwickshire (01926 425812)

Echinacea A. Brooks, c/o Elton Hall, Elton, Ludlow, Shropshire and Mrs L. Raynor, The Herb Garden, Chesterfield Road, Hardstoft, Pilsey, Derbyshire (01246 854268)

Lavandula H. Head, Norfolk Lavender Ltd., Caley Mill, Heacham, Norfolk (01485 570384)

Mentha D. Barrett, Pen y Braich, Cesarea, Caernarfon, Gwynnedd (01286 881156) and Mrs R. Titterington, Iden Croft Herbs, Staplehurst, Kent (01580 891432)

Monarda C. Skinner, Culpeper Supervisor, Leeds Castle Enterprises Ltd, Leeds Castle, Maidstone, Kent (01622 765400)

Origanum Mrs R. Titterington, Iden Croft Herbs, Staplehurst, Kent (01580 891432) and Mrs S. White, Hexham Herbs, Chesters Walled Garden, Chollerford, Hexham, Northumberland (01434 681483)

Pelargonium Fibrex Nurseries Ltd., Honeybourne Road, Pebworth, Stratford-on-Avon, Warwickshire (01789 720788)

Rheum Northern Horticultural Society, Harlow Carr Botanical Gardens, Harrogate, Yorkshire (01423 565418)

Rosmarinus S.J. Charlesworth, Downderry Nursery, Pillar Box Lane, Hadlow, Tonbridge, Kent (01732 810081) and Mrs P. Thoresby, Yorkstock, Clifford, Wetherby, Yorkshire (01937 541387)

Salvia Mr & Mrs B.D. Yeo, Pleasant View Nursery, Two Mile Oak, Newton Abbott, Devon (01803 813388)

Sambucus J.H. Ellis, The National Trust, Wallington Garden, Cambo, Morpeth, Northumberland (01670 774389)

Thymus K.A. White, Hexham Herbs, Chesters Walled Garden, Chollerford, Hexham, Northumberland (01434 681483)

BOTANIC GARDENS

All Botanic Gardens are worth visiting for herbs. Some have special herb gardens, others have sections devoted to economic plants; medicinal plants from many parts of the world can also be found in their collections.

Acorn Bank Garden, Penrith, Cumbria (017683 61893) walled herb garden

Barnsley House, Barnsley, Gloucestershire (01285 740281; www.barnsleyhouse.com) knot garden, potager

Barwinnock Herbs, Barrhill, Ayrshire (01465 821338; www.barwinnock.com) organic herb garden

Chelsea Physic Garden, 66 Royal Hospital Road, London SW3 (020 7352 5646; www.cpgarden.demon.co.uk) traditional domestic herbs

Congham Hall Hotel, Grimston, Norfolk (01485 600250) culinary and medicinal herb gardens

Cottage Herbery, Mill House, Boraston, Tenbury Wells, Worcestershire (01584 781575) display herb garden

Hardwick Hall, Chesterfield, Derbyshire (01246 850430) large formal garden

Harlow Carr Botanical Gardens, Harrogate, Yorkshire (01423 565418; www.rhs.org.uk) herb garden, national *Rheum* collection

Hatfield House, Hatfield, Hertfordshire (01707 262823) knot gardens, scented gardens

Herb Farm, Reading, Berkshire (0118 972 4220) Saxon maze, knot gardens, borders, containers

Herb Garden, Hardstoft, Derbyshire (01246 854268) medicinal, potpourri, and formal gardens

Hexham Herbs, Hexham, Northumberland (01434 681483) Roman garden, national *Thymus* and *Origanum* collections in walled garden

Iden Croft Herbs, Staplehurst, Kent (01580 891432; www.herbs-uk.com) various herb gardens, including a garden for the disabled; national *Origanum* collection

Norfolk Lavender, Caley Mill, Heacham, Norfolk (01485 570384; www.norfolk-lavender.co.uk) national *Lavandula* collection

Old Hall Plants, The Old Hall, Barsham, Beccles, Suffolk (01502 717475) unusual herbs, display garden

Queen's Garden, Royal Botanic Garden, Kew, Surrey (020 8332 5000; www.kew.org.uk) 17th-century herbs

Royal Horticultural Society's Garden, Wisley, Surrey (01483 224234; www.rhs.org.uk) formal herb garden

Sissinghurst Castle, Cranbrook, Kent (01580 712850) herb garden, thyme lawn

QUICK INDEX OF COMMON NAMES

The common names here are sorted letter-by-letter. Page references are to main (or only) entries in the text. For full information on the plant in question, please use the subject index (*see* pp.434–447).

A

Aaron's rod *see Verbascum thapsus* 401
abata cola *see Cola acuminata* 175
abele *see Populus alba* 328
abscess root *see Polemonium reptans* 326
acajou see Anacardium occidentale 118
achiote see Bixa orellana 144
aconite *see Aconitum* 100
acuyo see Piper auritum 320
adrue *see Cyperus articulatus* 189
African cherry *see Prunus africana* 332
African horned cucumber *see Cucumis metuliferis* 185
African marigold *see Tagetes erecta* 379
African serpentwood *see Rauvolfia vomitoria* 341
Africa potato *see Hypoxis hemerocallidea* 29
agar/agar-agar *see Gelidium amansii* 221
agnus castus *see Vitex agnus-castus* 406
agrimony *see Agrimonia eupatoria* 107
  hemp *see Eupatorium* 208
  water *see Bidens tripartita* 143
ailanto *see Ailanthus altissima* 108
aji see Capsicum baccatum 155
ajowan/ajwain *see Trachyspermum ammi* 392
alang-alang see Imperata cylindrica 242
alder *see Alnus* 114
alder buckthorn *see Rhamnus frangula* 343
alderleaf buckthorn *see Rhamnus alnifolia* 343
alecost *see Tanacetum balsamita* 381
alehoof *see Glechoma hederacea* 225
Aleppo pine *see Pinus halepensis* 318
alexanders *see Smyrnium olusatrum* 371
Alexandrian senna *see Senna alexandrina* 365
alfalfa *see Medicago sativa* 273
alkanet *see Alkanna* 111
alligator pear *see Persea americana* 308
allspice *see Pimenta dioica* 316
  wild *see Lindera benzoin* 263
almond *see Prunus dulcis* 332
  Indian *see Terminalia catappa* 384
aloewood *see Aquilaria malaccensis* 126
alpine lady's mantle *see Alchemilla alpina* 110
alpine lovage *see Ligusticum* 260
aluka see Dioscorea quaternata 194
alumroot *see Geranium maculatum* 223; *Heuchera americana* 234
amalaki see Phyllanthus emblica 313
amaranthus, two-toothed *see Achyranthes bidentata* 98
ambrette *see Abelmoschus moschatus* 96
American angelica *see Angelica atropurpurea* 122
American arbor-vitae *see Thuja occidentalis* 386
American aspen *see Populus tremuloides* 328
American blackberry *see Rubus villosus* 350
American boxwood *see Cornus florida* 181
American bugbane *see Actaea podocarpa* 102
American cranesbill *see Geranium maculatum* 223
American dittany *see Cunila origanoides* 186
American duppy basil *see Ocimum campechianum* 290

American feverfew *see Parthenium integrifolium* 303
American ginseng *see Panax quinquefolius* 300
American ground pine *see Lycopodium complanatum* 268
American hellebore *see Veratrum viride* 401
American holly *see Ilex opaca* 241
American larch *see Larix laricina* 251
American liquorice *see Glycyrrhiza lepidota* 226
American mandrake *see Podophyllum peltatum* 325
American mint *see Mentha arvensis* var. *villosa* 276
American papaya *see Asimina triloba* 156
American pennyroyal *see Hedeoma pulegioides* 231
American red osier *see Cornus stolonifera* 181
American sanicle *see Heuchera americana* 234
American spikenard *see Aralia racemosa* 126
American styrax *see Liquidambar styraciflua* 264
American valerian *see Cypripedium parviflorum* var. *pubescens* 189
American white elm *see Ulmus americana* 395
American wild lettuce *see Lactuca canadensis* 250
amla see Phyllanthus emblica 313
ammoniac *see Dorema ammoniacum* 196
Amur cork tree *see Phellodendron amurense* 311
Andean *aji see Capsicum baccatum* var. *pendulum* 155
anemone, Chinese *see Pulsatilla chinensis* 337
angelica tree, Chinese *see Aralia chinensis* 126
angled Solomon's seal *see Polygonatum odoratum* 327
angostura *see Galipea officinalis* 218
anise *see Pimpinella anisum* 317
aniseed *see Pimpinella anisum* 317
aniseed myrtle *see Backhousia anisata* 139
anise hyssop *see Agastache foeniculum* 105
anise marigold *see Tagetes anisatum* 379
anise mint *see Agastache foeniculum* 379
aniseroot *see Osmorhiza longistylis* 298
anise sweet Cicely *see Osmorhiza claytonii* 298
anise tree *see Illicium* 242
anise verbena *see Lippia alba* 264
anisillo see Tagetes lucida 379
annatto *see Bixa* 144
annual clary *see Salvia viridis* 356
aonla see Phyllanthus emblica 313
apamarga see Achyranthes aspera 99
apothecary's rose *see Rosa gallica* var. *officinalis* 347
apple-bearing sage *see Salvia pomifera* 355
apple geranium *see Pelargonium odoratissimum* 306
apple guava *see Psidium guajava* 334
applemint *see Mentha suaveolens* 278
apricot *see Prunus armeniaca* 332
apricot vine *see Passiflora incarnata* 303
Arabian coffee *see Coffea arabica* 175
Arabian jasmine *see Jasminum sambac* 246
Arabian tea *see Catha edulis* 158
arbor-vitae *see Thuja* 386
arbutus, trailing *see Epigaea repens* 202
archangel *see Lamium album* 250
areca palm *see Areca catechu* 127
arnica *see Arnica montana* 130
arrowroot, Japanese *see Pueraria lobata* 336

artichoke, globe *see Cynara cardunculus* subsp. *cardunculus* 188
arugula *see Eruca vesicaria* subsp. *sativa* 204
asafoetida *see Ferula assa-foetida* 213
asatsuki see Allium ledebourianum 112
ash *see Fraxinus* 216
  bitter *see Picrasma excelsa* 315
  northern prickly *see Zanthoxylum americanum* 409
  prickly *see Zanthoxylum* 409
  wafer *see Ptelea trifoliata* 335
  winged prickly *see Zanthoxylum planispinum* 409
Ashanti pepper *see Piper guineense* 319
ash pumpkin *see Benincasa hispida* 142
ashwagandha see Withania somnifera 408
Asian mint *see Persicaria odorata* 309
Asian plantain *see Plantago asiatica* 322
asparagus *see Asparagus officinalis* 135
  Japanese *see Aralia cordata* 126
aspen, lemon *see Acronychia* 39
asthma weed *see Euphorbia hirta* 210; *Lobelia inflata* 265
Atlas cedar *see Cedrus libani* 160
Australian mint *see Mentha australis* 276
Australian peppermint *see Eucalyptus dives* 207
Australian pepper tree *see Tasmannia lanceolata* 24
Australian quinine *see Alstonia constricta* 116
autumn crocus *see Colchicum autumnale* 176
autumn sage *see Salvia greggii* 355
avens *see Geum* 224
Avignon berry *see Rhamnus infectoria* 343
avocado *see Persea americana* 308
awl tree *see Morinda citrifolia* 282
Azores thyme *see Thymus caespititius* 387
Aztec marigold *see Tagetes erecta* 379
Aztec sweet herb *see Phyla scaberrima* 312
azure monkshood *see Aconitum carmichaelii* 100

B

babchi see Psoralea corylifolia 334
bachelor's buttons *see Centaurea cyanus* 161
badian see Illicium verum 242
Baikal skullcap *see Scutellaria baicalensis* 364
bai zhu see Atractylodes macrocephala 137
baker's garlic *see Allium chinense* 112
balloon flower *see Platycodon grandiflorus* 323
balm of Gilead *see Abies balsamea* 97; *Cedronella canariensis* 160; *Commiphora gileadensis* 177; *Populus × jackii* 328
balmony *see Chelone glabra* 165
balsam, orange *see Impatiens capensis* 242
  wild *see Eriodictyon californicum* 204
balsam fir *see Abies balsamea* 97
balsam of Peru *see Myroxylon balsamum* var. *pereirae* 285
balsam pear *see Momordica charantia* 280
balsam poplar *see Populus balsamifera* 328
bamboo *see Phyllostachys* 313
Bamenda cola *see Cola anomala* 175
baneberry *see Actaea* 102
Barbados aloe *see Aloe vera* 115
Barbados nut *see Jatropha curcas* 246
barbed skullcap *see Scutellaria barbata* 364
barbeen see Lepidium sativum 'Persian' 259
barberry *see Berberis* 142
barley *see Hordeum* 236

419

Q

R

SUBJECT INDEX

Pelargonium (continued)
P. 'Mabel Grey' 307
P. *odoratissimum* 305, **306**, *306*
P. 'Old Spice' 307, *307*
P. 'Prince of Orange' 307, *307*
P. *radens* 306, **306–7**
P. 'Radula' 305, 307, *307*
P. 'Radula Rosea' 307, *307*
P. *rapaceum* 305
P. *reniforme* 305
P. 'Rober's Lemon Rose' 307, *307*
P. 'Royal Oak' 307, *307*
P. *sidoides* 305
P. 'Sweet Mimosa' 307, *307*
P. *tomentosum* 59, 305, *306*, **307**
P. *triste* 305
Pemberton, John 17
pepper harvesting *43*
perfumes 46–7
Perilla **307–8**
P. *crispa* 307
P. *frutescens* 58, **307–8**, *308*
P. f. 'Aka Shiso' see P. f. 'Red'
P. f. 'Ao Shiso' see P. f. 'Green'
P. f. var. *crispa* 48, 78, 308, *308*
P. f. 'Green' 308
P. f. 'Hojiso' 308
P. f. 'Kkaennip' 308
P. f. var. *nankinensis* see P. f. var. *crispa*
P. f. 'Purple Cumin' 308
P. f. 'Red' 308
P. *ocimoides* see P. *frutescens*
perilla in food 42
Persea **308–9**
P. *americana* **308**, *308*
P. a. 'Hass' 308
P. a. 'Little Cado' see P. a. 'Wurtz'
P. a. 'Pollock' 308
P. a. 'Wurtz' 308
P. *borbonia* 252, **308–9**
P. *humilis* 308
P. *palustris* 308
Persia 10, 47, 346, 353
Persicaria **309**
P. *aviculare* 309
P. *bistorta* 81, *81*, **309**, *309*
P. b. 'Superba' 309, *309*
P. *hydropiper* 309
P. *minus* 309
P. *odorata* 37, **309**
P. *tinctoria* 244
Peru 394, 397
Pestalotiopis 384
pests and diseases 59
Petiver, James 15
Petiveria **309–10**
P. *alliacea* **309–10**, *310*
Petroselinum **310**
P. *crispum* 27, 49, *53*, 55, 58, 62, 63, 69, *72*, *76*, 85, 88, 90, **310**, *310*
P. c. 'Afro' 75, 78, 85, 90, 310, *310*
P. c. 'Clivi' 88, 310
P. c. var. *neapolitanum* 310, *310*
P. c. var. *tuberosum* 310, *310*
Peucedanum graveolens see *Anethum graveolens*
Peumus **310–11**
P. *boldus* 25, **310–11**, *311*

Pfaffia **311**
P. *paniculata* 25, **311**
Pharbitis hederacea see *Ipomoea hederacea*
Phaseolus vulgaris 'Purple Teepee' 76
Phellodendron **311**
P. *amurense* **311**, *311*
P. *chinense* 311
Philadelphus 'Belle Etoile' 87
Phormium tenax 39
Phragmites **311–12**
P. *australis* 311, **312**, *312*
Phygelius capensis 88
Phyla **312**
P. *alba* see *Lippia alba*
P. *dulcis* see P. *scaberrima*
P. *nodiflora* 312
P. *scaberrima* **312**, *312*
Phyllanthus **312–13**
P. *debilis* see P. *niruri*
P. *emblica* 32, 312, **313**, *313*
P. *niruri* 312, **313**
P. *reticulatus* 312
P. *urinaria* 312
Phyllostachys **313**
P. *nigra* 55, **313**
P. n. 'Boryana' 313
P. n. 'Henonis' see P. n. var. *henonis*
P. n. var. *henonis* 313
P. *pubescens* 313
Phylloxera vastratrix 407
Physalis **313–14**
P. *alkekengi* **313–14**, *314*
P. *ixocarpa* 313
P. *peruviana* 313
P. *philadelphica* 313
physic gardens 11
Physiomedical Movement 22, 44, 265, 364
Physostigma **314**
P. *venenosum* 28, 29, *29*, **314**
Phytolacca 41, **314–15**
P. *acinosa* 314, *314*
P. *americana* 23, **314–15**, *315*
Picraenia excelsa see *Picrasma excelsa*
Picrasma **315**
P. *excelsa* **315**, *315*
P. *quassioides* 315
Picrorhiza **315**
P. *kurrooa* 33, **315**, *315*
P. *scrophulariiflora* see *Neopicrorhiza scrophulariiflora*
Pilocarpus **316**
P. *jaborandi* 316
P. *microphyllus* 25, **316**
P. *pinnatifolius* 316
P. *trachylophus* 316
Pilosella **316**
P. *officinarum* **316**
Pimenta **316–17**
P. *acris* see P. *racemosa*
P. *dioica* 25, **316–17**, *316*
P. *racemosa* **317**, *317*
P. r. var. *racemosa* 316
Pimpinella **317–18**
P. *anisum* 27, **317**, *317*
P. *major* 317
P. m. 'Rosea' 317
P. *saxifraga* **317–18**, *318*
P. s. var. *nigra* 317
Pinelli, Giovanni 318
Pinellia **318**
P. *ternata* **318**, *318*

Pinguicula grandiflora 197
P. *vulgaris* 197
Pinus 22, **318–19**
P. *halepensis* 318
P. h. subsp. *brutia* 30
P. *massoniana* 318
P. *mugo* **318**
P. m. 'Mops' 319, *319*
P. m. Pumilio Group 55, 319, *319*
P. m. var. *pumilio* see P. m. Pumilio Group
P. *nigra* 318
P. *palustris* 318, **319**, *319*
P. *pinaster* 318
P. *strobus* 318
P. *succinifera* 318
P. *sylvatica* 318
P. *sylvestris* 26, **319**, *319*
P. s. 'Aurea' see P. s. Aurea Group
P. s. Aurea Group 55, 319, *319*
P. s. 'Fastigiata' 319, *319*
P. *tabuliformis* 318
Piper **319–21**
P. *angustifolia* 319
P. *auritum* 319, **320**, *320*
P. *betle* 319, **320**, *320*
P. *cubeba* **320**, *320*
P. *guineense* 319
P. *lolot* 37, 319
P. *longum* 319, **320–1**, *320*
P. *methysticum* 319, 320, **321**
P. *nigrum* 33, 319, 320, **321**, *321*
P. *retrofractum* 320
P. *sarmentosum* 319
pips, growing from 63
Piscidia **321**
P. *erythrina* see P. *piscipula*
P. *piscipula* 25, **321**
Pistacia **321–2**
P. *lentiscus* 26, 321, *321*, **322**
P. *terebinthus* **322**, *322*
pitta 44
pituri 38, 39
plan of garden 51
plant breeding 16
plant ingredients 19
Plantago **322–3**
P. *arenaria* 322
P. *asiatica* **322**, *323*
P. a. 'Variegata' 322, *323*
P. *indica* 33, 322
P. *lanceolata* 322
P. *major* 27, *27*, **322–3**, *323*
P. m. var. *asiatica* see P. *asiatica*
P. m. 'Rosularis' 323, *323*
P. m. 'Rubrifolia' 60, 323, *323*
P. *ovata* 322
P. *psyllium* 322, **323**, *323*
planting herbs 53, *53*
containers 54–5
Plants Naturally Nursery 11
Platycladus orientalis see *Thuja orientalis*
Platycodon **323–4**
P. *grandiflorus* **323–4**, *323*
P. g. var. *albus* 323, 323
P. g. 'Apoyama' 324, *324*
P. g. var. *apoyama* see P. g. 'Apoyama'
P. g. 'Mother of Pearl' see P. g. 'Perlmutterschale'
P. g 'Perlmutterschale' 324

Plectranthus **324**
P. *amboinicus* **324**, *324*
P. a. 'Variegated' 324
P. a. 'Well-Sweep Wedgewood' 324, *324*
P. *patchouli* 325
Pliny 15, 165, 247, 330, 346, 349, 354, 371, 382, 395
Podophyllum **324–5**
P. *emodi* see P. *hexandrum*
P. *hexandrum* 32, 33, 324
P. *peltatum* 23, 324, **325**, *325*
Pogostemon **325**
P. *cablin* 59, 64, **325**, *325*
P. *heyneanus* 325
P. *parviflorus* 325
P. *patchouli* see P. *cablin*
P. *plectranthoides* 325
poisonous herbs 41, 53
Polchresia Herba Veronica 402
Polemonium **325–6**
P. *caeruleum* 325, *325*, **326**
P. c. 'Album' see P. c. f. *album*
P. c. f. *album* 326
P. c. 'Blanjou' 325, 326
P. c. 'Brise d'Anjou' see P. c. 'Blanjou'
P. *reptans* 325, **326**, *326*
P. r. 'Album' see P. r. 'Virginia White'
P. r. 'Pink Dawn' 326
P. r. 'Virginia White' 326
Poliomintha **326**
P. *bustamanta* 230, **326**
P. *incana* 326
P. *longiflora* see P. *bustamanta*
Polygala **326**
P. *amarella* 326
P. *senega* **326**
P. *tenuifolia* **326**
P. *vulgaris* 326
Polygonatum **326–7**
P. *biflorum* 326
P. *odoratum* 59, 326, **327**, *327*
P. o. 'Flore Pleno' 327
P. o. 'Gilt Edge' 327
P. o. 'Variegatum' 327, *327*
P. *pubescens* 326
Polygonum bistorta see *Persicaria bistorta*
P. *multiflorum* see *Fallopia multiflora*
P. *odoratum* see *Persicaria odorata*
P. *tinctorium* see *Persicaria tinctoria*
Polynesians 39
Polypodium **327**
P. *glycyrrhiza* 327
P. *vulgare* **327**, *327*
P. v. 'Cornubiense' 327, *327*
Poncirus trifoliata 171
ponds, herbs for 53
Populus **327–8**
P. *alba* **328**, *328*
P. a. 'Richardii' 328, *328*
P. *balsamifera* 328
P. × *candicans* see P. × *jackii*
P. *gileadensis* see P. × *jackii*
P. × *jackii* **328**, *328*
P. × j. 'Aurora' 328, *328*
P. *nigra* 328
P. *tremuloides* 328
Poria cocos see *Wolfiporia cocos*
Porophyllum **328–9**
P. *coloratum* 328
P. c. subsp. *coloratum* 328
P. c. subsp. *obtusifolium* 329

Porophyllum (continued)
P. *ruderale* 328, *328*, **329**
P. r. subsp. *macrocephalum* 328
P. r. subsp. *ruderale* 328
Porteranthus trifoliatus see *Gillenia trifoliata*
Portulaca **329**
P. *grandiflora* 329
P. *oleracea* 54, **329**, *329*
P. o. var. *aurea* 88, 329, *329*
potager 71, *71*, 76–7
Potawatomi 339
Potentilla **329**
P. *anserina* 329
P. *erecta* **329**, *329*
P. *reptans* 329
P. *tormentilla* see P. *erecta*
Poterium officinalis see *Sanguisorba officinalis*
pot-herbs 42
potpourri herb garden 82–3
Pouch of Pearls 298
poultices 45
Practice of Aromatherapy 45
prairies 57
prana 44
preserving herbs 68–9
Preslia cervina see *Mentha cervina*
Primula **330**
P. *veris* 41, 69, **330**, *330*
P. *vulgaris* 41, 52, 62, **330**, *330*
P. v. 'Alba Plena' 330, *330*
P. v. 'Double Sulphur' 330
P. v. 'Double White' see P. v. 'Alba Plena'
P. v. 'Jack in the Green' 330, *330*
Prinos verticillatus see *Ilex verticillata*
propagating herbs 62–5
Propertius 350
Prostanthera 39, **330–1**
P. *cineolifera* 330
P. *rotundifolia* 330, **331**
Proteum altissimum 148
Prunella **331**
P. *vulgaris* **331**, *331*
prunes 331, 332
pruning 61
Prunus 60, 61, **331–4**
P. *africana* 29, 331, **332**
P. *armeniaca* 10, 47, 331, **332**, *332*
P. a. 'Hemskirke' 332, *332*
P. a. 'Moorpark' 332, *332*
P. *avium* 331
P. *cerasus* 331
P. *domestica* **332**, *332*
P. d. subsp. *domestica* 331
P. d. 'Mirabelle' 332
P. d. 'Prune d'Agen' 332, *332*
P. *dulcis* 10, 31, 47, **332–3**, *332*
P. d. 'All-in-One' 332
P. d. 'Amara' 332
P. d. 'Macrocarpa' 332
P. *japonica* 333
P. *laurocerasus* 331, 332, **333**
P. l. 'Castlewellan' 332, 333
P. l. 'Marbled White' see P. l. 'Castlewellan'
P. l. 'Otto Luyken' 333, *333*
P. l. 'Schipkaensis' 333, *333*
P. *mume* 331, 332, **333**, *333*
P. m. 'Beni-chidori' 333, *333*
P. m. 'Benishidore' see P. m. 'Beni-chidori'
P. m. 'Microcarpa' 333
P. m. 'Peggy Clarke' 333

ACKNOWLEDGEMENTS

1	2	3	4	5	6
7	8	9	10	11	12
13	14	15	16	17	18
19	20	21	22	23	24
25	26	27	28	29	30
31	32	33	34	35	36

The publisher would like to thank the following for their kind permission to reproduce their photographs:

AKG London British Museum 10bl;
The Art Archive Asciano Museum, Italy/Daglo Orti 12bl; Bibliotheque Nationale Paris 43b; Topkapi Museum 10tc;
Art Directors & TRIP 30bl, 31tr; A. Gasson 24tr;
A–Z Botanical Collection 257tr, 360/2, 386bl; Andrew Ackerley 407/32; Ron Bass 326bl; David Hughes 404/33, 404/36; Jiri Loun 242bc; T.G.J. Rayner 395tc; Dan Sams 383/29, 383/35; Derek Shimmin 215/27; Adrian Thomas 388/3; A. Young 391/7;
Deni Bown 4/36, 5/31, 5/36, 6, 25tc, 28br, 53c, 75/31, 76/15, 79br, 80t, 81cl, 81bl, 82/5, 83/1, 83/3, 83/30, 86tr, 87/13, 89/31, 89/34–35, 96br, 96bl, 97tc, 97tr, 98tc, 98tr, 99bc, 99br, 100bl, 100bc, 100br, 100/29, 100/30, 101/6, 101/11, 101/12, 102tc, 102bc, 102bcl, 105tr, 106tc, 107bl, 108tl, 108c, 108cr, 108bc, 108bcr, 108br, 109bl, 109br, 110tc, 110bc, 111tc, 112br, 114bc, 114br, 115tl, 115tr, 116bl, 116bc, 117tl, 118bl, 119tl, 119bc, 120tl, 120br, 121tc, 122tl, 122br, 123tc, 123bc, 123br, 124bc, 124br, 125tc, 125tr, 126tl, 126tc, 126br, 127tr, 127bl, 128tl, 128bc, 129tc, 130tr, 130bl, 131cb, 131br, 131/22, 134tc, 135tr, 135bl, 136tl, 138tr, 139tl, 140tl, 140tc, 140tl (inset), 141tc, 141tr, 141br, 142tl, 142tc, 142br, 143/35, 144tr, 145tr, 146bl, 147bl, 147bc, 148tl, 148tc, 149tr, 149/33–34, 150/24, 150/31–32, 150/34, 151/35–36, 153/5–6, 154/21–22, 156tr, 156/1, 156/33–34, 156/35–36, 157/3–4, 157/5–6, 160tl, 160tc, 160tr, 161tc, 164/4, 164/8, 165/32, 165/34, 165/36, 166bc, 168tl, 169tr, 170/27, 171/36, 172crb, 172bcl, 172bcr, 172cbl, 176br, 176tc, 176/6, 176/12, 177tr, 178/1–2, 178/34, 178/35, 178/36, 180/4–6, 181bl, 181bc, 182bl, 182/28, 184/3–4, 184/5–6, 184/15, 186/31–32, 187/25–26; 187/31, 189/3–6, 192tl, 193/31–32, 194/5–6, 195tr, 197tc, 198tc, 198bl, 199tl, 201bc, 202tc, 202bc, 202br, 203tc, 204tc, 204/3–4, 204/5–6, 205/31–32, 205/35–36, 206/5–6, 208tl, 209tr, 210/31–32, 210/35–36, 211/5–6, 212tc, 212tr, 212bc, 213tc, 213br, 214/3, 214/5, 214/11, 214/12, 216/1–7, 216/21–22, 216/33, 216/34, 217/1–2, 217/5–6, 218/11–12, 219/3–4, 219/5–6, 222tl, 222tc, 224tc, 224tr, 225tc, 225tr, 226tl, 227tl, 228tr, 229tl, 229br, 230cr, 231tl, 232br, 233bl, 234bc, 236/3–4, 236/36, 237/3–4, 237/15, 237/16, 238/3–4, 238/5–6, 238/35–36, 240bcr, 243bc, 245/28, 245/33, 246/35–36, 248tr, 248bl, 249tl, 250/35–36, 251/1–2, 251/3–4, 252tl, 252/8, 252/21, 256/24, 256/36, 258tr, 262br, 263tr, 264bl, 264/36, 265tc, 266tc, 267bc, 267br, 268bc, 268bl, 269tl, 269/27, 269/36, 270bc, 271/13, 272bl,

272tr, 273tr, 273bl, 275tl, 275br, 275/13, 275/14, 276/34, 277/27, 279tl, 280tl, 280/10, 282bc, 283tl, 283bl, 284tl, 284tr, 285bc, 285br, 285bl, 286tl, 286/9, 286/15, 286/16, 287tc, 287br, 288tl, 288bl, 288tr, 289bl, 291br, 292/31, 293/31, 295/31, 296/26, 296/29, 296/34–35, 297/25, 297/35, 298tc, 299/27, 299/33, 301tl, 302tr, 302/2, 302/13, 302/25, 302/26, 303tl, 304tr, 305/25, 305/26, 305/27–28, 305/31, 306/5–6, 306/33, 306/36, 307/28, 309tc, 310tl, 310/28, 311tl, 311tr, 312tl, 312bc, 312/22, 313tl, 314tr, 315tl, 315br, 316br, 317tr, 318tc, 319/19, 319/20, 319/21, 319/31, 319/32, 320bl, 320tr, 320bc, 320br, 321/36, 323br, 323/7, 324tr, 324tl, 324bc, 325tl, 325bc, 325/23, 327tl, 327tr, 327bl, 328/28, 328/33, 328/35, 329tc, 329br, 330/3, 330/4, 331tc, 335tr, 335bl, 336br, 337/1, 337/33, 337/34, 339/35, 340bc, 340/19, 340/31, 341tl, 341bc, 342tl, 342bc, 342/28, 343bc, 345bl, 345/11, 346/28, 346/30, 346/35, 347/25, 347/31, 349tr, 349/31, 349/32, 350tl, 350/27, 350/28, 350/35, 351/36, 352tr, 352/11, 352/12, 353tr, 353/25, 353/31, 353/32, 354/20, 354/25, 354/31, 354/33, 354/36, 355/25, 355/28, 355/32, 356/25, 357tl, 357br, 357/4, 357/9, 357/10, 358tr, 358bc, 359tl, 359bl, 360/1, 360/7, 360/10, 360/11, 360/12, 361br, 362/1, 362/7, 363bc, 364bl, 364bc, 365bl, 367bl, 368tc, 368tr, 369tc, 369br, 370bl, 371tr, 373bc, 373br, 374tr, 374/31, 374/33, 376tl, 377/27, 378tl, 379/35, 379/36, 380br, 381/28, 381/33, 382/2, 382/8, 382/10, 384br, 384tc, 385tr, 386/6, 386/11, 387tl, 387/13, 388/8, 390/2, 390/12, 391tr, 391bl, 391bc, 391/8, 393tc, 393bl, 393br, 394tl, 394/7, 394/28, 394/29, 394/34, 394/35, 396tl, 396tr, 396bc, 397bc, 398br, 400bl, 400/18, 401bc, 401tc, 403tl, 403tc, 404/1, 404/7, 404/13, 404/22, 404/24, 404/30, 405/27, 406/36, 407/31, 408tl, 409br; 411tc;
Bridgeman Art Library, London / New York 18cla;
Pat Brindley 117br, 351tr;
© The British Museum 12tr, 15tr;
Jonathan Buckley 131/33;
R.B. Burbridge 163tc;
Neil Campbell-Sharp 11tr, 52bl, 58bl, 70tc, 314tl;
Jean-Loup Charmet 23bl;
Cherikoff–The Rare Spice Company, Australia 39;
Bruce Coleman Collection 27tl; George Bingham 38tr; Gerald Cubitt 28cla, 28tr, 32tr; Michael Freeman 32bl, 46bl; Frank Lanring 20tc; Luiz Claudio Marigo 21bl; Hans Reinhard 66bl; Kevin Rushby 7; Norbert Schwirtz 26tr; Michel Viard 26cla;
Colorific! Michael Yamashita 34bc, 37bl;
Corbis Earl and Nazima Kowall 43tr; Enzo and Paolo Ragazzini 33tr;
Eric Crichton Photos 74tl, 76/6, 77/1, 77/18, 78/29, 109/23;
Tom Croat 152/3–4, 223tc;
James Davis Travel Photography 20cl;
C.M. Dixon 17cra;
Frank Dobson 163tr;
Mary Evans Picture Library 34tl;
John Fielding 102bfr, 103tc, 106br;
Werner Forman Archive 44tl;
Steven Foster Group Inc 137bl, 137bc, 166br, 170/28, 214tr, 300tr, 366bl, 397tl.
M.P. Frankis 30cl, 31c;
Andrew Gagg 144bl, 239br, 240cbr;
Garden Picture Library 70cl, 209tc, 256/22; Mark Bolton 232/14, 241/15; Philippe Bonduel 215/28; Clive Boursnell 49br; Lynne Brotchie 48bl; Linda Burgess 6; Chris Burrows 150/27, 206/18; Brian Carter 253/35, 255/24, 269/19, 374/32, 380tc; David Cavagnaro 292/25; Bob Challinor 60br; Densey Clyne 235c; Eric Crichton 248tc; John Glover 231/5, 231/12, 232/15, 239/1–2, 241/12, 251/33–34, 256/35, 281/1, 281/7, 306/33; Sunniva Harte 171/22, 171/24; Neil Holmes

199/29, 253/21, 253/26, 253/36, 254/29, 390/5; A.I. Lord 232/3; Mayer/Le Scanff 259tc; Jerry Pavia 243tl, 291/25; Howard Rice 220tr, 223/30, 241/5, 245/29, 266bc, 350/36; Kevin Richardson 206/17; Gary Rogers 278/22; Christel Rosenfeld 48tc; J.S. Sira 150/33, 199/35, 254/23, 254/32, 276/36; Michel Viard 300bl; Juliette Wade 71bl; Didier Willery 164/7, 270tr, 297/31, 333/36;
Garden Exposures Photo Library 161br, 171/35;
John Glover 49tr, 50bl, 59tr;
Robert Harding Picture Library 23tr, 35, 42bl; Fiore 67tr; Robert Frerck/Odyssey, Chicago 41tr; T. Gervis 47;
Jerry Harpur Edwina Von Gal USA 56/6;
Hutchison Library 25, 30tr; Felix Green 45br; Liba Taylor 41br;
Anne Hyde 131/21;
Andrew Lawson 75/19, 131/34;
Charles Mauzy 383/36;
Miranda Morris 31cl, 31bl;
Natural Visions Heather Angel 21tr, 40br, 207/6;
N.H.P.A. David Middleton 56/13; Kevin Schafer 24bl; Mirko Stelzner 36bl; Dave Watts 38b;
Clive Nichols 51bl, 55tc, 233tc; Glazely Old Rectory 71tr; Lucy Huntington 55cr; Le Manoir Aus Quat 77/5; Old Rectory, Shropshire 50tr;
Oxford Scientific Films 304tl; ; Deni Bown 40tc, 149/19–20, 149/25, 149/31, 176/4, 221, 222bc, 293/3, 306/28–29; Aldo Brando 20br; 222bc; Jack Dermid 336bl; Geoff Kidd 57c; James Robinson 289br; Karen Ross/Partridge Films Ltd. 289tr; Peter Ryley 27tc; Alastair Shay 57t; Claude Steelman 22tr;
Panos Pictures Victoria Keble-Williams 29tr;
Photos Horticultural 140tl, 140tcb, 198tc, 214/1, 249tr, 251/5–6, 330br, 394/36, 405/33;
Royal Horticultural Society, Wisley 14tr, 15bl, 59/26–31–32;
Ann Ronan Picture Library 18tr;
Royal Botanic Gardens Kew 279tr, 287tl;
Royal Botanic Garden Edinburgh 29tl, 29b, 31br; (David Rae) 230tr
The Royal Photographic Society Robinson 13bc;
Science Photo Library Jean-Loup Charmet 44br; John Greim 16bl;
Harry Smith Collection 16tr, 26br, 54tr, 233br, 252/20, 253/33, 253/34, 255/20, 255/21, 255/32, 255/33, 255/34, 256/26, 256/31, 256/34, 260bc, 261br, 264/33, 269/13, 269/14, 269/20, 271/7, 271/14, 277br, 278/25, 278/31, 280/3, 280/11, 280/17, 281/5, 281/13, 281/15, 281/16, 290tl, 290/29, 290/30, 291/31, 291/33, 292/27, 296/28, 306/28, 308tr, 310/27, 317bl, 319/33, 322tl, 323/10, 325/35, 330/9, 332/29, 333/25, 333/29, 333/35, 334bc, 337/7, 338/31, 338/32, 340/22, 342tr, 345/17, 347/33, 354/32, 354/34, 355/29–30, 359/36, 360/5–6, 382/3–4, 409tl; Ivan Tolunix 223tl;
South American Pictures 11crb;
Still Pictures Nigel Dickinson 37tr;
Telegraph Colour Library Colorific/Patrick Morrow/Blackstar 34tr;
John Vander-Plank, National Collection of Passiflora 303bc;
Dave Watts 38b;
Steve Wooster 1, 2–3, 70br, 113br; Anthony Park 85bl, 90tr.

All other images © Dorling Kindersley.
For further information see www.dkimages.com

Indexer Michèle Clarke
Dorling Kindersley would also like to thank the following for their assistance in the preparation of this revised edition: Lynn Bresler, Sarah Duncan, Stephanie Farrow, Jude Garlick